THE
MARYLAND CAMPAIGN
OF SEPTEMBER 1862

Brevet Brigadier General Ezra A. Carman (courtesy of Antietam National Battlefield).

THE
MARYLAND CAMPAIGN
OF SEPTEMBER 1862

Ezra A. Carman's Definitive Study of the Union
and Confederate Armies at Antietam

EDITED BY
JOSEPH PIERRO

Routledge
Taylor & Francis Group
New York   London

Cover: *Artillery Hell* by James Hope. Courtesy of Antietam National Battlefield.

Routledge
Taylor & Francis Group
270 Madison Avenue
New York, NY 10016

Routledge
Taylor & Francis Group
2 Park Square
Milton Park, Abingdon
Oxon OX14 4RN

© 2008 by Taylor & Francis Group, LLC
Routledge is an imprint of Taylor & Francis Group, an Informa business

Printed in the United States of America on acid-free paper
10 9 8 7 6 5 4 3 2 1

International Standard Book Number-13: 978-0-415-95628-4 (Hardcover)

Library of Congress Cataloging-in-Publication Data

Carman, Ezra Ayers, 1834-1909.
 The Maryland Campaign of September 1862 : Ezra A. Carman's definitive study of the Union and Confederate armies at Antietam / edited by Joseph Pierro.
   p. cm.
 Includes index.
 ISBN 0-415-95628-5 (hardback : alk. paper)
 1. Antietam, Battle of, Md., 1862. 2. United States. Army--History--Civil War, 1861-1865. 3. United States. Army of the Potomac--History. 4. Confederate States of America. Army--History. 5. Maryland--History--Civil War, 1861-1865--Campaigns. 6. United States--History--Civil War, 1861-1865--Campaigns. I. Pierro, Joseph. II. Title.

E474.61.C37 2007
973.7'336--dc22
                                                                                    2006037347

Visit the Taylor & Francis Web site at
http://www.taylorandfrancis.com

and the Routledge Web site at
http://www.routledge.com

Contents

Acknowledgments

When I first decided to assume the responsibility of editing this manuscript, I little appreciated the enormity of the task I had set for myself. What was envisioned as a pleasant academic diversion of several weeks' duration turned out to require a year of my attention. My own labors, however, pale in significance to those of Ezra A. Carman. Indeed, the demands placed upon me in finalizing his work for publication only strengthened my already-healthy admiration for all that he had accomplished in crafting *The Maryland Campaign of September 1862*.

The following institutions were generous with their time and resources: the Library of Congress, the National Archives, the Fenwick Library at George Mason University, the Library of Virginia, Antietam National Battlefield, the Fairfax County (Virginia) Public Library System, the New Jersey Historical Society, the Eleanor S. Brockenbrough Library at the Museum of the Confederacy, Arlington National Cemetery, the Virginia Historical Society, the Pamunkey Regional (Virginia) Library System, the New York Public Library, the Maryland State Archives, the Washington County (Maryland) Historical Society, the McGraw-Page Library at Randolph-Macon College, and the Caroline Meriwether Goodlett Library at the United Daughters of the Confederacy Memorial Building in Richmond, Virginia. The respective staffs of all have my deepest thanks for their kindness.

A particular debt of gratitude is owed to the following individuals:

John R. Sellers of the Manuscript Division of the Library of Congress granted me permission to examine the actual manuscript pages of Carman's text whenever the limitations of archival microfilm were reached. Around the corner in the Serial and Government Publications Division, his colleague G. Travis Westly was equally helpful in locating individual issues of rare nineteenth century newspapers. At the National Archives, Jill Abraham and Trevor K. Plante of the Old Military and Civil Records Division were kind enough to allow me access to Carman's original correspondence with survivors of the campaign when the microfilmed edition proved unavailable, and on several occasions they volunteered to unearth long-undisturbed documents in order to allay my doubts concerning the accuracy of published versions. Robert K. Krick, John M. Coski, Richard J. Sommers, and Robert E. L. Krick, gifted historians all, were gracious in sharing their expertise, no matter how arcane or convoluted my questions. Ezra Carman's modern-day successor at Antietam National Battlefield, Ted Alexander, was an early champion of this book. His enthusiasm cemented the decision to commit myself to a daunting editorial task. He not only placed both the park's vertical files and his own encyclopedic knowledge at my disposal but also provided the cover art and frontispiece for this volume. My longtime friend and fellow Civil War enthusiast Dennis A. Buttacavoli was open with his time and his substantial private collection, fielding a barrage of e-mail queries with the diligence of any reference librarian. Daniel S. Levy volunteered much needed logistical assistance in obtaining materials located in New York City, while John J. Fox III shared his insights into the fate of the 35th Georgia in Maryland.

Dave Grabarek of the Library of Virginia's Inter-Library Loan Division routinely performed miracles on my behalf, locating items of such obscurity that in a number of instances the eventual lenders did not at first believe they owned the materials in question. His persistence and exactitude assured that my every research need was met. Without his aid, this project would have foundered long ago, and the extent of my debt to him is incalculable.

William C. Davis and Crandall Shifflett shared their expertise on the economics and customary practices of the academic publishing market and provided much-appreciated guidance in deciphering the arcana of contract boilerplate.

At Routledge, Kimberly Guinta was as quick to recognize the uniqueness of this project as she was willing to read an unsolicited proposal from someone not possessed of the traditional curriculum vitae. She allowed the work to speak for itself, for which I shall be forever grateful. Takisha L. Jackson and Mimi Williams managed the Herculean labor of shepherding more than 400,000 words through production despite my constitutional inability to stop making changes, and Matthew Kopel eased my passage through the numerous administrative stages of the publishing process. Having spent more than a few years on their side of the desk, I have a keen appreciation of the amount of labor *The Maryland Campaign of September 1862* demanded from them all.

Finally, there is my wife, Kimberly, who permits my dallying behind a keyboard. *Sola in me semper credidit.*

Joseph Pierro
Hanover County, Virginia

About the Author

Ezra Ayers Carman was born in Middlesex County, New Jersey, on February 27, 1834. He received a B.A. from the Western Military Institute in Drennon Springs, Kentucky, in 1855, and remained with the institution as an associate professor of mathematics when it relocated to Tennessee that same year and became the University of Nashville. He received his M.A. from the university in 1858 and then returned to New Jersey, where he worked as a bookkeeper until the outbreak of the Civil War.

Ill health and family responsibilities led Carman to refuse a proffered captaincy during the initial call for volunteers, but his interest in the Union cause was strong enough to draw him to the outskirts of Washington, D.C., in time to witness the war's first major engagement at Bull Run on July 21, 1861. Returning to his native state, Carman accepted a commission in September as lieutenant colonel of the 7th New Jersey and served with the regiment until May 5, 1862, when he received a gunshot wound to his right arm during the fighting near Williamsburg, Virginia. He returned home to recuperate, and while there he accepted on July 8, 1862, the colonelcy of a new regiment still in the process of recruitment, the 13th New Jersey.

Carman led his green troops into their first battle at Antietam that September, and he remained on the rolls of the regiment for the remainder of the war. He was twice detached to serve as temporary brigade commander and from February to March 1864 was again separated from his unit to serve as post commander at Tullahoma, Tennessee. While supporting a battery of artillery at Kennesaw Mountain, Georgia, on June 27, 1864, Carman was injured in the line of duty once more, when a nearby explosion of shells caused him to suffer a loss of hearing in his left ear. By the time he was mustered out of Federal service on June 8, 1865, he had participated in twenty-three battles, and for his "gallant and meritorious services during the war" he was awarded the brevet of brigadier general in the U.S. Volunteers (to rank March 13, 1865).

Returning to civilian life, he pursued a living in the New Jersey lumber trade until 1870, when he obtained a series of state government posts. In 1877 he was appointed chief clerk in the U.S. Department of Agriculture, a position he retained until 1885. Throughout these two decades, he was an active member of numerous veterans' organizations and began assembling material for a number of projects (none of which were ever published), including a study of the 1861 campaign in western Virginia, a history of the Twentieth Corps, and an account of the Atlanta campaign.

It was Antietam, however, that would come to occupy the largest share of his efforts as a historian. Within weeks of the fighting he toured various sections of the field, interviewed local inhabitants and Confederate prisoners, and began the barest preparations for a map and narrative of the battle—projects he would continue to perfect for nearly half a century. His interest assumed an official character in the immediate aftermath of the war when, on April 23, 1866, he was appointed by the governor of New Jersey to serve as that state's trustee in the Antietam National Cemetery Association, a multistate entity formed under the direction of the Maryland legislature to purchase and develop a suitable section of the battlefield for the interment of Union dead who fell in the surrounding counties. Carman remained on the board of trustees until 1877, when ownership and maintenance of the cemetery were transferred formally to the U.S. War Department.

In 1890 the Federal government authorized an expansion of the Cemetery Association's earlier work, establishing Antietam National Battlefield and authorizing a new "Antietam Board" to mark the battle lines of the two armies. Carman's initial attempt to gain a position on the two-man panel was unsuccessful. When an opening appeared in 1894, he reapplied and on October 8 was appointed by the secretary of war as one of four commissioners on an expanded board and given the title of historical expert. His primary mission was to gather as much information from survivors as possible, and over the ensuing years he carried on a tremendous correspondence with hundreds of fellow veterans of the battle, supplemented by oral interviews and walking tours of the field with his subjects. Completion of the congressional mandate proved more costly than was expected, and by August 1895 the Antietam Board had exhausted its appropriated funds. The War Department economized by discharging Carman and one other commissioner, but such was Carman's dedication that he successfully petitioned the secretary of war to continue working in a volunteer capacity. The following year, Congress appropriated additional funding, rehiring the two commissioners from July 1 to December 31, 1896, to finalize any outstanding tasks.

The final report of the Antietam Board was presented to the secretary of war on March 18, 1898. Under Carman's direction, the text for 238 historical markers had been written. Erected near the unit positions established by his research, these iron tablets continue to this day to narrate the actions of the Union and Confederate commands. In 1904, the War Department published the *Atlas of the Battlefield of Antietam*: fourteen plates detailing the course of the fighting, with "Positions of troops by Gen. E. A. Carman." (A second edition, incorporating corrections and new findings by Carman, was released in 1908.) These maps form the basis of all subsequent understandings of the tactical evolutions during what remains the bloodiest day (in terms of American casualties) in U.S. history.[1]

Although Carman maintained an interest in Antietam (continuing to make changes to the markers as late as 1906), his official focus shifted to the western theater of the war. In June 1905 he was appointed to one of three seats on the Chickamauga-Chattanooga Park Commission, then was named its chairman in 1908. He died of complications from pneumonia on Christmas Day the following year in Washington, D.C. He is buried in Arlington National Cemetery.[2]

---

[1] The noticeable absence of any maps in Carman's original manuscript likely is due to his expectation that cartographic needs would be met by the publication of the *Atlas*. Both editions are long out of print and hard to locate today, though the Library of Congress has recently scanned the entirety of the 1904 original as part of its "American Memory" digital archive. Library of Congress, "Atlas of the Battlefield of Antietam," http://hdl.loc.gov/loc.gmd/g3842am.gcw0247000 (last accessed June 18, 2007). The library's Digital Reference Team has assured the editor that the second edition will be scanned and included in "American Memory" eventually.

[2] Information for this sketch was drawn from the following: typescript biography of Ezra A. Carman, folder 6, Ezra Ayers Carman Papers, New Jersey Historical Society, Newark, N.J.; Carman, "The Battle of Williamsburg: A Personal Account," Ezra Ayers Carman Papers; diary of Carman (1862–63), Ezra Ayers Carman Papers; Compiled Service Record of Carman, 7th New Jersey Infantry, Carded Records Showing Military Service of Soldiers Who Fought in Volunteer Organizations During the American Civil War, 1890–1912, Record Group 94, National Archives; Compiled Service Record of Carman, 13th New Jersey Infantry; Survivor's Pension Record of Carman (application no. 203,511; certificate no. 141,349), Case Files of Approved Pension Applications of Veterans Who Served in the Army and Navy Mainly in the Civil War and The War With Spain ("Civil War and Later Survivors' Certificates"): Nos. SC 9,487– 999,999, 1861–1934, Record Group 15, National Archives; Widow's Pension Record of Carman (application no. 932,937; certificate no. 695,625), Case Files of Approved Pension Applications of Widows and Other Veterans of the Army and Navy Who Served Mainly in the Civil War and The War With Spain ("Civil War and Later Widows' Certificates"): Nos. WC 2–1,651,647, 1861–1934; Record Group 15, National Archives; General Correspondence, 1859–1899, boxes 1 and 2, Ezra A. Carman Papers, Manuscripts and Archives Division, New York Public Library; Charles W. Snell and Sharon A. Brown, *Antietam National Battlefield and National Cemetery: An Administrative History* (Washington, D.C.: U.S. Department of the Interior/National Park Service, 1986), 1–113.

Editor's Note

Despite its immense size and scope, little is known about the editorial history of *The Maryland Campaign of September 1862* itself. The bulk of Carman's research presumably occurred after his appointment to the Antietam Board in 1894, though his interest in writing a history of the battle can be traced to the weeks immediately following the event, and surviving letters among his papers show that he began soliciting memoirs from other Antietam participants as early as 1877. Nor can a terminal date be established for his writing. Carman is known to have been collecting unpublished material for this project as late as December 1902 (see p. 301 n. 7). Quotations from works copyrighted in 1905 appear at several points in the narrative, but no references to its completion have been found in Carman's surviving correspondence. Internal evidence demonstrates that the manuscript passed through a number of drafts, and it may not even be the case that Carman considered the book to be in its final form at the time of his death.

For purposes of this edition, the more than 1,400-page manuscript deposited at the Library of Congress in 1912 has been treated as the author's final draft of a secondary source intended for publication. The result, therefore, is not a mere transcription of Carman's work. It has undergone editing consistent with the treatment routinely afforded final text submitted by an author to a publisher. Scrupulous care has been taken in this process to balance enhanced readability with the preservation of Carman's intent and meaning.

Punctuation and spelling have been standardized throughout Carman's writing; in quotations they reflect the idiosyncrasies of the original source material. Numbers have been rendered according to modern editorial practices. Forenames and ranks have been inserted upon the introduction of participants in the narrative. Unwieldy run-on sentences have been broken up by periods or semicolons. Digressions have been placed in parentheses. Some paragraph breaks have been inserted or removed as necessary. Imprecise pronouns have been replaced in a few instances with their specific antecedents. Some of Carman's more opaque constructions of grammar have necessitated the shifting of clauses within a sentence, and his fondness for the endless strings of participles has at times been replaced with the judicious substitution of a verb in the perfect active indicative. In a handful of places, a synonym has been inserted into repetitious phrases. The only sizeable excision from the entire manuscript as originally written is one block quotation of approximately one and a half pages, which Carman inserted again to better effect in its entirety in the very next chapter. (The specifics of this excision are discussed in a note at the relevant point in the text.) A responsible editor in Carman's own time would have done no less.

Unit and geographic designations have been standardized through the text; explanation of any resulting alterations has been made in the notes. Regiments and battalions are assumed to be infantry units unless otherwise designated. As batteries, battalions, brigades, and divisions of the Army of Northern Virginia were identified formally by the name of their commanders at the time of the Maryland campaign, these have been capitalized in the text (Jackson's Division), while similar designations for components of the Army of the Potomac have been rendered in lowercase (Hooker's corps). Only when the unit type forms a part of the formal designation of a Federal unit (Fifth Corps, Kanawha Division) has it been capitalized. Niggling questions of precision aside, it is hoped that this cosmetic alternation will render the text more manageable to readers who have not committed the tables of organization of the two armies to memory.

The fifteen appendices that conclude this volume represent a change from Carman's initial ordering of the work. These sections (largely statistical and tabular data) were interspersed throughout the original manuscript. The editor is confident that this decision provides a more coherent and uninterrupted flow to Carman's narrative while assigning this supporting material a single, easy to find location. The original positions of each appendix are marked in the notes.

The editor has made every effort to double check all quotations against their source material. Slight errors in transcription by Carman have been corrected without comment; those of a more substantive nature have been addressed in the notes. Quotations running eight or more lines in the editor's typescript have been rendered here as block quotations. For the purpose of editorial consistency, Carman's habit of beginning quotations with a capital letter if the quotation forms a complete sentence (even if only part of a sentence in the original source) has been retained without employing square brackets. Similarly, his habit of ending the final sentence of all quotations with a single full stop, even when the sentence continues in the original, has been retained—though not before the editor ensured that the omission did not change the meaning of the quoted portion. (In the few instances where such changes of meaning occur, they are addressed in an appropriate note.) Excisions from within a quotation, however, have been marked with ellipses (a practice Carman frequently omitted), using the three-dot rule throughout.

With regard to explicit citations, the conventions of scholarship in Carman's time were far less exacting and rigorous than prevail today—a fact regrettable but unchangeable. To attempt to reconstruct the precise chain of evidence employed by the author for every sentence nearly a century after his death was deemed an impossible chore. In the absence of a complete bibliography, a definitive accounting of each source employed by Carman cannot be constructed. Further, it must be borne in mind that Carman was not only a participant in the campaign but that he also conducted innumerable interviews (formal and informal) with others in the decades that followed. The cumulative weight of the data gathered in nonwritten forms, and its impact upon the final product, is likely as significant as it is immeasurable.

What the editor has done instead is endeavor to locate the source of all materials quoted directly within the manuscript or referenced by the author. (Instances of the latter range from explicit mentions in marginal notes of authors, titles, and page numbers to cryptic messages such as "A biographer says …" or "One soldier writes ….") Whenever he has been successful, he has provided a citation in keeping with the standards of modern scholarship. Carman's explanatory notes (as separate from those of the editor) are designated "—EAC," though any complete citations to sources within them are the product of the editor. Citations are also provided for passages where the editor has discovered language so similar to that found in another work that the latter is obviously the unique source for Carman's statement.

Despite exhaustive searching, the source of some quotations has proved elusive; it is hoped that these will be uncovered in the future. (It may also be the case that they are from correspondence no longer extant, the product of Carman's oral interviews, or—as is discussed further in the notes—that these "quotations" are in fact paraphrases by Carman of statements that appeared in the third person in the source material.) Having weighed carefully the absence of such citations in a published manuscript against the continued absence of Carman's entire work from library shelves, the editor concluded that withholding the release of the book until every last source could be unearthed would contradict the very reason he began this project: his surety that Carman's narrative is an essential resource for any examination of the Maryland campaign and that the present difficulty in accessing the manuscript, even with its flaws, is an obstacle to scholarship.

Finally, the editor has not sought to use Carman's work as a springboard for engaging the totality of primary sources pertaining to the Maryland campaign—to say nothing of the extensive historiography since generated. Both tasks are admirable and could well engage the attention of a lifetime, but they transcend the scope of this effort. Neither has he intended to deconstruct Carman's entire manuscript in the context of a comprehensive critical study. His wish from the beginning has been merely to make Carman's text readily available for scholars and enthusiasts alike to engage on its own terms: as the definitive account of how the campaign was understood by the man who literally cast its official history in iron.

1
Maryland

In the early days of the War of the Rebellion, Maryland was represented by the Southern people as a weeping maiden, bound and fettered, seeking relief from the cruel fate that had deprived her of liberty and forced her to an unholy and unnatural alliance with the North. Southern orators and writers debated largely and eloquently on her wrongs, sentiment and song were invoked to save her, and General Robert E. Lee records that one of the objects of his campaign of September 1862 was, by military succor, to aid her in any efforts she might be disposed to make to recover her liberties.[1] It is well, therefore, before entering upon the narrative of the military campaign, to consider the condition of the state and see what liberties had been taken from her and wherein she had been oppressed.

Maryland was at heart a loyal state, although she had much sympathy with her Southern sisters. Her position was a peculiar one. Bounded on her entire southern border by Virginia, having the same interest in slavery, closely connected with her by business interests and family ties, she watched the course of that state with great anxiety. Slavery was the source of much of her wealth, and she had a greater financial interest at stake in the preservation of the Union, with slavery, than any other Southern state. It is estimated that the value of the slaves in the state in 1861 was fully fifty million dollars, and her proximity to free territory made them a very precarious kind of property. The largest slaveholding counties were those adjacent to Washington and in the southern part of the state. Like Virginia, a part of her territory was bordered by free states, and the free state of Pennsylvania had the same effect on Maryland that free Ohio had on western Virginia. After the secession of the cotton states, many, believing the Union hopelessly divided, favored a grand Middle Confederacy stretching from the Atlantic to the Pacific, leaving out the seceded states and New England. The best men of Baltimore and of the state opposed secession; they as strongly opposed coercion. They desired to be strictly neutral. Many were ready to make common cause with the seceded states should North Carolina, Kentucky, Tennessee, and Virginia take a position of resistance to the Federal government. Like the other border states and states north and west, a majority of her people could not and did not appreciate the impending crisis and fondly hoped that the Union might be preserved. The state had been faithful in the observance of all its constitutional obligations, was conciliatory in all its actions, and had kept aloof from the extreme schemes of the Southern leaders. It was as little disposed to take political lessons from South Carolina as from Massachusetts, and it is safe to say that four-fifths of her people regarded the action of South Carolina and other cotton states as rash and uncalled for. But they were almost unanimous against coercion.

Immediately after the election of Abraham Lincoln, Maryland governor Thomas H. Hicks[2] was solicited to call an extra session of the legislature to consider the condition of the country and determine what course should be taken. The secessionists had made a careful canvass and found that a majority of that body were in full sympathy with them and would act according to their dictation, could they be convened. Their intention was to have a convention similar to those by which South Carolina and other states had been declared out of the Union. Hicks well knew the designs of these men and refused to convene the legislature, again and again refusing when repeatedly urged and threatened. It was also urged upon him by those who honestly believed that Maryland, by a wise and conservative course, could control events, that she had influence with the North and South, and that this influence could be exercised to promote harmony. But the greatest pressure came from those who desired an expression of sympathy with the South, those who would have the state follow the example of South Carolina.

---

1   Robert E. Lee to Samuel Cooper, August 19, 1863, reprinted in U.S. War Department, comp., *War of the Rebellion: A Compilation of the Official Records of the Union and Confederate Armies* (Washington, D.C.: Government Printing Office, 1880–1901), ser. 1, vol. 19, pt. 1, 144 (hereafter *OR*; all subsequent citations are to series 1 unless noted otherwise). See also Lee to Jefferson Davis, September 3, 1863, reprinted in *OR*, vol. 19, pt. 2, 590–91; Lee to Davis, September 5, 1862, reprinted in *OR*, vol. 19, pt. 2, 593–94.

2   The son of a prosperous farmer from Maryland's Eastern Shore, Thomas Holliday Hicks (1798–1865) spent nearly the whole of his adult life in public service. A former county sheriff, registrar of wills, state assemblyman, and delegate to the state's 1850 constitutional convention, Hicks had begun his political career as a Democrat before moving (with many of his fellow Maryland slaveholders) into the Whig camp in the 1840s. When that party collapsed during the political realignments of the 1850s, Hicks then joined the American or "Know-Nothing" Party and, as its standard-bearer, was elected governor in 1858.

On the twenty-seventh of November, Hicks, in a letter to ex-governor Thomas G. Pratt[3] and others, replied to these urgent appeals, declining to convene the legislature for reasons that he fully set forth. He did not consider the election of Lincoln, who was fairly and constitutionally chosen, a sufficient cause for the secession of any state, and he purposed to give the Lincoln administration proper support. He knew from personal observation that an immense majority of all parties were decidedly opposed to the assemblage of the legislature. He would at least wait until Virginia acted. He would await the action of the national executive, whose duty it was to look not to Maryland alone, but to the entire Union. He believed that to convene the legislature would have the effect to increase and revive the excitement pervading the country, then apparently on the decline.[4]

A large and influential body of the people believed in the governor and confided in his judgment. He was born and lived in a slaveholding county of the state, was himself a slave-holder, and had always identified himself with the extreme southern wing of the Whig party. In hearty sympathy with those who were defending Southern rights, he was opposed to the policy of secession and distrusted those who were leading in that direction. With some apparent inconsistencies, he was, however, a Union man, and his persistent refusal to call an extra session of the legislature at that time doubtless prevented the secession of Maryland and performed an estimable service to the Union and to the cause of humanity.

In the appointment of commissioners by the seceding states, Maryland was specially remembered. On December 19, 1860, the commissioner from Mississippi, Alexander Handy,[5] addressed the citizens of Baltimore on the object and purposes of the secessionists.[6] Upon his arrival in Maryland, he had asked the governor to convene the legislature for the purpose of counseling with the constituted authorities of Mississippi, as represented by himself. The very day Handy was addressing the citizens of Baltimore on the peculiar designs of the secessionists, Hicks was writing him that the state, though "unquestionably identified with the Southern States, in feeling[,] … is also conservative, and, above all things devoted to the Union of these States under the Constitution." The people intended "to uphold that Union," and he could not consent, "by any precipitate or revolutionary action," to aid in its dismemberment.[7]

Handy was a native of Maryland, and his speech to the people of Baltimore on the nineteenth made a deep impression— of which those in sympathy with the South took quick advantage. They called a meeting for December 22 at the Universalist Church to "take some action in regard to convening the legislature." The meeting was fully attended, and a free interchange of opinion resulted in the appointment of a committee to wait upon the governor. The committee discharged this duty on Christmas Eve and urged him to convene the legislature.[8] They used taunts and threatened him. They intimated fears for his personal safety should he decline their request, said that blood would be shed and Lincoln not permitted to be inaugurated. To which, the governor responded that he was a Southern man but could not see the necessity for shedding blood or convening the legislature.

Following this there were meetings in Anne Arundel, Prince George's, Queen Anne, St. Mary's, Charles and other counties of the state, with resolutions demanding an extra session. Public meetings and strong resolutions were supplemented by personal appeals and social blandishments, but all to no purpose. The governor would not yield.

---

3   Thomas George Pratt (1804–69) served as governor from 1845 to 1848, where he demonstrated such devotion to the national government's policy of war with Mexico that Maryland raised more troops than the United States could accept into service. Following his governorship he served in the U.S. Senate for seven years, only to be denied re-election in 1856 when the "Know-Nothings" (whose nativist policies he opposed) came into power in the state. Initially a Whig, the years after the collapse of that party saw him gravitate toward the southern Democrats, and he supported the candidacy of John C. Breckinridge in the election of 1860.

4   See Thomas H. Hicks to Thomas G. Pratt, Sprigg Harwood, J. S. Franklin, N. H. Green, Llewellyn Boyle, and J. Pinkney, November 27, 1860, reprinted as "Letter from Governor Hicks, Refusing to Convene the Maryland Legislature," *Baltimore Sun*, November 29, 1860.

5   Seeking greater opportunity than was available to him as a lawyer in Maryland, Alexander Hamilton Handy (1809–83) moved to Mississippi in 1836 and there built up a successful law practice before winning election as a Democrat to the state's High Court of Errors and Appeals in 1853.

6   See "Mississippi to Maryland," *Baltimore Sun*, December 19, 1860, 2; "Mississippi to Maryland—Meeting at the Maryland Institute Hall," *Baltimore Sun*, December 20, 1860, 1; and Frank Moore, ed., *The Rebellion Record: A Diary of American Events*, vol. 1 (New York: G. P. Putnam, 1861), Diary of Events, 3.

7   In his original manuscript, Carman amalgamated these phrases and presented them as a single, direct quotation. See Hicks to Alexander H. Handy, December 19, 1860, reprinted as "Reply of the Governor of Maryland to the Commissioner from Mississippi," in Moore, Documents and Narratives, 1. See also "Reply of Gov. Hicks to the Commissioner of Mississippi," *Washington Star*, December 22, 1860; "The National Crisis," *Baltimore Sun*, December 24, 1860.

8   See "A Demonstration in Baltimore," *Baltimore Sun*, December 24, 1860.

From Alabama came as commissioner Jabez L. M. Curry, a minister, former member of Congress, and a man of character and ability.[9] Hicks was absent from the capital, but Curry informed him that, as a commissioner from the sovereign state of Alabama to the sovereign state of Maryland, he came to advise and consult with the governor and legislature as to what was to be done to protect the rights, interests, and honor of the slaveholding states; to secure concert and effectual cooperation between Maryland and Alabama; to "'secure ... a mutual league, united thought and counsels,' between those whose hopes and hazards" were "alike joined in the enterprise of accomplishing deliverance from Abolition domination"; and to oppose that anti-slavery "fanaticism," that "sentiment of the sinfulness of slavery ... embedded in the Northern conscience," that "infidel theory" corrupting "the Northern heart." "To unite with the seceding States," said the sanguine commissioner, "is to be their peers as confederates and have an identity of interests, protection of property and superior advantages in the contests for the markets, a monopoly of which has been enjoyed by the North. To refuse union with the seceding States is to accept inferiority, to be deprived of an outlet for surplus slaves, and to remain in a hostile Government in a hopeless minority and remediless dependence."[10]

On the sixth day of January, 1861, the governor appealed to the people in these words:

I firmly believe that a division of this Government would inevitably produce civil war ... We are told by the leading spirits of the South Carolina Convention, that neither the election of Mr. Lincoln nor the non-execution of the Fugitive Slave law, nor both combined, constitute their grievances. They declare that the real cause of their discontent dates as far back as 1833. Maryland, and every other State in the Union, with a united voice, then declared the cause insufficient to justify the course of South Carolina. Can it be that this people, who then unanimously supported the cause of General [Andrew] Jackson, will now yield their opinions at the bidding of modern Secessionists? ... That Maryland is a conservative Southern State all know who know any thing of her people or her history. The business and agricultural classes—planters, merchants, mechanics, and laboring men—those who have a real stake in the community, who would be forced to pay the taxes and do the fighting, are the persons who should be heard in preference to excited politicians, many of whom, having nothing to lose from the destruction of the Government, may hope to derive some gain from the ruin of the State. Such men will naturally urge you to pull down the pillars of this "accursed Union," which their allies in the North have denominated a "covenant with Hell."

The people of Maryland, if left to themselves, would decide, with scarcely an exception, that there is nothing in the present causes of complaint to justify immediate secession; and yet, against our judgments and solemn convictions of duty, we are to be precipitated into this revolution, because South Carolina thinks differently. Are we not equals? Or shall her opinions control our actions? After we have solemnly declared for ourselves, as every man must do, are we to be forced to yield our opinions to those of another State, and thus, in effect, obey her mandates? She refuses to wait for our counsels. Are we bound to obey her commands?

The men who have embarked in this scheme to convene the Legislature will spare no pains to carry their point. The whole plan of operations in the event of assembling the Legislature is, as I have been informed, already marked out, the list of Embassadors [sic] who are to visit the other States is agreed on, and the resolutions which they hope will be passed by the Legislature, fully committing this State to secession, are said to be already prepared.

In the course of nature I cannot have long to live, and I fervently trust to be allowed to end my days a citizen of this glorious Union. But should I be compelled to witness the downfall of that Government inherited from our fathers, established, as it were, by the special favor of God, I will at least have the consolation, at my dying hour, that I neither by word or deed assisted in hastening its disruption.[11]

---

9 Jabez Lamar Monroe Curry (1825–1903) was born in Lincoln County, Georgia, and spent his teens in Talladega County, Alabama. He studied law at Harvard College (where his classmates included future general and president Rutherford B. Hayes). A self-described "adherent of the Calhoun school of politics," he returned to Alabama after graduation and served at different times during the pre-war years in both the Alabama legislature and the U.S. House of Representatives. (A stint as a private with the Texas Rangers during the Mexican War was curtailed due to ill health.) With Alabama's secession, Curry left his congressional seat in Washington to help form the new Confederate States government in Montgomery.

10 Jabez L. M. Curry to Hicks, December 28, 1860, reprinted in OR, ser. 4. vol. 1, 38–42.

11 Selections from Hicks's remarks, including all of the passages quoted by Carman, appear in "Union Address of the Governor of Maryland," Harper's Weekly, January 19, 1861, 39. See also "An Address to the People of Maryland by Governor Hicks," Baltimore Sun, January 7, 1861; "Extract from Gov. Hicks' Address," in Moore, Documents and Narratives, 17–18.

The governor had a powerful supporter in the person of Henry Winter Davis, a representative in Congress from the city of Baltimore.[12] On the second of January, Davis issued a strong appeal to the voters of his district, taking ground against the calling of the legislature or the assembling of a border state convention. He denied that Maryland had been wronged by the general government and asserted that her interests were indissolubly connected with the integrity of the United States. She had not an interest that would survive the government under the Constitution. "Peaceful secession is a delusion," said Davis,

and if you yield to the arts now employed to delude you, the soil of Maryland will be trampled by armies struggling for the national capital ...

If the present government be destroyed, Maryland slaveholders lose the only guarantee for the return of their slaves. Every commercial line of communication is severed. Custom-house barriers arrest her merchants at every frontier. Her commerce on the ocean is the prey of every pirate, or the sport of every maritime power. Her great rail-road loses every connection which makes it valuable ...

Free trade will open every port, and cotton and woolen factories, and the iron and machine works of Maryland would be prostrate before European competition.

The hope held out to them by the secessionists that Baltimore would be the emporium of a Southern republic was a delusion too ridiculous to need refutation; nothing intended for the South would ever pass Norfolk. He opposed the calling of the legislature because the halls of legislation would immediately become the focus of revolutionary conspiracy. "Under specious pretexts, the people will be implicated, by consultations with other States, by concerted plans, by inadmissible demands, by extreme and offensive pretensions, in a deeply-laid scheme of simultaneous revolt, in the event of the inevitable failure to impose on the free States the ultimatum of the slave States. Maryland will find herself severed from more than half the States, plunged in anarchy, and wrapped in the flames of civil war, waged by her against the government in which we now glory." In the face of such circumstances, he contended, there was no justification, no excuse, for convening the legislature. Within its constitutional powers it would do nothing, and there was nothing for it to do.

As to a meeting of the border states, Davis was utterly opposed to it; the Constitution forbade any agreement between Maryland and any other states for any purpose. He warned his constituents against the agitation of subjects in which they had no earthly interest, which was of no practical purpose to them:

If by common consent any change can be made which will silence clamor, or soothe the sensibilities, or satisfy the jealousies excited by the recent contest, let *that* change be made. But that is the only interest you have in any change; and if none can be obtained of *that character*, it is our policy to let the question alone, and to make others let it alone ...

The firm attitude of Maryland is now the chief hope of peace. If you firmly adhere to the United States against all enemies, resolved to obey the Constitution and see it obeyed, your example will arrest the spirit of revolution, and greatly aid the government in restoring, without bloodshed, its authority. If Maryland yield [sic] to this revolutionary clamor, she will be overcome in a few months in the struggle for the national capital; and her young men, torn from the pursuits of peace, excluded from the closed work-shop and counting-house, must shoulder the musket to guard their homes at the cost of fraternal blood.[13]

---

[12] The life and career of Henry Winter Davis (1817–65), the son of an Episcopalian minister, was influenced dramatically by the ouster of his outspokenly Federalist father from his post as president of St. John's College (Maryland) in 1828 by trustees loyal to Democrat Andrew Jackson—an act that engendered a deep antipathy for the Democratic Party in the young Davis. With family fortunes strained by the removal, Davis struggled to assemble the funds necessary to study law at the University of Virginia. Successful in this endeavor, he moved to Alexandria, Virginia, in 1840 and set up a soon-thriving practice. He campaigned for Winfield Scott, the Whig nominee for president, in 1852, and in 1855 was elected to Congress as a "Know-Nothing." He steered a middle course on the issue of slavery in the territories for as long as possible, but the increasing polarization of national politics and the demise of the American Party left him less and less room in which to maneuver. In January 1860 he had his revenge against the Democrats by voting with the Republicans to break a seven-week deadlock in the elections for Speaker of the House. Later that year he campaigned for the Bell-Everett Constitutional Union ticket and was instrumental in assuring the victory of pro-Union Thomas H. Hicks as governor. Bitterly opposed to the proposition that secession was legal, Davis gained national fame for his outspoken defense of the Union and the need to place Federal forts in the hands of avowedly loyal men.

[13] See "Address to the Voters of the Fourth Congressional District," in Henry W. Davis, *Speeches and Addresses Delivered in the Congress of the United States, and on Several Public Occasions* (New York: Harper & Brothers, 1867), 187–98.

Much in the same vein wrote another of her patriotic sons:

Maryland has no future out of the Union. It is impossible, in the event of a separation, that she should go with the South or with the North. As a member of a Southern Confederacy she would be a slave State without a single slave in her borders, and a Southern State on the wrong side of the division line. As a member of a Northern Confederacy, her fellowship would be far away from her sympathies … It is indeed by no means certain that her territory would not be split in two, and the parts of it go off in opposite directions. Baltimore would be a provincial town, with the grass growing in her streets, and the fox looking out of the window … Maryland has in her keeping the capital of the nation. It was confided to her by George Washington. To the great duty of its safe keeping she has been consecrated by an authority but one remove a little lower than the Divine. Like the sons of Aaron and the tribe of Levi, she has the charge of the tabernacle and the holy things of the temple; and let the storm come, let the earthquake come, and they will find her faithful and true to her charge.[14]

The progress of affairs in Maryland was watched with the keenest interest in the North, and Hicks was urged by many of its prominent men to resist every attempt of those who were seeking to have the legislature convened. Among these was Governor Charles S. Olden of New Jersey, who wrote early in January imploring him not to yield to the demands of the "secessionists" and expressing the belief, shared by many others, that "the peaceful inauguration of Mr. Lincoln depends on the firmness of your Excellency."

The secession element grew stronger and the leaders more and more impatient at the governor's refusal to convoke the legislature. They insisted that their representatives should, in body assembled, give expression to the will of the state. "They insisted," one prominent secessionist recalled, "that their representatives should meet, so as to act for them as occasion might require. If Virginia seceded, then to join Maryland to Virginia in one common destiny, for weal or for woe. If the Middle States submitted, then to place Maryland side by side with them in protecting the Gulf States from war."[15]

It was anticipated by these men that any expression would be that of full sympathy with the South and a call for a state convention. As the governor was immovable, some of the most ardent friends of the South hit upon the plan of holding what they pleased to term a sovereign convention. St. Mary's, Prince George's, and Charles Counties, the three strongest slave counties in the state, elected delegates to a convention to be held in January. Citizens of Frederick County, led by some of the young men—prominent among whom was Bradley T. Johnson[16]—held a meeting on January 8, issued an address to the people, called a convention for February 22, and elected delegates to it. Meanwhile, the Union men of the state were not inactive. They held Union meetings in country, town, and city, and five thousand citizens of Baltimore united in a letter to Hicks approving his course in declining to convene the legislature. On the evening of January 10, an immense Union meeting was held at the Maryland Institute, which was addressed by Reverdy Johnson,[17] Augustus W. Bradford, W. H. Collins, and others. Resolutions were adopted expressive of Maryland's love for the Union, of her hopes of peace by concession and compromise, and in support of the position assumed by Hicks. This meeting, the most important as to numbers and respectability that had ever assembled in Baltimore, quickened the Union sentiment.[18]

On the same day that this imposing Union meeting was held, a conference took place in the Law Building "relative to the threatening condition of public affairs." All parts of the state were represented, and after a conference of two days the Crittenden compromise measures were approved and a committee appointed to wait on the governor and solicit him to

---

[14] As of this writing, Carman's source for this unattributed quotation has not been identified.

[15] Bradley T. Johnson, "Memoir of First Maryland Regiment," *Southern Historical Society Papers* 9 (1881): 346.

[16] The grandson of a Revolutionary War officer, Bradley Tyler Johnson (1829–1903) was born in Frederick, Maryland. Educated at Princeton, he returned south, studied law, and was admitted to the Maryland Bar in 1851. He became active in Democratic politics, holding a number of offices in the pre-war years, including the chairmanship of the state Democratic Committee. His subsequent participation in the war, as it relates to the scope of this study, is treated in the text.

[17] Reverdy Johnson (1796–1876) was born in Annapolis, read law under his father's guidance, and was admitted to the Maryland Bar in 1815. He moved to Baltimore two years later and spent the better part of the next sixty years as an active member of that city's legal community. Frequently retained as counsel in constitutional cases, his most famous appearance before the Supreme Court came from his successful appearance for the defense in *Dred Scott v. John F. A. Sandford*, 60 U.S. 393 (1856). He was a passionate Whig for the duration of that party's existence, then spent the rest of his life as a moderate southern Democrat and an opponent of the right of secession. He served in the U.S. Senate and then as attorney general under Zachary Taylor, resigning upon the president's death. During the antebellum crisis, he urged compromise and was a member of the abortive Washington Peace Conference of 1861. Elected to the Maryland House of Delegates in 1861, he worked to keep Maryland in the Union.

[18] See "Great Union Demonstration at Maryland Institute Hall," *Baltimore Sun*, January 11, 1861.

issue a proclamation calling on the people to vote whether a convention should, or should not, be called.[19] The committee went to Annapolis on the twelfth, where they had a long interview with the governor and urged his immediate action on this request.[20] They were sure that the position of Maryland was misunderstood, both at the South and at the North, that the failure of the people to declare themselves was construed in the South as a determination to make no further struggle against the advance of abolitionism, while at the North it was construed as an admission of the justice of Republicanism and an acquiescence in its teachings. They magnified the importance of their state by suggesting that, through the influence of Maryland, "the extremists of the South might be persuaded to be more moderate, and the fanatics of the North compelled to be more just." But the governor turned a deaf ear to their entreaty; he declined to issue the proclamation. Meanwhile, prominent men took sides, openly declaring for and against secession, and again on the thirtieth of January the governor was appealed to, to convene the legislature in response to public meetings. The request came from the president of the Senate and the speaker of the House of Delegates, but was refused.

As we have seen, much of the pressure for the secession of Maryland came from outside the state. The revolutionary spirits at the national capital, seeking to control events, advanced and maintained the idea that, if Maryland should secede, the District of Columbia would revert to the state by which it had been ceded to the general government. That the secession of Maryland was confidently relied upon by them is well known, and it was hoped that Washington could be seized before the inauguration of Lincoln. So at this time, increased pressure was brought to bear by outside parties.

At a large and enthusiastic meeting at Maryland Institute Hall on the evening of February 1, called by the citizens of Baltimore who were "in favor of restoring the Constitution of the Union of the States" and "who desire the position of Maryland in the existing crisis to be ascertained by a Convention of the People,"[21] resolutions were passed denouncing Hicks and calling a sovereign convention. Robert M. McLane declared, "By the Living God, if the administration shall dare to bring its Black Republican cohorts to the banks of the Susquehanna to coerce the South, that river shall run red with blood before the first man shall cross it. I for one pledge here my life and means to march with you to the banks of the Susquehanna to forbid the passage of these invaders." (Although a graduate of West Point, the speaker did not enter the military service on either side during the war.) Ex-governor Enoch L. Lowe insisted that Maryland should link her destiny with Virginia and at the proper time take possession of the District of Columbia. If the governor refused the demand for the assembling of the legislature and a convention of the people, he would raise the banner of revolt. He said, "If after Virginia and Tennessee have spoken and the loyal men of Maryland have spoken, he refuses, we will gibbet him."[22]

Pursuant to the action of this meeting, a convention was held by the states-rights men in the Universalist Church at Baltimore on the eighteenth of February to take advisory action on the state of the country. All the counties of the state were represented by able and influential men. The sense of the convention as expressed in resolutions offered by McLane and adopted was that "the secession of the seven slaveholding States from the Federal Union was induced by the aggression of the non-slaveholding States, in violation of the constitution of the United States." The moral and material interest and the geographical position of the state demanded that it should act with Virginia in the crisis, cooperating with that state "in all honorable efforts to maintain and defend the constitutional rights of its citizens in the Union, and failing in that, to associate with her in confederation with our sister States of the South." It further resolved that the honor of the state required that it should not permit its soil to be made a highway for Federal troops, sent to make war upon sister states of the South, and it was the expressed opinion of the convention that an attempt on the part of the Federal government to coerce the states that

---

[19] See "The Position of Maryland in the National Crisis—The Counties in Conference at the Law Buildings—Gov. Hicks and a Convention—Counter Resolutions, &c.," *Baltimore Sun*, January 11, 1861; "The Conference of the Counties on the National Crisis—The Resolutions Adopted—Committee to Request Gov. Hicks to Call a Convention—Speech of Hon. Isaac D. Jones on Coercion, &c.," *Baltimore Sun*, January 12, 1861.

On December 18, 1860, Senator John J. Crittenden of Kentucky introduced a series of Federal laws and irrevocable constitutional amendments in an attempt to fix a permanent solution to questions surrounding the institution of slavery and thereby prevent the breakup of the Union. Known as the "Crittenden Compromise," the major components of the plan called for a re-establishment of the Missouri Comprise line, congressional non-interference with slavery in the states, and strengthening of the Fugitive Slave Act. *Joint Resolution Proposing certain Amendments to the Constitution of the United States*, S. 50, 36th Cong., 2d sess., 1860 (*Congressional Globe*, 114). A prescient analysis of the objections likely to be raised by adherents of the various political parties to Crittenden's plan appeared the next day as "The New Compromise," *New York Times*, December 19, 1860.

[20] See "Interview with Gov. Hicks," *Baltimore Sun*, January 15, 1861.

[21] See *Speech of S. Teackle Wallis, Esq., as Delivered at the Maryland Institute on Friday Evening, February 1, 1861* (Baltimore: Murphy & Co., [1861]), 1.

[22] As of this writing, Carman's source for these statements is not known. They do not appear in any of the published addresses consulted by the editor.

had seceded would necessarily result in civil war and the destruction of the government itself.[23] After a session of two days the convention adjourned, to reassemble on March 12 unless in the meanwhile Virginia should take decided action; in that event the convention was to reassemble as soon as possible. While this conference was in session in Baltimore, a meeting was held in Howard County that was addressed by the speaker of the House of Delegates, and a resolution was adopted that "immediate steps ought to be taken for the establishment of a Southern Confederacy, by consultation and co-operation with such other Southern and slave States as may be ready therefore."[24]

Ambrose R. Wright, commissioner from Georgia, arrived at Baltimore on February 18, and one week thereafter, after two failures, succeeded in obtaining an interview with the governor and left for his consideration a long and able communication stating that he came to Maryland to urge upon her people the policy of secession from the power known as the United States and cooperation with the state of Georgia and other independent Southern states in the formation of a new confederation. In language that reads like a parody of the Declaration of Independence, he laid at the door of the Republican Party every political crime known to modern times and warned the governor and people of Maryland that "the irrepressible conflict with them is just begun. Their mission is to annihilate slavery from the American continent." Referring to the presence of U.S. troops in and around Washington and the adjoining states of Maryland and Virginia, he said:

> These are the overtures of peace extended to us now by the Northern Federal Government—[General-in-Chief Winfield] Scott and scorpions, cannon and cartridge …
>
> … By what bonds can such a people be held? They ignore the Bible, violate oaths, nullify the laws, and pharisaically [sic] call upon Jehovah to guide and support them in their infamous course.
>
> … [To redress and resist the wrongs committed by these people, Georgia offers to make common cause with Maryland.] She is not unmindful of the past history of your noble State … The wealth, population, and commercial importance of her great metropolis, Baltimore, point out that city as the great commercial and financial center of the Southern Republic.

In glowing sentences he depicted the future of Baltimore—that with her natural advantages no less than from her varied and extended commercial relations with the civilized world, "she will become the great importing agent for the entire South, whilst her facilities for and her great proficiency in the art of ship building will make her the carrier of our immense productions of rice, grain, cotton, and sugar." He hoped that the descendants of Chase, Carroll, and McHenry would no longer be deterred by a consultation with their fears. "Georgia warns Maryland against any patched-up adjustment of existing difficulties."[25]

The ambassador from Georgia was not more successful with Hicks than were those from Mississippi and Alabama. Wright was obliged to report to his governor[26] that, though he had received no written reply to his communication, for which he had long waited, he regretted to inform him that as a result of a personal interview he found Hicks not only opposed to the secession of Maryland from the Federal Union, but that if she should withdraw from the Union, Hicks would advise and urge her to confederate with the middle states in the formation of a new confederacy, and that he had already, in his official capacity, entered into a correspondence with the governors of those states, including New York, Pennsylvania, New Jersey, Delaware, Virginia, Missouri, and Ohio, with a view, in the ultimate disruption of the Federal Union, to the establishment of such a central confederacy. Hicks would interpose no objection to the march of troops through the state to coerce the Southern states, nor would he convene the legislature to take action in the matter. The governor went so far as to declare that the seceded states were attempting to coerce Maryland. But from those with whom he associated, the ambassador was led to believe that the gallant, patriotic and brave people of Maryland were "true to the memories of

---

[23] In Carman's original manuscript, the quoted portions of the resolutions vary slightly from what appears herein. The above presents the resolutions as they were printed in *Addresses and Resolutions Adopted at the Meeting of the Southern Rights Convention of Maryland, Held in the Universalist Church, in the City of Baltimore, February 18th and 19th, 1861* (Baltimore, J. B. Rose & Co., 1861), 10. Carman used as his source a copy of the resolutions sent to the president of Georgia's secession convention by its ambassador to Maryland, which contained minor stylistic differences. See Ambrose R. Wright to George W. Crawford, March 13, 1861, reprinted in *OR*, ser. 4, vol. 1, 151–52.

[24] As of this writing, a copy of the resolution has not been found.

[25] Wright to Hicks, February 25, 1861, reprinted in *OR*, ser. 4, vol. 1, 153–60. Carman presents the bracketed sentence as a direct quotation from Wright's letter; it does not appear in the published version of Wright's text, but it conveys the meaning of the deleted portion accurately.

   Samuel Chase (1741–1811) and Charles Carroll (1737–1832) were two of Maryland's signers of the Declaration of Independence. James McHenry (1753–1816) volunteered for service in the Continental forces at the outbreak of hostilities in New England in 1775 and later served on the staffs of both George Washington and the Marquis de Lafayette. He became a member of the Continental Congress, a signer of the Constitution, and secretary of war under Presidents Washington and Adams.

[26] Carman errs as to the recipient. The letter was sent to the president of the Georgia secession convention (who had previously served as governor), not to the sitting chief executive of the state.

the past," and should Virginia withdraw from the Union, they would, "in the shortest possible period of time, assume the responsibility, assemble in spontaneous convention, and unite their destinies with the Confederate States of the South."[27]

Meanwhile, a recruiting office was opened in Baltimore and enlisted men sent to join the forces besieging Fort Sumter in Charleston Harbor. This office was in the charge of Louis T. Wigfall—a U.S. senator from Texas—and authorized by Jefferson Davis, to whom Wigfall reported that he would meet with great success.[28]

From the day of Lincoln's arrival in Washington until the day of his inauguration on the fourth of March, 1861, Baltimore was a quiet city and Maryland a peaceful state. Rumor, it is true, peopled her borders with banded conspirators who threatened to seize the public buildings and archives of the government, proclaim the Southern Confederacy at Washington, and prevent the inauguration of Lincoln, but in truth such things were seriously thought of only by a few, and then only in case Maryland should first secede. (Many who sympathized with the South, particularly those without family, left the state and entered the service of the Southern Confederacy.) There was a pause on all sides, an anxious waiting to see what was to come next, a suspense that hung on the tone of the president's inaugural address. It was hoped that through his conservative nature a peaceful solution of difficulties would be reached. His promised peace gave strength to the Union sentiment of the state. His appointment of Montgomery Blair, a citizen of the state, to a seat in the cabinet cleared the political atmosphere and soothed the apprehensions of all parties.

On March 12, the states-rights convention reassembled at Baltimore. As Virginia had not yet seceded (an event that had been hoped for by the delegates meeting on the eighteenth of February) it again adjourned—not, however, before appointing a committee of influential gentlemen to visit the Richmond convention and urge that body to recommend a convention of the border states. This duty the committee performed by laying before that body a communication inviting such action "to secure, as far as it may be done, a full, fair and accurate expression of the popular will, in such form as to leave no doubt either of its character, or of the authority of those who may be selected as its agents and representatives."[29] Virginia was not then prepared to act in this direction, and the committee returned without any success in the accomplishment of its mission.

The younger members of the convention were not satisfied with this conservative action. They were, in Bradley T. Johnson's opinion,

> convinced that Virginia would eventually be forced into the war; insisted on preparing the people, organizing minute-men, collecting and distributing arms and ammunition, and placing affairs in such a train that the blow once struck in Maryland would rouse the neighboring States and involve them all in one common cause. The older and more cautious portion were opposed to this and only suggested waiting for Virginia. They had no other plan.
>
> They were told that Virginia might linger until Maryland was overpowered, and then it would be too late, but they were unable to perceive the crisis, and refused to co-operate. But the more ardent spirits threw their energies into the work. They organized companies, formed bands of minute-men and prepared for action as quickly and rapidly as possible.[30]

The unmistakably hostile intention of the secessionists, the knowledge that recruiting for the armies of the Southern Confederacy was being carried on under the auspices of a U.S. senator backed by the financial aid of one of the wealthiest businessmen of Baltimore, and the fact that bodies of men were nightly drilling in out-of-the-way halls and rooms impressed Hicks that he should prepare for the worst. On March 18 he asked Secretary of War Simon Cameron if, in case of necessity to put down rebellion in Maryland, he could be furnished arms for two thousand men. "I am," said the governor, "strongly inclined to believe that a spirit of insubordination is increasing, and that any unfortunate movement on the part

---

[27] Wright to Crawford, 151–53.

[28] For evidence of his Confederate recruiting efforts while still a member of the U.S. Senate, see Louis T. Wigfall to Davis, February 18, 1861, reprinted in Lynda Lasswell Crist and Mary Seaton Dix, eds., *The Papers of Jefferson Davis*, vol. 7 (Baton Rouge: Louisiana State University Press, 1992), 51–53; Wigfall to Davis, February 25, 1861, reprinted in Crist and Dix, 60–62. Although the voters of Texas ratified the state's ordinance of secession on February 21, Wigfall never resigned his seat, continuing to vote through most of the special session of the 37th Congress (March 4–28, 1861) before heading south to cast his lot with the Confederacy. See *Senate Journal*, 37th Cong., special sess., March 23, 1861, 425–26. He was expelled in absentia from the Senate on July 11, 1861. See *Senate Journal*, 37th Cong., 1st sess., July 11, 1861, 29–30; *Congressional Globe*, 37th Cong., 1st sess., 1861, 62–63.

[29] See W. Mitchell, E. F. Chambers, William Henry Norris, Isaac D. Jones, and J. Hanson Thomas to "the Honorable, the President of the Convention of the People of Virginia [John Janney]," no date [presented to the Virginia state convention on March 18, 1861], reprinted in *Journals and Papers of the Virginia State Convention of 1861*, vol. 3 (Richmond: Virginia State Library, 1966), document no. 15. Various reactions by Virginia delegates to the intrusion of Marylanders upon their deliberations can be seen in George H. Reese, ed., *Proceedings of the Virginia State Convention of 1861, February 13–May 1*, vol. 2 (Richmond: Virginia State Library, 1965), 26–27.

[30] Bradley T. Johnson, "Memoir of First Maryland Regiment," 347.

of the Virginia convention … may cause an outbreak in Maryland." Cameron assured the governor that his requisition, should the emergency arise, would be complied with.[31]

The attack upon and fall of Fort Sumter caused great excitement in Baltimore and throughout the state of Maryland, which was intensified by the president's call for troops. Opinion was sharply divided and Union men and secessionists gave expression to their views. Breaches of the peace were frequent and angry threats were heard on all sides. Peaceful men armed themselves and the lawless became defiant. But overall there was a strong Union feeling. The thoughtful and influential saw for Maryland no place but in the Union, and men sharing this view sustained Hicks.

Excitement increased on the morning of the eighteenth, when reports came from Harrisburg that Pennsylvanians were on the way to Washington and would arrive at Baltimore early in the afternoon. Crowds assembled on the streets and threats were freely made that no "Yankee" troops should pass through Baltimore to coerce the South. Thanks to the efficiency of the Baltimore police, the Pennsylvanians passed safely through the city and reached Washington in the evening.

The news that Virginia had finally seceded, the passage of troops through Baltimore, collisions in the streets, and two secession meetings held during the day (in which armed resistance to the Federal government was advised) increased the excitement in the city to fever heat. Business was entirely suspended, the streets were crowded until late at night, and, under the stress of circumstances, Unionism was nearly crushed out. Opposition to the passage of Northern troops through Baltimore was unanimous. One observer noted, "The staidest and soberest were infected by it. Men who all along had been opposed to secession now openly advocated armed resistance, and it was declared over and over again in the most public manner that no Northern troops should be permitted to enter Baltimore, or if they did enter, to leave the city alive."[32]

Moved by the events of the day, Hicks issued an address to the people of Maryland, counseling moderation of speech and invoking them to obey the laws and aid the constituted authorities in preserving the peace. He promised them that no troops should be sent from Maryland, unless for the defense of the national capital, and assured them of an opportunity "in a special election for Members of the Congress of the United States, to express their devotion to the Union, or their desire to see it broken up."[33] Mayor George W. Brown of Baltimore followed the governor in issuing a proclamation to the people of the city, concurring in the governor's determination to preserve the peace and "maintain inviolate the honor and integrity of Maryland" and expressing his satisfaction at Hicks's resolution that no troops were to be sent from the state to the soil of any other state.[34]

On the morning of the nineteenth, feeling was intensified by news from Harper's Ferry that the Virginians had driven the U.S. garrison from that place and seized the government property. Quick upon the heels of this came the 6th Massachusetts, its march through the city, rioting, and bloodshed in the streets. The story has been so often told that it is too well known to require repetition.[35]

Immediately after the riot, Hicks and Brown united in advising that all troops *en route* to Washington be sent back to the Maryland line, and Lincoln was appealed to send no troops through the city.[36] Early on the morning of the twentieth, the bridges on the railroads running north from Baltimore were burned.

---

[31] Carman is mistaken as to the person of whom Hicks made his request. The governor wrote his appeal for two thousand stands of arms to General Scott, who in turn forwarded it to Secretary Cameron two days later with a favorable endorsement. Hicks's letter, Scott's reaction, and Cameron's reply are all reprinted in *OR*, vol. 51, pt. 1, 317–18.

[32] As of this writing, Carman's source for this unattributed quotation has not been identified.

[33] See Hicks to "the People of Maryland," April 18, 1861, reprinted as "Proclamation of the Governor of Maryland," in Moore, *Documents and Narratives*, 76–77.

[34] Ibid., 77.

Born in Baltimore, George William Brown (1812–90) was educated at Dartmouth and Rutgers before returning to his native city for admission to the Maryland Bar. Devoted to orderly and democratic government, he was alarmed by the increasingly chaotic and thuggish tactics of the "Know-Nothing" Party in Baltimore, which controlled the city for much of the 1850s. Running as an independent, he broke their power in Baltimore with his election in 1859. As opposed to mob rule as he was Federal coercion, Brown labored to keep the city in Union hands while preventing usurpation of civilian rights and authority by the military.

[35] The 6th Massachusetts, en route to Washington, arrived by train in Baltimore late on the morning of April 19. Having reached the southern terminus of the Philadelphia, Wilmington, and Baltimore Railroad, the cars ferrying the Union soldiers were uncoupled from their locomotive and attached individually to teams of horses for transfer to the Baltimore and Ohio Railroad, approximately a mile and a half distant. When a crowd of pro-Confederate residents of the city attempted to block their passage, then began pelting the makeshift convoy with whatever missiles the surroundings afforded (bricks, bottles, paving stones, etc.), the Massachusetts men responded by firing into the mob. The resulting street battle ended when the soldiers reached the B&O and departed the city, but not before scores of men had been killed and wounded on both sides. For a sampling of contemporary accounts, see *OR*, vol. 2, 7–21; "Transit of Massachusetts Volunteers and Other Troops Through Baltimore," *Baltimore Sun*, April 20, 1861.

[36] See George William Brown, *Baltimore and the Nineteenth of April, 1861: A Study of the War* (Baltimore: Johns Hopkins University, 1887), 56–57.

When, on the fifteenth, Lincoln called for Maryland's quota of troops (four regiments) for the defense of the capital, Hicks called upon the secretary of war and General Scott to have an explicit understanding where these troops were to be used "for the defense of the United States Government, the maintenance of the Federal authority, and the protection of the Federal capital"—and whether their services would be required out of the state. Two days later he asked that the president reduce the agreement to writing,[37] and the secretary of war replied, "The troops called for from Maryland are destined for the protection of the Federal capital and the public property of the United States within the limits of the State of Maryland, and it is not intended to remove them beyond those limits except for the defense of this District."[38] Three days later, on the twentieth, while his militia was under arms in the city of Baltimore to prevent troops from other states going through that city to the defense of the nation's capital, and while he, in person, at the capital of his state was vainly beseeching Brigadier General Benjamin F. Butler not to land Massachusetts men at Annapolis (to reach Washington by going around Baltimore), Hicks wrote to Secretary Cameron declining, for the present, to furnish the four regiments of infantry.[39] He had passed under the influence of the mob.

Governor Hicks was not the only Union man that bent before the storm. It seemed that, for the time being, the lovers of the Union should acquiesce in the preparations to resist the passage of Northern troops. It was thought better to go with the current than endeavor to stem it. The leading Union papers appealed to the people to sustain Hicks and Brown in their determination that no Northern troops should pass through Baltimore or "unharmed through the State of Maryland for the purpose of subjugating the South."[40] Reverdy Johnson visited Lincoln and requested him to bring no more troops through Maryland; if he did so, all Union sentiment would be annihilated.[41] Other Union men gave the same counsel, and, at the moment, it appeared that all Union sentiment was crushed.

There was yielding too on the part of the national government. Sincerely desirous of avoiding any pretext for a collision, Lincoln and Scott assured the Baltimore authorities that no more troops should be passed through that city and those en route were turned back to Pennsylvania.[42] This concession emboldened a suggestion and then a demand that no troops should be brought through Maryland, but to this the president would not consent.[43] He must have troops for the defense of the capital.

Immediately following the rioting in the streets of Baltimore, volunteer companies of infantry and cavalry came from various parts of the state and, on the afternoon of April 21, George H. Steuart, in command of the pro-Southern troops in the city, sent special messengers to then-Colonel Robert E. Lee, informing him that "the people of Baltimore and, indeed, the citizens of Maryland generally, are united in one thing at least, viz, that troops volunteering for Federal service against

[37] Hicks to Abraham Lincoln, April 17, 1861, reprinted in *OR*, ser. 3, vol. 1, 79–80.

[38] Simon Cameron to Hicks, April 17, 1861, reprinted in *OR*, ser. 3, vol. 1, 80.

[39] Hicks to Cameron, April 20, 1861, reprinted in *OR*, vol. 2, 581.

[40] See J. Thomas Scharf, *The Chronicles of Baltimore: Being a Complete History of "Baltimore Town" and Baltimore City from the Earliest Period to the Present Time* (Baltimore: Turnbull Brothers, 1874), 598.

[41] Johnson did not meet with Lincoln, but rather expressed his concerns in a letter dated April 22, 1861. When Lincoln—who feared committing his opinions in such matters to paper lest they furnish "new grounds for misunderstanding"—made no reply, Johnson sent a second note on the twenty-fourth pressing the president for an answer to his early communication. Lincoln finally responded with a confidential letter on the same day. Lincoln to Reverdy Johnson, April 24, 1861, reprinted in Roy P. Basler, ed., *The Collected Works of Abraham Lincoln*, vol. 4 (New Brunswick, N.J.: Rutgers University Press, 1953), 342–43. A footnote on p. 343 contains excerpts from Johnson's original note of the twenty-second.

[42] Lincoln wrote to Hicks and Brown on the twentieth that while troops must be brought to the national capital, it was not required that they march through Baltimore en route. Although he intended to leave the details to General Scott, the president expressed his hope that the general-in-chief would find a movement bypassing Baltimore to be "practical and proper"; from the instructions he had already heard Scott issue, Lincoln believed that the general was in full accord. Lincoln to Hicks and Brown, April 20, 1861, reprinted in Basler, 340. The president later telegraphed Hicks in Baltimore on the twentieth, asking him and Brown to take a special train to Washington "immediately" (the president offered to have one sent if none were available) in order to "consult ... relative to preserving the peace of Maryland." Lincoln to Hicks, April 20, 1861, reprinted in *OR*, vol. 2, 581. The same telegram was sent directly to Brown; see Basler, vol. 4, 341 n. 1. Hicks by this time had already left Baltimore for Annapolis, but Brown traveled to Washington immediately and met with the president. Earl Schenck Miers, ed., *Lincoln Day by Day: A Chronology*, vol. 3, *1861–1865* (1960; reprint, 3 vols. in 1, Dayton, Ohio: Morningside, 1991), 36–37; and Basler, 341 n. 1.

Separate orders issued by Cameron and Scott on the twenty-first to the Pennsylvania volunteers at Cockeysville, Maryland (en route to Baltimore), calling for their return to Harrisburg, Pennsylvania, for re-transport by water to Annapolis are reprinted in *OR*, vol. 2, 584.

[43] See "Interview between the Mayor of Baltimore and the President and Cabinet at Washington," *Richmond Enquirer*, April 25, 1861. Hicks was more realistic than his associates in his understanding of both the situation and the president's circumstances. "I hoped," Hicks replied from Annapolis to Brown on the twentieth, "they would send no more troops through Maryland, but as we have no right to demand that, I am glad no more are to be sent through Baltimore." Hicks to Brown, April 20, 1861, reprinted in *OR*, vol. 2, 581.

Virginia and other sister Southern States shall not, if they can keep it, pass over the soil of Maryland."[44] Colonel Isaac R. Trimble of the city militia, who had but recently resigned from the U.S. Army, was looked to as the leader of all military movements, a military dictator in fact. He allowed no boat, vehicle or person to leave the city without his permission.[45] It is well for Baltimore that his rule was absolute. The unruly and riotous element began to show itself. Theft was common and the law-abiding became timid. The militia (which had been called out on the nineteenth) and the volunteer companies paraded the streets under the state flag of Maryland and repressed disorder and turbulence as fully as they could, but still there was an element which, once let loose in those hot hours, was more feared by the thoughtful than the march of all Massachusetts through Baltimore.

The weakness of the secession cause in Baltimore was soon made evident. A special election was held on April 24 to choose members of the legislature.[46] To the dismay of the secessionists and the great joy of the Union men, out of 30,000 voters in Baltimore only 9,244 votes were cast.[47] They represented the full strength of rebellion in the city. From that day the Union element asserted itself. The secessionists lost heart. The showing was too plain to be disputed. On the next day, the Police Board directed all police officers and others in the employ of the Board, and all other parties whatsoever, to offer no obstruction to the running of the trains to Washington. The railroad and telegraph lines were repaired and vessels were allowed to leave port.

Meanwhile, stirring events were taking place in the state outside the city of Baltimore. Prevented from coming through that place, troops en route for Washington went by way of Annapolis, and the credit for opening that route belongs to General Butler with the 8th Massachusetts. Butler, who reached Perryville, on the Susquehanna River, by rail on the twentieth, embarked on the steamer *Maryland* and arrived in Annapolis early on the morning of the twenty-first. Hicks advised him not to land his men on account of the great excitement and informed him that he had telegraphed to that effect to the secretary of war.[48] But the most surprising act of the governor was to request the president to order the troops elsewhere and ask Lord Richard Lyons, the British minister to the United States, to act as mediator between the North and South.[49] After some sharp correspondence between Butler and Hicks,[50] the troops were landed without opposition and two or three days later arrived in Washington. Many regiments followed by the same route.

Horace Greeley insisted (and many others in the North agreed with him) that practically, on the morning of April 20, Maryland was a member of the Southern Confederacy and that Hicks was in full sympathy and confidence of the secession leaders. To this charge Mayor Brown replies:

It is true that the city then, and for some days afterwards, was in an anomalous condition, which may be best described as one of "armed neutrality"; but it is not true that in any sense it was, on the 20th of April, or at any other time, a member of the Southern Confederacy. On the contrary, while many, especially among the young and reckless, were doing their utmost to place it in that position, regardless of consequences, and would, if they could, have forced the

[44] L. P. Bayne and J. J. Chancellor to Lee, April 22, 1862, reprinted in *OR*, vol. 2, 774.

Unbeknownst to Steuart, Lee had submitted his resignation as colonel in the U.S. Army on April 20. A few days later he was commissioned major general in both the Provisional Army of Virginia and the Volunteer Forces of Virginia and made commander of the state's military and naval forces. (Although the Virginia state convention passed an ordinance of secession on April 17, it required ratification by the citizens, which did not occur until some weeks thereafter. Virginia was not admitted formally into the Confederate States of America until May 7.) Once Virginia's military was consolidated into that of the Confederacy, Lee received a brief demotion to brigadier general (the highest rank authorized under Confederate law initially), then was appointed subsequently to the rank of general on August 31, 1861. See *Journal of the Provisional Congress of the Confederate States of America*, vol. 1 of *Journal of the Congress of the Confederate States of America, 1861–1865*, 58th Cong., 2d sess., 1904, S. Doc. 234, serial 4610, 223, 464.

[45] See Bradley T. Johnson, *Maryland*, vol. 2 of *Confederate Military History*, ed. Clement A. Evans (Atlanta: Confederate Publishing Co., 1899), 23; James Green and E. J. Smithers to Henry H. Lockwood, July 11, 1861, reprinted in *OR*, vol. 2, 740.

[46] "Ten members from Baltimore were elected at a special election held in that city on the 24th, in the place of the delegation returned as elected in 1859, but unseated on account of fraud and violence at the election." Bradley T. Johnson, *Maryland*, 25.

[47] The slate of candidates from Baltimore ran unopposed. In his interpretation of the election returns, Carman assumes that all who supported its pro-secession tenor went to the polls, and that any votes not cast represent expressions of Unionist sentiment. The fallacy of this reasoning is exposed in the following: "The election was a mere form yesterday, there being no opposition and the conclusion certain, consequently the vote is without significance. In a casual meeting of five citizens last evening at about six o'clock, all firm supporters of Southern Rights, the question was made one of the other who had voted, and it turned out that only one of the five had done so. From this fact, and the general appearance of the precincts during the day, we did not look for so large a return as appears." "The Election Yesterday," *Baltimore Sun*, April 25, 1861. The *Sun* article also provides vote totals for all twenty wards.

[48] For the administration's response, see Seward to Hicks, April 22, 1861, reprinted as "Maryland and the Troops for the Capital," *Richmond Enquirer*, April 25, 1861.

[49] Hicks to Lincoln, April 22, 1861, reprinted in *OR*, vol. 2, 588–89.

[50] For a sampling, see Hicks to "the Commander of the Volunteer Troops on Board the Steamer [Benjamin F. Butler]," April 21, 1861, reprinted in *OR*, vol. 2, 586–87; Butler to Hicks, April 22, 1861, reprinted in *OR*, vol. 2, 589–90; Hicks to Butler, April 22, 1861, reprinted in *OR*, vol. 2, 591.

hands of the city authorities, it was their conduct which prevented such a catastrophe. Temporizing and delay were necessary. As soon as passions had a time to cool, a strong reaction set in and the people rapidly divided into two parties—one on the side of the North, and the other on the side of the South; but whatever might be their personal or political sympathies, it was clear to all who had not lost their reason that Maryland, which lay open from the North by both land and sea, would be kept in the Union for the sake of the national capital, even if it required the united power of the nation to accomplish the object.[51]

The riot in Baltimore and the enforced isolation of Washington from the North and West gave great encouragement to secessionists elsewhere and fostered the belief and hope that Maryland would secede and demand Washington, as South Carolina had demanded Fort Sumter. The secessionists in Maryland were urged to persevere in the work they had undertaken. Arms and ammunition were promised, some of the former reaching Baltimore from Harper's Ferry on the twenty-third. Everywhere in the South the great importance of Baltimore was recognized, but vigorous action did not follow.

Prominent among many Southern men whom Secretary of State William H. Seward had taken into his confidence was John A. Campbell of Alabama,[52] an associate justice of the Supreme Court of the United States. Campbell had acted as intermediary between the government and the commissioners of the Southern Confederacy during the negotiations regarding Fort Sumter and, although from the South, was regarded as a Union man, and so trusted. He remained in Washington, drawing his pay from the U.S. Treasury—while also acting as an advisor for the Southern Confederacy. He gave his opinion of the importance of Baltimore to the Confederates in these words to Jefferson Davis:

Maryland is the object of chief anxiety with the north & the administration. Their fondest hope will be to command the Chesapeake and retain this. Their pride and their fanaticism would be sadly depressed by a contrary issue. This will be the great point of contest in all negotiations …

… I incline to think that they are prepared to abandon it south of the Potomac. But not beyond. Maryland is weak. She has no military men of talents & I did hear that Col. [Benjamin] Huger was offered command & declined it, because his resignation had not been accepted. [George W.] Hughes is plainly not competent for such a purpose. Lee is in Virginia. Think of the condition of Baltimore & provide for it, for there is the place of danger.

The events at Baltimore have placed a new aspect upon everything to the north. There is a perfect storm there. While it has to be met, no unnecessary addition should be made to increase it.[53]

The *Richmond Examiner* was especially pleased:

The glorious conduct of Maryland decides the contest at hand. With a generous bravery, worthy of her ancient renown, she has thrown herself into the pathway of the enemy, and made of her body a shield for the South … She stands forth in one day the leader of the Southern cause … The heart of all Maryland responds to the action of Baltimore, and that nursery of fine regiments, instead of being the camping ground of the enemy, preparing to rush upon the South, will speedily become the camping ground of the South, preparing to cross the line of Mason and Dixon.

It is impossible to estimate the moral effect of the action of Maryland …

To have gained Maryland is to have gained a host. It insures Washington City, and the ignominious expulsion of Lincoln … from the White House. It makes good the words of Secretary [of War Leroy P.] Walker at Montgomery in regard to the Federal Metropolis. It transfers the line of battle from the Potomac to the Pennsylvania border. It proclaims to the North that, except abolitionized Delaware, the South is a unit against them … It gives us the entire waters of the Chesapeake. It rounds out the fairest domain on the globe for the Southern confederation … Maryland is the Louisiana of the East. Baltimore and Richmond will be the New York and Philadelphia of the South, and Norfolk her Boston and Portland combined. Maryland completes our geographical and commercial unity …

---

[51] Brown, 77.

[52] Born in Wilkes County, Georgia, John Archibald Campbell (1811–89) was admitted to Franklin College (today the University of Georgia) at the age of eleven and, upon his graduation three years later, was admitted to the U.S. Military Academy by Secretary of War John C. Calhoun, a close family friend. The death of his father and the tangled condition of his estate forced Campbell to leave West Point prematurely and return home. There he undertook the study of law and at the age of eighteen was admitted to the Georgia Bar by a special act of the state legislature. Within a year he moved to Alabama and rose quickly within its legal community. He served two terms as a state legislator, twice declined appointments to the Alabama supreme court, and in June 1850 served as a delegate to the Nashville Convention, where he was responsible for drafting many of the resolutions adopted by that body. In March 1853 Franklin Pierce named him to the U.S. Supreme Court, where he voted with the majority in *Dred Scott*.

[53] John A. Campbell to Davis, April 23, 1861. An error-filled transcription of this letter appears in John G. Nicolay and John Hay, *Abraham Lincoln: A History*, vol. 4 (New York: Century Co., 1890), 148–49, and it was from this source that Carman copied in his original manuscript. A true copy appears in Crist and Dix, 117–18, and this text is used in the portion cited above.

The South could not have spared Maryland. Her territory, her waters, her slaves, her people, her soldiers, her sailors, her ship-builders, her machinists, her wealth, enterprise and bravery were all essential to it.[54]

The *Richmond Enquirer* called upon Virginia to disregard state lines and hold both sides of the Potomac. "*The Marylanders must not be left without instant and efficient aid. We must not allow them to be crushed* by the powerful army which is coming upon them! We must rush to their aid. We must send them men and arms—and we must do it at once."[55] Jefferson Davis, Virginia governor John Letcher, and other southern officials and leaders urged instant relief and assistance to Baltimore. The whole Southern press re-echoed the cry. But no action was taken.

The grave events transpiring in Baltimore and the excitement throughout the state impelled the governor to convene the legislature. The immediate cause of this action was the issuance of a call by a single senator, Coleman Yellott, for that body to meet at Baltimore. Knowing that such a meeting in that city, filled with secessionists, would lead inevitably to the secession of the state and more bloodshed in its streets and on the soil of Maryland, the governor forestalled such action by convening it at Frederick, a loyal part of the state.[56]

The legislature assembled at Frederick at noon on April 26 and received the governor's message. After reciting the steps taken to maintain order in Baltimore, to prevent the passage of troops through Maryland, and his unsuccessful effort to have Lord Lyons act as a mediator between the loyal and seceded states, Hicks said that events satisfied him that the War Department had concluded to make Annapolis its point for landing troops and had resolved to open and maintain communication between that place and Washington. His convictions were that the only safety of Maryland was in preserving a neutral position between the people of the North and the South. Maryland had violated no rights of either section. She had been loyal to the Union. He counseled Maryland to take no side against the general government until it should commit outrages that would justify resistance to its authority. He was for union and peace; this was the sole groundwork of his policy.[57]

On the twenty-seventh the state Senate, by a unanimous vote, issued an address to the people of Maryland soliciting their confidence in the fidelity with which they proposed to discharge their duties and disclaiming all idea, intention or authority to pass any ordinance of secession.[58] Two, at least, of the senators who by their votes thus assured the people of Maryland that all fears of secession were without just foundation were, on that same day, carrying on an intrigue with Brigadier General Daniel Ruggles, looking to a cooperation with Virginia troops, on Maryland soil, for the capture of Fort Washington and a dash on the national capital.[59]

Every shade of opinion was represented by the resolutions proposed as to Maryland's duty. These were all referred, as were those proposing the reorganization of the militia, to the Committee on Federal Relations in both houses. On the ninth of May, the committee of the House of Delegates presented an exceedingly able and elaborate report drawn by Severn T. Wallis, reviewing all the constitutional points involved in the question of secession and the "coercion" of "sovereign States"; denouncing Lincoln for what they considered his illegal act in calling out the militia to wage war against the Southern Confederacy; and criticizing Hicks for the stand he had taken, regretting that in acknowledging the president's call for troops, "the response of his Excellency, the Governor, should have fallen so far short, in this regard, of the manly and patriotic

---

[54] *Richmond Examiner*, April 23, 1861.

[55] "Glorious Old Maryland—Baltimore Gloriously Redeemed," *Richmond Enquirer*, April 25, 1861 (italics in original). Carman continues the quotation as follows: "Maryland is ours by ties of blood, by the memories of the past, by the deeds of her past, by a common and indissoluble interest … Washington is southern soil, and we must have it." The article does not, however, contain these last sentences, nor do they appear anywhere in the specified issue of the *Enquirer* (either in the daily or semiweekly editions published on April 25). Absent these final sentences, one cannot sustain Carman's charge that its editors advocated disregarding the state line (not, at least, as of April 1861). Yet such sentiments did hold currency among a number of Virginia fire-eaters at the time, leading one to suspect that Carman drew these concluding lines either from another Virginia newspaper or a later issue of the *Enquirer* and conflated them in his note-taking.

[56] See Bradley T. Johnson, *Maryland*, 25.

[57] See Hicks to "Gentlemen of the Senate and House of Delegates," April 25, 1861, Governor's Letterbooks, February 1854–January 1866, *Records of the States of the United States of America: A Microfilm Compilation* (Washington, D.C.: Library of Congress Photoduplication Service, 1949–51), Maryland E.2, reel 5. See also "Message of Governor Hicks," Moore, "Documents and Narratives, 159–61. Moore's version is drawn from the *New York Herald*, which appears to have taken the text in turn from a Baltimore newspaper. Thus, Moore's copy is datelined incorrectly "Baltimore, April 27, 1861."

[58] See *Journal of Proceedings of the Senate of Maryland, in Extra Session, April, 1861* (Frederick, Md.: Beale H. Richardson, 1861), 8–9.

[59] Carman's original text says "Confederate General Daniel Ruggles." Like Lee, Ruggles would accept a commission in Confederate service eventually, but at the time in question he was a member of the Virginia state forces.

   As of this writing, Carman's source for this charge and the identity of the Maryland senators in question has not been identified, but see E. W. Bell to "Steuart," April 25, 1861, as contained in Philip S. G. Cocke to Lee, April 25, 1861, reprinted in *OR*, vol. 2, 779.

spirit with which the Governors of Virginia and North Carolina, Tennessee, Kentucky and Missouri, threw back the insulting proposition of the Administration."[60]

The spirit of the legislature is shown in the above quotation. The majority of the members would gladly have voted for immediate secession, but they feared the consequences. They argued up to the point of resistance, but they did not resist. They protested but, under all the circumstances, reached the conclusion that the only feasible attitude of the state toward the Federal government was of submission, "voluntary and cheerful submission on the part of those who can persuade themselves that the Constitution remains inviolate and the Union unbroken, or that the Union can survive the Constitution—unwilling and galling submission on the part of those who think and feel differently; but still, peaceful submission upon both sides."[61] As to calling a sovereign convention and arming the militia, they favored both, but these things could not be done when the state was prostrate and the Constitution silenced by Federal bayonets.

Following this report the committee proposed the adoption of resolutions protesting against the war which the Federal government had declared upon the Confederate States and the state of Virginia; asking the Federal government, in the name of God and humanity, to cease the "unholy" and "unprofitable strife"; demanding the peaceful and immediate recognition of the Confederate States; denouncing the military occupation of Maryland; and calling on all good citizens to abstain from violent and unlawful interference with the troops in transit through or quartered in the state.[62] These resolutions passed the House of Delegates on May 10 by a vote of forty-five to twelve. The Senate added a resolution providing for the appointment of four members of each house, four of whom should wait upon the president of the United States and four upon the president of the Southern Confederacy, to obtain, if possible, a cessation of hostilities with a view to an adjustment of existing troubles by means of negotiations rather than the sword.[63]

Among the measures proposed, and one which caused much discussion in the South and great uneasiness throughout the state, was a bill presented by Coleman Yellott, state senator from Baltimore, entitled "An Act to Provide for the Safety and Peace of the People of Maryland." This bill provided for a board (to be appointed by the legislature) vested with extraordinary powers and had for its object the transfer of the executive power from the governor to a body of men of well known secession sympathies. It authorized the expenditure of five million dollars for the defense of the state and gave the entire control of the military into the hands of the board, including the appointment and removal of commissioned officers. As soon as the features of the bill became generally known, vigorous protests against its passage came from every part of the state. It was denounced as unconstitutional, despotic, and fatal to the interests of Maryland. Some petitions favored its passage, but sentiment was so overwhelmingly against it that its friends became alarmed and abandoned it. Bradley T. Johnson, who was constant and ardent in pressing the measure, says:

> The plan of the projectors of the committee of safety was to arm the militia. They expected to equip forty thousand men as promptly as the Northern States had armed and equipped their volunteers, and they knew that Maryland volunteers would take arms as quickly as those of Massachusetts and Ohio. They did not propose to carry the State out of the Union, but they intended to arm their young men and command the peace in the State. When that failed, as fail they knew it would, the State would be represented by forty thousand armed and equipped volunteers who would carry her flag in the front line and would make her one of the Confederate States in fact, if not in name.[64]

When Johnson saw that the bill could not be carried through the legislature he arranged with Captain James Ashby, then at Point of Rocks, to dash into Frederick, seize Hicks and carry him into Virginia, and thus break up the state government and throw it into the hands of the legislature, which would be obliged to take charge during the interregnum. When notice of this intention was given to the leaders in the legislature, they promptly demanded that Johnson desist from the enterprise, and he dropped the matter.[65]

On the fourteenth of May, the legislature adjourned until the fourth of June. When it had first assembled on the twenty-sixth of April, it was ripe for secession. Three-fourths of its members were ready to call a "sovereign convention," as secession bodies were then termed, vote the state out of the Union, and form an alliance with Virginia. But events moved too rapidly. Annapolis was held by a strong Union force, Washington was secured, Pennsylvania threatened the northern border of the state, the North demanded a thoroughfare to the national capital, and the cry of commercial distress came up from Baltimore.

---

[60] *Report of the Committee on Federal Relations in Regard to the Calling of a Sovereign Convention* (Frederick, Md.: E. S. Riley, 1861), 9.

[61] Ibid., 19.

[62] Ibid., 21–22.

[63] *Journal of Proceedings of the Senate*, 23.

[64] Bradley T. Johnson, *Maryland*, 36.

[65] Ibid., 36–37.

Nor was Virginia all powerful. The secessionists had looked to her action with much interest. From the secession of South Carolina down to the meeting of the Maryland legislature, they had squared their actions with those of Virginia. She was looked upon as an exemplar and a guide. Above all things, an alliance with her was the most popular. It will be remembered that a committee that visited Richmond about the middle of March did not find the Virginians prepared for a decided step, but after the secession of the state the Virginians became very active in bringing influence to bear on the deliberations of the Maryland legislature. Many self-constituted agents came across the border to instill lessons of states-manship into the heads of the Maryland legislators, while Governor Letcher sent, as special commissioner, ex-U.S. senator James M. Mason to assure the legislature of the sympathy of Virginia and to say that should they think it proper "to commit the power and authority of the State of Maryland, in co-operation with Virginia and the Confederate States, in resistance to the aggressions of the Government at Washington, then and in that case Virginia will afford all practicable facilities for the furtherance of such object, and will place such arms at the disposal of the Maryland authorities as she may have it in her power to give."[66]

At first Mason was greatly encouraged and reported that the legislature was probably for secession, but he soon ascertained that he could not enter into a compact committing Maryland to secession and an alliance with Virginia. The time had passed. The sober second thought of the people had asserted itself, and the U.S. government had quartered forty thousand soldiers on her soil and overlooking it. She was securely moored to the Union.

On the night of May 13, General Butler marched into Baltimore and camped on Federal Hill, completely controlling the city. The next morning he issued a proclamation in which he promised protection to all law-abiding citizens and gave notice that all traitorous acts must cease.[67] From the nineteenth of April to the fourteenth of May, a great change had taken place in the attitude of the city toward the general government. In spite of the activity and energy of the secessionists it was apparent that the Union men were largely in the majority. Many causes contributed to this result.

Encouraged by the growth of the Union feeling in Baltimore and throughout the state, and strengthened by the arms of the national government, Hicks thought of complying with the requisition of the secretary of war for four regiments but was deterred by the menacing attitude of the legislature. But immediately upon the adjournment of this body on May 14, he issued his proclamation calling for four regiments of infantry to serve within the limits of the state or for the defense of the capital of the United States.[68] The proclamation and the occupation of Baltimore by Butler on the same day dates the death of secession in Maryland and the complete ascendancy of the national government.

Meanwhile, there were those who, doubting the loyalty of Hicks or despairing of prompt and decided action on his part, made direct overtures to the national authorities to volunteer for the defense of the national capital. One of these was James Cooper, a native of the state but a resident of Pennsylvania, who on April 10 asked the secretary of war if the U.S. government had authority to commission the officers of a brigade or regiment raised in Maryland independent of state authority, and whether, possessing the authority, it could be relied upon to do so.[69] The response was favorable. Cooper was appointed by the president a brigadier general of volunteers, assigned to duty in Maryland, and authorized to accept volunteers (under the call of May 2) for three years or the duration of the war, and by the middle of May reported that he had filled Maryland's quota and awaited muster into service. Under the circumstances the secretary of war did not need the services of the four regiments for three months' service and so advised the governor, and also of the fact that General Cooper had been authorized to accept Maryland's quota under the call of May 2.[70] The 1st Maryland, raised principally in Baltimore, was mustered into the U.S. service before the end of May. Recruiting for the 2d Maryland began in June and for the 3d Maryland in July.

Maryland's contribution to the army of the Union was large. From the beginning of the war to its close she furnished twenty regiments and one independent company of infantry; four regiments, one battalion, and one independent company of cavalry; and six batteries of light artillery. The records of the War and Navy Departments show that, from 1861 to 1865, she furnished 50,316 white troops, 8,718 colored troops, and 3,925 sailors and marines, or a grand total of 62,959

[66] "Extracts from the proceedings of the Advisory Council of the State of Virginia," May 2, 1861, reprinted in OR, vol. 2, 794.

[67] Butler to Winfield Scott, May 15, 1861, reprinted in OR, vol. 2, 29–30; Butler to E. C. Parker, May 14, 1861, reprinted in OR, vol. 2, 30–32.

[68] See Headquarters Maryland Militia, General Orders No. 2, May 14, 1861, reprinted in OR, ser. 3, vol. 1, 199; Cameron to Hicks, May 17, 1861, reprinted in OR, ser. 3, vol. 1, 210; General Orders No. 1, May 14, 1861, Governor's Letterbooks, Records of the States, Maryland E.2, reel 5; General Orders No. 4, May 14, 1861, ibid.; Hicks to "the Hon. Secretary of War of the United States [Simon Cameron]," May 14, 1861, ibid.

[69] James Cooper to Cameron, April 30, 1861, reprinted in OR, ser. 3, vol. 1, 138.

[70] Cameron to Hicks, May 17, 1861, reprinted in OR, ser. 3, vol. 1, 210.

men[71]—nearly one-tenth of the entire population, or over 15 percent of the male population, and more than one-half of her available military population[72]—good men and true.

Maryland contributed liberally to the Southern cause also; many of her sons attained high rank and made brilliant records in the Confederate Army. When it became apparent that Maryland would not join her fortunes with the South, many of her younger sons thought they had but one honorable course, and that was to carry the flag of Maryland with the Southern army and rally around it such Maryland men as could be collected. First to move in this direction was Bradley T. Johnson of Frederick. He was an ardent secessionist and one of the first to lead a company into Baltimore after the riot of April 19. When the legislature convened, he intently watched its movements and essayed to direct them. He looked with contempt upon conservative action within the forms of the law and advocated revolutionary methods. When he saw that Maryland would not act, he applied to James M. Mason, the commissioner from Virginia, and procured from him authority to raise troops for the Southern army, then proceeded to Harper's Ferry to obtain Colonel Thomas J. Jackson's permission to rendezvous and ration his men at Point of Rocks, the most available point for that section of Maryland. On the eighth of May, Johnson marched his company out of Frederick, crossed over to Virginia, and reported to Captain Turner Ashby.[73] Some sons of Maryland preceded Johnson; many more followed him. From the secession of Virginia until the surrender of Appomattox, it is estimated that more than fifteen thousand of them served the Confederate cause, and they served it bravely.

It is known to the student of the history of the time under consideration that slavery had but little share in determining Maryland's position at the outbreak of rebellion. Political lines of separation did not run between opposing opinions on that subject, nor were the advocates of freedom confined to one party. Many of the heaviest slaveholders in the state were uncompromising Union men and most of the secessionists had no pecuniary interest in slavery. In fact, slavery was not an appreciable factor in Maryland politics. In Baltimore and in the northern part of the state, there were but few slaveholders and slavery was of a nominal character. All state legislation had been in the direction of improved conditions for the slave.

The Maryland legislature resumed its sitting on June 4, and G. W. Goldsborough, from the committee sent to intercede with the Federal government, reported that the purposes of the committee were defeated "by the movement of Federal troops on Virginia and an active commencement of hostilities" and that they had not felt authorized on the part of the sovereign state of Maryland in presenting a request which had in advance been repudiated. The dignity of the state and the self-respect of the committee, he claimed, demanded this course.[74] The committee appointed at the preceding session to visit Montgomery, Alabama, laid before the Senate and House a letter of Jefferson Davis, in which he expressed the hope "that at no distant day, a State whose people, habits and institutions are so closely related and assimilated with theirs, will seek to unite her fate and fortunes with those of this Confederacy," but, as to a cessation of all hostilities, that depended on the action of the Federal Government. As to the Confederacy, "its policy cannot but be peace: peace with all nations and people."[75]

Petitions poured in from all parts of the state demanding the immediate adjournment of the legislature *sine die*, that the public welfare would be promoted thereby, that they could do no good for the people—whose sentiments they failed to represent. They expressed alarm at the propositions before the legislature and declared their fixed purpose to resist, by force if necessary, any attempt to drag Maryland into collision with the general government. They solemnly protested against the appointment by the legislature of ambassadors and demanded that the delegates chosen under the reign of terror in Baltimore should at once retire from the positions they held. They protested against the so-called "Bill of Ratification" of outrages in Baltimore and, also, against the call for a convention to determine whether the people of Maryland should remain citizens of the United States.[76]

[71] "Abstract from official records showing the forces called for by the President of the United States, the quotas assigned, and the number furnished (i.e., credits allowed) for the military and naval services from 1861 to 1865," OR, ser. 3, vol. 4, 1269; "Classification of the forces credited," OR, ser. 3, vol. 4, 1270. Carman misread his source material, however, in regard to white troops. In the "Abstract," 50,316 represents the total number of men—white or black—who were either furnished by the state *or* who paid a commutation fee. The "Classification" specifies that the number of white troops provided by Maryland was 33,995. Adding this figure to the totals given for colored troops and naval personnel (33,995 + 8,718 + 3,925) yields a total of 46,638—which is precisely the total number of enlistments of all races, across all branches of service, credited to Maryland in the "Abstract."

[72] William F. Fox, using the correct number of men furnished (46,638) estimates that the percentage of the state's military population furnished to the Union was 48.9 percent. He points out, however, that the census of 1860 did not include blacks in its calculation of the military population—resulting in an artificially high percentage. Fox, *Regimental Losses in the American Civil War, 1861–1865: A Treatise on the Extent and Nature of the Mortuary Losses in the Union Regiments, with Full and Exhaustive Statistics Compiled from the Official Records on File in the State Military Bureaus and at Washington* (Albany, N.Y.: Albany Publishing Co., 1889), 534–36.

[73] Bradley T. Johnson, "Memoir of First Maryland Regiment," 349.

[74] *Journal of the Proceedings of the [Maryland] House of Delegates, in Extra Session* (Frederick, Md.: Elihu S. Riley, 1861), 161–62.

[75] Davis to "Messrs. McKaig, Yellot, and Harding, Committee of Maryland Legislature," May 25, 1861, reprinted in *Journal of the Proceedings of the House of Delegates*, 270–71.

[76] *Journal of Proceedings of the Senate*, 140–43.

Notwithstanding the angry protests of the people from all parts of the state, the legislature proceeded with its hostility to the Union cause. The Senate on June 5 asked the governor why he had taken the arms from certain military companies in Baltimore and deposited them for safe keeping in Fort McHenry and what security he had for their return.[77] The governor promptly replied that he did so because he was satisfied that many of them had been carried beyond the limits of the state and that more of them were likely to be used for disloyal purposes. He had ordered them deposited in Fort McHenry because other arms belonging to the state had previously been stolen from depositories selected in Baltimore and he did not deem it prudent to again incur a similar risk. The security he had for them was the honor of the U.S. government and of its loyal officers; he deemed it absurd and insulting to ask for more.[78]

On June 11, Severn T. Wallis, chairman of the Committee on Federal Relations of the House of Delegates, made a report on the "arbitrary proceedings of the United States authorities." The governor was charged with neglect of duty in not protecting John Merryman, "a prisoner at Fort McHenry, the victim of military lawlessness and arbitrary power," and Ross Winans, a venerable and prominent citizen, a useful and respected member of the Maryland House, "arrested by military force, without color of lawful authority, and hurried into illegal imprisonment within the walls of a Federal fortress." The committee offered for consideration resolutions declaring "their earnest and unqualified protest against the oppressive and tyrannical assertion and exercise of military jurisdiction, within the limits of Maryland, over the persons and property of her citizens, by the Government of the United States, and do solemnly declare the same to be subversive of the most sacred guaranties of the Constitution and in flagrant violation of the fundamental and most cherished principles of American free government." These resolutions, passed on the twenty-second, were sent to the senators from Maryland in the Senate of the United States, with the request that they "present the same to the Senate, to be recorded among its proceedings, in vindication of the right and in perpetual memory of the solemn remonstrance of this State against the manifold usurpations and oppressions of the Federal Government."[79]

On the same day the Maryland Senate concurred in resolutions, passed by the House of Delegates, protesting against the acts of the U.S. government in quartering large standing armies upon the soil of Maryland, in seizing and using her railroads and telegraphs, in depriving her citizens of arms and subjecting them to arrest, and declaring that "the right of separation from the Federal Union is a right neither arising under, nor prohibited by the Constitution, but a sovereign right, independent of the Constitution to be exercised by the several states upon their own responsibility." They demanded that the war should cease and that the Southern Confederacy be recognized, and they viewed with the utmost alarm and indignation the exercise of the despotic power that dared to suspend the writ of Habeas Corpus and hold John Merryman within the walls of Fort McHenry.[80]

On June 25 the legislature adjourned until July 30. Its whole session had been marked by hostility to the national government and an intense dislike of Hicks, who stood as a bulwark against its disunion schemes and who, after its adjournment, continued the work (in which he had been some time engaged) of disarming the disloyal militia.

While the legislature was in session, secessionists in the state and beyond its borders looked for assistance from the Confederate troops at Harper's Ferry, and both Davis and Lee were appealed to, to take position in Maryland. It was hoped that Confederate occupation would counteract the effect of Federal possession and revive the waning secession feeling. Particularly it was desired to lay strong hold on western Maryland. On June 4, the day that the legislature assembled, Isaac R. Trimble, now an officer in the Confederate service stationed at Norfolk, Virginia,[81] addressed an elaborate communication to Lee suggesting a strong movement to Hagerstown, Maryland, it being a better point to defend Virginia than Harper's Ferry. He was particularly anxious that this movement should be made before the election in Maryland, and he urged a simultaneous movement on Baltimore, which would revolutionize the state of Maryland, bring six thousand armed men into the Confederate ranks, and probably have the effect of driving Lincoln out of Washington and down the Potomac.[82]

Plans were proposed for organizing secretly a military force for the liberation of the state. Companies, regiments, and brigades were to be recruited at different parts of the state and sworn into Confederate service. Rendezvous were to be designated for each, and certain trustworthy persons in Maryland were to be appointed to organize this force and arm it with

---

[77] Ibid., 143.

[78] Ibid., 152.

[79] *Report of the Committee on Federal Relations upon the Messages of the Governor, in Regard to the Arbitrary Proceedings of the United States Authorities, and the Governor's Correspondence with the United States Government* (Frederick, Md.: Elihu S. Riley, 1861). See also *Journal of the Proceedings of the House of Delegates*, 228–31; Resolution Number 13, *Laws of the State of Maryland, Made and Passed at a Special Session of the General Assembly, Held at Frederick, April 26, 1861* (Annapolis: Elihu S. Riley, 1861), n.p.

[80] Resolution Number 14, *Laws of the State of Maryland*, n.p.

[81] In his original text, Carman refers to Trimble as "a native of Maryland." Though associated closely with that state due to his years of service in the antebellum period with a number of Baltimore-based railroads, he was in fact a native of Culpeper County, Virginia.

[82] Isaac R. Trimble to Lee, June 4, 1861, reprinted in *OR*, vol. 51, pt. 2, 129–30.

shotguns, rifles, pistols, and anything else calculated to destroy the enemy, then strike for Baltimore or Washington, as should be determined by the authorities at Richmond.[83] The great advantage of the proposed plan was that "when Maryland does turn upon her oppressors she will have a regularly organized force, and not a mere rabble without organization."[84]

On the tenth of June, Major General Nathaniel P. Banks was appointed to the command of the Department of Annapolis, with headquarters at Baltimore. On the twenty-seventh he arrested police marshal George P. Kane, committed him to Fort McHenry, and suspended the commissioners of police. Four days later he arrested and imprisoned the police commissioners and revolutionized the entire city government. The removal of the municipal authorities and the substitution of military rule was excused on the plea of military necessity.[85] Baltimore had sinned on the nineteenth of April; it might sin again, and the risk was too great of having a barrier placed on one of the principal routes connecting the capital of the nation with the North. In a lesser degree, the whole state was under suspicion, and it was the mailed hand that was offered her. The legislature, which re-assembled on the thirtieth of July, continued in session until the seventh of August. It spent its days in talking and resolving, and after adopting a vigorous protest against the "unconstitutional and illegal acts of President Lincoln,"[86] it adjourned to meet on the seventeenth of September.

As the time approached for the adjourned meeting, there were apprehensions that the passage of an ordinance of secession was contemplated, and on September 11 the secretary of war instructed Banks, then in command of troops at Darnestown, Maryland, that such action must be prevented and, if necessary to that end, all or any number of the members should be arrested.[87] On the twelfth Major General George B. McClellan advised Banks that the seizure of the members would be made on the seventeenth and instructed him to "have everything prepared to arrest the whole party, and be sure that none escape." If successfully carried out McClellan thought it would "go far toward breaking the backbone of the rebellion."[88] (Preliminary to the arrest of the legislature, Mayor Brown and several prominent citizens of Baltimore were quietly arrested and committed to Fort McHenry. Among the number were members of the legislature from the city.)[89]

Both houses of the legislature were called at noon on the seventeenth; as no quorum appeared, an adjournment was effected until next day. Meanwhile, the military surrounded the city and permitted none to leave it. On the eighteenth several officers and members of the Senate and House of Delegates were arrested and the legislature broken up.[90] It was stoutly maintained by the national authorities that the legislature intended passing an ordinance of secession; it was quite as earnestly denied by those who had means of knowing. Brown says, "The apprehension that the Legislature intended to pass an act of secession, as intimated by Secretary Cameron, was, in view of the position in which the state was placed, and the whole condition of affairs, so absurd that it is difficult to believe that he seriously entertained it. The blow was no doubt, however, intended to strike with terror the opponents of the war, and was one of the effective means resorted to by the Government to obtain, as it soon did, entire control of the State."[91] The action was met with approval from Hicks, who two days later congratulated Banks, saying he concurred in all he had done, that the good fruit produced by the arrests was already apparent, and that there could be no longer any mincing matters with "these desperate people."[92]

For five months the legislature, sustained and encouraged by less than one-fifth of the people, had kept the state in a turmoil and filled the national authorities with grave apprehensions. It was well known that it did not reflect or represent the wishes or interests of the state; when finally broken up, there was much relief and great satisfaction to all who had at heart the true interest of the state. A large majority of her people had the good sense to see that the welfare of Maryland was inseparably blended with the Union, but such had been the fraudulent and violent spirit and course of the secessionists that they were overawed. The dispersal of the legislature and the determination of the national government that no more should

---

[83] James D. McCabe to Leroy P. Walker, July 6, 1861, and "A plan for the effectual organization of a military force in the State of Maryland to co-operate with the Army of the Confederate States against the U.S. troops," no date, reprinted in *OR*, vol. 51, pt. 2, 155–57.

[84] McCabe to Severn T. Wallis, July 6, 1861, reprinted in *OR*, vol. 51, pt. 2, 157.

[85] See Scott to Nathaniel P. Banks, June 24, 1861, reprinted in *OR*, vol. 2, 138–39; Banks to Scott, July 1, 1861, reprinted in *OR*, vol. 2, 139; Banks to Scott, July 1, 1861, reprinted in *OR*, vol. 2, 139–40; Banks to "the People of the City of Baltimore," June 27, 1861, reprinted in *OR*, vol. 2, 140–41; Banks to "the People of the City of Baltimore," July 1, 1861, reprinted in *OR*, vol. 2, 141–42.

[86] Resolution Number 15, *Laws of the State of Maryland*, n.p.

[87] Cameron to Banks, September 11, 1861, reprinted in *OR*, vol. 5, 193.

[88] George B. McClellan to Banks, September 12, 1861. A copy of this letter appears in Stephen W. Sears, ed., *The Civil War Papers of George B. McClellan: Selected Correspondence, 1860–1865* (New York: Ticknor & Fields, 1989), 99.

[89] See John A. Dix to John E. Wool, September 13, 1861, reprinted in *OR*, vol. 5, 194; Allen Pinkerton to William H. Seward, September 23, 1861, reprinted in *OR*, vol. 5, 195–96; John E. Wool to "the Commanding Officer, Fort Lafayette, New York Harbor," September 24, 1861, reprinted in *OR*, vol. 5, 196–97.

[90] See Banks to Seward, September 18, 1861, reprinted in *OR*, vol. 5, 194; Banks to Randolph B. Marcy, September 20, 1861, reprinted in *OR*, vol. 5, 194–95.

[91] Brown, 103.

[92] Hicks to Banks, September 20, 1861, reprinted in *OR*, vol. 5, 197.

that body stir up strife in the state, nor Baltimore threaten the security of Washington, gave encouragement to Union men everywhere and strengthened the growth of Union expression in Maryland. Volunteering became brisk, and confidence grew that the Union men could take care of the state.

On November 6 a state election was held, resulting in the choice of Augustus W. Bradford (the candidate of the Union Party) for governor by a majority of 31,438 and a legislature largely Union. Ten days thereafter Hicks called for the newly elected legislature to convene in extra session, beginning on December 3, "to consider and determine the steps necessary to be taken to enable the State of Maryland to take her place with the other loyal States, in defense of the Constitution and the Union."[93]

It is beyond our purpose to pursue the subject further. The struggle of the Union majority for supremacy had been bitter and agitated the state from the mountains to the sea, but with the national and state authorities in accord, peace was assured and tranquility restored. Many secessionists and the turbulent left the state, and only those who essayed to provoke disorder or encourage revolution felt "the despot's heel" or complained of oppression. Those who walked or lived within the law were in the full enjoyment of all their rights and liberties.[94]

---

[93] See Proclamation of Thomas H. Hicks, November 16, 1861, Proceedings of the Governor, June 1861–January 1869, *Records of the States*, Maryland E.1, reel 12.

[94] Inexplicably, Carman chose to conclude this chapter with a short essay on the ardently pro-Confederate ballad "My Maryland." (Adopted in 1939 as the official state song of Maryland, it remains so as of this writing.) This discordant close to Carman's declaration of Unionist ascendancy is reprinted herein as Appendix C.

2
The Confederate Invasion of Maryland

In the preceding chapter, we have noted the efforts of prominent individuals, mass meetings, city and county conventions, and the legislature to ally Maryland with the Southern Confederacy. We have noted also the great desire of the South for such an alliance to round out the fair proportions of the new Confederacy. There were some proposed military movements to that end, but these were to be made in connection with legislative action and, measurably, to influence it.

When the Confederate army began to gather in front of Washington, more specific measures were canvassed and proposed. On July 18, 1861, Brigadier General Pierre G. T. Beauregard, commanding the (Confederate) Army of the Potomac, sent Colonel James Chesnut Jr. of his staff to Richmond with a suggestion to President Davis that Brigadier General Joseph E. Johnston's Army of the Shenandoah (then at Winchester) and Beauregard's force be united at Manassas, advance upon and crush Brigadier General Irvin McDowell in the vicinity of Fairfax Court House, then turn upon and defeat Major General Robert Patterson near Winchester.[1] Brigadier General Robert S. Garnett was to be reinforced sufficiently to defeat McClellan in West Virginia and then join Johnston at Winchester, "who was forthwith to cross the Potomac into Maryland with his whole force, arouse the people as he advanced to the recovery of their political rights and the defense of their homes and families from an offensive invader, and then march to the investment of Washington in the rear," while Beauregard resumed the offensive in front.[2] The complicated plan was not seriously considered, and Beauregard's official report, in which the subject is mentioned, bears the endorsement of Davis that "the plan was based on the improbable and inadmissible supposition that the enemy was to await everywhere, isolated and motionless, until our forces could effect junctions to attack them in detail."[3]

There was much disappointment in the South at the failure of Johnston and Beauregard to follow the defeat of McDowell at Manassas, on July 21, 1861, by an advance on Washington and into Maryland. A few weeks later both Johnston and Beauregard, joined by Major General Gustavus W. Smith (commanding Johnston's old corps), favored an immediate offensive campaign beyond the Potomac—provided an adequate force could be concentrated for this purpose. These three senior generals of the Confederate army threatening Washington were satisfied that the number of men "present for duty" in the army, about forty thousand, was not sufficient for making an active campaign of invasion, and thought if Davis would come to the headquarters of the army—away from the interruption caused by disturbing elements surrounding him in Richmond—he too would be satisfied that the best policy at the time would be to concentrate in that vicinity, as rapidly as possible, all the available forces of the Southern Confederacy; cross the Potomac with the army thus reinforced; and, by pressing the fighting in the enemy's country, make a determined effort in the autumn of 1861 to compel the Northern states to recognize Confederate independence, the campaign to be sharp and if possible decisive, before active operations would have to be suspended because of approaching winter.[4]

In furtherance of this idea, Beauregard wrote Davis on September 6, suggesting an advance of the army beyond the Potomac and arguing the good results of such a movement in relieving the pressure upon other points. Davis replied on the eighth, "It is true that a successful advance across the Potomac would relieve other places; but, if not successful, ruin would befall us." He regretted that he had not arms to place in the hands of the volunteers, necessary to the purpose. Besides, Missouri and Kentucky demanded his attention and the southern coast needed additional defense.[5]

---

[1] Johnston and Beauregard were promoted to general on the same day as Lee—August 31, 1861. See *Journal of the Provisional Congress of the Confederate States of America*, vol. 1 of *Journal of the Congress of the Confederate States of America, 1861–1865*, 58th Cong., 2d sess., 1904, S. Doc. 234, serial 4610, 464.

   The Confederacy's Army of the Potomac formed the nucleus of what would become by 1862 the Army of Northern Virginia.

[2] Pierre G. T. Beauregard to Samuel Cooper, August 26 [October 14—*OR* editors], 1861, reprinted in *OR*, vol. 2, 485.

[3] Endorsement of Jefferson Davis on Beauregard to Cooper, 505. No date is given for Davis's endorsement.

[4] Gustavus W. Smith, *Confederate War Papers: Fairfax Court House, New Orleans, Seven Pines, Richmond and North Carolina* (New York: Atlantic Publishing and Engraving Co., 1884), 29, 32.

[5] Jefferson Davis to Joseph E. Johnston, September 8, 1861, reprinted in *OR*, vol. 5, 833–34. Beauregard's letter of the sixth was actually written to Johnston, who in turn forwarded it to Davis. This letter is now lost, but mention is made of it at the start of Davis's September 8 communication to Johnston.

On September 26, Johnston reported to the new secretary of war, Judah P. Benjamin, that he had made preparations "to remove the troops from the unhealthy atmosphere of the valley of Bull Run and to be ready to turn the enemy's position and advance into Maryland, when the strength of this army would justify it." He followed with the suggestion that the president be induced to visit the army, or send a representative, to confer upon the matter of an advance.[6] (This letter was sent by Captain Thomas L. Preston of Johnston's staff, who was instructed to make a statement to the secretary and answer such questions as should come up.) Benjamin replied on the twenty-ninth, "It is extremely difficult, even with the aid of such information as Captain Preston has been able to give us orally, as suggested by you, to determine whether or not we can furnish you the further means you may deem necessary to assume the active offensive."[7]

A few days thereafter, Davis arrived at Fairfax Court House and a conference was held, at which were present Davis, Johnston, Beauregard and Smith. It was the unanimous opinion that the military force of the Confederacy was at the highest point it could attain without arms from abroad, that the army grouped around Fairfax Court House was in the finest fighting condition, and that if kept inactive it must retrograde immensely in every respect during the winter—the effect of which was foreseen by all. On the other hand, the enemy were daily increasing in numbers, arms, discipline, and efficiency. A sad state of things was anticipated at the opening of the spring campaign. Davis was asked, "Is it not possible to increase the effective strength of this army, and put us in condition to cross the Potomac and carry the war into the enemy's country? Can you not by stripping other points to the last they will bear, and, even risking defeat at all other places, put us in condition to move forward?" The generals sought to impress upon Davis that success, at that time, would save everything. Defeat would lose all.[8]

Smith says:

> In explanation, and as an illustration of this, the unqualified opinion was advanced, that, if for want of adequate strength on our part in Kentucky, the Federal forces should take military possession of that whole state, and enter and occupy a portion of Tennessee, a victory gained by this army beyond the Potomac would, by threatening the heart of the Northern States, compel their armies to fall back, free Kentucky—and give us the line of the Ohio, within ten days thereafter. On the other hand should our forces in Tennessee and Southern Kentucky be strengthened, so as to enable us to take, and to hold, the Ohio River as a boundary, a disastrous defeat of this army would at once be followed by an overwhelming wave of Northern invaders, which would sweep over Kentucky and Tennessee, extending to the northern part of the cotton States, if not to New Orleans.
>
> Similar views were expressed in regard to ultimate results in North-Western Virginia, being dependent upon the success or failure of this army, and various other special illustrations were offered. Showing, in short, that success here was success everywhere—defeat here, defeat everywhere,— [sic] and that this was the point upon which all the available forces of the Confederate States should be concentrated.

It was acknowledged by all that the army at Fairfax Court House was not strong enough to carry a campaign beyond the Potomac, that ten to twenty thousand additional men were required—seasoned men. These Davis could not spare from other points, nor had he arms to put into the hands of recruits. The whole country was demanding protection at his hands and praying for arms and troops for defense. Want of arms was the great difficulty; without these from abroad, he could not reinforce the army.[9]

Davis then proposed some operations of a partisan character, especially an expedition by a detachment against Brigadier General Joseph Hooker's division in lower Maryland, opposite Evansport. Johnston objected to this proposition because he had no means of transporting a sufficient body of men to the Maryland shore quickly, and (the Potomac being controlled by Federal vessels-of-war) such a body, if thrown into Maryland, would inevitably be captured or destroyed in attempting to return—even if successful against the land forces. Upon Johnston's declining such an enterprise, the conference terminated.[10]

On the eighth day of October, Smith again called the attention of Davis to the necessity of an offensive movement and to the fact that the morale of the army was suffering because of enforced idleness, to which Davis replied on the tenth:

[6] Johnston to Judah P. Benjamin, September 26, 1861, reprinted in *OR*, vol. 5, 881–82.

[7] Benjamin to Johnston, September 29, 1861, reprinted in *OR*, vol. 5, 883.

[8] Gustavus W. Smith, 14–16. Nearly all of the first chapter of Smith's book consists of a reprinted memorandum of the meeting, drafted by Smith on January 31, 1862, and countersigned by Johnston and Beauregard as to the authenticity of its contents. The memorandum also appears as "Council of war at Centreville," in *OR*, vol. 5, 884–87. The *OR* version bears a date at top of October 1, 1861—the editors' approximation of the date of the meeting, not of the document's drafting.

[9] Gustavus W. Smith, 17–18.

[10] Johnston, *Narrative of Military Operations, Directed, during the Late War between the States* (New York: D. Appleton & Co., 1874), 77.

Your remarks about the moral effect of repressing the hope of the volunteers for an advance are in accordance with the painful impression made on me, when in our council it was revealed to me that the Army of the Potomac had been reduced to about one-half the legalized strength, and that the arms to restore the number were not in depot. As I then suggested, though you may not be able to advance into Maryland and expel the enemy, it may be possible to keep up the spirits of your troops by expeditions, such as that particularly spoken of against [Brigadier General Daniel E.] Sickles' brigade, on the Lower Potomac, or Banks', above, by destroying the canal, and making other rapid movements whenever opportunity presents to beat detachments or to destroy lines of communication.[11]

Three days later Secretary Benjamin wrote to Johnston, "I had hoped almost against hope that the condition of the army would justify you in coming to the conclusion that some forward movement could be made, and that the roofs to shelter the troops during the approaching winter would be found on the other side of the Potomac; but our destitute condition so far as arms are concerned renders it impossible to increase your strength."[12]

A few days after the Fairfax Court House conference, Brigadier General Thomas J. "Stonewall" Jackson proposed that the Confederates should invade the North in two columns, winter at Harrisburg and, in the spring of 1862, advance directly upon Philadelphia. As preliminary to this he would move into northwestern Virginia with ten thousand men, reclaim that country from Federal sway, and summon the inhabitants to his standard. Of these he thought he could recruit fifteen to twenty thousand, which would place his command to at least twenty-five thousand. He would then rapidly move his entire force across the Monongahela, into Monongalia County, march upon Pittsburgh, seize that place and destroy the arsenal there, and then—in cooperation with a column crossing the Potomac near Leesburg and forming a junction with his own column—advance upon Harrisburg and occupy it. From Harrisburg he proposed that the united columns should advance, in the spring, upon Philadelphia. Smith gives the argument presented by Jackson:

McClellan … with his army of recruits, will not attempt to come out against us this autumn. If we remain inactive they will have greatly the advantage over us next spring. Their raw recruits will have then become an organised [*sic*] army, vastly superior in numbers to our own. We are ready at the present moment for active operations in the field, while they are not. We ought to invade their country now, and not wait for them to make the necessary preparations to invade ours. If the President would reinforce this army by taking troops from other points not threatened, and let us make an active campaign of invasion before winter sets in, McClellan's raw recruits could not stand against us in the field.

Crossing the Upper Potomac, occupying Baltimore, and taking possession of Maryland, we could cut off the communications of Washington, force the Federal Government to abandon the capital, beat McClellan's army if it came out against us in the open country, destroy industrial establishments wherever we found them, break up the lines of interior commercial intercourse, close the coal mines, seize and, if necessary, destroy the manufactories and commerce of Philadelphia, and of other large cities within our reach; take and hold the narrow neck of country between Pittsburg and Lake Erie; subsist mainly on the country we traverse, and making unrelenting war amidst their homes, force the people of the North to understand what it will cost them to hold the South in the Union at the bayonet's point.

(Jackson at this time commanded a brigade in Smith's corps and, in presenting his plan and the argument for it, urged Smith to use his influence with Johnston and Beauregard and with the authorities at Richmond to have it approved. When informed by Smith of the substance of the Fairfax Court House conference, Jackson was sorely disappointed, and dropped the matter.)[13]

Considering the circumstances it is not so certain that the Confederates would have achieved such success as to compel the North to recognize their independence before winter set in. Indeed, the probabilities are to the contrary. The fighting quality of Northern troops was underestimated and their quick recovery from defeat not appreciated. Nor was it taken into account that the patriotism of the people of the North was not to be quenched by a temporary reverse and that they had come to the determination, cost what it would, to preserve the government. Davis knew all this and appreciated it at its worth; he saw, too, the political reasons against the step—conditions of the South which he could not disregard in weighing the subject and coming to a conclusion. As he says, "The whole country was demanding protection at his hands, and praying for arms and troops for defence."[14] The opinion is a correct one that "he could not have consolidated his people for the

[11] Jefferson Davis to Gustavus W. Smith, October 10, 1861, reprinted in *OR*, vol. 5, 893–94. The entirety of Smith's October 8 letter has been lost, but a portion appears in Gustavus W. Smith, 20.

[12] Benjamin to Johnston, October 13, 1861, reprinted in *OR*, vol. 5, 896.

[13] G. F. R. Henderson, *Stonewall Jackson and the American Civil War*, vol. 1, (London: Longmans, Green, and Co., 1898), 213–15 (quoting a letter from Smith to Henderson). See also Gustavus W. Smith, 30–31.

[14] Such at least is what Davis is reported to have said. Gustavus W. Smith, 18.

long struggle which had to come, if he had denied defense to all, for the sole purpose of an invasion from Virginia."[15] There might have been temporary success, but not such as would have held Maryland, discouraged the North, or compelled the recognition of Confederate independence.

However far the military arm fell short of consummating the hopes of the Confederate secessionists of Maryland and the people of the Southern Confederacy, the Confederate Congress was quick to express itself in favor of "speedy and efficient exertion" for the relief of the people of Maryland. On December 21, 1861, it passed these resolutions:

Whereas, the State of Maryland has suffered the same wrongs which impelled these Confederate States to withdraw from the United States, and is intimately associated with these States by geographical situation, by mutual interests, by similarity of institutions, and by enduring sentiments of reciprocal amity and esteem; and

Whereas, it is believed that a large majority of the good people of Maryland earnestly desire to unite their State with the Confederate States, a desire which is proved to exist even by the violent, extraordinary, and tyrannical measures employed by our enemy to restrain the expression thereof; and

Whereas, the Government of the United States, by imprisoning members of the Legislature of Maryland, by establishing powerful armies of foreign troops within that State and along her borders, and by suppressing with armed force the freedom of speech and of elections, has prevented the people and their representatives from adopting the political connection which they prefer, and in revenge of their preference has inflicted upon them many outrages and established over them a foreign despotism; and

Whereas, the accession of Maryland to this Confederation will be mutually beneficial, and is essential to the integrity and security of the Confederate Union: Be it therefore—

First. *Resolved by the Congress of the Confederate States of America,* That the sufferings of the good people of Maryland under the oppression of our enemy excite our profound sympathy and entitle them to speedy and efficient exertions on our part for their relief.

Second. That it is the desire of this Government, by appropriate measures, to facilitate the accession of Maryland, with the free consent of her people, to the Confederate States.

Third. That no peace ought to be concluded with the United States which does not insure to Maryland the opportunity of forming a part of this Confederacy.[16]

This idea was constantly kept in view by the Confederate executive. When it was thought that the Confederate government was about to be recognized by Great Britain and France and intervention resorted to, to end the war, Davis was prompt to inform his representatives abroad that there were certain conditions that would be insisted upon by the Confederate government, and these were expressed in a communication prepared by Secretary of State Robert M. T. Hunter. After debating upon the great advantages that would accrue to Great Britain and France by the recognition of the Southern Confederacy and its establishment as one of the powers of the world, which the signs of the time indicated were near at hand, he laid down conditions upon which intervention would not be deprecated:

No treaty of peace can be accepted which does not secure the independence of the Confederate States, including Maryland, Virginia, Kentucky, and Missouri, the States south of them, and the Territories of New Mexico and Arizona.

The union of the States of Maryland, Kentucky, and Missouri with the Southern Confederacy might be contingent upon a fair vote of the citizens of those States, to be uninfluenced by force or the presence of the troops either of the Confederate or of the United States.[17]

He set forth the inducements to such an arrangement and the great interest Great Britain and France had in the increase of the supply of cotton and sugar and the enlargement of markets, in which and for which they could exchange their manufactures upon convenient and easy terms. For this purpose the Southern Confederacy ought to be so constituted as to

---

[15] As of this writing, Carman's source for this unattributed quotation has not been identified.

[16] Resolutions of the Confederate Congress Relating to Maryland, December 21, 1861, reprinted in *OR*, ser. 4, vol. 1, 805–6.

[17] Robert M. T. Hunter to James M. Mason, February 8, 1862. A copy also appears in U.S. Navy Department, comp., *Official Records of the Union and Confederate Navies in the War of the Rebellion* (Washington, D.C.: Government Printing Office, 1894–1927), ser. 2, vol. 3, 333–34 (hereafter *ORN*; all subsequent references are to series 2 unless noted otherwise). A nearly identical dispatch was sent to John Slidell, the Confederate commissioner to France.

As his fragmentary notations suggest, Carman worked from captured manuscript originals (or letterbook copies) of the correspondence to and from the Confederate State Department. Publication of these documents in series 2 of the *ORN* did not begin until 1921—more than a decade after Carman's death. See Alan C. and Barbara A. Aimone, *A User's Guide to the Official Records of the American Civil War* (Shippenburg, Pa.: White Mane Publishing Co., 1993), 31.

enable the states growing cotton and sugar to devote their labor almost exclusively to these objects and to draw their provisions from other states better suited to the production of such supplies. He held that:

> The union of North Carolina, Virginia, Maryland, Kentucky, and Missouri with the cotton-growing States south of them is essential to constitute such a confederacy. By such a union we should enlarge the area in which agriculture would be the principal employment, and increase greatly the number of customers who would desire to purchase British manufactures at as low a rate of duty as would be consistent with their revenue wants. The value of that market would be enhanced, too, from the fact that it would then include in the circle of its exchanges not only cotton, sugar, and rice, but tobacco, naval stores, timber, and provisions, the articles most sought after by Great Britain in her foreign trade. Such a confederacy would be independent of its Northern neighbors in all respects. Its people would find within themselves the means of supplying all their wants except those of manufactures and of transportation by sea, which they would seek abroad … Such a confederacy, too, would be able to take care of itself, and to protect its own independence and interests against all assault from its neighbors. But if Maryland, Kentucky, and Missouri should be united to the Northern Confederacy, all hope of a balance of power between the two would be gone, and the Confederate States would be in constant danger of aggression from its Northern neighbor. A temptation would thus be held out to the formation of a party for a reconstruction of the old political union not only for the purpose of peace, but to secure the trade of the border slave States which is so advantageous if not indispensable to them.
>
> At least they would probably seek to restore the old connection in trade by means of treaties which might favor their Northern neighbors beyond all other foreign nations. Such an arrangement of boundaries would either lead to this state of things or else to frequent wars, and the intervening parties would find that they had given not a peace but a hollow truce. This state of things would prove a constant source of expense, trouble, and turmoil to all concerned. The simple and natural plan of uniting all the slave-holding States would avoid these difficulties. Although nominally inferior to the United States, it is easy to see from their position on the map and a comparison of their resources that there would be no uneven balance between them …
>
> In this connection it may be proper to show the immense importance of the Chesapeake Bay to the Confederate States. In the new Confederacy by means of railroad and water lines its streams of commerce will flow from sources far west of the Mississippi and range in their northern and southern boundaries from St. Louis to New Orleans. By the concentration of so much commerce at such a point the European shipping is saved the tedious and sometimes dangerous circumnavigation of the Southern Atlantic coast and the Gulf of Mexico.[18]

The secretary then went on to say that when the union of all the slaveholding states, save Delaware, was once established, its commercial and industrial development would be "unparalleled in the past"—but such a union was necessary for this purpose. Without it, "constant war must arise from the efforts of those States to get together again." There was "no other road to a solid and permanent peace which the highest interests of mankind" seemed to demand. At the same time, it was declared that intervention was not sought and that the government had no doubt of its ability to achieve independence and drive the invader from its soil. It might require time and sacrifices, blood and money, but effort should not cease until it was accomplished.[19]

In his inaugural address to the Confederate Congress on February 22, 1862, Davis said, "Maryland, already united to us by hallowed memories and material interests, will, I believe, when enabled to speak with unstifled voice, connect her destiny with the South."[20] Yet there were those who would not wait on the voice of the people of Maryland, and no sooner had the Confederate Congress assembled than there arose a hot clamor for an immediate movement into Maryland to redeem Baltimore and Annapolis and cut off railroad communication with the North. Not into Maryland only did they demand an advance; they insisted on a movement farther north, to compel the men and wealth of New York, Philadelphia, Boston, and other cities to pay the South for the losses she had sustained. But these visionary schemes were not shared by the majority, which was held to a strict defensive by the personal influence of Davis.

On the contrary, there were some extremists who did not want Maryland as a member of the Southern Confederacy upon any consideration. They had not welcomed Virginia, because she had a habit of absorbing all the offices. Their ideal was a Confederacy of cotton-growing states. Judah Benjamin assured Congressman Reuben Davis of Mississippi, early in March 1862, that there was no doubt of the recognition of the Southern Confederacy by England within ninety days,

---

[18] Ibid., 334–35.

[19] Ibid., 335.

[20] See "Inauguration of Jeff. Davis," reprinted in Frank Moore, ed., *The Rebellion Record: A Diary of American Events*, vol. 4 (New York: G. P. Putnam, 1862), Documents and Narratives, 201. Until this date, Davis had been serving as president under a provisional constitution. February 22—Washington's birthday—was chosen as the day on which the permanent Confederate government would come into being.

and that would end the war. When questioned what measures meanwhile would be taken to drive the Union forces from Tennessee, Benjamin replied that such measures were not necessary, that the South would hold from the Memphis and Charleston Railroad south, and the Northern states could keep what was north of that line.[21]

The great majority, however, would not listen to any proposition that did not embrace Maryland as one of the Confederate States, and unceasing efforts were exerted to impress upon civil and military authorities the high and solemn duty of liberating her. These efforts were seconded by many prominent men and women of Maryland, who, leaving their state, crossed the Potomac and journeyed to Richmond. Here, like exiled Stuarts, they held court, thronged the official residences, mingled in the gayeties of the capital, and poured their sorrows into the sympathetic ears of the influential. Expressions of sympathy for them and for their state were manifest at all times and on all occasions, shared by the highest and the lowest. "Maryland, My Maryland" was the popular air of the day and was heard everywhere.

When it was known that McClellan had transferred the (Union) Army of the Potomac from in front of Washington to the York Peninsula, Johnston was assigned to command the army for the defense of Richmond, and he advised that it be concentrated behind defensive works around that place. There was a difference of opinion among the Confederate chiefs as to the advisability of this plan and, about the middle of April 1862, a conference was held at which were present Davis, Lee, Johnston, Smith, and Major General James Longstreet. Among the propositions brought forward was one offered by Smith, which was to garrison Richmond, occupy McClellan in besieging that place, move the larger part of the Confederate army rapidly across the border, and make an active offensive campaign beyond the Potomac, striking Baltimore and Washington, if not Philadelphia and New York, before McClellan could take the works around Richmond. Both Davis and Lee opposed this plan as well as that of Johnston (to hold the army in the defenses of Richmond), and the result of the conference was an order to Johnston to occupy the line selected by Major General John B. Magruder on the Peninsula—the Warwick River and Yorktown line.[22]

McClellan set himself down before this line and made elaborate preparations to break it. Johnston saw the impossibility of preventing this or successfully resisting the march of the Army of the Potomac up the Peninsula to the gates of Richmond, and on April 29 wrote Lee, "The fight for Yorktown, as I said in Richmond, must be one of artillery, in which we cannot win. The result is certain; the time only doubtful … We must abandon the Peninsula soon." As two or three days more or less would signify little, Johnston considered it best for the sake of the capital to abandon Yorktown and put his army in position to defend Richmond, and he notified Lee of his intention to do so as soon as it could be done conveniently.[23] On the next day he renewed the suggestion, made by Smith two weeks before, in a letter to Lee:

> We are engaged in a species of warfare at which we can never win.
>
> It is plain that General McClellan will adhere to the system adopted by him last summer, and depend for success upon artillery and engineering. We can compete with him in neither.
>
> We must therefore change our course, take the offensive, collect all the troops we have in the East and cross the Potomac with them, while Beauregard, with all we have in the West, invades Ohio.
>
> Our troops have always wished for the offensive, and so does the country. Please submit this suggestion to the President. We can have no success while McClellan is allowed, as he is by our defensive, to choose his mode of warfare.[24]

Lee replied on May 1, "The feasibility of the proposition … has been the subject of consideration with him [Davis] for some time, so far as advancing a column to the Potomac with all the troops that can be made available. The proposed invasion of Ohio by General Beauregard, however desirable, it is feared at this time is impracticable, though it will also be considered. He concurs in your views as to the benefits to be obtained by taking the offensive, and is very desirous of being able to carry it into effect."[25]

Johnston abandoned Yorktown and McClellan advanced up the Peninsula and fronted Richmond. At the same time, Jackson (now a major general) was conducting his brilliant campaign in the Shenandoah Valley, resulting in the defeat of Banks, Major General John C. Frémont, and Brigadier General James Shields. As he saw Banks's troops retreating across the Potomac above Harper's Ferry, Jackson's thoughts again turned to an invasion of the North, and at Halltown on May 30 he instructed a member of his staff to proceed to Richmond and tell the authorities that, if his army could be increased to forty thousand men, a movement might be made beyond the Potomac which would raise the siege of Richmond and transfer the

---

[21] Reuben Davis, *Recollections of Mississippi and Mississippians* (Boston: Houghton, Mifflin and Co., 1889), 431–32.

[22] See Gustavus W. Smith, 41–44.

[23] Johnston to Robert E. Lee, April 29, 1862, reprinted in *OR*, vol. 11, pt. 3, 473.

[24] Johnston to Lee, April 30, 1862, reprinted in *OR*, vol. 11, pt. 3, 477.

[25] Lee to Johnston, May 1, 1862, reprinted in *OR*, vol. 11, pt. 3, 485.

campaign from the banks of the James to those of the Susquehanna. Jackson's staff officer was delayed in reaching Richmond; meanwhile, Frémont was disposed of at Cross Keys on June 8 and Shields at Port Republic the next day, and Jackson took position at Brown's Gap, from which place he again sent his staff officer to Richmond to make formal application to the government to increase his command to forty thousand men in order that he might carry into effect the movement he had proposed at Halltown more than a week previous. "By that means," he said, "Richmond can be relieved and the campaign transferred to Pennsylvania." In making the proposed counter-movement northward, he would advance toward the Potomac along the eastern side of the Blue Ridge, masking his march as much as possible, and "by rapidly crossing the mountain at the most available gap," he could, by getting in the rear of Banks (who had returned to Winchester), quickly dispose of him and "thereby open up the road to western Maryland and Pennsylvania" by way of Williamsport and Hagerstown.[26]

Jackson's messenger arrived at Richmond on the fourteenth of June and laid his messages before the new secretary of war, George W. Randolph, who referred him to Davis, who, in turn, referred him to Lee. The general listened attentively as Jackson's plans were unfolded, inquired as to the condition of his army and the crop prospects of the Valley, and finally expressed an opinion that it would be better for Jackson to come down to Richmond and help drive McClellan's "troublesome people" away from it.[27] Two days later Lee said the movement proposed by Jackson "will have to be postponed." The reason was the necessity for the use of his command in giving a crushing blow to McClellan.[28]

Jackson moved down to Richmond and joined Lee. McClellan was attacked and driven to Harrison's Landing on the James River, where his impregnable position forbade further Confederate action in that quarter. Jackson was for aggressive action; he would give the North no time to reorganize its armies or to drill the new levies flocking to its camps. He would give not a day's respite, but would strike heavy blows at every favoring opportunity. Above all he would invade the North.

While the army lay near Westover, resting from its toils, General Jackson called his friend, the Honorable Mr. [Alexander R.] Boteler, to his tent, to communicate his views of the future conduct of the war, and to beg that on his next visit to Richmond, he would impress them upon the Government. He said that it was manifest by every sign, that M'Clellan's [sic] was a thoroughly beaten army, and was no longer capable of anything, until it was reorganized and reinforced. There was danger, he foresaw, of repeating the error of Manassa's [sic] Junction; when the season of victory was let slip by an ill-timed inaction, and the enemy was allowed full leisure to repair his strength. Now, since it was determined not to attempt the destruction of M'Clellan where he lay, the Confederate army should at once leave the malarious district, move northward, and carry the horrors of invasion from their own borders, to those of the guilty assailants. This, he said, was the way to bring them to their senses, and to end the war. And it was within the power of the Confederate Government to make a successful invasion, if their resources were rightly concentrated. Sixty thousand men could march into Maryland, and threaten Washington City, producing most valuable results. But, he added; while he wished these views to be laid before the President, he would disclaim earnestly the charge of self-seeking, in advocating them. He wished to follow, and not to lead, in this glorious enterprise: he was willing to follow anybody; General Lee, or the gallant [Major General Richard S.] Ewell. "Why do you not at once urge these things," asked Mr. Boteler, "upon General Lee himself?" "I have done so;" replied Jackson. "And what," asked Mr. Boteler, "does he say to them?" General Jackson answered: "He says nothing." But he added; "Do not understand that I complain of this silence; it is proper that General Lee should observe it: He is a sagacious and prudent man; he feels that he bears a fearful responsibility: He is right in declining a hasty expression of his purposes, to a subordinate like me." The advice of Jackson was laid before the President.[29]

---

[26] Alexander R. Boteler, "Stonewall Jackson in Campaign [sic] of 1862," *Southern Historical Society Papers* 40 (September 1915): 164–68, 172–73. Although Carman provides no citation, the language of this passage (including the quotation from Jackson) makes it clear that Boteler's essay—published posthumously—was made available to Carman in some form years before its *SHSP* appearance.

[27] Ibid., 173–74.

Johnston was wounded badly on May 31, 1862, near the end of the first day's fighting at the battle of Seven Pines (Fair Oaks). For the extent and duration of his injuries, see Jack D. Welsh, *Medical Histories of Confederate Generals* (Kent, Ohio: Kent State University Press, 1995), 120. Though the army endured a second day of combat under the nominal leadership of Smith, Lee—who had been serving since March in an anomalous position as military advisor to Davis—was named that same day to command of the Army of Northern Virginia. See Jefferson Davis to Lee, June 1, 1862, reprinted in *OR*, vol. 11, pt. 3, 568–69; Headquarters Richmond, Special Orders No. 22, June 1, 1862, reprinted in *OR*, vol. 11, 570. For Lee's assignment within Davis's military family, see Douglas Southall Freeman, *R. E. Lee*, vol. 2 (New York: Charles Scribner's Sons, 1934), 4–7.

[28] Boteler, "Stonewall Jackson in Campaign of 1862," *Southern Historical Society Papers* 42 (September 1917): 174; Lee to Thomas J. Jackson, June 16, 1862, reprinted in *OR*, vol. 11, pt. 3, 602. Although the 1917 version of Boteler's memoir contains a few paragraphs deleted (whether deliberately or in error) from the 1915 essay cited earlier—including the phrase quoted above—it duplicates most of the second half of the earlier text.

[29] R. L. Dabney, *Life and Campaigns of Lieut.-Gen. Thomas J. Jackson, (Stonewall Jackson.)* (New York: Blelock & Co., 1866), 486–87.

The Confederate president had looked with disfavor upon all projects for an invasion of the North, and Jackson's suggestions were apparently unnoticed. Yet, that the offensive policy had been considered was evident from the fact that Davis, in a July 5, 1862, address to the army, after reciting the great deeds it had successfully accomplished in expelling McClellan from in front of Richmond, said, "Let it be your pride to relax in nothing which can promote your future efficiency, your one great object being to drive the invader from your soil and carry your standards beyond the outer boundaries of the Confederacy, to wring from an unscrupulous foe the recognition of your birthright, community independence."[30] Thus was publicly announced the project of an aggressive campaign. Two weeks later Benjamin, now secretary of state, wrote Confederate commissioner John Slidell at Paris, "This Government and people are straining every nerve to continue the campaign with renewed energy before the North can recover from the shock of their bitter disappointment; and if human exertion can compass it, our banners will be unfurled beyond the Potomac in a very short time."[31]

The policy of concentration forced upon the administration by Lee and the sweeping conscription law that "robbed the cradle and the grave"[32] gave the Southern Confederacy two powerful armies to accomplish the object—the Army of Northern Virginia, under Lee, and the Army of Tennessee, under General Braxton Bragg. Lee was to clear Virginia of Union troops and advance beyond the Potomac; Bragg was to recover Tennessee and Kentucky, redeem Missouri, and invade Ohio. Those things accomplished, it was fondly hoped that the U.S. government, as well as England and France, would acknowledge the independence of the Southern Confederacy.

It has been noted that the Southern leaders were extremely eager for the accession of Maryland, and they taught themselves to believe that the majority of the people of that state were loyal to the cause of the South and would welcome the armies of the Confederacy. The same delusion prevailed as to Kentucky. It was believed, especially by the government at Richmond (where the belief was a mania) that the people of both states stood ready to receive the Confederates with open arms, feed them with their substance, rally to their standards to throw off Union domination, and assist in conquering a peace beyond the Ohio.

The advance of the Union armies on Chattanooga and Knoxville in June and July 1862 was a serious menace to the South. Both cities were reinforced, and Bragg, commanding the Western Department, was authorized by Davis to make a counter-movement into middle Tennessee and Kentucky. The time seemed ripe: McClellan had been driven from Richmond, and the Confederate government had passed from its defensive policy and listened to the voice of its people that the war should be carried into the enemy's country.

Bragg was then at Tupelo, Mississippi, whither the Confederate army had retreated from Corinth on May 29, 1862; Major General Edmund Kirby Smith was in command of the department embracing Chattanooga and Knoxville. These two officers had a conference at Chattanooga on July 31 and arrived at an understanding to cooperate in freeing Tennessee and Kentucky from Union domination. Information led them to believe that, if properly armed, the people would rise and assist them. At the same time, Major Generals Earl Van Dorn and Sterling Price were to make a simultaneous advance from Mississippi into West Tennessee, and Bragg trusted that all would unite in Ohio. Isham G. Harris, the refugee governor of Tennessee, was to accompany the army, and Bragg assured him that he would carry him into Nashville before the last of August.

Bragg, who had begun the movement of his army from Tupelo to Chattanooga on the twenty-first of July, took a very rosy view of the situation, and wrote, "Everything is ripe for success, the country is aroused and expecting us."[33] The Kentucky delegation in the Confederate Congress were sanguine that the movement would result in the overthrow of the Union state government of Kentucky and "give to the people of the State an opportunity of establishing such a government as they may desire."[34] On the twenty-fifth of August, Bragg issued orders at Chattanooga for the forward movement, closing with these words: "Soldiers, the enemy is before you and your banners are free. It is for you to decide whether our brothers and sisters of Tennessee and Kentucky shall remain bondmen and bondwomen of the Abolition tyrant or be restored to the freedom inherited from their fathers."[35]

---

[30] Jefferson Davis to the "Army of Eastern Virginia," July 5, 1862, reprinted in *OR*, vol. 11, pt. 3, 690.

[31] Benjamin to John Slidell, July 19, 1862. A copy appears in *ORN*, vol. 3, 466.

[32] The first Confederate conscription act provided that white male citizens between the ages of eighteen and thirty-five were eligible to be drafted. "An act to further provide for the public defense," April 16, 1862, as contained in Adjutant and Inspector General's Office, General Orders No. 30, April 28, 1862, reprinted in *OR*, ser. 4, vol. 1, 1095. Amended subsequently as Confederate fortunes and manpower dwindled, by 1864 these parameters would be expanded to between the ages of seventeen and fifty. "An Act to organize forces to serve during the war," February 17, 1864, as contained in Adjutant and Inspector General's Office, General Orders No. 26, reprinted in *OR*, ser. 4, vol. 3, 178.

[33] Braxton Bragg to Edmund Kirby Smith, August 15, 1862, reprinted in *OR*, vol. 16, pt. 2, 759.

[34] John W. Crockett, Henry E. Read, George W. Ewing, W. E. Simms, H. C. Burnett, W. B. Machen, Robert J. Breckinridge, George B. Hodge, E. M. Bruce, and James S. Chrisman to Jefferson Davis, August 18, 1862, reprinted in *OR*, vol. 16, pt. 2, 772.

[35] Headquarters Department No. 2, General Orders No. 124, August 25, 1862, reprinted in *OR*, vol. 16, pt. 2, 779.

Meanwhile, Smith had left Knoxville and marched through Big Creek and Roger's Gap into Kentucky to carry out his part of the programme, in cooperation with Bragg, in the movement to the Ohio. He routed the Union forces at Richmond, Kentucky, on August 30 and advanced to Lexington on September 2, from which place Brigadier General Henry Heth, with about six thousand men, was sent to threaten Cincinnati.[36] Smith remained at Lexington to collect supplies, gather in recruits, and await Bragg's movements. He informed Bragg that he could add twenty-five thousand Kentuckians to his army in a few days,[37] reported to Richmond that "the heart of Kentucky is with the South" and that its people were rallying to his ranks, and urged upon the government the importance of supporting the movement into Kentucky by sending all the men and arms that could be spared.[38] A few days dispelled the dreams indulged in by Smith, and on September 18 he reported to Bragg, "The Kentuckians are slow and backward in rallying to our standards. Their hearts are evidently with us, but their blue-grass and fat-grass are against us."[39]

Bragg crossed the Tennessee River near Chattanooga, and on August 28 his column took up its march over the Cumberland Mountains and threatened Nashville, upon which Union forces under Major General Don Carlos Buell, advancing on Chattanooga, fell back to cover Nashville and their communications with Louisville. Finding that Buell had done so, Bragg crossed the Kentucky line and reached Glasgow on September 13, thus throwing his army between the forces of Buell and Smith and between Buell and Louisville. Munfordsville surrendered to Bragg's forces on September 17 (the day McClellan and Lee were in deadly struggle at Antietam), and Bragg issued an order of congratulation at the crowning success of the campaign and the redemption of Tennessee and Kentucky.[40]

Bragg took up a strong position barring the road to Louisville. Buell, advancing from Bowling Green, made dispositions for attack—when it was discovered that Bragg had withdrawn. Bragg had found it impossible to remain in a country destitute of supplies and turned his head of column where he expected to find them. He ordered Smith to march from Lexington to Shelbyville, that their combined operations might be immediately undertaken against Louisville, and marched his own column to Bardstown. This left the way open to Buell; the proposed junction of Bragg and Smith was not promptly made. Buell reached Louisville and proceeded to organize an army that marched out in October and on the eighth fought Bragg at Perryville. On the thirteenth Bragg began his retreat from the state he had sought to redeem, seeking shelter in east Tennessee. The day preceding the beginning of his retreat through Cumberland Gap, Bragg wrote to the adjutant general of the Confederate Army, "The campaign here was predicated on a belief and the most positive assurances that the people of this country would rise in mass to assert their independence. No people ever had so favorable an opportunity, but I am distressed to add there is little or no disposition to avail of it. Willing perhaps to accept their independence, they are neither disposed nor willing to risk their lives or their property in its achievement. With ample means to arm twenty thousand men and a force with that to fully redeem the State we have not yet issued half the arms left us by casualties incident to the campaign."[41] Bragg entered Kentucky with high hopes of marching through the state to and beyond the Ohio River and of occupying the cites of Louisville and Cincinnati. He was to redeem the state and establish a Confederate state government. He retreated sadly disappointed and thoroughly disgusted. He had won barren victories at Richmond and Munfordsville; otherwise, he had been outgeneraled. He had taken neither Louisville nor Cincinnati, nor had he caught a distant glimpse of the Ohio. The "blue-grass and fat-grass" Kentuckians did not rally to his colors, and the governor he had inaugurated at Frankfort was a fugitive before the ceremonies had been fully completed. His campaign in Kentucky was paralleled by that of Lee in Maryland, to which we now return.

Lee had not utterly destroyed McClellan's army on the Peninsula as he hoped and expected to do (and, as he asserts, under ordinary circumstances should have been done[42]), but he had saved the capital and paralyzed McClellan. On the eighth of July, he fell back to Richmond; on the nineteenth, Jackson, marching to meet a new threat from Major General John Pope and the Army of Virginia, reached Gordonsville. On the ninth of August, Jackson defeated a portion of that force, under Banks, at Cedar Mountain but was obliged to fall back behind the Rappahannock and await reinforcements, which could not be immediately given in view of the uncertain intentions of McClellan's army on the banks of the James and the report that he was being reinforced to resume the offensive. As soon as it was known that McClellan was being withdrawn from the Peninsula to reinforce the Army of Virginia, Lee put his army in motion to overthrow Pope before McClellan's forces could reach him. His point of concentration was Gordonsville. On the fifteenth of August, Jackson—with his division and

---

[36] See Edmund Kirby Smith to Cooper, September 6, 1862, reprinted in *OR*, vol. 16, pt. 1, 933.

[37] Edmund Kirby Smith to Bragg, September 3, 1862, reprinted in *OR*, vol. 16, pt. 1, 932.

[38] Edmund Kirby Smith to Cooper, 933.

[39] Edmund Kirby Smith to Bragg, September 18, 1862, reprinted in *OR*, vol. 16, pt. 2, 846.

[40] Headquarters Army of the Mississippi, General Orders No. 6, September 17, 1862, reprinted in *OR*, vol. 16, pt. 2, 841–42.

[41] Bragg to "the Adjutant-General [Cooper]," October 12, 1862, reprinted in *OR*, vol. 16, pt. 1, 1088.

[42] "Under ordinary circumstances the Federal Army should have been destroyed." Lee to Cooper, March 6, 1863, reprinted in *OR*, vol. 11, pt. 2, 497.

those of Major Generals Richard S. Ewell and Ambrose P. Hill (the Light Division) of the infantry and James E. B. "Jeb" Stuart of the cavalry—led the advance, crossing the Rapidan on the twentieth and the Rappahannock on the twenty-fourth. Then followed the battles of Groveton, Second Manassas, and Chantilly, the resultant defeat of Pope's army, and its retreat to Washington. The proximity of the fortifications around Alexandria and Washington, thanks to McClellan's foresight, rendered further pursuit useless, and Lee's army rested on the second of September near Chantilly, Pope being followed only by the cavalry, which continued to harass him until he reached the defensive lines near the Potomac.

When Lee was acting in an advisory capacity to Davis, he united with his chief in opposing the suggestion of Johnston, G. W. Smith, and Longstreet to defend Richmond by an advance of the main Confederate army into the North. But when the fortune of war—in the wounding of Johnston—placed him in command, he formed and steadfastly held the opinion, till the close of his military career, that the proper defense of Richmond and the Confederacy lay in the transfer of its army to the vicinity of Washington and, preferably, in an entrance into Maryland. This idea he pressed upon Davis. So, when McClellan was driven back to the James River, Lee's thoughts instantly turned to dislodging him from that position and from the entire Peninsula by an advance northward to overthrow Pope and menace Washington, with the result known to history. Lee was not averse to bearing heavy burdens and in his plans embraced other fields than the one in which he was operating or over which he had command. He aimed not only to relieve the pressure on Richmond and the Peninsula but upon the whole of Virginia and upon other parts of the Confederacy. When prisoners were taken on the Rappahannock from Major General Ambrose E. Burnside's men from North Carolina and Brigadier General Jacob D. Cox's from western Virginia, showing that troops had been drawn from these points, he pointed to the fact as proof of the correctness—or, rather, of the success—of his plan. Failing to demolish Pope between the Rapidan and the Rappahannock, as he had planned to do (and, it is contended, he might have done but for the failure of Brigadier General Fitzhugh Lee's cavalry[43]), Lee then pursued Pope with the determination to cut him off from Washington or drive him into it. This would open the way to another campaign, which from the necessities of the case must be conducted outside of Virginia. He did not cut Pope off from Washington, but he fought him back to its defenses.

The condition of affairs was now favorable for an invasion of the North, and Lee saw the way clear to carry out the understanding between Davis and himself that, when opportunity presented, the Confederate army should enter Maryland and demand recognition of Confederate independence.

There were those who agreed with Lee, as the conditions were then presented, that he had no great risk to face in the prosecution of a campaign beyond the Potomac and as far north as Pennsylvania and that the time and opportunity had come to strike a blow in the enemy's country, which would go far toward securing the independence of the South. Many victories in Virginia had raised the spirit of the army to the highest point, and it felt equal to any task. It could be relied upon to put forth its greatest efforts; that done, the result was not doubted, and it was reasonably considered that such a grievous stroke as had been given Pope in Virginia would have been well nigh fatal had it been administered in Maryland (within easy reach of Washington) or in Pennsylvania (near the pulse of manufacture and trade). To crown their brilliant victories in Virginia, the colors of the Southern Confederacy must be carried to the banks of the Susquehanna in Pennsylvania and, fortune favoring, displayed in Philadelphia's Independence Square. Dreams of this kind were indulged in on those early September days.

Beyond considerations of a purely military nature, there were those of a political character, domestic and foreign, that called for an invasion of Northern territory at this time. One of the delusions of the South was an abiding faith in the words and promises of many of the leaders of the Democratic Party of the North. That party has produced many of the great names of American history, names that will live so long as patriotism is recognized as a virtue and loyalty to American principles, as laid down in the Declaration of Independence, is regarded as a duty to humanity. But in the few years preceding the outbreak of the rebellion, the party of Thomas Jefferson and Andrew Jackson had sadly degenerated, and its broad principles of early days narrowed to the single idea of the perpetuation and extension of human slavery. Everything else was secondary and subordinate to this. That the Southern man should contend for this was, considering his environment, very natural, but the pity of it is that many Democrats of the North followed blindly the leaders of the extremists of the South. They yielded to the views of these extremists in the construction of political platforms and, by their votes, supported slave legislation in Congress. Their whole course led the South to believe that it would receive their support, and that of their followers, in any course it chose to pursue. On more than one occasion, Northern members of Congress asserted, on the

---

[43] Pursuing Pope's army on its northward retreat, the Confederates came upon the Army of Virginia in a vulnerable position between the two rivers. Delays on the part of Fitzhugh Lee's much needed brigade of cavalry, as well as the weakened condition it displayed upon arrival, necessitated a delay in the plan of attack—during which Pope's army extricated itself from the danger. See James E. B. Stuart to Robert H. Chilton, February 5, 1863, reprinted in *OR*, vol. 12, pt. 1, 726; John J. Hennessey, *Return to Bull Run: The Campaign and Battle of Second Manassas* (New York: Simon & Schuster, 1993), 50–51, 54–55.

floor of the House of Representatives, that should the incoming administration of Abraham Lincoln undertake to coerce the South, it would first have to deal with the Democracy of the North, and, after the beginning of hostilities, there were some parties in Massachusetts, Connecticut, Illinois, Indiana, and elsewhere who offered volunteer companies to Jefferson Davis to fight in the ranks of the Confederate Army.

As early as January 6, 1860, Franklin Pierce of New Hampshire, ex-president of the United States, wrote to Davis complaining that, in the debates in Congress, full justice had not been done to the Democracy of the North. He said, "Without discussing the question of right, of abstract power to secede, I have never believed that actual disruption of the Union can occur without blood, and if, thro the madness of northern abolitionism that dire calamity must come, the fighting will not be along Mason's and Dixon's line merely. It [will] be within our own borders in our own streets between two classes of citizens to whom I have referred. Those who defy law and recent constitutional obligations will, if we ever reach the arbitrament of arms, find occupation enough at home."[44]

It is not strange[45] that after such an expression from high Democratic authority, Lawrence M. Keitt, speaking at Charleston, South Carolina, in November 1860, said, "Let me tell you, there are a million of Democrats in the North who when the Black Republicans attempt to march upon the South, will be found a wall of fire in the front."[46] In the South Carolina secession convention the following month, Julius A. Dargan said, "It is not true, in point of fact, that all the Northern people are hostile to the rights of the South. We have a Spartan band in every Northern State."[47]

That these secessionists correctly gauged the attitude of their Democratic brethren of the North, we have evidence from the action of the Democratic Party of Ohio at a state convention held on January 8, 1861—the anniversary of the battle of New Orleans. Jacob Cox says:

On the 8th of January the usual Democratic convention and celebration of the battle of New Orleans had taken place, and a series of resolutions had been passed, in which, professing to speak in the name of "200,000 Democrats of Ohio," the convention had very significantly intimated that this vast organization of men would be found in the way of any attempt to put down secession until the demands of the South in respect to slavery were complied with. A few days afterward I was returning to Columbus from my home in Trumbull county, and meeting upon the railway train with David Tod, then an active Democratic politician, but afterward one of our loyal "war governors," the conversation turned on the action of the convention which had just adjourned. Mr. Tod and I were personal friends and neighbors, and I freely expressed my surprise that the convention should have committed itself to what must be interpreted as a threat of insurrection in the North, if the Administration should, in opposing secession by force, follow the example of Andrew Jackson, in whose honor they had assembled. He rather vehemently reasserted the substance of the resolution, saying that we Republicans would find 200,000 Ohio Democrats in front of us, if we attempted to cross the Ohio River.[48]

On the sixth of January, 1861, Fernando Wood, the Democratic mayor of New York City, sent a message to the common council suggesting that New York should be made a "free city," and the proposition met with much favor among his followers. The idea was advanced that, when secession of the South became a fixed fact, not only the city but the states of New

---

[44] When Union troops moved through Mississippi in 1863, many of Davis's antebellum papers were discovered in the home of a Davis family friend, where they had been placed for safekeeping. As a result, Pierce's letter made its way into a number of Republican newspapers as evidence of Democratic perfidy in the late antebellum period. The text above reflects the grammar and spelling as given in a printed facsimile of Pierce's manuscript original. Franklin Pierce to Jefferson Davis, January 6, 1860, series 3, Franklin Pierce Papers (preservation microfilm, reel 6), Manuscript Division, Library of Congress. It is clear, however, that Carman's source for this passage is John A. Logan, *The Great Conspiracy: Its Origin and History* (New York: A. R. Hart & Co., 1886), 261. Logan writes "through" instead of Pierce's usage—"thro"—and incorrectly gives the last sentence as "Those who defy law and *scout* constitutional obligations [emphasis added]." Both of these errors appear in Carman's original manuscript.

The letter is also reprinted in Dunbar Rowland, ed., *Jefferson Davis, Constitutionalist: His Letters, Papers and Speeches*, vol. 4 (Jackson: Mississippi Department of Archives and History, 1923), 118–19. Rowland errs in his transcription of Pierce's admittedly poor handwriting, however, misplacing the terminal punctuation and thereby altering the meaning of a key sentence. In his version the letter reads, "I do not believe that our friends at the South have any just idea of the state of feeling, running at this moment to the pitch of intense exasperation, between those who respect their political obligations, and those who have apparently no impelling power but that which fanatical passion on the subject of domestic slavery imparts *without discussing the question of right—of abstract power to secede. I have never believed ...* [emphasis added]," and then continues as in the original. As Carman's version properly reflects, the subject of the participial phrase "discussing the question of right" in the original letter was Pierce, not the opponents of slavery.

[45] Although Carman's original manuscript reads, "It is strange ...," the context suggests he intended this to be a negative.

[46] See Henry Wilson, *History of the Rise and Fall of the Slave Power in America*, vol. 3 (Boston: James R. Osgood and Co., 1877), 69.

[47] Ibid.

[48] Jacob D. Cox, "War Preparations in the North," in *Battles and Leaders of the Civil War*, vol. 1 (New York: Century Co., 1887), 86.

York, New Jersey, and other Middle States would withdraw from the Union and unite with the insurgent South.[49] Following in the footsteps of Wood was Rodman M. Price, formerly a Democratic governor of New Jersey, who published a letter urging his state to "go with the South from every wise, prudential, and patriotic reason."[50] In public speech and private conversation, he denounced the idea of coercion and advocated armed resistance to it. The actions of Wood and Price were undisguised treason, but they truly represented the feeling of a great majority of their party in 1860–61, who, opposed to coercion and favorable to an abject surrender to the South, encouraged Southerners in their course. Henry Wilson is correct in saying, "Had they not found auxiliaries out of the South ready to lend their aid, they would never have ventured upon the rash experiment."[51]

There was encouragement to secession in the tone of the *New York Tribune*—the leading Republican paper of the country, edited by Horace Greeley. On November 9, 1860, the *Tribune* said, "If the Cotton States consider the value of the Union debatable, we maintain their perfect right to discuss it. Nay: we hold with Jefferson to the inalienable right of communities to alter or abolish forms of government that have become oppressive or injurious; and if the Cotton States shall become satisfied that they can do better out of the Union than in it, we insist on letting them go in peace. The right to secede may be a revolutionary one, but it exists nevertheless, and we do not see how one party can have a right to do what another party has a right to prevent."[52] On December 17, 1860, just three days before the secession of South Carolina, Greeley again said in the *Tribune*, "If it [the argument contained in the Declaration of Independence] justified the secession from the British Empire of Three Millions of colonists in 1776, we do not see why it would not justify the secession of Five Millions of Southrons from the Federal Union in 1861. If we are mistaken on this point, why does not some one attempt to show wherein and why?"[53] On February 23, 1861, five days after the inauguration of Jefferson Davis at Montgomery, Greeley argued once more, "We have repeatedly said, and we once more insist, that the great principle embodied by Jefferson in the Declaration of American Independence, that governments derive their just power from the consent of the governed, is sound and just and that if the Slave States, the Cotton States, or the Gulf States only, choose to form an independent nation, they have a clear moral right to do so"[54]

Although Greeley did not correctly represent the sentiment of the great body of the Republican Party of the North, it must be admitted that many of that party, without conceding the right of secession, looked with complacency upon a peaceful separation of the States. General Scott, the veteran commander of the Army of the United States, advised that the "wayward sisters" be permitted to "depart in peace."[55] The *New York Herald*, an independent Democratic paper, said on November 9, 1860, "Each State is organized as a complete government, holding the purse and wielding the sword, possessing the right to break the tie of confederation as a nation might break a treaty, and to repel coercion as a nation might repel invasion … Coercion, if it were possible, is out of the question."[56] While conceding the right of secession and deprecating coercion, the *Herald* did not go so far as to countenance an alliance with the secession leaders for a forcible opposition to the course of the government, but the acknowledged leaders of the Democratic Party gave no uncertain indication of their designs.

On January 31, 1861, a Democratic state convention was held in Tweddle Hall in Albany, New York. The convention was large in numbers, a representative one, and embraced the talent of the party. Reuben H. Walworth made a speech in which he asserted that "it would be as brutal … to send men to butcher our own brothers of the Southern States as it would be to massacre them in the Northern States."[57] He was followed by James S. Thayer, who said, "The public mind will bear the avowal, and let us make it—that if a revolution of force is to begin, *it shall be inaugurated at home.* And if the incoming Administration shall attempt to carry out the line of policy that has been foreshadowed, we announce that, when the hand of Black Republicanism turns to blood-red, and seeks from the fragment of the Constitution to construct a scaffolding for coërcion—another name for execution—we will reverse the order of the French Revolution, and save the blood of the

---

[49] In his original manuscript, Carman says "the ninth," but the full text of Wood's message to the Common Council—dated the sixth—appears in "City Government for 1861," *New York Times*, January 8, 1861. A lengthy editorial opposing Wood's plan ("Secession Gone to Seed") also is contained in the same issue.

[50] See Wilson, 68.

[51] Ibid., 70. In his original manuscript, Carman quotes this incorrectly as, "If the South had not found auxiliaries out of the North ready to lend their aid, they would never have ventured into the rash experiment."

[52] "Going to Go," *New York Tribune*, November 9, 1860.

[53] "The Right of Secession," *New York Tribune*, December 17, 1860.

[54] "Self-Government," *New York Tribune*, February 23, 1861.

[55] Winfield Scott to William Seward, March 3, 1861, reprinted in Scott, *Memoirs of Lieut.-General Scott, LL.D.*, vol. 2 (New York: Sheldon & Co., 1864), 628.

[56] "The Effect in the South of the Election of Lincoln—Manifest Duty of the President Elect," *New York Herald*, November 9, 1860.

[57] See Wilson, 64.

people by making those who would inaugurate a reign of terror the first victims of a national guillotine."[58] The sentiments of the speaker were greeted with enthusiastic and long continued applause. He had fairly expressed the views of the Democratic leaders of New York.

The action of this convention—a declaration against coercion and a demand for concession to the South—was hailed by secession leaders and those who sympathized with them, South and North, as evidence that "if [the] President should attempt coercion, he will encounter more opposition *at the North* than he can overcome."[59] All through the South was repeated the expression of Dargan and Keitt that "a Spartan band in every Northern State" was true to their interests and that a "million Democrats in the North" would stand like a wall of fire to beat back the Black Republicans should they attempt to "march upon the South." It was published widely that the action of the Democratic conventions of Ohio and New York showed that the party of human slavery and secession had loyal and devoted followers in the North—those who would see that no Union troops crossed to the south bank of the Ohio or left the limits of New York without becoming the "victims of a national guillotine." It was a firm reliance upon the division of the North and an active alliance of the Democracy that impelled a senator in the Confederate Congress to boast that he would soon quaff wine from golden goblets in the palaces of New York and that caused the boast of Robert Toombs that he would call the roll of his slaves at the foot of Bunker Hill Monument.[60]

On January 26, 1861, the *Detroit Free Press* said, "If troops shall be raised in the North to march against the people of the South, *a fire in the rear will be opened upon such troops which will either stop their march altogether or wonderfully accelerate it.* In other words, if, in the present posture of the republican party towards the national difficulties, war shall be waged, *that war will be fought in the North* … We warn it that the conflict which it is precipitating will not be with the South, *but with tens of thousands of people in the North.* When civil war shall come, it will be a war here in Michigan and here in Detroit, and in every northern State."[61] When Lincoln was inaugurated, he recognized the fact that the seed of treason had been so broadly sown in the North and that any immediate attempt to apply force against the people of the South would be followed by riots and civil war in some of the Northern cities. Therefore, he hesitated to reinforce Fort Sumter and sought to reunite the divided North.

In his history of the Confederacy, Jefferson Davis reviews the condition of affairs in the North in 1860–61, as shown in the utterances of public men and the press of devotion to the South and a fixed determination to oppose by force any attempt of the administration to enforce the laws, then says, "And here the ingenuous reader may very naturally ask, What became of all this feeling? How was it that, in the course of a few weeks, it had disappeared like a morning mist? Where was the host of men who had declared that an army marching to invade the Southern States should first pass over their dead bodies?"[62] The answer is to be found in the order of Davis and his cabinet to open fire upon a U.S. fort and the flag of the Union. The attack upon Fort Sumter caused a rude awakening. It united the North, party lines were obliterated, and the great party upon which the South depended for moral and physical support was found true to the principle of its fathers and loyal to the Union. Leading men were prompt to declare themselves; many entered the Union service and rose to high position and enduring fame. The masses, who were expected to form mobs and resist authority in the North, crowded recruiting offices and, later, left their patriotic blood, in generous measure, on every battlefield of the war.

There were Southern men who correctly measured the effect of opening fire upon Fort Sumter. Among them was Robert Toombs, the first Confederate secretary of state. Although he had boasted that he would call the roll of his slaves at the foot of Bunker Hill Monument, when the cabinet met to consider the propriety of firing upon Fort Sumter, he said, "Mr. President … at this time, it is suicide, murder, and will lose us every friend at the North. You will wantonly strike a hornet's nest which extends from mountains to ocean, and legions, now quiet, will swarm out and sting us to death. It is unnecessary; it puts us in the wrong; it is fatal."[63]

Early to recognize the true state of affairs was John Campbell. Although a Southern man, he had not resigned his seat on the Supreme Court, and on April 28 he wrote from Washington to Davis, "The Northern States are in the wildest condition of excitement. Some of the truest friends of the South have given in their adhesion to the policy of 'defending the capital.'

[58] See Horace Greeley, *The American Conflict: A History of the Great Rebellion in the United States of America, 1860–65; Its Causes, Incidents, and Results: Intended to Exhibit Especially Its Moral and Political Phases, with the Drift and Progress of American Opinion Respecting Human Slavery from 1776 to the Close of the War for the Union*, vol. 1 (Hartford, O. D. Case, 1867), 392.

[59] Ibid., 396.

[60] Although the sentiment has the ring of Toombs's bombast, one of Carman's own sources reports that, in an 1856 letter, Toombs denied ever having made such a claim. See Pleasant A. Stovall, *Robert Toombs: Statesman, Speaker, Soldier, Sage* (New York: Cassell Publishing Co., 1892), 119.

[61] "The Attitude of Michigan," *Detroit Free Press*, January 26, 1861, 2. In his original manuscript, Carman says this was printed on February 2, 1861, but that is likely the date of its subsequent reprint in another newspaper.

[62] Jefferson Davis, *The Rise and Fall of the Confederate Government*, vol. 1 (New York: D. Appleton and Co., 1881), 257.

[63] Stovall, 226.

General [Franklin] Pierce, General [Caleb] Cushing and Mr. [Daniel S.] Dickinson will occur to you at once, as men not likely to yield to a slight storm … We cannot get along at all by looking only to our own side of the question, or to the emanations of our own people … New York, Boston, & Philadelphia will pour out its capital even for subjugation. The impression that we had firm, staunch friends North who would fight for us is a delusion. Oh! I pray you do not rest upon it."[64]

Davis was not convinced that the Southern cause had lost all its friends in the North. Indeed, he knew to the contrary, and he kept up constant communication during the entire war with many who still adhered to it and who opposed the national administration. He was kept well informed of the temper of the North and the dissensions of the people. He was advised that the reverses of the Union army, before Richmond and elsewhere, were having a dispiriting effect upon some sections of the North and upon the great money and commercial centers, and that the element demanding peace was growing in strength. Nor was it necessary that he should depend upon this source of information; the papers of the great cities, in their news columns and on their editorial pages, told him of the increasing discontent of factions in the party of the administration, of the great unpopularity of the draft, of the difficulties in recruiting for the army, and of the growing desire for peace—"Peace for the North and independence for the South." Nor were these indications confined to Democratic politicians and the Democratic press. They were shown in carping criticism and wanton attacks by prominent Republican journals upon the administration and its policy. That the summer of 1862 was a gloomy one for loyal men of the country is well known, and Horace Greeley has put on record this opinion: "It is quite probable that, had a popular election been held at any time during the year following the Fourth of July, 1862, on the question of continuing the War or averting it on the best attainable terms, a majority would have voted for Peace; while it is highly probable that a still larger majority would have voted against Emancipation."[65] Davis knew all this and recognized the fact that the appearance of the Confederate army in Maryland and Pennsylvania would go far to intensify the peace feeling at the North, strengthen the opponents of the national administration, and have a signal effect upon the elections to be held in many Northern states in October for members of Congress. This idea was partially shared by Lee and runs through his correspondence.

There were urgent reasons, beyond those of a purely military character or the effect upon sentiment at the North, that impelled the Confederate government to pass from the defensive and assume the offensive, with the intention of winning new victories and securing Maryland, Kentucky and Missouri to the Southern Confederacy. These have a direct bearing upon the campaign now under consideration and must be noted.

For more than a year the Confederate leaders had been anxiously awaiting the recognition of the Confederacy by foreign powers and their intervention to raise the blockade and give its cause moral and physical support; for more than a year they had been told that recognition would follow their decided success in the field. They had not looked to war as the outcome of secession and from the first had no doubt of a speedy recognition by the European powers; any hesitation in that direction was expected to be overcome by King Cotton.[66] The Confederate leaders reasoned that the cotton-spinning powers of Europe must have cotton or a famine, and, as they could not have cotton without slavery, they would swallow slavery and find some pretext for intervention. John Bigelow says that prominent Southerners were firm "in the conviction that cotton was king in Europe as well as in the United States, and that an interruption of its supply would be so serious in its consequences that a new republic, where cotton was to be king and slavery its corner-stone, would be welcomed into the family of nations as the surest possible guaranty against the recurrence of such a disaster."[67] It was argued that, in any event, Great Britain must have American cotton to keep her spindles moving, and it was expected that, in exchange for this, the South would be supplied with such manufactured goods as she had been in the habit of purchasing in Northern markets. To secure political recognition and commercial advantages were the first objects of Confederate diplomacy, and this diplomacy rested entirely upon cotton. Many opposed the policy of endeavoring to force recognition by cotton; among these was Vice President

---

[64] John A. Campbell to Jefferson Davis, April 28, 1861. As before (see p. 12 n. 53), Carman's original manuscript draws upon an inaccurate copy found in John G. Nicolay and John Hay, *Abraham Lincoln: A History*, vol. 4 (New York: Century Co., 1890), 261–62. A true copy appears in Lynda Lasswell Crist and Mary Seaton Dix, eds., *The Papers of Jefferson Davis*, vol. 7 (Baton Rouge: Louisiana State University Press, 1992), 137–38, and this text is used in the portion cited above.

[65] Greeley, *The American Conflict*, vol. 2, 254–55.

[66] "We can live, if need be, without commerce. But when you shut out our cotton from the looms of Europe, we shall see whether other nations will not have something to say and something to do on that subject. 'Cotton is King,' and it will find means to raise you blockade and disperse your ships." Senator Alfred Iverson (Sr.) of Georgia, January 28, 1861, reprinted in *Congressional Globe*, 36th Cong., 2d sess., 1861, 589. In the campaign in West Virginia (July 1861), the colors of a Georgia regiment were captured. Under the representation of the state arms was the inscription, in letters of gold, "Cotton is King."—*EAC*

[67] John Bigelow, *Retrospections of an Active Life*, vol. 1 (New York: Baker & Taylor Co., 1909), 527. Presumably, Carman was privy to the work in manuscript form.

Alexander H. Stephens, who said it was a very serious mistake at the beginning of the war to consider cotton as a political instead of a commercial power.

As early as February 13, 1861, the Confederate Congress authorized Davis to appoint three persons as commissioners to Great Britain, France, and other European powers.[68] William L. Yancey, Pierre A. Rost, and A. Dudley Mann were named and directed to proceed first to London and seek an interview with Queen Victoria's secretary of state for foreign affairs, Lord John Russell. They were instructed to inform the secretary of the secession of several states and the formation of an independent government, which presented itself for admission into the family of independent nations and asked for that acknowledgement and friendly recognition "due to every people capable of self-government and possessed of the power to maintain their independence." They were to assure the secretary that under no conditions would they consent to a re-union with their late associates and that they had a well organized government capable of taking care of itself, even to the taking up of arms if necessary—which they did not anticipate, as the United States was in no condition to make war upon them. The commissioners were instructed also to inform the secretary that the high protective tariff, forced upon them by the North, was the prime cause of secession. They were empowered to negotiate a treaty of friendship, commerce, and navigation, and impress upon the British mind that wise maxim of political economy: "Buy where you can buy cheapest, and sell where you can sell dearest." Then the subject of cotton was to be presented. Davis rested foreign policy of the Confederacy on the absolute supremacy of cotton, and upon this point the instructions to the commissioners reads:

> The Confederate States produce nearly nineteen-twentieths of all the cotton grown in the States which recently constituted the United States. There is no extravagance in the assertion that the gross amount of the annual yield of the manufactories of Great Britain from the cotton of the Confederate States reaches $600,000,000. The British Ministry will comprehend fully the condition to which the British realm would be reduced if the supply of our staple should suddenly fail or even be considerably diminished. A delicate allusion to the probability of such an occurrence might not be unkindly received by the minister of foreign affairs [Russell], an occurrence, I will add, that is inevitable if this country shall be involved in protracted hostilities with the North.[69]

During the month of May 1861, the Confederate commissioners had two conferences with Lord Russell, from whom they received the impression that the British Ministry had no settled policy as to the recognition of the Southern Confederacy. It would adhere to the declaration of neutrality but postpone a decision as to recognition as long as possible, "at least until some decided advantage is obtained by [the Confederate States], or the necessity for having cotton becomes pressing."[70] They were sanguine of success "when the cotton crop is ready for market," but were doubtful of recognition before it was picked and a favorable military event was announced.[71] Such a military success they thought had been achieved at Bull Run, and they addressed a communication to Russell in which they discussed the causes leading to secession; went into labored arguments of states rights and sovereignty; called attention to the resources of the South, especially in cotton and tobacco; criticized the English stand of neutrality; pointed to the fact that they had achieved a signal victory over the forces of the United States; insisted they were able to maintain their independence and possessed all "the elements of a great and powerful nation, capable not only of clothing, feeding, and defending themselves, but also of clothing all the nations of Europe under the benign influence of peace and free trade"; and asked for recognition. The morality of slavery they would not discuss, but they called attention to the fact that the "cotton-picking season" had commenced and that an average crop would be placed, as usual, on the wharves at Southern ports, "when there shall be a prospect of the blockade being raised and not before."[72] The reply to this communication was that the British government would not acknowledge the independence of the seceding states "until the fortune of arms or the more peaceful mode of negotiation shall have more clearly determined the respective positions of the two belligerents."[73]

The summer had passed away when the Confederate Congress came to the conclusion to send abroad commissioners of greater reputation (though of less ability), James M. Mason of Virginia being named for England and John Slidell of Louisiana for France. The instructions given to each were similar to those under which Yancey, Rost, and Mann were acting: the keynote was cotton and free trade.[74]

---

[68] *Journal of the Provisional Congress*, 49.

[69] Robert Toombs to William L. Yancey, Pierre A. Rost, and A. Dudley Mann, March 16, 1861. A copy appears in *ORN*, vol. 3, 191–95.

[70] Yancey, Rost, and Mann to Toombs, June 1, 1861. A copy appears in *ORN*, vol. 3, 220.

[71] Yancey and Mann to Toombs, June 10, 1861; Yancey and Mann to Toombs, July 15, 1861. Respective copies appear in *ORN*, vol. 3, 221, 223.

[72] Yancey, Rost, and Mann to John Russell, August 14, 1861. A copy appears in *ORN*, vol. 3, 238–46.

[73] Russell to Yancey, Rost, and Mann, August 24, 1861. A copy appears in *ORN*, vol. 3, 248.

[74] See Hunter to Mason, September 23, 1861, reprinted in *OR*, ser. 2, vol. 2, 1207–14; Hunter to Slidell, September 23, 1861, reprinted in *OR*, ser. 2, vol. 2, 1214–22.

The English masses—the plain people, those who earned their living by the sweat of their faces—and those of modest trade were friendly to the North and free institutions. They saw that the cause of the North was the cause of democracy in their own land. On the other hand, the governing class was favorable to the slave confederacy. Its views can be stated in two quotations. Henry John Temple, Viscount Palmerston, the prime minister of Great Britain, said to August Belmont of New York in July 1861, "We do not like slavery, but we want cotton, and we dislike very much your Morrill tariff."[75] The *Times* (London) said, "It is for their trade that the South are resolved to fight. They dissolved the Union to create more slave states—that is, to make more cotton. They undertook the war for the very object that we have most at heart."[76]

The religious middle class, those one would naturally suppose to be strong in support of human liberty and free institutions, sympathized with a government whose cornerstone was African slavery and lent influence to perpetuate and extend it. They had departed from the humane and lofty teachings of Clarkson and Wilberforce[77] and others prominent in English history. The governing class—the aristocracy, the sordid commercial class, the established church, and the religious middle class—agreed in opinion that the South was entitled to and was certain to achieve its independence, and the sooner the fact was acknowledged the better for all.

From early in March, France's minister at Washington had been advising his government of the complete disintegration of the Union and suggesting the recognition of the Southern Confederacy. He dwelt somewhat on the necessity of raising the blockade to supply cotton for the French manufacturers, for its scarcity was producing much distress. The French government was favorable and approached Russell on the subject, who on October 17 wrote Palmerston, "It will not do for England and France to break a blockade for the sake of getting cotton." But Russell proposed to offer fair and equitable terms of pacification and, if either belligerent rejected them, harsh measures were to be resorted to. Palmerston thought that the time had not yet come to act and replied to Russell's note, "Our best and true policy is to go on as we have begun and to keep quite clear of the conflict."[78] About this time a Liverpool paper declared that the supply of cotton was the greatest question of the civilized world.

The emperor of France was awaiting, with some impatience, the action of the English government and, at the same time, maturing his Mexican schemes. The failure of Palmerston to respond favorably to his proposition was a keen disappointment. He could not act alone because he was bound by an agreement to act jointly with Great Britain. The Confederate commissioners were duly informed of the agreement between France and England and of the attitude of the English Ministry and were advised that the temper of both North and South was such that action was not politic, but that "an important military success might determine the period for their action."[79]

Charles Francis Adams, the American minister to England, was kept quite in the dark as to these exchanges of diplomatic opinion but, from the utterances of public men, the hostile tone of the press, and other indications, came to the conclusion that recognition was imminent and so advised his government. His biographer writes, "It is not going too far to assert that, between May and November, 1861, the chances in Europe were as ten to one in favor of the Confederacy and against the Union."[80] The seizure of the *Trent* and the capture of Mason and Slidell increased the chances against the Union. Taking advantage of the intense feeling in England, the commissioners promptly lodged with Russell a protest against

---

[75] See James Ford Rhodes, *History of the United States from the Compromise of 1850*, vol. 4 (New York, Harper & Brothers Publishers, 1899), 433. Passed in early 1861, the Morrill Tariff doubled the average ad-valorem tax on imports.

[76] Although Carman places this passage in quotation marks, it is in fact a paraphrase. The relevant passage of the original source reads, "It is for their trade, in fact, that they may be said to fight. They have dissolved the Union, and taken up arms for the right of carrying their slaves into fresh territories; but the only object of this privilege is to create fresh Slave States, or, in other words, to grow more Cotton. The value of slave labour in America is expressed in Cotton only. If Cotton were not to be grown and exported more freely than before, it would have been of no use for the Southern States to claim territory, to uphold slavery, or to leave the Union when their wishes were opposed. The war itself, therefore, may be in some sense regarded as undertaken for the very object which we have most at heart." "Evils Often Diminish In Magnitude As We Approach," *Times* (London), May 2, 1861. Such garbling of quotations is not uncommon in Carman's manuscript, but it may be the case in this instance (as was true of many newspaper articles he references) that he was not working from the original source, but had found it reprinted in whole or in part in another newspaper or a secondary source.

[77] Thomas Clarkson (1760–1864) and William Wilberforce (1759–1833) were two of the leading figures in the successful movement to end slavery throughout the British Empire.

[78] See Spencer Walpole, *The Life of Lord John Russell*, vol. 2 (London: Longmans, Green, and Co., 1889), 344.

[79] Yancey, Rost, and Mann to Hunter, October 28, 1861. A copy appears in *ORN*, vol. 3, 287–88.

[80] Charles Francis Adams [Jr.], *Charles Francis Adams* (Boston: Houghton, Mifflin, and Co., 1900), 148.

such "an infamous act"[81] and, three days later,[82] under express directions from Davis, presented the foreign secretary with evidence showing that the blockade was ineffectual and that further observance of neutrality was an injustice to parties "who are so deeply interested in a ready and easy access to the cheapest and most abundant sources of cotton supply."[83] The feeling against the United States was now so intensely bitter that the commissioners were sanguine of a favorable response and early recognition of the Confederacy, but, to their great surprise, Russell replied to their notes of November 27 and 30 that, in the present state of affairs, he "must decline to enter into official communication with them."[84]

Thanks to the great common sense of Abraham Lincoln, peaceful relations were preserved between the United States and England, but the incident and the hostile feeling it engendered was a distinct gain to the Southern Confederacy.

Mason, on being given up by the United States, made his way to London, where he arrived January 29, 1862, and was not favorably impressed with the aspect of affairs.[85] He was coldly received, and he found the Foreign Ministry averse to raising the blockade of the Southern ports or recognizing the Confederacy and apparently anxious to avoid any further broil with the United States. Slidell, at Paris, found the sentiment quite as strong as it was in England, and the French minister for foreign affairs refused to discuss the subject of recognition.

On February 8, 1862, Hunter, who by this time had replaced Toombs as secretary of state, instructed Mason that no terms of agreement would be entered into, as the result of English intervention, that did not concede Maryland, Kentucky, and Missouri to the South.[86]

The Union victories of Mill Springs, Roanoke Island, and Fort Donelson clouded Confederate prospects and produced a feeling throughout England that the South would fail unless sustained by outside help, and the Richmond authorities were notified that, if these reverses were not counterbalanced by success elsewhere, the South must "bid adieu to all hopes of ... recognition."[87] A little later Russell's prediction of an early termination of the war, by the establishment within three months of two mighty republics in the territory of the late United States, heightened the prospect of speedy recognition, and the Confederate government was so advised. It was, however, cautioned not to place too much reliance upon the foreign minister's words, but to work out its own salvation by winning victories in the field.[88] Upon this situation came the fall of New Orleans. Confederate sympathizers minimized the reverse, and Mason and Slidell hastened to inform the powers that it would in no degree change the determination of the Confederacy to carry on the war.

England gave no official sign. Slidell was given to understand that France was becoming dissatisfied with the tortuous course pursued by England, but that there was a seeming change in the tone of the English ministry; that if New Orleans had not fallen Confederate recognition could not have been much longer delayed; and that, even after that disaster, if the Confederates obtained decided successes in Virginia and Tennessee, or could hold the enemy at bay for a month or two, the same results would follow. At the same time the emperor of France was reported to have said that he "would at once dispatch a formidable fleet to the mouth of the Mississippi," that England would send an equal force, and that they would demand free egress and ingress for their merchantmen, with their cargoes of goods and supplies of cotton, which were essential to the world.[89]

The fall of New Orleans and other Confederate reverses were soon followed by Confederate successes, and the tide of hope turned. The brilliant campaign of Jackson in the Shenandoah Valley and the initial victories of Lee in front of Richmond

81 Yancey, Rost, and Mann to Russell, November 27, 1861, reprinted in OR, ser. 2, vol. 2, 1231–33. On November 8, 1861, the British mail steamer Trent, carrying the two new Confederate commissioners, was stopped and boarded by a U.S. warship (the "Trent Affair"). To avoid a possible military response by England over this affront to its sovereignty, Mason and Slidell were released from U.S. custody on January 1, 1862.

82 Carman writes "two days later" in his original manuscript and gives the dates of their notes as November 27 and 29. The reply from the Foreign Office, however, dates the second message as November 30. British Foreign Office, "Memorandum," December 7, 1861, reprinted in OR, ser. 2, vol. 2, 1236.

83 The text of the communication to be given to Russell was laid out in detailed instructions sent by the secretary of state. For these, see Hunter to Mason, September 23, 1861, 1207–14.

84 British Foreign Office, "Memorandum," 1236.

85 "They [Mason, Slidell, and their two secretaries] are here for their own interest, in order, if possible, to drag us into their own quarrel and ... rather disappointed, perhaps, that their detention has not provoked a new war ... They must not suppose, because we have gone to the very verge of a great war to rescue them, that therefore they are precious in our eyes. We should have done just as much to rescue two of their own Negroes ... Let the Commissioners come up quietly to town, and have their say with anybody who may have time to listen to them. For our part, we cannot see how anything they have to tell can turn the scale of British duty and deliberation." "London, Saturday, January 11, 1862," Times (London), January 11, 1862.—EAC

86 Hunter to Mason, February 8, 1862. A copy appears in ORN, vol. 3, 333–36. A nearly identical message was sent to Slidell in Paris.

87 Slidell to Mason, March 10, 1862, A copy appears in ORN, vol. 3, 356.

88 See Mason to Hunter, March 11, 1862. A copy appears in ORN, vol. 3, 358–60.

89 Slidell, "Memorandum of Dispatch No. 5," [c. April 14, 1862]. A copy appears in ORN, vol. 3, 393–95. See also Slidell to Benjamin, May 15, 1862; Slidell to Mason, May 14, 1852; Slidell to Benjamin, June 1, 1862; Mason to Benjamin, June 23, 1862. Respective copies appear in ORN, vol. 3, 419–20, 422–23, 428–29, 444–46.

intensified the determination of the government to put forth new efforts and work out the salvation of the cause by military success. Benjamin, having moved from the War Department to State in March, wrote both Mason and Slidell on July 19, 1862, that the government was to push the offensive and cross the Potomac. He concluded his letter in a confident strain:

> Our sky is at last bright and is daily becoming more resplendent. We expect (we can scarcely hope the contrary possible) that this series of triumphs will have at least satisfied the most skeptical of foreign Cabinets that we are an independent nation, and have a right to be so considered and treated. A refusal by foreign nations now to recognize us would surely be far less than simple justice requires and would indicate rather settled aversion than impartial neutrality. On this theme, however, I think it hardly necessary to say more than to assure you of the entire reliance felt by the President and the Department that you will spare no effort to avail yourself of the favorable opportunity presented by our recent successes in urging our right to recognition. We ask for no mediation, no intervention, no aid. We simply insist on the acknowledgement of a fact patent to mankind. Of the value of recognition as a means of putting an end to the war, I have spoken in a former dispatch. In our finances at home the effect would be magical, and its collateral advantages would be innumerable. It is not to be concealed that a feeling of impatience and even resentment is beginning to pervade our people, who feel that in the refusal of this legitimate demand the nations of Europe are in point of fact rendering active assistance to our enemy and are far from keeping to the promise of strict neutrality which they held out to us at the beginning of the war.[90]

This communication, conveying the declaration of the intention of the Confederates to recover lost ground and move into Maryland, was sent by special messenger, who was instructed to inform Mason and Slidell that Kentucky, Tennessee, and Missouri were to be redeemed, McClellan destroyed or captured, Pope overthrown, and the North invaded. Close upon these expected successes, the envoys were to demand immediate recognition.

France was becoming still more anxious to intervene but was restrained by its understanding with England. The French emperor, Napoleon III, was encouraging the South with the view of neutralizing the power of the United States. On July 3, 1862, he wrote to General Elie Frédéric Forey, "In the present state of the civilization of the world, the prosperity of America is not a matter of indifference to Europe, for it is the country which feeds our manufactures and gives an impulse to our commerce. We have an interest in the Republic of the United States being powerful and prosperous, but not that she should take possession of the whole Gulf of Mexico, thence commanding the Antilles as well as South America, and being the only dispenser of the products of the New World."[91]

The cotton famine now made itself felt in Britain. None could be had, the mills were closed, and thousands were thrown out of employment and obliged to seek municipal relief. In France the situation was about the same; in one district alone "no less than 130,000 persons, aggregating with those dependent upon them a total of some 300,000 souls, were absolutely destitute, all because of the cotton famine."[92]

The starvation of the English workingman did not appeal so strongly to the sympathy of the English government as did the losses of the commercial and manufacturing classes, and from these came strong pressure for recognition and the raising of the blockade. Members of the ministry began to give serious thought to the propriety and necessity for such action. These thoughts were strengthened by the success of the Confederates in the field. The defeat of McClellan's army on the Peninsula and the reverses of Pope's in front of Washington intensified the pressure, and close upon the disaster of Second Manassas both France and England took measures for intervention, which were checked by the failure of Lee's Maryland campaign. We have made this digression in narrative to bring before the reader the momentous importance of the campaign under consideration and to show the imminence of the crisis when Lee, after defeating Pope in front of Washington, turned his victorious columns toward the Potomac.

---

[90] Benjamin to Slidell, 467. A nearly identical letter was sent to Mason.

[91] See Napoleon III to Elie Frédéric Forey, July 2, 1862, reprinted in John William Draper, *History of the American Civil War*, vol. 2 (New York: Harper & Brothers, 1868), 521–22. A soldier of the Bourbon Restoration, the Second Republic, and the Second Empire, Forey (1804–72) commanded the French expedition against Mexico in 1862.

"At this period the French government, discarding all the traditions of national policy, had openly extended its sympathies to the enemies of the American Union, and that under the name, sometimes of recognition, sometimes of mediation, it had already been several times anxious to intervene in their favor. The wisdom of the English government, which refused to participate in these measures, had prevented France from pursuing so fatal a policy. But the numerous friends of the Confederates did not despair of dragging England into this course, and thus securing them the support of these two great European powers. In order to accomplish this, they only asked of their clients some success which could be adroitly turned to advantage; a victory achieved beyond the Potomac would have enabled them to maintain that the North, beaten on her own soil, would never be able to conquer those vast States which had rebelled against her laws." Comte de Paris (Louis-Phillippe-Albert d'Orléans), *History of the Civil War in America*, vol. 2 (Philadelphia: Porter & Coates, 1876), 309.—*EAC*

[92] Adams [Jr.], 265–71.

In the Confederate camps, for more than a year, events in Europe had been watched with the keenest interest; in all ranks, from the general to the private, there was an abiding faith in the intervention of England and France. This was strengthened as the army approached the Potomac, and, as it neared the boundary line of the Confederacy, officers and men were confident that the time had come and doubted not that the entrance into Maryland would bring the matter to a speedy and favorable issue. This was believed not only by the army, but throughout the Confederacy, and there was good reason for the belief. Therefore, when Lee concluded to cross the Potomac, he was "playing for a great stake," according to Bradley T. Johnson, and thought he held a winning hand. Lee "had the possibility of ending the war and achieving the independence of his people by one short and brilliant stroke of genius, endurance and courage."[93]

Lee's orders were issued on September 2, and the movement began next morning.[94] He had been joined by the troops ordered up from Richmond ten days before—the infantry divisions of Major Generals Daniel H. Hill and Lafayette McLaws, Brigadier General Wade Hampton's brigade of cavalry, and a number of batteries. These commands had numbered, at Richmond, about nineteen thousand men, but they had been diminished by the severity of the march made to join Lee. Putting his columns in motion toward the Potomac, to gain a footing in Maryland before the Union army could recover from its defeat and reorganize to meet him, Lee paused at the end of the first day's march to write this letter:

> Headquarters Alexandria and Leesburg Road
> Near Dranesville, September 3, 1862

His Excellency President Davis
Richmond, Va.

Mr. President: The present seems to be the most propitious time since the commencement of the war for the Confederate Army to enter Maryland. The two grand armies of the United States that have been operating in Virginia, though now united, are much weakened and demoralized. Their new levies, of which I understand 60,000 men have already been posted in Washington, are not yet organized, and will take some time to prepare for the field. If it is ever desired to give material aid to Maryland and afford her an opportunity of throwing off the oppression to which she is now subject, this would seem the most favorable.

After the enemy had disappeared from the vicinity of Fairfax Court House, and taken the road to Alexandria and Washington, I did not think it would be advantageous to follow him farther. I had no intention of attacking him in his fortifications, and am not prepared to invest them. If I possessed the necessary munitions, I should be unable to supply provisions for the troops. I therefore determined, while threatening the approaches to Washington, to draw the troops into Loudoun, where forage and some provisions can be obtained, menace their possession of the Shenandoah Valley, and, if found practicable, to cross into Maryland. The purpose, if discovered, will have the effect of carrying the enemy north of the Potomac, and, if prevented, will not result in much evil.

The army is not properly equipped for an invasion of an enemy's territory. It lacks much of the material of war, is feeble in transportation, the animals being much reduced, and the men are poorly provided with clothes, and in thousands of instances are destitute of shoes. Still, we cannot afford to be idle, and though weaker than our opponents in men and military equipments, must endeavor to harass if we cannot destroy them. I am aware that the movement is attended with much risk, yet I do not consider success impossible, and shall endeavor to guard it from loss. As long as the army of the enemy are employed on this frontier I have no fears for the safety of Richmond, yet I earnestly recommend that advantage be taken of this period of comparative safety to place its defense, both by land and water, in the most perfect condition. A respectable force can be collected to defend its approaches by land, and the steamer Richmond, I hope, is now ready to clear the river of hostile vessels.

Should General Bragg find it impracticable to operate to advantage on his present frontier, his army, after leaving sufficient garrisons, could be advantageously employed in opposing the overwhelming numbers which it seems to be the intention of the enemy now to concentrate in Virginia.

I have already been told by prisoners that some of Buell's cavalry have been joined to General Pope's army, and have reason to believe that the whole of McClellan's, the larger portion of Burnside's and Cox's, and a portion of [Major General David] Hunter's, are united to it.

What occasions me most concern is the fear of getting out of ammunition. I beg you will instruct the Ordnance Department to spare no pains in manufacturing a sufficient amount of the best kind, and to be particular, in

---

93 Address of Bradley T. Johnson, contained in "Reunion of the Virginia Division Army Northern Virginia Association," in *Southern Historical Society Papers* 12 (1884): 506.

94 Chilton to Daniel H. Hill, September 2, 1862, reprinted in *OR*, vol. 19, pt. 2, 588.

preparing that for the artillery, to provide three times as much of the long-range ammunition as of that for smooth-bore or short-range guns. The points to which I desire the ammunition to be forwarded will be made known to the Department in time. If the Quartermaster's Department can furnish any shoes, it would be the greatest relief. We have entered upon September, and the nights are becoming cool.

I have the honor to be, with high respect, your obedient servant,

R. E. Lee,
General[95]

Again, on the following day, he wrote:

Headquarters
Leesburg, Va., September 4, 1862

His Excellency President Davis
Richmond, Va.

Mr. President: I am extremely indebted to Your Excellency for your letter of the 30th ultimo, and the letter from Washington, which you inclosed to me. You will already have learned all that I have ascertained subsequently of the movements of McClellan's army, a large part, if not the whole, of which participated in the battle of Saturday last, as I have good reason to believe.

Since my last communication to you, with reference to the movements which I propose to make with this army, I am more fully persuaded of the benefit that will result from an expedition into Maryland, and I shall proceed to make the movement at once, unless you should signify your disapprobation. The only two subjects that give me any uneasiness are my supplies of ammunition and subsistence. Of the former, I have enough for present use, and must await results before deciding to what point I will have additional supplies forwarded. Of subsistence, I am taking measures to obtain all that this region will afford; but to be able to obtain supplies to advantage in Maryland, I think it important to have the services of some one known to, and acquainted with, the resources of the country. I wish, therefore, that if ex-Governor Lowe can make it convenient, he will come to me at once, as I have already requested by telegram. As I contemplate entering a part of the State with which Governor Lowe is well acquainted, I think he could be of much service to me in many ways. Should the results of the expedition justify it, I propose to enter Pennsylvania, unless you should deem it unadvisable upon political or other grounds. As to the movements of the enemy, my latest intelligence shows that the army of Pope is concentrating around Washington and Alexandria in their fortifications. Citizens of this county report that Winchester has been evacuated, which is confirmed by the Baltimore Sun of this morning, containing extracts from the *Washington Star* of yesterday. This will still further relieve our country and, I think, leaves the valley entirely free. They will concentrate behind the Potomac.

I have the honor to be, with high respect, your obedient servant,

R. E. Lee,
General[96]

These two communications reveal Lee's intention at the beginning of his Maryland campaign. He proposed to free Virginia of the presence of Federal troops, gather for himself the rich supplies of the Shenandoah Valley and Maryland, and, should it not be unadvisable upon political or other grounds, enter Pennsylvania. His reasons are more fully set forth in his official report, here quoted:

The enemy having retired to the protection of the fortifications around Washington and Alexandria, the army marched on September 3 toward Leesburg. The armies of Generals McClellan and Pope had now been brought back to the point from which they set out on the campaigns of the spring and summer. The objects of those campaigns had been frustrated and the designs of the enemy on the coast of North Carolina and in Western Virginia thwarted by the withdrawal of the main body of his forces from those regions. Northeastern Virginia was freed from the presence of Federal soldiers up to the intrenchments of Washington, and soon after the arrival of the army at Leesburg information was received that the troops which had occupied Winchester had retired to Harper's Ferry and Martinsburg. The war was thus transferred from the interior to the frontier, and the supplies of rich and productive districts made accessible to our army. To prolong a state of affairs in every way desirable, and not to permit the season for active operations to pass without endeavoring to inflict further injury upon the enemy, the best course appeared to be the

[95] Lee to Jefferson Davis, September 3, 1862, reprinted in *OR*, vol. 19, pt. 2, 590–91.
[96] Lee to Jefferson Davis, September 4, 1862, reprinted in *OR*, vol. 19, pt. 2, 591–92.

transfer of the army into Maryland. Although not properly equipped for invasion, lacking much of the material of war, and feeble in transportation, the troops poorly provided with clothing, and thousands of them destitute of shoes, it was yet believed to be strong enough to detain the enemy upon the northern frontier until the approach of winter should render his advance into Virginia difficult, if not impracticable. The condition of Maryland encouraged the belief that the presence of our army, however inferior to that of the enemy, would induce the Washington Government to retain all its available force to provide against contingencies, which its course toward the people of that State gave it reason to apprehend. At the same time it was hoped that military success might afford us an opportunity to aid the citizens of Maryland in any efforts they might be disposed to make to recover their liberties. The difficulties that surrounded them were fully appreciated, and we expected to derive more assistance in the attainment of our object from the just fears of the Washington Government than from any active demonstration on the part of the people, unless success should enable us to give them assurance of continued protection.

Influenced by these considerations, the army was put in motion, D. H. Hill's division, which had joined us on the 2d, being in advance, and between September 4 and 7 crossed the Potomac at the fords near Leesburg, and encamped in the vicinity of Fredericktown.

It was decided to cross the Potomac east of the Blue Ridge, in order, by threatening Washington and Baltimore, to cause the enemy to withdraw from the south bank, where his presence endangered our communications and the safety of those engaged in the removal of our wounded and the captured property from the late battlefields. Having accomplished this result, it was proposed to move the army into Western Maryland, establish our communications with Richmond through the Valley of the Shenandoah, and, by threatening Pennsylvania, induce the enemy to follow, and thus draw him from his base of supplies.[97]

On September 8, after reaching Frederick, Maryland, Lee said to Brigadier General John G. Walker, one of his division commanders:

"In ten days from now … if the military situation is what I confidently expect it to be after the capture of Harper's Ferry, I shall concentrate the army at Hagerstown, effectually destroy the Baltimore and Ohio road, and march to this point," putting his finger on the map at Harrisburg, Pennsylvania. "That is the objective point of the campaign. You remember, no doubt, the long bridge of the Pennsylvania railroad over the Susquehanna, a few miles west of Harrisburg. Well, I wish effectually to destroy that bridge, which will disable the Pennsylvania railroad for a long time. With the Baltimore and Ohio in our possession, and the Pennsylvania railroad broken up, there will remain to the enemy but one route of communication with the West, and that very circuitous, by way of the [Great] Lakes. After that I can turn my attention to Philadelphia, Baltimore, or Washington, as may seem best for our interests …

"You doubtless regard it hazardous to leave McClellan practically on my line of communication, and to march into the heart of the enemy's country?"

Walker acknowledged that he did regard the movement as hazardous, upon which, Lee continued, "He [McClellan] is an able general but a very cautious one … His army is in a very demoralized and chaotic condition, and will not be prepared for offensive operations—or he will not think it so—for three or four weeks. Before that time I hope to be on the Susquehanna."[98]

Jackson moved from Chantilly on the morning of the third, crossed the Loudoun and Hampshire Railroad at Vienna and Hunter's Mill, struck the Leesburg and Alexandria Turnpike, and followed it through Dranesville in the direction of Leesburg, camping that night on Sugarland Run. On the fourth he passed through Leesburg and went into camp near Big Spring, nearly two miles from town. Longstreet followed Jackson. He left Chantilly on the third, the divisions of Major General Richard H. Anderson and Brigadier General David R. Jones marching by way of Dranesville, while McLaws took the Green Spring Road, the three divisions being concentrated at Leesburg on the night of the fourth, where they remained

---

97 Lee to Cooper, August 19, 1863, reprinted in *OR*, vol. 19, pt. 1, 144–45. Longstreet says, "When the Second Bull Run campaign closed we had the most brilliant prospects the Confederates ever had. We then possessed an army which, had it been kept together, the Federals would never have dared attack. With such a splendid victory behind us, and such bright prospects ahead, the question arose as to whether or not we should go into Maryland. General Lee, on account of our short supplies, hesitated a little, but I reminded him of my experience in Mexico, where sometimes we were obliged to live two or three days on green corn. I told him we could not starve at that season of the year so long as the fields were loaded with 'roasting ears.' Finally he determined to go on, and accordingly crossed the river and went to Frederick City." James Longstreet, "The Invasion of Maryland," in *Battles and Leaders*, vol. 2, 663.—EAC

98 John G. Walker, "Jackson's Capture of Harper's Ferry," in *Battles and Leaders*, vol. 2, 605–6.

until the morning of the sixth. John B. Hood's Division[99] and Nathan G. Evans's Brigade, both unassigned, followed Longstreet from Chantilly and arrived at Leesburg on the evening of the fourth. Longstreet says, "As our columns approached Leesburg, 'Maryland, My Maryland' was in the air, and on the lips of every man from General Lee down to the youngest drummer. Our chief could have safely ordered the ranks to break in Virginia and assemble at Fredericktown."[100]

Lee's army was made up of Longstreet's command—the four divisions of McLaws, Anderson, Jones, and Walker—containing eighteen brigades; Jackson's command—the three divisions of Ewell (commanded by Brigadier General Alexander R. Lawton), A. P. Hill, and Jackson (commanded by Brigadier General John R. Jones)—containing fourteen brigades; D. H. Hill's Division of five brigades; Hood's Division of two brigades; and the unassigned brigade of Evans. In all, Lee had forty brigades of infantry, Stuart's cavalry division of three brigades, and seventy-three batteries of artillery aggregating 318 guns.

The strength of this army is disputed. Longstreet says that it numbered "sixty thousand men encouraged, matured, and disciplined by victory."[101] Other Southern writers do not admit this number; it is safe to say that, including D. H. Hill's and Walker's Divisions, Lee's effective force was not far from forty-eight thousand men—men whose superiors could not be found on the planet, whose spirits were raised to the highest pitch by the victories they had achieved and by the prospect of a successful invasion of the North.

Lee states that he was not properly equipped for invasion, lacking much of the matériel of war, feeble in transportation, and thousands of his men destitute of shoes.[102] He knew, however, that the country north of the Potomac was rich in horses and supplies for his men and, writes Longstreet, "that his army was equal to any service to which he thought to call it, and ripe for the adventure; that he could march into Maryland and remain until the season for the enemy's return into Virginia for autumn or winter work had passed, improve transportation[,] supplies, and the clothing of his army, and do that, if not more, for relief of our Southern fields and limited means, besides giving his army and cause a moral influence of great effect at home and abroad."[103]

The invasion of Maryland being determined, the army was stripped of all encumbrances and transportation reduced "to a mere sufficiency" to carry cooking utensils and the absolute necessities of a regiment. Surplus artillery was turned in and all animals not actually employed for artillery, cavalry, or draught purposes were left to be "recruited." Batteries were to select the best horses for use, turning over all others. As the army was "about to engage in most important operations," where any excesses committed would "exasperate the people, lead to disastrous results, and enlist the populace on the side of the Federal forces," quartermasters and commissaries were directed to make all arrangements for purchase of supplies needed by the army, "thereby removing all excuse for depredations" upon a people whose friendship was desired. A provost guard was organized to "follow in rear of the army, arrest stragglers, … punish summarily all depredators, and keep the men with their commands."[104] Stringent orders were issued against straggling and plundering, orders which were strictly enforced throughout the campaign, "but it was found impossible," writes William Allan, "to prevent the straggling of half sick and barefooted men."[105] He continues, "Many thousands of the men were ill clad and barefooted. The shoes, captured or supplied, had been altogether insufficient to keep the army shod, and now they were about to march through a stony country and over turnpike roads. In addition to this, the effect of the insufficient food and the green corn diet of the past week or two were telling in the large number of men weakened by diarrhoea [sic] and other similar complaints, whom a day's march would convert into stragglers."[106]

---

[99]   As an administrative unit, the division of Brigadier General John B. Hood was effectively disbanded for the first two weeks of the campaign. Prior to crossing the Potomac, his two brigades formed a part of a larger, provisional division under Brigadier General Nathan G. Evans. Almost immediately thereafter, Hood ran afoul of his new superior and was placed under arrest. As Evans's force was marching to join in the fighting at South Mountain on September 14, Lee ordered Hood's release, restored him to command of the two brigades, and detached them (and Hood) from further service under Evans. See John B. Hood, *Advance and Retreat: Personal Experiences in the United States and Confederate States Armies* (n.p., 1880), 38–40.

[100] Longstreet, *From Manassas to Appomattox: Memoirs of the Civil War in America* (Philadelphia: J. P. Lippincott Co., 1896), 199.

[101] Ibid., 279.

[102] Lee to Cooper, August 19, 1863, 144.

[103] Longstreet, *From Manassas to Appomattox*, 200–201.

[104] Headquarters Army of Northern Virginia, General Orders No. 102, September 4, 1862, reprinted in *OR*, vol. 19, pt. 2, 592–93.

[105] William Allan, *The Army of Northern Virginia in 1862* (Boston: Houghton, Mifflin and Co., 1892), 325. Carman's paraphrase of Allan at the beginning of this sentence is at variance with Allan's intended meaning and implies a greater measure of success by officers in keeping their men to these orders than Allan (who himself overstates the situation) intended to convey. Allan's original text reads, "Stringent measures were authorized to keep the men in the ranks, and the most careful instructions were issued to prevent depredations upon private property. *These last were in the main effectual*, but it was found impossible to prevent the straggling of half sick and barefooted men [emphasis added]."

[106] Ibid., 324.

At Leesburg, the commanding general learned that Brigadier General Julius White, commanding a brigade of Union troops at Winchester, had abandoned the place, whereupon Lee gave orders to occupy the town as a depot of supplies for his army.[107] Crippled and feeble soldiers, wending their way to the army, were directed to march through the Shenandoah Valley and join him in Maryland, and he suggested to the secretary of war that conscripts and deserters be gathered from the counties of Virginia wrested from Federal occupation and sent to Richmond to swell the garrison for the defense of that place.[108] Another suggestion was that Major General William W. Loring, then operating in the Kanawha Valley, should make short work with the Union forces in that quarter and then move to the lower Valley, about Martinsburg, and guard approach in that direction, but Loring found full employment on the Kanawha, and Lee's flank and rear in the great valley were entrusted to a few squadrons of Virginia cavalry detached from Stuart's cavalry division.

On the eve of crossing the Potomac, Lee again addressed Davis:

As I have already had the honor to inform you, this army is about entering [sic] Maryland, with a view of affording the people of that State an opportunity of liberating themselves. Whatever success may attend that effort, I hope, at any rate, to annoy and harass the enemy. The army being transferred to this section, the road to Richmond, through Warrenton, has been abandoned as far back as Culpeper Court-House, and all trains are directed to proceed by way of Luray and Front Royal from Culpeper Court-House to Winchester. I desire that everything coming from Richmond may take that route, or any nearer one turning off before reaching Culpeper Court-House. Notwithstanding the abandonment of the line, as above mentioned, I deem it important that as soon as the bridge over the Rapidan shall be completed, that over the Rappahannock should be constructed as soon as possible, and I have requested the president of the road to have timber prepared for that purpose. My reason for desiring that this bridge shall be repaired is, that in the event of falling back it is my intention to take a position about Warrenton, where, should the enemy attempt an advance on Richmond, I should be on his flank; or, should he attack me, I should have a favorable country to operate in, and, bridges being repaired, should be in full communication with Richmond.

I have had all the arms taken in the late battles collected as far as possible, and am informed that about 10,000 are now at Gainesville. All empty trains returning to Rapidan are ordered to take in arms at Gainesville to transport to Rapidan. They should be sent at once to Richmond to be put in order, as arms may be needed in Maryland. I desire that Colonel [Josiah] Gorgas will send some one to take charge of these arms at once, as the cavalry regiments now on duty in the vicinity of Gainesville will have to be withdrawn.

We shall supply ourselves with provisions and forage in the country in which we operate, but ammunition must be sent from Richmond. I hope that the Secretary of War will see that the Ordnance Department provides ample supplies of all kinds. In forwarding the ammunition it can be sent in the way above designated for the other trains, or it can be sent to Staunton, and thence by the Valley road to Winchester, which will be my depot. It is not yet certain that the enemy have evacuated the valley, but there are reports to that effect, and I have no doubt that they will leave that section as soon as they learn of the movement across the Potomac. Any officer, however, proceeding toward Winchester with a train will, of course, not move without first ascertaining that the way is clear. I am now more desirous that my suggestion as to General Loring's movements shall be carried into effect as soon as possible, so that with the least delay he may move to the lower end of the valley, about Martinsburg, and guard the approach in that direction. He should first drive the enemy from the Kanawha Valley, if he can, and afterward, or if he finds he cannot accomplish that result, I wish him to move by way of Romney toward Martinsburg and take position in that vicinity.[109]

The movement into Maryland was covered by a threatened advance on Washington; this was confided to Stuart's cavalry division. The battle of Chantilly or Ox Hill was fought on the evening of the first of September. On the second, Fitzhugh Lee's Brigade occupied Fairfax Court House, where, on the same day, it was joined by Hampton's Brigade, just arrived from Richmond, where it had been on duty guarding the retirement of the army and its march north from that place. During the day the 2d Virginia Cavalry (Colonel Thomas T. Munford) of Brigadier General Beverly H. Robertson's Brigade advanced to Leesburg, drove Captain Samuel C. Means and his independent company of cavalry from the town, and pursued them to Waterford—a distance of seven miles. On the same day, Hampton made a reconnaissance and came upon a rear-guard of Major General Edwin V. Sumner's corps at Flint Hill. After some firing of sharpshooters and artillery, the Federals retired—followed by Hampton and his entire brigade, with two guns in charge of Captain John Pelham. Sumner's men were soon overtaken and Pelham opened on them with one of his rifled guns, creating some confusion. It was now growing dark;

---

[107] See Lee to George W. Randolph, September 7, 1862, reprinted in OR, vol. 19, pt. 1, 140.

[108] Lee to Randolph, September 3, 1862, reprinted in OR, vol. 19, pt. 2, 589–90.

[109] Lee to Jefferson Davis, September 5, 1862, reprinted in OR, vol. 19, pt. 2, 593–94.

the pursuit was slow and cautious. Hampton was finally checked by artillery and infantry commanding the road on which he was advancing, and he withdrew.

On the morning of the third, Fitzhugh Lee, with his brigade and some horse artillery, made a demonstration toward Alexandria, while Hampton, moving by way of Hunter's Mill on the Leesburg Turnpike below Dranesville, encamped near that place. Robertson's Brigade, at Chantilly since the first, crossed over from the Little River Turnpike and camped near Hampton. Demonstrations were kept up toward Groveton and the Chain Bridge, but these did not impose on the latest general-in-chief of the Union armies, Major General Henry W. Halleck, who cautioned McClellan on the third that there was every probability that the Confederates would cross the Potomac and make a raid into Maryland and Pennsylvania.[110] McClellan's cavalry commander, Brigadier General Alfred Pleasonton, who was at the front, came to the same conclusion—that "the enemy is only making a show of force to conceal his movements on the Upper Potomac."[111]

On the morning of the fourth, Robertson, moving in the direction of Falls Church, encountered Pleasonton's cavalry pickets between Vienna and Lewinsville and drove them in. Posting a part of his command and one gun of Captain Roger P. Chew's (Virginia) Battery near Lewinsville to prevent surprise, Robertson opened fire with two guns from the hill overlooking the church, to the right of the main road, where he had drawn up his cavalry in a conspicuous position. Pleasonton replied with two guns, and the firing was kept up until nearly sundown, when, perceiving that Pleasonton was about to advance on him in force, Robertson retired in the direction of Leesburg, near which place Stuart was concentrating his division to cover the rear of Lee's main army, now crossing the Potomac.

---

[110] Henry W. Halleck to George B. McClellan, September 3, 1862, reprinted in *OR*, vol. 19, pt. 2, 169.

[111] Alfred Pleasonton to Randolph B. Marcy, September 4, 1862, 1:30 p.m., reprinted in *OR*, vol. 19, pt. 2, 178.

3

The Confederate Army Crosses the Potomac

The Confederate advance into Maryland was led by D. H. Hill's Division, which had left Petersburg on the twenty-first of August and joined Lee at Chantilly on the second of September. On the morning of the third it marched up Pleasant Valley in the direction of Dranesville to strike the turnpike at that place, or between it and Leesburg, and reached the vicinity of Leesburg the same day. From there, on the morning of the fourth, one of Hill's brigades, under Brigadier General George B. Anderson, was pushed to the Potomac opposite Point of Rocks to demonstrate on the Baltimore and Ohio Railroad, interrupt communication with Baltimore and Washington, and divert attention from the fords below. While Anderson was engaged in this duty and amusing Colonel Henry B. Banning (who—with the 87th Ohio, some Maryland troops, and two guns of Captain John H. Graham's battery of New York artillery—had been sent from Harper's Ferry to guard the crossings of the river at and below Point of Rocks), Hill, with two brigades, brushed away a detachment of thirty men commanded by Lieutenant Jerome B. Burk[1] of the 1st Maryland, Potomac Home Brigade, at Cheek's Ford (at the mouth of the Monocacy), crossed over, and spent that night and next day in an attempt to destroy the locks and banks of the Chesapeake and Ohio Canal. (The aqueduct, carrying the canal over the Monocacy, could not be destroyed for want of powder and tools.) While so engaged, Hill was directed on the fifth by Jackson, then crossing at White's Ford, to push forward that evening and unite with him where the Baltimore and Ohio Railroad crossed the Monocacy, near Frederick, to save or destroy the bridge as circumstances should determine. But Hill could not see his way clear to carry out Jackson's instructions (Jackson, too, was delayed) and remained near the mouth of the Monocacy until the morning of the sixth, when he followed Jackson's Division to a point near Frederick.

Jackson left Leesburg on the morning of the fifth, marched to White's Ford on the Potomac, and began to cross before noon. The water was not deep and the passage was effected without much difficulty, though the progress was slow. An army correspondent writes, "When our army reached the middle of the river, … General Jackson pulled off his hat, and the splendid band of music struck up the inspiring air of 'Maryland, my Maryland,' which was responded to and sung … by all who could sing; and the name of all who could then and there sing was legion."[2] What took place at the head of the column occurred its entire length. Each band, as it came to the Potomac or emerged from its waters, struck up the inspiring air; every regiment gave it vocal expression. The entire army was in the highest state of enthusiasm. Its historian says, "Its spirit at this time was high. A series of brilliant successes had given it unbounded confidence in itself and in its leaders, and the ragged and dirty soldiers hailed with joy the advance to the Potomac. The weather was fine, and on those splendid September days when the crossing was effected, the broad and placid river, with the long columns of wading infantry, and the lines of artillery and wagons making their way through it, and the men shouting and singing 'My Maryland' to give vent to their noisy delight, made a picturesque and animated scene."[3] One of Lee's biographers writes, "The fare of green apples and green corn, and the continuous bivouac and battle engaged in by the two corps of Jackson and Longstreet left thousands of stragglers behind. Clad in fluttering rags and with feet either bare or only half-shod, the depleted Confederate army moved forward in high spirit, with shout and song. They looked like a band of scarecrows … The groves and green fields of Maryland were made vocal with laughter as the gray-jackets marched toward Frederick."[4]

Jackson's spirits were as exuberant as those of a schoolboy. For months he had advocated a movement into Maryland and Pennsylvania, and as he saw before him fair fields laden with grain, orchards full of fruit, and his columns heading northward, he felt that the Confederate cause was brightening and looked forward to happy results. Not that he had any sentimental feeling regarding Maryland, but every step northward was taking him nearer the great industrial establishments, coal mines, and railroads of Pennsylvania that he would destroy and the manufactures and commerce of Philadelphia and other cities and towns that he would annihilate. He was where he could subsist on the country and, once in

---

[1] In his original manuscript, Carman gives the name incorrectly as "J. A. Burk."

[2] John Esten Cooke, *The Life of Stonewall Jackson: From Official Papers, Narratives, and Personal Acquaintance* (New York: C. B. Richardson, 1863), 196–97.

[3] William Allan, *The Army of Northern Virginia in 1862* (Boston: Houghton, Mifflin and Co., 1892), 325–26.

[4] Henry A. White, *Robert E. Lee and the Southern Confederacy, 1807–1870* (New York: G. P. Putnam's Sons, 1905), 199.

Pennsylvania, would make unrelenting war upon her people at their homes and force them to understand the cost of holding the South in the Union at the point of the bayonet.

On the afternoon of the fifth, Stuart followed Jackson across the Potomac, Fitzhugh Lee's Brigade in the advance, and moved to Poolesville, near which place was encountered Captain Samuel E. Chamberlain with a detachment of one hundred men of the 1st Massachusetts Cavalry. (This regiment had served in South Carolina and landed at Alexandria, Virginia, on the second. Crossing the Potomac on the fourth, it pushed out to Tennallytown, Maryland, from whence, on the morning of the fifth, Chamberlain was sent to watch the fords of the Potomac.) As they marched through the principal street of Poolesville, some citizens, in sympathy with the Confederates, placed obstacles of stones and other articles in the road behind the blue-clad horsemen. Chamberlain encountered Fitzhugh Lee and his men just west of the town and was soon borne back by superior numbers. As the Union cavalry retreated rapidly through town, they were thrown into confusion by the falling of their horses over the obstacles, resulting in the capture of Chamberlain and thirty of his men. (None were killed; eight or nine were wounded. Fitzhugh Lee's loss was three killed and four wounded.) The victorious Confederates went into camp about two miles east of Poolesville, and Hampton followed to the same point. Fitzhugh Lee, impressed no doubt by the kindly assistance given by the citizens in overthrowing the Massachusetts cavalry, reported that the reception of the Confederate troops in Maryland, "was attended with the greatest demonstrations of joy, and the hope of enabling the inhabitants to throw off the tyrant's yoke stirred every Southern heart with renewed vigor and enthusiasm."[5]

On September 6, after paroling the Massachusetts prisoners, the brigades of Fitzhugh Lee and Hampton (the latter in advance) marched from Poolesville in the direction of Frederick. Fitzhugh Lee occupied New Market, on the Baltimore and Ohio Railroad, and felt out in the direction of Ridgeville (nestled in a gap in Parrs Ridge). Hampton took position at Hyattstown, with advanced posts at Damascus and Clarksburg in Parrs Ridge. Robertson's Brigade, now under the command of Colonel Munford,[6] joined the command during the day; it proceeded to hold the right at Sugar Loaf Mountain and extended pickets as far as Poolesville. In this position—from the mouth of the Monocacy on the right to the Baltimore and Ohio Railroad on the left—Stuart covered the front toward both Washington and Baltimore. This position was maintained until the eleventh, Hampton being engaged in light skirmishing near Hyattstown and Munford in more serious affairs at Poolesville and between that place and Sugar Loaf. Meanwhile, the main body of Lee's army took position behind the Monocacy and, covered by Stuart's enterprising cavalry, enjoyed a much needed rest.

When Jackson crossed the Potomac on the fifth, it was his intention to make a rapid march and seize the Baltimore and Ohio Railroad bridge over the Monocacy near Frederick that night (as noted, either to hold it or destroy it), and he called upon Hill, then engaged in the attempted destruction of the canal near the mouth of the Monocacy, to join him, but so much time was consumed in the crossing that Jackson could not accomplish the march. He halted at Three Springs, near Buckeystown, six miles from the bridge and about nine miles from Frederick, a company of cavalry under Captain Robert Randolph moving in advance and scouting to the right to observe any Union movement and keep connection with Stuart's cavalry. After going into bivouac, Jackson sent orders to his division and brigade commanders to let their men gather green corn for two days, which was all they now had to eat. He then sent for Captain Elijah V. White of the cavalry and directed that officer to accompany him in a ride. Starting after dark, they went back over the road marched that day nearly to the Potomac, then back again to the bivouac, Jackson not speaking a word during the entire ride.

Jackson resumed his march by the Frederick Road on the morning of the sixth, arriving at the Frederick junction of the Baltimore and Ohio Railroad in the afternoon. Ewell's Division was put in position covering the railroad and the approaches from the direction of Baltimore and A. P. Hill's Division those from the direction of Washington; Jackson's old division went into camp on the Best farm, between the railroad junction and Frederick. Ewell's Division seized the railroad bridge over the Monocacy (which had been held by the 14th New Jersey until, under an order of Major General John E. Wool, it retired in the direction of Baltimore). D. H. Hill's Division followed Jackson's and camped near it. Jones's Brigade (commanded temporarily by Colonel Bradley T. Johnson) of Jackson's Division occupied Frederick as a provost guard, and

5 The closing sentiment, credited by Carman to Fitzhugh Lee, was penned instead by Stuart. James E. B. Stuart to Robert H. Chilton, February 13, 1864, reprinted in *OR*, vol. 19, pt. 1, 815.

6 Before the brigade crossed into Maryland, Robertson was relieved from duty with the Army of Northern Virginia and re-assigned to the Department of North Carolina, where his services were deemed "indispensably necessary for the organization and instruction of cavalry troops." Headquarters Department of Northern Virginia, Special Orders No. 188, September 5, 1862, reprinted in *OR*, vol. 19, pt. 2, 595.

   In Carman's original narrative, he alternates the designation of this unit from this point out, referring to it sometimes as "Robertson's Brigade" and at others as "Munford's Brigade." Because Munford was not retained in permanent command of the unit subsequently, the editor feels the former is the more appropriate designation and for the purpose of editorial consistency has standardized the references throughout. Indeed, Munford's own report of the action at Crampton's Gap is headed, "Headquarters Robertson's Brigade." Thomas T. Munford to James T. W. Hairston, October 3, 1862, reprinted in *OR*, vol. 19, pt. 1, 826.

Johnson—a former resident of the place—proclaimed to the citizens that he and his men came as their deliverers from a tyrannical oppression.

Frederick was held by a company of the 1st Maryland, Potomac Home Brigade, commanded by Captain William T. Faithful. There were about six hundred sick and wounded men in hospitals throughout the town. When Faithful heard of the approach of Jackson, he removed the convalescent, set aside stores for those who could not be moved, sent all supplies possible to Pennsylvania, and burned the remainder. Joined by Lieutenant Burk's detachment, which had fallen back from the mouth of the Monocacy, he led the party—about one hundred men—on the Harper's Ferry Road through Jefferson, Petersville, and Knoxville, joining his regiment at Sandy Hook, a short distance east of Harper's Ferry, on the afternoon of the sixth.

Longstreet's command crossed the Potomac at White's Ford on the morning of the sixth and, marching by way of Buckeystown and Frederick Junction, arrived at Frederick on the seventh; Hood's Division and Evans's Brigade followed. General Lee accompanied Longstreet.

Walker's Division had been left on the James River for the defense of Richmond. When it was ascertained that McClellan was leaving Harrison's Landing, Walker was ordered northward to reinforce Lee in his campaign against Pope, but when he reached the field of Second Manassas he found that the campaign in northeastern Virginia was closed and that Lee was pushing into Maryland. Walker followed and arrived at Leesburg on the evening of September 6. The next morning he crossed the Potomac at Cheek's Ford, at the mouth of the Monocacy about three miles above White's Ford. Here he overtook G. B. Anderson's Brigade, which had been demonstrating at Point of Rocks, and, marching with it, reached Buckeystown the same evening. On the eighth Walker marched his division to Frederick Junction and, riding ahead, reported to Lee, by whom he was informed of the plan to capture Harper's Ferry, in which he was to cooperate under orders not yet matured. On the morning of the ninth, he was ordered by Lee to return to the mouth of the Monocacy and destroy the aqueduct of the Chesapeake and Ohio Canal—the duty which had been assigned previously to D. H. Hill and not performed. Walker's men arrived at the aqueduct a little before midnight and found it occupied by some cavalry pickets. These were driven away by the 24th and 25th North Carolina, which crossed the stream. Working parties were at once detailed and set to work drilling holes for blowing up the arches, but after several hours' labor, Walker met with no more success than had Hill; the aqueduct was so admirably constructed and cemented that it was found virtually a solid mass of granite. Not a seam or crevice could be discovered in which to insert the point of a crow-bar, and the drills were too dull and the granite too hard, so he was compelled to abandon the effort. Before daylight of the tenth, the division went into bivouac west of the Monocacy, having lost Captain George T. Duffy of the 24th North Carolina, mortally wounded, and a few men taken prisoner.[7]

The high spirits with which the Southern army entered Maryland were intensified by cheering news from Bragg's army in Kentucky, essaying to carry the colors of the Confederacy to the Ohio River. Lee made the announcement in General Orders on the sixth:

> The general commanding takes pleasure in announcing to the brave soldiers of the Army of Northern Virginia the signal success of their comrades in arms in the West. The Confederate forces, under the command of Maj. Gen. E. Kirby Smith, defeated on August 30 the Federal forces commanded by [Major] General [William] Nelson, capturing General Nelson and his staff, 3,000 prisoners, and all his artillery, small-arms, wagons, &c. This great victory is simultaneous with your own at Manassas. Soldiers, press onward! Let each man feel the responsibility now resting on him to pursue vigorously the success vouchsafed to us by Heaven. Let the armies of the East and the West vie with each other in discipline, bravery, and activity, and our brethren of our sister States will soon be released from tyranny, and our independence be established upon a sure and abiding basis.[8]

On September 7 Lee was holding the line of the Monocacy. He reported that he found plenty of provisions and forage in the country; that the community received his army with kindness but hesitated to receive Confederate currency in payment for supplies; and "notwithstanding individual expressions of kindness that have been given, and the general sympathy in the success of the Confederate States, situated as Maryland is, I do not anticipate any general rising of the people in our behalf. Some additions to our ranks will no doubt be received, and I hope to procure subsistence for our troops."[9] At the same time, Lee could not conceal the fact that there was great and urgent necessity to correct some evils in his army, especially as it was in a state whose citizens it was his purpose to conciliate and bring to his cause; every outrage upon their feelings and property should be checked. The evils he complained of were "backwardness in duty, tardiness of movement, and neglect of orders" on the part of officers, and straggling from the ranks among the men, and he begged Davis to find

[7] See John G. Walker to Gilbert Moxley Sorrel, October 7, 1862, reprinted in *OR*, vol. 19, pt. 1, 912–13.

[8] Headquarters Army of Northern Virginia, General Order No. 103, September 6, 1862, reprinted in *OR*, vol. 19, pt. 2, 596.

[9] Robert E. Lee to Jefferson Davis, September 7, 1862, reprinted in *OR*, vol. 19, pt. 2, 596–97.

some tribunal under the law that could take cognizance of and punish such offenses. He wrote again to Davis on the same day:

> I find that the discipline of the army, which, from the manner of its organization, the necessity of bringing it into immediate service, its constant occupation and hard duty, was naturally defective, has not been improved by the forced marches and hard service it has lately undergone. I need not say to you that the material of which it is composed is the best in the world, and, if properly disciplined and instructed, would be able successfully to resist any force that could be brought against it. Nothing can surpass the gallantry and intelligence of the main body, but there are individuals who, from their backwardness in duty, tardiness of movement, and neglect of orders, do it no credit. These, if possible, should be removed from its rolls if they cannot be improved by correction.
>
> Owing to the constitution of our courts-martial, great delay and difficulty occur in correcting daily evils. We require more promptness and certainty of punishment. One of the greatest evils, from which many minor ones proceed, is the habit of straggling from the ranks. The higher officers feel as I do, and I believe have done all in their power to stop it. It has become a habit difficult to correct. With some, the sick and feeble, it results from necessity, but with the greater number from design. These latter do not wish to be with their regiments, nor to share in their hardships and glories. They are the cowards of the army, desert their comrades in times of danger, and fill the houses of the charitable and hospitable in the march. I know of no better way of correcting this great evil than by the appointment of a military commission of men known to the country, and having its confidence and support, to accompany the army constantly, with a provost-marshal and guard to execute promptly its decisions.[10]

Six days later, Lee wrote that his movement was much embarrassed by the reduction of his force by straggling, which it seemed impossible to prevent with the present regimental officers. Although he had reason to hope that his casualties in battle in the recent campaign in Virginia did not exceed five thousand men, his ranks were much reduced—he feared anywhere from one-third to one-half of the original numbers.[11] After the battle of Antietam, he reported that the efficiency of his army "was greatly paralyzed by the loss to its ranks of the numerous stragglers … A great many men belonging to the army never entered Maryland at all; many returned after getting there, while others who crossed the river kept aloof."[12]

G. F. R. Henderson, in his elaborate biography of "Stonewall" Jackson, says:

> Many a stout soldier, who had hobbled along on his bare feet until Pope was encountered and defeated, found himself utterly incapable of marching into Maryland. In rear of the army the roads were covered with stragglers. Squads of infantry, banding together for protection, toiled along painfully by easy stages, unable to keep pace with the colours, but hoping to be up in time for the next fight; and amongst these were not a few officers. But this was not the worst. Lax discipline and the absence of soldierly habits asserted themselves … Not all the stragglers had their faces turned towards the enemy, not all were incapacitated by physical suffering. Many, without going through the formality of asking leave, were making for their homes, and had no idea that their conduct was in any way peculiar. They had done their duty in more than one battle, they had been long absent from their farms, their equipment was worn out, the enemy had been driven from Virginia, and they considered that they were fully entitled to some short repose. And amongst these, whose only fault was an imperfect sense of their military obligations, was the residue of cowards and malingerers shed by every great army engaged in protracted operations.[13]

The sympathy of Jackson's biographer was with the Southern cause, and the picture here presented of the straggling of Lee's army is in fortification of an argument for the comparatively small number engaged at Antietam. Yet the picture is not much overdrawn, and it may be said in addition that many of the Confederate officers and men were opposed to an invasion of the North or an incursion beyond the borders of the Southern Confederacy. They had been taught to believe that their duty lay entirely in defending their own soil from invasion.

As soon as it was known that Lee was across the Potomac, the Confederate authorities at Richmond rose to a high state of exaltation; many believed that in ten days he would be dictating peace from the steps of the Capitol at Washington. Davis went so far as to prepare a mission to propose terms of peace, and Henry S. Foote, in the Confederate House of Representatives, offered this resolution: "That the signal success with which Divine Providence has so continually blessed our arms for several months past would fully justify the Confederate Government in dispatching a commissioner or commissioners to

---

[10] Lee to Davis, September 7, 1862, reprinted in *OR*, vol. 19, pt. 2, 597 (second message).

[11] Lee to Davis, September 13, 1862, reprinted in *OR*, vol. 19, pt. 2, 605–6.

[12] Lee to Davis, September 21, 1862, reprinted in *OR*, vol. 19, pt. 1, 143.

[13] G. F. R. Henderson, *Stonewall Jackson and the American Civil War*, vol. 2, (London: Longmans, Green, and Co., 1898), 251–52.

the Government at Washington, empowered to propose the terms of a just and honorable peace." By a vote of fifty-nine to twenty-six the resolution was laid on the table.[14]

There was not entire unanimity in Confederate councils. When Davis communicated to the House of Representatives Lee's dispatches announcing his intention to cross the Potomac and the news that he had done so subsequently, the following resolution was offered: "That Congress has heard with profound satisfaction of the triumphant crossing of the Potomac by our victorious army, and assured of the wisdom of that masterly movement, reposes with entire confidence on the distinguished skill of the commanding general and the valor of his troops to achieve, under favor of the Great Ruler of Nations, new triumphs, relieve oppressed Maryland, and advance our standard into the territory of the enemy." As we have seen, the Confederate Congress had resolved in December 1861 that no peace ought to be concluded with the United States which did not ensure to Maryland the opportunity of forming a part of the Confederacy. We have elsewhere noted the fact that in February 1862 (when the Confederate government began to congratulate itself that it had convinced England and France that cotton was king and that those two great powers were on the eve of armed intervention in American affairs) the Confederate commissioner in London was advised that no treaty of peace or settlement would be considered that did not secure the independence of the Confederate States, including Maryland, Kentucky, and Missouri. The liberation of Maryland and her alliance with the Confederacy had become the settled purpose of the South, and its Congress was willing to express and confirm it in the resolution before the House. But a formidable minority would not go beyond that point and favor an invasion of Pennsylvania, and objection was made to the closing words of the resolution: "… and advance our standard into the territory of our enemy." A motion to strike out those words was warmly debated by those who were not prepared to take the responsibility of going so far; they had not been invited even to enter Maryland—but had been invited to enter Kentucky and had been driven out by Kentucky steel. Others insisted that the North should taste some of the bitterness of war; the people demanded it. Congressman William P. Miles of South Carolina was sanguine that Jackson, with half the Army of Northern Virginia, could scatter six hundred thousand of the enemy and gain peace. The motion to strike out the concluding words of the resolution was defeated by a vote of twenty-nine to sixty-one, and the entire resolution as originally offered—committing the government to an invasion of the North—was adopted on September 12, 1862, by a vote of sixty-three to fifteen.[15]

About the same time, to help Bragg's operations in Kentucky, it was proposed to make peace with the states of the northwest and detach them from the Union by offering them the free navigation of the Mississippi River. A committee made a favorable report on the proposition that "such a proclamation … it is confidently believed, would have a tendency greatly to strengthen the efforts of the advocates of peace in the Northwestern States, be calculated to bring those States quickly into amicable relations with the States of the South, withdraw them ultimately altogether from their present injurious political connection with the States of the North and East, with which they have really so little in common, and thus enable us to dictate the terms of a just and honorable peace from the great commercial emporiums of that region through whose influence mainly has this wicked and unnatural war been thus far kept in progress."[16] A minority report was submitted, contending that the reported desire for peace in the Northwest was delusive, and it advanced the opinion that "the most effective mode of conquering a peace is not to be found in extending to the enemy propositions of reconciliation, but in the vigorous prosecution of the war."[17] These reports were submitted on September 19, 1862. Lee's army had then recrossed the Potomac, and dreams of conquering a peace—at that time—vanished.

The tone of the Southern press and what was expected to be accomplished by an invasion of the North is shown in the following editorial of the *Richmond Dispatch*:

The road [to Pennsylvania] lies most invitingly open. There are no regular soldiers on the route, and it would be a task of little difficulty to disperse the rabble of militia that might be brought to oppose him [Lee].

… The country is enormously rich. It abounds in fat cattle, cereals, horses, and mules. Our troops would live on the very fat of the land. They would find an opportunity, moreover, to teach the Dutch farmers and grazers, who have

---

[14] See *Journal of the House of Representatives of the House of Representatives of the First Congress of the Confederate States of America*, vol. 5 of *Journal of the Congress of the Confederate States of America, 1861–1865*, 58th Cong., 2d sess., 1904, S. Doc. 234, serial 4614, 385–86.

[15] Ibid., 371–72. On the motion to strike out the closing phrase, Carman states incorrectly in his original manuscript that sixty-two votes were cast in the negative. Both the tabulation and the roll call show sixty-one votes. The original manuscript contains a similar error in regard to the final vote on committing to an invasion of the North, stating that it passed fifty-six to thirteen (instead of sixty-three to fifteen). Carman confuses final passage of the relevant resolution with a subsequent amendment to add the words "Congressional General Order No. 1" to its title (which, if passed, undoubtedly would have incurred Davis's wrath as an unconstitutional encroachment on his powers as commander-in-chief).

[16] Ibid., 405.

[17] Ibid., 406–7.

been clamorous for this war, what invasion really is. If once compelled to take his own physic, which is a great deal more than he has ever bargained for, Mynheer [Mein Herr] will cry aloud for peace in a very short time. For our own part, we trust that the first proclamation of Pope, and the manner in which his army carried it out, will not be forgotten. We hope the troops will turn the whole country into a desert, as the Yankees did the Piedmont country of Virginia. Let not a blade of grass, or a stalk of corn, or a barrel of flour, or a bushel of meal, or a sack of salt, or a horse, or a cow, or a hog, or a sheep, be left wherever they move along. Let vengeance be taken for all that has been done, until retribution itself shall stand aghast.—This is the country of the smooth-spoken, would-be gentleman, McClellan. He has caused a loss to us, in Virginia, of at least thirty thousand negroes, the most valuable property that a Virginian can own. They have no negroes in Pennsylvania. Retaliation must therefore fall upon something else, and let it fall upon everything that constitutes property. A Dutch farmer has no negroes; but he has horses that can be seized, grain that can be confiscated, cattle that can be killed, houses that can be burnt. He can be taken prisoner and sent to Libby's warehouse, as our friends in Fauquier, and Loudoun, and Culpepper [*sic*], and Stafford, and Fredericksburg, and the Peninsula, have been sent to Lincoln's dungeons in the North. Let retaliation be complete, that the Yankees may learn that two can play at the game they have themselves commenced.

… By advancing into Pennsylvania with rapidity, our army can easily get possession of the Pennsylvania Central Railroad, and break it down so thoroughly that it cannot be repaired in six months. They have already possession of the Baltimore and Ohio Railroad and the York Railroad. By breaking down these and the railroad from Philadelphia to Baltimore, they will completely isolate both Washington and Baltimore. No reinforcements can reach them from either the North or West, except by the Potomac and the bay.[18]

Up to the eighth, Lee could not ascertain that any Union movement was being made to oppose him in Maryland, only that the entire Union army was concentrating about Washington. He was still purchasing ample supplies of provisions in the country and endeavoring to break up his line of communication as far back as Culpeper Court House and turn everything into the Valley of Virginia, in accordance with the plan communicated to Davis earlier.[19] Firmly established behind the Monocacy, he held the Baltimore and Ohio Railroad and the principal roads to Baltimore, Washington, Harper's Ferry, and the upper Potomac—and could operate on several of them. Those toward Harper's Ferry, Baltimore, and Pennsylvania were unoccupied, while that in the direction of Washington was held by the Union army, now concentrating in his front.

Lee now felt himself strong enough to develop one of the political objects of his Maryland campaign. Edward A. Pollard says, "Mr. Davis had been persuaded that at the moment the Confederate armies were so visibly superior as to carry the war into the enemy's country, if he would then make any proposition showing the moderation of the designs of the South, it would furnish capital to the Democratic party in the North, widen the divisions of party there, and excite a political division in favor of the South, besides making a moral exhibition to the world of great advantage to its cause." It was for these reasons—to work on the feelings of the North and strengthen the hands of Northern Democrats—that Davis gave the most stringent orders that Lee's army was to protect every right of private property in the North, to abstain from retaliation and to show the utmost regard for the humanities of war. "It was not," observes Pollard, "so much to sentimentalism of 'Christian warfare' as the calculation of political effect … of operating on the division of parties in the North, and thus weakening its resolution and temper in the contest."[20]

In his review of the Maryland campaign, Longstreet says, "It had been arranged that the Southern President should join the troops, and from the head of his victorious army call for recognition," and he indulges in roseate views of the effect:

---

[18] "Our Army in Maryland," *Richmond Dispatch*, September 17, 1862. "Mein Herr" is a reference to the prosperous farmers of German descent, overwhelmingly Republican in sympathy, who made up a sizeable portion of the population of western Pennsylvania. For the "first proclamation of Pope," see Headquarters Army of Virginia, General Orders No. 5, July 18, 1862, reprinted in *OR*, vol. 12, pt. 2, 50; General Orders. No. 6, July 18, 1862, reprinted in *OR*, vol. 12, pt. 2, 50; General Orders No. 7, July 10 [18?], 1862, reprinted in *OR*, vol. 12, pt. 2, 51.

As for losses to slave property, the writer's ire is misdirected. Interference with the "peculiar institution" was antithetical to McClellan's entire conception of the war and its aims. His attitude toward the question of slavery is illustrated best in a letter he wrote only days after replacing Scott as general-in-chief: "Help me to dodge the nigger—we want nothing to do with him. *I* am fighting to preserve the integrity of the Union & the power of the Govt—on no other issue. To gain that end we cannot afford to raise up the negro question—it must be incidental & subsidiary." George B. McClellan to Samuel L. M. Barlow, November 8, 1861, reprinted in Stephen W. Sears, ed., *The Civil War Papers of George B. McClellan: Selected Correspondence, 1860–1865* (New York: Ticknor & Fields, 1989), 128.

[19] Lee to Davis, September 8, 1862, reprinted in *OR*, vol. 19, pt. 2, 600–601 (second message).

[20] Edward A. Pollard, *Life of Jefferson Davis, with a Secret History of the Southern Confederacy, Gathered "Behind the Scenes in Richmond": Containing Curious and Extraordinary Information of the Principal Southern Characters in the Late War, in Connection with President Davis, and in Relation to the Various Intrigues of His Administration* (Philadelphia: National Publishing Co., 1869), 237–39.

Maryland would have put out some of her resources, and her gallant youth would have helped swell the Southern ranks,—the twenty thousand soldiers who had dropped from the Confederate ranks during the severe marches of the summer would have been with us. Volunteers from all parts of the South would have come, swimming the Potomac to find their President and his field-marshal, while Union troops would have been called from Kentucky and Tennessee, and would have left easy march for the Confederate armies of the West to the Ohio River.

Even though the Confederates were not successful, the fall elections were against the Federal administration. With the Southern armies victorious, the result of the contest at the polls would have been so pronounced as to have called for recognition of the Confederacy.[21]

To what extent Lee shared these views is not definitely known, but we have Longstreet for authority that it was Lee's "deliberate and urgent advice to President Davis to join him and be prepared to make a proposal for peace and independence from the head of a conquering army."[22] But Davis had not joined the army, and Lee, flushed with his victories in Virginia and quietly seated in the richest part of Maryland, wrote this letter:

Headquarters
Near Fredericktown, Md., September 8, 1862

His Excellency Jefferson Davis,
President of the Confederate States, Richmond, Va.:

Mr. President: The present position of affairs, in my opinion, places it in the power of the Government of the Confederate States to propose with propriety to that of the United States the recognition of our independence. For more than a year both sections of the country have been devastated by hostilities which have brought sorrow and suffering upon thousands of homes, without advancing the objects which our enemies proposed to themselves in beginning the contest. Such a proposition, coming from us at this time, could in no way be regarded as suing for peace; but, being made when it is in our power to inflict injury upon our adversary, would show conclusively to the world that our sole object is the establishment of our independence and the attainment of an honorable peace. The rejection of this offer would prove to the country that the responsibility of the continuance of the war does not rest upon us, but that the party in power in the United States elect to prosecute it for purposes of their own. The proposal of peace would enable the people of the United States to determine at their coming elections whether they will support those who favor a prolongation of the war, or those who wish to bring it to a termination, which can but be productive of good to both parties without affecting the honor of either.

I have the honor to be, with high respect, your obedient servant,

R. E. Lee,
General[23]

It was expected by Davis that when Lee entered Maryland, the general would be joined by persons of influence who would advise with him upon the political condition of the state and upon other matters of import, but Lee found no such persons awaiting his arrival or coming forward to advise him. It was a matter of grave concern to Lee how he should supply his army without money. The farmers of western Maryland had no use for Confederate currency and lent little faith in the promises of the Confederate Quartermaster, and Lee reported that he anticipated some embarrassment in paying for necessities for the army, as it was probable that many individuals would hesitate to receive Confederate currency. He wrote to Davis:

I shall endeavor in all cases to purchase what is wanted, and, if unable to pay upon the spot, will give certificates of indebtedness of the Confederate States for future adjustment. It is very desirable that the chief quartermaster and commissary should be provided with funds, and that some general arrangement should be made for liquidating the debts that may be incurred to the satisfaction of the people of Maryland, in order that they may willingly furnish us what is wanted. I shall endeavor to purchase horses, clothing, shoes, and medical stores for our present use, and you will see the facility that would arise from being provided with the means of paying for them. I hope it may be

---

[21] James Longstreet, *From Manassas to Appomattox: Memoirs of the Civil War in America* (Philadelphia: J. P. Lippincott Co., 1896), 285. Although Carman is correct to question the overly-optimistic scenario presented by Longstreet, he misstates the former Confederate's meaning slightly. A full reading of the paragraphs leading up to this passage shows that Longstreet was speculating as to what the army might have accomplished "had it been held in hand and refreshed by easy marchings and comfortable supplies." Ibid., 284. That, not the presence of Davis with the army, was what Longstreet identified as the key to assured victory.

[22] Ibid., 204.

[23] Lee to Davis, September 8, 1862, reprinted in *OR*, vol. 19, pt. 2, 600 (first message).

convenient for ex-Governor Lowe, or some prominent citizen of Maryland, to join me, with a view of expediting these and other arrangement necessary to the success of our army in this state.[24]

Lee refrained from inducing men of prominence to come forward and openly, actively espouse the Confederate cause and expressed himself as averse to doing so. He was not confident of his ability to hold the state and was too considerate to compromise those who would suffer the moment his army failed to protect them. As none came forward, and finding that the citizens were embarrassed as to the intentions of the army, he determined to delay no longer in making known the purpose of Confederate invasion[25] and issued this proclamation:

Headquarters Army Of Northern Virginia
Near Fredericktown, Md., September 8, 1862

To the People of Maryland:

It is right that you should know the purpose that brought the army under my command within the limits of your State, so far as that purpose concerns yourselves. The people of the Confederate States have long watched with the deepest sympathy the wrongs and outrages that have been inflicted upon the citizens of a commonwealth allied to the States of the South by the strongest social, political, and commercial ties. They have seen with profound indignation their sister State deprived of every right and reduced to the condition of a conquered province. Under the pretense of supporting the Constitution, but in violation of its most valuable provisions, your citizens have been arrested and imprisoned upon no charge and contrary to all forms of law. The faithful and manly protest against this outrage made by the venerable and illustrious Marylander, to whom in better days no citizen appealed for right in vain, was treated with scorn and contempt; the government of your chief city has been usurped by armed strangers; your legislature has been dissolved by the unlawful arrest of its members; freedom of the press and of speech has been suppressed; words have been declared offenses by an arbitrary decree of the Federal Executive, and citizens ordered to be tried by a military commission for what they may dare to speak. Believing that the people of Maryland possessed a spirit too lofty to submit to such a government, the people of the South have long wished to aid you in throwing off this foreign yoke, to enable you again to enjoy the inalienable rights of freemen, and restore independence and sovereignty to your State. In obedience to this wish, our army has come among you, and is prepared to assist you with the power of its arms in regaining the rights of which you have been despoiled.

This, citizens of Maryland, is our mission, so far as you are concerned. No constraint upon your free will is intended; no intimidation will be allowed within the limits of this army, at least. Marylanders shall once more enjoy their ancient freedom of thought and speech. We know no enemies among you, and will protect all, of every opinion. It is for you to decide your destiny freely and without constraint. This army will respect your choice, whatever it may be; and while the Southern people will rejoice to welcome you to your natural position among them, they will only welcome you when you come of your own free will.

R. E. Lee,
General, Commanding[26]

This address was received with cold indifference. The "ancient freedom of thought and speech" of the people of Maryland had not been so much curtailed as to anger them to the fighting point, and they doubted the power of Lee's ragged army to regain even the small moiety of the rights of which they were told they had been despoiled. Those of Frederick and adjoining counties were a thrifty people, entirely willing to dispose of a reasonable share of their products at unreasonably high prices, but were not easily moved to rise and avenge the "wrongs and outrages" that had been inflicted upon them. They were not aware of the fact that they had been "deprived of every right and reduced to the condition of a conquered province." The temper of the people was misjudged.

Bradley T. Johnson was an ardent Confederate and prone to judge others' thoughts by his own. He was sanguine of a Confederate rising and used his gift of oratory to that end. Upon his entrance into Frederick as provost marshal with Jackson's advance on the sixth, he proclaimed himself and his men as deliverers and called upon all to throw off the yoke of oppression and subjugation. In the evening Colonel Johnson addressed a public meeting and assured his hearers that the Confederates had come into western Maryland to stay, predicted that Washington and Baltimore would fall into their

---

[24] Lee to Davis, September 7, 1862, reprinted in *OR*, vol. 19, pt. 2, 596.
[25] Lee to Davis, September 12, 1862, reprinted in *OR*, vol. 19, pt. 2, 605.
[26] Lee to "the People of Maryland," September 8, 1862, reprinted in *OR*, vol. 19, pt. 2, 601–2.

hands, and was sanguine that Lee would dictate terms of peace in Independence Square, Philadelphia.[27] On the day that Lee issued his address to the people of Maryland, Johnson put forth this appeal:

To the People of Maryland:

After sixteen months of oppression more galling than the Austrian tyranny, the victorious army of the South brings freedom to your doors. Its standards now wave from the Potomac to Mason and Dixon's line. The men of Maryland, who during the last long months have been crushed under the heel of this terrible despotism, now have the opportunity for working out their own redemption, for which they have so long waited and suffered and hoped. The government of the Confederate States is pledged by the unanimous vote of its Congress, by the distinct declaration of its President, the soldiers and statesman Davis, never to cease this war until Maryland has the opportunity to decide for herself, her own fate, untrammeled and free from Federal bayonets. The people of the South, with unanimity unparalleled, have given their hearts to our native state, and hundreds of thousands of her sons have sworn with arms in their hands that you shall be free.

You must now do your part. We have the arms here for you. I am authorized immediately to muster in for the war, companies and regiments, the companies of one hundred men each, and the regiments of ten companies. Come, all who wish to strike for their liberties and homes! Let each man provide himself with a stout pair of shoes, a good blanket and a tin cup. Jackson's men have no baggage.

Officers are in Frederick to receive recruits, and all companies formed will be armed as soon as mustered in. Rise at once. Remember the cells of Fort McHenry! Remember the dungeons of Fort Lafayette and Fort Warren! the insults to your wives and daughters! the arrest! the midnight searches of your houses! Remember these wrongs! and rise at once in arms, and strike for liberty and right!

Bradley T. Johnson, Colonel, C.S.A.
Frederick, September 8, 1862[28]

The appeal was but feebly answered. A few enlisted. Some who came to enlist, upon seeing their liberators (officers as well as men) barefoot, ragged, and filthy, changed their minds and went home. The result was disappointing to Johnson, who had impressed his optimistic views upon his superiors that, in that part of the state, the Southern cause would find recruits to march under its colors, that—freed from Federal bayonets and given the opportunity—they would decide for the South. Fewer than five hundred recruits were obtained, not enough to compensate for deserters. It is said, "Lee expected volunteers to enroll themselves under his standard [twenty-five thousand or more, says Longstreet—EAC], tempted to do so by the hope of throwing off the yoke of the Federal Government, and the army certainly shared this expectation. The identity of sentiment generally between the people of the States of Maryland and Virginia, and their strong social ties in the past, rendered this anticipation reasonable, and the feeling of the country at the result afterward was extremely bitter."[29]

Had Lee entered Maryland by the southern counties or had his army reached the vicinity of Baltimore—where the secession sentiment was strong—many would have flocked to his standards, but he was in a section of the state where there was an almost complete indifference, if not open hostility, to the Confederate cause; instead of being received with smiles, his ragged troops were regarded with aversion and ill concealed dislike. The bad condition of the men had much to do with the character of their reception. J. R. Jones, the commander of Jackson's Division, reported that "never has the army been so dirty, ragged, and ill-provided for as on this march."[30] In his life of Lee, John Esten Cooke thus writes:

The condition of the army was indeed forlorn. It was worn down by marching and fighting; the men had scarcely shoes upon their feet; and, above the tattered figures, flaunting their rags in the sunshine, were seen gaunt and begrimed faces, in which could be read little of the "romance of war." The army was in no condition to undertake an invasion; "lacking much of the material of war, feeble in transportation, poorly provided with clothing, and thousands of them destitute of shoes," is Lee's description of his troops. Such was the condition of the better portion of the force; on the opposite side of the Potomac, scattered along the hills, could be seen a weary, ragged, hungry, and confused multitude, who had dragged along in rear of the rest, unable to keep up, and whose miserable appearance said little for the prospects of the army to which they belonged.

---

[27] See "Confederates in Maryland," *Montgomery County (Md.) Sentinel*, September 12, 1862.

[28] See Bradley T. Johnson, *Maryland*, vol. 2 of *Confederate Military History*, ed. Clement A. Evans (Atlanta: Confederate Publishing Co., 1899), 90–91.

[29] Cooke, 127–28. Carman's authority for Longstreet's statement about an expected twenty-five thousand Marylanders has not been identified.

[30] John R. Jones to Alexander S. Pendleton, January 21, 1863, reprinted in *OR*, vol. 19, pt. 1, 1008.

From these and other causes resulted the general apathy of the Marylanders, and Lee soon discovered that he must look solely to his own men for success in his future movements. He faced that conviction courageously; and, without uttering a word of comment, or indulging in any species of crimination against the people of Maryland, resolutely commenced his movements looking to the capture of Harper's Ferry and the invasion of Pennsylvania. The promises of his address had been kept. No one had been forced to follow the Southern flag; and now, when the people turned their backs upon it, closing the doors of the houses in the faces of the Southern troops, they remained unmolested.[31]

Lee was able to obtain forage for his animals and some provisions for his men, but there was some difficulty about the latter. Many of the farmers had not yet threshed their wheat, and there was reluctance on the part of millers and others to commit themselves in his favor or to receive pay in Confederate scrip. He obtained some cattle, but the inhabitants had driven most of their stock into Pennsylvania.[32]

Reports reached Lee on the ninth that led him to believe that the Union forces were pushing a strong column up the Potomac by Rockville and Darnestown, and by Poolesville toward Seneca Mills.[33] Again he informed Davis that he was endeavoring to break up the line through Leesburg, which was no longer safe, and turn everything off from Culpeper Court House toward Winchester; that he would move in the direction originally intended (toward Hagerstown, Maryland, and Chambersburg, Pennsylvania) for the purpose of opening the line of communication through the Shenandoah Valley in order to procure supplies of flour; and that his plan was to move on the tenth or eleventh.[34]

Lee now heard of Davis's intention to visit the army and was quick to inform the president that, while he "should feel the greatest satisfaction" in having an interview with him and consulting upon all matters of interest, he could not but feel great uneasiness for his safety. Davis would not only encounter the hardship and fatigue of a very disagreeable journey but also run the risk of capture. Lee went so far as to send Major Walter H. Taylor of his staff to explain how very hazardous would be the proposed visit.[35] Taylor left Frederick at noon on the ninth with dispatches and verbal messages to Davis and suggestions to ex-governor Lowe of Maryland, both of whom he expected to meet at Warrenton, but, on Taylor's arrival on the tenth, Davis had returned to Richmond and Lowe did not put in an appearance.

Enoch Lowe was an ardent sympathizer with the South, zealous in promoting and encouraging secessionist feeling in the state and in urging armed effort against the U.S. government. He was one of those who longed for the appearance of the "liberating army of the South," and he was looked to, to give it moral and substantial assistance in its "holy mission" to redeem the soil from the foot of the "vandal invader." Before entering Maryland, Lee (as we have seen) asked Davis to have Lowe meet him, as he thought the former governor could be of service in many ways and make arrangements necessary to the success of the army in its liberating march through the state. Lowe failed to meet Lee's messenger at Warrenton on the tenth, but three days later he made a speech at Winchester in which he said Maryland, long disappointed, had been perfectly taken by surprise on the entrance of the Confederate army and that when it was seen to be no mere raid, "25,000 men would flock to our standard, and a provisional government would be formed."[36]

But the twenty-five thousand men did not flock to the standard. A storm of indignation swept over the South at the cold and indifferent treatment accorded the liberators, and Lowe rushed into print with an explanation of how it came about. He said that no notice had been given the Maryland people of Lee's intention; the Confederates' entrance into the state was a surprise to them, and it was impossible for Marylanders to know whether it was a mere raid or they intended permanent occupation. Lee's army had entered the state where the "Black Republican" feeling was the strongest, but, even in western Maryland, a free expression at the ballot-box would show a decided majority for the secession cause. Besides, the stay in Maryland was so short that the people had no chance to rally to the support of their liberators. Maryland wanted more time; how much time, measured in days, he could not say. "All that she asks," Lowe insisted, "is to be set free and admitted into the Southern Confederacy. She wants such an occupation of her soil by the Southern army, and for such a reasonable length of time as will enable her people to dissolver their connection with the Federal Government, obtain admission into the Southern Confederacy, and arm and organize her quota of the Confederate army."[37]

We have said that Lee shared the sanguine views of Davis as to the result of an invasion of Maryland. The statement needs qualification. While it is quite true that Lee was convinced of military success in its initiative, he was fully aware of the immense resources of the North and the ability of the Union government—should time be given to it—to concentrate

---

[31] Cooke, 131–32.

[32] Lee to Davis, September 9, 1862, reprinted in *OR*, vol. 19, pt. 2, 602 (first message).

[33] Ibid.

[34] Lee to Davis, September 9, 1862, 603.

[35] Ibid., 602–3.

[36] "Our Army Correspondence," *Richmond Dispatch*, September 20, 1862.

[37] Enoch L. Lowe, "Maryland—Her Sympathies and Situation," *Richmond Dispatch*, October 1, 1862.

an overwhelming force against him. His enforced delay at Frederick and the failure to arouse the people of Maryland dashed even those hopes that he shared, in a lesser degree, with Davis, who, not looking at the obstacles in the way, was desirous of a speedy issue, with results much more important than those foreshadowed by Lee (which he has given us in his official report). Davis favored and hoped for a prompt march into Pennsylvania or on Baltimore or Washington. Lee did not feel that he was free to make any advance with his army—north or east—until Harper's Ferry was reduced, and in reply to Davis's suggestion as to the movement of his army said, "I wish your views of its operations could be realized, but so much depends upon circumstances beyond its control and the aid that we may receive, that it is difficult for me to conjecture the result. To look to the safety of our own frontier and to operate untrammeled in an enemy's territory, you need not be told is very difficult. Every effort, however, will be made to acquire every advantage which our position and means may warrant."[38]

The incursion of the Confederates into Maryland caused intense excitement in Baltimore and throughout the state; it also spread dismay beyond the border, extending into Pennsylvania as far northward as Harrisburg and Philadelphia. General Wool ruled Baltimore with a firm hand. Volunteers were enrolled for the defense of the city and the forts surrounding it were strengthened. Governor Andrew G. Curtin of Pennsylvania called for fifty thousand militia to defend the state and appealed to Lincoln, Halleck, and Secretary of War Edwin M. Stanton (who had replaced Simon Cameron in January) for competent generals and eighty thousand disciplined men. The reply was given that the men could not be furnished, that Harrisburg and Philadelphia were in no danger, and that the true defense of Pennsylvania lay in the strengthening of the Army of the Potomac, then marching after Lee in Maryland.[39]

Before crossing the Potomac, Lee considered the advantages of entering Maryland east or west of the Blue Ridge Mountains. (In either case, it was his intention to march on Hagerstown and Chambersburg.) By crossing east of the Blue Ridge, both Washington and Baltimore would be threatened, which he believed would ensure the withdrawal of the mass of the Union army north of the Potomac and the evacuation of Martinsburg and Harper's Ferry, thus opening his line of communication through the Shenandoah Valley. But for reasons that will hereafter appear, Harper's Ferry was not abandoned. It was a great surprise to Lee when he reached Frederick to know that the place was still garrisoned (instead of being abandoned as he fully expected and as it should have been, had correct military principles been observed). It was more than a surprise to him; it was a keen disappointment, and it became necessary to dislodge the garrison from that post—on the direct line of communication of his army—before concentrating his army west of the Blue Ridge. Yet to reduce it was to retard his projected campaign and required a separation of his army, for were he to use his whole force for the service and recross the Potomac, there was more than a strong probability that McClellan, now in his immediate front, would prevent his return to Maryland. Lee came to the decision to divide his army and capture the Union forces at Martinsburg and Harper's Ferry. He says:

> To accomplish this with the least delay, General Jackson was directed to proceed with his command to Martinsburg, and, after driving the enemy from that place, to move down the south side of the Potomac upon Harper's Ferry. General McLaws, with his own and R. H. Anderson's division, was ordered to seize Maryland Heights, on the north side of the Potomac, opposite Harper's Ferry, and Brigadier-General Walker to take possession of Loudoun Heights, on the east side of the Shenandoah, where it unites with the Potomac. These several commands were directed, after reducing Harper's Ferry and clearing the Valley of the enemy, to join the rest of the army at Boonsborough [sic] or Hagerstown.
>
> The march of these troops began on the 10th, and at the same time the remainder of Longstreet's command and the division of D. H. Hill crossed the South Mountain and moved toward Boonsborough. General Stuart, with the cavalry, remained east of the mountains, to observe the enemy and retard his advance.[40]

Two days before coming to a decision to send Jackson on this duty, Lee confided his plan for the capture of Harper's Ferry and its garrison to Longstreet. Upon this point, Longstreet says:

> Riding together before we reached Frederick [September 6—EAC], the sound of artillery fire came from the direction of Point of Rocks and Harper's Ferry, from which General Lee inferred that the enemy was concentrating his forces

---

[38] Lee to Davis, September 13, 1862, 605–6.

[39] Andrew G. Curtin to Abraham Lincoln, September 11, 1862, reprinted in *OR*, vol. 19, pt. 2, 268 (second message); Lincoln to Curtin, September 12, 1862, 10:35 a.m., reprinted in *OR*, vol. 19, pt. 2, 276. See also message of Curtin, September 6, 1862, as contained in John E. Wool to Edwin M. Stanton, September 7, 1862, 2:00 a.m.; Stanton to Curtin, September 7, 1862 (first message); Curtin to Stanton, September 7, 1862, 5:00 p.m.; Stanton to Curtin, September 7, 1862, 7:30 p.m. These are reprinted sequentially in *OR*, vol. 19, pt. 2, 203–4.

[40] Lee to Samuel Cooper, August 19, 1863, reprinted in *OR*, vol. 19, pt. 1, 145.

from the Valley, for the defense at Harper's Ferry, and proposed to me to organize forces to surround and capture the works and the garrison.

I thought it a venture not worth the game, and suggested, as we were in the enemy's country and presence, that he would be advised of any move that we made in a few hours after it was set on foot; that the Union army, though beaten, was not disorganized; that we knew a number of their officers who could put it in order and march against us, if they found us exposed, and make serous trouble before the capture could be accomplished; that our men were worn by very severe and protracted service, and in need of repose; that as long as we had them in hand we were masters of the situation, but dispersed into many fragments, our strength must be greatly reduced. As the subject was not continued, I supposed that it was a mere expression of passing thought, until, the day after we reached Frederick, upon going over to head-quarters, I found the front of the general's tent closed and tied. Upon inquiring of a member of the staff, I was told that he was inside with General Jackson. As I had not been called, I turned to go away, when General Lee, recognizing my voice, called me in. The plan had been arranged …

As their minds were settled firmly upon the enterprise, I offered no opposition.[41]

Two facts are here revealed. First, the conception of surrounding Harper's Ferry and capturing the garrison was Lee's and not Jackson's (as has been claimed by some of Jackson's biographers). Second, Jackson was selected to execute the movement because Longstreet was not in favor of it (had virtually refused it) and because Lee recognized the military impropriety of committing an important movement to a doubting commander.[42]

Referring to this period of the campaign, one of Jackson's biographers says:

General Lee now assembled his leading Generals in council, to devise a plan of operations for the approaching shock of arms. Harper's Ferry had not been evacuated, as he hoped. His first design, of withdrawing his army in a body toward Western Maryland, for the purpose of threatening Pennsylvania, and fighting M'Clellan upon ground of his own selection, was now beset with this difficulty: that its execution would leave the garrison at Harper's Ferry to re-open their communications with their friends, to receive an accession of strength, and to sit upon his flank, threatening his new line of supply up the valley of Virginia. Two other plans remained: the one was to leave Harper's Ferry to itself for the present, to concentrate the whole army in a good position, and fight M'Clellan as he advanced. The other was to withdraw the army west of the mountains, as at first designed, but by different routes, embracing the reduction of Harper's Ferry by a rapid combination in this movement; and then to re-assemble the whole at some favorable position in that region, for the decisive struggle with M'Clellan. The former was advocated by Jackson; he feared lest the other system of movements should prove too complex for realizing that punctual and complete concentration which sound policy required. The latter, being preferred by the Commander-in-Chief was adopted.[43]

As reports indicated that McClellan was advancing cautiously but firmly, Lee impressed upon his officers in command of the columns the necessity for prompt action. The final orders were as follows:

---

[41] Longstreet, *From Manassas to Appomattox*, 201–2. A similar account appeared earlier in Longstreet, "The Invasion of Maryland," in *Battles and Leaders of the Civil War*, vol. 2 (New York: Century Co., 1887), 663.

[42] Carman is simply too accepting of his source in this instance. Longstreet's most rabid detractors (both in his own time and ours) exaggerate wildly when they label all of his postwar writings as self-serving fictions, but it must be conceded that he had a tendency to place himself always at the center of the army's strategic planning in his recollections. Given Jackson's historic success at maneuver while in independent command in the Valley and in the Second Manassas campaign, it seems unlikely that Longstreet would have been Lee's initial choice for conducting the multi-pronged envelopment of Harper's Ferry. It is worth noting that Longstreet makes no mention of being offered the assignment or objecting to the plan in his official report. See Longstreet to Chilton, October 10, 1862, reprinted in *OR*, vol. 19, pt. 1, 839–43. Nor does Lee speak of a proposed role for Longstreet in the investment of the garrison. In fact, the most detailed explanation of his planning suggests strongly that he had always intended Jackson to oversee the movement: "It had been supposed that the advance upon Fredericktown [*sic*] would lead to the evacuation of Martinsburg and Harper's Ferry, thus opening the line of communication through the Valley. This not having occurred, it became necessary to dislodge the enemy from those positions before concentrating the army west of the mountains. *To accomplish this with the least delay*, General Jackson was directed to proceed with his command to Martinsburg, and, after driving the enemy from that place, to move down the south side of the Potomac upon Harper's Ferry [emphasis added]." Lee to Cooper, 145.

[43] R. L. Dabney, *Life and Campaigns of Lieut.-Gen. Thomas J. Jackson, (Stonewall Jackson.)* (New York: Blelock & Co., 1866), 548–49.

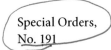

Hdqrs. Army of Northern Virginia
September 9, 1862

. . . III. The army will resume its march to-morrow, taking the Hagerstown road. General Jackson's command will form the advance, and, after passing Middletown, with such portion as he may select, take the route toward Sharpsburg, cross the Potomac at the most convenient point, and by Friday morning take possession of the Baltimore and Ohio Railroad, capture such of them as may be at Martinsburg, and intercept such as may attempt to escape from Harper's Ferry.

IV. General Longstreet's command will pursue the main road as far as Boonsborough, where it will halt, with reserve, supply, and baggage trains of the army.

V. General McLaws, with his own division and that of General R. H. Anderson, will follow General Longstreet. On reaching Middletown will take the route to Harper's Ferry, and by Friday morning possess himself of the Maryland Heights and endeavor to capture the enemy at Harper's Ferry and vicinity.

VI. General Walker, with his division, after accomplishing the object in which he is now engaged, will cross the Potomac at Cheek's Ford, ascend its right bank to Lovettsville, take possession of Loudoun Heights, if practicable, by Friday morning, Keys' Ford on his left, and the road between the end of the mountain and the Potomac on his right. He will, as far as practicable, co-operate with Generals McLaws and Jackson, and intercept retreat of the enemy.

VII. General D. H. Hill's division will form the rear guard of the army, pursuing the road taken by the main body. The reserve artillery, ordnance, and supply trains, &c., will precede General Hill.

VIII. General Stuart will detach a squadron of cavalry to accompany the commands of Generals Longstreet, Jackson, and McLaws, and, with the main body of the cavalry, will cover the route of the army, bringing up all stragglers that may have been left behind.

IX. The commands of Generals Jackson, McLaws, and Walker, after accomplishing the objects for which they have been detached, will join the main body of the army at Boonsborough or Hagerstown.

X. Each regiment on the march will habitually carry its axes in the regimental ordnance wagons, for use of the men at their encampments, to procure wood, &c.

By command of General R. E. Lee:

R[obert] H. Chilton,
Assistant Adjutant-General[44]

Not satisfied with the organization of McLaws's column, Longstreet asked and obtained permission, on the morning of the tenth, to strengthen it with three brigades (Wilcox's, Featherston's, and Pryor's) from Anderson's Division. The different columns proceeded as ordered. "It was a rollicking march," says Longstreet, "the Confederates playing and singing, as they marched through the streets of Frederick, 'The Girl I left behind me.'"[45]

All movements were made as ordered, but before following them we must see what the Union government was doing to meet this Confederate invasion of Maryland and why the garrison at Harper's Ferry was retained at that hazardous point.

[44] Headquarters Army of Northern Virginia, Special Order 191, September 9, 1862, reprinted in *OR*, vol. 19, pt. 2, 603–4.
[45] Longstreet, *From Manassas to Appomattox*, 205.

4

General McClellan and the Army of the Potomac

When George McClellan transported the Army of the Potomac to the Virginia Peninsula in April 1862, he left for the protection of Washington the commands of Banks and McDowell, to which was subsequently added the army commanded by Frémont. On June 26 Jackson—after defeating these three independent commands and driving them from the Shenandoah Valley—joined Lee for that remarkable campaign which, in seven days, forced McClellan from the front of Richmond to Westover, on the banks of the James. On this same twenty-sixth of June, the defeated commands of Banks, McDowell, and Frémont were consolidated into one army—the Army of Virginia—and Major General John Pope was assigned to the command.[1] With this army of about forty-five thousand men, Pope was to cover Washington, assure the safety of the Shenandoah Valley, and so operate upon the enemy's lines of communication in the direction of Gordonsville and Charlottesville as to draw off, if possible, a considerable force of the enemy from Richmond, thus relieving the operations of the Army of the Potomac against that city.[2]

There was much objection in Washington to the removal of McClellan's army to the Peninsula, and, after its defeat, the government was not entirely willing to reinforce it at the expense of troops thought necessary to ensure the safety of the capital. Beyond this there was distrust of McClellan's capacity as a general and of his ability to take Richmond. These views were honestly entertained by some; by others they were put forward to shelve McClellan. There had grown up a hostility against him soon after he was placed in command of the armies of the Union,[3] with the result that, when he set out for the Peninsula, he left behind him in Washington hardly a friend among public men, with the exception of Lincoln and two members of his cabinet. (Secretary of War Stanton, though profuse in expressions of friendship, was not friendly.) Beyond all this it was manifest that the cooperation of the two armies acting in Virginia could not be relied upon and that they should have a common head. For this and other reasons, personal and political, Halleck was assigned to the command of the land forces of the United States on July 11, 1862, and ordered to Washington,[4] where he arrived on the twenty-second.

In many respects the selection of Halleck was an unfortunate one for the country. He soon perceived what action would be most agreeable to Stanton and those who sided with him. On the twenty-fifth Halleck visited the Army of the Potomac at Harrison's Landing. He came to the conclusion to withdraw McClellan from the Peninsula and unite his army with that of Pope in front of Washington; on August 3 orders were issued to that effect.[5] McClellan made an earnest protest, setting forth the depressing effect which would follow the withdrawal of the army. He claimed that troops not necessary to the defense of Washington and Harper's Ferry were available to reinforce him, and he contended that the fate of the nation should be decided on the banks of the James: "Here, directly in front of this army, is the heart of the rebellion. It is here that our resources should be collected to strike the blow which will determine the fate of this nation. All points of secondary importance elsewhere should be abandoned and every available man brought here. A decided victory here, and the military strength of the rebellion is crushed. It matters not what partial reverses we may meet with elsewhere; here is the true defense of Washington."[6]

But McClellan's argument and protest made no impression on Halleck, who replied on the sixth, refusing to rescind the order. In a private letter to McClellan, Halleck said:

> I fully agree with you in regard to the manner in which the war should be conducted …
>
> I deeply regret that you cannot agree with me as to the necessity of reuniting the old Army of the Potomac. I, however, have taken the responsibility of doing so, and am to risk my reputation on it. As I told you when at your camp, it is my intention that you shall command all the troops in Virginia as soon as we can get them together, and with

---

[1] Abraham Lincoln to Lorenzo Thomas, June 26, 1862, reprinted in *OR*, vol. 12, pt. 1, 169.

[2] John Pope to George W. Cullum, January 27, 1863, reprinted in *OR*, vol. 12, pt. 2, 21.

[3] McClellan served as both general-in-chief of the Union Army and commander of the Army of the Potomac beginning November 1, 1861. On March 11, 1862, he was relieved of the former responsibility. Adjutant General's Office, General Orders No. 94, November 1, 1861, reprinted in *OR*, vol. 5, 639; President's War Order No. 3, March 11, 1862, reprinted in *OR*, vol. 10, pt. 2, 28.

[4] Order of Abraham Lincoln, July 11, 1862, reprinted in *OR*, ser. 3, vol. 2, 217.

[5] Henry W. Halleck to George B. McClellan, August 3, 1862, 7:45 p.m., as contained in McClellan to Thomas, August 4, 1863, reprinted in *OR*, vol. 11, pt. 1, 80–81.

[6] McClellan to Halleck, August 4, 1862, 12:00 p.m., reprinted in *OR*, vol. 12, pt. 2, 8–9.

the army thus concentrated I am certain that you can take Richmond. I must beg of you, general, to hurry along this movement. Your reputation as well as mine may be involved in its rapid execution.

I cannot regard Pope and Burnside as safe until you re-enforce them. Moreover, I wish them to be under your immediate command for reasons which it is not necessary to specify.[7]

McClellan very reluctantly withdrew from the Peninsula to unite his army with that of Pope in front of Washington but did not implicitly believe in the sincerity of Halleck's promise that the troops to be united would be placed under his command.[8] On August 23, while on his way up the Potomac, McClellan wrote these prophetic words to his wife: "I take it for granted that my orders will be as disagreeable as it is possible to make them, unless Pope is beaten, in which case they will want me to save Washington again. Nothing but their fears will induce them to give me any command of importance or treat me otherwise than with discourtesy."[9]

McClellan arrived at Alexandria on the evening of August 26 and reported by telegraph to Halleck the next morning.[10] As fast as his troops arrived they were virtually taken from him and he was reduced to the command of a few orderlies, camp guards, and construction parties instead of being put in command of the combined forces of himself and Pope (as General Halleck had indicated on more than one occasion). He assured Halleck of his readiness to lend any assistance in his power but complained of the extreme difficulty of doing anything while his power was curtailed and his position undefined.[11] Meanwhile, Stanton and some of his associates in the cabinet had formed a resolution that no more should McClellan command any army of the Union, and they were jubilant when Pope reported a great victory on the field of Second Manassas. They looked upon Pope as the coming man and could not conceal their intense pleasure at the apparent utter downfall of McClellan.

Then there was a sudden transformation. Early on the morning of September 1, it began to dawn upon Halleck's mind that Pope's reported victories were defeats. This impression was confirmed by a dispatch from Pope that the enemy was evidently feeling for his right,[12] upon which he telegraphed Pope, "If the enemy moves as your last telegram indicates, and you engage him to-day without a decisive victory, I suggest a gradual drawing in of your army to Fairfax Court-House, Annandale or, if necessary, farther south, toward Alexandria."[13] He then sent for McClellan and gave him verbal directions to take charge of the defenses of Washington, expressly limiting his jurisdiction to the works and their garrisons and prohibiting him from exercising any control over the troops actively engaged under Pope.[14]

During the day and night of September 1, alarming news from Pope's army reached Washington, and on the morning of the second, between seven and eight o'clock, Lincoln, accompanied by Halleck, called at McClellan's home. The president informed McClellan that he had received alarming news: affairs were in a very bad condition (much worse than had been reported to Halleck on the preceding day), Pope's army was in confusion and in full retreat, and the roads were full of stragglers. Lincoln desired him to resume command and do the best he could to restore confidence and defend Washington. McClellan assured the president that he could save the capital and bring order out of chaos. This assurance was a great relief to the president, who then verbally placed McClellan in entire command of the city and of the troops falling back upon it, with instructions to take immediate steps to stop and collect the stragglers, place the works in a proper state of defense, go out to meet and take command of the army when it approached the vicinity of the works, and then to place the troops in the best positions. Everything was committed to his hands.[15] This action of the president was cordially approved (or at least accepted) by Halleck, who seemed glad to be rid of a great responsibility. Secretary of the Navy Gideon Welles later made

7   Halleck to McClellan, August 7, 1862, reprinted in *OR*, vol. 11, pt. 3, 359–60.

8   "Halleck writes that all the forces in Virginia, including Pope, Burnside, etc., are to be placed under my command; I doubt it." McClellan to Mary Ellen McClellan, August 10 [11], 1862, midnight, reprinted in McClellan, *McClellan's Own Story: The War for the Union, the Soldiers Who Fought It, the Civilians Who Directed It, and His Relations to It and Them* (New York: Charles L. Webster & Co., 1887), 466. For similar expressions, see also those letters reprinted on pp. 467, 468, and 470.—EAC

9   McClellan to Mary Ellen McClellan, August 23, 1862, 9:30 p.m., reprinted in McClellan, *Own Story*, 471.

10 McClellan to Halleck, August 27, 1862, 9:45 a.m., reprinted in *OR*, vol. 12, pt. 3, 688.

11 McClellan to Halleck, August 31, 1862, 10:25 p.m., reprinted in *OR*, vol. 12, pt. 3, 773.

12 Pope to Halleck, September 1, 1862, 11:00 a.m., reprinted in *OR*, vol. 12, pt. 2, 84. See also Pope to Cullum, 45.

13 Halleck to Pope, September 1, 1862, reprinted in *OR*, vol. 12, pt. 3, 785.

14 McClellan to Thomas, August 4, 1863, reprinted in *OR*, vol. 11, pt. 1, 104.

15 McClellan, *Own Story*, 535. See also McClellan to Thomas, August 4, 1863, reprinted in *OR*, vol. 11, pt. 1, 105.

Many of the narrative portions of *Own Story* quoted by Carman also appear in McClellan, "From the Peninsula to Antietam," in *Battles and Leaders of the Civil War*, vol. 2 (New York: Century Co., 1887), 545–55. Based on the marginalia in Carman's original manuscript, he appears to have worked largely from McClellan's autobiography, although in two instances he cites the *Battles and Leaders* article explicitly.

the statement that Lincoln had said to him, "Halleck had no plan or views of his own, proposed to do nothing himself, and fully approved [of] calling upon McClellan."[16]

The president's verbal order to McClellan was supplemented, late in the day, by this written one:

General Orders,
No. 122

War Department, Adjt. Gen's Office
Washington, September 2, 1862

Major-General McClellan will have command of the fortifications of Washington and of all the troops for the defense of the capital.

By command of Major-General Halleck:

E[dward] D. Townsend,
Assistant Adjutant-General[17]

As originally drawn the order was worded as follows:

Headquarters of the Army
Adjutant-General's Office
Washington, September 2, 1862

By direction of the President, Major-General McClellan will have command of the fortifications of Washington and of all the troops for the defense of the capital.

By order of the Secretary of War:

E. D. Townsend,
Assistant Adjutant-General[18]

There was no change in the substance of the order but a modification in form. Stanton would not permit it to be promulgated "By order of the Secretary of War," nor would he have it appear that it was made "By direction of the President," and the order was issued with Halleck as its responsible author. He was made to assume the responsibility, though he had no knowledge that morning of Lincoln's intention. In a letter to Pope, Halleck later said, "The assignment of General McClellan to this command, or rather his retention in it, was not my act nor that of the War Department, it was the act of the President alone. I did not even know of his decision on the matter till he himself announced it to General McClellan."[19]

There has been much discussion upon the matter and manner of McClellan's restoration to full command. We here note only the views expressed by the biographers of Lincoln. John G. Nicolay and John Hay write:

The majority of the Cabinet were strongly opposed to it. The Secretary of War and the Secretary of the Treasury [Salmon P. Chase] agreed, upon the 29th of August, in a remonstrance against McClellan's continuance in command of any army of the Union. They reduced it to writing; it was signed by themselves and the Attorney-General [Edward Bates], and afterwards by the Secretary of the Interior [Caleb B. Smith]. The Secretary of the Navy concurred in the judgment of his colleagues, but declined to sign it, on the ground that it might seem unfriendly to the President. In the cabinet meeting of the 2d of September the whole subject was freely discussed. The Secretary of War disclaimed any responsibility for the action taken, saying that the order to McClellan was given directly by the President, and that General Halleck considered himself relieved from responsibility by it, although he acquiesced and approved the order. He thought that McClellan was now in a position where he could shirk all responsibility, shielding himself under Halleck, while Halleck would shield himself under the President. Mr. Lincoln took a different view of the transaction, saying that he considered General Halleck as much in command of the army as ever, and that General McClellan had been charged with special functions, to command the troops for the defense of Washington, and that he placed him there because he could see no one who could do so well the work required.[20]

The writers here quoted advance other reasons for Mr. Lincoln's action:

It was not alone for his undoubted talents as an organizer and drill-master that he was restored to his command. It was a time of gloom and doubt in the political as well as in the military situation. The factious spirit was stronger among the

[16] Gideon Welles, *Lincoln and Seward: Remarks upon the Memorial Address of Chas. Francis Adams, on the Late Wm. H. Seward, with Incidents and Comments Illustrative of the Measures and Policies of the Administration of Abraham Lincoln, and Views as to the Relative Positions of the Late President and Secretary of State* (New York: Sheldon & Co.: 1874), 196.

[17] Adjutant General's Office, General Orders No. 122, September 2, 1862, reprinted in *OR*, vol. 12, pt. 3, 807.

[18] Adjutant General's Office, Draft of General Orders No. 122, September 2, 1862, reprinted in McClellan, *Own Story*, 546.

[19] Halleck to Pope, October 10, 1862, reprinted in *OR*, vol. 12, pt. 3, 820.

[20] John G. Nicolay and John Hay, *Abraham Lincoln: A History*, vol. 6 (New York: Century Co, 1890), 21–22.

politicians and the press of the Democratic party than at any other time during the war. Not only in the States of the border, but in many Northern States, there were signs of sullen discontent among a large body of the people that could not escape the notice of a statesman so vigilant as Lincoln. It was of the greatest importance, not only in the interest of recruiting, but also in the interest of that wider support which a popular Government requires from the general body of its citizens, that causes of offense against any large portion of the community should be sedulously avoided by those in power. General McClellan had made himself, by his demonstrations against the President's policy, the leader of the Democratic party. Mr. Lincoln, for these reasons, was especially anxious to take no action against McClellan which might seem to be dictated by personal jealousy or pique; and besides, as General Pope had himself reported, there was a personal devotion to McClellan among those in high command in the Army of the Potomac which rendered it almost impossible for any other general to get its best work out of it. [Major] General Ethan Allen Hitchcock, one of the most accomplished officers of the old army, gave this as the reason for his declining that command.[21]

The true reason for the restoration of McClellan was the unfitness of Halleck. One would naturally suppose that when the forces of McClellan, Pope, and Burnside were concentrated in front of Washington, Halleck, as commander-in-chief, would have seized the opportunity of putting himself at their united head and assume supreme control of affairs in the field. But he was either unequal to the responsibility or conscious of his lack of nerve and avoided the task. It does not appear that the president urged the matter upon him, although when, at the instance of Pope,[22] he appointed Halleck to the command of the army, he expected that Halleck would exercise command in the field over operations in Virginia. This, however, evidently was not Halleck's idea, for when he visited the Peninsula on July 25 he promised McClellan that, if the armies were speedily united, he should command them.

This promise to McClellan was studiously kept from the knowledge of Lincoln and Stanton—and also from Pope, who, as late as August 25 (while opposing Lee on the Rappahannock and vainly endeavoring to join hands with Burnside at Fredericksburg), dispatched Halleck, "I certainly understood that as soon as the whole of our forces were concentrated you designed to take command in person."[23] This was the understanding of the president and the secretary of war as well. Somebody was being deceived, for Halleck had from the beginning determined to manage the armies from his office at Washington. Lincoln soon saw this, the feebleness of Halleck's management, and the influences other than military that were surrounding the general-in-chief, and in his perplexity the president turned to McClellan as one at least who was willing to accept responsibility and do what was required to bring order out of chaos. For whatever may have been the opinion of his military ability or his failure properly to support Pope, it was well know that he alone had the power to restore confidence to the Army of the Potomac and that as an organizer he had no superior in the army. Halleck assented to the arrangement with great good grace (if he did not actually court it), for he thought it relieved him of all responsibility—too obtuse in mind to comprehend that he held at arm's length an opportunity that most ambitious soldiers would have given half a lifetime to have met and embraced. Nevertheless Halleck took upon himself the credit of saving Washington from capture, writing to his wife on September 5, "I hope and believe I have saved the capital from the terrible crisis brought upon us by the stupidity of others. Few can conceive the terrible anxiety I have had within the last month."[24]

When the conference between Lincoln and McClellan terminated, Halleck hastened to inform Stanton of what had taken place. What occurred in Stanton's room we do not know, but we have the testimony of eyewitnesses as to what took place at the cabinet meeting that morning. Treasury Secretary Chase says:

The Secretary of War came in. In answer to some inquiry, the fact was stated by the President or the Secretary, that McClellan had been placed in command of the forces to defend the Capital—or, rather, to use the President's own words, "he had set him to putting these troops into the fortifications about Washington," believing that he could do that thing better than any other man. I remarked, that this could be done equally well by the engineer who constructed the forts … The Secretary of War said that no one was now responsible for the defense of the Capital; that the order to McClellan was given by the President direct to McClellan, and that General Halleck considered himself relieved from responsibility, although he acquiesced and approved the order; that McClellan could now shield himself, should anything go wrong, under Halleck, while Halleck could and would disclaim all responsibility for the order given. The president thought General Halleck as much responsible as before, and repeated that the whole scope of the order was, simply, to direct McClellan to put the troops into the fortifications, and command them for the

---

[21] Ibid., 23–24.

[22] For evidence of Pope's role in the selection of Halleck as general-in-chief, see Welles, 192.

[23] Pope to Halleck, August 25, 1862, reprinted in OR, vol. 12, pt. 2, 66.

[24] Halleck to Elizabeth Halleck, September 5, 1862, reprinted in James Grant Wilson, "Types and Traditions of the Old Army: II. General Halleck—A Memoir," *Journal of the Military Service Institution of the United States* 36, no. 135 (May–June 1905): 558.

defense of Washington. I remarked that … I could not but feel that giving command to him was equivalent to giving Washington to the rebels. This, and more, I said …

The President said it distressed him exceedingly to find himself differing on such a point from the Secretary of War and the Secretary of the Treasury; that he would gladly resign his place; but he could not see who could do the work wanted as well as McClellan. I named Hooker, or Sumner, or Burnside, either of whom could do the work better.[25]

In his account, Navy Secretary Welles says:

At the stated Cabinet meeting on Tuesday, the 2d of September, while the whole community was stirred up and in confusion, and affairs were gloomy beyond anything that had previously occurred, Stanton entered the council-room a few moments in advance of Mr. Lincoln and said, with great excitement, he had just learned from General Halleck that the President had placed McClellan in command of the forces in Washington. The information was surprising, and, in view of the prevailing excitement against that officer, alarming. The President soon came in, and in answer to an inquiry from Mr. Chase, confirmed what Stanton had stated. General regret was expressed, and Stanton with some feeling remarked, that no order to that effect had issued from the War Department. The President, calmly but with some emphasis, said the order was his, and he would be responsible for it to the country. With a retreating and demoralized army tumbling in upon us, and alarm and panic in the community, it was necessary, the President said, that something should be done, but there seemed to be no one to do it. He therefore had directed McClellan. who knew this whole ground, who was the best organizer in the army, whose faculty was to organize and defend, and who would here act on the defensive, to take this defeated and shattered army and reorganize it. He knew full well the infirmities of McClellan, who was not an affirmative man; was worth little for an onward movement; but beyond any other officer he had the confidence of the army, and he could more efficiently and speedily reorganize it and put it in condition than any other general. If the Secretary of War, or any other member of the Cabinet, would name a general that could do this as promptly and well, he would appoint him. For an active fighting general he was sorry to say McClellan was a failure; he had "the slows"; was never ready for battle, and probably never would be; but for this exigency, when organization and defense were needed, he considered him the best man for the service, and the country must have the benefits of his talents though he had behaved badly. The President said he had seen and given his opinion to General Halleck, who was still General-in-Chief; but Halleck had no plan or views of his own, proposed to do nothing himself, and fully approved his calling upon McClellan.

… A long discussion followed, closing with acquiescence in the decision of the President, but before separating the Secretary of the Treasury expressed his apprehension that the reinstatement of McClellan would prove a national calamity.[26]

On the following Friday, Welles had an interview with the president, which he has put on record. The secretary says:

The President said most of our troubles grew out of military jealousies. Whether changing the plan of operations (discarding McClellan and placing Pope in command in front) was wise or not, was not now the matter in hand. These things, right or wrong, had been done. If the Administration had erred, the country should not have been made to suffer nor our brave men been cut down and butchered. Pope should have been sustained, but he was not. These personal and professional quarrels came in. Whatever may have been said to the contrary, it could not be denied that the army was with McClellan. He had so skillfully handled his troops in not getting to Richmond as to retain their confidence. The soldiers certainly had not transferred their confidence to Pope. He could, however, do no more good in this quarter. It was humiliating, after what had transpired and all we knew, to reward McClellan and those who failed to do their whole duty in the hour of trial, but so it was. Personal considerations must be sacrificed for the public good. He had kept aloof from the dissensions that prevailed, and intended to; "but," said he, "I must have McClellan to reorganize the army and bring it out of chaos. There has been a design, a purpose, in breaking down Pope, without regard to the consequences to the country that is atrocious. It is shocking to see and know this, but there is no remedy at present. McClellan has the army with him."[27]

Montgomery Blair, postmaster general in Lincoln's cabinet, later wrote, "The bitterness of Stanton on the reinstatement of McClellan you can scarcely conceive. He preferred to see the capital fall … McClellan was bound to go when the

---

[25] Diary entry of Salmon P. Chase, September 2, 1862, reprinted in Robert B. Warden, *An Account of the Private Life and Public Services of Salmon Portland Chase* (Cincinnati: Wilstach, Baldwin & Co., 1874), 459–60.

[26] Welles, 194–96.

[27] Ibid., 197–98.

emergency was past, and Halleck and Stanton furnished a pretext."[28] In another letter, Blair said, "The folly and disregard of public interests thus exhibited would be incredible but that the authors of this intrigue, Messrs. Stanton and Chase, when the result of it came, and I proposed the restoration of McClellan to command, and to prevent the completion of ruin by the fall of this capital, *actually declared that they would prefer the loss of the capital to the restoration of McClellan to command.* Yet these are the men who have been accounted by a large portion of our countrymen as the civil heroes of the war, whilst McClellan, who saved the capital, was dismissed."[29]

After the president's departure from McClellan's house, the general stepped to the door of the room where his staff had assembled and said, with evident satisfaction, "Gentlemen, I am reinstated in command," then followed this announcement with orders to several members of the staff, who were sent in various directions.[30] McClellan's first step in complying with the president's instructions was a communication to Pope, wherein he advised him that he had been requested by Halleck to repeat the order given in the morning to withdraw the army to Washington without unnecessary delay. McClellan suggested the roads by which the withdrawal should be made and where the divisions should be posted: "[Major General Fitz John] Porter's corps upon Upton's Hill, that it may occupy Hall's Hill, &c.; McDowell's to Upton's Hill; [Major General William B.] Franklin's to the works in front of Alexandria; [Major General Samuel P.] Heintzelman's to the same vicinity; [Major General Darius N.] Couch to Fort Corcoran, or, if practicable, to the Chain Bridge; Sumner either to Fort Albany or to Alexandria, as may be most convenient."[31] This order to Pope was carried by Lieutenant John M. Wilson, who found Pope at Fairfax Court House. Pope was greatly surprised and cast down, betraying in the expression of his countenance his pain and deep mortification.

In a very short time, McClellan had made all requisite preparations and (while the cabinet was still in angry session) was about to start to the front to assume command as far out as possible, when a message came from Halleck informing him that it was the president's order that he should not assume command until the troops had reached the immediate vicinity of the fortifications. McClellan therefore deferred the matter. (Meanwhile, Halleck, as we have noted, had ordered Pope to fall back to the fortifications and advised him that McClellan had been put in charge of the defenses.) That afternoon, McClellan crossed the Potomac and rode to the front and, at Upton's Hill, met the advance of McDowell's corps and with it Pope and McDowell. He gave Pope directions on how best to place the respective divisions in the defensive works, made other dispositions, and at a late hour of the night returned to Washington.[32]

The assumption of command by McClellan was a grievous blow to Pope, who could not understand it. He thought it a great injustice to himself. He could not understand how the officer whom he held responsible for the reverses at Second Manassas (by McClellan's failure to forward help when help was so much needed) should be entrusted with command. Pope urged Halleck, if nothing else could be done, to command the army himself.[33] Halleck could but reply that McClellan commanded all troops in the fortifications. A reorganization for the field would immediately be made; till then, McClellan, as senior, would exercise general authority. As soon as Pope's troops arrived within McClellan's command, Pope was to report in person to Halleck's headquarters.[34]

Halleck's functions were now reduced to mere routine work. The president assumed the entire responsibility not only of McClellan's assignment but of all military affairs and, with his own hands, wrote this order for the reorganization of an army for the field:

Washington, D. C., September 3, 1862

Ordered, that the General-in-Chief, Major-General Halleck, immediately commence, and proceed with all possible dispatch, to organize an army for active operations, from all the material within and coming within his control, independent of the forces he may deem necessary for the defense of Washington, when such active army shall take the field.

By order of the President:

Edwin M. Stanton,
Secretary of War[35]

---

[28] Letter of Montgomery Blair, April 22, 1870, reprinted in McClellan, *Own Story,* 545.

[29] Letter of Blair, April 3, 1879, reprinted in McClellan, *Own Story,* 545

[30] See McClellan, *Own Story,* 53. No source has been discovered in which McClellan is quoted directly as speaking the above sentence, but it does capture the essential nature of the event. This may be case in which Carman, paraphrasing a third-person account, placed words in the mouth of a subject.

[31] McClellan to Pope, September 2, 1862, as contained in McClellan to Thomas, August 4, 1863, reprinted in *OR,* vol. 11, pt. 1, 105.

[32] McClellan, *Own Story,* 536–37; McClellan to Thomas, August 4, 1862, reprinted in *OR,* vol. 11, pt. 1, 105.

[33] Pope to John C. Kelton, September 3, 1862, reprinted in *OR,* vol. 12, pt. 3, 808.

[34] Halleck to Pope, September 3, 1862, reprinted in *OR,* vol. 12, pt. 3, 809.

[35] Order of "Edwin M. Stanton," September 3, 1862, reprinted in *OR,* vol. 19, pt. 2, 169. However, the editors of the *OR* note, "The original is in President Lincoln's handwriting."

A copy of this order was delivered to Halleck at ten o'clock that night,[36] upon which he prepared this communication:

Washington, September 3, 1862

Major-General McClellan, Commanding, &c. :

There is every probability that the enemy, baffled in his intended capture of Washington, will cross the Potomac, and make a raid into Maryland or Pennsylvania. A movable army must be immediately organized to meet him again in the field. You will, therefore, report the approximate force of each corps of the three armies now in the vicinity of Washington, which can be prepared in the next two days to take the field, and have them supplied and ready for that service.

H. W. Halleck,
General-in-Chief[37]

Meanwhile, Pope's army had fallen behind the defenses of Washington, McClellan was concentrating everything for the defense of the capital and bringing order out of confusion, Burnside (with the remainder of his command) was ordered up from Aquia Creek, and new regiments streamed in from the North.

Pope's defeat startled Washington and the country and partially stunned the national authorities. Halleck was dazed; a member of Lincoln's cabinet says both Stanton and Halleck were "filled with apprehensions beyond others."[38] By direction of the president, the clerks and employees of the departments were organized for the defense of the capital, the money in the Treasury and the contents of the arsenal were ordered to be shipped to New York, and a gunboat with steam up lay in the river off the White House, giving the impression that Lincoln was about to take flight.[39] These things were seen by and known to the public, and a partial panic resulted. "Never before," says William Swinton, "had the national capital been in such peril—not even when, the year before, the fugitive mob of McDowell rushed in panic under its walls."[40]

In view of this acute panic, it may surprise the reader to know that at this time (September 1) there stood before the defenses of the capital 40,000 veterans that had not fired a shot in Pope's campaign. Behind them in the defenses were another 30,000 men of the garrisons and reserves, of whom quite two-thirds were well disciplined (though all were untried in battle). Adding to these the 40,000 men Pope was leading back gave McClellan 110,000 men for the defense of Washington on September 2.[41] New regiments increased the number daily, so that, by September 7, when McClellan led an army of 74,000 men to meet Lee in Maryland, he left for the defense of Washington over 73,000 men, with 120 field guns and about 500 heavy guns in position. Included in this number were the troops of the Third, Fifth, and Eleventh Corps (commanded respectively by Heintzelman, Porter, and Major General Franz Sigel) covering the fortified line on the Virginia side of the Potomac and numbering about 47,000 for duty; the garrisons of the works, 15,000; and the city guard and Brigadier General Silas Casey's provisional brigades of newly arriving regiments, about 11,000—"in brief, nearly one half of McClellan's entire army; a force a fourth or a third larger than Lee's; indeed, to all appearance, the identical command designed for General McClellan himself, before the defense of the capital had made it necessary for him to resume operations in the field by the pursuit of Lee."[42] And this force was increasing daily by the arrival of volunteers from the North.

On June 28 (when it had been known that McClellan had suffered severe reverses on the Peninsula), Lincoln, in a communication to Seward, said, "I expect to maintain this contest until successful, or till I die, or am conquered, or my term expires, or Congress or the country forsake me."[43] He was sanguine that there was strength enough in the country to put down rebellion, and he would bring it out. He accepted a tender of three hundred thousand men from the governors of the loyal states.[44] He was not mistaken in the reserve strength of the country, and the call for volunteers brought it out. The governor of Connecticut replied, "Our losses before Richmond only stimulate this people to increased efforts and a

[36] Endorsement of Edward D. Townsend, September 3, 1862, reprinted in *OR*, vol. 19, pt. 2, 169.

[37] Halleck to McClellan, September 3, 1862, reprinted in *OR*, vol. 19, pt. 2, 169.

[38] Welles, 194.

[39] Richard B. Irwin, "Washington Under Banks," in *Battles and Leaders*, 542.

[40] William Swinton, *The Twelve Decisive Battles of the War: A History of the Eastern and Western Campaigns, in Relation to the Actions That Decided Their Issue* (New York: Dick & Fitzgerald, 1867), 149–50.

[41] Irwin, 541.

[42] Ibid., 542. Carman adopts all of Irwin's figures save for the number of men who marched out from Washington with McClellan on September 7. Where Carman gives a figure of 74,000, Banks reports this number at 87,000. The larger figure represents a close approximation of what McClellan reported his "present for duty" strength to be at Antietam. McClellan to Thomas, August 4, 1863, reprinted in *OR*, vol. 19, pt. 1, 67. As Carman makes clear in his narrative, however, some commands joined the Federal army during its march through Maryland.

[43] Lincoln to William H. Seward, June 28, 1862, reprinted in *OR*, ser. 3, vol. 2, 180.

[44] Lincoln to McClellan, July 2, 1862, reprinted in *OR*, vol. 11, pt. 3, 286.

firmer purpose to preserve the Union entire. Our armies may be checked and destroyed, but others will be organized and success is sure."[45] Governor John A. Andrew of Massachusetts reported that men swarmed the camps and that he would raise regiments until the government cried, "Hold!"[46] Charles S. Olden, the Quaker governor of New Jersey, promptly responded, "I will hurry forward every available man in the shortest possible time."[47] In four weeks twenty-five thousand men volunteered in Illinois; her governor urged greater animus and energy into military movements and demanded that the president "summon to the standard of the Republic all willing to fight for the Union," including the colored men of the South.[48] Ohio was ready with her men, and her sturdy governor, David Tod, recognizing the injury being done the cause of the Union by unseemly and disgraceful cabals at Washington, telegraphed Stanton, "For God's sake, stop the wrangling between the friends of McClellan and yourself in Congress."[49] Other states were not behind in sending men to the front, by which it came about, in the first days of September 1862, that many thousands of these new volunteers had reached Washington and many thousands more were on the way to guard the capital of the republic and strengthen the advance against Lee in Maryland.

The fact that the Confederates had withdrawn from the front on the third, coupled with information received during the day from Harper's Ferry and the signal officers on Sugar Loaf Mountain in Maryland, led McClellan to believe that Lee intended to cross the upper Potomac into Maryland. "This," says McClellan, "materially changed the aspect of affairs and enlarged the sphere of operations; for, in case of a crossing in force, an active campaign would be necessary to cover Baltimore, prevent the invasion of Pennsylvania, and clear Maryland."[50] Therefore McClellan that same day ordered the Second Corps, under Sumner, and the Twelfth Corps, under Brigadier General Alpheus S. Williams, to withdraw from the Virginia side of the Potomac and move to Tennallytown on the Maryland side, and the Ninth Corps, then disembarking from the transports that had brought it from Aquia Creek, to a point on the Seventh Street Road near Washington. Pleasonton's cavalry was sent to the fords near Poolesville, Maryland, to watch and impede the enemy in any attempt to cross the river in that vicinity. The Second and Twelfth Corps crossed the Potomac by the Aqueduct Bridge on the fourth and marched through Georgetown to Tennallytown, where they were joined by Couch's division of the Fourth Corps, and on the next day the Second and Twelfth were advanced to Rockville.[51] The Ninth Corps crossed the Potomac by the Long Bridge during the night and went into camp on Meridian Hill early in the morning of the fifth.

When McClellan reported to Halleck that he had moved these troops into Maryland, he was asked what general had been placed in command of them. To McClellan's reply that he made no such detail, as he should take command in person if the enemy appeared in that direction, Halleck reminded him that his command included only the defenses of Washington and did not extend to any active column that might be moved out beyond the line of works. No decision had yet been made as to the commander of the active army. McClellan says, "He repeated the same thing on more than one occasion before the final advance to South Mountain and Antietam took place."[52]

McClellan made no effort to force a decision as to who should command in the field. The present was in his own hands; he was hopeful that things would come his way as the work of organization progressed and his prestige increased.

On the fifth, Halleck sent to McClellan the following confidential note:

The President has directed that General Pope be relieved and report to War Department; that Hooker be assigned to command of Porter's corps, and that Franklin's corps be temporarily attached to Heintzelman's. The orders will be issued this afternoon. Generals Porter and Franklin are to be relieved from duty till the charges against them are examined. I give you this memorandum in advance of the orders, so that you may act accordingly in putting forces in the field.[53]

Notwithstanding the fact that as yet no decision had been made as to the commander of the active army and that McClellan's command was expressly limited to the defense of Washington, the responsibility that should have rested with Halleck was thrust upon McClellan. Halleck would not order but proffered suggestions. On the fifth he wrote McClellan, "I think there can now be no doubt that the enemy are crossing the Potomac in force, and that you had better dispatch

---

[45] William A. Buckingham to Lincoln, July 10, 1862, reprinted in *OR*, ser. 3, vol. 2, 213.

[46] John A. Andrew to Lincoln, August 11, 1862, reprinted in *OR*, ser. 3, vol. 2, 353.

[47] Charles S. Olden to Lincoln, July 3, 1862, reprinted in *OR*, ser. 3, vol. 2, 202.

[48] Richard Yates to Lincoln, July 11, 1862, reprinted in *OR*, ser. 3, vol. 2, 218.

[49] David Tod to Stanton, July 11, 1862, reprinted in *OR*, ser. 3, vol. 2, 219.

[50] McClellan to Thomas, August 4, 1863, reprinted in *OR*, vol. 19, pt. 1, 38.

[51] Ibid.

[52] McClellan, *Own Story*, 549.

[53] Halleck to McClellan, September 5, 1862, reprinted in *OR*, vol. 19, pt. 2, 182. The same order is reprinted again in *OR*, vol. 12, pt. 3, 811, but in this instance the third sentence contains a misprint and begins, "*Reynolds*, Porter, and Franklin are to be relieved [emphasis added]."

General Sumner and additional forces to follow. If you agree with me, let our troops move immediately."[54] McClellan had already placed Sumner north of the Potomac, with the Ninth and Twelfth Corps in support, preparatory to a movement northwards.

At the same time, McClellan ordered Pope to have his command ready to march with three days' rations, to which Pope gave answer that he did not know what his command was nor where it was, as McClellan had ordered his troops to take post at various places and he had not been notified in a single instance of their positions.[55] He then asked Halleck if he was "to take the field and under McClellan's orders,"[56] to which Halleck replied the same day, "The armies of the Potomac and Virginia being consolidated, you will report for orders to the Secretary of War."[57] Halleck also lifted from his shoulders responsibility for the safety of Harper's Ferry, telegraphing General Wool at Baltimore, "I find it impossible to get this army into the field again in large force for a day or two. In the mean time Harper's Ferry may be attacked and overwhelmed. I leave all dispositions there to your experience and local knowledge."[58]

The president's order of September 3 directed Halleck to "proceed with all possible dispatch" to organize an army for active operations, and Halleck in turn had advised McClellan that a movable army "must be immediately prepared to meet the enemy in the field." It was not the original intention that McClellan should command this army, and an intense bitterness developed in the cabinet and among the higher officers of the army in the discussion of the matter of who should command it. Rivalries, petty jealousies, and deep-seated antipathies and animosities were active in all circles, especially among prominent general officers. Halleck thus wrote to Pope on September 5, "The differences and ill feeling among the generals are very embarrassing to the administration, and unless checked will ruin the country … We must all act together or we shall accomplish nothing, but be utterly disgraced."[59] On the same day, Halleck wrote to his wife, "The generals all around me are quarreling among themselves, while I am doing all in my power to conciliate and satisfy. It is sad to witness the selfishness of men at this time of sore trial … I want to go back to private life as soon as possible and never again to put my foot in Washington."[60] It was at this time that Lincoln remarked to the secretary of the Navy that most of their troubles grew out of military jealousies.

The bitterness of feeling was not confined to the generals; it existed among the politicians, especially between what were known as the "radical" and "conservative" wings of the Republican Party. The eastern press took sides, and both factions seemed more intent upon political advantages than success in the field. Back on January 20, 1862, Halleck, who was then assigned to command in the West, wrote McClellan, "I take it for granted, general, that what has heretofore been done has been the result of political policy rather than military strategy, and that the want of success on our part is attributable to the politicians rather than to the generals … to pepper-box strategy … movements having been governed by political expediency and in many cases directed by politicians in order to subserve particular interests."[61] This feeling was observed by Halleck when he came to command the Army; on July 30 he wrote to McClellan, "There seemed to be a disposition in the public press to cry down any one who attempted to serve the country instead of party."[62]

Nor was this feeling confined to the politicians at large and the press. It was among the president's advisors and at the cabinet meetings, where personal ambition fought for partisan advantage and control of the administration. One of the first to recognize and criticize this political tendency of military direction was Stanton, who, immediately after McDowell's defeat at Manassas and the arrival of McClellan from West Virginia to assume command of the army in front of Washington, wrote to ex-president James Buchanan, "Will not [General-in-Chief] Scott's jealousy, cabinet intrigues, and Republican interference thwart [McClellan] at every step?"[63] A few weeks later we find Stanton urging McClellan to arrest then-Secretary of War Simon Cameron for inciting to insubordination, because he had heartily endorsed an emancipation speech made by Colonel John Cochrane.[64] McClellan says, "He [Stanton] often advocated the propriety of my seizing the government and taking affairs into my own hands."[65] Alexander K. McClure writes, "It is an open secret

---

[54] Halleck to McClellan, September 5, 1862, reprinted in *OR*, vol. 19, pt. 2, 182 (second message).

[55] Pope to Randolph B. Marcy, September 5, 1862, 12:05 p.m., reprinted in *OR*, vol. 19, pt. 2, 182–83.

[56] Pope to Halleck, September 5, 1862, 12:05 p.m., reprinted in *OR*, vol. 19, pt. 2, 183.

[57] Halleck to Pope, September 5, 1862, reprinted in *OR*, vol. 19, pt. 2, 183.

[58] Halleck to John E. Wool, September 5, 1862, reprinted in *OR*, vol. 19, pt. 2, 189.

[59] Halleck to Pope, September 5, 1862, reprinted in *OR*, vol. 12, pt. 3, 813.

[60] Halleck to Elizabeth Halleck, October 7, 1862, reprinted in Wilson, 558.

[61] Halleck to McClellan, January 20, 1862, reprinted in *OR*, vol. 8, 509.

[62] Halleck to McClellan, July 30, 1862, reprinted in *OR*, vol. 11, pt. 3, 343.

[63] Stanton to James Buchanan, July 26, 1861, reprinted in McClellan, *Own Story*, 67 n.

[64] McClellan, *Own Story*, 152. On November 13, 1861, Colonel John Cochrane, 1st U.S. Chasseurs, made a speech to his regiment, in which he took strong ground for arming the slaves in the War for the Union and for emancipation. Secretary Cameron was present and in a short speech endorsed the advanced view presented by Cochrane.—*EAC*

[65] Ibid.

that Stanton advised the revolutionary overthrow of the Lincoln government, to be replaced by General McClellan as military dictator."[66] Elsewhere McClure says, "Stanton was then the close friend and adviser of General McClellan, and it was well know in the Administration circles and to Lincoln himself that Stanton earnestly urged McClellan to overthrow the constitutional Government because of weakness and incapacity, and declare himself dictator."[67] Stanton wrote freely of the "painful imbecility" of Lincoln and of the "venality and corruption" of the government, expressing his belief that no better condition of things was possible "until Jeff Davis turns out the whole concern."[68] All this was before Stanton was called into the cabinet, and up to that time he was in close and confidential relations with McClellan. When he entered the cabinet in January 1862, he believed that upon his shoulders rested the duty and responsibility of crushing the rebellion, and it was with reluctance that he deferred to the authority of the president. Stanton soon became a pronounced enemy of McClellan and aspired to the dictatorship that he had once urged the general to assume. Under the president's order of March 11, 1862, McClellan was relieved from the command of the armies of the United States, his command being limited to the Department of the Potomac. No one was named as his successor as commander-in-chief. All department commanders were ordered to report "severally and directly to the Secretary of War," by which order the president virtually assumed command, with the secretary of war acting as his chief of staff.[69]

At the beginning of the war, members of the cabinet believed themselves capable of managing military affairs and giving directions for the movement of armies in the field, but, recognizing the prestige of General Scott, they refrained from an undue intrusion upon his prerogative and contented themselves with recommending and urging the appointment of general officers and those of lower grade. When Scott was relieved and McClellan came to the command, the latter was tendered any amount of advice, which was coolly received, and he went so far as to snub the president when he inquired into proposed military movements. (This was one of the primary, underlying causes of his removal from the chief command.) Then Lincoln's advisors came forward with their various plans and pushed their diverse views upon the president's attention, much to the annoyance and disgust of Stanton, who as secretary of war was specially charged with the conduct of military affairs.

Prominent among these cabinet officers were William H. Seward and Salmon P. Chase. Seward assumed many duties outside of those connected with the foreign affairs of the government and was especially active in all things pertaining to the military arm. In the spring of 1861, he wrote, "I am consulting with the cabinet one hour, with the Army officers the next, the Navy next, and I visit all the troops as fast as they come" A year later he continued in this vein: "I dare not, because I cannot safely, leave this post from which all supplies, all directions, all inquiries must radiate, to armies and navies at home and to legations abroad."[70] He had entered upon the duties of his office with the idea that he was to be the ruling spirit of the administration and was to direct the affairs of the country in the name of the president. In carrying out this idea, he trenched very largely and sometimes very offensively upon duties that pertained to other members of the cabinet, notably the secretary of war and secretary of the Navy. Within a month after the inauguration of Lincoln, we find that Seward, in the words of Gideon Welles, "exhibited his loose ideas of government, his want of system and defect of correct executive and administrative talent by preparing and sending out an irregular military expedition for the relief of Fort Pickens, without consulting the Secretary of War and without his knowledge or that of any of his associates."[71] Welles further says, "He took upon himself, as Secretary of State, to perform secretly and improperly the duties of Secretary of War without the knowledge of that officer. On one or two occasions when he attempted, in total disregard of good government and correct administration, to intermeddle with naval matters, the proceedings were, as with the War Department, disapproved as irregular, improper, and reprehensible."[72]

Seward continued to take great interest in military affairs and pressed his views upon the president. He visited armies in the field and accompanied Lincoln to the camps and grand reviews. He was particularly active in hastening the organization of New York volunteers and forwarding them to Washington and elsewhere in the field (and here he really did much good service), and he did not fail to see that New York had its fair and generous share of military appointments, from major

---

[66] Alexander K. McClure, *Abraham Lincoln and Men of War-Times: Some Personal Recollections of War and Politics during the Lincoln Administration* (Philadelphia: Times Publishing Co., 1892), 173.

[67] McClure, *Colonel Alexander K. McClure's Recollections of Half a Century* (Salem, Mass.: Salem Press Co., 1902), 206.

[68] Ibid., 172.

[69] Lincoln, President's War Order No. 3, March 11, 1862, reprinted in *OR*, vol. 10, pt. 2, 28–29.

[70] Frederic Bancroft, *The Life of William H. Seward*, vol. 2 (New York: Harper & Brothers, 1900), 350. In his original manuscript, Carman presents these two quotations as a single entry; in actuality, they come from two different letters written by Seward. Bancroft notes this fact and presents them as two distinct quotations, but positions them one immediately after the other in the identical manner as Carman. Assuredly, Bancroft's work was Carman's source.

[71] Welles, 54–55.

[72] Ibid., 46.

generals down to military store-keepers. But his interest grew less as the delicate condition of foreign affairs began to impress his attention, and his subsequent intrusion upon the duties of the secretary of war was not offensive. His influence was cast in favor of harmonizing the various elements of support to the administration by retaining McClellan in command.

His conservative course and friendship for McClellan brought upon him the condemnation of the radical wing of the administration and its supporters, one of whom wrote, "McClellan in the field and Seward in the cabinet have been the evil sprits that have brought our grand cause to the very brink of death."[73] McClellan's reverses on the Peninsula increased the severe criticisms on Seward, and efforts were made by his former political supporters in New York, as Seward himself says, "to sow the seeds of disunion" in the relations between him and his colleagues in the cabinet. The matter went so far that, after McClellan had taken the field against Lee in Maryland, a committee from New York journeyed to Washington early in September to insist upon Seward's enforced retirement from the cabinet because of his friendliness to McClellan and his conservatism upon the emancipation question, which was then agitating the cabinet and the country. The efforts of this self-constituted committee were met by Lincoln's very plain reply, "There is not one of you who would not see the country ruined if you could turn out Seward."[74]

Chase was exceedingly active. He appeared to think that he had a peculiar and particular aptitude for military leadership. At the beginning of Lincoln's administration, he was looked upon as the representative of the West and as especially qualified to deal with the western Border States; in Virginia and what became West Virginia he exercised a semi-military responsibility. "In fact," says Alfred B. Hart, "until Stanton became Secretary of War, Chase continued to consider himself … the special administrator of operations in the West."[75] He looked to the appointment, assignment, and promotion of western officers, and these and western politicians were especially fond of seeking his military influence. For many months, he felt quite as much responsibility for the military affairs of the country as he did for its finances, proof of which is found in his diaries and correspondence with officers in the field. As early as May 1861, he urged Scott to occupy Manassas and compel the Virginians to evacuate Harper's Ferry. He similarly urged McDowell to advance and give battle in July 1861. When McClellan was called to the command of the army, Chase requested a conference with him regarding proposed military movements. On January 11, 1862, McDowell inquired of Chase as to McClellan's plans and Chase gave him what he knew in strict confidence. On the following day, at a cabinet meeting to which McClellan was invited, Chase insisted that the general-in-chief should explain his military plans in detail, that they might be submitted to the approval or disapproval of the cabinet members. McClellan refused to discuss his plans and from that hour lost Chase's support. Hart notes examples of Chase's further involvement in military affairs:

In 1862, he began a correspondence with Colonel James A. Garfield, with whom he maintained intimate relations throughout the war. General Morgan asked him for regular troops; General Shields wanted him to confer in his behalf with the President; he was in direct and confidential correspondence with General Butler in New Orleans; General Banks sent him a message saying that he should like to join forces with Chase, the two to be "head and arm"; to General McDowell, in March, 1862, he sent an article from the "Cincinnati Commercial" criticizing McClellan, who was then superior in rank to McDowell; to Colonel [Thomas M.] Key [of McClellan's staff] he expressed his reasons for approving Lincoln's orders to McDowell before McClellan's campaign of 1862.[76]

Hart admits that, occasionally, Chase tried giving unasked counsel. He cites that in June 1862, "when McClellan was engaged in the Peninsula, Chase strongly urged the President to direct a column of troops under McDowell to Charlottesville, and was much pained that his judgment was not followed. A little later he was writing to General Pope and General Butler on the slavery question, as affected by the military situation, and was trying to impress upon the President the necessity of a campaign against Vicksburg."[77]

Chase favored the advancement of Republican officers who had real merit to counterpoise the too great weight already given to Democratic officers possessing little, who he felt had been more pushed than Republicans and to whom the administration had been more than generous—lavish even. Chase complained that generals had been placed and continued in command who never manifested the slightest sympathy with the Union cause as related to the controlling question of

---

[73] As of this writing, Carman's source for this unattributed quotation has not been identified, but the editor has found a variation of it reprinted in a later study of Lincoln's cabinet, attributed to a letter of *Chicago Tribune* editor Joseph Medill to Indiana congressman Schuyler Colfax. See Burton J. Hendrick, *Lincoln's War Cabinet* (Boston: Little, Brown and Co., 1946), 327.

[74] Diary of Chase, September 10, 1862, reprinted in Warden, 468.

[75] Alfred Bushnell Hart, *Salmon Portland Chase* (Boston: Houghton, Mifflin and Co., 1899), 213.

[76] Ibid., 295–96. In Carman's original manuscript, this block quotation is not placed within quotation marks, making it appear as though these are his own words. However, a footnote by Carman at the end of the paragraph directs the reader to Hart's biography.

[77] Ibid., 294.

slavery. "These," he said, "naturally have never been more than half in earnest; and, instead of *their* being impelled to the most vigorous action, their influence has been suffered to paralyze, in a great degree, the activity of the administration."[78]

At the beginning Chase was very friendly toward McClellan. Indeed, the secretary claimed a large share of credit for his appointment and suggested a plan of campaign for him, but after McClellan's refusal to divulge his own plans and the failure of the Peninsula campaign, Chase was very anxious to get rid of him. To a suggestion by Pope that McClellan might be retained in command (and retrieve himself) by advancing on Richmond, Chase replied that if the movement were made and proved successful it "would only restore underserved confidence and prepare future calamities."[79] He did not regard McClellan as "loyal to the administration," although he did not question his "general loyalty to the country."[80] On July 27, Chase spoke to the president "of the financial importance of getting rid of McClellan."[81]

When Halleck was summoned to Washington and assigned to the command of the army, there was a partial repression of military suggestions from those members of the cabinet not specially charged with the conduct of the war, and it was sought to confine the discussion and direction of military affairs to the president, Stanton, and Halleck. Chase tried hard to have it otherwise, and complained that, in the movements of the army, "We [the cabinet] have as little to do with it as if we were heads of factories, supplying shoes or clothing,"[82] and when he called upon Halleck "judged it prudent not to say much of the war."[83] He would have the war conducted upon intense anti-slavery lines and was much pained to hear Halleck say that he did not "think much of the negro."[84]

In the midst of these jealousies and contentions, and the increasing pressure that the war should be conducted on anti-slavery lines by anti-slavery generals, grew the alliance of Chase, Stanton, and other members of the cabinet for McClellan's downfall—followed by the defeat of Pope, the order to McClellan of September 2, and the scene at the cabinet meeting, upon which occasion the president expressed his distress to find himself differing from the secretaries of war and the Treasury and said that he would gladly resign his place.

Events did not move by the path desired by Chase, Stanton, and the radical anti-slavery men of the country. Strange as it may appear, the general they had most mistrusted, the only general of the Union army who had publicly declared against emancipation, was the chosen instrument that made emancipation possible within twenty days by the expulsion of the Confederate army from Maryland.

McClellan having been assigned to the defenses of the capital and an order being given on September 3 for the organization of the army to take the field against Lee, there began a great pressure upon the president for the command of the movable army. Many names were presented and urged by members of the cabinet and others, and various military, political, and personal arguments were advanced for their selection. In the midst of the diverse views and insistence of his advisors, the president kept his own counsel and seems, at first, to have considered Pope for the command.[85] The idea was quickly abandoned if ever seriously entertained, and the command was offered to Burnside, by whom it had been refused in July and who now did so again. Burnside urged that McClellan be retained in command and earnestly pled that good relations be restored between him and the War Department. He thought no one could do as well with the army as McClellan, if matters could be so arranged as to remove the objections held against him by the president and the secretary of war.[86] General Hitchcock was then offered the command and declined it, for reasons given elsewhere.

This brings us to the evening of September 5, when Halleck wrote Pope that the ill feelings and differences among the generals were very embarrassing to the administration and when the president said to Welles that most of their troubles

---

[78] Chase to A. S. Latty, September 17, 1862, reprinted in Warden, 454. See also diary of Chase, September 13, 1862, reprinted in Warden, 474.—*EAC*

[79] Diary of Chase, July 26, 1862, reprinted in Warden, 441.

[80] Diary of Chase, July 22, 1862, reprinted in Warden, 440. Nor was Chase himself loyal to the administration. He was, writes Alexander K. McClure, "the merest plaything of the political charlatans who crossed his path, and he was thus made to do many things which were unworthy of him, and which, with any other than Lincoln to judge him, would have brought him to absolute disgrace. He wrote many letters to his friends in different parts of the country habitually complaining of Lincoln's incompetency and of the hopeless condition of the war." McClure, *Abraham Lincoln and Men of War-Times*, 138. "From the day that Chase entered the Cabinet he seems to have been consumed with the idea that he must be Lincoln's successor in 1864, and to that end he systematically directed his efforts, and often sought, by flagrant abuse of the power of his department, to weaken his chief." Ibid., 133.—*EAC*

[81] Warden, 442.

[82] Hart, 294.

[83] Diary of Chase, August 1, 1862, reprinted in Warden, 444.

[84] Diary of Chase, August 3, 1862, reprinted in Warden, 448.

[85] "Pope came over and talked with the President, who assured him of his entire satisfaction with his conduct; assured him that McClellan's command was only temporary; and gave him reason to expect that another army of active operations would be organized at once, which he (Pope) would lead." Diary of Chase, September 3, 1862, reprinted in Warden, 460.—*EAC*

[86] *Report of the Joint Committee on the Conduct of the War*, 37th Cong., 3d sess., 1863, S. Rep. 108, pt. 1, serial 1152, 650. Carman presents much of this sentence as a direct quotation in his original manuscript, but it is instead a close paraphrase of Burnside's statement to the committee.

grew out of military jealousies. As the Confederate army was now crossing into Maryland and a decision was necessary, the president, accompanied by Halleck, walked over to McClellan's residence about nine o'clock on the morning of September 6. After a short discussion upon the condition of affairs and the necessity for an immediate movement, Lincoln said to McClellan, "General, you will take command of the forces in the field." Until that moment, Halleck did not know who was to command.[87]

To the contrary, McClellan asserts that he was not placed in command of the forces in the field, but conducted the Maryland campaign with a halter around his neck.[88] It is well to examine the record on this point. In his examination before the Committee on the Conduct of the War, McClellan said, "I asked the question, two or three times, of General Halleck, whether I was to command the troops in the field? and he said it had not been determined; and I do not think it ever was. I think that was one of those things that grew into shape itself. When the time came I went out."[89] In his *Own Story*, McClellan says, "As the time had now arrived for the army to advance, and I had received no orders to take command of it, but had been expressly told that the assignment of a commander had not been decided, I determined to solve the question for myself, and when I moved out from Washington with my staff and personal escort I left my card, with P.P.C. written upon it at the White House, War Office, and Secretary Seward's house, and went on my way."[90]

The assertion by McClellan that he moved from Washington without orders and with no assignment to command the army in the field is disputed by Halleck's testimony and contradicted by McClellan's autobiography. Halleck later testified before a court of inquiry that, some days before going to the front, McClellan had been directed to take the field against the enemy in Maryland.[91] In his official report, Halleck says, "General McClellan was directed to pursue him with all the troops which were not required for the defense of Washington."[92] Before the Committee on the Conduct of the War, Halleck said:

> The order was given verbally to General McClellan by the President, at General McClellan's house, about 9 o'clock in the morning, previous to General McClellan leaving the city for Rockville … The question was discussed by the President for two or three days as to who should take command of the troops that were to go into the field. The decision was made by himself, and announced to General McClellan in my presence …
>
> The day the President gave General McClellan directions to take command of the forces in the field we had a long conversation in regard to the campaign in Maryland. It was agreed between us that the troops should move up the Potomac, and, if possible, separate that portion of General Lee's army which had crossed the Potomac from the remainder on the Virginia side. There were no definite instructions, further than that understanding between us, as to the general plan of the campaign.[93]

This testimony reveals the fact that not only was McClellan ordered to take command, but that the campaign was considered. That harmony prevailed is attested by a letter written by McClellan to his wife on the afternoon of the seventh, in which he said, "I leave here this afternoon to take command of the troops in the field. The feeling of the Government towards me, I am sure, is kind and trusting. I hope, with God's blessing, to justify the great confidence they now repose in me, and will bury the past in oblivion."[94] In his preliminary report of the Maryland campaign, submitted before relief from command embittered his feelings, he said, "The disappearance of the enemy from the front of Washington and their passage into Maryland enlarged the sphere of operations, and made an active campaign necessary to cover Baltimore, prevent the invasion of Pennsylvania, and drive them out of Maryland. Being honored with the charge of this campaign, I entered at once upon the additional duties imposed upon me with cheerfulness and trust, yet not without feeling the weight of the responsibilities thus assumed and being deeply impressed with the magnitude of the issues involved."[95]

In the face of Halleck's testimony and McClellan's own letter and official report, it is difficult to understand how he could make that statement that he fought the battles of South Mountain and Antietam with a halter around his neck, unless we unhesitatingly accept the opinion advanced by McClellan and some of his friends some years later that, had the Maryland

---

[87] Ibid., 451. Early in the following October, Lincoln told William D. Kelley that the command was given to McClellan on September 2 to reorganize a broken and demoralized army and that his direction to take command of the forces in the field was due more to Lee than to himself. William D. Kelley, *Lincoln and Stanton: A Study of the War Administration of 1861 and 1862, with Special Consideration of Some Recent Statements of Gen. Geo. B. McClellan* (New York: G. P. Putnam's Sons: 1885), 72–74.—EAC

[88] McClellan, *Own Story*, 551.

[89] *Report of the Joint Committee*, 438–39.

[90] McClellan, *Own Story*, 551. "P.P.C." stands for *pour prendre conge*—"to take leave."

[91] "Record of the Harper's Ferry Military Commission," October 29, 1862, reprinted in *OR*, vol. 19, pt. 1, 786.

[92] Halleck to Stanton, November 25, 1862, reprinted in *OR*, vol. 19, pt. 1, 4.

[93] *Report of the Joint Committee*, 453–54.

[94] McClellan to Mary Ellen McClellan, September 7, 1862, 2:50 p.m., reprinted in McClellan, *Own Story*, 567.

[95] McClellan to Thomas, October 15, 1862, reprinted in *OR*, vol. 19, pt. 1, 25.

campaign ended in disaster to the Union arms, McClellan's enemies in the War Department would have taken advantage of the irregularity of his assignment to the command to bring charges against him.[96] This idea is adopted by the Comte de Paris, who writes that "the idle allegations which, at a later period, were made the pretext for deposing him give the impartial historian the right to entertain such a supposition."[97]

This view is also entertained by George Ticknor Curtis, who writes:

General McClellan fought the battles of South Mountain and Antietam without any written order defining his command, excepting the ambiguous one of September 2d—ambiguous, that is to say, after the date on which it was issued from the War Department. What, then, would have been his fate if he had lost those battles, and especially the last? We must carry the reader back to a period when mean rivalries, deep hatreds, and vengeful prejudices had their sway. It cannot be doubted that, if McClellan had been defeated in the battle of Antietam, he would have had to answer for it before a court-martial, and that his blood would have been demanded. We know what deeds were done in that period under the forms and mockeries of military justice. McClellan's bitterest enemies were among those who, from their official stations, would have had the power, which they would not have scrupled to use, to arraign him for having assumed a command to which he had not been legally assigned. They could have pointed to the narrow scope of the order of September 2d, and they would have pointed to the lives of brave men that had been lost and the public property that had been destroyed beyond what, they would have contended, was the scope of the only authority that he had received which could avail him as a legal order. In suffering McClellan to be thus exposed, President Lincoln would seem to have been unconscious of what a strain might be brought upon his own sense of executive justice if any disaster should befall the General who had taken the command at his earnest personal entreaty, and who had been left without a proper legal authority for the acts which he was expected to perform.[98]

It is admitted that Lincoln gave McClellan a verbal order on the morning of September 6 to assume command of the army in the field. Why that verbal order was not supplemented by a written one, as was done September 2, can be explained only upon the supposition that in the dazed condition of Halleck and the confused state of affairs in the War Department it was forgotten. McClellan says he was fully aware of the risk he ran; if so, he was certainly very remiss in not asking for written orders. In after days, when asked why he had not requested written orders, he replied, "It was no time for writing, and in fact I never thought of it."[99]

But why orders of any kind were necessary is not apparent. McClellan had never been relieved from command of the Army of the Potomac, and Halleck, when he ordered that army from the Peninsula, assured McClellan of his intention to have him assigned to the command of the consolidated armies. McClellan brought the Army of the Potomac to Alexandria, and a part of it was sent to Pope. On September 5 Pope was relieved from command of the Army of Virginia, and it was consolidated with the Army of the Potomac, which McClellan commanded. In addition thereto he had been put in command of the defenses of Washington on September 2. Naturally and legally, therefore, McClellan was in full command and in control of all the troops inside the defenses of Washington as well as those outside of them belonging to the Army of the Potomac, including those formally of the Army of Virginia.

It cannot be doubted that, had McClellan been unsuccessful, his enemies would have pursued him unrelentingly and endeavored upon any pretext to inflict upon him the severest penalties, but we do not share the opinion that Lincoln would have been unable to save him from any punishment due to his taking the field without written orders. He would not have permitted an act of such gross injustice. The president would have assumed all the responsibility for any irregularity.

Be it as it may, whether McClellan had or had not reason to anticipate severe punishment should his campaign end in failure, he entered upon it with a full and patriotic determination to do his full duty and save the capital and the nation. Candor compels us to say that his efforts were not encouraged by those in authority who "actually declared that they would prefer the loss of the capital to the restoration of McClellan to command."

The consolidation of the Army of the Potomac and the Army of Virginia, the relief of Pope, and the assumption of command by McClellan were followed by other changes. General McDowell, commanding a corps in the Army of Virginia, was relieved to await an investigation (self-sought) of most cruel and unjust charges affecting his loyalty to the country, and

[96] "I was afterward accused of assuming command without authority, for nefarious purposes, and in fact I fought the battles of South Mountain and Antietam with a halter around my neck, for if the Army of the Potomac had been defeated and I had survived I would, no doubt, have been tried for assuming authority without orders, and, in the state of feeling which so unjustly condemned the innocent and most meritorious General F. J. Porter, I would probably have been condemned to death." McClellan, "From the Peninsula to Antietam," 552.—EAC

[97] Comte de Paris [Louis-Phillippe-Albert d'Orléans], History of the Civil War in America, vol. 2 (Philadelphia: Porter & Coates, 1876), 305–6.

[98] George Ticknor Curtis, "McClellan's Last Service to the Republic," North American Review 130, no. 281 (April 1880): 336–37.

[99] W. C. Prime, "The Life, Services, and Character of George B. McClellan," in McClellan, Own Story, 14.

Generals Fitz John Porter and William B. Franklin, commanding the Fifth and Sixth Corps of the Army of the Potomac, were ordered to be relieved, pending an investigation into their loyalty to Pope.

Major General Joseph Hooker, commanding a division of the Third Corps, was at first assigned to command Porter's corps, and Major General Jesse L. Reno, commanding a division of the Ninth Corps, was designated to command McDowell's; Franklin's corps was ordered to be attached to Heintzelman's Third Corps. On September 6, McClellan suggested to Halleck that it would save a great deal of trouble and invaluable time if the investigation of the charges against Porter and Franklin was deferred until he could see his way out of the difficulties then confronting him. He desired to move Franklin's corps to the front at once and, to avoid a change in the Ninth Corps while on the march by taking Reno from it, urged that Hooker be given command of McDowell's corps,[100] to all of which Halleck promptly and properly assented—an act characterized by the enemies of McClellan as an abject surrender of the administration.

Halleck's actions in yielding to the request of McClellan had the sanction of the president, who reasoned logically that as, under the stress of circumstances, he had condoned the apparent remissness of McClellan in sustaining Pope, the pardon should extend to his subordinates. Lincoln's self-abnegation, his personal feeling, was nothing as weighed against the great interests of the country, and he undoubtedly felt at this time as when, upon a previous occasion, protest was made against his patient endurance of McClellan's exasperating conduct and sometimes absolute disrespect, he replied, "I will hold his horse if he will only conquer the rebellion."[101] The restoration of McClellan was hailed with joy by the army.

McClellan had under his command, exclusive of the forces left for the defense of Washington, the First Corps (Hooker), the Second Corps (Sumner), a division of the Fourth Corps, under Couch, the Sixth Corps (Franklin), the Ninth Corps (Burnside), and the Twelfth Corps (Williams). Brigadier General George Sykes's division was an independent command at the beginning of the campaign; it was joined on the march near Frederick by Major General George W. Morell's division—the two comprising the Fifth Corps, under Porter. In addition to this infantry force there was the cavalry division led by Pleasonton and an artillery reserve of seven batteries. Including the two divisions (Sykes's and Morell's) of the Fifth Corps, and excluding Brigadier General Andrew A. Humphreys's division of the same (which did not leave Washington until September 14), the Army of the Potomac in the field numbered 75,800 infantry and artillery and 4,300 cavalry. The artillery had sixty batteries aggregating 326 guns. Nearly 30,000 men were new recruits, fresh from the stores, workshops, and farms of the North. Over 48,000 were tried, seasoned veterans who had seen service on the Peninsula, in the Shenandoah Valley, in North Carolina, in West Virginia, and in front of Washington.

Before McClellan took the field, there was an arrangement between Halleck and himself: the army would be divided into two wings and a reserve; Sumner would command one wing of two corps and Burnside another (with Franklin's corps as a reserve); and the two corps of the Army of Virginia would be separated, one to the right wing and one to the left.[102] In the general advance, McClellan observed this arrangement, but he did not announce the formation of the wing commands in orders until September 14[103]—only to suspend it within twenty-four hours. Why, we shall tell elsewhere.

The right wing, commanded by Burnside, was composed of the First and Ninth Corps (in the latter was included Brigadier General Jacob D. Cox's Kanawha Division from West Virginia). The center, under Sumner, was composed of the Second and Twelfth Corps. The left, under Franklin, was composed of the Sixth Corps and Couch's division of the Fourth Corps. Of the Fifth Corps, only Sykes's division took the field as early as the sixth, and to this was attached the reserve artillery. Morell's division joined on the thirteenth. (Humphreys's division of the Fifth Corps did not join until September 18.) The Fifth Corps, under the command of Porter, constituted the army reserve.

Joseph Hooker, the commander of the First Corps, was one of the most positive and conspicuous characters of the War of the Rebellion and enjoyed the admiration of soldiers and of his countrymen. He was born at Hadley, Massachusetts, on November 13, 1814, graduated from the U.S. Military Academy in 1837, and was commissioned a second lieutenant in the 1st U.S. Artillery. He passed his first year of service in the Florida War. On November 3, 1838, he was promoted to the rank of first lieutenant. In 1841 he was adjutant at West Point and for the next five years was adjutant of his regiment. In 1846, at the beginning of the war with Mexico, he was assigned to staff duty, and his brilliant services during the war won for him the brevets of captain, major, and lieutenant colonel. After the war with Mexico, he served on staff duty on the Pacific coast and in 1851 resigned his commission in the Army and settled in California. When war broke out, he hastened to Washington and offered his services to the government but met with but little encouragement. Finally he concluded to

[100] McClellan to Halleck, September 6, 1862, reprinted in *OR*, vol. 19, pt. 2, 189–90.

[101] Carman's source for this statement is unknown, but Lincoln's secretaries give the president's words as, "I will hold McClellan's horse if he will only bring us success." Nicolay and Hay, vol. 4, 469 n. 1.

[102] Carman's language here is somewhat imprecise. As he details properly in the next paragraph, the "wing command" that eventually was adopted in the campaign was tripartite, consisting of right, center, and left wings, with the Fifth Corps forming the army reserve.

[103] Headquarters Army of the Potomac, Special Orders of September 14, 1862, reprinted in *OR*, vol. 19, pt. 2, 290.

call upon Lincoln, to whom he stated his case and said that he was about to return to California, adding, "But before going, I was anxious to pay my respects to you, Sir, and to express my wish for your present welfare, and for your success in putting down this rebellion. And while I am about it, Mr. President, I want to say one thing more, and that is, that I was at the battle of Bull Run the other day, and it is neither vanity nor boasting in me to declare that I am a better General than you, Sir, had on that field."[104]

This frank and characteristic declaration impressed Lincoln, and Hooker was commissioned a brigadier general of volunteers (to date from May 17, 1861). In the autumn and winter of 1861–62, he was in command of the Second Division, Third Corps, Army of the Potomac, stationed on the lower Potomac in Maryland. In April 1862 his division went to the Peninsula and, with the First Division (under Brigadier General Philip Kearny), formed Heintzelman's corps. These three commanders, all skillful and self-reliant, never awaited a second order to get into a fight. On May 5, 1862, occurred the battle of Williamsburg—conducted principally by Hooker, sustained by Kearny. This battle established the fame of Hooker as a fighting commander, and he was justly rewarded by promotion to major general of volunteers (to date from May 5, 1862). In the battles before Richmond, Hooker bore a prominent part. At Fair Oaks (Seven Pines), Glendale, and Malvern Hill, his division was ably led and did heavy fighting. While the army lay at Harrison's Landing, Hooker led a reconnaissance toward Richmond, the success of which was so marked that he maintained, if properly supported, the Army of the Potomac could be placed at Richmond before the Confederates in Pope's front could return to prevent it. His suggestion was not acted upon, which caused him to express himself very freely and openly upon the incapacity of McClellan. Before the army withdrew from Harrison's Landing, Hooker urged McClellan to march again on Richmond, believing it could be taken, and told McClellan "that if we were unsuccessful it would probably cost him his head, but that he might as well die for an old sheep as for a lamb" and that he knew of no better place to put an army than between the enemy in Pope's front and the defenses of Richmond.[105] McClellan seems to have imbibed Hooker's spirit, for on August 10 he wrote his wife that he hoped to move on Richmond next day, crush or thrash Longstreet, and follow into Richmond while they were hammering at Pope, but he was apprehensive that they would be too quick for him in Washington and relieve him before he had the chance of making the dash.[106] At the last moment, McClellan shrank from the movement. When the army was transferred from the Peninsula to Alexandria, Hooker was among the first to report to Pope. He needed no urging to find the enemy; when the latter was encountered at Bristoe Station on August 27, a severe engagement resulted in a victory for Hooker. However much he may have criticized McClellan and however little the confidence he had in Pope, his loyalty to country made him loyal in action to his commanders; "he was by instinct and by education too much of a soldier to injure his cause or his commanders by inefficient performance or disloyal deeds." He was handsome and knew it; had confidence in himself; was full of life, skillful on the field, of brilliant courage; was dead earnest in his fighting, and always on that part of the line where there was most of it; was courteous to those under him, and his gentle kindliness to the private soldiers will not be forgotten by those who served under him. "Lofty patriotism, high conception of duty, and the loyal performance of it, conscientiously exerted and faithfully sustained by candid effort and fearless execution—this was Hooker."[107] He was by far the best fighting corps commander of the army that McClellan was leading against Lee.

Edwin V. Sumner, the commander of the Second Corps, was a veteran officer of the regular Army and the oldest of high rank in the Army of the Potomac (being over sixty-five years of age, though still vigorous and active). He was born at Boston, Massachusetts, on January 30, 1797, entered the Army from civil life as a second lieutenant in 1819, and served in the Black Hawk War. Upon the organization of the 2d U.S. Dragoons in 1833, he was appointed captain in that regiment and was employed on the western frontier, where he took high rank as an Indian fighter. He was promoted major in 1846 and served in the Mexican War with great distinction. He led the famous cavalry charge at Cerro Gordo in April 1847, where he was wounded and obtained the brevet of lieutenant colonel. He commanded the reserves at Contreras and Churubusco, where he won high honors. At Molino del Rey he commanded Scott's entire cavalry force and at its head checked the advance of a very superior force of Mexican lancers, for which he was brevetted colonel. In 1848 he became lieutenant

---

[104] It is impossible to determine Carman's particular source for this passage. As Walter H. Hebert notes in his biography of Hooker, the quotation appears in "many newspaper and all articles concerning Hooker." Walter H. Hebert, *Fighting Joe Hooker* (Indianapolis: Bobbs-Merrill Co., 1944), 312 n. 7. On p. 49, Hebert—drawing from an unidentified clipping found among Hooker's papers—renders the sentiment in precisely the same language as does Carman.

[105] *Report of the Joint Committee*, 579.

[106] McClellan to Mary Ellen McClellan, August 10, 1862, 4:00 p.m., reprinted in McClellan, *Own Story*, 465.

[107] Carman's source for the first of these two unattributed quotations regarding Hooker has not been identified. The second appears to come from the report of Edward L. Welling, secretary of the Third Army Corps Union, at its 1888 meeting. A fellow officer of that organization records Welling's concluding remarks as follows: "Lofty patriotism, high conception of duty and the loyal performance of it, conscientiously understood, and faithfully performed,—this was Joe Hooker." William P. Shreve, *The Story of the Third Army Corps Union* (Boston: privately printed, 1910), 57.

colonel of the 1st U.S. Dragoons. In 1851–53 he was governor of New Mexico. In 1855 he was commissioned colonel of the 1st U.S. Cavalry. He was in command of the Department of the West in 1858, and conducted affairs with great discretion during the Kansas border troubles. In March 1861 he was promoted to brigadier general in the regular Army and ordered to San Francisco, California, to relieve Brigadier General Albert Sidney Johnston in command of the Department of the Pacific, and his courage and loyalty did much to hold California true to the cause of the Union. He was recalled from California and was one of the five corps commanders designated by President Lincoln for the Army of the Potomac in March 1862[108] and commanded the left wing of the army at the siege of Yorktown. At Fair Oaks, where McClellan's army was attacked when divided by the Chickahominy, on the first sound of the battle Sumner hurried the heads of his columns down to the bridges of the stream in anticipation of orders to cross, and when orders came he was ready to cross and do great service. The Comte de Paris says that the army was saved "by the indomitable energy of old Sumner."[109] In the Seven Days campaign near Richmond he was twice wounded.

Sumner was of fine presence. Consciousness of his high rank showed in all his movements. He was courageous as a lion and assertive—whether for himself or his men, yet never arrogant or unkind and always accessible to his soldiers, who believed in and loved to follow him. Those who followed him testify to Sumner's honor, his courage, his chivalry, his patriotism, his magnanimity, and his kindness. Meanness, falsehood, and duplicity were more hateful than death to him. "If," says Francis A. Walker, "the Second Corps had a touch above the common; if in the terrible ordeals of flame and death through which, in three years of almost continuous fighting, they were called to pass[,] these two divisions [those of Major Generals John Sedgwick and Israel B. Richardson] showed a courage and tenacity that made them observed among the bravest; if they learned to drop their thousands upon the field as often as they were summoned to the conflict, but on no account to leave a color in the hands of the enemy, it was very largely through the inspiration derived from the gallant old chieftain who first organized them and led them into battle." The same writer, while awarding praise and only praise to his transcendent soldierly virtues, says, "Much may be said upon either side of the question whether, with his mental habits and at his advanced age, he should have been designated for the command of twenty thousand new troops in the field, against a resolute and tenacious enemy skillfully and audaciously led."[110] Francis W. Palfrey says that "he was a most excellent and every way respectable man" and "had in the highest degree the courage of a soldier, but was wanting in the courage of a general. He was apt to be demoralized by hard fighting, and to overestimate the losses of his own side and the strength of the enemy, and he seems to have possessed no judgment as a tactician. It is probable that his training as a cavalry officer had done him positive harm as a leader of infantry."[111] McClellan pays him this tribute: "He was an old and tried officer; perfectly honest; as brave as a man could be; conscientious and laborious. In many respects he was a model soldier. He was a man for whom I had a very high regard, and for his memory I have the greatest respect. He was a very valuable man, and his soldierly example was of the highest value in a new army. A nation is fortunate that possesses many such soldiers as was Edwin V. Sumner."[112]

Fitz John Porter, the commander of the Fifth Army Corps, was born at Portsmouth, New Hampshire, on June 13, 1822, the son of Captain John Porter, U.S. Navy. He graduated from West Point in 1845 and was assigned to the 4th U.S. Artillery, in which he became second lieutenant a year later. He served in the Mexican War, particularly in the siege of Vera Cruz, the battles of Cerro Gordo, Contreras, and Molino del Rey, the storming of Chapultepec, and the capture of the city of Mexico. For gallantry at Molino del Rey he was brevetted captain on September 8, 1847, and major for Chapultepec five days later. During the assault on the city of Mexico, he was wounded at the Belen Gate. On July 9, 1849, he was detailed as assistant instructor of artillery at West Point and in 1853–54 served as adjutant at the Academy. From May 1, 1854 to September 11, 1855, he was instructor of cavalry and artillery. In 1856 he was appointed to assistant adjutant general with the rank of captain. He served on the staff of Major General Persifer F. Smith in the Kansas troubles of 1856 and in 1857 reported to A. S. Johnston, under whom he served in the Utah expedition. In November 1860 he inspected the defenses of Charleston Harbor and advised against the occupation of Fort Sumter and Castle Pinckney by U.S. troops. In April 1861 he was ordered by the secretary of war to superintend the protection of the railroad between Baltimore and Harrisburg against the Baltimore rioters, and his services on this occasion were marked by great energy and tact. He was then assigned as chief of staff to General Patterson near Harper's Ferry (and was in fact the most potent influence surrounding Patterson, remaining with him until the close of that officer's time of service). He was appointed colonel of the 15th U.S. Infantry (to date from

[108] Lincoln, President's General War Order No. 2, March 8, 1862, contained in McClellan to Lorenzo Thomas, August 4, 1863, reprinted in *OR*, vol. 5, 18.

[109] Comte de Paris, 73.

[110] Francis A. Walker, *History of the Second Army Corps in the Army of the Potomac* (New York: Charles Scribner's Sons, 1887), 11–13.

[111] Francis Winthrop Palfrey, *The Antietam and Fredericksburg*, vol. 5 of *The Army in the Civil War* (New York: Charles Scribner's Sons, 1882), 54.

[112] McClellan, *Own Story*, 138.

May 14, 1861) and at the request of McClellan was made brigadier general of volunteers (to date from May 17, 1861) and assigned to duty at Washington. McClellan says of him:

> Fitz-John Porter was on duty with Gen. Patterson, as adjutant general, when I assumed command. As soon as possible I had him made a brigadier-general and gave him the command vacated by [Brigadier General] W[illiam] T. Sherman. Take him for all in all, he was probably the best general officer I had under me. He had excellent ability, sound judgment, and all the instincts of a soldier. He was perfectly familiar with all the details of his duty, an excellent organizer and administrative officer, and one of the most conscientious and laborious men I ever knew. I never found it necessary to do more than give him general instructions, for it was certain that all details would be cared for and nothing neglected. I always knew than an order given to him would be fully carried out, were it morally and physically possible. He was one of the coolest and most imperturbable men in danger whom I ever knew—like all his race.[113]

In the spring of 1862, Porter was in command of a division of the Third Corps and went to the Peninsula with it, where, on April 27, McClellan appointed him director of the siege of Yorktown. On May 18th, with the consent of the president, McClellan formed two provisional corps, one for Porter and one for Franklin. Porter's was denominated the Fifth and to it was attached the artillery reserve of the Army of the Potomac. McClellan's partiality for Porter had been observed by the older officers of the army and the fact was communicated to Lincoln, who, a few days before assenting to the formation of the new corps, wrote McClellan, "I am constantly told that you consult and communicate with nobody but General Fitz John Porter, and perhaps General Franklin. I do not say these complaints are true or just; but at all events it is proper you should know of their existence."[114] He fought the battle of Mechanicsville on June 26, made a splendid defense of his position at Gaines's Mill on June 27, and commanded the left wing of the army at Malvern Hill on July 1. In all these actions, he displayed rare ability and unflinching courage. He was brevetted brigadier general in the regular Army on June 27, and on July 4 was made major general of volunteers. He was actively engaged and his corps fought nobly at Second Manassas on August 30, but charges were brought against him for his inaction on the twenty-ninth and he was deprived of his command. Porter was restored to duty at the request of McClellan and took part in the Maryland campaign. The historian of the Fifth Corps says of him, "Born a patriot; ambitious, but unselfish; self-respecting and self-denying; thoroughly equipped and void of ostentation; imperturbable and unflinching; self-reliant, but never egotistic; prudent without trace of fear; reserved, yet sympathetic; quiet, but quick to see, decide, and act; courteous and careful to avoid offense, if possible, yet without 'strange oaths' or other foreign aid, conveying with an order given the conviction that obedience must follow, his influence was ever present and controlling."[115] Yet conceding his eminent ability as a soldier, it is questionable under the circumstances if he should have been restored to command on the eve of an important campaign and if he gave strength to McClellan and the cause of the Union.

William B. Franklin, the commander of the Sixth Corps, was born at York, Pennsylvania, on February 27, 1823. He graduated from West Point in 1843 at the head of his class and was assigned to the topographical engineers, in which he was commissioned second lieutenant on September 21, 1846. He accompanied the army to Mexico, served on the staff of Major General Zachary Taylor as engineer, and for gallantry at Buena Vista received the brevet of first lieutenant (to date from February 23, 1847). After the close of the Mexican War, he was engaged on surveys in the West, was for a time an assistant professor at the Academy, and when the War of the Rebellion broke out was at Washington in charge of the construction of the Capitol and other public buildings. Meantime he had been promoted first lieutenant on March 3, 1853, and captain on July 1, 1857. On May 14, 1861, he was appointed colonel of the 12th U.S. Infantry, and three days later was commissioned brigadier general of volunteers. He commanded a brigade in Heintzelman's division at Manassas on July 21, 1861, and in April 1862 went to the Peninsula in command of a division. He was engaged at the siege of Yorktown and the affair at West Point on the York River, and on May 18, when two provisional corps were authorized, Franklin was given one, which was denominated the Sixth. It was a great corps in many respects. At its head he fought at White Oak Bridge, Savage Station, and Malvern Hill. For distinguished services in these engagements, he was brevetted brigadier general in the regular Army (to date from June 30, 1862) and was made major general of volunteers (to date from July 4, 1862). On the transfer of the Army of the Potomac from the Peninsula to Alexandria, Franklin fell under the displeasure of Pope and, after Pope's defeat, was relieved (with Porter) from duty under serious charges. At the request of McClellan, Franklin was restored to his command and led it in the Maryland campaign. McClellan says of him, "Franklin was one of the best officers I had; very

113 Ibid., 139.

114 Lincoln to McClellan, May 9, 1862. A copy appears in Roy P. Basler, ed., *The Collected Works of Abraham Lincoln*, vol. 5 (New Brunswick, N.J.: Rutgers University Press, 1953), 208.

115 William H. Powell, *The Fifth Army Corps (Army of the Potomac): A Record of Operations during the Civil War in the United States of America, 1861–1865* (New York: G. P. Putnam's Sons, 1896), 6.

powerful. He was a man not only of excellent judgment, but of a remarkably high order of intellectual ability. He was often badly treated, and seldom received the credit he deserved. His moral character was of the highest, and he was in all respects an admirable corps commander; more than that, he would have commanded an army well. The only reason why I did not send him to relieve Sherman, instead of Buell, was that I could not spare such a man from the Army of the Potomac."[116]

Ambrose E. Burnside, the commander of the Ninth Corps, was born at Liberty, Indiana, on May 23, 1824, and graduated from West Point in 1847. He was commissioned a second lieutenant of artillery (to date from July 1, 1847[117]) and proceeded to Mexico. At the close of the war there, he was ordered to Fort Adams in Newport, Rhode Island, and in 1849 transferred to New Mexico as first lieutenant of the battery commanded by Braxton Bragg. After some service in repressing Indian troubles, he returned to Newport and married. On November 1, 1853, he resigned his commission in the army and entered into arrangements with the national government to manufacture and furnish an improved rifle, a breech loader. The enterprise failed, Burnside lost his all and was heavily in debt, and went west to retrieve his fortunes. Early in 1858 he obtained a position in the land department of the Illinois Central Railroad, of which his old friend and classmate, George B. McClellan, was vice president. "He made his quarters with … McClellan," Augustus Woodbury writes, "and around a common fireside the two friends renewed the intimacy of former days. Mr. Burnside, limiting his expenses to a certain amount, devoted the remainder of his salary to the payment of his debts; and, when afterwards he was enabled to free himself entirely from the claims of his creditors, his unblemished integrity in business was as conspicuous as his fidelity in the field."[118]

He had experienced poverty, disappointment, failure, then success, and was "well and favorably known," says Woodbury, "for his energy and his skill in affairs, his geniality in social intercourse, his high sense of honor, and his honest simplicity."[119] Though politically opposed to the administration of Lincoln, he was intensely loyal to his country, and, when war broke out, he entered the Union service. On April 16, 1861, he was commissioned colonel of the 1st Rhode Island Militia and on the twenty-sixth was in Washington with his regiment. At Bull Run on July 21, he commanded a brigade in Hunter's division, which was severely engaged. On August 6, 1861, he was appointed brigadier general of volunteers and given a command composed of three-year regiments then assembling in Washington. In January 1862, with Brigadier Generals John G. Foster, Jesse L. Reno, and John G. Parke as brigade commanders, he landed a division at Roanoke Island, North Carolina, and, after some brilliant movements and severe fighting, took possession of it. New Bern was taken on March 14, the surrender of Fort Macon and Beaufort soon followed, and Burnside was hailed as the most successful of the Union leaders. (This campaign was probably the most successful of any with which he was connected, and much of this success was undoubtedly due to the skill of his subordinates.) For his service in this campaign, he was promoted to major general of volunteers (to date from March 18, 1862) and assigned to command the Department of North Carolina, where he administered its affairs in a business-like and conciliatory manner. When McClellan was defeated before Richmond and the army was ordered withdrawn from the Peninsula, Burnside was ordered to Aquia Creek and Fredericksburg. He visited McClellan to consult in regard to future operations and found him surrounded by discord, petty jealousy, and discouragement. He did not approve of Halleck's determination to evacuate the Peninsula, told McClellan frankly that he had enemies to contend with in the cabinet, and, after a full and free exchange of views, went to Washington convinced that McClellan had not been given a fair show and hoping that the differences between Stanton and McClellan might be composed. Upon his arrival at Washington, he was offered command of the Army of the Potomac, but declined it. After the defeat of Pope and the withdrawal of the army to Washington, Burnside was called into consultation with Lincoln and Halleck. Again he was offered the command of the army and again declined it, using his best endeavor to have McClellan retained.

He was a tall and handsome man, of striking appearance, had fine eyes and a winning smile that showed a fine row of teeth. He was frank, sincere, captivating, and true to his friends, which won their confidence and esteem. He had a jovial, dashing way with him as he rode through the camps or along the lines, a good humored cordiality toward everybody that raised the enthusiasm of his soldiers to the highest degree. His personal character was without reproach and his patriotism unquestioned. He was brave when under fire and his courage was never doubted. He was modest and shrank from

[116] McClellan, *Own Story*, 138. In October 1861 Sherman was named commander of the Department of the Cumberland. Overwhelmed by the responsibility of keeping Kentucky securely in the Union, he suffered a nervous collapse after little more than a month.

[117] Carman makes a slight error. July 1, 1847, was the date of rank for Burnside's commission as brevet second lieutenant. The date at which Burnside took rank as second lieutenant was September 8, 1847. Cullum, *Biographical Register of the Officers and Graduates of the U.S. Military Academy, at West Point, N.Y., from its Establishment, March 16, 1802, to the Army Re-Organization of 1866-67*, vol 2., 2d ed. (New York: D. Van Nostrand, 1868), 191.

[118] Augustus Woodbury, *Major General Ambrose E. Burnside and the Ninth Army Corps: A Narrative of Campaign in North Carolina, Maryland, Virginia, Ohio, Kentucky, Mississippi and Tennessee, during the War for the Preservation of the Republic* (Providence, R.I.: Sidney S. Rider & Brother, 1867), 10.

[119] Ibid.

responsibility because he had doubts of his ability to handle operations of magnitude. It is not going too far to say that the Union cause would have received no hurt and saved much blood had Burnside's own estimate of his ability been accepted by the administration.

When Burnside was given command of the right wing (the First and Ninth Corps of the army), Jesse L. Reno was assigned to the command of the Ninth Corps. Reno was born at Wheeling, Virginia, on June 20, 1823, and when quite young removed to Pennsylvania. He entered West Point in 1842, graduated in 1846, and received his commission as second lieutenant of ordnance on July 1, 1846.[120] He accompanied the army to Mexico and was at the battle of Cerro Gordo, where his gallantry won him the brevet of first lieutenant. He was at Contreras and Churubusco. At the storming of Chapultepec, he was in command of a howitzer battery, severely wounded, and brevetted captain for his gallantry. On January 9, 1849, he was detailed as an assistant professor of mathematics at West Point and in July was assigned as secretary of a board to prepare a system of instruction for heavy artillery. He was on topographical duty in Minnesota in 1853–54 and chief of ordnance in the Utah expedition in 1857–59. He was in command of Mount Vernon Arsenal, Alabama, from 1859 until its seizure by the state authorities in January 1861. From February 2 until December 6, 1861, he was in charge of the arsenal at Fort Leavenworth, Kansas. He was commissioned brigadier general of volunteers on November 12, 1861, and assigned to the command of one of the brigades composing the Burnside expedition to North Carolina. For distinguished gallantry at Roanoke Island and New Bern, he was promoted major general of volunteers on April 26, 1862. From April to August 1862, he was in command of a division in the Department of North Carolina. In Pope's August campaign, he was at the head of the Ninth Corps in the field and was engaged at Second Manassas and Chantilly. His services in this campaign were warmly eulogized by the commanding general, who says, "I cannot express myself too highly of the zealous, gallant, and cheerful manner in which General Reno deported himself from the beginning to the end of the operations. Ever prompt, earnest, and soldierly, he was the model of all accomplished soldier and a gallant gentleman."[121]

He was warm hearted and cordial, yet quick-tempered, and always just and ready to recognize and reward merit. "In person," Woodbury writes, "Reno was of middle stature, stout, well knit and compact in frame. His forehead was high and broad, his face wore a genial expression, his eye beamed upon his friends with rare and quick intelligence, or, kindled in the excitement of conflict, flashed out in brave defiance of the foe. He had a magnetic kind of enthusiasm, and when leading on his men, he seemed to inspire his followers and make them irresistible in action. A dauntless soldier, whose like we rarely see!"[122] His death at South Mountain on September 14, 1862, was a distinct loss to the army and a national misfortune.

Alpheus S. Williams, the commander of the Twelfth Corps, was born at Saybrook, Connecticut, on September 20, 1810. He was of Puritan stock and his ancestors were men of note in the early days of the colonies. In 1827 he entered Yale College and graduated in 1831. He then entered the Yale law school, where he spent three years, and then traveled two years in Europe, returning in 1836 and settling in Detroit, Michigan, where he began the practice of law. In 1839 he was elected judge of the court of probate of Wayne County, which position he held until 1844, when he was elected recorder of Detroit. Meantime he became connected with the press and conducted one of the leading journals of the city for about four years, when his editorial career was interrupted by the breaking out of the war with Mexico and his entering the volunteer service of his country as lieutenant colonel of the 1st Michigan. At the end of the war, he returned to Detroit and resumed his law practice. At the close of 1849, he was appointed postmaster of that city, which position he held until 1853, when a change in the politics of the national administration was followed by his removal. In 1861, when the secession war broke out, Williams was one of the first to offer his services to the government, and as he had always been an active member of the Democratic party, his example had great influence for good in a city where it was much needed. He first served as president of the State Military Board, then as commander of the military camp of instruction at Fort Wayne. On December 17, 1861, he was appointed brigadier general of volunteers and joined the Army of the Potomac. He was assigned to the command of a brigade in Banks's division on the upper Potomac. In March 1862 he was given command of a division in Banks's corps and in the operations in the Shenandoah Valley displayed great skill and courage. When Jackson's aggressive movement on Banks's flank compelled him to fall back from Strasburg, Virginia, Williams had full charge of covering the retreat and did so skillfully, retiring on May 24 and, in a series of brilliant engagements, checking Jackson's advance at Newtown, Kernstown, and Winchester long enough to save a part of the trains. The retreat was a disastrous and humiliating one; it would have been much more so had Williams not shown greater skill and judgment as a soldier than his immediate superior. At Cedar Mountain he handled his division admirably and in the subsequent campaign around Manassas was active and

---

[120] Carman again errs in the date of commissioning. Reno took rank as brevet second lieutenant on July 1, 1846, and as second lieutenant on March 3, 1847. Cullum, *Biographical Register*, 145.

[121] Pope to Cullum, 47.

[122] Woodbury, 131.

unsparing in effort. When Banks assumed command of the defenses of Washington on September 8, Williams succeeded to the command of the corps in which he had served as a brigade and division commander.

Throughout his long and arduous service, which began with the beginning of the war and ended only when the final surrender was made, he never was taken by surprise and when in action was cool and quick to see a faulty disposition or movement in his own army or in that of the enemy. He was not a brilliant soldier, but a safe one; he never sacrificed his men for the mere sake of winning to himself the attention of the newspaper correspondents and the plaudits of the public, but whenever hard work was to be done or hard knocks to be received he was ready. He was social in his habits, kind and considerate to officers and men, ever alive to their needs and comforts, and always with them from the beginning to the end. He never received a furlough; his life was in camp with his men. He never received the promotion to which his long and faithful service entitled him, but this did not lessen his honesty of purpose or diminish the energy with which he performed duty. His ambition was more concerned in the welfare of his country and the triumph of her armies than his own promotion and advancement, and he was never above the work to which he was assigned, whether commanding a corps, a division, or a brigade. It has been truly said of him, "He was content that he did his duty, and in the satisfaction that he never committed an error, never misrepresented an order, never relaxed his careful watchfulness and disinterested devotion to his country." Although this devotion to duty was not recognized by the government, he never complained; "he never said ought in derogation of a fellow soldier; he was charitable even toward those who supplanted him or when advanced when seemingly he justly was entitled to the promotion. He was a noble man as well as a gallant solder."[123]

All these corps commanders had served in the Mexican War. Five were graduates of West Point, two had resigned from the service and been reappointed, and three had been in the service continuously. (Sumner had not attended the Academy but had been many years a soldier; Williams was appointed from civil life.) Among the division and brigade commanders were many who subsequently rose to high command and fame: George G. Meade to the command of a corps and the Army of the Potomac, Henry W. Slocum to the command of a corps and the Army of Georgia, and Oliver O. Howard to the command of a corps and the Army of the Tennessee.

We have already stated that McClellan was the only general of the Union Army who had publicly declared against the policy of emancipation. It is a noteworthy fact that every one of his corps commanders—six of whom were Democrats and one a Republican—shared his views and were opposed to the attitude of the administration and to the actions of Congress touching the question of slavery. More than two-thirds of the division and brigade commanders were of the same view.

---

[123] As of this writing, Carman's source for these unattributed quotations regarding Williams has not been identified.

5

The Advance of the Army of the Potomac from Washington to Frederick and South Mountain

The general theatre of operations lay in eastern Virginia and western Maryland. The Potomac River crosses this area from northwest to southeast and (with the Chesapeake and Ohio Canal, which runs along it on the east) forms a military obstacle of some magnitude in the front of a vigilant enemy. The Monocacy and the Antietam enter the Potomac from the east and the Shenandoah from the west (its waters, in turn, mingling with those of the Potomac at Harper's Ferry). During the summer and early fall, the Potomac is fordable at several places above Conrad's Ferry and presents no serious obstacle (when low) to the strategic conduct of a campaign.

The immediate theatre of operations was western Maryland, the physical features of which are determined by the great Appalachian system which crosses that section nearly due north and south. The Blue Ridge, the eastern range of this system, is here broken into two defined ranges separated by a fertile valley of entrancing beauty, seven to nine miles in width, known as the Catoctin or Middletown Valley. The eastern range is known as Catoctin Mountain, the western as South Mountain. West of South Mountain and crossing the Potomac at Harper's Ferry is a lesser range known in Maryland as Elk Ridge. (Where it borders the Potomac, it presents a cluster or aggregation of lofty hills known as Maryland Heights.) Elk Ridge extends northeast from the Potomac about ten miles and descends into and is lost in the general undulation of the country about one and a half miles southwest of Keedysville. The valley between it and South Mountain is happily known as Pleasant Valley and varies in width from one to three miles.

The three ranges are pierced by several gaps or passes, presenting opportunities for good defense against superior numbers. The roads, both in the valleys and leading over the mountains by the gaps, are generally good, most of them macadamized turnpikes not excelled anywhere. The great number of roads gives easy access to all parts of the country. The entire field of operations is well wooded, springs and streams of pure, cool water abound, and there are no natural obstacles (save in the mountain gaps) to hinder the movements of troops in any direction. The climate is healthy, the air invigorating, and supplies of all kinds, for men and animals, abundant.

The movement of the Union army northward from Washington was initiated by the 1st Massachusetts Cavalry. This regiment had been in service in South Carolina and disembarked from steamers at Alexandria on September 2. Early that day Pope telegraphed Halleck from Fairfax Court House and said that it would be well for him to look out for his communications, as "the enemy from the beginning has been throwing his rear toward the north, and every movement shows that he means to make trouble in Maryland,"[1] whereupon orders were given that this Massachusetts regiment should move up the Potomac, watching all the fords between Great Falls and Harper's Ferry. Not a moment was to be lost in the execution of the order, as it was probable that the enemy might attempt to cross that night.[2] Such was the confusion at Alexandria that the officers of the regiment could not be found on the second and the orders were repeated on the third, with the advice that it was not expected the regiment would engage the enemy but simply watch carefully his operations and give timely notice should he appear on the Potomac above Great Falls. Three times was this order repeated on the third, but not until the morning of the fourth did the regiment cross the Potomac by the Aqueduct Bridge and push out beyond Tennallytown, where it was halted for orders.[3]

On the morning of the fourth, Pleasonton (then in camp at Fort Albany, on the Virginia side of the Potomac) was ordered to Falls Church to ascertain, if possible, the intentions of the enemy. With the 6th U.S. Cavalry (Captain William P. Sanders) and two companies of another regiment, he reached the village, where he was joined by the 8th Illinois Cavalry and the 8th Pennsylvania Cavalry. (The two last named skirmished with Robertson's Brigade about a mile north of the village.) Cox, commanding the Kanawha Division at Upton's Hill, reported early in the morning an accumulation of evidence that the

---

[1] John Pope to Henry W. Halleck, September 2, 1862, 7:30 a.m. reprinted in *OR*, vol. 12, pt. 3, 797.

[2] Randolph B. Marcy to Robert Williams, September 2, 1862, 11:10 p.m., reprinted in *OR*, vol. 51, pt. 1, 781.

[3] Seth Williams to H. L. Higginson, as contained in Seth Williams to C. B. Ferguson, September 3, 1862, 11:52 p.m., reprinted in *OR*, vol. 51, pt. 1, 783.

main body of the enemy had gone in the direction of Leesburg and that the movements in his front were feints.[4] Pleasonton came to the same conclusion and, around noon, dispatched his opinion that the Confederates were only making a show of force in his front to conceal their movements on the upper Potomac.[5]

Pleasonton was now ordered to withdraw from Falls Church and, with such forage and subsistence as could be carried on his horses, cross the Aqueduct Bridge, proceed to Tennallytown, and await orders.[6] He moved promptly with two regiments, and on reaching Tennallytown received orders to move up the Potomac. Early on the fifth, he was in motion, marching by way of Rockville to Darnestown, reconnoitering all the fords of the river as far north as Seneca Mills. Captain Chamberlain's detachment of the 1st Massachusetts, pushing ahead, encountered Fitzhugh Lee's cavalry beyond Pooles-ville and came to grief, as we have seen. Exploration of the various fords south of Seneca Creek showed them to be unoc-cupied, and small parties were left to observe them. Pleasonton with his main force took position on Muddy Branch, where it is crossed by the road from Rockville to Darnestown.[7]

On the fifth, the 1st New York Cavalry, which had come up from Aquia Creek on the third, marched through Washing-ton and bivouacked near Rockville, reporting early next day to Pleasonton. It was immediately marched to Middlebrook, and four companies were advanced to occupy Clarksburg and picket the line of the Seneca, scouting at the same time the country toward Hyattstown, near which place Hampton's Brigade was encountered. On the same day, a squadron of the 1st U.S. Cavalry moved to Brookeville and scouted to Unity, Goshen, and Cracklintown in the direction of the Baltimore and Ohio Railroad, while the 8th Illinois Cavalry and the 3d Indiana Cavalry pushed beyond Darnestown, picketing the roads in the direction of Poolesville and the fords of the Potomac.[8]

Stuart's cavalry pickets were encountered in every direction and, from information obtained, Pleasonton reported on Sep-tember 6 that Lee's entire army had crossed the Potomac with the evident intention of moving on Washington—Jackson by the Frederick Road and another column by the road running through Poolesville and Darnestown.[9] Late in the day, his informa-tion was that Jackson was to lead an advance upon Baltimore by way of Damascus, Clarksburg, and Cooksville, whereupon he extended his right as far as Mechanicsville and called for reinforcements. Pleasonton had the 3d Indiana Cavalry and the 8th Illinois Cavalry in Darnestown, the 1st New York Cavalry at Middlebrook, and the 1st U.S. Cavalry at Brookeville and Mechanicsville, picketing and scouting the country thoroughly from the Potomac and Seneca Mills to Cooksville, on the Bal-timore and Frederick Turnpike. Sumner, with his own corps and that of Williams, was but a short distance in his rear.

On the seventh, a squadron of the 1st New York Cavalry moved from Middlebrook to reinforce the 1st U.S. Cavalry and assist in scouting the country to Damascus and Cooksville. Two squadrons each of the 3d Indiana Cavalry and the 8th Illinois Cavalry, under the command of Major George H. Chapman of the 3d, made a dash on Poolesville and captured two cavalry videttes. On the next day, Pleasonton sent Colonel John F. Farnsworth, with the 3d and the 8th and two guns of Battery M, 2d U.S. Artillery (the last under Lieutenant Robert H. Chapin), to occupy Poolesville and picket the roads to Conrad's Ferry, Barnesville, and the Monocacy. As Farnsworth approached Poolesville, Stuart's cavalry pickets were seen retreating on the road to Barnesville. Some of the 3d pushed after them and soon came upon the 7th and 12th Virginia Cavalry and two guns, all under Colonel Munford.[10]

Advised by the pickets of Pleasonton's advance on the evening of the seventh and divining his intention to occupy Pooles-ville, Stuart the next morning had ordered Munford to advance from his camp near Sugar Loaf Mountain and drive the enemy from the place. Munford's advance guard had barely entered the town when Farnsworth appeared and drove it back to where Munford was drawn up to check further pursuit. Munford opened on Farnsworth with two guns of Chew's Bat-tery. Lieutenant Chapin soon silenced these, and a charge of the 3d Indiana Cavalry broke the 12th Virginia Cavalry and sent it to the rear in some confusion, thus imperiling Chew's two guns, which were rescued by a gallant counter-charge of the 7th Virginia Cavalry, led by Captain Samuel B. Myers, that checked the Indiana men and enabled Chew to get off his pieces. Munford retreated toward Barnesville, closely pursued by Farnsworth as far as Monocacy Church, where, about dark, Farnsworth was checked by the sharpshooters of the 2d Virginia Cavalry that had hastened from Barnesville to

[4] Jacob D. Cox to George B. McClellan, September 4, 1862, 2:30 a.m., reprinted in *OR*, vol. 19, pt. 2, 176.
[5] Alfred Pleasonton to Marcy, September 4, 1862, reprinted in *OR*, vol. 19, pt. 2, 178.
[6] Marcy to Pleasonton, September 4, 1862, reprinted in *OR*, vol. 51, pt. 1, 786–87.
[7] Pleasonton to Marcy, September 19, 1862, reprinted in *OR*, vol. 19, pt. 1, 208.
[8] Ibid.
[9] Pleasonton to Marcy, September 6, 1862, 8:30 a.m., reprinted in *OR*, vol. 19, pt. 2, 192.
[10] Pleasonton to Marcy, September 19, 1862, 208.

Munford's assistance. Munford's loss was one killed and ten wounded, eight of whom were of the 12th. Farnsworth had one killed and twelve wounded, the loss, with one exception, falling upon the 3d.[11]

On the morning of the ninth, Farnsworth resumed his advance. His men overtook, roughly handled, and dislodged the 12th Virginia from its position near Monocacy Church, capturing its battle-flag and a few prisoners. After a slight skirmish on the edge of Barnesville, Farnsworth's command entered that place and pursued the Virginians two miles beyond, the net result of the day's work being the capture of one flag and twenty-seven prisoners.[12] On the same day, a battalion of the 1st New York Cavalry under the command of Major Alonzo W. Adams made a dash into Hyattstown and drove out some of Hampton's cavalry. Hampton's men returned next day with artillery and a sharp encounter took place, the New York men being supported by a squadron of the 1st U.S. Cavalry under Captain Marcus A. Reno. Hampton's men were repulsed and the Union cavalry fell back to Clarksburg.

While Pleasonton was feeling the Confederate lines and seeking information of Lee's movements, McClellan was getting his army well in hand, supplying its needs (which were many), reorganizing the commands, and providing for the defense of Washington. His corps on the Maryland side of the Potomac were moving cautiously in rear of Pleasonton and within supporting distance of him and each other.

On the sixth, the First Corps, moved from Upton's Hill, crossed the Potomac by the Long Bridge and marched through Washington to Leesborough. Cox's Kanawha Division of the Ninth Corps moved from Upton's Hill, crossed the Potomac by the Aqueduct Bridge, and, marching through Washington, went out on the Seventh Street Road to the Soldiers' Home. The Sixth Corps moved from the Alexandria Seminary, crossed the Potomac by the Long Bridge, and encamped near Georgetown. Sykes's division of the Fifth Corps (designated as a reserve under the personal direction of McClellan) crossed the Potomac by the Long Bridge and took the road to Rockville. On the night of the sixth, the army was thus distributed: the First Corps was at Leesborough; the Second and Twelfth were at Rockville, with Sykes' division of the Fifth on the march for that place; three divisions of the Ninth Corps were on Meridian Hill, with Cox's division at the Soldiers' Home; the Sixth Corps was between Georgetown and Tennallytown; and Couch's division of the Fourth Corps was thrown forward to Offutt's Cross-Roads by the river road, thus covering that approach and watching the fords of the Potomac. (Couch ultimately moved as a support to the Sixth Corps.)

Cox's division took the advance of the Ninth Corps on the seventh, marching from the Soldiers' Home to Leesborough; Reno followed from Meridian Hill with the corps' other three divisions. The Sixth Corps moved from near Tennallytown to Rockville and was followed by Sykes's division. The First Corps remained at Leesborough, the Second and Twelfth at Rockville, and Couch's division at Offutt's Cross-Roads.

McClellan's avowed purpose in advancing from Washington was "simply to meet the necessities of the moment by frustrating Lee's invasion of the Northern States, and, when that was accomplished, to push with the utmost rapidity the work of reorganization and supply, so that a new campaign might be promptly inaugurated with the army in condition to prosecute it to a successful termination without intermission."[13] With this in view, McClellan left Washington on the afternoon of September 7, arriving at Rockville in the evening, where he established headquarters and was joined by the Sixth Corps, which he had advanced from Tennallytown. Before leaving Washington, however, he received this dispatch from Halleck: "I have just seen General Pleasonton's dispatch of 2.30. Until we can get better advices about the numbers of the enemy at Dranesville, I think we must be very cautious about stripping too much the forts on the Virginia side. It may be the enemy's object to draw off the mass of our forces and then attempt to attack from the Virginia side of the Potomac. Think of this. I will see you as soon as I can."[14] (Pleasonton's dispatch was to the effect that paroled prisoners said Lee's army was moving on the road to Frederick, tearing up the rails on the road as it went; that Pleasonton had heard that, on the night of the fifth, the Confederates had fifty thousand men at Dranesville that might be kept there to cross the Potomac in the direction of Rockville after the Union advance had become engaged elsewhere; and that the enemy had already possessed themselves of Sugar Loaf Mountain, upon which they had established a signal station.[15])

[11] Ibid.; Thomas T. Munford to "Major," [October 16?—OR editors], 1862, reprinted in OR, vol. 19, pt 1, 825; James E. B. Stuart to Robert H. Chilton, February 13, 1864, reprinted in OR, vol. 19, pt. 2, 815. Munford reports the losses in his command at eight killed, wounded, and missing in the 12th Virginia Cavalry and two killed and wounded in the 2d. Stuart, writing much later, gives the casualties as fifteen killed, wounded, and missing.

[12] Pleasonton to Marcy, September 19, 1862, 208–9.

[13] McClellan, McClellan's Own Story: The War for the Union, the Soldiers Who Fought It, the Civilians Who Directed It, and His Relations to It and Them (New York: Charles L. Webster & Co., 1887), 553.

[14] Halleck to McClellan, September 7, 1862, reprinted in OR, vol. 19, pt. 2, 201.

[15] Pleasonton to Marcy, September 7, 1862, 2:30 p.m., reprinted in OR, vol. 19, pt. 2, 200–201.

In his official report, McClellan says:

At this time it was known that the mass of the rebel army had passed up the south side of the Potomac in the direction of Leesburg, and that a portion of that army had crossed into Maryland; but whether it was their intention to cross their whole force with a view to turn Washington by a flank movement down the north bank of the Potomac, to move on Baltimore, or to invade Pennsylvania, were questions which at that time we had no means of determining. This uncertainty as to the intentions of the enemy obliged me, up to the 13th of September, to march cautiously, and to advance the army in such order as continually to keep Washington and Baltimore covered, and at the same time to hold the troops well in hand, so as to be able to concentrate and follow rapidly if the enemy took the direction of Pennsylvania, or to return to the defense of Washington if, as was greatly feared by the authorities, the enemy should be merely making a feint with a small force to draw off our army, while with their main forces they stood ready to seize the first favorable opportunity to attack the capital.[16]

On September 8 the Ninth Corps advanced from Leesborough to Brookeville, the Second and Twelfth Corps from Rockville to near Middlebrook, and the Sixth Corps from Rockville to near Darnestown. The First Corps remained at Leesborough, Couch's division at Offutt's Cross-Roads, and Sykes's at Rockville.

McClellan says elsewhere:

Partly in order to move men freely and rapidly, partly in consequence of the lack of accurate information as to the exact position and intention of Lee's army, the troops advanced by three main roads: that near the Potomac by Offutt's cross-roads and the mouth of the Seneca, that by Rockville to Frederick, and that by Brookeville and Urbana to New Market. We were then in condition to act according to the development of the enemy's plans, and to concentrate rapidly in any position. If Lee threatened our left flank by moving down the river road or by crossing the Potomac at any of the forks [fords] from Coon's Ferry upward, there were enough troops on the river road to hold him in check until the rest of the army could move over to support them; if Lee took up a position behind the Seneca near Frederick, the whole army could be rapidly concentrated in that direction to attack him in force; if he moved upon Baltimore the entire army could rapidly be thrown in his rear and his retreat cut off; if he moved by Gettysburg or Chambersburg upon York or Carlisle we were equally in position to throw ourselves in his rear.[17]

On the seventh Halleck cautioned McClellan not to strip the defenses on the Virginia side of the Potomac; on the eighth he became satisfied that Lee was not to be feared in that quarter and suggested that McClellan should move rapidly forward to meet the enemy on the Maryland side, leaving a reserve in reach of his army and Washington at the same time.[18] To which, McClellan replied that he was by no means satisfied that the enemy had crossed into Maryland in any large force; that his information was "entirely too indefinite to justify definite action"; and that he was prepared to attack anything crossing south of the Monocacy, prevent any attack in force on Baltimore, and at the same time cover Washington. He was ready to move in any direction, and, as soon as he found out where to strike, he would be after the enemy without an hour's delay. He did not feel sure that there was no force in front of Washington on the Virginia side of the river.[19]

During the evening, however, he became satisfied that Lee had crossed his entire army into Maryland, upon which he determined on a general advance for the morrow—the right wing to Goshen and Cracklintown, with the cavalry well out on the right and front; the center near Middlebrook; and the left by Darnestown and Gaithersburg—the intention being to occupy the line of the Seneca.[20] The movement was made on the ninth as ordered. The cavalry pushed out in front, and on the right occupied Damascus and marched through Cooksville to Lisbon on the main road to Ridgeville and New Market. The Ninth Corps camped at Goshen and Cracklintown, with Hooker's First Corps in reserve at Brookeville and Mechanicsville. The Second and Twelfth Corps remained at Middlebrook, the Sixth Corps at Darnestown. Couch's division (leaving the 98th Pennsylvania at Offutt's Cross-Roads) marched to the mouth of Seneca Creek. The Confederate pickets fell back without offering much resistance. Some who were taken prisoner reported that Stuart was at Urbana and Jackson at New Market (indicating that a movement on Baltimore was intended), upon which McClellan dispatched Halleck that Jackson

[16] McClellan to Lorenzo Thomas, October 15, 1862, reprinted in OR, vol. 19, pt. 1, 39. McClellan submitted two complete reports of the Maryland campaign; in his original manuscript, Carman identifies the source of this passage incorrectly as McClellan's second, "elaborate" report of August 4, 1863.

[17] McClellan, Own Story, 553.

[18] Halleck to McClellan, September 8, 1862, 1:05 p.m., reprinted in OR, vol. 19, pt. 2, 210.

[19] McClellan to Halleck, September 8, 1862, 8:00 p.m., reprinted in OR, vol. 19, pt. 2, 211.

[20] McClellan to Halleck, September 8, 1862, 10:00 p.m., reprinted in OR, vol. 19, pt. 2, 211.

and Longstreet had about 110,000 men of all arms near Frederick, covered by Stuart's cavalry. He was "well prepared for anything except overwhelming numbers," but wanted more cavalry.[21]

The position taken by McClellan on the ninth—the ridge bordering Seneca Creek—was a defensive one. He had no intention of attacking Lee, his sole object being to interpose such a force in front of Washington as might best defend against an advance from Lee at the head of overwhelming numbers. These last dispatches to Halleck show McClellan's serious defect as a commander in overestimating the numbers of the enemy. It was so in West Virginia in 1861, so on the Peninsula in the spring and summer of 1862, and so in the Maryland campaign—from the day he set out from Washington to the day that Lee's army, much inferior in numbers, recrossed the Potomac. At Rich Mountain McClellan was convinced that he was greatly outnumbered. While in front of Washington in 1861, he thought the enemy had three or four times his own force and for many days was apprehensive that Beauregard would attack Washington or cross into Maryland with very superior numbers. On the Peninsula he constantly contended that the Confederates outnumbered him two to one. His corps commanders accepted the estimate, and the Army of the Potomac was taught implicitly to believe the fiction. Nor was the falsehood dispelled when Lee crossed into Maryland; McClellan reported his belief that Lee had at least 120,000 men.[22] It was a saying of Napoleon that the general who is ignorant of his enemy's strength and disposition is ignorant of his trade. Judged by this standard, McClellan was not a great general.[23]

We have noted Lee's complaint of the prevalence of straggling from the ranks of the Army of Northern Virginia. The evil prevailed to a still greater extent in the Army of the Potomac. When it crossed from Virginia into Maryland, many remained behind at Alexandria; when it moved from Washington, many remained in the city or went to their homes, and the country through which the march was made was overrun by stragglers. Halleck expressed the opinion that the straggling and demoralization were caused by the incapacity of officers, the want of proper discipline, and the action of Congress in the abolition and confiscation measures, which were very distasteful to the western armies and, as he understood, to the Army of the Potomac. There were many men belonging to the army that could not, from absolute want of muscular tone, follow its marches. Moreover, men never known to fall behind on previous marches did so in Maryland, and what prevailed in the ranks of the old regiments to a great extent occurred in the more than twenty new regiments that joined the army at Washington. The straggling was not confined to those who had lost muscular tone by hard service, nor to those who were dissatisfied with political ideas of the administration and Congress, but affected the entire organization. (Yet while some of the divisions and brigades lost a large fraction of their numbers in their daily marches, falling so far behind as to appear more numerous on the roadside than the marching column, there were other brigades and divisions in which the evil was almost unknown.)

So great was the straggling that on the ninth, before the army had moved far from Washington, McClellan issued stringent orders designed to abate it. He characterized the evil as habitually associated with cowardice, marauding, and theft, and laid down stringent rules for numerous roll calls during a march. None would be allowed to leave the ranks save for necessary purposes or extenuating causes. McClellan also observed that the evil was viewed without the least apparent concern by the officers of both high and low grades, and he issued a circular calling attention to the fact of the frequent absence of superior officers from their command while in camp and from their columns on the march—laxities that had to be remedied. Inattention and carelessness on the part of those high in rank had been "one fertile source of the straggling and want of discipline" then obtaining in the various camps. Attention was called to the fact that the safety of the country depended upon what the Army of the Potomac should achieve in the campaign; it could not be successful if the soldiers were "one-half skulking to the rear" while the brunt of battle was borne by the other half and "its officers inattentive to observe and correct the grossest evils which were daily occurring under their eyes." He entreated all general officers to lend every energy to "the eradication of the military vice of straggling" and felt assured that their united determination could break up the practice in a single week.[24] But it was not broken up in a week; the orders were but partially and indifferently observed and the army moved slowly to the front, leaving behind a swarm of stragglers who did more damage to the property of friendly citizens than did the Confederates. So while a host of Lee's stragglers were wandering around in Virginia, a larger number of McClellan's men were wandering over Maryland.

Late in the evening of the ninth, Burnside had his scouts at Ridgeville (within three miles of New Market) and obtained information that the main Confederate force was still at Frederick, but that Jackson was at New Market with a considerable

[21] McClellan to Halleck, September 9, 1862, 7:30 p.m., reprinted in *OR*, vol. 19, pt. 2, 219; McClellan to Halleck, September 9, 1862, 8:15 p.m., reprinted in *OR*, vol. 19, pt. 2, 219.

[22] McClellan to Halleck, September 13, 1862, 11:00 p.m., reprinted in *OR*, vol. 19, pt. 2, 281.

[23] When King Joseph wrote to Napoleon that he could not ascertain the position and strength of the enemy's army, the emperor replied, "Attack him and you will find out."—*EAC*

[24] Headquarters Army of the Potomac, General Orders No. 155, September 9, 1862, reprinted in *OR*, vol. 19, pt. 2, 226–27; Circular of September 9, 1862, reprinted in *OR*, vol. 19, pt. 2, 225.

body, threatening an advance on Baltimore.[25] McClellan ordered Burnside to push a reconnaissance beyond Ridgeville, using cavalry and artillery for that purpose. Should the enemy make any demonstration toward Baltimore, Burnside was to allow him to get the column well in motion and then attack him vigorously on the flank. McClellan assured him of his support with everything available.[26]

McClellan's intentions for the tenth were to occupy Ridgeville with a sufficient force to check an advance of the Confederates toward Baltimore. In view of this, early in the morning, the army was ordered to advance to the line of Parrs Ridge and along it from Ridgeville, through Damascus and Clarksburg; the extreme left was to move to Poolesville and Barnesville, on the same high ridge.[27] As these movements were "such as to uncover Washington slightly in the direction of Baltimore," McClellan ordered Banks, who had been left in command at Washington, to put his troops and works on the Maryland side of the Potomac in a good position for defense.[28]

The movement began early in the morning. Cox's division had gone but one mile on the road from Goshen to Ridgeville, the First Corps but a short distance on the road from Brookeville to Poplar Springs and Cooksville, the Second to within three miles of Clarksburg, and the Twelfth to within two miles of Damascus, when the entire movement on the right and center was suspended because McClellan received information that the mass of the enemy was still at Frederick, and he wished to verify this information by further reconnaissance.[29] He would not press his advance until satisfied whether the enemy intended to move toward Baltimore or Washington. (In fact, the whole Confederate army was then on its "rollicking march" from Frederick to Harper's Ferry and Hagerstown.)

No further advance was made by the right and center that day. The First Corps remained near Brookeville, the Ninth at Goshen, Seneca Ridge, and Cracklintown, with an advance guard (the 30th Ohio and a section of Captain James R. McMullin's Ohio battery) at Damascus. The Second Corps was halted within three miles of Clarksburg and the Twelfth about two miles of Damascus. Sykes's division remained at Rockville. On the left, the Sixth Corps, preceded by the 6th U.S. Cavalry, pushed forward from Darnestown to Barnesville, covering the road from the mouth of the Monocacy to Rockville, and in position to connect with and support the center should it become necessary to force the line of the Monocacy. Leaving the 7th Massachusetts at the mouth of the Seneca, Couch's division marched to Poolesville, Brigadier General John Cochrane's brigade being advanced to Bells's Cross-Roads (a short distance north of the town), while the 55th New York of Brigadier General Albion P. Howe's brigade was sent to the mouth of the Monocacy to support the 1st Massachusetts Cavalry in preventing the destruction of the aqueduct at that point.

About three miles north of Barnesville, Sugar Loaf Mountain rises from the Monocacy Valley, in the shape indicated by its name, to a height of 1,281 feet above the level of the sea and about 750 feet above the general level of the surrounding area. It commands a view of the entire country east of Catoctin Mountain watered by the Monocacy and looks far into Virginia on the west. From its summit can be seen Frederick and the road over the Catoctin to Middletown, and no body of troops could move in any direction without being plainly seen and its numbers correctly determined. Banks had early recognized its importance as a signal station and used it for that purpose. From one of his signal parties came the first authentic news that Lee had crossed the Potomac into Maryland,[30] and one of the first acts of the Confederates upon entering Maryland was to possess themselves of the mountain and establish a signal party on it. McClellan recognized the importance of its possession. On the morning of September 9, he called Pleasonton's attention to the fact that as a signal station it was of great value not only to him but to the enemy and should be taken if not incurring too much risk.[31] Late in the day, McClellan received information that Pleasonton had carried Barnesville and Sugar Loaf, but early on the morning of the tenth he found that he had been wrongly informed as to the latter, upon which he renewed his order to take it.[32]

Munford's cavalry covered the right of the Confederate line and was specially charged with the defense of Sugar Loaf. The brigade was greatly reduced by detachments for service elsewhere. The 6th Virginia Cavalry and the 17th Virginia Cavalry Battalion had been left in Virginia; on the morning of the tenth, the 7th Virginia Cavalry accompanied Jackson on his march to Harper's Ferry. This left the 2d and 12th Virginia Cavalry (about two hundred men each) and Chew's Battery of four guns—in all less than five hundred men. The 2d, under Lieutenant Colonel Richard H. Burks,[33] was in position at the

[25] McClellan to Abraham Lincoln, September 10, 1862, 12:00 p.m., reprinted in *OR*, vol. 19, pt. 2, 233.

[26] Marcy to Ambrose E. Burnside, September 9, 1862, 10:00 p.m., reprinted in *OR*, vol. 19, pt. 2, 222.

[27] McClellan to Lincoln, September 10, 1862, 233.

[28] McClellan to Nathaniel P. Banks, September 10, 1862, reprinted in *OR*, vol. 19, pt. 2, 234.

[29] Ibid.

[30] "Miner, signal officer, Banks' Division" to Banks, September 5, 1862, 9:00 a.m., reprinted in *OR*, vol. 19, pt. 2, 184.

[31] Marcy to Pleasonton, September 9, 1862, 10:00 a.m., reprinted in *OR*, vol. 51, pt. 1, 802–3.

[32] Marcy to Pleasonton, September 10, 1862, 11:15 a.m., reprinted in *OR*, vol. 51, pt. 1, 810–11.

[33] At this point in his original manuscript, Carman gives the name incorrectly as "J. S. Burks," but renders it properly in his table of organization.

cross-roads southeast of the base of the mountain, covered by rail barricades. The 12th, under Colonel Asher W. Harman, was on its right and rear.

In the early forenoon of the tenth, Captain Sanders, with a small cavalry force and two guns, attempted to dislodge the 2d Virginia Cavalry from its position but found it too strongly posted to be driven by the force at his disposal and, after a loss of one man killed and four wounded, withdrew as soon as the Sixth Corps came up and took position at Barnesville.[34] During the engagement the 9th Virginia Cavalry of Fitzhugh Lee's Brigade came to Munford's assistance. (It did not become engaged and was held in reserve.)

Pleasonton reported to McClellan that he had made three attempts to dislodge the enemy. He believed the Confederates had a very strong position and evidently intended to hold it, but he noted that Franklin held an opposite opinion.[35] McClellan was greatly disappointed and ordered Franklin to support Pleasonton with a brigade of infantry. At noon Couch, who was at Poolesville, was directed to aid Pleasonton with a brigade (if necessary, with his entire division) and to assume charge of the movement. An hour later, Couch was ordered to hasten the movement and advised that the mountain must be taken if it should require all his available command and that of Franklin also.[36] Three urgent messages were sent to Pleasonton, impressing upon him the great importance of carrying the position and informing him that both Couch and Franklin had been ordered to give him all the support required.[37] At 3:00 p.m. Franklin was ordered to take control of the movement and accomplish the important object, if it could be done without incurring the risk of losing his command.[38]

Notwithstanding these urgent orders to Pleasonton, Couch, and Franklin, no serious effort was made to carry Sugar Loaf Mountain on the tenth. Had Pleasonton put more force and persistence into his attack and carried the mountain, his lookout could have seen from its summit on that clear, bright morning of September 10 the long columns of Jackson, Longstreet, D. H. Hill, and McLaws as they marched out of Frederick and over Catoctin Mountain; Walker's Division would have been seen marching down from the mouth of the Monocacy northward to Point of Rocks; and the mystery of Lee's whereabouts would have been solved. Or had one of the nine brigades of available infantry supported Pleasonton on the afternoon of the tenth, the less than eight hundred cavalry at Munford's disposal could have been driven away before night. McClellan would have known the movements of his enemy and could have made dispositions for a rapid advance on the morrow. At 11:15 p.m. Franklin was ordered to put himself in communication with Sumner at Clarksburg and to carry Sugar Loaf Mountain if possible, but if the enemy appeared too strong he was authorized to await the result of Sumner's advance on Hyattstown. (Franklin was also told that "the earlier we gain the Sugar Loaf the better.") After midnight the order was repeated, and Franklin was advised that Sumner had been directed to cooperate with him.[39]

Partly if not wholly owing to the failure to carry Sugar Loaf Mountain on the tenth, McClellan's movements on September 11 were extremely cautious. Sumner, in the center, was directed to occupy Clarksburg and Damascus as soon after daylight as possible. Burnside, on the right, was ordered to push a strong reconnaissance across the Frederick and Baltimore Turnpike and along the Baltimore and Ohio Railroad toward New Market and, if he learned that the enemy had moved toward Hagerstown, to press on rapidly to Frederick, keeping his troops constantly ready to meet the enemy in force—but he was not to occupy New Market at the expense of an engagement. A corresponding movement was ordered on the left. These movements were made as ordered: in the center the Second Corps moved three miles and occupied Clarksburg, and the Twelfth Corps marched two miles to Damascus; on the right the Ninth Corps occupied Ridgeville and New Market, Brigadier General John F. Reynolds's division of the First Corps marched from Brookeville by way of Cooksville and Lisbon to Poplar Springs, Brigadier General Rufus King's division to Lisbon, and Brigadier General James B. Ricketts's to Cooksville. Sykes's division advanced from Rockville to Middlebrook.

While these cautious and deliberate movements were made in the center and on the right on the morning of the eleventh, the left was held back, but after the occupation of Damascus by the Twelfth Corps and Clarksburg by the Second, a movement was made by Franklin. In the afternoon Colonel John F. Farnsworth's brigade of cavalry, supported by Brigadier General Winfield S. Hancock's infantry brigade of the Sixth Corps, dislodged Munford's rear-guard from Sugar Loaf Mountain. The Confederate horsemen retired by the Buckeystown Road in the direction of Frederick, bivouacking three

[34] Carman's source for the four wounded is not known, but Pleasonton reported one soldier mortally wounded. Pleasonton to Marcy, September 10, 1862, 4:45 p.m. (first message), as contained in Marcy to McClellan, September 10, 1862, reprinted in *OR*, vol. 19, pt. 2, 238.

[35] Ibid.

[36] Marcy to Darius N. Couch, September 10, 1862, 12:30 p.m., reprinted in *OR*, vol. 51, pt. 1, 808; Marcy to Couch, September 10, 1862, 1:45 p.m., reprinted in *OR*, vol. 51, pt. 1, 808–9.

[37] Marcy to Pleasonton, September 10, 1862, 11:15 a.m., 810; Marcy to Pleasonton, September 10, 1862, 12:00 p.m., reprinted in *OR*, vol. 51, pt. 1, 811; Marcy to Pleasonton, September 10, 1862, 1:40 p.m., reprinted in *OR*, vol. 51, pt. 1, 811.

[38] Marcy to William B. Franklin, September 10, 1862, 3:00 p.m., reprinted in *OR*, vol. 51, pt. 1, 807.

[39] McClellan to Marcy, September 10, 1862, reprinted in *OR*, vol. 19, pt. 2, 238; Marcy to Franklin, September 11, 1862, 1:00 a.m., reprinted in *OR*, vol. 51, pt. 1, 815.

miles from the last named place, with the 9th Virginia Cavalry pushing on through Urbana to New Market, where it rejoined its brigade. With the exception of Hancock's brigade, the Sixth Corps remained at Barnesville and Couch's division at Poolesville. The 23d Pennsylvania, 1st New York Cavalry, and a section of artillery relieved the 55th New York at the mouth of the Monocacy.

At noon McClellan consulted Franklin as to the propriety and possibility of throwing a column over the Monocacy at its mouth to cut off Lee's retreat, but information received shortly thereafter by Cox at Ridgeville and Hooker at Cooksville, being to the effect that Lee had abandoned Frederick and was moving northward (which information was confirmed by dispatches received from Governor Curtin of Pennsylvania that Jackson's command had already reached Hagerstown with the evident intention of moving into Pennsylvania[40]), orders were given for a rapid movement on Frederick—the Ninth Corps, under Reno, by the direct road from New Market, the First Corps by way of Ridgeville and New Market (following Reno), and a corresponding movement of all the troops in the center and on the left in the direction of Urbana. McClellan reported that, up to this time, his movements were for the purpose of feeling the enemy—"to compel him to develop his intentions— at the same time that the troops were in position readily to cover Baltimore or Washington, to attack him should he hold the line of the Monocacy, or to follow him into Pennsylvania if necessary."[41]

Cautious and deliberate as was McClellan's advance, there were reasons for it beyond Halleck's warnings: the condition of the transportation and artillery, the vigilance and superb handling of the Confederate cavalry, and the consequent ignorance of the Confederate movements.

The quartermaster department was sadly disorganized. The trains of the Army of the Potomac brought from the Peninsula were not promptly disembarked and, when disembarked, were not properly distributed to the divisions to which they belonged; the Army of Virginia had lost much of its transportation; and there was not that systematic and perfect organization that, in general, characterized the quartermaster service in the Army of the Potomac. In fact, no information could be obtained as to the number of wagons belonging to that army or what quartermasters were on duty. In consequence, when the troops of both armies moved from Washington there was some confusion, the trains were slow in coming up, and some brigades and divisions suffered accordingly, but under the energetic and intelligent direction of Brigadier General Rufus Ingalls, aided by his corps and division chiefs, order was brought out of chaos—there was a uniform and efficient system, and good service. This was done on the march, and by the time the army reached Frederick it was well supplied, though its transportation was less than the usual allowance.[42]

The artillery was much disorganized. A number of batteries of the reserve were separated from their command and attached to troops not only of the Army of the Potomac but also to those of the Army of Virginia. Brigadier General Henry J. Hunt, who was designated chief of this arm of the service on September 5, as the army was entering Maryland, was "compelled to obtain on the roads the names and condition of the batteries and the troops to which they were attached." Not only were the batteries of the Army of the Potomac, brought from the Peninsula, dispersed and serving with other divisions than their own, but he had no knowledge of the artillery of the corps that had joined from the other armies other than what he could pick up on the road. "Many had not been refitted since the August campaign [under Pope]; some had lost more or less guns; others were deficient in men and horses, and a number were wholly unserviceable from all these causes combined." Hunt was an energetic and efficient chief and threw his whole soul into the work assigned him. His first measures were directed to procuring supplies of ammunition, of which several hundred wagon loads were ordered from the arsenal at Washington and reached the army at various points on its advance. Batteries were supplied from the artillery reserve to the corps and divisions deficient in guns, horses taken from the baggage train, and men temporarily detailed from the infantry. By the time the artillery reached the Antietam it was, all things considered, in very good condition. "Like the rest of the army," Hunt notes of this period that "the artillery may be said to have been organized on the march and in the intervals of conflict."[43]

The Confederate cavalry completely masked Lee's movements. It occupied every avenue of approach and resisted every attempt to drive it. From the Potomac on its right to the Baltimore and Ohio Railroad on the left, it covered Lee's entire front and no scout could penetrate it. Consequently there was a want of reliable information, and McClellan knew neither the strength, position, nor purpose of his adversary. Rumors of the most conflicting character came to him hourly, upon which he and his lieutenants built theories of the most plausible and irreconcilable kind. While a movement on Baltimore was regarded as entirely too hazardous, it was nevertheless borne in mind that Lee and his able lieutenants were prone

---

[40] Andrew G. Curtin to John A. Wright, September 11, 1862, 11:00 a.m., reprinted in *OR*, vol. 19, pt. 2, 267; Curtin to Lincoln, September 11, 1862, 3:30 p.m., reprinted in *OR*, vol. 19, pt. 2, 268; Curtin to Lincoln, September 11, 1862, reprinted in *OR*, vol. 19, pt. 2, 268.

[41] McClellan to Thomas, October 15, 1862, 25–26.

[42] Rufus Ingalls to Marcy, February 17, 1863, reprinted in *OR*, vol. 19, pt. 1, 94.

[43] Henry J. Hunt to Marcy, February 6, 1863, reprinted in *OR*, vol. 19, pt. 1, 205.

to make hazardous movements with great success. Lee's masterly movements in front of Richmond, by which McClellan had been driven to the James River, were keenly remembered, and Jackson's movement upon Manassas, in defiance of all ordinary rules of strategy, was not forgotten. There was nothing regarded as impossible to the Confederate leaders, who were men of military genius, quick to win campaigns by means not laid down in the art of war rather than suffer defeat by following systems laid down in the books. It is true that the Union army had able generals, but they were not the equals of the Confederate chiefs in singleness of purpose, fertile resource, and swiftness of execution. It is not venturing too much to assert that McClellan felt this; therefore we say that there were reasons for his deliberate advance.

Beyond the necessity for a reorganization of the artillery and the supply department and the ignorance of Lee's movements (which were so effectively screened by Stuart's cavalry), it should be borne in mind that the question of relieving Harper's Ferry was an embarrassing one, giving some occasion for delay. It should also be borne in mind that the orders and suggestions of Halleck were confusing—at times contradictory and unintelligible—and not easy to obey. McClellan's movements would have been much more rapid had he not been so tied to the telegraph wire that led from Halleck's office in Washington. Yet we see no good reason why he might not have advanced to the Monocacy as early as the tenth.

When McClellan took command in the field, he was careful to leave in the defenses of Washington a force sufficient to ensure its safety and quiet the fears of the administration. He had not forgotten his experience earlier in the year, when he was called to account for leaving what others thought to be an insufficient force on the Virginia side of the Potomac. He had not forgotten how his army had been sliced off by divisions and corps to rectify the errors attributed to him or to enlarge the commands of aspiring rivals, so when he left Washington on September 7, it was with the intention to leave intact those troops he had assigned for the defense of the capital. Nor had he asked for the troops under General Wool (in whose department he was now operating), including the garrison at Harper's Ferry and detachments at Baltimore and at other points in Maryland. Now he had come to the point where he thought he needed more men. His information led him to believe that Lee had not less than 120,000 men and was intent on giving battle. So, abandoning his purpose to ask no more men from the defenses of Washington, at noon of the eleventh he telegraphed Halleck to order Major General John J. Peck's division (from Major General John A. Dix's command at Fort Monroe) to move at once to Rockville upon its arrival from the Peninsula.[44] He also asked that one or two of the three corps on the Potomac opposite Washington be sent him.[45] In the following elaborate communication, McClellan sums up the situation and advises that Colonel Dixon S. Miles's force at Harper's Ferry be ordered to join him:

Headquarters
Camp near Rockville, Md., September 11, 1862

Maj. Gen. H. W. Halleck,
General-in-Chief:

General: At the time this army moved from Washington, it was not known what the intentions of the rebels were in placing their forces on this side of the Potomac. It might have been a feint to draw away our troops from Washington, for the purpose of throwing their main army into the city as soon as we were out of the way, or it might have been supposed to be precisely what they are now doing. In view of this uncertain condition of things, I left what I conceived to be a sufficient force to defend the city against any army they could bring against it from the Virginia side of the Potomac. This uncertainty, in my judgment, exists no longer. All the evidence that has been accumulated from various sources since we left Washington goes to prove most conclusively that almost the entire rebel army in Virginia, amounting to not less than 120,000 men, is in the vicinity of Frederick City. These troops, for the most part, consist of their oldest regiments, and are commanded by their best generals. Several brigades joined them yesterday, direct from Richmond, two deserters from which say that they saw no other troops between Richmond and Leesburg. Everything seems to indicate that they intend to hazard all upon the issue of the coming battle. They are probably aware that their forces are numerically superior to ours by at least 25 per cent. This, with the prestige of their recent successes, will, without doubt, inspire them with a confidence which will cause them to fight well. The momentous consequences involved in the struggle of the next few days impels me, at the risk of being considered slow and overcautious, to most earnestly recommend that every available man be at once added to this army.

I believe this army fully appreciates the importance of a victory at this time, and will fight well; but the result of a general battle, with such odds as the enemy now appears to have against us, might, to say the least, be doubtful; and if we should be defeated the consequences to the country would be disastrous in the extreme. Under these

[44] McClellan to Halleck, September 11, 1862, 12:00 p.m., reprinted in OR, vol. 19, pt. 2, 253.

[45] McClellan to Halleck, September 11, 1862, 3:45 p.m., reprinted in OR, vol. 19, pt. 2, 253.

circumstances, I would recommend that one or two of the three army corps now on the Potomac, opposite Washington, be at once withdrawn and sent to re-enforce this army. I would also advise that the force of Colonel Miles, at Harper's Ferry, where it can be of but little use, and is continually exposed to be cut off by the enemy, be immediately ordered here. This would add about 25,000 old troops to our present force, and would greatly strengthen us.

If there are any rebel forces remaining on the other side of the Potomac, they must be so few that the troops left in the forts, after the two corps shall have been withdrawn, will be sufficient to check them; and, with the large cavalry force now on that side kept well out in front to give warning of the distant approach of any very large army, a part of this army might be sent back within the intrenchments to assist in repelling an attack. But even if Washington should be taken while these armies are confronting each other, this would not, in my judgment, bear comparison with the ruin and disaster which would follow a signal defeat of this army. If we should be successful in conquering the gigantic rebel army before us, we would have no difficulty in recovering it. On the other hand, should their force prove sufficiently powerful to defeat us, would all the forces now around Washington be sufficient to prevent such a victorious army from carrying the works on this side of the Potomac, after they are uncovered by our army? I think not.

From the moment the rebels commenced the policy of concentrating their forces, and with their large masses of troops operating against our scattered forces, they have been successful. They are undoubtedly pursuing the same now, and are prepared to take advantage of any division of our troops in future. I, therefore, most respectfully, but strenuously, urge upon you the absolute necessity, at this critical juncture, of uniting all our disposable forces. Every other consideration should yield to this, and if we defeat the army now arrayed before us, the rebellion is crushed, for I do not believe they can organize another army. But if we should be so unfortunate as to meet with defeat, our country is at their mercy.

Very respectfully, your obedient servant,
Geo. B. McClellan,
Major-General[46]

To McClellan's request for Peck's division, Halleck replied within an hour that it would not arrive from the Peninsula for some days, but that Brigadier General Max Weber's brigade of the Seventh Corps, just arrived from Suffolk, Virginia, would be sent forward as soon as it could get transportation. Halleck also made this suggestion: "Why not order forward Porter's corps, or Sigel's? If the main force of the enemy is in your front, more troops can be spared from here."[47] McClellan was quick to act on the suggestion, and sent this dispatch to Halleck: "Please send forward all the troops you can spare from Washington, particularly Porter's, Heintzelman's, Sigel's, and all the other old troops. Please send them to Brookville [sic], via Leesborough, as soon as possible. General Banks reports 72,000 troops in and about Washington. If the enemy has left for Pennsylvania, I will follow him rapidly."[48] Halleck replied that Porter would be on the march next day to join him.[49] As for the rest, Lincoln himself dispatched, "This is explanatory. If Porter, Heintzelman, and Sigel were sent you, it would sweep everything from the other side of the river, because the new troops have been distributed among them, as I understand. Porter reports himself 21,000 strong, which can only be by the addition of new troops. He is ordered to-night to join you as quickly as possible. I am for sending you all that can be spared, and I hope others can follow Porter very soon."[50] Porter's two divisions—Morell's and Humphreys's—were put in motion. (Morell joined before the battle of Antietam, Humphreys the day after.)

Early on the eleventh, McClellan had sent this dispatch to Halleck:

Camp near Rockville
September 10, 1862—9.45 a.m.

Colonel Miles is at or near Harper's Ferry, as I understand, with 9,000 troops. He can do nothing where he is, but could be of great service if ordered to join me. I suggest that he be ordered at once to join me by the most practicable route.[51]

---

[46] McClellan to Halleck, September 11, 1862, reprinted in *OR*, vol. 19, pt. 2, 254–55.

[47] Halleck to McClellan, September 11, 1862, 1:00 p.m., reprinted in *OR*, pt. 19, pt. 2, 253.

[48] McClellan to Halleck, September 11, 1862, 3:45 p.m., 253.

[49] Halleck to McClellan, September 11, 1862, 9:00 p.m., reprinted in *OR*, pt. 19, pt. 2, 255.

[50] Lincoln to McClellan, September 11, 1862, 6:00 p.m., reprinted in *OR*, vol. 19, pt. 2, 253–54.

[51] McClellan to Halleck, September 11, 1862, 9:45 a.m., as contained in McClellan to Thomas, August 4, 1863, reprinted in *OR*, vol. 19, pt. 1, 43. In McClellan's report, he says this dispatch was sent on the morning of the tenth, but the compiler of the [*OR*] says it was September 11, according to the files of Headquarters of the Army.—*EAC*

To this Halleck would not consent. He would not retire Miles from Harper's Ferry, nor would he permit his transfer to McClellan's command until the forward march of the army opened communication with him. Halleck replied to McClellan, "There is no way for Colonel Miles to join you at present. His only chance is to defend his works till you can open communication with him. When you do so he will be subject to your orders."[52]

Had Halleck acceded to McClellan's request at this time and placed Miles under his command, this history would not be called upon to narrate the fall of Harper's Ferry and the loss of an army. Miles would have had orders to abandon the place and join McClellan in the field. Failing in that, he would have been ordered to concentrate everything on Maryland Heights, fortify, and hold out to the last—and he could have defied all effort of the Confederates to dislodge him until relieved by the advance of McClellan. But it was not to be.

The general advance ordered by McClellan for the twelfth was not made with the spirit demanded. Early in the day, the 6th New York Cavalry (Colonel Thomas C. Devin), attached temporarily to the Ninth Corps, was sent from New Market off to the right to cover that flank and to investigate the truth of reports that the enemy's cavalry were north of the column. Reno, moving directly from New Market with the advance of the Ninth Corps, arrived at Monocacy Bridge in the afternoon, and Cox's Kanawha Division was ordered to carry it. (The bridge was defended by two squadrons of Hampton's cavalry and a section of artillery.) Cox brought up a battery and engaged the Confederate guns while a regiment of infantry forced the cavalry back from the bridge, another regiment crossing the river by a ford a quarter of a mile to the right. As Cox had the advantage of position, opposition was soon overcome and the bridge carried and crossed. Colonel Augustus Moor's brigade, in the advance, was deployed on the right and left of the road, and Colonel Eliakim P. Scammon's brigade deployed in the second line, with Moor's 11th Ohio in column in the road.

We turn to the Confederates. When Lee marched from Frederick on the tenth, Stuart's cavalry was directed to remain south of the Monocacy to cover his movement and observe McClellan, but upon the general advance of the Union army (its right on the Baltimore and Ohio Railroad), Stuart was obliged to retire. On the morning of the eleventh, Fitzhugh Lee's Brigade fell back from New Market to Liberty and crossed the Monocacy above Frederick on the morning of the twelfth. Hampton's Brigade, falling back from Hyattstown and Urbana, occupied Frederick, with pickets thrown out on the various roads leading in the direction of the Union advance and two squadrons with artillery at Monocacy Bridge. About noon Hampton was notified of Cox's approach on the National Road and placed a squadron of the 2d South Carolina Cavalry to support the squadrons and battery at the bridge. This squadron was under the command of Lieutenant John Meighan, who now began skirmishing with Cox's advance, the Kanawha men replying with a fire that killed two of Meighan's men. Hampton withdrew his advance squadrons slowly to the town, sending his guns to occupy a position commanding the road from Frederick to the foot of Catoctin Mountain. As Hampton's men retired, they were followed by Moor's brigade, deployed on either side of the turnpike (Moor himself, with Captain Frederick Schambeck's troop of Chicago Dragoons and a gun of Captain Seth J. Simmonds's Kentucky battery, being in the road abreast his line). Moor's movement was too deliberate to suit the views of a young staff officer attached to corps headquarters, who volunteered some criticism that angered Moor. Thinking the criticism came from corps headquarters, Moor dashed ahead "at a gallop, with escort and staff, and the gun."[53] As he came to where the road turned, in the suburbs of town, he was brought to quick grief.

Hampton had seen Moor's movement; it was necessary to check it to ensure the orderly withdrawal of his brigade, and Colonel Matthew C. Butler of the 2d South Carolina Cavalry was ordered to make a counter-charge. Lieutenant Meighan's squadrons attacked (supported by the brigade provost guard of forty men, under Captain Joseph F. Waring), rode down, unhorsed, and captured Moor and seven others. Simmonds's gun was fired during the melee and capsized into a ditch, two men were killed, and the survivors of staff and escort went back in disorder. This sharp encounter protected Hampton's rear, and his brigade was slowly withdrawn to Middletown, leaving the Jeff Davis Legion and two guns, under Lieutenant Colonel William T. Martin, to hold the gap in Catoctin Mountain. As the rear of Hampton's cavalry went out at one end of the street, Cox's infantry came in at the other, passing through the town amid joyous shouts and the waving of miniature Union flags and handkerchiefs. It encamped in the suburbs, and other divisions of the corps moved up and bivouacked about the town.

Reynolds's division of the First Corps moved from Poplar Springs to Monocacy Bridge, King's division from Lisbon to New Market, and Ricketts's division from Cooksville to Ridgeville. The 3d Pennsylvania Cavalry pushed north to Unionville. The Second Corps moved from Clarksburg to Urbana, the Twelfth Corps from Damascus to Ijamsville Cross-Roads. On the left, Farnsworth's brigade of cavalry, with the regular horse batteries of Lieutenant Peter C. Hains and Captain James M. Robertson, pushed past Sugar Loaf Mountain and through Urbana to Frederick, Munford's Virginia cavalry

---

[52] Halleck to McClellan, September 11, 1862, as contained in "Record of the Harper's Ferry Military Commission," October 17, 1862, reprinted in *OR*, vol. 19, pt. 1, 758.

[53] Cox, "Forcing Fox's Gap and Turner's Gap," in *Battles and Leaders of the Civil War*, vol. 2 (New York: Century Co., 1887), 584.

falling back to the gap in the Catoctin at Jefferson. The Sixth Corps marched from Barnesville to Licksville Cross-Roads, Couch's division from Poolesville to Barnesville, and Sykes's division from Middlebrook to Urbana. Colonel Andrew T. McReynolds of the 1st New York Cavalry was put in charge of a brigade (consisting of his own regiment, the 8th Pennsylvania Cavalry, and a section of Hains's Battery M, 2d U.S. Artillery) and ordered to Gettysburg, for which place a body of Stuart's cavalry was reported moving.[54] Morell's division of the Fifth Corps, moving from Upton's Hill and Arlington, crossed the Potomac and, marching through Georgetown, went out on the Seventh Street Road as far as Silver Springs, where it bivouacked. The two brigades of Humphreys's division, those of Brigadier General Erastus B. Tyler and Colonel Peter H. Allabach, were ordered to start from their camps in Virginia and follow Morell.

Halleck directed Heintzelman, whom he had put in charge of the defenses on the Virginia side of the river, to ascertain by his cavalry the probable strength of the enemy south of the Potomac: "Should there be no immediate danger of an attack on that side of the river, I wish to send more forces to General McClellan."[55] Heintzelman could find no trace of an enemy near Washington nor could he hear of any considerable force south of the Potomac, but when McClellan ordered Banks (whom he had left in command of the defenses of Washington) to send from that place eight new regiments to relieve parts of Couch's command left at Offutt's Cross-Roads, Seneca Mills, and Conrad's and Edward's Ferries (their presence at these points being deemed "very necessary" to guard his left and rear),[56] Halleck interposed an objection and informed McClellan that Banks could not spare the regiments for that purpose, as nearly all new ones were being used to guard the railroad. In the same communication, he cautioned McClellan against moving from the river and thus uncovering the capital.[57]

Earlier in the day, McClellan advised Halleck that his columns were pushing on rapidly to Frederick and that he was confident that the enemy were "moving in two directions, viz., on the Hagerstown and Harper's Ferry roads."[58] Halleck dispatched in reply, "Is it not possible to open communication with Harper's Ferry, so that Colonel Miles' forces can cooperate with you?"[59] At 5:30 p.m. McClellan reported the movements of the day and said that cavalry had been sent toward Point of Rocks to ascertain whether there was any force of the enemy in that direction. "Should the enemy go toward Pennsylvania," he continued, "I shall follow him. Should he attempt to recross the Potomac I shall endeavor to cut off his retreat … The troops have marched to-day as far as it was possible and proper for them to move."[60] In a later dispatch, he informed Halleck that, in his orders of movement for the morrow, he had arranged so that he could go to or send to Miles's relief if necessary, but that he had heard no firing in that direction. If Miles made any resistance whatsoever, McClellan could relieve him and place his assailants in great peril of capture.[61]

If McClellan had any doubts as to Lee's movements, these were partially dispelled by the following dispatch:

> Washington City, D.C.
> September 12, 1862—5.45 p.m.
>
> Major-General McClellan:
> Governor Curtin telegraphs me:
>
>> I have advices that Jackson is crossing the Potomac at Williamsport, and probably the whole rebel army will be drawn from Maryland.
>
> Receiving nothing from Harper's Ferry or Martinsburg to-day, and positive information from Wheeling that the line is cut, corroborates the idea that the enemy is recrossing the Potomac. Please do not let him get off without being hurt.
>
> A. Lincoln[62]

McClellan replied that the main body of his cavalry and horse artillery were ordered after the enemy's main column with instructions to check its march as much as possible, in order that he might overtake it. If Harper's Ferry was still held, he

---

[54] In his manuscript, Carman says incorrectly that it was "Battery M, 5th U.S. Artillery." See Peter C. Hains to A. J. Cohen, September 26, 1862, reprinted in *OR*, vol. 51, pt. 1, 137.

[55] Halleck to Samuel P. Heintzelman, September 12, 1862, reprinted in *OR*, vol. 19, pt. 2, 274.

[56] McClellan to Halleck, September 12, 1862, 5:30 p.m., reprinted in *OR*, vol. 19, pt. 2, 271.

[57] Halleck to McClellan, September 13, 1862, 10:45 a.m., reprinted in *OR*, vol. 19, pt. 2, 280.

[58] McClellan to Halleck, September 12, 1862, 10:00 a.m., reprinted in *OR*, vol. 19, pt. 2, 270–71.

[59] Halleck to McClellan, September 12, 1862, 1:45 p.m., reprinted in *OR*, vol. 19, pt. 2, 271.

[60] McClellan to Halleck, September 12, 1862, 5:30 p.m., 271.

[61] McClellan to Halleck, September 12, 1862, 6:00 p.m., reprinted in *OR*, vol. 19, pt. 2, 272.

[62] Lincoln to McClellan, September 12, 1862, 5:45 p.m., reprinted in *OR*, vol. 19, pt. 2, 270.

thought he could save the garrison; if the enemy were really marching into Pennsylvania, he should "soon be up with them," but his apprehension was that they would make for Williamsport and get across the river before he could catch them.[63]

In explanation of the slowness and deliberation of his march to this point, McClellan says, "During these movements I had not imposed long marches on the columns. The absolute necessity of refitting and giving some little rest to troops worn down by previous long-continued marching and severe fighting, together with the uncertainty as to the actual position, strength, and intentions of the enemy, rendered it incumbent upon me to move slowly and cautiously until the headquarters reached Urbana, where I first obtained reliable information that the enemy's plan was to move upon Harper's Ferry and the Cumberland Valley, and not upon Baltimore, Washington, or Gettysburg."[64]

Referring to the position of affairs at Harper's Ferry and the orders to McClellan of the twelfth, Halleck reports:

As this campaign was to be carried on within the department commanded by Major-General Wool, I directed General McClellan to assume control of all troops within his reach, without regard to departmental lines. The garrisons of Winchester and Martinsburg had been withdrawn to Harper's Ferry, and the commanding officer of that post had been advised by my chief of staff to mainly confine his defense, in case he was attacked by superior forces, to the position of Maryland Heights, which could have been held a long time against overwhelming numbers. To withdraw him entirely from that position, with the great body of Lee's forces between him and our army, would not only expose the garrison to capture, but all the artillery and stores collected at that place must either be destroyed or left to the enemy. The only feasible plan was for him to hold his position until General McClellan could relieve him or open a communication so that he could evacuate it in safety. These views were communicated both to General McClellan and to Colonel Miles.[65]

In this same connection, McClellan reports:

It seems necessary for a distinct understanding of this matter to state that I was directed on the 12th to assume command of the garrison of Harper's Ferry as soon as I should open communications with that place, and that when I received this order all communication from the direction in which I was approaching was cut off. Up to that time, however, Colonel Miles could, in my opinion, have marched his command into Pennsylvania by crossing the Potomac at Williamsport or above, and this opinion was confirmed by the fact that Colonel [Benjamin F.] Davis marched the cavalry part of Colonel Miles' command from Harper's Ferry on the 14th, taking the main road to Hagerstown, and he encountered no enemy except a small picket near the mouth of the Antietam.

Before I left Washington, and when there certainly could have been no enemy to prevent the withdrawal of the forces of Colonel Miles, I recommended to the proper authorities that the garrison of Harper's Ferry should be withdrawn, via Hagerstown, to aid in covering the Cumberland Valley, or that, taking up the pontoon bridge and obstructing the railroad bridge, it should fall back to the Maryland Heights and there hold out to the last. In this position it ought to have maintained itself for many days.

It was not deemed proper to adopt either of these suggestions, and when the matter was left to my discretion it was too late for me to do anything but endeavor to relieve the garrison. I accordingly directed artillery to be fired by our advance at frequent intervals, as a signal that relief was at hand. This was done, and, as I afterwards learned, the reports of the cannon were distinctly heard at Harper's Ferry. It was confidently expected that Colonel Miles would hold out until we had carried the mountain passes and were in condition to send a detachment to his relief. The left was therefore ordered to move through Crampton's Pass in front of Burkittsville, while the center and right marched upon Turner's Pass in front of Middletown.[66]

On the night of the twelfth, McClellan knew that Harper's Ferry was in great danger and that Jackson, for some purpose not clearly known, had recrossed the Potomac near Williamsport. With this information in his possession, what did McClellan do on the thirteenth? Captain Sanders of the 6th U.S. Cavalry, who had reported his impression that Jackson was marching on Harper's Ferry,[67] was directed to push his scouts in the direction of that place. The 1st Rhode Island Cavalry, which had been sent from Arlington on the eleventh and arrived at Frederick on the twelfth, was sent to Seneca Mills and Poolesville early on the thirteenth to "watch all the fords from Seneca to the mouth of the Monocacy."[68]

---

[63] McClellan to Lincoln, September 12, 1862, 9:00 p.m., reprinted in *OR*, vol. 19, pt. 2, 272.

[64] McClellan to Thomas, October 15, 1862, 26–27.

[65] Halleck to Edwin M. Stanton, November 25, 1862, reprinted in *OR*, vol. 19, pt. 1, 4.

[66] McClellan to Thomas, August 4, 1863, 44.

[67] Marcy to Pleasonton, September 12, 1862, 8:45 p.m., reprinted in *OR*, vol. 51, pt. 1, 824.

[68] Marcy to "Commanding Officer, First Rhode Island Cavalry," September 13, 1862, 7:30 a.m., reprinted in *OR*, vol. 51, pt. 1, 830.

Before withdrawing from Frederick, Stuart ordered Fitzhugh Lee to feel the right and rear of McClellan's army to ascertain the strength and meaning of its movements, and that enterprising officer was now heard from at Liberty. Reports then came of his presence at Westminster, on the march to Gettysburg, upon which Pleasonton (as we have seen) detached McReynolds's brigade with a section of artillery to follow Fitzhugh Lee in the direction of the latter place. The 6th Pennsylvania Cavalry (Rush's Lancers), supported by Colonel Harrison S. Fairchild's brigade of Brigadier General Isaac P. Rodman's division of the Ninth Corps, was sent to Jefferson as reinforcement for Franklin's column, with which the 6th U.S. Cavalry and a battery of horse artillery were then acting. With the remainder of his command, Pleasonton pushed out of Frederick on the National Road at daylight and had gone some three or four miles when Colonel Martin—who, with the Jeff Davis Legion and two guns of Captain James P. Hart's (South Carolina) Battery, had been left the night before on the road, where it passes over the Catoctin at Fairview—opened on Pleasonton's advance with his artillery, supported on either side of the road by his dismounted cavalry, favorably posted on the crest of the ridge. Two sections from Robertson's and Hains's batteries were run forward and opened on Hart's two guns. Some squadrons of the 3d Indiana Cavalry and the 8th Illinois Cavalry were dismounted and sent up the ridge to the right as skirmishers, with the 1st Massachusetts Cavalry in support on the road.

McClellan's movements on the twelfth were not understood by Stuart, who was watching him and guarding Lee's rear. All means were taken to ascertain their character—whether it was a reconnaissance, feeling for an opening, or an aggressive movement of the entire army. What information he did receive—notice of the occupation of Frederick by Burnside's advance and his probable forward movement the next day—was promptly conveyed to D. H. Hill (then at Boonsboro), and Stuart added to the information the suggestion that the gap over the Catoctin, held by Martin, was a very strong position for infantry and artillery. The orders under which Stuart was acting, in common with other subordinate commanders, contemplated the capture of Harper's Ferry on the twelfth or thirteenth, and, as the garrison was not believed to be strong at that point, he supposed it had already fallen—and then no importance would attach to the mountain gaps. But, as he had received no intelligence from Harper's Ferry, he felt it important to check McClellan as much as possible and develop his force. So, on the morning of the thirteenth, he ordered Hampton to return from Middletown and support Martin in holding the gap in Catoctin Mountain while Fitzhugh Lee was feeling McClellan's right. Hampton moved as ordered, but it does not appear that he became actively engaged, leaving the fight to Martin, who conducted it with great skill, spirit, and persistency. Martin's skirmishers became actively engaged, and Hart's guns annoyed the Union batteries, causing them to make many changes of position.[69]

After some severe artillery firing and much brisk skirmishing, Pleasonton's skirmishers gained a position commanding Hart's guns as well as the road at about 2:00 p.m., upon which Hampton retired the two guns to near Middletown, barricaded the road in several places, and drew up his entire brigade in rear of the guns. Pleasonton followed in pursuit, taking a number of prisoners, and came up to Hampton's second stand east of Middletown. Captain Horatio G. Gibson's regular battery was brought up and indulged in a hot exchange of artillery fire. The skirmishers also became engaged once more and the action continued a few minutes, when Stuart, having held his enemy in check sufficiently long to accomplish his purpose (to give Hill time to occupy Turner's Gap), again fell back, his rear covered by Colonel Lawrence S. Baker's 1st North Carolina Cavalry. Farnsworth's entire brigade then advanced and drove Baker through Middletown and down the long slope, which terminated at Catoctin Creek, a lovely stream winding through the valley to the Potomac. Here Baker made a stand. A section each of Gibson's and Hains's batteries engaged him and there was some skirmishing, but, in a few minutes, Baker blew up and destroyed the bridge over the creek and retreated rapidly to Turner's Gap in South Mountain. As the creek was easily fordable, the destruction of the bridge did not long delay Pleasonton's advance to the foot of the mountain, which he found too strong a position to be carried by his cavalry. He sent back to Burnside for some infantry and while awaiting its arrival pushed some dismounted men ahead to reconnoiter.

When Stuart arrived at the east foot of Turner's Gap, he found—much to his relief—that Hill had occupied it with infantry (Colonel Alfred H. Colquitt's Brigade) in response to his suggestion, whereupon Stuart ordered Hampton's Brigade, with the exception of the Jeff Davis Legion and the two guns of Hart's Battery, to reinforce Colonel Munford at Crampton's Gap. (This was considered by Stuart to be the weakest part of his line—and necessary to be held for the protection of the rear of McLaws, who had gone through Brownsville Gap, one mile south, into Pleasant Valley on the way to Maryland Heights.) Stuart remained at Turner's Gap to put Colquitt's Brigade in position on the eastern slope of South Mountain. Colonel Thomas L. Rosser (who, with the 5th Virginia Cavalry and two guns of Pelham's [Virginia] Battery, had left New Market on the morning of the eleventh, and moved through Liberty, Unionville, New Windsor, Westminster, Union, Middleburg, Utica, and Hamburg, reaching Boonsboro after dark on the thirteenth) was thrown forward during the night to Fox's Gap

---

[69] Stuart to Chilton, 816.

on Colquitt's right. Meanwhile, Fitzhugh Lee, with three regiments of his brigade, was north and west of Frederick, endeavoring to ascertain the strength and intention of McClellan's movements.

Munford (who, on the afternoon of the twelfth, had been ordered to occupy the gap in the Catoctin near Jefferson) had only two regiments—the 2d and the 12th Virginia Cavalry, the rest of the brigade being on detached service. (Two regiments had not crossed the Potomac with him, and, two days before, the 7th Virginia Cavalry went with Jackson in his movement against Harper's Ferry.) Union troops began skirmishing with him on the morning of the thirteenth and continued the entire day. Captain Sanders and the 6th U.S. Cavalry advanced by the main road from Licksville. Later in the day, the 6th Pennsylvania Cavalry, supported by Fairchild's brigade of infantry and the battery of the 9th New York,[70] moved from Frederick by the road, leading over a gap, that intersects the one leading to Middletown about one mile and a half north of Jefferson. Fairchild deployed the 89th and 103d New York and advanced skirmishing, with the 9th New York in reserve. At the same time, Sanders on the left made his presence known on the Licksville Road. Munford was too feeble to resist this pressure and fell back to Burkittsville, encumbered with his brigade train and pursued nearly the whole way by the Union cavalry. Colonel Harman was hastened to Burkittsville with the 12th Virginia Cavalry to protect the main road leading directly from Jefferson to that point and to ensure the passage of the wagon train over Crampton's Gap, while Munford, with the sharpshooters of the 2d Virginia Cavalry (under Captain Thomas B. Holland), disputed the Union advance. Holland gradually yielded ground, then finally made a dash at his pursuers and checked them until an advantageous position had been secured for the artillery on the mountainside beyond Burkittsville. Getting his train safely over Crampton's Gap, Munford placed three guns in position and awaited the Union approach, which was expected momentarily.

While Pleasonton, with the main body of his cavalry, was advancing to the foot of Turner's Gap, a detachment of Farnsworth's brigade consisting of one squadron of the 8th Illinois Cavalry and a part of the 3d Indiana Cavalry (all under the command of Major William H. Medill of the 8th) left Middletown to reconnoiter in the direction of Harper's Ferry. The detachment took the road leading through Burkittsville. At the same time, Hampton, with his cavalry brigade, was moving from Turner's Gap to Crampton's Gap by the road running near the foot of the mountain—unaware of the pressure under which Munford was laboring and of the presence of an enemy near his own line of march. When near Crampton's Gap, he saw the Union cavalry on a road parallel to the one on which he was moving. Hampton ordered Lieutenant Colonel Pierce M. B. Young to charge it with the cavalry battalion of Cobb's Legion. The order was carried out in gallant style, Young dispersing the body and capturing prisoners from both the 3d and the 8th. Hampton's loss was four killed and nine wounded; the Union loss was about the same. This attack gave needed relief to Munford. Fairchild's brigade withdrew under orders from Reno and was returning to Frederick, and the 6th Pennsylvania Cavalry moved to the vicinity of Broad Run Village. The road was now clear for Hampton, who, as he drew near from the direction in which Munford was looking for an attack, was not recognized by him. Waiting until the head of Hampton's column was within easy range, Munford's guns were shotted and the lanyards applied when, fortunately, Hampton perceived the intention and, raising a white flag, made himself known as a friend. He bivouacked at the foot of the gap.

The 3d Pennsylvania Cavalry, which had advanced to Unionville on the twelfth in pursuit of Fitzhugh Lee's cavalry, marched on the thirteenth to Woodsborough, Creagerstown, and Emmitsburg, returning to Frederick on the fourteenth.

While the Union cavalry was pushing the Confederates from Catoctin Mountain and across the valley to South Mountain, the infantry columns slowly and cautiously advanced. The Ninth Corps, following Pleasonton, marched to and near Middletown; King's and Ricketts's divisions of the First Corps closed up to Reynolds's on the Monocacy (a distance of sixteen miles); the Second Corps moved from Urbana to Frederick; and the Twelfth Corps from Ijamsville Cross-Roads to Frederick (five miles)—all these covering the direct road from Frederick to Washington. The Sixth Corps, continuing its movement by way of Barnesville, reached Buckeystown. Couch's division replaced Franklin at Licksville and went into camp after a march of five miles. Sykes's division and the reserve artillery, which habitually moved with it, pushed on from Urbana to Frederick. Morell's division marched through Rockville to Middlebrook, and its advance pushed on to Seneca Creek.

The welcome extended by the citizens of Frederick to the Union army was not confined to the enthusiastic demonstration given the Ninth Corps. The Second Corps marched through the town on the morning of the thirteenth, and its reception is told by its gifted historian:

> Probably no soldier who entered Frederick on the morning of the 13th will ever forget the cordial welcome with which the rescuing army was received by the loyal inhabitants. For five months the Second Corps had been upon the soil of Virginia, where every native white face was wrinkled with spite as the "invaders" passed; marching through or

---

[70] One company of the 9th New York (Company K) was actually a battery of naval howitzers under the command of Captain James R. Whiting. Carman makes this clearer in Chapter 20. See pp. 338–39 passim.

encamping in a region which, to a Northern eye, was inconceivably desolate and forlorn, barren fields affording the only relief to the dreary continuity of tangled thickets and swampy bottoms. Here, in the rich valley of the Monocacy, shut in by low mountains of surpassing grace of outline, all nature was in bloom; the signs of comfort and opulence met the eye on every side; while, as the full brigades of Sumner, in perfect order and with all the pomp of war, with glittering staffs and proud commanders, old Sumner at the head, pressed through the quaint and beautiful town, the streets resounded with applause, and from balcony and window fair faces smiled, and handkerchiefs and scarfs [*sic*] waved to greet the army of the Union. Whether the ancient and apocryphal Barbara Fritchie had sufficiently recovered from the sentimental shock of a poetical shower of imaginary musket-balls to appear again on this occasion may be doubted; but many an honest and many a fair countenance of patriot man and patriot woman looked out upon the brave array of Sumner's corps with smiles and tears of gratitude and joy. Amid all that was desolate and gloomy; amid all that was harsh and terrible, in the service these soldiers of the Union were called to render, that bright day of September 13, 1862, that gracious scene of natural beauty and waving crops, that quaint and charming Southern city, that friendly greeting, form a picture which can never pass out of the memory of any whose fortune it was to enter Frederick town that day.[71]

McClellan's deliberate marches during this campaign have been severely (and, in many cases, unjustly) criticized, but, slow and deliberate as they were, they were too rapid to please Halleck, who trembled for the safety of Washington as McClellan's columns receded from it. So while McClellan's cavalry was driving Stuart's from Fairview Gap in Catoctin Mountain, Halleck, in his office at Washington, was preparing this dispatch, which was received by McClellan during the day: "Until you know more certainly the enemy's force south of the Potomac, you are wrong in thus uncovering the capital. I am of opinion that the enemy will send a small column toward Pennsylvania, so as to draw your forces in that direction; then suddenly move on Washington with the forces south of the Potomac and those he may cross over. In your letter of the 10th [11th?—*OR* editors] you attach too little importance to the capital. I assure you that you are wrong. The capture of this place will throw us back six months, if it should not destroy us. Beware of the evils I now point out to you."[72] Halleck repeated his caution on the fourteenth: "Scouts report a large force still on the Virginia side of the Potomac … I fear you are exposing your left and rear."[73] (Not as affecting the immediate movements of McClellan, but to show the apprehension of Halleck, we anticipate our narrative by giving in this place a dispatch received by McClellan on the afternoon of the sixteenth, when he was facing Lee on the Antietam: "As you give me no information in regard to the position of your forces, except that at Sharpsburg, of course I cannot advise. I think, however, you will find that the whole force of the enemy in your front has crossed the river. I fear now more than ever that they will recross at Harper's Ferry or below, and turn your left, thus cutting you off from Washington. This has appeared to me to be a part of their plan, and hence my anxiety on the subject."[74])

Halleck denies that he cautioned McClellan that he was moving too precipitately or too far from Washington. In his testimony before the Committee on the Conduct of the War, he says, "In respect to General McClellan going too fast or too far from Washington, there can be found no such telegram from me to him. He had mistaken the meaning of the telegrams I sent him. I telegraphed him that he was going too far, not from Washington, but from the Potomac, leaving General Lee the opportunity to come down the Potomac and get between him and Washington. I thought General McClellan should keep more on the Potomac, and press forward his left rather than his right, so as the more readily to relieve Harper's Ferry."[75]

McClellan retorts that he can find no telegram from Halleck ordering him to keep his left flank nearer the Potomac, nor do the records show such instructions. Commenting upon Halleck's dispatches, McClellan says:

> The importance of moving with all due caution so as not to uncover the National Capital until the enemy's position and plans were developed was, I believe, fully appreciated by me, and as my troops extended from the Baltimore and Ohio Railroad to the Potomac, with the extreme left flank moving along that stream, and with strong pickets left in rear to watch and guard all the available fords, I did not regard my left or rear as in any degree exposed. But it appears from the foregoing telegrams that the General-in-Chief was of a different opinion, and that my movements were, in his judgment, too precipitate, not only for the safety of Washington but also for the security of my left and rear.

[71] Francis A. Walker, *History of the Second Army Corps in the Army of the Potomac* (New York: Charles Scribner's Sons, 1887), 93–94.

[72] Halleck to McClellan, September 13, 1862, 10:45 a.m., reprinted in *OR*, vol. 19, pt. 2, 280–81.

[73] Halleck to McClellan, September 14, 1862, contained in McClellan to Thomas, August 4, 1863, 41. Carman leaves an important qualifier out of the quotation. As reported by McClellan, Halleck's second sentence reads, "*If so*, I fear you are exposing your left and rear [emphasis added]." McClellan himself also misquotes the message. The original dispatch appears elsewhere in the *OR* and reads, "Scouts report a large force still on Virginia side of the Potomac, near Leesburg. If so, I fear you are exposing your left *flank, and that the enemy can cross in your rear* [emphases added]." Halleck to McClellan, September 14, 1862, 1:30 p.m., reprinted in *OR*, vol. 19, pt. 2, 289.

[74] Halleck to McClellan, September 16, 1862, 12:30 p.m., as contained in McClellan to Thomas, August 4, 1863, 41.

[75] *Report of the Joint Committee on the Conduct of the War*, 37th Cong., 3d sess., 1863, S. Rep. 108, pt. 1, serial 1152, 451–52.

… My left, from the time I left Washington, always rested on the Potomac, and my center was continually in position to re-enforce the left or right, as occasion might require. Had I advanced my left flank along the Potomac more rapidly than the other columns marched upon the roads to the right, I should have thrown that flank out of supporting distance of the other troops and greatly exposed it, and if I had marched the entire army in one column along the bank of the river, instead of upon five different parallel roads, the column, with its trains, would have extended about 50 miles, and the enemy might have defeated the advance before the rear could have reached the scene of action. Moreover, such a movement would have uncovered the communications with Baltimore and Washington on our right and exposed our right and rear. I presume it will be admitted by every military man that it was necessary to move the army in such order that it could at any time be concentrated for battle and I am of opinion that this object could not have been accomplished in any other way than the one employed. Any other disposition of our forces would have subjected them to defeat in detached fragments.[76]

Elsewhere McClellan writes, "Very few in the Army of the Potomac doubted the favorable result of the next collision with the Confederate army, but in other quarters not a little doubt prevailed, and the desire for very rapid movements, so loudly expressed after the result was gained, did not make itself heard during the movements preceding the battles; quite the contrary was the case, as I was more than once cautioned that I was moving too rashly and exposing the capital to an attack from the Virginia side."[77]

Considering the uncertainty of Lee's movements, the overestimate of his strength, and the apprehensions of Halleck and his warning dispatches, McClellan's excuses for deliberate movements are valid, but on the thirteenth, by good fortune, he was put in possession of information that made everything clear—he emerged from the darkness in which he had been groping. Upon his arrival at Frederick, he was handed a copy of Lee's Special Orders No. 191, giving in detail the movements and position of every division of Lee's army and above all that Jackson, McLaws, and Walker were surrounding the garrison at Harper's Ferry. How that order came into his possession and the means taken by McClellan to relieve Harper's Ferry shall be told elsewhere.

The appearance of the Confederate army in Maryland caused intense excitement throughout the state and beyond its borders. Baltimore was in a fever when it became known that the Potomac had been crossed, and excitement increased when it was reported that Lee had reached Frederick and that the scouts of Stuart's cavalry were on the roads heading to Baltimore. There were apprehensions on the part of Union men and hopes indulged in by the secessionists that Lee would march on the city. (Rumors to that effect were freely circulated.) Collisions on the street were frequent and more serious trouble was anticipated. Four hundred special policemen were sworn in, and the mayor requested the citizens to assemble and form themselves into military companies for the defense of the city. Prominent citizens published a request to all those who desired to join an independent military company, to be called the "Maryland Line," to register their names at the Post Office, and on September 8 Governor Bradford issued a proclamation stating that the Confederates had crossed the border and calling upon the citizens of the state to organize and assist in defending "our homes and firesides against the assault of the invader." The governor could arm and equip all the cavalry that would probably be offered but was short of arms for infantry. He hoped that the loyal citizens would not wait for arms but organize everywhere without delay and "assist in driving from the State the invading host that now occupies its soil, armed with any weapon which opportunity may furnish."[78]

General Wool, commanding the military department which included Baltimore, was instructed by Halleck that he had "full power for every emergency, and must exercise it for the maintenance of order in the city."[79] Brigadier General John R. Kenly was ordered to report to Wool "to organize and command a brigade of new troops."[80] (Under this order, Kenly was assigned the duty of organizing the 1st, 4th, 6th, 7th, and 8th Regiments of Maryland volunteers, then in process of formation near the city, and Captain Frederick W. Alexander's Baltimore Light Artillery.) Wool was not apprehensive that Lee would march on Baltimore, but took all precautionary measures, planned some additional works, and reported to that there were four roads by which the enemy could enter the city; if they did enter, he would prevent their occupying it "longer than to pass through it."[81] (The explanation of the latter part of Wool's report is found in the fact that the forts of Baltimore, as

---

[76] McClellan to Thomas, August 4, 1863, 41–42.

[77] McClellan, *Own Story*, 551.

[78] Carman's particular source is unknown, but the full text is reprinted as "Proclamation of Gov. Bradford," *Baltimore Sun*, September 9, 1862.

[79] W. P. Jones to John E. Wool, September 6, 1862, reprinted in *OR*, vol. 19, pt. 2, 198.

[80] Headquarters of the Army, Adjutant General's Office, Special Orders No. 225, September 6, 1862, reprinted in *OR*, vol. 19, pt. 2, 199.

[81] Wool to McClellan, September 9, 1862, reprinted in *OR*, vol. 19, pt. 2, 231. See also Wool to Stanton, September 9, 1862, 7:50 p.m., reprinted in *OR*, vol. 19, pt. 2, 232.

well as some war vessels, were in readiness to lay the city in ashes in case of a secession outbreak or its occupation by the Confederate army.)

Notwithstanding the loyal resolutions and acts of the legislature, the action of the patriotic citizens of the state in swelling the ranks of the army of the Union, and the patriotic responses made by the citizens of Baltimore to the appeal of Governor Bradford and the mayor of the city, the military authorities had much mistrust of the strength of that loyalty. Wool, whom it was proposed to transfer to Pennsylvania to concert measures for the defense of that state, thought his absence from the city would lead to the most serious consequences.[82] General Dix, who was more than two months in command in the city, suggested that Federal Hill and other points should be more strongly fortified, as there was "no city in the Union" in which domestic disturbances had been "more frequent or carried to more fatal extremes." Although the great body of the people were "eminently distinguished for their moral virtues," there was in its midst "a mass of inflammable material" liable to ignite "on the slightest provocation." A city so prone to burst into flames should be controlled by the strong arm of the Federal government.[83] But there was no trouble in Baltimore. The increase in the police force, free enrollment of citizens in volunteer companies, and the repressive measures of Wool[84] gave quiet to the city. General Lee, meanwhile, was preparing to move in an opposite direction.

Lee's entrance into Maryland was the signal for intense excitement in Pennsylvania, particularly on her southern border and in the cities of Harrisburg and Philadelphia. The farmers, who had well-filled barns and fine livestock, trembled for their safety, and every effort was made to remove everything as far as possible from the grasp of the invader. Governor Curtin appealed to Washington for assistance and was assured that the military authorities would see to it that the Confederates should be checked long before they could reach Harrisburg.[85] To the request that disciplined troops should be sent from the Army of the Potomac, Baltimore, or Washington, the reply was made that it was not possible to send them. Lincoln argued that the true defense of Harrisburg was to strengthen the column that, under McClellan, was marching on the enemy in Maryland,[86] and the suggestion was made that the men of the state should be called out and concentrated at or near Chambersburg.[87] Brigadier General Andrew Porter was ordered to report to Governor Curtin to organize volunteers and take measures for the defense of Harrisburg.[88]

The citizens of Philadelphia were thoroughly alarmed and appealed for help. Prominent men asked the president to send them a general of known energy and capacity, "one who combines the sagacity of the statesman with the acuteness and skill of the soldier,"[89] to which Stanton gave answer, "If you know or have heard of any officer coming up anywhere near your description of the one you need, please make me happy by naming him, and I will make you happy by assigning him to your city."[90] Major General Ormsby M. Mitchell was then suggested as the very man for the emergency,[91] but Stanton thought he "would not begin to fill the bill"—and besides, he was required with his command in the South. However, General Wool, whose command embraced Pennsylvania, was ordered to Philadelphia.[92] Wool objected; he thought that Philadelphia was in no danger whatever, while Baltimore was threatened from within and without, and it would be extremely hazardous to relinquish his command of the city under the intense excitement then prevailing. His objection availed and General Reynolds was then asked for. Halleck inquired of McClellan if he could be spared.[93] McClellan objected to the detachment of one of his best division commanders, then on important service in the very face of the enemy,[94] but his objection was overruled by Halleck's curt dispatch: "General Reynolds' division can be commanded by some one else. He has been designated for

---

[82] Wool to Halleck, September 10, 1862, 9:55 p.m., reprinted in *OR*, vol. 19, pt. 2, 246.

[83] John A. Dix to Halleck, September 15, 1862, reprinted in *OR*, vol. 19, pt. 2, 304–5.

[84] Carman is ungenerous to Wool, who during this time was complaining to Halleck about military arrests of civilians in Baltimore on "mere suspicion." See Wool to Halleck, September 13, 1862, reprinted in *OR*, vol. 19, pt. 2, 286; Headquarters Eighth Army Corps, Middle Department, General Orders No. 30, September 1, 1862, reprinted in *OR*, vol. 19, pt. 2, 286–87.

[85] Carman here may have overstated the confidence of the Washington authorities. A message from Stanton told the governor that it was "*now more than probable* the enemy will be *struck* long before they can reach Harrisburg [emphasis added]." Stanton to Curtin, September 7, 1862, 7:30 p.m., reprinted in *OR*, vol. 19, pt. 2, 204. The secretary of war's qualifier as to likelihood aside, attacking an army is not synonymous with stopping it.

[86] Stanton to Wool, September 8, 1862, reprinted in *OR*, vol. 19, pt. 2, 215.

[87] McClellan to Curtin, September 10, 1862, 10:30 p.m., reprinted in *OR*, vol. 19, pt. 2, 248.

[88] See John C. Kelton to Andrew Porter, September 7, 1862, and McClellan's endorsement of the same date, reprinted in *OR*, vol. 19, pt. 2, 203.

[89] Thomas Webster, Morton McMichael, and John W. Forney to Stanton, September 10, 1862, 10:02 a.m., reprinted in *OR*, vol. 19, pt. 2, 251.

[90] Stanton to Webster, McMichael, and Forney, September 10, 1862, reprinted in *OR*, vol. 51, pt. 1, 813.

[91] Webster, McMichael, and Forney to Stanton, September 10, 1862, 2:45 p.m., reprinted in *OR*, vol. 19, pt. 2, 251. See also B. Gerhard and William H. Allen to Lincoln and Stanton, September 10, 1862, 1:20 p.m., reprinted in *OR*, vol. 19, pt. 2, 251.

[92] Stanton to Webster, McMichael, and Forney, September 10, 1862, reprinted in *OR*, vol. 19, pt. 2, 251.

[93] Halleck to McClellan, September 11, 1862, 10:20 a.m., reprinted in *OR*, vol. 19, pt. 2, 252.

[94] McClellan to Halleck, September 11, 1862, 10:45 a.m., reprinted in *OR*, vol. 19. pt. 2, 252.

other duty, and must report here immediately."[95] Reynolds was commanding a division in Hooker's corps, and that impetuous officer made a vigorous protest and advised McClellan not to heed Halleck's order, that "a sacred Governor ought not to be permitted to destroy the usefulness of an entire division of the army, on the eve of important operation ... It is only in the United States that atrocities like this are entertained." Hooker expressed an emphatic belief that the rebels "had no more intention of going to Harrisburg than they have of going to heaven."[96]

On September 10 Governor Curtin called for fifty thousand men to rally for the defense of the state; on the morning of that same day, Jackson left Frederick, moving northward. Swift-footed rumor ran that the Confederates, two hundred thousand strong, "ragged and filthy, but full of fight," were moving on Harrisburg and Philadelphia.[97] Consternation and dismay reigned on the border and panic took possession of the governor, who advised Lincoln to put strong guards on the railway lines between Washington and Harrisburg, send "not less than 80,000 disciplined men" over to the last named place, and order from New York and the eastern states every available man to hasten to Harrisburg, where Curtin would concentrate in a few days as many of the Pennsylvania militia as he could muster. It was the "only hope to save the North and crush the rebel army." The governor did not wish it supposed for one instant that he was unnecessarily alarmed; he believed Harrisburg in great danger, as his engineers, who had examined west of the Susquehanna, reported that defensive works could not be erected to stand against fifty thousand men—and the enemy would bring against the city not less than 120,000, with much artillery. He concluded by advising the president that "the time for decided action by the National Government has arrived."[98] To which, Lincoln promptly replied that he did not have in excess of eighty thousand disciplined troops east of the mountains, and most of them, with many of the new regiments, were then close in the rear of the enemy supposed to be invading Pennsylvania. "Start half of them to Harrisburg," the president warned, "and the enemy will turn upon and beat the remaining half, and then reach Harrisburg before the part going there, and beat it, too, when it comes. The best possible security for Pennsylvania is putting the strongest force possible into the enemy's rear."[99] The mayor of Philadelphia shared in the dire apprehensions of the governor of the state and wanted a general to command in the city. He was assured by Lincoln that Halleck had made the best provision he could for generals in Pennsylvania, and the president hoped he would not take offense at his assurance that Philadelphia was in no danger. It was "more than 150 miles from Hagerstown. and could not be reached by the rebel army in ten days, if no hindrance was interposed."[100]

Nor was the partial panic confined to Pennsylvania and its chief cities. The mayor of New York City was apprehensive of a visit of one or two Confederate ironclads from Europe at any moment and requested heavy guns for the defense of the harbor and men to handle them.

[95] Halleck to McClellan, September 11, 1862, 1:55 p.m., reprinted in *OR*, vol. 19, pt. 2, 252.
[96] Joseph Hooker to Seth Williams, September 12, 1862, reprinted in *OR*, vol. 19, pt. 2, 273–74.
[97] Curtin to McClellan, September 10, 1862, 10:00 a.m., reprinted in *OR*, vol. 19, pt. 2, 248.
[98] Curtin to Lincoln, September 11, 1862, reprinted in *OR*, vol. 19, pt. 2, 268.
[99] Lincoln to Curtin, September 12, 1862, 10:35 a.m., reprinted in *OR*, vol. 19, pt. 2, 276.
[100] Lincoln to Alexander Henry, September 12, 1862, *OR*, vol. 19, pt. 2, 278.

Harper's Ferry is beautifully situated at the confluence of the Potomac and Shenandoah rivers, where these streams, uniting, burst through the barriers of the Blue Ridge and roll their waters to the ocean. Thomas Jefferson said that the boldness and beauty of the view was worth a voyage across the Atlantic. At an early period, the government established an arsenal and armory at this point, and much importance was attached to it as a military post. It was thought to be of great strategic value. The town itself is on the tongue of land at the junction of the Potomac and the Shenandoah, which gradually rises to a table of land about five hundred feet above the river level. It is completely commanded by Maryland Heights beyond the Potomac, Loudoun Heights across the Shenandoah, and by Bolivar Heights on the west—these three heights being separated from each other by a distance of nearly three miles. Although regarded during the first two years of the war as a place of great strategic importance, it was in fact a death trap. It was not defensible and could not be held by a garrison that did not absorb more men than could be spared for such a purpose. It was urged that its occupation was necessary for the protection of the railroad and the canal running through it; both of these could have been cut elsewhere and whenever necessary. It was considered highly important to hold it because it was the debouch from Virginia into Maryland, but the Confederates had no occasion to pass through it, as good roads and fords led into Maryland above and below it. Its defects and dangers as a military position were recognized early by the Confederate officers. The Union authorities came to the same conclusion at a later day, after much dear and mortifying experience.

Simultaneously with the secession of Virginia, Harper's Ferry—with the U.S. arsenal, armory, arms, and munitions of war—was seized by Virginia troops. Jackson, who came to the command, determined to hold possession "with the spirit which actuated the defenders of Thermopylae," but he saw that Maryland Heights was the key to the position.[1] This he proceeded to occupy and fortify in the face of the caution of Lee, then commanding the Virginia troops, who wrote him that it was "considered advisable not to intrude upon the soil of Maryland," lest it might interrupt the friendly relations with that state and arouse a spirit of hostility to the Confederate cause.[2] But Lee was of Jackson's opinion that Harper's Ferry should be strongly held; he opposed the suggestion of abandoning it as a measure depressing to the Southern cause.[3] He was aware that the position could be easily turned by crossing the Potomac at Williamsport and Shepherdstown, thus threatening the communications of the garrison with Winchester, but he would be prepared to take a strong offensive against any such movement.

Joseph E. Johnston succeeded Jackson in command in the latter part of May 1861 and promptly reported the place as untenable against a large force moving on it. He proposed to abandon it and take position at Winchester, but Davis objected. A few days later, when Patterson advanced from Chambersburg, Pennsylvania, toward the Potomac, Johnston, not intending to be caught in a trap, promptly abandoned the position and retired to Winchester. At the same time, he destroyed all the bridges on the Potomac as far up as Williamsport.

After the Confederates abandoned the place, it was reoccupied by the Union forces, the military authorities attaching much importance to its retention as a protection to the railroad and the canal passing through it and as the eastern debouch of the Shenandoah Valley. On March 29, 1862, Colonel Dixon S. Miles (2d U.S. Infantry) was assigned to the protection of the Baltimore and Ohio Railroad from Baltimore to the western limits of the Department of the Potomac, with headquarters at Harper's Ferry. This assignment by McClellan was continued by Wool when he came to the command of the Eighth Army Corps, with headquarters at Baltimore. Wool soon relieved Miles of the care of the railroad from Baltimore to Point of Rocks but put him in special charge of Harper's Ferry, the railroad immediately west of it, and the railroad east to Point of Rocks. Miles had disgraced himself at the first battle of Bull Run, where he was in command of one of the reserve divisions and had shown an utter lack of military capacity.[4] Wool says, "I did not think he had the capacity to embrace so large a command as

---

[1] Thomas J. Jackson to Robert E. Lee, May 7, 1861, reprinted in *OR*, vol. 2, 814.

[2] Lee to Jackson, May 9, 1861, reprinted in *OR*, vol. 2, 822.

[3] Lee to Joseph E. Johnston, June 3, 1862, reprinted in *OR*, vol. 2, 901.

[4] Accused of being intoxicated during the battle of Manassas, Miles requested and received a court of inquiry into the matter, which held that, although a fellow officer was "justified in applying the term drunkenness" to Miles's condition, evidence sufficient for a conviction in a court-martial could not be found. Headquarters Army of the Potomac, General Orders No. 42, November 6, 1861, reprinted in *OR*, vol. 2, 438–39.

he had there; but he appeared to be very zealous … Indeed, he was the only one I could place there, the only regular officer."[5] Why a confessedly incompetent regular officer should be preferred to a good volunteer does not appear.

While McClellan was operating on the Peninsula and Pope in front of Washington, outposts were kept at Winchester and Martinsburg to hold the lower Valley and protect the Baltimore and Ohio Railroad. There was only a small force at Martinsburg but a brigade under the command of Brigadier General Julius White was stationed at Winchester. White had been assigned to this command by Pope on July 26; on the thirty-first his brigade numbered 3,600 men and he had fifteen pieces of artillery. His brigade consisted of the 39th New York (Colonel Frederick G. D'Utassy), 32d Ohio (Colonel Thomas H. Ford), 60th Ohio (Colonel William H. Trimble), 9th Vermont (Colonel George J. Stannard), 7th Squadron, Rhode Island Cavalry (Major Augustus W. Corliss), 1st Independent Indiana Battery (Captain Silas F. Rigby), and Captain Benjamin F. Potts's Ohio battery. There was added to this command on August 20 a battalion of the 1st Maryland Cavalry under Captain Charles H. Russell.

The troops at both Winchester and Martinsburg were kept constantly on the alert by three or four small detachments of Virginia cavalry that, when Jackson marched from the Shenandoah Valley to join Lee before Richmond, had been left to observe the movements of the Union army. These small detachments, numbering less than one hundred men each, ran in White's outposts, captured and burned railroad cars, and caused some uneasiness. On August 11, twenty-five men of the 12th Virginia Cavalry dashed into Front Royal and captured two officers. On the twenty-third, a detachment of the same regiment captured a train of cars on the Winchester and Potomac Railroad about two miles south of Summit Point, with ten prisoners and eight thousand dollars. The train was burned and the telegraph line cut. On the same day, the command of Lieutenant Robert H. Milling (part of Captain Henry A. Cole's battalion of Maryland cavalry) was captured by Captain George Baylor's company of the 12th Virginia Cavalry at Smithfield, east of Winchester. These and other spirited attacks gave credence to reports that a column of Confederates was marching up the Valley, leaving Winchester to the left.

Miles had no adequate force on the railroad between Harper's Ferry and Point of Rocks to resist an attack of any considerable body of men. There was one company of infantry at Sandy Hook, one at Berlin, one at Point of Rocks, and another ten miles south at Edward's Ferry, these four companies belonging to Colonel William P. Maulsby's 1st Maryland, Potomac Home Brigade. On the twenty-seventh of August, Wool ordered Miles to increase the force at Point of Rocks with infantry and two guns, which Miles did by sending about two hundred men of the 87th Ohio and two guns of Graham's New York battery.

There was but one small regiment, the 11th New York Militia, to keep open communication between Harper's Ferry and Winchester, and the term of service of this regiment was about to expire. On the twenty-eighth of August, Wool ordered the 8th New York Cavalry, then at the Relay House, to report to Miles, who, on the thirty-first ordered it to Summit Point on the Winchester Railroad to watch the Confederate cavalry (especially the 12th Virginia Cavalry) operating in that vicinity and to give timely notice should White be attacked at Winchester—but the primary duty of the regiment was to protect the Winchester Railroad. If cut off from Harper's Ferry, the regiment was to retreat to Martinsburg, cross the Potomac at Shepherdstown, and join Miles by the left bank of the river. Four companies of the 12th Illinois Cavalry were ordered from Martinsburg to Smithfield, six miles north of Summit Point. Cole's cavalry battalion and Captain Means's company of Virginia partisans were to operate in Loudoun County from Hillsboro and Leesburg to Snicker's Ferry. If too heavily pressed by the enemy, Captain Cole was to fall back with the entire command on Berlin or Point of Rocks. One infantry regiment, the 3d Maryland, Potomac Home Brigade, held Kearneysville and Shepherdstown, with orders to cross the Potomac at Shepherdstown Ford[6] and occupy Maryland Heights if attacked.

Halleck was looking for a movement of the Confederates into the Shenandoah Valley and instructed White to keep him advised of any information coming from that quarter, upon which White replied on the twenty-fifth (before the arrival of the New York horsemen) that want of cavalry prevented him from obtaining information of importance, but that Union men at and around Winchester constantly informed him that the movements of the Confederates on Pope's right were to keep the Valley clear for the "real attack on Maryland."[7] Subsequent movements of Lee's army brought it nearer the Valley and, on the morning of September 2, Halleck telegraphed White, "You will immediately abandon the fortifications at Winchester, sending the heavy guns under escort by rail to Harper's Ferry. If this cannot be done, they should be rendered unserviceable. Having sent off your artillery, you will withdraw your whole force to Harper's Ferry."[8] Simultaneously with this order came Pope's defeat and information that a column of twenty thousand Confederates was coming down the

---

5   "Record of the Harper's Ferry Military Commission," October 30, 1862, reprinted in *OR*, vol. 19, pt. 1, 792.

6   Shepherdstown Ford is also known as "Blackford's Ford" and "Boteler's Ford," and Carman uses all three at different points in his original manuscript. Since the first is most prevalent in Carman's work, the editor has chosen to standardize reference to this location as "Shepherdstown Ford" throughout the narrative (save for references to other descriptors appearing within direct quotations).

7   Julius White to Halleck, August 25, 1862, 11:15 a.m., reprinted in *OR*, vol. 12, pt. 3, 665.

8   Halleck to White, September 2, 1862, reprinted in *OR*, vol. 12, pt. 3, 800.

Valley. (This column of twenty thousand was, in fact, the 17th Virginia Cavalry Battalion, moving for Snicker's Gap in the Blue Ridge.) White was not deceived by this report and sent out some cavalry to assure himself if there was anything in it to hasten his movements; meanwhile, he telegraphed Halleck that if rapid movement was necessary much ammunition would be abandoned and suggested that time be given him to remove it.[9] He waited for an answer until ten o'clock that night. None coming,[10] he evacuated Winchester—abandoning four siege guns, blowing up his magazines, and burning some buildings containing military stores—and fell back to Harper's Ferry, the retreat being covered by the 7th Squadron, Rhode Island Cavalry. The four siege guns, a few prisoners, and some supplies fell into possession of the Confederates the next day, when Lieutenant Colonel John H. S. Funk, commanding a detachment of Virginia cavalry, entered the town. Miles immediately notified Wool that White had abandoned Winchester, but he assured him that he had everything in readiness for any demonstration on Harper's Ferry,[11] to which Wool replied, "I must leave the course you ought to pursue to your own sound direction. Take care of your position and not expose it to surprise. Watchfulness, vigilance, and a sound discretion must be your guide at the present moment."[12]

On the third Wool was directed by Stanton to send all paroled prisoners then at Point of Rocks to Cumberland and was advised that there were strong indications that the Confederates intended "to cross the Potomac below and cut off Harper's Ferry."[13] On the evening of the same day, Wool was notified by the officer commanding a detachment of the 87th Ohio at Point of Rocks of the dispersion of Cole's and Means's cavalry at Leesburg and of Munford's dash into Waterford on the afternoon of the second.[14] It was also that same evening that White arrived at Harper's Ferry from Winchester with his brigade. Reports came to Miles that Confederate cavalry were at Lovettsville, Hillsboro, and on the Potomac below him and that infantry and artillery were approaching Leesburg.[15] Similar reports came in on the fourth. Colonel Henry B. Banning, who had been sent to Point of Rocks with the greater part of the 87th Ohio, abandoned that place upon hearing that D. H. Hill had crossed the Potomac below, and Miles promptly ordered him back from Berlin with instructions to retreat only when compelled and to obstruct the advance of the enemy as much as possible.[16]

Wool was informed by Miles on the fifth and again on the sixth that Lee's army was crossing the Potomac, and Wool promptly responded that Miles must "be energetic and active, and defend all places to the last extremity. There must be no abandonment of a post, and shoot the first man that thinks of it, whether officer or soldier."[17] In another message that day, Wool directed, "The position on the heights ought to enable you to punish the enemy passing up the road in the direction of Harper's Ferry. Have your wits about you, and do all you can to annoy the rebels should they advance on you. Activity, energy, and decision must be used. You will not abandon Harper's Ferry without defending it to the last extremity."[18] To all of which, Miles replied on the seventh, "The enemy is steadily pressing on my pickets, and is establishing batteries on the plateau opposite Point of Rocks, but I am ready for them."[19] This was the last communication Wool had from Miles—for the telegraph was now cut and the Baltimore and Ohio Railroad obstructed near Frederick.

When Stanton and Halleck realized the fact that their administration of military affairs had endangered the safety of the capital, they sought to unload their responsibility upon the shoulders of others. Lincoln took direction of affairs and

9 White to Halleck, September 2, 1862, 3:00 p.m., reprinted in *OR*, vol. 12, pt. 3, 801.

10 Blinded perhaps by his antipathy to Halleck, Carman neglects to mention that Halleck *did* reply: "The orders given you about the withdrawal of your forces were based on the supposition that the entire force of the enemy was now engaged with General Pope's army, near Fairfax Court-House, and that you would have plenty of time to remove everything. It is impossible, from the conflicting reports of the different generals as to the position of the enemy, to give special instructions. As a general rule, public property should be destroyed only when absolutely necessary. You must exercise your own discretion in this matter from the facts as you ascertain them; but don't be deceived by mere rumors. Take measures to ascertain facts, and act accordingly." Halleck to White, September 2, 1862, as contained in "Record of [the Winchester] Military Commission," October 17, 1862, reprinted in *OR*, vol. 12, pt. 2, 768. Unfortunately for all concerned, the final leg of the telegraph was inoperative at the time, and the message was not transmitted beyond Harper's Ferry. Confirming testimony from the telegraph operator at Harper's Ferry can be found in "Record of [the Winchester] Military Commission," October 20, 1862, 789–90.

11 Dixon S. Miles to John E. Wool, September 3, 1862, reprinted in *OR*, vol. 51, pt. 1, 784 (first message).

12 Wool to Miles, September 3, 1862, reprinted in *OR*, vol. 51, pt. 1, 784.

13 Halleck to Wool, September 3, 1862, reprinted in *OR*, vol. 19, pt. 2, 173.

14 John Faskin to Wool, September 3, 1862, 9:25 p.m., reprinted in *OR*, vol. 19, pt. 2, 173.

15 Miles to Halleck, September 3, 1862, 8:30 p.m., reprinted in *OR*, vol. 19, pt. 2, 174.

16 Henry M. Binney to White, September 18, 1862, reprinted in *OR*, vol. 19, pt. 1, 533.

17 Wool to Miles, September 5, 1862, reprinted in *OR*, vol. 19, pt. 1, 523.

18 Wool to Miles, September 5, 1862, as contained in "Record of the Harper's Ferry Military Commission," October 30, 1862, 790.

19 Wool included this passage in his report, presenting it as a direct quotation from Miles's dispatch. Wool to Halleck, September 27, 1862, reprinted in *OR*, vol. 19, pt. 1, 520. The copy entered into evidence at the Harper's Ferry inquiry, however, reads, "The enemy is steadily pressing on my pickets from Point of Rocks; has driven them in to Sandy Hook, and is putting batteries in position on a plateau opposite. I am ready for them." Miles to Wool, September 7, 1862, 2:30 a.m., as contained in "Record of the Harper's Ferry Military Commission," October 30, 1862, 791.

assumed the responsibility of placing McClellan in command of the army to save Washington, notwithstanding the protest of Stanton and Chase that "they would prefer the loss of the capital to the restoration of McClellan to command." Halleck, in the following paper, abdicated direction of affairs in Maryland and the Shenandoah Valley to Wool:

Headquarters of the Army
Washington, D.C., September 5, 1862

Major-General Wool, Baltimore, Md.:

I find it impossible to get this army into the field again in large force for a day or two. In the mean time Harper's Ferry may be attacked and overwhelmed. I leave the dispositions there to your experience and local knowledge.

I beg leave, however, to suggest the propriety of withdrawing all our forces in that vicinity to Maryland Heights. I have no personal knowledge of the ground, and merely make the suggestion to you.

H. W. Halleck,
General-in-Chief[20]

We have quoted McClellan as saying that before he left Washington, when there was no enemy to prevent the withdrawal of Miles, he recommended that the garrison at Harper's Ferry should be withdrawn via Hagerstown to aid in covering the Cumberland Valley, or that, taking up the pontoon bridge and obstructing the railroad bridge, it should fall back to Maryland Heights and there hold out to the last. Halleck did not deem it proper to adopt either suggestion, unless the dispatch of September 5 was the result. The matter was again brought to Halleck's attention in the manner and with the result as here given in McClellan's words:

Before I went to the front Secretary Seward came to my quarters one evening and asked my opinion of the condition of affairs at Harper's Ferry, remarking that he was not at ease on the subject. Harper's Ferry was not at that time in any sense under my control, but I told Mr. Seward that I regarded the arrangements there as exceedingly dangerous; that in my opinion the proper course was to abandon the position and unite the garrison (ten thousand men, about) to the main army of operations, for the reason that its presence at Harper's Ferry would not hinder the enemy from crossing the Potomac; that if we were unsuccessful in the approaching battle Harper's Ferry would be of no use to us, and its garrison necessarily lost; that if we were successful we would immediately recover the post without any difficulty, while the addition of 10,000 men to the active army would be an important factor in ensuring success. I added that if it were determined to hold the position the existing arrangements were all wrong, as it would be easy for the enemy to surround and capture the garrison, and that the garrison ought, at least, to be withdrawn to the Maryland Heights, where they could resist attack until relieved.

The secretary was much impressed by what I said, and asked me to accompany him to Gen. Halleck and repeat my statement to him. I acquiesced, and we went together to Gen. Halleck's quarters, where we found that he had retired for the night. But he received us in his bed-room, when, after a preliminary explanation by the secretary as to the interview being at his request, I said to Halleck precisely what I had stated to Mr. Seward.

Halleck received my statement with ill-concealed contempt; said that everything was all right as it was; that my views were entirely erroneous, etc., and soon bowed us out, leaving matters at Harper's Ferry precisely as they were.[21]

On the day that McClellan left Washington to take command in the field, Halleck—notwithstanding his telegram on the fifth that he had no knowledge of the topography around Harper's Ferry and that Wool must look to the safety of that place—telegraphed directly to Miles, "Our army is in motion. It is important that Harper's Ferry be held to the latest moment. The Government has the utmost confidence in you, and is ready to give you full credit for the defense it expects you to make."[22] To this order and the strict construction put upon it by Miles is due the loss of Maryland Heights and Harper's Ferry, or, as Halleck officially states it, "the disgraceful surrender of the post and army."[23]

---

[20] Halleck to Wool, September 5, 1862, as contained in "Record of the Haper's Ferry Military Commission," October 17, 1862, 757. In his testimony before the Miles court of inquiry, General Wool said that he had no recollection of this dispatch of September 5. Even if he had received it, he would not have approved it, because he thought Miles's troops could have defended themselves where they were, in Harper's Ferry, particularly after he had ordered a block-house to be constructed on Maryland Heights. "Record of the Harper's Ferry Military Commission," October 30, 1862, 793.—EAC

[21] McClellan, *McClellan's Own Story: The War for the Union, the Soldiers Who Fought It, the Civilians Who Directed It, and His Relations to It and Them* (New York: Charles L. Webster & Co., 1887), 549–50.

[22] Halleck to Miles, September 7, 1862, as contained in "Record of the Harper's Ferry Military Commission," October 17, 1862, 757.

[23] Halleck to Edwin M. Stanton, November 25, 1862, reprinted in *OR*, vol. 19, pt. 1, 5.

On the fourth White, who had come in from Winchester the preceding day, was ordered to the command of Martinsburg, his brigade remaining at Harper's Ferry. On the fifth, the troops at Harper's Ferry were thus brigaded:

First Brigade (right wing, line of battle Bolivar Heights, Va.), Col. F. G. D'Utassy (Thirty-ninth New York) commanding: Thirty-ninth New York (Garibaldi Guard) Infantry; One hundred and eleventh New York Volunteers, Colonel [Jesse] Segoine; One hundred and fifteenth New York, Colonel [Simeon] Sammon; battery Fifteenth Indiana Volunteers, Capt. [John C. H.] von Sehlen.

Second Brigade (left wing, line of battle Bolivar Heights, Va.), Colonel Trimble (Sixtieth Ohio) commanding: Sixtieth Ohio Volunteers, Colonel Trimble; One hundred and twenty-sixth New York, Colonel [Eliakim] Sherrill; Ninth Vermont Volunteers, Colonel Stannard; Potts' battery (substituted Rigby's subsequently).

Third Brigade, commanding on Maryland Heights (including the heavy siege guns thereon), Md., Col. Thomas H. Ford (Thirty-second Ohio) commanding: Thirty-second Ohio Volunteers, Colonel Ford; battalion First Maryland Potomac Home Brigade, Maj. John A. Steiner; Captain [Eugene] McGrath, Company F, Fifth New York Heavy Artillery; Major Corliss' battalion Rhode Island cavalry; detachment First Maryland Cavalry, Captain [Charles H.] Russell.

Fourth Brigade (commanding the intrenchments on Camp Hill, Va.), Col. W[illiam] G. Ward (Twelfth New York State Militia) commanding (three months): Twelfth New York State Militia, Colonel Ward; Captain Graham's company (A), Fifth New York Heavy Artillery; Captain Rigby's battery (Potts' substituted afterward); Eighty-seventh Ohio Volunteers, Colonel Banning (three months).

Independent commands: First Maryland Potomac Home Brigade Regiment, Colonel Maulsby, Sandy Hook, Md.; Eighth New York Cavalry, Col. B[enjamin] F. Davis, Harper's Ferry, Va.; detachments companies [sic] First Maryland Potomac Home Brigade Cavalry, under Captain Cole, Sandy Hook.[24]

On September 6 Colonel Maulsby at Sandy Hook was ordered to the utmost vigilance in guarding the fords below Harper's Ferry and to concentrate five companies of his regiment as near the ford at Sandy Hook as he could get, to command it and the roads leading to Maryland Heights. He was advised that Captain Faithful, who had abandoned Frederick, was on the march to join him and that the position of Sandy Hook was to be held if it took half of the force at Harper's Ferry. Under no circumstances must it be abandoned.[25] Colonel Banning of the 87th Ohio, then at Berlin, was ordered to defend that point as long as possible, but if obliged to fall back he was to stop at Sandy Hook, which was to be defended at all hazards.[26] The commanding officer of three companies of the 29th Pennsylvania at Hagerstown was ordered by Wool to send all stores and two Parrott guns to Chambersburg, Pennsylvania,[27] and on the same day the orders were repeated to Lieutenant Franklin B. Crosby (Battery F, 4th U.S. Artillery), who was directed to hasten the movement, but in the same dispatch was permitted to use his discretion in the matter, governed by movements of the enemy.[28]

Banning, who had been ordered to return to Point of Rocks on the fourth, and who took with him two howitzers of Captain Graham's Battery A, 5th New York Heavy Artillery, was shelled from the opposite side of the Potomac on the sixth by G. B. Anderson's command and pressed on the Monocacy Road by Longstreet's skirmishers. He again fell back to Berlin and thence to Sandy Hook, where he formed a junction with Colonel Maulsby's 1st Maryland, Potomac Home Brigade. On the seventh Miles visited Sandy Hook and Weverton and directed cavalry reconnaissances on the different roads. Some of the detachments started out, heard rumors, and returned, but Lieutenant Hanson T. C. Green, with a small party of Cole's cavalry, pushed through Petersville and Middletown to within two and a half miles of Frederick, ran into the Confederate pickets, took some prisoners, and returned without loss to report that Lee's army was at Frederick.[29]

This definite information inspired Miles with much energy, and he was now constantly in the saddle. On the eighth he visited Colonel Ford (who, three days before, had been sent to Maryland Heights) and instructed him and his officers as to the importance of the position, giving them to understand that they must retain it at all hazards; with them held, he could defy an army of twenty-five thousand men on his front. Finding himself short of forage and subsistence, he seized all the flour in the stores and mills in the vicinity and sent out foraging parties on various roads. Major Corliss of the Rhode Island cavalry made a reconnaissance into Solomon's Gap on Elk Ridge, thence down through Jefferson, driving in the enemy's pickets, capturing twenty-five prisoners, and pushing on to within two miles of Lee's army at Frederick. Again, on the

24 Binney to White, 533.
25 Miles to William P. Maulsby, September 6, 1862, reprinted in OR, vol. 51, pt. 1, 794.
26 Miles to Henry B. Banning, September 6, 1862, reprinted in OR, vol. 51, pt. 1, 795.
27 Wool to Michael Scott, September 6, 1862, reprinted in OR, vol. 51, pt. 1, 796.
28 Wool to Franklin B. Crosby, September 6, 1862, reprinted in OR, vol. 51, pt. 1, 796.
29 Binney to White, 534.

ninth, Miles was at Sandy Hook, Weverton, Maryland Heights, and Bolivar Heights, and rumors of the enemy were heard in every direction.[30]

On the tenth, authentic reports came in thick and fast that the Confederates had crossed South Mountain and were in motion northward. Lieutenant Colonel Stephen W. Downey of the 3d Maryland, Potomac Home Brigade, with Captain Francis Shamburg's company (twenty men) of the 1st Maryland Cavalry, encountered Jackson's advance near Boonsboro while scouting in Pleasant Valley and suffered a loss of one man killed and three wounded.[31] He ascertained that the whole Confederate army was on the move, but whether on Hagerstown or to recross the Potomac below he could not tell. White, who received the same information at Martinsburg, reported it to Halleck at Washington[32] and Wool at Baltimore[33] and telegraphed to Miles, "The enemy will be whipped in Maryland, and we will be boggled up in their retreat." But from his lookout or observatory on Maryland Heights, White could see no indications of the enemy in any direction. On the eleventh Miles again went onto Maryland Heights and soon ascertained that the Confederates had come into Pleasant Valley by Brownsville Gap and made a lodgment at Solomon's Gap. Later came the startling news from White at Martinsburg that he was surrounded.[34]

When Halleck ordered White to evacuate Winchester and retire to Harper's Ferry on September 2, he consulted neither Wool nor Miles about the matter—Halleck was simply stampeded. Nor did he advise either of the step. Wool received his first information from Miles and, naturally, was greatly surprised that such an important outpost, generally regarded as the key to the Valley, had been abandoned "without the approach or presence of an enemy."[35] As White ranked Miles, his presence at Harper's Ferry was not agreeable to Wool, who wanted a regular officer at that place. He promptly detached White from his brigade and ordered him to the command of the small garrison at Martinsburg with instructions to guard the Baltimore and Ohio Railroad, to exercise "sleepless energy," and take "active and energetic measures" to defend the place to the last extremity.[36] White could not see that Martinsburg was of more importance than Winchester (from which place he had been ordered to beat a somewhat precipitate retreat) nor could he see how the position could be any better held against a superior force. The assignment was much to his astonishment and extremely distasteful, and he asked to be returned to his rightful command of the brigade that he had organized at Winchester,[37] but this was denied him, and he was ordered to remain at Martinsburg. Wool repeated the admonition to defend himself to the last extremity and that there must be "no running before the enemy is coming."[38] When Halleck was appealed to, he informed White that no orders had been sent by him to go to Martinsburg,[39] but as in falling back from Winchester to Harper's Ferry he had come under Wool's orders, White must be governed by them.[40]

On September 6 Miles advised White that communication with Baltimore and Washington was cut off, that Frederick was occupied by the Confederates in force, that rumor said a column was moving on Williamsport, and to "look out for squalls."[41] On the same day, White informed both Wool and Halleck that his outposts had been attacked that morning; to Wool, he made an additional remark that he should obey the order to fight, "though with no hope of support."[42] Later that day he reported the repulse of the attack, which gave Stanton an opportunity to commend him and to say, "It is expected that no post will be surrendered, but that every officer and every man shall fight as if the fate of the Government depended upon him."[43]

The orders of Wool and Stanton to hold on to Martinsburg to the last extremity—that there must be "no running before the enemy is coming" and that "no post will be surrendered"—may be taken as criticism of Halleck's order for the abandonment of Winchester.

---

[30] Ibid., 534–35.

[31] Ibid., 536.

[32] White to Halleck, September 10, 1862, 11:00 p.m., reprinted in OR, vol. 19, pt. 2, 249.

[33] White to Wool, September 10, 1862, 9:00 p.m., reprinted in OR, vol. 19, pt. 2, 249.

[34] Binney to White, 535–36.

[35] Wool to Miles, September 4, 1862, reprinted in OR, vol. 19, pt. 2, 182.

[36] Wool to White, September 4, 1862, reprinted in OR, vol. 19, pt. 2, 181.

[37] White to George W. Cullum, September 6, 1862, reprinted in OR, vol. 19, pt. 2, 198.

[38] Wool to White, September 6, 1862, as contained in "Record of the Harper's Ferry Military Commission," October 30, 1862, 791.

[39] Cullum to White, September 6, 1862, reprinted in OR, vol. 19, pt. 2, 199.

[40] Halleck to White, September 8, 1862, reprinted in OR, vol. 19, pt. 2, 218.

[41] Miles to White, September 6, 1862, reprinted in OR, vol. 51, pt. 1, 794.

[42] White to Wool, September 7, 1862, 10:00 a.m., reprinted in OR, vol. 19, pt. 2, 205. The phrase "on the same day" is a maddeningly representative example of Carman's imprecise grammar. If by this he means September 6 (referring to the previous sentence), the assertion is contradicted by the date of the message containing the phrase "though with no hope of support." More likely, Carman meant to convey the fact that the message to Halleck and the one to Wool were sent on the same day.

[43] Stanton to White, September 7, 1862, 9:15 p.m., reprinted in OR, vol. 51, pt. 1, 798.

White's outposts were daily attacked and the 12th Illinois Cavalry and a detachment of the 8th New York Cavalry were active in repelling these assaults, all of which was reported to Wool with a request for reinforcement of four regiments of infantry and two batteries (as he had but a small force of cavalry and infantry and three 6-pounder guns).[44] Wool could not spare the reinforcement nor would he permit Miles to give it, but he telegraphed White, "If 20,000 men should attack you, you will of course fall back. Harper's Ferry would be the best position I could recommend, but be sure that you have such a force against you or any other that would overwhelm you."[45]

On the eighth, two companies of the 8th New York Cavalry scouted to Bunker Hill, Smithfield, and Summit Point, capturing a few pickets but ascertaining no general movement of the enemy in that direction. Colonel Downey, who scouted from Kearneysville and returned without incident, was ordered to remain there and protect the road and the bridge over the Opequon unless severely pressed by the enemy, in which case he would retreat to Shepherdstown, cross the Potomac to Maryland Heights, and report for duty to Colonel Ford.[46] Two days later the 8th made a reconnaissance toward Winchester and saw nothing, and Downey, crossing the Potomac, ran into Jackson's advance near Boonsboro (as we have seen) and gave White information of the danger menacing him. What action White now took is told in his official report:

On the 11th instant reports reached me, through scouts and others, that the enemy were crossing the Potomac into Virginia at or about Williamsport and Cherry Run in force; also, that they were passing to the west of Martinsburg, between it and North Mountain, thus cutting off our retreat in that direction.

It being ordered by Major-General Wool that the place should be held to the last extremity, at noon on the 11th instant I sent out one section of Captain [John C.] Phillips' battery and four companies of the Sixty-fifth Illinois, together with half a company of cavalry and two teams, with axes, &c., the whole under command of Colonel [Daniel] Cameron, of the Sixty-fifth Illinois, with orders to proceed out upon the Williamsburg [Williamsport—*OR* editors] road, as far as practicable, and to obstruct the roads, tear up the bridges, and, in every way possible, retard the advance of the enemy.

At night-fall, it having been well ascertained that the enemy were between us and North Mountain, and were in very large force near Falling Waters, on the Williamsport road, some 7 miles from Martinsburg, and were still crossing, it became evident that with the small force at my disposal the position could not longer be held.

Colonel Cameron's party was accordingly recalled, and every exertion made to convey the public property to Harper's Ferry, that being the only line of retreat left open …

The railroad train was loaded to the extent of its capacity and sent to Harper's Ferry, where it arrived in safety. The transportation was then employed to haul the most valuable property remaining, and the troops and wagons took up their line of march at 2 o'clock on the morning of the 12th.

But little public property was abandoned, consisting mostly of tents and camp equipage, which could not be conveyed with the means at disposal.

Upon the march, the pickets of the enemy were encountered at Halltown, but they were driven back to Charlestown, the command arriving safely at Harper's Ferry on the afternoon of the 12th.[47]

On the twelfth a detachment of the 8th New York Cavalry was observing Knott's Ford near the mouth of the Antietam, but upon the approach of Jackson's column from Martinsburg it withdrew to Harper's Ferry. On the same day, the 7th Squadron, Rhode Island Cavalry, set out from Maryland Heights on a reconnaissance to Sharpsburg. It passed the mouth of the Antietam, saw the New York cavalry at Knott's Ford, and advanced nearly to Sharpsburg when, finding that its retreat by the road was cut off by the occupation of Solomon's Gap by the brigades of Brigadier Generals Joseph B. Kershaw and William Barksdale, returned to camp by way of the canal tow-path.

As ranking officer, White was entitled to the command of all the forces now assembled and should have assumed it, but believing the intention and desire of both Halleck and Wool was that Miles should retain it, he waived his rights, at least for the present, and put himself and his staff at Miles's disposal and gave him loyal help. This action was more to the credit of his heart than his head, but he justified himself in the fact that fighting had already commenced, Miles knew the topography of the vicinity, and that there was no probability that the interests of the service would suffer.[48]

[44] White to Wool, September 7, 1862, 11:00 a.m., reprinted in *OR*, vol. 19, pt. 2, 205.

[45] Wool to White, September 8, 1862, as contained in Wool to Halleck, September 27, 1862, reprinted in *OR*, vol. 19, pt. 1, 520. This order appears in a slightly altered form in "Record of the Harper's Ferry Military Commission," October 30, 1862, 791.

[46] Binney to White, 535.

[47] White to William D. Whipple, September 20, 1862, reprinted in *OR*, vol. 19, pt. 1, 524.

[48] White actually stated all this in writing to Miles the day after arriving at Harper's Ferry. White to Miles, September 13, 1862, reprinted in *OR*, vol. 19, pt. 1, 525.

When White arrived, skirmishing had begun on Maryland Heights and distrust was growing as to Miles's capacity. (Brigade and regimental commanders generally approved White's course under the circumstances, yet wished that he had done otherwise.) Immediately upon his arrival, White asked Miles what his plans were but received no definite reply. He had no specific plan beyond the defense of Bolivar Heights and the bridges; that these positions being defended, Harper's Ferry was secure; and that his orders were to hold Harper's Ferry. White then suggested that Maryland Heights appeared to be the key to the position and offered the only feasible line of retreat, should this become necessary, as well as the most defensible position should it become necessary to concentrate the entire force at any one point. It should be defended at all hazards and with the entire force if necessary. In the main Miles agreed with White but thought Camp Hill best commanded the bridges and the approach from that side. He stated there was no water on Maryland Heights, that the objection to taking the entire force over there was that and the difficulty of getting up subsistence and artillery.[49] But Miles's great objection was the orders he had received to hold Harper's Ferry to the last extremity. To leave Harper's Ferry—even to go to Maryland Heights—would be disobeying the instructions he had received from both Halleck and Wool. Other officers made like suggestions, but to one and all he made the same reply: he had been ordered to hold Harper's Ferry.

The defenses of Harper's Ferry comprised an unfinished line of rifle-pits on Bolivar Heights. These heights, two miles and more beyond the town, form a low ridge extending from near the Potomac southward to the Charlestown Road, where a small work for the protection of a battery was thrown up. Thence, the line dropped to a lower plateau near the Winchester Road, then rose again into a slight eminence, finally sloping steeply to the Shenandoah. This line was over one and a half miles long and was held by about seven thousand men. In the rear of this line, eastward, in the upper part of the town, was an earthwork on elevated ground known as Camp Hill, and in this work were about eight hundred men. About one thousand men guarded the bridges and other points on the river.

Maryland Heights, beyond the Potomac and rising over one thousand feet above it, completely commands Harper's Ferry; looking up from this town the heights seem ready to drop upon it. On the crest, one and a half miles north of the railroad bridge, there was a small work called the "stone fort." Well down its western slope, was a battery of heavy guns that could throw shot down upon Bolivar Heights and beyond it; a line of entrenchments ran across this slope, terminating at a work near the Potomac called Fort Duncan, but this line was not occupied except at the upper end. For the defense of these heights, Miles assigned about two thousand men.[50]

The eastern approaches to Maryland Heights were guarded by Colonel Maulsby and his 1st Maryland, Potomac Home Brigade, at Sandy Hook, where the railroad and the canal hugging the Potomac and the country roads leading down Pleasant Valley united. (A zig-zag and difficult road leading from Harper's Ferry over the southern end of the heights came into Pleasant Valley at the hamlet of Sandy Hook.) Maulsby had under his command five companies of his own regiment, eight companies of the 87th Ohio, Cole's cavalry, and three pieces of artillery under Captain Potts. These forces were placed to prevent surprise and repel attack upon the eastern side of Maryland Heights from the direction of Pleasant Valley, as well as to guard the approach to the ferry around the bend of the Potomac. On the eleventh the greater part of this command was withdrawn to the slope of Maryland Heights and one gun added to the three already under Potts's charge.

We now return to the Confederates, who, in high feather, left Frederick on the morning of the tenth on their "rollicking march" to surround and capture the prey that Halleck had already corralled for them. To repeat the orders under which they were acting, Jackson, with fourteen brigades, was to march on the morning of the tenth by way of Middletown and Boonsboro in the direction of Sharpsburg, cross the Potomac at the most convenient point, and, by Friday morning (September 12), take possession of the Baltimore and Ohio Railroad, capture such of the enemy as were at Martinsburg, and intercept those attempting escape from Harper's Ferry. After destroying the Monocacy viaduct, Walker, with his two brigades, was to cross the Potomac at Cheek's Ford (near the mouth of the Monocacy), ascend the west bank of the river to Lovettsville, and take possession of Loudoun Heights (overlooking Harper's Ferry from the Virginia side of the Potomac,

---

[49] "Record of the Harper's Ferry Military Commission," October 15, 1862, 716.

[50] Much of this paragraph and the one preceding it is taken from a postwar article by White. Julius White, "The Surrender of Harper's Ferry," in *Battles and Leaders of the Civil War*, vol. 2 (New York: Century Co., 1887), 612. In addition to commonalities in word choice and troop figures, White's article contains two anachronisms that also appear in Carman's work. Mention is made of the "stone fort" at the top of Maryland Heights and "Fort Duncan" at its base. Neither structure was in place during the Maryland campaign of 1862; they were constructed afterwards in response to the events described in the rest of this chapter. That these structures were not yet erected during the time described herein is evidenced by a message sent by McClellan at the conclusion of the campaign: "I have just returned from Maryland Heights, *and have determined to fortify them*, as well as the heights on the opposite side of the river, in order to avoid a similar catastrophe to the one which happened to Colonel Miles. In view of this, I shall be glad to have contrabands sent to Harper's Ferry from Washington to perform a portion of the necessary labor, if there are any disposable [emphasis added]." McClellan to Halleck, September 26, 1862, 10:30 p.m., reprinted in *OR*, vol. 19, pt. 2, 360–61. Elsewhere in his narrative, Carman makes note of the fact that no fortification had been built on the summit of Maryland Heights (see pp. 112–13).

but separated from the town by the Shenandoah). Walker was to be in place by the morning of Friday the twelfth, Keys's Ford on his left and the road between the end of the mountain and the Potomac on his right. As far as possible, he was to cooperate with Jackson and McLaws and intercept the retreat of the enemy. McLaws, with his own division and that of Anderson (ten brigades in all) was to turn to the left on reaching Middletown, cross South Mountain, traverse Pleasant Valley, and seize Maryland Heights (overlooking Harper's Ferry from the Maryland side of the river). He also was to be in place by that same Friday morning. Although separated from both Maryland Heights and Loudoun Heights by the Potomac and Shenandoah respectively, Harper's Ferry was commanded by both and at the mercy of a plunging fire from them. Jackson was to prevent the escape of the garrison in the direction of Martinsburg and close in on it from the west; McLaws and Walker were to prevent escape across the Potomac and Shenandoah. After the capture of Harper's Ferry, Jackson, Walker, and McLaws were to rejoin Lee at or near Hagerstown.

The divisions of D. H. Hill, D. R. Jones, and Hood, the brigade of Nathan G. Evans (in all, fourteen brigades), and the greater part of Stuart's cavalry were retained by Lee to watch and delay the march of McClellan until Harper's Ferry should be taken (a matter considered as requiring not more than three days). Then the army, reunited at Hagerstown, would continue its advance into Pennsylvania or, if possible and advisable, give McClellan battle west of South Mountain. There was such absolute confidence in the continued slow and cautious movement of McClellan that Lee apprehended no serious interference with his plans. He had not entertained the intention of offering or receiving battle at Frederick or delaying McClellan at the passes of South Mountain—quite the contrary. His plan was to draw him beyond South Mountain and give battle in the valley west of it, where the Army of the Potomac would be farther removed from its reserves of men and supplies at Washington and where a disaster to it would be well nigh irretrievable.

When the order for this movement was issued, Walker's Division was on detached service in a vain effort to destroy the aqueduct of the Chesapeake and Ohio Canal at the mouth of the Monocacy. (D. H. Hill, as mentioned previously, had been instructed to do this when he crossed into Maryland on the fourth, but finding it impracticable, he abandoned it, whereupon Walker was ordered back to do it effectively.) He worked from 11:00 p.m. of the ninth to early morning of the tenth but with no better success than Hill. The work was one of days instead of hours, and as he had been informed by Lee that the army would march from Frederick toward Hagerstown on the tenth (thus leaving his small division in the immediate presence of a strong force of the enemy), he determined to rejoin his chief by way of Jefferson and Middletown as he had been instructed. Before marching, however, he received Lee's order to cross the Potomac at Cheek's Ford and proceed toward Harper's Ferry to cooperate with Jackson and McLaws.[51] When ready to move on the morning of the tenth, he found that the aqueduct and its approaches, as well as Cheek's Ford, were commanded by artillery supported by the 1st Massachusetts Cavalry, upon which he marched up the east bank of the Potomac and crossed at Point of Rocks during the night of the tenth—but with much difficulty, owing to the destruction of the bridge over the canal and the steepness of the river banks. A heavy rain now set in, and as his men were exhausted by their night march, Walker allowed them to rest during the eleventh and resumed march on the morning of the twelfth, camping at Hillsboro that night.

At ten o'clock on the morning of the thirteenth, Walker arrived at the east foot of Loudoun Heights. Reconnaissance disclosed that they were unoccupied, upon which Colonel John R. Cooke, with the 27th North Carolina and the 30th Virginia, took possession of them and held them during the night. Upon his arrival in the morning, Walker was joined by a detachment of signal men and Captain Elijah V. White's independent company of cavalry. The former went with Cooke to open communication with Jackson; the latter scouted the approaches from Harper's Ferry and the Maryland side. Cooke, on reaching the summit of Loudoun Heights, put his men in hiding from the view of the garrison at Harper's Ferry. Meanwhile, McLaws had gained the summit of Maryland Heights (which commanded Loudoun Heights as well as Harper's Ferry). Walker's entire division, except that portion of it occupying Loudoun Heights, was placed in a strong position to prevent the escape of the Union forces down the west bank of the Potomac.

Jackson left his bivouac near Frederick early on the morning of the tenth, passed through Frederick and Middletown, and, with his own division and that of A.P. Hill, went over Turner's Gap and bivouacked one mile from Boonsboro, Ewell's Division bivouacking between Middletown and the gap. A staff officer riding with Jackson that day writes:

> In Frederick he asked for a map of Chambersburg and its vicinity, and made many irrelevant inquiries about roads and localities in the direction of Pennsylvania … Having finished this public inquiry, he took me aside, and after asking me about the different fords of the Potomac between Williamsport and Harper's Ferry, told me that he was

---

[51] "September 9, 1862. Marched four miles to within two miles of Frederick. After sunset marched to the aqueduct across Monocacy River. This regiment, with the 25th N.C., was thrown across the river. In a slight skirmish with the enemy's pickets, Capt. Duffy (Co. B) was mortally wounded, and two privates of Co. K. missing supposed to have been taken prisoners. During the night withdrew to the position occupied the evening before." Muster Roll of the 24th North Carolina Infantry, October 31, 1862.—*EAC*

ordered to capture the garrison at Harper's Ferry, and would cross either at Williamsport or Shepherdstown, as the enemy might not withdraw from Martinsburg …

On the march that day, the captain of the cavalry advance, just ahead, had instructions to let no civilian go to the front, and we entered each village we passed before the inhabitants knew of our coming.[52]

Jackson had now to determine whether to go on to Williamsport or turn toward Shepherdstown, and Captain Henry Kyd Douglas of his staff was directed to ride into Boonsboro and make inquiries as to the whereabouts of the Union troops—more especially, whether White was still at Martinsburg. As Douglas, with but a single cavalryman, rode into the village, he encountered Captain Shamburg's detachment of the 1st Maryland Cavalry and was quickly driven back without obtaining the desired information.[53]

The next morning, the eleventh, having learned that the Union troops still held Martinsburg, Jackson marched through Boonsboro and, taking the direct road to Williamsport, recrossed the Potomac into Virginia at Light's Ford during the afternoon, the troops singing and the bands playing "Carry Me Back to Ole Virginia." A. P. Hill's Division took the direct road to Martinsburg, while Jackson, to prevent the escape of White from Martinsburg westward and northward, led his division and Ewell's by a side road to North Mountain Depot on the Baltimore and Ohio Railroad (about seven miles northwest of Martinsburg), where they bivouacked that night. (Captain Samuel B. Myers, commanding the cavalry, sent a detachment of his command as far south as the Berkeley and Hampshire Turnpike.)[54] White, advised of Jackson's approach, abandoned Martinsburg during the night (as we have seen) and joined Miles at Harper's Ferry.

On the morning of the twelfth, Jackson's cavalry entered the town, followed during the day by the entire command. They took a large quantity of abandoned quartermaster and commissary stores and, moving on, camped that night on the banks of the Opequon. On the morning of the thirteenth, the march was resumed on Harper's Ferry, and at eleven o'clock A. P. Hill's Division, in the advance, came into view of Miles's forces drawn upon Bolivar Heights. Hill went into camp near Halltown about two miles from Miles's position, with Jackson's and Ewell's Divisions encamping nearby. The reasons why Jackson delayed attack are thus stated in his official report:

The commanding general having directed Major-General McLaws to move, with his own and General R. H. Anderson's divisions, to take possession of the Maryland Heights, overlooking Harper's Ferry, and Brig. Gen. J. G. Walker, pursuing a different route, to cross the Potomac and move up that river on the Virginia side and occupy the Loudoun Heights, both for the purpose of co-operating with me, it became necessary, before making the attack, to ascertain whether they were in position. Failing to learn the fact by signals, a courier was dispatched to each of those points for the required information. During the night the courier to the Loudoun Heights returned with a message from General Walker that he was in position. In the mean time General McLaws had attacked the Federal force posted to defend the Maryland Heights; had routed it and taken possession of that commanding position. The Potomac River flowed between the positions respectively occupied by General McLaws and myself, and the Shenandoah separated me from General Walker, and it became advisable, as the speediest mode of communication, to resort to signals. Before the necessary orders were thus transmitted the day was far advanced. The enemy had, by fortifications, strengthened the naturally strong position which he occupied along Bolivar Heights, extending from near the Shenandoah to the Potomac. McLaws and Walker, being thus separated from the enemy by intervening rivers, could afford no assistance beyond the fire of their artillery and guarding certain avenues of escape to the enemy, and, from the reports received from them by signals, in consequence of the distance and range of their guns, not much could be expected from their artillery so long as the enemy retained his advanced position on Bolivar Heights.[55]

Longstreet followed Jackson from Frederick, bivouacking on the night of the tenth between Middletown and Turner's Gap. Next morning he marched over South Mountain and, with Jones's and Hood's Divisions and Evans's Brigade, moved on the road to Hagerstown to procure some needed supplies and to meet a force of Pennsylvanians reported to be advancing from Chambersburg. D. H. Hill, who had followed Longstreet from Frederick, was left at Boonsboro with five brigades

---

[52] Henry Kyd Douglas, "Stonewall Jackson in Maryland," in *Battles and Leaders*, 622.

[53] Ibid., 622–23.

[54] Ibid., 623; Jackson to Lee, April 23, 1863, reprinted in *OR*, vol. 19, pt. 1, 953.

In his original manuscript, Carman refers to Myers at this point as "Major." At the time of the Maryland campaign, Myers held the rank of captain, which Carman notes correctly elsewhere in his narrative and in his table of organization. Myers was promoted to major on October 30, 1862. Compiled Service Record of Samuel B. Myers, Compiled Service Records of Confederate Soldiers Who Served in Organizations from the State of Virginia (National Archives Microfilm Publication M324, reel 78), Record Group 109, National Archives. Jackson's report, cited above, was written nearly six months later—hence its mention (copied subsequently by Carman) of "Major Myers" as the officer responsible for sending cavalry to the Berkeley and Hampshire Turnpike.

[55] Jackson to Lee, April 23, 1863, 953.

to guard the immense wagon train of the entire army, support Stuart's cavalry in holding the passes in rear, and to prevent the escape of any part of the garrison from Harper's Ferry by the road up Pleasant Valley.

Hagerstown is pleasantly situated in the center of a rich farming country abounding in supplies and is a place of considerable local importance. Good roads radiate from it in every direction, and the fords over the upper Potomac were accessible over routes not likely to fall into possession of the enemy. It was sufficiently far from Harper's Ferry and South Mountain to enable Lee to concentrate his army in the event of disaster at any of these places and a good point from which to conduct offensive operations in Maryland or into Pennsylvania—therefore, a place of considerable strategic value. (Longstreet indulges in the criticism that the change of his position from Boonsboro to Hagerstown further misled Stuart and the commanders of the divisions at Boonsboro and Harper's Ferry into a feeling of security that there could be no threat by the Union army moving from Washington.[56])

On the morning of the ninth, McLaws received verbal instructions from Lee as to the part he was to play in this complicated yet simple movement. He was to follow with his own division and that of R. H. Anderson in the rear of the army as it marched from Frederick. On reaching Middletown he would take the left-hand road leading to Harper's Ferry and by the morning of the twelfth possess himself of Maryland Heights and endeavor to capture the garrison at Harper's Ferry. When informed by McLaws that he had never been to Harper's Ferry and knew nothing of the surrounding country, Lee replied to the effect that it did not matter, but that seven or eight thousand of the enemy were there, their capture was a matter of some importance, and troops enough would march with him to accomplish the purpose.[57] Following these verbal instructions, there came to McLaws that evening his written orders—Special Orders No. 191.

Late on the morning of the tenth, McLaws marched out of Frederick.[58] If he had had a clear road, he could have reached Pleasant Valley early on the eleventh and Maryland Heights next day; as it was, he moved in the rear of a slow march, turned to the left on reaching Middletown, and, passing through Burkittsville, bivouacked between that place and Brownsville Gap. On the next day, he marched through Brownsville Gap to Pleasant Valley and bivouacked near the foot of the pass.

Pleasant Valley is appropriately named. It is rolling and highly cultivated, the home of a very prosperous and contented farming community where good stock and well filled barns give evidence of intelligent thrift. The valley runs north and south and is bounded on the east by South Mountain and the west by Elk Ridge (the distance across in a line between the summits of the ridges being about two and a half or three miles), narrowing as it approaches the Potomac and widening as it extends north to Keedysville. A main road runs along or near the foot of South Mountain and another along the base of Elk Ridge (at the time very much out of repair and not much used).

South Mountain is a continuous ridge from eight hundred to one thousand feet high and abuts the Potomac in a lofty, almost perpendicular mass of rocks overhanging the small hamlet of Weverton, the canal to Washington, the Baltimore and Ohio Railroad, and the turnpike from Harper's Ferry to Frederick, there being just enough space for them between the mountains and the river. Four miles north of Weverton Pass is Brownsville Gap, by which the road through Burkittsville debouches into Pleasant Valley, and one mile north of this is another pass known as Crampton's Gap. Six miles north of Crampton's Gap is Turner's Gap, through which the National Road pursues its way from Frederick to Hagerstown; the turnpike from Frederick to Harper's Ferry passes through Weverton, as already stated. About halfway between Weverton and Harper's Ferry is Sandy Hook. A road from Sandy Hook runs about the middle of Pleasant Valley and joins the main road along the foot of South Mountain about two miles from the Potomac. Passing from the valley going west were two roads: one along the south end of Maryland Heights and another through Solomon's Gap—a slight depression in Elk Ridge—about five miles north of the first.

Elk Ridge bounds Pleasant Valley on the west; its southern extremity is more specially designated and generally known as Maryland Heights, dominating both Harper's Ferry and Loudoun Heights. Its northern extremity dips down into and is lost in the rolling country about a mile southwest of Keedysville. Where the railroad, canal, and turnpike (after passing Weverton) go under the south end of Maryland Heights, the crowded space made for them was gained by blasting the almost-perpendicular rocks for a considerable distance. The railroad bridge crosses the Potomac (here about four hundred yards wide) just under the frowning precipice of Maryland Heights, and about fifty yards above the bridge was a pontoon

[56] James Longstreet, *From Manassas to Appomattox: Memoirs of the Civil War in America* (Philadelphia: J. P. Lippincott Co., 1896), 219–20.

[57] Lafayette McLaws, "The Capture of Harper's Ferry," *Philadelphia Weekly Press*, September 5, 1888.

[58] In Carman's original manuscript, this sentence reads, "Late on the morning of the tenth, McLaws marched out of Frederick *in rear of D. H. Hill* [emphasis added]." McLaws's march was delayed by another command to his front that day, but D. H. Hill's was not the offending division. The mistaken reference to it here by Carman is assuredly inadvertent, for he was aware that Hill's men were the last Confederate infantry to leave Frederick. Special Orders No. 191, which Carman quotes at length earlier (see p. 57), states clearly in its seventh paragraph that "General D. H. Hill's division will form the rear guard of the army, pursuing the road taken by the main body." In his official report (upon which Carman draws heavily throughout the narrative), Hill confirms that this was the case: "On the 10th, my division constituted the rear guard, and had charge of the immense wagon-train moving in the direction of Hagerstown." Daniel H. Hill to Robert H. Chilton, 1862 [no day or month given], reprinted in *OR*, vol. 19, pt. 1, 1019.

bridge for wagons and infantry by which communication was kept up between Harper's Ferry and the Maryland shore. The railroad bridge was defended by cannon placed on the farther end; the narrow causeway along the river under Maryland Heights by guns placed under the precipice and on the road. The Potomac thus runs along the south ends of both South Mountain and Elk Ridge, and between it and these high ridges run the Baltimore and Ohio Railroad, the Chesapeake and Ohio Canal, and the Frederick Turnpike—all centering on Harper's Ferry, on the Virginia side of the river.

Harper's Ferry is at the confluence of the Potomac and Shenandoah, but it is commanded by Maryland Heights. So long as Maryland Heights was occupied by Union troops, Harper's Ferry could not be occupied by the Confederates; if McLaws gained possession of these heights, Harper's Ferry was not tenable to Miles. With this view in mind, McLaws made his dispositions. Ascertaining that there was a rugged road running from the top of Solomon's Gap along Elk Ridge to the heights commanding Harper's Ferry, he directed Kershaw, with his brigade and Barksdale's, to ascend the ridge, march along its summit, and carry the heights using infantry alone, as the character of the ground forbade the use of either cavalry or artillery. Brigadier General Ambrose R. Wright's Brigade[59] was directed to ascend South Mountain with two pieces of artillery and move down it to the point overlooking Weverton to command the approaches to the pass there—the route by which McClellan's left column might be expected to attempt the relief of the garrison at Harper's Ferry. The brigade of Brigadier General Howell Cobb was directed to cross the valley and, marching along the base of Elk Ridge, keep in communication with Kershaw above and up to his advance, to support it if necessary and to serve as a rallying force in case of disaster. Those of Brigadier Generals Paul J. Semmes and William Mahone (the latter commanded by Lieutenant Colonel William A. Parham) were left at the west foot of Brownsville Gap to protect the rear of Kershaw and guard the approaches over South Mountain by Crampton's and Brownsville gaps.

These dispositions made and columns in motion early on the morning of the twelfth, McLaws, with the four brigades of Brigadier Generals Cadmus M. Wilcox (commanded by Colonel Alfred Cumming), Lewis A. Armistead, Roger A. Pryor, and Winfield S. Featherston, moved down the valley toward the Potomac by the road along the base of South Mountain, keeping in advance of Kershaw on Elk Ridge. As McLaws marched down the valley, its citizens impressed him with the idea that the crest of Maryland Heights was lined with cannon for a mile or more overlooking Harper's Ferry.

Kershaw, marching early, reached Solomon's Gap without opposition, when he discovered Union cavalry pickets under Captain Russell of the 1st Maryland Cavalry. It behooved Kershaw to advance cautiously with skirmishers thrown well out to the right and left, for the ground was favorable to an ambuscade and a stout resistance; this being done and an advance made, Russell withdrew after a few scattering shots, his object being not so much to resist a Confederate movement as to observe it. Upon reaching the summit of the ridge, Kershaw's skirmishers were thrown well down its side on the right, the main column filing to the left along the ridge, which in places was not more than twenty-five yards in width. The skirmishers on the right soon received a volley from a party under the command of Major Hugo Hildebrandt of the 39th New York, and upon the return fire Hildebrandt's men fell back with slight loss. About a mile farther on, Major John M. Bradley of the 13th Mississippi, commanding the skirmishers in advance of the main column, reported an abatis across the ridge, from which he had been fired upon. He was ordered forward and passed the obstruction without resistance, the Union pickets—some men of the 32d Ohio and the Potomac Home Brigade—falling back upon the main body. Leaving the path, which at this point passed down the ridge to the right, the Confederates filed along the crags on the ridge, the natural obstacles being so great that the soldiers only reached a point a little more than a mile from the point of the mountain at about 6:00 p.m. Here another abatis was encountered, extending across the narrow ridge and flanked on either side by ledges of precipitous rocks. A sharp skirmish ensued. Kershaw became satisfied that the enemy occupied the position in force, ordered Bradley to withdraw his skirmishers (not before they had been quite roughly handled, however), and deployed his own brigade in two lines extending across the entire practicable ground on the summit of the mountain, with Barksdale's Brigade immediately in rear. It was now dark, and further operations were suspended.

Wright, moving down South Mountain, his two mountain howitzers drawn by one horse each, gained his position on the bold heights overlooking Weverton without opposition. At sunset, Pryor's Brigade was pushed forward from McLaws's main column, took possession of Weverton, and deployed to close and defend the pass between the mountain and the river. The brigades of Armistead and Cobb were moved up and formed a line across the valley, commanding the road from Sandy Hook, upon which Colonel Maulsby (who, with 1,100 men and four guns, was holding that place as an outpost) fell back to Harper's Ferry and disposed his command to guard both the railroad bridge and the pontoon crossing. McLaws had now closed well in on all sides, and Kershaw was about to grasp the key to Harper's Ferry.

It is about time to consider what dispositions had been made to defend these heights and what had been left undone.

General Wool, while on an inspection visit to Harper's Ferry early in August, gave verbal orders to Colonel Miles to build a block-house on the heights, but Miles did not do so, as he thought it unnecessary, and appears not to have visited

---

[59] Wright has been encountered previously in this narrative as the commissioner from Georgia to Maryland in the early days of 1861.

the heights until September 7, when he inspected the position but gave no orders to throw up works, contenting himself by directing the officers in command to hold the heights at all hazards, as he considered them the key to his entire position. Colonel Ford of the 32d Ohio, who had withdrawn from Winchester two days before, was on the fifth put in command on Maryland Heights and over the troops there stationed: the 32d Ohio (Major Sylvester M. Hewitt now commanding); the 7th Squadron, Rhode Island Cavalry, under Major Corliss; three companies of the 1st Maryland, Potomac Home Brigade, under Major John A. Steiner; two companies of the 1st Maryland Cavalry under Captain Russell; about twelve men of Means's Rangers; and Captain Eugene McGrath's battery of the 5th New York Heavy Artillery. This last was nearly halfway up the west slope of the heights and had two 10-inch Columbiads (which could throw shot into Halltown, about two miles beyond Bolivar Heights) and one 50-pounder rifled gun. To these three guns were subsequently added four 12-pounder howitzers. In all, Ford had 1,150 men and seven guns.

Ford found that no preparation had been made for defense and the eastern and northern slopes of the mountain open and easy of access by way of Solomon's Gap, where a battery might be so placed as to repel a large force. (Repeated applications for guns to be placed at that point were refused by Miles.) Examination of the top of the mountain, at a point known as the Lookout, satisfied him that, if he could procure two guns, he could make a stand at that point and possibly prevent an enemy from ascending the mountain, either on the eastern or northern slope through the gap, but a second earnest appeal for two guns was met with the remark that if Ford and McGrath (his acting artillery officer) had their way, all the artillery would be withdrawn from Harper's Ferry to Maryland Heights, whereupon Ford abandoned this project and utterly neglected to throw up any defensive works—seemingly content with a small picket a short distance north of the Lookout and a few cavalry in observation at Solomon's Gap. On the eleventh Ford was informed that the Confederates were in Pleasant Valley, directly opposite Solomon's Gap. He reinforced the picket at the Lookout by one company of the 32d Ohio and two companies of the 1st Maryland, Potomac Home Brigade. Captain Russell, who was observing Solomon's Gap, reported Kershaw's advance. Ford called upon Miles for reinforcements, and a battalion of the 39th New York under Major Hildebrandt; the 126th New York, under Colonel Sherrill; and one company of the 111th New York were sent to him. Hildebrandt came up early enough to skirmish with Kershaw near Solomon's Gap. Sherrill arrived just before night and became partially engaged in front of the barricade beyond the Lookout.

A short mile above where the railroad crosses the Potomac, there leads up around the western slope of the mountain a rather difficult road. (It was about halfway up this road that McGrath's guns were placed.) Along the ridge of a mountain ran a rough path for nearly a mile to the highest point, where the Lookout was constructed, and north of this was a log-work partway across the crest of the mountain, thrown up by Captain John T. Whittier of the 1st Maryland, Potomac Home Brigade, when he heard of Kershaw's appearance in Pleasant Valley. A company of the 32d Ohio and two companies of the 126th New York were disposed to guard the approach from Pleasant Valley by the Sandy Hook Road, and Hildebrandt, with a part of the 39th New York and two companies of the 32d Ohio, was to support McGrath's guns. Sherrill, with eight companies of his regiment, one company of the 111th New York, and five companies of the 32d Ohio under Major Hewitt, was sent to the top of the mountain to reinforce Captain Whittier at the barricade of chestnut logs—before which Kershaw had been brought to a halt and lay down within five hundred yards of its defenders, whose advance pickets could hear the talk of his men and the rattling of their canteens.

It was apparent that the contest would be renewed in the morning, and Ford was apprehensive of the result. He made a pressing call on Miles for reinforcements—at least three regiments during the night, or all would be lost in the morning. He enforced repeated messages to that effect by sending Major Hewitt, who had been over the ground and knew the situation, to press upon Miles the importance of immediate help, and Miles promised to have reinforcements on the ground at daybreak—two regiments and two guns to report to Ford and one regiment to go up the west side of the mountain and come in on the enemy's right flank. (The heights are very rugged, unsuitable for the movements of troops, and in great part covered with dense woods and undergrowth, impeding movement and obscuring the vision.)

We left Kershaw at dark, on the twelfth, in check some distance north of the barricade. At sunrise of the thirteenth, he advanced his first line, the 7th South Carolina (Colonel David W. Aiken) on the right, the 8th South Carolina (Colonel John W. Henagan) on the left. Henagan's regiment soon came to a ledge of rocks that cut him off from further participation in the attack at that point, but Aiken's men, moving forward briskly through the dense woods under a heavy and telling fire of musketry, forced some slashings, and at the end of little more than a half-hour drove the skirmish line and its supports (consisting of nearly the whole force on the summit) back three hundred to four hundred yards to the barricade, behind which they confusedly rallied under the immediate command of Sherrill, an inexperienced but gallant officer, and some of the subordinate officers.

At the beginning of the attack, Kershaw had directed Barksdale to form his brigade down the eastern face of the mountain to his left (in prolongation of the two lines of the South Carolina brigade on the summit) to oppose that part of the Union line extending down this slope of the mountain. When Aiken had forced the slashings, Barksdale was ordered to advance and attack the Union line on that flank and in rear, and the two Carolina regiments again pressed forward in front. The Carolinians met with a most obstinate resistance, and a fierce and destructive fire was kept up for some time, entailing a heavy loss, which fell principally on the 7th South Carolina. It became necessary to send in the 3d South Carolina (Colonel James D. Nance) to its support. This gallant regiment marched over their not less gallant comrades of the 7th to carry the barricade and met the same stout resistance—and severe loss—from both those who had held the barricade and its approaches since early morning and a valiant reinforcement just arrived.

About ten o'clock, Lieutenant Colonel Stephen W. Downey, at the head of eight companies of the 3d Maryland, Potomac Home Brigade, came over from Harper's Ferry and reported to Ford, who retained four companies to go around on the eastern slope of the mountain and ordered Downey (with the other four companies and three companies of the 32d Ohio under Captain William A. Palmer) up the western slope to the assistance of the troops engaged. Downey marched up by a difficult bypath and, just as he reached the Lookout, came under a rattling fire that wounded several of his men. Pressing on, he came up to the barricade, ranged his men behind it, and, with others there, began his work. The firing was very brisk and heavy and brought the South Carolinians to check. Colonel Nance, seeing the difficulty of forcing the position by direct attack, suggested a flank movement by the 8th South Carolina on the Union left, but before his suggestion could be acted on, resistance ceased and the Union men were in retreat.

Meanwhile, word had come from Barksdale that, after much difficulty and hard labor, he had reached the desired position on the Union right flank but could not bring his men to the crest of the mountain without coming under the fire of the South Carolinians, as he was partially in rear of the Union line. Upon which, Kershaw (hoping to capture the enemy before him, if Barksdale could get up) ordered a cessation of firing, but before the order had been carried to all parts of the line, the right company of the 17th Mississippi of Barksdale's Brigade fired into a body of the 126th New York posted on a rocky and inaccessible position. A small fusillade began along the whole line. Sherrill was badly wounded and carried from the field, a partial panic followed, and many of the Union troops left in wild disorder despite all effort to stay them. William H. Nichols of the 7th Squadron, Rhode Island Cavalry, writes, "After Colonel Sherrill was wounded there appears to have been no field officer in responsible command on the heights, and contradictory and confusing orders followed one another … The larger portion of the men were just from home and had not had their arms long enough to have learned to load and fire." It was "a bad place in which to match green troops against veterans," and though some of the green troops went to the rear rather precipitately, there were many instances of conspicuous bravery among them.[60]

The defense of the heights was badly managed. Colonel Ford did not go to the top of the mountain where the contest was carried on and entrusted the direction of affairs to Major Hewitt, of his regiment, who, far in the rear, saw the stricken fugitives and judged it time to abandon the heights. Without making a personal examination, he sent orders for those at the barricade to retreat. This order, conveyed to the troops nearest him, was promptly obeyed. The remaining troops, either hearing that an order had been given to retreat or judging from the general retrograde movement that such had been given, began to fall back down the mountain, crowding to and past McGrath's battery. This was about eleven o'clock, and the Confederates, seeing the first indications of the retreat, gave a joyous shout, poured in a parting volley, and advanced to the possession of the barricade that had cost them dear, for they lost thirty-five killed and nearly two hundred wounded before it.

In the meantime, a stand had been made south of the Lookout by some companies of the 126th New York, 32d Ohio, and parts of other regiments, and a line was formed across the ridge and down the west side. It was at this critical state of affairs that Miles came on the field with reinforcements and endeavored to stem the tide of retreat and rally the fleeing troops, but, says Ford, "as fast as we forced them up one mountain path they returned by another until all seemed to be lost."[61] There were, however, some who had not lost head and heart. By the exertions of many officers, partial order was restored and part of the retreating troops, men of all regiments, returned to the front and formed on the line near the Lookout. Orders were given to retake the barricade, but an advance in that direction was met by the fire of the enemy, who had taken possession of the abandoned work and were in the act of moving forward. Miles now returned to Harper's Ferry. Ford understood him to say that if it became necessary to abandon the heights, the guns were to be spiked, dismounted, and rolled over the crags, so they could not be used against Harper's Ferry.

About twelve o'clock, Colonel Simeon Sammon arrived on the heights with seven companies of the 115th New York. Five companies, under the command of the colonel, were placed on the side of the hill near an old house and spring, beyond McGrath's battery, and two companies were sent to the mountaintop. Severe skirmishing continued at all points on the mountain as McLaws's two brigades cautiously advanced without pressing the fighting. When, about 3:30 p.m., it was discovered that the Confederates were advancing on both flanks as well as in front, Ford, it is said, "in obedience to the positive

[60] William H. Nichols, *The Siege and Capture of Harper's Ferry by the Confederates, September, 1862* (Providence, R.I.: Rhode Island Soldiers and Sailors Historical Society, 1889), 26.

[61] Thomas H. Ford to White, September 1862 [no day given], reprinted in *OR*, vol. 19, pt. 1, 543.

orders of Colonel Miles ... ordered the guns to be spiked and dismounted and the forces withdrawn to the opposite side of the river, all of which was done in good order."[62] Ford rode down the mountain at the head of the 126th New York. Nichols records, "It is said that McGrath, who commanded the battery, upon receiving orders to spike his guns refused to obey and would not do so until he saw the infantry deserting him ... It was supposed that Ford had orders to hold the heights to the last extremity, which had not then arrived. Colonel Miles told General White immediately after the evacuation that he gave no orders to withdraw from the heights."[63]

Barksdale was now directed to occupy the point of the heights, which he did without encountering more than a retiring skirmisher, and by 4:30 p.m. McLaws's two brigades had possession of the entire heights, the Union troops retiring down a road invisible to the Confederates in the valley and fired on by their skirmishers from high ground as they crossed the bridge to the Harper's Ferry side of the Potomac. The western slope of the heights was so fully swept by artillery fire from Camp Hill in Harper's Ferry that the Confederates did not occupy it, from which it resulted that, on the next day, a detachment of the 39th New York and the 65th Illinois under the command of Major John Wood (of the latter regiment) crossed the bridge and recovered the four abandoned field guns, with a load of ammunition and other stores.

Most of the Union troops engaged in the defense of Maryland Heights behaved well, some of them most gallantly. Heavy and undeserved censure fell upon a great part of the 126th New York—a new regiment, raw and undrilled, suddenly placed in a trying position, where it suffered severe loss. Its subsequent record was a good and honorable one.[64]

Miles was justly censured for the loss of Maryland Heights and Ford was dismissed from the service. Ford did not personally direct the movements of his men, many of whom were raw recruits, nor did he ascend the mountain while they were engaged. In fact, he never went to the crest where the barricade was thrown up (before, during, or after the engagement) but, remaining near McGrath's battery on the west slope of the mountain, entrusted the conduct of affairs to Hewitt, a venerable gentleman with a long white beard who had exchanged the practice of medicine for the profession of arms. It was this nervous officer who, from the vicinity of the Lookout, heard the rattle of musketry, saw wounded officers and men borne past him, was unduly impressed by the usual confusion in rear of a fighting line, and, believing that the time had come for retreat, ordered the abandonment of the barricade. This order was fatal to the further possession of Maryland Heights and sealed the fate of Harper's Ferry.

With Maryland Heights secured, the Confederate troops in Pleasant Valley were advanced. Cobb's Brigade occupied Sandy Hook, Colonel Maulsby's infantry and four guns having abandoned the place and fallen back to Harper's Ferry. At the same time, the main Confederate column near South Mountain moved down to close all avenues of escape from Harper's Ferry and tighten their grasp on that place.

Up to this time, McLaws had received no notice of the advance of either Jackson or Walker, except that a courier from Jackson brought a dispatch to the effect that his leading division would be near Harper's Ferry about 2:00 p.m., and some firing in that direction led to the belief that he was advancing. During the day, heavy cannonading was heard to the east and northeast, and cavalry scouts were constantly reporting the advance of Union troops from various directions.[65] At night on the thirteenth, McLaws had the two brigades of Semmes and Mahone guarding the passes at Brownsville and Crampton's gaps, Wright's and Pryor's at Weverton, Cobb's and Armistead's at Sandy Hook, Kershaw's and Barksdale's on Maryland Heights, and Featherston's in Pleasant Valley as a reserve.

During the night, McLaws received a dispatch from Lee with information of his belief that McClellan was moving toward Harper's Ferry to relieve Miles. Lee urged him to expedite matters and, when they were completed, to move to Sharpsburg. McLaws was also told that Longstreet would move down from Hagerstown the next day (September 14) and take position on Beaver Creek, and that Stuart had been directed to keep McLaws informed as to the enemy's movements.[66] On the same night came another dispatch from Lee that he had not heard from McLaws since he left the main body of the army; that the enemy had abandoned Martinsburg and retreated to Harper's Ferry, 2,500 to 3,000 strong; and that Stuart occupied Middletown Valley, D. H Hill was a mile or two west of Boonsboro at the junction of the Boonsboro and Hagerstown roads, and Longstreet at Hagerstown. This dispatch directed him to watch well the main road from Frederick to

[62] Ibid., 544.

[63] Nichols, 27–28.

[64] For a time the 126th New York was derided as the Harper's Ferry Cowards. This undeserved stain was removed from its reputation permanently the following July, when the regiment—at a cost of more than 50 percent casualties over two days of fighting at Gettysburg—captured three Confederate battle-flags, acts that earned three members of the regiment the Medal of Honor. See John W. Busey and David G. Martin, *Regimental Strengths and Losses at Gettysburg* (Hightstown, N.J.: Longstreet House, 1982), 244; Wayne Mahood, *"Written in Blood": A History of the 126th New York Infantry in the Civil War* (Hightstown, N.J.: Longstreet House, 1997), 154–57.

[65] McLaws to Chilton, October 18, 1862, reprinted in *OR*, vol. 19, pt. 1, 854.

[66] Thomas M. R. Talcott to McLaws, September 13, 1862, 10:00 p.m., reprinted in *OR*, vol. 19, pt. 2, 607.

Harper's Ferry, through Weverton, and to communicate freely. Above all, Lee hoped that Harper's Ferry would be speedily disposed of and the various detachments returned to the main body of the army.[67]

When it became known that Ford had abandoned Maryland Heights, there was much astonishment among officers and men in Harper's Ferry and on Bolivar Heights. Miles was appealed to by White and others to reoccupy them at any cost, but he pleaded the orders under which he was acting and also argued that, as the guns had been spiked and dismounted, the heights across the Potomac were of no further consequence. The troops withdrawn from Maryland Heights were put in position on Bolivar Heights.

It was evident to Miles and his officers that they could not hold out much longer in the position where the troops were now crowded. Hearing nothing from McClellan (yet believing him near), Miles sent for Captain Russell of the 1st Maryland Cavalry and asked if he could not go with two or three men, pass the enemy's lines, and "try to reach somebody that had ever heard of the United States Army, or any general of the United States Army, or anybody that knew anything about the United States Army, and report the condition of Harper's Ferry." Russell was willing to make the trial, upon which Miles told him that if he could get to any general of the U.S. Army, to any telegraph station, or, if possible, to General McClellan (whom he supposed was at Frederick), to report that Maryland Heights had been lost, that he thought he could hold out forty-eight hours, and that he had subsistence for forty-eight hours, but if not relieved in that time he would have to surrender. Russell selected nine men, went through the Confederates on the Virginia side, moved across fields near the river, and crossed the Potomac near the mouth of the Antietam, where he dashed past a Confederate picket and, by by-roads and trails, reached South Mountain, where another picket was met and avoided. Russell crossed South Mountain by a wood road, reached Middletown, and informed General Reno of his mission. Passing on, by nine o'clock of the morning of the fourteenth, he had delivered his message to McClellan, by whom he was informed that General Franklin was on the way to relieve Miles.[68] Nearly three hours later, McClellan wrote Franklin from Middletown that he had heard from Miles, who had abandoned Maryland Heights, and said in concluding his dispatch, "Continue to bear in mind the necessity of relieving Colonel Miles if possible."[69] This dispatch was delivered to Franklin while he was making leisurely arrangements to force Crampton's Gap. What other measures McClellan took to relieve Miles shall appear elsewhere.

On the morning of the fourteenth, Miles held the bridges across the Potomac, Camp Hill, and the line of Bolivar Heights, along with the ridge on the prolongation of the heights between the Charlestown Turnpike and the Shenandoah River. The bridges were guarded by eight companies of the 1st Maryland, Potomac Home Brigade, the 87th Ohio, and one section of Captain Potts's battery, all under the command of Colonel Maulsby.

Bolivar Heights forms the base of a triangle, of which the Potomac and Shenandoah are the other two sides. It rises quite abruptly from the town on the west, spreads out into a plain, and, again rising, forms a sort of parapet, sloping down to the surrounding country, the level of which is of much lower grade. The right of Bolivar Heights was held by the 39th New York (Major Hildebrandt), 111th New York (Colonel Segoine), 115th New York (Colonel Sammon), 65th Illinois (Colonel Cameron), and six rifled guns each of Phillips's Illinois battery and von Sehlen's Indiana battery. (These troops were brigaded under the command of Colonel D'Utassy of the 39th New York.) The 65th Illinois was on the extreme right of the brigade (where the bluff descended abruptly to the Potomac), von Sehlen's battery about the center of the brigade, and Phillips's on its left, slight earthworks being thrown up for their protection. On the forenoon of the fourteenth, three heavy guns of Graham's battery moved from Camp Hill and took position on the extreme right, supported by the Illinois regiment. The left of Bolivar Heights was held by the brigade commanded by Colonel Trimble of the 60th Ohio, consisting of that regiment, the 9th Vermont (Colonel Stannard), 126th New York (now commanded by Captain Philo D. Phillips), and Rigby's battery. Rigby was on the left of the line about fifty yards from the Charlestown Turnpike, and a slight earthwork was constructed to shelter the men. The 60th Ohio was on the immediate right of the battery.

Miles had utterly neglected to entrench the heights and failed to cut down the woods in front, which gave good shelter and cover to an enemy's advance. Axe-men were now set to felling trees, and, without orders from superior officers, regimental and company commanders began to throw up entrenchments. They were thrown up on the morning of the fourteenth, made of logs and earth and filled in with tents, cast-off clothing, army blankets, and anything else that would break the force of a ball.

The ground to the southwest of the Charlestown Turnpike and between it and the Shenandoah, full of ravines and quite heavily wooded, was held by the 3d Maryland, Potomac Home Brigade, under the command of Colonel Downey. Other troops were placed upon the plateau adjacent to Bolivar Heights and, as much as possible, under cover of ravines.

[67] Armistead L. Long to McLaws, September 13, 1862, reprinted in *OR*, vol. 19, pt. 2, 606.

[68] "Record of the Harper's Ferry Military Commission," October 16, 1862, 720–21.

[69] McClellan to William B. Franklin, September 14, 1862, 11:45 a.m., reprinted in *OR*, vol. 51, pt. 1, 833.

Camp Hill, rising immediately from the town of Harper's Ferry, was surrounded by an inner line of entrenchments to fall back on in the event of being driven from the more advanced position of Bolivar Heights. This reserve position was occupied by Captain Graham's Battery A, 5th New York Heavy Artillery, and four guns (two 24-pounder howitzers and two 20-pounder Parrott guns) of Captain Potts's Ohio battery, supported by the 12th New York State Militia under the command of Colonel Ward. As we have seen, three of Graham's guns were sent on the morning of the fourteenth to the extreme right of the line on Bolivar Heights; the remainder, on the precipice overhanging the Shenandoah, commanded the approaches by the Shenandoah Road and also up the Potomac from Sandy Hook. They commanded also the position on Bolivar Heights and raked the whole plain across which troops must approach to the inner entrenchments, and they had the range of Maryland Heights and Loudoun Heights. Potts's guns were north of the main road running from Harper's Ferry to Bolivar. In addition to the batteries of Graham and Potts, a number of howitzers were mounted along the entrenchments.

Jackson (as we have seen) encamped on the evening of the thirteenth two miles in front of Miles's position on Bolivar Heights. This was after McLaws had possession of Maryland Heights and had driven the Union forces from them and into the blind alley, of which Jackson had the key and had but to advance and gather the fruit of McLaws's enterprise. Before moving, however, Jackson wished to satisfy himself that all avenues of escape were closed to Miles and deferred attack until he could communicate with McLaws and Walker. Early in the morning, he acknowledged receipt of McLaws's dispatch of the thirteenth; informed him that Loudoun Heights were in possession of Walker; directed McLaws to take complete possession of Maryland Heights; and hoped that McLaws could establish batteries to fire upon Miles and, if so, to let him know when they were ready so that he could make a demand for the surrender of the place before opening fire on it.[70] There was much difficulty in communicating with McLaws and Walker. McLaws did not receive this dispatch until late in the day, and forenoon on the fourteenth passed with but little movement on Jackson's part, partly attributable to the fact that he could not be made to believe that McClellan's whole army was in movement and partly because Bolivar Heights was so strong that he desired to remain quiet until McLaws and Walker drew attention from him. The following were the orders of the day:

SPECIAL ORDERS

No. —.

Headquarters Valley District

September 14, 1862

I. To-day Major-General McLaws will attack so as to sweep with his artillery the ground occupied by the enemy, take his batteries in reverse, and otherwise operate against him, as circumstances may justify.

II. Brigadier-General Walker will take in reverse the battery on the turnpike, and also sweep with his artillery the ground occupied by the enemy, and silence the battery on the island in the Shenandoah should he find a battery there.

III. Maj. Gen. A.P. Hill will move along the left bank of the Shenandoah, and thus turn the enemy's left flank and enter Harper's Ferry.

IV. Brigadier-General Lawton will move along the turnpike for the purpose of supporting General Hill and otherwise operating against the enemy on the left of General Hill.

V. Brigadier-General Jones will, with one of his brigades and a battery of artillery, make a demonstration against the enemy's right; the remaining part of his division will constitute the reserve and move along the turnpike.

By order of Major-General Jackson:

W[illia]m L. Jackson,

Acting Assistant Adjutant-General[71]

These orders were prepared in the morning and sent to the signal officer near midday; they were not received by McLaws and Walker until action had been opened.

We left Walker, on the evening of the thirteenth, in possession of Loudoun Heights and closing all avenues of escape down the west bank of the Potomac. At daylight of the fourteenth, he ordered Captain Thomas B. French, with three Parrott guns of his own (Virginia) battery and two rifled pieces of Captain James R. Branch's (Virginia) Battery under Lieutenant Melvin A. Martin, to ascend Loudoun Heights. (Walker accompanied him to place the guns in a good yet masked position.) This was done by eight o'clock, and Walker sought to open communication by signal with Jackson, but it was after ten o'clock before he could advise him of his readiness to attack and ask whether he should wait for McLaws before opening fire. "Wait," replied Jackson,[72] who then prepared the following, which was signaled to both McLaws and Walker:

---

[70] Jackson to McLaws, September 14, 1862, 7:20 a.m., reprinted in *OR*, vol. 19, pt. 2, 607.

[71] Headquarters Valley District, Special Orders of September 14, 1862, as contained in the report of Joseph L. Bartlett, September 14, 1862, reprinted in *OR*, vol. 19, pt. 1, 959.

[72] Bartlett, 958.

If you can, establish batteries to drive the enemy from the hill west of Bolivar and on which Barbour's house is, and any other position where he may be damaged by your artillery, and let me know when you are ready to open your batteries, and give me any suggestions by which you can operate against the enemy. Cut the telegraph line down the Potomac if it is not already done. Keep a good lookout against a Federal advance from below. Similar instructions will be sent to General Walker. I do not desire any of the batteries to open until all are ready on both sides of the river, except you should find it necessary, of which you must judge for yourself. I will let you know when to open all the batteries.[73]

The sound of heavy guns was now heard by Walker in the direction of Turner's Gap, and McLaws signaled him that the enemy was in his rear, upon which he again communicated with Jackson, giving him the information he had received from McLaws and again reporting that his guns were ready to open,[74] to which Jackson replied, "Do not open until General McLaws notifies me what he can probably effect. Let me know what you can effect with your command upon the enemy."[75]

As the sound of artillery in the direction of South Mountain grew louder and apparently nearer at noon, indicating McClellan's advance, Walker again asked permission to open fire and about the same time signaled that he had information that the enemy were advancing on his own rear by way of Purcellville and had possession of the passes from the valley.[76] About this time, Jackson signaled both McLaws and Walker to "fire at such positions of the enemy as will be most effective,"[77] but before receipt of this (indeed, Walker says that he never received it), Walker had opened fire. The signal station and two North Carolina regiments under Colonel Matt W. Ransom (who had relieved Colonel Cooke's men) had attracted the attention of the batteries on Camp Hill and Bolivar Heights, which opened their guns upon them. Walker construed Jackson's order not to fire until it became necessary as now operative.[78] Fully impressed with the idea that McClellan was advancing with much more speed than either Lee or Jackson had anticipated and anxious to expedite matters with Miles, he opened his five guns on the batteries on Bolivar Heights and Camp Hill, disabling some of them and stampeding their infantry supports. Colonel George L. Willard of the 125th New York reports, "The fire was rapid and all the troops on the plateau made a speedy and somewhat disorderly retreat. My regiment, in spite of my efforts, and subjected for the first time to a hot fire, retreated in a good deal of disorder toward the ravine running south from the battery on Bolivar Heights."[79] The long-range guns near the Barbour house on Camp Hill and von Sehlen's battery on Bolivar Heights answered the fire ineffectively and were soon silenced. An hour after Walker opened his batteries, those of Jackson joined in from the right and left of his line, and, still an hour later, McLaws's added to the attack—the combined fire disabling four of Miles's guns, blowing up two caissons, and discouraging the cavalry and infantry, who were helpless to defend themselves against a heavy fire of artillery in front and a plunging fire from the rear.

---

[73] Jackson to McLaws and John G. Walker, September 14, 1862, as contained in Bartlett, 958.

[74] Walker to Jackson [September 14, 1862], as contained in Bartlett, 958.

[75] Jackson to John G. Walker [September 14, 1862], as contained in Bartlett, 958.

[76] Walker to Jackson [September 14, 1862], as contained in Bartlett, 959.

[77] Jackson to John G. Walker and McLaws [September 14, 1862], as contained in Bartlett, 959.

[78] Two days after this, Jackson and Walker were riding from the Potomac to join Lee at Sharpsburg. Walker says, "As we rode along, I mentioned my *ruse* in opening fire on Harper's Ferry. Knowing the strictness of Jackson's idea in regard to military obedience, I felt a little doubtful as to what he would say. When I had finished my confession, he was silent for some minutes, and then remarked, 'It was just as well as it was; but I could not believe that the fire you reported indicated the advance of McClellan in force. It seemed more likely to be merely a cavalry affair.' Then, after an interval of silence as if to himself, he continued, 'I thought I knew McClellan … but this movement of his puzzles me.'" John G. Walker, "Jackson's Capture of Harper's Ferry," in *Battles and Leaders*, 611.—EAC

Walker's emphasis in this postwar article on having disobeyed orders stems from a claim he made therein to the effect that Jackson had signaled him that the bombardment was not be opened for twenty-four hours after all three commands were in position, in order to give the garrison time to surrender. John G. Walker, "Jackson's Capture of Harper's Ferry," 609. The notion that Jackson would have delayed a time-sensitive (and already behind-schedule) operation by a full day was no less plausible in its day than it is to modern readers. Upon its appearance in print, two contemporaries issued written refutations of this claim. Bradley T. Johnson, "Stonewall Jackson's Intentions at Harper's Ferry I," in *Battles and Leaders*, 615–16; Douglas, "Stonewall Jackson's Intentions at Harper's Ferry II," in *Battles and Leaders*, 617–18. It is noteworthy that Walker makes no mention of any such admonition to withhold fire for twenty-four hours (or violating the same) in his report of the battle. See John G. Walker to Elisha F. Paxton, October 7, 1862, reprinted in *OR*, vol. 19, pt. 1, 912–14. Of greater significance is the fact that Carman, who accepted other portions of Walker's account, did not include this particular story in his narrative. In the very next sentence, however, Carman appears to support Walker's larger contention: that both Jackson and Lee had underestimated McClellan and that he (Walker) rectified the error by taking decisive action on his own initiative. See John G. Walker, "Jackson's Capture of Harper's Ferry," 609–10.

In fairness to Walker, however, the controversy lies not in the notion of a truce by Jackson but rather in the duration. Evidence of Jackson's intention regarding the former is irrefutable: "So soon as you get your batteries all planted, let me know, as *I desire*, after yourself, Walker, and myself have our batteries ready to open, *to send in a flag of truce, for the purpose of getting out the non-combatants, should the commanding officer refuse to surrender* [emphasis added]." Jackson to McLaws, September 14, 1862, 7:20 a.m., reprinted in *OR*, vol. 19, pt. 2, 607.

[79] George L. Willard to William H. Trimble, September 21, 1862, reprinted in *OR*, vol. 19, pt. 1, 540.

We return to McLaws.[80] The engineers that had been examining the ground during the evening of the thirteenth had reported that it was impractical to carry cannon to the top of the heights, owing to the steepness of the ascent and the numerous walls of rock that could not be passed, but Major Abram H. McLaws, quartermaster of the division, in coming from Kershaw's command that evening, had accidentally struck an old wood road which wound up a part of the way. By using that as far as it went, the men could, by lifting the guns over the ledges and hauling them by hand in other places, get the guns up. So General McLaws employed the morning of the fourteenth in cutting and improving this wood road to the top of the heights and overcoming the difficulties of the ascent. Between two and three o'clock in the afternoon, Captains John P. W. Read and Henry H. Carlton, commanding Georgia batteries with Kershaw's and Barksdale's Brigades, had (under the direction of Major Samuel P. Hamilton, divisional chief of artillery) two Parrott guns from each battery in position overlooking Bolivar Heights, Camp Hill, and the town. Fire was opened at once, driving the Union troops from Camp Hill and their works on the right of Bolivar Heights. This, in connection with Walker's fire from Loudoun Heights and from Jackson's advancing line, was kept up all the afternoon.

A. P. Hill, on the right, was ordered to move along the left bank of the Shenandoah around the base of the hill, turn Miles's left, and enter Harper's Ferry. Lawton, commanding Ewell's Division, was directed to move along the turnpike in support to Hill and also to operate against Miles's line to the left. J. R. Jones, commanding Jackson's Division, was directed to take one brigade and a battery of artillery and make a demonstration against Miles's right, while the remaining brigades of the division moved along the turnpike as a reserve. Major Thomas B. Massie, who with two companies of the 12th Virginia Cavalry had joined Jackson while on the road from Martinsburg, was instructed to keep upon the left flank for the purpose of preventing the escape of the Union forces in that direction.

The movement began late in the afternoon by the advance of Brigadier General Charles S. Winder's (Stonewall) Brigade, under Colonel Andrew J. Grigsby, on the Union right, by which a cavalry detachment was quickly dispersed and a commanding hill secured near the Potomac (and from which the Virginia batteries of Captain William T. Poague and Captain John C. Carpenter did admirable execution subsequently). Toward night, Jones moved nearer the Potomac and, when darkness concealed the movement, Brigadier General William E. Starke's Brigade was moved in still closer proximity, resting on the river road and overlooking the water to prevent the Union troops from making their escape.

Having first shelled the woods through which his route lay and flushed out the Union skirmishers, Hill, in execution of his orders, moved obliquely to the right until he struck the Shenandoah. Observing an eminence crowning the extreme left of the Union line—occupied by infantry but without artillery, bare of all earthworks, and protected only by an abatis of slashed timber—the brigades of Brigadier General William Dorsey Pender, Brigadier General James J. Archer, and Colonel John M. Brockenbrough were directed to gain the crest of this hill, while those of Brigadier Generals Lawrence O'Bryan Branch and Maxcy Gregg were directed to march along the river road during the night, take advantage of the ravines cutting the precipitous banks of the river, and establish themselves on the plain to the left and rear of the Union line. Colonel Edward L. Thomas's Brigade was to follow in reserve.

The execution of the movement on the hill by the three brigades of Pender, Archer, and Brockenbrough was entrusted to Pender (his own brigade being commanded by Lieutenant[81] Richard H. Brewer of his staff). Pender moved forward

---

80 In Carman's original manuscript, the prior paragraph concluded with the sentence, "Leaving Hill for a moment, now in motion closing in from the Charleston [*sic*] road, we return to McLaws." The "Hill" in this case is A. P. Hill—whose actions on this day have not yet been treated in the narrative. Examination of the physical page shows that the paragraph in question was cut from a different sheet of paper and glued into place here. The reference to the as yet unmentioned A. P. Hill demonstrates that this portion appeared originally at a later point in one of Carman's earlier drafts.

81 Carman lists him "Colonel R. H. Brewer," and he appears as such in the table of organization for the Army of Northern Virginia in the Maryland campaign created by the compilers of the *OR*. "Organization of the Army of Northern Virginia, General Robert E. Lee, commanding, during the Maryland Campaign," *OR*, vol. 19, pt. 1, 807. Strictly speaking, this is incorrect—but understandable. In his official report, Pender makes two references to Brewer: "Colonel Brewer was in command of the brigade at this time, and did himself great credit in the manner in which he handled it," and then, "I would beg leave to bring to the notice of the major-general the distinguished gallantry and efficiency of First Lieut. R. H. Brewer, volunteer aide on my staff, whom I recommend for promotion." William Dorsey Pender to "General" [Ambrose P. Hill], October 14, 1862, reprinted in *OR*, vol. 19, pt. 1, 1004–5. As a serving U.S. officer, Brewer was extended and accepted a commission in the regular Confederate Army as lieutenant in March 1861. By June 1862, he had risen to the rank of colonel in the provisional Army, commanding a mixed regiment of Mississippi and Alabama horsemen in the western theater, at which time he requested to be relieved from further field service in the cavalry due to ill health. The request was granted, voiding his provisional Army commission. Thus, when he agreed to serve as a volunteer aide-de-camp under Pender some weeks later, he was operating under his regular commission as lieutenant. Pender's use of "colonel" in his report is a courtesy. Compiled Service Record of Richard H. Brewer, Compiled Service Records of Confederate General and Staff Officers, and Non-Regimental Enlisted Men (National Archives Microfilm Publication M331, reel 32), Record Group 109, National Archives. See also Robert E. L. Krick, *Staff Officers in Gray: A Biographical Register of the Staff Officers of the Army of Northern Virginia* (Chapel Hill: University of North Carolina Press, 2003), 82.

briskly, his own brigade in advance, and soon encountered the skirmishers of Colonel Downey's 3d Maryland, Potomac Home Brigade, and drove them. General White was on this part of the field and, perceiving the danger of Pender's movement, ordered the 9th Vermont to support Downey and subsequently reinforced the two regiments with the 32d Ohio and one section of Rigby's battery. (One of Rigby's guns opened fire with good effect; the other was unable to limber.) Later, the 125th New York was put on a cross-road extending from Bolivar Heights to the Shenandoah as a reserve and to extend the left of the line as far as the railroad and connect with the 87th Ohio, and two guns of Potts's battery were hastened from Camp Hill and placed on the turnpike.

Pender continued the engagement until after dark but did not gain the coveted ground, although within one hundred yards of it. No troops being within supporting distance, he ordered his brigade back a few yards. (White claims that it was repulsed, the Union troops behaving very handsomely.[82]) Major[83] Reuben Lindsay Walker, chief of artillery of A. P. Hill's Division, brought up the batteries of Captains William J. Pegram (Virginia), David G. McIntosh (South Carolina), Greenlee Davidson (Virginia), Carter M. Braxton (Virginia), and William G. Crenshaw (Virginia) and during the night established them on the ground gained by Pender's advance. Branch and Gregg, moving down the Winchester and Potomac Railroad, the 7th North Carolina in advance, drove some sharpshooters from a high point overlooking the railroad and gained the position indicated for them. This was not accomplished until after midnight, and daylight found them in rear of the Union line, between Bolivar Heights and the Shenandoah.

As directed, Lawton led Ewell's Division, in the center, along the turnpike in three columns—one on the road and the others on either side of it—until he reached Halltown, where he formed line of battle. Lawton's and Trimble's Brigades (commanded by Colonels Marcellus Douglass and James A. Walker, respectively) were on the right of the turnpike and that of Brigadier General Harry T. Hays on the left. Brigadier General Jubal A. Early's Brigade was in rear of Lawton. In this order, Lawton advanced to School House Hill, fronting Bolivar Heights and in easy range of artillery. The troops lay on their arms during the night.

While engaged in getting his guns in position on Maryland Heights on the fourteenth, McLaws was startled by news that McClellan was forcing Crampton's Gap in his rear.[84] This he communicated to Jackson,[85] but Jackson could not credit the information; he thought only of cavalry affairs in that quarter.[86] Jackson directed McLaws to notify D. H. Hill of the enemy's position and request him to protect his rear—and to send the same message to Lee near Hagerstown. At the same time, he requested McLaws to let him know what he could probably effect with his artillery and also with his entire command.[87] Earlier in the day, McLaws had received a message from Lee that Longstreet would move back from Hagerstown to occupy the "Boonsborough" (Pleasant) Valley so as to protect his flank until the operations at Harper's Ferry were finished and that Lee desired McLaws to push those operations as rapidly as possible and join the main army by way of that same valley.[88] McLaws knew later that Crampton's Gap had been forced, so when night came he withdrew Kershaw and Barksdale from Maryland Heights and hastened to form line across Pleasant Valley, leaving only the 13th Mississippi and two guns of Read's Battery on the heights overlooking Harper's Ferry.

---

[82] White to Whipple, September 22, 1862, 527.

[83] In his original manuscript, Carman gives Walker's rank here as "Lieutenant Colonel." However, in his table of organization for the Army of Northern Virginia he gives it as "Major." Walker also appears at this lower rank on the War Department tablet (no. 372) erected for this unit, under Carman's supervision, at Antietam National Battlefield. The editors of the OR list him as "Lieutenant Colonel" in their table of organization for the campaign. "Organization of the Army of Northern Virginia," 807. Walker signs his official report of the campaign as "Lieutenant Colonel," and the only other two reports for the campaign that mention him (Jackson's and A. P. Hill's) refer to him this way. Reuben Lindsay Walker to Richard C. Morgan, March 1, 1863, reprinted in OR, vol. 19, pt. 1, 985; Jackson to Lee, April 23, 1863, reprinted in OR, vol. 19, pt. 1, 952; Ambrose P. Hill to Charles J. Faulkner, February 25, 1863, reprinted in OR, vol. 19, pt. 1, 979. However, all three documents are from the following year; this appears to be the source of the confusion. As it happened, Walker was recommended for promotion to lieutenant colonel by the president on September 8, 1862, and was confirmed by the Senate on October 4. Journal of the Senate of the First Congress of the Confederate States of America, vol. 2 of Journal of the Congress of the Confederate States of America, 1861–1865, 58th Cong., 2d sess., 1904, S. Doc. 234, serial 4611, 365, 422.

[84] McLaws later reported that he heard the sound of cannon fire from the gaps, but believed the Confederate rear-guard was in no danger of collapse behind him because Stuart had arrived from there with the news that there was only one brigade of the enemy probing South Mountain. His surprise was understandable when, a short time later, one of his staffers returned with the news that "the enemy had forced the gap." McLaws to Chilton, October 18, 1862, reprinted in OR, vol. 19, pt. 1, 854. The absence of this detail in Carman's narrative points again to his overly positive assessment of the performance of Stuart's cavalry.

[85] John G. Walker to Jackson [September 14, 1862], as contained in Bartlett, 958.

[86] John G. Walker, "Jackson's Capture of Harper's Ferry," 609–10. Here again is evidenced Carman's acceptance of Walker's self-serving and inaccurate claims to have saved the Harper's Ferry operation from Jackson's lack of due concern.

[87] Jackson to McLaws [September 14, 1862], as contained in Bartlett, 958.

[88] Lee to McLaws, September 14, 1862, reprinted in OR, vol. 19, pt. 2, 608.

While in the execution of this movement, McLaws received this dispatch from Lee:

The day has gone against us and this army will go by Sharpsburg and cross the river. It is necessary for you to abandon your position to-night. Send your trains not required on the road to cross the river. Your troops you must have well in hand to unite with this command, which will retire by Sharpsburg. Send forward officers to explore the way, ascertain the best crossing of the Potomac, and if you can find any between you and Shepherdstown leave Shepherdstown Ford for this command. Send an officer to report to me on the Sharpsburg road, where you are and what crossing you will take. You will of course bring Anderson's division with you.[89]

Later in the night, McLaws received another dispatch from the commanding general:

In addition to what has already been stated in reference to your abandonment of Weverton, and routes you can take, I will mention you might cross the Potomac, below Weverton, into Virginia. I believe there is a ford at the Point of Rocks, and at Berlin below, but do not know whether either is accessible to you. The enemy from Jefferson seem to have forced a passage at Crampton's Gap, which may leave all on the river clear. This portion of the army will take position at Centreville, commonly called Keedysville, 2½ miles from Boonsborough, on the Sharpsburg road, with a view of preventing the enemy that may enter the gap at Boonsborough turnpike from cutting you off, and enabling you to make a junction with it. If you can pass to-night on the river road, by Harper's Ferry, or cross the mountain below Crampton's Gap toward Sharpsburg, let me know. I will be found at or near Centreville, or Keedysville, as it is called.[90]

McLaws reasoned that to obey these orders would leave open a way for Miles to escape and that Lee did not know the real condition of affairs in Pleasant Valley, so he sent a courier to inform Lee that his position was a strong one. McLaws would take the risk of remaining where he was and rely upon Lee to get him out of the difficulty he was in by maneuvering McClellan away from the support of Franklin, who had come through Crampton's Gap (McLaws considering himself able to take care of Franklin). McLaws says in his report:

The enemy having forced Crampton's Gap, thereby completely cutting off my route up the valley to join the forces with General Lee, as Solomon's Gap, the only road over Elk Ridge, was just in front of the one over the Blue Ridge occupied by the enemy, I had nothing to do but to defend my position. I could not retire under the bluffs along the river, with the enemy pressing my rear and the forces at Harper's Ferry operating in conjunction, unless under a combination of circumstances I could not rely on to happen at the exact time needed; could not pass over the mountain except in a scattered and disorganized condition, nor could have gone through the Weverton Pass into the open country beyond to cross a doubtful ford when the enemy was in force on the other side of the Blue Ridge and coming down in my rear. There was no outlet in any direction for anything but the troops, and that very doubtful. In no contingency could I have saved the trains and artillery. I therefore determined to defend myself in the valley, holding the two heights and the two lower passes in order to force a direct advance down the valley, to prevent co-operation from Harper's Ferry, and at the same time to carry out my orders in relation to the capture of that place.[91]

Lee's instructions to Jackson were similar to those given McLaws; he informed Jackson of McClellan's advance and impressed upon him the necessity of completing the work at Harper's Ferry and hastening to join him. Jackson replied, "Through God's blessing, the advance, which commenced this evening, has been successful thus far, and I look to Him for complete success to-morrow. The advance has been directed to be resumed at dawn to-morrow morning. I am thankful that our loss has been small. Your dispatch respecting the movements of the enemy and the importance of concentration has been received."[92]

The tenor of this characteristic dispatch indicated that Jackson did not fully realize the fact that McClellan's entire army was abreast both passes of South Mountain and that Lee and all his detachments were in great jeopardy. Had he so thought, it is inconceivable how he could have run the risk of remaining another hour in front of Harper's Ferry; he would have abandoned operations and immediately marched to rejoin his chief. But he correctly reasoned that to relinquish the opportunity of gaining the prize before him and march to join Lee would make his brilliant movement a vain one and, knowing that it was with McClellan that Lee had to deal, concluded that instead of marching to join Lee that night he would hold on a few hours longer and reap the fruits of his enterprise.

---

[89] Chilton to McLaws, September 14, 8:00 p.m., reprinted in *OR*, vol. 51, pt. 2, 618–19.

[90] Chilton to McLaws, September 14, 1862, 11:15 p.m., reprinted in *OR*, vol. 19, pt. 2, 608.

[91] McLaws to Chilton, October 18, 1862, 856.

[92] Jackson to Chilton, September 14, 1862, 8:15 p.m., reprinted in *OR*, vol. 19, pt. 1, 951.

Jackson worked with great energy to get his guns in position by daylight to crush out all resistance. During the night Colonel Stapleton Crutchfield, his chief of artillery, crossed ten guns from the batteries of Captain William D. Brown (Maryland), Captain William F. Dement (Maryland), Lieutenant Asher W. Garber[93] (Virginia), and Captain Joseph W. Latimer (Virginia) over the Shenandoah at Keys's Ford and, moving on the west side, established them on a plateau at the foot of Loudoun Heights so as to enfilade the entire position on Bolivar Heights and take the nearest and most formidable work—an embrasure battery for four guns, but open in the rear—in reverse. These ten guns were of Ewell's Division; the other guns of this division were placed in position on the crest of School House Hill on either side of the road.

When night came on the fourteenth, Miles's officers felt that they were in desperate straits, and many of them favored an attempt to cut a way out or retake Maryland Heights. Of what use was it, they argued, to remain there and be butchered, and they made their views known to Miles, who drew from his pocket and read to them Halleck's order to defend Harper's Ferry to the last extremity. This order, he emphatically declared, he intended to obey to the letter. When the suggestion was offered to make the defense on Maryland Heights (assuming it could be retaken), Miles insisted that it was not Maryland Heights he had been ordered to defend but Harper's Ferry. White then secured approval of his suggestion to mass all the artillery on Bolivar Heights and fight it out there, but when the batteries were about to be moved to that point, two obstacles presented themselves: there were no horses to haul the guns, and Miles had changed his mind and countermanded the order. Miles then yielded to a suggestion that the cavalry might attempt escape.

During the afternoon of the thirteenth, Colonel Benjamin F. Davis of the 8th New York Cavalry and Lieutenant Colonel Hasbrouck Davis of the 12th Illinois Cavalry waited upon White, then in temporary command of all the cavalry, and suggested that, as the cavalry was of no use there and forage short, it cut its way out (if obliged to surrender, the horses and equipments would be a great prize to the enemy) and that an effort to reach McClellan ought to be made. That evening, a conference of the cavalry commanders was held at Miles's headquarters, and Miles agreed that, if they would consult together and propose means of getting out and a road to go by, he would consider the matter and, if he deemed proper, issue orders. The question whether the whole force—cavalry, infantry, and artillery—might not escape was considered, but the discussion came to a negative conclusion on the grounds that the infantry and artillery could not march fast enough and by an objection of Miles that, under his orders, he had no right to abandon the post.[94]

There was considerable disputation as to the road to be taken. B. F. Davis desired to go up on the western or Virginia side of the Potomac as far as Kearneysville and then cross the river at Shepherdstown; others favored a crossing of the Shenandoah and a march down the Potomac in the direction of Washington, or to recross at or below Point of Rocks and join McClellan by way of Frederick. Miles represented that there was extreme danger in both these routes. He and Davis had much talk about it, and there were some sharp words between them, which were finally cut short by a decision of Miles to issue an order directing the column to go across the pontoon bridge and then up the Maryland side of the river by what was known as the Sharpsburg route. All were cautioned by Miles to preserve secrecy from the infantry officers because, if they became aware of the intention, it would cause a stampede among them and their men. White preferred to go with the cavalry, as most of it had been under his command, but under the circumstances thought it his duty to remain at Harper's Ferry, so the command devolved upon the senior officer, Colonel Arno Voss of the 12th Illinois Cavalry.

The following order was issued and sent late in the afternoon to each cavalry commander:

Headquarters, Harper's Ferry, September 14, 1862

Special Order No. 120.

The cavalry force at this post, except detached orderlies, will make immediate preparations to leave here at eight o'clock to-night, without baggage-wagons, ambulances, or led horses, crossing the Potomac over the pontoon bridge, and taking the Sharpsburg road. The senior officer, Colonel Voss, will assume command of the whole, which will form the right at the quartermaster's office, the left up Shenandoah Street, without noise or loud command, in the following order: Cole's Cavalry, Twelfth Illinois Cavalry, Eighth New York Cavalry, Seventh Squadron Rhode Island

---

[93] At this point in his original text, Carman lists this unit (also known as the Staunton Artillery), as the battery of "Garber." For the remainder of his narrative, however, he alternates between "Garber's Battery" and "Balthis's Battery." The commanding officer of the battery, Captain William L. Balthis, had been wounded at the battle of Malvern Hill on July 1, 1862, and left the unit in September to convalesce at home. Garber served as acting commander until Balthis finally resigned his commission three month's later due to continuing ill health, at which point Garber was promoted to fill the vacancy. Compiled Service Record of William L. Balthis, Virginia (M324, reel 297); Compiled Service Record of Asher W. Garber, Virginia (M324, reel 297). See also Robert J. Driver Jr., *The Staunton Artillery—McClanahan's Battery* (Lynchburg, Va.: H. E. Howard, 1988), 21–27. Although Carman uses the descriptor "Balthis's Battery" more frequently, the editor has chosen to standardize the unit's designation throughout this work according to Carman's first and more accurate rendering.

[94] White, "The Surrender of Harper's Ferry," 613.

Cavalry, and First Maryland Cavalry. No other instructions can be given to the Commander than to force his way through the enemy's lines and join our own army.

By order of Colonel Miles.

H. C. Reynolds,
Lieutenant and A.A.G.[95]

There was not much preparation required, so as soon as it was dark and the Confederate fire had ceased, supper was eaten, forage divided among the horses, and the several commands moved silently down to the rendezvous in the main street, running close to the Shenandoah, and took places in the column, which was ready to march at the designated time. The command numbered about 1,500 officers and men in good condition, well mounted and armed.

William M. Luff writes, "Although the enemy was believed to be in strong force on the road chosen, and there were unknown dangers to be met in the darkness of night, it was an immense relief to be once more in motion with a chance for liberty. Hemmed in on all sides as they had been, harried by shot and shell without being able to strike back, and with the gloomiest forebodings for the future, the spirits of officers and men had been depressed to the point of despondency; but all now recovered their cheerfulness, and pressed forward, full of hope and courage, and equal to any emergency."[96]

The command was formed in column of twos and led by Lieutenant Green of Cole's cavalry,[97] who knew the country, and another experienced guide, the two Davises riding at the head of the column and giving it immediate direction. It took up the line of march in intense darkness, crossed the pontoon bridge, turned to the left, passed up between the canal and Maryland Heights for nearly a mile, and then turned to the right into the woods and by a narrow road moved in the direction of Sharpsburg, closing up as rapidly as possible into column of fours. Near the road leading up Maryland Heights from the river, the head of the column encountered a picket guard, which was scattered by a charge, the Confederate shots doing no damage. The pace was now increased and the movement was rapid, sometimes at a trot, sometimes at a gallop, at times in the road, at times across fields, with an occasional picket shot to accelerate speed and increase confusion. The last of the Confederate pickets were cleared near the Antietam Iron Works, just beyond which the stone bridge near the mouth of the Antietam was crossed and the direct route to Sharpsburg followed, which place was reached near midnight and a halt made in the quiet street of that sleepy place for the rear to close up and the horses to gain breath.

Here the officers heard of new dangers that increased their caution and shortened their stay. Lee's army had fallen back from South Mountain; some of it was at Keedysville, but three miles distant, and advance parties still nearer, with some scouts in the town. Commanders were quietly informed of this, and a reconnoitering party was sent out on the Boonsboro Road, which was fired upon from the hill just beyond the town. The column was now massed as closely as possible, and the march resumed on the Mercerville Road, west of the Hagerstown Pike. Once on the road, they broke into a brisk trot and went through New Industry and Mercerville (on the Potomac), traversing hills and ravines, through cornfields and meadows, over fences and water courses, with an occasional halt to breathe the horses and determine the route.

Before it was yet day, the column came out near St. James College, and a halt was made to blow the horses and close up, then the march was resumed, and the advance entered the woods skirting the turnpike from Hagerstown to Williamsport. It was now in the gray of the morning, the bivouac fires of the Confederate camps near Winchester were plainly visible, and the column was on the point of crossing the turnpike about two and a half miles from Williamsport when the low, rumbling sound of heavy carriage wheels was heard. The column was halted, and the leader of the advance reported a large wagon train in sight coming from Hagerstown. It was promptly decided to surprise and capture the train. The 8th New York Cavalry and the 12th Illinois Cavalry were formed in line near the turnpike, the Maryland and Rhode Island cavalry in reserve, while B. F. Davis, with a squadron of the 8th, quietly advanced and took possession of the turnpike to intercept the passing of the train to Williamsport. When the head of the train came up, it was discovered that four or five infantrymen guarded each wagon. The first wagon was halted and the guard ordered to surrender, which it did without much parley or the firing of a shot on either side. With but a short halt, the foremost wagon was turned to the right, driven a short distance over a dirt road to the Greencastle Turnpike, and then driven northward on that road at a rapid pace.

[95] William M. Luff, "March of the Cavalry from Harper's Ferry, September 14, 1862," in *Military Essays and Recollections: Papers Read before the Commandery of the State of Illinois, Military Order of the Loyal Legion of the United States*, vol. 2 (Chicago: A. C. McClurg and Co., 1894), 39.

[96] Ibid., 40.

[97] In his original manuscript, Carman here gives the name incorrectly as "Greene" and the regiment as the "1st Maryland Cavalry"—despite having introduced the officer correctly at an earlier point in his narrative (see p. 105). For evidence that the two passages refer to the same officer, see L. Allison Wilmer, J. H. Jarrett, and George W. F. Vernon, *History and Roster of Maryland Volunteers, War of 1861–5*, vol. 1 (Baltimore: Guggenheimer, Weil, & Co., 1899), 666.

Luff continues:

As each wagon successively reached the point where Colonel Davis was posted, it shared the fate of its predecessors. Its escort was noiselessly captured, and, with scarcely another halt or check of the column, the whole train was transferred to the Greencastle road and traveling northward faster than a wagon train ever moved before.

The capture was effected so quietly that after the foremost wagons had been taken and turned toward Greencastle the escorts of the remainder were in complete ignorance of what had taken place until they reached the point where the change of direction was made ...

Many of the drivers rebelled against driving into captivity; but with a trooper on each side with drawn revolver, they had little opportunity to hesitate. Several wagons were purposely ditched by their drivers, but these were promptly set on fire and destroyed.

After the whole train had passed, and was on the road to Greencastle, the cavalry formed in its rear to prevent recapture. The Rebel cavalry escort had not before ventured to attack; but being reinforced, they now several times charged the rear of our column,—without effect, however, as they were in each instance met and driven back.[98]

The Confederate cavalry followed as far as the Pennsylvania line, and two light guns which they brought up annoyed the Union rear. It was now broad day, and as the sun rose bright and warm the scene upon the road is described as very enlivening. Luff says, "The long train of heavily loaded wagons rumbling over the hard smooth road as rapidly as they could be urged forward, enveloped by throngs of cavalry-men with a solid column in their rear, the clouds of dust, the cracking of whips, the cries of the drivers, and the shouts of officers and men, formed a striking contrast to the long march in the silence and darkness of the previous night."[99] The column reached Greencastle, Pennsylvania, between nine and ten o'clock on the morning of the fifteenth with the captured train of ninety-seven wagons, about six hundred prisoners, and a goodly supply of beef-cattle. The wagons proved to be those of Longstreet's ordnance train, which, under the charge of Lieutenant[100] Francis W. Dawson, had left Hagerstown during the night to cross into Virginia.

The escaping cavalry narrowly missed a rather novel encounter with the reserve artillery of Lee's army, under the command of Brigadier General William N. Pendleton, which crossed its track between eight and nine miles north of Sharpsburg about sunrise on the fifteenth. On the fourteenth, Pendleton had accompanied Longstreet on the march back from Hagerstown to Boonsboro but was halted on reaching Beaver Creek (four miles northwest of the latter place) and ordered to put his guns in position on the heights covering the National Road and the crossings of the stream. After the day had gone against Lee at South Mountain, Pendleton was ordered to take two battalions of the artillery by the shortest route to Williamsport and recross the Potomac to guard the fords of that river. He started during the night and thus reports:

By sunrise, Monday, 15th, we had reached the intersection of the Hagerstown, Sharpsburg, Boonsborough, and Williamsport roads, and there received reliable intelligence of a large cavalry force of the enemy not far ahead of us. I immediately posted guns to the front and on the flank, sent messengers to [Brigadier] General [Robert A.] Toombs, understood to be at Sharpsburg, for a regiment or two of infantry, set to work collecting a band of armed stragglers, and sent scouts to the front. These latter soon returned and reported the road clear for some 2 miles. I therefore determined to advance cautiously, without waiting for infantry, in order to protect the large wagon train proceeding by the Hagerstown road through Williamsport. The cavalry, which consisted of three regiments, escaped from Harper's Ferry, crossed our road perhaps less than an hour ahead of us. We thus narrowly missed a rather strange encounter. My purpose was, of course, if we met, to attempt the destruction of those retiring invaders.[101]

The escaping Union cavalry narrowly missed another encounter—with a regiment of Confederate cavalry and a light battery of six guns. When Hampton's Brigade marched from Burkittsville on the morning of September 14, part of it went along the east base of South Mountain to Knoxville, on the Potomac, and picketed the roads leading to Berlin and Frederick. Two regiments crossed Brownsville Gap into Pleasant Valley. One of these, the Jeff Davis Legion, with Hart's Battery of six guns, was placed at Solomon's Gap in Elk Ridge. Colonel Martin, commanding the regiment, threw out pickets in the direction of the Potomac; some of these were encountered and brushed away by the Union cavalry about 10:00 p.m., as it neared the bridge spanning the Antietam near its mouth. This information was quickly carried to Martin, who was surprised at news of an enemy in that direction, and, after a hasty conference with some of his officers, the conclusion was

[98] Luff, 44–45.

[99] Ibid., 45.

[100] In his original manuscript, Carman gives Dawson's rank incorrectly as "Captain." See Krick, 112.

[101] William N. Pendleton to Lee, September 24, 1862, reprinted in *OR*, vol. 19, pt. 1, 830. Prior to receiving a general officer's commission, Toombs had served briefly as the Confederacy's first secretary of state.

reached that McClellan's left wing had interposed between Jackson's forces besieging Harper's Ferry and the Confederates at Turner's Gap, Boonsboro, and Hagerstown.

Martin did not know the result of the day's fighting at South Mountain, and, as his scouts reported a large Union force south and west, he decided to fall back toward Hagerstown and quickly set out in that direction, throwing scouts on the cross-roads to the left, which reported the Union column (the cavalry from Harper's Ferry) moving parallel to him up the Potomac. Hart placed some of his guns in advance to cover all cross-roads and kept one or more at the rear of the column. Skirting the east base of Elk Ridge, the column, leaving Keedysville to the right, went over the Antietam by the bridge above Pry's Mill and, going through Smoketown and Bakersville, came to Downsville, where just before sunrise it was learned that the Union cavalry had passed that point. From Downsville, Martin followed rapidly after the retiring force and soon after sunrise saw the explosions from the burning of part of Longstreet's ordnance train, which had been intercepted. He was too late to afford any relief, even if his force had been sufficient. After a short pursuit past the burning wagons, Martin withdrew to Williamsport, crossed the Potomac, went down the Virginia side, recrossed the river at Shepherdstown Ford on the afternoon of the sixteenth, and rejoined his brigade at Sharpsburg on the seventeenth. When Jackson heard that the cavalry had escaped from Harper's Ferry, he was much disappointed, saying, "I would rather have had them than everything else in the place."[102]

We return to the beleaguered garrison at Harper's Ferry. When it became known that the cavalry had passed out, some of the leading officers of the infantry waited upon Miles and suggested that the entire force be withdrawn to Maryland Heights. (As we now know, it would have been found held by but one regiment of Confederate infantry and two guns.) Colonel Willard of the 125th New York thought that by falling back during the night to the town there would be found many old walls, stone fences, and rocks which could be made available for a stout resistance; others thought a retreat by the road through Sandy Hook possible, but Miles negatived all such suggestions. Still later in the night, when it was reported that Jackson was placing batteries in position beyond the Shenandoah and also opposite the right of the line, these suggestions were earnestly renewed, and Miles emphatic reply was, "No, I cannot listen to any such proposition; I am ordered to hold Harper's Ferry at all hazards."[103] If Miles had not been tied down by his orders to hold Harper's Ferry at all hazards, his twelve thousand infantry could have followed the cavalry and escaped. McLaws could not have barred their passage, and their junction with Franklin in Pleasant Valley could have been readily accomplished.

William Allan writes:

After dark on Sunday (14th), the various batteries that were then in position, especially those from Loudoun and Maryland Heights, continued their fire on Harper's Ferry, and this, together with the Federal guns replying from Bolivar, constituted a magnificent display of fireworks, which was visible for many miles. All night were Jackson's troops making … movements …, and his artillery officers placing guns in position. The devoted garrison awaited with apprehension and without hope the fearful hail of fire which the day would surely bring. The Confederates were spurred to prompt action by the important events of the 14th elsewhere. The advance on that day of McClellan, the battle of South Mountain, and the seizure of Crampton's Gap and of Pleasant Valley in rear of McLaws …, all showed the vigorous efforts making to relieve Harper's Ferry, and earnest dispatches from Lee represented to his lieutenants the necessity of speedy success and of a speedy reunion of his scattered forces, to make head against the overwhelming advance of McClellan's army.[104]

Before daylight, Starke's Brigade fell back from its close proximity to the Potomac to its position of the evening before, in support of Captain John B. Brockenbrough's (Maryland) Battery, which re-opened fire with telling effect. In the near vicinity, the batteries of Poague and Carpenter poured an incessant fire upon the right of Bolivar Heights and the batteries of von Sehlen and Phillips. Lawton advanced Ewell's Division to the front of the woods to support the advance of A. P. Hill, and Major Walker, Hill's chief of artillery, opened a rapid enfilade fire from all his batteries at about one thousand yards' range, the batteries on School House Hill firing upon Miles's line in front.

As Colonel Crutchfield was obliged to cut a road for his guns beyond the Shenandoah, he did not get them into position by daybreak as intended, but in a short time after Major Walker's guns had opened, the ten guns of Brown's, Garber's,

---

[102] As of this writing, Carman's source for this quotation has not been identified. It is difficult to imagine, however, that Jackson seriously believed the escape of some 1,500 cavalry outweighed the capture of the artillery, stores, and infantry taken at Harper's Ferry—let alone the neutralization of the threat to Lee's line of communications in the Shenandoah Valley. One wonders why Carman accepted the statement so uncritically.

[103] This appears to be an instance where Carman transformed a third-person statement into a first-person quotation. In sworn testimony, Colonel Trimble recalled, "He [Miles] said, 'No; he could not listen to any such proposition; he was ordered to hold Harper's Ferry at all hazards.'" "Record of the Harper's Ferry Military Commission," October 20, 1862, 745.

[104] William Allan, *The Army of Northern Virginia in 1862* (Boston: Houghton, Mifflin and Co., 1892), 339.

Dement's, and Latimer's Batteries poured an accurate fire upon the left and rear of Miles's defenses. This concentrated fire from many guns, bearing most heavily upon Rigby's battery on the left of the line near the Charlestown Turnpike and upon Potts's battery nearby (which White had ordered up and placed in position to reply to Hill's and Lawton's guns in front), soon silenced the Union guns—the men running from them and returning as the fire slackened, only to abandon them again as the fire strengthened.

The artillery upon Loudoun Heights, under Captain French, which had silenced the guns on Camp Hill and near the Barbour house on the afternoon of the fourteenth, again opened fire, but as it was foggy their shots were at random. The two guns on Maryland Heights joined in the attack by a plunging fire, which added to the Union discomfort and demoralization. For more than a full hour, this heavy direct, enfilading, and plunging fire from front, flanks, and rear was responded to by all the Union guns that could be brought to bear, but Phillips and von Sehlen soon ran out of ammunition. Captain Graham, on Camp Hill, exhausted the ammunition for the 20-pounder Parrotts, but Rigby and Potts, moving nearer the Shenandoah, still kept up a sharp and effective fire, which availed but little, however, against the superior weight of the Confederate fire. At this point, White says, "The long-range ammunition had now almost entirely failed, and it became evident that, from the great preponderance of the enemy's artillery and his ability to keep up a fire at long range to which we were no longer able to reply, our ability to hold the position became a mere question of time, and that our defense could only be continued at a great sacrifice of life without any corresponding advantage."[105]

The Union fire now slackened, for ammunition was momentarily running lower. Believing resistance nearly at an end, Hill's batteries were ordered to cease their fire, which was the signal for the infantry to storm the works. Pender had moved his three assaulting brigades (his own, Archer's and Brockenbrough's) to within 150 yards of Miles's works, sheltered as much as possible from fire by the inequalities of the ground, and had commenced to advance to the assault when the Union fire again opened with full force. Pegram and Crenshaw pushed their batteries to within four hundred yards of Miles's works and poured a rapid fire into them over the heads of their own infantry, in which they were joined by the guns beyond the Shenandoah (which, since the return of the battery men to their guns, had been paying particular attention to Rigby's battery on the Charleston Road and Potts's guns between it and the Shenandoah). Under this fire, Hill was gathering for a determined assault; when the white flag was seen on Miles's works, his guns ceased their fire and his infantry came to a halt.

When Miles saw the circle of fire by which he had been surrounded and felt the effects when the Confederate guns had opened up on him, he realized that it was only a question of time as to the final result unless aid came from McClellan, but when one battery commander after another reported ammunition running low and then exhausted, he knew that the time had come earlier in the day than he had anticipated. White says, "During the afternoon of the 14th our guns at Harper's Ferry, engaged with Jackson's forces, were cheeringly responded to by those of General Franklin at Crampton's Gap; but after 4 o'clock of that day, and on the morning of the 15th, there was no sound of conflict in that direction, and the hope of relief from McClellan, which the proximity of the firing had inspired, was abandoned."[106] Without ammunition for his guns, much of the infantry disorganized and demoralized, and all hope lost of help from McClellan, Miles at 8:30 a.m. called a council of the brigade commanders and conferred with them upon the propriety of an immediate surrender. There was some opposition to this course, but an interchange of opinion resulted in the unanimous conclusion that it was useless to continue the contest and that, if reasonable terms could be obtained, it was best to stop further waste of life by surrender. Accordingly, the white flag was raised on Bolivar Heights, and White was directed to arrange terms of capitulation.

The Confederate batteries across the Shenandoah and those in front on the Charlestown Road ceased firing upon the display of white flags, but the men of Brockenbrough's Battery did not see them and continued their fire until a courier stopped them. The gunners on Loudoun Heights did not immediately see the signals through a heavy fog and powder smoke and continued their work for some minutes. From Maryland Heights the white flag was seen on Bolivar Heights and the U.S. flag on Camp Hill, and the two Confederate guns there were then trained on the latter until it was replaced by a white flag. From one of these points a shell was thrown that struck Miles in the leg, inflicting a mortal wound.

When the white flag was displayed and the firing ceased, Jackson was at the church in the wood on the Bolivar and Halltown Turnpike. He sent Captain Douglas of his staff up the turnpike and into the Union lines to ascertain the purpose of the white flag. On his way, and when near the top of the hill, Douglas met White and staff and told his mission. White replied that Miles had been mortally wounded and that he was in command and desired an interview with Jackson. At that moment, A. P. Hill came up from the direction of his line, and the whole party went back to the church, where Jackson was found sitting on his horse. Douglas recounts the scene: "He was not, as the Comte de Paris says, leaning against a tree asleep, but exceedingly wide-awake. The contrast in appearances there presented was striking. General White, riding

---

[105] White to Whipple, September 22, 1862, 528.
[106] White, "The Surrender of Harper's Ferry," 614–15.

a handsome black horse, was carefully dressed and had on untarnished gloves, boots, and sword. His staff were equally comely in costume. On the other hand, General Jackson was the dingiest, worst-dressed, and worst-mounted general that a warrior who cared for good looks and style would wish to surrender to. The surrender was unconditional, and then General Jackson turned the matter over to General A. P. Hill."[107] Hill granted liberal terms. The officers were allowed to go on parole with side arms and private property and the privates with everything except equipments and guns.

Jackson sent a brief dispatch to Lee announcing the surrender[108] and then rode up to Bolivar and down into Harper's Ferry. The Union prisoners lined the sides of the road, and their curiosity to see him was keen and kindly. Many of them uncovered as he passed, and he invariably returned the salute. Some cheered him, and, says Douglas, "One man had an echo of response all about him when he said, 'Boys, he's not much for looks, but if we'd had him we wouldn't have been caught in this trap.'"[109]

There were surrendered, including the wounded, over 12,000 officers and men, 73 pieces of artillery, 13,000 small arms, about 200 wagons, and a large amount of quartermaster and commissary stores.[110] Of the 217 Union killed and wounded, four-fifths are chargeable to the defense of Maryland Heights on the twelfth and thirteenth. The Confederate loss was 41 killed and 247 wounded, of which McLaws had 35 killed and 178 wounded on Maryland Heights, Walker 1 killed and 3 wounded on Loudoun Heights, and Jackson 5 killed and 66 wounded in front of Bolivar Heights.[111]

Miles would not permit the destruction of the government property, which fell into the hands of the enemy. He would not destroy the pontoon bridge across the Potomac after the abandonment of Maryland Heights, and by its use McLaws was enabled to cross and reach the field of Antietam some hours earlier than he could otherwise have done (and in time to deliver that telling blow upon Sedgwick's flank in the Dunkard church woods).

Lee's necessities did not permit much rest to Jackson's troops. Leaving Hill to receive the surrender of the Union troops and take the requisite steps for securing the captured stores, Jackson moved to rejoin Lee with the remaining divisions of his command. By a severe night march he reached the vicinity of Sharpsburg on the morning of the sixteenth. Walker followed Jackson. He crossed Loudoun Heights, the Shenandoah, and the Potomac, reached the neighborhood of Sharpsburg on the sixteenth, and reported to Lee.

So far Lee's plans had been carried out with complete success, but with a delay that he did not anticipate and that was nearly fatal to that part of his army north of the Potomac. McLaws was but little behind time, Walker was a day late, and Jackson more than a day late in closing in on Harper's Ferry, and nearly two days more were consumed in reducing the place. What it was thought could be accomplished by the evening of the thirteenth was not consummated until the morning of the fifteenth. Meanwhile, events were taking place at the South Mountain passes, threatening not only the operations at Harper's Ferry, but imperiling the entire Confederate army.[112]

---

107 Douglas, "Stonewall Jackson in Maryland," 626.

108 Jackson to Lee, September 15, 1862, "near 8:00 a.m.," reprinted in *OR*, vol. 19, pt. 1, 951.

109 Ibid., 627.

110 In his original manuscript, Carman inserts at this point a table of the losses sustained by the Union at Maryland Heights and Harper's Ferry. It is reproduced herein as Appendix D.

111 McLaws, "The Capture of Harper's Ferry," September 12, 1888; John G. Walker to Paxton, 913; Ambrose P. Hill to Faulkner, 981.

112 In Carman's original manuscript, this chapter concludes with a lengthy note in which he discusses the results of the court of inquiry convened to examine the circumstances surrounding the surrender of Harper's Ferry. It is reprinted herein as Appendix E.

7

South Mountain (Crampton's Gap)

September 14, 1862

James Longstreet followed "Stonewall" Jackson from Frederick on the morning of September 10 and bivouacked that night near the east foot of Turner's Gap. On the morning of the eleventh, he resumed his march by the National Road to Hagerstown, with D. H. Hill's Division of five brigades being left near Boonsboro. Longstreet's advance, the 1st Virginia Cavalry (Lieutenant Colonel Luke Tiernan Brien), dashed into Hagerstown about midday, followed in the afternoon by Toombs's Brigade, which passed through the town and encamped a short distance southeast of town, between it and Funkstown.

Lee accompanied Longstreet and awaited the result of the operations upon Martinsburg and Harper's Ferry; if successful, he proposed to concentrate his army at Hagerstown for a further advance into Pennsylvania or to give battle to McClellan should he follow west of South Mountain. On the twelfth he sent Davis copies of his proclamation of September 8 and Special Orders No. 191. He reported that his advance pickets were at Middleburg, on the Pennsylvania line; that his army had been received with sympathy and kindness; and that he had found in the town about 1,500 barrels of flour and had hopes of a further supply from the mills in the surrounding country, though he feared he should have to haul more from the Valley of Virginia. His supply of beef was small and he had not been able to procure bacon. One thousand pairs of shoes had been obtained at Frederick, 250 pairs in Williamsport, and about 400 pairs in Hagerstown, but they "were not sufficient to cover the bare feet of an army."[1] The thirteenth found him still waiting for news from McLaws and Walker; to the first named he expressed his anxiety for the speedy accomplishment of the duty assigned him and the quick return of the various detachments to the main body of the army. He informed him that Stuart with his cavalry occupied Middletown Valley, D. H. Hill was near Boonsboro, and that by noon Jackson would be at Harper's Ferry.[2] Lee wrote Davis the next day that every effort would be made to acquire all advantages which his position and means might warrant and called attention to the great embarrassment in the reduction of the army by straggling. Lee's ranks were very much diminished. "I fear," Lee wrote, "from a third to one-half of the original numbers."[3]

Meanwhile, events were transpiring beyond South Mountain that culminated in the entire failure of Lee's campaign and its expected results: the liberation of Maryland and its alliance with the South, English and French intervention, and the recognition of the independence of the Southern Confederacy. On the night of September 12, the Twelfth Army Corps, under Williams, bivouacked at Ijamsville Cross-Roads, five miles from Frederick. On the morning of the thirteenth, it marched in the direction of that place and, at early noon, reached the outskirts of the city, where the converging columns of other commands caused it to halt in a meadow. The weather was warm and the march had been tiresome; arms were stacked, and the men threw themselves on the grass for rest. Sergeant John M. Bloss and Corporal[4] Barton W. Mitchell of the 27th Indiana were separated by a few feet, and Bloss noticed near Mitchell a long envelope, one end showing above the tall grass. At his request Mitchell handed it to him. The envelope was not sealed, and as it passed into Bloss's hands two cigars and a paper fell out. The cigars were properly divided and the two men were about to indulge in a quiet smoke when Bloss picked up, opened, and proceeded to read the paper that had fallen from the envelope. As the reading progressed, he recognized its great value. Barely completing the reading, he hastened with it to his captain, Peter Kop. The captain, accompanied by Bloss and Mitchell, went to Colonel Silas Cosgrove, commanding the regiment, and Bloss explained how the paper came into his possession. Cosgrove, who had not yet dismounted from his horse, rode over to Williams's headquarters not far distant and handed the paper to Captain Samuel E. Pittman, acting adjutant general of the corps. It was

---

[1] Robert E. Lee to Jefferson Davis, September 12, 1862, reprinted in *OR*, vol. 19, pt. 2, 604–5.

[2] Armistead L. Long to Lafayette McLaws, September 13, 1862, reprinted in *OR*, vol. 19. pt. 2, 606.

[3] Lee to Davis, September 13, 1862, reprinted in *OR*, vol. 19, pt. 2, 606.

[4] In his original manuscript, Carman gives Mitchell's rank incorrectly as "Private." This is a common mistake in discussions about the discovery of the lost order. Mitchell entered Federal service in September 1861 as a corporal and held that rank during the Maryland campaign. Beginning with his company's muster roll for September–October 1863, and on every subsequent roll for the remainder of his enlistment, Mitchell appears as a private. No explanation for the demotion is given in his service record. Compiled Service Record of Barton Warren Mitchell, 27th Indiana Infantry, Carded Records Showing Military Service of Soldiers Who Fought in Volunteer Organizations During the American Civil War, 1890–1912, Record Group 94, National Archives.

addressed to Major General D. H. Hill and signed by Lieutenant Colonel Robert H. Chilton, assistant adjutant general. Pittman recognized the signature of Chilton as genuine; as a teller in the Michigan State Bank at Detroit where a few years before Chilton had kept his account as a paymaster in the U.S. Army, Pittman had paid many of his checks and thus became well acquainted with his signature. Pittman wrote a brief note to McClellan's adjutant general to accompany the transmission of the paper and was about to copy the paper itself, recognizing that the finding of such an important document was likely to become an interesting fact of history, but Williams would not permit a moment's delay. The paper was immediately taken by Pittman to McClellan's headquarters and delivered to the commanding general. (Sergeant Bloss states that he found the paper not later than ten o'clock; he thinks it was really an hour later. In this he is evidently mistaken. Accounts generally agree that Williams's corps arrived near Frederick and halted about noon—very early noon—and this agrees with the recollection and papers of the writer.)

The effect that the paper had upon McClellan is shown in the telegram that was immediately sent to Lincoln:

I have the whole rebel force in front of me, but am confident, and no time shall be lost. I have a difficult task to perform, but with God's blessing will accomplish it. I think Lee has made a gross mistake, and that he will be severely punished for it. The army is in motion as rapidly as possible. I hope for a great success if the plans of the rebels remain unchallenged. We have possession of Catoctin. I have all the plans of the rebels, and will catch them in their own trap if my men are equal to the emergency. I now feel that I can count on them as of old. All forces of Pennsylvania should be placed to co-operate at Chambersburg. My respects to Mrs. Lincoln. Received most enthusiastically by the ladies. Will send you trophies. All well, and with God's blessing will accomplish it.

Geo. B. McClellan[5]

At 3:00 p.m. a copy of the order found was sent to Pleasonton, who was directed to ascertain whether the order of march as given in it had been followed, and he was cautioned to approach the pass through the Blue Ridge (South Mountain) with circumspection, as his advance might be disputed with two columns.[6] At 3:35 p.m. Cox was ordered to march his division to Middletown and support Pleasonton;[7] two hours later Captain Sanders of the 6th U.S. Cavalry was ordered to send one company to Noland's Ferry, on the Potomac, to assist Couch in guarding it and with his main body push out from Licksville to Jefferson, using his discretion whether to go by way of Point of Rocks or Adamstown. From Jefferson, he would throw out scouts as far as possible toward Harper's Ferry, and he was to open communication with Pleasonton, who could be found on the National Road between Middletown and South Mountain.[8]

When Lee's order was taken to McClellan, there still remained seven hours of good daylight. His troops had done but little marching during the day; quite half of them were in bivouac by noon. They were in good condition, well fed and well clothed, the weather was clear and pleasant, and the broad roads excellent. Yet beyond the orders given Pleasonton, Cox, and Sanders, not a move was made, nor was an order of movement prepared until 6:20 p.m., and this was very far short of the requirement of the occasion.

The order of 3:00 p.m. to Pleasonton is suggestive that McClellan had suspicions that the lost order was not a genuine one, that it was not lost in reality, that it was left where he would find it, that it was intended to deceive. Upon no other theory can his inaction be accounted for, yet the order confirmed the reports he was receiving from Governor Curtin and others of the movement and position of the Confederate army, and these reports should have been promptly accepted as guarantees of the genuine character of the order.

However, if for a moment, a few minutes, an hour, or nearly a full afternoon he doubted, the truth was finally accepted—and there were revealed to him Lee's designs and knowledge of his intended movement for days to come. It told him that Lee's army was divided, where its divisions were and what they were doing, that Walker was on Loudoun Heights beyond the Potomac, that Jackson also was on the Virginia side of the Potomac, facing Bolivar Heights, that McLaws was on Maryland Heights, on the Maryland side of the Potomac, and that Walker, Jackson, and McLaws were surrounding—indeed had surrounded—Harper's Ferry. It also told him that Lee, Longstreet, and D. H. Hill were just beyond South Mountain and that with them were the reserve artillery and the trains, that in his immediate front was Stuart's cavalry to delay his advance, and that all were awaiting the issue at Harper's Ferry preparatory to the concentration of the army at Boonsboro or Hagerstown. It was a revelation that permitted him to smile at Halleck's fears of a sudden dash on Washington and to exult that Lee had put himself in great peril, and this unquestionably Lee had done.

---

[5] George B. McClellan to Abraham Lincoln, September 13, 1862, 12:00 p.m., reprinted in *OR*, vol. 19, pt. 2, 281.

[6] Randolph B. Marcy to Alfred Pleasonton, September 13, 1862, 3:00 p.m., reprinted in *OR*, vol. 51, pt. 1, 829.

[7] Marcy to Jacob D. Cox, September 13, 1862, 3:35 p.m., reprinted in *OR*, vol. 51, pt. 1, 827.

[8] Marcy to William P. Sanders, September 13, 1862, 5:45 p.m., reprinted in *OR*, vol. 51, pt. 1, 830. In his original manuscript, Carman states incorrectly that this was sent "one hour" after the message to Cox.

There has been much criticism of Lee's conduct of the campaign against Harper's Ferry and the danger in which he put the various divisions of his army, all of which has been ably answered by William Allan:

> Lee has been severely criticized for dividing his army at this time, and in one sense he is fairly exposed to it. But at bottom, the criticism in this case is but the common one to which a bold leader is always exposed, who attempts by superior energy and skill to make up for inferiority of men and resources. General Lee's whole course during the summer of 1862, and indeed during the war, is open to this kind of criticism. There were no aggressive movements possible to an army so inferior in strength as was the Confederate that may not be condemned as rash, while on the other hand a strictly defensive war against the resources and facilities of attack possessed by the North, pointed to certain and not distant collapse.
>
> Lee's expectation in regard to the reduction of Harper's Ferry was a reasonable one, and the risk he assumed in dividing his army to effect it was less than the risk he incurred in the operations against Pope three weeks before. A single day's more time would probably have rendered unnecessary the struggle at the South Mountain passes; two days would certainly have done so, and the Confederate army, loaded with the spoils of Harper's Ferry, would have reunited at Hagerstown without difficulty. No one can read the history of that campaign, no one can study McClellan's career, no one can see the doubt, the anxiety, of the Federal administration as shown by Halleck's dispatches, without feeling that these two days and more would have been Lee's had the course of events not been affected by the accident of the lost dispatch.[9]

Longstreet says that the copy of Special Orders No. 191 sent him was carefully read, "then used as some persons use a little cut of tobacco, to be assured that others could not have the benefit of its contents."[10] When Walker received his copy, he was "so impressed with the disastrous consequence which might result from its loss" that he pinned it securely in an inside pocket.[11] There has been much discussion as to how and by whom Lee's order was lost. It was addressed to D. H. Hill, and the statement of that officer is conclusive so far as he is concerned. He says, "I went into Maryland under Jackson's command. I was under his command when Lee's order was issued. It was proper that I should receive that order through Jackson and not through Lee. I have now before me the order received from Jackson … My adjutant-general made affidavit, twenty years ago, that no order was received at our office from General Lee. But an order from Lee's office, directed to me, was lost and fell into McClellan's hands. Did the courier lose it? Did Lee's own staff-officers lose it? I do not know."[12] Jackson was so careful that no one should learn the contents of the order that the copy he furnished Hill was written by his own hand and entrusted to a careful member of his staff for delivery. Charles S. Venable of Lee's staff says, "One copy was sent directly to Hill from headquarters. General Jackson sent him a copy … in his own handwriting, which General Hill has. The other was undoubtedly left carelessly by some one at Hill's headquarters."[13]

But however lost, the find was a valuable one. The possibilities it opened to McClellan were great, possibilities that come to a commander but seldom, and not to one man more than once in a lifetime. How did he approach them? Did he even meet them halfway? He had three courses presented to him: he could move to the relief of Harper's Ferry by the road leading through Jefferson and Knoxville and thence up the east bank of the Potomac; he could force his left under Franklin by way of Burkittsville through Crampton's Gap, then come directly upon the rear of McLaws on Maryland Heights and interpose between him and Lee; or he could press his right, under Burnside, and his center, under Sumner, by way of Middletown through Turner's Gap, thus interposing between Lee, Longstreet, D. H. Hill, and all the reserve trains and artillery on one side and the troops beyond the Potomac on the other—and the chances were that these fifty-five thousand Union soldiers would utterly rush the fifteen thousand men that the Confederates had to oppose them. All depended, however, on celerity of movement and vigor of attack.

McClellan determined not to move by the direct road through Jefferson and Knoxville, and he gives his reasons in his official report:

> It may be asked by those who are not acquainted with the topography of the country in the vicinity of Harper's Ferry why Franklin, instead of marching his column over the circuitous road from Jefferson via Burkittsville and Brownsville, was not ordered to move along the direct turnpike to Knoxville and thence up the river to Harper's Ferry. It was

9   William Allan, "Strategy of the Campaign of Sharpsburg or Antietam, September, 1862," in *Campaigns in Virginia, Maryland, and Pennsylvania, 1862–1863*, vol. 3 of *Papers of the Military Historical Society of Massachusetts* (Boston: Griffith-Stillings Press, 1903), 85–86.

10   James Longstreet, *From Manassas to Appomattox: Memoirs of the Civil War in America* (Philadelphia: J. P. Lippincott Co., 1896), 213.

11   John G. Walker, "Jackson's Capture of Harper's Ferry," in *Battles and Leaders of the Civil War*, vol. 2 (New York: Century Co., 1887), 611.

12   Daniel H. Hill, "The Battle of South Mountain, or Boonsboro'," in *Battles and Leaders*, 570 n. 1.

13   Long, *Memoirs of Robert E. Lee: His Military and Personal History, Embracing a Large Amount of Information Hitherto Unpublished* (New York: J. M. Stoddard & Co., 1886), 213.

for the reason that I had received information that the enemy were anticipating our approach in that direction, and had established batteries on the south side of the Potomac which commanded all the approaches to Knoxville. Moreover the road from that point winds directly along the river bank at the foot of a precipitous mountain, where there was no opportunity of forming in line of battle, and where the enemy could have placed batteries on both sides of the river to enfilade our narrow approaching columns. The approach through Crampton's Pass, which debouches into Pleasant Valley in rear of Maryland Heights, was the only one which afforded any reasonable prospect of carrying that formidable position. At the same time the troops upon that road were in better relation to the main body of our forces.[14]

McClellan was informed wrongly that the enemy had batteries on the south side of the Potomac, commanding the approaches to Knoxville, and he imagined the difficulties of reaching Harper's Ferry by that route. In the main his reasons for not choosing it are sound. It is enough to say that they were convincing to him and that he chose a route promising better results.

The plan that he adopted had two purposes: the controlling one to relieve Harper's Ferry as speedily as possible by moving through Crampton's Gap and breaking the line of investment that McLaws had thrown across Maryland Heights and the foot of Pleasant Valley; the other to force Turner's Gap, then fall upon and destroy that part of the Confederate army Lee had retained at Boonsboro. The plan was a good one, and in the hands of an able general and enterprising subordinates it should have produced great results. McLaws had ten brigades, and these were not concentrated, nor were they in close supporting distance, and there remained to Lee beyond South Mountain but fourteen brigades aggregating, according to D. H. Hill, about fifteen thousand men. Five brigades, under Hill, were at Boonsboro; nine brigades, under Longstreet, were twelve miles in the rear near Hagerstown. (This division of command was an advantage to McClellan had he known it, but he did not, as the lost order indicated that Lee, Longstreet, Hill, and all the reserve artillery and trains were at Boonsboro.)

Having concluded to move by Crampton's Gap, McClellan sent this letter of instruction to Franklin, then at Buckeystown:

I have now full information as to movements and intentions of the enemy. Jackson has crossed the Upper Potomac to capture the garrison at Martinsburg and cut off Miles' retreat toward the west. A division on the south side of the Potomac was to carry Loudoun Heights and cut off his retreat in that direction. McLaws, with his own command and the division of R. H. Anderson, was to move by Boonsborough and Rohrersville to carry the Maryland Heights. The signal officers inform me that he is now in Pleasant Valley. The firing shows that Miles still holds out. Longstreet was to move to Boonsborough and there halt with the reserve corps, D. H. Hill to form the rear guard, Stuart's cavalry to bring up stragglers, &c. We have cleared out all the cavalry this side of the mountains and north of us.

The last I heard from Pleasonton he occupied Middletown, after several sharp skirmishes. A division of Burnside's command started several hours ago to support him. The whole of Burnside's command, including Hooker's corps, march this evening and early to-morrow morning, followed by the corps of Sumner and Banks and Sykes' division, upon Boonsborough, to carry that position. Couch has been ordered to concentrate his division and join you as rapidly as possible. Without waiting for the whole of that division to join, you will move at daybreak in the morning, by Jefferson and Burkittsville, upon the road to Rohrersville. I have reliable information that the mountain pass by this road is practicable for artillery and wagons. If this pass is not occupied by the enemy in force, seize it as soon as practicable, and debouch upon Rohrersville, in order to cut off the retreat of or destroy McLaws' command. If you find this pass held by the enemy in large force, make all your dispositions for the attack, and commence it about half an hour after you hear severe firing at the pass on the Hagerstown pike, where the main body will attack. Having gained the pass, your duty will be first to cut off, destroy, or capture McLaws' command and relieve Colonel Miles. If you effect this, you will order him to join you at once with all his disposable troops, first, destroying the bridge over the Potomac, if not already done, and, leaving a sufficient garrison to prevent the enemy from passing the ford, you will then return by Rohrersville on the direct road to Boonsborough if the main column has not succeeded in its attack. If it has succeeded, take the road by Rohrersville to Sharpsburg and Williamsport, in order either to cut off the retreat of Hill and Longstreet toward the Potomac, or prevent the repassage of Jackson. My general idea is to cut the enemy in two and beat him in detail. I believe I have sufficiently explained my intentions. I ask of you, at this important moment, all your intellect and the utmost activity that a general can exercise.[15]

McClellan appears to have intended the completion of the letter at this point, but before signing he received a dispatch from Franklin that the enemy was in some force at Petersville, whereupon he continued to write:

---

[14] McClellan to Lorenzo Thomas, August 4, 1863, reprinted in *OR*, vol. 19, pt. 1, 44–45.

[15] McClellan to William B. Franklin, September 13, 1862, 6:20 p.m., as contained in McClellan to Thomas, August 4, 1863, 45–46.

Knowing my views and intentions, you are fully authorized to change any of the details of this order as circumstances may change, provided the purpose is carried out; that purpose being to attack the enemy in detail and beat him. General Smith's dispatch of 4 p.m. with your comments is received. If, with a full knowledge of all the circumstances, you consider it preferable to crush the enemy at Petersville before undertaking the movement I have directed, you are at liberty to do so, but you will readily perceive that no slight advantage should for a moment interfere with the decisive results I propose to gain. I cannot too strongly impress upon you the absolute necessity of informing me every hour during the day of your movements, and frequently during the night. Force your colonels to prevent straggling, and bring every available man into action. I think the force you have is, with good management, sufficient for the end in view. If you differ widely from me, and being on the spot you know better than I do the circumstances of the case, inform me at once, and I will do my best to re-enforce you. Inform me at the same time how many more troops you think you should have. Until 5 a.m. to-morrow general headquarters will be at this place. At that hour they will move upon the main road to Hagerstown.[16]

This letter is here given in full because of its importance in showing the information McClellan had in his possession and how he proposed to profit by it, and it invites attention. As far as it went it was good, but it did not go far enough. It did not set Franklin and the entire army in instant motion, and there were no valid reasons why this should not have been done. The army had not been wearied by long marches nor exhausted for want of sleep. It was well clothed, well fed, and ready to respond to any call upon it. It had confidence in most of its officers and idolized McClellan.

On the day in question, September 13, Hooker's First Corps moved from Lisbon to Cooksville by the National Road to the Monocacy, the average march of the divisions being about sixteen miles; no other divisions covered half this distance. Sumner's Second Corps marched from Urbana to Frederick, about six miles; Williams's Twelfth Corps from Ijamsville to Buckeystown, about six miles; and Couch's division from Barnesville to Licksville, about five miles. Farnsworth's cavalry brigade marched out of Frederick by the National Road on the morning of the thirteenth, drove Hampton's cavalry from Fairview Gap of the Catoctin, followed through Middletown, overtook Hampton's rear-guard on Catoctin Creek, brushed it away, and pursued nearly to the foot of Turner's Gap of South Mountain. A detachment of Farnsworth's brigade scouted in the direction of Burkittsville and was roughly handled by Hampton's cavalry. The 1st and 6th U.S. Cavalry advanced from Licksville to Jefferson and threw out scouts in the direction of Crampton's Gap and Petersville, and the 6th Pennsylvania Cavalry, supported by Fairchild's brigade (Rodman's division, Ninth Corps), moved from Frederick to near Burkittsville, skirmished with Munford's cavalry (which was driven to Burkittsville, at the foot of Crampton's Gap), and then drew off to near Broad Run Village, with Fairchild's brigade—by some singular misapprehension of orders—returning to Frederick. The 1st Rhode Island Cavalry examined the fords of the Potomac below Point of Rocks. Cox's Kanawha Division of the Ninth Corps moved from Frederick to Middletown and thence a mile beyond (a total of seven miles), and Sturgis's and Willcox's divisions of the same corps marched to within one mile of Middletown. With the exception of some of the cavalry and Fairchild's brigade of infantry, none of the army had come in touch with the enemy, more than two-thirds had marched less than seven miles, and all save the cavalry, the First Corps, and a part of the Ninth Corps was in bivouac by noon—consequently, well rested by sunset.

The cavalry was close up to Turner's Gap and the Ninth Corps but a few miles in its rear. The Second and Twelfth Corps and Sykes's division of the Fifth were at Frederick, twelve miles from Turner's Gap and the same distance from Crampton's Gap; the First Corps was on the Monocacy, a short distance east of Frederick. Franklin's Sixth Corps was at Buckeystown, twelve miles from Crampton's Gap and ten from Burkittsville, and Couch's division at Licksville was the same distance from these two places by roads running nearer the Potomac, either through Jefferson or Petersville.

From Frederick the broad National Road had been cleared to the foot of Turner's Gap by the cavalry, and they had cleared the road to Burkittsville to within two miles of that place. On the left Sanders's regular cavalry had marched to Jefferson and beyond, and there was nothing to prevent a rapid advance of the entire army. Nothing was wanting but the order to march. The afternoon had been practically lost; the loss should have been retrieved by an order to march at sunset. The roads were good, the nights were cool, and the evening dews, which fell early, partially laid the dust. A night march would have been welcomed by the soldier, and the twelve miles between Frederick and the foot of Turner's Gap were over a broad road as smooth as the floor. The ten miles from Frederick to Burkittsville, and the ten miles from Buckeystown and Licksville to Burkittsville, could have been comfortably made before midnight, and all would have had a good rest and been in good condition to begin work at daylight of the fourteenth. As far as McClellan and Franklin supposed then, and as we know now, there was nothing to oppose or in any way interfere with this night march save a few Confederate cavalry scouts thrown out

[16] McClellan to Franklin, reprinted in *OR*, vol. 51, pt. 1, 826–27. Though appearing in widely separated volumes of the *OR*, this passage and those covered in the previous note come from the same document. The first selection appeared verbatim in vol. 19 as a part of McClellan's official report, so the editors chose to reprint only the conclusion in vol. 51—wherein many of his other dispatches of September 13 appear—rather than give the communication in its entirety.

in front of Burkittsville that could have been brushed away without halting the column, and this night march would not have been as severe a one as Jackson was to make on the night of the fifteenth from Harper's Ferry to Sharpsburg.

Had the Ninth, Second, and Twelfth Corps marched that night and reached the foot of Turner's Gap by midnight and rested until morning, they would have found to oppose them one of Stuart's cavalry regiments, the small infantry brigades of Colquitt and Brigadier General Samuel Garland Jr., and eight pieces of artillery. The gap could have been forced before D. H. Hill could have brought up his support from beyond Boonsboro, five miles away. Or, had Franklin marched at the same time, he could have taken Crampton's Gap next morning with but little opposition and descended into Pleasant Valley early in the forenoon, with the consequent result of relieving Miles at Harper's Ferry, interposing between Lee and McLaws, and, moving on the flank and rear of the Confederate forces, engaging the main body at Turner's Gap—providing always that he took advantage of opportunity. McLaws might have rejoined Lee by descending the west side of Maryland Heights and marching north by Antietam Furnace and Sharpsburg, which would have permitted Miles to reoccupy the heights and join Franklin; he might have recrossed into Virginia by Knott's Ford at the mouth of the Antietam and joined Jackson; or he might have descended the southeastern extremity of the height and, uniting his command at Weverton, marched by Knoxville and recrossed the Potomac by some of the fords below (which would have been hazardous). In fact, all three movements would have been attended with great risk and entailed the loss of many stragglers and much material. In any event, the abandonment of Maryland Heights would have been imperative.

But McClellan did not rise to the occasion. He did not take full advantage of the long afternoon, he did not order the night march—and thereby missed the opportunity of his life. At noon he dispatched Lincoln that his army was "in motion as rapidly as possible" and that, knowing the plan of the rebels, he would "catch them in their own trap" if his men were "equal to the emergency." As a matter of fact, nearly the entire army at that hour was at a dead halt, and McClellan did not rise to the situation to lead it forward. The failure to be "equal to the emergency" was on the part of the commander of the army and not on the part of the men.

We turn from the contemplation of what might or should have been done to the narration of what actually was done. Before this, however, we shall note what occurred after the order was prepared for Franklin at 6:20 p.m., how Lee came to the knowledge that McClellan had a copy of some important paper that had been found, and the preparations made to meet and delay the Union advance.

Pleasonton was ordered to occasionally fire a few artillery shots, even though no enemy appeared in his front, so that Miles at Harper's Ferry would know that the Union army was near,[17] and, after orders were issued for the advance of the several corps at daylight the next day, McClellan's time was occupied in receiving reports from the front, writing a letter to the adjutant general of the Army about the artillery service in the regular Army,[18] and preparing a long and by no means clear dispatch to Halleck. He told Halleck that he had found Lee's order addressed to D. H. Hill, that its authenticity was unquestionable, that the order disclosed that the main Confederate army was before him, and that the genuineness of the order was attested by the fact that "heavy firing has been heard in the direction of Harper's Ferry this afternoon, and the columns took the roads specified in the order." McClellan had good reason for believing that Lee had 120,000 men or more and that it was his intention to penetrate Pennsylvania. He informed Halleck that the army would make forced marches on the morrow to relieve Miles, but he feared it was too late. McClellan then proceeded to allay Halleck's fears for the safety of Washington. He assured him that there was very small probability of the enemy being in much force south of the Potomac. He agreed with Halleck that the holding of Washington was of great consequence but insisted that the fate of the nation depended upon the success of his army, and it was for this reason he had said that everything else should be made subordinate to placing his army in proper condition to meet Lee's large army in his front. In conclusion, McClellan said, "Unless General Lee has changed his plans, I expect a severe general engagement to-morrow. I feel confident that there is now no rebel force immediately threatening Washington or Baltimore, but that I have the mass of their troops to contend with, and they outnumber me when united."[19]

When McClellan came into possession of the lost order, a citizen friendly to the Southern cause was present and observed the great satisfaction it gave him and the exuberant spirit of his staff. He listened to some talk of what was to be done by the

---

[17] Marcy to Pleasonton, September 13, 1862, 9:00 p.m., reprinted in *OR*, vol. 51, pt. 1, 829.

[18] McClellan to Thomas, September 13, 1862, reprinted in *OR*, vol. 19, pt. 2, 282–83. That McClellan devoted any thought on this day to suggesting administrative reorganizations for the War Department (even if, as is possible, this letter was written before Special Orders No. 191 were brought to his attention) speaks volumes as to the general's priorities and his sense of urgency.

[19] McClellan to Henry W. Halleck, September 13, 1862, 11:00 p.m., reprinted in *OR*, vol. 19, pt. 2, 281–82. Halleck had telegraphed McClellan that day, "Until you know more certainly the enemy's force south of the Potomac, you are wrong in thus uncovering the capital. I am of opinion that the enemy will send a small column toward Pennsylvania, so as to draw your forces in that direction; then suddenly move on Washington with the forces south of the Potomac and those he may cross over." Halleck to McClellan, September 13, 1862, 10:45 a.m., reprinted in *OR*, vol. 19, pt. 2, 280–81.—*EAC*

Union army and noted the activity of aides and orderlies. He did not know the character of the paper, whether it was an order to McClellan or some report from one of his corps commanders, but he knew that it was of some importance and that a rapid forward movement of the army was to be ordered. It was but a few minutes till he was speeding out of Frederick in the direction of Stuart's cavalry outposts, and before sunset he had found Stuart near Turner's Gap and told him what he had seen and heard. Stuart hastened a swift courier with the news to Lee at Hagerstown, fifteen miles away, and was able to confirm it by reporting increased activity on the part of Pleasonton's cavalry during the afternoon, that cavalry affairs had taken place near Burkittsville and Jefferson, and that Pleasonton had driven him back and was then in the immediate front of the gap. All this unlooked for and unpleasant information Lee received early in the evening, and he acted promptly. He concluded that McClellan was acting with energy for the relief of Harper's Ferry, and he determined to press matters there to a conclusion, to protect and support the troops he had detached to reduce it, and to thwart McClellan in his efforts to divide his army and beat it in detail (as he rightly determined McClellan was endeavoring to do).

Longstreet argued against this course and advised an immediate withdrawal behind the Antietam of all forces north of the Potomac. Lee was not prepared to yield his grasp on Harper's Ferry (the surrender of which was looked for hourly), nor was he willing to risk the march of McLaws to join him by the Boonsboro Pike or Pleasant Valley. His position at Turner's Gap would not only give support to McLaws, but it would check the advance of McClellan long enough to ensure the surrender of Harper's Ferry, so he concluded not to yield his hold on that place and concentrate behind the Antietam as Longstreet advised. Longstreet says:

> It seems that up to the night of the 13th most of the Confederates were looking with confidence to the surrender of Harper's Ferry on the 13th, to be promptly followed by a move farther west, not thinking it possible that a great struggle at and along the range of South Mountain was impending; that even on the 14th our cavalry leader thought to continue his retrograde that day. General Hill's attention was given more to his instructions to prevent the escape of fugitives from Harper's Ferry than to trouble along his front, as the instructions covered more especially that duty, while information from the cavalry gave no indication of serious trouble from the front.
>
> A little after dark of the 13th, General Lee received, through a scout, information of the advance of the Union forces to the foot of South Mountain in solid ranks. Later information confirmed this report, giving the estimated strength at ninety thousand. General Lee still held to the thought that he had ample time. He sent for me, and I found him over his map. He told of the reports, and asked my views. I thought it too late to march on the 14th and properly man the pass at Turner's, and expressed preference for concentrating D. H. Hill's and my own force behind the Antietam at Sharpsburg, where we could get together in season to make a strong defensive fight, and at the same time check McClellan's march towards Harper's Ferry, in case he thought to relieve the beleaguered garrison by that route, forcing him to first remove the obstacle on his flank. He preferred to make the stand at Turner's Pass, and ordered the troops to march next morning, ordering a brigade left at Hagerstown to guard the trains … The hallucination that McClellan was not capable of serious work seemed to pervade our army, even to this moment of dreadful threatening.[20]

Lee sent a note of warning to Jackson and ordered him to press his attack at Harper's Ferry. D. H. Hill, who had been left near Boonsboro, was informed of the condition of affairs and directed to see that Turner's Gap was defended. Longstreet, who had taken position near Hagerstown to gather supplies and keep an eye on Governor Curtin's militia, was ordered to march at an early hour in the morning to Hill's support, while Stuart, holding the gaps over South Mountain, was ordered to delay McClellan's advance as much as possible and to keep McLaws informed of his movements. At 10:00 p.m. this communication was sent to McLaws:

> General Lee directs me to say that, from reports reaching him, he believes the enemy is moving toward Harper's Ferry to relieve the force they have there. You will see, therefore, the necessity of expediting your operations as much as possible. As soon as they are completed, he desires you, unless you receive orders from General Jackson, to move your force as rapidly as possible to Sharpsburg. General Longstreet will move down to-morrow and take a position on Beaver Creek, this side of Boonsborough. General Stuart has been requested to keep you informed of the movements of the enemy.[21]

Early the next morning, Lee transferred his headquarters from Hagerstown to Boonsboro, but before doing so he sent another dispatch to McLaws:

---

[20] Longstreet, 219–20.
[21] Thomas M. R. Talcott to McLaws, September 13, 1862, 10:00 p.m., reprinted in *OR*, vol. 19, pt. 2, 607.

General Longstreet moves down this morning to occupy the Boonsborough Valley, so as to protect your flank from attacks from forces coming from Frederick, until the operations at Harper's Ferry are finished. I desire your operations there to be pushed on as rapidly as possible, and, if the point is not ultimately taken, so arrange it that your forces may be brought up the Boonsborough Valley. General Stuart, with a portion of General D. H. Hill's forces, holds the gap between Boonsborough and Middletown, and Hampton's and Munford's brigades of cavalry occupy Burkittsville and the pass through the mountains there. If Harper's Ferry should be taken, the road will be open to you to Sharpsburg. Around the mountains from Sharpsburg the road communicates with Boonsborough and Hagerstown.[22]

It would appear from this dispatch that Lee was not aware of the fact that McLaws had any infantry at Crampton's Gap. The dispatch was received by McLaws when his troops were in touch with Franklin's advance.

Franklin's orders were to move at daybreak on the morning of the fourteenth by Jefferson and Burkittsville, gain Crampton's Gap as soon as practicable, and debouch upon Rohrersville (in Pleasant Valley) in order to cut off the retreat of or destroy McLaws's command. He started from Buckeystown at six o'clock and marched to Jefferson, where he halted to await the arrival of Couch from Licksville. At the end of an hour, he learned that Couch was still some distance in the rear and resumed the march to within two miles of Burkittsville, where he arrived at noon and, thinking that Crampton's Gap was occupied by the enemy in strong force, made elaborate preparations for an attack. He says, "The enemy was strongly posted on both sides of the road, which made a steep ascent through a narrow defile, wooded on both sides, and offering great advantages of cover and position. Their advance was posted near the base of the mountain, in the rear of a stone wall, stretching to the right of the road at a point where the ascent was gradual, and for the most part over open fields. Eight guns had been stationed on the road, and at points on the sides and summit of the mountain to the left [south] of the pass."[23]

It was evident to Franklin that the position could be carried only by an infantry attack, and Major General Henry W. Slocum, a splendid soldier commanding the First Division, was assigned that duty. He was directed to move his division through and to the right of Burkittsville and begin the attack on the right. Captain John W. Wolcott's Battery A, Maryland Light Artillery, was put in position on the left of the road and to the rear of the village, where it maintained a steady fire until the close of the engagement. Battery F, 5th U.S. Artillery (of Major General William F. Smith's division), was posted on commanding ground on the right of the road, some distance in Wolcott's rear and near Franklin's headquarters, where it kept up an uninterrupted fire upon the Confederate artillery on the side of the mountain, nearly two miles distant. Smith's division was held in reserve on the east side of the village, ready to cooperate with Slocum or support his attack as occasion might require.

Slocum's skirmishers met the pickets of the enemy at twelve o'clock noon near Burkittsville, upon which he deployed the 96th Pennsylvania (Colonel Henry L. Cake) of Colonel Joseph J. Bartlett's brigade and ordered it forward. Cake drove in Munford's cavalry pickets and advanced to the village, drawing the fire of Captain Cary F. Grimes's (Virginia) Battery and Chew's Battery on the road to Crampton's Gap and that of Captain Basil C. Manly's (North Carolina) Battery in Brownsville Gap, one mile south, which was kept up during the greater part of the afternoon—the shots being divided between the skirmishers and the main body of the regiment, drawn up in line on the road leading out of Burkittsville southwest to Knoxville. The other regiments of Slocum's division were advanced to a position about half a mile east of the village, where they were completely concealed from the view of the enemy and covered from the fire of his artillery. Here the command halted quite two hours while the men ate their rations and the officers considered preparations for attack. Colonel Bartlett writes:

Here everything was halted, and while the men were taking their midday meal, the General commanding came up and established his headquarters in the edge of the little wood, at a point from which he could overlook the intervening valley, which stretched up to the base of the mountain, and had the road leading to the Pass and the Pass itself plainly in vision. After resting perhaps an hour in this position, the Adjutant-General of the division, Maj. H[iram] C. Rodgers, came to me with a message from Gen. Slocum, saying he would like to see me at Gen. Franklin's headquarters, where I immediately reported.

I found grouped there, resting upon the ground, in as comfortable positions as each one could assume, after lunch, smoking their cigars, Gen. Franklin, commanding the corps; Gen. Slocum and W. F. Smith (Baldy), commanding respectively the First and Second Divisions; Gen. Hancock, commanding First Brigade, Smith's Division; [Brigadier] Gen. W[illiam] T. H. Brooks, commanding Vermont Brigade, Smith's Division, and [Brigadier] Gen. John Newton, commanding Third Brigade, Slocum's Division. After a little preliminary conversation, not touching

[22] Lee to McLaws, September 14, 1862, reprinted in OR, vol. 19, pt. 2, 608.

[23] Franklin to Seth Williams, September 30, 1862, reprinted in OR, vol. 19, pt. 1, 375.

upon the battle before us, Gen. Slocum suddenly asked me on which side of the road leading through and over the pass I would attack. Without a moment's hesitation I replied, "On the right." "Well, gentlemen, that settles it," said Gen. Franklin. "Settles what, General," I exclaimed. "The point of attack." I was naturally indignant that I should be called upon to give even an opinion upon such an important matter without previously hearing the views of such old and experienced officers upon such an important question. Gen. Slocum then explained the situation. In discussing the situation, it seems that they were equally divided in their opinions between the right and left of the road for the main attack. Gen. Franklin then asked Gen. Slocum who was going to lead the attack. Gen. Slocum replied, "Bartlett." "Then," said Gen. Franklin, "send for Bartlett and let him decide; he has carefully looked over the ground from the right, and Gen. Brooks has done the same on the left, and as Bartlett is to lead the assault, let him decide." This settled the question as to where the principal attack was to be made; and later, when we were alone together, I asked Gen. Slocum what formation he intended to make with the division. He said: "As Gen. Franklin has allowed you to decide the point of attack, on the ground that you were to lead it, it is no more than fair that I should leave to you the formation." I suggested the formation of the three brigades in column of regiments deployed, two regiments front, at 100 paces interval between lines (that would give us six lines); that the head of the column should be directed toward a point I indicated to him, at nearly right angles to the road which crossed the mountain, and in a direction to strike the highest point the road reached at the crest, it being the shortest line; that I would deploy the 27th N. Y. (his old regiment and mine also) as skirmishers at the head of the column, and skirmish into the teeth of their line of battle, following with the head of the column at 100 paces; that I would not halt after giving the order forward until we reached the crest of the mountain, if possible. These suggestions met with the General's approval, and he based his written order upon them. I was to attack at the point and in the manner indicated, take the crest of the mountain, and throw out a picket line for the night.

The enemy's artillery had now opened upon everything in sight.[24]

The road from Burkittsville to Rohrersville and Pleasant Valley runs northwest from Burkittsville a good half-mile, when it begins to ascend the mountain in a northerly direction by a laborious grade. It runs this way another good half-mile when it turns gradually to the west and reaches the summit of the gap at an elevation of four hundred feet above the level of Burkittsville. (Though of heavy grade, the road is good.) At the time, the mountain on either side of the road was heavily wooded from base to summit. About one-third of a mile west of Burkittsville and 250 yards short of where the road turns northerly in ascending the mountain, a narrow country road leads from the right, northerly, along the base of the mountain. On both sides of this narrow road were stone walls or fences, not continuous on both sides nor continuous on either side, but on one side or the other they furnished good cover for infantry and were skillfully utilized for the defense of the gap. On the west side of this road were several houses, behind which the mountain slope was well wooded.

McLaws did not share in the belief (entertained by Lee, Jackson, Stuart, and others) that McClellan would give them no serious trouble while in the execution of their plans, although he did not anticipate the prompt movement that was made. He had been informed by Lee at Frederick that Stuart would take care of the mountain gaps after he had passed them, but was rightly minded to look to this matter himself. So when he marched through Brownsville Gap on the eleventh and moved on Elk Ridge and Maryland Heights, he left Semmes (with his brigade and Mahone's) in Pleasant Valley, opposite the gap, to guard both Crampton's and Brownsville gaps and gave instructions to send a regiment to protect the rear of Kershaw, who had ascended Solomon's Gap in Maryland Heights. (As we have seen, Wright's Brigade of Anderson's Division proceeded down South Mountain and took position on the heights above Weverton Pass as ordered the night before.) Cobb was directed to cross Pleasant Valley and, marching along the eastern base of Elk Ridge, keep in communication with Kershaw above and up to his advance, ready to give him support if needed and serve as a rallying force should Kershaw be worsted (which McLaws asserts Cobb failed to do because of some misconception of orders). R. H. Anderson pushed forward Pryor's Brigade, took possession of Weverton, and disposed of the troops of Wright and Pryor to defend that pass.

McLaws ordered a picket of one company posted in Brownsville Gap, which, on the twelfth, Semmes increased to three regiments and five pieces of artillery, thus employing his entire brigade except the 10th Georgia (which was picketing the Rohrersville Road and other avenues leading down Pleasant Valley in the direction of Harper's Ferry). On the thirteenth Colonel Parham (commanding Mahone's Brigade) reported to Semmes, and the 41st Virginia was sent as a picket to Solomon's Gap to cover Kershaw's rear. Having familiarized himself with the roads and passes, Semmes, on the morning of the fourteenth, ordered Parham (with his skeleton brigade and Grimes's Battery) to support Munford's cavalry at Crampton's Gap and instructed Parham, if he needed support, to call upon Major Willis C. Holt (10th Georgia) for his

---

[24] Joseph J. Bartlett, "Crampton's Pass," *National Tribune*, December 19, 1889.

regiment, then posted on the Rohrersville Road. (Munford had been gradually forced back to the gap on the thirteenth by Pleasonton's cavalry and late the same day had been joined by the horsemen of Hampton's Brigade.)

Believing that Crampton's Gap was the weakest point in his line, Stuart left Colonel Rosser, with the 5th Virginia Cavalry, at Fox's Gap, saw that two brigades of D. H. Hill's Division were put in Turner's Gap, and, early on the morning of the fourteenth, rode down to Crampton's Gap. Here he saw no signs of a Union advance in force and, fearing a movement along the Potomac toward Harper's Ferry, sent Hampton in that direction, thus leaving Munford with but two small cavalry regiments (the 2d and 12th Virginia Cavalry) and a part of Mahone's infantry brigade at Crampton's Gap. Hampton went down the east side of South Mountain, halted at the south end at Knoxville, and threw out pickets on the roads to Point of Rocks and Frederick. Stuart proceeded to McLaws's headquarters to acquaint him with the situation of affairs and rode with him to Maryland Heights to assist in the reduction of Harper's Ferry, as he was familiar with the topography of the county from his connection with the John Brown raid. He says, "I explained to him the location of the roads in that vicinity … and repeatedly urged the importance of his holding with an infantry picket the road leading from the Ferry by the Kennedy farm toward Sharpsburg; failing to do which, the entire cavalry force of the enemy at the Ferry, amounting to about 500, escaped during the night by that very road, and inflicted serious damage on General Longstreet's train in the course of their flight."[25]

While Stuart was thus prompting McLaws on Maryland Heights, trouble was brewing for Munford, who as senior officer had been ordered to take command at Crampton's Gap and hold it at all hazards. The morning was rife with rumors of the Union advance, and Munford prepared to receive it. He posted the 6th, 12th, and 16th Virginia of Mahone's Brigade behind the stone walls and rail fences of the road at the eastern base of the mountain and running parallel with it; the 2d and 12th Virginia Cavalry were dismounted and disposed on the flanks of the infantry as sharpshooters (the 2d on the right, the 12th on the left). Chew's Battery and a section of Navy howitzers of Grimes's were placed in rear about halfway up the slope of the mountain, in the most eligible position that could be found. Major Holt and the 10th Georgia were ordered by Semmes to Munford's support and took position at the base of the mountain, but were almost immediately ordered by Semmes to fall back and take position at the colored church on the road to Rohrersville. Holt had reached the summit of the mountain when Parham halted him, allowed him to send two companies to the church at the junction of the roads, and gave him peremptory orders to return and go into position on the left of the line he had formed. Colonel Edgar B. Montague and the 32d Virginia of Semmes's Brigade, holding Brownsville Gap, one mile south of Crampton's Gap, stationed a picket of 200 men at the base of the mountain and a line of skirmishers along his whole front, connecting with Munford's right. (These were more spectators than participants in the action about to ensue, as they were not engaged.) Including the 300 men of Semmes's Brigade on the right of his command, Munford had about 1,200 men to meet the advance of five brigades of Franklin's corps, numbering nearly 12,000 men, but he had the advantage of position and thirteen pieces of artillery.

As elsewhere stated, reconnaissance had decided that the Union attack should be made on the right and flank of the road leading over the mountain, and Bartlett was to direct and lead the advance. Bartlett conducted his brigade as secretly as possible to a large field near the base of the mountain, where the formation was to be made in a ravine screened from view by a hedge and a large cornfield. (About this time, Captain Russell arrived upon the field with a dispatch from McClellan to Franklin, and Russell informed Franklin of the condition of affairs at Harper's Ferry.)

It was three o'clock before the column of attack was formed in this order: the 27th New York (Lieutenant Colonel Alexander D. Adams) was deployed as skirmishers, to be followed at a distance of two hundred yards by two regiments in line of battle—the 16th New York (Lieutenant Colonel Joel J. Seaver) on the right and the 5th Maine (Colonel Nathaniel J. Jackson) on the left. These three regiments were of Bartlett's brigade. Newton's brigade was to follow Bartlett's and was formed in two lines. In first line, the 32d New York (Colonel Roderick Matheson) was on the right and the 18th New York (Lieutenant Colonel George R. Myers) on the left; in second line, the 31st New York (Lieutenant Colonel Francis E. Pinto of the 32d New York) was on the right and the 95th Pennsylvania (Colonel Gustavus W. Town[26]) on the left.

The New Jersey brigade (Colonel Alfred T. A. Torbert) was also formed in two lines. In first line, the 1st New Jersey (Lieutenant Colonel Mark W. Collet[27] of the 3d New Jersey) was on the right and the 2d New Jersey (Colonel Samuel L. Buck) on the left; in second line, the 3d New Jersey (Colonel Henry W. Brown) was on the right and the 4th New Jersey (Colonel William B. Hatch) on the left. Including the skirmish line, the column was six lines deep, the four leading lines being separated by intervals of 200 yards (the New Jersey brigade took intervals of 150 yards). The 96th Pennsylvania of

---

[25] James E. B. Stuart to Robert H. Chilton, February 13, 1864, reprinted in *OR*, vol. 19, pt. 1, 818.

[26] At this point in his original manuscript, Carman gives the name incorrectly as "George W. Town," but it appears properly in his table of organization.

[27] As above, Carman here gives the name incorrectly as "M. W. Collett," but it appears properly in his table of organization.

Bartlett's brigade, which had advanced into the village, joined the column as it went forward, following the Jerseymen. The 121st New York was held as a reserve.

McClellan's order to Franklin was to seize the pass immediately upon his arrival before it, if not occupied by the enemy in force. If it was held in force, he was to make his dispositions and begin the attack half an hour after hearing severe fighting at Turner's Gap. The sound of heavy fighting at Turner's Gap came down the valley before Franklin had reached Burkittsville and continued during his leisurely preparations; it was not necessary to wait, and the day was well spent when the orders were given to advance. As soon as it began, the Confederates opened a heavy and well directed fire from their artillery halfway up the mountain and in Brownsville Gap, but the troops advanced steadily, preceded by the skirmishers that soon drew the fire of the Confederate infantry and dismounted cavalry posted behind the stone fences and houses (which afforded them admirable cover). Having thus developed the Confederate position, Slocum withdrew the skirmishers. The first line (the 5th Maine and the 16th New York) moved to a rail fence on a rise of ground within three hundred yards of the Confederates, an open field intervening, and a severe engagement ensued in which the two regiments lost heavily, while the Confederates, having greatly the advantage of position, took few casualties.

Bartlett advanced his line promptly and in good order, but for some unexplained and unaccounted reason Newton did not promptly follow, and there was more than six hundred yards' interval between the two lines. When Newton did come up, Bartlett's men, who had been engaged nearly an hour, had suffered severely and were out of ammunition. Newton advanced the 32d and 18th New York to relieve Bartlett's two regiments, which fell slightly to the rear, and his second line (the 31st New York and the 95th Pennsylvania) soon came up and formed on the left.

When first examined, the position of the pass and its approaches made it evident to Slocum that the attempt to carry it must be made by infantry alone; therefore, the artillery had been left behind. But the stone walls covering the enemy presented such an obstacle to the advance of his lines that further effort was suspended until the artillery could be brought up and used against them. A battery was sent for. It came at a gallop, but before fairly in position there was no use for it: the Confederate position at the base of the mountain had been carried.

While awaiting the arrival of artillery, Torbert's brigade came up on the left in two lines (the 1st and 2d New Jersey in advance), opening a rapid and accurate fire. The 96th Pennsylvania took position on the extreme right, but no impression seemed to be made on the enemy, while the Union line, much exposed, was severely suffering. It was apparent to everyone, officer and private, that nothing but a quick rush—a united charge of the entire line—would dislodge the enemy and win the day. Bartlett and Torbert, young and gallant soldiers, had a moment's consultation and, as the artillery was not yet in sight, decided to charge immediately without waiting for it or further orders from Slocum. Everything was in readiness. The 96th Pennsylvania of Bartlett's brigade was on the right of the whole line; on its left were the 32d and 18th New York of Newton's brigade, and on the left of these two New York regiments the 16th and 27th New York and the 5th Maine of Bartlett. On the left of Bartlett's three regiments were the 31st New York and the 95th Pennsylvania of Newton, and on the left of the 95th Pennsylvania was Torbert's Jersey brigade—the left of the division. The left of Torbert's line was about two hundred yards north of the Burkittsville Road. From right to left, the length of the line was about a mile.

Thus formed, the order was passed along the line to cease firing and the command given to charge double-quick. Instantly the troops were in motion, and the sight was a grand and thrilling one. The mile of brightened muskets glistened in the evening sun, and the regimental colors, stirred by a gentle breeze, waved proudly over the well aligned ranks as they went forward over mostly open fields swept by musketry and ploughed by shot and shell.

The fields through which the 96th Pennsylvania charged on the extreme right presented many obstacles, and in order not to meet the enemy with disordered lines, Colonel Cake twice halted for a moment under cover of the stone fences to reform. The last of the many fields over which it had to charge was marshy meadow and tall standing corn, and as it emerged from the corn and came into the open field—officers all in place and cheering the men onward, the men well aligned on the colors, which were proudly carried by a stalwart bearer—it received a murderous fire from the stone-walled road but twenty paces distant that laid low a large number of men and, for a moment, staggered it. The men threw themselves flat on the ground to avoid as much as possible the distinctive rain of Minié balls pouring into the ranks, but it was for a moment only. They rose as one man, the colors pointed forward. The road was gained and the enemy sent in confused retreat up the mountain. The left of the Confederate line was routed, and, without stopping, the Pennsylvanians pressed on in eager pursuit. To the left of the 96th Pennsylvania, the men of Bartlett's and Newton's brigades had less natural obstacles to contend with, but the rain of musketry was severe and thinned the charging lines, though it did not stop them. They swept over the open field, drove the Virginians from cover, and followed them up the mountain side.

When the order to advance was given, the 3d and 4th New Jersey were in second line to the 1st and 2d New Jersey and about one hundred yards distant, protected by a slight rise in the ground. The 1st and 2d ceased firing, and the 3d and 4th, with wild cheers, went forward on a run, jumped the rail fence behind which the 1st and 2d had been fighting, and faced the leaden storm that swept over the grass field between them and the stone wall bordering the road. When they had come about 150 yards, the 1st and 2d charged in the same handsome manner as did their comrades, both lines reaching the stone wall about the same time, the Virginians breaking and retreating up the side of the mountain, closely pursued by Jerseymen.

While Slocum's men were making their successful charge on the right of the road, Brooks's Vermont brigade of Smith's division moved on the left. After passing through Burkittsville under the fire of the artillery in Brownsville Gap, the Confederate skirmish line was encountered. Brooks deployed the 4th Vermont as skirmishers, with the 2d Vermont in support (the other three regiments remaining as a reserve on the edge of the village), and advanced. The Confederates quickly retreated, leaving some of their number as prisoners.

While the Virginians are retreating up the mountain, closely pursued by the Union lines, we must see what dispositions were made to relieve them at the top and meet the Union pursuit.

When McLaws had descended into Pleasant Valley three days before, he had ordered Semmes to take care of his rear by occupying both Crampton's and Brownsville gaps, and two brigades were placed at his disposal—Semmes's own and Mahone's. Brownsville Gap seemed to Semmes of the first importance, and he placed there three regiments of his own brigade and a battery of artillery, leaving Mahone's Brigade, under Colonel Parham, in the valley west of the mountain. Becoming familiar with the roads and passes, he recognized the great importance of Crampton's Gap, and on the morning of the fourteenth ordered Parham to move into it with three regiments and a battery and authorized him in case of need to call upon the 10th Georgia, then on the Rohrersville Road. By this time Semmes had become so thoroughly impressed by what he had heard of the Union advance in heavy force that he rode in hot haste to acquaint McLaws of the danger threatening his rear. He found him on Maryland Heights about noon, told him that scouts were constantly reporting the Union advance from Frederick, and suggested an increase of forces at Crampton's Gap whereupon McLaws sent an order to Cobb, near Sandy Hook, to march back to the camp near the foot of Brownsville Gap and directed Semmes to withdraw the regiment of Mahone's Brigade from Solomon's Gap, leaving a small rear-guard to give notice should a force of the enemy approach that position. Semmes was instructed also to tell Cobb, on his arrival in the vicinity, to take command at Crampton's Gap. Semmes rode back to his command and disposed his brigade for action. Cobb—receiving McLaws's order at one o'clock—set out on the return march from Sandy Hook, reaching his old camp (about two miles from Crampton's Gap) at four o'clock, where he was immediately waited upon by Semmes, who gave him the instructions he had received from McLaws. But Cobb was sluggish and remained a full hour without making the least effort to acquaint himself of what was going on, nor did he give sign of interest until he was spurred to action by a message from Munford recommending him to move up to the gap, as the enemy were pressing his small force. McLaws says:

> General Cobb was inexperienced enough not to realize that as ranking officer he was responsible for everything that might happen in the rear, where his inferiors in rank were stationed, unless they were under the immediate orders of others superior to himself. He was sent to the camp ground upon which I camped on the evening of the 11th, when my command came into the valley, so as to be able to throw his troops either to Brownsville Gap or to Crampton's, or to any other forces in this area where they were most needed, and of this he was to be the judge, as he was superior in rank to General Semmes and to all others in that neighborhood. If he had had more experience as to the responsibility which rank confers he would not have waited an hour in camp upon contingencies, but would have gone in person in advance to inform himself as to the best way to provide against misfortune.[28]

Cobb was finally moved by the advice of Semmes and the appeals of Munford, and he sent two of his strongest regiments to Munford's support. These had hardly taken up the line of march when a message was received from Parham to the effect that the enemy was pressing him hard with overwhelming numbers. Parham appealed for all the support he could bring him, upon which Cobb ordered the two remaining regiments of his brigade to march and accompanied them in person. As he started, he received McLaws's orders to hold the gap if it cost the life of every man in his command.[29] Thus impressed with the importance of the position, Cobb went forward as rapidly as possible. When he went by the road to the top of the mountain, Munford and Parham were still engaged. Through an opening in the woods where he stood and over the tops of the trees below him could be seen the long Union line charging and overlapping the Confederate flanks. Munford explained the position of his troops and yielded the command; as he did so, the Virginians broke and began to come up

---

[28] McLaws, "The Capture of Harper's Ferry," *Philadelphia Weekly Press*, September 12, 1888.

[29] In his official report, McLaws says, "I was on Maryland Heights, directing and observing the fire of our guns, when I heard cannonading in the direction of Crampton's Gap, but I felt no particular concern about it, as there were three brigades of infantry in the vicinity, besides the cavalry of Colonel Munford, and General Stuart, who was with me on the heights and had just come in from above, told me he did not believe there was more than a brigade of the enemy. I, however, sent my adjutant-general to General Cobb, as also Major [James M.] Goggin, of my staff, with directions to hold the gap if he lost his last man in doing it, and shortly afterward went down the mountain and started toward the gap." McLaws to Chilton, October 18, 1862, reprinted in *OR*, vol. 19, pt. 1, 854.—EAC

the mountain. The Cobb Legion and the 24th Georgia were now up, and Cobb requested Munford to put them in position (which he promptly did) on the road just east of the summit and where it turns to the right in descending the mountain to Burkittsville. The 15th North Carolina and the 16th Georgia came up, and at Cobb's request Munford placed them on the road running to the left after crossing the gap, but, says Munford, "they behaved badly and did not get in position before the wildest confusion commenced, the wounded coming to the rear in numbers and more well men coming with them."[30]

The unsteadiness in the ranks of these two regiments was caused by the retreat of the Virginians through them and the oncoming of Slocum's line. The 96th Pennsylvania and other regiments on the right and center did not halt—even for breath—at the foot of the mountain, but, scaling the stone walls and fences, went on close upon the heels of the Virginians, and as the most long-winded and fleet-footed neared its summit, they saw this new line of battle on the road and, taking cover of rocks and trees, immediately engaged it. As the Union firing line increased by others coming up, the two regiments broke and retreated, leaving many prisoners in the hands of their enemy, and were pursued as rapidly as Slocum's men could climb the hill to its summit and then down it. Like disaster overtook the Cobb Legion and the 24th Georgia at the hands of Torbert's brigade and the left of Newton's. As the Jerseymen climbed up the shingly side of the mountain, they took many prisoners from among the Virginians. When they reached near the crest, on the left side of the road, it was seen that the Georgians were forming a new line on their right, upon which the right regiment wheeled to the right and poured a murderous volley into them that dispersed them and sent them in disorder through the gap and down the west side of the mountain, closely followed by the Jerseymen, the 31st New York, and the 95th Pennsylvania.

Cobb—aided by Semmes, Munford, Parham, and others—made great effort to rally his men; the 10th Georgia and the Virginia cavalry and infantry (a few being collected) endeavored to stay them, but without the least effect. Munford says, "It would have been as useless to attempt to rally a flock of frightened sheep," and as it was evident that the gap could no longer be held, he formed his own command and moved down the Rohrersville Road to where his horses had been left, "the infantry still running in great disorder on the Harper's Ferry road," with no apparent idea of stopping until met by McLaws and Stuart coming from Maryland Heights.[31] Stuart says, "Hearing of the attack at Crampton's Gap, I rode at full speed to reach that point, and met General Cobb's command just after dark, retreating in disorder down Pleasant Valley. He represented the enemy as only 200 yards behind, and in overwhelming force. I immediately halted his command, and disposed men upon each side of the road to meet the enemy, and a battery, which I had accidentally met with, was placed in position commanding the road. The enemy not advancing, I sent out parties to reconnoiter, who found no enemy within a mile. Pickets were thrown out, and the command was left in partial repose for the night."[32]

The Union pursuit was halted by darkness, the weariness of the men, and the dislocation of the commands consequent upon the broken character of the field. Slocum's division gathered along the road to Rohrersville, at the western foot of the gap. Brooks's Vermont brigade, which participated in the charge up the mountain, moved on Slocum's left. When the summit was reached, the 4th Vermont followed the crest of the mountain to the left, where Manly's Battery had been, and the 2d Vermont continued on down the western slope and reached the base of the mountain just as Slocum's men had scattered the enemy. The 4th Vermont proceeded along the crest about a half-mile and captured the battle-flag, Major Francis D. Holliday, and many men of the 16th Virginia, and then descended the west side of the mountain, where it was joined by the other regiments of the brigade. All bivouacked in the valley at the point where Slocum's division ceased pursuit—on the Harper's Ferry Road about a half-mile south of the gap. In Smith division, Colonel William H. Irwin's brigade went over the mountain by the gap and bivouacked on Brooks's right. Hancock's brigade was held in reserve, did not participate in the engagement, and remained east of the mountain.

The operations of the day resulted in a Union victory and the capture of six hundred prisoners, seven hundred stands of arms, a piece of artillery from the Troup (Georgia) Artillery, and four colors. (The piece of artillery had been abandoned at the foot of the mountain because of the hot pursuit of the 95th Pennsylvania and was captured by the skirmishers of the Vermont brigade.) The victory was purchased at the expense of 113 killed, 418 wounded, and 2 missing—an aggregate of 533.[33]

The defense of the Confederates at the east foot of the mountain against the heavy odds they faced was a brilliant one. Outnumbered eight to one, they held position until fairly overwhelmed. Nor must the action of the men of Cobb's Brigade be too harshly criticized. They came upon the field when it was practically lost, pursued and pursuers nearly commingled; they were then thrown into some disorder by the unexpected, murderous fire poured into them from front and flank and

---

[30] Thomas T. Munford to James T. W. Hairston, October 3, 1862, reprinted in *OR*, vol. 19, pt. 1, 827.

[31] Munford to Hairston, 827.

[32] Stuart to Chilton, 819.

[33] In Carman's original manuscript, the casualty tabulations for the Union forces appear at this point. For the sake of clarity and convenience, this chart is reprinted herein as Appendix F.

yielded only when one-fourth of their number were killed and wounded and the survivors nearly surrounded. Their severe losses attest to their gallantry.[34]

Night was falling fast as McLaws, hastening from Maryland Heights, drew near Cobb's retreating forces. On the way he met his adjutant general, who informed him that Franklin had carried the gap and that Cobb needed help, upon which he at once ordered up Wilcox's Brigade from down the valley and rode on to Cobb's camp, where there was much apprehension, notwithstanding that Stuart had averted a panic and measurably allayed fear. McLaws remarked to Stuart that it looked very much as if he had been caught in a trap and asked what he thought of the situation. Stuart advised that an effort be made to retake Crampton's Gap, but McLaws would not consider the proposition and instead came to a conclusion to make preparations to resist an advance down Pleasant Valley, to keep guard over the passes below, and to push the attack on Harper's Ferry from Maryland Heights. R. H. Anderson concurred in McLaws's views, and they were carried out. McLaws says:

> Fortunately, night came on and allowed a new arrangement of the troops to be made to meet the changed aspect of affairs. The brigades of Generals Kershaw and Barksdale, excepting one regiment of the latter and two pieces of artillery, were withdrawn from the heights … overlooking the town, and formed line of battle across the valley about 1½ miles below Crampton's Gap, with the remnants of the brigades of Generals Cobb, Semmes, and Mahone, and those of Wilcox, Kershaw, and Barksdale, which were placed specially under command of General Anderson. Generals Wright and Pryor were kept in position guarding the Weverton Pass, and Generals Armistead and Featherston that from Harper's Ferry. That place was not yet taken, and I had but to wait and watch the movements of the enemy. It was necessary to guard three positions: First, to present a front against the enemy advancing down the valley; second, to prevent them from escaping from Harper's Ferry and acting in conjunction with their troops in front; third, to prevent an entrance at Weverton Pass.
>
> The loss in those brigades engaged was, in killed, wounded, and missing, very large, and the remnant collected to make front across the valley was very small. I had dispatched Lieutenant [Thomas S. B.] Tucker, my aide-de-camp, with a courier and guide, to report to General Lee the condition of affairs, but, on getting beyond our forces, he rode suddenly on a strong picket of the enemy, was halted, and fired on by them as he turned and dashed back. The courier was killed, but Lieutenant Tucker and the guide escaped. General Stuart had, however, started couriers before that, and sent others from time to time during the night, and I, therefore, was satisfied that General Lee would be informed before morning.[35]

None of these couriers ever reached Lee, and McLaws was left to work out his own salvation. Meanwhile, we turn to affairs at Turner's Gap.

---

[34] Casualty tabulations for the Confederate forces appear at this point in Carman's original manuscript. This chart is reprinted herein as Appendix G.

[35] McLaws to Chilton, 855.

8

South Mountain (Turner's Gap)

September 14, 1862

While William Franklin's Sixth Corps was forcing Crampton's Gap, the First and Ninth Corps, under the overall command of Ambrose Burnside, were severely engaged at Turner's Gap, six miles to the northeast. The engagement was most severe at and south of Fox's Gap, a mile and more to the south, and there was a sharp and fierce contest north, but as these were both for possession of the main road that ran through Turner's Gap, this place has given the Union name to the battle. (The Confederates call it the battle of Boonsboro.)

At this point South Mountain runs, in a general direction, northeast and southwest, and its crests are about 1,300 feet above sea level and 1,000 feet above the general level of the Catoctin, or Middletown, Valley. The National Road, the turnpike between Frederick and Hagerstown, crosses the mountain at Turner's Gap some three hundred feet below the crests on either side. The mountain on the north side of the turnpike is divided into two crests and ridges by a narrow valley that, though deep at the gap, becomes a slight depression about a mile to the north. There are country roads both to the right of the gap and to the left, giving access to the crests overlooking the National Road. The principal one on the left (or south), called the Old Sharpsburg Road, is nearly parallel to and about three-fourths of a mile distant from the road through the gap, until it reaches the crest of the mountain at Fox's Gap, when it bends to the left and, leaving Boonsboro far to the right, goes to Sharpsburg. A road on the right, known as the Old Hagerstown Road, passes up a ravine in the mountain about a mile from the National Road and, bending to the left over and along the first crest, enters the National Road just east of the Mountain House, a famous hostelry of the older days, when stagecoach and wagons formed the chief means of communication between Baltimore and Wheeling.[1] By the National Road, the summit of the gap is reached by easy grades. On the east side of the mountain, on either side of the road, almost to the very summit, the land was cleared and under cultivation. At the summit, on the south side of the road, is the Mountain House.

From the opposition displayed by the Confederates to his advance from Frederick on the thirteenth, Pleasonton was convinced that they would make a determined stand at Turner's Gap with an accession of force and called upon Burnside for infantry support. Awaiting its arrival, he utilized the declining hours of the day by sending some dismounted cavalry up the mountain, on the right of the National Road, to examine the position. This brought on some skirmishing and caused the Confederates to concentrate on that flank. Pleasonton learned of the two roads (one on the right and one on the left of the gap, both entering the National Road beyond it) favoring the movement of turning both flanks of the Confederate position. As the infantry support requested of Burnside did not come up on the thirteenth, however, Pleasonton made no effort to force the gap and bivouacked in the valley near its foot.

Early on the morning of the fourteenth, Pleasonton renewed his reconnaissance of the gap and soon ascertained that the Confederates were in some force, upon which he continued to await the arrival of infantry. Meanwhile, Lieutenant Samuel N. Benjamin's regular battery and Gibson's battery had come up to within a short distance of Bolivar, Maryland, and took position to the left of the National Road on a high knoll (about half a mile beyond the fork of the Old Sharpsburg Road with the turnpike) commanding a portion of the gap, and they began an engagement with the Confederate artillery well up in the gap. Later in the day, McMullin's Ohio battery came up and engaged the Confederates about a mile distant.

Jacob Cox, commanding the Kanawha Division of the Ninth Corps, bivouacked a little west of Middletown on the night of the thirteenth. He did not receive an order from Burnside to support Pleasonton on the evening of the thirteenth (as Pleasonton was led to believe) but was ordered that evening to support him with a brigade next morning. Cox detailed the brigade, commanded by Colonel Scammon, to report to Pleasonton, and at 6:00 a.m. on Sunday, September 14, it left camp and marched out on the National Road. The brigade consisted of the 12th, 23d, and 30th Ohio and numbered nearly 1,500 men.

---

[1] Some years after the war, Madeleine Dahlgren, widow of Rear Admiral John A. Dahlgren, purchased the Mountain House and much of the surrounding field and forest. The house was renovated, the field and forest improved, and a charming summer home established. North of the road and nearly opposite the house, a modest memorial chapel was erected, in which were placed the remains of Admiral Dahlgren and Colonel Ulric Dahlgren. In May 1898 the remains of Mrs. Dahlgren were laid at rest by the side of those of her husband and son.—*EAC*

Cox was on the road when Scammon marched out and, impelled by a laudable curiosity to know how Pleasonton intended to use the brigade, rode forward with Scammon. Just after crossing Catoctin Creek, Cox was greatly surprised to see, standing at the roadside, Colonel Augustus Moor, who two days before had been taken prisoner in the streets of Frederick. Cox asked for an explanation, and Moor replied that he had been paroled and was on the way back to the Union camps. Upon learning that the object of Scammon's movement was a reconnaissance into the gap, Moor made an involuntary start and uttered an unintended note of warning, then—remembering that he was under parole—checked himself and turned away.[2]

The incident was not lost upon Cox, who now realized that there was more serious work to be done by his brigade than merely supporting a cavalry reconnaissance. He says:

> I galloped to Scammon and told him that I should follow him in close support with [Colonel George] Crook's brigade [formerly Moor's], and as I went back along the column I spoke to each regimental commander, warning them to be prepared for anything, big or little,—it might be a skirmish, it might be a battle. Hurrying back to the camp, I ordered Crook to turn out his brigade prepared to march at once. I then wrote a dispatch to General Reno, saying I suspected we should find the enemy in force on the mountain-top, and should go forward with both brigades instead of sending one. Starting a courier with this, I rode forward to find Pleasonton, who was about a mile in front of my camp, where the old Sharpsburg road leaves the turnpike. I found that he was convinced that the enemy's position in the gap was too strong to be carried by a direct attack, and that he had determined to let his horsemen demonstrate on the main road, support-ing the batteries [Benjamin's and Gibson's—EAC], … while Scammon should march by the Sharpsburg road and try to reach the flank of the force on the summit. Telling him of my suspicion as to the enemy, I also informed him that I had determined to support Scammon with Crook, and if it became necessary to fight with the whole division I should do so, in which case I should assume the responsibility myself as his senior officer. To this he cordially assented.
>
> One of my batteries [Captain Seth J. Simmonds's—EAC] contained a section of 20-pounder Parrots, and as these were too heavy to take up the rough mountain road, I ordered them to go into action beside Benjamin's battery, near the turnpike, and to remain with it till further orders. Our artillery at this time was occupying a knoll about half a mile in front of the forks of the road, and was exchanging shots with a battery of the enemy well up toward the gap. It was about half past 7 o'clock when Crook's column filed off on the old Sharpsburg road, Scammon having perhaps half an hour's start. We had fully two miles to go before we should reach the place where our attack was made, and, as it was a pretty steep road, the men marched slowly with frequent rests. On our way up we were overtaken by my courier who had returned from Reno with approval of my action, and the assurance that the rest of the Ninth Corps would come forward to my support.[3]

The engagement about to be opened by Cox was confined entirely to the south of the National Road. It began early in the day and continued until after dark, and it shall be first considered.

When Cox left the column to order out Crook's brigade, Scammon continued the march and reported to Pleasonton on the National Road, about a mile beyond the Catoctin. By this time Pleasonton had come to the conclusion to send him to the left, by the Old Sharpsburg Road, to feel the enemy and ascertain whether they held the crest of South Mountain on that side in any considerable force. About 7:00 a.m. Scammon turned off the National Road at the Ripp house and, tak-ing a cross-road past a schoolhouse, entered the Old Sharpsburg Road, which was followed for a quarter of a mile beyond Mentzer's Mill, when an artillery shot from the summit of the mountain revealed the presence of an enemy and compelled more caution in movement. A detachment of the 30th Ohio continued the direct movement up the mountain by the main road, and the main column turned off (at what is now the Reno Schoolhouse) into a country road leading still farther to the left and running nearly parallel to the crest of the mountain. (It had the advantage of cover of the forest.) When the head of the column reached the extreme southern limit of the open field south of the gap, on the east slope of the mountain, the 23d Ohio, under Lieutenant Colonel Rutherford B. Hayes, was deployed to the left to move through the woods and up to the crest of the mountain in order to gain the enemy's right, attack, and turn it. The remainder of the brigade advanced on Hayes's right and rear, the 12th Ohio (Colonel Carr B. White) in the center and the 30th Ohio (Colonel Hugh Ewing) on the right. The entire line soon became engaged with the enemy, whose preparation we now note.

We have seen that D. H. Hill, with five brigades, was halted near Boonsboro on the night of the tenth to guard the wagon trains and park of artillery of the Confederate army and to watch all the roads leading from Harper's Ferry up Pleasant Val-ley. This required a considerable separation of his command on the various roads; his headquarters were about the center of his five brigades and not less than three miles from Turner's Gap. As Stuart and his cavalry had been charged with the duty of observing the movements and checking the advance of the Union army, Hill did not consider it necessary to leave any

---

[2] Jacob D. Cox, "Forcing Fox's Gap and Turner's Gap," in *Battles and Leaders of the Civil War*, vol. 2 (New York: Century Co., 1887), 585–86.
[3] Ibid., 586.

infantry to defend the gap. When, on the forenoon of the thirteenth, he received a message from Stuart that he was being pushed back by two brigades of infantry and requesting that a brigade of infantry be sent to check the Union pursuit at Turner's Gap, Hill sent him the two brigades of Garland and Colquitt and the four-gun batteries of Captains James W. Bondurant (Alabama) and John Lane (Georgia). It was the presence of this force that caused Pleasonton to pause in his advance of the evening of that day and call upon Burnside for a brigade of infantry.

At the same time, Hill ordered the three other brigades to be drawn in nearer to Boonsboro and directed Brigadier General Roswell S. Ripley to send, at daylight next morning, a regiment to hold the Hamburg Pass Road, between two and three miles north of Turner's Gap. About midnight Hill received a note from Lee saying that he was not satisfied with the condition of things on the National Road and directing him to go in person to Turner's Gap next morning and assist Stuart in its defense. Hill made an early start and, upon reaching the Mountain House (at the summit of the gap) between daylight and sunrise of the fourteenth, received a message from Stuart that he had gone to Crampton's Gap. The cavalry pickets had been withdrawn and, as far as Hill then knew, Stuart had taken all his command with him. Garland's Brigade was found at the Mountain House and Colquitt's at the foot of the mountain on the east side—without cavalry videttes in front and with no information of the Union forces, but under the impression that they had retired. In reality, says Hill, "General Cox's Federal division was at that very time marching up the old Sharpsburg or Braddock's road, a mile to the south, seizing the heights on our right and establishing those heavy batteries which afterward commanded the pike and all the approaches to it."[4] Nor did Hill know of or suspect this movement, and he was ignorant of the topography of the country. He has been criticized as being slow to learn the character of his surroundings and for not accompanying his two brigades to the mountain on the afternoon of the thirteenth and examining the ground upon which it was probable he would be called upon to fight. He had, however, depended entirely upon Stuart to defend his rear.

Stuart parries criticism by reporting that the gap was no place for cavalry operations. He had put Hill's two brigades in position, directed Colonel Rosser, with a detachment of cavalry and the Stuart Horse Artillery, to occupy Fox's Gap, and then started to join the main portion of his command at Crampton's Gap. Stuart says:

> I had not, up to this time, seen General D. H. Hill, but about midnight he sent General Ripley to me to get information concerning roads and gaps in a locality where General Hill had been lying for two days with his command. All the information I had was cheerfully given, and the situation of the gaps explained by map. I confidently hoped by this time to have received the information which was expected from Brig. Gen. Fitz. Lee. All the information I possessed or had the means of possessing had been laid before General D. H. Hill and the commanding general. His troops were duly notified of the advance of the enemy, and I saw them in line of battle awaiting his approach, and, myself, gave some general directions concerning the location of his lines during the afternoon, in his absence.[5]

Once on the ground, it took Hill but a hasty examination to decide that the gap could only be held by a force larger than he had at his disposal and was wholly indefensible by a small one. Robert E. Lee was so informed, and Hill ordered up G. B. Anderson's Brigade and proceeded to form a defensive line. Considering that the foot of the gap was not the proper place to defend it, he brought Colquitt's Brigade back near the summit and ordered it in line of battle on either side of the National Road, three regiments on the right and two on the left. Having posted Colquitt across the road, he then rode to the right on a ridge road to reconnoiter and, much to his surprise, found Rosser with the 5th Virginia Cavalry and two guns of Pelham's Battery guarding Fox's Gap on the Old Sharpsburg Road. Rosser had been ordered to that point by Stuart, who had not informed Hill of the fact, nor had Rosser been told that he would have infantry support. While here, Hill became convinced that there were movements of troops on the mountainside below, screened from view by the forest. At the foot of the mountain, Cox's men could be seen advancing.

This was a menacing condition of affairs, and Hill took measures to meet it. He rode back to the Mountain House and found Garland prepared for action. That gallant and enterprising officer had heard the report of a gun on the right front and the hurtling of a shell and put his brigade under arms. Hill explained the situation to him and ordered him to sweep through the woods on the right to the Old Sharpsburg Road and hold it at all hazards, as the safety of Lee's large train depended upon its retention. He had already ordered up G. B. Anderson to assist Colquitt and Garland, but was reluctant to order up Ripley or Brigadier General Robert E. Rodes from the important points held by them near Boonsboro until something definite was known of the strength and designs of the Union advance.

From the National Road at the Mountain House (where Garland was drawn up), a rough road runs southerly, first on the east slope and then along the crest of the mountain nearly a mile, when it is intersected at right angles by a road diverging from the National Road about a mile west of Middletown. (This road was followed by Major General Edward Braddock in

---

[4] Daniel H. Hill, "The Battle of South Mountain, or Boonsboro'," in *Battles and Leaders*, 561.
[5] James E. B. Stuart to Robert H. Chilton, February 13, 1864, reprinted in *OR*, vol. 19, pt. 1, 817.

his march on Fort Duquesne in 1755 and for many years was known as the Braddock Road; later it became known as the Old Sharpsburg Road.) The point where this road intersects the road on the crest of the mountain is generally known as Fox's (sometimes as Braddock's) Gap.

About three-quarters of a mile beyond Fox's Gap, another road reaches the mountaintop and connects with the crest road. This road branches from the Old Sharpsburg Road at the foot of the mountain, runs southerly some distance along its base, and reaches the crest by a northwest course. From Fox's Gap the road runs southerly for a half-mile, then follows the trend of the mountain westerly a quarter of a mile and intersects the road reaching the crest by the northwest course. At the point of this intersection on the crest, several wagon roads and trails lead down the west side of the mountain into the valley south of Boonsboro. West of the crest road there is a slight depression, beyond which are spurs and ridges covered by a dense forest. In front of Fox's Gap, and between it and the road farther south, is a plateau of open ground. (At the time, some was wheat stubble, some in corn, and some in grass.) The ground sloping eastward from this plateau was open and under cultivation, and heavy stone fences separated many of the fields.

Garland's orders were to move quickly to the right and defend Fox's Gap and the road south of it, where it crossed the mountain. He was immediately in motion and, passing through the first belt of woods south of the National Road, found Rosser and, after a short conference with him, formed line. He had five regiments of North Carolina infantry (aggregating about one thousand men) and Bondurant's Battery of four guns. The 5th North Carolina was placed on the left, north of the farther road and quite near it. The 12th and 23d North Carolina were on the left of the 5th, on the mountain or crest road, the 12th on open ground and the 23d behind a low stone wall. These three regiments filled the line between the two roads crossing the mountain road south of Turner's Gap. Then came the 20th and 13th North Carolina on the left, north of Fox's Gap. From the nature of the ground and the duty to be performed by an inadequate force, the regiments were not in contact with each other, the 13th being 250 yards to the left of the 20th. (There were intervals between the regiments south of Fox's Gap also, but this part of the line was strengthened by Bondurant's Battery, which took position near the right in a small clearing, with a stone fence on either flank. Later, as we shall see, the 20th and 13th were moved to the right, south of the gap, but the interval between them was not closed.) Garland and Colonel Duncan K. McRae (5th North Carolina) went forward to reconnoiter. McRae reports:

> Immediately in front of the ridge road were stubble and corn fields, and, for about 40 paces to the front, a plateau, which suddenly broke on the left into a succession of ravines, and, farther beyond and in front, a ravine, of greater length and depth, extended from the road which ran along the base of the mountain far out into the field, and, connected with the ravine on our left, formed natural parallel approaches to our position. Between and beyond these ravines to our right was a dense growth of small forest trees and mountain laurel, through which this intersecting road ran for some distance, and on the mountain side to the top this growth was continued. General Garland and I had been but a few moments in the field when our attention was directed to persons moving at some distance upon this road, and, apprehending that the enemy might be preparing to make a lodgment upon the mountain side, he ordered me to advance a body of 50 skirmishers into the woods to our right oblique front, to go as far as possible and explore. This was done, and they had not passed 50 steps from where we then stood when they encountered the enemy's skirmishers and the fight commenced.[6]

The skirmishers then encountered were those of the 23d Ohio and the time was 9:00 a.m. Colonel Hayes's men were moving through the woods on the left of the road by the right flank—one company deployed in front as skirmishers and one each on the right and left as flankers.

As soon as the skirmishers became engaged, Garland ordered McRae to support those of the 5th North Carolina, and McRae led his entire regiment forward. The forest growth of small trees was so dense that it was almost impossible to advance in line of battle, and as he cleared some of it—coming into partly open ground and approaching the near edge of another woods—McRae was met by the advance of the 23d Ohio. Hayes had seen McRae coming downhill on his right and, while yet in the woods, faced his regiment by the rear rank and pushed through the thicket and over the rocky, broken ground to meet the advancing North Carolinians. The skirmishing at close quarters was very severe, many falling on both sides. As the skirmishing soon involved the whole regiment, Hayes ordered an advance, and his men responded quickly. Some conscripts on the right of the North Carolinians, never before under fire, fled from the field, upon which McRae fell back a short distance. Hayes halted, re-formed line, and the engagement was soon resumed and became so hot that he ordered a charge, which was made in gallant style, driving the Confederates clear out of the woods. The 5th North Carolina fell back to its original position.

---

6 Duncan K. McRae to "Major," October 18, 1862, reprinted in OR, vol. 19, pt. 1, 1040.

While this was transpiring, the 12th North Carolina (numbering about seventy men) came to the support of the 5th North Carolina, gave one wild volley, and retreated in disorder; about half the regiment halted on the line of the 13th North Carolina and continued with it the remainder of the day. The 23d North Carolina now advanced from the crest road about forty yards into the field in front of the 23d Ohio and, under cover of a hedgerow and an old, partly fallen-down stone fence, opened with some effect upon it and upon the 12th Ohio, on the right of the 23d Ohio. This advance of the 23d North Carolina was followed by Garland's order to the 20th and 13th North Carolina to move from the left to the right to support the 5th.

The 23d Ohio halted at a stone fence just out of the woods and kept up a brisk fire upon the 23d North Carolina, which was behind the old stone fence on an opposite hill not more than one hundred yards distant. The Ohioans' loss was heavy; among the wounded was its gallant commander. Soon after giving the command to charge and when but a few yards out of the woods, Hayes was severely wounded, a musket ball shattering the bone of his left arm above the elbow, but he remained in command. Weak from loss of blood, he was compelled to lie down. Fearing an attack on the left, he ordered his regiment to leave the stone fence and fall back to the edge of the woods. In falling back he was left in the field, requesting to be carried back. A few men stepped out of the woods for that purpose, but drew upon themselves such a heavy fire from the 23d North Carolina that Hayes ordered them back. A few moments later, Lieutenant Benjamin W. Jackson ran forward, brought his wounded commander back into the woods, and laid him down behind a log, where he relinquished the command to Major James M. Comly, had his wound dressed, walked to the house of the widow Coogle nearly a mile distant, and was then taken to Middletown.[7]

On the right of the 23d Ohio and in the center of the brigade line was the 12th Ohio, which after moving nearly a fourth of a mile through a pine wood was obliged to advance over open pasture ground under a most galling fire from the 23d North Carolina. It was halted and ordered to lie down for shelter and await the coming of the 30th Ohio on its right, when a general advance of the entire brigade was to be made.

These movements convinced McRae that a strong Union force had been massed in the woods with the intention to turn his right, and he suggested that the woods be shelled, but there were no guns available. (Bondurant's Battery had been so heavily pressed by the Ohio skirmishers, who advanced to the stone fence on its right and opened fire on its flank, that Garland ordered it away.) Garland now rode to the left to bring up the 20th and 13th North Carolina, which he had ordered to the support of the 5th. He met these two regiments after they had crossed the Old Sharpsburg Road and, perceiving that some of the skirmishers of the 30th Ohio were apparently endeavoring to turn the left of his line, he halted the 13th North Carolina at the farmhouse of Daniel Wise and the 20th North Carolina 250 yards farther to the right. The 13th was in an open field upon the brow of a hill, and immediately in front of it in a dense wood were the Ohio skirmishers, some of whom, farther to the left, were threatening the flank of the 13th. Not being able to see those in the immediate front, the whole fire of the 13th was directed upon those on the left, who were soon driven from that part of the field. While thus engaged, the Ohio skirmishers in its front poured in a hot fire, by which Garland was mortally wounded. (He was a fine soldier, of whom D. H. Hill says, "I never knew a truer, better, braver man. Had he lived, his talents, pluck, energy, and purity of character must have put him in the front rank of his profession, whether in civil or military life."[8]) Not deeming it prudent to advance down the hill into the woods in the face of an enemy supposed to be very strong, and being very much exposed, the 13th North Carolina was withdrawn about fifty yards from the brow of the hill, which brought it in advance and to the right of the Wise house.

Upon the fall of Garland, the command passed to Colonel McRae. As soon as he saw the condition of affairs and had become convinced of the enemy's determination to turn both his flanks, he notified D. H. Hill that the force at his disposal was wholly inadequate to hold the position. Very soon thereafter Colonel Charles C. Tew, with the 2d and 4th North Carolina of G. B. Anderson's Brigade, reported to McRae. The units were about to take position on the immediate left of the 13th North Carolina when Tew received an order from Anderson to move off to the left. Hill was advised of this movement and of the wide gap made in the line, and McRae, believing that his division commander would immediately respond by sending troops to fill it, ordered the 13th North Carolina to follow Tew to the left and keep connection with him in anticipation of their arrival. McRae then rode to the right, intending (if time allowed) to move the 5th North Carolina to the left and with it fill the vacant space in the line, but found that, under a previous order given by him, this regiment had already been advanced into the field on the right of the 23d North Carolina, and it was then dangerous to withdraw it.

While dispositions were being made on both sides (during which there was a comparative lull), a section of McMullin's battery under Lieutenant George L. Crome was advanced by hand to the top of the slope in front of the 12th Ohio and

---

[7] Lieutenant Colonel Hayes subsequently rose to the rank of major general of volunteers and became president of the United States. The 23d Ohio has the unique distinction of graduating from its ranks two presidents: Rutherford B. Hayes and William McKinley.—*EAC*

[8] Hill, "The Battle of South Mountain," 562.

opened fire upon the 20th North Carolina, in position behind a stone fence about four hundred yards distant. The position of the section was an exposed one, and the men were soon struck down; the skirmishers of the North Carolina regiment, under Captain James B. Atwell, killed the gallant Crome as he was sighting a gun. After firing but four rounds of canister, the guns were abandoned, but the Confederates were unable to capture them.

Of the Confederates at this time, Colonel McRae reports:

The Fifth [North Carolina], on the extreme right, was nearest to the intersecting road, which was threatened. It was advanced into the field, sheltered in some degree by a fence which ran perpendicularly to its line. Next, in the field, under cover of the piles of stone, was the Twenty-third. Back on the ridge road, to the left and rear of the Twenty-third, was the Twentieth. This regiment could not be advanced with the others because of the exposed position, and because this would discover to the enemy at once the vacuum in our line. Between this and the Thirteenth was the open space of 250 to 300 yards, which I had been so anxious to fill.[9]

The skirmishers of the 30th Ohio, after persistent efforts against those of the 13th North Carolina, had now come up on the right of the 12th Ohio. Crook's brigade, led by Cox, came up in close support to Scammon. The division was united, and Cox gave the order for a general advance of the whole line. Scammon moved promptly with the 1,400 men of his brigade, the whole line giving a loud and prolonged yell. On the left the 23d Ohio, led by Major Comly, sprang out of the woods, passed through a cornfield, and, under a deadly volley of musketry, struck the 23d North Carolina. Many of both regiments were killed and wounded in a hand-to-hand contest over the stone fence, through an opening of which the Ohio men passed. Many met death or wounds at the very muzzle of the musket. Bayonets were freely used, and men on both sides fell under their cutting thrusts; among these were three North Carolinians and Sergeant Major Eugene L. Reynolds of the Ohio regiment. The contest was most obstinate and sanguinary, but the North Carolina men were finally driven from the field, followed by the 23d Ohio, which established itself firmly on the crest.

On the right of the 23d Ohio, the 12th Ohio charged up the slope with the bayonet. The 20th North Carolina, in its front, stood firm and kept up a steady fire until the Ohio men were within a few yards, then it broke and fled over the crest into the shelter of a dense laurel thicket skirting the other side, leaving fifteen to twenty dead and wounded on the field. The 12th Ohio dashed over the crest and into the thicket in pursuit, halted three hundred yards beyond the crest, and lay for some time under a severe fire of shell and canister.

The quick overthrow of the center of Garland's Brigade and the Union pursuit cut off the 5th and part of the 23d North Carolina, which escaped by moving to the right and rear, thence by a circuitous route to the turnpike, where they reported to D. H. Hill. The 20th and the greater part of the 23d North Carolina rallied on the west side of the mountain and, at Rosser's request, occupied an adjacent height to support a battery that he proposed to put in position to command the Old Sharpsburg Road. Four regiments of Garland's Brigade were now out of the fight; Hill says they had been "too roughly handled to be of any further use that day."[10] The commander of the brigade reports:

The enemy …, with a long-extended yell, burst upon our line, surrounding the Twentieth [North Carolina] on both flanks, and passing to the rear of the Twenty-third. The distance was so short that no opportunity was given for more than a single fire, which was delivered full in the enemy's face, and with great effect, for his first line staggered and some of his forces retreated. A portion of the Twenty-third received his advance upon their bayonets, and men on both sides fell from bayonet wounds; but the enemy's strength was overpowering, and could not be resisted. The Twentieth and a portion of the Twenty-third, finding themselves surrounded, were compelled to retreat, and this they did, under a severe fire, down the mountain side.[11]

It remains to note the movements of the 30th Ohio on the right of the brigade. This regiment was ordered to attack and turn the left of Garland's Brigade (held by the 13th North Carolina) and to seize Bondurant's Battery on that part of the line. It succeeded in driving back the heavy skirmish line and reaching the top of the slope in the face of showers of canister and spherical case from Bondurant's guns. Line was formed to charge the battery and its supports, and the 36th Ohio (of Crook's brigade) was rushed forward as a support and formed on the right of the 30th Ohio. An advance was made, but the 13th North Carolina was so advantageously posted, so skillfully handled, and made such a determined resistance that the Ohio men could not reach the battery (which was, however, soon driven away by the 12th Ohio), nor could they pass the plateau that lay between them and the mountain road in front.

9 McRae to "Major," 1041–42.
10 Hill, "The Battle of South Mountain," 566.
11 McRae to "Major," 1042.

When the 12th Ohio stopped its pursuit of the Confederates in the woods, about three hundred yards west of the ridge road, it came under a heavy fire from Bondurant's guns, and as these could not be reached by the 30th and 36th Ohio, the 12th was ordered to charge them. (The guns were near a stone fence about six hundred yards to the front and right.) The regiment pushed through the dense thicket under a heavy fire and gained the flank of the battery at a garden enclosed by a stone fence, when a severe fight occurred, with the result that the Confederate infantry supporting the battery were driven away, leaving many prisoners with the Ohio men, but the battery escaped by the road leading to the Mountain House.

While engaged in checking the advance of the 30th and 36th Ohio, the commander of the 13th North Carolina, Lieutenant Colonel Thomas Ruffin Jr., sent his adjutant to the right to see what was transpiring in that quarter. The adjutant returned with information that the center and right of the brigade had disappeared and that the Union troops had gained the ridge and were coming down from that direction. Ruffin now discovered that his left was in the air (Colonel Tew, with the two regiments of G. B. Anderson's Brigade, having been ordered away), upon which he marched his regiment to the Old Sharpsburg Road and joined Anderson (who had now come on to the field with the remainder of his force), taking position on Anderson's right and acting under his orders the rest of the day.

Hill, believing that Cox was about to advance to the Mountain House by the road running south from it on the summit of the mountain and having nothing else with which to oppose him, ran two guns down from the Mountain House and opened a brisk fire on the advanced Ohio skirmishers. A line of dismounted staff officers, couriers, teamsters, and cooks was formed behind the guns to give the appearance of battery supports. (Hill states that some of the advancing Union skirmishers encountered Colquitt's skirmishers, under Captain William M. Arnold, and were driven back.[12]) Had Cox pressed his advantage, there is little room to doubt that he could have seized and held Fox's Gap and the Old Sharpsburg Road, but he knew nothing of the enemy's strength and did not know what he might encounter in the woods and dense thickets lying beyond the ridge road. He naturally supposed that his enemy was in force to hold the position against his small division, and he was ignorant of the fact that he had thoroughly disposed of four regiments of Garland's Brigade and that there was scarcely anything to oppose him. Cox was further moved to caution by threatening movements on both flanks. Therefore the advance parties were recalled from the woods, the line made more compact, and the expected reinforcements awaited.

To meet the movement on his left, where the enemy (principally Rosser's cavalry and artillery and a few of Garland's rallied men) extended beyond the flank of the 23d Ohio and poured canister into the line, the 11th Ohio of Crook's brigade had been moved to the left of the 23d and skirmished toward the woods beyond the open field. On nearing them the 11th received a heavy fire on its right and rear from the enemy in the woods and behind a stone fence, upon which it charged into the woods, suffering severely until relieved by the advance of the 23d Ohio. This was near the northwest corner of the open field and the opposing force was Rosser's, concerning which Hill says, "Rosser retired in better order, not, however, without having some of his men captured, and took up a position from which he could still fire upon the old road, and which he held until 10 o'clock that night."[13] This position was across the ravine by which the Old Sharpsburg Road went down the west side of the mountain and on a hill in rear of the heights at the Mountain House where there was some open ground. On the right two 10-pounder Parrott guns of Simmonds's battery under Lieutenant Daniel W. Glassie were pushed forward to an open spot in the woods in front of the 30th Ohio, where they remained until the close of the battle. (Later in the day these guns were supported by Lieutenant Horatio Belcher and one hundred men of the 8th Michigan, who became separated from their brigade during the confusion of the battle and reported to Cox for duty, with the request for an assignment where they could render service.)

Cox reports, "The enemy made several attempts to retake the crest, advancing with great obstinacy and boldness. In the center they were at one time partially successful, but the Thirty-sixth Ohio, of the Second Brigade, Lieut. Col. [Melvin] Clarke commanding, was brought forward, and, with the Twelfth, drove them back by a most dashing and spirited charge. The whole crest was now held by our troops, as follows: The left by the Eleventh and Twenty-third Ohio, the center by the Twelfth Ohio, supported by the Thirty-sixth formed in line in reserve, and the right by the Thirtieth Ohio, supported by the Twenty-eighth, Lieut. Col. [Gottfried] Becker commanding."[14] The line thus formed ran diagonally across the mountaintop, conforming somewhat to the shape of the ground and making the formation a hollow curve. The 11th and 23d Ohio, on the left, clung to the hill that the 23d had first carried, their line nearly parallel to the Old Sharpsburg Road; the right was in the air, exposed to an annoying artillery fire from Pelham's guns on a hill to the northwest, from some guns near the Mountain House, and also from a battery on a hill north of the turnpike. Referring to this stage of the action, Cox says:

We had several hundred prisoners in our hands, and learned from them that D. H. Hill's division, consisting of five brigades, was opposed to us, and that Longstreet was said to be in near support. Our own losses had not been trifling,

[12] Hill, "The Battle of South Mountain," 566.

[13] Ibid.

[14] Cox to Lewis Richmond, September 20, 1862, reprinted in OR, vol. 19, pt. 1, 459.

and it seemed wise to contract our lines a little, so that we might have some reserve and hold the crest we had won till the rest of the Ninth Corps should arrive. Our left and center were strongly posted, but the right was partly across Fox's Gap, at the edge of the woods behind Wise's house, around which there had been a fierce struggle. The 30th and 36th [Ohio] were therefore brought back to the crest on the hither side of the gap, where we still commanded the Sharpsburg road, and making the 30th our right flank, the 36th and 28th were put in second line. My right thus occupied the woods looking northward into Wise's fields. About noon the combat was reduced to one of artillery, and the enemy's guns had so completely the range of the sloping fields behind us that their canister shot cut long furrows in the sod, with a noise like the cutting of a melon rind.[15]

In this position Cox awaited reinforcements. Meanwhile, the Confederates were gathering in his front. First to arrive was G. B. Anderson's Brigade. A part of this had engaged the right of Cox's line and given some assistance to the 13th North Carolina, which, as we have seen, fell in on Anderson's right in the Old Sharpsburg Road. Anderson's men did not become seriously engaged; they did some skirmishing late in the forenoon during which a few men of the 30th North Carolina were wounded.

Ripley followed Anderson. At 9:00 a.m., while occupying a position northeast of Boonsboro, he received an order from Hill to send forward his artillery. A few minutes later came an urgent order to march his brigade to Turner's Gap. Upon Ripley's arrival at the Mountain House with the 1st and 3d North Carolina and the 44th Georgia, Hill directed him to move on the ridge road and form on Anderson's left. He found Anderson in the Old Sharpsburg Road, his left at the Wise house, and it was arranged that Anderson should extend farther to the right and make room for Ripley on his left. The two were then to advance and attack the Union line then occupying the crest of the ridge to the south. While making these dispositions, Hill came up with the brigades of Colonel George T. Anderson and Brigadier General Thomas F. Drayton— the advance of Longstreet's command, which had arrived at the Mountain House about 3:30 p.m. and reported to Hill. (The two brigades aggregated about 1,900 men.) As Hill was very anxious to dispose of the Union force on his right before the main attack, which he apprehended would be made on his left (north of the National Road), these brigades were ordered to move to the right until they came to Rosser's first position or reached Ripley's left, when they were to come to a front and, marching in line of battle with Ripley on their right, sweep everything before them. (To facilitate the movement, a battery was brought forward and shelled the woods in various directions.) After these directions had been given and the column was moving off by the flank, Hill concluded to accompany it and, upon reaching Ripley's position in the Old Sharpsburg Road, called Ripley, G. T. Anderson, and Drayton together and again gave the nature of the movement that he wished executed. He ordered G. B. Anderson and Ripley to extend still farther to the right to make room in the Old Sharpsburg Road for G. T. Anderson and Drayton and then returned to the Mountain House to await the coming of Lee and Longstreet, leaving Ripley in command of the four brigades (G. B. Anderson's, Ripley's, G. T. Anderson's, and Drayton's—in the order named from right to left) with instructions to advance and make a vigorous attack as soon as the brigades were properly formed. G. B. Anderson and Ripley had moved some distance to the right; G. T. Anderson was moving to overtake Ripley's left and had opened an interval of nearly three hundred yards between his left and Drayton's right when Drayton, not yet in position, was attacked.

We return to the Union preparations for this attack. When Cox notified Reno early in the morning that he was going forward with his entire division (instead of one brigade, as had been ordered) and that there was a probability that the enemy would be encountered at the mountaintop, he was promptly assured by Reno that the rest of the Ninth Corps would move forward to his support. The first to move was Brigadier General Orlando B. Willcox's division, which, on the night of the thirteenth, bivouacked a mile and a half east of Middletown; at 8:00 a.m. it was on the march by the National Road. When near Bolivar, Cox advised Willcox to consult Pleasonton as to taking position. Pleasonton indicated an attack along the slope of the mountain north of the National Road, and Willcox marched on and formed for an attack upon the wooded spur southeast of the Mountain House when Burnside rode up and ordered him to withdraw, cross over to the Old Sharpsburg Road, march up it, and take position near Cox.[16]

Much valuable time was lost, and it was two o'clock when Willcox came up and found Cox's division a few hundred yards to the left of the road skirmishing with the enemy on the wooded slope. Willcox halted his command on the road where it turns to the left and where the mountain slopes down toward the National Road on the right, upon which he looked down. His left was covered by the eastern slope of the mountain. Under Cox's direction Willcox sent the 8th Michigan (Lieutenant

[15] Cox, "Forcing Fox's Gap," 587.

[16] In stating this movement, we have followed Willcox's report. Orlando B. Willcox to Richmond, September 21, 1862, reprinted in OR, vol. 19, pt. 1, 427–28. Cox says Willcox's movement to the north of the National Road was because of "a mistake in the delivery of a message to him" and that he was "recalled and given the right direction by Reno, who had arrived at Pleasonton's headquarters." Cox, "Forcing Fox's Gap," 587–88.—EAC

Colonel Frank Graves) and the 50th Pennsylvania (Major Edward Overton) to follow up Cox's line on the left. The rest of Willcox's division was in the process of taking position on the immediate right of Cox, facing the summit, when Willcox received an order from Reno to take position overlooking the National Road on the right, which order he executed by forming line along the Old Sharpsburg Road—his left near Cox's right, but his line drawn back at nearly right angles to it.

Meanwhile, a section of Captain Asa M. Cook's Massachusetts battery had been advanced near to the turn of the road and at the angle of the line made by Cox and Willcox, about four hundred yards from the summit, and opened fire upon Lane's Battery, about a mile distant across the National Road. After a few good shots, one of Cook's guns became disabled and another was going up the road to replace it when the Confederates opened a rapid and heavy fire of canister and shell from Bondurant's Battery, positioned near the Wise house in a small field partially surrounded by woods. This sudden and unexpected fire at less than six hundred yards drove some of Cook's men from their guns. The drivers with the limbers went wildly to the rear, down the narrow, gullied road and through the ranks of the 17th Michigan and other troops in it, creating great confusion (which was increased by the exploding shells that followed the sudden stampede). Cook and some of his men stood some time by the guns but, unable to save them after a loss of one killed and four wounded, they were abandoned. Cook ordered his men to the shelter of the woods on the slope of the hill.

This sudden attack came when the entire division was in motion and changing position. A temporary panic was the result, stayed only by the exertion of the officers and the prompt transfer of the 79th New York and the 17th Michigan from the left to the right to face the enemy, which was so close that it was thought a charge on Cook's guns was contemplated. Cox, who was senior officer on the line, ordered Willcox to close in on his (Cox's) right and make the line continuous, at the same time holding strongly the Old Sharpsburg Road, upon which Willcox made a new disposition of his division. The 79th New York (Lieutenant Colonel David Morrison) was advanced to a stone fence on the left of the road and of Cook's guns; the 17th Michigan (Colonel William H. Withington) was in great part to the right of the road and a little to the rear of the guns. Colonel Thomas Welsh's brigade formed on the left of the road, with the right of the 45th Pennsylvania (Lieutenant Colonel John I. Curtin) resting on the road while the 46th New York (Lieutenant Colonel Joseph Gerhardt) took position on its left, extending to the right of Cox's division. Colonel Benjamin C. Christ's brigade formed on Welsh's right, across the Old Sharpsburg Road. (The 100th Pennsylvania, coming up later, was held in reserve.) The entire division was now under cover of the hillside at the edge of the wood looking into the open ground at Fox's Gap, and two companies of the 45th Pennsylvania went forward to reconnoiter preparatory to swinging forward the right of the line up to the wooded hill running south from the Mountain House. Upon reaching the top of the hill, the Pennsylvanians saw the Confederates in force: a battery commanding the approach and infantry—covered by trees and stone fences—supporting the battery.

The Confederate force was Drayton's Brigade (which we left coming on the field), which had taken position at and around the Wise house, availing itself of the stone fences at and on both sides of the dwelling. (The road from the Mountain House comes into the Old Sharpsburg Road at the Wise house.) From the house northward, for about 550 yards, this road was bounded on the east by a stone fence three feet high overlooking cleared fields on the east (the summit of the mountain being in these fields), beyond which was another stone fence running northeast from the Old Sharpsburg Road but not visible from the first fence, the slight ridge forming the summit intervening. On the south side of the Old Sharpsburg Road, forty yards east from where the Mountain House road comes into it, commences a lane or ridge road running southerly. For about five hundred yards, this narrow lane was flanked on both sides by stone fences, then a single stone fence ran nearly its entire length, separating the woods from the cleared fields. East of the double stone-walled lane was a cleared field of about four acres, bounded on the north by the Old Sharpsburg Road and on the east and south by forest. West of the lane was a garden of about one acre, bounded on the east, south, and west by a stone fence and on the north by an ordinary rail fence running along the Old Sharpsburg Road. In this garden was the Wise house—a small log cabin a few feet from the road. Directly north of the Wise house, across the Old Sharpsburg Road, was a partially cleared spot of about an acre, in which was Bondurant's Battery. It was behind these stone fences, running north and south from the Old Sharpsburg Road at the Wise house and behind the garden fences, that Drayton formed and sent a heavy body of skirmishers well to the front—to the stone fence beyond the field north of the Old Sharpsburg Road and into the woods east of the small field south of it (the Wise field).

Meanwhile, the Confederate guns had kept up a furious fire of canister and shell, to escape which their opponents lay close to the ground. The shot rattled against the stone wall that the 79th New York lay behind, knocking the stones about, and those which went over made gaps here and there in the lines of the reinforcing troops as they came up. Willcox soon received an order to silence the guns in his front and proposed to do so by a charge of the 79th New York directly upon them, but on seeing the thin line of the regiment and recognizing the fact that a strong infantry force was supporting the guns, concluded to relieve the 79th New York with the 45th Pennsylvania (a larger regiment) and deploy the 17th Michigan (a new, large regiment) on the right of the road and move it on the flank of the guns—the movement to be supported with the entire division. His dispositions were made quickly: the 45th Pennsylvania took its place behind the stone fence, the 79th New York faced to its rear as a support, the 17th Michigan formed on the right of the road, and the advance was ordered. The 45th Pennsylvania leaped over the stone fence and double-quicked up the hill, the 46th New York advancing *en echelon* on its left. As the Pennsylvanians came to the crest of the hill, they met the advancing Confederate skirmishers and the action began.

After a sharp contest, the Confederates were driven back to their main line behind the stone fences in front of the Wise house, where a determined stand was made and many Pennsylvanians laid low, for the latter were on open ground and at close quarters. The fighting was fast and furious, extending on the left to the center of Cox's division. On the right the 17th Michigan went forward in gallant style. The Michigan men had lain a long time exposed to fire without being able to reply and were impatient at the delay; the order to advance was received with shouts of enthusiasm. The tangle of dense undergrowth in which they lay and through which they had to pass somewhat destroyed formation, but they went forward rapidly a short distance, and as they came to the edge of the woods they saw a stone fence in the open ground in front, behind which were Drayton's skirmishers, who at once opened a heavy and accurate fire that inflicted much loss. At the same time, artillery on the right opened upon them, but under the fire of musketry and artillery they pressed on and drove Drayton's men from the fence and across the open ground, back to the stone fence bordering the forest and the ridge road north of the Wise house. The batteries in the direction of the Mountain House now fairly swept the open field into which the regiment had advanced, and this caused the line to crowd to the left, across the Old Sharpsburg Road and into the woods on the right of the 45th Pennsylvania, where the contest was maintained with the enemy square in front behind the double stone fence in front of the Wise house.

The Confederate guns now played upon the woods, bringing down broken limbs, and the discharge of musketry from the stone fences was a continuous blaze. The artillery fire soon relaxed, and the greater part of the Michigan regiment moved back into the open field across the road and advanced upon the stone fence north of the Wise house, which was quickly abandoned by Drayton's men. This enabled the right wing of the Michigan troops to swing to the left and open an enfilading fire upon Drayton's command behind the stone fences south of the Old Sharpsburg Road. This was more than Drayton's men could stand. They had maintained a most heroic fight against great odds, but with the fire of the left wing of the 17th Michigan and the 45th Pennsylvania (supported by the 79th New York) in front, the 46th New York and the right of Cox's line on their right, and this terrible enfilade fire of the Michigan men on their left, they broke in disorder and went streaming to the rear down the west side of the mountain, leaving many dead, wounded, and prisoners in the hands of the Union men, who closely pursued down the slope far into the woods. The battery, for the capture of which the charge had been made, escaped by the road to the Mountain House.

Before the order for the advance had been given, the 46th New York (on the left of the 45th Pennsylvania) was under cover of a stone fence. When the order was given, it sprang forward under a heavy fire to the woods where the right of Cox's division was engaged and joined in the fight, which it kept up until the 9th New Hampshire charged past it. Then the New Yorkers again advanced over an open field on the extreme left of the division and joined the 9th New Hampshire in pursuit of the enemy beyond the stone-walled lane and into the woods. The right of Cox's division participated in this charge, but its center and left were not seriously engaged, coming under skirmishing fire only. It was early in this engagement that the head of Brigadier Samuel D. Sturgis's division came up.

Sturgis had moved from near Middletown about 1:00 p.m.; it was 3:30 p.m. when he reached the field. The 2d Maryland and the 6th New Hampshire had been sent along the National Road in the direction of Turner's Gap, and at the foot of the mountain the battery of Captain Joseph C. Clark Jr. (Battery E, 4th U.S. Artillery) was detached and sent to the support of Cox's left. Arriving near the crest of the mountain while the contest was still raging, the brigade of Brigadier General Edward Ferrero was deployed on either side of the Old Sharpsburg Road and, coming under fire, suffered some loss. The 48th Pennsylvania and the 9th New Hampshire of Colonel James Nagle's brigade were held in reserve for a time, but soon went forward and participated in the final charge. Captain George W. Durell's Pennsylvania battery was put in position on the right of the road and quickly silenced Lane's Battery, which had been enfilading the Union line from a point near the Mountain House. About the same time, Cook's guns—abandoned earlier in the day—reopened fire upon the Confederates at Turner's Gap. The right of the Union line was refused to avoid the enfilading fire from the Confederate artillery near the Mountain House and presented to D. H. Hill's view the appearance of an inverted V. He says, "The V afforded a fine target from the pike, and I directed Captain Lane to open on it with his battery. His firing was wild, not a shot hitting the mark. The heavy batteries [Durell's and Cook's] promptly replied, showing such excellent practice that Lane's guns were soon silenced."[17]

---

[17] Hill, "The Battle of South Mountain," 571.

Referring to the action just described, Cox, in his official report, says:

About 4 o'clock p.m., most of the re-enforcements being in position, the order was received to advance the whole line and take or silence the enemy's batteries immediately in front. The order was immediately obeyed, and the advance was made with the utmost enthusiasm. The enemy made a desperate resistance, charging our advancing lines with fierceness, but they were everywhere routed and fled with precipitation. In this advance the chief loss fell upon the division of General Willcox, which was most exposed, being on the right …; but it gallantly overcame all obstacles, and the success was complete along the whole line of the corps.[18]

Elsewhere Cox says:

Their strongest attack fell upon the angle of Willcox's command, and for a little while there was some confusion there, due to the raking artillery fire which came from the right; but Willcox soon reformed his lines, and after a very bloody contest, pushed across the Sharpsburg Road, through Wise's fields, and into the wooded slope beyond. Along the front of the Kanawha Division the line was steadily maintained and the enemy was repulsed with severe loss. At nearly 4 o'clock, Sturgis's division arrived and relieved the left wing of Willcox's division, the latter taking ground a little more to the right and rear.[19]

When Sturgis relieved the left of Willcox, he formed line just at the top of the mountain, facing Fox's Gap and on the left of the Old Sharpsburg Road. Ferrero's brigade was on the right and two regiments of Nagle's on the left, "occupying," as Cox reports, "the new ground gained on the farther side of the slope."[20]

The division of Brigadier General Isaac P. Rodman came on the field after Sturgis's. It marched from Frederick at 3:00 a.m. and arrived at Middletown at 10:00 a.m., where it remained four hours. The march was resumed at 2:00 p.m. and the field reached between 4:00 and 5:00 p.m. The division was now split: Colonel Edward Harland's brigade, under the supervision of Rodman, was posted on the extreme right in support to Willcox, while Colonel Fairchild's brigade was sent by Cox to the extreme left to strengthen the flank of the Kanawha Division and support Clark's battery of four guns, which had been ordered in that direction. Fairchild arrived at the designated place and proceeded to take position in rear of the guns—the 9th New York on the right, the 103d New York in the center, and the 89th New York on the left.

It is now time to return to the Confederate movements. When the Union line struck Drayton, the brigade of G. T. Anderson, over four hundred yards to the right, was moving by the right flank, following Ripley's Brigade down the Old Sharpsburg Road. Upon the first sound of the firing, Ripley ordered Anderson to move by the left flank into the woods south of the road. The skirmishers, having no orders to the contrary, continued moving to the right, thus uncovering the front of the brigade, which having moved some distance up the wooded mountainside came to a halt. Anderson, finding his front uncovered and that the firing was more to the left than to the front, changed front forward on the left and ordered Colonel William J. Magill to deploy half of the 1st Georgia Regulars as skirmishers, feel forward, and locate the enemy. But before Magill could get in motion, it was ascertained that Drayton's right had been completely turned and that the Union troops pursuing Drayton were on his own left and rear. At the same time, Anderson learned that Ripley was more than four hundred yards to the right and rear. Finding that he was unsupported and almost isolated, Anderson recrossed the Old Sharpsburg Road to the left, re-formed his line, and was advancing to find the right of Drayton when his skirmishers reported that the Union troops were crossing the road and were already on his left. Upon learning this Anderson again moved by the left diagonally to the rear to intercept them and met General Hood's two brigades coming up through the tangled forest to recover the ground lost by Drayton. Anderson reported to Hood for orders and formed on his left. (Anderson's Brigade had not yet been engaged, the skirmishers only firing a few shots.)

Ripley, who had been left by D. H. Hill in command of four brigades, appears to have been unequal or disinclined to the task. Upon the rout of Drayton, he concluded that he was entirely cut off from Hill and, upon a report from the skirmishers of his own brigade that a heavy body of troops was moving across his front (supposed to be those of the enemy; in reality those of G. B. Anderson, from his own command), he ordered an immediate retreat down the mountain—without coming in contact with an enemy or firing a shot, leaving the commanders of the other brigades (placed by Hill under Ripley's orders) to wonder what had become of him. Hill says that Ripley uselessly employed his brigade in marching and countermarching, for some cause was not engaged, and "did not draw trigger."[21] After stating that Drayton and G. T. Anderson had been placed on Ripley's left and a forward movement ordered, Hill continues, "In half an hour or more I received a

---

[18] Cox to Richmond, 460.

[19] Cox, "Forcing Fox's Gap," 588.

[20] Cox to Richmond, 460.

[21] Hill to Chilton, 1862 [day and month illegible], reprinted in *OR*, vol. 19, pt. 1, 1021.

note from Ripley saying that he was progressing finely; so he was, to the rear of the mountain on the west side. Before he returned the fighting was over, and his brigade did not fire a shot that day."[22]

G. B. Anderson, whose movement across Ripley's front caused the latter's withdrawal, was not so remiss in duty. After he had moved by the right flank some distance down the Old Sharpsburg Road, he recognized the fact that he was moving far away from his enemy and, without prompting, faced to the left and moved up the mountain. He had the 2d, 4th, and 30th North Carolina of his own brigade and the 13th North Carolina of Garland's. (The 14th North Carolina had become detached earlier in the day and had fallen in with Ripley.) It was an arduous march up a mountainside covered with huge boulders, laurel thickets, and tangled vines. When the top was reached, it was at the crest road and some distance beyond Cox's left. Finding nothing in his immediate front, he sent the 2d and 4th North Carolina to reconnoiter. Captain Edwin A. Osborne, commanding the skirmishers of the 4th, on coming to the open ground on the left saw Clark's battery and its infantry support all facing nearly north. He hastened back to his regimental commander and told him that they could deliver a flank fire upon the infantry support before it could change position to meet them. Upon which, the 2d, 4th, and 13th North Carolina were marched along the ridge road to the left until they came to a dense cornfield on the right of the road, where they saw the guns and the infantry in support. An instant charge was ordered. The North Carolinians sprang out of the laurel thicket and over the fence into the open—at the moment that the 89th New York, its left in the corn, was just coming into position on the left of its brigade. The 89th New York and the battery opened fire, and the North Carolinians were quickly repulsed with great loss and fell back into the woods, leaving their dead, wounded, thirty prisoners, and 150 stand of arms in the hands of the 89th, which had but one wing engaged and lost two killed and eighteen wounded. The 9th and 103d New York reported no casualties.[23] It was now sunset, and the fighting on the left was over.

This encounter on the left was quickly followed by an affair on the right, near the Wise house. Hood, with his two brigades, arrived at the Mountain House about 4:00 p.m. and took position on the left of the National Road, but was soon ordered to the right to support the troops there, who were reported as giving way. On his way he met Drayton's men coming out and reporting that the enemy had succeeded in passing to their rear. Hood then inclined more to the right over very rugged ground, came up to G. T. Anderson's Brigade, and took position to engage and check the Union advance, with Anderson forming on his left. No enemy appearing, he fixed bayonets and swept through the woods, drove back a few Union stragglers, and, regaining part of the ground lost by Drayton, came to the stone fence running north from the Wise house. Fire was opened by him and upon him, but he held his ground with small loss; among his mortally wounded was Lieutenant Colonel Owen K. McLemore of the 4th Alabama.

In this encounter, as the shades of night were falling, the gallant and loved Jesse L. Reno, commander of the Ninth Corps, lost his life. It will be remembered that when Sturgis relieved the left of Willcox, he formed on the left of the Old Sharpsburg Road, Nagle's two regiments (the 48th Pennsylvania and the 9th New Hampshire) on the right and Ferrero's brigade on the left in column of regiments: the 51st Pennsylvania in front, 51st New York second, 35th Massachusetts third, and 21st Massachusetts in rear. The head of the column was on the west edge of the woods overlooking the field of four acres separating the woods from the Wise house. Near sunset the 35th Massachusetts was sent into the woods north and west of the Wise house to reconnoiter. It went some distance, came back, reported that no enemy was in the immediate front, and resumed its place in the third line of its brigade.

Up to this time, Reno had not been up the mountain, but had remained with McClellan and Burnside at Pleasonton's position near the heavy batteries in the valley. He now rode up to see why it was that the right of the line could not get forward to the summit at the Mountain House. After a brief conference with Cox, during which Reno was informed of the condition of affairs and the obstacles in the way to an advance to the Mountain House, he rode out to where Sturgis had formed his division, went forward to examine the ground in the immediate vicinity of the Wise house, saw a few men

---

[22] Hill, "The Battle of South Mountain," 569.

[23] The historian of the 9th New York gives an account of the action: "The brigade was formed like the letter L, the 9th being the base line, while the 103d and 89th New York were formed at right angles to it, extending toward the rear. The battery faced down the line toward the left. The Ninth and 103d, with about two companies of the 89th, had arrived on the line when the enemy, who were concealed in a close thicket of laurel on the west slope of the mountain, suddenly dashed from their cover, and made an impetuous charge on the battery, yelling and discharging their muskets as soon as the forces were sighted. Without hesitation Colonel [Edgar A.] Kimball gave the order: 'Right wing, attention! Fix bayonets! By the right flank by file left, double quick. March!' and led the way through and between guns and limbers into the thick brush on the right of the battery beyond the view of the remainder of the regiment, to a position where he could strike the flank of the charging rebels. Meanwhile the battery was firing double charges of canister at point-blank range, the enemy being so close that it was unnecessary to aim but simply point the guns after each discharge. The 103d after a momentary unsteadiness, stood up to the work like good fellows, firing volley after volley, while the two companies of the 89th opened a steady, well-directed fire, the other companies joining in as each arrived on the line, the entire movement being so coolly and methodically performed as though on drill in winter camp." Matthew J. Graham, *History of the Ninth New York Volunteers (Hawkins' Zouaves): Being a History of the Regiment and Veteran Association from 1860 to 1900* (New York: E. P. Coby & Co., 1900), 271–72.—EAC

around the house and in the small opening across the road from it succoring the wounded, and was told by some of these men that there seemed to be a movement of some kind in the woods out of which the 35th Massachusetts had just come. He rode back to Ferrero's brigade, ordered the 51st Pennsylvania to the right of the Old Sharpsburg Road, and directed its skirmishers to the stone fence (north of the Wise house) and into the woods beyond. His order was being promptly executed—the 51st Pennsylvania was crossing the road and its skirmishers pushing obliquely to the front—when Hood's men opened fire from behind the stone fence. The fire was returned, but the sudden rain of bullets from the woods, where no enemy was expected, came as a surprise, and one of Sturgis's regiments became panic stricken, broke, and opened indiscriminate fire. Reno and others hastened to rally the men; while so doing, Reno received a mortal wound.

The 51st Pennsylvania had now crossed to the right of the road. The men of the 51st New York sprang to their feet and advanced to the crest of the plateau, on a line with the Pennsylvanians, and the entire front opened upon the enemy. The contest ceased only when darkness came on, but a desultory fire was kept up all along the line until 10:00 p.m.

On the Confederate side, G. T. Anderson had come up on Hood's left. G. B. Anderson still held ground on the right, and Ripley, returning to the front after the fighting was over, filled the interval between G. B. Anderson and Hood. This line was held until the retreat was ordered.

The casualties in the Ninth Corps numbered 157 killed, 691 wounded, and 41 missing—a total of 889. The Confederate loss in killed and wounded in front of the Ninth Corps was about six hundred men; many others were captured, the Kanawha Division alone claiming the capture of six hundred men (in which, however, must be included some of the wounded). Cox had started from camp in the morning to support a cavalry reconnaissance, became engaged at 9:00 a.m. with an enemy whose presence was only suspected, carried the crest of the mountain early in the forenoon, and was left unaided till 2:00 p.m. (when Willcox came up), followed an hour and more later by Sturgis and Rodman. It was not until 3:00 p.m. that any movement was made on the right of the National Road, at which hour Hooker, at the head of the First Corps, reached the eastern base of the mountain at Mount Tabor Church and began his deployment.

Let us return briefly to the Confederates at Hagerstown, whom we left on the night of the thirteenth under orders to march back to Turner's Gap next morning. At daybreak, the column—the brigades of Drayton, Brigadier General James L. Kemper, Brigadier General Richard B. Garnett, G. T. Anderson, Evans (commanded by Colonel Peter F. Stevens), Brigadier General Micah Jenkins (commanded by Colonel Joseph Walker), Colonel William T. Wofford,[24] and Colonel Evander M. Law, with artillery—marched as ordered, leaving Toombs's Brigade, the 11th Georgia of G. T. Anderson's (which had been all night on picket), and the 1st Virginia Cavalry at Hagerstown. The day was very hot and the roads dusty; the march, consequently, was a severe one, and nearly one-half of the command became stragglers and did not reach the field of action. The artillery battalions of Colonel Stephen D. Lee, Colonel John Thompson Brown, and Major William Nelson were left on the heights of Beaver Creek, four miles north of Boonsboro. The brigades of G. T. Anderson, Drayton, Wofford, and Law engaged the Ninth Corps, as we have seen; the remaining four brigades of Kemper, Garnett, Evans, and Jenkins went to the north to make head against Hooker's advance.

At daybreak of the fourteenth, Hooker marched from his camp on the Monocacy by the National Road, passed through Frederick and Middletown, and about 1:00 p.m. halted on Catoctin Creek, one mile west of Middletown, where the men were directed to rest and make coffee. Hooker rode forward to examine the country in the neighborhood of where it was proposed to make an attack on the north side of Turner's Gap. He says:

> In front of us was South Mountain, the crest of the spinal ridge of which was held by the enemy in considerable force. Its slopes are precipitous, rugged, and wooded, and difficult of ascent to an infantry force, even in absence of a foe in front. The National turnpike [running northwest and southeast—*EAC*] crosses the summit of this range of mountains through a gentle depression, and near this point a spur projects from the body of the ridge, and running nearly parallel with it about a mile, where it is abruptly cut by a rivulet from the main ridge, and rises again and extends far to the northward. At and to the north of the pike this spur is separated from the main ridge by a narrow valley, with cultivated fields, extending well up the gentle slope of the hill on each side. Here the enemy had a strong infantry

---

24 In his original manuscript, Carman here refers to the unit as the brigade of "Hood." In the rest of the narrative, however, he calls it "Wofford's." His reason for favoring the latter designation is unclear, as Wofford served only as acting brigade commander. (Jerome B. Robertson was named its permanent commander in the beginning of November 1862, and three weeks later Wofford and his regiment, the 18th Georgia, were transferred to another brigade. See Headquarters Army of Northern Virginia, Special Orders No. 234, November 6, 1862, reprinted in *OR*, vol. 19, pt. 2, 699; Headquarters Army of Northern Virginia, Special Orders No. 253, November 26, 1862, reprinted in *OR*, vol. 21, 1033.) The War Department tablets (no. 324 and 331) erected for this unit, under Carman's supervision, at Antietam National Battlefield also list it as "Wofford's Brigade." Therefore, the editor has decided to standardize references throughout this edition to match Carman's preference.

force posted, and a few pieces of artillery. Through the break in the spur at the base of the principal ridge were other cleared fields, occupied by the enemy.[25]

For convenience sake we shall call the main ridge the north ridge and the spur projecting from it the south spur. At the summit of Turner's Gap and eighty yards east of the Mountain House a road branches from the National Road and runs in a northeasterly direction along the southeast slope of the north ridge. At the distance of nearly a mile it inclines to the right, passes down a gorge (dividing the south spur from the eastern part of the north ridge) and, curving around to the right at the hamlet of Frosttown, goes south by Mount Tabor Church and enters the National Road by Bolivar, at the eastern foot of the mountain (two miles east of where it leaves the summit, near the Mountain House). This is the Old Hagerstown Road. There are other roads branching from this and leading over the mountain; these shall be noted as occasion requires.

Before Hooker had completed his reconnaissance, Brigadier General George G. Meade's division (formerly Reynolds's) was ordered at 2:30 p.m. to make a movement north of the National Road to divert attention from Reno, who was operating south of it. Brigadier Generals John P. Hatch (who had replaced Brigadier General Rufus King that day) and James B. Ricketts were ordered to follow Meade with their divisions and support him. The three divisions moved from the Catoctin, turned to the right at Bolivar, and marched by the Old Hagerstown Road to the vicinity of Mount Tabor Church, where they turned into the fields west of the road and took position to support Captain James H. Cooper's Pennsylvania battery, which it was proposed to establish on an adjoining eminence near the base of the mountain. As soon as the divisions arrived, they were successfully deployed for action: Meade on the right, Hatch to the left, and Ricketts in reserve. (The 3d Pennsylvania Reserves, under Lieutenant Colonel John Clark, was detached from the Second Brigade of Meade's division to watch a road running to the right, from the Old Hagerstown Road, about three-fourths of a mile north of Mount Tabor Church. It remained there until it was relieved late in the day by the movement of the 1st Massachusetts Cavalry higher up the valley.)

The Confederates, perceiving these movements, opened fire from a battery on the mountainside, but without inflicting any injury, upon which Cooper's battery was quickly put in position on elevated ground and opened on such bodies of the enemy as were visible. At the same time, the 13th Pennsylvania Reserves (the Bucktails[26]) deployed as skirmishers and advanced to feel for the enemy. Becoming satisfied that the mountain was held in force, Hooker ordered Meade to extend his division to the right, outflank the Confederates, and then move to the attack. Hatch and Ricketts followed Meade's movement to the right. The right of Meade's division now rested a mile and a half from the National Road, at a point where, a mile beyond Mount Tabor Church, a road branching to the right from the Old Hagerstown Road runs over the mountain, coming out to the National Road at Zittlestown, about a half-mile west of the Mountain House. Brigadier General Truman Seymour's brigade was on the right of this road, with those of Colonels Thomas F. Gallagher and Albert L. Magilton between it and the Old Hagerstown Road.

In front of Meade was a succession of parallel ridges, alternating with deep, irregular valleys and broken ravines. Those nearest him were wooded; beyond those, it was quite open all the way to the summit. The hills increased in height, and their eastern slopes became more abrupt and rugged as they neared the crest of the mountain, which was of irregular crescent front, in many places jutting out in rugged prominences of different access. Gorges or small ravines bisected the ridges, running parallel to the crest. Favorable positions were occupied by small Confederate outposts, well protected by rocks, trees, and the numerous stone fences separating the fields.

Early in the morning, Rodes's Brigade (the 3d, 5th, 6th, 12th, and 26th Alabama) relieved G. B. Anderson's North Carolinians a half-mile west of Boonsboro. As it neared noon, Rodes was ordered to follow Ripley up the mountain. Upon arriving at the Mountain House, Rodes was ordered by D. H. Hill to occupy the south spur immediately to the left of the National Road. He held this position about three-quarters of an hour under artillery fire from the batteries of Benjamin, Gibson, and McMullin near Bolivar, when he was ordered to occupy a bare hill on the north ridge about three-quarters of a mile to the left. The entire brigade was moved to the hill, and in doing so crossed a deep gorge that separated the north ridge from the south spur. This left a large interval between the right of the brigade (which rested in the gorge) and the rest of the division; this was filled by sending back the 12th Alabama, under Colonel Bristor B. Gayle, to cover the ground to the National Road and support Lane's Battery.

By this time Hooker's lines were well developed and in full view; it was evident to Hill and Rodes that it was Hooker's intention to attack the main ridge, the south spur, and the gorge between them and that from the length of his line it would extend a half-mile beyond Rodes's left. Immediately upon his arrival on the extreme left, Rodes had discovered that the hill there was accessible to artillery and that a good road, passing by its left from Hooker's line, continued immediately in his rear and entered the National Road about a half-mile west of the Mountain House. Therefore, he sent for artillery and determined upon

---

[25] Joseph Hooker to Richmond, November 7, 1862, reprinted in *OR*, vol. 19, pt. 1, 214.

[26] In his original manuscript, Carman refers to this regiment by its nickname in much of his narrative. To maintain consistency, the editor has chosen to use its formal designation throughout.

the only promising plan by which Hooker could be prevented from taking immediate possession of this road and thus marching in his rear: to extend his own line as far as possible to the left, keeping his right in the gorge, and to send for reinforcements to fill out from his right to the National Road—an interval of three-fourths of a mile. Skirmishers were sent to the left, and Lieutenant Robert E. Park of the 12th Alabama led forty men to the foot of the mountain to delay Hooker's advance.

Hooker was very deliberate in making his dispositions, and it was nearly 5:00 p.m. before the assault on the mountain was ordered.[27] It began by throwing forward heavy skirmish lines, which Meade and Hatch were to support with their entire divisions. The battle that ensued resolved itself into two attacks: one, led by Meade, for the possession of the north ridge, the other, led by Hatch, for the possession of the south spur. Ricketts assisted each with a brigade.

We follow the assault led by Meade upon Rodes. Seymour's brigade on the right, under cover of the forest at the base of the mountain, was ordered to move on and near the road over the mountain to Zittlestown (the road watched by Rodes). The 275 men of the 13th Pennsylvania Reserves commanded by Colonel Hugh W. McNeil, advanced as skirmishers, supported by the 2d Pennsylvania Reserves and two companies of the 1st Pennsylvania Reserves moving fifty yards in rear, with the remainder of Seymour's brigade closely following. Soon after advancing through open woods and over cultivated ground on the right of the road, Seymour could see the two detached heights on which Rodes was posted—the 12th Alabama on one and the 3d, 5th, 6th, and 26th Alabama on the other—and reported to Meade that he could take the north ridge (along which the road ran) and then advance across the ravine to the south spur, taking it in flank. Meade directed him to do so.

The two brigades of Gallagher and Magilton advanced on the left of Seymour and simultaneously with him. As Meade's entire division swept into the open, Rodes was convinced that his own 1,200 men were opposed to a force that would flank them completely on either side. Particularly did he fear the danger menacing the peak on the Zittlestown Road, a danger so imminent that he ordered his left regiment, the 6th Alabama (Colonel John B. Gordon) to move along the brow of the hill under fire still farther to the left, which was done in good order. Once, during the movement, Gordon essayed a charge that checked Seymour's onward progress, and a severe skirmish fire followed, which on the Confederate side was assisted by the fire of artillery up the mountain to the left. Some of Seymour's men, greatly exposed on open ground, fell under this fire.

While Seymour was moving on the right to take Rodes in reverse, Gallagher and Magilton went straight to the front. At first Gallagher moved obliquely to the right and front to keep in touch with Seymour, by which he came under a harmless artillery fire. The 9th Pennsylvania Reserves, on the right of the brigade, gained a stone wall near the foot of the mountain, behind which it remained some twenty minutes, engaged with Confederate skirmishers sheltered by a log house in the ravine. Finally, a charge was made, the house carried, and a few prisoners captured, when the 9th was relieved by the 10th Pennsylvania Reserves. In advancing on the left of the 9th, the 11th Pennsylvania Reserves, when approaching the ravine, received a volley that laid low more than half its commissioned officers and many men. The 12th Pennsylvania Reserves, on the left of the brigade, crossed the ravine and came under the fire of an unseen enemy but did not suffer as severely as the 11th. In this spirited affair, Gallagher was wounded, and Lieutenant Colonel Robert Anderson of the 9th succeeded to the command of the brigade. Of this affair in the ravine, Rodes says, "In the first attack of the enemy up the bottom of the gorge, they pushed on so vigorously as to catch Captain [Edward S.] Ready and a portion of his party of skirmishers, and to separate the Third from the Fifth Alabama Regiment. The Third made a most gallant resistance at this point, and had my line been a continuous one it could never have been forced."[28] (In the movement to the ravine, Magilton advanced on the left of Gallagher, his three regiments deployed in one line. With Gallagher he engaged the Confederates at the foot of the mountain and was opposed also by Lieutenant Park and his forty skirmishers.)

Meade's men were very persistent. When they drove the Alabamians from the bottom of the ravine, they followed them closely up the mountainside, pushed them from every point of vantage—behind trees, rocks, and stone walls—penetrated their thin and broken line, worked in and on their flanks, and continued swinging around their left. Rodes's efforts to meet and repel Meade's steady advance are well told in his admirable report:

> By this time the enemy, though met gallantly by all four of the regiments with me, had penetrated between them, and had begun to swing their extreme right around toward my rear, making for the head of the gorge, up the bottom and sides of which the whole of my force, except the Sixth Alabama, had to retreat, if at all. I renewed again, and yet again, my application for re-enforcements, but none came. Some artillery, under Captain [Thomas H.] Carter, who was moving up without orders, and some of [Lieutenant] Colonel [Allen S.] Cutts', under a gallant lieutenant, whose name I do not now recollect, was reported by the last-named officer to be on its way to my relief; but at this time the enemy had obtained possession of the summit of the left hill before spoken of, and had command of the road in rear

---

[27] "I had to order him [Hooker] four separate times to move his command into action, and … I had to myself order his leading division (Meade's) to start before he would go." Ambrose E. Burnside to Seth Williams, September 30, 1862, reprinted in *OR*, vol. 19, pt. 1, 422–23.—*EAC*

[28] Robert E. Rodes to James W. Ratchford, October 13, 1862, reprinted in *OR*, vol. 19, pt. 1, 1035.

of the main mountain. The artillery could only have been used by being hauled up on the high peak, which arose upon the summit of the ridge just at the head of the gorge before mentioned. This they had not time to do, and hence I ordered it back.

Just before this, I heard that some Confederate troops had joined my right very nearly. Finding that the enemy were forcing my right back, and that the only chance to continue the fight was to change my front so as to face to the left, I ordered all the regiments to fall back up the gorge and sides of the mountain, fighting, the whole concentrating around the high peak before mentioned. This enabled me to face the enemy's right again, and to make another stout stand with Gordon's excellent regiment (which he had kept constantly in hand, and had handled in a manner I have never heard or seen equaled during this war), and with the remainder of the Fifth, Third, and Twelfth Alabama Regiments. I found the Twelfth had been relieved by other troops and closed in toward my right, but had passed in rear of the original line so far that, upon re-establishing the line on the main peak, I found that the Third Alabama came upon its right. The Twenty-sixth Alabama, which had been placed on my right, was by this time completely demoralized; its colonel ([Edward A.] O'Neal) was wounded, and the men mingled in utter confusion with some South Carolina stragglers [of Evans's Brigade—*EAC*] on the summit of the hill, who stated that their brigade had been compelled to give way, and had retired. Notwithstanding this, if true, left my rear entirely exposed again (I had no time or means to examine the worth of their statements), I determined, in accordance with the orders I received about this time, in reply to my last request for re-enforcements, to fight on the new front.

My loss up to this time had been heavy in all the regiments except the Twelfth Alabama. The Fifth Alabama, which had occupied the left center, got separated into two parts in endeavoring to follow up the flank movement of Gordon's regiment. Both parts became engaged again before they could rejoin, and the right battalion was finally cut off entirely. The left and smaller battalion, under Major [Edwin L] Hobson's gallant management, though flanked, wheeled against the flanking party, and, by desperate fighting, silenced the enemy so far as to enable his little command to make its way to the peak before mentioned … Having re-established my line, though still with wide intervals, necessarily, on the high peak (this was done under constant fire and in full view of the enemy, now in full possession of the extreme left hill and of the gorge), the fight at close quarters was resumed, and again accompanied by the enemy throwing their, by this time apparently interminable, right around toward my rear.[29]

Seymour, while advancing and still working on Rodes's flank, saw as he looked to the left an extended field of corn leading directly to the position Rodes had taken and determined to carry it. The 13th Pennsylvania Reserves continued on in the direction they were then moving (straight for the 6th Alabama, to turn its left), while the 1st, 2d, and 5th Pennsylvania Reserves changed direction to the left and, supported by the 6th Pennsylvania Reserves, ascended the slope. After a stubborn resistance the whole division line—Seymour, Anderson, and Magilton—gained the crest of the north ridge, the loss being severe on both sides. (Among the Confederates, Colonel Gayle of the 12th Alabama was killed.) Seymour was first to gain the crest and follow the Confederates to the left, where the latter came under the fire of Anderson and Magilton.

Soon after the action began, Meade, having reason to believe that the Confederate line was being extended to the left to flank Seymour's right, sent to Hooker for help. Brigadier General Abram Duryee's[30] brigade of Ricketts's division was sent him. (Owing to the distance to be marched, Duryee's men did not arrive until just at the close of the engagement and were then thrown in on Seymour's left and in front of the right wing of Anderson's brigade. It was now dark, and the Confederates retreated.)

Magilton, moving up the mountain on the left of Anderson, faced the National Road somewhat and met an obstinate resistance. The 8th Pennsylvania Reserves, on the extreme left, fought its way at every step and sustained a heavier loss than that of all the other regiments of the brigade combined. Because of this stout resistance made by Evans's Brigade, Magilton's force did not gain the crest quiet as early as the brigades on the right. When it did get up, it was quite dark, the Confederates had fallen back, and, with the other two brigades of the division (but separated from them by Duryee's brigade), it bivouacked on the commanding eminence won.

The effort made by the Confederates to defend their last position is told in the report of Rodes:

The Sixth Alabama and the Twelfth suffered pretty severely. The latter, together with the remainder of the Third Alabama, which had been well handled by Colonel [Cullen A.] Battle, was forced to retire, and in so doing lost heavily. Its colonel (Gayle) was seen to fall, and its lieutenant-colonel ([Samuel B.] Pickens) was shot through the lungs; the former was left on the field, supposed to be dead; Pickens was brought off. Gordon's regiment retired slowly, now being

---

[29] Ibid., 1034–35.

[30] His last name appears throughout the *OR* as "Duryea," and this is how Carman gives it in his original manuscript. Examination of his signature on a number of documents, however, shows the spelling as "Duryee."

under an enfilading as well as direct fire and in danger of being surrounded, but was still, fortunately for the whole command, held together by its able commander. After this, I could meet the enemy with no organized force except Gordon's regiment. One more desperate stand was made by it from an advantageous position. The enemy by this time were nearly on top of the highest peak, and were pushing on, when Gordon's regiment, unexpectedly to them, opened fire on their front and checked them. This last stand was so disastrous to the enemy that it attracted the attention of the stragglers, even, many of whom Colonel Battle and I had been endeavoring to organize, and who were just then on the flank of that portion of the enemy engaged with Gordon, and for a few minutes they kept up a brisk enfilading fire upon the enemy; but, finding his fire turning from Gordon upon them, and that another body of Federal troops were advancing upon them, they speedily fell back. It was now so dark that it was difficult to distinguish objects at short musket range, and both parties ceased firing. Directing Colonel Gordon to move his regiment to his right and to the rear, so as to cover the gap, I endeavored to gather up stragglers from the other regiments. Colonel Battle still held together a handful of his men. These, together with the remnants of the Twelfth, Fifth, and Twenty-sixth Alabama Regiments, were assembled at the gap, and were speedily placed alongside of Gordon's regiment, which by this time had arrived in the road ascending the mountain from the gap, forming a line on the edge of the woods parallel to and about 200 yards from the main road. The enemy did not advance beyond the top of the mountain, but, to be prepared for them, skirmishers were thrown out in front of the line.[31]

Rodes's loss was 61 killed, 157 wounded, and 204 missing. He sums up the result of his fight: "We did not drive the enemy back or whip him, but with 1,200 men we held his whole division at bay without assistance during four and a half-hours' steady fighting, losing in that time not over half a mile of ground."[32] Although Rodes reports that he had no assistance, he refers to the fact that he heard that some Confederate troops had nearly joined his right and that some South Carolina stragglers were on the peak with him. D. H. Hill says that Evans's Brigade, which was supporting Rodes, "fought gallantly and saved him from being entirely surrounded, but they got on the ground too late to effect anything else."[33] Evans's Brigade had about 550 men.

Nathan G. Evans marched that day from Hagerstown in command of a provisional division, comprising the two brigades of Hood's Division and his own South Carolina brigade. When nearing the Mountain House, he was informed that Hood's two brigades were to be detached to support the right at Fox's Gap, and that he, with his own brigade (still commanded by Colonel Stevens) was to support Rodes and hold the position assigned him on the left of the National Road; reinforcements would be sent him. When Stevens arrived at the summit of Turner's Gap, about 4:00 p.m., he was ordered by Longstreet (who had just come up) to report to D. H. Hill and was conducted to that officer by Major John W. Fairfax of Longstreet's staff. Hill ordered Stevens to the position held by Rodes, but when the brigade had gone halfway and was on the slope of the mountain, Stevens was overtaken by an order from Evans to halt. At about the same time came a message from Rodes to press on to his assistance. While awaiting new instructions from Evans, Stevens discovered that the Union forces were in the valley below, on his right. Throwing the Holcombe Legion to the right as skirmishers, he disposed the brigade along the brow of the hill, the left regiment (the 23d South Carolina, under Captain S. A. Durham) very nearly joining Rodes's right. Before Stevens received further instructions from Evans, his skirmishers were driven in and his brigade engaged with that of Magilton. The 23d South Carolina was on the left of the Old Hagerstown Road, its left extending along the summit of the ridge. It advanced a short distance, met the skirmishers coming in, was quickly driven back, and rallied on the left of the 22d South Carolina (Lieutenant Colonel Thomas C. Watkins). The two regiments made an effort to stop the Union advance, but were soon driven in some disorder. Watkins endeavored to rally his regiment and was killed. The men became confused and were partially rallied three times by Major Miel Hilton, but the Union pressure upon them was so persistent that they fell back to the National Road. The 23d, after being twice rallied, finally fell in with the 6th Alabama and marched off the field with it. The 18th South Carolina (Colonel William H. Wallace), in the right center, shared much the same fate as the 22d. Wallace reports that, when it arrived near Rodes's Brigade, that unit was retiring:

Under orders from Colonel Stevens, commanding the brigade, the Eighteenth was then ordered to change front forward on first company and advance, with the view of taking a column of the enemy in flank which was advancing upon the point first occupied by the Eighteenth, and which it had left to go to Rodes' support. A sharp engagement ensued, when, a heavy column of the enemy appearing upon our left flank, and the enemy, continuing to press upon Rodes' brigade, were gaining ground toward our rear, the Eighteenth was ordered to face back toward the top of the mountain and form on the right of the Twenty-second South Carolina Volunteers. The enemy advancing, we engaged

[31] Rodes to Ratchford, 1035–36.
[32] Ibid., 1036.
[33] Hill, "The Battle of South Mountain," 574.

them in this position until, the troops upon the left giving away, the enemy gained a point from which they enfiladed us again. Whereupon the regiment fell back to the turnpike, where it remained until the march to Sharpsburg began.[34]

The 17th South Carolina (Colonel Fitz W. McMaster), on the extreme right, beyond the gorge road leading down the mountain, was tenaciously holding ground against the 7th and 8th Pennsylvania Reserves, but seeing the left of its brigade go in disorder, pressed in front by the 8th, and flanked by the 7th, it retired to form a new line some three hundred yards to the rear. Again flanked by the steady Union advance, it continued its retreat with but thirty-six men in its ranks. McMaster was now ordered to form on the left of Jenkins's Brigade. Before being able to do so, night came, and, under Evans's order, he fell back to the National Road, the brigade having been rallied there near the Mountain House. The Holcombe Legion was thrown to the front as a picket and deployed about a skirt of woods on the south foot of the hill from which the brigade had been driven. Of the 550 men taken into action, it lost 171 killed and wounded and 45 missing.

When Evans was sent to help Rodes, he was given to understand that the interval between his right and the National Road would be filled. The only troops available for the purpose were the brigades of Kemper, Garnett, and Jenkins (under Colonel Joseph Walker) of Jones's Division. When the two brigades of Drayton and G. T. Anderson were detached and sent directly up the mountain to report to D. H. Hill, these three small brigades were ordered by Longstreet to march from Boonsboro in a southerly direction and then ascend the mountain to assist in the defense of Fox's Gap, which, it was reported, Reno was about to carry. After much marching and countermarching, it was finally ascertained that the Confederates on that part of the line were fairly holding their own, but that north of the National Road affairs were more threatening and needed more attention. Thus, D. R. Jones was ordered to move his three brigades as speedily as possible back to the main road and thence to the mountaintop. When, after more blind marching, he reached the main road—not more than a third of a mile from where he left it—his men were well nigh exhausted by miles of useless travel, added to the hot, dusty, and fatiguing march from Hagerstown. He lost many men by straggling; beyond this, he lost much valuable time. Under Longstreet's orders, he placed the brigades of Kemper and Garnett, supported by Jenkins's, in position on the ridge to the right of Rodes and Evans. Hill says, "Major-General Longstreet came up about 4 o'clock with the commands of Brig. Gens. N. G. Evans and D. R. Jones. I had now become familiar with the ground, and knew all the vital points, and, had these troops reported to me, the result might have been different. As it was, they took wrong positions, and, in their exhausted condition after a long march, they were broken and scattered."[35]

Kemper's Brigade formed chiefly across the Old Hagerstown Road. Garnett's followed and took position about two hundred yards to its right, the 8th Virginia (only thirty-four men under Colonel Eppa Hunton) on the right, resting in a thick wood, the ground descending quite abruptly in front. The left, which at first was held by the 56th Virginia (Colonel William D. Stuart), then by the 28th Virginia (Captain William L. Wingfield), was in a field of standing corn. In front of Colonel John B. Strange's 19th Virginia, the left center was an open space, beyond which, about fifteen yards, was a stone fence.

As soon as the line had been formed, Garnett sent out skirmishers to ascertain the position of the enemy. It was near sunset when he received an order to send the 56th Virginia from his left to strengthen the right of Kemper, about two hundred yards distant, and to withdraw the rest of the brigade to a wooded ridge a little to the left and rear. The 56th Virginia had scarcely been detached (leaving the 28th Virginia on the left) and Garnett was about to move to the position designated for him when the Union skirmishers of Hatch's division made their appearance, immediately followed by their main body, and at once the action became general.

Before considering this, we briefly note the position and formation of Kemper's Brigade on Garnett's left. When leaving the National Road at the Mountain House, Kemper's Brigade moved to the left by the Old Hagerstown Road, Kemper and staff riding ahead some distance to see the lay of the ground. He had gone about one hundred yards, beyond the backbone of a ridge running nearly north and south, when he was fired upon by the advancing enemy, upon which he galloped back and formed his brigade across the Old Hagerstown Road. The brigade had come up under a severe shelling from Durell's battery on Reno's line south of the National Road, this enfilading fire causing some loss. The brigade was formed from right to left in the following order: the 17th Virginia (Colonel Montgomery D. Corse), 11th Virginia (Major Adam Clement), 1st Virginia (Captain George F. Norton), 7th Virginia (Major Arthur Herbert of the 17th Virginia), and 24th Virginia (Colonel William R. Terry[36]). The 24th and 7th Virginia and part of the 1st were in rocky woods on the left of the road, the remainder of the brigade on the right of it. On the extreme right, the 17th Virginia advanced about one hundred yards to the far edge of a cornfield with a wood in front and sent out skirmishers. Then it moved to the left in the corn to connect

[34] William H. Wallace to Asa L. Evans, October 21, 1862, reprinted in *OR*, vol. 19, pt. 1, 947.

[35] Hill to Chilton, 1021.

[36] Throughout his original manuscript, Carman gives the name incorrectly as "W. R. Perry."

with the 11th Virginia as the 56th Virginia of Garnett's Brigade closed in on its right, the three regiments being in the same cornfield. The combined strength of the two brigades of Garnett and Kemper did not exceed 850 men, and they were about to be struck by Hatch's fine division.

When Hatch left the National Road at Bolivar to follow Meade to the right, he had the three brigades of Brigadier General Marsena R. Patrick, Colonel Walter Phelps Jr., and Brigadier General Abner Doubleday—an effective force of about 3,500 men. He arrived in the vicinity of Mount Tabor Church about 3:30 p.m. and formed on Meade's left. The general order of battle was for two regiments of Patrick's brigade to precede the main body as skirmishers, supported by the two remaining regiments of the brigade, these to be followed at two hundred paces by Phelps's brigade, and Phelps's in turn by Doubleday's at the same interval.

Following this arrangement, Patrick deployed the 21st New York (Colonel William F. Rogers) as skirmishers, with orders to move up a ravine on the right leading to a depression on the mountaintop, and the 35th New York (Colonel Newton B. Lord) to move on the left of the 21st directly to the summit of the south spur. The 21st was supported by Lieutenant Colonel Theodore B. Gates's 80th New York, and the 35th by Colonel Henry C. Hoffman's 23d New York. The objective point was the south spur, and all the movements of the division were on the left, south of the Old Hagerstown Road, with Meade's division operating at the same time on the right of that road.

Colonel Rogers and the 21st New York, supported by the 80th, ascended the ravine that partially divided the eastern slope of the mountain, throwing skirmishers to the right and left. The 35th New York, supported by the 23d, was on the left. (Eventually it diverged so much further to the left as to overlook the National Road at the foot of the south spur.) These movements were made with some deliberation, under a fire of artillery described by D. H. Hill "as harmless as blank-cartridge salutes in honor of a militia general" and which "the enemy did not honor by so much as a dodge." Hill states that the advance of Hatch's division in three lines, a brigade in each, was grand and imposing. Hatch's general and field officers were on horseback, his colors were all flying, and the alignment of the men seemed to be perfectly preserved. (Hooker, looking at it from the foot of the mountain, describes it as a beautiful sight.) From the top it was grand and sublime. Hill also states, "There was not a single Confederate soldier to oppose the advance of General Hatch." Hill obtained some guns from the reserve artillery of Colonel Cutts to fire at the three imposing lines,[37] but the cannonade, owing to the large angles of depression and the limited practice of the gunners, was "the worst I ever witnessed."[38] It was while this harmless cannonade was going on that Longstreet appeared with three small brigades and assumed direction of affairs, Evans's Brigade being sent to aid Rodes and those of Garnett and Kemper to meet and check Hatch, advancing so far without opposition.

Before these brigades had fairly taken position, Hatch was well on his way up the south spur. When nearing a road part way up the spur, parallel to its crest and just at the edge of a wood, it was discovered that there was a considerable interval between the right of the 35th New York and the left of the 21st New York, upon which the 80th New York was brought up to the left of the 21st. The left wing of the brigade (the 35th and 23d New York), reaching the road at about the time that the 21st struck it, was ordered to change direction to the right to close the opening, which had not been accomplished when Phelps's brigade came up in column of divisions and passed through it. Phelps saw that no skirmish line was in front, halted, and advised Hatch of the situation. Hatch, who was close at hand, came up, rode to the front, and saw that the gap was closed. The skirmishers and the entire line again pushed ahead, Phelps following thirty yards in rear of the skirmishers. Soon the ascending column came under fire of Garnett's and Kemper's skirmishers. Phelps deployed his brigade in line of battle; the skirmishers of the 35th New York and their support (the 23d), which had again drifted far to the left, were again drawn in to the right and merged in the general line of battle, now moving steadily toward the summit of the south spur under a galling fire from the Confederates above, posted behind trees, among rocks, and under the shelter of stone walls. The steepness of the ascent and the heat of the day, added to the long march of the morning, caused a slow advance up the rough side of the spur.

The skirmishers soon developed the position of Garnett's Brigade—behind a stone fence on the summit of the spur running north and south, fronted by a wood and backed by a cornfield full of rock ledges. Phelps now ordered his men to attack, and Hatch rode through the lines to urge them forward, but they needed no urging. They leaped forward with a hearty cheer, poured in a hot fire, and were given a hot volley in return, followed by a heavy and continuous fire that was as heavily responded to. After a contest of about fifteen minutes, in which Garnett's men displayed much courage and obstinacy, the

---

[37] Hill, "The Battle of South Mountain," 573–74. The statement attributed to Hooker is referenced on p. 573. Hill's source for Hooker's opinion is not entirely clear. It is probably Hill's own interpretation of this passage from Hooker's official report: "From its great elevation and the dense smoke which rose over the top of the forest, the progress of the battle on this part of the field was watched with anxious interest for miles around, and while it elicited the applause of the spectators, they could not fail to admire the steadiness, resolution, and courage of the brave officers and men engaged." Hooker to Richmond, 215.

[38] Hill to Chilton, 1020.

line began to yield. The 28th Virginia, on the left, gave way and fell back on Kemper's right, and the 8th Virginia, on the right, was obliged to yield ground (despite all efforts of Colonel Hunton) and form on Jenkins's Brigade, just then coming into position as Garnett's support. Phelps now ordered a charge. The stone fence was carried and the entire line of Garnett driven back some two hundred yards, leaving many prisoners in Phelps's hands. In this contest at the fence, Colonel Strange of the 19th Virginia was killed and General Hatch wounded. Doubleday succeeded to the command of the division.

Captain Henry T. Owen of the 18th Virginia (Garnett's Brigade), after a graphic account of the march to the field and the appearance of the steadily advancing Union line, says:

> A heavy fire was soon opened upon the enemy, but they neither paused nor faltered, and a brief, fierce contest took place along the ridge until the enemy brought up a second line of reinforcements[,] when the Confederates, being greatly outnumbered, suddenly gave way and rushed back down the hill and out in the open field. There was great confusion, and the broken ranks were hard to rally and re-form, so that had the enemy followed up closely behind they could have taken the gap without any difficulty, as this brigade were the only troops at that time on that side of the gap; but the enemy halted …, and this gave the Confederates time to rally and re-form in separate squads and detachments behind the rocks and fences and reopen a brisk fire … Still falling back and fighting as we retreated, we reached the fence across the field, and although half of the brigade had disappeared, the survivors made a stand along the fence and endeavored to hold the enemy back until reinforcements could be brought up.
>
> There were now, probably, not more than two hundred men left in the brigade, and these were fighting in squads of a dozen or more, with great gaps between them, and were scattered along behind the fence and bushes for half a mile, while the enemy had a strong line in front and outflanked our position on both the right and left. On the right of our line Colonel Eppa Hunton, with some thirty or forty men, was trying to keep the enemy back, then a gap in the line, perhaps of fifty yards, and a dozen men were found together, and then another gap and another squad, then a gap of two or three hundred yards, and on the other side, but in line, came Major [George C.] Cabell [18th Virginia] and General Garnett with, perhaps, a hundred men more. The sun was now behind the mountains and the sombre shadows of night were settling down over the smoky, blood-stained field.[39]

While the main fight was in progress at the stone fence between Phelps and Garnett, Patrick's divided brigade came up on either side of Phelps—the 21st and 80th New York on his right, the 35th and 23d New York on his left. Colonel Rogers, with his two regiments (the 21st and 80th New York), cooperated with Phelps by cautiously advancing his right, forcing back part of Kemper's skirmishers and seizing and holding the fence bordering the northeast side of the cornfield. Phelps's fierce attack upon Garnett did not extend to Kemper's Brigade on Garnett's left, between whose right and Garnett's left there was an interval of quite two hundred yards. Kemper's skirmishers were driven in, but the brigade front was not seriously engaged. Fearing, however, for the right flank (threatened by the fierce attack upon Garnett), the 56th Virginia, which had joined Kemper's right, changed front, with its right wing prepared to meet the Union advance in that direction. It was now quite dark and almost impossible to see anything of Phelps's men, or of Garnett on Kemper's right front. When, at the end of a few minutes, Garnett's 28th Virginia fell back onto Kemper's right, and it was ascertained that the Union troops (the 21st and 80th New York) were advancing and forcing back the left, Colonel Corse, who was commanding the right wing (the 56th, 17th, and 11th Virginia), fell back about twenty yards to the shelter of a fence separating the cleared field and the cornfield, which position was held until long after dark under a severe fire of musketry obliquely on his right and upon his front.

On the left the 23d and 35th New York came up to the fence that Phelps had carried and opened fire through the cornfield. After a few rounds, Confederate fire slackened. The two regiments were ordered to cease firing and the alignment corrected about five yards back of the fence. It was then quite dark and there was much confusion, which was increased by the renewal of the Confederate fire. Doubleday, coming up, ordered the regiments back to the fence.

At this time Phelps's brigade, much reduced in number by casualties and meeting a determined resistance from the Confederates, was relieved by Doubleday's brigade, now under the command of Colonel William P. Wainwright of the 76th New York. This brigade had ascended the spur in close support to Phelps and numbered about one thousand men. It took position behind the stone fence from which Garnett had been driven. (Garnett's men subsequently rallied in knots and squads in the cornfield—still showing a determined, although broken, front.) Wainwright's left extended beyond Garnett's right and was threatened by Jenkins's Brigade.

This unit, under the temporary command of Colonel Walker, followed Garnett, reached the field shortly after 4:00 p.m., and formed on Garnett's right, though some distance in rear and but a short distance beyond the Mountain House. When the attack developed upon Garnett, it moved, under Jones's order, farther up the mountain obliquely to the right and

[39] Henry T. Owen, "Annals of the War—Chapters of Unwritten History: South Mountain," *Philadelphia Weekly Times*, July 31, 1880.

formed line, still on Garnett's right and rear. The 1st South Carolina Volunteers and the 6th and 5th South Carolina were quickly advanced two hundred yards to the front behind a stone fence, where the 8th Virginia of Garnett's Brigade, driven from its position at the front, fell in on their left. Small parties of Kemper's and Garnett's men rallied upon the line and kept up an irregular fire upon the 23d and 35th New York and Wainwright's brigade, which had relieved Phelps.

It was the movement of Jenkins's Brigade in the fading light that led Wainwright to believe that an effort was being made to turn his left (though no such movement was intended), upon which he changed front with the 76th New York and the 7th Indiana. A severe fire was kept up for some time by both sides—Garnett's and Jenkins's position being known only by the flashes of fire from their muskets—when, almost out of ammunition, Wainwright was relieved by Colonel William A. Christian's brigade of Ricketts's division and fell back a few paces. Christian's brigade fired a few volleys and, in about a half-hour, the Confederates withdrew. Brigadier General George L. Hartsuff's brigade of Ricketts's division was brought up after dark and formed line across the gorge, connecting Doubleday's right with Meade's left, and the entire corps was ordered to sleep on its arms.

While the contest was at its height on the crest of the south spur, the brigades of Brigadier General John Gibbon and Colonel Colquitt were severely engaging each other on the National Road, which ran past the south foot of the spur. (Colquitt, as has been noted, had been withdrawn from the east foot of the mountain nearer to the summit and placed in line on either side of the road.) About 700 yards in a direct line from the Mountain House, or about 850 yards by the winding road, the 23d Georgia (Colonel William P. Barclay) and the 28th Georgia (Major Tully Graybill), each with about three hundred men, were on the left—north of the road. The 23d Georgia, its right resting on the road, was under cover of a stone fence and a channel or shallow ravine worn by water down the slope of the south spur. The 28th Georgia, on the left of the 23d, was about one-fourth behind the same stone fence, the remainder in the woods higher up the spur. The position held by the two regiments was a very strong one. The 23d was under cover and out of sight until the enemy mounted a gentle rise of ground about forty yards in front, of which—and the ground to its right front—it had complete command. The 28th, on the wooded slope of the spur, had command of the approaches to the front of the 23d and, by advancing its left, could enfilade any line attacking it. Two companies of each regiment were detached as skirmishers.

The 6th and 27th Georgia and the 13th Alabama were on the right of the road (on lower ground than the 23d Georgia), nearly the entire line in woods, extended across a deep ravine, and under instructions to connect with Garland on the right. But the force in the three regiments was not sufficient to reach that distance; there was a gap of about four hundred yards between the two brigades, and this gap Colquitt was to cover should it become necessary to do so. Upon the right of the road, about four hundred yards in advance of Colquitt's right, was a thick growth of woods, with fields in front and around them. In these woods were concealed four companies of Colquitt's skirmishers under the command of Captain Arnold. The strength of Colquitt's Brigade was about 1,350 officers and enlisted men.

When Hatch's division had turned to the right at Bolivar, Gibbon's brigade was detached from it and, moving on the National Road a short distance, was halted. After two hours (or about 5:00 p.m., when the general advance was made by Hooker on the right and Reno on the left), Gibbon was ordered by Burnside to move directly up the road and attack the Confederates in position at Turner's Gap. One section of Captain Joseph B. Campbell's regular battery under the command of Lieutenant James Stewart accompanied the brigade. The 7th Wisconsin (Captain John B. Callis) formed on the right of the road and the 19th Indiana (Colonel Solomon Meredith) formed on the left, with Captain William W. Dudley's company of the 19th being thrown to the left as flankers. One company each from the 2d and 6th Wisconsin under the overall command of Captain Wilson Colwell of the 2d was thrown one hundred yards to the front. The two advance regiments followed (formed in double column at half distance), with the section of artillery in the road a short distance in rear of the infantry. The 7th Wisconsin was supported by the 6th Wisconsin (Lieutenant Colonel Edward S. Bragg) and the 19th Indiana by the 2d Wisconsin (Colonel Lucius Fairchild), each following about two hundred yards in rear.

When Colquitt saw these well regulated movements, he sent an urgent request for support, but D. H. Hill had none to give, and Colquitt was left to his own resources. The Wisconsin skirmishers (closely supported by the 7th Wisconsin and the 19th Indiana) soon encountered those of Colquitt, while Lieutenant Stewart's two guns moved on the road until within range of the Confederate guns firing from the summit of the gap, when they opened with good effect. The 19th Indiana, advancing on the left of the road, was much annoyed by a skirmish fire from a house and outbuildings surrounded on the southwest and north by woods. This fire was soon silenced by a few shots from Stewart's guns, but the Georgians, seeking the cover of the woods, reopened fire, upon which Colonel Meredith ordered his regiment forward and engaged them at close quarters. The Georgians soon yielded and were closely followed; when coming to a stone fence, they rallied on Arnold's skirmish battalion, and the Indianans were checked by a severe fire. The 19th Indiana's Company G, under command of Captain John R. Clark, was wheeled to the left and, gaining a position enfilading the line behind the fence, speedily dislodged Arnold's skirmishers, capturing eleven prisoners (including three officers). The 2d Wisconsin supported the 19th Indiana by moving up on its right, the right of the 2d resting on the National Road.

On the right of the road, the 7th Wisconsin moved about one hundred yards in rear of the skirmishers and went by the right of companies to the front, through a cornfield nearly half a mile, and emerged into an open field, where the skirmishers met such a sharp fire from those of the 23d and 28th Georgia that farther progress was checked, the open field affording no shelter from the fire of the Georgians behind one of the stone walls bounding the winding road. The regiment now formed line of battle and advanced, its left touching the road, the right extending north to the edge of the woods on the slope of the south spur. It immediately came under the fire of the enemy from the stone fence on the left of the road (from which as yet they had not been driven by the 19th Indiana and 2d Wisconsin), which fire was returned by a left oblique volley followed by a scattering fire. When the 19th Indiana and 2d Wisconsin came up on that side of the road and dislodged the Confederates (as we have seen), the 7th Wisconsin kept on until an enfilading fire from the 28th Georgia (in the woods on the right) and a direct fire at forty yards from the 23d Georgia behind the stone fence in the ravine again checked it. The 7th Wisconsin did not fall back, however, and the firing on both sides was rapid and deadly. Colquitt says, "Confident in their superior numbers, the enemy's forces advanced to a short distance of our lines, when, raising a shout, they came to a charge. As they came full into view upon the rising ground, 40 paces distant, they were met by a terrific volley of musketry from the stone fence and hillside. This gave a sudden check to their advance. They rallied under cover of the uneven ground, and the fight opened in earnest. They made still another effort to advance, but were kept back by the steady fire of our men."[40]

Meanwhile, the 19th Indiana and 2d Wisconsin had come up on the left and, having driven the Confederates from their own front, opened a right oblique fire on the 23d Georgia (then engaging the 7th Wisconsin). The 2d Wisconsin, with its right wing, changed front to the right, parallel to the road, and opened fire. Its ammunition was soon exhausted, and it was relieved by the left wing, which was relieved in turn by the 19th Indiana. From the fact that the 23d Georgia was well protected by the stone fence and that the 19th Indiana and 2d Wisconsin were on much lower ground, their firing was not effective, and the 7th Wisconsin could make no progress. Captain Callis made an effort to drive the Georgians from behind the fence by advancing the 7th's right wing and getting an enfilade fire upon them, but there burst from the woods on the right a flame of musketry from the 28th Georgia, followed by such a shower of bullets into the rear of the right wing that it was driven back. This reinforced the impression that the Confederates were making an effort to flank the line, upon which Colonel Bragg, who was but a few yards in rear, was ordered to form the 6th Wisconsin on the right of the 7th and check the movement. Bragg moved double-quick and became engaged with the 28th Georgia. He used some effective tactics, the details of which he gives in his official report:

The skirmishers soon found the enemy in front, and an irregular fire commenced. This was past twilight. The Seventh moved to the support of the skirmishers, and was soon engaged with the enemy, who was concealed in a wood on their left and in a ravine in front. So soon as the Seventh received the fire of the enemy and commenced replying, I deployed the Sixth, and with the right wing opened fire upon the enemy concealed in the wood upon the right. I also moved the left wing by the right flank into the rear of the right wing, and commenced a fire by the wings alternately, and advancing the line after each volley.

At this time I received an order from the general, directing me to flank the enemy in the wood. The condition of the surface of the ground, and the steepness of the ascent up the mountain side, rendered this movement a difficult one; but without hesitation the left wing moved by the flank into the wood, firing as they went, and advancing the line. I directed Major [Rufus R.] Dawes to advance the right wing on the skirt of the wood as rapidly as the line in the wood advanced, which he did. This movement forward and by the flank I continued until the left wing rested its right on the crest of the hill, extending around the enemy in a semicircular line, and then moved the right wing into the wood so as to connect the line from the open field to the top of the hill. While this was being done, the fire of the enemy, who fought us from behind rocks and trees, and entirely under cover, was terrific, but steadily the regiment dislodged him and kept advancing. Ammunition commenced to give out, no man having left more than four rounds, and many without any. It was dark, and a desperate enemy in front.

At this moment I received an order from General Gibbon to cease fire and maintain the position, and the battle was won. I directed my men to reserve their fire, unless compelled to use it, and then only at short range, and trust to the bayonet. No sooner did the time of fire cease than the enemy, supposing we were checked, crept close up in

---

[40] Alfred H. Colquitt to Ratchford, October 13, 1862, reprinted in *OR*, vol. 19, pt. 1, 1053.

the wood and commenced a rapid fire. I directed a volley in reply, and then, with three lusty cheers for Wisconsin, the men sat cheerfully down to await another attack; but the enemy was no more seen.[41]

Gibbon held his ground until late in the evening, when all his command (except the 6th Wisconsin, which occupied the field all night) was relieved by Brigadier General Willis A. Gorman's brigade from the Second Corps. He lost 37 killed, 251 wounded, and 30 missing; among the killed was Captain Colwell of the 2d Wisconsin, an officer of rare merit, who commanded the skirmishers with signal ability and bravery. Colquitt's loss was about 110 killed, wounded, and missing, falling principally on the 23d and 28th Georgia. He closes his official report with the statement, "The fight continued with fury until after dark. Not an inch of ground was yielded. The ammunition of many of the men was exhausted, but they stood with bayonets fixed."[42] He quietly withdrew at about 10:00 p.m. and marched for Sharpsburg.

When night put an end to the day's conflict, the Confederates still held the National Road leading over Turner's Gap, but both flanks had been forced back. On the right, Fox's Gap was held, but Cox held the crest in front and south of it and the roads leading into Pleasant Valley south of Boonsboro. North of the National Road, Hooker had completely turned the position, seized the commanding heights from which he had driven the brigades of Rodes and Evans and their supports, and was waiting for daylight to advance to the rear of the Mountain House—to which Lee's entire left wing had been driven.

It was an anxious and disheartened group that gathered at Lee's headquarters that night. D. H. Hill, who was more conversant with the situation than either Lee or Longstreet, expressed his decided opinion that the position was no longer tenable and advised an immediate retreat. Longstreet concurred with Hill. Lee had not entirely abandoned hope and, before giving orders for a retreat, ordered a small detachment back to the ground on the left to ascertain whether it was still held by Hooker or whether he had retired, as reported. A picket officer, Lieutenant William P. Dubose of the Holcombe Legion, was charged with the duty, went forward, and was captured. Hooker's pickets were found alert and strongly posted on the heights overlooking the Mountain[43] House, and a prisoner gave information that Sumner had arrived at Bolivar and that the Twelfth Corps was on the march for that place. Lee then ordered a retreat. Longstreet reports, "It became manifest that our forces were not sufficient to resist the renewed attacks of the entire army of General McClellan. He would require but little time to turn either flank, and our command must then be at his mercy. In view of this, the commanding general ordered the withdrawal of our troops to the village of Sharpsburg."[44]

In a letter to Jefferson Davis, written at Sharpsburg on September 16, 1862, Lee reports:

My letter to you of the 13th instant informed you of the positions of the different divisions of this army. Learning that night that Harper's Ferry had not surrendered, and that the enemy was advancing more rapidly than was convenient from Fredericktown, I determined to return with Longstreet's command to the Blue Ridge, to strengthen D. H. Hill's and Stuart's divisions, engaged in holding the passes of the mountains, lest the enemy should fall upon McLaws' rear, drive him from the Maryland Heights, and thus relieve the garrison at Harper's Ferry. On approaching Boonsborough, I received information from General D. H. Hill that the enemy in strong force was at the main pass on the Frederick and Hagerstown [i.e., National] road, pressing him so heavily as to require immediate re-enforcements. Longstreet advanced rapidly to his support, and immediately placed his troops in position. By this time Hill's right had been forced back, the gallant Garland having fallen in rallying his brigade. Under General Longstreet's directions, our right was soon restored, and firmly resisted the attacks of the enemy to the last. His superior numbers enabled him to extend beyond both of our flanks, and his right was able to reach the summit of the mountain to our left, and press us heavily in that direction. The battle raged until after night; the enemy's efforts to force a passage were resisted, but we had been unable to repulse him.

Learning later in the evening that Crampton's Gap (on the direct road from Fredericktown to Sharpsburg) had been forced, and McLaws' rear thus threatened, and believing from a report from General Jackson that Harper's Ferry would fall next morning, I determined to withdraw Longstreet and D. H. Hill from their positions and retire to the vicinity of Sharpsburg, where the army could be more easily united. Before abandoning the position, indications led me to believe that the enemy was withdrawing, but learning from a prisoner that Sumner's corps (which had not been engaged) was being put in position to relieve their wearied troops, while the most of ours were exhausted by a fatiguing march and a hard conflict, and I feared would be unable to renew the fight successfully in the morning,

[41] Edward S. Bragg to Frank A. Haskell, September 20, 1862, reprinted in *OR*, vol. 19, pt. 1, 253–54.

[42] Colquitt to Ratchford, 1053.

[43] In his original manuscript, Carman here writes "Mansion House." This is assuredly inadvertent. The Mansion House is a luxurious Georgian-style dwelling built in 1846 near Hagerstown, approximately fifteen miles northwest of Turner's Gap.

[44] James Longstreet to Chilton, October 10, 1862, reprinted in *OR*, vol. 19, pt. 1, 840.

confirmed me in my determination. Accordingly, the troops were withdrawn, preceded by the trains, without molestation by the enemy, and about daybreak took position in front of this place.[45]

In his official report, written the following year, Lee says:

The effort to force the passage of the mountains had failed, but it was manifest that without re-enforcements we could not hazard a renewal of the engagement, as the enemy could easily turn either flank. Information was also received that another large body of Federal troops had during the afternoon forced their way through Crampton's Gap, only 5 miles in rear of McLaws. Under these circumstances, it was determined to retire to Sharpsburg, where we would be upon the flank and rear of the enemy should he move against McLaws, and where we could more readily unite with the rest of the army.[46]

The retreat began about ten o'clock. The troops near the Mountain House retired by the National Road and Boonsboro, those confronting Cox generally by the Old Sharpsburg Road to the foot of the mountain and thence to Boonsboro. Jenkins's Brigade, under Colonel Walker, covered the withdrawal from Turner's Gap. When Colquitt was withdrawn from the foot of the mountain, about ten o'clock, the 2d South Carolina went down the National Road from near the Mountain House and threw out a strong line of skirmishers on either side of it. Walker remained at the Mountain House with the other regiments of the brigade until 4:00 a.m. of the fifteenth, when the 2d South Carolina was withdrawn and the entire brigade was relieved by Fitzhugh Lee's cavalry; it marched to Sharpsburg, where it rejoined its division. Colonel Rosser, with the 5th Virginia Cavalry, covered the withdrawal of the troops from Fox's Gap.

During the day of the fourteenth, the Union troops in the rear closed up on the First and Ninth Corps. The Second Corps moved from near Frederick by the Shookstown Road (north of the National Road) to Middletown, thence by the National Road to Bolivar. Major General Israel B. Richardson's division was pushed ahead to Mount Tabor Church to the support of the First Corps. One brigade of Major General John Sedgwick's division was ordered to relieve Gibbon; the other two brigades and Brigadier General William H. French's division remained at Bolivar.

The Twelfth Corps, near Frederick, was ordered to move at 7:00 a.m.; it was somewhat later when it drew out on the road. It marched through Frederick as the church bells were calling to worship the followers of the Prince of Peace. The Stars and Stripes floated over the most prominent buildings, were hung from windows, and were waved by fair hands, demonstrating that the brief Confederate occupation of the ancient borough had not impaired its love for the old flag, nor diminished its sympathies for its defenders. Through the streets of Frederick-town, "green-walled by the hills of Maryland," rendered immortal by Whittier's undying verse, on that beautiful Sabbath morning, amid the ringing of church bells and the waiving of flags, thousands of men were pressed on to conquer a peace and to illustrate to all coming time, to all Christian nations, the truth of Julia Ward Howe's most beautiful sentiment that as Christ died to make men holy, the highest duty of a citizen-soldier is to die to make men free. Presently a voice strikes up the song "John Brown's Body," the bands join in, it is taken up by regiment after regiment, is carried from the leading brigade through the whole division, from one division to another, until the grand chorus, swelling from thousands of voices, fills the whole air and produces an effect beyond the comprehension of those who know not, from experience, the capability, power, and richness of a man's voice when a man's heart is in it.[47]

It was thus that the Twelfth Corps marched through and out of Frederick; thus it climbed the Catoctin Mountain and saw from its summit the beautiful Middletown or Catoctin Valley, bathed in a flood of sunlight. Beyond this peaceful and charming valley, a garden in the highest state of cultivation, could be seen the powder smoke as the shells exploded in air at and near Turner's Gap. Descending into the valley, the corps went into bivouac, but after a brief rest was again ordered forward. The road was crowded with artillery, ordnance, and baggage wagons, and the troops were compelled to take to the fields and through corn higher than the heads of the men. It was now dark, and the march was through fields and woods and over ditches and fences—north, south, east, and west. In fact, if there is a point of the compass toward which the head of the column did not march that evening (and in the darkness) it is unknown to us. Finally the advance struck a road that led to Middletown. Thence it took the road leading back to Frederick, went some distance, found somebody had blundered, and marched back to Middletown, where, worn out by the unnecessary marching, the men lay down in the street awaiting orders, and while doing so they slept (not the sleep of the righteous, for they swore worse than the army in Flanders). Again they were urged forward and about midnight halted in some fields near Bolivar; the organizations were there, but more than one-half the men were sleeping in cornfields, along fences, and in the tortuous trail of the march. Sykes's division and the reserve artillery marched from Frederick on the fourteenth and halted for the night at Middletown. "Thus," reports

---

[45] Robert E. Lee to Jefferson Davis, September 16, 1862, reprinted in *OR*, vol. 19, pt. 1, 140.

[46] Lee to Samuel Cooper, August 19, 1863, reprinted in *OR*, vol. 19, pt. 1, 147.

[47] The sudden change of tense and tone in this passage is attributable no doubt to a genuine expression of the author's own emotional recall. His regiment, the 13th New Jersey, was attached to the Third Brigade, First Division, Twelfth Corps during the Maryland campaign.

McClellan, "on the night of the 14th the whole army was massed in the vicinity of the field of battle, in readiness to renew the action the next day or to move in pursuit of the enemy."[48]

The Confederates indulged in many regrets that affairs at South Mountain were not differently managed. Longstreet, speaking only of his own troops, says, "Had the command reached the mountain pass in time to have gotten into position before the attack was made, I believe that the direct assaults of the enemy could have been repulsed with comparative ease. Hurried into action, however, we arrived at our positions more exhausted than the enemy."[49] D. H. Hill contends that had Longstreet's men been directed to report to him, the result might have been different, and he further says, "Had Longstreet's division been with mine at daylight in the morning, the Yankees would have been disastrously repulsed; but they had gained important positions before the arrival of re-enforcements. These additional troops came up, after a long, hurried, and exhausting march, to defend localities of which they were ignorant, and to fight a foe flushed with partial success, and already holding key-points to further advance. Had our forces never been separated, the battle of Sharpsburg never would have been fought, and the Yankees would not have even the shadow of consolation for the loss of Harper's Ferry."[50]

These are vain regrets and apologies for defeat, but Hill derives some consolation from the satisfactory work of his own division and makes it the subject of official report:

Should the truth ever be known, the battle of South Mountain, as far as my division was concerned, will be regarded as one of the most remarkable and creditable of the war. The division had marched all the way from Richmond, and the straggling had been enormous in consequence of heavy marches, deficient commissariat, want of shoes, and inefficient officers. Owing to these combined causes, the division numbered less than 5,000 men the morning of September 14, and had five roads to guard, extending over a space of as many miles. This small force successfully resisted, without support, for eight hours, the whole Yankee army, and, when its supports were beaten, still held the roads, so that our retreat was effected without the loss of a gun, a wagon, or an ambulance. Rodes' brigade had immortalized itself; Colquitt's had fought well, and the two regiments most closely pressed (Twenty-third and Twenty-eighth Georgia) had repulsed the foe. Garland's brigade had behaved nobly, until demoralized by the fall of its gallant leader, and being outflanked by the Yankees. [G. B.] Anderson's brigade had shown its wonted gallantry. Ripley's brigade, for some cause, had not been engaged, and was used with Hood's two brigades to cover the retreat.[51]

A Confederate historian makes this criticism:

Hill's troops were badly handled. The field was not understood, and the troops not promptly enough put into position. Though with such odds against the Confederates as demanded the services of every man, Ripley's brigade was not engaged at all, and the half of G. B. Anderson's very slightly. The condition of affairs was not improved after Longstreet's arrival, though of course it should be remembered that he came hurriedly upon an unknown battlefield in the midst of a fight. Three of his brigades lost valuable time and valuable strength in marching first two or three miles towards the south side of the battlefield, and then retracing their steps. Others seem to have been badly placed. G. T. Anderson's brigade was not engaged, and Jenkins's but slightly. It seems probable that had Hill's troops been in position in the early morning, and had Longstreet arrived some hours sooner, the Federal army would not have succeeded in taking and holding any of the Confederate positions.[52]

On the other hand, McClellan cannot escape criticism. His movements were so slow that he failed in the object of his movement—the relief of Harper's Ferry. We have referred to his failure to take advantage of his knowledge of Lee's plans and press forward on the afternoon and night of the thirteenth. Affairs were not better conducted on the morning of the fourteenth. Cox went forward promptly and engaged the enemy on the summit of the mountain at nine o'clock. Notwithstanding the assurance given him that the entire corps would follow promptly, it was five hours later—at 2:00 p.m.—when Willcox came to his support. (He had camped one mile east of Middletown and had but six miles to march, yet in doing so consumed six hours of most valuable time.) Sturgis's division, which had camped near Middletown, was not ordered forward until 1:00 p.m. and arrived on the field at 3:30 p.m. We now know that had Willcox and Sturgis joined Cox before noon, as they could and should have done, Cox could have carried Fox's Gap and flanked the position at Turner's Gap before the arrival of Lee's footsore men from Hagerstown. Hooker's movements on the right were entirely too deliberate for the occasion. Burnside never went beyond his headquarters at Bolivar and (from what McClellan says) was listless and

[48] George B. McClellan to Lorenzo Thomas, August 4, 1863, reprinted in *OR*, vol. 19. pt. 1, 52–53.

[49] Longstreet to Chilton, 841.

[50] Hill to Chilton, 1022.

[51] Ibid, 1021–22.

[52] William Allan, *The Army of Northern Virginia in 1862* (Boston: Houghton, Mifflin and Co., 1892), 360–61.

indifferent.[53] McClellan was late on the field and fairly responsible for the delay of his subordinates in not energetically pushing matters and for Burnside's neglect to reinforce Cox and carry the passes before night.

The result of the day's work was that the Confederate invasion of the North was thwarted. Lee ordered McLaws to recross the Potomac by the most practicable ford. The reserve artillery, which had been halted on Beaver Creek, was (except for S. D. Lee's Battalion) ordered back to Virginia by way of Williamsport. Lee led that part of the army with him to cross the Potomac by Shepherdstown Ford, and Jackson was ordered up from Harper's Ferry to cover his crossing.

The Union troops engaged in the battle of Turner's Gap (including the fighting at Fox's Gap) numbered about 26,000 men, and their loss was 1,813 killed, wounded, and missing. According to William Allan, "The Confederates engaged consisted of one cavalry regiment under Rosser, of the five brigades under D. H. Hill, and of eight brigades which came up with Longstreet. Hill's division numbered 5,000. It is doubtful if Longstreet's brigades were as strong as Hill's, but averaging them at the same, the Confederates had in all some 13,000 or 14,000 men on the field."[54] Their loss was about 1,950 killed, wounded, and missing.

Though tactically defeated in the two engagements at Crampton's Gap and Turner's Gap, the Confederates were strategically successful, and D. H. Hill was correct in his statement that they had "accomplished all that was required—the delay of the Yankee army until Harper's Ferry could not be relieved."[55]

---

[53] "Burnside never came as near the battle as my position. Yet it was his command that was in action! He spent the night in the same house that I did." McClellan, *McClellan's Own Story: The War for the Union, the Soldiers Who Fought It, the Civilians Who Directed It, and His Relations to It and Them* (New York: Charles L. Webster & Co., 1887), 583.—*EAC*

[54] Allan, 360.

[55] Hill to Chilton, 1021.
In Carman's original manuscript, the casualty tabulations for the Union and Confederate forces comprise the conclusion of Chapter 8. For the sake of clarity and convenience, these appear herein as Appendices H and I, respectively.

9

From South Mountain to the Antietam

When Robert E. Lee, after nightfall of September 14, realized that the action at Turner's Gap had gone against him, he abandoned (temporarily, at least) his idea of a further invasion of the North into Pennsylvania, or even of remaining in Maryland, and took immediate measures to reunite with McLaws and recross the Potomac into Virginia. Those who were with Lee say that he gave no sign of disappointment and depression that his campaign had ended in failure, but we can imagine it was with a swelling heart that, at 8:00 p.m., he sent this dispatch to McLaws:

> The day has gone against us and this army will go by Sharpsburg and cross the river. It is necessary for you to abandon your position to-night. Send your trains not required on the road to cross the river. Your troops you must have well in hand to unite with this command, which will retire by Sharpsburg. Send forward officers to explore the way, ascertain the best crossing of the Potomac, and if you can find any between you and Shepherdstown leave Shepherdstown Ford for this command. Send an officer to report to me on the Sharpsburg road, where you are and what crossing you will take. You will of course bring Anderson's division with you.[1]

At about the same hour, he sent a dispatch to Jackson to march up from Harper's Ferry and cover his passage of the Potomac at Shepherdstown Ford. (These orders to McLaws and Jackson contemplated the abandonment of operations against Harper's Ferry, but these had so far progressed that the place was then, virtually, in the grasp of Jackson and McLaws.) Longstreet and D. H. Hill were directed to push such of their commands and trains as were at and near Hagerstown across the Potomac at Williamsport. The three reserve artillery battalions at Beaver Creek (four miles north of Boonsboro) were ordered to move—two battalions by Williamsport into Virginia, one battalion to Keedysville.

Two hours later, about 10:00 p.m., Lee had information that Franklin had forced Crampton's Gap and interposed between himself and McLaws, upon which he sent McLaws a message to make a way, if practicable, over Elk Ridge to Sharpsburg; if not practicable, to cross the Potomac near Weverton. At about the same time, 10:15 p.m., he sent this order to Colonel Munford, near Rohrersville: "Hold your position at Rohrersville, if possible, and if you can discover or hear of a practicable road below Crampton's Gap by which McLaws, at Weverton at present, can pass over the mountains to Sharpsburg, send him a messenger to guide him over immediately."[2] Munford knew no road by which McLaws could escape over the mountain and so informed Lee. He gave the same information to McLaws when he forwarded Lee's dispatch to him.

Up to 10:30 p.m. Lee had no idea of departing from his intention to cross the Potomac as speedily as possible, but the unwelcome news that Franklin had interposed between him and McLaws necessitated a change in his plans. McLaws could not now join him by the road up Pleasant Valley, and it would not do to leave him to his fate; his extrication was of grave necessity. To accomplish this, Lee concluded to halt on the road to the Potomac at Keedysville, five and a half miles from Turner's Gap and three miles southwest of Boonsboro, for the purpose of covering McLaws's movement from Pleasant Valley by way of Weverton, or across Elk Ridge to Sharpsburg, thence by some ford across the Potomac. Then he proposed an immediate crossing of the army he had with him (Longstreet and D. H. Hill) by Shepherdstown Ford. To this end, before he received Munford's reply to his dispatch of 10:15 p.m., he again wrote McLaws at 11:15 p.m.:

> In addition to what has already been stated in reference to your abandonment of Weverton, and routes you can take, I will mention you might cross the Potomac, below Weverton, into Virginia. I believe there is a ford at the Point of Rocks, and at Berlin below, but do not know whether either is accessible to you. The enemy from Jefferson seem to have forced a passage at Crampton's Gap, which may leave all on the river clear. This portion of the army will take position at Centreville, commonly called Keedysville, 2½ miles from Boonsborough, on the Sharpsburg road, with a view of preventing the enemy that may enter the gap at Boonsborough turnpike from cutting you off, and enabling you to make a junction with it. If you can pass to-night on the river road, by Harper's Ferry, or cross the mountain below Crampton's Gap toward Sharpsburg, let me know. I will be found at or near Centreville, or Keedysville, as it is called.[3]

---

[1] Robert H. Chilton to Lafayette McLaws, September 14, 1862, 8:00 p.m., reprinted in *OR*, vol. 51, pt. 2, 618–19.
[2] Chilton to Thomas T. Munford, September 14, 1862, 10:15 p.m., reprinted in *OR*, vol. 19, pt. 2, 609.
[3] Chilton to McLaws, September 14, 1862, 11:15 p.m., reprinted in *OR*, vol. 19. pt. 2, 608.

How McLaws received these instructions and his actions in regard to them have already been noted and shall again be referred to. Meanwhile, we follow the withdrawal of Lee's immediate command.

At 10:00 p.m. General Toombs, at Hagerstown, received an order from D. R. Jones, his division commander, to march immediately to Sharpsburg, leaving the 11th Georgia of G. T. Anderson's Brigade to conduct the large wagon train across the Potomac at Williamsport. Toombs started from beyond Hagerstown about midnight and, marching by the Hagerstown Turnpike, reached Sharpsburg before daybreak of the fifteenth and took position on the high ground southeast of the town. Upon the arrival of his division commander a few hours later, he was ordered to detail two regiments from his brigade and direct them to march immediately and in haste to Williamsport for the protection of the wagon train crossing over into Virginia. Toombs selected the 15th and 17th Georgia and placed them under the command of Colonel William T. Millican, a brave and energetic officer, who reached Williamsport after a severe march of thirteen miles to find that the train had already crossed into Virginia. He followed it across the river, overtook it, and remained with it until the seventeenth, when, with the two regiments and five companies of the 11th Georgia, he recrossed the river at Shepherdstown Ford and rejoined his brigade while it was in action on the fields south of Sharpsburg.

Longstreet's reserve ammunition train was near Hagerstown and started for the Potomac at midnight without apprehension of danger and very lightly guarded. Near Funkstown was a train of supplies collected in Maryland and other commissariat and quartermaster stores. There were also many wagons belonging to D. H. Hill's Division that had been pushed forward from near Boonsboro to Funkstown late in the evening, and with these were cooking details from the several brigades. Longstreet's ordnance train moved directly from Hagerstown toward the Potomac; the general supply train—about fifty wagons guarded by the 11th Georgia (Major Francis H. Little)—moved west from Funkstown by the Williamsport Road and, intercepting Longstreet's train at the intersection of the Hagerstown and Williamsport roads, fell in behind it. The men were scattered along behind what they supposed to be the regimental or brigade wagons and in the confusion of haltings and startings became weary, sleepy, and listless. Apprehending no danger, they paid no attention to the wagons and overlapped Longstreet's train as they neared Williamsport, when Colonel Benjamin F. Davis with his cavalry was upon them and turning a part of Longstreet's train off the Williamsport Road onto the road leading to Greencastle, Pennsylvania.

The historian of the 11th Georgia writes that the regiment, with the 1st Virginia Cavalry, was detailed to guard the transportation train and

> accordingly moved back [from Hagerstown—*EAC*] to Functown [*sic*], in order to meet a portion of the returning wagons, and take the Williamsport road from that place. The train extended for several miles, and our small force was of necessity wholly inadequate to cover the line of its movements. But Major Little made the best possible disposition of his men. He divided the regiment, placing Captain [William H.] Mitchel[l] in command of the right wing towards the front, and moving himself with the left, in rear of the wagons. Before day next morning the right wing was in motion. About the time of their starting, two brigades (so reported) of fugitive Yankee cavalry from Harper's Ferry crossed the track of the train at the junction of the Functown [Greencastle—*EAC*] and Hagerstown roads, and began to conduct the wagons in the direction of the former place. At first the wagoners thought they were Confederate soldiers and obeyed instructions with their usual cheerfulness. But as daylight was dawning the secret soon leaked out, and a messenger was hurried off to communicate the intelligence to Captain Mitchell. Knowing it was impossible, with his handful of men, to contend against such a force, the Captain (after consultation with his officers,) wisely resolved to fall back and connect with the left wing. But the Federals meditated nothing more than a passing notice, they were too thoroughly panic-stricken to tarry, and he had not, consequently, retreated a great way before information came that the road was again clear, and he resumed his march, and reached Williamsport without further interruption. We had lost a number of wagons, and some valuable stores by this raid.[4]

The train, save the wagons captured by Colonel Davis, crossed the Potomac at Williamsport. Later, Colonel Millican, with the 15th and 17th Georgia, came up and took charge of the train and added the 11th Georgia to his command. The rations cooked for D. H. Hill's men near Boonsboro on the night of the fourteenth were given them on the field of Sharpsburg on September 17.

Lee made this report of the loss of a part of Longstreet's train:

> I regret ... to report that on the night of the 14th instant, when I determined to withdraw from the gap in front of Boonsborough to Sharpsburg, a portion of General Longstreet's wagon-train was lost. When his division was ordered

---

[4] Kittrell J. Warren, *History of the Eleventh Georgia Vols., Embracing the Muster Rolls, together with a Special and Succinct Account of the Marches, Engagement, Casualties, etc.* (Richmond: Smith, Bailey & Co., 1863), 50.

back from Hagerstown to the support of D. H. Hill, his train was directed to proceed toward Williamsport, with a view to its safety, and, if necessary, to its crossing the river. Unfortunately, that night the enemy's cavalry at Harper's Ferry evaded our forces, crossed the Potomac into Maryland, passed up through Sharpsburg, where they encountered our pickets, and intercepted on their line of retreat to Pennsylvania General Longstreet's train on the Hagerstown road. The guard was in the extreme rear of the train, that being the only direction from which an attack was apprehended. The enemy captured and destroyed 45 wagons, loaded chiefly with ammunition and subsistence.[5]

The 1st Virginia Cavalry, which had been detached from its brigade at New Market on the tenth to accompany Jackson and protect his flank and rear from a possible movement from Pennsylvania, remained in the vicinity of Hagerstown, scouting and picketing up to the Pennsylvania line until the fourteenth, when its scouts and pickets were withdrawn. The regiment concentrated at Hagerstown and followed the trains across the river after daybreak of the fifteenth, encamping that night at Hainesville. On the sixteenth it marched through Martinsburg to Shepherdstown Ford, where it recrossed the river and rejoined Fitzhugh Lee's Brigade on the left of the Confederate line.

Late at night the commander of the reserve artillery, General Pendleton (who with three battalions had, late in the afternoon, taken position on the heights of Beaver Creek, four miles north of Boonsboro) was summoned to Lee's headquarters and directed to send S. D. Lee's Battalion to Keedysville and to move with the battalions of Brown and Nelson by the shortest route to Williamsport and across the Potomac to guard the fords of the river. Pendleton hastened back to his camp, moved promptly to the Boonsboro and Williamsport Road, and by sunrise reached Jones's Cross-Roads, where the Williamsport Road intersects the Hagerstown and Sharpsburg Turnpike. Here he was informed that a large force of Union cavalry was not far ahead of him, upon which he placed some guns in position commanding the road leading to Williamsport and the Hagerstown Pike on either flank, sent to Toombs (who had passed down to Sharpsburg) for a regiment or two of infantry, and set to work collecting a band of armed stragglers to support his guns. Meanwhile, he had sent out scouting parties. These soon returned with information that the road was clear for some two miles, upon which (without waiting for infantry from Toombs) he resumed the road to destroy the "retiring invaders" with his artillery and protect the large wagon train proceeding by the Hagerstown Road through Williamsport.[6] Colonel Davis's cavalry had passed on the road and attacked Longstreet's train, and Pendleton—without meeting an enemy or further delay—reached Williamsport and crossed the Potomac by Light's Ford into Virginia.

Colonel Brown, with his battalion of five batteries, was ordered to guard Light's Ford and a ford two miles below. Major Nelson's battalion of five batteries went down the river road to Shepherdstown, which he reached on the sixteenth, and took position on the heights commanding Shepherdstown Ford a mile below town.

D. H. Hill's Division was the first to retire from South Mountain. At 10:00 p.m. Colquitt's Brigade, relieved by the 2d South Carolina of Jenkins's Brigade, withdrew from the east foot of the mountain. Uniting with Rodes's Brigade at the Mountain House, the two brigades (with Rodes in command) began the descent of the mountain at 11:00 p.m., passed through Boonsboro, and, marching on the Boonsboro and Sharpsburg Turnpike, reached Keedysville about 1:00 a.m. of the fifteenth, where, under Lee's orders, Rodes halted. After resting about an hour, he was ordered to proceed to Sharpsburg with the two brigades under his command to drive out a Union cavalry force reported there. He was soon on the road and quickly overtaken by Colonel Chilton of Lee's staff with contrary orders, which required him to send only a part of his force. (He selected the 5th and 6th Alabama, under Colonel Gordon.) In a few minutes, however, he received an order from Longstreet to go ahead and did so with the two brigades, but found no cavalry at Sharpsburg; it had passed through the town. Colquitt's Brigade pushed through the town to Shepherdstown Ford on the Potomac. Rodes halted his brigade on the high ground southwest of the town and cooked breakfast at a very early hour, for both brigades arrived at Sharpsburg some time before daylight.

The three brigades of Garland, Ripley, and G. B. Anderson, in the order named, moved on by-roads from the Old Sharpsburg Road to the vicinity of Boonsboro, then followed Rodes on the Boonsboro and Sharpsburg Pike to Keedysville, where they were halted an hour, then, continuing the march, crossed the Antietam between daybreak and sunrise and formed line on the high ground a short mile beyond the stream and north of the Boonsboro Pike. D. H. Hill, who accompanied the three brigades, placed the right of his line (G. B. Anderson's Brigade) on the Boonsboro Pike, Ripley's Brigade a short distance to the rear, and Garland's Brigade (now commanded by Colonel McRea of the 5th North Carolina) on the high ground and in the sunken road (now known as Bloody Lane), with its left resting on the lane running north from the sunken road to the Roulette house. Rodes and Colquitt were now brought back from beyond the town and placed on the line, Rodes on a plateau on the right of Garland and at right angles to it. In his immediate rear was the Piper cornfield. "Here," says Rodes,

[5] Robert E. Lee to Jefferson Davis, September 21, 1862, reprinted in OR, vol. 19, pt. 1, 142.
[6] William N. Pendleton to Lee, September 24, 1862, reprinted in OR, vol. 19, pt. 1, 830.

"subsisting on green corn mainly and under an occasional artillery fire, we lay until the morning of the 17th."[7] Colquitt took position on Garland's left in the sunken road, between the mouth of the Roulette lane and the Hagerstown Pike. The brigades of G. B. Anderson, Ripley, and Rodes faced the Antietam and the east. Garland's and Colquitt's faced north, looking upon groves and fields in grass and luxuriant corn freshly plowed for seeding. Captain Thomas H. Carter's (Virginia) Battery was placed in the interval between Rodes and Garland and in Garland's front—two guns on Rodes's left (facing the Antietam), two guns in front of Garland's right, and one in front of his center (the last three guns facing north). Captain William B. Jones's (Virginia) Battery and Captain Robert A. Hardaway's (Alabama) Battery were in reserve. Bondurant's Battery, still east of the Antietam, was (when it arrived) kept with the reserve artillery beyond the town and not brought to the front until the seventeenth.

Following D. H. Hill's Division came the trains of the army—quartermaster, commissary and ordnance wagons, ambulances, and some of the reserve artillery. These passed through Sharpsburg and beyond more than half way to the Potomac, where they halted for rest near Shepherdstown Ford, still under instructions to cross the Potomac (for as yet Lee had not come to the determination to give battle at Sharpsburg). With the trains came S. D. Lee with his battalion of six batteries. Colonel Lee had been unable to reach Keedysville from Beaver Creek by the road through Boonsboro and was obliged to go across fields and on by-roads to reach the main road, about midway between Boonsboro and Keedysville, which was found crowded with infantry, artillery, and wagons making their confused way to the rear. It was with difficulty he gained a place in the road. This done, he proceeded on his way to Keedysville. Here he was ordered to push on to Sharpsburg. He crossed the Antietam at 8:00 a.m. and, under Longstreet's orders, went into position with five batteries on the ridge north of the Boonsboro Pike, on D. H. Hill's line facing the Antietam. The left of his line was near Rodes's Brigade and the right extended toward the Boonsboro Pike, occupying positions most favorable for artillery. John L. Eubank's (Virginia) Battery was detached from the battalion and reported to Toombs, who about this time was moving to his position to cover the Rohrbach Bridge (now known as the Burnside Bridge).[8]

Longstreet did not follow D. H. Hill closely. It was necessary to give time for the wagon train and other impedimenta to get on the road, and this delayed Longstreet's withdrawal until midnight and later. Drayton's Brigade, on the Old Sharpsburg Road near the foot of Fox's Gap, marched in lanes and on by-roads and across fields to Boonsboro; Kemper's and Garnett's Brigades, leaving Jenkins's to retire last, took the National Road down the mountain and then marched by the Boonsboro Turnpike to Keedysville. G. T. Anderson's Brigade, being ordered to report to Hood for rear-guard, was left near Fox's Gap. The retreat was not effected without much disorder and some demoralization, and the number of stragglers was very large—particularly in Longstreet's command, which had made a severe march from Hagerstown, been needlessly moved about the field, some of it very roughly handled by the enemy, and all of it much jaded.

Hood had under his command, for rear-guard, the two brigades of his own division and the brigades of Evans and G. T. Anderson. Evans's men descended the mountain by the National Road to Boonsboro, then followed the main army to Keedysville. Hood's two brigades and G. T. Anderson's withdrew from Fox's Gap about 1:00 a.m. on the fifteenth and by roads and farm lanes reached the road to Keedysville a mile southwest of Boonsboro and halted until after daylight, when the march was resumed. The roads were filled with stragglers and broken-down and belated wagons, which made the march slow and tedious. Colonel Walker (commanding Jenkins's Brigade), who had been ordered by D. R. Jones to cover the withdrawal of the troops from the vicinity of the Mountain House, remained until 4:00 a.m. on the fifteenth, when he descended the mountain, passed through Fitzhugh Lee's cavalry brigade, and followed the route taken by the army.

When Robert E. Lee withdrew from Turner's Gap, it was with the intention of halting his entire army at Keedysville for the purpose of assisting McLaws out of Pleasant Valley and forming a junction with him at Keedysville or at Sharpsburg, and this he had in view when, just as he was leaving his headquarters, he dispatched McLaws at 11:15 p.m. that the army would take position at Keedysville "with a view of preventing the enemy that may enter the gap at Boonsborough turnpike from cutting you off, and enabling you to make a junction with it." Soon after this dispatch was written, Lee started from his headquarters at the foot of South Mountain. He had been disabled by a fall on the field of Second Manassas and was unable to use his bridle arm, so he rode in an ambulance, officers of his staff riding in front, guiding him through the troops, artillery, and trains that were moving toward the Potomac. He arrived at Keedysville about an hour before daybreak. Not hearing from McLaws, and doubtful if the dispatches already sent had reached him, Lee immediately sent another dispatch: "We

---

[7] Robert E. Rodes to James W. Ratchford, October 13, 1862, reprinted in *OR*, vol. 19, pt. 1, 1036.

[8] Here, at its first mention in the text, is one of the few times Carman refers to the span by its period name: the Rohrbach Bridge. In nearly all other references to the span in his original manuscript, Carman designates this structure as the "Burnside Bridge." Although the latter name had entered common parlance by the time of Carman's writing, the editor finds its use anachronistic—especially when describing events prior to the Ninth Corps' assault upon the span. Accordingly (and after much reflection), its period name has been substituted throughout the manuscript in all but a few instances.

have fallen back to this place [Keedysville] to enable you more readily to join us. You are desired to withdraw immediately from your position on Maryland Heights, and join us here. If you can't get off any other way, you must cross the mountain. The utmost dispatch is required. Should you be able to cross over to Harper's Ferry, do so and report immediately."[9]

After this dispatch had been sent, Lee heard from Munford that McLaws could not come up the valley and that the difficulties in getting over Elk Ridge and Maryland Heights were very great. Upon the receipt of this communication, Lee determined not to make a stand at Keedysville, and there were sound reasons for his conclusion. First, as McLaws could not come up the valley (thus exposing his flank to Franklin), the position at Sharpsburg was as good a one to help McLaws over the mountain (or through it, by Weverton Pass) as was that at Keedysville. Second, it was a better defensive one against McClellan's large army. Later, Lee was confirmed in his conclusion by additional information from Munford, upon which he ordered that officer to hold his position near Rohrersville until morning and then follow the army beyond the Antietam. (Prior to Munford's news, Lee had heard nothing from McLaws. Hoping to hear from him, and hoping too that by some means McLaws would be able to elude Franklin and join him at Keedysville, Lee had remained there, while Longstreet was closing up, until eight o'clock in the morning.)

There can be no question that when the sun rose that morning, it was an anxious hour for Lee. He had not heard from either McLaws or Jackson and was in profound ignorance of how they were progressing and when and by what route they could join him. It was understood that, Harper's Ferry being reduced, both were to come up Pleasant Valley and join him at Hagerstown. Circumstances had changed all this. Lee was reasonably sure that some time during the day he would hear from Jackson, who would come to his relief by the Virginia side of the Potomac in response to his urgent dispatch of the night before, but of McLaws nothing was assured.

While resting here in a meadow by the roadside on the high ground nearly a mile west of the village, near where McClellan afterwards had his headquarters, a farmer's kindly wife sent Lee a pot of hot coffee. A few minutes later, a courier rode up with this belated dispatch from Jackson, dated 8:15 p.m. of the fourteenth: "Through God's blessing, the advance, which commenced this evening, has been successful thus far, and I look to Him for complete success to-morrow. The advance has been directed to be resumed at dawn to-morrow morning. I am thankful that our loss has been small. Your dispatch respecting the movements of the enemy and the importance of concentration has been received."[10] Both the coffee and the dispatch had an invigorating effect upon Lee. He looked southward, where, fourteen miles away, he could see Maryland and Loudoun Heights sloping west and east down to the Potomac, but he could not hear the sound of Jackson's guns. Then, turning to the east, he saw, by the aid of his glass, the head of the Union column coming down the slope of South Mountain. To the west, beyond the Antietam, he saw D. H. Hill's Division going into position and the wagon train moving over Cemetery Hill and down into Sharpsburg. When the train had passed, Lee, leaving Longstreet to bring up his command, was assisted into his ambulance and driven across the Antietam, where Hill was forming his command. He stopped on Cemetery Hill, examined the ground, and gave general directions for the formation of the line and the placing of the artillery. Longstreet followed Lee, crossed the Antietam about 9:30 a.m., and joined his chief on Cemetery Hill.

Jones's Division, the advance of Longstreet's command, crossed the Antietam at 10:00 a.m., and as the brigades arrived on the field they were put into position under Longstreet's direction on the south side of the Boonsboro and Sharpsburg Turnpike, on the high ground just east and southeast of Sharpsburg. This high ground or ridge, rising 185 feet above the Antietam and running nearly north and south, is very commanding. South of the turnpike and very near the highest point of the ridge is an old burying ground or cemetery, in which stood, but a few feet from the turnpike, a modest log-built house of worship, the Lutheran church. (We shall call the ridge south of the turnpike Cemetery Hill and the ridge running north from the turnpike, on which there is now a citizen's cemetery, Cemetery Ridge.[11])

At first Jones's Division (except Toombs's Brigade) was formed in double line on Cemetery Hill facing east and southeast, Kemper's, Jenkins's, and Drayton's Brigades in first line, Garnett's in second line. (G. T. Anderson's Brigade, being with Hood as rear-guard, had not yet arrived.) Toombs's Brigade—reduced to only the 2d and 20th Georgia by previous detachments—was ordered to occupy the most eligible position that could be found on the Antietam near the Rohrbach Bridge to prevent the enemy from crossing it and to hold it for the passage of McLaws, should he cross Elk Ridge near Solomon's Gap and approach Sharpsburg by the roads coming from the east and south. From this position Toombs was ordered to fall back, when it should become necessary, by his right flank, and hold a hill about four hundred yards below the bridge and immediately on the Antietam as long as practicable, then fall back and take position to the right of Jones's Division, in the line of battle of the other brigades. With these orders, Toombs took place on the ground indicated, with the 20th Georgia

9 Armistead L. Long to McLaws, September 15, 1862, reprinted in *OR*, vol. 19, pt. 2, 609–10.
10 Thomas J. Jackson to Chilton, September 14, 1862, 8:15 p.m., reprinted in *OR*, vol. 19, pt. 1, 951.
11 At the close of the war, a national cemetery was laid out a short distance east of the old Lutheran church and cemetery, in which rest the remains of 4,742 Union dead. Just opposite the national cemetery, on the north side of the road, has been laid out a citizens' cemetery.—*EAC*

(Colonel John B. Cumming) and the 2d Georgia (Lieutenant Colonel William R. Holmes)—about four hundred muskets in total—under the immediate command of Colonel Henry L. Benning of the 17th Georgia, who had remained with the brigade. Eubank's Battery took position on the high ground in Toombs's rear and commanded the approaches to the bridge. The Wise (Virginia) Artillery (Captain James S. Brown's Battery) was put on the high ground south of the town and west of the road running from Sharpsburg to the Rohrbach Bridge.

Colonel James B. Walton's[12] Washington (Louisiana) Artillery Battalion of four batteries crossed the Antietam about 11:00 a.m. and took position on the line held by Longstreet on Cemetery Hill (on the south side of the Boonsboro Pike). The 1st Company (Captain Charles W. Squires's Battery) was on the left and close to the pike, the 3rd Company (Captain Merritt B. Miller's Battery) to the right of Squires. (The position occupied by these two batteries is now in the enclosure of the national cemetery, between the entrance gate and the state of the American soldier.) To the right of Miller, across a ravine (down which runs the road to the Rohrbach Bridge), the 2nd Company (Captain John B. Richardson's Battery) and the 4th Company (Captain Benjamin F. Eshleman's Battery) were placed in an apple orchard. Squires and Miller commanded the Middle Bridge over the Antietam, Richardson and Eshleman the Rohrbach Bridge and its approaches. As the batteries came up and took position, Longstreet said, "Put them all in, every gun you have, long range and short range,"[13] the object being to make as formidable a showing as possible and impress the enemy that they were going no further backward and were at bay.

Hood, having halted with the rear-guard of four brigades of infantry and four batteries of artillery near Boonsboro until after daybreak, crossed the Antietam a little after 11:00 a.m. and at noon took position on Cemetery Hill. G. T. Anderson's Brigade formed in rear of Squires's and Miller's Batteries, its left resting on the Boonsboro Road. Evans's Brigade formed on the north side of the Boonsboro Road, opposite Anderson's left. Captain Robert Boyce's (South Carolina) Battery of Evans's Brigade was held in reserve in a ravine on the right side of Anderson. Law's and Wofford's Brigades[14] of Hood's Division formed on D. R. Jones's right. Two of Hood's batteries also were on Cemetery Hill—Captain William K. Bachman's (South Carolina) Battery on the right of Miller's, with its guns pointing to the bridge by which the army had crossed the Antietam, and Captain James Reilly's (North Carolina) Battery facing the Rohrbach Bridge. Captain Hugh R. Garden's (South Carolina) Battery was held in reserve at the west foot of the hill, close to the road running from Boonsboro and Sharpsburg to the Rohrbach Bridge, prepared to resist the advance of the enemy by the road crossing the bridge.

Colonel Rosser, with the 5th Virginia Cavalry, and Captain Pelham, with two guns of his Virginia battery, were ordered to cover the withdrawal from Fox's Gap of South Mountain. At daybreak they moved down the Old Sharpsburg Road to the foot of the mountain, thence to Boonsboro, passing through the western outskirts of the town to the Boonsboro and Sharpsburg Pike just as Fitzhugh Lee entered the place by the National Road. Rosser pushed before him many stragglers and, as no cavalry pursued him, moved back leisurely, detaining the Union advance (Richardson's division) by causing it to deploy repeatedly and thus spend a good part of the time in covering only a few miles. On reaching Keedysville all the Confederate infantry had gone and the road was clear. He sent frequent written reports to Robert E. Lee as he fell back on the character of McClellan's advance, informed him of Fitzhugh Lee's misadventure (which we shall discuss shortly) and that he had been cut off, and without incident of note crossed the Antietam about noon, leaving a few skirmishers east of the stream. As his was the only cavalry command on the field, Rosser threw out detachments on both flanks of the army (south beyond the Rohrbach Bridge and north on the Hagerstown Pike, beyond the Dunkard church) and down the Smoketown Road in the direction of the upper crossings of the Antietam.

Colonel Munford, who was at Rohrersville and near the intersection of the Rohrersville and Old Sharpsburg roads with the 2d and 12th Virginia Cavalry, had been ordered by Robert E. Lee to hold his position until daylight. It was after sunrise when, menaced by Franklin, he started to withdraw. He marched by the Old Sharpsburg Road over the nose of Elk Ridge and through Porterstown to the Rohrbach Bridge, crossing which, he formed on Toombs's right and covered all the approaches to Sharpsburg from the east and south, his right being at Antietam Furnace, beyond the stone bridge at the mouth of the Antietam.

Cutts's Battalion of the reserve artillery and Bondurant's Battery of D. H. Hill's Division were actively engaged at Turner's Gap. They were relieved just before nightfall and sent to the train near Boonsboro to replenish ammunition and bivouac for the night. When evening came the train had gone, and they were without orders. Soon it was learned that the army had retreated and that Fitzhugh Lee was covering the retreat. He was found just at the time that some of Richardson's skirmishers were reported on the Boonsboro Road, west of the town, and he ordered the batteries to make their way to Sharpsburg

---

[12] In his original manuscript, Carman gives the name incorrectly as "John B. Walton."

[13] William Miller Owen, *In Camp and Battle with the Washington Artillery: A Narrative of Events during the Late Civil War, from Bull Run to Appomattox and Spanish Fort* (Boston: Ticknor and Co., 1885), 138.

[14] In his original manuscript, Carman refers to the latter unit as "Wofford's Brigade" in all but one or two instances (wherein it is styled "Hood's Brigade"). For narrative consistency, the editor has chosen to standardize the designation to the former usage throughout.

by the best practicable route and as speedily as possible. They took a settlement road running nearly parallel with the Boonsboro and Sharpsburg Pike and, after an exciting and rapid march, crossed the Antietam at a ford near Pry's Mill, traveling thence by the Williamsport Road to the Hagerstown Pike, down which they proceeded. Cutts's Battalion came to a halt near the Dunkard church. Bondurant's Battery went through Sharpsburg to the Grove farm, more than a mile beyond town, where it remained until the seventeenth.

By mid-noon all the Confederate infantry and artillery (except Cutts's Battalion and Bondurant's Battery), Rosser's 5th Virginia Cavalry, and Munford's cavalry were across the Antietam. Their retreat had been conducted without loss, except in stragglers. But Fitzhugh Lee, who covered the retreat from Turner's Gap, was not so fortunate.

After a week spent among the rich pastures and generous cornfields of Frederick County and the adjoining country, Fitzhugh Lee, then at New Market, received orders on September 11 to operate with his cavalry on the right and rear of McClellan's army and ascertain what his advance indicated. He moved at 11:00 a.m. and marched that day to Liberty, where he bivouacked for the night. On the twelfth he moved toward Frederick, hovered in the vicinity all day, and, marching all night, reached the foot of Catoctin Mountain at Shookstown early in the morning of the thirteenth. Here he remained until 2:00 p.m., when he moved north along the base of the mountain to the entrance to Hamburg Pass, which was reached at sunset. He bivouacked at dark partway up the pass. At dawn the march was resumed over the Catoctin and down its western slope to the beautiful valley below, through which the peaceful Catoctin Creek (bordered on either side with well-tilled farms) winds gracefully. After a march of several hours, the brigade halted near a large grist mill and rested under the shade of an apple orchard until 4:00 p.m., when the march was resumed over South Mountain to Boonsboro which was reached after nightfall. A halt was ordered to rest and feed horses. Here Fitzhugh Lee soon received an order to report to Robert E. Lee, who told him that he was about to withdraw his army from South Mountain and Boonsboro and directed him to move his brigade up as close as possible to the front and relieve by dismounted cavalry the infantry pickets, cover the retreat of the infantry from Turner's Gap, and resist and retard as much as possible the advance he anticipated McClellan would make in the morning. It was near midnight when Fitzhugh Lee marched out of Boonsboro on the National Road in the direction of Turner's Gap. The disaster to the Confederate arms was apparent as infantry (in detached parties of from ten to two hundred, apparently without organization), artillery, wagons, and ambulances were met in a confused retreat down the mountain. The brigade was halted about a mile and a half out of Boonsboro and remained in readiness for a charge until daylight of the fifteenth.

The nature of the ground was not favorable to the operations of cavalry, but formation was made to command the road down the mountain. A good position, on a swell of ground, was selected for the artillery (two guns of Pelham's Battery) and dismounted skirmishers were pushed well to the front. A mounted force of the 3d Virginia Cavalry (Lieutenant Colonel John T. Thornton) held the front and flanks, the 9th Virginia Cavalry (Colonel William H. F. "Rooney" Lee) was in column on the road a little in rear of the guns, and the 4th Virginia Cavalry (Colonel Williams C. Wickham), in the same formation, was in rear of the 9th nearer Boonsboro. A little before daybreak, Jenkins's Brigade filed down the road from the Mountain House—the last of the Confederate infantry—and there was nothing between Fitzhugh Lee and the advance of the Union army.

When the contest was closed by darkness on the fourteenth, McClellan had good reasons for believing that when morning came the Confederate army would not be seen in his front. Evidently the reasons, so apparent to others, did not so impress him (or orders would have been given for an immediate pursuit), but beyond orders to his corps commanders to press forward their pickets at early dawn he gave no instructions for an energetic, aggressive movement.

At dawn of the fifteenth, the skirmishers of Hartsuff's brigade of the First Corps, overlooking the Mountain House, went forward and discovered that the Confederates had fallen back towards Boonsboro, leaving their dead and badly wounded. Soon after Hartsuff's advance, Richardson's division of the Second Corps came up and was ordered to take the place of Hartsuff and give pursuit, leaving Hooker's First Corps to make coffee and draw sustenance, of which they had had none since leaving the Monocacy twenty-four hours before (save a cup of coffee at Catoctin Creek).

At night of the fourteenth, Richardson's division had been ordered to report to Hooker and did so, halting at Mount Tabor Church. At 9:00 p.m. Hooker was ordered to hold his position on Lee's flank, commanding the Mountain House, at all hazards and was advised that Richardson was placed under his orders. At the same hour, Sumner was advised of these orders and directed to notify Richardson to obey them. Hooker, knowing that there would be a fight or a foot race early in the morning, ordered Richardson to move at daybreak up the Old Hagerstown Road to support him in either case. And this, as far as we know, was the only order given on the night of the fourteenth to prepare for the work to be done early on the fifteenth.

Richardson moved promptly, as ordered, up the sometimes very steep and always rough and very rocky road from Mount Tabor Church to the Mountain House, seeing nothing of the Confederates except their dead and wounded. With Brigadier General Thomas F. Meagher's Brigade in the fore, the division passed Hartsuff's advance and descended the mountain towards Boonsboro. Fitzhugh Lee's officers say it was about sunrise when the head of Richardson's column descended from the gap and engaged the cavalry skirmishers, who were slowly driven back until the position held by Pelham's guns was uncovered. (The fire of the guns was withheld until the head of the Union column was within easy range, then shells exploded in it so rapidly as to cause it to halt.) Richardson now formed line of battle on either side of the road, extending beyond both of Fitzhugh's Lee's flanks, again advanced, and again halted.

In the march that morning, the 5th New Hampshire (Colonel Edward E. Cross) was rear-guard. This excellent regiment was now brought to the front, and Richardson ordered Cross to deploy it as skirmishers and cover the advance. Four companies were deployed on either side of the road and two marched in it. Before the steady advance and rattling fire of this line, the Confederate guns were retired, followed by their supports—the 4th Virginia Cavalry leading, the 9th Virginia Cavalry following, and the 3d Virginia Cavalry in the rear, nearest Richardson. The 4th and 9th continued on to Boonsboro and, passing beyond the center of the town, halted in the narrow street. As the 3d was retiring through the town, the ranks of Richardson's infantry suddenly opened and six companies of the 8th Illinois Cavalry, led by their brigade commander, Colonel John F. Farnsworth, dashed past at a gallop, charging down the road and into the street. The 3d, led by Fitzhugh Lee in person, met the charge and checked it handsomely, forcing the Illinois men back upon the infantry. (Pleasonton had bivouacked near Bolivar on the night of the fourteenth, and at daylight of the fifteenth he galloped to the front with the 8th Illinois Cavalry, 1st Massachusetts Cavalry, and 3d Indiana Cavalry, the 8th Illinois in front. Four companies of the Illinois regiment were ordered to take a road to the left, Farnsworth leading the six companies on the National Road, as we have stated, beyond Richardson's infantry.)

Farnsworth's check was but momentary. His men quickly faced about, made another charge, and the 3d Virginia Cavalry was driven pell-mell down the street, closely followed by the Illinois horsemen. The men of the 4th and 9th Virginia Cavalry had been so long in the saddle during the four days past that when they halted in the street they were permitted to dismount and for some time remained in this way, standing by their horses or sitting on the curbstones and holding the bridle reins. Suddenly the cry, "Mount! Mount!" resounded down the street and simultaneously a rapid fire of pistols and carbines was heard near at hand. "Rooney" Lee ordered the rear squadron of the 9th to face about, but before the order could be executed—even before the men could mount—the rear-guard 3d, retreating at full speed, dashed into the already confused column, and in an incredibly short time the street became packed with a mass of horses and horsemen so jammed together as to make motion impossible. Had the 4th promptly fallen back, there would have been some relief, but it did not do so. Very soon a pistol fire was opened upon the Virginians from the upper windows of some of the houses, and clouds of dust covered everything. The Illinois cavalry, quickly taking in the situation, dashed up boldly and discharged their carbines into the struggling and helpless mass of humanity and horse.

Meanwhile, the 4th Virginia Cavalry had gotten under way and thus opened an avenue for the 9th and 3d, upon which a general stampede ensued, the whole force—closely followed by the Illinois men, who were using their carbines—rushing from the town along the Hagerstown Road at the highest speed, many escaping through the fields. This disorderly movement was increased by the report that some of Richardson's infantry skirmishers were moving upon their flank and threatening to cut off their retreat. The fleeing men of the 9th had scarcely cleared the town when "Rooney" Lee tried to rally them, but his horse was killed and, in falling, severely injured his rider. Dirt-covered and bruised, he lay some time on the ground unable to move, ridden over by friend and foe, finally to escape through the fields and find shelter in a cornfield. Captain John Hughlett's horse fell in like manner at the edge of the town, and Hughlett, leaping the rail fence on the roadside, found concealment in a cornfield, from which he emerged after dark and rejoined his regiment the next day. In the middle of the turnpike were piles of broken stone, placed there for repairing the roadway. On these, amidst the impenetrable dust, many horses blindly rushed and, falling, piled with their riders one on another, crushing, mangling, and killing many. Here and there in the pell-mell race, blinded by the dust, horses and horsemen dashed against telegraph poles and fell to the ground, to be trampled by those behind.

When the open fields were reached, beyond the range of infantry, a considerable part of the 9th Virginia Cavalry was rallied by Lieutenant Colonel Richard L. T. Beale, who led a charge with the saber, when his horse was killed within a few paces of the Union cavalry line, deployed across the pike and the field on the Confederate left. Captain Thomas Haynes assumed command and, continuing the charge, forced back the Illinois men a short distance and brought out three or four prisoners. The charge was participated in by a squadron of the 4th Virginia Cavalry and cost it several killed and wounded. Among the latter was the sergeant major of the regiment.[15]

This gallant charge checked the ardor of the Illinois men and gave Fitzhugh Lee an opportunity to rally his command around the colors of the three regiments. This was about a mile and a half beyond town and near the intersection of a road

---

[15] In the preparation of the few preceding pages, free use was made of Richard L. T. Beale, *History of the 9th Virginia Cavalry in the War between the States* (Richmond: B. F. Johnson, 1899), 39–40 and G. W. B. [George Washington Beale], "Maryland Campaign," *Southern Historical Society Papers* 25 (1897): 276–80.—*EAC*

running to Keedysville. He then withdrew, followed by a few shells from a section of Captain John C. Tidball's regular battery, which Pleasonton had brought up. Finding that he was not pursued, Fitzhugh Lee turned to the left and, following by-roads, crossed the Antietam north of Keedysville and reached the left of Robert E. Lee's line (near the Dunkard church) that evening. Some of his men fell in with Cutts's Battalion and Bondurant's Battery on their march.

Pleasonton, in obedience to instructions, moved across country and came up with Richardson's division in line of battle beyond Keedysville. He reported a loss of one killed and fifteen wounded, "among the latter … the brave Captain [Elisha S.] Kelley, of the Eighth Illinois Cavalry, who was shot while gallantly charging at the head of his squadron." He also reported that he captured two guns and a very large number of prisoners, among whom were several hundred stragglers, and that Fitzhugh Lee left thirty dead on the field and some fifty wounded. He claimed that the Confederates outnumbered him two to one and that the number of personal encounters demonstrated the superiority of the Union cavalry. He commended Colonel Farnsworth; Major Medill, Captain Kelley, and Lieutenant Dennis J. Hynes of the 8th Illinois Cavalry; and Captain George A. Custer of McClellan's staff for conspicuous gallantry.[16]

The Confederate loss is not definitely known. That of the 9th Virginia Cavalry was two lieutenants and sixteen privates killed and mortally wounded and ten privates captured. Many of the killed and mortally wounded were trodden to death; several slightly wounded and bruised are not numbered. The 4th Virginia Cavalry had several killed and wounded, and there was some loss in the 3d Virginia Cavalry.

Richardson's division did not become engaged at Boonsboro. When Pleasonton's cavalry uncovered the road turning west to Keedysville (the Boonsboro and Sharpsburg Pike, on which it was learned the Confederate infantry had retreated), Richardson—without a cavalryman or gun in advance—followed the trail of the enemy. Fairly out of town, two companies of the 5th New Hampshire were deployed as skirmishers on either side of the road, Captain Charles H. Long commanding on the right and Captain John W. Bean on the left. Rosser's cavalry skirmishers were encountered and gradually forced back from one position after another and by 2:00 p.m. had all fallen back beyond the Antietam, closely followed by the New Hampshire men, who ascended the bluff bordering the east bank of the Antietam and skirmished with the enemy beyond. They were soon joined by the skirmishers of Meagher's brigade and a lively fusillade kept up, during which Richardson's entire division went into position on the north side of the Boonsboro Pike and at the east foot of the bluff bordering the Antietam.

Pleasonton soon came up, and as none of Richardson's artillery had arrived, he ordered Tidball's battery to reply to the enemy's (the guns of S. D. Lee), which had opened from four different points of their line. Tidball quickly ascended the bluff on the right of the road and opened fire. He was soon followed by the six guns of Captain Rufus D. Pettit's (New York) battery, and both engaged the Confederate artillery until nearly dark. Colonel Lee's engaged guns were two rifles of Captain William W. Parker's (Virginia) Battery, two of Captain Andrew B. Rhett's (South Carolina) Battery, and one of Captain Tyler C. Jordan's (Virginia) Battery. Colonel Lee reports that "they were exposed to a hot fire, several men slightly wounded and several horses disabled."[17]

On the night of the fourteenth, McClellan's headquarters were at Bolivar, two miles east of Turner's Gap. The next morning he gave Pleasonton an early start, but gave no other order until 8:00 a.m., when he ordered Burnside to advance upon Boonsboro by the Old Sharpsburg Road as far as the intersection of the Boonsboro and Rohrersville roads; place himself in communication with the troops advancing by the Boonsboro Pike (and also with Franklin, if he had reached Rohrersville); and lend assistance to either if required or else advance straight upon Keedysville and Sharpsburg to cut off the retreat of the enemy. After writing this, but before delivery, McClellan heard that Richardson had taken the advance from the Mountain House, and he added a postscript directing Burnside to keep the head of his column as near parallel as possible to Richardson's and to move promptly, keeping his skirmishers well to the front and flanks until he came to open ground.[18] An hour later McClellan advised Burnside that Fitz John Porter would follow on the same road to support him, and the commanding general desired to impress upon Burnside "the necessity for the utmost vigor" in the pursuit.[19] How Burnside obeyed these orders shall be shown later.

At 8:45 a.m. McClellan ordered Sumner to move with the Second Corps (Sedgwick's and French's divisions) and the Twelfth Corps from Bolivar, on the National Road, to Boonsboro, following Pleasonton and Richardson. He informed him that Burnside had been ordered to advance on his left. McClellan directed Sumner, should Boonsboro be abandoned, to take a strong position in the vicinity. Before sending this order, he heard from citizens and from Hooker that Lee was

[16] Alfred Pleasonton to Randolph B. Marcy, September 19, 1862, reprinted in *OR*, vol. 19, pt. 1, 210. In the passage wherein the officers are commended, Pleasonton refers to Medill as "Captain." At other points in the same report, his rank is given as "Major." Pleasonton's confusion likely stems from the fact that Medill's promotion had taken place less than two weeks previously. See Abner Hard, *History of the Eighth Illinois Cavalry Regiment, Illinois Volunteers, during the Great Rebellion* (Aurora, Ill: privately printed, 1868), 171, 331.

[17] Stephen D. Lee to Gilbert Moxley Sorrel, October 11, 1862, reprinted in *OR*, vol. 19, pt. 1, 844.

[18] George D. Ruggles to Ambrose Burnside, September 15, 1862, 8:00 a.m., reprinted in *OR*, vol. 51, pt. 1, 836–37.

[19] Ruggles to Burnside, September 15, 1862, 9:00 a.m., reprinted in *OR*, vol. 51, pt. 1, 837.

making a demoralized retreat for the Potomac, whereupon he gave additional orders that, should such be the case, Sumner was to pursue the enemy as rapidly as possible.[20] Hooker was ordered to get rations from his train and, if Sumner was closed up when he reached Turner's Gap, to allow him to pass. Hooker would then follow Sumner.[21]

Sumner and Hooker moved as ordered, the advance of the column reaching Keedysville about 3:00 p.m. Instead of massing the brigades and divisions on either side of the road as they came up, the entire column was halted in the road and remained there. Consequently, the road was congested for miles back. Some of the troops did not get up until midnight, some not until next morning. The Twelfth Corps, starting from Bolivar late in the forenoon, after marching through Boonsboro and a short distance beyond, turned into the fields and bivouacked at Nicodemus's Mill, nearly two miles southeast of Keedysville, on the Old Sharpsburg Road.

Hearing that the Confederates had made a stand beyond Keedysville, Hooker rode forward and found Richardson and Pleasonton at the front, with Tidball's and Pettit's guns replying to those of the Confederates beyond the Antietam. He saw the Confederate infantry ostentatiously deployed, with many batteries posted to resist the passage over the bridge crossing the Antietam, and estimated that thirty thousand men were then deployed and that his own command was too weak in numbers and morale to attack them. Meanwhile, Major David C. Houston of the engineers had gone up the stream in search of bridges and fords by which a crossing could be made. He found a practicable bridge and two fords, which with a little labor were made practicable for infantry, but it was now five o'clock, the infantry column had not closed up, and Hooker decided that he could not cross. In this opinion Sumner concurred.

Leaving the column strung along the road at 5:30 p.m., at a halt, awaiting orders, we turn to the movements of Burnside and Fitz John Porter. McClellan's early orders to Burnside to pursue with the "utmost vigor" have been noted. On the night of the fourteenth, Porter was at Middletown with Sykes's division and the reserve artillery; Morell's division was at Frederick. Sykes was ordered to march at daybreak and Morell at 3:00 a.m. of the fifteenth.[22] Porter, with Sykes's division and the artillery, moved from Middletown about 9:00 a.m., then passed through Bolivar and up the Old Sharpsburg Road to Fox's Gap, where he arrived about noon. To his great surprise, he found that Burnside—whom he had been ordered to follow—had not yet moved, nor displayed any intention of so doing. McClellan now rode up, and Porter reported the condition of affairs and asked for orders to pass Burnside and take the advance. McClellan gave the orders at 12:30 p.m.[23] Burnside was ordered to follow Porter as closely as possible and give the reason for delay in not marching under the orders of the morning.[24] So far the official records indicate; McClellan, in his *Own Story*, says:

> Early in the morning I had directed Burnside to put his corps in motion upon the old Sharpsburg road, but to wait with me for a time until more detailed news came from Franklin. About eight o'clock he begged me to let him go, saying that his corps had been some time in motion, and that if he delayed longer he would have difficulty in overtaking it; so I let him go. At about midday I rode to the point where Reno was killed the day before, and found that Burnside's troops, the 9th corps, had not stirred from its bivouac, and still blocked the road for the regular division. I sent for Burnside for an explanation, but he could not be found. He subsequently gave as an excuse the fatigued and hungry condition of his men.[25]

---

[20] Ruggles to Edwin V. Sumner, September 15, 1862, 8:45 a.m., reprinted in *OR*, vol. 51, pt. 1, 834–35.

[21] Marcy to Joseph Hooker, September 15, 1862, 9:30 a.m., reprinted in *OR*, vol. 51, pt. 1, 834.

[22] Ruggles to Fitz John Porter, September 14, 1862, 9:30 p.m., reprinted in *OR*, vol. 51, pt. 1, 832. A separate message was sent directly to Morell a half-hour later. Ruggles to George W. Morell, September 14, 1862, 10:00 p.m., reprinted in *OR*, vol. 51, pt. 1, 832.

[23] A footnote by Carman at this point consists of the text of the following order, as reprinted in *OR*, vol. 19, pt. 2, 296:

Headquarters Army Of The Potomac
September 15, 1862—12.30 p.m.

Major-General Porter:

General: General McClellan desires me to say that Burnside's corps has not yet marched. Should the march of Sykes' division be obstructed by Burnside's troops, direct General Sykes to push by them and to put his division in front.

I am, general, very respectfully, your obedient servant,

R. B. Marcy,
Chief of Staff

[Endorsement]

Burnside's corps was not moving three hours after the hour designated for him, the day after South Mountain, and obstructed my movements. I, therefore, asked for this order, and moved by Burnside's corps.

F. J. P. [Fitz John Porter]

[24] Ruggles to Burnside, September 15, 1862, 12:30 p.m., reprinted in *OR*, vol. 51, pt. 1, 837.

[25] George B. McClellan, *McClellan's Own Story: The War for the Union, the Soldiers Who Fought It, the Civilians Who Directed It, and His Relations to It and to Them* (New York: Charles L. Webster & Co., 1887), 586.

It appears that part of the corps had marched without rations on the preceding day and during the night had sent back for them. Burnside took the responsibility of allowing the corps to wait until these supplies came up and the men could be fed before marching again. Meanwhile, orders were given to bury the dead and send the wounded and prisoners to Middletown. Thus it was nearly noon when Cox (who was in immediate command of the corps) got his orders to march, and then Porter had come up. Porter filed past Burnside and, taking the Old Sharpsburg Road, at 5:30 p.m. reached Porterstown and the intersection of the turnpike from Boonsboro to Sharpsburg. He found Richardson in position and formed Sykes's division on his left, at the base of the bluff bordering the Antietam. Skirmishers were sent to the left, also to the top of the bluff, and the 3d U.S. Infantry (Captain John D. Wilkins) was advanced and deployed on either side of the Boonsboro Pike, near the Antietam, to guard the stone bridge, which it was apprehended the enemy might attempt to destroy. The reserve artillery (having been cut off by Burnside's corps) arrived later and was massed in rear of the right of Sykes's division.

The Ninth Corps, following Porter's infantry, marched down the mountain and was soon overtaken by the orders to move on Rohrersville, connect with Franklin, and attack and defeat McLaws (or, if Franklin could hold his own against McLaws, then to move on and join in the attack on Sharpsburg). Under these orders Burnside halted near the junction of the Rohrersville and Old Sharpsburg roads. Here he heard that McLaws was leaving Franklin's front; at 4:30 p.m. Burnside was ordered to resume his march to Sharpsburg. He passed through Springvale and over the nose of Elk Ridge, his head of column halting at sunset close to the hills on the southeast side of Antietam Valley and on the left of the Old Sharpsburg Road, in rear of the left of Sykes's division.

Richardson, delayed in his advance by Rosser's cavalry, arrived in front in reasonably good time. Pleasonton, after a severe affair, promptly followed Richardson. Porter, marching from Middletown and delayed by Burnside, made a good day's work. These three officers escape criticism. Sumner and Hooker were very remiss in halting their commands on the road instead of massing them as they came up—thus delaying the arrival of the center of the column until long after dark, the rear until next morning, and the trains until late in the day.

McClellan says, "It had been hoped to engage the enemy during the 15th. Accordingly, instructions were given that if the enemy were overtaken on the march, they should be attacked at once; if found in heavy force and in position, the corps in advance should be placed in position for attack, and await my arrival."[26] Where was McClellan during the advance of his divisions to the Antietam and when his columns arrived there and awaited orders? In the morning he was at Bolivar, where in addition to the orders issued to his corps commanders he dispatched Halleck at 8:00 a.m. that he had just learned from Hooker that Lee was "making for Shepherdstown in a perfect panic" and that he (McClellan) was hurrying everything forward to press Lee's retreat to the utmost.[27] In another dispatch of the same hour, he reported Franklin's success at Crampton's Gap as complete as that at Turner's Gap and that "the *morale* of our men is now restored."[28] At 9:00 a.m. he sent a dispatch to General Banks, whom he had left in command of the defenses of Washington, that under the present circumstances it would be well to move the greater part of his command to the south side of the Potomac, as he did not consider that any danger to Washington was to be feared from the north side of the river.[29] At 9:30 a.m. he sent a second telegram to his wife that he had won a glorious victory,[30] and a half-hour later he sent a second dispatch to Halleck confirming the reports of the rout and demoralization of Lee's army and giving some further details.[31] At Bolivar he heard that Miles had probably surrendered and awaited news from Franklin. He left Bolivar about noon and rode to Fox's Gap, saw where Reno had been killed, ordered Porter to pass Burnside, rode over to Turner's Gap, passed over Hooker's battlefield of the previous day, and talked to the wounded.[32] From Turner's Gap he rode on to Boonsboro and telegraphed General Scott at West Point of the battle of the fourteenth and that he was pursuing Lee closely, taking many prisoners.[33] Here he received a report

[26] McClellan to Lorenzo Thomas, August 4, 1863, reprinted in *OR*, vol. 19, pt. 1, 53.

[27] McClellan to Henry W. Halleck, September 15, 1862, 8:00 a.m., reprinted in *OR*, vol. 19, pt. 2, 294 (first message).

[28] McClellan to Halleck, September 15, 1862, 8:00 a.m., reprinted in *OR*, vol. 19, pt. 2, 294 (second message).

[29] McClellan to Nathaniel P. Banks, September 15, 1862, 9:00 a.m., reprinted in *OR*, vol. 19, pt. 2, 294.

[30] McClellan to Mary Ellen McClellan, September 15, 1862, 9:30 a.m., reprinted in McClellan, *Own Story*, 612.

[31] McClellan to Halleck, September 15, 1862, 10:00 a.m., reprinted in *OR*, vol. 19, pt. 2, 294–95.

[32] "More than one will remember the morning after the battle of South Mountain …, when head-quarters of the army moved westward over the mountain by the turnpike road through Turner's Gap to Boonesboro' and Keedysville. As the cavalcade was riding rapidly up the eastern approach to Turner's Gap they came to a two-story farm-house on the right of the road, which had been occupied as a hospital, and some wounded men were lying outside on the grass because the house was entirely taken up by the surgeons with the more serious cases. In front of this house McClellan suddenly halted, dismounted, and accompanied by General Marcy walked among the men lying on the grass outside, taking the hands of many and telling them how valuable and timely a victory their bravery had won, and that he thanked them in the name of their country. He then went into the house and remained some minutes, and when he reappeared and passed rapidly to the road, though his face was unmoved, tears were trickling down his cheeks, and as he came to his horse he dashed them away with his hand, mounted hastily and rode on." William F. Biddle, "Recollections of McClellan," *United Service* 9, no. 5 (May 1894): 462.—EAC

[33] McClellan to Winfield Scott, September 15, 1862, reprinted in *OR*, vol. 19, pt. 2, 295.

from the signal station near the Washington monument on South Mountain that the forces of the enemy were visible near Sharpsburg, forming line of battle beyond the Antietam. At 4:30 p.m. he was yet at Boonsboro, sending messages and orders to Franklin, in Pleasant Valley, to hold his own without attacking McLaws and to Burnside, on the Old Sharpsburg Road, to move at once on Sharpsburg and that he would be at the front to meet him. It was quite five o'clock when he mounted his horse and rode out of Boonsboro on the road to Sharpsburg. When he overtook the rear of the column (either at a halt or laboriously creeping to the front) and his presence became known, the wearied men parted a way for him, threw up their caps, and cheered and yelled until their throats were sore. An eyewitness, a gallant officer of the 20th Massachusetts, thus writes of what took place near the head of the column:

> On the afternoon of the hot fifteenth of September, while the long columns of the Federal army were resting along the Boonsboro' road, General McClellan passed through them to the front, and had from them such a magnificent reception as was worth living for. Far from the rear the cheers were heard, faintly at first, and gradually the sound increased and grew to a roar as he approached. The weary men sprang to their feet and cheered and cheered, and as he went the cheers went before him and with him and after him, till the sound receding with the distance at last died away.[34]

When McClellan emerged from this tumult of enthusiasm, he was at the foot of a hill nearly a mile beyond Keedysville, on which, subsequently, he had his headquarters. Here he was met by Sumner and others and ascended the hill. This he reports as the condition of affairs:

> I found but two divisions, Richardson's and Sykes', in position. The other troops were halted in the road, the head of the column some distance in rear of Richardson. The enemy occupied a strong position on the heights on the west side of Antietam Creek, displaying a large force of infantry and cavalry, with numerous batteries of artillery, which opened on our columns as they appeared in sight on the Keedysville road and Sharpsburg turnpike …
>
> … After a rapid examination of the position, I found that it was too late to attack that day, and at once directed the placing of the batteries in position in the center, and indicated the bivouacs for the different corps, massing them near and on both sides of the Sharpsburg turnpike. The corps were not all in their positions until the next morning after sunrise.[35]

In his *Own Story*, McClellan says, "Near Keedysville I met Sumner, who told me that the enemy were in position in strong force, and took me to a height in front of Keedysville whence a view of the position could be obtained. We were accompanied by a numerous staff and escort; but no sooner had we shown ourselves on the hill than the enemy opened upon us with rifled guns, and, as his firing was very good, the hill was soon cleared of all save Fitz-John Porter and myself."[36]

The natural inference from this plain statement that "the hill was soon cleared of all save Fitz-John Porter" and McClellan himself is that *they* only braved the fire and that the rest—Hooker, Sumner, Burnside, and Cox (for all were there)—sought safety elsewhere. The fact is that McClellan directed that all but Porter should retire behind the ridge, while he and Porter continued the examination of Lee's position. The discarded officers did not hear what passed between McClellan and Porter, but one, at least, came to the quick conclusion that there would be no aggressive action that night or next day should McClellan listen to the advice of Fitz John Porter.[37] Others looked upon the notorious partiality of McClellan for Porter as disrespectful to them and as bad for McClellan and the Union cause, for however brilliant Porter's services on the Peninsula had been, there was a strong feeling that he had acted badly toward General Pope. He was known to be intensely hostile to the administration, and by many his loyalty was distrusted.

Late in the evening, McClellan was considering the advisability of sending a large force of Pleasonton's cavalry with artillery to Jones's Cross-Roads (the intersection of the Keedysville and Williamsport Road with the Hagerstown and Sharpsburg Turnpike), four miles north of Sharpsburg, but finally concluded not to send them so far off. Instead he ordered Benjamin F. Davis (who had escaped from Harper's Ferry) to return from Greencastle to that point and unite with about three hundred Pennsylvania cavalry under Colonel William J. Palmer, which had marched through Hagerstown during the day and awaited orders at the cross-roads. Governor Curtin was requested to send all the troops he could spare from the Cumberland Valley to the same place.

The First Corps marched to the right, crossed the Little Antietam by a stone bridge, and bivouacked, under McClellan's direction, in the forks of the Big and Little Antietam. The divisions of French and Sedgwick,[38] of the Second Corps, went

[34] Francis Winthrop Palfrey, *The Antietam and Fredericksburg*, vol. 5 of *The Army in the Civil War* (New York: Charles Scribner's Sons, 1882), 56.

[35] McClellan to Thomas, 53–54.

[36] McClellan, *Own Story*, 586.

[37] General Hooker, who made this statement to the writer.—*EAC*

[38] In a slip of the pen, Carman's original manuscript reads, "The divisions of French and *Richardson*, of the Second Corps, went into position … in rear of *Richardson* [emphasis added]."

into position after dark in rear of Richardson and on either side of the Boonsboro Turnpike, Sedgwick on the right and French on the left. The Twelfth Corps remained at Nicodemus's Mill until the next day. Burnside was directed to move still further to the left, and McClellan sought headquarters at Keedysville with the satisfactory belief that he had "delivered Pennsylvania and Maryland."[39]

We sum up the operations of the day: Harper's Ferry was surrendered early in the morning, Franklin lay inactive in Pleasant Valley while McLaws quietly withdrew from his front, and McClellan moved the main body of his army from the east side of Turner's Gap to the banks of the Antietam.

In his *Antietam and Fredericksburg*, Palfrey says:

> The fact of the surrender [of Harper's Ferry], and the hour at which it took place, were speedily made known to McClellan. It was reasonably certain that the troops assigned by Lee's special order No. 191 to the duty of capturing the garrison at Harper's Ferry, were then around that place, and most of them far from Lee, and all of them separated from him either by distance and the Potomac, or by Union troops, or both. Whatever his estimate may have been of the amount of the force so employed, he knew that it comprised all or part of Jackson's command, and the divisions of McLaws, R. H. Anderson, and Walker. If he looked for no aggressive action on the part of Franklin and Couch, he could at least look to them to hold in check and neutralize the forces of McLaws and R. H. Anderson, and this left him free to use his First, Second, Ninth, and Twelfth Corps, with all of the Fifth Corps that was with him, and Pleasonton's cavalry command, against Longstreet and D. H. Hill. In other words, in fine country and in fine weather, he had thirty-five brigades of infantry to use against Longstreet's nine brigades and D. H. Hill's five brigades. Pleasonton's cavalry and the reserve artillery were probably as numerous as Stuart's and Rosser's cavalry and their artillery. We assume this, in the absence of figures … Here again was a great opportunity. With a long day before him, a force that outnumbered his opponent as five to two, and probably as six to two, and the knowledge that the large detachments his opponent had made could not join him for twenty-four hours, and might not join him for forty-eight or more, it was a time for rapid action. It would seem that he ought to have pressed his troops forward unrestingly till they reached cannon-shot distance from the enemy, and made his reconnoissances [*sic*] as his columns were advancing. He would speedily have learned the length of the enemy's line, and as the distance from the summit of Turner's Gap to Sharpsburg is only seven or eight miles, it is not easy to see why he might not have attacked in force early in the afternoon. He had every reason for believing that delay would strengthen the enemy much more proportionally than it would strengthen him, and he might be sure that delay would be at least as serviceable to the enemy as to him in acquiring knowledge of the ground, and much more so in putting that knowledge to account. But it was not to be. With all his amiable and estimable and admirable qualities, there was something wanting in McClellan. If he had used the priceless hours of the 15th September, and the still precious, though less precious hours of the 16th as he might have, his name would have stood high in the roll of great commanders; but he let those hours go by.[40]

In his admirable *History of the Second Army Corps*, Francis A. Walker commends Palfrey's views. He shows that not one of Lee's detached divisions could, by the most strenuous exertion, be brought up through the long, roundabout way which was open to them to support Lee on the Antietam before the morning of the sixteenth, while a portion could not be expected before the seventeenth. In this situation the most strenuous exertions should have been made to carry the four corps (First, Second, Ninth, and Twelfth) and Sykes's division, constituting the right and center, clean and fast across the space (not more than seven miles, as the line of march was) that intervened between the base of South Mountain and the banks of the Antietam. The staff should have been out upon the road all day, full of life and all alert to prevent delays, to keep the columns moving, to crowd the troops forward, and to bend everything to the encounter. Instead of all this, the army moved uncertainly and slowly for lack of the inspiration and direction which general headquarters should always supply.[41]

There was one cause of the delay in getting to the front and the want of action when the leading divisions arrived there that must now be noted, and that was the suspension of the order by which Burnside commanded the right wing of the army, composed of the First and Ninth Corps. It will be remembered that before McClellan left Washington it was arranged with Halleck that Burnside and Sumner were to command wings of at least two corps each, and this was done at the suggestion of Lincoln. The arrangement was observed from the beginning of the campaign and worked well, but the formal orders were not published until September 14:

---

[39] McClellan to Mary Ellen McClellan, September 16, 1862, 7:00 a.m., reprinted in McClellan, *Own Story*, 612.

[40] Palfrey, 46–47.

[41] Francis A. Walker, *History of the Second Army Corps in the Army of the Potomac* (New York: Charles Scribner's Sons, 1887), 96–97.

Special Orders,   Headquarters Army of the Potomac
No. —.   In the Field, September 14, 1862

Maj. Gen. A. E. Burnside is assigned to the command of the right wing of this army, which will be composed of his own and Hooker's corps.

The Second Corps (Banks'), late Army of Virginia [i.e., the Twelfth Corps], is placed, until further orders, under the command of Maj. Gen. E. V. Sumner, commanding Second Corps, Army of the Potomac.

By command of Major-General McClellan:

S[eth] Williams,
Assistant Adjutant-General[42]

Before the advance was resumed on the morning of the fifteenth, these orders were suspended by the following:

Special Orders,   Headquarters Army of the Potomac
No. —.   In the Field, September 15, 1862

I. The operation of the Special Orders of yesterday's date, assigning General Burnside to the command of the right wing, owing to the necessary separation of the Third [First] Corps, is temporarily suspended. General Hooker will report direct to these headquarters.

II. Brig. Gen. J[oseph] K. F. Mansfield is temporarily assigned to the command of Banks' corps.

By command of Major-General McClellan:

S. Williams,
Assistant Adjutant-General[43]

It is claimed that the detachment of the First Corps was at Hooker's request. This may be true; it is altogether probable, for Hooker was prone to ask such things, but this was no sufficient reason for such action as thwarted the intention of Halleck and the administration (that Burnside should have command of the two corps), nor was there any military necessity for the separation. The First and Ninth Corps acted practically as a unit on the march and at South Mountain; they were in their proper positions as the right of the army, and it was easy to continue the advance keeping Burnside's right wing intact (and the same as to Sumner's). But by this order, Sumner's and Hooker's corps became entangled on the road to Sharpsburg. In fact the framework of the army became disjointed, and its divisions reached the Antietam much later than they should have and in no relation to each other for quick cooperation, had such been needed.

Burnside was at McClellan's headquarters when the orders were issued and protested against them, but the protest was of no avail. There were influences at work too powerful for him to overcome, and, grieved at the turn of affairs, he asked McClellan's permission to go forward and join his corps, which had been ordered to move. There are good reasons for believing that the motive in detaching Hooker and thus reducing Burnside's command was purely personal and that it was influenced by Porter.

Of all his corps commanders, Fitz John Porter stood highest in McClellan's estimation, and his partiality for Porter was common talk.[44] He had been appointed a brigadier general of volunteers at McClellan's request and was favored by him to the exclusion of others. At the siege of Yorktown in April 1862, he was designated as the director of the siege although McClellan had with him the best engineering talent of the army, and he was consulted and his advice taken on every important step, though junior to many others in years, length of service, and rank. Naturally, this was offensive to his seniors and discourteous to them, and it resulted in much bad feeling. That he was the confidential advisor of McClellan was well known in Washington, and Lincoln warned McClellan of the mischief likely to ensue when, in May, he authorized McClellan to form two "provisional corps," one to be commanded by Porter.

On the eighth of March, the president ordered the organization of five army corps and designated the senior division generals to command them. These were McDowell, Sumner, Heintzelman, Banks, and Brigadier General Erasmus D. Keyes. McClellan made an earnest protest, arguing that it was his intention to postpone the formation of army corps until service in the field had indicated the general officers best fitted to exercise those most important commands. McDowell's and Banks's corps were detached from McClellan's immediate command, and he renewed his objection to the formation of

---

[42] Special Order of September 14, 1862, reprinted in *OR*, vol. 19, pt. 2, 290.

[43] Special Order of September 15, 1862, reprinted in *OR*, vol. 19, pt. 2, 297.

[44] "Take him [Porter] for all in all, he was probably the best general officer I had under me." McClellan, *Own Story*, 139.—*EAC*

the corps of Sumner, Heintzelman, and Keyes. He proposed the formation of two provisional corps, the troops to be taken from the corps then organized. Lincoln yielded to his importunities, but in doing so gave McClellan a piece of his mind:

> I now think it indispensable for you to know how your struggle against it is received in quarters which we cannot entirely disregard. It is looked upon as merely an effort to pamper one or two pets, and to persecute and degrade their supposed rivals. I have had no word from Sumner, Heintzelman, or Keyes. The commanders of these Corps are of course the three highest officers with you, but I am constantly told that you consult and communicate with nobody but General Fitz John Porter, and perhaps General Franklin. I do not say these complaints are true or just; but at all events it is proper you should know of their existence. Do the Commanders of Corps disobey your orders in any thing?
>
> … Are you strong enough—are you strong enough, even with my help—to set your foot upon the necks of Sumner, Heintzelman, and Keyes all at once? This is a practical and very serious question for you.
>
> The success of your army and the cause of the country are the same; and of course I only desire the good of the cause.[45]

The warning was lost upon McClellan, who still continued to maintain closer relations to Porter than to any other officer in the army. That an officer who stood in such close relations to his chief as did Porter to McClellan should have much influence over him is very natural, and this influence was now used to humble and if possible injure Burnside for an act that unintentionally was threatening to injure Porter.

The circumstances are these: when the Army of the Potomac was withdrawn from the Peninsula, both Burnside and Porter were landed at Falmouth, on the Rappahannock River, Porter being pushed forward to join Pope while Burnside remained at Falmouth. Pope by this time had been cut off from communication with Washington, and all that could be heard from him was through Burnside, to whom Porter reported Pope's movements and those of the enemy, as far as they could be ascertained. In these dispatches of Porter, running from August 25 to 30, there was much matter of an indiscreet character—sneers at the strategy of the campaign, a great lack of confidence in its management, and expressions of a desire to get ordered out of Pope's command.[46] As the president and Halleck were very anxious for news, Burnside sent copies of these dispatches. It was all that he had to send, not supposing that they would do Porter any harm but might do the service some good.[47] In fact, in the most objectionable dispatch, Porter said, "Most of this is private … Make what use of this you choose, so it does good."[48] So, without editing the dispatches, copies of them were forwarded to the president, Halleck, and McClellan. After the close of the campaign, Porter became aware of the transmission of these dispatches in their entirety—indiscreet utterances and all—and that they were to be used against him in the trial by court-martial then impending. Not unnaturally, he was greatly incensed at Burnside, held him responsible for furnishing damaging testimony against him, and joined McClellan on the fourteenth of September with the determination to even up matters with him.

As McClellan also was involved in the charges of disloyalty to Pope and the administration, it was easy for him to sympathize with Porter and share his feelings toward Burnside. So, putting aside all remembrance of what Burnside had done for him in twice refusing to take command of the army and insisting that McClellan should be retained, he joined hands with Porter and from that hour became Burnside's enemy. (This does not show in the official records of that period, but it does show in *McClellan's Own Story*.) Porter joined McClellan at Middletown near noon of the fourteenth; after that, McClellan ceased to send orders to Burnside as wing commander, but sent them directly to Hooker and Reno, the two corps commanders. The pursuit of revenge and the effort to make a record against Burnside was renewed the next day, when Porter asked for written orders to pass the Ninth Corps and endorsed them with an unnecessary criticism of Burnside's delay in marching.[49] McClellan or someone at his headquarters continued the nagging on the sixteenth and seventeenth. Subsequently, both he and Porter filed incorrect and misleading reports as to Burnside and his command at the battle of the seventeenth. Such a spirit shown toward a faithful officer of high rank could have but one effect. Burnside did not openly complain, but the facts were known to his brother officers and did not serve to strengthen confidence in McClellan or respect for Porter.

Other reasons have been advanced for the tardiness of movement on the fifteenth of September. The Comte de Paris says, "The obstructions of the road, the fatigue of the soldiers, want of exactitude on the part of some of the commanders and

---

[45] Abraham Lincoln to McClellan, May 9, 1862. A copy appears in Roy P. Basler, ed., *The Collected Works of Abraham Lincoln*, vol. 5 (New Brunswick, N.J.: Rutgers University Press, 1953), 208–9.

[46] See particularly Porter to Burnside, August 27, 1862, 4:00 p.m., reprinted in *OR*, vol. 12, pt. 3, 699–700; Burnside to Halleck, August 29, 1862, 5:15 p.m., reprinted in *OR*, vol. 12, pt. 3, 733.—*EAC*

[47] Testimony of Burnside, "The Fitz John Porter Court-Martial," December 31, 1862, reprinted in *OR*, vol. 12, pt. 2, supp., 1003.

[48] Porter to Burnside, 700.

[49] See [p. 178 n. 23].—*EAC*

the indifference of others, had kept back the rest of the army [except Richardson and Porter—*EAC*], which stretched out in interminable column between Boonesboro' and Antietam."[50] Oliver O. Howard writes:

> Eager as McClellan was to engage him [Lee] before the return of Jackson and the other Harper's Ferry detachments, he was forced to postpone his attempt at least till the next morning. Taking into account all the sickness, discouragement, disgust, envies and contentions which followed in the wake of the second Bull Run and the Harper's Ferry disaster, it will not seem strange that much of our army was strung along the thoroughfares between Washington and South Mountain. Even the reaction from our small successes at the South Mountain Passes produced additional weariness, willfulness, slowness, and indifference on the part of some officers—and some of them, too, holding responsible commands.
>
> These suggestions will account for strange delays in the marches which were ordered and the comparatively small number which we actually had in position in front of Lee as late as the morning of the 16th of September.[51]

Palfrey says, "The success of our army was undoubtedly greatly lessened by jealousy, distrust, and general want of the *entente cordiale*."[52]

There is evidence that, in starting from Washington on the Maryland campaign, McClellan and some of his prominent lieutenants would have been satisfied with checking the invasion of Pennsylvania and expelling Lee from Maryland without risking a general engagement. They did not consider the army in proper condition as to morale and organization. Upon this point we quote McClellan:

> The Army of the Potomac was thoroughly exhausted and depleted by its desperate fighting and severe marches in the unhealthy regions of the Chickahominy and afterward, during the second Bull Run campaign; its trains, administration services and supplies were disorganized or lacking in consequence of the rapidity and manner of its removal from the peninsula as well as from the nature of its operations during the second Bull Run campaign … The divisions of the Army of Virginia were also exhausted and weakened, and their trains were disorganized and their supplies deficient by reason of the movements in which they had been engaged.
>
> Had General Lee remained in front of Washington [south of the Potomac—*EAC*] it would have been the part of wisdom to hold our own army quiet until its pressing wants were fully supplied, its organization was restored, and its ranks were filled with recruits—in brief, until it was prepared for a campaign. But as the enemy maintained the offensive and crossed the Upper Potomac to threaten or invade Pennsylvania, it became necessary to meet him at any cost notwithstanding the condition of the troops, to put a stop to the invasion, save Baltimore and Washington, and throw him back across the Potomac. Nothing but sheer necessity justified the advance of the Army of the Potomac to South Mountain and Antietam in its then condition, and it is to the eternal honor of the brave men who composed it that under such adverse circumstances they gained those victories … It must then be borne constantly in mind that the purpose of advancing from Washington was simply to meet the necessities of the moment by frustrating Lee's invasion of the Northern States, and, when that was accomplished, to push with the utmost rapidity the work of reorganization and supply so that a new campaign might be promptly inaugurated with the army in condition to prosecute it to a successful termination without intermission.[53]

From McClellan's tardiness in reaching the front and other surrounding circumstances, we are led to the conclusion that he had no serious intention of giving Lee battle on the fifteenth. Indeed, there were many camp rumors that McClellan and some of his most trusted lieutenants were well satisfied that Lee had fallen back behind the Antietam and that they would have been still further satisfied had he continued an unmolested retreat beyond the Potomac. McClellan had around him a large circle of officers who were his partisans against what in army parlance was called "the politicians." Some of these officers were on his staff and openly characterized the war as a politicians' war for the abolition of slavery. Some of these, before the campaign opened, publicly declared that the time had come for McClellan to proclaim himself dictator, and this idea was prevalent when the army began its march from Washington. There was as much discussion in the army about politics as there was at Washington and elsewhere, and it was a shade of political discussion antagonistic to the administration and indulged in unceasingly. Those who visited headquarters at this time were astonished at the more or less disloyal talk, the disloyal influences at work, and the assurance given McClellan that the people had assumed that the army was so devoted to him that they would as one man enforce any decision he should make as to any part of the war policy. "It would seem,"

[50] Comte de Paris [Louis-Phillippe-Albert d'Orléans], *History of the Civil War in America*, vol. 2 (Philadelphia: Porter & Coates, 1876), 333.

[51] Oliver O. Howard, "Gen'l O. O. Howard's Personal Reminiscences of the War of the Rebellion," *National Tribune*, March 24, 1884.

[52] Palfrey, 59 n. 1.

[53] McClellan, "From the Peninsula to Antietam," in *Battles and Leaders of the Civil War*, vol. 2 (New York: Century Co., 1887), 553–54.

says Cox, "that treasonable notions were rife about him to an extent that was never suspected, unless he was made the dupe of pretenders who saw some profit in what might be regarded as a gross form of adulation. He must be condemned for the weakness which made such approaches to him possible; but we are obliged … to accept as one of the strange elements of the situation a constant stream of treasonable suggestions from professed friends in the army and out of it."[54]

The press, hostile to the administration, were editorially advising McClellan to insist upon a reconstruction of the cabinet by the expulsion of the Radical element from it. The *New York Herald*, in discussing the situation and McClellan's relation to it, said:

> The political vultures still hover over Washington …, waiting for their opportunity to give him a stab in the back, like stealthy Indians, and then raise their hideous warwhoop against him once more.
>
> Under these circumstances, what is the duty of General McClellan? His position is like that of Wellington in the Spanish peninsula, when he was interfered with by the British Cabinet; and it is a duty which he owes to the country, no less than to himself, to follow the example of that illustrious and patriotic general. When "the iron Duke" found that the administration were bent on his destruction and the defeat of the army which he was leading, he firmly took his stand and insisted that the cabal should be broken up. His country was in danger, and he was in a position to dictate terms. His remonstrances had the desired effect: the meddling Cabinet was overthrown, and thenceforward victory crowned the British arms. Now this is the ground which McClellan ought to take in reference to that portion of the administration at Washington which is responsible for the present condition of things. He ought to insist upon the modification and reconstruction of the Cabinet, in order to have it purged of the radical taint which may again infuse its poison over the whole. Now is the time for him to prove himself not only a great general, but a statesman worthy of the occasion and of the responsibility which he has assumed. The safety of the country is entrusted to him. He is bound to see that no insidious enemy lurks behind about his base of operations. His own security and the security of his army are involved, and the fate of the republic itself is at stake. He is master of the situation. He is the only man in whom the troops and the country have confidence as a general for the chief command of the army in the field. He has a right to demand indemnity for the past and security for the future, and he ought not to rest satisfied till he is assured by facts, not mere promises, that his plans shall not be interfered with hereafter. The game is now in his hands and unless he plays his best trump and disposes effectually of the radicals, as he has the power to do, they will soon dispose of him by striking him down in the very crisis of the campaign now opened in Maryland, on which hang the destinies of the American republic and of millions of the human race yet unborn.[55]

On the next day, September 12, the *Herald* said, "Let President Lincoln keep our abolition disorganizers from intermeddling any more with the plans of General McClellan, and R. E. Lee will never get his ragged liberating rebel army back to Richmond."[56]

The sentiments expressed in the *Herald* of the eleventh were fully shared by those who surrounded McClellan, and they were not slow to discuss matters of that kind. A correspondent of the *New York Tribune* writes:

> Three days before the battle of Antietam I had quarters one night in a farm house. Judge [Thomas M.] Key, of Cincinnati, whom Chase had got appointed Judge Advocate General on McClellan's staff, rode up about dark and told me he felt too ill to sleep in a tent or on the ground. I offered to share my room with him. A headache prevented him from sleeping, and he talked a large part of the night. He told me that a plan to countermarch to Washington and intimidate the President had been seriously discussed the night before [September 13] by the members of McClellan's staff, and that his [Key's] opposition to it had, he thought, caused its abandonment. Judge Key …, was a lawyer of unusual ability and of high social standing in Cincinnati. I did not doubt the entire accuracy of his statement. Indeed I was not greatly surprised at the time, for I knew that the men McClellan had gathered around him were nearly all Copperheads who had no heart in the war.[57]

The plan was to expel Stanton from the war office and compel Lincoln to change his war policy. In taking this course, these officers did not consider their actions treasonable. They considered the administration as entirely wrong and would check its unconstitutional acts. There is good reason to believe that McClellan was ignorant of this design, though listening

54 Jacob D. Cox, *Military Reminiscences of the Civil War*, vol. 1 (New York: Charles Scribner's Sons, 1900), 363–64.
55 "The Important Position of General McClellan—The Attitude He Ought to Assume," *New York Herald*, September 11, 1862, 4.
56 "The Campaign in Maryland—General Lee's Proclamation," *New York Herald*, September 12, 1862, 4. It is unclear whether Carman miscopied the sentence or worked from a secondary source, but in his original manuscript the sentence ends, "… Lee will *soon* get his ragged … army back to Richmond [emphasis added]."
57 "Unwritten History of the War," *New York Tribune*, March 14, 1880, 5.

to much adverse criticism of his civilian superiors. He himself admits that he was urged to put himself in open opposition to the political tendencies of the administration, but he was the last man that would have listened to the use of the army for such a purpose, and the Army of the Potomac could not have been so used. But the fact remains that the Army of the Potomac was officered by that class of men who, yet true to the national flag, limited their efforts to the strict requirements of duty, solicitous that no disaster should come to the country, and more than willing that the Confederates should get away without battle.

Under all these circumstances, it is easy to understand why, now that the battle of South Mountain had been fought and the army leisurely marched to the Antietam, there was a hesitation to attack. Those in high command (and McClellan shared their views to some extent) thought that the expulsion of Lee from Maryland had been accomplished by the success at South Mountain. The risk of a battle was discussed with some misgivings, and there was a hope that Lee would recross the Potomac without further bloodshed.

When Lee disposed his command on the heights east of Sharpsburg, fronting the Antietam, on the morning of the fifteenth, it was for the purpose of delaying McClellan and forming a junction with McLaws. He had no present intention of giving battle north of the Potomac. But events decided otherwise. Before his dispositions were fairly completed, he received this dispatch from Jackson, dated near 8:00 a.m.: "Through God's blessing, Harper's Ferry and its garrison are to be surrendered. As Hill's troops have borne the heaviest part in the engagement, he will be left in command until the prisoners and public property shall be disposed of, unless you direct otherwise. The other forces can move off this evening so soon as they get their rations. To what point shall they move?"[58]

It will be remembered that soon after sending the dispatch to McLaws at 8:00 p.m. of the fourteenth, Lee advised Jackson of the reverse at South Mountain and ordered him to march to Shepherdstown to cover his crossing into Virginia. When Jackson sent the dispatch just quoted, that Harper's Ferry was to be surrendered and asking where he should go, this dispatch of Lee's ordering his march to Shepherdstown had not been received, but it came later. Jackson lost no time, and without comment on the dispatch he folded and endorsed it, "I will join you at Sharpsburg," then handed it to a courier for swift delivery.[59] By midday it was in Lee's hands at Sharpsburg. It was this message from Jackson that determined Lee to accept battle north of the Potomac and on the banks of the Antietam. He was now certain that Jackson, closely followed by Walker, would be with him on the morning of the next day, and he had the best of reasons for the belief that McLaws would not be far behind.

Henry Alexander White, in his life of Lee, says, "Noonday (September 15) brought him a note from Jackson, written at an early morning hour: 'Through God's blessing, Harper's Ferry and its garrison are to be surrendered.' Not until the receipt of this news, with the additional knowledge that 'Stonewall' was making all speed to join him, did Lee determine to stand and give battle at Sharpsburg."[60] (The "additional knowledge" that Jackson was making all speed to join Lee was derived from Jackson's subsequent dispatch that he would join Lee at Sharpsburg.) Longstreet says, "A few minutes after our lines were manned, information came of the capitulation of Harper's Ferry,"[61] and that up to that time Lee had no intention of giving battle at Sharpsburg.

Longstreet opposed a battle at Sharpsburg. He had opposed the movement from Hagerstown back to Turner's Gap the day before, and he suggested the withdrawal of his own force from Hagerstown and D. H. Hill's from South Mountain and their concentration behind the Antietam at Sharpsburg, where they could get together in season to make a strong defensive fight and at the same time check McClellan's advance toward Harper's Ferry in case he thought to relieve Miles by that route. Now that Miles had surrendered, Longstreet was opposed to giving battle at Sharpsburg and proposed that the army cross over into Virginia. He gives his reasons:

> As long as the armies were linked to Harper's Ferry, the heights in front of Sharpsburg offered a formidable defensive line, and in view of possible operations from Harper's Ferry, through the river pass, east of South Mountain, formed a beautiful point of strategic diversion. But when it transpired that Harper's Ferry was surrendered and the position was not to be utilized, that the troops there were to join us by a march on the south side, its charms were changed to perplexities. The threatening attitude towards the enemy's rear vanished, his line of communication was open and free of further care, and his army, relieved of entanglements, was at liberty to cross the Antietam by the upper fords and bridges, and approach from vantage-ground General Lee's left. At the same time the Federal left was reasonably

[58] Jackson to Lee, September 15, 1862, "near 8:00 a.m.," reprinted in *OR*, vol. 19, pt. 1, 951.

[59] Statement to the writer by Henry Kyd Douglas of Jackson's staff. See also John Codman Ropes, *The Story of the Civil War: A Concise Account of the War in the United States of America between 1861 and 1865*, vol. 2 (New York: G. P. Putnam's Sons, 1898), 348.—EAC

[60] Henry Alexander White, *Robert E. Lee and the Southern Confederacy, 1807–1870* (New York: G. P. Putnam's Sons, 1897), 207.

[61] James Longstreet, *From Manassas to Appomattox: Memoirs of the Civil War in America* (Philadelphia: J. P. Lippincott Co., 1896), 228.

secured from aggression by cramped and rugged ground along the Confederate right. Thus the altered circumstances changed all of the features of the position in favor of the Federals.[62]

Again Longstreet writes:

That night [September 15], after we heard of the fall of Harper's Ferry, General Lee ordered Stonewall Jackson to march to Sharpsburg as rapidly as he could come. Then it was that we should have retired from Sharpsburg and gone to the Virginia side of the Potomac.

The moral effect of our move into Maryland had been lost by our discomfiture at South Mountain, and it was then evident we could not hope to concentrate in time to do more than make a respectable retreat, whereas by retiring before the battle [of Sharpsburg] we could have claimed a very successful campaign.[63]

It is quite true, as Longstreet here argues (and as he argued that day with Lee), that in recrossing the Potomac Lee would have avoided all chances of a disaster and would have been observant of recognized principles of war. But, at the same time, he would have lost prestige by retiring from Maryland without trying conclusions with McClellan in a general engagement. He had entered Maryland for the purpose, among others, of relieving Virginia from the ravages of war and Maryland from the despotism of the Union. He had not found that Union despotism was particularly distasteful to Maryland people and could have dismissed this phase of the campaign from his mind without any compunction, but he was averse to carrying back to Virginia the horrors of war that he knew would follow his retreat beyond the Potomac. He knew that if he recrossed into Virginia he would be giving time to McClellan to reorganize and discipline his army for an advance into Virginia at his convenience. Lee considered his wiser policy to be to give McClellan no time in reorganize his army and drill and discipline his new recruits, but force him to a battle before his troops had fully recovered from the disastrous defeat on the plains of Manassas, and he had such a sublime confidence in his men that he doubted not the result.

It is also true that the moral effect of the move into Maryland had been lost by the discomfiture at South Mountain. Yet that loss had its compensation in the success at Harper's Ferry, and still other successes were possible. Beyond military considerations there were those of a political character to be considered, political causes which had rendered the invasion of Maryland and the North an imperative necessity, and to which we have already referred at some length in a previous chapter. To abandon the friends of the South who were fighting her battle in the North at the ballot box was not to be thought of, nor could the dreams and hopes of foreign intervention be dashed by a return to Virginia without trying the fortune of arms on Maryland soil. All these things Lee had to consider. He was upon the defensive. He had been foiled in strategy and forced from the road by which he proposed to enter Pennsylvania back to the banks of the Potomac and within the angle formed by that stream and the Antietam, compelled to give battle with a river at his back or go back to Virginia with a loss of prestige. It required a resolute commander to accept battle under all the circumstances, and Lee was a resolute commander. His front was covered by the Antietam, a stream presenting many difficulties for an enemy to cross, and behind it he concluded to challenge a contest that must be decisive. If victorious, he could force McClellan out of the Antietam Valley and back to South Mountain (the fears of the administration would probably have carried him back to Washington), and the way would be open to Pennsylvania. If defeated, he could recross the Potomac by Shepherdstown Ford. His army had been elated by many successes. The victory at Harper's Ferry gave it, says Lee, "renewed occasion for gratitude," and he believed in its invincibility.[64] He counted much on the supposed demoralization of the Army of the Potomac.

Lee well knew Jackson's views. He knew that this trusted lieutenant had, from the beginning, favored active operations in the enemy's country and that a return to Virginia under the circumstances would be greatly disappointing to him. If he had any reason to doubt Jackson's views, it was dispelled by Jackson's dispatch of that morning that he would join Lee at Sharpsburg. In a letter written to Mrs. Jackson, Lee says, "When he [Jackson] came upon the field [September 16], having preceded his troops, and learned my reasons for offering battle, he emphatically concurred with me. When I determined to withdraw across the Potomac, he also concurred; but said then, in view of all the circumstances, it was better to have fought the battle in Maryland than to have left it without a struggle."[65]

But Lee had a most critical condition to face. His daring was never more fully shown than when he made up his mind to fight at Antietam, and it has been much cited by his admirers as the test of his great generalship and as an expression of the sublime confidence he reposed in his army and of his ability to reunite his detachments before the enemy could strike

[62] Ibid., 228–29.

[63] Longstreet, "The Invasion of Maryland," in *Battles and Leaders*, 666–67.

[64] Lee to Davis, September 16, 1862, reprinted in *OR*, vol. 19, pt. 1, 141.

[65] Lee to Mary Anna Jackson, January 25, 1866, reprinted in G. F. R. Henderson, *Stonewall Jackson and the American Civil War*, vol. 2 (London: Longmans, Green, and Co., 1898), 583.

him. McClellan's large army was already filling the valley of the Antietam; could Jackson march sixteen miles and ford the Potomac before Lee was struck? Walker was twenty miles distant, beyond the Shenandoah. McLaws and R. H. Anderson were in Pleasant Valley, and no way was open to them save by way of Harper's Ferry—more than twenty-five miles. Was it possible for them to come up before McClellan attacked in overwhelming force? Lee, knowing McClellan's caution and relying upon the energy of his own lieutenants, answered in the affirmative.

Having concluded to receive battle on the Antietam, Lee replied to Jackson's dispatches by ordering Jackson to join him as quickly as possible. Then, with his field glass, he inspected the wooded heights to the northeast, as if to discover whether or not troops were being passed through them. While thus engaged, Stuart came up from the rear, just from Harper's Ferry, his horse covered with foam. Dismounting, he said to Lee, "We got 11,000 prisoners and all their commissary and quartermaster stores, including wagons and teams." Lee, before making any reply, told the orderly to keep Stuart's horse moving, not to let him cool off too soon, and then turning to Stuart said, "General, did they have many shoes? These good men are barefoot," referring to the men of the 6th North Carolina of Hood's Division, drawn up in line about ten paces in his rear.[66]

This was about noon. Stuart soon rode away to the left and Lee continued his examination of the field with a view to a better disposition of his forces. It was seen that the left, near the Dunkard church, was the weakest point and most likely to be attacked, and Hood's two brigades were moved from Cemetery Hill to guard and hold that point. In moving to the position, Hood lost a few men from the fire of the guns beyond the Antietam. S. D. Lee's artillery battalion (except for Captain George V. Moody's [Louisiana] Battery and Eubank's Battery) was ordered to the left also. The right of the line was extended by the transfer of the brigades of Garnett, Jenkins, Drayton, and Kemper from Cemetery Hill across the road leading to the Rohrbach Bridge.

This bridge, as we have said, was assigned to the care of Toombs. Its surroundings and how he utilized them are described in his official report:

> The Antietam River runs comparatively straight from a point about 100 paces above the bridge to a point about 300 paces below the bridge, and then curves suddenly around a hill to a ford on a neighborhood road. About 600 yards to my right and rear the road from Sharpsburg to Harper's Ferry from the foot of the bridge over the Antietam turns suddenly down the river, and runs nearly upon its margin for about 300 paces; then leaves the river nearly at right angles. Upon examining the position, I found a narrow wood upon the margin of the river just above the bridge (an important and commanding position) occupied by a company of Texans from Brigadier-General Hood's command. I then ordered the Twentieth [Georgia] to take position, with its left near the foot of the bridge, on the Sharpsburg side, extending down the river near its margin, and the Second Georgia on its right, prolonging the line down to the point where the road on the other side from the mountain approached the river. This required a more open order than was desirable, on account of the smallness of the regiments, both together numbering but a little over 400 muskets.[67]

Meanwhile, the Union divisions, numbering 50,000 men, were arriving in the valley of the Antietam, presenting to the Confederates, "then shattered by battles and scattered by long and tiresome marches," an awe-inspiring spectacle.[68] What did Lee have with which to oppose this force? Of Longstreet's command, D. R. Jones's and Hood's Divisions (eight brigades) and the brigade of Evans; of Jackson's, the division of D. H. Hill (five brigades)—fourteen brigades in all, say 12,000 men, with the cavalry and reserve artillery less than 4,000—an aggregate of about 16,000 men. When night came and Lee knew that not a Union skirmisher had approached the Rohrbach Bridge, not an enemy appeared at the Upper Bridge and the adjacent ford, he was much relieved. He knew that Jackson and Walker soon would be with him. His only solicitude was for McLaws. Let us see what has become of McLaws, whom we left in Pleasant Valley.

---

[66] Samuel M. Tate to John M. Gould, April 15, 1891, John M. Gould Collection of Papers Relating to the Battle of Antietam (preservation microfilm, reel 3), Rauner Special Collections Library, Dartmouth College, Hanover, N.H. Gould assembled a sizeable collection of veterans' accounts of the opening phase of the battle in the course of his own historical research, and readily lent both his expertise and his material to Carman over a number of years.

[67] Robert Toombs to David R. Jones, October 25, 1862, reprinted in *OR*, vol. 19, pt. 1, 889.

[68] Longstreet, "The Invasion of Maryland," 667.

10
McLaws and Franklin in Pleasant Valley

When Lafayette McLaws lost Crampton's Gap and was cut off from Lee on the evening of September 14, he found himself in a critical and perplexing situation. After consultation with R. H. Anderson, it was decided to bring from Maryland Heights the brigades of Kershaw and Barksdale (save for the 13th Mississippi, of the latter brigade) and all the artillery but two rifled guns and form a line of battle across Pleasant Valley about one and a half miles below Crampton's Gap, to make head against Franklin's advance down the valley. The line was formed with the remnants of the brigades of Cobb, Mahone, and Semmes; Kershaw and Barksdale were marched down from Maryland Heights; and Wilcox was brought back from near the mouth of the valley. These commands were disposed in two lines, and artillery (under the direction of Major Samuel Hamilton) was placed on swells of ground in the rear and on the left flank. So formidable was the appearance of this line that it deterred Franklin from attacking it. This line was placed specially under the command of Anderson.

Wright and Pryor were kept in position guarding Weverton Pass and Armistead and Featherston that from Harper's Ferry, the Sandy Hook Road. Harper's Ferry had not yet been taken. McLaws had to watch and wait the movements of his enemy—had to present a front against Franklin (marching down Pleasant Valley) and prevent Miles's escaping and attempting an advance (in conjunction with Franklin) on Weverton. (McLaws was in constant expectation of an attack on Weverton because, by doing this, the Union commander would give ocular evidence to Miles at Harper's Ferry that relief was near.)

During the night, McLaws received several dispatches from Lee ordering him to abandon his position, including Maryland Heights, and join him at Keedysville or Sharpsburg. The first dispatch was that of 8:00 p.m., by which he was ordered to recross the Potomac. This McLaws considered as clearly impracticable as his command was then situated: a regiment and two pieces of artillery on top of the high and precipitous Maryland Heights, two brigades and a battery on top of South Mountain (overlooking Weverton) and the remainder in line of battle against Franklin. He could not have assembled his command before daylight, and it was also impracticable (as it was contemplated) that he should go up the valley; that route Franklin had closed by his entrance into it. Nor could McLaws go up the river with his trains and artillery. It is true that he might have passed his infantry under the precipice at the foot of Maryland Heights by going up the bed of the canal (the water having been let out), but his wagons and artillery could not have gone that way.

Later came Lee's dispatches of 10:30 and 11:15 p.m. (the former to Munford, who forwarded it to McLaws), the purport of both being that McLaws should leave Pleasant Valley and Maryland Heights and go by way of the river road past Harper's Ferry or over Elk Ridge to Sharpsburg. McLaws contends, and his contention is a good one, that had he desired to leave the valley he could not have done so that night, for there was but one way to go with his artillery, wagons filled with nearly four hundred wounded, and trains of supplies—and that way was down the river. To do this his troops had to be well in hand to meet a probable attack from Franklin, who was but a short distance—not two miles—above him. To have attempted a retreat, unless he was prepared to fight if pursued, would have resulted in a helter-skelter movement and in all probability ended in a complete rout, disgraceful to everyone concerned in it, especially to the responsible commander. Franklin may not have attacked if he saw McLaws compact and ready for it (and such was the case), especially if he were moving away from Harper's Ferry and Lee, but he may have done so, and if McLaws went he would have rapidly advanced to the relief of Harper's Ferry and at once crossed the river with his whole force. Assuming the offensive, he would force Jackson to retire precipitately from the front of Bolivar Heights and cut off Walker. This done, McClellan, with his army on one side, and Franklin, with the nearly twelve thousand reinforcements at Harper's Ferry, could have had the disposal of events in their own hands, as there would have been Franklin with a larger force than Lee could assemble in Lee's rear, on his line of retreat, and McClellan himself, with a very superior force, in his front. All this McLaws feared would happen if he abandoned his position on the night of the fourteenth (as Lee twice ordered him most positively to do) or even if he complied with the order early on the morning of the fifteenth.

McLaws could not reason to his own satisfaction otherwise than that, while he was saving his own command by retreating (was even under orders to do so), a possible disaster might happen to himself and that great disaster might result to the whole army. If he remained and boldly faced Franklin, there was a possibility of good results to follow, so he notified Lee that he had a strong position and would defend himself where he was, and he relied upon Lee's operations to relieve him.

"At any rate," he says, "I would wait and see what fortune the morrow would bring me."[1] (The repeated messages sent by McLaws to Lee during the night of the fourteenth never reached Lee, and their non-receipt gave him much concern.)

It was after daylight on the morning of the fifteenth when McLaws had completed all his arrangements to resist Franklin's advance, and he was both surprised and satisfied to see, as the hours advanced, that Franklin gave no sign of molesting him. Although more concerned how his own command could escape capture than he was whether Miles could be made to surrender, he did all in his power that his force would permit to prevent Miles's escape, as his orders directed him to do. To this end his guns on Maryland Heights were ordered to continue their plunging fire upon Harper's Ferry and its garrison.

About 10:00 a.m. it was signaled to McLaws from Maryland Heights that the garrison at Harper's Ferry had hoisted a white flag and ceased firing. He at once ordered the troops defending Weverton Pass and those on the Sandy Hook Road to advance skirmishers along the road to the bridge at Harper's Ferry, or until they were fired on, and directed all his trains to be sent to the bridge. He still watched Franklin and kept his line of battle in his front. About this time also it was reported to him that Franklin was putting batteries in position on South Mountain, near Brownsville Gap, to operate against his artillery on the other side of the valley. This, apparently, gave him but little concern.

Early in the day he had sent Lieutenant Tucker of his staff to communicate with Jackson. Tucker returned about 1:00 p.m. with a message to McLaws that Jackson desired to see him. As Franklin showed no disposition to be aggressive, McLaws left the command to Anderson, with directions to push the trains down the valley and across the river as soon as possible and follow with the infantry when the trains were well over. At 2:00 p.m. Anderson began to withdraw down the valley toward Weverton and accomplished the withdrawal deliberately and without molestation. (Franklin reports that General Smith went in pursuit with a brigade and battery but could not catch him.[2] Anderson could see no evidence that Smith was in pursuit.) Anderson halted at the foot of the valley, about three miles from the first position, formed a second line (still holding Weverton and Maryland Heights), and awaited the passage of the trains over the bridge into Harper's Ferry—the bridge which Miles would not permit to be destroyed when he abandoned Maryland Heights.

When McLaws reported to Jackson at Harper's Ferry, he gave the situation of affairs in Pleasant Valley and suggested that if Jackson would cross over, or send even a potion of his force, they could dispose of Franklin. Jackson did not think it of sufficient importance to warrant a non-compliance of his orders to go to Sharpsburg and ordered McLaws to follow him as soon as possible. When asked if he could go around the mountain from where he was, Jackson made no reply. "It was well," says McLaws, "I did not try, as McClellan was already ahead of me."[3]

When McLaws returned to his command, he found that Anderson had skillfully withdrawn it and was waiting for the wagon train to pass over the river. Although some of this had gone over by noon, much of it was prevented from doing so because the paroled prisoners were being sent over it from Harper's Ferry, thus occupying it to the exclusion of McLaws's wagons and troops. By dark McLaws's command had been in line all day expecting attack, and his wagons were full of wounded men. It was not until 2:00 a.m. of the sixteenth that the bridge was clear for his crossing. He moved out of the valley by Sandy Hook, thence up the river road and passed rapidly over, marched through Harper's Ferry, and camped at Halltown, about four miles distant. His entire command did not cross over until 11:00 a.m., no advance or interruption being offered by Franklin. Had he been permitted the use of the bridge during daylight of the fifteenth and provisions allowed his men, his forces could have been rested and refreshed, and he would have been at Sharpsburg early on the sixteenth. As it was, his men were allowed rest whilst he went in search of provisions for them, for Jackson's men had already appropriated everything that was captured at Harper's Ferry. Regarding his operations in Pleasant Valley, McLaws made this report to Lee's adjutant general:

> The enemy having forced Crampton's Gap, thereby completely cutting off my route up the valley to join the forces with General Lee, as Solomon's Gap, the only road over Elk Ridge, was just in front of the one over the Blue Ridge [South Mountain—*EAC*] occupied by the enemy, I had nothing to do but to defend my position. I could not retire under the bluffs along the river, with the enemy pressing my rear and the forces at Harper's Ferry operating in conjunction, unless under a combination of circumstances I could not rely on to happen at the exact time needed; could not pass over the mountain except in a scattered and disorganized condition, nor could have gone through the Weverton Pass into the open country beyond to cross a doubtful ford when the enemy was in force on the other side of the Blue Ridge and coming down in my rear. There was no outlet in any direction for anything but the troops, and that very doubtful. In no contingency could I have saved the trains and artillery. I therefore determined to defend myself in the valley, holding the two heights and the two lower passes in order to force a direct advance down the valley, to prevent co-operation from Harper's Ferry, and at the same time to carry out my orders in relation to the capture of

---

[1] Lafayette McLaws, "The Maryland Campaign," in *Addresses Delivered before the Confederate Veterans Association, of Savannah, Ga., to which is Added the President's Annual Report* (Savannah: George N. Nichols, 1896), 18.

[2] William B. Franklin to George B. McClellan, September 15, 1862, 3:00 p.m., reprinted in *OR*, vol. 19, pt. 2, 296.

[3] McLaws, "The Maryland Campaign," 18.

that place. I received several communications from your headquarters in relation to my position, which were obeyed so far as circumstances permitted, and I acted, in departing from them, as I believed the commanding general would have ordered had he known the circumstances. The force in Harper's Ferry was nearly, if not quite, equal to my own, and that above was far superior. No attempt was made to cooperate from Harper's Ferry with the force above, and the force above did not press down upon me, because, I believe, General Lee offered battle at Sharpsburg. The early surrender of Harper's Ferry relieved me from the situation, and my command joined the main army at Sharpsburg on the morning of the 17th.[4]

We return to Franklin. About noon of the fourteenth, McClellan, then at Middletown, advised Franklin of what was transpiring at Turner's Gap, gave word that Miles had abandoned Maryland Heights and occupied Bolivar Heights, and reminded him to keep in view "the necessity of relieving Colonel Miles if possible."[5] Two hours later he dispatched Franklin to mass his troops and carry Crampton's Gap "at any cost," and that if he (McClellan) succeeded in carrying Turner's Gap, it would clear the way for Franklin to go through Crampton's Gap, whereupon Franklin was to follow the enemy as rapidly as possible.[6] About the same time, McClellan sent from Middletown this dispatch to Miles:

> The army is being rapidly concentrated here. We are now attacking the pass on the Hagerstown road over the Blue Ridge. A column is about attacking the Burkittsville and Boonsborough Passes. You may count on our making every effort to relieve you. You may rely upon my speedily accomplishing that object. Hold out to the last extremity. If it is possible, reoccupy the Maryland Heights with your whole force. If you can do that, I will certainly be able to relieve you. As the Catoctin Valley is in our possession, you can safely cross the river at Berlin or its vicinity, so far as opposition on this side of the river is concerned. Hold out to the last.[7]

Three copies of this were sent by three different messengers on different roads. It is not known that any of them ever reached Miles, but the dispatch is here given to show what McClellan desired Miles to do and what he believed Miles was doing while he was pushing Franklin to his relief.

At 1:00 a.m. of the fifteenth, when he knew that Crampton's Gap had been carried, he ordered Franklin to occupy the road from Rohrersville to Harper's Ferry, placing a sufficient force at Rohrersville to hold that position should it be attacked by the enemy from the direction of Boonsboro. He was to open communication with Miles at Harper's Ferry by attacking and destroying such of the enemy as should be found in Pleasant Valley. If he succeeded in opening communications with Miles, he was directed to withdraw him from Harper's Ferry with all the guns and public property he could carry, destroy what he could not remove, attach him to his own command, and then proceed to Boonsboro (which place McClellan intended to attack on the morrow, September 15) and join the main body at that place. Should he find, however, that the enemy had retreated from Boonsboro toward Sharpsburg, he should endeavor to fall upon him and cut off his retreat.[8]

When this order was received by Franklin, it was not possible to relieve Miles; we believe that possibility had passed with the setting sun of the fourteenth. But it was possible to crush McLaws before anyone could come to his relief, and it is possible that an engagement very early on the fifteenth might have been heard by Miles and encouraged him to a more determined resistance. Exclusive of Hancock's brigade (which was left near Burkittsville) and the 121st New York (which was burying the dead and caring for the wounded), Franklin had, in his two divisions, 11,000 men, which number had been augmented by the arrival of Couch's division with over 7,000 more. It is safe to say that he had "present for duty" 18,000 men—as good men as the Army of the Potomac could muster. To oppose them McLaws had not to exceed 10,000 (6,000 in Franklin's front and 4,000 at and near Weverton), and many of these had been sadly demoralized the night before. But Franklin did not feel sufficient confidence in the result to make an attack. He says that as he was crossing the mountain, about seven o'clock on the morning of the fifteenth, he had a good view of McLaws's force below, which seemed to be well posted on hills stretching across the valley (about two miles wide). When he reached Smith's headquarters, an examination was made of the position, and both he and Smith came to the conclusion that it would be suicidal to attack it. The whole breadth of the valley was occupied, and batteries swept the only approaches to the position. They estimated McLaws's force as quite as large as their own and in a position that, properly defended, would require a much greater force than they could command to carry.[9]

---

[4] McLaws to Robert H. Chilton, October 18, 1862, reprinted in *OR*, vol. 19, pt. 1, 856.

[5] McClellan to Franklin, September 14, 1862, 11:45 a.m., reprinted in *OR*, vol. 51, pt. 1, 833.

[6] McClellan to Franklin, September 14, 1862, 2:00 p.m., as contained in McClellan to Lorenzo Thomas, August 4, 1863, reprinted in *OR*, vol. 19, pt. 1, 46.

[7] McClellan to Dixon S. Miles, September 14, 1862, as contained in McClellan to Thomas, 45.

[8] George D. Ruggles to Franklin, September 15, 1862, 1:00 a.m., reprinted in McClellan to Thomas, 47.

[9] Franklin, "Notes on Crampton's Gap and Antietam," in *Battles and Leaders of the Civil War*, vol. 2 (New York: Century Co., 1887), 596.

At 8:50 a.m., apparently before he had made this examination and in response to McClellan's order of 1:00 a.m., Franklin reported from his position three miles from Rohrersville:

My command started at daylight this morning, and I am waiting to have it closed up here. General Couch arrived about 10 o'clock last night. I have ordered one of his brigades and one battery to Rohrersville or to the strongest point in its vicinity. The enemy is drawn up in line of battle about 2 miles to our front, one brigade in sight. As soon as I am sure that Rohrersville is occupied, I shall move forward to attack the enemy. This may be two hours from now. If Harper's Ferry has fallen, and the cessation of firing makes me fear that it has—it is my opinion that I should be strongly re-enforced.[10]

At the hour this dispatch was penned, McClellan prepared an order to Franklin to communicate with Burnside at the intersection of the Rohrersville and Boonsboro roads and, if the intelligence of the retreat of the enemy toward Shepherdstown Ford was confirmed, to push on with his whole command (cautiously keeping up communication with Burnside) to Sharpsburg and endeavor to fall upon the enemy and cut off his retreat, and to use the cavalry with the utmost vigor in following up the pursuit.[11] There was not a word in the dispatch regarding McLaws's force in front, and a strict obedience to the instructions contained in it would have been the abandonment of Pleasant Valley to McLaws and permission for him to retire unmolested and at his leisure (which, later, he actually did, with Franklin still in his front).

Franklin asserts that he never received this order.[12] We know that he did not act upon it. But apparently he did receive this or a similar order after he had made an examination of McLaws's position, and this he answered at 11:00 a.m.:

I have received your dispatch by Captain O'Keeffe. The enemy is in large force in my front, in two lines of battle stretching across the valley, and a large column of artillery and infantry on the right of the valley looking toward Harper's Ferry. They outnumber me two to one. It will, of course, not answer to pursue the enemy under these circumstances. I shall communicate with Burnside as soon as possible. In the mean time I shall wait here until I learn what is the prospect of re-enforcement. I have not the force to justify an attack on the force I see in front. I have had a very close view of it, and its position is very strong.[13]

It was this dispatch of Franklin's that caused the order to Burnside and Porter, elsewhere noted, to halt at the Rohrersville Road or march on Rohrersville and join Franklin. McClellan replied to it at 1:20 p.m.:

Burnside's corps and Sykes' division are moving on Porterstown and Sharpsburg by the road about one mile south of Hagerstown pike, with orders to turn and attack a force of the enemy supposed to be at Centerville [Keedysville—EAC]. I will instruct them to communicate with you at Rohrersville, and if necessary re-enforce you. It is important to drive in the enemy in your front, but be cautious in doing it until you have some idea of his force. The corps of Sumner, Hooker, and Banks [i.e., Mansfield] are moving to Boonsborough on the main pike. At least one division has already passed down toward Centerville [Keedysville—EAC]. I will direct a portion to turn to the left at the first road beyond the mountain (west), so as to be in a position to re-enforce you or to move on Portersville [Porterstown—EAC]. Sykes will be at the Boonsborough and Rohrersville road in about one hour and a half, Burnside following close. Thus far our success is complete, but let us follow it up closely, but warily. Attack whenever you see a fair chance of success. Lose no time in communicating with Sykes and Burnside.[14]

After McClellan arrived at Boonsboro and his troops had occupied Keedysville (thus covering Franklin's rear), he ordered Franklin to withdraw the brigades at Rohrersville to join his main body and to hold his position without attacking McLaws unless presented with a very favorable opportunity. He advised him of his efforts to concentrate everything during the evening on the enemy at or near Sharpsburg and said that he would be satisfied if Franklin could keep the enemy in his front without anything decisive until the Sharpsburg affair was settled, when he would at once move directly to Franklin's assistance and also endeavor to cut off the enemy in Franklin's front.[15] He was spared the effort, for even then McLaws had escaped.

Smith, whose division was Franklin's advance, made a demonstration from his left late in the forenoon on Brownsville Gap with two regiments of infantry and a section of horse artillery. Later the Confederates were observed to be withdrawing,

[10] Franklin to McClellan, September 15, 1862, 8:50 a.m., as contained in McClellan to Thomas, 47.

[11] Ruggles to Franklin, September 15, 1862, 8:45 a.m., reprinted in OR, vol. 51, pt. 1, 836.

[12] As of this writing, Carman's source for this assertion has not been identified.

[13] Franklin to McClellan, September 15, 1862, 11:00 a.m., reprinted in McClellan to Thomas, 47.

[14] McClellan to Franklin, September 15, 1862, 1:20 p.m., reprinted in OR, vol. 51, pt. 1, 836.

[15] Randolph B. Marcy to Franklin, September 15, 1862, 4:30 p.m., reprinted in OR, vol. 51, pt. 1, 836.

but this (very correctly) was not attributed to the demonstration. Smith started in pursuit with a brigade of infantry and a battery and soon reported to Franklin that McLaws was drawing off through the valley too fast for him. McLaws says that his movement down the valley, of but three miles, was not so rapid as to prevent its being overtaken by Smith, "and if a pursuit was made it is strange that none of my commanders, nor any of my staff, nor anyone else reported or mentioned that there had been seen at any time any evidence of any advance."[16]

Before hearing from Smith, who had gone in languid pursuit of McLaws, Franklin had written McClellan that, under his order of 1:20 p.m., he did not feel justified in putting his whole command in motion to the front (toward Sharpsburg) but should act according to the dictates of his judgment as circumstances occurred, and that he had sent a squadron of the 6th Pennsylvania Cavalry to communicate with Burnside. If they succeeded in getting to him, the information that Burnside might give should determine his action. After preparing this dispatch, but before sending it, he heard from Smith that McLaws was retiring, upon which he added a postscript to his dispatch that he should start for Sharpsburg at once.[17] Before he was ready to move, he received McClellan's dispatch from Boonsboro of 4:30 p.m. to hold his position until the Sharpsburg affair was settled. Franklin held his position, with no enemy in front, until the morning of the seventeenth. It does not appear that at any time during the fifteenth Franklin got near enough to McLaws for serious skirmishing. Convinced of McLaws's overwhelming numbers, Franklin was well content to observe him at a respectful distance. For nearly two whole days he was kept in position where he was doing no service, when his presence was much needed elsewhere.

There has been much criticism upon the course of both McClellan and Franklin in the conduct of affairs in Pleasant Valley on the fifteenth and the detention of Franklin there, with no enemy in front, on the sixteenth. Franklin briefly replies to some of this criticism:

> The evidence before the court of inquiry on the surrender of Harper's Ferry shows that the white flag was shown at 7:30 a.m., on the 15th, and the firing ceased about one hour afterward. It is evident, therefore, that a fight between General McLaws's force and mine could have had no effect upon the surrender of Harper's Ferry. Success on my part would have drawn me farther away from the army and would have brought me in dangerous nearness to Jackson's force, already set free by the surrender. McLaws's supports were three and a half miles from him, while my force was seven miles from the main army.[18]

It is all very true that an attack after eight o'clock on the morning of the fifteenth would have had no effect upon the situation of affairs at Harper's Ferry, but why was McLaws not attacked very early on the morning of the fifteenth as intended by the spirit of all the orders given by McClellan—not only for the purpose of relieving Miles but also of destroying McLaws? And why was it necessary to suspend that effort when it was known that Miles had surrendered? Then it was that a supreme effort should have been made to crush McLaws or keep so close to him that he could not get away, but it was not done, nor an attempt made to do it, unless Smith's feeble efforts are taken seriously.

John C. Ropes defends Franklin. In his *Story of the Civil War*, he says, "In considering the caution exhibited by Franklin in this affair, we must remember that he had been warned to provide against an attack on his right rear by way of Rohrersville, which might be made for the purpose of relieving his pressure on McLaws, and that Couch's division was accordingly occupying that place, and also, that, for all he knew, Jackson might send a portion of his command across the river to the assistance of McLaws."[19] Up to noon of the sixteenth, this defense is a good one. McClellan's advance to the Antietam on the afternoon of the fifteenth had rendered the presence of Couch at Rohrersville unnecessary, but there was danger that Jackson might cross from Harper's Ferry, join McLaws, and gain McClellan's left and rear, thus interposing between him and Washington. Of this danger McClellan was almost daily cautioned by Halleck (especially on the sixteenth), who, after he had been informed by McClellan that he had reached the Antietam and that Lee confronted him, dispatched, "I think, however, you will find that the whole force of the enemy in your front has crossed the river. I fear now more than ever that they will recross at Harper's Ferry or below, and turn your left, thus cutting you off from Washington. This has appeared to me to be a part of their plan, and hence my anxiety on the subject."[20]

This was not a part of Lee's plan, but it suggested itself to some of his subordinates and doubtless was in Lee's thoughts. We have noted McLaws's suggestion to Jackson that he join him in Pleasant Valley and attack Franklin. It is quite probable that Jackson had already thought of this or a similar movement. Indeed, some of his staff officers have assured us that

---

[16] McLaws, "The Capture of Harper's Ferry," *Philadelphia Weekly Press*, September 12, 1888.

[17] Franklin to McClellan, September 15, 1862, 3:00 p.m., reprinted in *OR*, vol. 19, pt. 2, 296.

[18] Franklin, "Notes on Crampton's Gap," 596.

[19] John Codman Ropes, *The Story of the Civil War: A Concise Account of the War in the United States of America between 1861 and 1865*, vol. 2 (New York: G. P. Putnam's Sons, 1898), 347.

[20] Henry W. Halleck to McClellan, September 16, 1862, 12:30 p.m., as contained in McClellan to Thomas, 41.

he discussed it and that without further orders from Lee he would have made it, thus carrying out the original intention that he should rejoin his chief by the north side of the Potomac. But when, under the changed condition of affairs and the uncertainty of Lee's position and his necessities, he asked for Lee's order where to go and received his instructions to join him at Sharpsburg, Jackson was no longer at liberty to follow his own inclination, and he answered to McLaws that he did not feel warranted in disregarding Lee's order to go to Sharpsburg. In fact, nothing could have justified such a movement by Jackson except Lee's direct order.

It is known that Longstreet was not favorable to joining battle at Sharpsburg but would have reunited the army beyond the Potomac, and there is a fair inference that he looked favorably upon a movement against McClellan's left and rear. In his *Manassas to Appomattox*, Longstreet says:

> The "lost order" directed the command of Generals Jackson, McLaws, and Walker, after accomplishing the objects for which they had been detached, to join the main body of the army at Boonsborough or Hagerstown. Under the order and the changed condition of affairs, they were expected, in case of early capitulation at Harper's Ferry, to march up the Rohrersville-Boonsborough road against McClellan's left. There were in those columns twenty-six of General Lee's forty brigades, equipped with a fair apportionment of artillery and cavalry. So it seemed to be possible that Jackson would order McLaws and Walker up the Rohrersville road, and move with his own corps through the river pass [at Weverton—*EAC*] east of South Mountain, against McClellan's' rear, as the speedier means of relief to General Lee's forces. But prudence would have gone with the bolder move of his entire command east of the mountain against McClellan's rear, with a fair field for strategy and tactics. This move would have disturbed McClellan's plans on the afternoon of the 15th, while there seemed little hope that McClellan would delay his attack until Jackson could join us, marching by the south side.
>
> The field, and extreme of conditions, were more encouraging of results than was Napoleon's work at Arcola.[21]

McLaws says:

> I could not help thinking, when looking over the country, that if when Harper's Ferry surrendered, Gen. Jackson had crossed to my side in Pleasant Valley with his divisions and Walker's, the forces of Gen. Lee could easily have joined us, and our army united could have held Harper's Ferry and Maryland Heights as our stronghold for the time, and perhaps have forced McClellan to have attacked us in some strong position of our own choosing, and with more chances for our success and with less wear and tear of our men, and less prospect of great disaster than now seemed imminent. But I supposed that Gen. Lee had weighed all these chances, and whatever seemed to him the best was the best, but nevertheless I could not but think that it would have been better for us than Sharpsburg, under the circumstances.[22]

It is not difficult to agree with McLaws in this matter. That a movement of Jackson, Walker, and McLaws through Weverton and east of South Mountain, promptly followed by Lee's recrossing the Potomac on the night of the fifteenth and uniting with them, would have played havoc with McClellan's campaign and led to results that are idle to speculate upon is evident to us now and was evident then to Halleck and McClellan. Their reasons for caution were sound. But when, on the morning of the sixteenth, it was known—or should have been known—that McLaws had entirely abandoned Pleasant Valley and crossed over to Harper's Ferry, that Lee was still on the Antietam, and that Jackson was believed to have joined him,[23] there seems to have been no reason why Franklin should not have marched for the Antietam at noon on the sixteenth ready for action the next day, Couch's division being left in Pleasant Valley.

Franklin remained in Pleasant Valley all day of the sixteenth. In the evening he received McClellan's order to march the next morning and join him before Sharpsburg.[24]

---

[21] James Longstreet, *From Manassas to Appomattox: Memoirs of the Civil War in America* (Philadelphia: J. P. Lippincott Co., 1896), 232–33.

[22] McLaws, "The Maryland Campaign," 27.

[23] Governor Andrew Curtin of Pennsylvania received the following dispatch on September 16: "I rode to General McClellan's headquarters at Keedysville at 12 o'clock last night, and have just returned, leaving there at noon. The general believes that Harper's Ferry surrendered yesterday morning, and that Jackson re-enforced Lee at Sharpsburg last night … Rebels appear encouraged at arrival of their re-enforcements." "Captain Palmer" to Andrew G. Curtin, no date, as contained in Curtin to Abraham Lincoln, September 16, 1862, 11:00 p.m., reprinted in *OR*, vol. 19, pt. 2, 311.—*EAC*

[24] In Carman's original manuscript, "McLaws and Franklin in Pleasant Valley" is followed immediately by a chapter containing the table of organization for both armies. It is reprinted herein as Appendices A and B.

No one who campaigned with Generals McClellan or Lee in September 1862 can ever forget the incomparable beauty of the valleys of western Maryland, through and across which they marched from the Monocacy to South Mountain and the Antietam. Loveliest of these is the Antietam Valley, extending from the South Mountain to the Potomac. As one descends the National Road from Turner's Gap, going westward, the valley spreads out before the vision in charming, graceful undulations to the north and west. To the southwest is seen the wavy outline of Elk Ridge, which bisects the valley from Harper's Ferry northward and sinks down upon its bosom near Keedysville. It has a width of eight to twelve miles. In this charming valley, soon to be stained yet hallowed with blood, marking a great battle of American history—of all history—war now stalked, and we follow its footsteps to the banks of the Antietam and the Potomac to note the ground of impending battle and the approaches thereto.

After descending from South Mountain to Boonsboro, the National Road divides into four branches. One, the continuation of the main road, runs a little west of northwest to Williamsport, on the Potomac; one, northwest to Hagerstown; one, south to Rohrersville and down Pleasant Valley; and another, southwest through Keedysville and Sharpsburg to the Potomac, at Shepherdstown. From Boonsboro to Keedysville, a distance of three miles, the road runs through a gently undulating country with fine farms and noble groves of oak. At Keedysville it strikes more swelling ground: the declining prolongation of Elk Ridge. Immediately after crossing the Little Antietam, which winds through and around the village, a road branches to the right and, crossing the main Antietam by a graceful stone bridge, runs northwest to Williamsport. Another road branching to the left runs a little east of south, along the eastern base of Elk Ridge to Rohrersville, while a third runs down the west side of Elk Ridge to the Rohrbach Bridge, where it intersects the Sharpsburg and Rohrersville Road.

The Boonsboro and Sharpsburg Road, continuing a southwest course, reaches the plateau of a prominent and commanding ridge at the distance of a short mile from Keedysville, upon which Lee rested on the morning of the fifteenth and McClellan established his headquarters on the evening of the sixteenth, and from which can be seen the ground upon which Lee disposed his army. From this point the road gradually descends another short mile to the east foot of the bluff behind which, on either side of the road, Richardson and Sykes deployed their divisions on the afternoon of the fifteenth. Passing through a gorge in the bluff, the Antietam was crossed by a stone bridge, similar to the one north of it on the Keedysville and Williamsport Road. From the western bank of the Antietam, the road ascends a ridge that reaches an elevation of 120 feet when 620 yards from the stream. Then it descends into a ravine that snakes up from the Antietam south of the bridge, then again ascends to a ridge (where Lee drew up his right and center) at an elevation of 185 to 190 feet above the Antietam and about a mile from it, and where the National Cemetery now crowns it in beauty.[2]

Lying close under this ridge to the west is Sharpsburg, the steeples of its churches just visible from the east bank of the Antietam, through which the road passes southwest three miles to the Potomac, opposite Shepherdstown. Before the war a stone bridge carried the road over the river, but this had been destroyed by Joseph E. Johnston when he abandoned Harper's Ferry in June 1861, and the crossing of the river was effected by a ford one mile below Shepherdstown known variously as Shepherdstown, Boteler's, and Blackford's Ford. The Potomac at this point is about two hundred yards wide and the ford is just below the breast of a mill dam. (In ordinary stages of water it is a good ford.) Where the road from Sharpsburg strikes the canal and river opposite Shepherdstown, a road ran south along the banks of the canal to the ford, and the ford was reached by another road branching off from the Harper's Ferry Road, about a mile south of Sharpsburg.

In reaching Shepherdstown from the west and north, the Potomac makes a series of remarkable curves. At Mercerville, two and a half miles west of north from Sharpsburg, it glides in gracefully from the west, strikes the foot of a bluff that it follows southerly five or six hundred yards to New Industry, then sweeps southwest over a mile and, curving to the right, flows southeast a mile and a half, strikes another bluff about a mile and a quarter west of Sharpsburg, and, turning, runs due west a mile. Here it again turns and runs southeast a mile and a quarter, then changes its course once more and flows southwest between high bluffs, curves gracefully at Shepherdstown, and pursues a southeast course nearly four miles, when it receives

---

[1] Carman divided his original manuscript into two volumes. The second volume begins with "The Field of Antietam."
[2] The elevations are computed from the level of the water at the Rohrbach Bridge, which is 375 feet above sea level.—*EAC*

the waters of the Antietam coming in from the north. The eastern bank of the river in this entire distance is followed by the Chesapeake and Ohio Canal, which at the time was dry, the water being let out by the Confederates.

From Mercerville on the north to the Antietam on the south, there is but one ford practicable for infantry and artillery—Shepherdstown Ford—entering on the Blackford farm, on the Maryland side, and coming out near Boteler's Mill, on the Virginia side. By this route, Jackson, Walker, McLaws, and R. H. Anderson joined Lee on the sixteenth and seventeenth, and by this the entire Confederate army retired during the night of the eighteenth.

The Antietam rises near Waynesboro, in Pennsylvania's Cumberland Valley, pursues a southerly course (flowing at times drowsily through meadows and then rippling over ledges, but more generally curving between bold bluffs) and empties into the Potomac about ten miles above Harper's Ferry and three miles south of Sharpsburg. Joining the Potomac at an acute angle, it encloses a peninsula or neck two to four miles broad and five to six miles in length. Nearly in the center of this peninsula lies Sharpsburg, then and now a sleepy, un-enterprising town of about 1,200 inhabitants, situated in a saucer-like depression between two ridges running parallel nearly north and south and bounded by hills both on the north and south. From the Antietam the ground rises gradually to Cemetery Ridge and the general course of the Hagerstown Road, running north. Beyond Sharpsburg it rises gradually to a beautiful plateau, then falls away in rough outlines of rocky ledges and deep ravines to the Potomac.

The only value of Sharpsburg itself was as a strategic point from which five important roads radiated. The road running northeast to Keedysville and Boonsboro has been noted, as also has that running southwest to the Potomac at Shepherdstown. From Sharpsburg, running nearly due north, a good turnpike runs to Hagerstown twelve miles away, which at a distance of a little less than three miles is crossed by the Keedysville and Williamsport Road. Branch roads run from the Hagerstown Turnpike, the most important of which (to us) is the Smoketown Road, running northeast from the Dunkard church, and which shall be further noted. Where the Hagerstown Turnpike leaves the town to go north, a road leads southeast to Rohrersville, crossing the Antietam by a stone bridge at a distance of a little more than a mile from the town square. A road runs due south from the town square, crosses the Antietam a few yards from its mouth (beyond the limits of the battlefield and three miles from Sharpsburg) and continues on its rough way along the banks of the Potomac to Harper's Ferry. At a mile from town a right-hand branch from this road runs to Shepherdstown Ford. (Of lesser importance than the five roads named was one running north from the town square about 1,400 yards, parallel to the Hagerstown Road and 700 yards distant from it, which then turned west and northwest to New Industry and Mercerville, on the Potomac. Stretches of this road were used by the Confederates in moving to and from the left of their line.)

The turnpike, country roads, and farm lanes gave ready access to all parts of the field upon which, save along the banks of the Antietam itself, there were no obstacles to the movement of troops and but few to the passage of artillery. The undulating character of the ground, rolling into eminences of all dimensions (from little knolls over which a horse can freely gallop to steep ascents) then sinking in places to broad and deep ravines or basins in which a corps could be hidden, made it possible to move large bodies of troops from one point to another with secrecy and comparative safety. The Confederates took full advantage of this peculiarity of topography before and during the battle.

From what has been said, it will be seen that the Antietam was spanned by four bridges. One was at the mouth of the stream, which during the engagement was used only by Munford's cavalry, but by which Jackson, McLaws, Anderson, and Walker might have come upon the field. Another was the bridge on the road leading to Keedysville and Boonsboro, which we shall call the Middle Bridge. A third, the Rohrbach Bridge, lay one mile south of this. (Since the day of the battle it has been called the Burnside Bridge.) The last was on the Keedysville and Williamsport Road, one and five-eighths of a mile east of north of the Middle Bridge, which we shall call the Upper Bridge. These gray-colored stone bridges were comparatively new, artistic in design, and added beauty to the picturesque stream they spanned.

Between the bridges there are fords, most of them very difficult and impracticable for the passage of infantry and artillery. A half-mile south of the Upper Bridge and three hundred yards below the mouth of the Little Antietam is a ford practicable for infantry and artillery, which was improved on the evening of the fifteenth by Major David C. Houston of the Federal engineers, who ordered his men to cut down the banks bordering it. This ford was used by Hooker on the afternoon of the sixteenth and by Sumner and others on the morning of the seventeenth and shall be known as Pry's Ford. There are one or two difficult fords between this and the Middle Bridge, difficult of access and egress and not practicable for the movement of troops in any considerable number. There is but one practicable ford between the Middle Bridge and the Rohrbach Bridge. This is four hundred yards above the Rohrbach Bridge, in a bend of the stream where the road from Sharpsburg closely approaches it, and was used by Colonel Crook to cross a part of his brigade of the Kanawha Division about noon of the seventeenth. Less than one hundred yards south of the Rohrbach Bridge is a ford practicable for infantry but strongly and closely commanded by the steep, wooded bluff above it. Still farther downstream, where it changes course from south to west, is another ford practicable for infantry and artillery, but difficult of access and—defended by one hundred men on the bluff that overhangs it—may be considered as impracticable. It was used by both infantry and artillery on the seventeenth, but neither were under fire. Six hundred yards below this is Snavely's Ford, practicable for infantry and artillery, and used by General Rodman of the Ninth Corps on the seventeenth. Seven hundred yards below Snavely's, in a great bend of the Antietam, is Myers's Ford, practicable for infantry and artillery. (Below this, to the mouth of the Antietam, are other fords beyond the limits of the battlefield, generally difficult of access, which need not be considered.) Generally speaking, we may say that the Antietam was fordable in many places, but with steep and rugged banks. Although constituting something of an impediment all along its course, it was only that part of it in front of Lee's right that proved really to be an obstacle in his favor.

In this position, his front covered by the line of the Antietam and an open road to Sharpsburg (by which, if hard pressed, he could cross the Potomac into Virginia), Lee prepared for action. His weakness was that he had a river at his back, in front of which was the additional obstruction of a canal, and his only ford—which was in rear of one of his flanks—was open to a determined movement in force either on his right flank (by the bridge at the mouth of the Antietam) or on his left (by crossing the Antietam at the Upper Bridge and ford and pressing vigorously southward). It was a fairly strong position for defense in front, but entirely open to an enterprising enemy on the left. Of this Lee was well aware, and it caused him some anxiety on the afternoon of the fifteenth, his glasses frequently being turned in that direction to see what might be coming from the upper crossings of the Antietam, which were beyond the ability of his small command to cover. In anticipation of a movement on his left, Lee strengthened it late in the afternoon of the fifteenth by moving Hood's Division and four batteries of S. D. Lee's artillery battalion to the Dunkard church, Hood being posted between D. H. Hill and the Hagerstown Road. The ground northwest from the Dunkard church to a bend in the Potomac was covered by Stuart's cavalry and horse artillery.

This part of the field was the first contested and required first attention. If we go from Sharpsburg northward on the Hagerstown Road, we pass in rear of Cemetery Ridge, on the western slope of which on the morning of the sixteenth were the four Virginia batteries of Major Hilary P. Jones's artillery battalion. A little to their left and front was the Louisiana battery of Captain Moody, the Irish gunners of which were at work throwing shell at the German (New York) batteries beyond the Antietam. At a distance of about one thousand yards from town, a narrow lane to the right gives access to the Piper farm buildings (prominent among which is a large stone barn), passing which the lane runs into the sunken road and thence to the Boonsboro Turnpike. From the Piper lane the Hagerstown Road ascends to a ridge, crossing the road in a northwest direction, and upon which, on the seventeenth, was posted the artillery of Anderson's Division and, at times, other batteries. About three hundred yards to the right, and north from the Piper lane, was an apple orchard, north and northeast of which was a large cornfield. (In this orchard and cornfield the Confederate divisions of D. H. Hill and Anderson contended with the Union divisions of French and Richardson during the middle hours of the seventeenth.) Descending the ridge and at a distance of nearly four hundred yards from the Piper lane is a farm lane or sunken road, running eastward from the road (along the northern edge of the Piper cornfield) and giving access to the farms of Samuel Mumma and William Roulette. The sunken road, after running eastward about 550 yards, runs southeast about 450 yards and reaches the plateau of the ridge overlooking the Antietam, then goes west of south 300 yards, then southeast another short 300 yards, then south down a steep hill a little over 300 yards to the bed of a water-washed ravine, which it follows southeast 200 yards to the Boonsboro and Sharpsburg Turnpike. From frequent rains this common dirt road in many places had been washed out (hence called the sunken road), and its depressed bed gave good cover for infantry. For all time to come it shall be known as the Bloody Lane.

Following the Hagerstown Road from the mouth of the sunken road northward, the ground gradually rises, and at a distance of four hundred yards we strike the southeasterly corner of a body of woods—the Dunkard church woods. The trees had been thinned out at this point, and the sword of bluegrass (with an occasional tree for shade) was used for picnic parties. One hundred and fifty yards further on, and a long mile from Sharpsburg, is the small brick building known as the Dunkard church. It stands in the edge of the woods on a slight elevation about forty feet west of the Hagerstown Road and became the central object of a great and bloody struggle. Toward it Hooker, as we shall see, directed his advance on the morning of the seventeenth, and behind it the Confederates retired when defeated and broken east of the Hagerstown Road. Those who knew not its tactical value, as they came on the field, made direct steps and bent all their energies to seize this modest brick building that stands in the woods by the roadside—the *La Haye Sainte* of Antietam.[3]

The Dunkard church woods (which, at the church, had a depth of 600 yards) ran along the road northward 450 yards, then there was a grass field, the edge of which, running west at right angles to the road for about 260 yards, made an elbow in the woods. The field then turned to the right and ran along the woods, nearly parallel to the road for about 370 yards, where it again turned square to the left and west and extended back 160 yards, making at this point another elbow. From

---

[3] Located on a cross-road in the center of the battlefield, the farmhouse of La Haye Sainte was one of the most heavily contested points during the fighting at Waterloo.

this elbow the eastern edge of the woods presented a concave appearance, extending northerly about two hundred yards, when it swept westward, still gradually curving until it ran south and then east, thus enclosing a body of woods connected with the woods surrounding and north of the church by a narrow neck. This entire body of woodland is known as the West Woods. This woodland is full of outcropping ledges of limestone, affording excellent cover for infantry. The most prominent of these ledges stands at or quite near the southwest corner of the field north of the church, runs northeast eight hundred yards, and crosses the Hagerstown Road at the David R. Miller farm. (The Miller house and barn stand on the ledge.) For its entire length it affords perfect cover for infantry, and it was to play an important part early on the seventeenth. The field enclosed by the West Woods and Hagerstown Road is a nearly level plateau, in grass at the time, and higher than the West Woods, which slope quite abruptly down from the western edge of the plateau.

Further north the ground is open immediately on the west of the road, and there are two good-sized woods detached from each other further to the west and quite near the Potomac. West and northwest of the West Woods is a prominent ridge (Hauser's Ridge), higher than the Hagerstown Road. Midway between the northwest corner of the West Woods and the Potomac, distant only 1,300 yards, this ridge reaches its greatest elevation, Nicodemus Hill—190 feet above the Antietam. (It commands a wide sweep of country to the north and east, and the Confederates put many batteries upon it to protect the left of their line, search the flank of the Union lines as they successfully advanced early on the morning of the seventeenth, and tear the body of Sedgwick's division as it passed to the west edge of the woods later in the forenoon.) Once taken and held by the Union forces, Hauser's Ridge would enable an opponent to take in flank and reverse the entire Confederate line. The neglect to seize it was one of the primal errors in the conduct of the battle.

The open ground west of the Hagerstown Road was beautifully diversified with fields of corn and grass, others that were freshly plowed, and still others that were in wheat stubble. These various fields were divided by fences largely of post-and-rail construction or the well known worm variety, though other fences were of stone. There were a few farm houses, numerous apple orchards, and many stacks of grain and hay.

Standing at the Dunkard church and looking to the northeast could be seen, about six hundred yards distant, an irregularly shaped body of woods covering about thirty-five acres. There were the East Woods, full of rock ledges and large boulders. Here General Seymour's Pennsylvania Reserves bivouacked on the night of the sixteenth, and here began the battle on the seventeenth. Looking northward could be seen, at a distance of nearly a mile, a belt of woods running east and west, crossing the Hagerstown Road. These were the North Woods and were occupied on the night of the sixteenth by two brigades of the Pennsylvania Reserves. The East Woods, the North Woods, and especially the West Woods were remarkably free from undergrowth. Timber of oak, walnut, and hickory—of great size—made grand groves, offering but slight impediment to the movement of troops.

At a distance of about forty yards north of the church, a country road leaves the Hagerstown Road and runs northeast to the East Woods, where—throwing off a branch to the right to the Samuel Poffenberger and Michael Miller farms, then one to the left to the Joseph Poffenberger farm—it emerges from the woods and continues on to Smoketown, two miles from the Dunkard church, where it strikes the Keedysville and Williamsport Road. This is known as the Smoketown Road, and at Smoketown a hospital was established.

Looking north from the church, and about 750 yards distant, was a field of corn running from the Hagerstown Road east to the East Woods. The field covered thirty acres and was known as the Miller cornfield. For years to come it shall be known as the Bloody Cornfield of Antietam.

North of the cornfield was a grass field of nearly forty acres of higher ground than the cornfield, upon which the Union batteries were posted on the seventeenth. In that part of the field bordering the Hagerstown Road stands the house of D. R. Miller, an apple orchard east and north of it, a garden in front, and in the southwest corner of the garden, close by the road, a spring of delicious water covered by a stone springhouse. Beyond the field containing the Miller house and orchard was another field, bounded on the north by the North Woods. South of the cornfield and bounded by the Hagerstown Road on the west and by the East Woods and the Smoketown Road on the east and south was a field of nearly eighty acres—most of it in luxuriant clover, some of it freshly plowed. In the East Woods and West Woods and the cornfield and grass fields between them is where the terrible struggle between the Union right and the Confederate left took place—the most sanguinary part of the whole field.

At the church and extending northward in the edge of the woods bordering the Hagerstown Road on the morning of the sixteenth was one of Hood's brigades, some of the men gathering corn from the Miller cornfield. (Since leaving Hagerstown on the morning of the fourteenth, they had had nothing to eat but green corn and green apples.) Out in this field in front of the church was Hood's other brigade, while in and on either side of the road on the right of the church was S. D. Lee's battalion of artillery, sheltered from view of the Union gunners beyond the Antietam by the high ground east of the road. Some guns of Cutts's Battalion were in and near the road north of the church. There were bodies of Stuart's cavalry in the adjacent fields both east and west of the church, and detachments could be seen coming down the turnpike from the north (which had been scouting in the direction of Hagerstown) and also coming and going on the Smoketown Road, watching the upper crossings of the Antietam and scouting the country between it and the Hagerstown Turnpike. On the rough stone steps of the church, Hood and Stuart were in earnest converse, the latter giving an animated account of his adventures in Pleasant Valley and on Maryland Heights and of the surrender of Harper's Ferry, and both concurring in opinion that before midday McClellan's entire army would be upon them by way of the upper crossings of the Antietam, which they were then watching.

Crossing the turnpike at the church and going east a little over two hundred yards is a plateau where, on the morning of the seventeenth, S. D. Lee placed his artillery battalion. It is 215 feet above the Antietam and commands an extensive and entrancing view. To the left and but a short distance were the Mumma buildings, and just beyond these a small Dunkard burying ground, with its modest headstones standing in pleasing contrast against the surrounding grass and plowed fields. At our feet is the Mumma cornfield, the stalks of corn beginning to wear the russet hues of autumn, and beyond this and a grass field (through which runs a spring branch from the Mumma place) are the farm buildings of William Roulette—a fine country house, a large barn, and some other outbuildings, including a stone house covering a noble spring of cool, pure water. Here were brought the wounded of French's and Richardson's divisions. Looking still eastward the ground descends to the Antietam, which cannot be seen, but whose winding can be traced by the willows and sycamores fringing the banks. Beyond is seen the high ridge or bluff bordering the east bank of the Antietam, upon which were placed those long-range guns that drove Colonel Lee's artillery from the spot on which we stand and furrowed the field with their 20-pounder Parrott shot and shell. Still beyond, at a distance of one and three-quarter miles, can be seen the red brick house of Philip Pry, which McClellan occupied as his headquarters, and still beyond a succession of farm houses, orchards, fields of grass and clover, and woodlands extending on rolling and gradually rising ground to the feet of Elk Ridge and South Mountain.

Turning to the south can be seen the sunken road and Piper cornfield, Sharpsburg and the high ground south and west of it, and Cemetery Hill, upon which are enemy batteries about to open upon the Union artillery across the Antietam. Almost with the naked eye could be seen, walking among the guns, Robert E. Lee.

The northern part of the field, upon which the battle is to open and wage the fiercest, is comparatively quite level, but south of Cemetery Hill it is rough, the valleys or ravines being deeper and the hills steeper. Looking to the southwest from General Lee's position on the hill could be seen Jones's Division—the right of the Confederate line—in one of these ravines. Twelve hundred yards in advance, to the southeast, was Robert Toombs's small command of not more than 450 men looking down upon the Rohrbach Bridge and the Antietam, employed in piling rails along the crest of the bluff bordering the stream and collecting stones which were heaped for protection.

With the exception of these few rails and stones hastily thrown together by Toombs's Georgians, and some similar defenses made by pickets generally, there were no entrenchments on either side. Not a spadeful of earth was turned, but some stone fences and outcropping ledges of rock in the vicinity of the Dunkard church afforded good cover for Jackson's and Longstreet's troops, and were taken advantage of by them. D. H. Hill had the advantage of a stone fence on the Hagerstown Road and used some rail fences to strengthen his position in the sunken road.

Excepting the woods in which the Confederate left rested and the East Woods, the battlefield was quite open, and most of it was visible from the ridges on the east side of the Antietam, including the one on which McClellan had his headquarters. There was probably no battlefield of the Civil War more free and open to the movement of troops and the oversight of commanders, none where more time was allowed for preparation (which, on the Confederate side at least, was complete), and none where the result depended so little upon purely accidental circumstances, but almost entirely and directly upon the ability of the generals and the conduct of the troops.

12
The Prelude to Antietam
September 16, 1862

General Lee was an early riser. On the night of the fifteenth, his headquarters were pitched in a body of open woods nearly three-fourths of a mile west of the Sharpsburg town square, on the right of the road leading to Shepherdstown. Very soon after daybreak of the sixteenth, he had breakfasted and was on Cemetery Hill, and after walking among the guns of the Washington Artillery—trying in vain to pierce the fog that hung over the course of the Antietam to see what McClellan was doing—he walked back to the roadside, where a campfire was smoldering. Here, about sunrise, a young officer of Longstreet's staff rode up, dismounted, and delivered a message to which Lee listened attentively, then, as in a soliloquy, said, "All will be right if McLaws gets out of Pleasant Valley."[1] Still earlier in the morning, he had heard that the head of Jackson's column had reached the Potomac and that, when Jackson left Harper's Ferry, McLaws was still in the valley, but had been ordered by Jackson to follow him as soon as possible.

We return to Jackson and Walker, whom we left at Harper's Ferry and Loudoun Heights on the morning of the fifteenth. We have noted the receipt by Jackson of Lee's orders to join him as speedily as possible, but Jackson's men were out of rations and these could not be immediately supplied. Late in the afternoon, Brigadier General Alexander R. Lawton (commanding Ewell's Division) was ordered to march to Sharpsburg, fourteen miles distant. Only two of Lawton's brigades—his own and Trimble's—were ready, and Lawton started with these near sunset, leaving Early (with his own brigade and Hays's) to follow as soon as possible. Lawton marched up the Virginia side of the Potomac until late in the night and went into camp about four miles from Shepherdstown Ford. Early was not promptly supplied with rations, and it was midnight when they had been cooked. At 1:00 a.m. he marched with his brigade and Hays's and, overtaking Lawton, the entire division was on the march at early dawn. It crossed Shepherdstown Ford at sunrise and, proceeding on the Sharpsburg Road, halted in a wood about a mile from town near Jackson's Division, which had preceded it in crossing the Potomac.

No sooner had the surrender of Harper's Ferry been assured than Walker descended Loudoun Heights, crossed the Shenandoah at Keys's Ferry, and marched to Halltown, where he halted for rations. At 1:00 a.m. he resumed his march, overtook the rear of Jackson's force about an hour later, and reached Shepherdstown Ford between daylight and sunrise. His division crossed the river early in the day and halted in a grove about midway from the ford to Sharpsburg, where it remained until 3:00 a.m. of the seventeenth. Then it moved to the right and took position to cover Snavely's and Myers's fords south of Sharpsburg. Jackson made this report: "Leaving General [A.P.] Hill to receive the surrender of the Federal troops and take the requisite steps for securing the captured stores, I moved, in obedience to orders from the commanding general, to rejoin him in Maryland with the remaining divisions of my command. By a severe night's march we reached the vicinity of Sharpsburg on the morning of the 16th."[2]

Some of Jackson's staff officers and others say that Jackson reported to Lee at daylight on Cemetery Hill. Walker says that he rode forward with Jackson from Shepherdstown Ford about eight o'clock.[3] He also says that after the troops had crossed the Potomac, he rode forward with Jackson about midday to report to Lee:

I expected to find General Lee anxious and careworn. Anxious enough, no doubt, he was; but there was nothing in his look or manner to indicate it. On the contrary, he was calm, dignified, and even cheerful. If he had had a well-equipped army of a hundred thousand veterans at his back, he could not have appeared more composed and confident. On shaking hands with us, he simply expressed his satisfaction with the result of our operations at Harper's Ferry, and with our timely arrival at Sharpsburg; adding that with our reënforcement [sic] he felt confident of being able to hold his ground until the arrival of the divisions of R. H. Anderson, McLaws, and A. P. Hill, which were still behind, and which did not arrive until the next day.[4]

---

[1] As of this writing, Carman's source for this quotation has not been identified.

[2] Thomas J. Jackson to Robert E. Lee, April 23, 1863, reprinted in *OR*, vol. 19, pt. 1, 955.

[3] John G. Walker, "Jackson's Capture of Harper's Ferry," in *Battles and Leaders of the Civil War*, vol. 2 (New York: Century Co., 1887), 611.

[4] John G. Walker, "Sharpsburg," in *Battles and Leaders*, 675.

Jackson and Walker brought to Lee about 10,300 officers and men. This was not a large reinforcement but, with 15,600 already in position, gave Lee an aggregate of infantry, cavalry, and artillery of 25,900—all veteran soldiers. It was a compact, well trained force. As the long September day wore on and gave the men time to rest, Lee became confident that he would not be called upon for any serious work that day and that by morning McLaws and Anderson would be with him, and his army (except A. P. Hill's Division) reunited and ready to give McClellan battle.

During the afternoon and night of the fifteenth, McClellan's forces moved to the positions assigned them, but it was not until after daybreak of the sixteenth that the great body of them were in their designated places. (Some brigades did not get up until noon.) Hooker's First Corps was in the forks of the Big and Little Antietam. Sumner's Second Corps was on both sides of the Boonsboro and Sharpsburg Road, with Richardson's division in advance near the Antietam on the right of the road and Sykes's division on the left of Richardson's. On Sykes's left and rear was Burnside's Ninth Corps. Mansfield's Twelfth Corps was at Nicodemus's Mill or Springvale. Pleasonton's cavalry division was just west of Keedysville.

Near midnight of the fifteenth, two companies each of the 61st and 64th New York, under the command of Lieutenant Colonel Nelson A. Miles, passed along the rear of Sedgwick's division and some distance along the bluff below the Middle Bridge, then turned back and reached the bridge just as a party of Union cavalry came riding sharply over it from the south bank. They informed Miles that the enemy had fallen back and that there were none in the immediate front of the bridge. Miles crossed the bridge to the west side of the creek and marched continuously along the highway. It was then daybreak. A heavy fog prevented vision for more than fifteen or twenty feet, the dust in the road deadened the sound of the footsteps, and silence was enjoined. Miles, who was in advance, had reached the crest of the ridge about six hundred yards beyond the Antietam and was about to descend into the broad ravine where the Confederates were in position when he ran upon a Confederate crossing the road, whom he captured and from whom he learned that he was very near the Confederate line. The command was faced about and moved back with as much silence and celerity as possible, and recrossed the bridge before the fog lifted but long after daylight of the sixteenth.

There has been much criticism for the failure of McClellan to attack Lee on the afternoon of the fifteenth or at least early on the morning of the sixteenth. We have referred to the failure to do so on the fifteenth. The situation, inviting prompt attack on the morning of the sixteenth, is well stated by Francis A. Walker in his *History of the Second Corps*:

> If it be admitted to have been impracticable to throw the thirty-five brigades that had crossed the South Mountain at Turner's across the Antietam during the 15th in season and in condition to undertake the attack upon Lee's fourteen brigades that day with success, it is difficult to see what excuse can be offered for the failure to fight the impending battle on the 16th, and that early. It is true that Lee's forces had then been increased by the arrival of Jackson, with Starke's [i.e., Jackson's] and Lawton's [i.e., Ewell's] divisions [also Walker's—*EAC*], but those of Anderson, McLaws … and A. P. Hill could not be brought up that day. A peremptory recall of Franklin, in the early evening of the 15th, would have placed his three divisions in any part of the line that might be desired. Even without Franklin, the advantage of concentration would have been on the side of McClellan. When both armies were assembled the Union forces were at least nine to six; of the Confederate six, only four could possibly have been present on the 16th. Without Franklin, the odds would still have been seven to four.[5]

It is evident that McClellan had no idea of fighting Lee on the fifteenth; there seems to have been no intention to do it on the sixteenth. Certainly no orders to that effect were issued, nor did he make any preparation. In fact he expected Lee to retreat during the night of the fifteenth.

At seven o'clock on the morning of the sixteenth, after telegraphing his wife that he had "no doubt delivered Pennsylvania and Maryland,"[6] McClellan dispatched Halleck, "The enemy yesterday held a position just in front of Sharpsburg … This morning a heavy fog has thus far prevented us doing more than to ascertain that some of the enemy are still there. Do not know in what force. Will attack as soon as situation of enemy is developed."[7] When the fog lifted he missed S. D. Lee's

---

5   Francis A. Walker, *History of the Second Army Corps in the Army of the Potomac* (New York: Charles Scribner's Sons, 1887), 97. In Francis Walker's original text, John G. Walker's Division is listed among those that could not have been brought up to Lee's defensive lines on the sixteenth.

6   McClellan to Mary Ellen McClellan, September 16, 1862, 7:00 a.m., reprinted in McClellan, *McClellan's Own Story: The War for the Union, the Soldiers Who Fought It, the Civilians Who Directed It, and His Relations to It and Them* (New York: Charles L. Webster & Co., 1887), 612.

7   McClellan to Henry W. Halleck, September 16, 1862, 7:00 a.m., reprinted in *OR*, vol. 19, pt. 2, 307. Halleck replied to this dispatch, "I think, however, you will find that the whole force of the enemy in your front has crossed the river. I fear now more than ever that they will recross at Harper's Ferry or below, and turn your left, thus cutting you off from Washington. This has appeared to me to be a part of their plan, and hence my anxiety on the subject." Halleck to McClellan, September 16, 1862, 12:30 p.m., as contained in McClellan to Lorenzo Thomas, August 4, 1863, reprinted in *OR*, vol. 19, pt. 1, 41. When this dispatch was read by McClellan during the afternoon of the sixteenth, contempt was written on his features as he remarked, "The idea of Halleck giving me lessons in the art of war!"—*EAC*

guns, which had been moved to the left, or as he reports, "It was discovered that the enemy had changed the position of his batteries. The masses of his troops, however, were still concealed behind the opposite heights. Their left and center were upon and in front of the Sharpsburg and Hagerstown turnpike, hidden by woods and irregularities of the ground, their extreme left resting upon a wooded eminence near the cross-roads to the north of [D. R.] Miller's farm, their left resting upon the Potomac. Their line extended south, the right resting upon the hills to the south of Sharpsburg, near Snavely's farm." This changed position of the batteries is given by McClellan as one of the reasons for not making the attack before afternoon, for he says he was "compelled to spend the morning in reconnoitering the new position taken up by the enemy, examining the ground, finding fords, clearing the approaches, and hurrying up the ammunition and supply trains, which had been delayed by the rapid march of the troops over the few practicable approaches from Frederick. These had been crowded by the masses of infantry, cavalry, and artillery pressing on with the hope of overtaking the enemy before he could form to resist an attack. Many of the troops were out of rations on the previous day, and a good deal of their ammunition had been expended in the severe action of the 14th."[8]

From the time of McClellan's arrival on the field until Hooker's advance in the afternoon of the sixteenth, nothing seems to have been done with a view to an accurate determination of the Confederate position. From the heights east of the Antietam, the eye could trace the right and center, but the extreme left could not be definitely located, nor was the character of the country on that flank known. It was upon this flank that McClellan decided to make his attack, and one would suppose that his first efforts would be directed to ascertain how that flank could be approached and what it looked like. This was proper work for cavalry, of which he had a good body available for the purpose. Pleasonton's cavalry division was in good shape, sated with its successful achievements (culminating in the discomfiture of Fitzhugh Lee's Brigade at Boonsboro the day before) and confident of its capacity for further good work. But it was not used. As far as we know, not a single Union cavalryman crossed the Antietam until Hooker went over in the afternoon of the sixteenth, when the 3d Pennsylvania Cavalry accompanied him. Nor can we discover that the cavalry did any productive work elsewhere. It did not ascertain that there were good fords below the Rohrbach Bridge leading directly to the right rear of the Confederate line, and we know of no orders given for its use, save a suggestion to Franklin to have his cavalry feel toward Frederick. The part taken by the cavalry this day is very briefly told by Pleasonton in his report: "On the 16th … my cavalry was engaged in reconnaissances, escorts, and supports to batteries."[9] If any part of his command, except the 3d Pennsylvania Cavalry, was engaged in reconnaissance and supporting batteries, we do not know it.

The first movement of the day was to crown the bluff east of the Antietam with artillery and cover the Middle Bridge. (This bluff, which almost overhangs the Antietam south of the bridge, recedes from it north of the bridge for a short distance, then approaches it. It rises 180 feet above the stream and commands nearly the entire battlefield.) The reserve artillery, which arrived late in the evening of the fifteenth, was put in position early in the morning by Brigadier General Henry J. Hunt, chief of artillery. Elijah J. Taft's New York battery and the German batteries of Lieutenant Alfred von Kleiser, Captain Robert Langner, and Lieutenant Bernhard Wever were placed on the bluff north of the Boonsboro Road (Taft's battery relieving Tidball's, which rejoined the cavalry division; Von Kleiser relieved Pettit's New York battery.) The four New York batteries had 20-pounder Parrott guns and were supported by Richardson's division. South of the Boonsboro Road, Captain Stephen H. Weed's battery (Battery I, 5th U.S. Artillery) and Benjamin's battery were run up the bluff in front of Sykes's division about 9:00 a.m.

Each battery, as it came into position, opened upon such bodies of Confederate infantry as could be seen: the Washington Artillery, the batteries of Hood's Division on Cemetery Hill, and the batteries on the ridge running north from it. The reply was prompt and spirited, during which Major Albert Arndt, commanding the German artillery battalion, was mortally wounded. As the Confederates were short of ammunition and the range too great for their guns, Longstreet ordered them to withdraw under cover of the hill. D. H. Hill says that the Confederate artillery was badly handled and "could not cope with the superior weight, caliber, range, and number of the Yankee guns … An artillery duel between the Washington Artillery and the Yankee batteries across the Antietam on the 16th was the most melancholy farce in the war."[10] At 1:00 p.m. Taft's and von Kleiser's batteries were moved from the north to the south of the Boonsboro Road, Taft relieving Benjamin (who went to the left, near the Rohrbach Bridge) and von Kleiser taking position about 120 yards on Weed's right. The 20-pounder Parrotts of Captain Charles Kusserow's New York battery relieved Taft north of the road, but not in the same position. From Taft's, von Kleiser's, and Weed's positions, one could look to the right (through the open space between the East and West Woods) and see Hood's men as they advanced to meet Hooker late in the day, and the artillerists' guns were brought to bear upon them. They were also turned upon Jackson's men as they took position near the Dunkard church

8 McClellan to Thomas, 54–55.
9 Alfred Pleasonton to Randolph B. Marcy, September 19, 1862, reprinted in *OR*, vol. 19, pt. 1, 211.
10 Daniel H. Hill to Robert H. Chilton, 1862 [no month or day given], reprinted in *OR*, vol. 19, pt. 1, 1026.

about sunset. From the bluff north of the Boonsboro Road, the gunners could look down the sunken road, and it appears but a stone's throw to the Piper cornfield, in and around which were the men of Rodes's Brigade. There were very few points of the Confederate line that these batteries could not reach, and on many they had an enfilade and reverse fire.

Early in the morning, a signal station was established on the crest of Elk Ridge. The extensive view from this position commanded Sharpsburg and Shepherdstown, the country in the vicinity, and the approaches in every direction. It communicated with signal stations at McClellan's headquarters, with some on the extreme right, and with Burnside's headquarters.

Sykes's division was on the south side of the Boonsboro Road, its right (Lieutenant Colonel Robert C. Buchanan's brigade) resting on the road, opposite Richardson's left. On the left of Buchanan was Major Charles S. Lovell's brigade, extending down toward the Rohrbach Bridge. Colonel Gouverneur K. Warren's brigade of two regiments (the 5th and 10th New York) was held in reserve; later in the day it, along with Lieutenant Alanson M. Randol's battery (Batteries E and G [consolidated], 1st U.S. Artillery), was moved to the left, out of the line of fire of the Confederate guns on Cemetery Hill. (Its new position was in a piece of woods, covering the approaches in the direction of Harper's Ferry.) At 7:00 a.m. Captain Hiram Dryer's 4th U.S. Infantry was ordered to take the Middle Bridge and establish part of his regiment on the west bank of the Antietam. Upon arriving within two hundred yards of the bridge, he passed the pickets of the 3d U.S. Infantry and detached Lieutenant John L. Buell with the 4th's Company G to advance rapidly to the bridge, which was done without opposition. Dryer then marched the regiment to the bridge and threw four companies across it, which were posted under cover of a stone bank and wall on the right of the road and of a rock ledge and barn on the left. In about two hours it was observed that the enemy was advancing a skirmish line on both sides of the road, upon which two companies under Buell and another lieutenant, Robert P. McKibbin, advanced on either side of the road to hold the Confederates in check. They advanced about three hundred yards up the ascending road and met the enemy, who after exchanging a few shots fell back under cover of the ridge (behind which lay G. B. Anderson's Brigade). About the same time, the Confederate batteries on Cemetery Hill began a vigorous shelling of Dryer's skirmishers and upon the batteries on the bluff in his rear, beyond the Antietam. (This firing was of short duration and did but little harm, wounding three of Dryer's men. Two others were wounded by the skirmishers.) At sunset Dryer was relieved by the 1st Battalion, 12th U.S. Infantry, under Captain Matthew M. Blunt, and recrossed the Antietam. As soon as the bridge had been taken by the regular infantry, two companies of the 5th New Hampshire under Captains Richard Cross and Charles Long were sent to destroy the mill dam a few yards below the bridge in the hope of lowering the waters of the creek above and make fording less difficult, but did not succeed in breaking the dam for want of proper tools. Several companies of Richardson's division were on picket during the night, and in the morning four companies of the 5th New Hampshire under Major Edward E. Sturtevant were detached to guard a small aqueduct crossing the Antietam near the Niekirk house, nearly a mile above the Middle Bridge.

During the forenoon the Twelfth Corps advanced from its bivouac near Nicodemus's Mill and massed in a field west of Keedysville and in rear of French's division. In the afternoon Morell's division of the Fifth Corps passed through Keedysville and bivouacked on the left of the Boonsboro and Sharpsburg Turnpike.

The valley of the Antietam at and near the Rohrbach Bridge is narrow. On the right of the stream the high bank was wooded below the bridge and about two hundred yards above it and commanded the approaches both to the bridge and the ford immediately below it. The steep slopes of the bank were lined with rifle-pits and breastworks of rails and stones. These, together with the woods, were filled with Toombs's infantry, while numerous batteries commanded and enfiladed the bridge and ford and their approaches.

McClellan seems to have had some apprehension that the Confederates might attack his left by this bridge and by the valley below it, and about noon ordered Burnside to move further to the left to a strong position in the immediate vicinity of the bridge and to reconnoiter the approaches to it carefully, as he would probably be ordered to attack there on the next morning. Later in the day, he rode to the left to satisfy himself that Burnside had properly placed his troops to secure his left flank from any attack made along the east bank of the Antietam, as well as to carry the bridge. He was not satisfied with the dispositions made by Burnside and found it necessary to order some changes, the result of which was that, late in the afternoon, Burnside's corps (except Willcox's division) was moved to the left and front in three columns and took position upon the rear slope of the ridges on the east bank of the Antietam, the center of the corps being nearly opposite the bridge. The batteries were placed on the crest of the hill near the bridge, the infantry in close support, with Benjamin's battery being on a knoll some distance to the left and back from the bridge.

Burnside's movement was not opposed nor disturbed, save for a few shots from Richardson's Battery south of Cemetery Hill, but Toombs's skirmish line (thrown across the bridge for observation) was seen near a cornfield southeast of the bridge, upon which Captain Hiram F. Devol and his company of the 36th Ohio went forward and drove it through the cornfield and back over the bridge. (About the same time, a detachment of the 48th Pennsylvania under Captain James Wrenn went a mile down the Antietam and saw nothing but Munford's cavalry on the west bank of the stream.) The 79th New York was detached and sent to guard the signal station on Elk Ridge, and the 28th Massachusetts and the 50th Pennsylvania, both under the command of Major Edward Overton, were sent to Elk Ridge (where the Rohrersville Road crosses it) to support some of Pleasonton's cavalry, which was keeping open the communication with Franklin in Pleasant Valley.

McClellan reports that the ground in front of the entire Confederate line consisted of undulating hills, their crests in turn commanded by others in their rear. "On all favorable points," he says, "the enemy's artillery was posted, and their reserves, hidden from view by the hills on which their line of battle was formed, could maneuver unobserved by our army, and, from the shortness of their line, could rapidly re-enforce any point threatened by our attack. Their position, stretching across the angle formed by the Potomac and Antietam, their flanks and rear protected by these streams, was one of the strongest to be found in this region of country, which is well adapted to defensive warfare."[11]

When McClellan made his rapid examination on the evening of the fifteenth, he concluded that an attack on the Confederate left offered better results than an attack elsewhere, and this conclusion was confirmed by a more extended examination on the morning of the sixteenth. (For reasons given elsewhere, which we consider entirely inadequate, he deferred the movement until afternoon.) The plan for the impending general engagement was to attack Lee's left with the corps of Hooker and Mansfield, supported by Sumner's corps (and, if necessary, by Franklin's corps), and as soon as matters looked favorable there, to move Burnside's corps against Lee's right, upon the ridge running to the south and rear of Sharpsburg. Having carried these positions, he then proposed to press with the right along the crest toward Sharpsburg and, when either of these flank movements should be successful, to advance the center across the Middle Bridge with all the forces then disposable. The plan was a good one, but its execution, from beginning to end, was miserable, though the fighting was splendid.

The first step in McClellan's plan was the transfer of Hooker's First Corps to the west bank of the Antietam. If this movement was not in itself a reconnaissance in force, it should have been preceded by such an examination of the ground as would have sufficed to determine where Lee's left was with some approach to accuracy, but this (as we have seen) was not done. This first step was a blunder, in that the movement was made in the afternoon of the sixteenth at an hour too late to accomplish anything before dark and serving no purpose, save to inform Lee where he was to be attacked.

It was 2:00 p.m. when McClellan gave Hooker orders to cross the Antietam by the Upper Bridge and the ford below to attack and, if possible, turn Lee's left. (Meade's and Ricketts's divisions were to cross the bridge and Doubleday's at the ford.) Later, Sumner was ordered to cross the Twelfth Corps during the night and hold the Second Corps in readiness to cross early next morning. It was nearly 4:00 p.m. when Hooker put his troops in motion, Meade's division in advance. He then rode to McClellan's headquarters for any further orders the commanding general might have to give, and was informed by McClellan that he was at liberty to call for reinforcements should he need them and that on their arrival they would be placed under his command, upon which he rode off and joined his troops on the march. His direction lay nearly perpendicular to the Antietam, his object being to gain the high ground or divide between the Antietam and the Potomac and then incline to the left (following the elevation toward Sharpsburg), feeling for Lee's flank, which it was believed would be found somewhere on the divide—its exact or even approximate position being unknown to either McClellan or Hooker that day or early on the next.

Meade's division led the advance across the bridge and on the Williamsport Road, two regiments being thrown forward as skirmishers, followed by a squadron of Lieutenant Colonel Samuel W. Owen's 3d Pennsylvania Cavalry (all closely supported by the division). Hooker, as was his custom, rode in advance, close to the skirmishers, and had not proceeded over half a mile when he was joined by McClellan and his staff, apparently to see how Hooker was progressing. "Among other subjects of conversation," reports Hooker, "I said to the general that he had ordered my small corps, now numbering between 12,000 and 13,000 (as I had just lost nearly 1,000 men in the battle of South Mountain), across the river to attack the whole rebel army, and that if re-enforcements were not forwarded promptly, or if another attack was not made on the enemy's right, the rebels would eat me up."[12] Soon after this conversation, McClellan recrossed the Antietam and rode to the Pry house, from which he could see across the Antietam and observe the effect of Hooker's march or any movement made to meet it. (From this time onward, the Pry house became his headquarters.) Ricketts's division followed Meade's over the bridge and on the Williamsport Road, and most of the artillery and all the ammunition train followed Ricketts.

Doubleday's division crossed at Pry's Ford, below the bridge, and drove some Confederate cavalrymen from a cornfield and strip of woods on the left, who hastened to inform Stuart at the Dunkard church that the Union army was crossing the upper Antietam. (Stuart, in turn, sent the information to Lee at Sharpsburg.) Doubleday first moved upstream a short distance, then, turning to the left, advanced over fields parallel with Ricketts and about eighty yards on his left. His entire

---

[11] McClellan to Thomas, 54.

[12] Joseph Hooker to Seth Williams, November 8, 1862, reprinted in *OR*, vol. 19, pt. 1, 217.

division was well closed up (Patrick's brigade in the advance), removing fences and filling their haversacks with apples from the numerous, well-laden orchards.

While Hooker's columns are in motion, we return to General Lee, whom we left congratulating Jackson and Walker upon the successful operations at Harper's Ferry and their timely arrival at Sharpsburg. It was with great satisfaction that he contemplated McClellan's delay in attacking his position—a delay he did not take advantage of to strengthen his position by the construction of any defenses. (The utility of hastily constructed entrenchments in the field was not yet appreciated.) However, it did give him an opportunity to make a thorough study of the field, to select and occupy the best defensive positions, to give Jackson's and Walker's men a good rest, and to concentrate more closely his widely separated commands.

During the afternoon, Lee, Longstreet, and Jackson held council in the house of Jacob A. Grove, at the southwest corner of the Sharpsburg town square. While they were examining a map of Maryland and a map of Washington County, the artillery on Cemetery Hill opened fire. Word came that there was a movement threatening the Rohrbach Bridge, and a cavalryman dashed up with the message from Stuart that the Union forces were crossing the Antietam near Pry's Mill. Lee at once ordered Longstreet to meet this advance on the left with Hood's Division, and Jackson was ordered to take position with his own division on Hood's left. Ewell's Division was ordered to the support of Toombs at the Rohrbach Bridge. Walker's Division remained in reserve near Lee's headquarters, west of the town.

Early in the day the greater part of Fitzhugh Lee's Brigade was in the fields near the Dunkard church, with detachments in advance on the Hagerstown Road and on the Smoketown Road and east of it, observing the crossings of the Antietam. The 9th Virginia Cavalry, which had spent a quiet night in an oak grove near Sharpsburg, moved up the Hagerstown Road during the day, passed Hood's men at and in front of the Dunkard church, went down the Smoketown Road beyond the East Woods, and drew up in rear of two guns of Pelham's battery near the southwest corner of the Samuel Poffenberger woods. The guns were masked by a clump of bushes, but the position commanded an extended view of open fields and the road leading to Smoketown and thence to the Antietam.

When the videttes came in and reported that the Union columns were crossing the Antietam by the bridge and ford, dispositions were made to delay their march, and Stuart and Hood, who were at the Dunkard church, were notified. Stuart prepared the rest of Fitzhugh Lee's Brigade to support the 9th Virginia Cavalry, should it be hard pressed, and Hood sent a company of the 2d Mississippi under Captain Richard E. Clayton and one of the 6th North Carolina under Lieutenant Jeremiah A. Lea[13] up the Hagerstown Road to the D. R. Miller farm. About one hundred men of the 4th Texas under the command of Captain William H. Martin went northeast from the church, through the thirty-acre cornfield and grass field beyond, and took position on the right of the two companies of Clayton and Lea and behind the fence overlooking the field between it and the North Woods (as well as the ground on the right and the Smoketown Road, beyond the East Woods). Other skirmishers of Hood's Division and some dismounted cavalry were behind the north fence of the East Woods, and on the right of those of the 4th Texas was a skirmish battalion of Colquitt's Brigade. S. D. Lee sent two howitzers of Rhett's Battery to the left of the Mumma house and quite near the Smoketown Road, and a section of Parker's Battery went up the Hagerstown Road nearly a mile to the toll-gate, soon returning without becoming engaged. D. H. Hill sent Lane's Battery of Cutts's Battalion to assist Hood, and it took position between the Smoketown and Hagerstown roads. Hood says he stationed "one or two batteries upon a hillock, in a meadow, near the edge of a corn field and just by the pike."[14] (One of these was Lane's; the other we cannot identify, but it was what Wofford reports as "a little battery."[15]) On the Hagerstown Road and about 180 yards south of the southwest corner of the cornfield was one gun of Captain James A. Blackshear's (Georgia) Battery under charge of Sergeant Major Robert Falligant. Later in the day, about sunset, three guns of Poague's Battery went into position on the left of Falligant and about forty yards west of the Hagerstown Road.

When the advance of Meade's division had gone less than a mile, Hooker saw at a distance the high ground he was seeking, upon which Meade's column turned to the left, off the road and across the Hoffman farm. Meanwhile, detachments of the 3d Pennsylvania Cavalry had been sent forward on the Williamsport Road (also due westward) to locate the Hagerstown Road; some of these men went down the Smoketown Road and were fired on by cavalry and artillery. The presence of the enemy was reported to Hooker just as he was leaving the road to march across the Hoffman farm, upon which he ordered the 13th Pennsylvania Reserves of Seymour's brigade to advance as skirmishers on the left and four companies of the 3d Pennsylvania Reserves to deploy to the right, the main column formed in battalions in mass division front, with the

---

[13] In his original manuscript, Carman reports that the company of the 6th North Carolina was commanded by "Captain Lea." The rosters for the regiment show two Leas who reached the rank of captain: Jeremiah A. Lea of Company H and James W. Lea of Company K. James resigned his commission on July 29, 1862, due to infirmities, while the date of rank for Jeremiah's captaincy was February 3, 1863. Weymouth T. Jordan Jr., comp., *North Carolina Troops, 1861–1865: A Roster*, vol. 4 (Raleigh: [North Carolina] Office of Archives and History, 1973), 356, 380.

[14] John B. Hood, *Advance and Retreat: Personal Experiences in the United States and Confederate States Armies* (n.p., 1880), 42.

[15] William T. Wofford to William H. Sellers, September 29, 1862, reprinted in *OR*, vol. 19, pt. 1, 927.

artillery moving over the open ground for the high ridge. At the same time, a squadron of the 3d Pennsylvania Cavalry under Lieutenant E. Willard Warren, moving to the left and by the farm lane running past the Miller house, had reached the southeast corner of the East Woods, where it was soon joined by a platoon of cavalry under Lieutenant William E. Miller. The platoon had advanced down the Smoketown Road, followed by the 13th Pennsylvania Reserves, upon which Warren charged into the woods, unmasked two Confederate guns, and was fired upon by Virginia cavalry. Feeling that the instructions to develop the enemy had been carried out, Miller and Warren fell back and awaited the infantry, now coming up.

Colonel McNeil, commanding the 13th Pennsylvania Reserves, had deployed four companies as skirmishers (the remaining six being held in reserve). Advancing steadily and cautiously on either side of the Smoketown Road, his men came upon the Confederate cavalry pickets in front of the East Woods, supported by troops in position behind the fence on the north edge of the woods. A body of Confederate cavalry dashed out of the woods and up the Smoketown Road toward the 13th's skirmishers but were quickly driven back. The Confederate infantry skirmishers were driven in, and the advancing Pennsylvanians came under a raking fire from the infantry and dismounted cavalry behind the fence, to which they replied (the reserve of six companies moving at once to the support of the skirmishers). No sooner had line been formed behind some haystacks in a plowed field when the Confederates opened on it with two batteries—Rhett's with shell and Lane's with solid shot and spherical case.

Up to this time, Hood's Division had remained near the Dunkard church, supporting the batteries that were firing beyond the East Woods. But when the cavalry was driven in at twilight, Hood went to the front to contest possession of the East Woods and the cornfield. Wofford's Brigade, which was in the field in front of the church, moved by the left flank and formed line on the south border of the cornfield, its left near the Hagerstown Road and its right (the 5th Texas) in the East Woods. Law's Brigade moved from the woods about the church directly to the front, its left wing on the left of the Smoketown Road (supporting Wofford) and its right wing on the right of the road and facing the eastern part of the East Woods. Scarcely had the division taken position when the cavalry and Pelham's two guns came back through the East Woods, passed through the deployed line of the division, and went to the rear. The 5th Texas then sent forward a skirmish company through the cornfield, over the fence, and across a narrow pasture to a rail fence overlooking a plowed field, and saw Hooker's men advancing (Seymour's brigade, with the 13th Pennsylvania Reserves leading).

McNeil, after forming line in the plowed field west of the Samuel Poffenberger farm (four companies on the right of the Smoketown Road and six on the left), rested some fifteen minutes, during which time the remainder of the brigade came up. He then gave the order to charge and drive the enemy from the woods. Placing himself at the front and on the left of the road, he led his command under a severe fire from the Texans and artillery to within fifteen yards of the East Woods, when he fell, pierced through the heart by a rifle ball. The regiment did not pause, but kept on, drove the enemy from the fence, and entered the woods, only to be checked when halfway through them by the 5th Texas and a battery on the south edge of the Miller cornfield. With the assistance of Cooper's guns and Captain Dunbar R. Ransom's regular battery of artillery, the Confederate battery was soon silenced, but the Texans held their ground. In this movement the 13th Pennsylvania Reserves was closely supported by the remainder of the brigade, with the 6th Pennsylvania Reserves advancing on its right, driving in the skirmishers of the 4th Texas and some of the 5th Texas, and following the 13th into the woods and to the fence separating the woods from the cornfield. An effort was made to penetrate the cornfield, but the right of Wofford's Brigade had pushed up into it and held its ground so tenaciously that the regiment withdrew about one hundred yards to the north part of the East Woods, leaving a heavy picket line along the fence in its front. The 1st Pennsylvania Reserves followed the 13th into the woods and formed on their right and rear. The 5th Pennsylvania Reserves, on the left of the brigade, remained some time on the open ground, but came up after dark and formed along the north fence of the woods, on the left of the 1st. Cooper's Pennsylvania artillery closely followed the 13th through the woods south of the Line farm by a wagon path, thence down the Smoketown Road, and went into battery west of the road (close to the northwest corner of the Samuel Poffenberger woods) with the 2d Pennsylvania Reserves in support, and opened fire upon Lane's Battery (which was firing at Seymour's men in the East Woods). While in this position and actively at work, the two brigades of Magilton and Anderson were swinging to the left and advancing past the right of the battery.

When the 13th Pennsylvania Reserves moved down the Smoketown Road to meet the enemy in that direction, Meade led the brigades of Magilton and Anderson toward the high ground and the Hagerstown Road. But soon after leaving the Line farm and crossing the Smoketown Road, he reached the crest of a gentle slope, wheeled to the left, and marched south, the column closed in mass with skirmishers well out, stopping occasionally to remove fences and make observations. When nearing the Joseph Poffenberger barn, the enemy's skirmishers were discovered in the North Woods, and a battery beyond the woods and quite near the Hagerstown Road opened fire, upon which four companies of the 3d Pennsylvania Reserves were deployed as skirmishers to the right and four companies directly to the front. These were followed by the 4th Pennsylvania Reserves in line of battle, closely supported by the two brigades. The Confederate skirmishers were quickly driven from the woods, and the two brigades pushed on and occupied them just at dusk, Anderson's right resting on the Hagerstown Road with Magilton on his left.

Upon approaching the North Woods, a Confederate battery was plainly seen in a field beyond them, supported by infantry, playing upon Seymour's men in the East Woods. Major John Nyce ordered the 4th Pennsylvania Reserves to fix bayonets and prepared to take it but was restrained by the order of his brigade commander (probably so directed by Meade, who says that as but one regiment, the 4th, was deployed, he was deterred from the endeavor to capture the battery by a charge.[16]) After Meade entered the woods, the battery was still continuing to fire upon Seymour; Ransom's Battery C, 5th U.S. Artillery, was ordered forward to silence it. Ransom went straight down from the field east of the Joseph Poffenberger barn, through the North Woods to the open field beyond, and into battery, opening upon the Confederate battery and supporting infantry an enfilade fire which, in addition to Cooper's fire and the musketry fire of the 13th Pennsylvania Reserves' skirmishers, caused the withdrawal of the offending guns. Wofford reports that he had one officer and some dozen men wounded by this fire, and that the enemy were informed of his position by the firing of a half-dozen shots from a little battery on the left of his brigade, which hastily beat a retreat as soon as the Union guns opened on it.[17]

About this time the three guns of Poague's Battery, west of the Hagerstown Road, began shelling Ransom's guns, the North Woods (occupied by Meade's men), and the hill beyond them. After a few shots at Poague's Battery, in which it was joined by Lieutenant John G. Simpson's Pennsylvania battery, Ransom was withdrawn and bivouacked a few yards north of the North Woods and east of the Joseph Poffenberger barn. Cooper remained in the position occupied at the beginning of the action, and Simpson remained on the ridge a little to the right and rear of Cooper.

The losses in this affair were not heavy. On the Union side, the principal loss fell upon the 13th Pennsylvania Reserves, in the death of their commander. Of Hood's Division, but three regiments and the division skirmishers were engaged (these lost very lightly) and the left of Wofford's Brigade suffered some from artillery fire. Colonel Philip F. Liddell of the 11th Mississippi was mortally wounded. (His regiment was in the south edge of the cornfield supporting Wofford's Brigade and was not engaged, when he was struck by a chance shot.)

While Hood was engaged, Jackson came on the field with his old division and formed on Hood's left. When he had received Lee's order to take this position, Jackson advanced from where he had been resting since morning (leaving Sharpsburg to the right), passed the Dunkard church, and formed partly in open ground and partly in woods, with his right on the Hagerstown Road opposite Hood's left. Winder's and Jones's Brigades were in front on open ground, those of Brigadier General William B. Taliaferro (commanded by Colonel James W. Jackson) and Starke in the edge of the woods a short distance in rear. Poague's Battery was on a slight knoll in advance of the first line and, as we have seen, became engaged with Ransom's battery, concerning which Poague says, "Upon this battery [Lane's], fire was opened, and in about twenty minutes it was silenced, our own battery on the right of the road in the mean time having retired. In this affair we were assisted by one gun of some unknown battery."[18] (This one gun, unknown to Poague, was Sergeant Major Falligant's gun of Blackshear's Battery.) John R. Jones, commanding Jackson's Division, reports that the skirmishers were "warmly engaged until night,"[19] and Major Hazael J. Williams of Winder's Brigade says of the Union artillery fire, "The display was grand and comparatively harmless, except to the stragglers in far rear."[20] But the second line suffered casualties. Colonel Edmund Pendleton of the 15th Louisiana (who succeeded to the command of Starke's Brigade the next day) reports that in taking position, "we encountered the shells from three of the enemy's batteries [Cooper's, Ransom's, and Simpson's—*EAC*], and had the misfortune about dark to lose several of our number, among whom was the gallant young [Archibald M.] Gordon, a lieutenant in the Ninth Louisiana Regiment and acting assistant adjutant-general of the brigade, who was killed by a shell which cut off both his legs at the thigh."[21]

At the time Jackson's Division was sent to the left, Lawton was ordered to support Toombs at the Rohrbach Bridge. It was soon seen that no serious work was to be looked for in that quarter, upon which Lawton was ordered to follow Jackson. He moved Ewell's Division through the fields to the west and north of Sharpsburg until he reached the Hagerstown Road at the Dunkard church. It was then growing dark. The troops in front were engaged, and Early's Brigade was formed on the left of Jackson's second line and at right angles to it to protect that flank. Hays's Brigade was put in Early's rear, and those of Lawton and Trimble were held in reserve near the church. About the time Jackson came up, Stuart's cavalry fell to the rear of Hood's Division, and for a time rested in the fields east of the church and observed the shells from two directions passing

---

[16] George G. Meade to Joseph Dickinson, September 22, 1862, reprinted in *OR*, vol. 19, pt. 1, 269.

[17] Wofford to Sellers, 927.

[18] William T. Poague to William H. Thomas, September 22, 1862, reprinted in *OR*, vol. 19, pt. 1, 1009.

[19] John R. Jones to Alexander S. Pendleton, January 21, 1863, reprinted in *OR*, vol. 19, pt. 1, 1007.

[20] Hazael J. Williams to Warner T. Taliaferro, January 15, 1863, reprinted in *OR*, vol. 19, pt. 1, 1012.

[21] Edmund Pendleton to Mann Page, October 20, 1862, reprinted in *OR*, vol. 19, pt. 1, 1016.

overhead, "their burning fuses making fiery streaks and gleaming like meteors, and the whole making a comparatively harmless but brilliant, spectacular performance."[22]

Of Hooker's corps, only Meade's division was engaged. The movement of this column to the left, closely followed by Ricketts's, interfered with the march of Doubleday's division. When Meade, moving south, had passed the head of Doubleday's column, Patrick's brigade was double-quicked west under a sharp artillery fire (by which some men were wounded) to a triangular piece of woods skirting the Hagerstown Road and formed line along the road fence, facing west. Before the other brigades of the division could be put in motion to follow Patrick, Ricketts's division crossed their line of march and moved into the Samuel Poffenberger woods (on both sides of the Smoketown Road) and bivouacked. After Ricketts had passed, the other three brigades of Doubleday resumed the march in the dark. Lieutenant Colonel John W. Hofmann's brigade (Doubleday's old command) halted on Patrick's left and close to the fence of the road, his left connecting with Meade's right at a right angle and resting within a few feet of a lane running from the Hagerstown Road to the Joseph Poffenberger farm. Phelps's small brigade followed Hofmann and bivouacked two hundred yards in rear of Patrick. Gibbon's brigade, closed in mass, bivouacked in rear of Hofmann. All of Doubleday's brigades faced west and were then at right angles to Meade, who faced south.

North of the Joseph Poffenberger house is a prominent hill or rounded ridge 220 feet above the Antietam and the highest point of the battlefield, dominating all the ground west of the Hagerstown Road and destined to play an important part in the battle of the seventeenth. It was on the western slope of this ridge that Doubleday's four brigades went into bivouac, and on its plateau were placed the division batteries. Campbell's Battery B, 4th U.S. Artillery, was about seventy yards north of the Joseph Poffenberger barn, Captain John A. Monroe's Battery D, 1st Rhode Island Light Artillery, on Campbell's right, and Captain John A. Reynolds's Battery L, 1st New York Light Artillery, on the right of Monroe. The 1st Battery, New Hampshire Light Artillery (Lieutenant Frederick M. Edgell), went into park in a cornfield about five hundred yards east of the ridge, where it remained until 3:30 a.m. on the seventeenth, when it advanced into position between Patrick's and Hofmann's brigades, close to the Hagerstown Road (one gun on the road prepared to be used in any direction).

Hooker's movement was barren of good results but prolific in bad ones. When darkness came and stopped his advance, he knew very little more of the enemy's position than when he crossed the Antietam. He had been ordered to turn Lee's flank and completed his day's work by posting his own command in such manner as to secure it from a flank attack of the enemy—a very proper thing to do under all circumstances, but a thing not contemplated when he started. He had given Lee complete and reliable information as to McClellan's intention for the morrow.

Pickets were thrown out to the front and on the right that were very close to those of the enemy, and, in the fore part of the night, the Confederate artillery kept up an annoying fire, particularly upon the brigades of Magilton and Anderson in the North Woods. About 9:00 p.m. Colonel Joseph W. Fisher of the 5th Pennsylvania Reserves, on the left of the line, had some apprehension for that flank and sent Lieutenant Hardman P. Petrikin with a detachment of twenty-four men to reconnoiter and establish a picket post to the left and about 180 yards to the front. After passing the northeast corner of the East Woods, Petrikin turned to the right and moved over a field east of the woods. It was so dark that objects were scarcely discernable, and as the party neared a fence running easterly from the southeast corner of the woods, smoldering campfires were seen, and some of the men cautioned Petrikin that the enemy were just beyond the fence. Petrikin ordered his party forward, and when about twenty-five feet from the fence, the 4th Alabama and part of the 6th North Carolina (both of Law's Brigade) fired a scathing volley. The detachment gave a partial volley in return and retreated, leaving Petrikin mortally wounded. He was taken by the Alabama men to the Dunkard church and cared for tenderly, but died during the night.

At his headquarters in the Joseph Poffenberger barn, Hooker heard the picket firing along the line in his immediate front and still farther to the left on Seymour's front, and, soon after the Petrikin incident, visited his pickets in order to satisfy himself concerning the firing. He found that the picket lines were so near each other that, though unseen, each could hear the other walk. Seymour's officers and men were keenly alive to their proximity to the enemy and appeared to realize the responsible character of their service for the night. Their conduct inspired Hooker with the fullest confidence. Upon returning to the barn, Hooker immediately dispatched a courier, informing McClellan of his surroundings and assuring him that the battle would be renewed at the earliest dawn and that reinforcements should be ordered forward in season to reach him before that moment.[23]

The 3d Pennsylvania Cavalry, after performing much detached duty during the day, was practically united soon after dark between the right of Seymour's brigade and the left of Magilton's. Late in the night, a squadron under the command of Captain J. Claude White was ordered on outpost duty. When giving White his instructions, Hooker said he could not give

[22] As of this writing, Carman's source for this unattributed quotation has not been identified.
[23] Hooker to Williams, November 8, 1862, reprinted in OR, vol. 19, pt. 1, 218.

any information about the roads, that he had taken position on the left flank of the enemy, and wanted White's men to move to the right and rear and use their eyes and ears so as to provide timely notice of any movement in that quarter on the part of the enemy. White moved north, more than a mile from Hooker's headquarters, to the intersection of the Williamsport Road and the Hagerstown Turnpike, placing his reserve in the angle of the two roads at the Schneibele house and picketing the turnpike and the roads west of it.

When darkness terminated the engagement, Stuart moved his cavalry still farther to the left, on Jackson's flank, and crowned the commanding hill between the West Woods and the Potomac with artillery ready for the attack in the morning. The greater part of Fitzhugh Lee's Brigade was massed in rear of this steep hill and near the river. It was quite late in the night when Fitzhugh Lee got into position, after which he went up the side of the hill, tied his horse to a small tree, and lay down to sleep. Jackson soon came up, lay down near him at the foot of a tree, and was soon asleep.

The 7th Virginia Cavalry of Robertson's Brigade had been detached on September 10 to accompany Jackson on his march to Harper's Ferry. On the afternoon of the sixteenth, it recrossed the Potomac at Shepherdstown Ford and marched by the Grove, Smith, and Rowe farms to the Coffman farm. Here the horses were left, and the men marched across the fields to Ground Squirrel Church and took position north of the woods that surround it and on both sides of the Hagerstown Turnpike. It was late at night, and they were not aware of the fact that they were but six hundred yards south of White's squadron of the 3d Pennsylvania Cavalry and but half a mile north of Doubleday's division. Nor did the Pennsylvania cavalrymen or Doubleday's men know of the near presence of the Virginians.

When it became evident to Robert E. Lee that Hooker's movement was but the advance of a much larger force and that his left was to be attacked early in the morning, he ordered D. H. Hill to extend his line to the left, which Hill did by moving Ripley's Brigade from the right (near the Boonsboro and Sharpsburg Turnpike) to the left and in support to Jackson and Hood and the batteries of S. D. Lee. Ripley passed in rear of the division and took position during the night about 150 yards west of the Mumma house, his right resting on the Mumma lane and his left extending northwest nearly to the Smoketown Road.

The officers and men of Hood's Division being without food for three days except a half-ration of beef for one day and green corn gathered from the fields, Hood rode back to Lee's headquarters and requested him to send two or more brigades to his relief (or at least for the night) in order that his men might have a chance to cook their meager rations of flour. Lee said that he would do so cheerfully, but he knew of no command that could be spared for the purpose. Instead, he suggested that Hood see Jackson and endeavor to obtain assistance from him. After riding a long time in search of Jackson, Hood finally found him alone, lying on the ground asleep by the foot of a tree. He aroused him and made known the half-starved condition of his troops, upon which Jackson ordered Lawton's and Trimble's Brigades to his relief. He exacted of Hood, however, a promise that he would move to the support of these brigades the moment he was called upon. It was now after ten o'clock. Hood's two brigades were relieved and fell back to a position about two hundred yards in rear of the Dunkard church, and Hood rode off in search of his wagons, that his men might prepare to cook their flour.

Lawton's Brigade relieved Wofford's. Two companies of skirmishers from the 31st Georgia were stationed about fifty feet into the south edge of the Miller cornfield, extending into the East Woods on the right and to the Hagerstown Road on the left. The other eight companies of the regiment were in support about 100 yards south of the corn, with the remainder of the brigade in line about 135 yards behind them. Trimble's Brigade, commanded by Colonel James A. Walker of the 13th Virginia, relieved Law. Walker's pickets were positioned in the edge of the East Woods (which was occupied but a short distance farther in by Seymour's men), and his main line was established in a plowed field east of the Smoketown Road, save for one regiment in a clover field west of the road and connecting (though not closely) with Lawton's Brigade on the left. The right connected with Ripley's Brigade, the latter forming nearly a right angle with Trimble's and fronting the Antietam. Lawton's Brigade faced north, Trimble's northeast; both brigades lay upon their arms during the night, with occasional skirmishing in front between the pickets.

There is nothing to show that when Hooker crossed the Antietam, it was the intention of McClellan that either the Twelfth or Second Corps should follow him that evening. (If there were such intentions, they were not shown in any orders to that end.) But when McClellan, after his march with Hooker, recrossed the Antietam, he ordered Sumner to send the Twelfth Corps to Hooker's support that evening and to hold his own Second Corps in readiness to march for the same purpose an hour before daylight.[24] Sumner, who was anxious to have his command of two corps act as a unit under his own eye (in so far as this was possible), asked permission to follow Mansfield's corps that night, but McClellan would not consent. He would give Sumner no authority to move till next morning. McClellan had broken up Burnside's wing command by detaching Hooker; he now dislocated Sumner's by detaching Mansfield.

---

[24] George D. Ruggles to Edwin V. Sumner, September 16, 1862, 5:50 p.m., reprinted in *OR*, vol. 51, pt. 1, 839.

Sumner sent the order to Mansfield (who, for reasons to be explained later, had superseded Alpheus Williams in corps command) late in the night. The Twelfth Corps crossed the Little Antietam and the main Antietam by the stone bridges, went up the Williamsport Road nearly a mile, then turned to the left, and about 2:30 a.m. went into bivouac on the Hoffman and Line farms, a mile in Hooker's rear. Sumner, anticipating the movement of his own corps, and impressed with the importance of having everything at the front at the earliest hour, sent five of his batteries across the Antietam during the night. They parked near the Twelfth Corps.

13
The Union and Confederate Armies

No battle of the Civil War has given rise to more discussion of the number of combatants engaged than Antietam. To those who weary of statistics, it may be sufficient to say that the Union force engaged numbered 46,146 infantry, 3,828 cavalry, 5,982 artillery—an aggregate of 55,956 men—and 301 guns. The Confederate army engaged numbered 29,222 infantry, about 4,500 cavalry (including the horse artillery), and 3,629 artillery—an aggregate of approximately 37,351 men—and 219 guns. (To those who desire to know how these figures are arrived at, and the strength of the various organizations, we present a detailed statement in a subsequent chapter.)

What kind of men were these 93,000 citizen soldiers who, before the setting sun of September 17, 1862, left 20,950 of their dead and wounded on the field? They were Americans of all classes, from every walk of life: farmers, mechanics, traders, laborers, students, ministers, teachers, and of all the learned professions. In the main they were of the very best of the country, and more than four-fifths of them were native-born Americans. At no other period of the war were both armies at so high a standard in the character of the men.

In the Union army, there were no substitutes and mercenaries (who later were attracted by large bounties). All had volunteered from patriotism and an intense desire to save the Union. The average age was between twenty-two and twenty-three. They represented in due proportion the various elements of the American population. Their morals were as good as those of any community in the broad land. Nearly every regiment had its chaplain, and prayer meetings were regular and well attended. With the exception of some new regiments, but a few days from home, it was a veteran army, whose services had been brilliantly if not always successfully performed in West Virginia, in the Shenandoah Valley, in Virginia, on the Peninsula, in front of Washington, and elsewhere. Its only weakness was in the new regiments, and of these many were thrown into action without an hour's drill or an hour's practice in firing—but the material of which they were composed was so superior that they stood their ground manfully, though more food for cannon and musket. The army was well fed and well clothed, and had confidence in its commander, George B. McClellan.

The Confederates were of the same high character as the Union troops. They were veterans of many a hard-fought battle, and there were among these comparatively few conscripts (and these were mixed with the old troops and had their moral support). The men were not as well armed nor as well clothed and fed as were their Union foes. Men who at home had been masters of many slaves, or who were wealthy and lived in affluence without doing a day's work in their lives, marched in the ranks barefooted, with ragged garments, carrying a musket and sleeping in rain and mud. Fitzhugh Lee writes:

> The picture of the private soldier of Lee's army at Sharpsburg, as he stood in the iron hail with the old torn slouch hat, the bright eye glistening with excitement, powder-stained face, rent jacket and torn trousers, blanket in shreds, and the prints of his shoeless feet in the dust of the battle, should be framed in the hearts of all who love true courage wherever found. He was a very tatterdemalion, loading and firing his rifle with no hope of reward, no promise of promotion, no pay, and scanty rations. If he stopped one of the enemy's bullets he would be buried where the battle raged, in an unknown grave, and be forgotten, except by comrades, and possibly a poor old mother who was praying in her Southern home for the safe return of her soldier boy.[1]

This army of "tattered uniforms and bright bayonets"[2] was probably "the strongest body of men of equal numbers that ever stood together upon the earth."[3] Its commander—Robert E. Lee—was one of the grandest military figures of the century.

---

[1] Fitzhugh Lee, *General Lee* (New York: D. Appleton and Co., 1894), 209.

[2] As of this writing, the origin of this phrase has not been determined. One of the first histories of the Army of the Potomac, quoting an unnamed source, referred to the Army of Northern Virginia as "that array of 'tattered uniforms and bright muskets'" William Swinton, *Campaigns of the Army of the Potomac: A Critical History of Operations in Virginia, Maryland and Pennsylvania from the Commencement to the Close of the War, 1861–5* (New York: Charles B. Richardson, 1866), 16. The descriptor appears in print in the same manner as Carman's version ("tattered uniforms and bright bayonets") in James Harrison Wilson, *The Life of Charles A. Dana* (New York: Harper & Brothers, 1907), 310. Like Swinton, however, Wilson presents it as an unattributed quotation.

[3] John W. Daniel, introduction to *Recollections of a Confederate Staff Officer*, by Gilbert Moxley Sorrel (New York: Neale Publishing Co., 1905), 11.

Before examining the particulars of the battle of Antietam, we note the following passage from Francis Palfrey's own study of the event:

Those who have been in battle know how much and how little they saw and heard. They remember how the smoke and the woods and the inequalities of ground limited their vision when they had leisure to look about them, and how every faculty was absorbed in their work when they were actively engaged; how the deafening noise made it almost impossible to hear orders; what ghastly sights they saw as men and horses near them were torn with shell; how peacefully the men sank to rest whom the more merciful rifle-bullet reached in a vital spot; how some wounded men shrieked and others lay quiet; how awful was the sound of the projectiles when they were near hostile batteries, how incessant was the singing and whistling of the balls from rifles and muskets; how little they commonly knew of what was going on a hundred yards to their right or left. Orderly advances of bodies of men may be easily described and easily imagined, but pictures of real fighting are and must be imperfect. Participants in real fighting know how limited and fragmentary and confused are their recollections of work after it became hot. The larger the force engaged, the more impossible it is to give an accurate presentation of its experiences.[4]

---

[4] Francis Winthrop Palfrey, *The Antietam and Fredericksburg*, vol. 5 of *The Army in the Civil War* (New York: Charles Scribner's Sons, 1882), 166. Though the passage occurs in Palfrey's examination of Fredericksburg, it is equally valid for Antietam. Indeed, if one makes allowance for the temporal specificity of the weapons described therein, Palfrey's statement expresses a universal truth about both the experience of combat and the inherent limits of tactical narratives.

14

The Battle on the Union Right and Confederate Left:
Daybreak to 7:30 a.m.

Antietam, September 17, 1862

The battle of Antietam (or Sharpsburg) was really three engagements, at different hours of the day, on entirely different parts of the field. The battle began on the Union right at daybreak and was practically over at 10:30 a.m. In the center it began at 9:30 a.m. and was over before 1:00 p.m. It began on the Union left at 10:00 a.m. and continued till sunset. No Union troops that fought on one part of the line were elsewhere engaged. With the Confederates it was different. Walter H. Taylor says, "With consummate skill were they maneuvered and shifted from point to point, as different parts of the line of battle were in turn assailed with greatest impetuosity."[1]

The engagement on the right began at daybreak with the advance of the First Corps, under Hooker, upon the divisions of Ewell and Jackson, resulting in the defeat of those two divisions and the check of Hood's Division. The next stage was the advance of the Twelfth Corps and its relief of the First at 7:30 a.m., its forcing back of Hood, and successful engagements with the brigades of Ripley, Colquitt, and Garland, driving them from the field at 8:40 a.m. The third stage, on the right, was the advance of the Second Corps at 9:10 a.m. and the engagement of Sedgwick's division and parts of the First and Twelfth Corps in the West Woods with Early's and G. T. Anderson's Brigades, the divisions of McLaws and Walker, and the remnants of Jackson's Division.

When Hooker crossed the Antietam on the afternoon of the sixteenth, it was his understanding that when he began the attack next morning on Lee's left, simultaneous attacks would be made upon Lee's center and right.[2] When he had taken position, he reported to McClellan that "the battle would be renewed at the earliest dawn," and suggested that he should be reinforced before that time.[3] There was no delay on Hooker's part. The stars were still shining when his skirmishers became engaged, and he and Meade left their quarters in the Joseph Poffenberger barn and went to the south edge of the North Woods to give direction to the attack. His examination determined him to continue a southward movement and seize what appeared to be the key point on that part of the field—the Dunkard church and the high ground adjacent on either side of the Hagerstown Road. Once gained, this position would take D. H. Hill's Division in left flank and rear and enfilade the Confederate batteries on Cemetery Hill. Orders were given holding Doubleday's division in readiness to move directly on the church and for batteries to be put in position to support the movement and silence S. D. Lee's guns, plainly seen on the plateau across the road from the church. While these examinations were being made, the battle was opened in the East Woods between Seymour's men and the Confederate brigades of Lawton and Trimble and by an artillery duel between Doubleday's batteries on high ground at the Joseph Poffenberger farm (Poffenberger Hill) and three Southern batteries on Nicodemus Hill. Ricketts's division was now ordered to support Seymour, Doubleday's was ordered forward, and Meade's division was held in the center to support the movements of Doubleday and Ricketts and go to the assistance of either when required.

The Confederate position was not exactly as Hooker expected to find it. It did not present its flank to him. The left was thrown back at nearly a right angle to the main Confederate line, with its left across the Hagerstown Road, Jackson's old division west of and perpendicular to the road, and two brigades of Ewell's Division east of it. General Lawton, commanding Ewell's Division, claims first attention.

Trimble's Brigade, under Colonel James A. Walker, was on the right of the division, its right resting on the Mumma graveyard and thence extending to the left across the Smoketown Road. From right to left were the 15th Alabama, 21st North Carolina, 21st Georgia, and 12th Georgia (the last named being on the left of the road). The brigade numbered about seven hundred men. Ripley's Brigade of D. H. Hill's Division was on the right and rear of Trimble's. On the left was Lawton's Brigade, but not in close connection, there being an interval of sixty-five to seventy yards. Commanded by

---

[1] Walter H. Taylor, *Four Years with General Lee: Being a Summary of the More Important Events Touching the Career of General Robert E. Lee, in the War between the States, Together with an Authoritative Statement of the Strength of the Army Which He Commanded in the Field* (New York: D. Appleton and Co., 1877), 73.

[2] *Report of the Joint Committee on the Conduct of the War*, 37th Cong., 3d sess., 1863, S. Rep. 108, pt. 1, serial 1152, 581.

[3] Joseph Hooker to Seth Williams, November 8, 1862, reprinted in *OR*, vol. 19, pt. 1, 218.

Colonel Marcellus Douglass of the 13th Georgia, this brigade had six Georgia regiments (the 13th, 26th, 31st, 38th, 60th, and 61st) numbering 1,150 men. When first in position, and until the battle had fairly opened, the left of the brigade was about 120 yards east of the Hagerstown Road, and the three left regiments—the 26th, 38th, and 61st, in order named from right to left—from 225 to 230 yards south of the Miller cornfield and practically parallel to it; the right wing of the brigade was refused and faced northeast. The 31st Georgia was thrown to the front and left of the right wing and to within 120 yards of the cornfield, its right about 100 yards from the East Woods fence. When taking position during the night of the sixteenth, two companies of the 31st under the command of Lieutenant William H. Harrison were advanced as pickets fifty feet into the corn, their right at the edge of the East Woods and their left extending to the Hagerstown Road. Before daybreak of the seventeenth, Harrison inadvertently stumbled upon the Union picket line, a few shots were fired, Harrison was captured, and his pickets were withdrawn from the corn and formed along its south border. The ground held by the brigade was somewhat lower than the cornfield, and in nearly its entire length was covered by low stone ledges and small protuberances that afforded some protection. In places a rail fence was thrown down and piled as a breastwork. In other places there was no protection of rock ledge, inequality of the ground, or fence rails, but as the action progressed and the line rapidly thinned, these exposed positions were abandoned for the more sheltered ones.

In rear of Lawton's two brigades, on the plateau nearly opposite and about 225 yards from the church, were four batteries of S. D. Lee's artillery battalion: the Ashland (Virginia) Artillery (Captain Pichegru Woolfolk Jr.); the Bedford (Virginia) Artillery (Captain Tyler C. Jordan); the Brooks (South Carolina) Artillery (better known as Rhett's Battery, under Lieutenant William Elliott); and Captain William W. Parker's (Virginia) Battery. There were also, in the vicinity of the church and on the ridge west and south of it, some guns of Cutts's artillery battalion. (This battalion consisted of the four Georgia batteries of Captains John Lane, Hugh M. Ross, George M. Patterson, and James A. Blackshear.[4] Lane's Battery was not engaged on the seventeenth. The other three batteries were engaged on various parts of the field in the vicinity of the church and on Hauser's Ridge, most of the time under the direction of General Stuart.)

There was some spiteful firing during the night by the opposing pickets, who in places were not over fifty feet apart. When not yet fairly dawn, the firing increased to the proportions of a severe engagement. Seymour's men soon advanced through the eastern part of the Miller cornfield and the East Woods to the fence bordering them on the west, drove in the right of the skirmish line, and fell upon the front and right flank of the eight companies of the 31st Georgia, who were driven back upon their brigade.

The 13th Pennsylvania Reserves now advanced in somewhat open order about one hundred yards to the left and front, still keeping in the woods and throwing its right forward, the left in this movement reaching and resting on the Smoketown Road. In this position, well covered by the large trees, it opened a steady and very accurate fire upon both Trimble's Brigade and the right of Lawton's, while the skirmish lines of the 1st and 6th Pennsylvania Reserves advanced to the edge of the corn and woods and gave their attention to the right and center of Lawton's Brigade. As the 13th became engaged with Trimble's Brigade, the 5th Pennsylvania Reserves, advancing through the eastern part of the East Woods, drove the Confederates out of them and came to the support of the 13th, the right wing of the 5th coming up behind the left of their comrades. The 5th was quickly obliqued beyond the Smoketown Road, its right twenty-five yards from it. Lining up behind the fence, it opened fire upon Trimble's Brigade, in line across the plowed field near the Mumma graveyard, three hundred yards distant. The fighting was severe—the Confederates suffering most, being on open ground, while the Pennsylvanians had the cover of trees. The ammunition of the 13th began to run out when it was relieved by the 2d Pennsylvania Reserves, which during the night had remained in support to Cooper's battery and had before day entered the woods. Now it moved up to support the 13th. The latter regiment fell back for ammunition, but some of the men, having cartridges, remained on the line. Colonel Fisher of the 5th, observing from his position on lower ground that the left of the 13th had fallen back, and not seeing that the 2d had taken its place (for it formed more to the right, out of his sight), and supposing that a heavy Confederate fire—heard at the time—had swept the troops from his right (thus exposing that flank), led his regiment off by the left flank down the east fence of the woods to the big spring at the Samuel Poffenberger farm and thence to the Poffenberger woods bordering the Smoketown Road. The 1st, 2d, 6th, and the greater part of the 13th still remained in East Woods.

While Trimble's Brigade was engaged with the Pennsylvania Reserves, two heavy batteries beyond the Antietam opened fire upon it, and very soon thereafter the Union artillery on the high ground east of the D. R. Miller farm joined in the fire. S. D. Lee now sent two guns of Jordan's Battery to his assistance, but these were soon silenced and withdrawn. Leaving Trimble's Brigade under the severe musketry fire of the 2d Pennsylvania Reserves and the crossfire of artillery, we note the arrival of reinforcements to Seymour.

---

[4] Elsewhere, Carman notes that a fifth unit, Captain Whitmel P. Lloyd's (North Carolina) Battery, was attached to the battalion temporarily but was not engaged (see p. 465).

At the same time Hooker ordered Ricketts to the support of Seymour, he also ordered that the batteries of the division should be hurried forward to the high ground between the D. R. Miller orchard and the East Woods. Captain Ezra A. Matthews's battery (Battery F, 1st Pennsylvania Light Artillery) immediately advanced from near the Samuel Poffenberger woods, passed in rear of the hill where Doubleday's guns were then engaged with Stuart's, and, being opened upon by S. D. Lee's guns, went into position near the extreme northwest corner of the East Woods. The battery soon advanced to a more favorable position in the same field, about twenty yards west of the woods, and fired over the corn at Lee's batteries near the church.

When, at dawn, Ricketts's division was ordered forward, Hartsuff's and Duryee's brigades were directed to flank to the right out of the Poffenberger woods and then advance south, Hartsuff leading in deployed line, with Duryee in column of divisions in close support on the right. Christian's brigade was to go directly on the left of the Smoketown Road. It was daybreak when Hartsuff and Duryee obliqued to the right, out of the woods, to the grass fields east of the Joseph Poffenberger barn. Hartsuff, who was in line, moved south, but was immediately halted. Duryee, passing to the right, went through the North Woods and over Magilton's brigade (which was lying in them), and halted in a plowed field, where a detail was made from the 105th New York to Captain James Thompson's Battery C, Pennsylvania Light Artillery, which had accompanied the brigade and was short of men. The advance was soon resumed under a terrific fire of shot and shell from S. D. Lee's guns, by which many were killed and wounded. Passing Matthews's battery, the brigade went down a gentle incline, deployed along the north fence of the Miller cornfield at about 5:45 a.m. (the 107th Pennsylvania on the right and the 97th, 104th, and 105th New York, in order named, on the left), and the 1,100 men lay down.

At the time Thompson halted his battery for a detail of men, Matthews was already engaged. When men were furnished him from the 105th New York, he opened fire upon S. D. Lee's guns, but finding that Jordan's section, on the line of Trimble's Brigade, had the correct range of his position, he turned his fire upon it until it was withdrawn. Thompson was then ordered to advance and go into action nearly on a line with Matthews twenty yards east of the D. R. Miller orchard and due east of his house. Thompson and Matthews now threw several charges of canister into the cornfield, and then at 6:00 a.m. Duryee's men sprang to their feet, went over the fence, and moved 245 yards through very dense corn (standing over their heads) to its south edge, the right of the line now about 145 yards east of the Hagerstown Road, the left about 100 yards from the East Woods. Simultaneously with the advance of Duryee's men into the corn, Thompson's battery went forward nearly to the fence and again opened upon S. D. Lee's guns.

The south edge of the corn was skirted by a row of broom corn, which the men began to poke to the right and left to discover what was in front. The left regiments saw Trimble's Brigade and the right of Lawton's engaged with Seymour's men in the East Woods, and the right regiments saw, 230 yards in their front, Lawton's left in rear of a low, partly thrown-down rail fence. As Lawton's Brigade had been instructed to watch for the Union line to reach the edge of the corn and for each man to fire down his "own corn row," Duryee's men were instantly fired upon, and there was a contest of the most deadly character. At first no attention was paid by either line to the rail fences in their respective fronts. Each stood and fired on the other, neither party endeavoring to advance. Soon, however, the severity of the fire dictated more caution, and most of the men on both sides lay down and sought cover. The 105th and 104th New York, on reaching the south edge of the corn, pushed out into the open field 160 and 180 yards, respectively, and were opened upon with such vigor by Lawton's right, the 12th Georgia (of Trimble's Brigade), and S. D. Lee's guns that they soon fell back to the corn, the 105th carrying with it its mortally wounded commander, Lieutenant Colonel Howard Carroll.

We return to the rest of Trimble's Brigade, which we left contending with the 2d Pennsylvania Reserves and annoyed by artillery fire. The 13th Pennsylvania Reserves having been withdrawn and the 5th having retired (because missing the 13th on its right), Colonel Walker paid particular attention to the 2d, which was obliged to fall back a short distance just as Duryee's men reached the south edge of the corn. Walker's skirmishers entered the East Woods but did not penetrate far, as the 2d had fallen back a short distance only, to a more advantageous and sheltered position. In the formation of Trimble's Brigade, the 12th Georgia, about one hundred men, was on the north side of the Smoketown Road, its right resting on the road twenty yards east of the lane running to the Mumma house. In this position it fired at the 2d Pennsylvania Reserves and the skirmishers of the 1st and 6th. Upon the falling back of the Pennsylvanians and the advance of the 105th and 104th New York south of the corn, the 12th Georgia wheeled to the left and took position behind a rock ledge parallel to the Smoketown Road and one hundred yards from it, and from this covered position delivered such an accurate fire upon the two regiments that they became much shaken and fell back. Walker, observing the effect of this cool and deliberate fire, now ordered the 21st Georgia and the 21st North Carolina to wheel to the left, cross the Smoketown Road, and—taking shelter under the same low rock ledge and the swelling ground on either side of it—open fire upon the left of Duryee's line with the view of breaking it. The movement was promptly executed, and after a few rounds Duryee's left yielded some ground. Observing that Hays's Brigade of Louisianans had now come on the field to the support of Lawton's and that, apparently, it was going forward to join the fight, Walker ordered his own line to advance. This it did for a short distance when, seeing that Hays did not advance with him (thus leaving Walker's own left exposed) and that his men could not advance farther with safety, he fell back to his original position. In this last advance, Walker noticed that the 12th Georgia did not go forward with the other regiments. (Only a handful had responded to the order, while the others were seen lying behind the rock ledge.) Surprised at the conduct of this tried and veteran regiment, he hastened to it and found that every man had gone forward who could do so. Those remaining were dead or wounded. Out of one hundred men carried into action, fifty-nine were killed and wounded. Among the killed was Captain James G. Rodgers, commanding the regiment.

Meanwhile, the struggle continued between Duryee's right (the 107th Pennsylvania and the 97th New York) and Lawton's left (the 26th, 38th, and 61st Georgia). At first the 26th Georgia was 120 yards east of the Hagerstown Road, but it obliqued to the left until it gained high ground about 50 yards from the road, and directed a right oblique fire upon the right of the 107th Pennsylvania (the left of the 107th and the entire 97th New York being under the fire of the 38th and 61st Georgia). On the west side of the road was Jackson's old division, not yet engaged, but a few of its skirmishers, at the fence of the road, were firing at the flank of the 107th Pennsylvania. The 38th Georgia made a desperate effort to gain the cover of a ledge in its front, near the corn, but was disastrously repulsed. The 61st Georgia was content with holding on, suffering terribly from a crossfire. Neither side gained any advantage of ground, but the men of Lawton's Brigade lost more heavily, as they were fired at from both front and right (the fire from Seymour's men in the East Woods enfilading the three left regiments at the same time Duryee's right partially enfiladed the right regiments). In addition, both Lawton's and Trimble's Brigades were then under artillery fire (and had been since daybreak) from the Union batteries in front and from the long-range guns beyond the Antietam, which with the infantry fire exposed these two brigades to "a terrible carnage," as General Early reports.[5]

The change of front and advance of the 21st Georgia and the 21st North Carolina caused the 2d Pennsylvania Reserves and the skirmishers of the 1st and 6th Pennsylvania Reserves to retire a short distance to a better position. An incorrect report reached Duryee that they had given way entirely and that the Confederates were filling the East Woods in pursuit, thus endangering his left flank. Without verifying the report, Duryee, after being in action thirty minutes, ordered his brigade to fall back. These orders met the 105th and 104th New York as they fell back from the pasture field and carried them to the northeast part of the cornfield. Parts of the 97th New York and the 107th Pennsylvania followed, but the right of the former and the left of the latter, failing to receive orders and, from the density of the corn, not perceiving that their comrades had retired, remained a little longer, until they discovered that they were alone. Then they fell back through the corn and, at its north side, met Hartsuff's brigade sweeping to the front. Under Hooker's orders they rallied as a support. (As these two detachments went back, the advance of Doubleday's division entered the northwest corner of the corn and moved to the attack.) In its action of about thirty minutes, Duryee's brigade lost 33.50 percent of its number. The most severe loss fell upon the 97th New York; out of 203 present, it had 107 killed and wounded, or 52.70 percent.

Immediately after Duryee's retirement, the skirmishers of Lawton's Brigade pushed into the corn in pursuit, and the entire line (supported by Hays's men) was ordered forward, when it was discovered that the advance of Doubleday's division on either side of the Hagerstown Road threatened to turn their left flank. The left of the brigade then obliqued toward the road and became engaged with the 6th and 2d Wisconsin of Doubleday's advance. At the same time, Jackson's old division, west of the road, became engaged. The battle now raged near and along the Hagerstown Road and west of the East Woods. We shall narrate later the action on the Confederate left of this line and now resume the telling of what followed Duryee's withdrawal.

We have stated that while Trimble's Brigade was engaged, Hays's Louisianans came on the field. They had bivouacked in the woods northwest of the church, and soon after daylight Lawton had ordered Hays to move quickly and fill the interval of 120 yards between the 26th Georgia and the Hagerstown Road. Hays crossed the road 120 yards north of the Dunkard church and was advancing due north to close the interval when he was directed by the acting division commander to bear to the right and take position immediately in rear of Lawton's own brigade. This was done, and Hays remained in this position until Colonel Douglass, commanding Lawton's Brigade, requested him to come to his assistance. With his 550 men, Hays advanced under a deadly fire from Matthews's and Thompson's guns, and he was still advancing when Hartsuff's brigade came down through the cornfield and the East Woods and opposed him.

When Hartsuff, after moving out of the Poffenberger woods to the right, at daybreak, halted his brigade, it was that he might go forward and examine the ground over which he was to move and see where Seymour was engaged, and thus lead his men to the most advantageous position for the work at hand. While in the performance of this most important duty, Hartsuff was severely wounded and borne from the field. The command of the brigade devolved upon Colonel Richard Coulter of the 11th Pennsylvania. The delay incident to the halt and change of command was about thirty minutes, but at the end of that

---

5 Jubal A. Early to Alexander S. Pendleton, January 12, 1863, reprinted in *OR*, vol. 19, pt. 1, 968.

time Coulter had received no orders to advance. (During these same thirty minutes, Duryee had become engaged, and the 90th Pennsylvania of Christian's brigade had been ordered to support Matthews's battery.)

When Coulter assumed command the brigade was in line north of the East Woods, in this order from right to left: the 12th Massachusetts, 11th Pennsylvania, 13th Massachusetts, and 83d New York. It numbered about one thousand men. Just as firing began on the Hagerstown Road, between the advance of Doubleday's division and the skirmishers of Jackson's Division, Coulter received orders to go forward and was instantly in motion. He advanced through the East Woods and over the open field west of them and, at Seymour's suggestion, obliqued a little to the right to clear Seymour's line. The 12th Massachusetts, on the right, went down the sloping ground. (The skirmishers of Lawton's Brigade had already entered the corn.) Bullets were flying fast and shells from S. D. Lee's and Stuart's guns were exploding. Two companies from the Massachusetts regiment were thrown out under command of Captain Benjamin F. Cook, and the line continued its advance.

As one company of skirmishers was found to be sufficient, the other fell in with the regiment, and Cook went on through the corn. Douglass's skirmishers slowly retired, while their opposite numbers from Massachusetts fell back into their regiment as it came up. The 12th Massachusetts, with Thompson's battery moving close on its right rear, proceeded to follow the Georgians to the south edge of the corn. Every step was marked by dead and wounded from the fire of the Confederate artillery, but there was not a straggler. The regiment advanced about fifty yards beyond the south edge of the corn to a swell of ground trending southwest, thus throwing its right ten or twelve yards farther from the corn than its left, which was about 150 yards from the East Woods. Douglass's main line was not seen until the regiment crowned the knoll and the battle smoke had drifted away, then it was discovered beyond some low ground—a scattering and irregular line to the right, but more compact in front. An advancing line was also seen on its left front. This was Hays's Brigade, and most bloody work began.

The 11th Pennsylvania, closely following on the left of the 12th Massachusetts, passed over the 6th Pennsylvania Reserves and through the corn to near its southeast corner, where, facing a little west of south, it opened fire. On the left the 13th Massachusetts and the 83d New York swept through the East Woods and, wheeling to the right, faced nearly west at the edge of the woods, where they became immediately engaged. The entire movement was executed in good order, the regiments coming into position in quick succession and opening fire before fairly halted. From the time the 12th Massachusetts crowned the knoll south of the corn to the time the 83d New York swung round to the edge of the woods, not more than three minutes elapsed, by which time Hays's Brigade—terribly depleted—had reached Douglass's line. Hays did not halt, but pushed right on against the 12th and 13th Massachusetts and the 11th Pennsylvania, a part of Lawton's Brigade going with him while the remainder obliqued to the left, toward the Hagerstown Road, only to be repulsed (as we shall see) by the 2d and 6th Wisconsin and parts of Colonel Phelps's brigade.

The weight of Hays's attack fell upon the 12th Massachusetts, 11th Pennsylvania, and the right wing of the 13th Massachusetts—all of which were on open ground and much exposed, the left wing of the 13th Massachusetts having the cover of the woods. S. D. Lee's guns tore great gaps in the ranks of the 12th Massachusetts as musketry fire rapidly thinned it. Major Elisha Burbank, its commander, was mortally wounded. The colors and the entire color guard went down in a heap. The men closed up on the colors, which still lay on the ground, and continued their fire. The 11th Pennsylvania and the 13th Massachusetts poured in a deadly fire and, struck in front and flank, Hays's men and those Georgians who had advanced with him were soon checked, then repulsed, and fell back slowly and sullenly to seek cover. (At this time Trimble's Brigade, nearly out of ammunition and gathering what it could from the cartridge boxes and pockets of the dead and wounded, was barely holding its ground; Douglass's left had been repulsed by Doubleday's advance along the Hagerstown Road.)

While all this was transpiring on the right of Jackson's line, east of the Hagerstown Road, bloody work was being done on the left (west) of it, and we now turn our attention to that part of the action. When Jackson's Division came upon the field at dusk of the sixteenth, it was formed in two lines. Winder's and Jones's Brigades were in first line on open ground, the right (Winder) resting on the Hagerstown Road on the left of Lawton's Brigade, though separated from it by an interval of 120 yards. (Lawton's Brigade was not in view, being beyond and below the ridge on which the road ran.) The left of this two-brigade line was about one hundred yards from the West Woods, and the entire line was under the direction of Colonel Andrew J. Grigsby (commanding Winder's Brigade). The second line (Starke's and Taliaferro's Brigades), under the command of Brigadier General William E. Starke, was in the north edge of the southern body of the West Woods, 210 yards in rear of the first line. Taliaferro's Brigade had its right resting on the Hagerstown Road, with Starke's Brigade, on the left, extending to the west edge of the woods. (These four brigades comprised what was popularly known as the Stonewall Division, commanded now by Brigadier General John R. Jones.)

The greater part of Jackson's artillery did not enter the West Woods but was in the open ground west of them, near the Alfred Poffenberger barn. However, the batteries of Poague, Brockenbrough, and the Louisiana battery of Captain Louis

E. D'Aquin followed the infantry and took position (Poague on Grigsby's line and Brockenbrough in front of Starke's, with D'Aquin near Brockenbrough). Before the action had fairly opened, Jackson saw that D'Aquin was in a very exposed position where, after the infantry became engaged, he could not use his guns to advantage, and Jackson ordered him out of the woods to the open ground on the west to act with Stuart's cavalry. Poague, who had done some work at dusk of the sixteenth, sent back his two Parrott guns and was given two howitzers from Captain Charles I. Raine's (Virginia) Battery, and at daybreak on the seventeenth he had three guns a few feet in advance of Grigsby's line and about thirty-five yards west of the Hagerstown Road. Skirmishers were well out in front, from the D. R. Miller house on the right to beyond the Nicodemus house on the left. The strength of Jackson's old division was about 1,600 men. J. R. Jones says, "Regiments were commanded by Capts. & Lieuts. and some companies by Sergts. Many of the men had shoes and many went into action barefooted. And fought with gallantry that has never been surpassed and rarely equaled. They were ragged, tired, hungry and barefooted, but they were soldiers, heroes who had marched hundreds of miles during the summer … and fought many battles under Jackson and Lee."[6]

At daybreak an artillery duel began across Jackson's front between Doubleday's and Stuart's guns, and soon after a storm of round shot and shell came from Matthews's and Thompson's batteries on the Miller farm. From the heavy guns beyond the Antietam came a fire that enfiladed Jackson's Division and took it in reverse. Poague's and Brockenbrough's guns replied to the artillery on the right front, but Brockenbrough was soon ordered to retire through the West Woods. (During this artillery fire, Jones was stunned by the explosion of a shell over his head and obliged to turn over the command of Jackson's Division to Starke and leave the field.) Lawton's and Trimble's Brigades were now at work on the right, and very soon Doubleday's advance was seen marching on the east of and close to the Hagerstown Road.

Before this, Grigsby had noticed the gap between his right and Douglass's left and had called attention to it. When Doubleday was seen advancing, Grigsby again sent a member of his staff to Starke with the request that the gap be filled in at once. It was just at this time that Lawton's order to the same effect came, and Jackson (who was with Starke) ordered Hays to move through the woods in Starke's rear, cross the road, and fill the gap. At the same time, Early was ordered to the left to support Stuart's cavalry and the artillery on Nicodemus Hill. How Hays executed his orders has been told; what Early did shall be told later. We now follow Doubleday.

It was nearly nine o'clock on the night of the sixteenth when Doubleday's division (infantry and artillery) went into bivouac on the hill north of the Joseph Poffenberger farm. At very early daybreak, Doubleday galloped along his line and ordered Gibbon and Phelps to move their brigades back at once, as they were on a hillside in open range of the Confederate batteries on Nicodemus Hill about one thousand yards distant. The men, most of whom were in a sound sleep, were awakened, and Gibbon hurriedly began moving back from the exposed slope. He had moved not more than ten rods when a shell burst over his brigade, then another, followed by a percussion shell that struck a threshing machine and exploded in the center of the moving mass, killing two men and wounding eleven of the 6th Wisconsin and disabling some men of the other regiments. Moving on, the brigade soon reached the shelter of the Poffenberger barn.

This fire directed at Gibbon came from the Virginia batteries of Garber and Captain George W. Wooding on Stuart's line and was the first artillery firing on the morning of the seventeenth of September. (The first shot was probably fired by Garber's Staunton, Virginia, battery.) Carpenter immediately joined his fire to that of Garber and Wooding, and they were promptly answered by Doubleday's guns—the first shot killing Lieutenant Colonel John T. Thornton, commander of the 3d Virginia Cavalry, who was in rear of Nicodemus Hill (where Fitzhugh Lee had massed the greater part of his cavalry brigade and on the west slope of which Jackson slept during the night of the sixteenth.)[7] This was the artillery prelude to the battle of Antietam, and was soon followed by S. D. Lee's guns near the Dunkard church, the Union guns beyond the Antietam, Poague's and Brockenbrough's guns, and those of Matthews and Thompson.

The Confederate guns on Nicodemus Hill were soon silenced, but resumed their fire soon after—not upon Doubleday's artillery alone, but upon his infantry and that of Ricketts's and Meade's divisions as they moved to the front, an enfilading fire

---

6   John R. Jones to Ezra A. Carman, February 25, 1896, folder 3, box 2, Ezra A. Carman Papers, Manuscripts and Archives Division, New York Public Library. In his original manuscript, Carman reconfigures this quotation to read: "Regiments were commanded by captains and lieutenants and some companies by sergeants. Many of the men had shoes and many went into action barefooted. They were ragged, tired, hungry and barefooted, but they were soldiers who had marched hundreds of miles during the summer and fought many battles under Jackson and Lee, and upon this field fought with a gallantry never surpassed and rarely equaled."

7   "I remember going up on the side of this steep ascent in my front, tying my horse during the night to a small tree, and going to sleep there. The next morning about light I was awakened by the firing of a Federal battery which seemed to have been run up during the night to a point above us, and about the first shell thrown from it exploded in one of my regiments (below us) doing much damage and killing one of my most promising Lieut. Cols. I think it was the opening gun of the battle. I remember Stonewall Jackson came up on the right side of the hill where I was, tied his horse and went to sleep near me. He was without staff or courier, as I was, and was awakened by the same shot and hastened to his command, as I did to mine." Fitzhugh Lee to the writer, February 18, 1896 [not found].—EAC

that was very annoying and that inflicted some loss. The fire from these guns ranged into the ranks of the 3d Pennsylvania Cavalry, which had bivouacked near the East Woods, causing it to change position. (The regiment was then broken up into detachments, serving on different parts of the field, supporting batteries and gathering stragglers.)

It was soon after the opening of this artillery fire that Doubleday was directed to get ready to move. (He had previously designated Gibbon to take the advance, followed in order by Phelps, Patrick, and Hofmann.) It was nearing 6:00 a.m. when Hooker ordered the advance—Gibbon to begin the attack along the Hagerstown Road, followed by Phelps as a support. About fifteen minutes later, Patrick went forward by Hooker's order, and by the same order Hofmann remained to support the artillery on Poffenberger Hill in his rear.

Gibbon's brigade consisted of the 2d, 6th, and 7th Wisconsin, and the 19th Indiana. It numbered 971 officers and men. It was a staunch organization, known as the Iron Brigade,[8] and had a good soldier as its commander. Gibbon advanced in column of divisions (the 6th Wisconsin, under Colonel Bragg, on the right) on the east of the Hagerstown Road, through the North Woods (which were being vigorously shelled by Stuart's guns), over Magilton's brigade of Pennsylvania Reserves, and into the open field south of the woods, where Hooker was directing affairs. Here the 6th Wisconsin was deployed in line and two companies thrown out as skirmishers. Under Hooker's order the regiment, followed by the rest of the brigade, obliqued to the right until it reached the road, then marched south. Upon reaching the D. R. Miller garden, the fire from that point was severe, the enemy still holding it as a picket post (although Duryee had passed it on the east). The skirmishers, under Captain John A. Kellogg, drove the Confederates out, and the regiment pushed on over the open field, which was swept by an artillery fire from Stuart's guns on the right and Poague's in front. The right wing passed to the right of the garden without trouble; the left was delayed in its advance by a picket fence surrounding it. (In moving over the flower beds and through the rose bushes, Captain Edward A. Brown was killed by a musket ball.) Beyond the garden, in a peach orchard, the two wings of the regiment were united just as the Confederate skirmishers disappeared into the cornfield, which was on rising ground, the corn stalks standing thick and high. (This was the western part of the Miller cornfield.) Bragg did not linger in the peach orchard, but ordered the regiment forward. It climbed the south fence of the orchard, moved across a shallow basin of seventy-five yards, and pushed into the corn. The three right companies were crowded into the road and across it on the right. The other regiments of the brigade followed the 6th Wisconsin and halted, closed in mass, in the open space between the orchard and cornfield, while the Wisconsin skirmishers were searching the corn.

Campbell's battery followed Gibbon through the North Woods and halted about one hundred yards south of them. A section under Lieutenant James Stewart was advanced and opened fire over the heads of the infantry in reply to S. D. Lee's and Poague's guns and also upon the woods north of the Dunkard church. (Reynolds's New York battery was subsequently ordered to the same field, and the position on the plateau north of the Joseph Poffenberger farm, vacated by Campbell and Reynolds, was filled by Cooper's and Simpson's batteries of Meade's division.)

Phelps's brigade followed Campbell's battery through the North Woods and into the open field in which Hooker and staff were seen (directly in rear of Campbell's battery), and Phelps was ordered by Hooker to move by the flank through the field and support Gibbon, who was seen advancing. The direct and cross artillery fire over the field was very heavy, but the brigade moved without loss to a point some ninety yards in advance of and on the right of the battery when column was deployed, the right resting on the Hagerstown Road, and the line moved forward some fifty yards in rear of Gibbon. Phelps had five regiments: the 22d, 24th, 30th, and 84th New York (also known as the 14th Brooklyn[9]) and the 2d U.S. Sharpshooters. The brigade numbered 425 officers and men. Patrick's brigade consisted of the 21st, 23d, 35th, and 80th New York and numbered about 824 men. It followed Phelps through the North Woods, open field, and peach orchard, halting in the shallow depression between the orchard and the cornfield as the 6th Wisconsin became engaged, closely supported by the rest of the brigade and Phelps.

We left the 6th Wisconsin advancing into the cornfield. Its skirmishers soon found the enemy mostly along the fence bordering the Hagerstown Road and under cover. These were rapidly driven across the road, and the regiment moved up steadily in support, closely followed by the 2d Wisconsin—the right of the 6th (under the immediate command of Bragg) on and to the right of the road, the left, under Major Rufus R. Dawes, in the corn. For some reason the right of the skirmish line failed to advance and clear that flank or discover what was in that direction, and the right wing reached a rise of ground in front of the Miller barn and some straw stacks on the right of the road, when it received an expected and severe fire upon

---

[8] There is some disagreement as to whether the nickname originated with the unit's performance at South Mountain or Antietam. See Alan T. Nolan, *The Iron Brigade: A Military History* (New York: Macmillan, 1961), 335 n. 50; Jeffry D. Wert, *A Brotherhood of Valor: The Common Soldiers of the Stonewall Brigade, C.S.A., and the Iron Brigade, U.S.A.* (New York: Simon & Schuster, 1999), 188–89.

[9] Carman alternates the designation throughout his original manuscript, but refers to the regiment as the "84th New York" in his table of organization. The editor has standardized all references to match the first appearance.

the flank from Captain Archer C. Page's Virginia skirmishers lying along the edge of the West Woods, nearly opposite the barn, and also under cover of the rock ledge between the road and the woods.

At this moment a Confederate gun (probably of Cutts's Battalion) passed into the road in front. Bragg ordered Captain Werner von Bachelle's company, which was in the road, to advance to a ridge crossing the road a few yards in front and open fire upon the horses attached to the gun. At the same time, he ordered the two companies on the right of the road to advance and occupy a shallow basin between two swells of ground and a few yards from the enemy (whom he had not yet seen, but of whose near presence he was well assured). As soon as this advance was attempted, the fire from the West Woods and the ledge upon his flank increased to a murderous enfilade. A fire from a skirmish line in front followed and, looking in that direction, Bragg saw Grigsby's line (Winder's and Jones's Brigades) lying along the fence and across the field to the West Woods and at right angles to the road. No sooner had he discovered it than the entire line rose to its feet and poured in a volley that struck down many of his men and swept over the field and into the cornfield held by the left companies. This rendered an advance on the right impracticable, and Bachelle's company, in the road, was ordered to lie down under cover of the fence. No sooner had he given this order than Bragg received a severe and painful wound in the left arm but was still able to direct the right companies to draw back under cover of the road fence and the left wing to halt and lie down in the corn. These orders were being executed when he fainted and was carried to the rear, Major Dawes succeeding to the command.

Early in the morning, Poague's Battery of three guns was a few yards in front of Grigsby's Virginians and was soon vigorously engaged with the Union batteries of Matthews and Thompson, and then with Lieutenant Stewart's two guns. It directed some of its fire upon Doubleday's advancing brigades and also upon Duryee and Hartsuff. When the skirmishers became engaged and Gibbon's line advanced through the corn, Poague withdrew to the rear of Grigsby's line and threw a few rounds of canister into the corn. When the Wisconsin companies appeared marching west of the road, the Union artillery (Stewart's guns now assisting) still keeping up a rapid and precise fire, he fell back to the Alfred Poffenberger barn. Grigsby held on with his less than 450 men, subjected to the same destructive artillery fire and to the severe fire of the Wisconsin skirmishers, who, creeping up along the fences of the road, did effective work upon his weak line. His men were falling fast. His left was threatened by the advance of a Union force through the West Woods. Grigsby sent Lieutenant James M. Garnett of his staff to Starke with the message that he could not hold on much longer. Garnett found Starke in the edge of the woods, delivered the message, and as he lifted his eyes saw the men retreating across the open field. Grigsby had used all effort to hold on, but the fire upon him was so destructive that Major Williams (commanding the 5th Virginia) suggested to him to move back into the woods. Grigsby would not take the responsibility, upon which Williams ordered the 5th Virginia to fall back and the other regiments of Winder's Brigade followed. Once started the retreat was rapid.

Jones's Brigade (commanded by Captain John E. Penn of the 42d Virginia) was on the left of Winder's and quickly followed it in retreat. (The left of this brigade rested about one hundred yards from the West Woods. It was very small, and the greater part of it was on the skirmish line under command of Captain Page.) When Gibbon was seen advancing through the Miller fields, the advance skirmishers near the Nicodemus house were recalled and the greater part of them posted in the east edge of the West Woods. Some of them were advanced to the shelter of the rock ledge running south from the Miller barn, and it was this body of skirmishers that opened fire upon Gibbon's flank as he advanced along the road and through the corn, which fire (with the direct fire of Grigsby in front) caused the 6th Wisconsin to halt and Gibbon to order the deployment of the 19th Indiana and the 7th Wisconsin to the right of the road and down to the West Woods. (At the same time, Gibbon ordered Stewart's two guns to the front.) About the same moment, Doubleday ordered Patrick, who had come up five minutes before, to cross the road with his brigade and support the movement of the 19th Indiana and the 7th Wisconsin.

The 19th Indiana crossed the Hagerstown Road between the Miller house and barn and formed line. Captain William W. Dudley, deploying his company as skirmishers, quickly dislodged the Virginians from their cover at the rock ledge and pushed on into the northern part of the West Woods. The Virginians fell back, and Dudley followed closely about 120 yards into the woods when, the opposition becoming very pronounced, he halted. The regiment, slowly following the skirmishers, halted at the edge of the woods, where the 7th Wisconsin came up and formed on its left at the extreme northeast corner of the woods and sent a company of skirmishers to assist Dudley. Patrick's brigade followed the 7th Wisconsin across the road and formed in rear of it and the 19th Indiana. The 19th Indiana and the 7th Wisconsin now pushed into the woods. Dudley again went forward. Captain Page, who had been forced back, was now reinforced by Captain Penn, who had been specially charged with the care of that flank. Penn was soon severely wounded, losing a leg, and the Virginians fell back to their brigade line just as Winder's Brigade was withdrawing. Jones's Brigade (now under the command of Page) quickly followed, the two brigades, reduced to less than 250 men, obliquing to the right in retiring and rallying in the woods in rear of Starke's left.

As the 19th Indiana and the 7th Wisconsin were sweeping through the West Woods, the 2d Wisconsin was moving in the corn to the left of the 6th Wisconsin. As it came up to the 6th, the commander of the 2d, Lieutenant Colonel Thomas S.

Allen, directed Major Dawes to advance. Dawes ordered his men up and, guiding on the right of the 2d, swung away from the road, ordering Captain John A. Kellogg to move the right companies obliquely to the left into the corn. Kellogg ordered his men up, but so many were shot down that he ordered them down again at once. The line did not wait for Kellogg, but pushed on through the corn, followed by Phelps's brigade twenty-five yards to the rear. (Farther to the left, Hartsuff's brigade was sweeping through the east part of the corn and the East Woods.) Up to this time, the 2d had not given or received a shot, nor had it seen an enemy, but as it reached the south edge of the corn, the men saw before them the left of Lawton's Brigade, about two hundred yards distant. There was no time for extended observation, for as the 2d Wisconsin and the seven companies of the 6th Wisconsin came into view, the 26th, 38th, and 61st Georgia rose from the ground. Both lines opened fire simultaneously. There was but a short halt at the south edge of the corn before the Wisconsin men bounded over the fence. Kellogg came up the road with his three companies, and all went forward firing and shouting, driving back and to the left the three Georgia regiments to the foot of the high ground, where—only a skirmish line now and under cover—they held on until Hood came up. (This encounter near the road was at the time Hays came up farther to the Confederate right and made the charge in which most of the officers in both his own and Lawton's Brigade were killed or wounded.)

At the moment the Georgians were driven back by the Wisconsin men, the latter saw a body of Confederates swarming out of the West Woods, just north of the Dunkard church, as though intent on turning the right of the Union line. Colonel Allen, on the left, changed front obliquely to the right to secure a better position for firing and directed his men to construct a rail barricade. This was on the high ground near the road, and his line faced southwest. The 6th Wisconsin formed on his right, its three right companies still in the road, many of the men lying down under cover of the fence.

The advancing Confederate line was Starke's, composed of his own brigade and that of Taliaferro. (Starke's Brigade numbered about 650 men, Taliaferro's about 500.) When Starke received Grigsby's appeal for help, his line was lying down in the woods about twenty yards from their edge, with the right of Taliaferro's Brigade resting on the Hagerstown Road. Starke immediately ordered the men up, waited until Grigsby's men had fallen back out of the way, then sprang to the front and led the advance, his objective point being the southwest corner of the Miller cornfield, where the Wisconsin men had made their appearance in pursuit of the Georgians. He led his own brigade obliquely to the right as Taliaferro's charged directly to the front. The right of one and the left of the other became mixed, causing some confusion, but both brigades pressed obliquely to the right. They soon received the fire of the Wisconsin men. Starke was mortally wounded (dying within an hour) about 160 yards north of the woods and 140 yards west of the road, and the two brigades—under a murderous fire, their ranks thinning at every step—reached the high and strong post-and-rail fence along the road and came face to face with the Wisconsin men across from it, only thirty to seventy-five yards away.

Fire was immediately opened. The 84th New York of Phelps's brigade rushed out of the corn and merged with the Wisconsin men, and the fighting was fast, furious, and deadly. The Union men fell on all parts of the line. Some ran back into the corn. Colonel Allen was wounded and, after a few minutes, the Union men fell back and lay down behind the low rail fence at the edge of the corn—but only for a moment—and the Confederates began to climb the fence into the road. Phelps's brigade, as we have seen, had moved up to within twenty-five yards of the Wisconsin men before they had left the corn. After the latter had gone forward and become engaged with Starke, the 84th New York rushed to their assistance. About the same time, the 2d U.S. Sharpshooters moved up to the fence and lay down. Phelps reports, "Having ascertained that the enemy's line was formed with their left advanced, … and that they were in position to partially enfilade our lines, I ordered the Second U.S. Sharpshooters, Colonel [Henry A. V.] Post, to move to the right and front, advancing his left, and to engage the enemy at that point."[10] Post's men went over the fence and about thirty yards beyond it, their right on or very near the Hagerstown Road and their left thrown forward (thus making an oblique line with the road), and engaged the left of Starke's line (the 1st Louisiana) in and beyond the road. The Wisconsin men and the 84th New York were slowly falling back when Post was taking this position. They quickly rallied in the corn and, with the remainder of Phelps's brigade, again went forward, formed on the left of the sharpshooters, and renewed the fight. Meanwhile, some of the Confederates had climbed the fence and got into the road and others were following, but the Union fire was so severe that no farther advance was attempted. They held on to the line of the fence, though suffering severely, and the contest had been maintained some fifteen minutes when new trouble came to them.

It will be remembered that when the advance of the 6th Wisconsin was checked by the fire on its right flank, Gibbon ordered Stewart with his two guns to the front from their position east of the D. R. Miller house, and he ordered the 19th Indiana, the 7th Wisconsin, and Patrick's brigade to the right, in and near the West Woods, where they drove back the Virginia skirmishers of Jones's Brigade. Stewart moved very promptly, came down the road at a dead run, and, wheeling to the right, put his two guns in position in front of some straw stacks south of the Miller barn and his limbers in rear of the stacks and between them and the barn to protect his horses. He was now ordered to move forward about 150 yards to the

---

[10] Walter Phelps to Captain Eminel P. Halstead, September 23, 1862, reprinted in *OR*, vol. 19, pt. 1, 233.

summit of the high ground, but objected, as he could see Starke's men coming out of the woods and the advanced position would bring him under their close fire. However, he went forward about fifty yards and came into battery about thirty yards west of the road. At the same time, the 80th New York (135 men) of Patrick's brigade came to his support, its right wing in rear of the guns, while the left wing (under Major Jacob B. Hardenburgh) advanced down the field close to the road. As the ground was undulating and not favorable for the use of canister, Stewart opened fire upon Starke's men with spherical case. The left of the 80th New York fired a few shots upon the left flank of the 1st Louisiana, the skirmishers of the 19th Indiana were seen cautiously coming up on the left and rear, and Starke's entire line retired rapidly (but in pretty good order) by the right flank to the woods from which it had advanced, Stewart's shrapnel following it.

At the moment of retiring, the color bearer of the 1st Louisiana was killed at the fence. The colors were seen to drop over the fence into the road, and adjutant Lewis C. Parmelee and others of the sharpshooters rushed forward to seize them. They received a galling fire from the left by which Parmelee was killed, but another secured the colors. Many of the sharpshooters crossed both fences of the road in eager pursuit of the Louisianans. Some went down the road but the greater part of the line (the Wisconsin men and Phelps's New Yorkers) moved down the east side and were rapidly approaching the Dunkard church when out from the woods around the church and into the open ground on the east swept Hood's Division, delivering such a business-like fire that the pursuing forces halted and then fell back in some disorder, those on the left to the corn, while the sharpshooters (flanked on the left and nearly surrounded) were crowded into the road, along which they retreated to the D. R. Miller farm. The left wing of the 80th New York fell back and joined its right wing in rear of Stewart's guns.

Starke's men had been engaged for less than thirty minutes and lost heavily. Starke (who at this point was commanding Jackson's Division) and nine other officers of his brigade were killed. Colonels Jesse M. Williams, Leroy A. Stafford, and Edmund Pendleton succeeded each other quickly in command, all being wounded, and, of the six hundred fifty men carried into action, nearly three hundred were killed and wounded. Taliaferro's Brigade lost heavily. Two officers commanding it were wounded, and of the five hundred carried into action, about one hundred seventy were killed and wounded. The Union loss was heavy.

The moment has now come to note the movement of Hood's Division, but before accompanying it to its brilliant and bloody advance, it is desirable to see in what position and condition the Union lines are to meet it. The 19th Indiana and the 7th Wisconsin (after having pushed into the West Woods and driven out the Virginians), along with Patrick's brigade, held the north part of the woods and the rock ledge running south from the D. R. Miller barn. Hofmann's brigade remained in position supporting the division batteries on Poffenberger Hill, which had silenced the Confederate batteries on Nicodemus Hill and compelled most of them to be withdrawn. Matthews's, Reynolds's, and four of Campbell's guns were in the field between the Miller farm and the East Woods, the brigades of Magilton and Anderson (with Ransom's battery) were moving from the North Woods to the front, and Christian's brigade had moved up in close support to Seymour and Hartsuff, who were still engaged in the southeast corner of the cornfield and in the East Woods.

Christian's brigade was composed of the 26th and 94th New York and the 88th and 90th Pennsylvania. Very early in the morning, the 90th Pennsylvania was detached to the support of Matthews's battery in the field west of the north part of the East Woods, and the other three regiments moved out of the Samuel Poffenberger woods and formed line south of them. After a halt of some minutes, they were formed in columns of divisions and advanced toward the East Woods, did an unnecessary amount of drilling under a wicked artillery fire that killed and wounded many men and demoralized one or two of the most prominent officers, and again halted near the East Woods. After a few minutes they were ordered to advance and support Hartsuff, then severely engaged. They entered the woods and again halted. Seymour now rode up and ordered the regiments to deploy in line and go forward. The 26th and 94th New York, moving south through the woods, crossed the Smoketown Road and formed behind the fence at the south edge of the woods. (The 94th rested its right on the Smoketown Road; the 26th was on its left.) As the two regiments made their appearance at the fence, they were greeted by a charge of canister from a battery about midway between the Mumma farm and the Smoketown Road and by a fire from Ripley's Brigade, which had now moved up on the right of Trimble's Brigade and was in line near the graveyard and along the fence of a cornfield to its right. The two New York regiments opened fire not only upon Ripley's men but also upon Trimble's, who could be seen behind the fences of the Smoketown Road engaging the left of Hartsuff's line (the 83d New York, now assisted by the 88th Pennsylvania). Some Pennsylvania Reserves were still on the line and carefully firing, but Christian's advance had relieved the 1st and 2d Pennsylvania Reserves, which now fell out of the woods.

When Christian's three regiments went into position, men of the 88th Pennsylvania saw to the right and front the brigades of Lawton and Hays engaged with Hartsuff, and still father to the front could be seen the fighting on the Hagerstown Road between Gibbon's and Phelps's men on one side and Starke's on the other. S. D. Lee's guns were searching the East Woods with round shot and shell and firing over the heads of Lawton and Hays at the Union batteries north of the cornfield. A little later could be seen Hood's advance from the church, and on the left both the 26th and 94th New York saw a

Confederate column (Colquitt's Brigade)—only the heads of the men visible—marching by fours toward the right through the low ground south of the Mumma house, then in flames. The hour was seven o'clock.

While Christian's three regiments were going into position on the left, the right and center of Hartsuff's brigade were melting away under the persistent and fatal fire of Hays's and Lawton's Brigades, which although repulsed were still holding on, waiting for help. The 12th Massachusetts had been reduced to less than forty men. The 11th Pennsylvania had suffered terribly. All were short of ammunition, and the 11th's colonel, Richard Coulter, rode into the East Woods looking for help. As he entered them, he met the 90th Pennsylvania moving to join its brigade. (It had been in support of Matthews's battery since early morning.) Coulter asked Colonel Peter Lyle (commanding the regiment) to come to his assistance. Lyle at once brought his regiment into line, passed out of the woods and over the ground held by the 13th Massachusetts, and swept into the pasture field about 160 yards west of the woods and 60 yards south of the corn. He ordered the colors planted on a rock ledge and, facing southwest, opened fire on Hays and Lawton. While so engaged he saw a body of Union troops near the Hagerstown Road go forward and then fall back.

During the not more than thirty minutes it had been engaged, Hartsuff's brigade suffered greatly. The 12th Massachusetts carried into action 334 officers and men and had 49 killed, 165 wounded, and 10 missing—an aggregate of 224, or 67 percent of those engaged.[11] When it saw help coming, the colors were raised from the ground where they had fallen, dead color bearers under and over them, and 32 men marched with them to the rear. The 11th Pennsylvania had 235 officers and men in action and lost 125 killed and wounded, over 53 percent. The losses in the 13th Massachusetts and the 83d New York were severe, but not in such proportion to numbers engaged.

The right and center of Hartsuff's brigade having fallen back, the Confederates now gave their undivided attention to the 90th Pennsylvania. As the 12th Massachusetts fell back, it saw the advance of Hood's men from the woods at the church and the 4th Alabama marching by the flank down the Smoketown Road. The 90th Pennsylvania saw the same, and Thompson's battery, still in the cornfield, opened upon them with shrapnel. (It could not use canister because so many Union wounded lay close in front of the guns.)

Soon after the retirement of the three right regiments of Hartsuff, the 83d New York fell back, and very soon thereafter—as everything on its right had gone and Hood's line was advancing—the 88th Pennsylvania was given orders to retire. Many protested and would have remained, but the order was repeated and the regiment fell back. Meanwhile, the 26th and 94th New York, on the extreme left, east of the Smoketown Road, were keeping up a desultory fire upon Trimble's and Ripley's Brigades, but soon the 94th New York saw that the 88th Pennsylvania, on its right, had gone. Hood's men were still advancing, the 4th Alabama was seen coming down the road from the church, and the regiment fell back in some confusion, closely followed by the 26th New York, which had gradually melted away. (Only a few remained to retire as Ripley's men began to advance and the 4th Alabama approached the woods on the right.) There was nothing now left south of the east part of the cornfield to resist Hood's advance but the 90th Pennsylvania.

As the Confederate brigades of Trimble, Lawton, and Hays did no more fighting after Hood's advance had relieved them, we may anticipate their withdrawal and count their losses. Colonel James A. Walker (commanding Trimble's Brigade), who had been painfully wounded and unfitted for further duty, ordered the commandants of regiments to conduct them to the rear to replenish ammunition and collect the stragglers. Captain Rodgers (commanding the 12th Georgia) and Captain Francis P. Miller (commanding the 21st North Carolina) were killed, and Major Thomas C. Glover (commanding the 21st Georgia) severely wounded. Of the less than 700 men carried by the brigade into action, 237 were killed, wounded and missing. Lawton's Brigade went off the field without a commander (Colonel Marcellus Douglass, its acting commander, had been killed in the last charge). When in the fields in the rear, Major John H. Lowe of the 31st Georgia, finding that he was the senior officer, re-formed it. The 38th Georgia carried 123 officers and men into action and lost 70 killed and wounded. Major Archibald P. McRae (commanding the 61st Georgia) and Captain William H. Battey (commanding the 38th Georgia) were killed, three regimental commanders were wounded, and 567 men—one-half of the brigade—were killed, wounded, and missing. In its gallant fight, Hays's Brigade suffered terribly, losing 60 percent in killed and wounded. Both of Hays's staff officers were disabled. Colonel Henry B. Strong and five other officers of the 6th Louisiana, as well as five more officers of the brigade, were dead on the field. Every regimental commander was either killed or wounded. Hays gathered the small

---

[11] William F. Fox, *Regimental Losses in the American Civil War, 1861–1865: A Treatise on the Extent and Nature of the Mortuary Losses in the Union Regiments, with Full and Exhaustive Statistics Compiled from the Official Records on File in the State Military Bureaus and at Washington* (Albany, N.Y.: Albany Publishing Co., 1889), 160. A statement made by George Kimball says the regiment had nine companies only on the fighting line, aggregating 262 officers and men, and that the loss in these nine companies was 49 killed, 163 wounded, and 10 missing—a total of 222, or 84.73 percent. George Kimball, "Highest Percentage of Loss in Any One Battle," *Annual Circular of the Secretary of the [Twelfth (Webster) Massachusetts] Regimental Association*, no. 2 (n.p., 1897), 6.—*EAC*

remnant of his brigade after they had fallen back to the West Woods and conducted them farther to the rear. None of these three brigades were again engaged during the day.

About the time Hays made his advance and was repulsed, Lawton (commanding Ewell's Division) was wounded and borne from the field. Jubal Early, who succeeded to the division's command, officially reports:

> The terrible nature of the conflict in which these brigades had been engaged, and the steadiness with which they maintained their position, are shown by the losses they sustained. They did not retire from the field until General Lawton had been wounded and borne from the field, Colonel Douglass, commanding Lawton's brigade, had been killed, and the brigade had sustained a loss of 554 killed and wounded out of 1,150, losing 5 regimental commanders out of 6; Hays' brigade had sustained a loss of 323 out of 550, including every regimental commander and all of his staff, and Colonel Walker and 1 of his staff had been disabled, and the brigade he was commanding had sustained a loss of 228 out of less than 700 present, including 3 out of 4 regimental commanders.[12]

From the Federal perspective, Hooker reports that "the slain lay in rows precisely as they had stood in their ranks a few moments before. It was never my fortune to witness a more bloody, dismal battle-field."[13]

Jackson, in his official report, says:

> About sunrise the Federal infantry advanced in heavy force to the edge of the wood on the eastern side of the turnpike, driving in our skirmishers. Batteries were opened in front from the wood with shell and canister, and our troops became exposed for near an hour to a terrific storm of shell, canister, and musketry … With heroic spirit our lines advanced to the conflict, and maintained their position, in the face of superior numbers, with stubborn resolution, sometimes driving the enemy before them and sometimes compelled to fall back before their well-sustained and destructive fire. Fresh troops from time to time relieved the enemy's ranks, and the carnage on both sides was terrific.[14]

In the midst of this terrific carnage, Hood came into action and added one-half of his division to the ghastly roster of dead and wounded. It consisted of two brigades, commanded by Colonel William T. Wofford (18th Georgia) and Colonel Evander M. Law (4th Alabama). Wofford's was Hood's old command, generally known as the Texas Brigade, comprising the 1st, 4th, and 5th Texas, 18th Georgia, and the Hampton Legion (South Carolina). Law's consisted of the 4th Alabama, 6th North Carolina, and the 2d and 11th Mississippi. The division numbered about two thousand men, their superior fighting quality not excelled in the army. Up to this day they had never known defeat. Hood was a lion-hearted soldier and his brigade commanders brave and skillful officers.

When Hood was relieved by Lawton on the night of the sixteenth and retired to the woods about 250 yards in rear of the Dunkard church, it was to get food for his men (who had been nearly famished for three days), and he rode in search of his wagons. It was with much difficulty that he found these in the darkness, and they contained flour only. Not until nearly dawn was this in the hands of the men, and they were without cooking utensils. It was dawn before the dough was prepared, which the men proceeded to cook on ramrods. About 4:00 a.m. Hood sent his aide to D. H. Hill to apprise him of Hood's condition and ask if he could furnish any troops to assist in holding the position on the left. (Hill replied that he could not.) As we have seen, the fighting began at dawn in and near the East Woods, and soon thereafter Hood received notice from Lawton that he would require all the assistance Hood could give him. Later, when Hartsuff and Gibbon advanced, an officer of Lawton's staff dashed up to Hood, saying, "General Lawton sends his compliments with the request that you come at once to his support," "To arms" was instantly sounded, and quite a number of Hood's men were obliged to go to the front, leaving their uncooked rations behind.[15] Some carried the half-cooked dough on their ramrods and ate it as they went forward.

At this time the Union artillery fire was very heavy from the batteries north of the cornfield as well as those beyond the Antietam (the latter fire directed at S. D. Lee's guns but going over them into the woods around the church). Shot and shell fell into the ranks of the division, killing and wounding many men, but it was quickly formed and went through the woods and to the Hagerstown Road under a heavy fire of shrapnel, shell, and round shot, and thence into the clover field nearly opposite the church. Law, on the right, went out by the flank. After crossing the road, he threw his brigade into line facing northeast and gave the order to advance, his objective being that portion of the East Woods south of the cornfield. The 4th Alabama, being crowded out of line, moved by the flank on the Smoketown Road. From right to left, the regiments were in this order: 4th Alabama, 6th North Carolina, 2d and 11th Mississippi. On reaching the field, Law saw but few Confederates. These were in much confusion, without commanders, but still fighting with much determination.

---

[12] Early to Pendleton, 968.

[13] Hooker to Williams, 218.

[14] Thomas J. Jackson to Robert E. Lee, April 23, 1863, reprinted in OR, vol. 19, pt, 1, 956.

[15] John B. Hood, *Advance and Retreat: Personal Experiences in the United States and Confederate States Armies* (n.p., 1880), 42–43.

Wofford's men moved through the woods and across the Hagerstown Road, about one hundred yards north of the church, formed up on Law's left almost if not quite as soon as Law had formed line, and faced nearly north. It was a general complaint against the Texas Brigade that it fought too fast. Whether well founded or not we do not know, but we do know that on this occasion, no sooner had it cleared the woods than it opened fire upon the two Wisconsin regiments and Phelps's men, who were following Starke's defeated and retreating command. In moving across the road, the brigade was thus formed from right to left: 5th, 4th and 1st Texas, 18th Georgia, Hampton Legion. Hood says that as he moved across the road in front of the church, "Lawton … was borne to the rear upon a litter," his command dispersed or fighting in small groups behind such shelter of rocks and ledges as the open field south of the cornfield afforded, and the only organized body of "Confederate troops, left upon that part of the field, were some forty men who had rallied round the gallant Harry Hays" on "the highest ground near the junction of the cornfield and meadow"[16]—and these were anxiously awaiting Hood's arrival. Hood crossed the Hagerstown Road at seven o'clock.[17]

There was no halting the division when the open field was reached, for now the ranks were plowed with artillery fire. Thompson, who was in the cornfield, opened upon them with spherical case as soon as he saw the leading regiment emerge from the woods. Matthews, who was on higher ground, fired over the heads of Hartsuff's men, who were just retiring, and the guns beyond the Antietam dropped heavy shell among them. Hood's men pressed on, unable to answer the musketry fire that was now striking them, for Hays and some of the Georgians were still in front and the dense smoke prevented a clear view of the enemy.

Meanwhile, Hood had ridden to the front and, finding that Hays was out of ammunition and his brigade practically destroyed or dispersed, advised him to withdraw his few remaining men, replenish ammunition, and reassemble his command. As Hays and a few Georgians with him (a mere handful) fell back through Hood's advancing line, then moving obliquely to the East Woods, fire was opened to the front and left. At the same time, it was observed that the left flank of the division was exposed to a flank attack from a body of men on the high ground near the Hagerstown Road. Hood ordered Wofford's Brigade, which had advanced about 150 yards after reaching the clover field, to move obliquely to the left. Law's Brigade continued its course to the northeast (which would have carried it into the East Woods), its left at the southeast corner of the corn. But a moment after the order was given to Wofford and promptly conveyed to his left regiment only, Law was ordered to change direction to the left to strike the southeast corner of the cornfield and a Union line south of it—the 90th Pennsylvania, which, in addition to a severe artillery fire, was rapidly firing and doing much harm.

With three regiments of his brigade on open ground, the 4th Alabama following in the woods on his right, and the 1st Texas of Wofford's Brigade on his left, Law—changing direction a little to the left—marched over ground covered with dead and wounded Georgians. Still under artillery fire, by which many men were struck down, they made directly for the 90th Pennsylvania, firing as they advanced and threatening both flanks of the regiment (particularly its left). The fire of four regiments in front and on the left flank, and gradually reaching the right flank, was more than the Pennsylvanians could stand. Everything on its left and immediate right (except Thompson's battery) had gone and the enemy was about to pass both its flanks. After a stand in which it had lost nearly one-half its men (having now only one hundred in the ranks), the 90th Pennsylvania fell back slowly to the East Woods, the color bearer walking backward and the men turning and firing, until it entered the woods, when it pushed hurriedly through them (closely followed to their farther edge by the 4th Alabama) and thence to the Samuel Poffenberger spring, where it halted and re-formed. Upon the retreat of the 90th Pennsylvania, Law advanced a short distance until near the corn and momentarily halted until the regiments on the left could be obliqued, and the 4th Alabama came up through the woods on the right.

In reaching the clover field as it came out of the woods at the church, the 4th Alabama was crowded out of the field and into the Smoketown Road, down which it went by the right flank, Trimble's men retiring as it went forward and the 26th and 94th New York and the 88th Pennsylvania falling back as it approached the East Woods. When it reached the point where the road struck a southwest projection of the woods, it came under a scattering fire from the woods, by which Captain Lawrence

---

[16] In his original manuscript, Carman presents everything from "Lawton was borne" to "cornfield and meadow" as a single, direct quotation from Hood. Most of it comes from Hood, *Advance and Retreat*, 43, but the phrase "the highest ground near the junction of the cornfield and meadow" is found in Hood to Carman, May 27, 1877, typescript copy, "Report Brig. Gen. J. B. Hood's Division—Artillery Battalion, Major F. W. Frobel" folder, box 2, Letters and Reports Concerning the Battle of Antietam, 1895–1900 ("Antietam Studies"), Record Group 94, National Archives. The passages placed outside the quotation marks have not been located in Hood's official report, his memoir, or in his correspondence with Carman. This may be another instance in which Carman intermingled source material with his own rephrasing.

[17] One of the most difficult things to determine in considering a great battle is the hour that particular events took place and the length of time troops were engaged. No two or more men will agree upon such points. Those of undoubted and equal courage will contend for largely varying periods. This difficulty confronts us at every step and upon nearly every page of the official reports of Antietam, but a close analysis of the movements up to this period of the action leads us to the conclusion that it was 7:00 a.m. when Hood crossed the Hagerstown Road at the church, and it was at this time that Colquitt was seen moving from the sunken road.—*EAC*

H. Scruggs was wounded, and the command of the regiment passed to Captain William M. Robbins. Here what was left of the 21st Georgia (under command of Captain James C. Nisbet[18]), which had not retired with its brigade, came over the field from the right and desired to continue in action, and Robbins advised it to fall in on his right.[19] All this occurred while pulling down the fence on the left of the road. With scarce a moment's delay, the 4th Alabama went forward into line and pushed into the woods, the Georgians on its right, all moving northward, yelling and firing at the 90th Pennsylvania as it went out of the woods. Then they turned upon the 6th Pennsylvania Reserves, which but a few minutes before had been moved from its earlier position into the woods and quite near where the Smoketown Road emerges from them. The regiment had been more or less severely engaged from the beginning of the battle. Its ammunition was well nigh exhausted, and Robbins's attack, reinforced by the fire of the right of Law's men in the open ground, forced it out of the woods northerly, to the Poffenberger woods bordering on the Smoketown Road. This part of the East Woods being cleared, Robbins rested his left on the fence separating the cornfield and the woods (about at the southeast corner of the corn), where, sheltered by trees and rocks, he kept up a skirmish fire to the front and obliquely to the left into the northeast corner of the corn and the woods adjacent. Soon after taking position, the 5th Texas came into the woods and formed on the right of the Georgians. All remained there—a staunch body on the Confederate right—until the advance of Brigadier General George S. Greene's division of the Twelfth Corps swept the Confederates from the East Woods and fields adjoining to the west side of the Hagerstown Road.

Thompson's battery held on until it was seen that the 90th Pennsylvania was moving out and that Hood's men were nearing the cornfield; then, its men and horses falling fast, Thompson gave the order to withdraw. It went back followed by a shower of bullets and gained the high ground east of the D. R. Miller farm, from which it had advanced into the corn. The moment it was halted eighteen horses fell dead, and the guns were temporarily abandoned until teams could be obtained to haul them off. The battery had eleven men wounded, twenty-three horses killed, and many wounded. As it went back, Ransom's battery was going into position.

Ricketts's division, with the exception of a few men of Duryee's brigade who had rallied in the northeast part of the cornfield and north part of the East Woods, had retired from the front to the open fields and woods beyond (the 90th Pennsylvania and Thompson's battery being the last to go), but Matthews still held on in the grass field north of the corn. The 6th Pennsylvania Reserves, the last of Seymour's brigade (save a few men who still clung to the north part of the woods), had just been pushed back by the right of Law's Brigade. Meade's two brigades (Magilton and Anderson), with Ransom's Battery C, 5th U.S. Artillery, were now in position to meet the farther advance of Hood's Division. On their right Stewart's guns, with Patrick's brigade, and the 19th Indiana and the 7th Wisconsin, with the remains of the 2d and 6th Wisconsin and Phelps's men, were still in the fight.

Soon after Doubleday became engaged along the Hagerstown Road and Ricketts in the East Woods and south of the corn, Hooker ordered Meade forward in the center with the brigades of Magilton and Anderson and Ransom's battery. Magilton, who was in the east part of the North Woods, closed in to the right on Anderson, Ransom moved from his position east of the Poffenberger barn, and all went out of the North Woods and halted on their south edge—the two brigades in column of battalions in mass, the battery on the left of the infantry. A short halt and all went forward, then came under a scattering fire from the cornfield and some of S. D. Lee's guns, which created some confusion in the ranks of Magilton's brigade. Passing to the left of the Miller orchard, the two brigades obliqued to the right and were massed in the shallow basin extending up to the Hagerstown Road—the ground over which Gibbon, Phelps, and Patrick had moved to the attack. Meade led the infantry and Hooker directed the movements of the battery, which he put in position on the ground vacated by Stewart's two guns, near the orchard. At this time Thompson's battery came out of the corn, and Hooker ordered Ransom to fire upon Hood. While advancing from the North Woods, the 10th Pennsylvania Reserves was detached from Anderson's brigade and sent beyond the Hagerstown Road to protect the flank of Patrick's brigade, which was in the West Woods in support of the 19th Indiana and the 7th Wisconsin. The 80th New York was in support of Stewart's two guns, Campbell being on the way to join him with the other four guns of the battery.

Meade thus reports his movement from the North Woods to the front:

Ransom's battery was advanced into the open ground between the two advancing columns, and played with great effect on the enemy's infantry and batteries. The brigades of Anderson and Magilton on reaching the corn-field were

[18] In his original manuscript, Carman gives the name incorrectly as "Nisbit."

[19] Statement to the writer of Captain William M. Robbins (4th Alabama) and Captain James C. Nisbet (21st Georgia). William M. Robbins to Carman, October 9, 1896, "Report Brig. Gen. J. B. Hood's Division" folder, "Antietam Studies." [The Nisbet letter has not been found.] Major John M. Gould (10th Maine) inclines to the belief that this body was the skirmish battalion of Colquitt's Brigade, composed of five companies (one from each regiment of the brigade). See John M. Gould, "At Antietam," Portland (Maine) Advertiser, August 11, 1892. This body had no flag; the 21st Georgia had a flag, and Robbins is confident that the body joining him had a flag. It is probable that the skirmish battalion did enter the woods and was engaged in the southern part of them.—EAC

massed in a ravine extending up to the pike. Soon after forming, I saw the enemy were driving our men from the corn-field. I immediately deployed both brigades, and formed line of battle along the fence bordering the corn-field, for the purpose of covering the withdrawal of our people and resisting the farther advance of the enemy. Just as this line of battle was formed, I received an order from the general commanding the corps to detach a brigade to re-enforce our troops in the woods on the left. I directed Magilton's brigade to move in that direction.[20]

Magilton's brigade was composed of the 3d, 4th, 7th, and 8th Pennsylvania Reserves. The 7th was on the right, the 3d and 4th in the center, and the 8th on the left. Immediately upon the receipt of Meade's order, the brigade started by the left flank, moving parallel and quite close to the north fence on the cornfield, and quickly came under a terrific fire from the cornfield (from Law's advancing brigade and probably from the 1st Texas also).

We left Law at a temporary halt near the south edge of the corn. Before his brigade reached this point, the 1st Texas, which had been moving on its immediate left (the 4th and 5th Texas having been crowded out of line), was ordered to oblique to the left, following the 18th Georgia and the Hampton Legion. At the moment of halting, the 4th Texas, which had by some means changed position with the 5th, came up in rear of the 11th Mississippi and lay down. The 5th Texas was found in rear of the 1st and was about to follow it into the cornfield when Hood rode up and, remarking that the 1st Texas could attend to the business in hand at that point, ordered the 5th to move to the right into the East Woods, where (as we have seen) it formed on the right of the 4th Alabama and the Georgians. The 4th Texas was ordered to the left to support the 18th Georgia and the Hampton Legion (then engaged near the Hagerstown Road with Stewart's two guns and the 80th New York). But before the 4th Texas had gotten to its feet, Law was in motion, and two companies of the Texans—mis-understanding orders—went with him.

Law's temporary halt near the south edge of the corn was by Hood's order and was of brief duration, not to exceed five minutes (probably not more than two or three minutes)—only sufficient time to allow Robbins with the 4th Alabama to come up on the right and the 1st Texas to gain a little ground to the left to form closer connection with the two regiments of Wofford near the Hagerstown Road. At the end of this time, the entire division advanced and the fighting became desperate from the East Woods on the right to the Hagerstown Road on the left. As Hood ordered the general advance, a staff officer came from Jackson to inquire as to the situation, to which Hood gave answer, "Tell General Jackson unless I get reinforcements I must be forced back, but I am going on while I can."[21]

We first follow the advance on the right. Law did not cease firing when he came to his brief halt, and as he swept into the corn he encountered the fire of about one hundred men of the 104th and 105th New York and some other organizations, but this did not materially check the advance. The Union men were soon driven out and, as Law's men neared the north fence of the corn, Matthews double-shotted his guns with canister and poured it in to them, thinning the ranks most terribly. Still they did not halt; as they approached the fence, Magilton's brigade was moving by the left flank across their front, and upon it they opened fire, breaking the 3d and 4th Pennsylvania Reserves, who retreated in some disorder. But the 8th Pennsylvania Reserves, though losing heavily, kept on and gained the cover of the woods, where with only fifty men it turned and opened effectively upon Law's men as they reached the north fence of the corn. Ransom too was training his guns upon them, and Matthews, giving them one more round of canister as some of them came over the fence, abandoned his guns. (Reynolds's New York battery went to the rear without being able to fire a shot.) The 6th North Carolina, upon reaching the fence, was so much exhausted and reduced in numbers that its aggressive force was gone; it held ground and returned the fire of the 8th Pennsylvania Reserves, in which it was assisted by Robbins in the East Woods. Those who crossed the fence were of the 2d and 11th Mississippi. As they did so, they caught sight of the 7th Pennsylvania Reserves upon their left (which had been cut off in the act of following the 3d and 4th) and immediately turned to the left and opened fire upon it. The Pennsylvanians had just begun their flank movement to the left when they saw the Mississippians coming over the fence, upon which they came into line nearly perpendicular to the fence, and with about 150 men returned the fire that was now poured upon them. It was going hard with the Pennsylvanians (nearly one-half were killed or wounded) when the enemy saw a large regiment of the Twelfth Corps approaching and fell back into the cornfield, the 7th Pennsylvania Reserves retiring to the ravine near the Hagerstown Road.

The Mississippians went over the fence without orders either from their brigade or regimental commanders. Colonel John M. Stone of the 2d Mississippi, observing that the right of the line had passed much beyond the 4th Alabama (which was still fighting in the woods and unable to advance), was unwilling to hazard the safety of his command by going beyond the corn and over the open ground to the woods on the right (where the 8th Pennsylvania Reserves was holding on). The

[20] George G. Meade to Joseph Dickinson, September 22, 1862, reprinted in *OR*, vol. 19, pt. 1, 269–70.

[21] Pendleton to Anzolette Elizabeth Pendleton, September 21, 1862, reprinted in Susan P. Lee, *Memoirs of William Nelson Pendleton, D.D.* (Philadelphia: J. B. Lippincott, 1893), 216.

11th Mississippi on the left was deterred from going forward because of the forbidding presence of Ransom's battery, which, but 150 yards on its left front, was turning its guns upon it. So, these two regiments, as well as the 6th North Carolina, were ordered to halt at the north fence of the cornfield, but as we have seen some of them would not be restrained and went over the fence, driving Matthews from his guns and the 7th Pennsylvania Reserves back to near the Hagerstown Road. When these impulsive men fell back (so that their comrades could open fire), all retired a few feet from the fence and to the right, where the lay of the ground gave more protection. While the 6th North Carolina was engaging the 8th Pennsylvania Reserves and some of the 3d and 4th (who had rallied on it), the two Mississippi regiments, with the 1st Texas on their left, paid particular attention to Ransom's guns, and with such effect that they were temporarily silenced. (Ransom says the musket balls cut several spokes from the wheels of his gun carriages.[22]) They also delivered a left oblique fire upon the heads and shoulders of Anderson's men (who were lying along the fence nearer the Hagerstown Road, engaged with Wofford) and upon the advance of the Twelfth Corps, then appearing on the high ground beyond. Particular attention was paid to a Union officer mounted on a white horse who was riding quietly about, sometimes in front of the line and sometimes in rear. An order was passed down the line of the 11th Mississippi, "Shoot the man on the white horse!"[23] Many shots were aimed at him, but when last seen by the Mississippians he and his horse were apparently untouched.

The man on the white horse was Hooker, who had risen early and mounted his favorite white horse. He was dressed with scrupulous care as usual, as though for a ceremonial parade, and his striking figure was indeed a good mark for the Mississippi riflemen. He was exceedingly active that morning, giving personal direction to the movements of every regiment, brigade, and division and the posting of every battery, and at all times he was at the extreme front under fire. He met the brigades of Doubleday's division as they emerged from the North Woods and gave orders in person for their deployment and advance. He rallied parts of Duryee's brigade as they were falling back under the orders of the brigade commander. He ordered Hartsuff forward. He rode with Ransom's battery, impetuously hastening it into position as Hood's men were seen coming through the corn, rallied the 3d and 4th Pennsylvania Reserves when their ranks were broken by Law's Brigade, and was seen by the Mississippians directing the advance of the Twelfth Corps into action. He was everywhere present, and everywhere his presence was an inspiration.

As Law was now threatened in front and on the right by the advance of Brigadier General Samuel W. Crawford's brigade of the Twelfth Corps, he gave orders to retreat. He makes this report:

> The … regiments of my command continued steadily to advance in the open ground, driving the enemy in confusion from and beyond his guns. So far, we had been entirely successful and everything promised a decisive victory. It is true that strong support was needed to follow up our success, but this I expected every moment.
>
> At this stage of the battle, a powerful Federal force (ten times our number) of fresh troops was thrown in our front. Our losses up to this time had been very heavy; the troops now confronting the enemy were insufficient to cover properly one-fourth of the line of battle; our ammunition was expended; the men had been fighting long and desperately, and were exhausted from want of food and rest. Still, they held their ground, many of them using such ammunition as they could obtain from the bodies of our own and the enemy's dead and wounded. It was evident that this state of affairs could not long continue. No support was at hand. To remain stationary or advance without it would have caused a useless butchery, and I adopted the only alternative—that of falling back to the wood from which I had first advanced.[24]

Meade makes this report of the action at the time Law retired: "Anderson's brigade still held the fence on the right, but the gap made by the withdrawal of Magilton was soon filled by the enemy, whose infantry advanced boldly through the cornfield to the woods. Seeing this, I rode up to Ransom's battery and directed his guns on their advancing column, which fire, together with the arrival of Magilton's brigade, … drove the enemy back, who, as they retreated, were enfiladed by Anderson, who eventually regained the crest of the ridge in the corn-field."[25]

Law's three regiments went back rapidly under a heavy fire of infantry and artillery and rallied for a moment on the south edge of the corn, where it was discovered that most of the officers had been killed or wounded, over half the men gone, and the colors of the 11th Mississippi left behind in the corn (the color bearer having been killed). The stricken regiments did not long halt, but went back to the rear of the Dunkard church. (Robbins and the 4th Alabama, with the 5th Texas and the Georgians, remained in the East Woods.) Of the three regiments that advanced through the cornfield, more than one-half of the men were killed and wounded; in some companies every man was struck. Nearly all the officers, including every field officer, were killed or wounded. The 2d Mississippi lost all its field officers and nearly every company commander, and

---

[22] As of this writing, Carman's source for this statement has not been identified.

[23] Ibid.

[24] Evander M. Law to William H. Sellers, October 2, 1862, reprinted in *OR*, vol. 19, pt. 1, 938.

[25] Meade to Dickinson, 270.

it came out of action under the command of a second lieutenant. In the 11th Mississippi, but one officer escaped unhurt, and it and the 6th North Carolina went out in charge of junior captains.

While Law was thus most deadly engaged on the right, Wofford was as bloodily engaged on the left, on and near the Hagerstown Road. We take up our narrative here where we left: Gibbon's and Phelps's men pressing the defeat of Starke and their sudden check by the appearance of Hood's Division swarming out of the woods at the church and opening fire upon them.

When Hood gave the order (soon after gaining the open field) for Wofford to oblique to the left, the Hampton Legion and the 18th Georgia were immediately set in motion in that direction, but the rest of the brigade did not receive the order, and the movement became a disjointed one. The Hampton Legion and the 18th Georgia moved obliquely to the rising ground bordering the Hagerstown Road, the left of the Legion resting on the crest near the road with the 18th Georgia on its right, and became engaged with the 2d and 6th Wisconsin and Phelps's men as they retired. Seeing the two regiments moving slowly forward—but rapidly firing—Wofford rode to them to urge a quicker pace when he saw two full regiments in their front. One of these was the 84th New York (with others of Phelps's brigade rallied on it); the other was the 2d Wisconsin. The Hampton Legion and the 18th Georgia advanced under a heavy fire of musketry in front and artillery on the right, three color bearers of the Legion being shot down in quick succession, when the colors were seized and carried by Major J. Harvey Dingle, who was himself killed when nearing the cornfield.

A little before this, the 4th Texas had been ordered by Hood to move from the rear of the 11th Mississippi to the left until its left rested on the crest of the high ground, in advance, near the road. Moving on the double-quick, the indicated position was occupied, and then it was ordered by Hood directly up the rise of ground on the left of the 18th Georgia and the Hampton Legion, then slowly advancing. Wofford, meanwhile, had seen that these two regiments were in danger of being cut off by a force threatening their left, and ordered the 1st Texas, which had advanced on Law's immediate left, to move by the left flank to their relief. This it did in a rapid and gallant manner just as the Union force on the east side of the road was driven back into the corn by the 18th Georgia, the Hampton Legion, and a part of Starke's line that had rallied, moved up the road and along the fence on the west side of it, and opened fire into the cornfield, threatening Stewart's guns. The two regiments were now checked by a terrific fire from Stewart's guns and the supporting infantry across the road. The 1st Texas, as it came up on their right by the left flank, fronted and charged into the cornfield in pursuit of the New York and Wisconsin men, who were quickly driven out of the corn and over Anderson's brigade (the colors of the 2d Wisconsin through the ranks of the 11th Pennsylvania Reserves, those of the 84th New York through the 9th Pennsylvania Reserves) and were rallied in Anderson's rear in the shallow basin or ravine between the cornfield and the Miller orchard.

The 1st Texas had been ordered to halt at the south edge of the corn in order that a proper alignment of the brigade could be made, but it either failed to get or heed the order and, as Hood afterwards explained, "slipped the bridle and got away from the command,"[26] and it could not be restrained until it had pushed far into the cornfield, its colors about 150 yards from the Hagerstown Road. Here its reception was a warm one. Ransom's battery opened upon it as it reached the highest ground in the corn, and when it approached to within thirty yards of the north fence corn it was met by the deadly fire of Anderson's brigade (which, as we have seen, Meade had deployed along the fence but a few minutes before); the 9th Pennsylvania Reserves (Captain Samuel B. Dick) on the right, its own right on and in the Hagerstown Road; the 11th Pennsylvania Reserves (Lieutenant Colonel Samuel M. Jackson) on the left of the 9th; and the 12th Pennsylvania Reserves (Captain Richard Gustin) on the left of the 11th. The regiments had not been long in this position when the New York and Wisconsin men began to come out of the corn in some confusion, reporting that the enemy were close behind them. The order was now passed along the line to fire as soon as all the Union men had come in. The Pennsylvanians steadied their guns on the lower rails of the fence, and when the legs of the Texans were seen about thirty yards from the fence in front of the 11th Pennsylvania Reserves, fire was opened by it and the 12th. The 9th Pennsylvania Reserves followed with a volley obliquely to the left, and at the same time Gibbon's men, beyond the Hagerstown Road, opened full upon its flank and rear, and the regiment was laid low. Only a squad remained to fall back, leaving their colors on the field—8 of the color-bearers being shot down in quick succession. Of the 226 officers and men taken into action, 170 were killed and wounded and 12 missing, or 80.52 percent of the number engaged.[27] A revised testament by an officer of the regiment, giving the loss in each of the twelve companies, shows 50 killed,

---

[26] As of this writing, Carman's source for this quotation has not been identified.

[27] Philip A. Work to William T. Wofford, September 23, 1862, reprinted in OR, vol. 19, pt. 1, 933. We have before us a letter of Colonel Work, in which he says, "The morning reports, by company commanders, on the morning of the 16th, showed (including field officers Major [Matt] Dale—[W. B.] Shropshire [Adjutant] and myself) a total regimental strength of 226 … After dark on the evening of the 16th, two men from each of the twelve companies of the regiment were detailed and sent to the rear for the purpose of roasting green corn as food for the regiment. Less than half of these had rejoined the regiment, when, just after day dawn, on the 17th, we were ordered forward—and by this means, we went into action with about 15 men less than 226." Work to Robert Burns, February 13, 1891, "Report Brig. Gen. J. B. Hood's Division" folder, "Antietam Studies." With this deduction the regiment had 211 in action and its loss of 182 was 86.25 percent.—EAC

132 wounded, and 4 missing—an aggregate of 186.[28] In two companies every officer and man was killed or wounded. Of 26 officers, 7 were killed and 11 wounded. Conceding the accuracy of Lieutenant Colonel Philip A. Work's statement that the 1st Texas had 211 in action,[29] its loss was 23.69 percent killed, 86.25 killed and wounded, and 88.15 percent killed, wounded, and missing.

The color lost was the Lone Star flag made from the wedding dress of Mrs. Louis T. Wigfall, whose husband—formerly Senator Wigfall—had been colonel of the 1st Texas. Its loss was not discovered until the regiment was moving out of the corn, when it was too late to hunt for it, as Patrick's men were pressing its flank and Anderson's were within a few yards of its rear. Work reports that he was "well convinced that had the Eighteenth Georgia and Hampton's Legion not met with the most obstinate and stubborn resistance from a superior force to their left, they would have supported me promptly and effectively upon my left, and that that portion of the enemy's force in our front would have been routed, the tide of battle there turned, and the day been ours."[30]

The 18th Georgia and the Hampton Legion could not go forward because they were checked by the fire of Stewart's guns and the supporting infantry. We left Stewart throwing spherical case at Starke's retreating men. When he saw Hood moving toward the cornfield, he turned his guns upon him and those swarming up the road and in the field close to the fence in which his guns were and threw canister as rapidly as his men could handle it. But still the Confederates pressed on and, under cover of the fences and the corn, some crept close to his guns, picking off gunners so rapidly that in less than ten minutes from the time he had taken position fourteen of his men were killed and wounded and the two guns were temporarily silenced—but not before they had done terrible execution to the ranks of the 18th Georgia and the Hampton Legion. Stewart's horse was killed and, in falling, threw him; as soon as Stewart could rise, he ran back to the stacks behind which the caissons had been left and ordered the drivers to accompany him to the front and take the places of the dead and wounded cannoneers. By the time he had returned with these to the guns, the battery commander, Captain Campbell, galloping down the road from the Miller field, brought the other four guns into battery on the left of Stewart's section and began firing canister into the cornfield and the field south of it, where the Confederates were seen near the east fence of the road. In a very short time, Campbell was severely wounded and the command fell to Stewart. Gibbon, seeing the danger threatening and observing the gunner of the left piece fall, ran into the battery and acted as gunner. What was left of Phelps's brigade and the 2d and 6th Wisconsin—not over 150 men in all—were brought across the road from where they had rallied when driven from the cornfield and, merging with the 80th New York, drew close to the guns. Those on the left opened fire into the cornfield; those on the right, with bayonets fixed, lay down behind the guns. In the full uniform of a general officer, his face begrimed by powder and perspiration running down his cheeks, Gibbon was still serving the guns of his old battery, declaring that they should not be taken, yet almost despairing of saving them. Double charges of canister were thrown into the corner of the cornfield. The aim was low; the stones and dirt on the road were plowed up, and the fence rails were splintered and thrown into the air. As the smoke and dust cleared away, groups of the enemy were seen running to the rear, and looking to the right there was seen a Union line sweeping across the front of the guns up to the road.

It was but a few minutes before this that the 4th Texas (Lieutenant Colonel Benjamin F. Carter), which had come from the right and halted at the brow of the ridge, moved up and received a scattering fire from the ledge 150 yards beyond the road. Carter wheeled his regiment to the left, drew up along the road fence, and replied to the fire from the ledge. About fifty men, catching sight of a Confederate flag in possession of Gibbon's men beyond the road, charged to retake it, but were checked before they had crossed the second fence, and they lay down on the west side of the road under shelter of the fence and ditch on that side. It was at this time that the officers of the Hampton Legion and the 18th Georgia saw that Law's men and the 1st Texas were falling back on their right and that on their left, not two hundred yards distant, a Union line, advancing in an oblique direction, covered their entire flank, threatening to cut them off, and the Confederates gave the order to fall back (simultaneously with Gibbon's last shot, which sent the fence rails flying into the air).

The five small regiments in this advancing Union line were the 19th Indiana, the 7th Wisconsin, and the 21st, 23d, and 35th New York. When the left of the skirmish line of the 19th Indiana, on the higher ground in the West Woods, saw the advance of Hood's Division passing their flank, they reported the fact to Lieutenant Colonel Alois O. Bachman, who, with the regiment, was still in the West Woods on much lower ground, and the information was conveyed to the 7th Wisconsin and Patrick's brigade. Bachman at once called in the skirmishers from his right and front and with his regiment, and the 7th Wisconsin, changed front to the left, moved out of the woods to the ledge, and opened fire upon the Confederates lying in the road and beyond it, and another line along the fence in an open field about one hundred yards distant, driving the latter line back. But the 4th Texas still held ground. Bachman, yielding to the urgent appeals of the men, gave the order to charge

[28] Carman, "1st Texas Infantry," no date, "Report Brig. Gen. J. B. Hood's Division" folder, "Antietam Studies."
[29] See n. 27.
[30] Work to Wofford, 934.

and—hand in hand, with drawn sword—led them on the double-quick, all cheering as they advanced. At the same time, the 7th Wisconsin sprung over the rock ledge and went forward on the left of the 19th Indiana, closely followed by Patrick's three regiments. (It was the sight of these advancing regiments that caused the retreat of the Hampton Legion and the 18th Georgia.) The 4th Texas, in danger of being cut off by the 19th Indiana, started to move off by the left flank before the 19th Indiana could intercept it, but it had moved only a few feet along the fence when its commander, seeing that the regiment was so much exposed and that it could not escape in that direction, ordered his men to halt and open fire on the 7th Wisconsin, which had nearly reached the road. Repulsing it, the Texans immediately fell back under the hill to re-form and were then ordered by Hood to move to the Dunkard church. The 19th Indiana was temporarily checked but finally went on, crossed the road, and followed the Confederates to the brow of the ridge, over which was seen a strong force of infantry (Ripley's Brigade), which opened fire. Bachman was mortally wounded and Captain William W. Dudley succeeded to the command. As soon as Bachman could be carried to the rear, the regiment fell back to the road and rallied on it. On its left were Patrick's regiments (the 21st, 23d, and 35th New York).

When the 19th Indiana and the 7th Wisconsin changed front to the left to strike Hood's flank, Patrick was in the north part of the West Woods in support to them. He also changed front and moved obliquely to the left with the 21st and 35th New York to the rock ledge, where he was quickly joined by the 23d New York (which early in the action had been sent to the right, but now had been relieved by the 10th Pennsylvania Reserves). The 21st and 35th New York reached the ledge just as the 7th Wisconsin went over it and the 19th Indiana farther to the right was making its charge. As the Wisconsin men fell back from the hot fire of the 4th Texas, the 21st and 35th New York (closely supported by the 23d) went forward through them under a severe fire from the retreating Texans and gained the road, the 21st New York going entirely across it and into the grass field beyond (but immediately falling back as the 19th Indiana, on its right, retreated and fell back to the road).

The venturesome Texans, who had been so eager to recapture the Confederate colors and who were in the road near the southwest corner of the corn, were cut off by this quick advance of the Union line and, perceiving that the Union troops were already in the corn, started directly down the road in the direction of the church and were fired upon. Some were killed or wounded, about twenty were captured, and a few escaped by climbing the east fence of the road.

The repulse of Wofford gave Gibbon an opportunity to retire Stewart's guns. Forty battery men had been killed or wounded, twenty-six horses were killed, and seven more disabled. Stewart was ordered to resume the position held by his two guns earlier in the day and the infantry supports, much reduced, were ordered to the North Woods.

When the 19th Indiana and other regiments took position in the road, no enemy was seen on their right, but they had been only a short time in the road when they were attacked in flank and rear by Starke's men, who had been driven into the woods. The Union line presented such a tempting opportunity that portions of the Louisiana brigade were led by Colonel Stafford out of the woods and, approaching unobserved to within one hundred yards of the 19th Indiana, gave it a rear and enfilade fire that caused it to fall back from the road, change front and engage them, and finally fall back to the rock ledge. The movement was followed by Patrick, all his regiments in succession changing front, engaging the enemy, finally driving them back to the woods, and then taking position behind the ledge.

The 19th Indiana and the 7th Wisconsin now moved to the rear near the West Woods and, after lying a short time under a severe artillery fire from "Jeb" Stuart's guns on their right, rejoined their brigade in the North Woods. Patrick held the ledge a few minutes longer, when, his ammunition being almost exhausted and his line attacked in flank and rear, he ordered his command to fall back to a low meadow near the D. R. Miller barn and behind a line of rock ledges at right angles to the road and about fifteen rods from the West Woods to await ammunition and reinforcement. He remained here between the fire of opposing batteries long enough to make coffee before (as we shall see) he was again engaged.

At the moment the Union line advanced to the road and saved Stewart's guns, Gibbon hastened across the road to Anderson's brigade to have it go forward. Meade could not be found (being on the left of his line), and Gibbon ordered Anderson to push through the corn in pursuit of the Confederates, advising him that a part of Gibbon's own brigade and Patrick's were still in and on the right of the road. Three of Anderson's regiments went forward, the 1st Texas and others retiring before them; the 9th Pennsylvania Reserves went clear through the corn to the open field where Wofford's men had been. The Union line, by this time, had been forced back from the road, and Stewart's guns were going to the rear, but the regiment advanced about seventy-five yards beyond the corn, when it saw Ripley's Brigade advancing across the low ground on its left front and immediately opened fire, to which Ripley's men promptly responded. Anderson rode back to get reinforcements; before he could return, Captain Dick, commanding the 9th Pennsylvania Reserves, learned that the 11th Pennsylvania Reserves, on his left, had fallen back. There was no support on his right, his men were falling fast, and Dick was obliged to fall back to the position from which he had advanced. The 11th and 12th Pennsylvania Reserves, on the left of the 9th, advanced about halfway through the corn, when they received such a severe fire that they were ordered to fall back—the 11th to the Hagerstown Road and thence to the rear, the 12th through the corn to the shallow basin near the road, where it was joined by the 9th. Subsequently the 9th and 12th were relieved by the Twelfth Corps, and Meade ordered them to join the division in support of the corps artillery.

While these three regiments were engaged in and near the cornfield, the 10th Pennsylvania Reserves (Lieutenant Colonel Adoniram J. Warner) was in action on the extreme right, beyond the north part of the West Woods. As its brigade moved to the front, this regiment was detached and, crossing the road just before reaching the D. R. Miller house, went across the low meadow and relieved the 23d New York, which rejoined its brigade in the advance to the road. Warner's skirmishers reported a Confederate brigade (Early's) moving behind a cornfield in the direction of the West Woods. Hooker was advised of the movement, and the regiment pushed on to a fence running northwest from the corner of the woods. (Part of the regiment deployed as skirmishers and went into the cornfield to annoy Early and if possible check and delay his movement.) In these operations Warner was wounded and the command fell to Captain Jonathan P. Smith. Early now detached the 13th Virginia to meet Warner's skirmishers; a battery was brought to bear upon the Union regiment, which was drawn to the left along the same fence, where for the present we leave it.

With the exception of Patrick's brigade, the 10th Pennsylvania Reserves on its right (west of the Hagerstown Road), and a few of Magilton's men in the north part of the East Woods, the infantry of Hooker's corps was out of the fight. Hood's Division, with the exception of the 4th Alabama and the 5th Texas (still in the East Woods), had withdrawn or was withdrawing to the woods at the Dunkard church. Ripley's' Brigade had become engaged with the advance of the Twelfth Corps.

Wofford had 854 in action and lost 560 killed, wounded and missing, or over 65.50 percent. Of the three regiments engaged at the road, the Hampton Legion had 77 in action and lost 55 killed and wounded, or 77.40 percent; the 18th Georgia had 176 engaged, of whom 101 were killed, wounded, and missing, or 57.38 percent; and the 4th Texas, with 200 engaged, had 107 killed and wounded, or 53.50 percent. (The 1st Texas, as stated, had 211 in action and lost 182 killed and wounded, or 86.25 percent.) After giving the names of twelve officers killed, Wofford says, "They deserved a better fate than to have been, as they were, sacrificed for the want of proper support."[31]

In *Advance and Retreat*, Hood writes of his division:

This most deadly combat raged till our last round of ammunition was expended. The First Texas Regiment had lost, in the corn field, fully two-thirds of its number; and whole ranks of brave men, whose deeds were unrecorded save in the hearts of loved ones at home, were mowed down in heaps to the right and left. Never before was I so continuously troubled with fear that my horse would further injure some wounded fellow soldier, lying helpless on the ground. Our right flank, during this short, but seemingly long, space of time, was toward the main line of the Federals, and, after several ineffectual efforts to procure reinforcements and our last shot had been fired, I ordered my troops back to Dunkard Church, for the same reason which had previously compelled Lawton, Hays and Trimble to retire.[32]

In his official report Hood says, "Fighting, as we were, at right angles with the general line of battle, and General Ripley's brigade being the extreme left of General D. H. Hill's forces and continuing to hold their ground, caused the enemy to pour in a heavy fire upon the rear and right flank of Colonel Law's brigade, rendering it necessary to move the division to the left and rear into the woods near the [Dunkard] church."[33] The complaint made by Hood and his officers that they were not properly supported is directed at both D. H. Hill and Ripley for not coming promptly to their assistance.

The events narrated in this chapter cover the period from daybreak to 7:30 a.m. Seymour's brigade and the artillery—of both sides—opened the engagement at daybreak. Duryee's brigade went to the assistance of Seymour and became actively engaged with the brigades of Lawton and Trimble at 6:00 a.m. and fell back a half-hour later. Hartsuff, later supported by Christian, became engaged at 6:40 a.m. with the brigades of Trimble, Lawton, and Hays, the last going to Lawton's assistance about 6:15 a.m. It was 6:30 a.m. when Gibbon, Phelps, and Patrick became engaged with Jackson's Division and the left of Ewell's, repulsing both. It was 7:00 a.m. when Hood's Division crossed the Hagerstown Road at the Dunkard church and relieved Lawton, Trimble, and Hays, then drove back the advance of Gibbon and Phelps, forced Hartsuff from the field, and was in turn checked and driven back by Gibbon, Patrick, Magilton, and the First Corps artillery, aided by the timely appearance of the Twelfth Corps.

[31] Wofford to Sellers, September 29, 1862, reprinted in *OR*, vol. 19, pt. 1, 929.

[32] Hood, *Advance and Retreat*, 44.

[33] Hood to Gilbert Moxley Sorrel, September 27, 1862, reprinted in *OR*, vol. 19, pt. 1, 923.

15

The Battle on the Union Right and Confederate Left: 7:30 a.m. to 9:00 a.m.

Antietam, September 17, 1862

About two o'clock on the morning of the seventeenth, Joseph Mansfield and the Twelfth Army Corps, after crossing the Antietam at the Upper Bridge, lay down to rest on the Hoffman and Line farms, a short mile in rear of Hooker's left. In the darkness a regular line was not formed. The men were informed that the enemy was in their immediate front and were ordered to rest on their arms (all of which was not conducive to sound sleep). The veteran commander spread his blankets in a fence corner near the Line house and had a fitful sleep. A few hours later he was brought back to the Line house to die.

Mansfield had assumed command of the corps on the fifteenth of September. He was fifty-nine years of age, of venerable appearance, white haired yet fresh and vigorous, with an open, intelligent countenance. He was an accomplished engineer officer but had limited experience in the handling of troops. His confidence in volunteer soldiers was not great, which may account for the fact that he insisted on leading his regiments into action closed in mass, contending (against the remonstrance of his division commanders) that if deployed they would run away. His two days' service with the corps had not impressed his immediate subordinates with great confidence in his military capacity, but he had endeared himself to the men. He was oppressed with the responsibility of his command, and this and other circumstances impelled him to give personal attention to the movements of regiments and batteries, regardless of division and brigade commanders.

The Twelfth was a small corps, its whole effective force less than 7,500 men—strangers for the most part in the Army of the Potomac. At Cedar Mountain, little over a month previous, the First Division had lost nearly all of the field officers and all the adjutants of one of its two brigades, and its ranks were so reduced that several of the old regiments numbered but little over one hundred men. There were in this division five new regiments not three weeks from home, which in the rapid marches from Frederick had been much reduced in numbers. The Second Division, 2,500 strong, had lost three general officers (wounded and prisoners) at Cedar Mountain, and its regiments were also much reduced. The whole corps, excepting the five new regiments, had been in continuous daily marches, and there was neither time nor opportunity to restore the spirit and vigor of the command. And yet, under all these adverse circumstances, this corps—as we shall see—repulsed the Confederates who were exultantly driving Hooker from the field, drove them out of the East Woods, back over the open fields and beyond the Hagerstown Road, and held these fields all day without yielding an inch of ground gained (except the woods it had seized around the Dunkard church).

It went into action without coffee or food and after an almost sleepless night. At the first sound of cannon at daybreak of the "misty, moisty morning," it was put in motion, crossed the Smoketown Road, moved west a short distance, swung to the left, and marched south in column of battalions in mass: the First Division, under Alpheus Williams, in advance (Samuel Crawford's brigade leading, Brigadier General George H. Gordon's following Crawford) and George Greene's Second Division bringing up the rear. From the moment of leaving the bivouac, the column marched directly in the line of fire of S. D. Lee's guns. The advance was slow and cautious, and the haltings (by Mansfield's orders) very frequent, but of sufficient time to allow the men to boil coffee. Regiments were detached to occupy woods on the flanks, brought back, and again detached. At 6:30 a.m. the head of the column was halted near the middle of an open field west of and adjoining the Samuel Poffenberger woods, and Mansfield rode forward to survey the ground and consult with Hooker. At the time of the halt, the old regiments of Crawford's brigade—the 10th Maine, 28th New York, and 46th Pennsylvania—were on the right, and the new regiments—the 124th, 125th, and 128th Pennsylvania—on the left. "It was the understanding," one regimental commander reports, "that the latter three regiments should move to the front when wanted, and the old ones (the Forty-sixth Pennsylvania, Tenth Maine, and Twenty-eighth New York) should follow at a proper distance in the rear, constituting, as it were, a reserve for the brigade."[1]

When coming to a halt, Williams observed that the regiments of his division had been moved up without deploying intervals. They were then under fire and liable at any moment to be called into action (as Hooker's corps was melting away,

---

[1] Joseph F. Knipe to H. B. Scott, October 1, 1862, reprinted in *OR*, vol. 19, pt. 1, 487.

much of it streaming to the rear). As Mansfield rode to the front, Williams ordered the deployment of the foremost brigade, and Crawford proceeded to execute the order. When nearly completed, Mansfield returned and ordered Crawford to suspend the deployment and again mass his command, although then exposed to artillery fire. Williams remonstrated, but Mansfield would not consent to a deployment in the open field, giving as a reason that if the new regiments were deployed in line they would run away, upon which Williams gathered the commanders of the old regiments under a large tree and gave instructions as to deployment, Colonel Joseph F. Knipe of the 46th Pennsylvania being directed to double-quick in advance and cover the deployment of the new regiments when the time came.

When Mansfield rode forward to report to Hooker, he was informed that the First Corps was hard pressed and that he would soon be called upon to relieve it. He had been back to his command but a few minutes, and Williams had scarcely concluded his conference with the three regimental commanders, when Hooker's order was received to deploy and advance. Directing Williams to lead the 124th and 125th Pennsylvania to the right as far as the Hagerstown Road, Mansfield advanced with the three old regiments and the 128th Pennsylvania, all still in column of divisions. It was then about 7:15 a.m.

The original intention to move the three new regiments in advance, followed by the three old ones, was now departed from. Knipe says, "The Tenth Maine, which had been on the right of the Forty-sixth Pennsylvania, by some means for which I cannot account got on the left of it, and both, with the Twenty-eighth New York, in advance of the One hundred and twenty-fourth, One hundred and twenty-fifth, and One hundred and twenty-eighth Pennsylvania."[2] The departure from the original intention was due to Hooker's direction to Mansfield to form the three new regiments of Crawford's brigade on the right (the right resting on the Hagerstown Road), the old regiments to extend the line to the left, where the danger was now most imminent. Gordon was to deploy in rear of Crawford's new regiments as a support, and Greene's division was to go in on the left of the old ones. It was in following these directions that Williams led the 124th and 125th Pennsylvania to the right and Mansfield led the three old regiments and the 128th Pennsylvania to the front, intending to form the 128th Pennsylvania on the right (connecting with the 125th), with the old regiments on the left of the 128th. How the movement was executed and the result we shall now tell.

Before the general advance was made, the 125th Pennsylvania had gone forward under the personal direction of Crawford. Colonel Jacob Higgins, commanding the regiment, says, "I was ordered by General Crawford to advance in close column, at daylight, through some fields to a piece of woods where there was heavy firing at that time going on. I was then ordered into the woods and then back again by General Crawford, then to throw out skirmishers and again advance through the woods until I reached the other side of the timber, and then deploy in line of battle and advance through the fields and there halt. At this place my command was exposed to a most terrific fire of musketry, shot, and shell. I then fell back a few rods, by order of General Crawford."[3] The regiment was in a slight depression in the ground about two hundred yards south from the Samuel Poffenberger woods, its left on the Smoketown Road and its right extending westerly nearly to the Joseph Poffenberger lane. It was now ordered to advance through a ten-acre cornfield and occupy a knoll, along which ran a fence separating the cornfield from the East Woods. A company of skirmishers passed through the corn and into the woods, closely followed by the regiment, and Captain Robbins's men—Alabamians, Georgians, and Texans—were seen in the far part of the woods. Before firing a shot the regiment and its skirmishers were recalled to the position from which they had been ordered forward. In its eccentric movements, exposed to a "terrific fire of musketry, shot, and shell," the loss was trifling; not until the regiment had fallen back was its first man killed that day—by a shot from the East Woods. The regiment had not fired a shot, but its movement in front and on the Confederate flank steadied Meade's left (what little there was of it), enabled Magilton to partially re-form his shattered brigade, held at bay Law's Brigade, and finally—with the appearance of the 10th Maine—compelled Law to withdraw. Meanwhile, the old regiments of the brigade came up, closely followed by the 128th Pennsylvania.

The advance of the old regiments was led by Mansfield in person, who rode with the 10th Maine on the left. The regiment marched in column of divisions, closed in mass, and entered the ten-acre cornfield east of the northern part of the East Woods, where it came under fire while deploying, by which a few men were killed and wounded by a fire from the East Woods. As the regiment was about to return the fire, it was ordered to oblique to the left the length of the regiment, and at once began the engagement with a regiment of the enemy. So far the official records indicate, but John M. Gould says the regiment did not deploy in the ten-acre cornfield, but moved—still closed in mass—across the Smoketown Road to a plowed field, where Mansfield left it. It was then 7:30 a.m.[4] The regiment now deployed and, while doing so, saw a

---

[2] Ibid.

[3] Jacob Higgins to Knipe, September 22, 1862, reprinted in *OR*, vol. 19, pt. 1, 491.

[4] John M. Gould, *History of the First-Tenth-Twenty-Ninth Maine Regiment: In Service of the United States from May 3, 1861, to June 21, 1866* (Portland, Maine: Stephen Berry, 1871), 235.

Confederate skirmish line (the 5th Texas) along the East Woods fence and, under the fire of these Texans (which also struck the 125th Pennsylvania), advanced and drove them back into the woods, and when reaching the fence saw before it the right of Hood's line—the 4th Alabama, the Georgians, and the 5th Texas—in the far edge of the woods. The eight companies of the 10th Maine went over the fence and, taking shelter of the trees and logs, opened fire upon the enemy. The right of the regiment rested on the Smoketown Road, seven companies and part of another behind or just over the fence, while two companies and part of a third were thrown back under cover of a rock ledge to guard the flank, as there were no Union troops on its left (it being, at the time and until relieved, the left of the corps line).

While the 10th Maine was thus getting into action on the left, the 28th New York and the 46th Pennsylvania moved through the small cornfield into the East Woods, deployed (part in the woods and part in open ground west of them), and then opened fire on the Confederates directly south. The 28th New York carried about 60 men into action, and the 46th Pennsylvania did not exceed 150 men. The deployment and advance of the two regiments and the near approach of the 128th Pennsylvania relieved some of the Pennsylvania Reserves who had held on to the woods, but some of them (mostly of the 8th Pennsylvania Reserves) still remained. The firing was now severe on both sides, during which Knipe and the 46th Pennsylvania were awaiting the arrival and deployment of the 128th Pennsylvania.

We consider Knipe's opponents. In the earlier period of Crawford's maneuvering, Hood's Division (save the 4th Alabama and 5th Texas, which, with some Georgians, remained in the East Woods) had retired. Anderson's brigade of Meade's division charged through the cornfield on the heels of the 1st Texas and was obliged to fall back upon the advance of Ripley's Brigade, with which (and the Confederates in the East Woods) Knipe was now contending. Ripley's Brigade was the left of D. H. Hill's Division, and on the night of the sixteenth bivouacked in the field south and west of the Mumma house and about 125 to 150 yards from it, in close support to Trimble's Brigade of Ewell's Division. The brigade was composed of the 1st and 3d North Carolina and the 4th and 44th Georgia, and numbered 1,349 officers and men. (The largest regiment, the 3d North Carolina, had 547 officers and men; the smallest, the 44th Georgia, had 162.) In the brigade formation, the 3d North Carolina was on the right, and on its left—in order named—the 1st North Carolina and the 44th and 4th Georgia. Ripley reports the early movements of the brigade:

> Early on the morning of the 17th, the skirmishers of Colonel Walker's [Trimble's—*EAC*] brigade, of Jackson's corps, immediately on my left, became engaged, and the enemy from his batteries on the eastern bank of the Antietam opened a severe enfilading fire on the troops of my command, the position which we had been ordered to occupy being in full view of nearly all of his batteries. This fire inflicted serious loss before the troops were called into positive action, the men lying under it, without flinching, for over an hour, while the enemy plied his guns unceasingly. During this while, a set of farm buildings [Mumma's—*EAC*] in our front were set on fire to prevent them being made use of by the enemy.
>
> At about 8 o'clock [7:00 a.m.—*EAC*] I received orders to close in to my left and advance. The troops sprung to their arms with alacrity and moved forward through the burning buildings in our front, reformed on the other side, and opened a rapid fire upon the enemy [the 26th and 94th New York—*EAC*].
>
> While engaged in reforming the brigade, I received a shot in the neck, which disabled me, and the troops moved forward under command of Colonel [George] Doles, of the Fourth Georgia Regiment.[5]

As soon as the line had been re-formed, Doles ordered an advance to the East Woods, and the brigade had gone about halfway when D. H. Hill rode up and word was passed down the line to change direction by the left flank, and in column of fours it was led by Hill across the Smoketown Road, just touching the projecting point of the East Woods, and subjected to quite a brisk fire (by which Major Robert S. Smith of the 4th Georgia and others were killed). Upon clearing the road, the leading regiments filed to the left in the direction of the Hagerstown Road, followed in succession by the others. All came into line facing nearly north, the right of the brigade resting near the southwest corner of the woods, as Hood's men were retiring in the direction of the church. (Robbins and his men were still fighting in the East Woods, his left very near the southeast corner of the corn.) In front of Ripley's Brigade was the cornfield, beyond which, on an elevation, was seen a Union line of infantry, with Ransom's battery of Napoleon guns.

The brigade now advanced, all in open ground. The left and center of the line (the 4th and 44th Georgia and part of the 1st North Carolina) making a slight wheel to the left engaged the 9th Pennsylvania Reserves on the high ground south of the corn and near the Hagerstown Road, while the 3d North Carolina and part of the 1st (moving straight ahead, the right along and near the East Woods), after some severe fighting, drove the 11th and 12th Pennsylvania Reserves from the corn but did not enter it (as the left had been checked by the resistance offered by the 9th Pennsylvania Reserves). When the 9th finally fell back, the left of Ripley's line advanced to the high ground near the road and halted about fifty yards south of the

---

5 Roswell S. Ripley to Archer Anderson, September 21, 1862, reprinted in *OR*, vol. 19, pt. 1, 1032–33.

cornfield fence. A part of the 1st North Carolina was now moved from the right center of the brigade to the left of the 4th Georgia and at nearly right angles to it, facing nearly west, to prevent a repetition of the Union tactics that had resulted so disastrously to the left of Wofford's Brigade. The skirmishers on the right now entered the cornfield and became engaged with the 28th New York and the 46th Pennsylvania. The 128th Pennsylvania now came up.

When Mansfield had conducted the 10th Maine across the Smoketown Road, he rode back to the 128th Pennsylvania and led it on the double-quick over the right of the 125th Pennsylvania and into the East Woods. The regiment was still in column of divisions. As it entered the woods, men of the 3d Pennsylvania Reserves and others of Magilton's brigade moved out. Upon reaching the woods, Mansfield ordered its commander, Colonel Samuel Croasdale, to deploy the 128th to the right, through the woods and into the open ground west of them, his evident intention being to bring the 28th New York and the 46th Pennsylvania on the left of the 128th and fill the interval between it and the 10th Maine (thus carrying out Hooker's instructions to have the three old regiments on the left of the brigade). Croasdale gave the order to deploy and was instantly killed, Lieutenant Colonel William W. Hammersly was severely wounded, and the command devolved upon Major Joel B. Wanner.

Meanwhile, the regiment was endeavoring to deploy to the right, but instead of moving each company in succession, nearly the entire mass crowded to the right in some disorder. In this condition the right and center went through the woods into open ground, passing in rear of the 28th New York and 46th Pennsylvania. Mansfield remained with the three left companies, which were deployed in the woods and on the knoll just east of them. About this time Mansfield was mortally wounded and carried from the field.[6] The entire regiment was now under the fire of Ripley's and Robbins's men; it was raw and inexperienced, and naturally there was much confusion in the deployment of the right and center, which Wanner endeavored to complete but found impossible. The greater part of the regiment had now gained the open ground and massed in disorder on the right of the 46th Pennsylvania, and some of the men had opened fire upon Ripley's men in and beyond the cornfield. Colonel Knipe, commanding the 46th, says of the 128th, "At this moment, seeing the uselessness of a regiment in that position, I took the responsibility of getting it into line of battle the best way circumstances would admit. When this was accomplished, I returned to my own regiment and ordered an advance, which was gallantly made as far as the fence of the corn-field."[7]

After he had succeeded in deploying his regiment, Major Wanner (at Knipe's suggestion) ordered a charge into the cornfield. The men started off in gallant style, cheering as they went down to the cornfield fence, the 46th Pennsylvania moving out of the way into the woods. Upon arriving at the fence, the regiment fired a few rounds into the corn and then charged nearly to its south edge, but was met by such a savage fire from Ripley's men (particularly from the 3d and part of the 1st North Carolina) that it was compelled to fall back to the fence in some disorder. With the 46th Pennsylvania, it was ordered into the woods, out of the line of fire of Gordon's brigade, and then to the rear of the woods to re-form.

The charge of the 128th Pennsylvania struck the 3d North Carolina as it was changing front to the right to meet Greene's division, seen in motion beyond the far edge of the East Woods and threatening its right. The Confederate regiment was thrown into some confusion; its colonel was wounded, many were killed and wounded, and it gave ground, but was rallied and steadied by Major Stephen D. Thruston.[8] After driving back the Pennsylvanians it completed its change of front, which brought it entirely out of the corn, its left near the south edge of it and about 290 yards from the Hagerstown Road. A strong line of brigade skirmishers re-entered the corn in pursuit of the Pennsylvanians, but the main line remained in the open ground south of the corn, exposed to the fire of Gordon's brigade.

We left General Williams moving to deploy the 124th Pennsylvania. He led it to the right and, passing through the eastern part of the North Woods, along the southern edge of which, starting one company after another by the flank, he formed the regiment in line, the right on the Hagerstown Road and the left extending along the south edge of the woods. Williams ordered Colonel Joseph W. Hawley, as soon as the deployment should be completed and the other regiments of the brigade come up on the left, to move forward with them. After he had gone to attend to the deployment of other regiments, however, it appears that Hooker or some other general officer rode up and gave orders to hold in the woods. It was after Williams had deployed the 124th Pennsylvania and was in quest of the 125th (which he had ordered Crawford to deploy on the left of the 124th) that he found the 125th had gone some distance to the left. At the same time, he heard that Mansfield had been mortally wounded. When this was reported to him, he did not know that all the old regiments had gone to the front and were then in action, so he sent orders for their deployment and advance and, riding to the front, reported to Hooker (whom he found alone in the plowed field on the D. R. Miller farm, east of the Hagerstown Road). Hooker's orders were to deploy in rear of the First Corps and relieve such portions of it as had not already retired from the field.

---

6 See [Appendix K].—*EAC*
7 Knipe to Scott, 487.
8 At this point in his original manuscript, Carman lists Thruston's rank incorrectly as "Lieutenant Colonel," but renders it properly in his table of organization.

While Williams was taking Hooker's instructions, Meade came from the left and Gibbon from the right, reporting that their batteries were in danger and would be lost unless they had instant support—and requested Williams to give it. Williams assured Hooker that Gordon's line of march would bring him to Meade's support, and that he would detach the rear brigade of Greene's division to Gibbon's support. Upon which, Hooker—turning to Meade and Gibbon, remarked, "Gentlemen, you must hold on until Williams's men get up,"[9] pointing at the same time to Gordon (then deploying south of the North Woods) and to Greene (hastening through the fields east of the Joseph Poffenberger house). Greene was ordered to detach Colonel William B. Goodrich's brigade and send it across the Hagerstown Road to report to Gibbon or any general officer on that part of the field. At the same time, an order was given the 124th Pennsylvania to push forward past the D. R. Miller farm, cross the Hagerstown Road and into the woods beyond, and hold the position as long as practicable—this on the supposition that Gibbon still held the right of the road, and not aware of the fact that Gibbon had already retired and that Patrick held the woods.

Having given his orders to Greene, Williams rode into the East Woods, where he saw that the 28th New York and the 46th and 128th Pennsylvania had been roughly handled. He informed Knipe that the colonel was now in command of the brigade and that Greene was to form on the left, and he ordered him to look up his command, get it in order, and support Greene's right. At this time Gordon's old regiments—the 2d Massachusetts, 3d Wisconsin, and 27th Indiana—were in line in the open field, in good order.

Gordon's brigade followed Crawford's from its bivouac on the Hoffman farm. Early in its movement, the 13th New Jersey was detached and thrown into the edge of a piece of woods to observe the right flank of the marching column in the direction of the Hagerstown Road, where—for the first time in its experience—its colonel [Ezra A. Carman] instructed it how to form line of battle by deploying it along the fences skirting the woods (much in the same manner as Williams had deployed the 124th Pennsylvania on the south border of the North Woods). After the long halt west of the Samuel Poffenberger woods, Gordon was ordered to support a battery on the right, but before reaching it the order was countermanded, and he was directed to move with all possible dispatch to the relief of the First Corps, which was then severely pressed, part of it giving way. Gordon moved double-quick, passed through the eastern part of the North Woods, and formed line—the 2d Massachusetts on the right, 3d Wisconsin in center, and 27th Indiana on the left. The 107th New York, by order of Hooker, was thrown along the edge of the Poffenberger woods on the left, to hold them and act as a reserve. It was while thus deploying south of the North Woods that Williams called Hooker's attention to his advance. Gordon had expected to come up in rear of Crawford's new regiments as a support to them, but he found nothing in his immediate front but fugitives and broken battalions of the First Corps, and with the instinct of a true soldier he moved on to fill the gap in the line. While moving, one of Hooker's aides galloped up and requested him to hurry forward. "It was apparent," says Gordon, "from the steady approach of the sound of musketry, that the enemy were advancing. Their shouts of exultation could be distinctly heard as the line of my deployed battalion, sustained on the right by Crawford's brigade [the 124th Pennsylvania only—EAC] and on the left by Greene's divisions, both of our own corps, advanced boldly to the front."[10]

The 3d Wisconsin and the 27th Indiana advanced to the crest of a swell of ground immediately east of the Miller orchard and between it and the East Woods, the left of the 27th Indiana almost fifty yards from the woods. Between the right of the 3d Wisconsin and the orchard was Ransom's battery of six guns, and on the line where the regiment halted were Thompson's abandoned guns. The 2d Massachusetts, in its advance on the right, passed through Ransom's battery, by which its movement was somewhat impeded, and going into the orchard was halted in its southeast corner some seventy-five yards in advance of the right of the 3d Wisconsin and formed in a broken line—the left perpendicular and the right parallel to the line of the other two regiments, both wings of the regiment being along the orchard fences. In front of the right wing and about fifty yards distant were two Union regiments (probably the 9th and 12th Pennsylvania Reserves) lying down obliquely to the Hagerstown Road in a depression of the ground.[11] The 3d Wisconsin was 150 yards from the cornfield fence and the left of the 27th Indiana 120 yards from the same fence. The strength of the three regiments was about 1,140 officers and men.

When the three regiments moved into position, the 128th Pennsylvania was retreating out of the corn, pursued by the enemy. The corn was on lower ground, was very heavy, and served to screen the enemy. Yet the colors and battle-flags clearly indicated their position, and Colonel Silas Colgrove of the 27th Indiana reports that he saw, immediately beyond the corn, upon open ground at the distance of about four hundred yards, three regiments in line of battle, and farther to the right,

---

9 As of this writing, Carman's source for this quotation has not been identified.

10 George H. Gordon to Alpheus S. Williams, September 24, 1862, reprinted in *OR*, vol. 19, pt. 1, 494–95.

11 Colonel George L. Andrews of the 2d Massachusetts reports, "In front of the right, about 50 yards distant, were two regiments lying down." George L. Andrews to Gordon, September 23, 1862, reprinted in *OR*, vol. 19, pt. 1, 500. These were subsequently relieved by the 124th Pennsylvania.—*EAC*

on a high ridge of ground, still another regiment in line diagonally to that of Gordon's brigade.[12] This accurately described the position of Ripley's Brigade, which now opened a terrific fire upon Gordon that could not be immediately returned (for the 128th Pennsylvania had not yet come out of the corn and there were still other Union men in front, about midway between the 27th Indiana and the cornfield fence). For more than five minutes, the 3d Wisconsin and 27th Indiana were compelled to stand a severe fire without replying, but when the Pennsylvanians came out of the corn and Williams rode up and ordered them into the woods, out of the way, Gordon's three regiments opened such a rapid and accurate fire that the pursuing enemy fell back and was soon reinforced by Colquitt's Brigade.

On the night of the sixteenth, Colquitt's Brigade bivouacked in the sunken road, near the Roulette lane. From right to left it was thus formed: the 6th, 27th, 28th and 23d Georgia and the 13th Alabama, which formation was preserved during the engagement. It numbered 1,320 officers and men. There was formed from this brigade a skirmish battalion of five companies, one from each regiment of the brigade, under command of Captain William M. Arnold of the 6th Georgia. The companies were from the right of each regiment and regularly drilled as skirmishers. Whenever skirmishing was required this battalion was deployed, each company covering the front of its own regiment. When the main line became engaged, these companies closed in to the right without further instruction or command than from the company commander, took their places upon the right of their respective regiments, and went into battle with them. This manner of using skirmishers was found both convenient and effective, and Arnold's battalion was noted for its efficiency and was sometimes used as an independent, detached command. As such, on the evening of the sixteenth, it was ordered forward from the left of D. H. Hill's Division, formed on the right of Hood's skirmishers in the edge of the East Woods, and engaged the 13th Pennsylvania Reserves of Seymour's brigade. At the close of the engagement, it withdrew to the Roulette orchard and bivouacked. Early on the morning of the seventeenth, the battalion again went forward and deployed along the fence running from the Mumma barn in the direction of the East Woods, where it engaged the 26th and 94th New York. Upon the retreat of Ricketts's division and the advance of Hood's Division, it entered the East Woods and engaged the advance of the Twelfth Corps. It claimed to have been in action an hour before its brigade became engaged, that it advanced into the woods with the 4th Alabama, and continued in action until driven out by Greene's division.

At about 7:00 a.m., Colquitt's Brigade moved a short distance along the sunken road by the flank, filed to the right, marched over a grass field along the east fence of the Mumma cornfield, then (moving north) went over the low ground between the Mumma and Roulette farms, passed the burning buildings and the small graveyard, and crossed the Smoketown Road at the southwest corner of the woods where Ripley's Brigade had crossed. Ripley's Brigade, though still firing at Gordon's line, was considerably broken, and D. H. Hill hastened Colquitt to its support. Still moving by the left flank, the 13th Alabama in advance, it passed the right of the 3d North Carolina and then obliqued to the left across its front, the 3d North Carolina at the same time obliquing to the left in its rear. When the 13th Alabama, moving in the open ground south of the corn, had gone what was judged a sufficient distance to bring the entire brigade in line in open ground west of the woods (and to clear the 4th Alabama, the Georgians, and the 5th Texas in the woods), the four leading regiments were fronted to the right and formed line, but part of the 27th Georgia was in the woods, as was also the 6th Georgia, which was the rear regiment and had entered the woods in crossing the road. Line formed, fire was immediately opened upon Gordon, which was participated in by the left and center of Ripley's Brigade. The greater part of the line had the protection of the rock ledges just south of the corn, but parts of the line were much exposed and suffered severely from Gordon's fire, which was delivered with great coolness and fatal accuracy. While Colquitt was thus engaged, two guns of Moody's Battery of S. D. Lee's Battalion came up in rear of the 13th Alabama and began firing. When Hood's Division became engaged, the contending lines were so close that Colonel Lee could not use his artillery, but he now advanced these two guns to the assistance of Ripley and Colquitt.

The 6th Georgia was the last to get on the brigade line. It came under fire and formed line in the East Woods, engaging the 10th Maine. It did not long tarry with the Maine men (leaving them to Captain Robbins and his mixed command) but went forward, and (as Robbins was in front) obliqued to the left, passed in rear of the 5th Texas, emerged from the woods, came up on the right of the brigade line (then engaged), and all pushed into the cornfield, followed by the 3d North Carolina and part of the 1st. Midway through the corn, passing over many dead and wounded men of both sides, it was met by such a terrific fire from Gordon's line that its advance was checked. Officers fell in every regiment and men went down by the score. To advance was impossible, and the entire brigade lay down and continued to fire.

Gordon's line, particularly the 3d Wisconsin and the 27th Indiana, was suffering severely. They stood on higher ground than the Confederates—the sky behind them, in good musket range, a good target—not yielding an inch, giving and taking punishment. When first coming into position, Ransom's battery had been silenced by the persistent and accurate fire of the 3d North Carolina and the gunners had gone to the rear, but when Gordon came up the gunners returned, charged the pieces with canister, and added their destructive work to that of the infantry.

---

12 Silas Colgrove to Gordon, September 22, 1862, reprinted in *OR*, vol. 19, pt. 1, 498.

Meanwhile, Lieutenant Stewart (under Gibbon's order to resume his position of the early morning) had come up and, seeing that Ransom occupied the ground, formed on his left, but the 3d Wisconsin being only a few feet in his immediate front, he could not use his guns. Recognizing the danger of the situation, he sent his limbers and horses to the rear and charged his guns with canister. The men lay down among them, protected by the slight swell of ground in front (on which stood the 3d Wisconsin) and awaited the further advance of the enemy. Captain George W. Cothran's New York battery of six guns came up and halted about 150 yards in rear of Ransom. Matthews's battery was still in position and ready for more work, about 160 yards in rear of the left of the 27th Indiana, and Reynolds's battery was near.

Colquitt's men were checked about midway in the cornfield, but they had not given up hopes of driving Gordon from the field, and when, after a halt of five to seven minutes, they heard that Garland's Brigade was coming up on the right, they again went forward. The right of the 6th Georgia moved along the edge of the East Woods, and it and the regiment on its left reached the north fence of the cornfield. (Some of the men went over it, but were quickly killed or driven back.) The three regiments on the left were met by such a rapid and accurate fire that they were checked before reaching the fence, and the entire brigade was ordered to lie down and continue the fight until Garland's men could come up on the right. Officers and men saw the dead and severely wounded of Law's Brigade lying along the fence in almost unbroken line. As Colquitt's men advanced, Ransom's battery poured canister upon them, the infantry rained bullets among them, and this fire was continued after the brigade had again been checked. From the higher ground where the 3d Wisconsin stood could be seen a steady stream of Confederate wounded—limping, crawling, or being helped to the rear. The 3d Wisconsin also was suffering severely, and the other regiments were hotly engaged. The 2d Massachusetts, which had moved into the orchard about seventy-five yards in advance of the other regiments, gave a crossfire across the front of the 3d Wisconsin and the 27th Indiana that was very effective upon the right of Colquitt's line.

The only Union forces at this time and place engaged—in fact, anywhere engaged on the entire field—were the 2d Massachusetts, 3d Wisconsin, 27th Indiana, and Ransom's battery on Gordon's line, and farther to the left, about 450 yards, the 10th Maine. At this time, the Confederate fire was terribly destructive. It seemed that the Wisconsin and Indiana regiments would be entirely destroyed (they could not be driven), but at this moment, after the 2d Massachusetts had opened its enfilade fire, a small body of Union men was seen to advance into the East Woods on the left and open full upon the right flank and front of the 6th Georgia. This fire, with that of Gordon's men, almost annihilated it, and drove the entire brigade from the field. The Union body so opportunely appearing was the advance of Greene's division, and it soon drove the entire Confederate line, with S. D. Lee's artillery, from the field and across the Hagerstown Road. Before treating of Greene's action and success, we must follow the movements of Garland's Brigade to this part of the field.

Garland's Brigade, commanded by Colonel Duncan K. McRae of the 5th North Carolina (Garland being killed at South Mountain), was composed of the 5th, 12th, 13th, 20th, and 23d North Carolina, and as near as we can estimate numbered 756 officers and men. It followed Colquitt from the sunken road and formed line near the small graveyard, where it halted a few minutes, subjected to a severe fire from the Union artillery beyond the Antietam, then advanced in line of battle (the 5th North Carolina on the right) across the plowed field and over the fences of the Smoketown Road and into the East Woods. Here great confusion ensued. Various conflicting orders were passed down the line, the men in ranks being allowed by the officers to repeat them, so that it became impossible to understand which came from proper authority, and it followed that the movements of the brigade were vacillating and unsteady, obliquing to the right and then to the left, coming finally upon a ledge of rock and swelling ground forming a fine breastwork. Under cover of this, the brigade sought shelter from a scattering fire. It was a little shaky and had not recovered from its severe experience at South Mountain, and when the right saw the 28th Pennsylvania coming up in the open field beyond the woods and somewhat on the flank, it became very uneasy. Where the right of the 5th North Carolina rested, the conformation of the ground was such that a few files were exposed, and Captain Thomas M. Garrett (now commanding the regiment) ordered these to deploy as flankers to the right and take shelter behind the trees. At this moment and while Garrett was directing the movement, Captain Thomas P. Thompson approached in a very excited manner and tone and cried out, "They are flanking us! See, yonder is a whole brigade!"[13] Garrett ordered him to keep silent and return to his place. At the same time, a cry ran along the line to cease firing, as Ripley's men were in front.

Some men were seen in front (not Ripley's, but those of the 4th Alabama and 5th Texas), and the idea that they were firing into them created a very unfavorable impression in the ranks and, added to the appearance of an enemy on the flank, stampeded the brigade. Some of the brigade retreated to the West Woods, some of it all the way to Sharpsburg. A part of it was rallied in the sunken road and, joined by a part of Colquitt's Brigade, formed on the left of Rodes's Brigade. D. H. Hill says that Garland's Brigade had been much demoralized by the fight at South Mountain, and that Thompson's indiscreet

---

[13] As of this writing, Carman's source for this quotation has not been identified.

cry that they were being flanked "spread like an electric shock along the ranks, bringing up vivid recollections of the flank fire at South Mountain. In a moment they broke and fell to the rear."[14]

In a letter written on December 27, 1870, McRae writes:

Line was formed facing a woods to our left in to which we were directed to advance being cautioned by Gen'l Hill not to fire upon Colquitt who might be in our front. Very soon after we entered the woods we encountered a fire of what appeared to be a slight skirmish line, when a cry went through the line that those were Colquitt's troops [they were the 10th Maine—*EAC*], and I gave the order for my men to desist firing until I could reconnoitre [*sic*] … I mounted a rock and looking over the slope for about a hundred yards I saw a line of what I suppose to be about a regiment with the flag of the U.S. flying and I ordered the brigade to fire and charge. But at this moment some scattering troops of the [enemy] were discovered on our extreme right, and a cry started from that position of my line, "They are flanking us," and in a moment the most unutterable stampede occurred. The whole line vanished and a brigade famed for previous and subsequent conduct of each of its Regts. fled in panic from the field leaving me with one or two officers to get off the field as well as I could.[15]

When Garland's Brigade fled the field, Hill was in the Smoketown Road, near the corner of the East Woods. Perceiving that Colquitt and Ripley could not make head against Gordon's staunch line, and satisfied of the truth of the report that a Union force was on his flank and that its movement indicated an attack on the flank and rear of his two brigades, he sent orders for their withdrawal to the Dunkard church, where he proposed to rally and make a stand. Almost immediately thereafter, he rode to the front and left to lead them from the field, but he was too late—for Greene's division was upon them. As he rode to the front, two guns of Woolfolk's Battery were coming into the plowed field between the Mumma farm and the East Woods.

As elsewhere stated, Greene's division consisted of three brigades and carried into action 2,504 officers and men. It followed Gordon's brigade from its brief bivouac on the Hoffman farm, its regiments in column by division—Lieutenant Colonel Hector Tyndale's brigade in advance, followed by those of Goodrich and Colonel Henry J. Stainrook. It halted two or three times to make coffee and was as often ordered forward without having time to do so (the last time Mansfield riding up with all speed, very much excited, and ordering them to move forward at once, as the enemy was driving Hooker back. Then he rode forward and conducted Crawford's brigade into action). As Greene followed Gordon, a steady stream of Hooker's men was met going to the rear, and when the leading brigade came nearly abreast the north part of the East Woods, Williams rode up, informed Greene that Mansfield had been wounded, and directed that Goodrich's brigade be sent across the Hagerstown Road to report to Gibbon. Greene was ordered to deploy the two brigades of Tyndale and Stainrook on the left of the Joseph Poffenberger lane and advance, swinging his left in the direction of the Mumma buildings, which were still burning. The detachment of Goodrich left Greene 1,727 officers and men in the two brigades, Tyndale having 1,191 and Stainrook 536. Tyndale's largest regiment was the 28th Pennsylvania, which went into action with 29 officers and 766 men. (The three Ohio regiments—the 5th, 7th, and 66th—had been so reduced by the casualties and hardships of Pope's campaign that they had an aggregate of 425 officers and men, and it was proposed, just before going into action, to throw the three Ohio flags in one cluster and fight them as a single regiment, but as the third flag would make some confusion and as no regiment was willing to go in without its own colors, the idea was not adopted, and each regiment preserved its organization and carried its flag.) The 28th Pennsylvania was full and strong, for though an old regiment, Antietam was its first field fight.

In advancing, the 7th Ohio was on the right, and to its left, in order named, the 66th Ohio, 5th Ohio, and 28th Pennsylvania. When reaching the northeast corner of the woods, the 28th Pennsylvania began swinging to the right, and also gaining ground to the left, and it was the sight of this large regiment and a scattering fire from the 10th Maine that caused the stampede of Garland's Brigade. While the 28th Pennsylvania was coming into position on the left, the three Ohio regiments, deploying to the right, moved toward the right of the line that the 28th Pennsylvania was to take, which brought the 7th and 66th Ohio into the East Woods and immediately in front of the right of Colquitt's Brigade, drawn up along the north fence of the cornfield. Lieutenant Colonel Eugene Powell of the 66th Ohio says the march "was now directed more to the right so as to pass by the strip of woods and into the field beyond," and as they rose up a slight hill in the woods and moved to within a few rods of the corner of them, still obliquing to the right, Powell (who was riding near the right of the line with Major[16] Orrin J. Crane, commanding the 7th Ohio) peered into the mist and battle smoke that hung low and

---

[14] Daniel H. Hill to Robert H. Chilton, 1862 [no day or month given], reprinted in *OR*, vol. 19, pt. 1, 1023.

[15] Duncan K. McRae to Gould, December 27, 1870, typescript copy, "Garland's Brigade, D. H. Hill's Division" folder, box 3, Letters and Reports Concerning the Battle of Antietam, 1895–1900: ("Antietam Studies"), Record Group 94, National Archives.

[16] At this point in his original manuscript, Carman gives Crane's rank incorrectly as "Captain," but renders it properly in his table of organization.

observed a line of the enemy about thirty yards distant that—looking steadily and intently to the left—had not yet observed the two regiments. He immediately gave orders to fire. "No," shouted Crane, "they are our men." Powell, sure that he was not mistaken, urged his horse into the ranks of the 66th Ohio and succeeded in getting the first volley into the close ranks of the enemy before they could prepare for it.[17]

It was but a moment before that the captain of the right company of the 6th Georgia approached Lieutenant Colonel James M. Newton and reported that they were being flanked, and instantly both the captain and Newton were killed by the first volley of the 66th Ohio. The 7th Ohio now joined in the fire, and Gordon's men poured in heavy volleys, but Colquitt's stood their ground most manfully. It was not for long, however, for soon they were struck on the right flank and in rear.

When the 28th Pennsylvania had swung to the right, so that it faced the east part of the woods, and when within about fifty yards of them, still closed in mass, it came under a severe fire from the woods and began its deployment (the 5th Ohio deploying on its right). Orders were sent to the 10th Maine to get out of the way. The Maine men fell back out of the woods and from the fence bordering them and went to the rear. Not a shot was fired by the Pennsylvania regiment until the fourth division was fully uncovered and the alignment perfected—then a volley was fired that "sounded like one gun,"[18] and the regiment, with the 5th Ohio on its right and the 111th Pennsylvania of Stainrook's brigade on its left, dashed into the woods and drove out Robbins's men, who since Hood's first advance had so stubbornly held their position, contending both with the 10th Maine on their right, and on their front and left with such Union troops as appeared in the north part of the woods and in the lower part of the field west of them. The 4th Alabama had come under a left oblique fire from the Ohio regiments, who were contending with Colquitt's right; it had already lost one-half of its men in killed and wounded, and it—with the Georgians on its right—fell back obliquely to the right and rear through the woods, soon followed by the 5th Texas. Captain Isaac N. M. Turner, commanding the 5th Texas, had four times sent to Hood for support, and had as often been informed that it could not be given and that he must hold on. About the time Hood's last message came, the right of Garland's Brigade came up and took position on his right. When the 28th Pennsylvania advanced, Garland's men fired their wild volley, then broke and ran. The Texans were now nearly out of ammunition, the 4th Alabama and the Georgians were giving way on the left, the Union line was closing in on the right, and as the volley of the 28th Pennsylvania was delivered, Turner gave the order to fall back, but not soon enough to prevent the capture of some of his men. In the charge into the woods, the 5th Ohio and the right wing of the 28th Pennsylvania pushed straight to the east fence of the cornfield, and after firing four or five volleys into the corn, which swept down Colquitt's line, charged into it as the 7th and 66th Ohio cleared the north fence of the cornfield. Powell says, "The sight at the fence, where the enemy was standing, when we gave our first fire, was awful beyond description: dead men were literally piled upon and across each other. We had been enabled to pour a volley into an entire line, at a few rods distance and striking them in flank at about the same time. No line of men in the world, of equal strength, could have done better than they tried to do, or have recovered from the situation. The circumstances were all against them, and they had to go down."[19]

The fighting in the northeast corner of the corn was now fast and furious and hand-to-hand, bayonets were used by those who had them, and those who had not used clubbed guns. The 6th Georgia, holding the right of the line, was almost wiped out of existence. The rest of the brigade was suffering severely. The left wing of the 28th Pennsylvania was swinging up in its rear, and it broke and went back, leaving many prisoners in the hands of its enemy and an appalling number of dead and wounded on the field, with the victors in close pursuit.

When Garland's men stampeded and D. H. Hill ordered Colquitt's and Ripley's Brigades to withdraw and rode to the left to conduct the movement, he succeeded in getting the left of Ripley's started for the Dunkard church in good order, but the 3d North Carolina and part of the 1st were involved in Colquitt's disaster. They had followed Colquitt into the corn and, in second line, had come under Gordon's fire. They were obliquing to the left with the intention of forming on the 13th Alabama (the left of Colquitt's line) when Tyndale's brigade made its attack and forced Colquitt from the field, the retreating men passing both flanks of the two North Carolina regiments. Effort was made to stay the precipitate retreat and make head against the enemy but it was unavailing, and the North Carolinians retreated to the woods around the Dunkard church.

While the 5th Ohio and the right wing of the 28th Pennsylvania went through the woods and into the corn, sweeping everything before them, the left wing of the 28th Pennsylvania and the 111th Pennsylvania, on its left, did not make such rapid progress, for the 4th Alabama and 5th Texas, falling back but a short distance, made a stand and poured in such an annoying fire on the flank of the line that it was momentarily checked. A short and sharp contest ensued, a half wheel was made to the left, and Robbins and his men were driven farther toward the southern part of the woods, where they came

---

[17] As of this writing, the source of these particular quotations has not been identified, but the disagreement with Crane over the identity of the troops to their front is also told in Eugene Powell, "Recollections of the Eastern Campaigns of the Fall of 1862," *National Tribune*, June 27, 1901.

[18] As of this writing, the source of this unattributed quotation has not been identified.

[19] As of this writing, the source of Powell's quotation has not been identified.

under the fire of the 3d Maryland and the 102d New York. The Pennsylvanians, going forward, came out of the woods and into the open ground south of the corn as the three Ohio regiments and the right wing of the 28th Pennsylvania broke Colquitt's line and started in pursuit. The brigade was now united (the 111th Pennsylvania still on the left), and it advanced. Colquitt's men made a stand at several points to resist them. Moody's two guns, which were near the south edge of the corn when the break came, fell back sullenly, going into position two or three times and opening full in the face and on the flank of their pursuers. Colquitt made several efforts to rally his men along the fences of the Smoketown Road and on the Mumma farm but was not successful. The three Ohio regiments, crossing the Smoketown Road about midway from the Mumma lane to the Dunkard church under a severe artillery fire, took shelter in the low ground between the Mumma house and the church. The 28th and 111th Pennsylvania crossed the Smoketown Road between the woods and the Mumma lane, captured the two guns of Woolfolk's Battery that had fired but two shots and then been abandoned, and, crossing the lane, joined the Ohio regiments. Here they awaited ammunition, and the 3d Maryland and the 102d New York came up and formed on their left.

While the 28th Pennsylvania was deploying north of the Smoketown Road preparatory to its advance into the East Woods, Stainrook's brigade was marching on its left to deploy south of the road. After crossing the road, the 111th Pennsylvania deployed in good shape, advanced firing (its right on the road), and came up to and went forward with the 28th Pennsylvania, but the 3d Maryland and the 102d New York, on the left, after crossing the road and being ordered to deploy under fire, became intermingled and confused. The right of the 102d New York was run into by the 3d Maryland; its left came under a severe skirmish fire from the woods. For a time, disorder reigned supreme, but some of the officers sprang to the front, the men were rallied, and at a run—with the 3d Maryland on its right—the regiment went over the fence and dashed into the East Woods, taking Texans, Georgians, and Alabamians prisoner. The 5th Texas escaped by going down the Smoketown Road before the Ohio men reached it. Robbins, with a remnant of the 4th Alabama, went south beyond the Mumma buildings, and thence to the Dunkard church, where Jackson, Hill, Hood, and others were endeavoring to rally the broken lines to dispute the possession of the woods about the church. After passing through the East Woods, the 102d New York and the 3d Maryland crossed the plowed field, until—nearing the Mumma farm—the Maryland regiment moved to the right and joined the 111th Pennsylvania, while the 102d New York, passing to the left of the burning barn, halted near the burning house. From this point, a greater part of the men, filled with the ardor of pursuit, followed the retreating enemy to the north fence of the Mumma cornfield and began to tear down the fence. Some went into the corn, but the great body of them halted at the fence and opened fire on Patterson's (Georgia) Battery to the right and front about thirty yards beyond the corn, playing energetically on the right of Greene's division line. The battery was soon silenced and driven beyond the Hagerstown Road, and the regiment, crossing the Mumma lane, took position on the left of its brigade.

General Greene was not popular with his men, but the signal ability with which he had handled his command won their admiration and confidence. The brilliant service performed by his division was surpassed by it later in the morning and shall be noted. Meanwhile, we return to Gordon's men and other commands, Union and Confederate.

When Greene's men charged into the corn on the left, Gordon was compelled to suspend firing. When the Confederate lines broke, the three regiments fixed bayonets, pursued, and went down through the corn. The 2d Massachusetts picked up the colors of the 11th Mississippi, and all, wheeling to the right, charged toward the Hagerstown Road with the intention of crossing it, but upon reaching the foot of the rise of ground near the road were halted and ordered to lie down. The 124th Pennsylvania, supported by the Purnell Legion, entered the corn on the right of Gordon. The 125th and parts of the 46th and 128th Pennsylvania charged through the East Woods close on the heels of Greene's men. The 13th New Jersey and the 107th New York, which were in reserve, were ordered to the front. Batteries were rushed forward and opened upon the West Woods, and Hooker made hurried preparation to follow up the advantage gained by the Twelfth Corps, but before this was completed he was wounded and borne from the field.

The advantage won by the Twelfth Corps was not without loss. Crawford's engaged regiments had suffered to some extent, as had the 2d Massachusetts. The 27th Indiana had 209 killed and wounded of the 443 carried into action, and of the 340 taken into action by the 3d Wisconsin, 27 were killed and 173 wounded—in the aggregate, nearly 59 percent of the number engaged. Greene's loss was not heavy.

On the Confederate side, Garland's Brigade got away with slight loss, but Ripley and Colquitt suffered greatly. Out of the 1,349 officers and men taken into action by Ripley, 110 were killed, 506 wounded, and 124 missing—an aggregate of 740, being over 50 percent of those engaged. The heaviest loss fell upon the 3d North Carolina, which is officially reported as having 46 killed and 207 wounded, but the muster rolls of the regiment say, "The regiment suffered severely, losing over 300 officers and men."[20]

---

[20] Colonel William L. DeRosset writes that of the 27 officers and 520 men taken into action, 7 officers were killed and 16 wounded, and 330 men killed and wounded. William L. De Rosset [sic], "Ripley's Brigade at South Mountain," *Century Magazine* 33, no. 2 (December 1886): 309.—EAC

In his official report, Colquitt says:

About 7 [8—EAC] o'clock in the morning my brigade entered the fight. It was moved to the front and formed on the right of General Ripley's brigade, which was then engaged. After a few rounds had been discharged, I ordered an advance, and at the same time sent word to the regiments on my left to advance simultaneously. The order was responded to with spirit by my men, and, with a shout, they moved through the corn-field in front, 200 [245—EAC] yards wide, and formed on the line of fence. The enemy was near and in full view. In a moment or two his ranks began to break before our fire, and the line soon disappeared under the crest of the hill upon which it had been established. It was soon replaced by another, and the fire opened with renewed vigor.

In the meantime Garland's brigade, which had been ordered to my right, had given way, and the enemy was advancing, unchecked. The regiments upon my left having also failed to advance, we were exposed to a fire from all sides and nearly surrounded. I sent in haste to the rear for re-enforcements, and communicated to General Hill the exposed condition of my men. With steady supports upon the right we could yet maintain our position. The support was not at hand and could not reach us in time. The enemy closed in upon the right so near that our ranks were scarcely distinguishable. At the same time his line in front advanced. My men stood firm until every field officer but one had fallen, and then made the best of their way out.

In this sharp and unequal conflict I lost many of my best officers and one-half of the men in the ranks. If the brigades upon the right and left had advanced, we should have driven the enemy from the field. He had at one time broken in our front, but we had not strength to push the advantage.[21]

Hill says, "Colquitt had gone in with 10 field officers; 4 were killed, 5 badly wounded, and the tenth had been stunned by a shell. The men were beginning to fall back, and efforts were made to rally them in the bed of an old road, nearly at right angles to the Hagerstown pike, and which had been their position previous to the advance. These efforts, however, were only partially successful. Most of the brigade took no further part in the action."[22]

It is not surprising that the brigade took no further part in the action, for the loss in some of the regiments was appalling, and the brigade was demoralized by it. It went into action with 1,320 officers and men, and from the official reports we gather that its loss was 111 killed, 444 wounded, and 167 missing—an aggregate of 732, about 55 percent of those engaged. (This includes Arnold's skirmish battalion engaged in the East Woods.) The heaviest loss fell upon the 6th Georgia, which held the right of the brigade line and was almost enveloped by the Union advance. James M. Folsom writes, "Our loss [in the 6th Georgia] on this field was almost incredible. We went into the battle with not more than two hundred and fifty men; and of this number eighty-one were left dead on the field, one hundred and fifteen were wounded, and about thirty taken prisoners," or over 81 percent.[23] The two field officers who led it into action were killed and nearly all the company officers killed or wounded. Company C had 27 men in action and lost 10 killed, 10 wounded, and 5 prisoners. Company E had 33 in action, of whom 13 were killed, 17 wounded, and 3 captured—not an officer or man escaped. Company K had 36 engaged: 15 were killed, 15 wounded, and 3 missing. The large proportion of killed is remarkable.[24]

The 23d Georgia had its colonel killed, its lieutenant colonel and major wounded, and half the entire regiment killed or wounded. The colonel of the 27th Georgia was killed, the lieutenant colonel wounded, every other commissioned officer but one killed or wounded, and lost over one-third of its enlisted men. The 28th Georgia lost nearly half of its 220 officers and men, and the 13th Alabama had its colonel and lieutenant colonel wounded and lost a large percentage of its three hundred men. The loss of the brigade was much greater than that given in the official report.

When the battle began that morning, S. D. Lee had four batteries of his battalion on the plateau opposite the Dunkard church, all of which opened fire at daylight over the heads of the Confederates upon the Union artillery and infantry with great effect. Two guns of Jordan's Battery, as we have seen, were very early sent to an advanced position on the line of Trimble's Brigade. Here, mixed in with the infantry, they were exposed to an infantry fire from the East Woods, not over two hundred yards distant, and to the fire of the heavy guns beyond the Antietam and of Thompson's and Matthews's guns near the Miller house. They were disabled in a half-hour and obliged to retire. Meanwhile, the other guns kept up a continuous fire upon the batteries of Thompson and Matthews and upon Hooker's infantry as it advanced to the attack and in position

[21] Alfred H. Colquitt to James W. Ratchford, October 13, 1863, reprinted in OR, vol. 19, pt. 1, 1053–54.

[22] Hill to Chilton, 1022–23.

[23] James M. Folsom, *Heroes and Martyrs of Georgia: Georgia's Record in the Revolution of 1861*, vol. 1 (Macon, Ga.: Burke, Boykin & Co., 1864), 26.

[24] These particulars have been given us by survivors of the companies named. When our attention was called to the statement made by Colonel Folsom, we communicated with surviving officers and men of the regiment. From three companies we obtained full and accurate information; from the other companies our information was conflicting, but what we did obtain leads to the conclusion that the loss of the regiment was nearly or quite 90 percent, mostly in killed and wounded, and that Colonel Folsom does not overstate it.—EAC

south of the corn, until Hood's Division advanced, when the contending lines were so close that the firing ceased. Lee's batteries were exposed to an enfilade fire of more the twenty rifled guns beyond the Antietam, from Thompson and Matthews in front, and from the fire of the Union infantry both from the front and the East Woods on the right. His men and horses suffered very heavily, and Rhett's Battery was ordered to the rear for ammunition; Parker's and Woolfolk's moved slightly to the rear to refit, many men and horses being killed. So many horses had been killed or disabled that the pieces could be moved only by leaving the caissons. About this time Moody's Battery, which had been engaged near the center of Hill's line, arrived and reported. Colonel Lee placed it in position on the ground previously occupied by Parker, and two guns of Blackshear's Battery of Cutts's Battalion (under Lieutenant Thomas Maddox) came up and went on the right of Woolfolk's Battery. Hood's Division now began to fall back, but the lines were so close that it was impossible for Lee to use his guns, and he advanced one of Moody's sections beyond the Smoketown Road and very nearly to the Miller cornfield, where he could use it. The section remained in this position and did good service for about twenty minutes under Captain Moody and Lieutenant John B. Gorey, exposed to a galling infantry fire, until Colquitt's Brigade gave way. Then it was ordered to the rear, Moody stopping several times to fire as he fell back. Gorey was shot in the head by a musket ball and instantly killed as he was sighting his guns for a last shot.

When D. H. Hill advanced his brigades, Lieutenant Maddox, commanding the section of Blackshear's Battery, had been wounded, and Sergeant Major Robert Falligant took charge of the section. He was ordered by Colonel Lee to advance to the right, where he fired until compelled to stop by Hill's advance, lest he should fire into his rear.

Very soon after Moody's two guns were ordered beyond the Smoketown Road to the assistance of Ripley and Colquitt, two guns of Woolfolk's Battery under command of Lieutenant William D. Terrell were ordered to the right. Terrell left his caissons behind the Mumma stacks and advanced his guns into the plowed field beyond the graveyard. He fired but two rounds of canister at Greene's men as they came out of the East Woods and abandoned the guns to the 28th Pennsylvania.

When Colquitt and Ripley began to give way, S. D. Lee's guns were ordered by Hill to the ridge west of the Hagerstown Road and about six hundred yards southwest of the church, where they fired for a short time at Greene's men, who had advanced to the ground just vacated by them. Here they remained until McLaws came up, when they moved back about a mile to refit. We shall see them again late in the day, but may here say that they had suffered so severely in this morning engagement that but twelve guns could be brought into action when they again went to the front on Cemetery Hill and Cemetery Ridge.

Early in the engagement, a section of Blackshear's Battery was in position on the right of the Hagerstown Road near the left of Lawton's Brigade, from which position it was driven by Gibbon's advance and formed on the right of Woolfolk's Battery nearly opposite the church. Patterson's guns were advanced to the same position, facing the Union line. A few minutes before Hill's line broke, he ordered Patterson to watch the line and, if it broke, to bring out the guns. It fell back as Hill's line began to give way and took position a few yards in rear of the Mumma cornfield, from which position it was soon driven by the 102d New York and fell back across the Hagerstown Road on the left of Rodes's Brigade, which had just formed in the sunken road.

All the Confederates north of the sunken road had now been driven across the Hagerstown Road, and we return to the movements that have occurred west of the latter road since the repulse of Starke's men and the fight of Gibbon, Patrick, and Hood around Stewart's guns near the straw stacks, and to some events still earlier in the day.

In the preceding chapter, we briefly noted the action, early in the morning, of the Confederate batteries on the left with the batteries of Doubleday's division. At this time Garber's, Wooding's, and Carpenter's Batteries were in or near the edge of the cornfield that crowned Nicodemus Hill—Garber's in the northwest corner of a field joining the cornfield on the south, Wooding's and Carpenter's in the cornfield. Pelham's Battery was some[25] yards to the right of Garber's. The Union fire upon these four batteries was very accurate and effective, and they were soon temporarily silenced. Wooding's was ordered to the rear about sunrise; Carpenter's was soon withdrawn to the cover of the ridge, as was Garber's, which was moved farther to the left. They were not permanently withdrawn from action, but as the Union fire slackened they would be run forward and open fire upon the advancing infantry of Hooker and Mansfield, again to be driven back. They had some assistance from Brockenbrough's and D'Aquin's Batteries (which by Jackson's orders had gone to the left) and by some guns of Cutts's Battalion. (Stuart reports that when the enemy had advanced too far into the woods near the Dunkard church for the fire to be continued without danger of harming his own friends, he withdrew the batteries farther to the rear,[26] but Early says they were withdrawn because a body of the enemy's troops were making their way gradually between the batteries and the left of the main infantry line.[27]) The position to which they were withdrawn was on Hauser's Ridge near the Hauser house,

[25] In his original manuscript, Carman writes that it "was   yards," leaving the distance blank.
[26] James E. B. Stuart to Chilton, February 13, 1864, reprinted in OR, vol. 19, pt. 1, 820.
[27] Jubal A. Early to Alexander S. Pendleton, January 12, 1863, reprinted in OR, vol. 19, pt. 1, 968–69.

nearly due west of the Dunkard church. Pelham's Battery, supported by the 13th Virginia and a small cavalry force, was left near the northwest corner of the West Woods. D'Aquin's Battery fell back to the Cox house for ammunition. Captain John R. Johnson's (Virginia) Battery, which encamped on the night of the sixteenth in open ground west of the south part of the West Woods, entered the woods about 4:00 a.m. of the seventeenth and remained there until Lawton had been repulsed, when it was ordered to the rear to find water for the horses. Raine's Battery fell back to Hauser's Ridge.

When Poague retired from the fight early in the morning to the Alfred Poffenberger barn and joined the other guns of his battery and those of Raine, he was exposed to a crossfire of heavy artillery on the right, by which one man was mortally wounded. Then, about 7:00 a.m., he moved his entire battery back about three hundred yards and to the left, near the crest of Hauser's Ridge, so as to command the West Woods in case the infantry should be compelled to abandon them. Having reported to Jackson, he was directed to advance toward the Hagerstown Road and see if a battery would be of any assistance in that direction or on the road, but finding all of the eligible positions already occupied, he proceeded to a position in rear of that occupied by him in the early morning and quite close to the woods and the Hagerstown Road. There was no infantry in the field, but a gap in the line of some two hundred yards between Early's right (who had just taken position) and the left of Hill's forces then engaged east of the road. Two guns were all he had with him. These opened fire to the front on the Union line, but with Ripley and Colquitt soon giving way and the Union line advancing on the flank, he withdrew the guns through the woods and resumed his position on Hauser's Ridge. This was after eight o'clock, and Jackson was making efforts to stop the stream of stragglers pouring out of the West Woods.

During the night of the sixteenth, the 7th Virginia Cavalry of Robertson's Brigade took position near Ground Squirrel Church on the Hagerstown Road, about nine hundred yards north of Doubleday's bivouac. Early in the morning, it discovered that it was in a false position—a squadron of the 3d Pennsylvania Cavalry in its front and Doubleday's infantry in its rear—upon which it retreated southwest to New Industry, on the Potomac. It remained there until late in the forenoon, when it moved south and joined its brigade near the Blackford house, about a mile south of Sharpsburg.

When Hooker's artillery opened fire upon the Confederate batteries on Nicodemus Hill, these were supported by Fitz-hugh Lee's cavalry, which had bivouacked in the valley in their rear near the Cox house, some of it in an orchard and some in open ground adjoining. Fitzhugh Lee remained in support of the guns until relieved by Early's Brigade, when he moved further to the left out of range of the artillery fire and massed his regiments near the river, picketing well to the left and guarding that flank, but was not actively engaged during the morning. The 9th Virginia Cavalry was detached early in the day and reported to Jackson near the Reel house, southwest of the church. He ordered it to stop the infantry stragglers who, singly and in groups, were going to the rear. Men without ammunition—and many with it—were leisurely retiring toward Sharpsburg, and some of the Confederate batteries, having shot their last round, were leaving the field at a gallop. All these Jackson ordered stopped and supplied with ammunition from the ordnance train near the Reel house and then marched back to the line of battle or conducted to their proper commands. Jackson, motioning to a captain of the 9th to give him his ear, directed him in a whisper not to halt any of Hood's men, as they had liberty to retire.[28] The regiment was on this duty the greater part of the day.

So soon as notified that Starke was killed, Grigsby, who succeeded to the command of Jackson's Division, endeavored to re-form the commands and restore order in the border of the woods near the Alfred Poffenberger buildings, and while so engaged Early came up. At the time that Hays's Brigade was ordered by Lawton to move to the assistance of the line east of the Hagerstown Road, Early was ordered by Jackson in person to march his brigade to the left and support Stuart's artillery, then engaged with Hooker's batteries on a hill at the Joseph Poffenberger farm. Early moved through a piece of woods northwest of the Alfred Poffenberger farm, a little back from the left of the line, then through some fields. As he was passing through these fields, he discovered Union skirmishers moving around the left, upon which he sent some from his own brigade to hold them in check until he had passed. He found Stuart nearly three-fourths of a mile to the left with several guns in position on Nicodemus Hill (supported by a squadron of the 5th Virginia Cavalry) and engaged with Hooker's guns. At Stuart's suggestion he formed his brigade in line in rear of the crest of the hill and remained there about an hour under artillery fire, by which some of his men were killed and wounded, when Stuart—his batteries suffering severely—having discovered that Patrick and Gibbon were gradually making their way between him and the left of the main line, determined to shift his position to an eminence nearer Jackson's line and a little to the rear, on Hauser's Ridge.

Under Stuart's instructions, Early moved back, taking a route in rear of the one by which he had moved out, and then into the skirt of woods through which he had passed an hour or more before, the woods about 425 yards northwest of the Alfred Poffenberger farm. Just as he was getting into line, Stuart informed him that Lawton had been wounded and that Jackson had sent for him to carry his brigade back and take command of the division. Leaving the 13th Virginia (numbering less than one hundred men) with Stuart at his request, to skirmish with the 10th Pennsylvania Reserves (which had

28 G. W. B. [George Washington Beale], "Maryland Campaign," *Southern Historical Society Papers* 25 (1897): 280.

relieved the 23d New York) and to support one of his batteries, Early moved to the rear of the woods and passed the south edge of a cornfield lying east of them. As he came near where he had bivouacked the night before, he found Grigsby and Stafford rallying some two or three hundred men of Jackson's Division where Starke's Brigade had lain the night before. As he came up, Grigsby advanced, and Early, forming his brigade in line, followed him, Patrick falling back from the ledge parallel to the road to one beyond the Miller barn and perpendicular to the road. Early halted at a ridge or rock ledge, remaining east and west in the woods that protected the right of his brigade, and Grigsby, who had advanced on open ground, was now moved to Early's left, forming a diagonal line, the left occupying a hollow in the south edge of the northern body of the West Woods. The 31st Virginia of Early's Brigade was put on Grigsby's right.

Early's line when thus formed was 130 yards from the north edge of the central body of the West Woods and perpendicular to the Hagerstown Road, his right resting near the open plateau between the woods and the road, concealed and protected by the rise of ground. The 49th Virginia, on the right, faced the Hagerstown Road, being formed at right angles to the main brigade line. Patrick's brigade was seen in the field in his north front threatening his flank and rear, and skirmishers were sent to the edge of the woods in which he lay and to the left.

These precautions taken, and as Patrick showed no disposition to advance (in fact he was making coffee), Early directed Colonel William Smith of the 49th Virginia to take command of the brigade and resist Patrick should he advance, and then he rode across the Hagerstown Road to take command of the rest of Ewell's Division and ascertain its condition. Early's Brigade was composed of seven Virginia regiments—the 13th, 25th, 31st, 44th, 49th, 52d, and 58th—and numbered 1,225 officers and men. As the approximately one hundred men of the 13th had been detached earlier, the rest of the brigade was now in line from right to left in this order: 49th, 44th, 58th, 25th, and 31st, the last named being on the right of Jackson's Division. In his report of the Maryland campaign, Early says, "I hope I may be excused for referring to the record shown by my own brigade, which has never been broken or compelled to fall back or left one of its dead to be buried by the enemy, but has invariably driven the enemy when opposed to him, and slept upon the ground on which it has fought, in every action, with the solitary exception of the affair at Bristoe Station, when it retired under orders, covering the withdrawal of the other troops."[29]

When Early rode in search of his division, he found that it had fallen back some distance to the rear to reorganize and heard that it was greatly shattered and would not probably be in condition to be engaged again, but he nonetheless sent a staff officer to find the brigades and order them up. While looking for Trimble's, Lawton's, and Hays's brigades, Early saw that Ripley and Colquitt were giving way. He rode to Jackson and informed him of the condition of his division and that the enemy was advancing on the west side of the Hagerstown Road—on the flank on which he had formed his brigade. Jackson assured him that he would send reinforcements and directed him to keep the enemy in check until they arrived, upon which Early returned to his brigade and resumed command. Soon after this, Goodrich's brigade of the Twelfth Corps, supported by Patrick, advanced. There was a short contest, and Early sent his chief of staff to inform Jackson that danger was imminent. The staff officer returned with Jackson's assurance that reinforcements should be given immediately, and just as he returned, Monroe's battery (Battery D, 1st Rhode Island Light Artillery) opened fire from a position on his right and rear. He took it for granted that it was a Confederate battery, but was soon undeceived when he saw that it was on the plateau opposite the church firing in the direction of Sharpsburg and supported by infantry. This convinced him that the Confederates had been driven back on the right and that the Union forces were in entire possession of the field east of the Hagerstown Road.

About this time the 124th Pennsylvania, which had advanced from the North Woods, followed Gordon's men and entered the Miller cornfield on their right, one company in and on the right of the Hagerstown Road, the entire regiment being under the fire of a Confederate battery beyond the West Woods. After going about twenty yards into the corn, it was halted and ordered to lie down. Here Colonel Hawley was wounded by a fire from beyond the road, and the regiment fell back to the north fence of the cornfield. In a few minutes, it again advanced, supported by the Purnell Legion. Three companies of the 124th under Major Isaac L. Haldeman, obliquing to the right, advanced to the right of the road, while seven companies continued the march through the corn. The left of the three companies moved close to the road, and when about 230 yards beyond the straw stacks the line was fired upon by Grigsby's men in the woods and by artillery beyond them, causing the right to swing back, thus forming an oblique line to the road. Lying down in this position, they returned Early's fire for a few minutes, then fell back into the road and then down it back to the straw stacks. (While lying in the road, sheltered by its bank, Sedgwick's division of the Second Corps crossed and went into the West Woods.) The seven companies went through the corn to the grass field beyond, were met by a shower of bullets from the west of the road, and lay down under cover of the ridge nearly parallel with the road. The Purnell Legion came up and formed on the right and rear of the seven companies.

---

[29] Early to Pendleton, 973.

When Patrick, after the repulse of Jackson's and Hood's Divisions, fell back to the ledge near the Miller barn to make coffee, replenish ammunition, and await reinforcements, he was soon thereafter fired upon by Pelham's Battery, and to shield his men as much as possible he was about to enter the woods some fifteen rods distant, when Goodrich's brigade of the Twelfth Corps came up. (It will be remembered that this brigade was detached from the rear of Greene's division as it approached the East Woods.) It moved quickly across the field in rear of Gordon's brigade, crossed the Hagerstown Road north of the Miller house (where the Purnell Legion was detached to support the 124th Pennsylvania), passed the Miller barn, and approached the West Woods. The brigade numbered 777 officers and men; by the detachment of the Purnell Legion, it was reduced to three regiments, aggregating 572 officers and men.

Goodrich had been detached in response to Gibbon's earnest request to save his battery and had been ordered to report to Gibbon or any other general officer on that part of the field. The battery had gone and so had Gibbon, and as soon as Goodrich was approaching the woods, Patrick and his officers cautioned him, advised him of the nature of the ground and the position of the enemy, and gave him some advice how to enfilade and drive Early from his strong position among the rocks in the woods. Patrick says, "Knowing the Ground well, I directed Col. Goodrich to advance cautiously, following his skirmishers, until I could get re-inforcements to go in on his left & front in sufficient force to drive through the Corner where the enemy appeared to hold in masses—Riding up the hill, to find Gen. Doubleday, & through the cornfield to the ploughed ground beyond, I found that the enemy had been driven down the road, but not by that point of wood [the corner of the middle wood, held by Early—*EAC*]."[30]

Goodrich did not wait for Patrick's return. He sent the 3d Delaware to the front and left as skirmishers and advanced, bearing more to the right than was proper, and entered the woods with the 60th and 78th New York, followed by the 21st, 23d, and 35th New York of Patrick's brigade as a support. In the advance Goodrich was killed; his regiments suffered severely from the fire of Early and Grigsby and were checked. When Patrick returned without reinforcements to find his fellow brigadier dead and the brigade, with difficulty, holding position, he ordered Goodrich's men and his own to hold on until further orders, confronting Early and Grigsby, who showed no disposition to advance. Concealed from view, the Confederates held their ground and kept up a desultory fire upon Goodrich's skirmishers and the few men of the 124th Pennsylvania in the Hagerstown Road.

Just before the Confederates were driven from the fields east of the Hagerstown Road, Lieutenant Colonel John W. Hofmann, whose brigade had been kept in support of the artillery on the hill at the Joseph Poffenberger farm, was ordered to send two rifled guns across the Hagerstown Road. He sent two guns of Cooper's battery under Lieutenant James S. Fullerton, supported by the 95th New York (Major Edward Pye). The guns and infantry support took position in a cornfield about two hundred yards west of the road and in front of the right of Hofmann's brigade. As soon as these guns were in position, they opened fire upon the enemy (who had withdrawn beyond the range of the howitzers) and soon drew the Confederate fire (which was partially the object in putting the guns in that position). During this time Hofmann's brigade remained in the position taken the night before, lying close to the fence and well sheltered.

When Colquitt and Ripley were repulsed, the Union batteries that had been engaged on the line were in no condition to follow and were ordered to the rear to refit. Monroe's Rhode Island battery and Edgell's New Hampshire battery were ordered to advance from Poffenberger Hill. They came down through the North Woods, and Hooker instructed Monroe to go beyond the cornfield and as near the woods at the Dunkard church as possible, saying that he would find Greene's infantry there to support him. Monroe, closely followed by Edgell, went down a path through the East Woods and into battery on open ground about 160 yards from the East Woods—his right near the corn, his left extending toward the Mumma gate on the Smoketown Road, the guns facing the Dunkard church and the plateau opposite. When taking position a regiment was seen on the right with its left refused (the 124th Pennsylvania), and still farther to the right in the corn was seen Gordon's brigade. This seemed to the officers a poor position for the battery, and it had scarcely taken position when the 125th Pennsylvania came out of the East Woods on its left and rear, and an officer of Hooker's staff rode up and ordered Monroe to go forward on the plateau opposite the church. The caissons were left and the guns went to the Smoketown Road and halted until the 125th Pennsylvania removed the fences, then went forward. As Monroe ascended the north slope of the plateau, he saw, a little to the left and front, Greene's infantry lying on the ground as though expecting an attack.

From their position Monroe judged that there must be a strong force of the enemy in the immediate front, and he was much in doubt whether it was judicious to put his battery in so advanced a position. He rode to the men and asked who they were. Greene now rode up and when asked to support the battery (which had now crossed the road) replied in a low tone that he had no ammunition but that most of his men had bayonets. Monroe thought it a strange place for men without ammunition, and that if they could hold on with empty cartridge boxes, he ought to be able to do it with well-packed limber

[30] A notation by Carman states that his source was Patrick's own journal, which has been published subsequently. David S. Sparks, ed. *Inside Lincoln's Army: The Diary of Marsena Rudolph Patrick, Provost Marshal General, Army of the Potomac* (New York: Thomas Yoseloff, 1964), 149.

chests. He gave the order "In battery!" which was instantly done, the right section being on the ground sloping toward the church and about seventy yards from the Hagerstown Road, the left being upon higher ground.[31] The line was perpendicular to the road, the guns pointing south toward Sharpsburg. Greene's men lay from three to five hundred yards behind the battery, and Edgell's battery came up on the left and about one hundred yards in rear. As the battery went into position, a Confederate battery was dropping its guns into battery not over 250 yards distant.

When Greene's division charged through the East Woods and then across the Smoketown Road in pursuit of Colquitt's men, the 125th Pennsylvania was lying in the open ground east of the East Woods. While here, Colonel Higgins says, "General Mansfield fell, some of my men carrying him off the field on their muskets until a blanket was procured." Some time after Greene's charge, the regiment was ordered forward, went through the East Woods (its right going through the southeast corner of the cornfield), and came into the open ground, where it halted for alignment, its left on and beyond the Smoketown Road. Higgins reports, "Here I took some prisoners, whom I sent to the rear. Again I was ordered to advance and halt in line with a battery. Before reaching the battery, though, I took a number of prisoners, some of whom came running back with white handkerchiefs tied on their guns and gave themselves up. At the battery I gave the command for my men to lie down whilst awaiting further orders. About this time the fire of the enemy slackened somewhat, only some shots from their sharpshooters being fired, and these at mounted officers and the artillery horses." It was while at this halt that the men removed the fences for the passage of Monroe's battery across the Smoketown Road, and it appears that they performed the same service for Edgell's battery. Hooker now rode up and asked Higgins if any troops were in the West Woods in front, to which Higgins replied, "None but rebels," and that the 125th Pennsylvania was in front of the Union line. While talking to Higgins, Hooker's horse was shot, and Higgins called his attention to it; Hooker turned and rode away in the direction of the East Woods.[32] The 107th New York, which had been deployed along the border of the Samuel Poffenberger woods, followed soon after the 125th Pennsylvania, charging in line of battle through the East Woods. It halted with its right wing in the Smoketown Road, west of the woods, and its left wing in the East Woods. The regiment faced southeast.

It was about this time that Hooker, riding back from the 125th Pennsylvania to get more artillery, was painfully wounded in the foot and obliged to give up his command. He says:

> At 9 o'clock that morning I had advanced steadily, but securely, to the point that I desired. I had at that time a battery of howitzers [Monroe's—EAC] on this high ground. I had sent for two additional batteries to double-quick up to that position. A number of my infantry regiments were well posted, to protect them on their arrival. While advancing, on the morning of the 17th, and about half-past 7 o'clock, Mansfield's corps, at my request, had been sent to my support, and as soon as all my reserves were engaged I ordered him forward, and about one-half of his command assisted in taking possession of this commanding position. [It was done by two brigades of Greene's division alone.—EAC] While looking for a point at which to post the batteries I had sent for, I was wounded. At that time my troops were in the finest spirits … Some of the commanding officers of the regiments were riding up and down in front of their men with the colors captured from the enemy in their hands; the troops almost rent the skies with their cheers; there was the greatest good feeling that I have ever witnessed on the field of battle.[33]

In his official report, Hooker says, "The whole morning had been one of unusual animation to me and fraught with the grandest events. The conduct of my troops was sublime, and the occasion almost lifted me to the skies, and its memories will ever remain near me. My command followed the fugitives closely until we had passed the corn-field a quarter of a mile or more, when I was removed from my saddle in the act of falling out of it from loss of blood, having previously been struck without my knowledge."[34]

Although Hooker had been open and unsparing—vehement even—in his criticism and denunciation of McClellan, that officer seems not to have stored it up against him. He had given Hooker charge of the attack upon Lee's left, and after the battle recommended his promotion to the rank of brigadier general in the regular Army and wrote him the following kindly and appreciative letter:

---

[31] John Albert Monroe, "Battery D, First Rhode Island Light Artillery, at the Battle of Antietam, September 17, 1862," *Personal Narratives of Events in the War of the Rebellion, Being Papers Read Before the Rhode Island Soldiers and Sailors Historical Society*, 3d ser., no. 16 (Providence: [Rhode Island Soldiers and Sailors Historical] Society, 1886), 21–22.

[32] Jacob Higgins to Joseph F. Knipe, September 22, 1862, reprinted in *OR*, vol. 19, pt. 1, 492. See [Appendix K].—EAC

[33] *Report of the Joint Committee on the Conduct of the War*, 37th Cong., 3d sess., 1863, S. Rep. 108, pt. 1, serial 1152, 581.

[34] Joseph Hooker to Seth Williams, November 8, 1862, reprinted in *OR*, vol. 19, pt. 1, 219.

Headquarters Army of the Potomac
Sharpsburg, September 20, 1862

Maj. Gen. Joseph Hooker,
  Commanding Corps:
    My Dear Hooker: I have been very sick the last few days, and just able to go where my presence was absolutely necessary, so I could not come to see you and thank you for what you did the other day, and express my intense regret and sympathy for your unfortunate wound. Had you not been wounded when you were, I believe the result of the battle would have been the entire destruction of the rebel army, for I know that, with you at its head, your corps would have kept on until it gained the main road. As a slight expression of what I think you merit, I have requested that the brigadier-general's commission rendered vacant by Mansfield's death may be given to you. I will this evening write a private note to the President on the subject, and I am glad to assure you that, so far as I can learn, it is the universal feeling of the army that you are the most deserving in it.
    With the sincere hope that your health may soon be restored, so that you may again be with us in the field, I am, my dear general, your sincere friend,

Geo. B. McClellan,
Major-General[35]

As Hooker was borne to the rear, Sumner's Second Corps was met. Sumner says that it was some distance to the rear where he passed Hooker, but that he saw nothing of the First Corps at all as he was advancing with his command; that it had been dispersed and routed, there was no question. He sent one of his staff officers to find where it was, and General Ricketts, the only officer he could find, said he could not raise three hundred men of the corps.[36] Had Ricketts confined the information given to his own division, he would have been nearer the truth. Hartsuff's brigade had been roughly handled by the enemy, but Duryee's and Christian's brigades had been feebly handled by their respective commanders and almost entirely neglected, when they were withdrawn from the front. The division commander seems to have lacked the disposition or the energy to gather his regiments, which were in the woods and fields in the rear. The division carried 3,158 officers and men into the action and lost 1,204 killed, wounded, and missing. Of the more than 1,900 remaining, less than 200 could be collected by noon; on the morning of the eighteenth, but 1,008 were reported, showing a loss by straggling of 946. Meade's division was in better shape. Out of the less than 3,000 carried into action, it had sustained a loss of 573 killed, wounded, and missing. It was not demoralized or routed. True it is that the brigades had been dislocated and the regiments withdrawn one after another, but these had preserved their organizations. Three of Seymour's were in the Samuel Poffenberger woods and had rallied and moved forward to the support of Crawford's men in the East Woods. Magilton's brigade had been badly punished, but had rallied in the North Woods, and there also was Anderson's brigade in good shape (upon which Sumner rallied a part of Sedgwick's division when driven from the West Woods an hour later). The reason that Sumner did not see these men was because they were to the right of his line of march. Of Doubleday's division, Gibbon's men lost heavily, but their staunch Iron Brigade was united in the North Woods, and Phelps's was near it. Hofmann's brigade was intact and had not been engaged. Patrick was still in the fight and, with Goodrich's small brigade of the Twelfth Corps, holding an advanced position in the West Woods and confronting Early. The greater part of two divisions was where it had started from in the morning, had suffered loss, but was not dispersed or routed. There was fight in the men yet, and they would have proven it had they been called upon.

Of the Twelfth Corps, Sumner says, "There were some troops lying down on the left which I took to belong to Mansfield's command. In the meantime General Mansfield had been killed, and a portion of his corps … had also been thrown into confusion."[37] Palfrey says, "At somewhere about nine o'clock, the Twelfth Corps seems to have about lost all aggressive force."[38] Neither of these gallant soldiers would willingly make a misstatement, and yet what they have to say is far from the truth. Of Williams's division, four regiments of Crawford's brigade had done some credible fighting and accomplished results. They had suffered loss, and were in and about the north part of the East Woods. Two regiments of this brigade, the 124th and 125th Pennsylvania, were in the open ground south of the corn and opposite the Dunkard church, and on their right were the Purnell Legion of Goodrich's brigade and the three old and tried regiments of Gordon's brigade, much

---

[35] George B. McClellan to Hooker, September 20, 1862, reprinted in *OR*, vol. 19, pt. 1, 219.

[36] *Report of the Joint Committee*, 368.

[37] Ibid.

[38] Francis Winthrop Palfrey, *The Antietam and Fredericksburg*, vol. 5 of *The Army in the Civil War* (New York: Charles Scribner's Sons, 1882), 81.

reduced in number but not a bit wanting in aggression. The 107th New York of Gordon's brigade was in second line in the East Woods, and the 13th New Jersey was approaching them. These two regiments, with the 125th Pennsylvania and seven companies of the 124th, had not been engaged, and their subsequent action showed that they had aggressive force. Greene's division on the left had done some brilliant work and was to do more of it. In fact the entire Twelfth Corps, then about six thousand strong, was preparing for an advance and soon would have advanced, had not Hooker been wounded and the approach of Sumner's corps been announced. It was high time. Had the Second Corps come two hours earlier and gone into action with the Twelfth Corps, Lee's left would have been crushed. Had it come an hour earlier and closely followed the advantage won by the splendid fighting of the Twelfth Corps, the West Woods would have been in its possession before McLaws reached them. Had it been on the field when the battle opened in the morning, the day would have been won before noon.

Williams's First Division became engaged at 7:30 a.m. and Greene's Second Division at about 8:15 a.m. Hood's Division fell back as the First Division was deploying, and by the united action of the two divisions, Ripley's, Colquitt's, and Garland's Brigades were driven from the field before 8:45 a.m.[39]

---

[39] In his original manuscript, Carman concludes this chapter with a lengthy note regarding Mansfield's wounding. It is reprinted herein in its entirety as Appendix K.

16
The West Woods and the Dunkard Church

Antietam, September 17, 1862
9:00 a.m. to 11:00 a.m.

The battle begun at daybreak had been waged with great determination and monstrous losses. It was nearing nine o'clock, and with the advance and success of the Twelfth Corps and the retreat of the Confederates into the West Woods and in the direction of Sharpsburg there was a grateful lull in the sanguinary contest, broken only by an occasional musket shot and then by the guns of Monroe's battery, which opened fire from the plateau opposite the Dunkard church. This fire was replied to by a battery of S. D. Lee's Battalion, in open ground south of the woods and west of the Hagerstown road.

The struggle that followed around the Dunkard church and in the West Woods was participated in by Greene's division (Twelfth Corps), three regiments (the 125th Pennsylvania, 2d Massachusetts, and 13th New Jersey) of Williams's division (Twelfth Corps), and Sedgwick's division (Second Corps) on one side and, on the other side, by Early's Brigade, the remnant of Jackson's Division, G. T. Anderson's Brigade of Jones's Division, three brigades (Kershaw's, Semmes's, and Barksdale's) of McLaws's Division, and Walker's Division of two brigades. The Union force numbered about 7,500 men, the Confederate force about 8,200. (This does not include the artillery on either side.)

The Second Corps was a veteran organization and had seen much hard service. Palfrey says it "contained some poor but many very excellent soldiers. The hard fate which its Second Division met in this battle may be an excuse for stating that up to May 10, 1864, the Second Corps never lost a gun nor a color, and that it was then and had long been the only corps in the army which could make that proud claim."[1] Francis A. Walker says the corps represented in an unparalleled degree the history of the war in the East:

That corps which, in fair fight with Lee's great army, had captured forty-four Confederate flags ere first it lost a color of its own; that corps which, under the command of Sumner, Couch, Warren, Hancock, and Humphreys—illustrious roll!—left nearly forty thousand men killed and wounded upon the battle-fields of Virginia, Maryland, and Pennsylvania; that corps among whose Generals of Division were numbered Sedgwick, Richardson, Howard, French, [Francis C.] Barlow, [David B.] Birney, [Nelson A.] Miles, [Gershom] Mott, Gibbon, [Alexander S.] Webb and Alexander Hays; the corps which crossed the Chickahominy to the rescue of the beaten left at Fair Oaks; which made the great assault at Marye's Heights; on which fell the fury of Longstreet's charge at Gettysburg; which was the rearguard, October 14th, at Auburn and at Bristoe; which stormed the Salient at Spottsylvania, and at Farmville fought the last infantry battle of the war against the Army of Northern Virginia.[2]

On the evening of September 16, when McClellan directed Sumner to send the Twelfth Corps across the Antietam that night, Sumner earnestly requested that the Second Corps should go also, but McClellan would not consent. He gave orders to hold the corps in readiness to march an hour before daybreak to support Hooker, but not to move until further orders. In anticipation of going that night Sumner had already sent some of his batteries across the Antietam. Sumner's men had all breakfasted before daybreak, filled their canteens, and rolled their blankets. They were ready to march, but no orders came, and after six o'clock Sumner, with his son Captain Samuel S. Sumner, of his staff, went to headquarters, but a few yards distant, for orders and personal instruction. McClellan had not yet awakened from sleep and none of his staff seemed disposed to disturb him, though the roar of battle was sounding in their ears. Sumner waited, walking to and fro on the veranda of the Pry house or sitting on the steps, the roar of battle increasing and the detonation of the heavy guns shaking the pane and shivering the sash of the windows, which let into McClellan's room the full sunlight, but McClellan did not make his appearance. Members of the staff were watching Hooker's struggle, which was in full view, yet McClellan could not be seen, and one of his staff remarked that Hooker's fight was only a rear-guard affair, as "Uncle Bobby Lee" was too

---

[1] Francis Winthrop Palfrey, *The Antietam and Fredericksburg*, vol. 5 of *The Army in the Civil War* (New York: Charles Scribner's Sons, 1882), 81–82.

[2] Francis A. Walker, *History of the Second Army Corps in the Army of the Potomac* (New York: Charles Scribner's Sons, 1887), 1–2.

much of a soldier to fight in that position with a river at his back. This opinion was expressed to McClellan also that morning; whether he shared it or not we do not know.

Finally, at 7:20 a.m., after waiting more than an hour, Sumner received his orders to cross the Antietam with two divisions, with Richardson to follow when relieved by Morell's division of the Fifth Corps.[3] He put Sedgwick in motion immediately, with French following, went down the hill in rear of McClellan's headquarters, and crossed the Antietam at Pry's Ford (where Doubleday had crossed the evening before). When across he ascended a gentle slope for about a quarter of a mile, halted, and formed his lines. He then moved in three parallel lines (brigade front) nearly due west, came to the field south of the East Woods, flanked to the right and, entering the woods, marched northward, then faced to the left, thus forming a column of three deployed brigades: Brigadier General Willis A. Gorman's in front, next, Brigadier General Napoleon J. T. Dana's, then Brigadier General Oliver O. Howard's. The column was now facing west, parallel to the Hagerstown Road 550 yards distant, and separated from it by the Bloody Cornfield, over which the tide of battle had ebbed and flowed since daybreak and in which, notwithstanding the struggle in it, Palfrey said "the corn was very high and very strong."[4] There was but a short halt while the east fence of the cornfield was being thrown down, and the men had time to see that "the ground beneath those great, fair Maryland oaks was strewn with the killed and wounded of the earlier battle."[5] It was nine o'clock when Sumner formed Sedgwick's division for the attack in the East Woods; it was at the same time that the 125th Pennsylvania, of the Twelfth Corps, crossed the Hagerstown Road and entered the West Woods at the Dunkard church.

Upon hearing of Sumner's approach, Alpheus Williams (once again commanding the Twelfth Corps) had sent a staff officer to apprise him of his position and the situation of affairs, and when Sumner came into the woods Williams rode up from the left, from near the Mumma farm, gave him the position and condition of his men, and made some precautionary suggestions as to the line of advance and care of his flanks, which were not well received. Sumner had already been informed by Ricketts that Hooker's corps had been dispersed and could not rally three hundred men, and he seems to have come to the conclusion that the Twelfth Corps was in not much better condition. Nor did he stop to satisfy himself on that point, or to make a reconnaissance,

or for anything more than a quick study of the field over which the 12th Corps had attacked. The enemy had been pushed back and a counter attack might be expected at any moment. As the only success which had attended the Union arms on that part of the field had been that just gained by the 12th Corps, it was obvious that that success should be followed up before the enemy could recover from its effects and resume the offensive. His resolution had to be taken, and was taken, on the instant … The emergency of the occasion would not permit him to await the arrival of French's division, which he expected to appear at any moment, for he had given the most positive orders to that officer to put and keep the head of his column abreast the division of Sedgwick, more than this he had sent several officers to reiterate the order, and had reasonable grounds for the belief that they had been obeyed.[6]

On the contrary, Walker intimates that Sumner neglected to give such orders to French: "So proud was he of his gallant troops, so full of fight, so occupied with the thought of engaging the enemy, that he did not even see to it that French was brought up within supporting distance—but allowed him, for want of proper direction, to diverge widely to the left. Be it as it may, Sumner did not wait. He felt so strong in these three brigades of Sedgwick's division that he could not imagine anything stopping them, and determined to crush the Confederate left with one terrific blow, then swung his column around with a grand, bold half-wheel to the left, and sweep down the Confederate line, driving it before him through Sharpsburg, and heaping it up in disorder before Burnside, who, crossing the lower bridge, will complete the victory."[7]

While Sumner is forming his column of attack and removing the fences, we note the condition of affairs around the church, where first the contest is to be waged, and the preparations being made by the Confederates to regain the ground lost by them, or at least to hold the Dunkard church and the West Woods.

[3] See Edwin V. Sumner to Seth Williams, October 1, 1862, reprinted in *OR*, vol. 19, pt. 1, 275.

[4] Palfrey, 82.

[5] Francis A. Walker, 101.

[6] George B. Davis, "The Antietam Campaign," in *Campaigns in Virginia, Maryland, and Pennsylvania, 1862–1863*, vol. 3 of *Papers of the Military Historical Society of Massachusetts* (Boston: Griffith-Stillings Press, 1903), 61–62.

[7] Francis A. Walker, 102–4. See also *Report of the Joint Committee on the Conduct of the War*, 37th Cong., 3d sess., 1863, S. Rep. 108, pt. 1, serial 1152, 368.—*EAC*

    The passage quoted here is perhaps Carman's most egregious lapse in transcription in the entire manuscript. The sentiments above are all contained in Walker, but an exact quotation from his original text (Carman's placement of the quotation marks notwithstanding) does not begin until the phrase "crush the Confederate left"—and even then Carman modifies the remaining passage slightly.

We left Monroe's Rhode Island battery in position on the plateau opposite the Dunkard church. Monroe says:

A battery of the enemy here opened upon me, but no attention was paid to it, and its fire was perfectly ineffective; but the battery with one section opened upon a body of the enemy [Colquitt's men—EAC], who was seen retreating at the left of their front, and about 125 yards distant, throwing them into great confusion. The other four guns opened with canister and case upon a large force advancing through the woods in front, which were very open, and, with the assistance of the other section, which had accomplished its object by a few shots, and the First New Hampshire Battery, checked the enemy, and he retired out of sight.

While engaged forcing back the enemy in the wood, a body of sharpshooters had, unobserved, crept along under a little ridge that ran diagonally to the front of the Rhode Island battery, and opened a most unerring fire upon it, killing and disabling many horses and men. As quick as possible, a section was directed to open upon them with canister, which, though it caused them no injury, they lying down under the ridge, kept them almost silent, they firing but an occasional shot, but without effect.

While this section was keeping the sharpshooters silent, the other four guns, with the guns of Lieutenant Edgell, opened upon the battery that was still firing, and soon silenced it. I then ordered my battery to limber to the rear. The sharpshooters took advantage of the opportunity thus afforded, and opened most briskly, severely wounding a number of men and killing and disabling a large number of horses.[8]

Perceiving the dangerous situation he was in and the great difficulty he would have in withdrawing his guns under this fire, Monroe sent a request to Greene to keep the sharpshooters down so that he could get the guns away, but the answer came that he could not for want of ammunition. The cannoneers were rapidly leaving their posts on account of wounds and the drivers were constantly employed in relieving disabled horses. When the order "Limber to the rear!" was given, it was executed almost in the twinkling of an eye, but the enemy behind the ridge, in the road south of the church, protected by fence rails thrown up and depressions in the ground, had them at their mercy, and right well did they improve the opportunity in showing the temper of it. They rose up in an unbroken line and poured a storm of lead into them. Five guns were gotten off with few losses, but the one remaining was less fortunate. As the horses made the turn to bring the limber to the trail of the gun, they were quickly shot down. Before a disabled horse could be disengaged from the team another would fall. Monroe was now short-handed for men and Lieutenant Ephraim Fiske rode off for some, soon returning with fifteen or twenty infantrymen, who ran the piece to the rear amid the cheers of friend and foe.[9] Four guns went back to near the corner of the East Woods. The right section went north to the cornfield and took position near the Hagerstown road and nearly opposite the Miller straw stacks, where it remained until its ammunition was exhausted and then retired to the position from which it had advanced earlier in the day.

Meanwhile, Battery A, First Rhode Island Light Artillery (Captain John A. Tompkins), had come up. This excellent battery was attached to Sedgwick's division and had crossed the Antietam by the Upper Bridge on the evening of the sixteenth and parked on the Hoffman farm. At 8:00 a.m. of the seventeenth, Tompkins was ordered to go to the front and report to Hooker. He passed the Michael Miller house, followed the road to and through the East Woods, and was ordered by Hooker to go into position on the plateau opposite the church. He made a circuit of the burning buildings at the Mumma farm (passing to their left), went at a gallop down the lane beyond, and came up as Monroe was retiring. He went into battery a little farther south from Monroe's position (and more under cover from the fire of the sharpshooters who had so annoyed Monroe), his right guns near where Monroe's left had been and the others on the ground descending to the left, all pointing south or nearly so. As soon as the six guns came into position, Tompkins opened fire upon a battery directly in his front across the Hagerstown Road and south of the West Woods and upon D. H. Hill's infantry in the sunken road (at the same time that the 125th Pennsylvania and the 34th New York were being driven out of the woods at the Dunkard church).

Very soon after the 125th Pennsylvania had assisted Monroe's battery to cross the Smoketown Road, and while lying down in the field about 350 yards from the Hagerstown Road awaiting orders, Lieutenant Edward L. Witman[10] of Crawford's staff rode up with Crawford's order to advance into the West Woods and hold them at all hazards. (Why such an order was given to this one regiment alone when the entire line was awaiting Sumner's preparations is not known; it was

---

8 John Albert Monroe to "Sir," September 26, 1862, reprinted in *OR*, vol. 19, pt. 1, 228.

9 Monroe, "Battery D, First Rhode Island Light Artillery, at the Battle of Antietam, September 17, 1862," *Personal Narratives of Events in the War of the Rebellion, Being Papers Read Before the Rhode Island Soldiers and Sailors Historical Society*, 3d ser., no. 16 (Providence: [Rhode Island Soldiers and Sailors Historical] Society, 1886), 24–25.

10 In his original manuscript, Carman gives Witman's rank incorrectly as "Captain." Crawford's own report of the battle praises "Lieutenant Witman, aide-de-camp, who conveyed my orders most intelligently, and often under circumstances of great personal exposure, from first to last." Samuel W. Crawford to Alpheus S. Williams, October 21, 1862, reprinted in *OR*, vol. 19, pt. 1, 486.

directed by neither Sumner nor Williams, but it was instantly obeyed.) The men sprang to their feet and went forward double-quick, driving before them a few Texans and Georgians, crossed the Hagerstown Road at nine o'clock, and halted on the edge of the woods just north of the Dunkard church. There was very little opposition to this advance. The Confederates, who were on the road in the immediate front, disappeared in the woods beyond the church, some of them to the south below the church (where, as we have seen, they remained, to the great annoyance of Monroe's battery).

When Hood fell back to the Dunkard church it was with the intention of collecting and re-forming everything that had gone back and contest further Union advance, and to that end Jackson, Hood, and others made great efforts. With the exception of Hood's men, but a few could be held. Wofford says, "After some time the enemy commenced advancing in full force. Seeing the hopelessness and folly of making a stand with our shattered brigade and a remnant from other commands, the men being greatly exhausted and many of them out of ammunition, I determined to fall back to a fence in our rear, where we met the long looked for re-enforcements, and at the same time received an order from General Hood to fall back farther to the rear to rest and collect our men."[11] Hood's men were retreating from the woods as the 125th Pennsylvania entered them at the church.

When the 125th Pennsylvania had crossed the Hagerstown Road, Captain John McKeage was ordered to deploy his company (Company G) as skirmishers and advance cautiously to a ridge in front, and Company B was formed (facing south) about twenty yards north of the church, its left opposite the northwest corner of it. The regiment then advanced about twenty yards and halted. As soon as Colonel Higgins entered the woods he saw that he was without support in rear and on his right. He was aware that an enemy was on his right front, and gave his horse to one of his officers with instructions to ride back to Crawford, inform him of the situation, and ask for support, as without it he would be unable to hold his position; the enemy would certainly flank him and cut him off, as he was far in advance of the corps.[12] The regiment then advanced and halted on the crest of a ridge about 120 yards from the road, its left west of and about twenty yards to the right of the church, its right beyond a ravine which, about two hundred yards north of the church, crosses the Hagerstown Road and runs west through the woods. The line was nearly parallel to the Hagerstown Road. Captain McKeage, who had halted his skirmishers on the ridge, was now ordered to advance and see what was in front. With little or no opposition, the skirmishers went to within twenty yards of the west edge of the woods, where fire was opened upon them from a ravine on the right by the 49th Virginia of Early's Brigade. Early's men gained the open ground in their front and advanced firing; the Pennsylvanians fell back in like manner. While at the front they saw not only Early's men but some troops (G. T. Anderson's) advancing on their left from the direction of Sharpsburg, and from these also they received fire, which was returned.

Leaving the 125th Pennsylvania for a moment, we return to Early, whom we left in the north part of the middle body of the West Woods confronting Patrick and Goodrich, keeping his eye on the three companies of the 124th Pennsylvania on the Hagerstown Road and anxious about the presence of Monroe's battery, Greene's division, and the 125th Pennsylvania on his right rear. He considered his condition as extremely critical, but recognized the great importance of holding his ground, "for, had the enemy gotten possession of this woods, the heights immediately in rear, which commanded the rear of our whole line, would have fallen into his hands."[13] He determined to wait for the reinforcements promised by Jackson, hoping that they would arrive in time to meet the 125th Pennsylvania before it entered the woods, and threw his right flank back quietly under cover of the woods and parallel to the Hagerstown Road (so as not to have his rear exposed in the event of being discovered), while still keeping an anxious eye on Greene's division, which he had seen disappear on the plateau opposite the church. Very soon he saw the 125th Pennsylvania enter the woods at the church. He looked to the rear for reinforcements but could not see them coming. He saw himself cut off from the main body of the army on the right and a force threatening his left. There was no time to be lost. He immediately ordered his brigade to move by the right flank, parallel to the Hagerstown Road, and directed Colonel Grigsby, who commanded what was left of Jackson's Division (about two hundred men) to move back in line so as to present front to Patrick and Goodrich. Early moved back along the rear of the ridge, concealed from view and in the belief that his presence was not suspected. Passing from behind the ridge, he came in full view of the skirmishers of the 125th Pennsylvania and made his presence known by directing the 49th Virginia (his leading regiment) to open fire upon them. They fell back, and Early continued to move by the flank until his entire line was exposed. Just at this time, he observed the promised reinforcements coming up at the southern corner of the woods and ordered his brigade to face to the front and open fire.

The reinforcement that Early saw was G. T. Anderson's Brigade of Jones's Division, closely followed by three brigades of McLaws's Division. Early in the morning, Anderson was lying on Cemetery Hill in support of the Washington Artillery.

[11] William T. Wofford to William H. Sellers, September 29, 1862, reprinted in OR, vol. 19 pt. 1, 928.

[12] See Jacob Higgins to Joseph F. Knipe, September 22, 1862, reprinted in OR, vol. 19, pt. 1, 492.

[13] Jubal A. Early to Alexander S. Pendleton, January 12, 1863, reprinted in OR, vol. 19 pt. 1, 970.

He was ordered by Lee to the left to support Hood, and without a guide or direction to find him moved off, directing his course by the sound of the musketry. By this means he succeeded in finding Hood, who pointed out the position he wished him to occupy. (Hood's men were retreating from the West Woods, and the position he ordered Anderson to take was the southwest face of the woods.) When within two hundred yards of the woods, Anderson was fired upon by the skirmishers of the 125th Pennsylvania, upon which he ordered his brigade sharpshooters forward. The Pennsylvanians, struck at the same time by Early, fell back, and Anderson advanced to the fence bounding the southwest face of the woods, which was torn down and piled for breastworks, behind which the men lay down. Just after Anderson reached the fence, Kershaw's Brigade marched up in his rear.

So far we have brought Early and Anderson to this part of the field, and while they are driving in the skirmishers of the 125th Pennsylvania, we accompany McLaws and Walker.

From his position on Cemetery Hill, Lee had watched the severe struggle on his left and observed Burnside on his right. Early in the morning, he had sent Walker's Division to guard the Antietam at Snavely's Ford, but perceiving that the weight of McClellan's attack was on the left, knowing that Sumner was in motion to augment it, and fully convinced that he had nothing to fear from Burnside, he concluded to throw Walker's and McLaws's Divisions to meet it. Yet, not sure of holding the ground around the Dunkard church, fearing in fact that he would lose it before they could reach it, Lee determined to take up a second line on the ridge nearer Sharpsburg, and walked from Cemetery Hill in that direction, at the same time ordering some batteries to the indicated position, behind which he proposed collecting his still-rallying infantry. In a field on the outskirts of town, Lee met Captain Thomas H. Carter, who was retiring his battery from Rodes's position in the sunken road. Carter says, "He seemed to fear that the whole left wing, then hard pressed and losing ground, would be turned, and that the enemy would gain possession of the range of hills some three-quarters of a mile to the left of Sharpsburg. He ordered me to this ground, with all the artillery that could be collected, to prevent this movement. Having communicated with Major [Scipio F.] Pierson, several batteries were gathered together on this part of the field. General Lee soon arrived there, in person."[14]

After giving some directions, General Lee was put on his horse and an orderly led it up the road toward the Dunkard church, soon meeting Colonel S. D. Lee, who, at the earnest solicitation of Hood, was on his way to Cemetery Hill to inform the commanding general of the critical state of affairs. Colonel Lee says:

> At the time Jackson and Hood were driven back and were with difficulty holding the ground near the Dunker Church, Hood came up to my … battalion of artillery …, which had been engaged during the entire morning and was pretty well wrecked, having lost thirty-five [over sixty-five—EAC] men and sixty horses, and ordered [m]e to turn over my artillery to the next officer in command and to go personally to find General R. E. Lee, and tell him the condition of affairs, and to say to him that unless reinforcements were sent at once the day was lost. I protested against leaving my artillery in its wrecked condition. He insisted, however, and I went. I soon met General Lee on horseback with one orderly, moving at a walk towards that part of the field and about half way between Sharpsburg and the Dunker church. I reported the condition of affairs on the left and reported General Hood's message. He quietly said, "Don't be excited about it, Colonel, go tell General Hood to hold his ground, reinforcements are now rapidly approaching between Sharpsburg and the ford; tell him that I am now coming to his support."
>
> I said, "General, your presence will do good, but nothing but infantry can save the day on the left." I started to return and had not gone over 100 yards when Lee called me and pointed to McLaws's division, then in sight and approaching at a double quick.[15]

Some Confederate writers have criticized McLaws for not arriving on the field on the sixteenth immediately following Jackson and for not reinforcing Jackson on the left earlier on the morning of the seventeenth—which if done, they contend, would have defeated McClellan's army. The criticism is an unjust one. It must be remembered that, though not marching as many miles as Jackson since the morning of the tenth, McLaws had been engaged in more arduous service and had done more fighting. He had been detained in Pleasant Valley until the morning of the sixteenth, and when he crossed the Potomac that morning and marched to Halltown he was without provisions. (As Jackson's men had already appropriated the stores captured at Harper's Ferry, he was obliged to hunt up provisions.) His command was very much fatigued. A large number of his men had no rations, and those who did had no time or opportunity to cook them. All had been without sleep during the night previous, except while waiting for the wagon trains to pass over the pontoon bridge at Harper's Ferry. His

---

[14] Thomas H. Carter to Henry A. Whiting, October 14, 1862, reprinted in *OR*, vol. 19 pt. 1, 1030.

[15] Dabney H. Maury, "Our Confederate Column," *Richmond Dispatch*, December 20, 1896. This source, from which Carman draws heavily at a number of points in the text, is not without its problems. For a full discussion, see p. 367 n. 7.

success in procuring provisions was very meager; he got one issue only. After vain effort to get supplies at Charlestown, some three miles distant, he returned to his command and, at 3:00 p.m. on the sixteenth, marched from Halltown, followed the route taken by Jackson and Walker, and halted only when it was too dark to see the road. He was within two miles of Shepherdstown Ford when, receiving urgent orders from Lee to hasten forward, he again took up the march at midnight, many of his regiments still without provisions. He crossed the Potomac before daylight; it was so dark that he used torches. Before sunrise on the seventeenth, the head of his column reached the vicinity of Lee's headquarters near Sharpsburg.

At this early hour he did not hear the sound of a gun, nor were there any noticeable indications that a battle had been fought, nor that one was imminent. He rode into town looking for Lee, but no one could give him any information. He rode back to halt his command and "look around" to find someone who could tell him where to go and met Longstreet and staff coming from the rear. Longstreet directed him to send Anderson's Division down the road to the hill beyond the town, where it would receive orders. Longstreet having informed him that he could find Lee in a small grove, he reported there for orders. Lee was dressing for the day, and said, as McLaws dismounted from his horse at the front of his tent, "Well general I am glad to see you, and have to thank you for what you have done, but we have I believe a hard days [sic] work before us, and you must rest your men. Do not let them come quite this far as the shells of the enemy fall about here, and halt them about ¼ of a mile back on the road and I will send for you when I want you." When told that but a few minutes before he had received an order from Jackson to go to the right, Lee replied, "Never mind that order but do as I told you and consider yourself as specially under my orders."[16] McLaws rode back and halted his division, hastened R. H. Anderson (who was in his rear), sent word along the lines for the men to rest and not to stray as they might soon be needed, dismounted, turned his horse loose, and in a very few minutes was asleep in the tall grass, as were most of his men.

McLaws's Division was composed of four brigades—Kershaw's, Cobb's (commanded by Lieutenant Colonel Christopher C. Sanders), Semmes's, and Barksdale's—and the batteries of Captains Basil C. Manly (North Carolina), John P. W. Read (Georgia), Miles C. Macon (Virginia), Edward S. McCarthy (Virginia), and Henry H. Carlton (Georgia). It was a veteran division and a good one, and had seen much hard service. Kershaw had 936 officers and men; Cobb, 398; Semmes, 709; and Barksdale, 891—an aggregate in the division of 2,934 officers and men, including the three batteries that became engaged. McLaws accounts for the small number carried into action by "the straggling of men wearied beyond … endurance and of those without shoes." Notwithstanding that he lost over 1,100 men on the seventeenth, his absentees—who joined before the morning of the eighteenth—made his force nearly as large as it was on the morning of the seventeenth.[17]

Somewhat more than an hour after McLaws had lain down and fallen asleep, Major Walter H. Taylor of General Lee's staff awakened him with the information that, as he had not been able to find McLaws previously (concealed as the general was in the tall grass), McLaws's adjutant-general had been ordered to go forward with the division. McLaws rode at once to the head of the column, which had left Lee's headquarters and Sharpsburg to the right, and struck the road leading from Sharpsburg to New Industry, on the Potomac. This they followed a short distance, stopped to pile knapsacks, then approached the southwest part of the West Woods. On the march were met the broken commands of Ewell and Hood retiring from the woods, with their tales of terrible fighting and great slaughter. Wounded men were being carried on stretchers to the rear or assisted by the stout arms of their comrades; guns were being hauled off by hand, the horses being killed or disabled; batteries that had saved their horses were dashing to the rear; and stragglers, without muskets, filled the fields. Manly's Battery and Macon's Richmond (Fayette) Artillery were ordered to prominent positions near the Reel house, which they held during the day without becoming engaged, and McLaws went forward with his four brigades and three remaining batteries.

An officer of D. H. Hill's staff pointed to the position that the division was expected to occupy. McLaws was ignorant of the ground and of the location of other troops, and at his request, Hood, who was riding by himself nearby, indicated the direction to advance. McLaws quickly resolved upon the formation of his line: Cobb's Brigade should move off to the right and advance north into the West Woods, Kershaw on Cobb's left, then Barksdale, with Semmes on the left of the line. McLaws, who had ridden ahead, realized the critical condition of affairs. Troops were seen retreating from the woods, but two hundred yards distant, very rapidly, and he saw that the 125th Pennsylvania was occupying them. He was anxious to cross the open space between himself and the woods before the latter were fully occupied by the enemy, and he ordered up an advance before his line had been entirely formed.

[16] Lafayette McLaws to Henry Heth, typescript copy, December 13, 1894, "Report of Gen. Lafayette McLaws, Comdg. Division—Division Artillery—Report of Gen. J. B. Kershaw" folder, box 2, Letters and Reports Concerning the Battle of Antietam, 1895–1900 ("Antietam Studies"), Record Group 94, National Archives.

[17] McLaws, "The Capture of Harper's Ferry," *Philadelphia Weekly Press*, September 19, 1888.

Meanwhile, a brigade was slipping from his hands. Cobb's Brigade, which had been ordered to the right to enter the woods from the south, marched so far to the right under a misapprehension of orders that it became entirely detached from the division and formed on the left of Rodes's Brigade in the sunken road, thus reducing McLaws to the three brigades of Kershaw, Barksdale, and Semmes (Kershaw on the right, and the first engaged). As McLaws's line was thus formed (or would have been formed, had all the brigades taken position before the advance was ordered), it faced northeast—Kershaw on the right about 150 yards from the southwest face of the woods, in rear of G. T. Anderson; Semmes on the left, in the direction of the Hauser house; and Barksdale in the center. Jackson now came up and ordered McLaws to send a brigade to support Stuart.[18] Kershaw was directed to form line while advancing and told that he must get to the woods before the enemy had full possession, and to do this he must not wait for his entire brigade to come up in line, but double quick his leading regiment, getting it in line as it went forward.

The 2d South Carolina was the leading regiment of Kershaw's Brigade. It was commanded by Colonel John D. Kennedy and numbered 253 officers and men. Kershaw made a brief speech of encouragement and ordered it forward to clear the woods and retake a battery beyond the church, which it was reported had been abandoned. It moved double-quick by the right flank, passed to the right of G. T. Anderson's recumbent men, moved up along the south edge of the woods, and began to climb the fence to enter the woods at a point about two hundred yards southwest of the church, when it was fired upon by the retiring skirmishers of the 125th Pennsylvania. Colonel Kennedy was wounded, and Major Franklin Gaillard succeeded to the command, but beyond this the regiment suffered very slightly. (Being on lower ground, the fire of the Pennsylvanians went over it.)

These Pennsylvanians were retiring before Early's advance. It had not been Early's intention to advance after his first fire and the falling back of the Pennsylvania skirmishers. He had observed some of the long-expected reinforcements preparing to advance into the woods from the direction of his right and was afraid of exposing his men to their fire. He feared also that the two movements would throw both attacking parties into confusion, as they would have been at right angles. In addition, another column was seen approaching his flank. He says, "The enemy in front, however, commenced giving way, and the brigade, which I have always found difficult to restrain, commenced pursuing."[19] This pursuit began as Kershaw was ordering the 2d South Carolina forward. Leaving that regiment where it was fired upon, and where, Kershaw says, it became "entangled in a rail fence,"[20] we follow Early's advance.

After firing at Early and the 2d South Carolina, the Pennsylvania skirmishers rallied upon their regiment, and it opened fire. Monroe's battery threw shrapnel, and Early's men were checked and thrown into some confusion. Some men in front were killed and wounded by their comrades in rear. Colonel Smith of the 49th Virginia was severely wounded but continued on the field, and Lieutenant Colonel John C. Gibson of the same regiment was disabled by a wound in the leg. Early's men were old soldiers and well disciplined; they quickly recovered from the confusion into which they had been thrown and returned the fire of the 125th Pennsylvania with great effect. Early led the 49th Virginia in two charges up the hill and then fell back—the better, it is said, to confuse the aim of Monroe's gunners. These movements had the effect of breaking the alignment of the brigade and again throwing it into confusion, to which there was now added the appearance of Sedgwick's division on his left, and to it we now return.

The fences skirting the cornfield had been thrown down. Williams ordered the regiments of his division to fall back out of the way, an order only partially obeyed, some remaining to be passed over. At 9:10 a.m., Sumner ordered Sedgwick's division forward. We quote Francis A. Walker:

It was a beautiful sight, those three lines of battle, as they emerged from the first belt of woods, passed through the corn-field, ripe almost to the harvest—and, moving steadily westward, crossed the Hagerstown pike. But, surely, they are not going to attack the enemy in that order! Other dispositions doubtless are to be made. The three lines are scarce seventy yards from front to rear. Two hundred men moving by the flank, in single file, would extend from the head of the column to its rear. Should these troops advance in this order, all three lines will be almost equally under fire at once, and their losses must be enormously increased. And where are the brigades that are to support them on the right and left, and protect the flanks of this perilously dense column? French is out of reach. The shattered brigades

---

[18] In his official report, McLaws says that Semmes was ordered to support Stuart, and Semmes in his report says the same, but in a letter before us, written by McLaws, he says Semmes was ordered to support Early. McLaws to "the Adjutant-General, Headquarters General Longstreet [Gilbert Moxley Sorrel]," October 20, 1862, reprinted in *OR*, vol. 19, pt. 1, 859; Paul J. Semmes to James M. Goggin, September 24, 1862, reprinted in *OR*, vol. 19, pt. 1, 874; McLaws to Heth, "Antietam Studies." As a matter of fact, Semmes preceded Early and charged some distance beyond him.—*EAC*

[19] Early to Pendleton, 971.

[20] Joseph B. Kershaw to Goggin, October 9, 1862, reprinted in *OR*, vol. 19, pt. 1, 865.

of the Twelfth Corps are holding stiffly on to their ground, under cover, but are hardly in numbers or in condition to undertake the offensive; and certainly, without a distinct effort to bring them forward, they will not be on hand if Sumner's column, in its forward rush, shall be assailed in flank. Richardson, indeed, could be up in forty minutes; and half that time would serve to draw French in toward Sedgwick's left. But Sumner does not wait ... All his life in the cavalry, he has the instincts of a cavalry commander ...

The order is still forward. Leaving the "Dunker Church" on their left and rear, Sedgwick's division, in close array, in three lines by brigade ... crossed the Hagerstown pike.[21]

In this advance, the left regiment of Gorman's brigade, the 34th New York, moved straight for the Dunkard church, its left clinging closely to the Smoketown Road. But when nearing the Hagerstown Road, orders were given to the brigade to oblique to the right, orders which were obeyed by three regiments but did not reach the 34th New York. It went straight ahead, crossed the road just north of the church, and came up in rear of the 125th Pennsylvania, then engaged. The other regiments of Gorman's brigade crossed the road 250 yards and more to the right.

It would be a simple matter to say that Sedgwick's division of five thousand men marched into an ambush; was attacked in front and on the flank by the brigades of Early, Semmes, Barksdale, and G. T. Anderson, the 2d and 3d South Carolina, and about two hundred men of Jackson's Division (in all, about 4,036 men), with some help from Stuart's artillery; and, as the historians of the Second Corps say, were "at the mercy of their enemy,"[22] "crushed by the ... fearful blow" and "driven out in disorder"[23] with "terrific slaughter,"[24] having "two thousand of them disabled in a moment"[25] and all the "successes of the morning ... lost."[26] This would be a very brief and accurate statement of what occurred, but we shall enter into some details of how all this occurred, so far as the meager, confused, and contradictory character of the official reports may enable us, with such assistance as is given in the most excellent histories of Palfrey and Walker, both gallant officers of Sedgwick's division. Palfrey says:

Sedgwick's division ... swept steadily forward ... Their march was rapid, and nearly directly west. There was very little distance between the lines. The recollections of the survivors range from fifty feet to thirty paces. Not a regiment was in column—there was absolutely no preparation for facing to the right or left in case either of their exposed flanks should be attacked. The total disregard of all ordinary military precaution in their swift and solitary advance was so manifest that it was observed and criticized as the devoted band moved on. A single regiment in column on both flanks of the rear brigade might have been worth hundreds of men a few minutes later, might indeed have changed the result of the battle. As the column pressed forward into the space between the pike and the West Woods, its left just reaching the Dunkard Church, it came under sharp artillery fire, and met with some loss. The lines were so near together that the projectile that went over the heads of the first line was likely to find its billet in the second or third. The swift shot were plainly seen as they came flying toward us. They came from Stuart's unseen guns, planted beyond the woods on or near the high ground which the Federal troops ought to have occupied. As the division entered the West Woods, it passed out of fire, and it moved safely through them to their western edge. There there was a fence, and, bordering it on the outside, a common wood road. The brigade of Gorman, followed by that of Dana, climbed this fence, and then their lines were halted. For some cause unknown, the left of the two brigades almost touched, while the line of Gorman's brigade diverged from the line of Dana's, so that there was a long interval from the right of the former to the right of the latter. It is doubtful whether the third line even entered the West Woods. If they did, they did not stay there long. There was a little, and only a little, musketry firing while the troops were in this position, but the Confederate guns to the right front of Sedgwick's position were active and efficient, firing now canister.[27]

---

[21] Francis A. Walker, 102–4.

[22] Palfrey, 86. In his original manuscript, Carman combines this phrase improperly with the one that follows to form a single quotation: "at the mercy of the enemy, crushed by the fearful blow."

[23] Francis A. Walker, 106.

[24] The phrase does not appear in either Palfrey's or Walker's account, though the latter writes of the event that the "slaughter" was "terrible." Ibid., 107.

[25] Palfrey, 87.

[26] Ibid., 88.

[27] Ibid., 83–84. Palfrey is in error in stating that all of Gorman's and Dana's brigades climbed the fence on the western border of the woods. Only the 1st Minnesota, the 82d New York, and two companies of the 15th Massachusetts went beyond it, the remainder of the 15th Massachusetts not crossing it, nor any of Dana's brigade.—EAC

Walker substantially follows Palfrey. He says:

Even when the leading brigade emerges from the further [*sic*] side of the grove, no enemy is seen in front. Only Stuart's horse-batteries, from some high, rocky ground on the right, search the woods, as they had the corn-field, with shell and solid shot. What means this unopposed progress? Is it well or ill, that this ground should not be disputed? Does it signify success or danger? It means that the Confederates have refused their left, and that Sedgwick is now pressing, in column, with his flank absolutely unprotected, past the real front of the enemy, and is aiming at that portion of their line which is drawn back. It is a position at once of power and of danger. If he will let Gorman go straight on until he strikes something, but hold Dana until the ground is cleared in front for a left half-wheel, to bring him facing south, and at the same time throw Howard's brigade into column of regiments, to be moved readily west to support Gorman or south to support Dana, the Second Division will have at least a chance—a small chance to achieve a victory against the superior forces which Lee is gathering to assail it, but large chance to make a strong resistance, to give a blow for every blow it must take, and, at the worst, to fall back without disaster.

But neither the chance of victory nor the chance of safety is to be taken. Without fronting so much as a regiment south, without increasing the intervals between the crowded brigades, two of which almost touch each other on the dangerously exposed left, Sumner, riding with the field-officers of the leading brigade, drives his column straight westward to find the enemy. As the leading brigade emerges from the grove last mentioned, fire is opened upon it from a line extended along the crest of a slight ridge in front, upon which stands a farmhouse, barn, and stacks of corn, while from the left and rear of this line one of Stuart's batteries plays upon Gorman's front. Our men drop like autumn leaves, but the regiments stand up to their work without a quiver; the colors are advanced and the battle begun with good set purpose.[28]

In the advance of Gorman's brigade, the 1st Minnesota was on the right, the 82d New York second in line, and the 15th Massachusetts on the left of the 82d New York. The 34th New York, on the extreme left, becoming detached, fought (as we shall see) at the Dunkard church. In its advance through the cornfield, the 1st Minnesota passed over the 27th Indiana, then over the three companies of the 124th Pennsylvania lying in the Hagerstown Road, and onto the narrow plateau a few yards south of the Miller barn. Sumner was riding with Colonel Alfred Sully of the 1st Minnesota, and, perceiving that the regiment had not removed the hood from its colors, exclaimed, "In God's name, what are you fighting for? Unfurl those colors!"[29] The regiment now descended the plateau to lower ground and the West Woods, swept across the front of Goodrich's brigade (almost touching it), pushed through the woods to a rail fence bordering them on the west, and halted at the fence, beyond which was a cornfield on ground gradually rising to the crest of Hauser's Ridge (on which was a small piece of woods concealing the 13th Virginia in support of Pelham's Battery). The Minnesota regiment was a little over five hundred yards west of the Hagerstown Road. There was no opposition when the fence was reached and no enemy in sight.

Immediately on the Minnesotans coming to a halt, the skirmishers of the 13th Virginia opened fire from the cornfield but were driven back to the woods about 220 yards distant, soon after which Pelham's Battery opened fire. The 82d New York, advancing on the left of the 1st Minnesota, gained the outer edge of the woods, its two right companies formed behind the fence, and the rest of the regiment, in open ground, faced more to the south (with the cornfield in front) and connected with the right of the 15th Massachusetts. The Massachusetts regiment, as it approached the Hagerstown Road, began obliquing to the right, crossed the road and open field beyond, descended the wooded slope, and came directly in front of the Alfred Poffenberger buildings, closing up to the 82d New York. As it gained the summit of a slight elevation, its left became hotly engaged with Jackson's Division, some of whose men were at the foot of the rise of the ridge near the Hauser farm, but many of them covered by the barn, stacks, and rock ledges, not over twenty-five yards beyond the wood road bordering the west edge of the woods. Raine's Battery, on the ridge five hundred yards distant, added its fire to that of Jackson's men and was momentarily silenced by the sharpshooters. The two right companies of the regiment crossed the wood road and took cover of a rock ledge in open ground, the remainder of the regiment in the edge of the woods, the left extending in the direction of the Dunkard church and about five hundred yards distant from it. The center and left were opposite the Alfred Poffenberger house and barn, the left being on the slope of the wooded ridge and about seventy yards from the wood road. The company of sharpshooters on the left was advanced to the wood road and barn.

Dana's brigade followed Gorman's. From right to left it was thus formed: the 19th and 20th Massachusetts, 59th New York, 42d New York, and 7th Michigan. Dana had been ordered to keep his line about seventy-five yards in rear of Gorman. On emerging from the East Woods, he saw part of Williams's division lying on the ground in front, which he took

[28] Francis A. Walker, 104–5.

[29] As of this writing, Carman's source for this quotation has not been identified.

to be Gorman's line, upon which he halted and ordered his men to lie down. They were hardly down when he received an order to move on, double quick, and enter the woods in front. The outline of the woods was irregular, presenting a salient point where the woods came to the road three hundred yards north of the church. Here his left regiment, the 7th Michigan, entered—and hardly had it done so when it became engaged with an enemy on its flank. Dana immediately ordered the 42d New York to change front to support the Michigan men in resisting this flank attack, and the three right regiments were permitted to move on, enter the middle woods, and halt very close to Gorman's now engaged line.

Howard's brigade was close upon Dana's. Its line was formed with the 71st Pennsylvania on the right, the 106th Pennsylvania right center, the 69th Pennsylvania left center, and the 72d Pennsylvania on the left. Howard reports that after passing out of the East Woods, by Sumner's order he detached the 71st Pennsylvania to the support of Mansfield's corps and halted his brigade, but Colonel Isaac J. Wistar of the 71st has no recollection of having received such an order or of halting his regiment.[30] "At this point," says Howard, "the musketry fire began to tell upon us, and I received an order from General Sedgwick to move up my entire line."[31] Howard says he delayed his line for the detached regiment to come up, then crossed the Hagerstown Road. The brigade was under severe artillery fire and struck the road obliquely (the right first reaching it and climbing the high rail fence on either side), then pushed on into the woods, the left of the line extending toward the church while the three right regiments continued across the open field beyond and into the woods in rear of Dana's right, where they came under fire of shell and solid shot. Howard says, "Just after passing the turnpike I noticed confusion on the left, and quite a large body of men falling back … I pushed the third line on a little farther, and into the woods beyond the turnpike, preserving about the distance first indicated … The second and third lines, as far as I could observe from my position near the center of the latter, were lying down as ordered."[32] Howard rode with the 106th Pennsylvania, the second regiment in line. Colonel Joshua T. Owen of the 69th Pennsylvania, next on the left, reports that as the brigade reached the top of the hill where the open field and woods join, he noticed many of the regiments to the left of the division falling back in great confusion and immediately suggested the propriety of moving the brigade obliquely to the left. Orders having been received, however, to dress to the right, the brigade entered the woods in good order and was dressed by the right of Dana's brigade.[33] This, however, was not done by the entire brigade; the left regiment was being swept from the field.

At the time, Sumner was in rear of the first line, Sedgwick was not seen, and Howard did not act as the occasion required. Had he taken the responsibility of changing front to the left with his three regiments when he saw the attack upon his flank, either by throwing forward his right or retiring his left, or both, and forming line perpendicular to the Hagerstown Road on high and very favorable ground, he would have formed a rallying point upon which other regiments could have been formed, and McLaws in all probability would have been checked—for we cannot doubt that the men who, in July following, held the Bloody Angle at Gettysburg against Pickett's Charge would have shown the same spirit here as they did on that occasion. But disregarding the attack on the left, Howard thought it of more importance to carry out an unimportant direction to dress on the line of Dana's brigade, and he went into the woods and ordered his men to lie down.

Thus, while the left of Dana's and Howard's brigades were crumbling away, the right and center of the two brigades advanced and entered the middle body of the West Woods and came up in rear of Gorman's line, then heavily engaged. This body of woods is 150 yards in depth, east to west, and in that space were crowded—*jammed*, one might say—the three lines on a sloping hillside, exposed to artillery and musketry fire, and the rear lines unable to fire a shot, unless over the heads of comrades in front.

We return to the 125th Pennsylvania at the Dunkard church and the Union regiments involved in its defeat and expulsion. The 34th New York, as we have seen, was advancing on the left of Gorman's brigade. As it approached the Hagerstown Road it double-quicked, crossed the road, and came up in rear of the left wing of the 125th Pennsylvania, its left going about thirty yards beyond the church. Perceiving that there was no support on his left, Colonel James A. Suiter, commanding the regiment, sent an officer to see what there was in that direction, and he learned that the 2d South Carolina was moving up the hill toward the church. The left of the 34th New York was now refused and faced southwest; the right wing, in rear of the left of the 125th Pennsylvania, faced nearly west. Almost as soon as the 34th New York came up, the 7th Michigan of Dana's brigade entered the woods to its right. This regiment was the left of its brigade and advanced into the woods about

---

[30] As of this writing, no such statement from Wistar has been found.

[31] Oliver O. Howard to "Colonel," September 20, 1862, reprinted in *OR*, vol. 19, pt. 1, 305.

[32] Ibid., 305–6.

[33] Joshua T. Owen to Eben T. Whittelsey, September 21, 1862, reprinted in *OR*, vol. 19, pt. 1, 318. Lieutenant James C. Lynch, in command of Company A, 106th Pennsylvania, "called the attention of Colonel Owen, of the Sixth-Ninth, to [the enemy] column, now plainly visible on our left flank; Colonel Owen said he saw them and had called General Howard's attention to them, and he replied that he knew it, but his orders were to move right oblique." Joseph R. C. Ward, *History of the One Hundred and Sixth Regiment, Pennsylvania Volunteers, 2d Brigade, 2d Division, 2d Corps, 1861–1865* (Philadelphia: Grant, Faires & Rodgers, 1883), 90.—EAC

sixty yards until nearly reaching the right of the 125th Pennsylvania, when it halted for alignment. It was but two minutes when Confederate colors and troops were seen advancing up the ravine in the old wood road on its left, but fire was not opened, as the men had been cautioned that a Union skirmish line was in front on that flank. Almost immediately two volleys in quick succession were poured into the right of the 125th Pennsylvania and left of the 7th Michigan, which broke the former and laid low one-half of the left wing of the latter. At the same time, the entire front of the 125th Pennsylvania and the 34th New York became involved. All these attacks were made by Barksdale's Brigade, a part of Early's, and the 2d South Carolina of Kershaw's. G. T. Anderson's Brigade was advancing to join the fray.

The 2d South Carolina had been pushed into the woods to check the advance of the 125th Pennsylvania (and troops supposed to be following it) until McLaws could form his command. This was soon accomplished, and McLaws gave the signal, by waving his handkerchief, for the movement to be made. Barksdale's Brigade entered the woods on their left edge to support the left of the 2d South Carolina; the 3d South Carolina entered the woods in rear of Barksdale's left. Semmes's Brigade, on the left, charged down from near the Hauser farm on the front of the 15th Massachusetts and the 82d New York. Kershaw led the 7th and 8th South Carolina over G. T. Anderson's men to support and form on the right of the 2d South Carolina, and Anderson followed and joined in the attack. These movements were made in the order stated, in quick succession. All report becoming engaged quickly, and all claim to have driven the enemy before them.

It will conduce to a clearer understanding of the somewhat complicated and confused movements of the attacking troops if we first consider the advance of Semmes's Brigade on the front of the 15th Massachusetts and the 82d New York, closely and severely engaging these regiments while others were working on the flank and rear of the entire division. Semmes's Brigade, as it came on the field, was ordered by McLaws to move forward in line to the support of Stuart's cavalry and artillery on the extreme left. The brigade was then on the high ground near the Hauser house, numbered 709 officers and men, and from right to left was thus formed: the 32d Virginia, 10th Georgia, 15th Virginia, and 53d Georgia. Semmes says, "Immediately the order was given, 'by company into line,' followed by 'forward into line,' both of which movements were executed, in the presence of the enemy, under a fire occasioning severe loss in killed and wounded." It advanced steadily two hundred yards, the left passing through the Hauser apple orchard under a severe fire from the 15th Massachusetts and the 82d New York, when orders were given to commence firing (as Semmes says, at long range for most of the arms in the brigade) for the purpose of encouraging the men and disconcerting the enemy, and the effect was visible in the diminished number of killed and wounded.[34] Crossing the fence which ran nearly north and south just east of the Hauser house, the brigade—under a murderous fire—charged across a stubble field, men falling at every step, and was brought to a halt, the right at a rocky knoll very near the Alfred Poffenberger barn (which gave some protection from the galling fire of the 15th Massachusetts on the hillside 130 yards distant) and the skirmishers at the barn and in the old wood road. The center and left of the brigade were under partial cover of the many projecting rock ledges. The conflict here was at close quarters and very severe, the entire brigade suffering heavily from the fire of the 15th Massachusetts, 130 to 190 yards in front, and an enfilading fire from the right. In advancing to this position and holding it a very few minutes, nearly one-half the brigade was killed and wounded, the loss being particularly severe in the 10th Georgia and 15th Virginia, each losing more than half their number. Three of the four regimental commanders were wounded.

The loss inflicted by Semmes upon the 15th Massachusetts and the two lines in its rear was severe, and to this was added the fire of several pieces of artillery that were run up on Hauser's Ridge and poured an incessant stream of canister and shrapnel along the entire front of the three right regiments of Gorman's brigade and upon the exposed and defenseless lines in rear. Two guns of the 1st Company, Richmond Howitzers, under Lieutenant Robert M. Anderson moved on Semmes's right, but the open, exposed field was no place for artillery. It could not live under the fire that swept it, and—under orders—Anderson withdrew his guns to the high ground in rear, south of the Houser farm.

Barksdale was nearing the woods when Semmes began his advance. He halted at the fence a short time until he saw that Semmes was under way across the field, then he went over the fence south of the barn and, entering the woods, immediately came under fire. (At this time, Early was making a vigorous attack upon the 125th Pennsylvania, advancing and falling back and again advancing, then lying down.) The left regiments were in some confusion, when Captain Robert D. Lilley of the 25th Virginia, observing a line coming up, called to his men to hold on a little longer, as help was coming, and in a moment Barksdale came up on the left and joined in the attack. Two of his regiments advanced up the ravine straight for the right of the 125th Pennsylvania, quickly followed by an advance covering its entire front, all firing with the precision of veterans at green troops. After firing six to eight rounds, the right of the 125th Pennsylvania gave way in disorder, carrying with it a few files of the 34th New York, and it was just before this that the 7th Michigan closed up on the right of the 125th Pennsylvania and had its left wing almost swept away by the terrific fire that had broken the Pennsylvanians. The left of the

---

[34] Semmes to Goggin, 874.

Pennsylvania regiment, having the moral support of the 34th New York in its rear, remained a little longer—but not much longer, for as the right gave way the 2d South Carolina appeared on its left. This regiment soon freed itself from the entanglement of the rail fence and, entering the south face of the woods, came into line as it advanced to the cover of some wood piles about 120 yards from the left of the 125th Pennsylvania, upon which it opened a very effective fire—"the most deadly fire," writes one of its officers, "the regiment ever delivered"[35]—full upon the exposed flank of the 125th Pennsylvania and the oblique front of the 34th New York. The effect of this fire was that the Pennsylvanians gave way and retreated, leaving the 34th New York exposed in front and on both flanks. The 2d South Carolina started in pursuit of the Pennsylvanians, but a well-directed volley from the 34th New York drove it back. A member of the South Carolina regiment says, "The first Union line was very quickly driven, but an oblique line [the 34th New York—EAC], apparently older soldiers, was not so easily moved and checked us."[36] The check was of very brief duration. Early had fallen back to change front and check Sedgwick, who was seen marching past his left, but Barksdale's Brigade was still advancing and G. T. Anderson's was moving on its front. As soon as the 7th and 8th South Carolina passed over his brigade, while it was lying down at the southwest face of the woods, Anderson started his regiments by the left flank, double-quick, along the fence about two hundred yards. They then faced to the right, went over the fence into the woods, passed to the right of the 3d South Carolina (which was swinging to the left), and went up the ridge as the 125th Pennsylvania was retreating. Soon they were on the left of the 2d South Carolina, though not connecting with it. Anderson's men poured in two or three volleys, the 2d South Carolina did the same, and the 34th New York was driven out of the woods just as the 72d Pennsylvania of Howard's brigade entered them near the church.

Howard's line advanced from the East Woods in some disorder. As it approached the Hagerstown Road, the right of the brigade began obliquing to the right, while part of the left wing (which had been halted) was attracted by the contest around the church and began to oblique in that direction. Part of the 69th Pennsylvania followed the 106th Pennsylvania, and part overlapped the 72d Pennsylvania but was soon moved to the right. Under a fire that struck down many, the 72d reached the road—somewhat broken by the rush of the retreating 125th Pennsylvania through it. It was aligned by dressing to the right and then advanced about ten yards into the woods. Its left, which was near the church, could not fire because some of the 34th New York were in front, but the right wing was uncovered and began firing. The 34th New York was almost instantly driven out and the 2d South Carolina, G. T. Anderson's Brigade, and a part of Barksdale's opened full upon the 72d Pennsylvania, which was ordered by Sumner to retire by the right flank. It had fired but a few rounds—some men had not fired a shot—and the regiment retreated to the right and rear under a heavy fire that inflicted much loss. It went back in some disorder, stampeded five of the seven companies of the new 124th Pennsylvania, and carried them back to the East Woods.

The 125th Pennsylvania had been in the woods no more than thirty minutes, and the 34th New York and the 72d Pennsylvania less than half that time. In that short period, and in their retreat, the losses were severe. The 125th Pennsylvania had over 140 killed and wounded, the 34th New York had 33 killed and 111 wounded (46 percent of the number engaged), and the 72d Pennsylvania lost over 200 killed and wounded. In falling back all went over the ground of the advance and rallied in rear of some batteries that had been put in position near the East Woods.

Early, Barksdale, and G. T. Anderson claim to have driven the three regiments from the woods; one does not note the presence of the others or that anyone was assisting. Early says, "The enemy in front … commenced giving way, and the brigade, which I have always found difficult to restrain, commenced pursuing, driving the enemy in front entirely out of the woods."[37] Barksdale says, "In a few moments I engaged them, and, after firing several volleys into their ranks, drove them through the woods and into an open field beyond."[38] Anderson makes the brief report that he "engaged the enemy and drove them for about half a mile, my men and officers behaving in the most gallant manner."[39] He did not pursue beyond the ground held by the right of the 125th Pennsylvania, about midway between the church and the open field northwest of the Hagerstown Road.

It was while engaged with the 125th Pennsylvania that both Early and Barksdale saw Sedgwick's line crossing the open plateau on their left. Early says he could not stop his men, who were in pursuit, and that they advanced until his left flank and rear "became exposed to a fire from the column on the left [Gorman—EAC], which had advanced past my former position. I also discovered another body of the enemy [Dana—EAC] moving across the plateau on my left flank, in double-quick time, to the same position, and I succeeded in arresting my command and ordered it to retire, so that I might change front and

[35] As of this writing, Carman's source for this quotation has not been identified.

[36] Ibid.

[37] Early to Pendleton, 971.

[38] William Barksdale to Goggin, October 12, 1862, reprinted in OR, vol. 19, pt. 1, 883.

[39] George T. Anderson to Asbury Coward, September 30, 1862, reprinted in OR, vol. 19, pt. 1, 909.

advance upon this force."[40] At this time, the left of Early's Brigade was in some confusion (he was on the right with the 49th Virginia), and the change in front was not effected with the precision one would expect from reading his official report.

Barksdale, when he discovered the enemy moving past his left, did not find it necessary to fall back to change front. He simply ordered his left wing (the 13th and 18th Mississippi) to wheel to the left and attack, while the 17th and 21st Mississippi—after assisting in driving out the 125th Pennsylvania, 34th New York, and 72d Pennsylvania—turned upon the 7th Michigan and the 42d New York. At this moment, the 3d South Carolina came to Barksdale's support. It entered the woods just to the right of the wood road that led past the church, and advanced under a severe fire drawn by Barksdale's Brigade, which had preceded it. When it had passed some distance through the woods, in the direction of the church, to form on the left of the 2d South Carolina, Sedgwick's lines were seen passing its left, upon which it changed direction to the left and came up in rear of the 17th Mississippi, and G. T. Anderson (as we have seen) came up and filled the gap between it and the 2d South Carolina.

It will be remembered that when the Mississippians struck and routed the right of the 125th Pennsylvania, they also struck down nearly half of the left wing of the 7th Michigan. The 7th fell back a few feet and, making a partial change of front, returned the fire, and while so engaged the 72d Pennsylvania came up on its left (but a little to the rear) and began firing. The contest was very short, and both regiments fell back badly shattered. The remnant of the 7th Michigan retreated across the road; one-half the regiment lay dead or wounded in the woods or on the road, and a rally was made on the colors in the open ground south of the Miller cornfield. Their line formed facing nearly south, with quite a number of the 72d Pennsylvania, as well as some of the 69th Pennsylvania and the 42d New York, rallying upon it.

The fate of the 42d New York was similar to that of the 72d Pennsylvania and the 7th Michigan. When the 7th Michigan was first attacked, Dana ordered the 42d New York—which was next in line from the left—to change front. As it advanced promptly on open ground to gain distance, it received a volley from the ravine inside the woods, which swept away every fifth man from the ranks before it had formed in a new position. It closed up on the colors and advanced obliquely toward the woods and another volley again thinned its ranks. The line began to waiver but soon steadied and reached the edge of the woods about fifty yards beyond the 7th Michigan, and was about to enter them when it received such murderous volleys from Barksdale's men and the 3d South Carolina that it retreated over the open field and across the Hagerstown Road with a loss of 181 officers and men, 52 percent of the number in action. Early in the engagement, Dana was painfully wounded, but remained with his two regiments until they were driven from the field. He pays them this tribute: "Although the shattered remnants of them were forced by overwhelming numbers and a crossfire to retreat in disorder, I bear them witness that it was after nearly half the officers and men were placed *hors de combat*."[41]

Barksdale's Brigade suffered very severely in the brief encounter but, with the 3d South Carolina, pursued to and beyond the fences both at the north and east edges of the woods, and poured their fire at the retreating regiments in the open fields beyond—the open fields over which the three Union lines had marched to the middle woods and where they were now exposed to a fire in the rear. Barksdale says, "The Seventeenth and Twenty-first [Mississippi] pursued the enemy across the open field, when, perceiving a very strong force moving to the right and attempting to flank them, and all of our forces having retired from that part of the field, they fell back, under protection of a stone fence, in good order."[42] The stone fence to which Barksdale fell back was beyond the southwest corner of the West Woods.

G. T. Anderson, who had come up and filled the interval between the 2d and 3d South Carolina, did not join Barksdale in the pursuit; there was no immediate enemy in his front after he had assisted in driving the 34th New York and the 72d Pennsylvania from the woods. While he was at another part of the line, a mounted officer dashed up to the brigade with a report that Kershaw had been repulsed on the right and ordered a retreat to prevent the brigade from being cut off. Some confusion ensued, but Anderson came up, re-formed his line, and moved the right and rear to the fence he had crossed in entering the woods, from which position he was soon ordered to the assistance of D. H. Hill at the sunken road.

Before this movement of Anderson's, and simultaneous with the pursuit made by the 17th and 21st Mississippi, the 13th and 18th Mississippi and the 3d South Carolina pushed northward along the edge of the wood and over the open field west of the Hagerstown Road and directly in rear of Sedgwick's three lines. Semmes was still contending with the front and left of Gorman's line, and Early was forming to attack the flank of the 15th Massachusetts. About the same time, Kershaw was advancing to the attack on Greene's division opposite the church.

While all this was transpiring at and near the Dunkard church, Sumner was riding in the rear of Gorman's right, encouraging it to a fresh advance. As he rode up to Lieutenant Colonel John W. Kimball of the 15th Massachusetts, he

---

[40] Early to Pendleton, 971.

[41] Napoleon J. T. Dana to the "Assistant Adjutant-General, Second Division, Second Corps, Army of the Potomac," September 30, 1862, reprinted in *OR*, vol. 19, pt. 1, 320.

[42] Barksdale to Goggin, 883.

asked, "Colonel, how goes the battle?" to which Kimball replied, "We are holding our ground and slowly gaining, but losing heavily as you can see."[43] At this moment both Colonel Kimball and Major Chase Philbrick discovered that the enemy had turned the left flank and was moving steadily upon the rear of the division and called Sumner's attention to it. He could not believe it, but when satisfied it was so exclaimed, "My God, we must get out of this!" and rode to the rear to change the position of the other brigades to meet the enemy.[44] From where Sumner left the 15th Massachusetts, it was but a few yards to where Howard had halted his men and ordered them to lie down, and it was soon after this that Sumner, appearing on the left of the brigade, his white locks stirred by the breeze, rode toward the right of the line, giving orders which—as first understood by the men—were for a charge. In response, the men rose up, gave him a cheer, and began to fix bayonets, but now Sumner was heard to say, "Back Boys, for God's sake move back; you are in a bad fix."[45] Howard, who was at the right of his line, says Sumner came riding rapidly, with his hat off and his arms stretched out, motioning violently while giving some unintelligible command, and that the noise of musketry and artillery was so great that he judged more by the gestures of the general as to the disposition he wished him to make than by the orders that reached his ears. He judged that his left had been turned, and immediately gave the necessary orders to protect his flank by changing front to the left with his brigade. "I think, even then," says Howard, "I could have executed such an order with troops which, like my old brigade, had been some time commanded by myself, and thoroughly drilled; but here, quicker than I can write the words, the men faced about and took the back track in some disorder."[46] In his official report Howard says, "The troops were hastily faced about, and moved toward the rear and right in considerable confusion."[47]

The 72d Pennsylvania had been crushed at the first onset. The 69th Pennsylvania went off in better order, and the 106th Pennsylvania, according to accounts given by some of its survivors, started to fall back by the right flank, "which soon became a hasty, disorganized and disgusting retreat."[48] The historian of the 106th makes a better showing:

> Arriving at the fence running at right angles to the Hagerstown road across the open field north of the Dunker Church, an effort was made to rally and check the advance of the now elated enemy, who were emerging from the woods in large numbers … [The colors were planted on the fence.—EAC] … Colonel [Turner G.] Morehead, though injured by the fall of his horse, remained on the field, at once took advantage of this opportunity, and, assisted by Major [John H.] Stover, ordered the men to stand by their colors; and stand they did. Detachments of other regiments joining them, they opened fire, pouring volley after volley in quick succession into the advancing enemy, who thinking they had struck our second line, checked their advance, and finally fell back under cover of the woods.[49]

A portion of this regiment fell back to some haystacks, where it was joined by the 15th Massachusetts.

In coming into position, the 71st Pennsylvania became somewhat out of touch with the 106th Pennsylvania on its left. It was not until the first two lines had given way in the vain effort to change front that it became engaged, and it suffered more from the fire on its left and rear than from that in its front. On ascending a projecting mass of rock to get a clearer understanding of affairs, Colonel Wistar perceived that the entire left was in full retreat, being already some distance to the rear, closely followed by the Confederates. The regiment seemed to be practically alone, was suffering severely, and in immediate danger of being enveloped and captured. It was quickly formed into column of companies (the better to effect a retreat through the Confederates, then in rear, but somewhat disordered by their own pursuit). In this movement, Wistar was wounded and captured, the regiment escaping in fairly good order.

Howard says his brigade was first to retreat, and Palfrey writes, "The third line, the Philadelphia brigade, so called, was the first to go."[50] Under the circumstances this would be very natural, and we cannot see that any particular stigma attaches to the men, however harshly we may criticize the superior officers, but the statement of Palfrey has been disputed and warmly resented.

When Dana endeavored to change front with the 7th Michigan and the 42d New York, he permitted the 59th New York, 20th Massachusetts, and 19th Massachusetts to go forward and halt in rear of Gorman, and very soon the 59th New York closed up on and began firing through the left wing of the 15th Massachusetts upon the enemy in front. By this fire, many of the Massachusetts men were killed and wounded, and the most strenuous exertions were of no avail either in stopping

[43] As of this writing, Carman's source for this quotation has not been identified.

[44] See Francis A. Walker, 106.

[45] Ward, 104.

[46] "Gen'l O. O. Howard's Personal Reminiscences of the War of the Rebellion," *National Tribune*, April 3, 1884.

[47] Howard to "Colonel," 306.

[48] As of this writing, Carman's source for this quotation has not been identified.

[49] Ward, 90–91.

[50] Palfrey, 87.

this murderous fire or in causing the second line to advance to the front. At this juncture, Sumner rode up and, his attention being called to the terrible mistake, he rode to the right of the 59th New York and ordered it to cease firing and retire, which it did in considerable confusion. Survivors of the regiment say they fired but seven or eight rounds and were subjected to a cross-fire. Sumner "cussed them out by the right flank,"[51] and they went out in much confusion and did not stop until they reached the Nicodemus house, where an officer directed them to the right, as the Confederate artillery was sweeping the ground directly to the north and a section of Cooper's battery, supported by Hofmann's brigade, was taking position near the toll-gate beyond Nicodemus's. As the regiment went out, some of the men saw a regiment moving by companies *en echelon* and delivering a fire that checked the enemy. This was probably the 71st Pennsylvania or the 19th Massachusetts.

The 20th Massachusetts was on the right of the 59th New York and stood some time under a very severe fire, when orders were given to face to the rear and fire. Palfrey, who was an officer of this regiment, and was wounded in the woods, says, "The only fire delivered by the Twentieth Massachusetts regiment of the second line was delivered faced by the rear rank. In less time than it takes to tell it, the ground was strewn with the bodies of the dead and wounded, while the unwounded were moving off rapidly to the north."[52] The regiment quickly broke; some parts of it went through the 19th Massachusetts (after that regiment had made a stand beyond the woods) and formed in its rear.

The 19th Massachusetts was the right of Dana's line. It suffered severely as it entered the woods under a fire of musketry, canister, and shell, which it could not return as the front line was in its front. Colonel Edward W. Hinks was wounded, a great number of officers and men were struck down, and a part of the 82d New York retreated in disorder through it. As soon as its front was partially cleared, the regiment advanced a short distance and opened fire, but had delivered a few rounds only when a fire came upon its left and rear, upon which it delivered a volley by the rear rank, then—changing front—moved out of the woods with the 1st Minnesota of Gorman's brigade.

The 82d New York of Gorman's brigade, when in line, was in a very exposed position and suffered severely from the fire of Raine's Battery in its front. Part of the regiment fell back through the 19th Massachusetts, but the greater part of it remained until the left and center of the two brigades in rear had gone. The regiment on its left was moving when the 82d was ordered back to the outer edge of the woods and formed on the right of the 1st Minnesota.

After Gorman had expended forty to fifty rounds of ammunition, it became evident that the enemy was moving in large force on the left, where the firing became terrific. Not five minutes after the regiments around the church had been driven out, the enemy's fire came pouring hotly on his left and rear. Being in front, without orders of any kind from anyone, and finding that the rear lines were changing position and had already moved from their original places, he gave an order (which reached no one but the 1st Minnesota's Colonel Sully) to move quickly by the right flank. Gorman says in his report:

> Shortly before this, I heard Major General Sumner directing the third line to face about, in order to repel the enemy, which had broken our left, supposing the design to be to take up a better position than the one just previously occupied, I having informed the general that my left must be supported or I could not hold the position. The attack of the enemy on the flank was so sudden and in such overwhelming force that I had no time to lose, for my command could have been completely enveloped and probably captured, as the enemy was moving not only upon my left flank but also forcing a column toward my right, the two rear lines having both moved from their position before either of my three right regiments changed theirs.[53]

As soon as Scully received Gorman's order to leave the woods and hold the enemy in check while the rest of the brigade retired, he faced the 1st Minnesota about and moved back at a double-quick under a shower of canister from a Confederate battery. The regiment went back in such manner that its left fell onto the right of the 19th Massachusetts in the second line (which was also falling back and changing front), and the two swung backward to a rock ledge about one hundred yards north of the woods and formed line nearly perpendicular to the Hagerstown Road. A part of the 82d New York joined the right of the 1st Minnesota, and for a time the pursuit of the enemy was checked, though with some loss.

We left the 15th Massachusetts at the moment Sumner rode to Howard. The firing had been incessant upon it for twenty minutes, but it stood resolutely to its work, the men falling rapidly from the fire in its front. Now a still more deadly fire came upon its left and rear from Early and Barksdale. Perceiving that the second and third lines had gone, Kimball ordered the regiment to move off by the right flank. It retired in fairly good order some 225 yards to the right and rear, faced about, and came under a severe artillery fire by which Captain Clark S. Simonds and others were killed and some wounded. It remained in this

---

[51] As of this writing, Carman's source for this quotation has not been identified.
[52] Palfrey, 87.
[53] Willis A. Gorman to Whittelsey, September 20, 1862, reprinted in *OR*, vol. 19, pt. 1, 311.

position a few minutes and then retired to the North Woods. In its brief encounter, the loss of the regiment was 315 killed, wounded, and missing—the greatest loss sustained by any regiment on the field—and 52.5 percent of those taken into action.

Not all the regiments of the second and third lines, which were broken by the attack upon the flank and rear, fell back without a halt or offering some resistance to the advancing enemy. We have already noted that the 106th Pennsylvania displayed its colors on the fence running from the northeast corner of the middle body of woods to the Hagerstown Road and opened a fire by which it is claimed pursuit was checked. The same was done by parts of the 71st Pennsylvania and the 20th Massachusetts and also by the 15th Massachusetts as it was leaving position. All this had an effect, but the pursuit by the 3d South Carolina and Barksdale's 13th and 18th Mississippi was checked in the open field between the woods and the road, about 225 yards from the south edge of the field where it began, by the appearance of infantry and artillery upon the right flank of the pursuing force.

The 3d South Carolina was on the right of Barksdale and of the pursuing line. After it had advanced 225 yards and come under fire of the 106th Pennsylvania at the fence, Colonel James D. Nance, its commander, discovered a Union force on his right—men of the 7th Michigan, 72d Pennsylvania, Purnell Legion, and others—who had rallied east of the road, and his advancing line was enfiladed by an artillery fire. All of this caused him to halt, changed front to the right and rear, and throw his line into a slight hollow in the southern part of the field, parallel to and 165 yards from the Hagerstown Road.

The artillery fire came from Lieutenant George A. Woodruff's battery (Battery I, 1st U.S. Artillery). Woodruff crossed the Antietam late on the sixteenth and parked near the Hoffman farm. Early on the seventeenth, he followed the route taken by Tompkins's Rhode Island battery and halted behind the East Woods. Major Francis N. Clarke, Sumner's chief of artillery, rode up, said that Sedgwick was having a hard time, and ordered the battery forward. It went through the East Woods at a gallop and over the fields straight for the Hagerstown Road through a stream of fugitives. One of the officers, preceding the guns, cleared the ground, and the battery dashed up, went into position about 150 yards from the road and 350 yards north of the church, and opened its six guns with canister upon the 3d South Carolina. This caused the regiment to change front, fall back, and seek cover as the same artillery fire ranged through Barksdale's ranks.

Woodruff was closely followed by Cothran's battery (Battery M, 1st New York Light Artillery) of the Twelfth Corps. Before Sumner's arrival, this battery had been ordered by Hooker to the front. (It was then in the field near the D. R. Miller farm and in rear of where Gordon's brigade and Ransom's battery had been engaged.) It went down through the East Woods to the Smoketown Road, where Cothran had been told he would be met by a staff officer to assign him a position. Meanwhile, Sedgwick's division had come up and gone forward. After a brief wait, the battery went down the Smoketown Road to the corner of the woods and turned into the field on the right as the 125th Pennsylvania and the 34th New York fell back. There was no staff officer—or other—to give orders, Cothran saw Woodruff engaged in front with infantry and, without awaiting or seeking orders, went forward and into position on Woodruff's right and opened with canister and spherical case not only upon the 3d South Carolina and Barksdale's men but upon the woods around the church.

Barksdale's 13th and 18th Mississippi advanced along the edge and in the woods on the left of the 3d South Carolina. At first, notes the historian of Kershaw's Brigade, they were staggered by the resistance of Dana's left, but, recovering, moved up the slope partly in open field and part among the straggling oaks, "while the … shell and canister thinned their ranks to such an extent, that when the infantry was met, their galling fire forced Barksdale to retire in great disorder."[54] Barksdale reports that his pursuit was for a considerable distance over ground covered with the dead and wounded of the enemy, but he did not deem it prudent to advance farther without more support, and ordered the two regiments to fall back to the woods in front of his first position.[55] McLaws says, "The ground over which the Mississippi Brigade (General Barksdale) advanced, and to his right, was thickly strewn with the dead and wounded of the enemy, far exceeding our own, and their dead were much more numerous than their wounded. The close proximity of the combatants to each other may account for the disproportion."[56] Barksdale's loss was 33 percent killed and wounded. His two regiments and the 3d South Carolina were checked and repulsed about 225 yards from the south edge of the field over which they charged when Dana's left gave way. On the left, Early went no farther, but halted at his first position under cover of the rocky ledges in the woods. Further pursuit was left to Semmes and the artillery under Stuart.

While the rear and flanks of Sedgwick's three lines were being pressed and crushed by the 3d South Carolina, Barksdale, and Early, Semmes, as we have seen, was heavily engaged in their front. When the line began to waiver, he poured in heavy volleys and advanced in a northeast direction, his right over the ground held by the right of the 15th and 20th

[54] D. Augustus Dickert, *History of Kershaw's Brigade, with Complete Roll of Companies, Biographical Sketches, Incidents, Anecdotes, Etc.* (Newbury, S.C.: E. H. Aull Co., 1899), 156.

[55] Barksdale to Goggin, 883.

[56] McLaws to "the Adjutant-General," 859.

Massachusetts and the 71st Pennsylvania, his left through the most northern body of the West Woods. Semmes had already lost heavily in his engagement with Gorman's front, and the more than seven hundred officers and men who had entered the fight had dwindled to less than five hundred. His advance was not in connected line, there being wide intervals between some of the regiments, and these became much scattered in the pursuit, some parts of them forging ahead of the others. Semmes reports that he drove the enemy "from position to position, through wood and field ..., expending not less than forty rounds of ammunition," and went "farther to the front than the troops on my right by about 300 yards, and for a time was exposed to a terrible front and enfilading fire, inflicting great loss."[57] It was this advance of Semmes that forced the front or turned the right flank of all the detachments that had united in checking the advance of Barksdale and the 3d South Carolina, and that finally expelled Goodrich and Patrick from the north body of the woods.

It will be remembered that when Sedgwick's division entered the West Woods, the right of Gorman's brigade swept past the front of Goodrich's brigade of the Twelfth Corps, which was closely supported by Patrick's brigade of the First Corps. As Sedgwick's fugitives went to the rear, they rushed through and over the three small regiments of Goodrich, carrying them along in their flight. Everything was in wild disorder. Patrick at once again threw his three small regiments under cover of the rock ledge beyond the woods and perpendicular to the road—partially to rally the retreating troops and partially to hold on with his few remaining cartridges until order could be restored and assistance come forward. The 21st New York (Colonel William F. Rogers), on the right, endeavored to check the retreating troops and form them on the right. Rogers says no heed was paid to his efforts, officers and men striving alike to reach the rear. "It was a complete route [*sic*] and they passed on out of our sight."[58] In front of the greater part of the line the pursued and pursuers were so close that Patrick's men could not fire.

In Semmes's advance, the 32d Virginia was on the right of the brigade. It charged over the ground held by the right of the 15th Massachusetts and, after a check of a few minutes (until the 10th Georgia came up on its left), pushed entirely through the woods, passing some of Barksdale's men but seeing none of Early's. It came into the open ground where Patrick was seen rallying his brigade and endeavoring to stem the tide of fugitives going to the rear.

The 10th Georgia and 15th Virginia advanced on the left of the 32d Virginia and halted ten or fifteen minutes in the wood road, beyond where the right of the 15th Massachusetts had been. At the end of this halt, they again advanced through a skirt of woods to the fence bounding the woods on the northeast; the Georgians in this advance claim to have "driven the enemy with heavy slaughter,"[59] and the Virginians captured many Pennsylvanians of Howard's brigade. The two regiments halted near the fence when they saw Patrick's men in front.

Patrick was a tenacious and resourceful fighter and undoubtedly would have checked the farther advance of Semmes's three regiments (now reduced to less than 250 men)—especially as the 1st Minnesota, 19th Massachusetts, and part of the 82d New York had now rallied to his right. But these were turned by the 53d Georgia, Stuart's artillery, and its infantry support (the 13th Virginia of Early's Brigade). The 53d Georgia was the left of Semmes's Brigade and the largest regiment in it, having double the number of any other regiment. In its advance it struck the 82d New York, 1st Minnesota, and 19th Massachusetts as they were retiring and changing front, and followed them nearly to the north edge of the woods when, perceiving the line they had formed under partial cover, it halted. Stuart, with artillery and the 13th Virginia, was advancing on its left.

There was not much opportunity for Stuart to use his cavalry. Much of it had been detached to gather the infantry stragglers, and the small body of Fitzhugh Lee's Brigade left to him was supporting artillery on the left that had been placed under Stuart's direction. Stuart was very active with his artillery. He had been given a very important position to hold—the high ground that lay between the left of the infantry and the river that, once occupied by the Union troops, would render the Confederate left untenable. He occupied it to good purpose aggressively. With the many batteries assigned him he had kept up a constant and very annoying fire, and with such effect as led to the belief that a continuous line extended from the Dunkard church to very near the Potomac—a belief that had its effect upon the Union movements early in the day. When Sedgwick's division approached, Stuart checked its advance at the west edge of the woods with some of this artillery and the 13th Virginia, aided by the few men of Jackson's Division, and gave time for McLaws to come up, make his dispositions, and attack. When Sedgwick's lines began to break, Poague's, Raine's, Brockenbrough's, and D'Aquin's Batteries started northerly along Hauser's Ridge and kept up an advancing fire from all favoring points, all the time under severe fire from the Union guns, but nevertheless advancing and firing. As these batteries continued moving to the left the guns were mixed up, D'Aquin's being generally in the lead. Some were halted in the Nicodemus cornfield, the highest point on the ridge, and opened fire upon the 59th New York, 15th Massachusetts, and detachments of other regiments that had halted near the

---

[57] Semmes to Goggin, 874.

[58] William F. Rogers, "Movement of the Twenty-first Regiment New York Volunteers at the Battle of Antietam September 17th, 1862," no date, typescript copy, "1st Corps—Doubleday—Hooker" folder, box 1, "Antietam Studies."

[59] Philologus H. Loud to Edmund B. Briggs, September 23, 1862, reprinted in *OR*, vol. 19, pt. 1, 878.

Nicodemus place, but one battery (supported by the 13th Virginia), moving between the woods and the cornfield, came to a knoll on the flank of the 1st Minnesota and about 260 yards from it, where it had an enfilading fire upon its line. At the same time, the 13th Virginia was seen working past the right of the line, threatening its rear, and an order was given for the entire line to fall back. In doing so, the 1st Minnesota and the 82d New York passed over the field in rear (in line with and almost in contact with the 13th Virginia on its right), facing about to repulse the 53d Georgia, which was now following them. The 1st Minnesota, rushing through the Nicodemus farmyard under a shower of canister, "tumbled over the stone fence beyond, and, in less than thirty seconds, formed on the colors in the Nicodemus lane, every man in his place,"[60] the fragment of the 82d New York with them, and immediately moved to the corner of that part of the North Woods extending west of the Hagerstown Road. The 19th Massachusetts fell back on the left of the 1st Minnesota, and both faced about to check the further Confederate advance as a section of Cooper's battery came up and went into position a short distance out in the open field on the right.

The artillery section was supported by Hofmann's brigade. When McLaws made his attack, this section, under Lieutenant Fullerton, was in the field to the right and in front of Hofmann's brigade, which lay along the Hagerstown Road in support to the artillery on the high plateau north of the Joseph Poffenberger farm. When it was seen that Sedgwick's men were falling back, Hofmann moved to the right and front with his entire brigade and the section of artillery and took position with his infantry behind the stone fences of the road leading west from the toll-gate on the Hagerstown Road. The two rifled guns were run into the open field beyond, between the road and the Nicodemus place and on the right of the 1st Minnesota. The enemy's battery was now quickly silenced and, for about twenty minutes, both the Minnesota and Massachusetts men exchanged fire with the sharpshooters of the 13th Virginia, supporting the Confederate battery, and silenced them. This was the limit of the Confederate pursuit; it was checked, reports Stuart, "by the enemy's reserve artillery coming into action."[61]

Meanwhile, Patrick had fallen back. When he saw the line on his right falling back and the colors of the 53d Georgia passing his right and others advancing in his front, he ordered his regiments to retire by the right flank. Colonel Rogers, commanding the 21st New York, on the right, says, "The enemys [sic] skirmishers continued warily to advance … There seemed to be no force to oppose them. My men had by this time exhausted their ammunition. I soon received orders to move to the rear and at once commenced to retire. This seemed to give greater encouragement to the advancing skirmishers, who quickly followed firing as they advanced causing many casualties during our retreat."[62] Patrick reports that the brigade "was withdrawn in an unbroken line,"[63] and Colonel Henry C. Hoffman of the 23d New York reports that his regiment retired in such perfect order as to attract the attention of Howard, who was vainly endeavoring to rally his men a short distance in rear. Pointing to the New York men, Howard said, "Men! that is the way to leave a field. That regiment are acting like soldiers. Do as they do, men, and we will drive them back again in ten minutes."[64] Patrick marched up the Hagerstown Road to the North Woods and joined Gibbon's brigade, which was deployed through the woods to arrest further retreat. In an article in the *National Tribune*, Howard writes, "When we reached the open space [where Patrick rallied—*EAC*], General Sumner and every officer of nerve made extraordinary efforts to rally the men and make head against the advancing enemy, but that was impossible till we had traversed the open space, for now we had the enemy's artillery and infantry both pursuing and flanking our broken brigades by rapid and deadly volleys."[65]

The retreat was arrested and the greater part of the division rallied at the North Woods. When the 7th Pennsylvania Reserves retired from its contest with a part of Hood's Division, it went up the Hagerstown Road and well into the North Woods, where it was joined by the 10th Pennsylvania Reserves, which after a few minutes before the advance of McLaws had been withdrawn from its position near the West Woods on Patrick's right. As Sedgwick's stragglers began to come back, Major Chauncey A. Lyman of the 7th deployed both regiments and endeavored to stop them. While so employed, Sumner rode up, inquired who they were, and ordered the two regiments forward. Promptly and prettily they advanced to the south edge of the woods and halted, where they came under an enfilading artillery fire by which Captain James L. Colwell of the 7th was killed and many wounded. The cool presence of these two small regiments was of great effect, and upon them Howard rallied a part of his brigade and the division retreated no farther, but took position in and about the woods.

[60] As of this writing, Carman's source for this quotation has not been identified.

[61] James E. B. Stuart to Robert H. Chilton, February 13, 1864, reprinted in *OR*, vol. 19, pt. 1, 820.

[62] Rogers, "Antietam Studies."

[63] Marsena R. Patrick to Eminel P. Halstead, September 21, 1862, reprinted in *OR*, vol. 19, pt. 1, 245.

[64] Henry C. Hoffman to Patrick, September 20, 1862, manuscript copy by Ezra A. Carman, "1st Corps" folder, "Antietam Studies."

[65] "Gen'l O. O. Howard's Personal Reminiscences."

Walker, in his *History of the Second Army Corps*, says:

> It is easy to criticize Sumner's dispositions at Antietam—the dangerous massing of Sedgwick's brigades, the exposure of the flank of the charging column, the failure of the commander to supervise and direct, from some central point, all the operations of the corps; yet no one who saw him there, hat in hand, his white hair streaming in the wind, riding abreast of the field officers of the foremost line, close up against the rocky ledges bursting with the deadly flame of Jackson's volleys, could ever fail thereafter to understand the furious thrust with which a column of the Second Corps always struck the enemy, or the splendid intrepidity with which its brigade and division commanders were wont to ride through the thickest of the fight as calmly as on parade.[66]

All this is conceded, yet the fact remains that these splendid troops of the Second Corps were much disorganized and many of them sadly demoralized when they fell back, and, unfortunately, that partial demoralization extended to their commander. We again quote Walker:

> If it is not profanation to say such a thing about Edwin V. Sumner, he had lost courage; not the courage which would have borne him calmly up a ravine swept by canister at the head of the old First Dragoons, but the courage which, in the crush and clamor of action, amid disaster and repulse, enables the commander coolly to calculate the chances of success or failure. He was heartbroken at the terrible fate of the splendid division on which he had so much relied, which he had deemed invincible, and his proximity to the disaster had been so close as to convey a shock from which he had not recovered.[67]

Nor had he recovered from this shock an hour or more later when Franklin came up.

As soon as Semmes's men saw that Patrick was retiring from his position behind the stone ledge, they rushed forward cheering and firing. The 32d Virginia, on the right, advanced to the stacks south of the D. R. Miller barn, where it was halted until supports could be brought up. It was reduced to less than eighty men, and these took cover behind the stacks. The 10th Georgia and the 15th Virginia, passing the left of the 32d Virginia and the barn, halted in rear of the rock ledge from which Patrick had withdrawn, where they engaged some Union troops that were under cover of the stone fences of the Hagerstown Road. Men of both regiments crossed the road to the Miller house, where they found a number of wounded and unwounded Union men, some of whom were captured and sent to the rear. These movements followed those of the 53d Georgia, which had been checked on the open ground to the front and left of the position taken by the 10th Georgia and the 15th Virginia. Semmes was now about 450 yards in advance of the point where Barksdale had been repulsed and Early had been halted.

When Stuart had driven the 1st Minnesota and 19th Massachusetts from the field, he came riding out of the woods to the 32d Virginia and inquired for Semmes. Just then a Union battery across the Hagerstown Road opened upon the barn, stacks, and infantry in sight, and Stuart told Semmes that the battery must be taken. Semmes replied that his men had been very severely engaged, had lost heavily, and were about out of ammunition, but that Barksdale was in the woods to the rear and not engaged, upon which Stuart dashed off after Barksdale.

The artillery fire that opened on Semmes came from the section of Campbell's battery under Lieutenant Stewart that had had such a serious and thrilling experience near these same stacks very early in the morning, and some of whose dead still lay near them. When Sedgwick's men passed to the rear through the woods, closely pursued by the enemy, this section was in position very near where Stewart had his section in the Miller field at the beginning of the fight, and Reynolds's New York battery was on its left. Both were under a heavy fire from the two Confederate batteries beyond the woods, which had their exact range. Stewart was unable to get his own range on account of the smoke of the musketry and so limbered to the rear and came up on Reynolds's left, when one of his men called attention to a body of Confederate infantry in front (apparently on the Hagerstown Road); the left or most-advanced part of the line, the 53d Georgia, appeared to be falling back. Stewart loaded his guns with canister, waited until he saw four stands of colors in their front, and began firing. It was at this time that Stuart came up and advised Semmes to capture the battery. Semmes remained but a short time after Stuart dashed off for Barksdale; no troops came to his support or to capture the battery, whose canister was very annoying as it enfiladed a part of his line. He ordered his regiments back into the woods, Stewart following them with canister until out of sight. They went back in good order to the position from which they had started, collected and buried their dead, and cared for the wounded. The loss of the brigade was severe: 314 killed, wounded, and missing—44 percent of those engaged, of which the 53d Georgia

---

[66] Francis A. Walker, 13.
[67] Ibid., 117–18.

lost 30 percent; the 32d Virginia, 45 percent; the 10th Georgia, 57 percent; and the 15th Virginia, 58 percent. Three of the four regimental commanders were wounded, and many of the best line officers killed or wounded.

It is difficult to determine the part taken by Early in the pursuit through the West Woods. He made a very elaborate and graphic report of the battle (covering four and a half pages of the *Official Records*) in which he shows all his earlier movements on the field, his great anxiety for reinforcements, and the advance made upon the 125th Pennsylvania, and then spares but five lines to a statement of his change of front and the expulsion of Sedgwick from the woods. He says, "Just as I reformed my line, Semmes', Anderson's, and part of Barksdale's brigades, of McLaws' division [*sic*], came up, and the whole, including Grigsby's command, advanced upon this body of the enemy, driving it with great slaughter entirely from and beyond the woods, and leaving us in possession of my former position."[68] His "former position" was perpendicular to the Hagerstown Road and 130 yards south of the north edge of the middle body of the woods. Some officers of the brigade state their impression that a part of the line went clear out of the woods and halfway to the Miller stacks, but instantly fell back to the woods. There is no question as to Early's engagement on the flank of the 15th Massachusetts and his advance over the ground held by it and the 20th Massachusetts to the position held by him earlier in the day, but he appears to have followed Semmes's right and Barksdale's left over this ground and was not closely engaged in the front line. This also appears from the record of losses. Semmes, in the short time during which he was engaged, lost 44 percent of his men. Barksdale lost 33 percent, while Early, who had been much longer engaged, suffered a loss of but 16 percent—the greater part of which was in his engagement with the 125th Pennsylvania. Semmes makes no mention of any troops preceding him and reported to McLaws that he was not supported by and did not see Early's Brigade.[69]

Early, after acknowledging the assistance rendered him by Semmes, Anderson, and Barksdale, says, "Major-General Stuart, with the pieces of artillery under his charge, contributed largely to the repulse of the enemy, and pursued them for some distance with his artillery, and the Thirteenth Virginia Regiment, under the command of Captain [Frank V.] Winston."[70] Stuart says the enemy broke in confusion and were pursued for half a mile along the road. Evidently he did not see Early, but "recognized in this pursuit part of Barksdale's and part of Semmes' brigades; and I also got hold of one regiment of [Brigadier General Robert] Ransom [Jr.]'s brigade, which I posted in an advantageous position on the extreme left flank after the pursuit had been checked by the enemy's reserve artillery coming into action. Having informed General Jackson of what had transpired, I was directed by him to hold this advance position, and that he would send all the infantry he could get in order to follow up the success. I executed this order, keeping the cavalry well out to the left, and awaiting the arrival of re-enforcements."[71]

Other affairs were taking place in and about the West Woods while Sedgwick's men were being driven through and after they had been expelled from them. It was but a short time after the 3d South Carolina had taken cover in the hollow parallel to the Hagerstown Road when Colonel Nance saw Kershaw's Brigade, about 380 yards to his right, advance "most beautifully" through the woods and up the open slope beyond—the slope to the plateau opposite the Dunkard church—and he thought he saw Greene's division break. His regiment belonged to Kershaw's Brigade and had become detached from it in advancing to the attack on Sedgwick's flank, and he thought now to advance and join it in pursuit of a routed enemy. He crossed the Hagerstown Road, "passed to the summit of a hill in a freshly plowed field" sixty yards beyond the road, and to his surprise found Union troops under cover of the hill or ridge and opened fire upon them. (These troops were the Purnell Legion, two companies of the 124th Pennsylvania, and a few men of Howard's brigade, remaining near Woodruff's battery.) These opened fire upon the South Carolinians as soon as they made their appearance on the high ground. Woodruff turned his guns on them and they were driven back to the road, where they remained but a moment (as Woodruff's canister was too much for them) before falling back to the ravine from which they had advanced. Colonel Nance reports that "under the heavy fire of artillery and the press of fresh troops, our line on my right [Kershaw—EAC] that had just before advanced in such admirable style fell back so far that I retired to the road I had just crossed. There I halted and fired for a time, until a further retirement required me to fall back to the hollow in which I had before changed my front. There I remained until the

---

[68] Early to Pendleton, 971.

[69] "Just as I was moving forward, General Jackson come up [*sic*] and directed me to send a Brigade to support Early and I directed General Semmes on my left to go with his brigade[.] [H]e, General S. came to me after awhile (himself and courier only) and I asked him where was his brigade? He replied[,] [']You ordered me to support Earl[y]. I went to the left a short distance and marched in line to the top of the hill ... [The enemy] gave way and I pursued, until I found myself and command in close proximity to a force in my front much greater than mine, with other forces of the enemy to my left and right and as no troops were supporting me I had no other way of getting out of the "cul de sac." I was in haste to give the order to the brigade to run back regardless of formation and form again in rear of these woods.['] ... I asked him where General Earley's [*sic*] command was[.] [H]e said[,] 'I never saw it[.]'" McLaws to Heth, "Antietam Studies."—*EAC*

[70] Early to Pendleton, 971.

[71] Stuart to Chilton, 820.

movements of the enemy and the absence of proper supports determined me to retire to the woods." These were the woods surrounding the Dunkard church and south of it. Finding no friends in them, Nance led his regiment near where he had first formed line and took position behind a rail fence running parallel to the woods.[72]

About this time, Walker's Division came upon the field and entered the West Woods. This division, as we have seen, remained near Lee's headquarters until 3:00 a.m. of the seventeenth, when it moved to the extreme right to guard Snavely's and Myers's fords, where it remained until nearly or quite 9:00 a.m., when an order from Lee directed it to hasten to the left. It moved left in front, Ransom's Brigade leading, marching rapidly. The division left Sharpsburg to the right and, after passing the Reel house, Ransom formed line by inversion, bringing the 49th North Carolina on the right. The line was formed under severe fire and in the presence of troops that had been driven back. As soon as this was done, the brigade was pushed rapidly forward, marching in column of regiments northerly along and near the west edge of the West Woods, when orders were given to "form to the right and resist the enemy in the woods."[73] The 49th North Carolina, on the right, made a right wheel that brought it up to the fence bordering the woods. The 35th North Carolina, marching straight on, wheeled to the right as soon as it cleared the 49th, passing on either side of the Alfred Poffenberger barn, and the 25th North Carolina, passing by the left of the 35th, made the same movement. The three regiments pushed eastward up the wooded slope, upon which had stood the 15th Massachusetts and lines in rear of it, and halted in the east edge of the woods overlooking the open field and the Hagerstown Road. The 24th North Carolina, on the extreme left, did not wheel to the right when it had passed the 25th but kept straight on and, joining some of the Confederates in pursuit, became engaged, lost heavily, went clear out of the woods to the north, and was caught up by Stuart and put in position on the extreme left.

Ransom reports that upon reaching the woods he "immediately encountered the enemy in strong force, flushed with a temporary success. A tremendous fire was poured into them, and, without a halt, the woods was cleared and the crest next the enemy [sic] occupied … The ground was piled with the dead and wounded of both sides."[74] What enemy Ransom encountered and drove from the woods is a mystery to us. As a matter of fact, Ransom came up just as McLaws had driven Sedgwick north and then swept eastward into the woods after McLaws had passed northward, and McLaws left no Union troops behind him west of the Hagerstown Road save dead, wounded, and prisoners.

In the line formed just inside the east edge of the woods, the 49th North Carolina faced the southwest corner of the open field, its right in the southern body of the woods. On its left was the 35th North Carolina, and on the left of it was the 25th North Carolina. All were well protected by a ledge of rock that ran along their entire front. The brigade numbered 1,600 men, but as the 24th North Carolina had gone too far to the left, Ransom had about 1,250 men in line. After taking this position, Ransom "determined to charge across a field in our front and to a woods [the East Woods—EAC] beyond, which was held by the enemy, but he again approached, in force, to within 100 yards, when he was met by the same crushing fire which had driven him first from the position."[75] This force approaching Ransom and staying his projected advance was two regiments—the 2d Massachusetts and the 13th New Jersey—of the Twelfth Corps.

When Sedgwick was being driven from the West Woods, Sumner called upon the Twelfth Corps for help, the staff officer delivering the order to Williams saying, "General Sumner directs you to send to the front all of your command immediately available."[76] Greene's division was then engaged at the Dunkard church; Williams had but few men available. Crawford's brigade had become scattered and some of it was roughly handled, and, as Gordon held his brigade in a manner most convenient for a movement to the point indicated, he was ordered to advance at once. Gordon says he "was to move up toward the woods in front, to support the troops there. The order, most urgent and imperative, furnished the only information I possessed that our forces had again entered the woods in our front. I deemed it of the utmost importance that my command should move forward with the least possible delay. I therefore in person gave the order to the regiments nearest me, without the formation of my entire brigade, intending to bring up other regiments to support or continue the line, as circumstances might require."[77] The regiments nearest Gordon were the 13th New Jersey and the 2d Massachusetts, which were in the East Woods. A staff officer rode up to the first and directed its colonel to go forward through the

[72] James D. Nance to Charles R. Holmes, September 22, 1862, reprinted in *OR*, vol. 19, pt. 1, 869.

[73] See Robert Ransom Jr. to William A. Smith, September 22, 1862, reprinted in *OR*, vol. 19, pt. 1, 920. Carman appears to have once again corrupted a statement into direct speech. What Ransom says in his report is, "I received orders to form to the right and resist the enemy, who were in possession of a piece of woods."

[74] Ibid. The last sentence, however, does not appear anywhere in Ransom's report and has not been found in any extant correspondence from Ransom.

[75] Ibid.

[76] See Alpheus S. Williams to Joseph H. Taylor, September 29, 1862, vol. 19, pt. 1, 477. The quotation seems to have been manufactured by Carman from Williams's statement.

[77] George H. Gordon to Alpheus S. Williams, September 24, 1862, reprinted in *OR*, vol. 19, pt. 1, 495.

cornfield, across the Hagerstown Road, and into the West Woods, where he was to report to the first general officer met. He was informed that a part of the 124th Pennsylvania and other Union troops might be on the road near the D. R. Miller barn and was twice cautioned not to fire upon troops in front as they were "our own men." The caution was communicated to the company officers and by them to their men. For the first time in their soldier experience, the men loaded their muskets and, the command being given, the regiment advanced in line of battle through the cornfield, becoming somewhat disordered as it neared the road, but it was ordered over the fence into the road, where it was thought it could be re-formed.

The right of the regiment was the first to reach the fence. No men could be seen on the road, there were a few men off to the right and front, and nothing was visible in the immediate front—where there was ominous silence. Part of the regiment climbed the fence into the road and the rest were following when puffs of white smoke were seen at the rock ledge 150 yards in front and a hail of musketry went through the regiment, killing some and wounding many. It was a trying experience for a new regiment, the first time in action, and there was some confusion, but officers and men soon rallied. On the right, Captain Hugh C. Irish crossed the second fence and called upon his men to follow; the gallant Irish fell dead a few yards beyond the fence, and the colonel, recognizing that a mistake had been made, ordered the men to form behind the first fence and hold the ground. This was soon found impossible. The men were being shot by a foe they could not see, so perfectly did the ledge protect them. The men of the 13th New Jersey scarcely knew how to load their muskets and were doing little or no execution. To hold them longer under fire would be murder, and they were ordered back to the East Woods, retiring in good order (under the circumstances) and rallying on the spot from which they had advanced.[78]

The 2d Massachusetts advanced on the left of the 13th New Jersey (but not in close connection with it) and a short distance in rear. It had a similar experience. Colonel George L. Andrews reports, "The regiment advanced in line, the Thirteenth New Jersey on its right, to a lane, fenced on both sides, which offered a partial cover, and which was about 100 yards from the wood held by the enemy. Here the regiment received a very heavy fire from a large body of the enemy posted in the woods. Our fire was opened in return; but the enemy having greatly the advantage, both in numbers and position, his fire became very destructive. Being unsupported, it was impossible to advance and a useless sacrifice of life to keep my position. The regiment was accordingly marched back in perfect order to the position from which it had advanced."[79]

The historian of the 2d Massachusetts gives more particulars:

While the 3d Wisconsin and 27th Indiana, both of which had suffered severely, lay behind a slight ridge, and the 107th New York was some distance yet to the left,—the Second [Massachusetts] and the 13th New Jersey … moved up to the road, crossed the fence, and formed behind the second one. Captain [Charles F.] Morse, with company B, crossed the second fence. This was but a few rods above the church, at the open ground. Sumner's corps was not visible. When soldiers appeared in the woods opposite, there was doubt who they were. "Show your colors!" said Colonel Andrews to the color bearer. Color-Sergeant [Francis] Lundy waved his flag. It was greeted by a shower of bullets. Fire was then opened and continued. But, as the smoke lifted, the small force found itself alone. On the left, no troops were visible: on the right, the left of the next corps had given way. The enemy were sheltered in woods and behind rocks, and were in great force … The flagstaff was broken, the flag riddled, the socket shot away from the color-bearer's belt. The brave [Lieutenant Colonel Wilder] Dwight was mortally wounded. A fourth of the men had soon fallen, and they were rapidly dropping. Suffering much more than the enemy could, and unsupported, the order was given, and the regiment fell back to the woods behind, thus uncovering the batteries. Cothran's and Woodruff's guns opened beautifully, and the advancing line of the enemy hastily took shelter again.[80]

The conduct of the two regiments was thus commended by General Gordon: "The Second Massachusetts and Thirteenth New Jersey pushed forward, with great alacrity, sufficiently far to find that the troops to be supported had retired, that a large force of the enemy lay concealed in the woods, while a not inconsiderable number showed themselves in the open field beyond. These regiments were received with a galling fire, which they sustained and returned for a brief period, then fell back upon their supports. So strong was the enemy, that an addition of any force I could command would only have caused further sacrifice, without gain."[81]

---

[78] "I was … ordered by General Gordon to advance through the corn-field on the right across the road and down into a thick wood to support General Sumner's corps. Advancing through the corn-field up to the road, I was fired into by the enemy, who had driven General Sumner's corps from the wood. Seeing that my whole command would be annihilated if I advanced, and knowing that General Sumner's corps had been driven from the wood, I formed my line and prepared to dispute the advance of the foe. Their fire into my line was heavy, and after a stand of a few minutes I was obliged to retire." Carman to "Captain Smith," September 24, 1862, reprinted in *OR*, vol. 19, pt. 1, 501–2.—*EAC*

[79] George L. Andrews to Gordon, September 23, 1862, reprinted in *OR*, vol. 19, pt. 1, 500–501.

[80] Alonzo H. Quint, *The Record of the Second Massachusetts Infantry, 1861–65* (Boston: James P. Walker, 1867), 137–38.

[81] Gordon to Alpheus S. Williams, 495.

As the two regiments went back, the 3d Wisconsin and the 27th Indiana were met coming to their support. These, upon being informed of the condition of affairs, moved back, and the four regiments took position in the edge of the East Woods in support to batteries. When the 2d Massachusetts and the 13th New Jersey were ordered to the front, the 107th New York (then in the southern part of the East Woods) was directed to close in to the right. While executing the movement, a general officer rode up and ordered the regiment to move out into the field and support Cothran's battery. This fine regiment moved with steadiness to the rear of the battery just as the 2d Massachusetts and the 13th New Jersey were falling back and maintained its ground for some hours until relieved, although exposed to a front fire from the enemy and a fire over its head from batteries in rear.

Besides the batteries of Woodruff and Cothran, there were others in front of the East Woods: Monroe's four guns at the southwest corner of the woods, Captain Joseph F. Knap's Pennsylvania battery at the southeast corner of the cornfield, the New York battery of Captain John T. Bruen on Knap's right, and Reynolds's and Stewart's guns in the field north of the corn. Under the impression that the West Woods concealed a large body of the enemy on the point of advancing, these batteries opened a furious fire upon the woods. McLaws says, "There was an incessant storm of shot and shell, grape and canister, but the loss inflicted by the artillery was comparatively very small. Fortunately, the woods were on the side of a hill, the main slope of which was toward us, with numerous ledges of rocks along it."[82] J. G. Walker says his brave men "lay upon the ground, taking advantage of such undulations and shallow ravines as gave promise of partial shelter, while this fearful storm raged a few feet above their heads, tearing the trees asunder, lopping off huge branches, and filling the air with shrieks and explosions, realizing to the fullest the fearful sublimity of battle."[83]

Meanwhile, there were stirring scenes—hard and brilliant fighting around the Dunkard church, where Greene's division signally repulsed the right of McLaws's Division (supported by Colonel Van H. Manning's Brigade[84] of Walker's Division) and, advancing across the Hagerstown Road, secured a footing in the woods beyond and south of the church. It will be remembered that when Early, Barksdale, and G. T. Anderson drove the 125th Pennsylvania, 34th New York, and 72d Pennsylvania from the woods at the church, they were assisted by the 2d South Carolina, but this regiment did not change direction to the left and pursue Sedgwick's division, nor did it halt and then fall back as did Anderson. After it fired its effective volley at the 34th New York and again at the 72d Pennsylvania, a part of it passed north of the church and, halting near the road, fired at the retreating troops, but the greater part, passing south of the church, crossed the road, went by an abandoned caisson, and gained a prominent rock ledge 110 yards east of the church and close to the Smoketown Road, where it fired upon the retreating troops and upon Monroe's battery, which, says a Confederate officer, "we thought was getting ready to fight or run away."[85]

Exultant at success and believing the Union line broken and driven entirely from this part of the field, Captain George B. Cuthbert, who was in command of that wing of the regiment, gave the order to form to the right, intending to advance a little farther to the higher ground on his right. Just as the movement began, and while most of the men were still facing north, Greene's men—some of whom had now replenished ammunition—rose up from behind the slight rise of ground that had concealed them and opened a fire that sent the surprised South Carolinians to the rear, across the road, and about 150 yards beyond the church. Here, under cover of the ridge, they rallied and moved to the right, out of the line of fire that the Union guns began pouring into the woods around the church. This lateral movement brought the regiment to within a few yards of the south edge of the woods, where it awaited the rest of the brigade.

It was about this time that Carlton's (Georgia) Battery of three guns came forward. When McLaws came up with his division, this battery advanced along Hauser's Ridge and near the Hauser farm. Stuart rode up and asked for a battery, which he proposed to push into the West Woods to hold them until McLaws could get up and be deployed. McLaws objected, but Jackson ordered him to turn the battery over to Stuart. Carlton was ordered by Stuart to go through the woods to the Dunkard church and hold that position until Kershaw came up, even if he lost every man and gun of the battery. (This was apparently before the 125th Pennsylvania had shown itself). As he started to go, Carlton heard the sound of firing in the woods. He

---

[82] McLaws to "the Adjusted-General," 858.

[83] John G. Walker to Gilbert Moxley Sorrel, October 14, 1862, reprinted in OR, vol. 19, pt. 1, 916.

[84] In his original manuscript, Carman refers to this unit as "Manning's Brigade" throughout his narrative. As with Hood's/Wofford's Brigade (see p. 155 n. 24), his reason for choosing this designation over "Walker's Brigade" is unclear, as Manning served only as acting brigade commander. (John R. Cooke was named its permanent commander in the beginning of November 1862, and three weeks later Manning and the 3d Arkansas were transferred to the Texas Brigade. See Headquarters Army of Northern Virginia, Special Orders No. 234, November 6, 1862, reprinted in OR, vol. 19, pt. 2, 699; Headquarters Army of Northern Virginia, Special Orders No. 253, November 26, 1862, reprinted in OR, vol. 21, 1033.) The War Department tablets (no. 367 and 388) erected for this unit, under Carman's supervision, at Antietam National Battlefield refer to it as "Manning's Brigade" as well. In the OR, however, it is designated—by both the editors and Walker's contemporaries—as "Walker's Brigade," except in a single instance in one of Walker's own after-action reports. John G. Walker to Sorrel, 915.

[85] As of this writing, Carman's source for this quotation has not been identified.

went down the Hauser lane, passing the Alfred Poffenberger farm, and thence by the cart road through the woods. As his battery reached the brow of the ridge on which the 125th Pennsylvania had stood and from which it had just been driven, it came under fire of Union artillery. Eighteen horses were almost instantly killed and Carlton was obliged to put his guns in by hand, which was done near the northwest corner of the church. Stuart followed Carlton, and as the two stood near the church they saw Greene's infantry and Tompkins's battery on the high ground to the right and artillery in position and coming into position in the field to the left and front. The Union batteries in front opened on Carlton's Battery; Tompkins, after the repulse of Kershaw, turned two guns upon it. In less than twenty minutes every one of Carlton's guns was disabled, and he was ordered to the rear. More than half his horses had been killed, and infantry assisted to withdraw the guns. He went into position after the 125th Pennsylvania and the 34th New York had been withdrawn from the woods; he withdrew immediately after Kershaw's repulse.[86]

---

[86] In Carman's original manuscript, the sentence above concludes, "… he withdrew immediately after Kershaw's repulse, which we now note." This is followed by several lines of a new paragraph: "Soon after the 2d South Carolina had fallen back, it saw advancing through the field to the south a body of troops supposed to be its own brigade, and the colors of the regiment were taken to the fence, unfurled, and waved, to warn them that they were friends, and when they came up it was seen that they were the 8th South Carolina. This regiment had not closely followed the 2d. It passed to the right of the 2d's route and, under a severe fire of canister from Tompkins's guns, approached the road, and was so [page ends here]."

After many months of work on this project, the editor was saddened to discover that the concluding pages of "The West Woods and the Dunkard Church" were missing. In the spring of 2006 he conducted a hand search of the entirety of the Carman manuscript—page by page—in the hope that they had simply fallen out of order. When this search proved fruitless, he did the same to each of the remaining twenty-three containers (ten linear feet in total) of the Ezra A. Carman Papers stored at the Manuscript Division of the Library of Congress. Similar searches were made subsequently in collections of Carman's papers at the National Archives and the New York Public Library. The pages could not be located. Nor do they appear in the microfilm copy of the manuscript created by the Library of Congress in 1998. It may be that the pages were mislaid when the manuscript was reprocessed for filming or when the Carman collection was first arranged in the 1940s. It is equally possible, however, that the pages were already missing when the collection was first deposited at the library in 1912. For the administrative history of this accession, see Michael Spangler, "Ezra Ayers Carman: A Register of His Papers in the Library of Congress" (unpublished finding aid, Manuscript Division, Library of Congress, 2003).

Internal evidence in the original manuscript (most notably, the sequence of numbers in the upper left corners of a succession of pages) reveals that no more than four handwritten pages are missing from the end of this chapter. Given the pattern established by Carman in his treatment of specific phases of the fighting on the seventeenth, the majority of the missing text likely recapped the action from 9:00 a.m. to 11:00 a.m., and then presented the numbers of troops involved and the casualties sustained on each side. If so, much of the missing material likely reappears in the extant portions. (The number of troops engaged by the various units mentioned in this chapter can be found in Appendix J and their losses in Appendix L.)

17

The Sunken Road ("Bloody Lane")[1]

Antietam, September 17, 1862

While John Sedgwick's division was being driven through the West Woods, a sanguinary struggle began for possession of the sunken road—a struggle so bloody that since that day the road has been known as the Bloody Lane. This lane or farm road, starting from the Hagerstown Road about six hundred yards south of the Dunkard church, runs in two courses, easterly and southeasterly about one thousand yards, then turns south and pursues a zig-zag course to the Sharpsburg and Boonsboro Road, which it strikes midway between the crest of Cemetery Hill and the Antietam. By rains and usage the roadway had been worn down to an ordinary depth of two to three feet (in many places to a much greater depth), thus giving protection to troops lying in it. It was in the easterly stretch of this road that Colquitt's Brigade lay on the night of the sixteenth, with Ripley's Brigade six hundred yards in front, and in the southeasterly course on Colquitt's right was Garland's Brigade, with Rodes's and G. B. Anderson's on the right and rear (Rodes's on Garland's immediate right and at right angles facing the Antietam, with Anderson's further to the right, also facing the Antietam). These five brigades constituted D. H. Hill's Division. While Ripley, Colquitt, and Garland were engaged to the left and front with the First and Twelfth Corps, Rodes was ordered to move to their assistance, and Anderson was directed to close in to the left and soon thereafter to form line on Rodes's right. Rodes reports that he received his orders about 9:00 a.m. (it was probably about a half-hour earlier), and he had hardly begun the movement before it was evident that the three brigades of the division engaged in front had met with a reverse and that the best service he could render them and the field generally would be to form a line in rear and endeavor to rally them before attacking or being attacked. Hill seems to have held the same view, for at the moment Rodes came to this conclusion he received an order from Hill to halt and form line of battle in the sunken road.[2] Rodes had then passed the mouth of the Roulette lane and halted in the road, his right eighty yards west of the Roulette lane, his left about 150 yards from the Hagerstown Road. Rodes had five Alabama regiments: the 6th (Colonel John B. Gordon) was on the right, and to the left, in order named, were the 5th (Major Edwin L. Hobson), 3d (Colonel Cullen A. Battle), 12th (Captain Exton Tucker), and 26th (Colonel Edward A. O'Neal). The brigade numbered 850 officers and men.

In a short time small parties of Garland's and Colquitt's Brigades, falling back in some disorder, were rallied and formed on his left, Rodes assuming command of them. This brought his left to the Hagerstown Road. Hill says he made an effort to rally all of Garland's and Colquitt's men at this point. He was not successful (most of them passed on to Sharpsburg), but the 23d North Carolina came off the field, led by Lieutenant Colonel Robert D. Johnston, and took position in the road, and some stragglers joined it. There were some men of the 13th North Carolina among those, characterized by Hill as stragglers,[3] and Rodes says that a small portion of Colquitt's Brigade formed on his left.[4] This part of his line received additional strength by the arrival of Cobb's Brigade of McLaws's Division, which took position in the Hagerstown Road at the mouth of the sunken road.

Carter's (Virginia) Battery, which had been on Rodes's left, was sent to the rear when the brigade moved to the left, and when the new position was taken Patterson's (Georgia) Battery of three guns occupied a knoll immediately in front about 250 yards, at the southwest corner of the Mumma cornfield, and was engaged firing at Greene's division of the Twelfth Corps, then taking position opposite the Dunkard church. Patterson's guns were quickly driven off, as we have seen, by the fire of the 102d New York, and then moved to the left.

G. B. Anderson now came up and formed on Rodes's right. During the night of the sixteenth, Anderson lay at the south end of the sunken road and astride the Sharpsburg and Boonsboro Road, his skirmishers thrown to the crest of the ridge crossing the road, watching the Middle Bridge over the Antietam. Early in the morning there was a severe artillery duel between the batteries east of the Antietam and the Confederate batteries in Anderson's rear (on Cemetery Ridge) and on

---

[1] Each chapter of Carman's original manuscript is introduced by its own title page, with the title restated again at the top of the first page of the chapter's text. In the case of this chapter, the title page reads "The Sunken Road," but the title above the text reads "The Bloody Lane."

[2] Robert E. Rodes to James W. Ratchford, October 13, 1862, reprinted in *OR*, vol. 19, pt. 1, 1036–37.

[3] Daniel H. Hill to Robert H. Chilton, 1862 [no day or month given], reprinted in *OR*, vol. 19, pt. 1, 1023.

[4] Rodes to Ratchford, 1037.

his left, after which he moved up the ravine to his left, halted and formed line, then moved up the same ravine and into the Piper cornfield and again formed line facing the Antietam (as at the previous halt). Then, moving into the sunken road, he formed line on Rodes's right, in this order from left to right: the 2d North Carolina (Colonel Charles C. Tew) joined the right of the 6th Alabama, the second company from the right being directly opposite the entrance to the Roulette lane; on the right of the 2d was the 14th North Carolina (Colonel Risden T. Bennett), under good shelter from a frontal attack; on the right of the 14th was the 4th North Carolina (Captain William T. Marsh); and the 30th North Carolina (Colonel Francis M. Parker) was on the right of the 4th. The line, which was not a continuous one, was mostly under good cover. There were places where the road was crossed by rock ledges; at these points there was great exposure, and they were not occupied. Along the entire front of Anderson and Rodes was high ground overlooking the sunken road, broken only by a ravine through which ran the Roulette lane. Behind Anderson's entire line and extending to the left, to the center of Rodes's Brigade, was a field of dense corn. In many places in rear this ground was much higher than the sunken road and looked directly down into it. The road was a natural rifle-pit.

G. B. Anderson's Brigade numbered 1,174 officers and men and was of most excellent material. A southern writer has said of it:

> The fondness of this brigade for prayer meeting and Psalm singing united with an ever readiness to fight, reminds one of Cromwell's Ironsides. It fought well at Seven Pines when one of its regiments, having carried in six hundred and seventy-eight officers and men, lost fifty-four per cent. in killed and wounded. At Malvern Hill it met with great loss … To see these poor devils, many of them almost barefooted and all of them half starved, approach a field where a battle was raging was a pleasant sight. The crack of Napoleons, the roar of Howitzers and crash of musketry always excited and exhilarated them, and as they swung into action they seemed supremely happy.[5]

Immediately upon taking position G. B. Anderson and Colonel Tew walked to the top of the hill in front and saw French's division forming at the East Woods and, following the example of Rodes's men, who had preceded them, the North Carolinians began to pile rails in their front. Rodes says, "A short time after my brigade assumed its new position, and while the men were busy improving their position by piling rails along their front, the enemy deployed in our front in three beautiful lines, all vastly outstretching ours, and commenced to advance steadily."[6] Hill says the enemy "advanced in three parallel lines, with all the precision of a parade day."[7] This enemy was French's division of the Second Corps, composed of the brigades of Brigadier Generals Max Weber and Nathan Kimball and a third containing three regiments of new troops, under the command of Colonel Dwight Morris of the 14th Connecticut. The three brigades were strangers to each other and had been thrown together as a division but the day before. French put his division in motion about 7:40 a.m., crossed the Antietam after Sedgwick, and at first followed him closely, but gradually fell behind. The division marched with Weber on the left, Morris in the center, and Kimball on the right. French says, "When my left flank had cleared the ford a mile, the division faced to the left, forming three lines of battle adjacent to and contiguous with Sedgwick's, and immediately moved to the front."[8]

French is in error in the statement that he formed his lines "adjacent to and contiguous with Sedgwick's." If such were the case he must have come up before Sedgwick's advance; evidence is to the contrary and to the effect that, when Sedgwick advanced from the East Woods, French had not come up. Upon the authority of Captain Samuel S. Sumner, son and staff officer of General Sumner, the statement was made by George B. Davis that the "emergency … would not permit him [Sumner] to await the arrival of French's division" (so Sedgwick was pushed forward without him), that French had been given most positive orders to put and keep the head of his column abreast of Sedgwick's division, and that these orders were reiterated by several staff officers.[9] It is hard to question such authority, and it is passing strange how French formed his lines contiguous to Sedgwick and then failed to move with him if he had such imperative and reiterated orders. As a matter of fact Sedgwick's division had advanced from the East Woods before the advance of French's three lines entered them, and there is no evidence that upon entering the woods he was met by Sumner's orders to follow Sedgwick, although it is highly probable such orders were given on the march from the Antietam.

French entered the East Woods about 9:15 a.m., halted, and fronted to the left, looking southward. On his right front, 750 yards distant, he could see a Union battery in action, firing south, and behind it infantry in position, the left of the line

---

5 W. R. Bond, *Pickett or Pettigrew?: An Historical Essay*, 2d ed. (Scotland Neck, N.C.: W. L. L. Hall, 1888), 52–53.

6 Rodes to Ratchford, 1037.

7 Hill to Chilton, 1023.

8 William H. French to Joseph H. Taylor, September 20, 1862, reprinted in *OR*, vol. 19, pt. 1, 323.

9 George B. Davis, "The Antietam Campaign," in *Campaigns in Virginia, Maryland, and Pennsylvania*, vol. 3 of *Papers of the Military Historical* (Boston: Griffith-Stillings Press, 1903), 62.

resting on the Mumma lane. He could also see the Confederates in the sunken road. Francis A. Walker says French, "for want of precise direction," was permitted to diverge widely to the left.[10] In the absence of orders for "precise direction," or for a movement in any direction, he came to the quick and proper conclusion: to advance and form on the left of the troops he saw in position (which he supposed to be from Greene's division) and engage the Confederates in the sunken road, whose presence there threatened the left and rear of the Union line. To have done otherwise under the circumstances, unless under specific orders, would have been highly reprehensible.

It required less than fifteen minutes to close up the columns and properly dress them. Then the brigades were ordered forward, Weber's in advance, followed by Morris's and Kimball's. Weber's brigade was composed of the 1st Delaware, 4th New York, and 5th Maryland. These were old regiments, well drilled and disciplined, but had never been in battle. The brigade numbered 1,800 officers and men. The 1st Delaware was on the right, the 5th Maryland in center, and the 4th New York on the left.

Weber ordered the colors of the 5th Maryland to be carried directly to the Roulette house, the regiments on the right and left dressing on the 5th. The line, emerging from the East Woods, went forward under the fire of a Confederate battery on the ridge south of the Piper house and one west of the Hagerstown Road—a fire which was very annoying, several shells falling into the ranks of the 1st Delaware. The color bearer of the 5th Maryland, who had been designated to give direction, was a very heavily built German, over six feet in height and weighing nearly three hundred pounds, very deliberate in movement. Hence, by the right and left color bearers moving a little more briskly, the brigade, as it approached the Roulette place, assumed a crescentic formation. The 1st Delaware disappeared in the Mumma cornfield on the right of the Roulette house, the 4th New York was separated from the left of the 5th Maryland by the Roulette lane (which ran from the barn to the sunken road), and the 5th Maryland advanced through the Roulette grounds, passed to the right of the dwelling, and entered the apple orchard, where the left of the regiment came under fire of a small Confederate outpost in the lane, near the Clipp house. The regiment, with the 4th New York, drove back this advanced party, a few men being killed and wounded on either side.

While driving back this Confederate outpost and brushing some skirmishers from the fences in front, the right of Weber's line was struck by the 8th South Carolina of Kershaw's brigade, which had (as mentioned previously) charged Tompkins's Rhode Island battery on the plateau opposite the Dunkard church. In this charge the 8th South Carolina passed the other regiments of it brigade and, as it mounted the crest overlooking the Mumma cornfield, saw troops moving through and beyond it and promptly halted and opened fire. The 8th was a very small regiment of not over forty muskets, but so sudden, unexpected, and well delivered was its fire that (with the fire of the artillery) it caused momentary confusion. (French says it was a "sudden and terrible fire."[11]) The South Carolinians remained but two or three minutes upon Weber's flank and then fell back with their brigade, which had been bloodily repulsed. At this time the 1st Delaware was in the Mumma cornfield, its right close to the fence of the lane; the 5th Maryland was in the Roulette orchard, its right connecting with the 1st Delaware, its left on the lane; and the 4th New York was beyond the lane. Weber now ordered bayonets fixed and the brigade went forward on a run to the ridge overlooking the sunken road and from fifty to eighty yards from it. As it reached the crest of the ridge, Rodes's and G. B. Anderson's men poured in a cool, accurate fire that caused the entire line to recoil, but it quickly rallied and opened fire. On the right the 1st Delaware advanced so far that its left was but fifty yards from the sunken road, and the fire from the road and from a line on higher ground beyond it was so severe that, after a vain effort to advance (during which, says Colonel John W. Andrews, "the second line [Morris's—EAC], composed of new levies, instead of supporting our advance, fired into our rear"), the regiment—having lost over one-fourth its men and eight officers commanding companies killed or wounded—fell back through the 14th Connecticut and the Mumma cornfield to the grass field beyond.[12] The color guard were all killed or wounded and the colors left on the field with Lieutenant Colonel Oliver Hopkinson, severely wounded, who afterwards brought them off. After the regiment had rallied in the field just beyond the corn, Major Thomas A. Smythe, Captain James Rickards, and Lieutenants James P. Postles, Charles B. Tanner, and Joseph C. Nichols, with about seventy-five to ninety men, went down the Mumma lane as far as the southwest corner of the cornfield, where, under shelter of rock ledges and the fencing, they remained, skirmishing until about noon. Here Captain Rickards was killed, and from this advantageous position they repulsed several attempted advances of the enemy upon Tompkins's battery, which was close to their right and rear.

On the left of the 1st Delaware, the 5th Maryland passed over the top of the ridge and was met by a murderous fire from the right of Rodes's Brigade and the 2d North Carolina of G. B. Anderson's—a fire so deadly that over one-fourth of the

---

[10] Francis A. Walker, *History of the Second Army Corps in the Army of the Potomac* (New York: Charles Scribner's Sons, 1887), 101. In his original manuscript, Carman misquotes this as "proper direction" here and in the next sentence.

[11] French to Taylor, 323–24.

[12] John W. Andrews to "Captain Burleigh," September 18, 1862, reprinted in *OR*, vol. 19, pt. 1, 337.

regiment was struck down instantly—but the survivors lay down and returned the fire. In the charge the colors were carried about thirty feet to the front and the men crawled forward and dressed on them, all the time maintaining a steady fire upon the enemy in the road at the foot of the hill about fifty yards distant. The 4th New York advanced on the left of the Roulette lane and, as it reached the crest of the hill overlooking G. B. Anderson's men in the sunken road about fifty yards distant, was met by a volley that laid low over 150 men, and the regiment recoiled and lay down under cover of the crest. Exultant at their success portions of G. B. Anderson's Brigade rushed forward, but were quickly driven back. In this short contest of not over five minutes, Weber lost one-fourth of his brigade.

Rodes says the Union line came to the crest of the hill overlooking his position, and for five minutes bravely stood a telling fire at about eighty yards delivered by his whole brigade.[13] Colonel Bennett of the 14th North Carolina, in whose immediate front the 4th New York advanced, says, "Their advance was beautiful in the extreme, and great regularity marked their column … [and] this precision of movement was preserved by the lines until a space not exceeding 50 yards separated the combatants. Then it was that a well-directed fire sent them in disorder some 50 paces rearward."[14]

Morris's brigade of three new regiments followed Weber. When it advanced out of the woods, Weber's brigade was about three hundred yards ahead of it. The 14th Connecticut, on the right, passed through the Mumma orchard, nine companies passed to the right of the Roulette house and one to the left, and the entire regiment moved into the Mumma cornfield, the right reaching to the Mumma lane and the left close to the east edge of the cornfield. The 130th Pennsylvania, on the immediate left of the 14th Connecticut, advanced through the small Roulette cornfield, passed between the house and barn, and then moved through the Roulette orchard with its left on the lane. The 108th New York moved on the left of the lane, its right resting on it. The advance was made under severe artillery and musketry fire, the latter being directed at Weber, in advance, who was being followed at a distance not exceeding two hundred yards. When the 14th Connecticut reached the south fence of the cornfield it came under the withering fire that was being poured upon the 1st Delaware in its front, but the men climbed the fence and with much difficulty advanced from fifty to sixty-five yards over the grass field, when, unable to advance further, they fell back to the cornfield. The 130th Pennsylvania advanced in line on the left of the 14th Connecticut. A part of it halted behind a stone fence that was a continuation of the south fence of the Mumma cornfield, some of the men advanced a few yards further, and many reached the line held by the 5th Maryland and remained upon it until relieved by the advance of Kimball's brigade. On the left of the Roulette lane the 108th New York moved up to the line held by the 4th New York, its left extending beyond it, and received such a severe fire from G. B. Anderson's North Carolinians that it recoiled in disorder and lay down upon the northern slope of the ridge. Again portions of Anderson's command advanced beyond the sunken road, and were quickly driven back.

It was about this time that Rodes, by Longstreet's direction, ordered an advance. A part of his line went forward and immediately came under such intense fire that it was checked. Tompkins's guns, from their fine position on the right and rear of the 14th Connecticut, opened fire with shell and case shot and the line fell back in some disorder and was with difficulty rallied in the sunken road. Rodes says:

> Receiving an order from General Longstreet to do so, I endeavored to charge them with my brigade and that portion of Colquitt's which was on my immediate left. The charge failed, mainly because the Sixth Alabama Regiment, not hearing the command, did not move forward with the others, and because Colquitt's men did not advance far enough. That part of the brigade which moved forward found themselves in an exposed position, and, being outnumbered and unsustained, fell back before I could, by personal effort, which was duly made, get the Sixth Alabama to move. Hastening back to the left, I arrived just in time to prevent the men from falling back to the rear of the road we had just occupied.[15]

Rodes lost quite severely in this effort, and among the killed was Captain Tucker, commanding the 12th Alabama.

Cobb's Brigade, on Rodes's left, took part in this movement. It will be remembered that when McLaws prepared for his attack upon Sedgwick, Cobb's Brigade moved too far to the right and was brought up on the left of Rodes, where it was covered from the Union musketry by a hill in front but suffered from the heavy shelling by the batteries beyond the Antietam. For an hour the brigade was inactive, then Longstreet ordered it forward with Rodes, and the men, "eager to meet the foe upon a more equal footing, gallantly pressed forward with a cheer, the top of the hill gained amid a galling and destructive shower of balls."[16] There it remained until the brigade's acting commander, Colonel Sanders, seeing that Rodes had fallen back and left him without support, fell back to the cover of the fence from which he had charged.

---

[13] Rodes to Ratchford, 1037.

[14] Risden T. Bennett to Ratchford, December 6, 1862, reprinted in OR, vol. 19, pt. 1, 1047.

[15] Rodes to Ratchford, 1037.

[16] William MacRae to Howell Cobb, September 23, 1862, reprinted in OR, vol. 19, pt. 1, 872

As Rodes was rallying the left of his brigade in the sunken road, a part of the 6th Alabama, under cover of the smoke, made a rush for the colors of the 5th Maryland, and the colors and that part of the line near them fell back about twenty yards. The Marylanders rallied in turn and the Alabama men were driven back to the road, the colors being advanced to their original position. In this affair Major Leopold Blumenberg, commanding the 5th Maryland, was severely wounded.

The two brigades of Weber and Morris had made spirited efforts to drive the enemy but were brought to a stand, had lost heavily, and—being new troops—had become confused and much broken. Many of the men had gone to the rear, but enough of them remained on the firing line to resist the enemy, though without sufficient aggressive force to advance. While the two brigades were thus engaged with Rodes and G. B. Anderson, Captain Sumner of the Second Corps staff rode up to French with an order from General Sumner to push on and make a diversion in favor of Sedgwick, who was being severely handled by McLaws. This order came when Kimball, following Morris from the East Woods, had passed the Roulette buildings and halted for alignment 350 yards in rear of Weber and Morris—the right wing (the 14th Indiana and the 8th Ohio) midway in the Roulette apple orchard, the left wing (the 132d Pennsylvania and the 7th West Virginia) beyond the Roulette lane. The 8th Ohio rested its left on the lane; on its right was the 14th Indiana. The 132d Pennsylvania was a new regiment; the others were veterans and had seen much service in western Virginia and on the Peninsula. Kimball was a stiff and tenacious fighter. He had thwarted Lee's efforts to force the Union position at Cheat Mountain in September 1861 and had defeated Jackson at Kernstown on March 23, 1862.

The brigade had not been long halted when Sumner's order to press the enemy was received, and Kimball was directed to pass Weber and Morris, carry the crest of the ridge, and drive the enemy from the sunken road with the bayonet. At this time the battle was raging 350 yards in front, and some officers and men of Kimball's brigade were killed and wounded while yet in the orchard. The men were lying down. Kimball called them to attention and as he went along the ranks said, "Boys, we are going in now to lick the rebels, and we will stay with them all day if necessary."[17] Knapsacks were taken off and piled under the apple trees, bayonets were fixed, and the entire line, starting at a double-quick, moved steadily and magnificently forward over the open plain under a heavy fire of shell and in the face of a sheet of musketry that dropped men here and there. The right wing swept past the left of the 14th Connecticut and over that part of the 130th Pennsylvania on its left. As it approached the 5th Maryland and some of the 130th Pennsylvania in front they cried, "Get to the rear, you fellows!"[18] and with a roar and a blaze passed over the ridge to receive such a staggering fire from artillery on the right and the musketry of Rodes and G. B. Anderson in front that it recoiled to the line held by the 5th Maryland. The right wing of the 14th Indiana was closed in to the left under cover of the ridge to avoid the artillery fire to which it was exposed, and in this position both the 14th Indiana and the 8th Ohio opened a steady fire that was continued until the Confederates were driven from the road or surrendered. Many of the 5th Maryland remained and fought with them. Kimball says, "Directly on my front, in a narrow road running parallel with my line, and, being washed by water, forming a natural rifle-pit between my line and a large corn-field, I found the enemy in great force, as also in the corn-field in rear of the ditch. As my line advanced to the crest of the hill, a murderous fire was opened upon it from the entire force in front. My advance farther was checked."[19]

As soon as Kimball's men recovered from the staggering blow under which they had recoiled, the color bearers of the 14th Indiana and the 8th Ohio crawled along the ground and planted their colors defiantly on the very crest of the ridge, the full color guard rallying around them. On these the men formed and, lying face to the ground, began their work, firing at the heads and shoulders of such of the enemy as exposed themselves in the sunken road and at others who were firing from the cornfield beyond. In this manner, says Kimball, "for three hours and thirty minutes the battle raged incessantly, without either party giving way."[20] Kimball overestimated the time; he was in action a little over two hours.

With the advent of Kimball and his firm hold on the ridge, the 5th Maryland, under direction of its company officers, began to withdraw by squads of a half dozen or more. There was some confusion in the withdrawal, and in endeavoring to check it and get his brigade in order Weber was wounded and lost his leg. Some men of the 5th Maryland remained on Kimball's line but the greater part of them were rallied at the Clipp house and near the Roulette barn, where they were joined by the 4th New York. A part of the 130 Pennsylvania fell back but the greater part remained in rear of the 8th Ohio, and the 14th Connecticut maintained its position in the south part of the Mumma cornfield, its left sixty-five yards in rear of the 14th Indiana. On the right of the 14th Connecticut, on high ground, well protected by the fences of the Mumma lane and the outcropping rocks, was the detachment of the 1st Delaware, and 280 yards to the right and rear was Tompkins's

---

[17] As of this writing, Carman's source for this quotation had not been identified.

[18] Ibid.

[19] Nathan Kimball to French, September 18, 1862, reprinted in *OR*, vol. 19, pt. 1, 327.

[20] Ibid.

battery, which poured a constant fire of shell and case shot upon the Confederates in the sunken road and in the cornfield beyond it.

In Kimball's advance the left company of the 8th Ohio was crowded beyond the Roulette lane and, with the 132d Pennsylvania and the 7th West Virginia, marched in good line up the hill and passed the 108th New York (which was retreating in some disorder). As these all mounted the crest they came under fire of Confederate artillery on Cemetery Ridge and received the fire of G. B. Anderson's men, who were waiting for them with guns resting on the rails in their front. This fire was terrific and deadly. Colonel Richard A. Oakford, commanding the 132d Pennsylvania, was killed, many officers and men of the two regiments and the company of the 8th Ohio were struck down, the advance was checked, and the line fell back under cover of the crest and lay down. When the company of the 8th Ohio reached the crest there were some men of the 4th New York still holding ground; these were relieved and joined their comrades near the Clipp house. The veteran Ohioans, crawling forward and getting such shelter as the ground afforded, opened a very cool and effective enfilading fire upon the 2d North Carolina and the right wing of the 6th Alabama, who were in that part of the sunken road west of the Roulette lane and in the immediate front of the right wing of the brigade.

The Roulette lane—dividing the wings of Kimball's brigade—requires a brief description. From the Hagerstown Road the sunken road runs easterly for 550 yards, then nearly turns southeast 450 yards to where it makes an angle and runs nearly south. For the first hundred yards the road is level, then rises to pass over a rock ledge, descends but little and again rises to another rock ledge, where it turns southeast. From this last rock ledge (the angle in the road) it descends eighty yards to the mouth of the Roulette lane, the descent in the eighty yards being twenty feet. From the mouth of the lane the road begins to ascend, and at 150 yards reaches the plateau upon which it runs to its southerly course. It will thus be seen that the mouth of the Roulette lane is in a depression, which is the beginning of a ravine or cleft that, running northerly, bisects the ridge or high ground overlooking the sunken road. In this ravine runs the narrow Roulette lane, the ground rising abruptly thirty to forty feet on either side of it.

The conformation of the ground determined the position of the troops. Kimball's right wing was west of the Roulette lane on a hill sloping south of the sunken road and east to the lane. Its right, the 14th Indiana, was about 80 yards from the angle of the sunken road in front; its left, the 8th Ohio, rested on the Roulette lane 105 yards from its mouth. This position gave a direct fire to the front upon the right of Rodes's Brigade and the 2d North Carolina of G. B. Anderson's, and an enfilading fire upon the left of the 14th North Carolina east of the mouth of the lane, from which it suffered terribly. Immediately east of the lane the ridge was higher, sloping both west and south, and on a grassy knoll one hundred yards from the mouth of the lane and overlooking it was the company of the 8th Ohio. From this point the crest of the ridge trends southeast, gradually nearing the sunken road, and on it, to the rear and left of the Ohio company, were the 132d Pennsylvania and the 7th West Virginia, the left of the latter about one hundred yards from the road.

Rodes and G. B. Anderson (including men from Colquitt's and Garland's Brigades who had rallied on the extreme left) had about 2,400 men. With these they had withstood the attack of French's 5,700 men without yielding a foot of ground. Being well protected (save near the Roulette lane), they had not suffered greatly but had inflicted great loss.

While all this was transpiring on his front, French was with Tompkins's guns on the right of his division. After the repulse of Sedgwick, Tompkins was ordered by Sumner to hold his position until properly relieved and not to retire on any account, even to the risk of losing his guns. Soon after this French came up and expressed some solicitation at the gap between his right and the left of Greene, a gap covered only by the battery and two small regiments of Greene. While in conversation, Major John S. Saunders's artillery battalion went into position in front, and soon thereafter R. H. Anderson's Division was seen coming over the fields toward the Hagerstown Road with the evident intention to charge the battery and attack French's right. Tompkins opened his guns upon Saunders's artillery and R. H. Anderson's infantry, and French impressed upon him the great necessity of holding his position, remarking that if the guns went his division would go too.

There were now several batteries of Confederate artillery on the high ground between the Reel farm and the Hagerstown Road, which had been gathered there under Lee's order to form a nucleus for a new line. Among them was Branch's Battery of Walker's Division, to which Jackson rode up and asked why it was not engaged. "No orders and no supports," was the reply. "Go in at once," was the curt rejoinder. "You artillery men are too much afraid of losing your guns."[21] The battery and another advanced but were quickly driven back with some loss.

Anderson's Division followed McLaws in crossing the Potomac and halted near Lee's headquarters. It had six brigades of infantry and an artillery battalion of four batteries. The brigades were those of Wright, Wilcox (commanded by Colonel

---

[21] Address of Bradley T. Johnson, contained in "Reunion of the Virginia Division Army Northern Virginia Association," in *Southern Historical Society Papers* 12 (1884): 531.

Alfred Cumming), Featherston (commanded by Colonel Carnot Posey), Pryor, Mahone (commanded by Lieutenant Colonel William A. Parham), and Armistead. Mahone's Brigade had been so badly broken at Crampton's Gap that it had but eighty-two men at Sharpsburg, was consolidated into a regiment, and acted with Pryor's Brigade. Armistead's Brigade was detached and ordered to the support of McLaws, on the left.

Saunders's artillery battalion was composed of Captain Frank Huger's (Virginia) Battery of four guns; the Portsmouth (Virginia) Artillery, four guns, commanded by Captain Cary F. Grimes; Captain Marcellus N. Moorman's (Virginia) Battery, four guns; and the Donaldsonville (Louisiana) Artillery, commanded by Captain Victor Maurin. (In the absence of Major Saunders, the battalion was under the command of Captain Grimes.) The battalion moved through Sharpsburg and up the Hagerstown Road and was put in position on the ridge running northwest from the Piper barn. Grimes, leading his own battery, went into position on the right of the road and about sixty yards from it, Moorman on Grimes's right and fifty yards west of the barn, and Huger and Maurin west of the road. This position was taken soon after Kimball had crowned the ridge overlooking the sunken road, and the four batteries opened fire upon him—a fire that was very effective upon the right of the 14th Indiana but of no particular effect upon other parts of his line. Tompkins turned four guns upon them, the 14th Indiana poured in a musketry fire at from six hundred to seven hundred yards, the long-range guns beyond the Antietam enfiladed them, and they were partially silenced in less than twenty minutes. Meanwhile, R. H. Anderson's infantry came up.

It was near 10:00 a.m. when Anderson's Division was ordered forward. It passed to the left of Sharpsburg and halted to pile knapsacks. The division then marched, left in front, Pryor's Brigade in advance, northeasterly across the open fields under a wicked and demoralizing fire of Tompkins's guns and reached the Hagerstown Road about one hundred yards south of the Piper lane. Pryor's Brigade marched up the road to the lane and then down the lane until it passed the Piper barn, when it filed to the left and went up the hill on the left of the orchard and was halted by a staff officer. Wilcox's Brigade followed Pryor's as far as the Hagerstown Road, which it crossed, and bearing to the right moved nearly to the crest of Cemetery Ridge (south of the Piper house), then halted and threw out skirmishers in the direction of the Antietam. Featherston's Brigade followed Wilcox's and formed near it on Cemetery Ridge.

Wright's Brigade did not follow Wilcox's and Featherston's to Cemetery Ridge. Instead, bearing to the left under fire from Tompkins's guns, it crossed the stone fences of the Hagerstown Road north of the Piper lane, passed the barn and the rear of Pryor's Brigade, and, facing to the left, was in rear of the Piper apple orchard. The orchard was enclosed by a close and strong oak picket fence, and in tearing it down the brigade suffered greatly from a crossfire of artillery—Tompkins in front and the guns beyond the Antietam on the flank. The 3d Georgia was on the right and, in order named, on its left were the 48th Georgia, 44th Alabama, and 22d Georgia.

As soon as the fence was torn down sufficiently to admit passage in place, the brigade moved through the orchard obliquely toward the northeast corner of the cornfield, all the time under artillery fire, and when it reached the high ground in the cornfield came under musketry fire and men fell by the score. While going through the orchard Wright's horse was torn in pieces by a shell and the general thrown to the ground. Disengaging himself from the fallen horse he led his brigade through the cornfield, and as he approached the sunken road his left came up in rear of the right wing of the 30th North Carolina, receiving such a severe and unexpected fire as it emerged from the corn that it was driven back, but soon rallied and took ground to the right. Wright was shot down and Colonel Robert H. Jones of the 22d Georgia (who succeeded to the command) was wounded and disabled by a musket ball that went through his breast. The brigade, reduced to about 250 men, reached the sunken road on G. B. Anderson's right and lay down in it, and Colonel William Gibson of the 48th Georgia assumed command.

In front and to the left, not over one hundred yards distant, was the 7th West Virginia, which now poured in its fire and began to gain ground to its left. There was some protection in the road from musketry fire; the brigade had passed out of the line of fire of Tompkins's guns but was subjected to a terrible enfilade fire of the guns beyond the Antietam that disheartened the officers and men, who were encouraged to hold on a little longer, as Pryor would soon join on the right and an advance be made. But Pryor did not come and there was an increasing fire in front. By the direction of Wright (who was still lying on the ground, twice wounded and unable to rise), Colonel Gibson ordered a charge upon the extended and exposed flank of the 7th West Virginia. The left and center of the brigade made little if any advance, but the 3d Georgia on the extreme right, led by Lieutenant Colonel Reuben B. Nisbet,[22] leaped out of the road and, making a slight left wheel, charged the 7th West Virginia, which changed front by refusing its left and advancing its right, and after a short but severe

---

[22] In his original manuscript, Carman first wrote "Colonel Nisbet," then added his given initials with a caret insertion. Nisbet, however, retired from duty at the rank of lieutenant colonel. See *Journal of the Senate of the Second Congress of the Confederate States of America*, vol. 4 of *Journal of the Congress of the Confederate States of America, 1861–1865*, 58th Cong., 2d sess., 1904, S. Doc. 234, serial 4613, 397.

fight drove the Georgians back to the road, leaving their colonel, badly wounded, on the field, to be taken prisoner a little later.[23]

Wright's Brigade had suffered greatly. Its commander had been badly wounded and disabled, Lieutenant Colonel Charles A. Derby (commanding the 44th Alabama) killed, Jones and Nisbet wounded, and a long list of line subordinate officers killed or wounded. One regiment had only one officer, and many companies of the brigade were in command of sergeants or corporals, but all remained in the road and kept up a warm fire.

It was about this time that G. B. Anderson—informed that a column of the enemy was approaching his right, threatening to envelop it—rode to the rear to report to Hill. Upon returning he was wounded at the south edge of the corn, near the northeast corner of the orchard, and sent his courier to Colonel Parker of the 30th North Carolina with instructions that adjutant Frederick Phillips be sent to Colonel Tew (commanding the 2d North Carolina) and inform him that he was in command of the brigade. Philips made his way under severe fire down the line to the left of the 14th North Carolina, and from that point word was passed along the line of the 2d North Carolina. Tew, who was lying down with his men, rose from the ground, acknowledged the receipt of the message by raising his cap, and was instantly killed. The command of the brigade fell to Colonel Bennett of the 14th North Carolina, who reports that at this time the brigade "appeared perfectly self-possessed" and that soon thereafter word came for the command to keep a lookout on the extreme right.[24] This was when Richardson's division was forming for attack.

Israel B. Richardson's division was composed of three brigades, commanded by Brigadier General John C. Caldwell, Brigadier General Thomas F. Meagher, and Colonel John R. Brooke of the 53d Pennsylvania. On the night of the sixteenth it was in position at the east foot of the bluff bordering the Antietam, its left on the Sharpsburg and Boonsboro Road. It received orders at 7:40 a.m. to march when relieved by Morell's division of the Fifth Corps, and it was not until 9:00 a.m. that Morell arrived from his bivouac on the suburbs of Keedysville, a mile distant. It was bad enough that Sumner did not receive his orders to march before 7:30 a.m.; it was worse that this fine division was delayed an hour and a half later, and there was no good reason for it. The events already narrated in this chapter are good proof that had Richardson closely followed French and joined in the advance upon the sunken road, Hill's men would have been driven from it before the arrival of Anderson's Division.

The division was put in motion at 9:00 a.m., went back a short distance on the road to Keedysville, filed to the left, descended the hill to the fords by which Sedgwick had crossed (which it went over about 9:30 a.m.), and made a brief halt to permit the men to wring the water from their socks. The march was resumed in a direction nearly parallel to the creek and, passing the Neikirk house, the division halted in a ravine through which ran a spring branch to the Antietam. Here the men piled knapsacks and blankets and the lines were then formed in a cornfield on the northeastern slope of high ground that overlooked the Roulette house, about 450 yards east of it and 700 yards northeast of the sunken road. Meagher's brigade, on the right, deployed from column into line of battle on the northeastern edge of the cornfield, marched through it for two hundred yards, and came to its southwestern edge under a scattering fire that clipped the corn and wounded a few men. From right to left the brigade was thus formed: the 69th New York, 29th Massachusetts, and 63d and 88th New York. Caldwell's brigade advanced through the same cornfield on Meagher's left, and Brooke's brigade followed in second line. The infantry strength of the division was 4,029 officers and men and it was not accompanied by its artillery. This had preceded it the evening before.

Owing to the smallness of the pioneer corps, which had become much reduced by service on the Peninsula, there was much embarrassment and delay in crossing the fence, during which many officers and men were killed or wounded. The same trouble occurred in passing a second fence, but here volunteers gave assistance, and the line went forward in fine order, ascended the rising ground overlooking the sunken road and advanced to within seventy-five to one hundred yards of it, then received a murderous fire from the Confederate line in the road and the artillery beyond. Meagher says, "On coming into this close and fatal contact with the enemy, the officers and men of the brigade waved their swords and hats and gave the heartiest cheers for their general, George B. McClellan, and the Army of the Potomac. Never were men in higher spirits. Never did men with such alacrity and generosity of heart press forward and encounter the perils of the battle-field."[25]

Meagher's brigade was known in the army and throughout the country as the Irish Brigade, and was even so designated in orders and reports of commanding officers. As a matter of fact the brigade at Antietam, and for months before and after that campaign, was not strictly an Irish brigade. Three regiments were composed mainly of Irishmen and men of Irish

---

[23] Kimball reports, "The enemy, having been re-enforced, made an attempt to turn my left flank by throwing three regiments forward entirely to the left of my line, which I met and repulsed, with loss, by extending my left wing, Seventh [West] Virginia and One hundred and thirty-second Pennsylvania, in that direction." Kimball to French, 327.—*EAC*

[24] Bennett to Ratchford, 1048.

[25] Thomas F. Meagher to John Hancock, September 30, 1862, reprinted in *OR*, vol. 19, pt. 1, 294.

parentage. These regiments, recruited in New York, marched and fought under the green flag of Ireland. The 29th Massachusetts, constituting one-fourth of the brigade, was not an Irish regiment. On the contrary, it was intensely American in its makeup. All its field officers were lineal descendants of the early colonists. With scarcely an exception, the line officers were thoroughbred Americans (nearly all of Revolutionary stock), and so with the men—mainly genuine Americans. It is doubtful if there was a regiment from Massachusetts with a larger percentage of Americans in its ranks. Every regiment of the brigade was superb, and the 29th Massachusetts prides itself upon its service in it, "and at no time during its four years war experience" writes a prominent officer of that regiment, "was fairer or better treatment accorded the regiment, from a gentlemanly and soldierly standpoint than that received while associated with the Irishmen of Meagher's Brigade."[26]

Notwithstanding the terrible punishment they had received from the first volley, these brave Irishmen and men of Massachusetts stood steadily and bravely to their work. Meagher's orders were that after the first and second volleys (delivered in line of battle by the brigade) it should charge with fixed bayonets upon the enemy. Relying upon the impetuosity and recklessness of Irish soldiers in a charge, he felt confident that before such a charge the enemy would give way and be dispersed. Meagher says:

Advancing on the right and left obliquely from the center, the brigade poured in an effective and powerful fire upon the column, which it was their special duty to dislodge. Despite a fire of musketry, which literally cut lanes through our approaching line, the brigade advanced under my personal command within 30 [60—EAC] paces of the enemy, and at this point, Lieut. Col. James Kelly having been shot through the face and Capt. Felix Duffy having fallen dead in front of his command, the regiment [69th New York] halted. At the same time Lieutenant-Colonel [Henry] Fowler and Maj. Richard Bentley, of the Sixty-third, on the left of our line, having been seriously wounded and compelled to retire to the rear, the charge of bayonets I had ordered on the left was arrested, and thus the brigade, instead of advancing and dispersing the column with the bayonet, stood and delivered its fire, persistently and effectually maintaining every inch of the ground they occupied.[27]

Meagher was close to the 69th New York, on the right of his brigade. This regiment in its advance marched over some troops lying on the ground under shelter of the brow of the hill, and when it ascended the ridge its right was eighty yards from the sunken road (its left much nearer), and the whole line on top of the ridge much exposed. Meagher permitted this regiment to fire five or six volleys, when it was ordered to stop firing and charge, and a like order was sent to the 63d and 88th New York on the left. After an advance of about thirty yards the order to charge was countermanded, and the 69th fell back to its first position and resumed firing. The left of the line was gradually advanced to within one hundred yards of the road, the right standing fast.

The 63d and 88th New York were drawn up beyond a slight depression in the ridge that was held by the 29th Massachusetts (of which we shall treat later). The 63d was on the right and received several deadly volleys without replying, by which it was greatly thinned. The charge it was ordered to make by Meagher failed owing to its heavy losses the first few minutes. The men began firing with round ball and buck shot, the brigade being armed with smoothbores, and an officer states that "it was give and take until ammunition ran out."[28] The nature and severity of the contest is graphically and touchingly told in the report of Colonel Fowler of the 63d:

It is now a solace to my mind, while suffering from my wound, to testify how gallantly and promptly each officer in his place and each company moved forward and delivered their fire in the face of the most destructive storm of leaden hail, that in an instant killed or wounded every officer but one and more than one-half the rank and file of the right wing. For a moment they staggered, but the scattered few quickly rallied upon the left, closing on the colors, where they nobly fought, bled, and died, protecting their own loved banner and their country's flag, until the brigade was relieved.

In the early part of the action Capt. P[atrick] J. Condon and Lieut. Thomas W. Cartwright, both of Company G, fell wounded while gallantly cheering on their men bravely at their post, as also Capt. M[ichael] O'Sullivan, Company F, while Lieut. P[atrick] W. Lydon, commanding Company D, Lieut. Cadwalader Smith, Company C, and Lieutenant [Henry] McConnell, of Company K, bravely rallying the gallant remaining few, fell pierced by bullets, instantly fatal.

As the right wing had fallen before me, I hastened to the left, where I found the major ([Richard C.] Bentley) close upon the line, and Capt. Joseph O'Neill, Company A, whose company had all fallen around him on the right, now assisting the major on the left. Here also was the stalwart Lieutenant [Joseph] Gleason, Company H, raising and

---

[26] As of this writing, Carman's source for this quotation has not been identified.
[27] Meagher to Hancock, 294–95.
[28] As of this writing, Carman's source for this quotation has not been identified.

supporting the repeatedly falling colors, with Lieut. John Sullivan commanding and pushing forward Company K; and here lay the slender form of Captain [John] Kavanagh, Company I, cold in death; the brave and enthusiastic Lieut. R[ichard] P. Moore, Company E, passing from right to left, boldly urging his men to stand firm, and the gallant Lieut. George Lynch, second lieutenant Company G, bravely pressing on until he too fell, mortally wounded. The killed died as brave men, sword in hand, and amid the thickest of the fight. Major Bentley was now wounded, and retired to have his wound dressed. Our number now left was less than 50 men; our colors, although in ribbons, and staff shot through, were still there, sustained at a bloody sacrifice, 16 men having fallen while carrying them. I now received a severe wound, and was compelled to retire just as the lines of the enemy were breaking.[29]

On the left of the 63d was the 88th New York. As it came into position it received the same deadly fire as had the 63d and returned it. During the engagement an aide rode up and ordered it to charge with the 63d and take the enemy's colors if possible. Lieutenant Colonel Patrick Kelly at once gave the order and the 88th advanced about twenty-five or thirty yards, but seeing that he had no support Kelly halted the regiment and inquired why the 63d had not advanced. (Colonel Fowler and Major Bentley of the 63d had been wounded.) Captain O'Neill of the 63d, who was on the left of his regiment, said he would advance with the 88th if he had anyone to command the regiment, but not knowing who was in command he did not wish to do so, upon which Kelly ordered the 88th to fall back a few feet.

We have stated that the 29th Massachusetts covered a depression in the ridge between the 69th and 63d New York. It had been under heavy infantry and artillery fire in its advance, which it returned, but on reaching its position about one hundred yards from the road ceased firing, for it could not see the enemy in the road nor could the enemy see it, as it was in the depression between the higher ground on its right and left, and the ridge along the sunken road completely sheltered it. But it had a good range upon the cornfield in rear of the road, which was on higher ground opening wide before it, its shots cutting down the stalks of green corn as would a scythe and having their effect upon the enemy who were hiding there or who came up as supports to those in the road. From these it received a severe fire.

When Meagher's brigade took position it was confronted by G. B. Anderson's North Carolinians and Wright's Georgians and Alabamians, but soon thereafter Anderson was reinforced by the brigades of Pryor, Featherston, and Wilcox, which made an effort to charge Meagher.

After Rodes had rallied his men (when repulsed in his attack upon French), he noticed troops (Wright's Brigade) going in to the support of G. B. Anderson, or to his right, and that a body of troops stopped in the hollow immediately in his rear and near the orchard instead of passing on to the front. As the fire between his own men and Kimball's was now desultory, he went to these troops and found that they belonged to Pryor's Brigade and that they had been halted there by someone other than General Pryor. Captain William D. Ballantine,[30] commanding the 2d Florida, says Pryor's Brigade had been halted some time (his own regiment very much exposed, being near the crest of a small hill) when Rodes came from the front and asked him to what command he belonged and why he was not engaged, to which Ballantine replied that he had no orders. Rodes said troops were needed at the front and ordered Ballantine to form line and go in, told him where to go, and then found Pryor—to whom he stated the conduct of his brigade and the necessity for it at the front. (R. H. Anderson had been wounded very soon after coming upon the field and Pryor, who succeeded to the command, was unaware of the orders under which Anderson was acting, and did not rise to the occasion. The consequent movement of his command was disjointed and without proper direction, but when apprised by Rodes of the condition of affairs he ordered his own brigade forward.)

Without waiting for this order from Pryor, Ballantine changed front forward on left company, the movement being in a measure masked by the orchard and cornfield in front, and the line of the 2d Florida was established fronting the cornfield, the right in the orchard and the left in open ground west of it. The other regiments executed the movement, forming double-quick on the right of the 2d Florida in this order, from left to right: the 8th Florida (Lieutenant Colonel Georges A. G. Coppens), 5th Florida (Colonel John C. Hately), 3d Virginia (Colonel Joseph Mayo), 14th Alabama (Major James A.

---

[29] Henry Fowler to Meagher, no date, reprinted in *OR*, vol. 19, pt. 1, 295–96. Carman cut the paragraphs quoted above from a copy of the *OR* and pasted them into his original manuscript. In so doing he placed the first paragraph at the end of the passage, either by accident or for dramatic effect. The sequencing contained herein represents the order in which the paragraphs appear in the *OR*.

[30] Carman gives Ballantine's rank as "Colonel" in his original manuscript, but he is in error. Although he frequently commanded the regiment, there is no evidence to suggest that he was promoted even to major until May 1863. See Florida Board of State Institutions, *Soldiers of Florida in the Seminole Indian, Civil and Spanish-American Wars* (Live Oak, Fla.: Democrat Book and Job Print, n.d.), 79; David W. Hartman, comp., *Biographical Rosters of Florida's Confederate and Union Soldiers, 1861–1865*, vol. 1 (Wilmington, N.C.: Broadfoot Publishing Co., 1995), 142. The leading authority on field officers in Lee's army notes that there is no official record of any promotion beyond the rank of captain. Robert K. Krick, *Lee's Colonels: A Biographical Register of the Field Officers of the Army of Northern Virginia*, 4th ed., rev. (Dayton, Ohio: Press of Morningside Bookshop, 1992), 44.

Broome), and the remains of Mahone's Brigade under Colonel Parham, now reduced to less than fifty men. Colonel Hately was now in command of Pryor's Brigade, and as soon as it formed he ordered it forward. It advanced through the orchard and as it entered the cornfield came under the fire of Tompkins's guns and the musketry of Kimball and Meagher. Colonel Coppens of the 8th Florida was killed and, immediately after, Captain Richard A. Waller, who succeeded him in command, fell dead with the colors of the regiment draped over his shoulders. Every regiment suffered great loss. Passing through the cornfield the left of the brigade came up in rear of the right wing of the 14th North Carolina, the right extending beyond the 4th North Carolina. When it reached the road it met with a severe fire that checked a part of the line. Another part of it went beyond the road a few yards but was quickly driven back with great loss, and all lay down with G. B. Anderson's men in the road and opened fire.

Featherston's Brigade was close on the heels of Pryor's. With Wilcox it had maneuvered some time on the ridge south of the Piper farm and then was recalled and formed line in the orchard in Pryor's rear, and it was at this time that Pryor went forward. From right to left the brigade was thus formed: the 2d Mississippi Battalion (Major William S. Wilson), 19th Mississippi,[31] 12th Mississippi (Colonel William H. Taylor), and 16th Mississippi (Captain Abram M. Feltus). As soon as it formed, it followed Pryor's Brigade through the orchard and entered the cornfield under a heavy artillery fire on both flanks and a sweeping fire of musketry in front, by which it suffered greatly, and came upon G. B. Anderson's and Pryor's men lying in the sunken road, its left behind the center of the 14th North Carolina and its right in rear of the left of the 30th North Carolina. It did not halt in the road but passed over those in it about thirty to forty yards and fiercely engaged Meagher, but in about five minutes was driven back to the road with great loss. Colonel Bennett of the 14th North Carolina says Featherston's men "flowed over and out of the road and many of them were killed in this overflow. The 16th Mississippi disappeared as if it had gone into the earth."[32]

By this time the ranks of Meagher's brigade had been greatly thinned. The 69th New York had nearly melted away and but a few Irishmen were left, huddling about the two colors, when one of the enemy shouted from the sunken road, "Bring them colors here!" upon which the two color bearers instantly advanced a few steps, shook their colors in the very face of the enemy, and replied, "Come and take them, you damn rebels!" This defiant challenge appeared to exasperate the enemy to another advance, and Lieutenant Colonel Joseph H. Barnes of the 29th Massachusetts, fearful that they might make a dash for the colors and possibly pierce the line and turn the right of his regiment, ordered three cheers to be given and a charge made. The historian of the 29th Massachusetts says:

An hour had nearly elapsed since the front had been reached; several of the captains had reported that the guns of their men were getting so hot that the rammers were leaping out of the pipes at every discharge. The men had already nearly expended their ammunition. Several times during the battle the enemy had undertaken to come forward, but as often as they attempted it, they were swept back by our fire. Since General Meagher had been disabled, there had been no general officer present, each colonel acting upon his own responsibility. The enemy were well covered and determined.

Up to this time neither regiment had known the fate of the others, nor the extent of their respective losses. Colonel Barnes now hastened to the right of the Twenty-ninth, for the purpose of taking a careful survey of the field. To his dismay, he perceived that the Sixty-ninth [New York], though holding on bravely, had lost nearly half their number; the Sixty-third [New York] had fared equally as hard, and the officers and men of both regiments were striving to keep up their formation. The Colonel, feeling a deep responsibility, saw at once that something must be done to prevent disaster; he knew, though he had received no orders since entering the fight, that from necessity the Brigade would soon be relieved, and was every moment expecting to hear the welcome shouts of fresh troops. Hastily giving his idea to Major Charles Chipman, his brave and worthy subordinate, he called upon the regiment for three cheers. The Major took the order to the left, and the boys gave the cheers with a will. Colonel Barnes then gave the order, "forward!" Instantly Sergeant Francis M. Kingman, the dauntless color-bearer, sprang to the front, the whole regiment promptly following him. Above the noise of the battle were heard the answering shouts of the brave Irishmen of the Brigade, their warlike spirit gaining fresh impulse as they started forward on the charge.

[31] In his original manuscript, Carman lists the commanding officer as Colonel Nathaniel H. Harris. He is in error both as to Harris's rank and his presence on the field that day (see p. 417 n. 15). The identity of the regiment's commander at Antietam is not known.

[32] One popular and well respected history of the campaign contains this identical quotation and cites as its source a letter from Bennett purportedly contained in Letters and Reports Concerning the Battle of Antietam, 1895–1900 ("Antietam Studies"), Record Group 94, National Archives. See Stephen W. Sears, *Landscape Turned Red: The Battle of Antietam* (New Haven, Conn.: Ticknor & Fields, 1983), 244, 394 n. 37. The editor was not able to locate it during his own examination of this collection, and although he accepts the probability that this was due to his own oversight, it should be noted that a number of documents identified as residing in this collection by the authors of works published during the 1980s and 1990s have since disappeared.

The crisis was over now; the bold forward movement had saved the Brigade from even one blot upon its bright record of fame. The shouts of our men, and their sudden dash toward the sunken road, so startled the enemy that their fire visibly slackened, their line wavered, and squads of two and three began leaving the road and running into the corn. Now the rush of troops was heard in the rear; now the air was rent with wild yells. It was altogether too much of a shock for the enemy; they broke, and fled for the corn-field. The next moment, Caldwell's brigade, led by General Richardson in person, with [Colonel Edward E.] Cross, [Colonel Francis C.] Barlow, and all its other heroes, came sweeping up behind the shattered lines of the Irish Brigade . . .

The flight of the enemy was now complete. In a few moments Caldwell's men were in possession of the road, and driving the Confederates through the corn-field and into the orchard beyond.[33]

When it was relieved and went to the rear, Meagher's brigade had been reduced to less than five hundred men. The loss in the 29th Massachusetts was comparatively light, but the three New York regiments had suffered heavily: the 88th New York, 33.80 percent; the 63d New York, 59.25 percent; and the 69th New York, 61.80 percent. The loss in officers was very large. With all the original officers and men of the Irish Brigade, Antietam was its great day, its crowing glory, though it brought no captured flags away. At Fredericksburg, where the brigade was nearly extinguished when charging over ground upon which the Confederate artillery officers boasted that "a chicken could not live" under the fire of their guns, the rallying cry of the officers was, "Come on, boys! This is nothing to Antietam!"

Before accompanying Caldwell's advance, we must note the condition of affairs within the Confederate lines. Since early morning there had been heavy artillery firing along the line south of the sunken road. For nearly two miles there was battery after battery on the high ground running south, aggregating nearly eighty guns. D. H. Hill says he had twenty-six guns of his own command, besides those of Cutts's Battalion temporarily under his command, and "positions were selected for as many of these guns as could be used, but all the ground in my front was completely commanded by the long-range artillery of the Yankees on the other side of the Antietam, which concentrated their fire upon every gun that opened and soon disabled or silenced it." Hill further says that the artillery was badly handled and "could not cope with the superior weight, caliber, range, and number of the Yankee guns; hence it ought only to have been used against masses of infantry. On the contrary, our guns were made to reply to the Yankee guns, and were smashed up or withdrawn before they could be effectively turned against massive columns of attack."[34]

Early in the morning Major Hilary P. Jones's artillery battalion of four Virginia batteries was on Cemetery Ridge, between the Piper farm and the Boonsboro Road, under orders to prevent the crossing of the Middle Bridge and was soon engaged with the Union batteries beyond the Antietam. Being inferior to these in weight of metal and range and threatened by an enfilade fire on the right by Weed's and Benjamin's batteries, Jones was ordered by Lee to withdraw under cover of the ridge to the lower ground between it and the Hagerstown Road. While Jones was on the ridge he was a witness to this incident, narrated by Longstreet:

During the progress of the battle of Sharpsburg General Lee and I were riding along my line and D. H. Hill's, when we received a report of movements of the enemy and started up the ridge to make a reconnaissance. General Lee and I dismounted, but Hill declined to do so. I said to Hill, "If you insist on riding up there and drawing the fire, give us a little interval so that we may not be in the line of the fire when they open upon you." General Lee and I stood on the top of the crest with our glasses, looking at the movements of the Federals on the rear left. After a moment I turned my glass to the right—the Federal left. As I did so, I noticed a puff of white smoke from the mouth of a cannon. "There is a shot for you," I said to General Hill. The gunner was a mile away, and the cannon-shot came whisking through the air for three or four seconds and took off the front legs of the horse that Hill sat on and let the animal down upon his stumps. The horse's head was so low and his croup so high that Hill was in a most ludicrous position. With one foot in the stirrup he made several efforts to get the other leg over the croup, but failed. Finally we prevailed upon him to try the other end of the horse, and he got down. That shot at Hill was the second best shot I ever saw.[35]

This incident occurred about twenty feet north of the Boonsboro Road, and the shot was fired by Captain Stephen H. Weed, commanding Battery I, 5th U.S. Artillery.[36]

After Jones withdrew from the ridge, Captain Thomas J. Peyton's Battery was detached and sent to the left, and Boyce's Battery passed from the Boonsboro Road along the ridge to the left. Later in the forenoon Jones reoccupied the ridge with

---

[33] William H. Osborne, *The History of the Twenty-Ninth Regiment of Massachusetts Volunteer Infantry, in the Late War of the Rebellion* (Boston: Albert J. Wright, 1877), 186–88.

[34] Hill to Chilton, 1022, 1026.

[35] James Longstreet, "The Invasion of Maryland," in *Battles and Leaders of the Civil War*, vol. 2 (New York: Century Co., 1887), 671.

[36] Ibid., 671 n.

three batteries. Two guns of Captain Richard C. M. Page's Battery were placed close to the Boonsboro Road (to fire to the front, in the direction of the Middle Bridge) and the others so arranged that their field of fire was off to the left. These opened fire upon Richardson's division, firing solid shot that struck the plowed ground in front of the column, Jones says, "with wonderful effect."[37]

Boyce's Battery of six guns bivouacked on the night of the sixteenth in a hollow in rear of Cemetery Hill. Captain Boyce reports that early on the seventeenth he was ordered by Colonel Walton "beyond the road north of the town of Sharpsburg" to meet and check the enemy. He marched about 150 yards on the Boonsboro Road, then turned to the left and marched along Cemetery Ridge to the vicinity he supposed he should occupy, and was placed by Colonel Stevens of Evans's Brigade on the slope of the second hill from the road, but finding his battery could be of no service in this position he was posted farther down in front of another battery. Here, discovering that he was still where he could not see the enemy, he moved his battery through a cornfield immediately in front, and on reaching the farther side of this field found the whole line of battle, for at least a mile, extending before him. He placed his guns in battery in easy range of a portion of the line but had to wait for an opportunity to fire, as his own friends, engaging the enemy, intervened. After a protracted struggle immediately in his front, the Confederate infantry abandoned the field to overwhelming numbers. Boyce says:

> My battery was at this time thrown forward, by your [Evans's] order, into an open field 200 or 300 yards in advance of its original position. The enemy then advanced through a corn-field to the field in which my battery had taken its position, showing a front of several hundred yards in extent, plainly on the right and center, but partly concealed by the corn on the left. The whole line of the enemy here was within canister range, and I opened upon him a destructive fire, cutting down two of his flags at the second or third discharge of the guns. The right and center soon gave way and retired. The battery was then turned upon the left, which held its position more obstinately. This portion of the line took shelter in a ravine at the base of the hill from which I was firing, and it was only with one or two guns that they could be reached. Having no support of infantry, and no other battery assisting me in resisting this large body of the enemy, and being exposed the whole time to a galling fire from the enemy's sharpshooters, after firing 70 rounds of canister and some solid shot I was forced to retire from this hazardous position. I retired, in order, to the corn-field from which I had advanced.[38]

It is difficult to locate the various positions held by Boyce but he appears to have been engaged with the advance of French's division and also with Richardson's, and to have fallen back into the cornfield from the open ground east of it.

About 9:15 a.m. Miller's Battery of four Napoleon guns (of the Washington Artillery) was ordered from its position on Cemetery Hill to the left. It went through Sharpsburg, then out on the Hagerstown Road, and was ordered by Longstreet up the hill through the Piper orchard to a position near the center of the orchard and about eighty yards south of the cornfield in front. In taking position a rain of bullets came showering over it from the right, left, and front, but it immediately opened fire upon Richardson's advance. In a very short time two gunners and several cannoneers were wounded, and Longstreet ordered the battery to cease firing and go under cover by withdrawing a few yards down the hill.

Very early in the morning Hardaway's (Alabama) Battery of three guns, under the command of Lieutenant John W. Tullis, was near the southwest corner of the Mumma cornfield (the position subsequently occupied by Patterson's [Georgia] Battery). It had rifled guns and fired to the front until the contestants were too close to distinguish the lines, when the guns were turned upon those beyond the Antietam near McClellan's headquarters. About 8:00 a.m. it crossed the Hagerstown Road and went into position opposite the mouth of the sunken road and one hundred yards from it, and from this position opened fire upon French's division in its advance, but was soon driven back by Tompkins[39] to a position three hundred yards west of the road and fifty yards south of the large cornfield. Here it remained until R. H. Anderson's artillery came up, when it fell back to a rock ledge with a depression in rear where the caissons were sheltered. This position was about 150 yards southeast of the Reel house and about the same distance from what is known as the Landing Road, and in this position the battery remained during the day and with its long-range guns assisted in resisting Richardson's advance. "Thus," says Longstreet, "when Richardson's march approached its objective, the Confederates had Boyce's battery, well out in the corn-field facing the march; Miller's section of Napoleons in the centre, and a single battery at McLaws's rear."[40]

---

[37] As of this writing, Carman's source for this quotation has not been identified.

[38] Robert Boyce to Nathan G. Evans, October 2, 1862, reprinted in *OR*, vol. 19, pt. 1, 943.

[39] A light pencil notation in Carman's hand inserts the words "or [illegible]" directly above the phrase "by Tompkins." Despite the editor's close familiarity with Carman's handwriting, his several attempts to decipher these words—even with the aid of a magnifying glass on the original manuscript page—proved fruitless. Further complicating matters is Carman's failure to mark with a caret the precise insertion point for this addition. Thus, it is not known which phrase he attempted to qualify: should it read "soon driven back or [illegible] by Tompkins" or "soon driven back by Tompkins or [illegible]"?

[40] Longstreet, *From Manassas to Appomattox: Memoirs of the Civil War in America* (Philadelphia: J. P. Lippincott Co., 1896), 249.

Saunders's artillery had been withdrawn. It had been engaged with Tompkins in front and had fired at French's men but was quickly silenced, and was inactive while Pryor's, Wright's, and Featherston's Brigades were advancing through the orchard and corn to the sunken road. About this time Captain Grimes advanced one gun of his battery to the left and front and fired at some infantry between the Dunkard church and the Mumma house. Men of the 14th Indiana saw the movement, several of them gaining favorable position on the right, and opened fire. Grimes was struck from his horse by a shot in the thigh, and his men were bearing him off the field when a second ball struck him in the groin and gave a mortal wound. Meanwhile, the other batteries had reopened fire but were quickly silenced and withdrawn. Moorman's Battery was badly used up and retired into park two miles from the field in the direction of Shepherdstown. Grimes's Battery followed, and Huger's Battery, abandoning one gun, followed Moorman and Grimes. This withdrawal was soon followed by the retreat of Rodes's Brigade from the sunken road.

We left Rodes after he had ordered Pryor's Brigade to the front. After he had found Pryor and informed him of the fact (Pryor had also sent an order for the brigade to go forward), Rodes started back to his own brigade and met Lieutenant Colonel James N. Lightfoot of the 6th Alabama looking for him. Colonel Gordon had been desperately wounded and Lightfoot was in command of the regiment. Upon his telling Rodes that the right of the 6th Alabama was being subjected to a terrible enfilading fire (which the enemy were enabled to deliver by reason of their gaining somewhat on G. B. Anderson) and that he had but few men left in that wing, Rodes ordered him to hasten back and throw his right wing back out of the sunken road, or rather from its exposed position on a ledge crossing the road immediately in front of the right of the 14th Indiana. Instead of executing the order as given by Rodes for the right wing to fall back, Lightfoot moved briskly to the rear of the regiment and gave the command, "Sixth Alabama, about face; Forward march!" Major Hobson of the 5th Alabama, seeing this, asked if the order was intended for the whole brigade. Lightfoot replied, "Yes," and thereupon the 5th, and immediately the other troops on their left, retreated.[41] Rodes says:

> I did not see their retrograde movement until it was too late for me to rally them, for this reason: Just as I was moving on after Lightfoot, I heard a shot strike Lieutenant [John] Birney, who was immediately behind me. Wheeling, I found him falling, and found that he had been struck in the face. He found that he could walk after I raised him, though he thought a shot or piece of shell had penetrated his head just under the eye. I followed him a few paces, and watched him until he had reached a barn [Piper's—*EAC*], a short distance to the rear, where he first encountered some one to help him in case he needed it. As I turned toward the brigade, I was struck heavily by a piece of shell on my thigh. At first I thought the wound was serious, but, finding, upon examination, that it was slight, I again turned toward the brigade, when I discovered it, without visible cause to me, retreating in confusion. I hastened to intercept it at the Hagerstown road. I found, though, that, with the exception of a few men from the Twenty-sixth, Twelfth, and Third [Alabama], and a few under Major Hobson, not more than 40 in all, the brigade had completely disappeared from this portion of the field. This small number, together with some Mississippians ... and North Carolinians, making in all about 150 men, I rallied and stationed behind a small ridge leading from the Hagerstown road eastward toward the orchard before spoken of, and about 150 [370—*EAC*] yards in rear of my last position ...
>
> ... After this, my time was spent mainly in directing the fire of some artillery and getting up stragglers.[42]

Rodes testifies to the gallantry of his brigade, which "finally fell back only when, as the men and officers supposed, they had been ordered to do so" and maintains that the troops on his right had already given way when his own men began to retreat.[43] On the contrary, Hill says G. B. Anderson "still ... held his ground, but the Yankees began to pour in through the gap made by the retreat of Rodes."[44] Colonel Bennett, then in command of G. B. Anderson's Brigade, says Rodes had retreated before he fell back with the two North Carolina regiments on his immediate right.[45] As a matter of fact, Rodes fell back at the time Wright's, Pryor's, and Featherston's Brigades, with the 4th and 30th North Carolina of G. B. Anderson's, retreated in confusion from the sunken road before Caldwell's advance, to which we now return.

Caldwell's brigade at first was on Meagher's left and rear but beyond the range of the immediate infantry contest and well sheltered, being on the reverse or northeast slope of the high ground where, farther to the right and front, Meagher was so mush exposed. Caldwell, finding no enemy in his immediate front, began to wheel his brigade cautiously to the right (which, had the movement been energetically continued, would have taken the Confederate position in the sunken road in flank very soon after Meagher had become engaged), but the movement was very slow and exasperating to those on

[41] Rodes to Ratchford, 1037–38.

[42] Ibid., 1038.

[43] Ibid.

[44] Hill to Chilton, 1024.

[45] As of this writing, Carman's source for this assertion has not been identified.

the right of the line, in plain view of Meagher's brigade, which was standing up under a galling fire. Colonels Barlow and Miles impatiently strode along the line making the air blue, cursing the fate or want of generalship that compelled slow and halting movement when dash was required. But an order was now received from Richardson to relieve Meagher, upon which the brigade moved by the right flank in rear of Meagher, then, facing to the left, passed his line to the front under a severe fire of musketry. The movement was not made with that precision described in the official reports (by breaking companies to the front, Meagher's regiments breaking by companies to the rear). The brigade was running when it reached Meagher's line and, without slacking pace, dashed through his ranks, passing the line by simply pushing its way through, Meagher's men readily conforming to the movement. Francis A. Walker says the movement "was effected with perfect composure, and Caldwell's brigade became the front line, and was soon involved in a most spirited contest, in which both the gallantry of the troops and the exceptional intelligence, skill and audacity of the regimental commanders were displayed to the highest advantage."[46] The brigade was thus formed: on the right, the 61st and 64th New York (temporarily consolidated under the command of Colonel Barlow), 7th New York (Captain Charles Brestel), 81st Pennsylvania (Major Henry B. McKeen), and 5th New Hampshire (Colonel Cross).

While Pryor's and Featherston's Brigades, after their repulse, were lying in the road with G. B. Anderson's men, they were subjected to a severe fire of artillery and musketry. The sudden advance ordered by Colonel Barnes started some of the men to the rear, and Colonel Posey, observing the crowded condition of the troops in the road (who were subjected to much loss), ordered Featherston's Brigade to retire. A scene of great confusion now ensued from the mingling of different brigades. Caldwell's men swept to the front and Pryor's and Featherston's men retreated, carrying with them the 4th and 30th North Carolina. Colonel Bennett reports that while he was observing the right of his brigade, "masses of Confederate troops in great confusion were seen, portions of Major-General Anderson's division as we then knew, for the Sixteenth Mississippi and Second Florida, of that command [the left regiments respectively of Featherston and Pryor—*EAC*], coming to our succor, broke beyond the power of rallying after five minutes' stay. In this stampede, if we may so term it, the Fourth North Carolina State Troops and Thirtieth North Carolina Troops participated."[47] An officer of the 4th North Carolina writes, "I think Featherston was started to the right, but instead of getting there came up behind us, where he was not needed, for we could have held our position indefinitely. He sustained great loss in killed and wounded and I have always thought was the cause of the line breaking, for when he found he was not needed there he gave an order to fall back, which was mistaken for a general order and all that could walk went back with him, which caused a general break in the line."[48]

Wright's Brigade had fallen back before the break occurred. Colonel Gibson, who was in command, says, "Seeing a new formation of the enemy in our front of a very large force ... I withdrew the brigade in order to a stone fence [the fence on the Hagerstown Road—*EAC*] in the rear."[49] Gibson's withdrawal was followed by that of Wilcox's Brigade. This brigade, as we have seen, had been sent to the ridge south of the Piper house. After observing the advance of Pleasonton's cavalry from the Middle Bridge to the ridge midway to the Antietam, and that it stopped there, the brigade recrossed the Hagerstown Road, then again crossed it east (north of the Piper lane), moved northeast through the orchard to the northeast corner of the cornfield, and became heavily engaged on Pryor's right —but the entire brigade did not succeed in reaching the sunken road. It lost heavily in its advance and when reaching position was confronted by "a heavy compact line of infantry about 120 yards in front," and a battery of artillery on its right flank "shelled it with terrible accuracy."[50] It remained until Pryor and Featherston gave way, when it retreated in some disorder, every man for himself, and rallied in the low ground south of the corn near the Piper lane and a few yards east of the lower part of the orchard. A few men remained in the sunken road and were captured.

As we have said, when the right of Caldwell's line rushed through Meagher's skeleton line and crowned the crest of the ridge overlooking the sunken road, the Confederates in front of the left were beginning to leave. The entire division of R. H. Anderson gave way, carrying with it the 4th and 30th North Carolina of G. B. Anderson's Brigade and exposing the right flank of the 14th and 2d North Carolina. Barlow had led the 61st and 64th New York up the ridge directly in front of these two regiments. As he crowned it he was met by a severe fire, upon which he quickly withdrew under cover of the ridge and moved rapidly to the left near the northeast corner of the cornfield, where he was quick to see the opportunity presented by the exposed flank of the North Carolinians. Advancing his left he poured an enfilading fire down the road just as the two regiments had been ordered to retreat. Colonel Bennett, commanding G. B. Anderson's Brigade, says, "Anderson's division had gone to the rear. Two regiments (Fourth and Thirtieth) of our own brigade were missing. The dark lines of

---

[46] Walker, 112–13.

[47] Bennett to Ratchford, 1048.

[48] As of this writing, Carman's source for this quotation has not been identified.

[49] Ibid.

[50] Ibid.

the enemy had swept around our right, and were gradually closing upon the ground of Rodes' brigade. They having gone to resist the lines in front was an easy task, to contend against front and rear attacks we were totally inadequate, and the bare alternative of retreat was presented. The command was ordered to make the retreat by the right-oblique, with frightful loss in some regiments, … [and] reformed at the road leading to Sharpsburg."[51] Barlow reports that he secured over three hundred prisoners in the road and, seeing no enemy in his immediate front, halted.[52] The 7th New York, 81st Pennsylvania, and 5th New Hampshire came up in quick succession on Barlow's left and entered the cornfield, where they were soon met by a severe fire of infantry and canister from Miller's guns in the orchard and shell from two guns of Maurin's Donaldsonville Artillery farther to the right, beyond the Hagerstown Road. The 81st Pennsylvania came up in rear of the 2d Delaware of Brooke's brigade, which had crossed the sunken road farther to the right. The 5th New Hampshire on the extreme left, advancing to a small depression about halfway through the corn, saw a body of Confederates advancing from the direction of the Piper house and lane, which was quickly driven back.

Colonel Barlow's success was shared by Kimball's brigade, the 132d Pennsylvania and parts of the 7th West Virginia and the 108th New York on Barlow's right joining in the fire on the enemy in the road and advancing to it, where they halted. But the 2d Delaware and the 52d New York, closely following, charged across the road and into the cornfield, driving everything out of it. The 2d Delaware came under a heavy fire from the Piper orchard that threw it into confusion, but it soon rallied as the 81st Pennsylvania came up in its rear. The 52d New York advanced to the crest of the hill in the cornfield. Its commander, Colonel Paul Frank, receiving information that two Confederate regiments were on his right on lower ground, marched the regiment to the high ground at the west end of the cornfield and opened fire upon the flank of these regiments, the 7th New York coming up on his left and supporting him most gallantly. Here he was joined by Barlow with the 61st and 64th New York.

After describing his movement on the flank of the Confederates in the sunken road and their capture, Barlow says, "After these events my regiments, with the rest of our line, advanced into the corn-field through which the enemy had fled … Our troops were joined together without much order—several regiments in front of others, and none in my neighborhood having very favorable opportunities to use their fire. Seeing quite a body of the enemy moving briskly on the right of our line, at no great distance, to attack us on the flank, my regiments changed front and moved to the crest of a hill on our right flank, occupying the only position where I found we could use our fire to advantage. This was to the right of the Fifty-second New York."[53] In this position the two regiments were behind a fence bordering the Piper cornfield on the west, the right of the 64th New York resting on the sunken road where the right of Rodes had been. At this time Kimball was resisting a flank attack on his brigade and Barlow gave him great assistance by opening an oblique fire to the right, on the edge of the Mumma cornfield.

As stated in the preceding pages, Kimball—west of the Roulette lane—had been severely engaged. Nearly half of the officers and men of the 14th Indiana and the 8th Ohio were killed or wounded. The men complained that their guns were foul and their ammunition exhausted. The ground was covered with arms and the men were ordered to change their pieces for these, and the officers busied themselves in gathering ammunition from the cartridge boxes of the dead and wounded and carrying it in their hats and pockets to the men. It was while thus engaged that Caldwell advanced and Kimball made a charge, which was followed by the retreat of Rodes, soon followed by that of the 2d and 14th North Carolina. Kimball says he drove the enemy "some distance into the cornfield beyond."[54] As a line, the 14th Indiana and 8th Ohio did not go beyond the sunken road, but Company A of the 14th and Company B of the 8th did cross close upon the heels of the 2d and 14th North Carolina, secured some prisoners, went some twenty to thirty feet into the cornfield, and were driven back. At this moment a galling artillery fire was poured upon Kimball's right flank, and lines of Confederate infantry were seen sweeping down upon it from the direction of the Dunkard church and the western end of the sunken road.

Longstreet, who was on this part of the line, perceived the pressure on the right of Anderson's Division and had ordered an attack on the flank of Kimball's brigade to relieve it. He directed the artillery west of the Hagerstown Road to concentrate its fire upon Kimball. Cobb's Brigade and Colonel John R. Cooke (commanding the 27th North Carolina and the 3rd Arkansas of Walker's Brigade) were ordered to charge upon his flank and rear. Cooke was then in the edge of a cornfield about three hundred yards west of the Hagerstown Road and two hundred yards south of the West Woods, and when the order was received had just ordered a charge for the capture of two guns that had moved into the woods near the Dunkard church, on the left of Greene's division. Cobb's Brigade was on Cooke's right. When this brigade fell back from the charge

---

[51] Bennett to Ratchford, 1048. In his original manuscript, Carman deleted the phrase "in some regiments," suggesting that the "frightful loss" was distributed evenly throughout the command.

[52] Francis C. Barlow to George H. Caldwell, September 22, 1862, reprinted in *OR*, vol. 19, pt. 1, 290.

[53] Barlow to George H. Caldwell, 290.

[54] Kimball to French, 327.

made in conjunction with Rodes's Brigade it was to a fence in the west end of the sunken road, where it remained until Rodes retreated; to prevent being flanked on the right it changed front to the rear, which brought it behind a stone fence on the Hagerstown Road, its left standing fast and resting on the sunken road. This movement had scarcely been executed when Hill rode up and ordered it forward. Colonel Sanders, though extremely ill, had retained command up to this time, but was now so much exhausted that he relinquished the command to Lieutenant Colonel William MacRae[55] of the 15th North Carolina, who led the brigade (about 250 men) up the hill in front and to the right to the board fences of the Mumma lane at a point just south of the cornfield. Cooke, abandoning his movement on the guns, charged across the Hagerstown Road close on the heels of Greene's division (which had just been driven from the West Woods), swept over the plateau opposite the church, and, wheeling to the right, made directly for the cornfield in the rear of Kimball's right.

Just before these movements were seen by Kimball, the 14th Connecticut (which had been in the cornfield on his right and rear) left its position, and there was now nothing to check Cooke, who was charging down on the flank and rear. Kimball promptly ordered a change of front. The colors of the 8th Ohio and the 14th Indiana were run to the right and rear to the adjoining plowed field south of the Clipp house and planted on a slight ridge that ran nearly parallel to the Roulette lane and about sixty feet from it. The fragments of the regiments rallied on their colors, the 14th Indiana on the right and a part of the 130th Pennsylvania on the left of the 8th Ohio. Barely had Kimball's men taken their new position than Cooke's 27th North Carolina and 3d Arkansas crossed the fences of the Mumma lane and entered the cornfield. Fire was immediately opened on both sides and Cooke was checked near the middle of the cornfield. Assistance now came to Kimball's right. Brooke's brigade, which had been second in line to Meagher, had started to move forward and relieve him, but Caldwell having moved by the flank and interposed, Brooke halted and ordered his men to lie down. Once Cooke was seen coming over the plateau opposite the church, Brooke "led the Fifty-seventh and Sixty-sixth New York and Fifty-third Pennsylvania to the right, to check any attempt the enemy might make to reach our rear."[56]

When Cooke reached the cornfield, the 53d Pennsylvania was ordered forward to check him and also to hold at all hazards the Roulette barn and orchard (the barn being used as a hospital). The regiment advanced under a shower of musketry, gained the barn, reached high ground in the orchard, and opened fire upon the left of the 27th North Carolina. At almost the same moment, the 7th Maine of Colonel William H. Irwin's brigade of the Sixth Corps approached the north fence of the cornfield and delivered a volley full upon its left flank. All this was more than Cooke could stand, and he ordered a retreat to the position from where he had started, a movement closely followed by Irwin's brigade. Cooke did not halt until he had recrossed the Hagerstown Road to his old position.

Very soon after Cooke had entered the Mumma cornfield, Cobb's Brigade, which had moved from the mouth of the sunken road about one hundred yards up the Hagerstown Road, charged up the hill on his right to the Mumma lane just south of the corn. It was not long in this position when Barlow came up and opened fire upon it and upon Cooke in the corn (the distance being about 350 yards). After firing about twenty rounds, Cobb's men, being now unsupported by Cooke (who had retreated), fell back in disorder across the Hagerstown Road and joined Cooke. Colonel MacRae, commanding Cobb's Brigade, reports that he held the enemy in check until his ammunition was exhausted and, seeing no sign of support, was compelled to give the command to fall back, leaving the field with not more than 50 of the 250 men he started with.[57]

Brigadier General William T. H. Brooks's Vermont brigade of the Sixth Corps had been ordered to the support of French's division. It came up after the flank attack had been repulsed and took position in the Mumma cornfield on the line that had been held by the 14th Connecticut. Kimball's brigade fell back near to the Roulette buildings. Kimball had been continuously engaged more than two hours, handling his brigade splendidly and losing 121 killed, 510 wounded, and 8 missing. The heaviest loss was sustained by the 14th Indiana and the 8th Ohio, the former losing 56.50 percent, the latter 48.67 percent.

Meanwhile, a desultory contest continued in the Piper cornfield, where (as Barlow reports) the "troops were joined together without much order."[58] Francis A. Walker writes, in his *History of the Second Army Corps*, "The colonels of the regiments of Caldwell's Brigade fought the battle pretty nearly at their own discretion in the absence of direction from the brigade commander, so that the regiments were not in continuous line much of the time. They faced in varying directions and at varying intervals from each other and sometimes were interspersed with regiments of the other brigades."[59] The like conditions, though worse, obtained on the Confederate side.

---

[55] In his original manuscript, Carman gives the name incorrectly as "McRae."

[56] John R. Brooke to William G. Mitchell, September 19, 1862, reprinted in *OR*, vol. 19, pt. 1, 299.

[57] MacRae to Cobb, 872.

[58] Barlow to George H. Caldwell, 290.

[59] Despite Carman's explicit author–title citation and use of quotation marks, what is presented is not from Walker's text, but instead appears to be Carman's own synopsis of a portion of it. See Walker, 112–15.

The Confederate line went back from the sunken road in some confusion, and when Caldwell followed into the corn the confusion was increased and disorder reigned supreme. Brigade and regimental commanders undertook to rally their broken commands but found it impossible to do so, and the greater part of Hill's and Anderson's Divisions fell back to the Piper buildings and under cover of the ridge running from the barn to the Hagerstown Road; some were rallied behind the stone fences of the road, and all this at the time Longstreet was counting on their holding the sunken road and cooperating in the attack upon Kimball's flank by a united movement on Richardson's front and flank. Cooke and Cobb had moved promptly and been repulsed, but when the time came for the assistance of Hill's and Anderson's Divisions they had been driven from the sunken road and were in disorder. After great effort parts of each division were rallied and charged northeast through the orchard and corn to attack Richardson's left, Miller's Battery (with a small infantry support) being left in the orchard to hold the right and center in check. It is impossible to say with any degree of certainty how the brigades were formed in line. There is a general agreement that regiments and brigades were intermingled one with another and considerably disorganized and demoralized by the loss of an unusually large number of officers and many of the men. In a general sense D. H. Hill's Division was on the left, but when the charge had reached its limit some of his men were on the extreme right of R. H. Anderson's.

At the time this advance was made the Union line was much extended and not continuous. The 5th New Hampshire was on the extreme left and front, somewhat detached from the 81st Pennsylvania, and Barlow with the 61st and 64th New York was still on the extreme right, where he was just repulsing Cobb's Brigade. The 52d New York on Barlow's left, after a half-hour's fighting, saw the enemy break in his front and, being without ammunition, fell back. Still in the corn between the 81st Pennsylvania and Barlow were the 2d Delaware and the 7th New York, both in a somewhat disordered condition. The 5th New Hampshire had repulsed an attempted advance of a body of Confederates from the direction of the Piper house and now—marching by the right flank obliquely to the rear under a heavy fire of shell and canister that killed or wounded many officers and men—had scarcely reached its position on the left of the 81st Pennsylvania and opened fire on the Confederates in the orchard when an officer of the regiment saw the Confederates moving through the corn, "cautiously attempting to outflank the entire division with a strong force concealed behind a ridge" in the cornfield. They had in fact advanced to within two hundred yards of the left of the 5th New Hampshire and were preparing to charge when Colonel Cross "instantly ordered a change of front to the rear, which was executed in time to confront the advancing line of the enemy in their center with a volley at very short range, which staggered and hurled them back." Cross says they rallied and attempted to gain his left, "but were again confronted and held, until, assistance being received, they were driven back with dreadful loss," leaving in the hands of the New Hampshire men the colors of the 4th North Carolina.[60] In this movement Cross had gained ground to the left and rear and held the sunken road at the northeast corner of the cornfield. The assistance he received was from the 81st Pennsylvania, commanded by Major McKeen. McKeen "noticed the enemy's flags approaching from the orchard, and engaging the Fifth New Hampshire," and the 5th having taken its position on the edge of the cornfield and in the sunken road, he immediately moved the 81st to the left and rear. Taking position on the right of the New Hampshire men, it opened fire on the Confederates and thus, says McKeen, "The Fifth New Hampshire and Eighty-first Pennsylvania thus completely frustrated an attempt to flank the division."[61] While thus engaged there was heard the rattle of musketry on the left and front, along the road to the Middle Bridge—the rattle of Pleasonton's carbines.

It was just as he had repulsed Cobb's Brigade that Barlow was attracted by the noise of the contest on the left, indicating an advance through the corn on his original front. As he was of no more use in his present position, he flanked to the left and filed left through the corn to the assistance of the other regiments of the brigade until he connected on the right of the 7th New York, when he came to a front and advanced. Brooke, who had held the 57th New York (Lieutenant Colonel Philip J. Parisen) and the 66th New York (Captain Julius Wehle) in hand until the attack on the right had been repulsed, now led them forward to fill the gap in the line of Caldwell's brigade, and swept across the sunken road and into the corn just as Barlow was closing in from the right. The 7th New York was crowded out of line, the 57th New York on the right connected with Barlow's left, and all swept forward through the corn under a very hot artillery fire and a scattering fire of musketry, by which Parisen was killed and many others struck down. Brooke's two regiments struck the Confederates that had been so signally repulsed by the 5th New Hampshire and the 81st Pennsylvania, drove them in disorder, and followed to the south edge of the cornfield. (Parts of them charged to the Piper lane but were quickly driven back.) In the advance through the corn the 57th New York captured the colors of the 12th Alabama and many prisoners, and the 66th New York captured a lieutenant of the 5th Florida with his whole company and a stand of colors. (All this was in the corn northeast of the orchard.) Barlow was brought to a stand before reaching the orchard by three guns of Miller's Battery and their infantry support.

---

[60] Edward E. Cross to George H. Caldwell, September 18, 1862, reprinted in *OR*, vol. 19. pt. 1, 288.

[61] Henry B. McKeen to John C. Caldwell, September 20, 1862, reprinted in *OR*, vol. 19, pt. 1, 292.

The cornfield ran east and west for 560 yards along the south of the sunken road, and from north to south had an average depth of 210 yards, being deepest in front of the apple orchard, which lay beyond its western end. The orchard joined the corn, was 225 yards in width east to west, and ran south 340 yards to the Piper lane. For 150 to 175 yards from the corn it was on high ground, then the ground descended abruptly thirty feet or more to a level bottom.

Early in the engagement Miller's four-gun battery of the Washington Artillery was in position in the northern part of the orchard on high ground about one hundred yards from the cornfield, but being exposed to a severe fire (which it was unable to return because of the Confederate line in its immediate front), Longstreet ordered it to take cover by withdrawing a few yards down the hill. Here it remained twenty minutes,

> when, the enemy again advancing, he ordered his battery again into position. Lieutenant [Andrew] Hero [Jr.] having been wounded and Lieutenant [Frank] McElroy having been left to watch the movements of the enemy on the right, Captain Miller found himself the only officer with his company, and, having barely men enough left to work a section effectively, he opened upon the enemy with two pieces with splendid effect. After an action of half an hour, he removed his section to a more advantageous position 100 yards to the front and right, placing the remaining section under Sergeant [William H.] Ellis, directing him to take it completely under cover. He then continued the action until the ammunition was nearly exhausted, when Sergeant Ellis brought up one of the remaining caissons. The enemy had made two determined attempts to force our line, and had been twice signally repulsed. They were now advancing the third time, and were within canister range, when Sergeant Ellis, who had succeeded in rallying some infantry to his assistance, brought one of the guns of his section into action on Miller's left, and gave them canister, with terrible effect. The three guns succeeded in checking the enemy's advance.[62]

Longstreet was with Miller's guns at this time and, as Miller was short-handed by reason of his loss of cannoneers, Longstreet's staff assisted in working the guns while their chief held their horses and directed the fire of their guns. Longstreet writes:

> Miller was short of hands and ammunition, even for two guns … Our line was throbbing at every point, so that I dared not call on General Lee for help.
>
> … As Richardson advanced through the corn he cut off the battery under Boyce, so that it was obliged to retire to save itself, and as Barlow came upon our centre, the battery on our left was for a time thrown out of fire lest they might injure friend as much as foe. Barlow marched in steady good ranks, and the remnants before him rose to the emergency. They seemed to forget that they had known fatigue; the guns were played with life, and the brave spirits manning them claimed that they were there to hold or to go down with the guns.
>
> As our shots rattled against the armored ranks, Colonel [sic] [John W.] Fairfax clapped his hands and ran for other charges. The mood of the gunners to a man was one of quiet but unflinching resolve to stand to the last gun. Captain Miller charged and double-charged with spherical case and canister until his guns at the discharge leaped in the air from ten to twelve inches.[63]

It was against these three guns firing double charges of spherical case and canister, and their infantry supports, that Barlow had led the 61st and 64th New York. Barlow says that from these pieces and others still further to the right the enemy had been pouring a destructive fire of shell, grape, and spherical case shot during the infantry engagement, and that while moving on the guns in the orchard he was wounded in the groin by a spherical case shot.[64] Lieutenant Colonel Nelson A. Miles then assumed command of the two regiments and "immediately deployed skirmishers forward through the field to [the] orchard."[65] Richardson now suspended the further advance of the division, partly because it had become somewhat dislocated, but more particularly because it was exposed to a heavy artillery fire that he could not silence, as he had no artillery.

At this time the Confederate left center under D. H. Hill was thoroughly broken up. Only a few scattered handfuls of Hill's Division were left and Anderson's was hopelessly confused and broken. The Confederate artillery, however, kept up a vigorous fire upon the right, left, and center of the Federals, and Hill, seeing that the center of Lee's position was in danger of being carried, exerted himself to the utmost, and successfully, to stop any further progress. He brought up Boyce's Battery and

---

[62] James B. Walton to Gilbert Moxley Sorrel, December 4, 1862, reprinted in *OR*, vol. 19, pt. 1, 849–50.

[63] Longstreet, *From Manassas to Appomattox*, 250–51. At the time of the battle, Fairfax held the rank of major, though he was promoted subsequently to lieutenant colonel. See Robert E. L. Krick, *Staff Officers in Gray: A Biographical Register of the Staff Officers in the Army of Northern Virginia* (Chapel Hill: University of North Carolina Press, 2003), 124.

[64] Barlow to George H. Caldwell, 290.

[65] Nelson A. Miles to George H. Caldwell, September 19, 1862, reprinted in *OR*, vol. 19, pt. 1, 291.

made it open vigorously, though itself exposed to a furious direct and reverse fire.[66] Hill says, "Affairs looked very critical. I found a battery concealed in a corn-field, and ordered it to move out and open upon the Yankee columns. This proved to be Boyce's South Carolina battery. It moved out most gallantly ... and with grape and canister drove the Yankees back."[67]

It was this fire of Boyce's Battery, in connection with Miller's guns in the orchard and from some batteries west of the Hagerstown Road and on the ridge south of the Piper farm, that caused Richardson to withdraw. Brooke's two regiments at the south edge of the corn were especially annoyed by this fire, and Brooke, "finding that the enemy made no attempt to regain the field, ... sought for and obtained the permission of General Richardson to withdraw ... from the now untenable position, being exposed to a cross-fire of the enemy's batteries."[68]

We have stated that parts of the 57th and 66th New York advanced to the Piper lane. Just before this advance was made G. T. Anderson's Brigade, which had been engaged in the West Woods earlier in the day, was behind the stone fence of the Hagerstown Road a short distance south of the sunken road. An enfilade fire of long-range artillery compelled Anderson to change position down the road toward Sharpsburg, under the crest of the hill and at the end of the Piper lane. "At this point," he says, "I found a 6-pounder gun, and, getting a few men to assist in placing it in position, a lieutenant of infantry, whose name or regiment I do not know, served it most beautifully until the ammunition was exhausted."[69]

This gun belonged to Huger's Battery and was abandoned when its battery left position west of the road and nearly opposite the Piper lane because its horses had been killed. The officer who served it was Lieutenant William M. Chamberlaine of the 6th Virginia of Mahone's Brigade. The gun was abandoned at a gate on the west side of the road a few yards south of the Piper lane. Chamberlaine, with others of the brigade and division who had been driven back, was assisting in rallying the men on the Hagerstown Road when he noticed this abandoned gun. With the aid of a few men (mostly of G. T. Anderson's Brigade, but some of the 6th Virginia), he ran it up the road about one hundred yards, nearly to the top of the ridge, where it opened fire upon Richardson's men moving through the cornfield, but the exposure here was so great that after two or three shots it was run back to the mouth of the Piper lane. Its first shot in this position was by Major Fairfax of Longstreet's staff, and was down the lane at the skirmishers of the 57th and 66th New York, who were crossing the lane to the Piper house. Two or three shots were fired in that direction, the New York men fell back, and the gun was then moved back up the road about fifty yards and turned upon Brooke's men with case shot as they were seen at the edge of the corn. Here several shots were fired and the gun continued in action until Richardson's line fell back.

It was after Boyce's Battery "with grape and canister drove the Yankees back" that Hill records, "I was now satisfied that the Yankees were so demoralized that a single regiment of fresh men could drive the whole of them in our front across the Antietam. I got up about 200 men, who said they were willing to advance to the attack if I would lead them. We met, however, with a warm reception, and the little command was broken and dispersed."[70] Rodes reports that about 150 of the 200 men were of his brigade and that they were led by Hill through the orchard, "the general himself handling a musket in the fight."[71] There was now no body of Confederate infantry that could have resisted a serious advance of Richardson's division, but the artillery fire rendered his position untenable, and the entire line was withdrawn across the sunken road and formed under cover of the ridge upon which Meagher had fought.

The serious infantry fighting on this part of the field ended with the withdrawal of Richardson's division about 1:00 p.m., at which time the Confederates reoccupied the Piper house and the adjoining buildings and advanced their skirmishers into the orchard, and their artillery "from the south end of the west woods round to the Boonesborough turnpike swept the country in Richardson's front with their fire."[72] Richardson's men suffered severely from this artillery fire in taking up their new position and it could not be replied to, for up to this time the division was without artillery. But now a section of Captain James M. Robertson's regular battery of horse artillery commanded by Lieutenant Albert O. Vincent of the 2d U.S. Artillery arrived on the ground and, taking position on Richardson's left, opened fire upon the Confederate batteries in its front and beyond the Hagerstown Road. Its fire was directed principally upon Miller's Battery in the Piper apple orchard, which was temporarily silenced. Vincent's section was relieved by the six brass guns of Captain William M. Graham's Battery K, 1st U.S. Artillery. (A rifled battery had been asked for, but there was none available on the right, and General Hunt, chief of artillery, was requested to furnish one. Hunt had none at his disposal. All were actively engaged or had been detached to other points, so Graham's light 12-pounders were sent instead.)

---

[66] William Allan, *The Army of Northern Virginia in 1862* (Boston: Houghton, Mifflin and Co., 1892), 418–19. The first four sentences of this paragraph are taken almost verbatim from Allan.

[67] Hill to Chilton, 1024.

[68] Brooke to Mitchell, 299.

[69] George T. Anderson to Asbury Coward, September 30, 1862, reprinted in *OR*, vol. 19, pt. 1, 910.

[70] Hill to Chilton, 1024.

[71] Rodes to Ratchford, 1038.

[72] Allan, 420.

Graham moved from his bivouac near Porterstown about noon, passed up behind the heavy batteries on the high ridge east of the Antietam, crossed the stream at Pry's Ford, went through the Neikirk place, and following the ravines, under cover, ascended to the high ground where Meagher had been engaged. Relieving Vincent's guns (which retired at once), Graham's battery took position about eighty yards north of the sunken road and on the left of Richardson's infantry, and engaged a section of Confederate artillery about seven hundred yards to the southwest behind a group of three haystacks in a field to the right of an orchard, which he silenced in about ten minutes. A very sharp fire of shot, spherical case, and shell was now opened upon Graham by several batteries, two of which had rifled guns. One of these (probably Hardaway's), situated on a rocky ridge beyond the Hagerstown Road, enfiladed his guns. Graham returned the fire as rapidly as possible, but after firing some twenty minutes found that they were beyond the range of his smoothbore guns, his solid shot falling short several hundred yards. Having called Richardson's attention to the fact, Graham was told by the general that he wished to save the battery as much as possible in order that it might advance with his division at a signal then expected from Sumner. While communicating this to Graham, Richardson was mortally wounded by a ball of a spherical case from the battery enfilading Graham. After this Graham continued his fire some five minutes and then, after losing 4 men killed, 5 severely wounded, and 17 horses killed and 6 severely wounded, withdrew two hundred yards under cover of the ridge. Graham's action was in plain view of McClellan's headquarters and is described by Lieutenant Colonel David H. Strother of the staff:

> About this time we witnessed one of the handsomest exhibitions of gallantry which occurred during the day. A battery of ours was seen entering the field in the vicinity of Richardson's Division; moving at a walk and taking position, apparently in advance of our line, it opened fire at short range, and maintained its ground for half an hour under the concentrated fire of at least forty guns of the enemy. As they moved in with the greatest deliberation I saw a number of shells strike and overthrow men and horses, and during the combat the battery sometimes appeared covered with the dust and smoke of the enemy's bursting shells. Unable to sustain the unequal contest they at length withdrew to shelter, and then we saw parties returning to the ground to bring off the wounded in blankets and to remove the limbers of two guns, the horses of which had been killed … The affair was observed from head-quarters with the greatest interest, and elicited the warmest commendation.[73]

The Confederate batteries engaging Graham were those of Miller in the orchard, the Donaldsonville Artillery (Maurin's Battery) near the haystacks beyond the Hagerstown Road, Carter's Battery (and others) of Hill's Division, and Cutts's Battalion. Captain Carter says, "I now received an order from General Rodes to plant my battery on the left of the Hagerstown road, near the Donaldsonville Artillery. With the consent of General Lee, I at once moved my battery to this point. On reaching it, I found several batteries engaged in driving off a Yankee battery [Graham's—*EAC*] posted near the spot occupied in the morning by my two howitzers. My battery at once took part in this fire, and continued firing until the battery was withdrawn. There was at this time a pause in the engagement."[74] Soon after the withdrawal of Graham's battery, Hill advanced his skirmishers to the upper part of the orchard and into the cornfield on its right and left.

Although Richardson's division had been withdrawn to the cover of the crest upon which it had begun its engagement, the center of the Confederate line, held by Hill and Longstreet, was still menaced by Franklin's Sixth Corps. Brooks's Vermont brigade had relieved French's division and was fresh, strong, and intact. On Brooks's right was Irwin's brigade. Both were in good condition and liable at any moment to be launched upon the Confederates—who were very much disorganized, partially demoralized, some of them out of ammunition, and not able to resist a serious onset of infantry. Parts of Hill's and Anderson's Divisions were under cover of the ridge from the Piper barn to the Hagerstown Road and along the stone fences of the road, while on their left, filling thinly the space to the south edge of the West Woods, was Colonel Cooke with the 27th North Carolina, 3d Arkansas, and the small remnant of Cobb's Brigade. Cooke was confronting Irwin and out of ammunition, and to repeated requests for it Longstreet replied that he had none to give him and that he must hold his position with the bayonet. Longstreet says, "Cooke stood with his empty guns, and waved his colors to show that his troops were in position."[75]

The Union troops engaged in the struggle for the sunken road numbered about 10,000 men—French's Division of 5,700 and Richardson's of 4,300. The Confederates opposing these were G. B. Anderson's Brigade of 1,174 men; Rodes's Brigade, 850; remnants of Colquitt's Brigade, about 200; G. T. Anderson's Brigade, about 500; Cobb's Brigade, 398; the 27th North Carolina, 325; the 3d Arkansas, 350; and R. H. Anderson's Division (excluding Armistead's Brigade), with its artillery,

---

[73] A Virginian [David H. Strother], "Personal Recollections of the War," *Harper's New Monthly Magazine* 36, no. 213 (February 1868): 284.
[74] Thomas H. Carter to Henry A. Whiting, October 14, 1862, reprinted in *OR*, vol. 19, pt. 1, 1030–31.
[75] Longstreet to Chilton, October 10, 1862, reprinted in *OR*, vol. 19, pt. 1, 840.

3,400 men—in all, with artillery, about 7,200 men, not including the artillery belonging to organizations other than D. H. Hill's and R. H. Anderson's.

The loss in French's division was 1,750 and in Richardson's 1,161; in all, 2,911 for the two divisions, to which must be added the loss in Graham's battery of 4 killed and 5 wounded—making an aggregate of 2,920, or 29.2 percent of the number engaged.

The Confederate loss was 1,243 in the five brigades and the artillery of Anderson's Division, 156 in Cobb's Brigade, 217 in the 3d Arkansas, about 150 in the 27th North Carolina, 50 in G. T. Anderson's Brigade, 203 in Rodes's Brigade, 475 in G. B. Anderson's Brigade, and about 50 in the remnant of Colquitt's Brigade. The batteries of D. H. Hill's Division lost about 30 men. The aggregate is 2,574, or about 30.5 percent of those engaged. Some of R. H. Anderson's regiments suffered a loss of over 50 percent (the 16th Mississippi over 63 percent), and the 3d Arkansas of Manning's Brigade of Walker's Division lost 62 percent.

18

The Dunkard Church
Antietam, September 17, 1862

Once more we return to the Dunkard church, which we left at 11:00 a.m. At that hour the divisions of the First Corps and Sedgwick's division of the Second were rallying in support of the artillery on Poffenberger Hill. Hofmann's brigade, which with two guns of Cooper's battery had advanced to the crossroad leading to the Potomac and assisted greatly in checking McLaws's pursuit, had remained in this position about half an hour, "when a large cavalry force was [seen] passing in rear of a narrow strip of wood," evidently intending to attack the brigade in flank. On the right a heavy body of infantry much larger than his brigade followed, upon which Hofmann retired to the small cornfield across the Hagerstown Road, where he could command the open field west of the road. He was soon ordered to the left, where he remained until late in the afternoon, when Sumner ordered him to join his division "just below the crest of a hill, and immediately in rear of a long line of infantry."[1]

Williams's division of the Twelfth Corps was holding the East Woods and supporting the batteries of Woodruff, Cothran, Knap, Bruen, and Captain John D. Frank (New York), which were in the open fields in front of the woods. Greene's five regiments were in the West Woods to the rear and left of the church. Soon after eleven o'clock the 13th New Jersey, moving from the East Woods through the batteries and over the open ground south of the cornfield, entered the West Woods at the church and relieved the 5th and 7th Ohio—these two small, gallant regiments, much reduced in number and entirely out of ammunition, retiring to the plateau east of the road, where they rejoined the 66th Ohio. (The 66th, with the 102d New York, had been left near Tompkins's guns.) Soon after this the Purnell Legion, two hundred strong, of Colonel Goodrich's brigade, which had been supporting the 124th Pennsylvania near the Hagerstown Road, entered the West Woods and formed line to the right of the church and about ninety yards beyond it, but not as far advanced as, nor forming close connection with, the 13th New Jersey. These regiments were sent Greene in response to his urgent request for more men to hold his important position. (He had asked for a much larger force, but Williams could not spare it. An appeal to Sumner was not successful, nor could Greene succeed in recalling the other regiments of Goodrich's brigade for the purpose.)

It will be remembered that when Manning's Brigade made its charge upon Greene's position, it moved in such a way as to be almost entirely covered from the fire of Woodruff's battery by the peculiar conformation of the ground. Woodruff found it impracticable to change front for want of time and the fact that while protecting one flank he should expose the other. Being without infantry support, his only course was to fall back about 240 yards to the edge of the East Woods, his left gun sweeping the Smoketown Road. Here he was supported on the right and could protect his left. After firing from this position a few rounds down the road in the direction of the church and observing that Manning's attack had been repulsed, Woodruff retired and was relieved by Batteries A and C (consolidated),[2] 4th U.S. Artillery, commanded by Lieutenant Evan Thomas. Thomas, who had been halted in the East Woods, ran his right section to the front and put it in position, then advanced his other guns, the left close to the Smoketown Road, and the entire battery remained some time without firing a shot. About the time Woodruff retired, Cothran moved his battery back a few yards and Thomas formed on his left, but not closely connecting. The 107th New York, supporting Cothran, fell back to the edge of the woods. For a short time Knap's battery remained in the southeast corner of the corn on Cothran's right and rear.

As it neared twelve o'clock, Tompkins, running out of ammunition, was relieved by Battery G, 1st Rhode Island Light Artillery (Captain Charles D. Owen), and withdrew to the position from which he had advanced early in the morning. It is doubtful if any battery on the field did more solid and effective work than Tompkins's. It took position on the plateau opposite the church at a most critical moment, contributed largely to the repulse of Kershaw and Manning, aided in the repulse of Rodes's attack on French, opened an effective and demoralizing fire upon R. H. Anderson's infantry as it approached the field, swept the Piper cornfield with terrible effect as it went through it, and silenced some of its artillery. During a great

---

[1] John W. Hofmann to Eminel P. Halstead, September 21, 1862, reprinted in *OR*, vol. 19, pt. 1, 236–37.

[2] In his original manuscript, Carman here designates the unit simply as "Battery A," but notes in his table of organization that it and Battery C were consolidated.

part of the time engaged, it had very little infantry support and was exposed on the right to an enfilading fire from the Confederate infantry. It expended 83 rounds of canister, 68 rounds of solid shot, 427 rounds of shell, and 454 rounds of case shot—1,032 rounds in all. With the exception of the shots fired at a battery on its right (which was hidden by a ridge), every shot was fired at a visible enemy, the guns pointed with care, and the accuracy of aim and the length of fuse noted. Its loss was 4 killed and 18 wounded.

On the night of the sixteenth, Owen's battery bivouacked a short distance east of the Smoketown Road, near Mansfield's corps, and about a mile and a quarter north of the East Woods. On the morning of the seventeenth it moved to the left and front in search of some position where it could be used to advantage. About 9:30 a.m. it passed through the East Woods and was about to take position in the field south of the Smoketown Road when the 125th Pennsylvania and the 34th New York came retreating from the Dunkard church, upon which Owen took position behind the burning Mumma buildings and reported to Major Francis N. Clarke (Sumner's chief of artillery) for orders. Clarke already had more batteries than could be used and directed Owen to get his battery under cover; it was moved to the open ground behind the Mumma orchard, where it remained until ordered to relieve Tompkins. It went forward and immediately engaged a battery a mile distant in the direction of Sharpsburg that was pouring in a heavy fire. In about twenty minutes the Confederate battery was silenced and Owen ceased firing.

About 11:30 a.m. the advance of the Sixth Corps arrived. (We left the Sixth Corps and Couch's division of the Fourth in Pleasant Valley, where they remained on the fifteenth and sixteenth.) During the night of the sixteenth, Franklin received orders to move toward Keedysville in the morning with his two divisions and to send Couch to occupy Maryland Heights.[3] Leaving the 121st New York to guard Crampton's Gap, bury the dead, and care for the wounded, Franklin started at 6:00 a.m. of the seventeenth, Smith's division in advance. Smith marched through Rohrersville to the Old Sharpsburg Road, thence to the nose of Elk Ridge, where he was met by an order of McClellan to mass his division near army headquarters, upon which he left the road on which he had been marching, struck across fields, and massed his command alongside of the Boonsboro Road not far from headquarters, ready to support the attack on the right or left as might be required.[4] McClellan says, "It was first intended to keep this corps in reserve on the east side of the Antietam, to operate on either flank or on the center, as circumstances might require, but on nearing Keedysville the strong opposition on the right, developed by the attacks of Hooker and Sumner, rendered it necessary at once to send this corps to the assistance of the right wing."[5] Smith massed his division at the road about 10:00 a.m. In a short time he was ordered to form his division to command the ford by which Sumner had crossed the Antietam, and shortly after was ordered to cross the creek and occupy a point in rear of where it was supposed the Union right was engaged. Smith went down the hill to the right of the Pry house, crossed the Antietam by the ford, and came up in rear of Sumner's right about 11:00 a.m., and was ordered to form his division in rear of the batteries on the extreme right. The division was then behind and to the right of the East Woods.

Before forming his division, Smith was informed by Lieutenant Colonel Joseph H. Taylor of Sumner's staff that a battery on the right center was unsupported, and he ordered two regiments of Hancock's brigade to its support. Shortly after, on visiting the ground, he ordered the remaining regiments and two batteries—the 1st Battery, New York Light Artillery (Captain Andrew Cowan), and Battery B, Maryland Light Artillery (Lieutenant Theodore J. Vanneman)—forward to the threatened point. Cowan went through the East Woods and took position in the grass field east of the D. R. Miller farm and north of the cornfield, the same field occupied earlier in the day by the guns of Stewart, Ransom, Thompson, and Matthews. Vanneman's battery relieved Knap's, which was moving to the left, the two guns going up the Smoketown Road to the Dunkard church (where we shall soon follow them). Hancock's disposition of his brigade is shown in his official report:

> Arriving on the ground, the regiments of my brigade were placed in position supporting three batteries—Cowan's, of Smith's division, on the right (3-inch guns); Frank's, of French's division, in the center (12-pounder brass guns), and Cothran's battery, of Banks' [i.e., Twelfth] corps (rifled guns), on the left, the regiments being placed in the following order: The Forty-ninth Pennsylvania Volunteers, under Lieut. Col. William Brisbane, on the right of Cowan's battery; the Forty-third New York Volunteers, under command of Maj. John Wilson, and a detachment of the One hundred and thirty-seventh Regiment Pennsylvania Volunteers, under Col. Henry M. Bossert, between Cowan's and Frank's batteries; the Sixth Maine Volunteers, under Col. Hiram Burnham, and the Fifth Wisconsin Volunteers,

[3] See William B. Franklin to Seth Williams, October 7, 1862, reprinted in *OR*, vol. 19, pt. 1, 376.
[4] See William F. Smith to Oliver D. Greene, September 30, 1862, reprinted in *OR*, vol. 19, pt. 1, 402.
[5] George B. McClellan to Lorenzo Thomas, August 4, 1863, reprinted in *OR*, vol. 19, pt. 1, 61.

under Col. Amasa Cobb, between Frank's and Cothran's batteries, the whole line being parallel to the woods in front, then occupied in force by the enemy, and at canister distance therefrom.[6]

Skirmishers were immediately thrown forward into the corn, who came under fire of those of the enemy lying behind the fences of the Hagerstown Road, and the D. R. Miller house and enclosures were occupied by detachments from the command. Very soon the Confederates placed two batteries in front of the West Woods, their infantry in the edge of it in support, and opened a heavy fire with shell, round shot, shrapnel, and grape. Hancock called upon Sumner for another regiment to place in the woods on his extreme right; the 20th Massachusetts was given him by Howard and posted in the west edge of the north part of the East Woods in support to a battery in its front. After a severe cannonade, the skirmishers assisting, the two batteries were silenced by Cowan's, Frank's, Vanneman's, and Cothran's guns and withdrawn from that part of the field.[7] Hancock's loss in infantry was very slight, but the batteries met some losses in men and horses.

To the left of Hancock's line was Thomas's battery of the Second Corps. Knap was taking position with four guns on Thomas's right, between him and Cothran. Battery F, 5th U.S. Artillery, under the command of Lieutenant Leonard Martin, was going forward to position on Thomas's left, and Smith was forming Irwin's brigade to support these batteries and extend Hancock's left when circumstances demanded more active duty. Leaving Smith for a moment, we return to Greene at the Dunkard church.

The left of Greene's line—held by two small companies of the 102d New York, 3d Maryland, and 111th Pennsylvania—was at the south fence of the West Woods, 168 yards to the left of the church, all facing south and engaged in sharp skirmishing with the 27th North Carolina and the 3d Arkansas. On the right of the 111th was the 28th Pennsylvania, now three hundred men strong, a part of its left facing south but the greater part of the regiment facing southwest, and firing into the corn and upon skirmishers who made their appearance in the woods in its front and to the right. On the right of the 28th Pennsylvania was the 13th New Jersey, facing west and firing obliquely to the left into the corn and to the front and right upon some skirmishers in the woods; its center was opposite to and about 190 yards west of the church. To the right and about eighty yards in rear of the 13th New Jersey was the Purnell Legion of about two hundred men. The left of this regiment rested to the right of the church and about ninety yards beyond it and faced a little north of west. In all Greene had about 1,350 men from four different brigades of the Twelfth Corps.

When he entered the woods at 10:30 a.m., Greene supposed that Sedgwick was still in the woods to his right and front and knew not to the contrary the whole time he was in them, but he knew there was a wide interval on his right, and it was to fill this interval that he had called urgently for reinforcements—a call only partially answered by sending him the 13th New Jersey and the Purnell Legion. Soon after taking position on Greene's right, the colonel of the 13th New Jersey, finding his flank in the air and knowing from his experience and that of the 2d Massachusetts on the Hagerstown Road about an hour before that the enemy were near his right, sent a message to Greene, who was on the extreme left, that his flank was exposed to the enemy, who were not far from his right. When this message was communicated to Greene he replied, "Tell your colonel not to be uneasy about his flank. The whole of Sedgwick's Division is in the woods on his right."[8] Greene had good reason for his belief; he had not been informed of Sedgwick's repulse. He himself had repulsed two brigades of McLaws's right. He had seen Barksdale's Brigade, the 3d South Carolina, and a stream of stragglers going through the woods to seek shelter beyond them. There was a cessation of infantry fire on the right, and he concluded that the whole Confederate line had been repulsed.

Men were now seen moving off toward the right, recognized as Confederate, and the adjutant of the 13th New Jersey was sent to Greene with the information and with the further information that the colonel of the regiment was thoroughly convinced—absolutely sure—that the identical position supposed to be held by Sedgwick was in fact held by the enemy. This brought Greene to the right. He made a hurried examination of the position, insisted that Sedgwick was on the right, told the colonel that he was surely mistaken in the idea that the enemy were in the woods on the right, and gave stringent

6 Winfield S. Hancock to Charles Mundee, September 21, 1862, reprinted in *OR*, vol. 19, pt. 1, 406.

7 We cannot identify these Confederate batteries. Early says that after Sedgwick's repulse and when he had placed his brigade behind the rock ledge, "some pieces of our artillery were moved into the angle of the plateau on my right and opened on the enemy, but were soon compelled to retire by the superior metal and number of guns opposed to them."—*EAC*

This passage can be found in Jubal A. Early, *Autobiographical Sketch and Narrative of the War between the States* (Philadelphia: Lippincott & Co., 1912), 150. Carman appears to have availed himself of a typewritten copy of a portion of the manuscript placed at his disposal by a former member of Early's staff. See John W. Daniel to Ezra A. Carman, December 1, 1902, folder 2, box 3, Ezra A. Carman Papers, Manuscripts and Archives Division, New York Public Library.

8 As of this writing, a textual source for this quotation has not been identified. Having been the recipient of the message, it is possible that he was working from memory.

orders that the men should under no circumstances be permitted to fire to the right.[9] After informing the colonel that the greatest danger was on the left and directing him to keep up an oblique fire in that direction (into the corn) and upon anything seen directly in front, Greene rode to the left, where an officer of the corps staff came up, to whom he stated that the officers on his right were laboring under the delusion that Sedgwick had been driven from the woods. "Why, yes, general," was the reply, "Did you not know it?"[10] Greene's response was more picturesquely sulphurous than polite. As Greene says, "The position of the division in the advanced woods was very critical. We were in advance of our line on the right and left of us … Guns were sent for … and [I] sought re-enforcements from General Williams. None were at the time available."[11] He was separated from French on the left by an interval of nearly six hundred yards, filled only by Tompkins's battery, supported by about three hundred infantry (most of whom had expended their ammunition). The nearest troops on his right were those of Williams's division, the nearest of whom were a half-mile in his rear.

Meanwhile, Confederate skirmishers were advancing—a company each of the 30th Virginia and the 46th North Carolina—on the front and on the right, up a ravine. These were driven back by the 28th Pennsylvania and the 13th New Jersey, and immediately thereafter the commanding officer of the Purnell Legion sent some skirmishers to the right, who, going but a few yards, saw a regiment (the 49th North Carolina) lying down in the woods, well concealed, very near the right and front, beyond a ravine, and where it had lain the entire time that Greene was in the woods. Other troops were seen moving stealthily and closing up on the left of this regiment. It was about this time that the two guns Greene had sent for were being placed in position in the woods near the church.

It was a little after half past eleven when Lieutenant Charles T. Greene, son and aide to the general, rode up to Knap with orders to advance two guns toward the church to assist in holding the woods. Lieutenant James D. McGill was sent with the right section. He had passed from the cornfield and along the west edge of the East Woods to and across the Smoketown Road, taking position on high open ground opposite the church, when Colonel Tyndale came up and ordered him into the woods beyond the church to dislodge the 27th North Carolina and 3d Arkansas from the cornfield, to which order McGill made earnest protest, stating among other reasons that the guns could be easily captured if a charge should be made and any of the horses shot. Tyndale insisted. McGill replied that the woods were no place for artillery in the face of concealed infantry but that he would obey orders. As the high post-and-rail fences of the Hagerstown Road were obstacles to an advance directly to the front, McGill moved back into the Smoketown Road and down it to the church, and thence about one hundred yards down the Hagerstown Road.[12] One gun went into the woods a short distance and halted, the other remaining on the road while McGill awaited more specific orders as to where his fire should be directed. At this time the limbs and branches were falling off the trees from the fire of the Confederate artillery. To the left was the cornfield, bounded by a fence skirted with trees, and concealed by this fence and the tall corn were the 27th North Carolina and 3d Arkansas, who were annoying the infantry in the woods.

Tyndale called McGill's attention to a group of horsemen and some dismounted officers gathered on a slight elevation southwest of the church and remarked, "Just take my glass, lieutenant, and you can see them."[13] McGill looked a moment, returned the glass, went to his advanced guns, moved it a short distance to rising ground in the woods, and ordered it to unlimber when the 27th North Carolina and the 3d Arkansas rose up from behind the cornfield fence and with a yell poured a volley at the guns. Two horses were shot, one cannoneer was killed, and another wounded. A cannon shot cut the limb of a tree, which, falling on the pole team, pinned the horses to the ground. Several infantrymen rushed to assist in extricating the gun when, on the extreme right, there was a crash of musketry and a wild yell, and at the same moment Colonel Cooke with his two regiments charged on the left and the gun was abandoned and lost—the only gun ever lost by the Twelfth Corps in action. Fortunately the second gun was still in the road and not yet unlimbered. It fired at the pursuing enemy as it fell back and quickly made its way by the Smoketown Road and rejoined its battery.

---

[9] "The events of that occasion are as distinctly impressed upon my mind as though the occurrence had been yesterday. Sergeant Edward Warren of the right company of the regiment, had taken position a little to the right and front of his company, where, behind a rock or tree, he was endeavoring to pick off a rebel wherever he could see one. As I passed up and down the regimental line, Warren beckoned to me and called my attention to the glistening of guns which could occasionally be seen through the trees, indicating a movement toward our right. I immediately reported this to you and you sent me to General Greene, to whose command we had been temporarily detailed. Greene immediately put to spurs to his horse and rode down the hill at our right. He soon returned and said to me, 'Adjutant, do not let the men fire to the right under any circumstances as Smith's Brigade [Sedgwick's Division—*EAC*] is in there and it is impossible to flank you.' I cautioned the men, but remained at the right, keeping a sharp lookout in that direction." Letter of Maj. (then adjutant) Charles A. Hopkins, January 15, 1900 [not found].—*EAC*

[10] George S. Greene's statement to the writer, two or three days after the battle.—*EAC*

[11] George S. Greene to Alpheus S. Williams, September 29, 1862, reprinted in *OR*, vol. 19, pt. 1, 505.

[12] As of this writing, Carman's source for this statement has not been identified.

[13] Ibid.

This simultaneous charge of Cooke and Colonel Matt W. Ransom on either flank of Greene's line was not a concerted one directed to be made at the same moment. Ransom, without orders, charged to capture the guns, and Cooke, when he saw the guns coming into position, had just received an order from Longstreet (who was engaged at the sunken road) to charge, in conjunction with Cobb's Brigade on his right, on the flank of French's division. These two movements on Greene's flank require separate treatment.

There are always two sides to a fight, and we must now look into the Confederate lines as they appeared immediately preceding the events above recited and at the hour Greene was attacked on both flanks, which was about a quarter past twelve. Kershaw's and Barksdale's Brigades, which had fallen back, were still in the fields beyond the West Woods under cover of rock ledges, stone and rail fences. Semmes was near them, and on their left, in the same open ground, were the 30th Virginia and the 46th and 48th North Carolina of Manning's Brigade, the 46th North Carolina being at the west fence of the woods. The 27th North Carolina and the 3d Arkansas were in line south of the woods opposing Greene, and Cobb's Brigade was on their right, opposite the mouth of the sunken road. Three regiments of Ransom's Brigade were under cover of the long rock ledge at the edge of the middle body of the West Woods, nearly parallel to and about 225 yards from the Hagerstown Road, which they faced. Early's Brigade was to their left and Armistead's Brigade was to the left and rear of Early. Armistead's Brigade belonged to Anderson's Division; it had acted as rear-guard to the infantry, was the last of the command to cross over the Potomac, and was not in the attack made by McLaws, although it had been detached from its division to join him. As it approached the Hauser farm it came under heavy artillery fire, by which Captain William G. Pollard, commanding the 53d Virginia, was killed and a few men wounded. It formed line east of there and moved into the West Woods in the rear of Ransom's Brigade. The adjutant of the 35th North Carolina was sent to pilot it into position, and as it entered the woods Armistead was wounded in the foot by a rolling ball. "He saw the ball as it came rolling down the hill, and could have moved out of its course with all ease but, probably thinking it a shell and likely to explode, stood as one transfixed and did not move his foot or a muscle."[14] There was a severe artillery fire at the time and some confusion in the ranks. Colonel James G. Hodges of the 14th Virginia assumed command and led the brigade to the left, where it took the position held by Early, who moved to the right, on the edge of the plateau facing the Hagerstown Road and on Ransom's left. Armistead's Brigade came up very soon after McLaws had fallen back and did not become engaged, but suffered some from artillery fire. Stuart, with cavalry, artillery, and the 13th Virginia and 24th North Carolina, was on the extreme left, where he had been checked, awaiting reinforcements that Jackson had promised to renew the battle. Hood's Division and Hays's Brigade, having replenished ammunition and partaken of some food, were approaching the West Woods to take position in them about midway west of the church.

But before Hood arrived there was no Confederate line in the woods immediately west of the church and there was a wide gap, which was now sought to be filled by the 46th North Carolina and a company of the 30th Virginia. It will be remembered that when Greene crossed the Hagerstown Road the 46th North Carolina was driven clear out of the woods. Here its colonel, Edward D. Hall, was met by Jackson, who ordered him to report to McLaws, by whom he was ordered to endeavor to hold the woods at all hazards. Hall says he then "advanced in line of battle to the edge of the woods, which by that time was filled with the enemy, and placed the regiment behind a ledge of rocks, throwing out Company A and the company from the Thirtieth Virginia, as skirmishers."[15]

The company of the 30th Virginia was commanded by Captain John M. Hudgin[16] and was not with the regiment in its disastrous charge across the Hagerstown Road at the church, having been left on picket at Snavely's Ford. When relieved and rejoining its regiment it was assigned as a support to a battery, and then ordered into the West Woods and deployed as sharpshooters, with orders if pressed by a heavy line to fall back on the 46th North Carolina. Hudgin's own company and the one of the 46th North Carolina advanced and were met by such a severe fire from the 28th Pennsylvania and the 13th New Jersey (by which many of the men were killed or wounded) that they fell back on the 46th North Carolina, "sheltered under a ledge of rock along the rear slope of the hill in the woods and at the west edge of them."[17] Just before these men went back Colonel Matt Ransom of the 35th North Carolina saw McGill with his two guns go from the Smoketown Road into the Hagerstown Road at the church and came to the quick conclusion to capture them. (At this time Brigadier General Robert Ransom Jr., in command of the brigade, had gone to the left to recall the 24th North Carolina, which was

---

[14] The exact quotation has not been found, but, in his notes on Armistead's Brigade, Carman records that John L. Latane of the 53d Virginia specified the spot at which the brigade formed line, at which time Armistead was wounded by a rolling solid shot coming down a hill. Carman therefore may be quoting from his conversation with Latane. Carman, "Armistead's Brigade," no date, "R. H. Anderson's Division—Saunders' Artillery Battalion" folder, box 2, Letters and Reports Concerning the Battle of Antietam, 1895–1900 ("Antietam Studies"), Record Group 94, National Archives.

[15] Edward D. Hall to William A. Smith, October 3, 1862, reprinted in OR, vol. 19, pt. 1, 918–19.

[16] In his original manuscript, Carman gives the name incorrectly as "Hudgins."

[17] As of this writing, Carman's source for this quotation has not been identified.

with Stuart, and Colonel Ransom was in temporary command of the brigade—the 25th, 35th, and 49th North Carolina.) The two regiments on the left of the brigade were behind the ledge in the edge of the middle woods and looking over the open ground west of the Hagerstown Road, across which Barksdale's Brigade and the 3d South Carolina had charged. The 49th North Carolina, on the right, was in the woods on a sloping hillside, well protected by the rock ledge and concealed by the foliage of the woods. Colonel Ransom ordered the 49th North Carolina to file down to the ravine, then change front forward on first company and charge for the church, the two regiments on the left to close in on the 49th and follow its movements—all of which was instantly done.

On level ground everything could be seen through the woods, but on the hillside and in the ravine the foliage of the treetops was so dense that nothing could be seen beyond the ravine, so the 49th North Carolina was not seen by the 13th New Jersey and the Purnell Legion until its right was nearly at the lowest depression of the ravine and its entire line was changing front forward on first company. When this was seen the three right companies of the 13th New Jersey were swung back at nearly a right angle to their former position. But even now, so impressed were the officers of the regiment by Greene's warnings (and he had not cautioned them otherwise) that the adjutant, immediately followed by an officer of the Purnell Legion, went forward to get a closer view and determine whether they were friends or enemies, for their uniforms could not be distinguished.[18]

The same uncertainty possessed the Confederates. When Colonel Ransom ordered the movement, it was for the purpose of capturing McGill's guns at the church, and he appears not to have been aware that there was any infantry between him and the Dunkard church (although he must have seen the 13th New Jersey and the Purnell Legion enter the woods at the church). Be this as it may, when the right of the 49th North Carolina came to a halt and began to change front to make a charge for the guns, they were surprised to see infantry in their front, and at the same time that the officers of the Union line were going forward to determine who the 49th North Carolina were, two officers of the 49th were sent out to ascertain who the Purnell Legion and the Jerseymen were, but before any of them returned a simultaneous fire was opened on both sides as though done by one order.[19] The 49th North Carolina, without waiting to complete its change of front, charged (after the right had fired two volleys)—not directly for the church, as at first intended, but, descending into the ravine, where it was under partial cover, made directly for the right and flank of the Purnell Legion, which fired three or four volleys and retreated out of the woods and across the Hagerstown Road. Its commander, Lieutenant Colonel Benjamin L. Simpson, reports that "the enemy appeared in overwhelming numbers and compelled it to retire."[20] The 13th New Jersey followed the Purnell Legion. It fired two or three volleys. Its right was pressed by the right of the 49th North Carolina, the left of that regiment was gaining its rear, and the 13th New Jersey retreated from the woods and across the road. (Its commanding officer reports, "Being flanked on the right, the whole brigade was obliged to retire."[21]) The 28th Pennsylvania did not come under the fire of this flank attack, but, perceiving the retreat of the troops on its right, hearing the Confederate yell in its rear and to the right, and feeling the pressure upon its left also, fell back out of the woods, followed by everything on its left. Major William Raphael reports that "the overwhelming force of the enemy, advancing in three columns on our right, left, and center, threatening annihilation to the small force in that position," compelled him to retire.[22] Greene, referring

---

18 "Soon I saw the glistening of the gun barrels again, and again reported to you, and then, on the strength of General Greene's instructions, ran down the hill to make sure as to whether the force was our men or not, although I had little doubt in my own mind as to their being rebels. The foliage of the trees prevented my getting a good view until they had nearly reached the extreme depression between the two hills. As soon as I discovered that they were Confederate, I started back, shouting 'They are rebs.' Our men immediately began firing and the rebels, deploying on their first division, opened fire simultaneously. Being caught between the two lines of fire, I dropped to the earth and remained there, until hearing the rebels cheering and yelling behind me, I looked back and saw them coming." Hopkins to the writer, January 15, 1900 [not found].—*EAC*

19 "We were drawn up in line near the church on the right of Ransom's Brigade and the 35th North Carolina was on the immediate left. The Union forces appeared in front across a ravine but we were undetermined whether they were enemies or not. Colonel [Lee M.] McAfee, commanding 49th, sent Captain Cicero Dunham to reconnoiter and he was called on to surrender, upon which he wheeled his horse and a hot fire was opened by both sides." Letter of Benjamin F. Dixon, 49th North Carolina [not found].—*EAC*

   "We discovered a column of men to our right … but being in the woods and so far off that we could not tell whether they were our men or not, and our Adjutant ran up on the side of plateau [sic] or hill to find out, and he shouted to us to fire into them." Letter of Charles P. Jetton, 49th North Carolina [not found].—*EAC*

20 Benjamin L. Simpson to unknown, September 27, 1862, reprinted in *OR*, vol. 19, pt. 1, 515.

21 Carman to "Captain Smith," September 24, 1862, reprinted in *OR*, vol. 19, pt. 1, 502.

22 William Raphael to "Maj. O. J. Crane," September 23, 1862, reprinted in *OR*, vol. 19, pt. 1, 509. In his original manuscript, Carman introduces this passage by saying, "Major William Raphael, commanding the regiment, reports." This is somewhat misleading. Major Raphael commanded the 28th Pennsylvania when he drafted the report, but that document begins by noting "Maj. Ario Pardee, jr." was in command on the seventeenth.

to his whole command, reports that "the enemy advancing in large force, threatening to envelop the small command, they were forced to retire."[23]

The 49th North Carolina, closely supported by a part of the 35th on its left, followed closely the left of the retreating troops, reached the Hagerstown Road about 120 yards north of the church, and continued fire upon the retreating troops as they went over the plateau opposite the church and upon McGill (who, driven from his position south of the church, was retiring with one gun and two caissons down the Smoketown Road). Some of the North Carolina men had crossed the road, but the main body had halted at a barricade at the edge of the woods, when Cothran's and Knap's guns (ten in all) opened upon them with a most savage fire—the heaviest artillery fire the regiment ever experienced—which ploughed up the ground around them, killing or wounding many officers and men, and the 49th fell back into the woods and to the left.

Some of Greene's men retreated across the road north of the church; the greater part of them crossed south of it. Officers of every grade made efforts to check the retreat on the plateau, where Greene had so successfully repulsed Kershaw and Manning, but effort availed nothing. The retreat was continued to the East Woods, Colonel Cooke with his two regiments, supported on the right by Cobb's Brigade, pursuing closely on the left flank and in the rear, the left of his line as far as the Mumma place. Owen's Rhode Island battery (which twenty minutes before had relieved Tompkins) had just ceased firing in the direction of Sharpsburg and the sunken road and was involved in the retreat. Owen was about to proceed toward the brow of the hill to engage the enemy's infantry (then in plain sight from that position, beyond the sunken road and around the Piper barn) when, he says, "a noise from my right attracted my attention, and I saw our infantry retreating in disorder toward me, and then about 150 yards off, closely followed by the rebels. I limbered up quickly and started on the trot into the road leading direct from the [Mumma] ruins, and when the last caisson left the ground the enemy were close upon us."[24]

When the 27th North Carolina and the 3d Arkansas first took position south of the Dunkard church woods, they were on a line of fence parallel to the woods; after skirmishing with Greene some time, all (save a few sharpshooters on the left) were drawn back about twenty paces in the corn, and the right was thrown back on a line with Cobb's Brigade and the end of the sunken road. The sharpshooters on the left kept up a lively fire upon Greene's men in the woods and the right engaged Tompkins's battery, which replied with an annoying fire of canister and shell. The regiments had been in position about half an hour when Tyndale ordered the two guns of Knap's battery into the woods south of the church. Colonel Cooke, who was observing the movement, ordered the four left companies up to the fence and directed them to fire at the two guns, both plainly seen, and particularly at the advanced gun and the horses. At the first fire the horses and some of the men were seen to fall, and the infantry, which had moved to support the guns, showed signs of wavering. At this moment came Longstreet's order to charge, in connection with Cobb's Brigade and D. H. Hill's command, upon the flank of French's division. Cooke ordered the charge, and the 27th North Carolina and the 3d Arkansas leaped the fence and made for the guns. McGill, who had one gun in the road, unlimbered and fired as he fell back past the church; the piece narrowly escaped capture by the 49th North Carolina as it turned into the Smoketown Road. The charging line had not proceeded over fifty yards when it was seen that this one gun had escaped and that Greene's men were crossing the road and retreating over the plateau, upon which Cooke, leaving the abandoned gun to his left, changed direction slightly to the right and pursued Greene, keeping up a running fire and taking some prisoners. In the pursuit the color bearers of the two regiments forged ahead of the line some distance, and Cooke cautioned the bearer of his own colors to go slower, as the regiment could not keep up with him, which brought the happy rejoinder, "Colonel, I can't let that Arkansas fellow get ahead of me."[25] It was in such rapid pursuit as this that Cooke reached the crest of the plateau, saw that Greene's men had reached the cover of artillery (which now opened upon him), and that he himself had gone entirely too far to the left, upon which he wheeled to the right, crossed the fences of the Mumma lane, and entered the cornfield in rear of where French's right had been but was now fronting him. Just before the line reached the lane, Captain William Adams and Lieutenant James A. Graham,[26] commanding the left companies of the 27th North Carolina, observed some Union officers and men behind the hay or grain stacks near the Mumma farm and double-quicked to the left and captured them. Ordering their prisoners to the rear, the two companies double-quicked back to their command, which had then gained the middle of the cornfield and been checked. Immediately in front, behind a ledge, were Kimball's men, who had changed front. On their left front were three regiments of Brooke's brigade. Barlow, with the 61st and 64th New York, was coming into position on their right front, and

[23] George S. Greene to Alpheus S. Williams, 505.

[24] Charles D. Owen to Francis N. Clarke, September 23, 1862, reprinted in *OR*, vol. 19, pt. 1, 326.

[25] James A. Graham, "Twenty-Seventh Regiment," in *Histories of the Several Regiments and Battalions from North Carolina in the Great War 1861–65*, ed. Walter Clark, vol. 2 (Goldsboro, N.C.: Nash Brothers, 1901), 436.

[26] In his original manuscript, Carman gives the company commanders as "Captains Adams and Graham." At the time of the Maryland campaign, however, Graham held the rank of lieutenant. He was not promoted to captain until November 1864. See Weymouth T. Jordan Jr., comp., *North Carolina Troops, 1861–1865: A Roster*, vol. 8 (Raleigh: [North Carolina] Office of Archives and History, 1973), 62. Carman later notes Graham's proper rank in his marginalia (see p. 462 n. 109).

soon after the skirmishers of Irwin's brigade appeared and opened fire on the left flank. The two Confederate regiments fell back at a double-quick, Irwin's brigade at their heels and on their flank, firing into them, killing or wounding many. They went back over nearly the same ground of their advance, to the position from which they had advanced and, with the few cartridges remaining, assisted in checking Irwin's pursuit, which did not reach the Hagerstown Road. Over one-half of the officers and men of the two regiments had fallen.

Cobb's Brigade supported Colonel Cooke's right. By its action earlier in the day it had been reduced to about 250 men. It advanced from the mouth of the sunken road to the board fences of the Mumma lane (striking the fences just south of the cornfield) and came under the fire of the 61st and 64th New York. Its loss was heavy; when the 27th North Carolina and the 3d Arkansas fell back it was left without support and was ordered back. Colonel MacRae, commanding the brigade, reports that it left the field with not more than 50 of the 250 men.[27] It fell back across the Hagerstown Road and joined the right of Cooke's command, remaining with it until relieved around 3:00 p.m.

As Greene's men retreated to the East Woods, Smith was about to form Irwin's brigade on Hancock's left, when it was observed that the enemy were advancing and that Lieutenant Thomas had turned his guns to the left upon the 27th North Carolina and the 3d Arkansas, opening with spherical case upon them as they crowned the crest of the plateau, and then with canister upon the two left companies of the 27th North Carolina as they approached the grain stacks. (As we have seen, these two companies quickly fell back and joined their regiment in the Mumma cornfield.) The 7th Maine and the 20th and 49th New York were in line of battle, with the 33d and 77th New York as skirmishers on the right. The 20th New York was the largest regiment in the brigade and led the advance, the 49th New York *en echelon* on its right and the 7th Maine *en echelon* on its left. The 20th New York cleared the East Woods and went forward south of the Smoketown Road in fine line, General Smith, Colonel Ernest von Vegesack, and his field officers riding close behind and pushing it on in the most spirited manner, the Confederate skirmishers falling rapidly back. Under Smith's order the regiment was to halt under cover of the crest that had sheltered Greene earlier in the day but, in the ardor of pursuit, the men passed the crest and immediately came under fire of Cooke's infantry and a four-gun battery south of the church, which opened with canister, inflicting much loss. The regiment was quickly recalled and ordered to lie down under cover, and the 49th New York came up and lay down on its right. The 7th Maine, moving *en echelon* on the left, charged a body of Confederates at the Roulette buildings, drove it out with the loss of 12 men, and double-quicked to the left of the 20th New York, joining it just as it halted, and lay down on its left.

Irwin had ordered the 33d and 77th New York to advance on the right as skirmishers; from some misunderstanding they both went forward by the right flank and passed through Thomas's guns. As they neared the church (the 33d on the right of the Smoketown Road and the 77th on the left), the 49th North Carolina (supported by the 35th), which had fallen to the left and rear, out of range of the batteries, saw them coming, reoccupied the rail barricade from which it had been driven, and poured a volley upon both regiments that "staggered them and threw both into momentary confusion."[28] Irwin says, "A severe and unexpected volley from the woods on our right struck full on the Seventy-seventh and Thirty-third New York, which staggered them for a moment, but they closed up and faced by the rear rank, and poured in a close and scorching fire, driving back ... the enemy."[29] Lieutenant Colonel Joseph W. Corning, commanding the 33d New York, reports that he "received orders from the commanding division general to support the right, and was ordered to march near the woods in front." His regiment was in column, marching by the right flank. "When near the woods the enemy suddenly and unexpectedly opened on the regiment a heavy fire from their infantry, who were in the woods ... This sudden and unexpected attack caused a momentary unsteadiness in the ranks, which was quickly rectified. The battalion faced by the rear rank and returned the fire, when, by order of the commanding general, the regiment retired a short distance, under cover of a ridge."[30] Captain Nathan S. Babcock, in command of the 77th New York, was at first ordered to support the 33d, but while advancing was ordered to the front "for the purpose of cutting off the flying enemy, already routed" by the left of the brigade, and while endeavoring to execute this order the position became critical and most of the casualties occurred, a "large force of the enemy" advancing on the right "under the cover of the woods." Babcock says it was "about to cut us off from the rest of [the] command" when the danger was discovered and the regiment ordered to fall back to the cover of a hill about fifty yards. According to Babcock, his men "only wavered a moment" and then retired and re-formed in good order "after delivering two well-directed volleys" into nearly if not quite a brigade of the enemy, so near the right of the regiment that "you could see the white of their eyes at the time of retiring."[31] The two regiments had come up a little to the right of

[27] William MacRae to Howell Cobb, September 23, 1862, reprinted in *OR*, vol. 19, pt. 1, 872.
[28] As of this writing, Carman's source for this quotation has not been identified.
[29] William H. Irwin to Mundee, September 22, 1862, reprinted in *OR*, vol. 19, pt. 1, 409.
[30] Joseph W. Corning to William H. Long, September 20, 1862, reprinted in *OR*, vol. 19, pt. 1, 414.
[31] Nathan S. Babcock to Irwin, September 20, 1862, reprinted in *OR*, vol. 19, pt. 1, 415–16.

the church, and Smith says, "At this point a severe flank fire from the woods was received …, which threw both regiments slightly into confusion. They were immediately rallied by their officers and faced by the rear rank, and ordered to lie down behind the crest of a slope facing toward the woods. The rest of the brigade was ordered to form behind a crest nearly at right angles to the other, facing to their proper front."[32]

A section of Owen's Rhode Island battery accompanied the advance of Irwin's brigade. The battery, when swept from its position by Greene's men, halted a few hundred yards in rear. After replenishing ammunition, Owen "took the pieces alone of the right section and proceeded up behind the advance that retook the field, but the infantry was quite unsteady on the right and broke the second time," and not deeming it prudent to risk his guns under such circumstances, he withdrew and reported to Sumner.[33]

It was the impression, if not the understanding, among the officers of Irwin's brigade that they were to retake the woods at the church, and this view was shared by Franklin, who in his testimony before the Committee on the Conduct of the War said, "General Smith made a charge with this brigade on the advancing enemy, and, after a severe musketry fight of fifteen or twenty minutes, drove them back into the woods. He attempted to follow them into the woods, but was met by a fire from a superior force in the woods, and halted just this side of the crest of the hill, where his troops were secure from that fire."[34]

On the contrary, Smith says that he never contemplated a movement into the woods; that when he had cleared the front of the enemy's skirmishers and put the 20th and 49th New York under cover of the crest of the hill near the church he had done—without orders—all he had set out to do; that he did not see Irwin and the other three regiments of the brigade; and that he supposed he had intimated to a staff officer that, when Irwin came up, he was to take position behind the crest to the left of the two regiments he had put in position.[35] In view of this statement and the fact that "Baldy" Smith was too good a soldier to put any part of his command in close action by the flank, we must conclude that the responsibility rests upon Irwin, who as events proved later in the day should not have been entrusted with any responsibility.

As soon as Irwin's brigade was formed and ordered to lie down, skirmishers were thrown out to the crest of the hill along its front. A Confederate battery advanced and played with severity along the flank of the brigade and through the line of the 20th New York, which from the nature of the ground was compelled to refuse its left and thus received the fire along its entire front. Irwin says, "Sharpshooters from the woods to the right and to the extreme left also opened upon us. Shell, grape, and canister swept from left to right. The practice of the enemy was rapid and very accurate, and in a short time our loss was very heavy, and the dead and wounded encumbered our ranks."[36]

Before the entire brigade had been established on the line held by Greene in the morning, Smith sent for Brooks's brigade to act as a support, but without his knowledge or consent it had been ordered by Sumner to support French. At first it was ordered to the support of Sedgwick on the extreme right, but before getting into position French reported his ammunition exhausted, and Brooks was ordered by Sumner to reinforce him. On gaining French's right, Brooks found the enemy had been checked and repelled, and the brigade took position in the south edge of the Mumma cornfield 170 yards from and parallel to the sunken road. This brought it on Irwin's left and the position was maintained until the close of the battle, the men lying on their arms and subjected to quite a galling fire of both artillery and sharpshooters, causing numerous casualties.

Meanwhile, Leonard Martin's Battery F, 5th U.S. Artillery went into position 110 yards south of the Smoketown Road and near the small graveyard, where it remained substantially in the same position until the close of the battle, firing at intervals during the afternoon of the seventeenth upon the enemy's artillery in the woods around the church and in the field south of it. Irwin records that to the excellent service of this battery the safety of his brigade "may be largely imputed" and that had it "not checked the heavy fire from the batteries of the enemy, they would have destroyed the greater part of my command."[37]

Soon after Martin had taken this position Slocum's division arrived and its artillery was put in position. Battery D, 2d U.S. Artillery (Lieutenant Edward B. Williston), on Martin's right, with its right gun about twelve yards from the Smoketown Road and seventy-five yards from the Mumma lane, opened fire at the Dunkard church and the woods surrounding it to drive there from the Confederate sharpshooters that were annoying Irwin. Battery A, Massachusetts Light Artillery (Captain Josiah Porter), relieved Thomas's and Knap's batteries, which after the advance of Irwin's brigade had opened fire

[32] William F. Smith to Oliver D. Greene, 402.

[33] Owen to Clarke, 326.

[34] *Report of the Joint Committee on the Conduct of the War*, 37th Cong., 3d sess., 1863, S. Rep. 108, pt. 1, serial 1152, 626.

[35] William F. Smith to Franklin, December 17, 1897, typescript copy, "6th Corps" folder, box 1, "Antietam Studies."

[36] Irwin to Mundee, 409–410.

[37] Ibid., 411.

upon the woods north of the church and upon Slocum's arrival had retired beyond the East Woods. Porter took position on Williston's right, north of the Smoketown Road and about one hundred yards in front of the East Woods. Cothran's battery, with its support (the 107th New York) was relieved by the eight guns of Battery A, Maryland Light Artillery (Captain John W. Wolcott), and retired to the fields beyond the East Woods. From the field east of the D. R. Miller buildings to the Mumma house, there were now seven batteries—Cowan's, Frank's, Vanneman's, Wolcott's, Porter's, Williston's, and Martin's—aggregating forty-four guns so closely placed that there was room for no more, and Captain William Hexamer's New Jersey battery was held in reserve in a depression in the East Woods, near the Smoketown Road.

Slocum had marched through Keedysville and crossed the Antietam by the Upper Bridge, and it was after noon when his advance reached the field. While the batteries were being put in position, Franklin, Slocum, and Smith were considering a charge upon the woods at the church. Newton's and Torbert's brigades had come up and been formed beyond the woods, and Bartlett's arrival was awaited to form a reserve, when it was found that Sumner had retained Bartlett to strengthen his own right in place of Brooks, whom he had sent to French. Franklin says:

> Immediately after [Slocum's] arrival two of his brigades (Newton's and Torbert's) were formed in column of attack, to carry the wood in the immediate vicinity of the white church. The other brigade (Bartlett's) had been ordered by General Sumner to keep near his right. As this brigade was to form the reserve for the column of attack, I waited until it came up. About the same time General Sumner arrived on the spot, and directed the attack to be postponed … Shortly afterward the commanding general came to the position and decided that it would not be prudent to make the attack, our position on the right being then considerably in advance of what it had been in the morning.[38]

In *Battles and Leaders of the Civil War*, Franklin writes:

> While awaiting the arrival of Slocum, I went to the right, held by Sumner. I found him at the head of his troops, but much depressed. He told me that his whole corps was exhausted and could do nothing more that day … About three hundred yards in its front, across an open field, was a wood … strongly held by the enemy. The corps had been driven back from an attack on this wood with great loss.
>
> When General Slocum arrived I placed two brigades of his division on General Sumner's left and was awaiting the arrival of his third brigade, which was to be in reserve. With the two brigades I intended to make an attack on the wood referred to, and General Sumner was informed of my intention. The two brigades were ready to move. Just as the third brigade arrived, General Sumner rode up and directed me not to make the attack, giving as a reason for his order, that if I were defeated the right would be entirely routed, mine being the only troops left on the right that had any life in them. Major [Herbert] Hammerstein, of McClellan's staff, was near, and I requested him to inform General McClellan of the state of affairs, and that I thought the attack ought to be made. Shortly afterward McClellan rode up, and, after hearing the statements of Sumner and myself, decided that as the day had gone so well on the other parts of the line it would be unsafe to risk anything on the right. Of course, no advance was made by the division.[39]

Palfrey says, "Wisely or unwisely, Sumner paralyzed the action of Franklin's corps, first detaching from Smith and then from Slocum."[40] But the responsibility rested upon McClellan for staying Franklin's advance. There was yet time to make it when he came upon this part of the field. McClellan says:

> Toward the middle of the afternoon, proceeding to the right, I found that Sumner's, Hooker's, and Mansfield's corps had met with serious losses. Several general officers had been carried from the field severely wounded, and the aspect of affairs was anything but promising. At the risk of greatly exposing our center, I ordered two brigades from Porter's corps … to re-enforce the right …
>
> General Sumner expressed the most decided opinion against another attempt during that day to assault the enemy's position in front, as portions of our troops were so much scattered and demoralized. In view of these circumstances, after making changes in the position of some of the troops, I directed the different commanders to hold their positions, and, being satisfied that this could be done without the assistance of the two brigades from the center, I countermanded the order, which was in course of execution.[41]

38 Franklin to Seth Williams, 377.
39 Franklin, "Notes on Crampton's Gap and Antietam," in *Battles and Leaders of the Civil War*, vol. 2 (New York: Century Co., 1887), 597.
40 Francis Winthrop Palfrey, *The Antietam and Fredericksburg*, vol. 5 of *The Army in the Civil War* (New York: Charles Scribner's Sons, 1882), 106.
41 McClellan to Lorenzo Thomas, 62.

Upon the abandonment of aggressive movement, Williams's division of the Twelfth Corps fell back into the East Woods and acted as a support to Franklin's corps. Smith's division retained its position. Newton's brigade of Slocum's division formed on Hancock's left and supported the two Maryland batteries. Torbert's New Jersey brigade formed on Newton's left and on either side of the Smoketown Road, supporting the batteries of Porter, Hexamer, Williston, and Martin. Bartlett's brigade was, for the present, held in reserve.

The remainder of the day was employed in collecting stragglers, straightening the line, filling the gaps in it, and relieving batteries that had been long in action by fresh ones. "The troops lay," writes Francis A. Walker, "with the bodies of the Union and Confederate slain all around, in momentary readiness to move forward …; now and then the bustle of the staff presaged new combinations, or the movement of troops to fill the gaps in the line of battle was taken to mean that hot work was at once to begin; at intervals the artillery broke out in furious cannonading all along the line, or here and there two ambitious battery commanders tested the range of their guns and the skill of their cannoneers in a duel across the crouching lines of infantry."[42]

Soon after Irwin had taken position under the crest of the plateau nearly opposite the Dunkard church, a Confederate battery south of the church became very active in throwing shot and shell at the two regular batteries south of the Smoketown Road and into the ranks of the New Jersey brigade supporting them, causing some casualties and much annoyance. The two batteries seemed unable to reach or silence it; Hexamer's battery was sent for and soon appeared. As he came up at a gallop, Hexamer said, "I'll silence that Battery, or cut down every tree in the woods."[43] The other batteries ceased firing. Hexamer passed them a few yards and opened fire. For fifteen or twenty minutes he rained shot and shell into and around that battery and it ceased to respond. He gave a few more shot and then withdrew amid the cheers of all who witnessed his fine practice.

Soon after this artillery duel, about 3:00 p.m., the 5th Maine and the 16th New York of Bartlett's brigade (then in second line in the edge of the East Woods) were ordered to the left as a support to Irwin and to fill an interval between him and Brooks. When in position their left rested on the Mumma lane and a little to the rear of Brooks's right. For the next hour there was comparative quiet on this part of the field; about 4:30 p.m. it was broken by the rapid roar of artillery on the extreme right, bringing every infantryman to his feet and the cannoneers to their guns in anticipation of a Confederate advance. For the cause of this we must go inside the Confederate lines.

At the hour when McClellan and Sumner came to the conclusion that further offensive movements were inadmissible and that the right wing of the army should remain on the defensive, Lee had ordered an attack by Jackson on McClellan's right in order to relieve his center from the pressure of Richardson's attack and the threatening movement of Pleasonton on the Boonsboro and Sharpsburg Road, and Stuart was then massing cavalry, artillery, and infantry for that purpose. McLaws says that, the enemy having abandoned their attempt to advance, he had an opportunity to examine the relative position of his own line and that of the enemy and soon "became convinced that we had nothing to gain by an advance of our troops."[44] But Lee, Longstreet, and Jackson had come to a different conclusion. Longstreet does not refer to it in his official report, but elsewhere says:

> At one or two points near our centre were dead angles into which I rode from time to time for closer observation of the enemy when his active aggression was suspended. General Burnside was busy at his crossing, but no report of progress had been sent me. One of my rides towards the Dunker chapel revealed efforts of the enemy to renew his work on that part of the field. Our troops were ordered to be ready to receive it. Its non-aggression suggested an opportunity for the Confederates, and I ordered McLaws and Walker to prepare to assault. Hood was back in position with his brigades, and Jackson was reported on his way, all in full supply of ammunition. It seemed probable that by concealing our movements under cover of the wood from the massed batteries of Doubleday's artillery on the north, and the batteries of position on the east, we could draw our columns so near to the enemy in front before our move could be known that we would have but a few rods to march before we could mingle our ranks with those of the enemy; that our columns massed and in goodly numbers, pressing severely upon a single point, would give the enemy much trouble, and might cut him in two, and break up his battle arrangements at the lower bridge; but just then General Jackson reported, with authority from General Lee, that he with the cavalry was ordered to march around and turn the entire position of the enemy by his right flank, and strike at his rear. He found that the march would be long and extremely hazardous, and abandoned his orders.[45]

---

[42] Francis A. Walker, 124–25.

[43] John P. Beech to Carman, August 29, 1899, "6th Corps" folder, "Antietam Studies."

[44] Lafayette McLaws to "the Adjutant-General, Headquarters General Longstreet [Gilbert Moxley Sorrel]," October 20, 1862, reprinted in OR, vol. 19, pt. 1, 859.

[45] James Longstreet, *From Manassas to Appomattox: Memoirs of the Civil War in America* (Philadelphia: J. P. Lippincott Co., 1896), 256–57.

John G. Walker was with Ransom's Brigade when the order was brought from Longstreet directing General Ransom to advance and capture the Union batteries in his front. Having been previously instructed by Jackson to hold his position in the woods until Stuart could turn the Union right and then advance, Walker directed Ransom to delay the execution of Longstreet's order until he could see Longstreet. Walker's action was approved; this was about three o'clock. Ransom says:

> About noon, General Longstreet sent me word to take the battery in our front, and the order to advance was given when General McLaws arrived and ordered me to postpone the attempt. Again, about 2 or 3 o'clock, I received instructions to advance and take the batteries. Just at this time the enemy was observed to have massed a strong force about the batteries, and General Walker, having arrived, forbade the movement until he could communicate with General Longstreet, in person. Shortly afterward, orders came to defer any attempt upon the enemy's position until General Jackson should have attacked him upon his right flank.[46]

It appears from an incident given by the adjutant of the 35th North Carolina that Jackson, in person, came to Ransom's Brigade and gave orders to be in readiness to join in an attack upon the Union right.

> [About 2 o'clock] Stonewall Jackson came along our lines … Stonewall remarked to Col. [Matt] Ransom, as he did to the other colonels along the line, that with Stuart's cavalry and some infantry he was going around the Federal right and get in their rear, and added "when you hear the rattle of my small arms, this whole line must advance." He wished to ascertain the force opposed, and a man of our regiment named Hood was sent up a tall tree which he climbed carefully to avoid observation by the enemy. Stonewall called out to know how many Yankees he could see over the hill and beyond the East Woods. Hood replied, "Whooee! there are oceans of them, General." "Count their flags," said Jackson. This Hood proceeded to do until he had counted thirty-nine, when the general told him that would do and to come down.[47]

Longstreet's idea was an attack directly to the front. Lee sought to relieve the pressure upon the center and right by turning McClellan's right.[48] Jackson contemplated both the turning movement and an attack in front.

As elsewhere stated, Jackson was disappointed at the partial success of McLaws's attack and directed Stuart (who, with his artillery, the 13th Virginia, and the 24th North Carolina, had been checked well to the left and front) "to hold this advance position, and … he [Jackson] would send all the infantry he could get in order to follow up the success." However, these reinforcements were, says Stuart, "diverted to another part of the field."[49] Jackson was not discouraged; he believed the enemy had done their worst, were sorely punished, and that there was still the chance of an opportunity to sweep the Union right from the field and gain a decisive victory.

General Walker says:

> The Federal infantry assaults having ceased, about half-past twelve I sought Jackson to report that from the front of my position in the wood I thought I had observed a movement of the enemy [Irwin's brigade—EAC], as if to pass through the gap where I had posted Colonel Cooke's two regiments. I found Jackson in rear of Barksdale's brigade, under an apple-tree, sitting on his horse, with one leg thrown carelessly over the pommel of his saddle, plucking and eating the fruit. Without making any reply to my report, he asked me abruptly: "Can you spare me a regiment and a battery?" I replied that Colonel Hill's 49th [48th—EAC] North Carolina, a very strong regiment, was in reserve, and could be spared, and that I could also give him both French's and Branch's batteries, but that they were without long-range ammunition, which had been exhausted at Harper's Ferry.
>
> Jackson then went on to say that, owing to the nature of the ground, General Stuart's cavalry could take no part in the battle and were in the rear, but that Stuart himself had reported for such duty as he could perform.
>
> Jackson added that he wished to make up, from the different commands on our left, a force of four or five thousand men, and give them to Stuart, with orders to turn the enemy's right, and attack him in the rear; that I must give orders to my division to advance to the front, and attack the enemy as soon as I should hear Stuart's guns—and that our whole left wing would move to the attack at the same time. Then, replacing his foot in the stirrup, he said with great emphasis: "We'll drive McClellan into the Potomac."
>
> After giving orders for the regiment and batteries to report to Stuart, I galloped down the line where I had posted Cooke … Soon returning to my command, I repeated General Jackson's order to my brigade commanders and

---

46 Robert Ransom Jr. to William A. Smith, September 22, 1862, reprinted in *OR*, vol. 19, pt. 1, 920.

47 Walter Clark, "Sharpsburg: Reminiscences of This Hard-Fought Battle," *Wilmington (N.C.) Messenger*, October 7, 1894.

48 "While the attack on our center was progressing, General Jackson had been directed to endeavor to turn the enemy's right." Robert E. Lee to Samuel Cooper, August 19, 1863, reprinted in *OR*, vol. 19, pt. 1, 151.—EAC

49 James E. B. Stuart to Robert H. Chilton, February 13, 1864, reprinted in *OR*, vol. 19, pt. 1, 820.

directed them to listen for the sound of Stuart's guns. We all confidently expected to hear the welcome sound by 2 o'clock, at least, and as that hour approached every ear was on the alert. Napoleon at Waterloo did not listen more intently for the sound of Grouchy's fire than did we for Stuart's. Two o'clock came, but nothing was heard of Stuart. Half-past two and then three, and still Stuart made no sign.

About half-past three a staff-officer of General Longstreet brought me an order from that general to advance and attack the enemy in my front. As the execution of this order would materially interfere with Jackson's plans, I thought it my duty before beginning the movement to communicate with General Longstreet personally. I found him in rear of the position in which I had posted Cooke in the morning, and upon informing him of Jackson's intentions, he withdrew his order.[50]

As soon as the order for the movement was given by Lee, Stuart massed his cavalry to lead in its execution. Fitzhugh Lee's Brigade was then in rear of Jackson's left and near it was the 7th Virginia Cavalry of Robertson's Brigade. Hampton's Brigade was brought from the right. (Hampton had acted as rear-guard to McLaws in the march from Harper's Ferry.) Crossing the Potomac partly by Knott's Ford (at the mouth of the Antietam) and partly at Shepherdstown Ford, he marched to the vicinity of General Lee's headquarters about the middle of the forenoon and remained until about 1:00 p.m., when he moved rapidly to the left (where Fitzhugh Lee had already massed three of his regiments at the Cox place, on the Mercerville Road). Hampton formed on Fitzhugh Lee's right, under cover of Nicodemus Hill, upon which were several batteries of artillery, slightly withdrawn from the crest of the hill.

In all Stuart had seven regiments of cavalry and nine guns from various batteries (one of which was from Poague's, two from Raine's, and three from Brockenbrough's) under Captain John Pelham, and in addition the batteries of French and Branch, supported by the 48th North Carolina Infantry of Walker's Division. The advance was made about 3:00 p.m., the 4th Virginia Cavalry leading. The column, starting from the Cox farm, passed up the road under cover of the high ground on its right until the advance reached New Industry, when it halted while the guns under Pelham, turning to the right and moving a short distance on the road leading to the Hagerstown Road at the toll-gate, turned to the left and went into position on the high ground nine hundred yards from and directly west of Doubleday's guns on Poffenberger Hill. Stuart's guns were greeted with such a heavy fire as they took position that they were quickly used up and forced to withdraw. Poague, who commanded one gun, says, "Along with six or eight other guns, under the direction of Major Pelham, an attempt was made to dislodge the enemy's batteries, but failed completely, being silenced in fifteen or twenty minutes by a most terrific fire."[51]

Hampton's Brigade moved but a short distance to the left before the head of the column was halted. Branch's and French's guns went into position on Nicodemus Hill about the time Pelham's guns were driven off and were almost instantly silenced, losing many killed or wounded by Doubleday's guns, which turned savagely upon them. The 48th North Carolina, which had moved double-quick to the left to support these guns, was not engaged. Stuart, after halting the head of his column an hour or more, withdrew and gave up the intended movement on McClellan's right, and the entire force fell back. Stuart reports, "In this movement I was honored with the advance. In endeavoring to pass along up the river bank, however, I found that the river made such an abrupt bend that the enemy's batteries were within 800 yards of the brink of the stream, which would have made it impossible to have succeeded in the movement proposed, and it was accordingly abandoned."[52] Jackson says, "In the afternoon, in obedience to instructions from the commanding general, I moved to the left with a view of turning the Federal right, but I found his numerous artillery so judiciously established in their front and extending so near to the Potomac, which here makes a remarkable bend, … as to render it inexpedient to hazard the attempt."[53]

When Jackson returned to near the Dunkard church he met Walker and told him of Stuart's failure, for the reason that he found the Union right "securely *posted on the Potomac*." Upon Walker's expressing surprise at this statement, "Jackson replied that he also had been surprised, as he had supposed the Potomac much farther away; but he remarked that Stuart had an excellent eye for topography, and it must be as he represented. He added: 'It is a great pity,—we should have driven

50 John G. Walker, "Sharpsburg," in *Battles and Leaders*, 679–80.
51 William T. Poague to William H. Thomas, September 22, 1862, reprinted in *OR*, vol. 19, pt. 1, 1010.
52 Stuart to Chilton, 820. Although the passage Carman quotes is applicable to the situation he describes, it has been detached from its original context. In Stuart's report this passage is preceded by the following sentence: "On the next day it was determined, the enemy not again attacking, to turn the enemy's right." Although Stuart did indeed have the responsibility for leading the advance in the proposed flanking move of the seventeenth, the quotation Carman employs refers to events that occurred the following day. Here again Carman violates modern standards of attribution and usage of historical evidence, though in his defense it must be conceded that the geographic obstacle Stuart describes—an abrupt bend of the river, narrowing the channel of advance around the Union right—was just as formidable twenty-four hours earlier. This is demonstrated in the very next quotation from Jackson, which described events on the seventeenth.
53 Thomas J. Jackson to Lee, April 23, 1863, reprinted in *OR*, vol. 19, pt. 1, 956–57.

McClellan into the Potomac.'"[54] (Considering the fact that Stuart had been two whole days on the left, within a half-mile of the Potomac and the great bend in it, one wonders that he had not informed himself of the situation on that flank. A single horseman could have gone unopposed a half-mile and viewed the ground at the bend, which was plainly to be seen from Nicodemus Hill—where Stuart had his batteries.)

As Stuart's unsuccessful movement ended Confederate operations on this part of the field and we shall have no occasion to return to it, we may as well briefly note such changes of position as were made during the afternoon. At half-past twelve Hood's Division, now reduced to less than eight hundred men, returned to the West Woods and occupied them about three hundred yards west of the church. Hays's small brigade formed in Hood's rear. The 49th North Carolina and part of the 35th, after the encounter with Irwin, fell back to the position from which they had charged Greene's flank. The 46th North Carolina advanced from the west edge of the woods and filled an interval between the 49th and Hood. Captain Hudgin's company of the 30th Virginia and other skirmishers were ordered to the east edge of the woods to pick off the Union cannoneers, who were tearing the treetops with shot and shell, but there was such a shower of canister poured upon them and the range being too great for their arms that they fell back into the woods under shelter. J. R. Johnson's Battery, which had fallen back with Trimble's Brigade early in the morning, returned to the field about 2:00 p.m. and took position three hundred yards to the right of and in advance of the Reel barn, a cornfield in its immediate front. It relieved Peyton's[55] Battery of Jones's Battalion, immediately became warmly engaged with Union artillery, and poured an incessant and annoying fire upon Irwin's and Brooks's brigades and upon Richardson's division; all effort to silence it was unavailing. For some time Johnson was alone but was afterwards joined by D'Aquin's Battery, which took position on his right. Both batteries were engaged until dark, with very little infantry for support. The batteries were on a point of a hill, the grass was burning around them, and when the engagement became very hot the caissons were moved to the foot of the hill to the left, near several haystacks. They retired at eight o'clock.

Kershaw's and Barksdale's Brigades, which since their repulse had been lying under cover of the fences and ledges beyond the woods, moved to the left, Barksdale forming on Early's right and Kershaw in the northern body of the woods, on the left of Armistead. Later in the day Major John H. Lowe, now commanding Lawton's Brigade, came up with about one hundred men and joined Early. Jackson's Division and Semmes's Brigade were in reserve. Between 3:00 and 4:00 p.m., Cooke's 27th North Carolina and 3d Arkansas and Cobb's Brigade—all out of ammunition—were relieved by Ripley's Brigade and fell back for food and ammunition. A little after 4:00 p.m. Hood and Hays moved from the West Woods and took position in the open ground opposite the mouth of the sunken road and supporting D. H. Hill, whose men were lying along the fences of the Hagerstown Road. About 5:00 p.m. the 27th North Carolina, 3d Arkansas, and Cobb's Brigade returned to the field. Cobb went to the left and joined Kershaw, and Cooke's two regiments remained near the southwest corner of the West Woods until sunset. The 48th North Carolina, returning from its participation in Stuart's movement, formed along the fence on their left. At sunset Ransom's Brigade moved from its position behind the rocky ledge to the right and bivouacked for the night beyond the Reel farm. Barksdale gained ground to the right and occupied the position vacated by Ransom; Manning's Brigade entered the woods and formed on Barksdale's right. As completed, from right to left, this was the disposition of the Confederate left for the night: Hood's Division and Hays's Brigade held the open ground opposite the sunken road; Ripley's Brigade held from Hood's left to the West Woods, at a point about three hundred yards west of the Hagerstown Road; Manning's Brigade held the woods west of the church; Barksdale's and Early's Brigades were behind the ledge that ran from the D. R. Miller barn, facing the Hagerstown Road; Armistead's Brigade was in the north part of the middle woods facing nearly north, his right in rear of Early's left; Kershaw's Brigade was in the north body of the woods, on the left of Armistead, facing northeast; and Cobb's Brigade was on Kershaw's left, facing north. Semmes's Brigade was in reserve near the Alfred Poffenberger place, and Ransom was in reserve in Hood's rear. Jackson's Division was supporting the artillery, which was under the cover of Hauser's Ridge, ready to run onto it at a moment's notice. Stuart's cavalry covered the interval between the left of the infantry and the Potomac.

After Stuart's brief affair on the left there was quiet on this part of the field, with the exception of some cannonading on the right and a movement of a regiment of Irwin's brigade, connected with operations on the line of the sunken road, to which we now return. Early in the afternoon, after Richardson had been grievously wounded, Hancock was directed by McClellan in person to take command of his division. Having received his orders from McClellan and some instructions from Sumner, Hancock proceeded to the ground. Francis A. Walker presents a graphic account of his ride:

---

[54] John G. Walker, 680.

[55] In his original manuscript, Carman here refers to the unit by the alternate designation of "Fry's Battery." For the sake of consistency, the editor has reverted here to the name employed by Carman in all other references to this battery.

Among the galloping staffs which cross that bloody field in the early afternoon, arousing the momentary expectation of renewed attack, is one of especially notable bearing, at which men gaze long as it passes down the jagged line of troops from right to left. At the head rides a general officer whose magnificent physique, bold air, and splendid horsemanship are well calculated to impress the beholder. Behind him ride a group of as dashing aids-de-camp [sic] as the army knows. It is Hancock, sent for in haste, from his brigade of the Sixth Corps, to take command of the division at whose head the gallant Richardson has fallen, never to mount horse or draw sword more. It is not amid the pomp of the review, with bands playing and well-ordered lines, but on the trampled battle-field, strewn with bloody stretchers and the wreck of caissons and ambulances, the dead and dying thick around, the wounded still limping and crawling to the rear, with shells shrieking through the air, that Hancock meets and greets the good regiments he is to lead in a score of battles. The lines are ragged from shot and shell; the uniforms are rent and soiled from hedge, fence, and ditch; the bands are engaged in carrying off the wounded, or assisting the regimental surgeons at their improvised hospitals; scarcely twenty-one hundred men remain with the colors of this fine, strong division.[56]

Hancock's instructions were to hold the position. He found the troops occupying one line of battle in close proximity to the enemy, who were then again in position near the Piper house. The 14th Connecticut and a detachment from the 108th New York, both under the command of Colonel Dwight Morris, were in reserve, the whole command numbering about 2,100 men, with no artillery. Finding a considerable interval at a dangerous point between Meagher's and Caldwell's brigades, the 14th Connecticut was placed there and the detachment of the 108th New York on the extreme left. Application was made for two batteries of artillery to the different commanders within reach, and to the chief of artillery, but none could be spared at that time. Morris was confident, however, of holding the position as he had been instructed, notwithstanding the absence of artillery and the fact that the men were already suffering from the shells of the enemy. He had a firm reliance upon the good qualities of the troops but was too weak to make an attack unless an advance was made on the right, as he had no reserves and his line was already enfiladed by the enemy's artillery in front of the right wing (which was screened from the fire of the Union guns on the right by the West Woods, then in Confederate possession). Soon after arriving on the ground a command of the enemy, probably G. T. Anderson's, was seen in line of battle, preceded by skirmishers advancing across his front, beyond the Piper house and toward Pleasonton's batteries and the regular infantry that had been thrown across the Antietam. He immediately sent a pressing message to Franklin for a battery, and Hexamer's battery of Slocum's division was ordered to report to him.

Hexamer was then in the East Woods, to which he had retired after his affair with the battery near the church. He quickly passed to the rear, went through the low ground around the Roulette farm, and then up and onto the open ridge, where most of the infantry were lying just behind its crest. The enemy had been sweeping the ridge with artillery, and Hexamer took position near its top, very near the spot from which Graham's battery had been driven, and opened fire. At each discharge of the guns the rebound sent them down the hill and they were rolled up again with the cheerful assistance of the infantry, more than willing to give a helping hand to the Jersey Dutchmen. In a very short time the enemy's infantry disappeared from view.

While Hexamer was thus engaged, perhaps a few minutes earlier, Captain Emory Upton, Slocum's chief of artillery, rode to Irwin's brigade and saw Hood's Division and Hays's Brigade marching toward the sunken road from the woods beyond the church. He suggested to Irwin that a battery should be placed in front of the left of his brigade, and Irwin, after examining the ground attentively, acquiesced. Not a moment could be lost, as "the enemy were massing in front with the evident design of throwing a powerful column against my left, and they could not be seen, except from that part of the line." Smith approved and Upton ordered up a battery, which opened with three rifled guns, "playing on the masses of the enemy with great effect for half an hour," when the three pieces were withdrawn.[57] These guns were relieved by Williston's battery of Napoleon guns, the fire of which Irwin reports as "terribly destructive."[58]

When Williston's battery was in full play, the Piper orchard on the left and front was occupied by D. H. Hill's skirmishers, whom Irwin says it was necessary to dislodge for the protection of the battery. He ordered Major Thomas W. Hyde (commanding the 7th Maine) to send a company and drive them away. Hyde acted promptly and had scarcely detached the company from the regiment when Irwin rode up and exclaimed in nearly these words, "That is not enough, sir; go yourself; take your regiment and drive them from those trees and buildings," pointing to the orchard and the Piper buildings. Hyde was perfectly astounded at an order to do, with his 181 officers and men, what Richardson's and French's divisions had

---

[56] Francis A. Walker, 125.

[57] Irwin to Mundee, 410. Hyde says these three guns were of a Maryland battery. Thomas W. Hyde, *Following the Greek Cross; Or, Memories of the Sixth Army Corps* (Boston: Houghton, Mifflin and Co., 1894), 99.—*EAC*

[58] Irwin to Mundee, 410.

failed to accomplish, and asked Irwin to repeat this order and point out the ground again. He did so, quite emphatically, in nearly the same words, and added with an oath, "Those are your orders, sir." Irwin repeated this several times.[59]

To the nearest point of the orchard was about six hundred yards; to the nearest of the Piper buildings—the barn—it was a half-mile. Hyde faced his regiment to the left and led it obliquely across the front of the skirmishers of Brooks's Vermont brigade on his left, then, coming to a front, sent out skirmishers, who drove the Confederate skirmishers from the edge of the cornfield and the hollow lying west of and near the orchard he was ordered to clear. The regiment closely followed the skirmishers and crossed the sunken road, which was so filled with dead and wounded that the mounted officers had difficulty in crossing without permitting their horses to step on them. (Hyde says his horse "had to step on them to get over."[60]) As soon as the road was crossed, the regiment was halted in the trampled corn to straighten the line, and, being now under fire from the front and left, Hyde gave the order to charge, directing the regiment on a point to the right of the Piper barn. The line dashed forward with a cheer, at a double-quick, down into the cup-shaped hollow. Hill's men in the orchard, on the left, being flanked and in danger of being cut off, broke and ran. Those directly in front, at the straw stacks and the Piper barn, retreated. At this moment a line of Confederates rose up from behind the stone fences of the Hagerstown Road, which were to the right and front, and poured in a volley, which, however, did not do much damage. At this Hyde ordered the regiment to oblique to the left, which brought it behind the ridge running from the barn to the Hagerstown Road (and somewhat protected from the fire coming from the stone fences) and then forward onto the ridge at the right of the barn. Hyde was riding a few feet in advance of his regiment, and as he neared the crest of the ridge he saw over it a line lying down, waiting for him at the ready, and another body double-quicking down the Piper lane and making for his left to cut off retreat.

It was but a short time before this that G. T. Anderson had led his brigade back from the ridge beyond the Piper house (out of the range of Hexamer's guns) and put it under cover of the ridge that Hyde was now mounting. Around him were the broken divisions of Hill and R. H. Anderson—some fragments with him under cover of the ridge and others on the Hagerstown Road and in the Piper lane—all in more or less disorder. Hill was walking up and down giving words of encouragement to his already twice-beaten command when he heard the fire of the skirmishers and, going to the rest of the ridge, saw his own skirmishers running in and Hyde advancing. Hill called G. T. Anderson's attention to it, and Anderson ordered his men to lie down and await orders as Hill sent some men down the lane to gain Hyde's left.

All this Hyde saw at a glance as his men were breasting the ridge. As he was greatly outnumbered and saw no support coming, to avoid being surrounded he ordered his regiment to move by the left flank before any of it had come in sight of Hill's men, and moving double-quick passed the Piper barn, went through an opening in the fence, into the orchard, and very close to the lane. Here a new danger confronted him. After Hill's fight at noon, Major Hilary A. Herbert (now commanding Wilcox's Brigade) and Lieutenant Colonel Philip Cook of the 4th Georgia (who had some of Ripley's men with him and some of Wright's) came to the conclusion that they could be of some service on the right, near the Boonsboro Road. They went in that direction, but did not become engaged. On returning along the ridge, they saw Hill's skirmishers retreating from the orchard, reached the Piper lane (east of the house and opposite the southeast corner of the orchard) just as Hyde passed through the fence and into its southwest corner, and opened fire. Hyde returned the fire, then faced about and retreated up the hill into the orchard and formed on a small crest, where he poured another volley into Herbert's men (who were hanging on the left) and faced G. T. Anderson's, who had now charged from the ridge behind which he had been secreted.

Hyde was now exposed to a severe fire from three directions and the enemy advancing upon him in force. He saw four battle-flags, and a battery opened up on his with grape. Although somewhat shielded by the apple trees he lost quite heavily here. Hexamer's and Williston's batteries shelled the orchard, which aided him some, but having expended most of his ammunition he ordered a retreat. His men gave the enemy another volley as they attempted to follow, got through the strong picket fence with difficulty and, closing up on the colors, went back through the corn and across the sunken road. The regiment received the hearty cheers of the Vermont brigade and resumed the position from which it had advanced. It had been gone about thirty minutes and lost 88 in killed, wounded, and missing.

When Irwin saw to what a serious engagement he had committed the Maine men, he was very anxious to support them, but his orders were positive not to advance his line, so he rode forward and requested the colonel of the right regiment of Brooks's brigade to support them, which he declined to do without orders from Brooks. He then returned to his own line

---

[59] Hyde to Mundee, September 19, 1862, reprinted in *OR*, vol. 19, pt. 1, 412. Hyde elsewhere says, "Colonel Irwin rode up … and said, 'Major Hyde, take your regiment and drive the enemy away from those trees and buildings.' I saluted, and said, 'Colonel, I have seen a large body of rebels go in there, I should think two brigades.' … 'Are you afraid to go, sir?' said he, and repeated the order emphatically. 'Give the order so the regiment can hear it and we are ready, sir,' said I, which he did, and 'Attention!' brought every man to his feet." Hyde, *Following the Greek Cross*, 99–100.—EAC

[60] Ibid., 100.

to ask for a support from the rear, but in a few minutes "had the extreme pleasure of seeing the shattered but bare remnant of the Seventh Maine in good order return to my lines." He adds, "No words of mine can do justice to the firmness, intelligence, and heroic courage with which this regiment performed its dangerous task. Their killed and wounded and their colors riddled by balls are the proud, yet melancholy, witnesses of their valor."[61] Hyde writes, "When we knew our efforts were resultant from no place or design at headquarters, but were from an inspiration of John Barleycorn in our brigade commander alone, I wished I had been old enough, or distinguished enough, to have dared to disobey orders."[62]

The Confederate reports of this affair are meager. Hill says that "a movement of a rather farcical character now took place. General Pryor had gathered quite a respectable force behind a stone wall on the Hagerstown road, and Col. G. T. Anderson had about a regiment behind a hill immediately to the right of this road. A Maine regiment … came down to this hill wholly unconscious that there were any Confederate troops near it. A shout and a volley informed them of their dangerous neighborhood. The Yankee apprehension is acute; the idea was soon taken in, and was followed by the most rapid running I ever saw."[63] G. T. Anderson says, "General Hill … called my attention to a line of the enemy advancing apparently to attack us. Suffering them to come near us, I ordered my command to charge them, which they did in splendid style and good order, killing and wounding many of the enemy, taking several prisoners, and routing the remainder. We could not pursue them as far as I wished, because of the severe fire of artillery directed against us from long-range guns that we could not reach. In this charge parts of Wilcox's, Featherston's, and Pryor's brigades participated with mine."[64]

The artillery fire referred to by G. T. Anderson, which checked his pursuit of the 7th Maine, came from the batteries of Hexamer and Williston in front, and from Hains's battery, just in advance of the Middle Bridge. Williston opened upon Anderson as he charged from the ridge and followed him into the orchard, firing over the heads of the Maine men when they rallied in the orchard. Hexamer saw the preparations made to meet Hyde and opened upon Herbert as he approached the Piper lane from the south and continued it when he pursued Hyde through the orchard. The fire of both Williston and Hexamer inflicted some casualties upon Hyde, but it did much to enable him to rally and make an orderly retreat.

Hexamer was now out of ammunition and, being relieved by Woodruff's battery, went back to the East Woods. Williston remained in position until dark and then went back to the Mumma orchard. When Woodruff took position it was on the right of Hancock's left brigade, with orders not to fire except in reply to a Confederate battery or in case of an attack by them. Late in the evening, Lieutenant Albert C. M. Pennington, with a section of Tidball's battery of horse artillery, took position on an elevated ridge on Hancock's left and engaged a Confederate battery near some stacks beyond the Hagerstown Road, doing material service by precision of fire in concealing the weakness of the position. Pennington was withdrawn about dark and all was quiet on Hancock's line. Pickets were thrown out as far as possible—a very short distance, for Hill's skirmishers were again advanced to the northern part of the orchard.

French's division, which had opened the fight in the forenoon on this part of the field, had gone by detachments to the rear and, with the exception of the 14th Connecticut and the 108th New York, was in the vicinity of the Roulette place as a reserve. Owen's Rhode Island battery, which from the vicinity of the Clipp house had been directed late in the day to fire a few shots toward the corner of the woods near the church, was advanced beyond Brooks's left and took position on the knoll where the right of Kimball's brigade had done its fighting.

On the extreme right, Sumner made dispositions to support the powerful line of artillery on Poffenberger Hill. Two guns of Captain Robert B. Hampton's Pennsylvania battery were moved from the barn farther to the right and front and Captain John G. Hazard's Rhode Island battery went into position at the northwest corner of the East Woods. When Williston's battery was sent to the front and left to strengthen Irwin, Wolcott's Maryland battery was moved from its position north of the Smoketown Road and took the ground vacated by Williston. Late in the day Wolcott sent four guns of his battery a little to the left to break up a cross-fire of the enemy upon him, by which several of his horses had been lost. About 5:30 p.m. Greene's division and Gordon's brigade of the Twelfth Corps were ordered by McClellan to the support of the left of Franklin's corps, south of the Smoketown Road. These movements completed the dispositions for the night from the extreme right of the Union line to its center, and the troops lay upon their arms amid the dead and wounded of the most bloody contest in history.

Hooker, with the First Corps, numbering 8,619 infantry, opened the battle at daybreak and was repulsed with a loss of 399 killed and 1,978 wounded—an aggregate of 2,377, or 27.50 percent of those engaged. Mansfield followed with the Twelfth Corps, numbering 7,239 infantry, and drove the enemy with a loss of 274 killed and 1,371 wounded—an aggregate of 1,645, or 22.72 percent of the number engaged. Sedgwick, with his division of 5,437 infantry, was then engaged and

---

[61] Irwin to Mundee, 410–11.
[62] Hyde, *Following the Greek Cross*, 104–5.
[63] Daniel H. Hill to Chilton, 1862 [day and month not given], reprinted in *OR*, vol. 19, pt. 1, 1025.
[64] George T. Anderson to Asbury Coward, September 30, 1862, reprinted in *OR*, vol. 19, pt. 1, 910.

repulsed with a loss of 369 killed and 1,572 wounded—an aggregate of 1,941, or 35.69 percent. All these losses were incurred in four hours, north and east of and at the Dunkard church, and mostly within a half-mile of it.

French's division went into action at the sunken road with 5,740 infantry and had 299 killed and 1,315 wounded—an aggregate of 1,614—28.11 percent of the number engaged. Richardson's division followed French's with 4,029 infantry and had 209 killed and 936 wounded—an aggregate of 1,145, or over 28.42 percent.

In these successive attacks the Union troops, not including Irwin's brigade, numbered 31,064 infantry, of whom 1,550 were killed and 7,172 wounded—an aggregate of 8,722 killed and wounded, 28.08 percent of the number engaged.[65]

The Confederate forces meeting these successive attacks, and attacking in return, were Jackson's Division of 1,784 infantry; Ewell's Division, 3,904; Hood's Division, 2,000; G. T. Anderson's Brigade, 590; McLaws's Division, 2,823; Walker's Division, 3,764; R. H. Anderson's Division, 3,672; and D. H. Hill's Division, 5,449—an aggregate of 23,986 infantry. The losses in these commands were: Jackson's Division, 597 killed and wounded, or 33.46 percent; Ewell's Division, 1,296, or 33.20 percent; Hood's Division, 915, or 40.75 percent; McLaws's Division, 1,068, or 37.83 percent; Walker's Division, 1,006, or 26.73 percent; R. H. Anderson's Division, 1,110, or 30.23 percent; D. H. Hill's Division, 1,716, or 31.49 percent; and G. T. Anderson's Brigade 85, or 14.41 percent. Of these, 1,304 were killed and 6,489 wounded—an aggregate of 7,793 killed and wounded, being 32.49 percent of the 23,986 engaged. Some regiments lost as low as 10 percent, others exceeded 50 percent, and at least two reached 85 percent.

In all, on both sides, 55,050 infantry were engaged on this part of the field with a loss of 2,854 killed and 13,661 wounded, an aggregate of 16,515, or 30 percent of the number engaged. Including the loss in the artillery and in Irwin's brigade, the killed and wounded numbered about 17,200. More than three-fourths of this loss occurred in less than four and a half hours' fighting—from 6:00 a.m. to nearly 10:30 a.m.—and within 1,100 yards of the Dunkard church; all of it occurred by one o'clock in the afternoon and within 1,200 yards of the church. Referring to this action, closing about half past ten, and of the field over which Hooker, Mansfield, and Sedgwick had fought (which was about 1,500 yards in length, with an average width of about 900 yards—an area of about 300 acres) and upon which 13,500 men had fallen, John C. Tidball truly says, "No other equal area on the American Continent has been so drenched in human blood."[66]

---

[65] In his original manuscript, Carman abruptly abandons exact percentages, reporting the losses for French, Richardson, and the attacking Union force as a whole at over 28 percent each. For the sake of editorial consistency, proper calculations have been inserted.

[66] John C. Tidball, "The Artillery Service in the War of the Rebellion, 1861–65," *Journal of the Military Service Institution of the United States* 12, no. 53 (September 1891): 968.

19

The Middle Bridge, the Fifth Corps, and the
Advance of Pleasonton's Cavalry Division[1]

Antietam, September 17, 1862

At daybreak of the seventeenth, the bold bluff bordering the east bank of the Antietam was crowned with forty-six heavy, long-range guns. North of the Boonsboro Road were the batteries of Wever, Langner, and Kusserow (20-pounder Parrott guns), and soon after daybreak Lieutenant Charles E. Hazlett's regular battery of Parrott guns was placed in the position occupied on the preceding day by Taft's New York battery, between Langner and Kusserow. South of the road were the batteries of Taft, von Kleiser, and Weed. Durell's battery was put on Weed's left early in the morning and Benjamin's was still farther to the left and rear, overlooking Sharpsburg and the country below it. They swept most of the ground between them and the Union troops. They were well served, especially the guns of Benjamin's battery, whose field of fire was extensive, reaching as far as the Dunkard church. From early morning until late in the day these batteries engaged the enemy's guns and fired upon their infantry. Their fire was very destructive upon the divisions of Ewell, Jackson, Hood, and D. H. Hill, and inflicted much loss upon the Confederates who were contending against the advance of French and Richardson at the sunken road. The batteries on the extreme left were supported by Burnside's Ninth Corps; those in the center and on the right by Porter's Fifth Corps.

Sykes's division held the line and supported the artillery south of the Boonsboro Road, three batteries of reserve artillery (Graham's and Lieutenants Marcus P. Miller's and William E. Van Reed's) being in rear of Lieutenant Colonel Robert C. Buchanan's brigade, which was on the right of the division. Major Charles S. Lovell's brigade was on the left of Buchanan's. Colonel Gouverneur K. Warren's small brigade of two New York regiments and Lieutenant Alanson M. Randol's regular battery were to the left and rear, covering the approaches in the direction of Harper's Ferry and connecting with the right of Burnside. About 9:00 a.m. Morell's division relieved Richardson, on the right of Sykes. Captain Richard Waterman's Rhode Island battery and Captain Augustus P. Martin's Massachusetts battery were thrown forward onto the bluff, the former joining in the fire of the heavy guns. Not including Humphreys's division, which did not reach the field until the morning of the eighteenth, Porter's strength as reported by McClellan was 12,930 and, including the reserve artillery, he had seventy-eight guns.

Pleasonton's cavalry division bivouacked on the night of the sixteenth in the west suburbs of Keedysville. While the battle was raging on the right, the heavy batteries were actively engaged, but Pleasonton's cavalry and Porter's infantry were idle. One of McClellan's staff says:

> During these operations the clamor of the artillery along the whole line of battle … was incessant. We could hear the distant muttering of musketry from the flanks, but Sumner's movement had evidently come to a stand. This produced a lull in the battle within our sight, and I had leisure to remark upon the head-quarters group immediately about me. In the midst was a small redan built of fence-rails, behind which sat General Fitz John Porter, who, with a telescope resting on the top rail, studied the field with unremitting attention, scarcely leaving his post during the whole day. His observations he communicated to the commander by nods, signs, or in words so low-toned and brief that the nearest by-standers had but little benefit from them. When not engaged with Porter, McClellan … [was] intently

---

[1] As with many portions of Carman's original manuscript, this chapter contains several differing sets of numbers for each page. The first page of extant text has a numeral "2" in its upper right corner, and unlike the first page of other chapters the text here does not begin with a repetition of the chapter number and title. This suggests that the first page of this chapter is missing. However, the folder containing this chapter of the manuscript contains two different title pages written in Carman's own hand: one reading "Chapter XX" (which is how Carman ultimately designated this chapter in his final ordering) and titled as it appears herein, and a photocopy of a now-missing page on which Carman had once written "Chapter XIX" and the title "Middle Bridge" before crossing out the latter portion and replacing it with the longer title. Between these two title pages and the first page of text are four maps (two printed, two hand-drawn) showing the section of the battlefield covered in this chapter; all are marked "Chapter XX" in Carman's hand.

After careful reading of the text, the editor has concluded that no text has been lost from this chapter. The peculiarity of the numbering and styling of its first page is a result of Carman's later consolidation of disparate material into a single chapter.

watching the battle ...; conversing with surrounding officers and giving his orders in the most quiet under-tones ... Every thing was as quiet and punctilious as a drawing-room ceremony.[2]

From this position McClellan viewed the progress of the action at the sunken road with a studied calmness of manner that scarcely concealed the underlying excitement, and when affairs seemed to be going well he exclaimed, "By George, this is a magnificent field, and if we win this fight it will cover all our errors and misfortunes forever!"[3] Up to this time not an infantry soldier or cavalryman had crossed the Middle Bridge that morning, nor had a demonstration been made beyond it, nor any action taken to relieve the pressure on the right, but Pleasonton had been ordered forward and was then moving on the road in the direction of the bridge with six regiments and a squadron of cavalry and the batteries of Gibson, Tidball, Hains, and Robertson. He was under orders to take a position beyond the bridge and support the left of Sumner's line. Finding the enemy had a crossfire of artillery on the bridge and sharpshooters covering it, he first threw forward cavalry skirmishers and then advanced Tidball's battery by piece to drive off the sharpshooters with canister.

The advance was led by Captain Samuel B. M. Young with a squadron of the 4th Pennsylvania Cavalry, followed by Lieutenant William N. Dennison's section of Tidball's battery. On nearing the bridge the column came under the fire of the Washington Artillery on Cemetery Hill and of Hilary P. Jones's batteries on the ridge to the north, but Young pushed on, dashed across the bridge, passed the pickets of the 12th U.S. Infantry that had crossed the night before, and charged up the long hill to its crest, 675 yards from the bridge. As he reached this point, still in the road, a shell was exploded in his ranks, killing or mortally wounding four men. Young immediately deployed on either side of the road and engaged the Confederate infantry near the west foot of the ridge, under cover of the stone fences lining the road.

This body of infantry was a detachment of G. T. Anderson's Brigade under the command of Captain Hansford D. D. Twiggs (1st Georgia Regulars). Late in the afternoon of the sixteenth, Twiggs had been ordered to take charge of this detail of eighty-five to one hundred men and do picket duty between Sharpsburg and the Antietam. He took position east of the town on a rise of ground about midway between the Antietam and the Boonsboro Road and threw out skirmishers. He was not recalled to join his brigade when it moved to the left on the morning of the seventeenth, and when an officer of the advance picket post reported the approach of cavalry and artillery he selected twenty of his best sharpshooters and hastened to the road, placing his men behind the stone fences on either side of it at the foot of the hill. When Young appeared Twiggs opened fire upon him with such effect as to drive him back. Young again advanced and attacked. By this time Dennison's section of artillery came up and was pushed forward to the highest point of the road; it had scarcely unlimbered when Twiggs, who had now called up his reserve and assembled his entire force behind the stone fences, drove the cannoneers from the guns. It was with much difficulty that they were withdrawn from their exposed position; while doing so the Confederate batteries on Cemetery Hill dropped shell and solid shot among the men and guns.

Meanwhile, Young was skirmishing with Twiggs, whose men were well protected, and Colonel James H. Childs came up with the main body of the 4th Pennsylvania Cavalry, which he had halted before reaching the crest of the ridge while he went forward on the right of the road to reconnoiter. Childs immediately saw that the place was not proper for cavalry and was returning to report the fact to Pleasonton and to bring up support to Young and the artillery when, on or very near the road a few yards east of the crest, he was struck by a [illeg.[4]] shot, fell from his horse, and died within an hour.

The other two sections of Tidball's battery had closely followed Childs and his regiment and, turning to the right, were run by hand up the ridge to a point about 160 yards from the road and immediately opened fire upon the enemy's batteries on the ridge beyond, Dennison's section following. Hains's battery followed Tidball and formed on his left, one section north of the road, the other on its left. It came into action under a heavy fire of artillery, directed particularly upon the right section, and was annoyed by Twiggs's men, who were in good rifle range. Robertson's battery followed Hains and went into position eighty yards to his left and rear, coming immediately under fire of the guns on Cemetery Hill. Gibson's battery followed Robertson and took position between him and Hains. Pleasonton says the plan of sending forward cavalry skirmishers and advancing Tidball's battery by piece "in a short time succeeded in clearing the front sufficiently to obtain positions for Gibson's, Robertson's, Tidball's, and Hains' batteries, who opened on the enemy with great effect, having a direct fire in front and an enfilading fire in front of Sumner's corps on the right, and supporting the right of Burnside's corps on the left, the distance to Sumner's corps being nearly a mile, and something greater to that of Burnside's, my force being the only one in front, connecting the two corps."[5] At the same time, Twiggs was keeping up his fire upon the batteries (especially Tidball's, which from its advanced and more exposed position presented a good target), until a battery beyond the Antietam—probably Weed's—enfiladed his position and he retreated precipitately, some of his men halting under

---

[2] A Virginian [David H. Strother], "Personal Recollections of the War," *Harper's New Monthly Magazine* 36, no. 213 (February 1868): 282.

[3] Ibid., 283.

[4] The word appears to be "cannst." Given the context, it appears that Carman meant to write that Childs was killed by a round of "canister."

[5] Alfred Pleasonton to Randolph B. Marcy, September 19, 1862, reprinted in *OR*, vol. 19, pt. 1, 211.

cover of some haystacks and a stone fence near the position from which he had advanced, where, joined by some of the 17th South Carolina, they renewed their fire and remained until driven back by the advance of the 2d and 10th U.S. Infantry (consolidated).

The cavalry followed the artillery across the bridge under a terrific fire of artillery (by which many saddles were emptied) and formed in rear of the horse batteries. The 4th Pennsylvania Cavalry, until relieved by the advance of the regular infantry, remained on the right of the road, and the 5th U.S. Cavalry formed on its left. On the left of the road were additional horsemen of the 6th Pennsylvania Cavalry and a squadron of the 8th Pennsylvania Cavalry, 3d Indiana Cavalry, 8th Illinois Cavalry, and 1st Massachusetts Cavalry. Some of the regiments were beyond the Newcomer barn and close up to Robertson's battery, others on the left and rear of the barn within a few yards of the Antietam. All were under fire; shell and spherical case exploded over them and solid shot, directed at the batteries and skipping over the elevation in front, dropped among them. One of the officers thought the round shot were endowed with military intelligence. "As they came to a certain point of the ridge in front and missed their mark, they evidently saw the cavalry under the hill and began to descend into the ranks, and everybody ducked their heads."[6]

The position of the cavalry was certainly an uncomfortable one. Most of the shot and shell directed at the batteries in front flew over the heads of the artillerymen and dropped in its ranks, while it could do absolutely nothing, not even see the enemy. Further, the nature of the ground, fences, and ravines was such as to have made efficient action as cavalry very difficult if it had been called on to repel an attack on the guns. Several times during the day the men mounted and drew sabers to charge (as all supposed), but were dismounted again without attempting anything. The fire of Lee's artillery was fierce, and together with that of the Union guns in the immediate front and rear made a noise that was infernal and deafening. The historian of the 1st Massachusetts Cavalry says, "The air was at times full of shot and shell, which had the curious effect of putting the men to sleep. Everywhere could be seen groups of men fast asleep."[7]

John C. Tidball says, "The cavalry that had crossed the bridge …, finding itself greatly exposed and without power of acting, took shelter in hollows and under the banks of the creek. At this period of the war the cavalry had not yet fallen into the hands of those who knew the proper use to make of it."[8] Another, a gallant young cavalry officer later in the war, says, "It is one of the surprising features of this surprising battle that the Federal cavalry, instead of being posted, according to the practice of the centuries, on the flanks of the infantry, was used throughout the day in support of its own horse batteries, in rear of the Federal centre, and in a position from which it would have been impossible for it to have been used as cavalry, or even to have emerged mounted."[9] The horse batteries crossed the Antietam and went into position just after Lee had given directions to his chief of artillery to put his most powerful batteries along the crest in front of Sharpsburg and engage those beyond the Antietam that were so annoying to his infantry, but before this could be effected the twenty-four pieces of Pleasonton opened such a spirited and accurate fire as not only to prevent the establishment of other batteries in their front but to drive under cover those already there, and as occasion offered they directed their fire to the right (upon the Confederates opposing Richardson and French) and to the left (upon the troops confronting Burnside).[10]

Although Twiggs had been driven from their immediate front, these batteries were still annoyed by sharpshooters of Evans's Brigade (under cover of the stone and rail fences, rock ledges in the fields, and other protection), who kept up a severe fire upon them (especially upon Tidball's) that the cavalry skirmishers were not able to silence. Pleasonton called upon Captain Matthew M. Blunt, commanding the 1st Battalion, 12th U.S. Infantry (then at the bridge), to advance a line of skirmishers and drive them away from Tidball's front, which was immediately done by Captain Frederick Winthrop. Soon after this Sykes ordered Blunt's battalion to advance to Tidball's support, and Winthrop deployed his company in skirmishing order down the road and in the fields south of it to the left of the battery, the battalion moving in the field as a support.

When Sykes ordered Blunt forward from the bridge, he ordered the 2d and 10th U.S. Infantry (consolidated), under the command of Lieutenant John S. Poland, to cross the Antietam and support Blunt. Poland crossed over, filed to the left, and came up to Blunt's battalion on the level near the stream. Advancing beyond Winthrop's skirmishers, he deployed seven companies as skirmishers to the left of the batteries, holding five companies in reserve. The entire battalion was south of the road.

---

[6] As of this writing, Carman's source for this quotation has not been identified.

[7] Benjamin W. Crowninshield, *A History of the First Regiment of Massachusetts Cavalry Volunteers* (Boston: Houghton, Mifflin, and Co., 1891), 79.

[8] John C. Tidball, "The Artillery Service in the War of the Rebellion, 1861–65," *Journal of the Military Service Institution of the United States* 12, no. 53 (September 1891): 965.

[9] George B. Davis, "The Antietam Campaign," in *Campaigns in Virginia, Maryland, and Pennsylvania, 1862–1863*, vol. 3 of *Papers of the Military Historical Society of Massachusetts* (Boston: Griffith-Stillings Press, 1903), 55.

[10] Tidball, 963.

While Poland was doing this, the horse batteries ran out of ammunition and were relieved by two batteries of Porter's corps, Robertson and Gibson being relieved by Randol's Batteries E and G (consolidated), 1st U.S. Artillery. Gibson, after replenishing ammunition, took position on the bluff east of the Antietam and on the north side of the road, where he remained during the day. One section of Robertson's battery under the command of Lieutenant Vincent moved northwest about 860 yards and took position on the left of Richardson's division, where, as we have seen, it became engaged and remained until relieved by Graham's battery, when it recrossed the Antietam. Lieutenant Van Reed's Battery K, 5th U.S. Artillery, relieved Tidball and Hains, taking position about seventy-five yards north of the road. Sykes reports that it was against his judgment that he sent Randol's and Van Reed's batteries across the Antietam, and with them four additional battalions of regular infantry under the command of Captain Hiram Dryer.[11]

We give place to an incident along Morell's line east of the Antietam. The historian of the 118th Pennsylvania (the Philadelphia Corn Exchange Regiment) says:

At noon the combat raged in all its fierceness. It was near this hour when General McClellan, with his large and imposing staff, rode upon the ground occupied by our division. The deep and abiding enthusiasm that habitually followed him promptly greeted him. Shouts, yells, and cheers of appreciation rent the air. This unusual noise, so loud that it was borne above the din of battle to the enemy's line, brought on a vigorous and persistent shelling. Regardless of the flying, bursting missiles, there he sat astride his splendid charger, glass in hand, calmly reviewing the mighty hosts, whose discomfiture with his trusted legions he was bent upon that day accomplishing. Intent, no doubt, on securing some permanent advantage at this particular point, he turned suddenly to Colonel [Alexander S.] Webb, … of his staff, who subsequently won imperishable fame in command of the Philadelphia Brigade at Gettysburg, and, after a few moments of hurried instructions, dispatched him on his mission down into the valley—down into the very jaws of death. The smoke of the conflict soon enveloped him and he was lost to view entirely.[12]

Where Webb went on his mission into the "very jaws of death," on the peaceful side of the Antietam, is not of record, but it was soon thereafter that Poland was seen leading his men down to the road from the left and thence across the bridge. Expectation ran high that now the Fifth Corps was to advance and engage the enemy, and thus relieve the pressure on the right and pierce the center, but these expectations were not realized.

Poland was soon followed by the 2d Battalion, 14th U.S. Infantry (Captain David B. McKibbin). McKibbin says he was ordered to move at 1:00 p.m. to support some batteries.[13] After crossing the stream he marched up the road some distance, filed to the right, halted his command under the crest of a knoll (relieving the 4th Pennsylvania Cavalry in support of a battery in front) and sent one company under Captain Horace K. Thatcher as skirmishers to relieve those of the 4th Pennsylvania Cavalry under Captain Young. These became engaged with the skirmishers of Twiggs and those of Evans's Brigade. (Upon being relieved by McKibbin, the Pennsylvania cavalry fell back to the Newcomer barn.)

As the advance of the regular infantry practically relieved the cavalry from any further duty on this part of the line, we shall here dispose of it and dismiss it from our narrative. At 1:00 p.m. the squadron of the 8th Pennsylvania Cavalry recrossed the bridge, marched up the east bank of the Antietam, recrossed to the west side at the Neikirk farm, and took position with a squadron of the 12th Pennsylvania Cavalry on high ground southwest of the Kennedy farm, near where Richardson formed for his advance. The two squadrons were here engaged in gathering stragglers, upon which duty they remained until night, when they rejoined their division near Keedysville. At 3:00 p.m. the 1st Massachusetts Cavalry moved across the road to the right and marched north about five hundred yards to the cover of a ridge, where it remained free from casualty or any apparent duty until late in the day, when it recrossed the upper Antietam. Under McClellan's order of 4:00 p.m. to send two squadrons to report to Meade,[14] the 3d Indiana Cavalry and the 8th Illinois Cavalry moved up the west bank of the Antietam and bivouacked in rear of the right wing of the infantry. The 5th U.S. Cavalry and the 4th and 6th Pennsylvania Cavalry remained until the horse batteries were withdrawn, and then accompanied them to the bivouac near Keedysville.

The cavalry was not as usefully employed as it should have been, and Pleasonton was disgusted at its enforced inaction. McClellan gives it these few words, and they tell the whole story: "The cavalry had little field for operations during the engagement, but was employed in supporting the horse-artillery batteries in the center, and in driving up stragglers, while awaiting opportunity for other service."[15]

[11] George Sykes to Fred T. Locke, September 30, 1862, reprinted in OR, vol. 19, pt. 1, 315.

[12] [John L. Smith], Antietam to Appomattox with 118th Penna. Vols., Corn Exchange Regiment (Philadelphia: J. L. Smith, 1892), 42–43.

[13] David B. McKibbin to William H. Powell, September 25, 1862, reprinted in OR, vol. 19, pt. 1, 360.

[14] George D. Ruggles to Pleasonton, September 17, 1862, 4:00 p.m., reprinted in OR, vol. 51, pt. 1, 845.

[15] George B. McClellan to Lorenzo Thomas, October 15, 1862, reprinted in OR, vol. 19, pt. 1, 31.

We return to the regular infantry. At 2:00 p.m. Sykes ordered Captain Dryer (4th U.S. Infantry) to cross the bridge with his regiment and the 1st Battalion, 14th U.S. Infantry (Captain Harvey W. Brown), and take command of the regular infantry on that side of the stream, consisting in all of the 2d and 10th, the 4th, the 1st Battalion of the 12th, and the two battalions of the 14th U.S. Infantry. The command aggregated about 1,640 men—400 in the 2d and 10th, 320 in the 4th, 280 in the 12th, and 640 in the 14th. Dryer's orders were to "support [the] batteries … and to dislodge the enemy from certain hay-stacks in a field on the right [left—EAC] of the pike."[16]

Meanwhile, Randol's battery had retired. As soon as it had taken position, relieving Gibson and Robertson, it opened a fire of spherical case upon the flank of a Confederate battery on Cemetery Hill, which soon retired out of range. Being somewhat annoyed by the enemy's skirmishers, who were behind stone fences and hidden in a cornfield in his front, Randol had Poland advance his skirmishers to the front of the guns, which was some relief. But as his position was an unfavorable one for the use of his guns, Randol was directed by Pleasonton to retire. (Sykes says he "very properly withdrew his battery."[17]) He was engaged but a short time, had no losses, and resumed his position with the reserve beyond the Antietam.

Dryer had now come up. It was nearly or quite three o'clock when he crossed the Antietam, and Van Reed's battery was the only one in position, but in a few minutes, Tidball, who had fed his men and horses and replenished ammunition, returned to his former position on Van Reed's right. Both became engaged with such Confederate batteries as had the temerity to show themselves, and fired at such bodies of infantry as came within view, especially upon D. H. Hill's men on the Piper farm, and those that were opposing Burnside, who had now crossed the lower bridge and was advancing on Sharpsburg. It was about three o'clock when Pleasonton asked McClellan for more infantry, and at 3:30 p.m. his request was thus answered by the chief of staff: "General McClellan directs me to say he has no infantry to spare. Confer with Major General Porter, and if he cannot support your batteries, withdraw them."[18]

About 3:30 p.m., under Pleasonton's order, the right section of Tidball's battery, in charge of Lieutenant Pennington, advanced about 650 yards to the right and front, took position on the left and front of Richardson's division, and engaged a battery west of the Hagerstown Road and a few yards north of where the Piper lane intersects it.

With the 4th U.S. Infantry and the 1st Battalion of the 14th, Dryer advanced over Newcomer Ridge in column (exposed to a severe fire) and halted on the right of Poland's command, which had been deployed as skirmishers, with the right resting on the road between the crest of the hill occupied by the artillery and the end of the sunken road. Dryer ordered Poland to advance with his skirmishers to the front and left and take possession of some haystacks in a field about 150 yards to the front and 300 yards to the left of the road. At the same time, Lieutenant Caleb H. Carlton was directed to deploy the three leading companies of the 4th, about 120 men, to the right of the road and advance near to the crest of a ridge about 250 yards in front, Dryer using the remaining five companies of the regiment as a support. Poland and Carlton moved promptly to their allotted work and Dryer deployed his five companies on the right of the road and the 1st Battalion of the 14th on the left, its right resting on the road.

Before following the advance of their line, let us note what had been transpiring in its front and what it has to encounter. Early in the morning, Cemetery Hill was occupied by the batteries of Squires, Miller, and Bachman, and on the extension of the ridge north of the road were the four batteries of Jones's Battalion. These seven batteries were supported by the brigades of G. T. Anderson, Garnett, and Evans. During the forenoon, Miller's Battery and a section of Bachman's, with G. T. Anderson's Brigade, were sent to the left. Jones's guns, which could not cope with the heavier guns beyond the Antietam, were retired under cover of the ridge. (One battery was sent to the left.) During the forenoon Jones again ascended the ridge with three batteries, and at noon there were Squires's Battery of four guns, one section of Bachman's, and the three batteries of Jones, with Boyce's Battery further to the left with D. H. Hill. This artillery was supported by Garnett's Brigade of 260 men and Evans's Brigade of 280 men. Garnett was on Cemetery Hill in rear of the artillery. He says, "As far as practicable the command was sheltered in a hollow in the rear of the artillery. For some four or five hours it was subjected to an almost uninterrupted fire of solid shot, shell, and spherical case, by which a number of men were killed and wounded, which casualties were borne by the troops with remarkable firmness and steadiness." All this was before noon, after which he was ordered forward on the brow of the hill to dislodge the Union skirmishers that began to annoy the artillery, and where he was more exposed to the Union artillery than in his former position, and suffered considerably. "At length," says Garnett, "for some cause unknown to me, a large portion of the pieces were withdrawn, and I moved my command farther back to a more secure place"[19]

---

[16] Hiram Dryer to Powell, September 25, 1862, reprinted in OR, vol. 19. pt. 1, 357.

[17] Sykes to Locke, 351.

[18] Marcy to Pleasonton, September 17, 1862, 3:30 p.m., reprinted in OR, vol. 51, pt. 1, 845.

[19] Richard B. Garnett to Asbury Coward, November 7, 1862, reprinted in OR, vol. 19, pt. 1, 896.

Evans's small South Carolina brigade was divided. On the evening of the sixteenth the Holcombe Legion and the 17th South Carolina (both under command of Colonel Fitz W. McMaster), not numbering over one hundred officers and men, were sent to the right and front of Cemetery Hill to the Sherrick lane, and Twiggs's detail from G. T. Anderson's Brigade took post on their left and front. Everything was quiet until about 1:00 p.m. of the seventeenth, when Twiggs and the skirmishers were driven in and rallied on the left, some of Twiggs's men stopping at the haystacks and at a stone fence near them. Soon after this McMaster was informed by an officer of Squires's Battery that a Union battery had proved quite destructive to Squires and that he would be compelled to discontinue firing unless it was silenced, upon which McMaster "immediately sent out about 25 volunteers, who silenced the battery of the enemy for some time."[20] Three regiments of Evans's Brigade (the 18th, 22d, and 23d South Carolina), under the command of Colonel Peter F. Stevens, were on the left of the road, supporting the batteries that from time to time were pushed forward to the crest of the ridge—and almost as quickly obliged to fall back before the fire of the guns beyond the Antietam and, later in the day, by those of the horse batteries. The 18th South Carolina (Colonel William Wallace) was on the left, acting as a support to Boyce's Battery. The 23d (Captain S. A Durham) and 22d (Major Miel Hilton) were near the road and in front of the artillery and for a great part of the time between the fires of the contending batteries, exposed to the heavy and continuous shelling of the Union guns, but, being deployed in skirmishing order, they sought cover and did not suffer much loss. When Pleasonton's horse batteries advanced and used canister upon them, the skirmishers fell back; as the fire ceased they again went cautiously forward—but not as far as the advanced position from which the canister had driven them.

D. H. Hill says it was about four o'clock (G. T. Anderson says it was earlier), "and Burnside's corps was massing to attack on our right. A heavy column was advancing up the Boonsborough pike, and I ordered up some 200 or 300 men, under command of Col. G. T. Anderson, to the hill ... commanding Sharpsburg, but they were exposed to an enfilade fire from a battery near the church, on the Hagerstown pike, and compelled to retire to another hill."[21] The position on the ridge vacated by Anderson was soon occupied by portions of Colquitt's and Garland's Brigades. It will be remembered that when Colquitt and Garland were disposed of by Greene's division early in the day, some of the men were rallied on Rodes's left in the sunken road, but many of them continued their retreat to Sharpsburg. Captain Thomas M. Garrett of the 5th North Carolina went into town hoping to get up with them and met Lee in the street, to whom he reported the misfortune that had befallen them, and asked for direction. Lee ordered him to rally all the stragglers he could, without regard to what command they belonged, and report with them to Evans. Only about 50 men of his own regiment could be found, but with the assistance of others about 150 were rallied and carried up to Evans, on the ridge north of the town.[22] These were formed into line under Garrett's command, along with other stragglers, and all placed under command of Colonel Alfred Iverson Jr. of the 20th North Carolina. Evans reports that with the assistance of his staff and after considerable exertion he succeeded in collecting about 250 men and officers, whom he formed into two commands and placed under Colonels Colquitt and Iverson of D. H. Hill's Division.[23] These small commands supported the three regiments of Evans's Brigade.

Meanwhile, Bachman's two guns, running out of ammunition, had withdrawn from Cemetery Hill, and the line of the ridge was held by Squires's Battery of four guns south of the road, supported by Garnett's Brigade of 260 men and McMaster's command of about 180 men (including Twiggs's detachment). On the left of the road were twelve guns of Jones's Battalion, Boyce's Battery (now reduced to two guns), and one gun of Bondurant's Battery. These fifteen guns were supported by Colquitt, Iverson, and Evans, with about 430 men. In all there were nineteen guns and about 870 infantry in Dryer's front when he was forming for an advance, but before the advance was ordered S. D. Lee came up with ten guns, under Longstreet's order to take position on the right and left of the road, relieving Walton's Washington Artillery. Four guns of Moody's Battery were placed on the right of the road, between it and Squires's Battery; two guns of Jordan's Battery on the left of the road and about 150 yards from it; two guns of Parker's some distance to the left of Jordan's; and two guns of Rhett's Battery on a ridge of the Hagerstown Road, about six hundred yards from the main street of the town. Parker's guns were somewhat late in coming up, and when moving into position some if not all of Jones's guns were retiring.[24] Jones's twelve guns were not all on the ridge at the same time. During the afternoon his batteries had relieved each other by turns, but all were available.

---

[20] Fitz W. McMaster to Nathan G. Evans, October 20, 1862, reprinted in OR, vol. 19, pt. 1, 946.

[21] Daniel H. Hill to Robert H. Chilton, 1862 [no day or month given], reprinted in OR, vol. 19, pt. 1, 1024. Anderson reported that it happened "about 2 or 3 p.m." George T. Anderson to Coward, September 30, 1862, reprinted in OR, vol. 19, pt. 1, 910.

[22] As of this writing, Carman's source for this statement has not been identified.

[23] Nathan G. Evans to Gilbert Moxley Sorrel, reprinted in OR, vol. 19, pt. 1, 939.

[24] Colonel Lee reports that he had twelve guns, but accounts for ten of them only. Stephen D. Lee to Sorrel, October 11, 1862, reprinted in OR, vol. 19, pt. 1, 845–46. Rhett's guns were not engaged on Evans's front, and Parker's two guns, under Lieutenant John Thompson Brown, appear to have arrived when the action was closing, or at least when the Confederate infantry and artillery were giving way.—EAC

Before S. D. Lee's guns took position on the east slope of Cemetery Hill, Garden's Battery of six guns crossed the Rohrbach Bridge Road from the west and took position on that part of the hill running west. These six guns faced south and commanded the Rohrbach Bridge Road. About the same time, Jenkins's Brigade of 755 officers and men, under command of Colonel Joseph Walker, crossed the Rohrbach Bridge Road from west to east and was held in support of Squires's Battery and the right section of Moody's. Garden's Battery and Jenkins's Brigade were engaged principally, if not wholly, with Burnside's troops, and are not to be included among those who opposed Dryer's advance, but by their presence on Garnett's right they gave his men moral support.

When S. D. Lee put Moody's guns in position on the edge of a cornfield, Garnett sent the 56th Virginia (forty men) to protect them from the Union sharpshooters. The Virginians advanced into the standing corn and became immediately engaged with Poland's skirmishers, now advancing. Dryer had halted in the ravine separating the two parallel ridges and ordered the two commands of Poland and Carlton to advance as skirmishers on either side of the road. Poland had 400 men and Carlton 120, and it was this thin line of 520 men that went forward over open ground against twenty to twenty-five guns favorably posted on a commanding ridge and supported by 870 infantry. The advance of Poland and Carlton was made at the same moment, but we first consider Poland.

When Poland was ordered to take the haystacks on his left and front, five companies of his command were in reserve. These he deployed on his right in skirmishing order, and the entire line (quite a long one) went forward, ascended the slope of a hill, and under a heavy fire of canister from Squires's and Moody's guns in front and some guns beyond the road on the right (and some additional fire from Garnett's skirmishers) pushed over the high ground, passed the haystacks (where some of Twiggs's men and others of the 17th South Carolina were captured), drove back McMaster (who at the same time was attacked on the right by Burnside), and, reaching the Sherrick lane, halted under cover of the fence and became closely and sharply engaged. He had advanced about 385 yards. The right of the line, not hearing the order to halt at the lane fence, went some distance beyond and, Poland reports, "by a well-directed fire compelled the enemy's cannoneers to leave their guns. At this juncture the fire from our own batteries compelled them to fall back to the fence, as their shells fell short."[25] Referring to this advance on Moody's guns, S. D. Lee says, "At one time their infantry was within 150 yards of our batteries, when, by a charge of our supporting infantry, they were driven back."[26] Poland's right rested on the road to Sharpsburg and extended to the left along the lane fence about 450 yards in the direction of the Sherrick house. After Poland reached this position, the Confederates in his front were reinforced. Garnett advanced his entire brigade, its left in front and on the flanks of the two guns of Moody's Battery, in the cornfield. The 56th Virginia, then in front, was recalled to a position on the left of the brigade, close to the road. The fighting now became general along the entire line of the brigade, which was in very open order, covering ground around to the southern slope of the hill.

Carlton deployed his three companies of the 4th U.S. Infantry as skirmishers on the right of the road, advanced through a small triangular-shaped cornfield of about three acres lying adjacent to the road, and, driving some of Evans's skirmishers before him, gained the crest of some high ground about 150 yards beyond the cornfield and on a line with Poland, who was on the left of the road. Here the skirmishers were momentarily halted until Dryer could position his supports.

When Poland and Carlton had gained some distance, Dryer advanced the five companies of the 4th to the west part of the small triangular cornfield and concealed them as much as possible in the tall corn. The 1st Battalion, 14th U.S. Infantry, advanced in line to the protection of a deep ravine on the south side of the road opposite the mouth of the sunken road. The 2d Battalion advanced beyond the batteries and took position in a ravine on the right of the 4th, with skirmishers thrown to the crest of the ridge in its front. It was under a heavy fire of shot and shell, but being well sheltered had only one man wounded. The 4th, on its left on higher ground, suffered some casualties. The 4th and the two battalions of the 14th made no further advance, and the fighting was done by Poland's and Carlton's skirmishers, whom Dryer with his three battalions has closely supported, and halted only when Poland was brought to a stand in front of the enemy's artillery and infantry.

When Evans saw the advance of Carlton's skirmishers (with a front of three hundred yards, followed by their support), he ordered Colquitt, Iverson, and his own men forward. Captain Garrett of the 5th North Carolina, who was near the left of Iverson's line, says D. H. Hill ordered the attack upon a regiment of the enemy, "which was maintaining a doubtful contest with a small body of our troops."[27] They had not advanced far before the skirmishers of the 22d South Carolina were driven in upon the main line, closely followed by Carlton's men, and the engagement became general. At first Carlton was compelled to yield some ground, but quickly recovered it and opened such a telling fire that Colquitt and Iverson were soon driven from the field. We again quote Garrett: "We moved up in line on the right and engaged them with spirit, and forced

---

[25] John S. Poland to Ephraim E. Sellers, September 22, 1862, reprinted in *OR*, vol. 19, pt. 1, 363.

[26] Stephen D. Lee to Sorrel, October 11, 1862, reprinted in *OR*, vol. 19, pt. 1, 846.

[27] Thomas M. Garrett to James M. Taylor, October 11, 1862, reprinted in *OR*, vol. 19, pt. 1, 1044.

them, for a moment, to give back. Very soon, however, the left of the line of which my command formed part gave way, and being left with but the men from my regiment, I ordered them to retire, and form behind a large rock in the field, about 50 yards distant. This was done, and, by the determined conduct of these few men, the regiment of the enemy was held in cheek for twenty-five or thirty minutes. After feeling our strength, however, he began to advance and I ordered the men to retreat."[28] They went entirely off the field and scattered in the streets of Sharpsburg, where the rest of Iverson's men and part of Colquitt's had preceded them. Colquitt refers to a small part of his command under Lieutenant Colonel William H. Betts (13th Alabama), which was "directed to deploy as skirmishers along the crest of a hill upon which the enemy was advancing. They did so with good effect, keeping back a large force by their annoying fire and the apprehension, excited by their boldness, that they were supported by a line in rear."[29] Under the elastic pen and poetic license of D. H. Hill, this state-ment of Colquitt's assumes these grotesque proportions: "About 30 men, under Lieutenant-Colonel Betts, … remained as supports to my division batteries … The Yankee columns were allowed to come within easy range, when a sudden storm of grape and canister drove them back in confusion. Betts' men must have given them a very hot fire, as Burnside reported that he had met three heavy columns on the hill. It is difficult to imagine how 30 men could so multiply themselves as to appear to the frightened Yankees to be three heavy columns."[30] As a matter of fact, Betts was detached on the left of Colquitt's line in support of some guns—beyond the right of Carlton's advance and opposed by only a few men who faced in his direc-tion. Carlton's right was refused to conform to the curvature of the hill over which he was advancing and connected on the right with the skirmishers of McKibbin's battalion, one company of which (under Captain Thatcher) was thrown forward from the ravine where it had halted and, as McKibbin reports, "were actively engaged during part of the afternoon."[31] As to Burnside, he was entirely beyond the road and his right never came within canister range of Hill's guns.

The three South Carolina regiments of Evans's Brigade soon followed Colquitt and Iverson. Colonel Stevens, who was with these regiments, seeing his men fall rapidly while Carlton was still advancing, and apprehensive of being flanked, ordered them to fall back to the stone fence on the Hagerstown Road. Colonel Wallace of the 18th South Carolina reports that Boyce's Battery (which it had been supporting) having retired under orders from Colonel Stevens, his regiment was deployed as skirmishers and advanced over the hill to repel the advance of a heavy body of skirmishers thrown forward by the enemy. The direction of his advance was toward the Boonsboro Road, and by a rapid movement he gained a rail fence running nearly parallel with the road. "This position," he says, "we held against a very largely superior force of the enemy for a considerable time, when Colonel Stevens, who was upon the left of our line, seeing the left was beginning to suffer severely, ordered the whole line to retreat to a stone fence some distance in our rear and upon the road running in a northwesterly [north—EAC] direction from Sharpsburg. This retreat was accomplished under a sharp fire of musketry and artillery, from which the regiment sustained some damage. Almost immediately the regiment was reduced to a handful of men."[32] Boyce's Battery, as stated by Wallace, fell back before engaging the infantry. Jordan's two guns were well protected by the ridge and did not suffer from infantry fire, but were so severely shelled by artillery that they remained in action not to exceed thirty minutes and withdrew as Carlton's men were advancing and the Confederate infantry was giving way. Everything was now clear in Carlton's immediate front. He had advanced to within 450 yards of the Lutheran church and partially crowned the crest of the ridge from which he could look into Sharpsburg, and Carlton was still advancing when he was opened upon by a fire of canister and musketry full upon his left flank from two of Moody's guns and Garnett's infantry south of the road. Garnett and S. D. Lee had been standing in the tall corn observing Poland's advance. They had not seen Carlton's approach on the left of the road and were not aware of it until their attention was attracted to the rattling skirmish fire. Looking in that direction, they saw the blue-coated regulars directly on their flank and the Confederates in retreat. Lee turned Moody's two guns upon them and Garnett faced a few men of the 56th Virginia to the left and sent a few rifle shots down the line. At the same moment, Carlton received an order from Dryer to fall back under cover on a line with Poland, who was still holding his position in the Sherrick lane, and to whom and Garnett we now return.

When Garnett advanced his brigade to the support of Moody's guns, the 56th and 28th Virginia (about one hundred men) were placed in the corn on the left and in advance of Moody's left section, which was on open ground just in rear of the corn. On the right of this section were the 19th and 18th Virginia (about 120 men) also in the corn and deployed from four to five feet apart in single line. In rear of Moody's right section (which was on the right and rear of the 18th Virginia) was the 8th Virginia, about twenty men only. The 56th, 28th, and part of the 19th Virginia were faced east and engaged Poland's right and the center; a part of the 19th and all of the 18th and 8th engaged Poland's left and the advance of

---

[28] Ibid., 1044–45.

[29] Alfred H. Colquitt to James W. Ratchford, October 13, 1862, reprinted in *OR*, vol. 19, pt. 1, 1054.

[30] Hill to Chilton, 1024–25.

[31] McKibbin to Powell, 360.

[32] William H. Wallace to Asa L. Evans, October 17, 1862, reprinted in *OR*, vol. 19, pt. 1, 948.

Burnside. Reports agree that the entire line was very severely engaged and lost heavily. Garnett reports that he was "called on to deplore the loss of many brave spirits."[33] Colonel Eppa Hunton (8th Virginia) says he lost one-half of his men.[34] Major George C. Cabell (18th Virginia) reported a loss of over one-third and said that the "entire color-guard was either killed or wounded."[35] The losses in the other regiments were large.

Some of Poland's men were quite well sheltered in the lane, under cover of the fence and the irregularities of the ground, but the greater part of them were much exposed. All kept up a cool and constant fire, and Dryer was about to charge Moody's Battery in Poland's front when he was ordered to withdraw.

Dryer had been ordered across the Antietam against the judgment of his division commander, Sykes, to support Pleasonton's guns, drive the enemy's skirmishers from their front, and take the haystacks on the left of the road. This was the extent to which it was intended his men should be employed. "They were, however," says Porter, "diverted from that service, and employed to drive the enemy's skirmishers to their reserves."[36] When it was seen that Dryer was exceeding his instructions and advancing on either side of the road with the evident intention of carrying the ridge upon which could be seen, from beyond the Antietam, eighteen guns and what appeared to be two full regiments, there was some apprehension. At this moment there came a note from Captain Matthew M. Blunt, commanding the 1st Battalion, 12th U.S. Infantry. Dryer had ordered Blunt to move forward and support him in an advance, and Blunt sent the note to Sykes, stating that Dryer was about to make an assault and that he did not understand that he (Blunt) had been sent over the Antietam for that purpose, and asked for instructions. Sykes was very much annoyed and immediately ordered Lieutenant William H. Powell of Colonel Buchanan's staff to ride over to Dryer with orders not only to suspend assault but to withdraw his troops to the ridge upon which were Pleasonton's batteries and maintain a defensive position. Powell rode fast and found Dryer in the road, at the intersection of the Sherrick lane (where the latter had just given an order to Poland to push forward), when Dryer saw the troops on the right of the road advance and was about to order the 4th U.S. Infantry forward. When Powell delivered his orders, Dryer asked if there might not be something left to his discretion; when informed that the order was imperative he ordered Carlton to withdraw, as we have seen, and wheeling his horse about rode off after Poland, whose left had now been joined by Burnside's advance from the Rohrbach Bridge.

When Powell gave the order for Dryer to withdraw, the Confederates had abandoned the ridge north of the road and were then abandoning Cemetery Hill. When Burnside's men approached from the Rohrbach Bridge, Garden's Battery left its position and went through Sharpsburg. Soon after, Squires's Battery, now coming under the fire of Burnside's skirmishers, went down a ravine southwest to the road leading to the Rohrbach Bridge, and turning to the right went through the streets of Sharpsburg. Jenkins's Brigade was driven back from the apple orchard on the southeastern slope of the hill. All on Garnett's left and right had gone, and it was but a few minutes after he had seen Carlton fall back that he discovered that the extreme right had been turned and was giving way and that "a number of the Yankee flags appeared on the hill in rear of the town and not far from our only avenue of escape."[37] Deeming the brigade in imminent danger of being captured he ordered a retreat. As the main street of the town was commanded by Union artillery, his infantry passed for the most part to the north of the town along the cross-streets, and in this direction he found "troops scattered in squads from various parts of the army, so that it was impossible to distinguish men of the different commands."[38] Moody's left section was withdrawn without difficulty and retreated through the main street of the town, but the right section had some difficulty and was slow in getting under way. Perceiving this, and that the guns were in danger from Poland's men and the advance of Burnside's corps, Major Cabell, who had moved back some fifty yards, halted his small regiment, faced it about, moved back into the corn, and waited until the guns were moved off, then rejoined his brigade. It is this movement that is thus referred to by Poland in his report: "The enemy advanced a regiment to protect the withdrawal of their guns from the hill directly in front of our left. This regiment was driven back, but their object had been effected."[39] While Poland was engaged with Garnett's retiring troops, the 79th New York and the 17th Michigan of Orlando Willcox's division of the Ninth Corps came up and fired a few shots at the retiring 18th Virginia. The left of his line being relieved by the 17th Michigan, Poland assembled his regiment on the center files. It was while thus engaged that Dryer came up and ordered him to withdraw a short distance, halt his command under shelter of the ridge over which he had charged, and await a supply of ammunition. He had lost 54 men killed and wounded; Carlton had lost about half that number. Together their losses were about 85 or 90 men killed,

[33] Garnett to Coward, 897.

[34] Eppa Hunton to Garnett, 1862 [no day or month given], reprinted in *OR*, vol. 19, pt. 1, 898.

[35] George C. Cabell to "General Garnett's assistant adjutant-general," October 14, 1862, reprinted in *OR*, vol. 19, pt. 1, 901.

[36] Fitz John Porter to Seth Williams, October 1, 1862, reprinted in *OR*, vol. 19, pt. 1, 339.

[37] Garnett to Coward, 897.

[38] Ibid.

[39] Poland to Sellers, 363.

wounded, and missing in the Fifth Corps. Garnett's loss was 78 killed and wounded, about one-third of the number he had engaged. The loss sustained by the Confederates opposing Carlton cannot be definitely stated.

As Pleasonton records it, it was nearing four o'clock—after his batteries, with "increased vigor and energy," had driven the enemy's batteries from their position in front—that a heavy column of dust, could be seen moving behind Cemetery Ridge toward Sumner's left. He directed the fire of the batteries into this dust, and "soon the development of the enemy's line of battle, fully a mile long, could be seen bearing down upon Richardson's division ..., then commanded by Hancock." Hancock called for some guns to assist him; none could be spared at that moment, but Pleasonton "directed the fire of some eighteen guns upon the enemy's line in front of him for twenty minutes," when he had the satisfaction of seeing "this immense line" first halt, deliver a desultory fire, and then "break and run to the rear in the greatest confusion and disorder." A section (Pennington's) of Tidball's battery was immediately advanced to the crest of a hill several hundred yards to the front, and in front of the infantry of Hancock's left.[40]

We cannot identify this immense column of Confederates moving to the left; the drift (if any) at this hour was in the opposite direction. We know that small bodies of D. H. Hill's men were keeping up a desultory affair with Richardson and that, about the time indicated by Pleasonton, G. T. Anderson with two hundred to three hundred men moved from the left to the right upon the ridge, but seeing (as he reports) no enemy, and being enfiladed by a battery on his left, Anderson moved back again to the ridge near the Piper barn.[41] But we cannot identify any body "fully a mile long," bearing down on Richardson. However, Pleasonton's success in breaking this "immense line," the additional success of Dryer in advancing far to the front on either side of the Boonsboro Road, and Burnside's advance, driving the enemy back, convinced Pleasonton that the field was open for an advance to Cemetery Ridge, to which point he desired to forward his batteries to obtain an enfilading fire upon the enemy in front of Burnside and enable Sumner to advance to Sharpsburg. So satisfied was he that this could be done that at four o'clock he sent a request to Porter for a division to support his advance, accompanied by a report that both Burnside and Sumner were driving the enemy and that he desired to take advantage of the opening and advance to the ridge. Porter could not spare the division; in fact he did not have it. Earlier in the day Warren's brigade had been sent to support Burnside, and at 4:00 p.m., while Pleasonton was framing his request, the brigades of Brigadier Generals Charles Griffin and Thomas B. W. Stockton of Morell's division had gone to the right to support Sumner. Parts of two other brigades were already with Pleasonton. Moreover, Porter says, "Between the dispatching and receiving of that call the tide of battle had changed. Our troops on the left under Burnside had been driven from the heights which they had so gallantly crowned, while those on the immediate right, under Sumner, were held in check. The army was at a stand. I had not the force asked for, and could not, under my orders, risk the safety of the artillery and center of the line, and perhaps imperil the success of the day by further diminishing my small command, not then 4,000 strong—then in the front line and unsupported, and protecting all our trains."[42] Palfrey justifies Porter's action in not "complying with the request of an officer who was not even a corps commander, who was his inferior in rank, and whose request had not received the approval of the general commanding."[43] It appears, however, that Porter at 5:00 p.m. sent this dispatch to Sykes: "Burnside is driving the enemy. Please send word to the command you sent to Pleasonton, to support his batteries, and let him drive them."[44]

Meanwhile, Van Reed's battery (which arrived on the field about two o'clock, relieving Hains's), after expending four hundred rounds of ammunition, was relieved in turn by Hains's at five o'clock and recrossed the Antietam. Hains put all his guns on the right of the road, directing their fire against Confederate infantry entirely, and principally against those on the Piper farm, who were then engaging the 7th Maine, by which fire they suffered severely both in advancing and falling back. At dusk both Tidball and Hains recrossed the Antietam. The 5th U.S. Cavalry and the 4th and 6th Pennsylvania Cavalry followed the artillery, and all joined their division near Keedysville. Dryer remained in his advanced position until the artillery had been withdrawn, when he marched back, waited until the cavalry had crossed, and then went over the bridge at 7:30 p.m., carrying with him his dead and wounded. Sykes reports that Dryer's troops "behaved in the handsomest manner, and, had there been an available force for their support, there is no doubt he could have crowned the Sharpsburg crest."[45] Before Dryer retired the Confederates reoccupied the ground from which they had been driven.

It will be remembered that early in the action, in fact before Carlton's and Evans's men had become engaged, Boyce's two guns had been retired under cover of the ridge and between it and the Hagerstown Road, but commanding the crests of the

---

[40] Pleasonton to Marcy, 211–12.

[41] George T. Anderson to Coward, 910.

[42] Porter to Williams, 339.

[43] Francis Winthrop Palfrey, *The Antietam and Fredericksburg*, vol. 5 of *The Army in the Civil War* (New York: Charles Scribner's Sons, 1882), 123.

[44] Porter to Sykes, September 17, 1862, 5:00 p.m., reprinted in *OR*, vol. 19, pt. 2, 316.

[45] Sykes to Locke, 351.

two hills in front. It appears that when Stevens with his South Carolinians was driven back to the Hagerstown Road he had forgotten Boyce and his guns, but he soon recalled the fact. He says:

> Perceiving that my retreat had left unsupported a section of Boyce's artillery, which I had not before seen, I again resumed my position, and, bringing up Boyce's battery, opened fire with musketry and artillery upon a line of the enemy advancing on the right of the road. The line was broken and driven back. Colonel Walker, of Jenkins' brigade, having sent for artillery, I ordered Captain Boyce to his support. It was now late in the evening, and, my men having nearly exhausted their ammunition, I left general instructions and sought the ordnance officer. Before I could get more ammunition my men had fallen back, in accordance with instructions, and, finding them scattering in town, I marched to the rear and bivouacked for the night.[46]

Captain Boyce reports:

> Colonel Stevens advanced, at this juncture, with a few skirmishers to the crest of the hill, and, finding the ground not occupied by the enemy immediately beyond, signaled me to advance. I went forward and placed my guns on the hill within canister range of the enemy. A few shots soon drove him beyond the reach of canister. I afterward used solid shot, cutting down his flag and driving him back. Having occupied this important position but a few minutes, an order came, from some source, for me to recross the road near the place occupied by me when I received my first order in the morning to go into the battle. I crossed over the road, as ordered, but could find no one there to give me any information as to who gave the order or what was required. This was late in the afternoon, and the battle soon after ended.[47]

Boyce went through the town and bivouacked with Evans's Brigade. Evans says his little command gallantly drove the enemy (the 4th U.S. Infantry) from its cover in the cornfield and caused him to retreat in confusion, leaving a number of dead and two stands of colors, the latter having been shot down by a well directed fire of Captain Boyce's battery.[48] It is difficult to reconcile this statement with the fact that the 4th did not leave their colors and that Dryer reported that he carried off his dead and wounded.

A two-gun section of Parker's Battery under Lieutenant John Thompson Brown appears to have come upon the field about the time the infantry and some artillery were in retreat.[49] Brown says he went about five hundred or six hundred yards north of the road and passed the major of two batteries, who had been unable to hold the hill and was then retiring. The officer inquired where he was going, and having been informed he ordered him back, saying that he had not been able to hold the hill and that it would be folly for his section to attempt it. Brown replied that he was under orders from S. D. Lee and passed on, taking position in a depression of the ground between two trees (an old excavation or ice-house in the ground) and firing over the hill at the 4th U.S. Infantry. "I remember," he writes, "seeing the standard bearer shot down and the staff shot off near the colors, and while he was lying down he raised the colors up on a corn-hill."[50]

When Dryer recrossed the Antietam, the 18th Massachusetts of Morell's division crossed to the west side, established headquarters and a reserve at Newcomer's Mill, and advanced a strong picket line to the ridge where the batteries had been engaged during the day.

Captain Thomas M. Anderson writes that, late in the afternoon of the seventeenth, he was talking with his brigade commander, Colonel Buchanan, when an orderly brought a note from the senior officer in command of the regular infantry beyond the Antietam, stating in effect that there was but one Confederate battery and two regiments in front of Sharpsburg connecting the wings of Lee's army, and that he proposed to charge the battery but asked instructions. Buchanan sent the note to Sykes, who at the time was talking with McClellan and Porter some yards away, sitting on their horses between Taft's and Weed's batteries. After the war Anderson asked Sykes why an advance was not made upon receiving Dryer's report. Sykes replied that he remembered the circumstance very well and that he thought McClellan was inclined to order in the Fifth Corps but that when he spoke of doing so, Porter said, "Remember, General! I command the last reserve of the

---

[46] Peter F. Stevens to Asa L. Evans, October 13, 1862, reprinted in *OR*, vol. 19, pt. 1, 942.

[47] Robert Boyce to Nathan G. Evans, October 20, 1862, reprinted in *OR*, vol. 19, pt. 1, 944.

[48] Nathan G. Evans to Sorrel, 940.

[49] In Carman's original manuscript, this sentence begins, "Parker's Battery of 2 guns, under Lieutenant J. Thompson Brown," implying that the battery was composed of only a pair of guns and that Brown and not Parker was the battery commander on the seventeenth. These suggestions are assuredly inadvertent, as he properly notes Parker's presence in his table of organization.

[50] Carman marked a footnote symbol at this point in his original manuscript, but no corresponding note appears at the bottom of the page. As of this writing, the source of the quotation has not been identified.

last Army of the Republic."[51] Porter says that no such note as "Captain Dryer's report" was seen by him and no such discussion for using the reserve took place between him and McClellan.[52]

In a private letter, Anderson says the incident occurred at sunset, two hours after the Pleasonton report and request, and recalls that while he was talking with Buchanan in front of his battalion a shell exploded in a pile of cracker boxes (Buchanan remarked that it was "the quickest distribution of hard tack he had ever seen") and that at the time they were watching the movement of a body of Confederate troops from their center to their left to attack Burnside. Buchanan received the note and, after reading it, said, "Dryer reports rebel center very weak & wants leave to attack," then sent the note to Sykes. He saw the note delivered to Sykes, and Buchanan said, "Fall in, you men. Our turn has come at last," but no order was given to advance. Anderson further says that when Dryer returned that evening he blamed Blunt for not making the attack with him, as he proposed, without orders.[53]

There is no record of such a paper being sent by Dryer, either in his own report or in those of his brigade and division commanders, nor elsewhere in the official records. William H. Powell, then a lieutenant and adjutant general of Buchanan's brigade, intimates that such a note may have been received by Buchanan, but if so it was after Sykes had ordered the withdrawal of Dryer and while he was carrying the order of withdrawal. Powell writes:

> Gallant and impetuous as Dryer always was, he could not remain idle, and it was soon observed that he was pushing his men forward on each side of the pike towards the crest occupied by the enemy, with a view, as it was afterwards understood, to charge and take a battery there.
>
> Having observed this, and knowing it was not the intention, nor could we afford, at that particular time, to make any forward movement on the center, I reported this to Generals Sykes and Buchanan, who were together at the time, and I was directed by General Sykes to proceed at once to the advanced position which Captain Dryer had obtained (being within three hundred or four hundred yards of the enemy's batteries) and direct him to withdraw his troops immediately to the original position at the head of the bridge, and then to report in person to General Sykes. During my absence at the front, I believe, the note in question was received. When Dryer reported, those who were present know that the interview was in no wise a subject of consultation.
>
> … It was confidently believed, however, by the two brigades of regular infantry that if they had been thrown forward at any time towards the close of the day of the 17th, supported by Morell's division, they could have carried the center, and thus could have enabled General Burnside to drive the enemy from the field on the left.[54]

Sykes comes to a similar conclusion. After paying a high compliment to the behavior of Dryer's men, he says, "Had there been an available force for their support, there is no doubt he could have crowned the Sharpsburg crest."[55]

Fitz John Porter has been severely and unjustly blamed for his inaction at Antietam. All the operations at the Middle Bridge were ordered by McClellan. He ordered Pleasonton across the stream; he ordered a part of Porter's infantry to Pleasonton's support. Being present, he was responsible for the action or want of action of Porter.

---

[51] Thomas M. Anderson, "The Reserve at Antietam," *Century Magazine* 32, no. 5 (September 1886): 783. Carman mistakenly cites this in his original manuscript as appearing in the October issue. He also refers to Anderson as "Lieutenant Colonel." This is the rank at which Anderson identified himself as the author of the *Century* article, but at Antietam he held the rank of captain.

[52] "Memoranda on the Civil War: 'The Reserve at Antietam'," *Century Magazine* 33, no. 3 (January 1887): 472.

[53] Thomas M. Anderson to George W. Davis, January 31, 1897, item 650, box 3, General Correspondence, Mainly Letters Received (Antietam Board), 1894–98, Record Group 92, National Archives.

[54] Powell, "Memoranda on the Civil War: More Light on 'The Reserve at Antietam'," *Century Magazine* 33, no. 5 (March 1887): 804.

[55] Sykes to Locke, 351.

20
The Rohrbach (Burnside) Bridge[1]
Antietam, September 17, 1862

We approach the concluding scenes of the day, the end of a disjointed battle. While Pleasonton's batteries and a few regulars of Porter's corps were engaged in advance of the Middle Bridge, Burnside's Ninth Corps was engaged at the Rohrbach Bridge and on the high ground between it and Sharpsburg, but there was no cooperation in the two movements. It is necessary to repeat the plan of battle. In his preliminary report of the battle, made on October 15, 1862, McClellan says, "The design was to make the main attack upon the enemy's left—at least to create a diversion in favor of the main attack, with the hope of something more by assailing the enemy's right—and, as soon as one or both of the flank movements were fully successful, to attack their center with any reserve I might then have on hand."[2] In his more elaborate report, dated August 4, 1863, but not made public until some months later, he says, "My plan for the impending general engagement was to attack the enemy's left with the corps of Hooker and Mansfield, supported by Sumner's and, if necessary, by Franklin's, and, as soon as matters looked favorably there, to move the corps of Burnside against the enemy's extreme right, upon the ridge running to the south and rear of Sharpsburg, and, having carried their position, to press along the crest toward our right, and, whenever either of these flank movements should be successful, to advance our center with all the forces then disposable."[3]

Burnside's understanding was that, when the attack by Hooker, Sumner, and Franklin should be progressing favorably, he was "to create a diversion in favor of the main attack, with the hope of something more."[4] Jacob Cox, to whom Burnside communicated his understanding of the part the Ninth Corps was to take in the action, says:

> It would also appear probable that Hooker's movement was at first intended to be made by his corps alone, taken up by Sumner's two corps as soon as he was ready to attack, and shared in by Franklin if he reached the field in time, thus making a simultaneous oblique attack from our right by the whole army except Porter's corps, which was in reserve, and the Ninth Corps, which was to create the "diversion" on our left and prevent the enemy from stripping his right to reenforce his left. It is hardly disputable that this would have been a better plan than the one actually carried out. Certainly the assumption that the Ninth Corps could cross the Antietam alone at the only place on the field where the Confederates had their line immediately upon the stream which must be crossed under fire by two narrow heads of column, and could then turn to the right along the high ground occupied by the hostile army before that army had been broken or seriously shaken elsewhere, is one which would hardly be made till time had dimmed the remembrance of the actual positions of Lee's divisions upon the field.[5]

William F. Biddle, in a highly laudatory article on McClellan, says that the movement "planned and persistently ordered for Burnside across the bridge" was "a forlorn hope."[6]

McClellan visited Burnside's position on the sixteenth and, after pointing out to him the proper dispositions to be made during the day and night, informed him that he would *probably* be required to attack the enemy's right on the following morning.[7] The Confederate artillery opened fire early in the morning of the seventeenth and was replied to by all of Burnside's guns in position and others on his right. Durell's Pennsylvania battery of Sturgis's division, supported by the 21st Massachusetts, was advanced to the corner of the bluff overlooking the Antietam and took position on the left of

---

[1] In his original manuscript, Carman entitled this chapter "The Burnside Bridge."

[2] George B. McClellan to Lorenzo Thomas, October 15, 1862, reprinted in *OR*, vol. 19, pt. 1, 30.

[3] McClellan to Thomas, August 4, 1863, reprinted in *OR*, vol. 19, pt. 1, 55.

[4] Jacob D. Cox, "The Battle of Antietam," in *Battles and Leaders of the Civil War*, vol. 2 (New York: Century Co., 1887), 634.

[5] Ibid.

[6] "No such bloody and obstinate fighting had then been seen as he gave on our right at Antietam, nor had there yet been planned and ordered such bold bayonet work, such a 'forlorn hope' charge as he planned and peremptorily ordered for Burnside across the bridge on our left early that morning, and that was not made (alas!) till afternoon." William F. Biddle, "Recollections of McClellan," *United Service* 9, no. 5 (May 1894): 465.—*EAC*

[7] McClellan, *McClellan's Own Story: The War for the Union, the Soldiers Who Fought It, the Civilians Who Directed It, and His Relations to It and Them* (New York: Charles L. Webster & Co., 1887), 589.

Weed's battery. The enemy's guns were soon silenced. The fire of Benjamin, Durell, and others was then directed to the right—at the Confederates engaged with Hooker and Mansfield around the Dunkard Church. Though the distance was from 3,200 to 3,600 yards, it was quite accurate and very effective. To meet what Sturgis reports as a heavy demonstration on the right and center, Clark's battery (Battery E, 4th U.S. Artillery) was sent forward to a position on Durell's left.[8] The batteries of McMullin, Cook, and Lieutenant Charles P. Muhlenberg's Battery A, 5th U.S. Artillery, advanced to positions on Benjamin's left and somewhat to the front, and to Benjamin's battery was added two guns of Simmonds's. Willcox's division was brought up and held in reserve.

While this artillery fire was going on and some of the troops were being shelled out of the exposed positions to which, owing to McClellan's fault, they had been conducted in darkness the night before, Burnside received this note from McClellan:

> Headquarters Army of the Potomac
> September 16, 1862
>
> Major-General Burnside,
> Commanding Ninth Corps, &c.:
>
> General: The general commanding has learned that, although your corps was ordered to be in a designated position at 12 m. to-day, at or near sunset only one division and four batteries had reached the ground intended for your troops.
>
> The general has also been advised that there was a delay of some four hours in the movement of your command yesterday. I am instructed to call upon you for explanations of these failures on your part to comply with the orders given you, and to add, in view of the important military operations now at hand, the commanding general cannot lightly regard such marked departure from the tenor of his instructions.
>
> —— ——,
> Lieutenant-Colonel, Aide-de-Camp, and Actg. Asst. Adjt. Gen.[9]

This was not, on McClellan's part, a very judicious or auspicious opening of the day on his left, and it probably had no bearing upon subsequent events, but we note it to show the state of mind at army headquarters. Burnside did not permit it to affect his determination to do all that the situation and the country required of him, and he replied:

> Headquarters
> September 17, 1862
>
> Brig. Gen. S. Williams, Assistant Adjutant-General:
>
> General: Your dispatch of yesterday this moment received. General Burnside directs me to say that immediately upon the receipt of the order of the general commanding, which was after 12 o'clock, he ordered his corps to be in readiness to march, and instead of having Captain [James C.] Duane post the division in detail, and at the suggestion of Captain Duane, he sent three aides to ascertain the position of each of the three divisions, that they might post them. These aides returned shortly before 3 o'clock, and they immediately proceeded to post the three columns. The general then went on an eminence above these positions to get a good view of them, and whilst there, during the progress of the movement of his corps, an aide from General McClellan came to him and said that General McClellan was not sure that the proper position had been indicated, and advising him not to hasten the movement until the aide had communicated with the general commanding. He (General Burnside) at once went to General McClellan's headquarters to inform him that he had seen large bodies of the enemy moving off to the right. Not finding the general commanding, General Burnside returned to his command, and the movement was resumed and continued as rapidly as possible. General Burnside directs me to say that he is sorry to have received so severe a rebuke from the general commanding, and particularly sorry that the general commanding feels that his instructions have not been obeyed; but nothing can occur to prevent the general from continuing his hearty co-operation to the best of his ability in any movement the general commanding may direct.
>
> I have the honor to be, general, very respectfully, your obedient servant,
>
> Lewis Richmond,
> Assistant Adjutant-General[10]

---

8   Samuel D. Sturgis to "Assistant Adjutant-General, Headquarters Ninth Corps, September 22, 1862, reprinted in *OR*, vol. 19, pt. 1, 444.

9   "Lieutenant-Colonel, Aide-de-Camp, and Actg. Asst. Adjt. Gen." to Ambrose E. Burnside, September 16, 1862, reprinted in *OR*, vol. 19, pt. 2, 308.

10 Lewis Richmond to Seth Williams, September 17, 1862, reprinted in *OR*, vol. 19. pt. 2, 314.

About seven o'clock Burnside received an order to make his dispositions to carry the stone bridge over the Antietam but to await further orders before making the attack. In accordance with these instructions, Cox was directed to advance the whole corps to the ridge nearest the stream and hold it, keeping the troops under cover as much as possible.

Early in the morning Rodman's division was northeast of the stone bridge. Colonel Edward Harland's brigade lay east of the road that ran past the Rohrbach house to Porterstown, its left opposite the Rohrbach orchard. It was in a hollow and somewhat protected from artillery fire. Colonel Harrison S. Fairchild's brigade, on the left of Harland's, was in the northeast part of a cornfield that ran down to the road skirting the Antietam. It had been put in position in the darkness and when morning came found itself exposed to the fire of Eubank's Battery across the Antietam, by which it suffered many casualties before it could change position, which was almost immediately done, the brigade moving up the ridge in the rear and under cover of the woods. (Harland followed later.) Sturgis's division was on the right of Rodman and on both sides of the road that led from the Rohrbach farm to Porterstown, with Colonel George Crook's Ohio brigade on its right front a short distance northeast of the farm. Willcox's division was in rear of Sturgis as a reserve, and Colonel Hugh Ewing's Ohio brigade was with Rodman. Burnside had directed that, in case of an attack on the bridge, Crook should make it, as a compliment to Cox's Kanawha Division for its brilliant conduct at South Mountain. Crook threw forward two companies as skirmishers, before whom some Confederate skirmishers, who had been sent across the bridge, retired, and all awaited orders to go forward.

Meanwhile, Burnside and Cox were watching the contest on the right. From the high ground occupied by them they saw the struggle between the East Woods and the West Woods and around the Dunkard church and cheered every well aimed shot that Benjamin sent in that direction. They saw the advance of French's division to the sunken road, and at this time Colonel Delos B. Sacket of McClellan's staff rode up and handed Burnside this order:

Headquarters Army of the Potomac
September 17, 1862—9.10 a.m.

Major-General Burnside:

General: General Franklin's command is within one mile and a half of here. General McClellan desires you to open your attack. As soon as you shall have uncovered the upper Stone bridge you will be supported, and, if necessary, on your own line of attack. So far all is going well.

Respectfully:

Geo. D. Ruggles,
Colonel, &c.[11]

In his official report, McClellan says, "Burnside's corps … was intrusted [sic] with the difficult task of carrying the bridge across the Antietam, near Rohrback's farm, and assaulting the enemy's right, the order having been communicated to him at 10 o'clock a.m."[12] Burnside says, "At 10 o'clock I received an order from the general commanding to make the attack."[13] Cox says the order was received at the time French was engaged at the sunken road, and "the manner in which we had waited, the free discussion of what was occurring under our eyes and of our relation to it, the public receipt of the order by Burnside in the usual and business-like form, all forbid the supposition that this was any reiteration of a former order."[14] Immediately upon receipt of the order, Burnside directed Colonel Henry W. Kingsbury to move forward his 11th Connecticut as skirmishers and drive the enemy from the head of the bridge. He also instructed Cox to detail Crook's brigade, supported by Sturgis's division, to make the assault and—when the bridge was carried—to deploy to the right and left and take the heights above it. Rodman's division was ordered to cross at a ford below and join the left of the column to be thrown over the bridge.

Directly opposite the east end of the bridge is a bluff rising at an angle of over thirty-five degrees to a height of 110 feet, wooded on the top and on the east but open on its western slope. About three hundred yards below the bridge, another hill, plowed at the time, rises at similar angle to a similar height above the Antietam. At a point on the road 260 yards below the bridge a farm road (the Rohrbach Road) runs northerly, through the ravine separating these two hills, to the Rohrbach farmhouse, thence to the Porterstown Road. East and south of the second hill and 375 yards below the bridge was a cornfield of some thirty to thirty-five acres on a sloping hillside, the southwest corner of which came down to the stream where the road leaves it to go southeast over a high ridge and on to Rohrersville. In this cornfield is a ravine from which the ground ascends southerly 180 to 190 feet above the stream, and on this elevation were placed the batteries of Benjamin, McMullin, Muhlenberg, Cook, and the New York battery of Captain Jacob Roemer, commanding a view of the entire field

[11] George D. Ruggles to Ambrose E. Burnside, September 17, 1862, reprinted in OR, vol. 51, pt. 1, 844.
[12] McClellan to Thomas, October 15, 1862, 31.
[13] Burnside to Williams, September 30, 1862, reprinted in OR, vol. 19, pt. 1, 419.
[14] Cox, "The Battle of Antietam," 649.

of battle and overlooking the bridge nine hundred yards distant. (From the southwest corner of the cornfield, which came down to the road where the Antietam begins to make a graceful sweep to the west, to the bridge is 375 yards.) The road turns square to the left to pass the bridge, which is 125 feet in length and but 12 feet wide. Cox gives an excellent description of the bridge and its surroundings:

> The bridge itself is a stone structure of three arches, with stone parapet above, this parapet to some extent flanking the approach to the bridge at either end. The valley in which the stream runs is quite narrow, the steep slope on the right bank approaching quite to the water's edge. On this slope the roadway is scarped, running both ways from the bridge end, and passing to the higher land above by ascending through ravines above and below; the other ravine being some 600 yards above the bridge, the turn about half that distance below. On the hillside immediately above the bridge was a strong stone fence running parallel to the stream. The turns of the roadway were covered by rifle-pits and breastworks, made of rails and stone, all of which defenses, as well as the woods which covered the slope, were filled with the enemy's infantry and sharpshooters. Besides the infantry defenses, batteries were placed to enfilade the bridge and all its approaches. The crest of the first hill above the bridge is curved toward the stream at the extremes, forming a sort of natural *tete-de-pont*. The next ridge beyond rises somewhat higher, though with less regularity, the depression between the two being but slight, and the distance varying in places from 300 to 700 yards.[15]

McClellan, after stating in his report that Burnside had been given a "difficult task," says, "The valley of the Antietam at and near this bridge is narrow, with high banks. On the right of the stream the bank is wooded, and commands the approaches both to the bridge and the ford. The steep slopes of the bank were lined with rifle-pits and breastworks of rails and stones. These, together with the woods, were filled with the enemy's infantry, while their batteries completely commanded and enfiladed the bridge and ford and their approaches."[16]

The bridge was defended by about four hundred men of Toombs's Brigade, supported on the right by a regiment of one hundred men of Drayton's Brigade and a company of Jenkins's Brigade. The 20th Georgia (Colonel John B. Cumming) rested its left about forty yards above the bridge with skirmishers on the left, some two hundred yards overlooking the Antietam. In a good position among some trees on the immediate bank of the stream was a company of the regiment. On the right of the 20th Georgia, about two-thirds of the way up the bluff and nearly opposite the head of the bridge, was a quarry from which the bridge could be raked its entire length. (Twenty-five to thirty men were in this quarry.) Also on the right of the 20th was the 2d Georgia (Lieutenant Colonel William R. Holmes), prolonging the line down the stream about three hundred yards below the bridge, where it curves sharply to the west opposite the point where the Rohrersville Road leaves it and ascends a sharp ridge. Then the greater part of the line was placed below the bridge. This disposition was adopted because the road to the bridge on the opposite side of the stream ran from below (up the bank, near the water) for about three hundred yards. Colonel Henry L. Benning of the 17th Georgia had immediate command of these two regiments. The line was on the crest of the bluff, well sheltered and hidden by the trees, and strengthened by rail fences, fallen trees, and everything that could give protection. Farther to the right was the 50th Georgia (Lieutenant Colonel Francis Kearse) of Drayton's Brigade, about one hundred men, which held a line on the right of the 2d Georgia. It was deployed in very open order to guard a blind plantation road leading to a ford in the bend of the Antietam between the right of the 2d Georgia and Snavely's Ford. Between the 2d and 50th Georgia was half a company of Jenkins's Brigade, and on the right of the 50th was the other half of this company, overlooking and observing Snavely's Ford. Toombs was in general command of the whole line. On a ridge about five hundred yards in rear was Richardson's Battery of the Washington Artillery; finding that it was too far in rear to render service in defending the passage of the bridge, Toombs obtained Eubank's Battery of S. D. Lee's Battalion, which took position in his rear about halfway between the stream and Richardson. (Until near noon Eshleman's Battery was on Richardson's right.) The batteries on Cemetery Hill had complete range of the bridge and the road to Sharpsburg, and after its passage they inflicted many casualties upon the troops that had crossed.

Toombs minimizes the strength of his position but says, "Its chief strength lay in the fact that, from the nature of the ground on the other side, the enemy were compelled to approach mainly by the road which led up the river for near 300 paces, parallel with my line of battle, and distant therefrom from 50 to 150 feet, thus exposing his flank to a destructive fire the most of that distance."[17] Cox says:

> I do not hesitate to affirm that the Confederate position was virtually impregnable to a direct attack over the bridge, for the column approaching it was not only exposed at pistol-range to the perfectly covered infantry of the enemy and

[15] Cox to Richmond, September 23, 1862, reprinted in *OR*, vol. 19, pt. 1, 424.

[16] McClellan to Thomas, October 15, 1862, 31.

[17] Robert Toombs to David R. Jones, October 25, 1862, reprinted in *OR*, vol. 19, pt. 1, 890.

to two batteries which were assigned to the special duty of supporting Toombs, and which had the exact range of the little valley with their shrapnel, but if it should succeed in reaching the bridge its charge across it must be made under a fire plowing through its length, the head of the column melting away as it advanced, so that, as every soldier knows, it could show no front strong enough to make an impression upon the enemy's breastworks, even if it should reach the other side. As a desperate sort of diversion in favor of the right wing, it might be justifiable; but I believe that no officer or man who knew the actual situation at that bridge thinks a serious attack upon it was any part of McClellan's original plan. Yet, in his detailed official report, instead of speaking of it as the difficult task the original report had called it, he treats it as little different from a parade or march across, which might have been done in half an hour.[18]

Cox had immediate command of the Ninth Corps during the battle. On the afternoon of the sixteenth, when expecting a battle, he remained with his division, desiring to lead it, and urged Burnside to assume the immediate command of the corps, to which Burnside "objected that as he had been announced as commander of the right wing of the army composed of two corps (his own and Hooker's), he was unwilling to waive his precedence or to assume that Hooker was detached for anything more than a temporary purpose," but he would assist Cox in every way he could till the crisis of the campaign should be over.[19]

Cox was an earnest and gallant soldier but new to the Army of the Potomac, and three of the divisions were strangers to him. He had conducted a very successful and brilliant campaign in the Kanawha Valley of present-day West Virginia in the summer of 1861 and had a well disciplined and good division that, under his command, had done good and brilliant service at South Mountain. To anticipate, he handled the Ninth Corps well at Antietam.

It would have been better had he handled it alone. It has been well said that "Burnside became a mere receiver and transmitter of orders to the commander of the Ninth Corps, and on the other hand it may easily be believed that so good a soldier as Cox would have shown more activity and accomplished more, if he had felt himself really the commander of the Ninth Corps. With Burnside close to him, he probably felt as if he were the mere tactical leader of the corps, not thinking for it, but simply seeing that it executed the orders which came to him from or through Burnside."[20] It can be stated upon unquestionable authority that, had he felt that he was in responsible command, he would not have depended upon reconnaissance made by McClellan's engineers and aides for knowledge of the crossings of the stream but would have ascertained the matter in person, and that he would have had two divisions at Snavely's Ford before ten o'clock on the morning of the seventeenth, ready to cross when McClellan gave the order to attack. However, this was not to be; we take things as we find them, and continue the narrative.

It had been determined that Crook's brigade should lead in the attack on the bridge and that Sturgis's division should support it. It was thought that by advancing part of Sturgis's command to the plowed hill below the bridge it could cover the advance of Crook, who could make a straight dash down the hill directly opposite the bridge and carry it. Orders were given accordingly for Crook, preceded by the 11th Connecticut as skirmishers, to assault the bridge. The 11th Connecticut was then detached from its brigade and went forward to the crest of the hill east of the Rohrbach Road, where it was halted and a battery put in position near it, which shelled the opposite bank of the Antietam. When the artillery firing ceased, the regiment went down the plowed hill, crossed the Rohrbach Road near the stream, and, in skirmishing order with a reserve, went over a wooded spur and pushed for the bridge under a severe fire. The left of the line reached the creek opposite the end of the Rohrbach Road and the right gained the level ground at the foot of the hill opposite the bridge. Captain John Griswold, on the left, endeavored to lead his men across the creek and was mortally wounded in the water; on the right Colonel Kingsbury was severely and then mortally wounded while leading the reserve toward the bridge. After a short but gallant effort, in which it lost over one-third of its men, the regiment fell back.

The 11th Connecticut was soon followed by Crook, who seems to have misunderstood the orders under which he was acting, as he says they were "to cross the bridge over Antietam Creek after General Sturgis had taken the bridge," but upon his arrival in the vicinity of the bridge he found that Sturgis had not arrived, so he sent the 11th Ohio ahead as skirmishers in the direction of the bridge.[21] Early in the morning, before the general advance had been ordered, two companies of the 11th Ohio were sent forward as skirmishers on the wooded bluff to watch the enemy closely and give notice of any movement made by them. They were fired upon as they made their appearance on the west side of the bluff, fell back under cover, and returned the fire upon the Georgians beyond the creek. This was prior to the advance of the 11th Connecticut, and when that advance was made the two companies were on the right of it, still skirmishing. Crook's brigade consisted of the

[18] Cox, "The Battle of Antietam," 650.

[19] Ibid., 631.

[20] Francis Winthrop Palfrey, *The Antietam and Fredericksburg*, vol. 5 of *The Army in the Civil War* (New York: Charles Scribner's Sons, 1882), 117.

[21] George Crook to Robert P. Kennedy, September 20, 1862, reprinted in *OR*, vol. 19, pt. 1, 471–72.

11th, 28th, and 36th Ohio. Attached to it was a battery of the Kentucky Light Artillery commanded by Captain Seth J. Simmonds. (One section of this battery had been attached to Benjamin; one remained with the brigade.) When Crook received his orders, he was a short distance northeast of the Rohrbach farm. He advanced, left the 36th Ohio in the Rohrbach orchard, and went down the road with the 11th and 28th Ohio, halting in the road about two hundred yards south of the house. Four companies of the 28th Ohio were sent over the wooded hill on the right as skirmishers, and, as they approached the open field looking down on the bridge, the fire from the opposite bank of the stream was so severe that they fell back and rejoined the regiment in the Rohrbach Road. Five companies of the 28th Ohio were now ordered to place in position (on the crest of the wooded hill, overlooking the bridge) two guns of Simmonds's battery, and Crook, ordering the 11th Ohio to advance on the bridge, led the other five companies of the 28th by the right flank over the wooded hill to cooperate with the 11th in a charge on the bridge, but lost direction and, instead of coming out at the bridge, went down the hill and came to within 50 yards of the creek at a point where there was a bend in the stream and a ford about 350 yards above the bridge. Here, seeking shelter under a low, sandy ridge and fence, Crook and his men engaged the Confederate skirmishers opposite and remained until the bridge had been carried by Sturgis's division.

When Crook led the five companies of the 28th Ohio to the right, the 11th Ohio was formed in line on the left of the road, on the side of the plowed hill, and advanced, but under conflicting orders it became broken, the right wing moving across the road to the wooded hill (where the two companies had remained as skirmishers) while the left wing moved straight down the open hill to its base, about one hundred yards from the creek, where it came under severe fire of infantry and artillery. Lieutenant Colonel Augustus H. Coleman, commanding the regiment, was mortally wounded, the ranks were thrown into confusion, and Major Lyman J. Jackson, finding himself in a useless and very exposed position, moved with a part of the regiment to the right, recrossed the field and the Rohrbach Road under cover of the fire of some of the 11th Connecticut (who had held on to the fences bordering the stream), and halted at a point of the hill opposite the bridge, where he reunited his command, formed under cover, and kept up fire until he was ordered to retire and join the 36th Ohio in the Rohrbach orchard. Crook handled his command badly, his loss was trifling, and he reported to Cox that he had his hands full and could not approach closer to the bridge.

Crook's movement having failed, Sturgis was ordered to take the bridge. Intending to act as a support to Crook and take advantage of any success gained by him, he had moved his division to the left and front, in such position that it could make a quick dash up the road skirting the stream to the bridge. Brigadier General[22] James Nagle's brigade lay nearest the bridge. The 2d Maryland (Lieutenant Colonel Jacob E. Duryee[23]) had marched down a stock lane from the Rohrbach farm and halted with its right at the southwest corner of the cornfield, 375 yards below the bridge; the 6th New Hampshire (Colonel Simon G. Griffin) was at the side of the stock lane, in rear of the 2d Maryland and under cover of the plowed hill immediately west; the 48th Pennsylvania (Lieutenant Colonel Joshua K. Sigfried) marched down through the corn to a small log building in its southwest corner, near the 2d Maryland; and the 9th New Hampshire (Colonel Enoch Q. Fellows) went down through the corn to the fence bordering the road and opened fire upon the enemy's skirmishers across the stream. Brigadier General Edward Ferrero's brigade followed Nagle's and took position in the cornfield (three regiments about two hundred yards from its western edge, with the 35th Massachusetts on their left and rear) on a hillside overlooking them. Some of the batteries were engaged when Crook was making his movement, but now all the guns that could be brought to bear opened a furious fire upon the west head of the bridge and the wooded heights below it, and further preparations were made to carry the span.

Rodman's division, supported by Ewing's brigade, had been directed to cross at the ford below the bridge. Cox says:

> Burnside's view of the matter was that the front attack at the bridge was so difficult that the passage by the ford below must be an important factor in the task; for if Rodman's division should succeed in getting across there, at the bend in the Antietam, he would come up in rear of Toombs, and either the whole of D. R. Jones's division would have to advance to meet Rodman, or Toombs must abandon the bridge … and Rodman was ordered to push rapidly for the ford.
>
> … We were constantly hoping to hear something from Rodman's advance by the ford, and would gladly have waited for some more certain knowledge of his progress, but at this time McClellan's sense of the necessity of relieving the right was such that he was sending reiterated orders to push the assault. Not only were these forwarded to me, but to give added weight to my instructions Burnside sent direct to Sturgis urgent messages to carry the bridge at all hazards.[24]

---

[22] For a discussion of Nagle's promotion, see p. 409 n. 40.

[23] Jacob E. Duryee was the son of Brigadier General Abram Duryee. In his original manuscript, Carman here and in his table of organization repeats the error made previously, giving the surname incorrectly as "Duryea." See p. 158 n. 30.

[24] Cox, "The Battle of Antietam," 650–51.

Nagle had taken position before the failure of Crook's attack; soon after its cessation, Sturgis ordered him forward up the road to the bridge. The movement was initiated by the 48th Pennsylvania, which left its place near the log building in the cornfield, moved to the right over the slope of the plowed hill, crossed the Rohrbach Road, and formed line on the wooded knoll in front of the bridge, near where the 11th Ohio had been engaged (and from which they were now retiring) and where five companies of the 28th Ohio were getting two of Simmonds's guns in position. Here the regiment opened fire upon the Confederates beyond the stream.

To lessen the long stretch of the road along which it was necessary to move under flank fire of the enemy, within easy pistol shot, the 2d Maryland was countermarched up the lane about two hundred yards to where the 6th New Hampshire had halted. Under cover of the plowed hill the two regiments, about 150 men each, were formed for the charge. It required but a few moments when—side by side, with bayonets fixed—they went down the hill at its southwest corner. The Rohrbach Road was fenced with stout chestnut posts and rails, which were quite high. The officers ran ahead and soon removed a short panel, and as the head of the 2d Maryland came to the opening it was met with such a withering fire that the leading files began to shrink and elbow out of the ranks, but the vehement commands and the examples of the officers steadied the men. The line straightened up and charged up the road toward the bridge under a severe front and flank fire. About midway from where they had struck the road and the bridge, the road bends slightly to the right; upon reaching this point, the head of the column came under the fire of the Georgians posted in the quarry just south of the head of the bridge and those on the brow of the bluff behind rail barricades and trees not over one hundred yards distant. Fully one-third of the Maryland men went down, but the regiment still went on and had reached to within 250 feet of the bridge when the right wing was so shattered that the few survivors fell back and sought such cover as the fences, logs, and trees afforded. The left wing essayed a farther advance, but it too was checked and sought cover. The 6th New Hampshire suffered severely before it cleared the opening in the fence. It was close on the heels of the 2d Maryland and met the same fate; it was badly shattered, sought cover and opened fire across the stream, in which it was joined by the Maryland men. The 9th New Hampshire followed the charging regiments as far as the Rohrbach Road, where it halted—its left about one hundred yards from the road that ran to the bridge, the right extending up the road in which it had halted, and all well covered from the fire beyond the creek, which was answered by crawling up the hillside and delivering an accurate and constant fire.

Cox now ordered Sturgis to take two regiments from Ferrero's brigade, which had not been engaged, and make a column by moving them by the flank, side by side, so that when they crossed the bridge they could turn to the right and left, forming line as they advanced on the run. As the effort along the main road had proven so disastrous, it was determined that these two regiments should charge from the hill opposite the bridge, where Crook had made his futile attempt. This charge was to be supported by artillery on the right, and on the left by the infantry lying along the road below the bridge—the 2d Maryland, 6th and 9th New Hampshire, and 21st Massachusetts, with the 35th Massachusetts to follow the two charging regiments. Under Cox's instructions Ferrero selected the 51st Pennsylvania (Colonel John F. Hartranft) and the 51st New York (Lieutenant Colonel Robert B. Potter). The two regiments piled their knapsacks in the cornfield, filled their canteens from the spring near the road, marched out of the corn, went over the lower part of the plowed hill, crossed the Rohrbach Road, ascended the eastern slope of the wooded knoll that looked down upon the entrance to the bridge, and formed behind the 48th Pennsylvania at a point where a dip in the ground concealed them from view (the 51st Pennsylvania on the right, the 51st New York on the left). The two regiments had about 335 officers and men each.

Meanwhile, Simmonds's two guns had been placed in position, supported by five companies of the 28th Ohio, and opened fire upon the heights above the far end of the bridge. Clark's battery of six guns was brought down the north side of the hill and opened fire at the same time, and a battery in rear of Clark's (probably Taft's 5th Battery, New York Light Artillery) added its fire. The 21st Massachusetts (Colonel William S. Clark), about 150 men, moved from the cornfield, took position behind the fence at the foot of the plowed hill, and engaged the enemy's skirmishers beyond the stream. When everything was ready, a heavy skirmishing fire was opened all along the bank of the stream, the guns were active with canister and shell, and the two regiments (led by Hartranft) sprang from cover. They passed over the 48th Pennsylvania and, side by side, went down the hill by the flank straight for the bridge, a little over three hundred yards distant, and were met by such a severe fire that the progress of the column was checked. When going down the hill, the company commanders (at least some of them) of the 51st Pennsylvania came to the conclusion that it would be impossible for the two regiments to charge in a body across such an exceedingly narrow structure as they now saw before them and changed their course to the right. Before Hartranft could stop them, they gained a stone fence running north from the bridge abutment and parallel to the creek, where, under good cover, they opened fire across the stream. Potter, at the head of the 51st New York, perceiving this movement and fearing that his exposed flank would lose very heavily under the concentrated fire of the enemy, brought his regiment forward into line, obliqued to the left down to the road on the edge of the stream below the bridge (where a rail fence offered some cover) and joined the 51st Pennsylvania in a rapid fire across the stream, principally upon the quarry near the far end of the bridge. When Colonel Clark of the 21st Massachusetts saw this condition of affairs, he double-quicked his regiment along the road and formed on the left of the 51st New York, where he was joined by Company A of the 35th Massachusetts.

After firing in this position a few minutes and perceiving a slackening in the Confederate fire and that some of them were leaving, Potter became satisfied that a rush would carry the bridge and suggested to Hartranft that it be made, but the latter replied that his men had received so heavy a fire that it would be very difficult to get them to leave cover, upon which Potter asked permission to lead his own regiment over. This was granted. Potter communicated his order to his nearest company commander on the right and, rushing toward the bridge, waved his sword for the regiment to follow. It started on the run. When it reached within a few feet of the bridge, the 51st Pennsylvania, which had seen the enemy in its front retiring by twos and threes, and spurred by the action of the New York men, ran by the left flank through a gateway in the fence close to the bridge, and the regiments, side by side, their colors close together, crossed the bridge amid the most enthusiastic cheering from every part of the field from which they could be seen. Upon clearing the bridge, the two regiments turned to the right and halted in the road leading to Sharpsburg. Toombs's men fell back; some were taken prisoners. A few sharpshooters, who could not make their escape, were found in the trees.

The 21st Massachusetts did not cross the bridge at this time, as it was out of ammunition, but the 35th Massachusetts was close upon the heels of the two charging regiments. It had followed them from the cornfield after a brief interval and, skirting the base of the plowed hill, passing along the rear of the 21st Massachusetts, crossed the Rohrbach Road, made a short halt on the wooded hill, then went out of the woods by the flank. Seeing the forces below engaged along the banks of the stream, it was ordered in line to join the firing, but the movement was scarcely completed when the charge for the bridge was seen, upon which it came at once into column and rushed across the bridge—the third regiment to cross. Turning to the right, it passed the two regiments and formed in the road on their right about 1:00 p.m. Nagle's brigade quickly followed. The 48th Pennsylvania, which had been on the bluff, and over which the 51st Pennsylvania moved in its charge, went down the hill close behind the 35th Massachusetts, crossed the bridge, turned to the left, ascended the heights by a very rough farm road, and threw out skirmishers to the front and left—those on the left going down the stream until they met the advancing skirmishers of Rodman's division, which had crossed the Antietam at Snavely's Ford. The 6th and 9th New Hampshire followed the 48th Pennsylvania across and up the road on the left, came under heavy artillery fire, and formed line under cover of the ridge beyond, upon which skirmishers were deployed, who became warmly engaged with those of the enemy about 350 yards distant and covered by a stone fence. Eubank's Battery had been driven from the field by the furious fire of the Union artillery about 9:00 a.m. Richardson's Battery remained until Toombs fell back, when it went down the Otto lane and then through Sharpsburg, but J. S. Brown's Battery, about nine hundred yards to the front and right of where Nagle's men had halted, poured in a rapid and incessant fire of shell and shrapnel. At the same time, the Confederate guns on Cemetery Hill threw their shell and shrapnel into the ranks of the men lying in the road near the bridge, killing and wounding many. (Among those killed was Lieutenant Colonel Thomas S. Bell of the 51st Pennsylvania.) About the time the bridge was carried, Crook crossed his five companies of the 28th Ohio at the ford 350 yards above and covered the road to Sharpsburg, where he was joined later by the rest of his brigade, which crossed at the bridge. Captain Hiram F. Devol's company of the 36th Ohio was sent to the right of the road, on the high ground overlooking the Sherrick farm, to dislodge some skirmishers, who were giving much annoyance.

Very soon after crossing the bridge, and while Nagle's brigade was going up the road on the left and taking position, the 35th Massachusetts was ordered to ascend the heights on the right. About seventy-five yards above the bridge is a ravine, beyond which is a very bold hill overlooking the road and stream. The regiment was ordered up this hill. It started in line of battle, the left in the ravine, climbing with difficulty the high rail fences and steep ground, but soon swung into column, moving by the right flank as it neared the top. When it reached the bare brow of the hill, J. S. Brown's Battery opened fire upon it, killing and wounding several, and it fell back under the brow of the hill and lay down in a grass field. Soon after, the 21st Massachusetts came up and formed on its left. The 51st Pennsylvania and 51st New York remained for a time in the road near the bridge.

Sturgis's artillery followed his infantry across the bridge. We left Durell's battery early in the morning engaged on the bluff overlooking the Antietam, from which position it went back to near where Benjamin was using his long-range guns. Two guns were advanced to assist Simmonds and Clark in silencing the enemy at the head of the bridge but did not get into action before the bridge was carried. They went down the hill, crossed the bridge, moved up the road to the right, and began to ascend the ravine by which the left of the 35th Massachusetts had gone up the bluff. No favorable position could be found for the guns and they returned to the bridge, advanced up the road to the left, and joined the other four guns that had crossed the bridge and taken position on a ridge 450 yards nearly west of the bridge and overlooking a deep valley, beyond which (about nine hundred yards from the battery) the ground rises from forty to sixty feet higher, and along which runs the road from Sharpsburg to the mouth of the Antietam and Harper's Ferry. At first two guns of the battery were on the right of Clark's; these were brought to the left and the battery united its left about twenty-five yards from the northeast corner of a forty-acre cornfield, through which ran a deep ravine south to the Antietam at Snavely's Ford. When the battery went into position it became hotly engaged with J. S. Brown's Battery on the right and front. Clark's battery, while going into position on the right of Durell's four guns (two of Durell's being on his right) was greeted with a rapid fire of spherical case from Brown's guns. Lieutenant William L. Baker was killed and Captain Clark severely wounded and compelled to leave the field. The command devolved upon Sergeant Christopher F. Merkle, who fought the battery the rest of the day with skill and courage.

In the several efforts to carry the bridge, the Union loss was about 500, that of the Confederates in defending it about 120—and they held it until the colors of the 51st Pennsylvania and 51st New York were upon it. Most of the Georgians then retreated, but the commander of the 2d Georgia, Colonel Holmes, appealing to some of his men to follow him, ran down to the bank of the stream. With a cry of defiance, he shook his sword in the faces of the Union men and fell, pierced by many bullets.

Thus died, says Colonel Benning, "a good officer, and as gallant a man, I think, as my eyes ever beheld." Benning also pays this tribute to his men: "During that long and terrible fire not a man, except a wounded one, fell out and went to the rear—not a man."[25]

Scant justice has been done the brave men who fought at what has become known as the Burnside Bridge. It is true that there was not such a holocaust of dead as on other parts of the field, but the fighting was brilliant. William Allan, the historian of the Army of Northern Virginia, writes, "There was no part of the bloody field of Sharpsburg which witnessed more gallant deeds both of attack and defense than did the Burnside bridge ... a fierce contest was waged for its possession ... The 500 Federal soldiers who lay bleeding or dead along the eastern approach to the bridge were witnesses to the courage of the assaults. On the Confederate side of the stream Toombs's two small regiments held their ground, and threw back assault after assault with a coolness and tenacity unsurpassed in history."[26]

There has been much unjust criticism at the delay in taking the bridge. The events narrated followed each other in quick succession and were as energetically pushed as were movements on any other part of the field. Cox says:

Nearly three hours had been spent in a bitter and bloody contest across the narrow stream. The successive efforts to carry the bridge had been made as closely following each other as possible. Each had been a fierce combat, in which the men, with wonderful courage, had not easily accepted defeat, and even when not able to cross the bridge had made use of the walls at the end, the fences, and every tree and stone as cover, while they strove to reach with their fire their well-protected and nearly concealed opponents. The lulls in the fighting had been short, and only to prepare new efforts. The severity of the work was attested by our losses.[27]

Confederate reports confirm Cox's statements and show the condition of affairs on that side. Benning, who was in immediate command of the 2d and 20th Georgia, after giving their position—without supports, and with the general line of battle nearly or quite three-quarters of a mile in rear—says:

In this forlorn condition were the two regiments ..., when the fight opened in earnest. At this time the enemy's infantry, aided by the fire of many pieces of artillery, advanced in heavy force to the attack; and soon the attack opened on our whole line as far up as the bridge. It was bold and persevering. The enemy came to the creek. The fire not only from their infantry, but from the artillery, was incessant, the artillery being so placed that it could fire over the heads of the infantry. It was met by a rapid, well-directed, and unflinching fire from our men, under which the enemy, after a vain struggle, broke and fell back. This attack was succeeded by two similar ones from apparently fresh bodies of troops, and with like results, the last of the two extending above the bridge to the upper part of our line. At length, toward 12 o'clock, the enemy made preparations for a still more formidable attack. A battery was placed in position

[25] Henry L. Benning to Dudley M. DuBose, October 13, 1862, reprinted in *OR*, vol. 51, pt. 1, 163.

[26] William Allan, *The Army of Northern Virginia in 1862* (Boston: Houghton, Mifflin and Co., 1892), 429–30.

[27] Cox, "The Battle of Antietam," 653. The quotation above is presented by the editor as it appears in the original source material. For some unknown reason, Carman re-arranged the order of the sentences. In his original manuscript, it reads, "The successive efforts to carry the bridge had been made as closely following each other as possible. Each had been a fierce combat, in which the men, with wonderful courage, had not easily accepted defeat, and even when not able to cross the bridge had made use of the walls at the end, the fences, and every tree and stone as cover, while they strove to reach with their fire their well-protected and nearly concealed opponents. The lulls in the fighting had been short, and only to prepare new efforts. ... Nearly three hours had been spent in a bitter and bloody contest across the narrow stream ... The severity of the work was attested by our losses." Carman's insertion of ellipses shows that this revision was deliberate, but his reason for doing so is not known.

from which it could command at almost an enfilade the whole face of the hill occupied by our troops. Soon it opened fire, and the infantry, in much heavier force than at any time before, extending far above as well as below the bridge, again advanced to the attack. The combined fire of infantry and artillery was terrific. It was, however, withstood by our men until their ammunition was quite exhausted, and until the enemy had got upon the bridge and were above and below it fording the creek. I then gave the order to fall back.[28]

The position to which the Georgians retired was a stone fence about nine hundred yards in rear. Some of them went farther to the south and skirmished with the advance of Rodman's division, which had crossed at Snavely's Ford.

There is no doubt that an earlier appearance of Rodman on this part of the field would have rendered unnecessary much of the great loss sustained in the successive attacks on the bridge. His delay is partly attributable to the want of knowledge of the fords. On the sixteenth McClellan's engineer officers made reconnaissances for fords and gathered information regarding them. Burnside was informed by them that there was a ford less than half a mile below the bridge, and when Rodman's division was led to its bivouac that night, Fairchild's brigade was supposed to be opposite this ford. Cox says that all the orders for the movement of troops were based on the reports of the engineer officers. Burnside reports that in the morning, after the preliminary movements were made and before the general advance was ordered, "Rodman's division, with Scammon's [i.e., Ewing's] brigade in support, [was] opposite the ford, some three-quarters of a mile below the bridge."[29] Cox reports that it was "about one-third of a mile below the bridge."[30] In reality the nearest ford below the bridge—the one referred to by the engineer officers—was two-thirds of a mile away and was impracticable. It was not properly situated, being at the foot of a steep bluff, rising more than 160 feet, over which it would have been almost impossible to deploy infantry against a skirmish line, and the passage of the ford would have consumed much time. It was not until after Rodman had been ordered to advance (about ten o'clock) from the heights to which he had retired early in the morning and had marched some distance that he became aware of the fact that the only ford by which he could cross was a mile distant from his starting point (as the crow flies) and that he would be required to march two miles over very rough ground to reach it. This was Snavely's Ford, 680 yards below the ford indicated in the orders of the day. It does seem probable that had one or two regiments of Pleasonton's cavalry been used on this flank some good results would have followed, not only in finding and crossing the ford but in protecting Rodman's flank from its surprise and disaster later in the day.

Rodman's division consisted of two brigades, commanded by Colonels Fairchild and Harland. Fairchild had the 9th New York (Hawkins's Zouaves), 89th New York, and six companies of the 103d New York. To this brigade was attached a battery of naval howitzers under the command of Captain James R. Whiting Jr. of the 9th New York. Harland had the 8th, 11th, and 16th Connecticut and the 4th Rhode Island. (Lieutenant Muhlenberg's Battery A, 5th U.S. Artillery, was attached to the division but did not accompany it to the left, nor did the 11th Connecticut.) The division was followed by the 12th, 23d, and 30th Ohio of what had initially been Colonel Eliakim P. Scammon's brigade. (Scammon being in command of the Kanawha Division in place of Cox, his brigade was now commanded by Colonel Ewing of the 30th Ohio.) The entire force numbered about 3,200 officers and men.

Rodman moved from his position on the high ridge at 10:30 a.m., crossed the Rohrersville Road about one thousand yards below the bridge, marched some eight hundred yards after crossing the road, and halted opposite the great bend in the Antietam where the course of the stream changes from due south to west. Whiting's five guns were put in position to shell the wooded bluff opposite the ford by which it was proposed to cross, and they shelled the road and woods on the opposite side of the creek, driving the enemy from their position. (This fire of Whiting's enfiladed the line of the Georgians at and below the bridge, and the annoyance it caused them is referred to in some of their reports.) Meanwhile, skirmishers had gone down to the creek, and Rodman had come to the conclusion that this ford was not one that could be crossed and directed Colonel Harland to make further reconnaissance. Harland says, "I then sent out two companies of skirmishers from the Eighth Regiment Connecticut Volunteers to discover, if possible, a ford by which the creek could be crossed."[31] These two companies were under the command of Captain Charles L. Upham. The bank of the stream was quite heavily wooded with dense undergrowth, but Upham soon reported that he had found a practicable ford, and the column, Fairchild's brigade in advance, marched down to it. Whiting's battery, supported by the 8th Connecticut, was put in position on a hill just below the ford to cover the crossing. Much time had been lost and it was nearly one o'clock. Cox says the winding of the stream made Rodman's march longer than was anticipated and that in fact he only approached the rear of Toombs's position from that direction about the time when the last and successful charge upon the bridge was made, between noon and one o'clock.[32]

[28] Benning to DuBose, 162–63.
[29] Burnside to Williams, 419.
[30] Cox to Richmond, 424.
[31] Edward Harland to Charles T. Gardner, September 22, 1862, reprinted in *OR*, vol. 19, pt. 1, 452.
[32] Cox, "The Battle of Antietam," 651.

From Snavely's Ford to the bridge, in a direct line a little east of north, it is 1,275 yards. When the head of the column halted on the hill overlooking the ford at an elevation of one hundred feet, it had an extensive view of a stretch of country toward the front and right, and above the bushes and over the trees could be seen the smoke of the contest at the bridge and the charge of the 51st Pennsylvania and the 51st New York. While this contest was in progress, Fairchild's brigade (the 9th New York leading) marched by the left flank down an old trail or wood road and entered the stream, which is about seventy-five feet wide, with a swift and strong current, the water hip-deep. At the far side was a meadow partly plowed, beyond which the ground rose gradually to a stone fence running parallel with the stream and about 165 yards from it, and on the right was the high, steep, wooded bluff, the eastern part of which commanded the ford 680 yards above Snavely's.

When partly across the ford, the 9th New York received the fire of Confederate skirmishers (the company from Jenkins's Brigade and some of the 50th Georgia) who were behind the stone fence, by which some men were wounded, but without replying to it the column moved on, reached the opposite bank, and, filing to the right, came under the shelter of the wooded bluff. The regiment then faced to the left and began the ascent of the bluff, which was very steep, rocky, and covered with a tangled undergrowth. Rodman was with the regiment, which broke into detachments right and left to avoid impassable places and to drive any of the enemy who might be secreted in the woods therefrom. In this manner, overcoming many difficulties, they reached the summit of the bluff, 185 feet above the Antietam, closely followed by the 103d and 89th New York, and the entire brigade, marching by the right flank near the bank of the stream, met the advancing skirmishers of the 48th Pennsylvania and made a junction with the troops that had forced the bridge. Under a very severe artillery fire from the enemy's guns in the direction of Sharpsburg, the brigade halted in a depression of the ground in rear of Durell's and Clark's batteries.

Harland followed Fairchild, and while the latter was making his difficult way up the bluff on the right, the 4th Rhode Island crossed the creek under fire of the enemy behind the stone fence, filed to the left on open ground, threw one company to the front and one to the left as skirmishers, and, advancing, drove the enemy from the stone fence and formed behind it. Almost immediately it received a musketry fire from the left, which was soon silenced by Whiting's guns across the creek. The 16th Connecticut followed the 4th Rhode Island and moved to support its left. Two companies were sent to the left beyond the Snavely buildings and were deployed behind the stone and rail fences of the road leading to Myers's Ford and at the foot of a bluff, upon which was a large cornfield. Here Munford had his cavalry skirmishers, which, advancing to the brow of the bluff, opened fire, while Eshleman's Battery, about six hundred yards to the right and front, dropped shrapnel among the Union men. Some casualties resulted and the skirmishers were ordered back to the regiment, which moved to the right along the rear of the 4th Rhode Island to a sheltered position. Eshleman's guns were now enfilading the left of the 4th Rhode Island, which, as soon as the 16th Connecticut had passed, moved to the right and formed under cover. The 8th Connecticut now came up and the brigade marched up the ravine and to the right, the two Connecticut regiments forming in Fairchild's rear and the 4th Rhode Island further to the left in the woods near the creek. Ewing's brigade followed Harland, came under the fire of Eshleman's guns, and, marching under cover, halted some distance below the bridge, thus forming the extreme left of the line. It was two o'clock.

After the infantry had crossed the ford, Whiting went over with his five guns under a fire of shrapnel from Eshleman's Battery, but found it impracticable to follow the infantry. His guns were brass Navy howitzers (12-pounders, two rifled and three smoothbores), each gun hauled by two horses and the trail guided by a man on each side with a rope fastened to it. (Going down the hill the men had to hold the guns back with a rope.) There were no limbers, the ammunition being carried in an Army wagon, together with the rifles of the men, who, when not acting as artillerymen, served as infantry. After crossing the stream, Whiting found the ground too rough for the movement of his guns. He could not supply them with ammunition and was ordered to recross the stream and rejoin the command by way of the bridge. He followed the bank of the stream under the bluff to the right and crossed at the ford 680 yards above Snavely's. When nearing the bridge, he met Burnside, who ordered Whiting to leave his guns behind under guard, get the rifles from the wagons, cross the bridge, and report to Cox, all of which was done. The company was thrown out as skirmishers on the extreme left, but it was late in the day.

Three divisions of the Ninth Corps had now been thrown across the Antietam and formed in one curved line, the left resting on the stream at its bend below the bridge, the right on the road to Sharpsburg, close to the stream, three hundred yards north of the bridge. Sturgis's division (supported by Crook's brigade) was on the right, Rodman's division (supported by Ewing's brigade) was on the left. It would have been well had they been in condition to go forward; both Burnside and Cox say they were not. The latter writes, "The ammunition of Sturgis's and Crook's men had been nearly exhausted, and it was imperative that they should be freshly supplied before entering into another engagement. Sturgis also reported his men so exhausted by their efforts as to be unfit for an immediate advance."[33] On this, Cox, who had accompanied the

---

[33] Ibid., 653.

troops across the bridge, sent to Burnside the request that Willcox's division be sent over with an ammunition train and that Sturgis's division be replaced by the fresh troops, remaining, however, on the west side of the stream as support to the others. "This was done as rapidly as was practicable," says Cox, "where everything had to pass down the steep hill road and through so narrow a defile as the bridge." Meanwhile, McClellan, abandoning effort on every other part of the field and holding Pleasonton in check, was sending Burnside pressing orders to advance but offered no assisting hand, although in his order of 9:10 a.m. he gave him the positive assurance that when he should have uncovered the Middle Bridge he would be supported, and, if necessary, on his own line of attack.[34] Pleasonton had crossed the Middle Bridge; there was no obstacle to the prompt support of Burnside. The way was open, but when Pleasonton suggested lending a helping hand, it was determined not to do so.

Willcox's division, which had now been joined by the three regiments detached the night before for service on Elk Ridge and was about three-fourths of a mile from the bridge, marched through the cornfield in which Sturgis had formed to assault the bridge, then went up the road, over the bridge, and along the road to near where it leaves the creek and turns northwest. The division had two brigades, commanded by Colonels Benjamin C. Christ and Thomas Welsh of the 50th and 45th Pennsylvania, respectively. In Christ's brigade were the 28th Massachusetts, 17th Michigan, 79th New York, and 50th Pennsylvania. Welsh had the 8th Michigan, 46th New York, and 45th and 100th Pennsylvania. Captain Asa M. Cook's 8th Battery, Massachusetts Light Artillery accompanied the division (Benjamin's battery remained east of the Antietam.) The head of the division crossed the bridge about two o'clock. Crook's brigade was in support. After Willcox had crossed the bridge, the 51st Pennsylvania and the 51st New York, which had remained in the road near the bridge, ascended the high ground and took position on the left of the 21st and 35th Massachusetts, the line being in rear of Rodman's right.

The road from the bridge to Sharpsburg runs along an open hollow or ravine that winds along to the village, overlooked by the heights to the right and left. Once on the heights, the country is rolling and dotted with many field fences, some of which were of stone. The Confederate skirmishers were posted behind these fences as well as haystacks, which also (with orchards and cornfields) served to conceal their lines. Batteries of field guns commanded the road and hollow down to the Antietam, and the whole plateau above was swept by a crossfire of artillery. Such was the character of the ground over which Willcox was obliged to pass, but we must now get a more extended view of the field over which the entire Ninth Corps is to move and the Confederate dispositions to hold it.

If the reader consults a map he will see that the portion of the field of battle south of Sharpsburg and west of the Antietam is included by the Boonsboro and Harper's Ferry roads, running at nearly right angles to each other, and the southeast quarter of the village lies in the angle. Cemetery Hill lies east of the village and descends sharply east and south (on the south, to a broad ravine or hollow, through which runs a spring branch from the village to the Antietam, which it reaches about 375 yards above the bridge). The road to the bridge runs over the southwest slope of the hill, then crosses the spring branch and follows it on the west side until it reaches the Antietam, which it follows and overlooks to the bridge. From the hollow south of Cemetery Hill, the ground again rises to a ridge running southwest, gradually widening to a plateau along which runs, to the south, the road from Sharpsburg to Harper's Ferry. From the hollow through which runs the branch and the road to the bridge are ravines running southwest, gradually narrowing and terminating before reaching the Harper's Ferry Road. These ravines are deep near the hollow, with rounded beds, and capable of concealing an entire army corps. The plateau along which runs the road to Harper's Ferry is forty to seventy feet higher than the ridge upon and behind which the Ninth Corps deployed, completely commands it, and is favorable to the movement of artillery. From this road to the Antietam, where the bridge crosses, it is 1,360 yards, and it is 940 yards from the road to where the batteries of Durell and Clark took position. The intervening space was open, with plowed ground, grass, and cornfields.

The defense of this part of the field was entrusted to Jones's Division of six brigades (Toombs's, Drayton's, Garnett's, Jenkins's, G. T. Anderson's, and Kemper's), the Washington Artillery (four batteries: Squires's, Miller's, Richardson's, and Eshleman's), Major Bushrod W. Frobel's Battalion of Hood's Division (three batteries: Garden's and Bachman's of South Carolina and Reilly's of North Carolina), Eubank's Battery of S. D. Lee's Battalion, and J. S. Brown's Battery (the Wise Artillery) of Jones's Division—in all nine batteries aggregating forty guns.

The position selected for Jones's Division and the artillery was Cemetery Hill and the ridge running southwest to the Harper's Ferry Road, the right of the division and of the entire army (Kemper's Brigade) being about 175 yards from the Harper's Ferry Road. There were some changes of position made earlier in the day, but at three o'clock, when the Ninth Corps was about to advance, Jones had on Cemetery Hill four guns of Moody's Battery, four guns of Squires's, six guns of Garden's, and the brigades of Garnett and Jenkins. Moody's guns and two of Squires's, with Garnett's Brigade, were

---

[34] The order speaks of the "upper Stone bridge," but the editor agrees with Carman's interpretation that this refers to the Middle Bridge (i.e., the bridge upstream from Burnside's position), which would be uncovered by a movement of the Ninth Corps westward after crossing the Rohrbach Bridge. For the full text of the order, see p. 331.

engaged with the Union advance from the Middle Bridge, while two of Squires's guns and all of Garden's were firing at the troops that had crossed the Rohrbach Bridge. In advance, on the southeast slope of the hill, were the 17th South Carolina and the Holcombe Legion of Evans's Brigade, with a detachment under Captain Twiggs of G. T. Anderson's Brigade. Across the Rohrbach Bridge Road and the spring branch, on the crest of the ridge running southwest and a short distance to the right of the southwest corner of the Avey orchard, were Brown's four guns and two of Reilly's, and about one hundred yards in rear of a stone and rail fence that ran on the crest of the ridge were the brigades of Drayton and Kemper in a deep ravine, and now on the point of advancing to the fence above them. The number of men at this time with these two brigades was about 560. The 15th South Carolina (Colonel William D. DeSaussure) of Drayton's Brigade was deployed as skirmishers, covering the ravine and the road to the bridge. In front of this position, about 750 yards to the southeast, near the middle of a forty-acre cornfield, were the 15th Georgia (Colonel William T. Millican) and 17th Georgia (Captain John A. McGregor) of Toombs's Brigade and five companies of the 11th Georgia (Major Francis H. Little) of G. T. Anderson's Brigade—all under the command of Colonel Benning. What was left of the 500 men who had defended the bridge joined Benning a few minutes later. About 450 yards in rear of Benning, deployed along a rail fence bounding a small cornfield on the east and about 230 yards from the Harper's Ferry Road, was the 7th Virginia (113 men under Captain Philip S. Ashby). Three hundred forty yards further to the right, behind a stone fence on the Harper's Ferry Road, was the 24th Virginia (150 men under Colonel William R. Terry). About 375 yards in front of the 24th Virginia was Eshleman's Battery of four guns. Richardson's Battery, which had been driven back at 1:00 p.m. and retreated through Sharpsburg when Toombs abandoned the bridge, had one gun disabled, but his section of howitzers was put in position on the west of the Harper's Ferry Road a short distance south of Sharpsburg, where a little later Richardson, having procured ammunition and repaired his disabled gun, joined his howitzer section and reported to Toombs. To the right and rear of the line was Robertson's Brigade (Munford having his headquarters at the Blackford house, where at this hour he greeted A. P. Hill, whose advance was coming upon the field). D. R. Jones had for the defense of his line the extreme right of the army: 2,785 infantry, 430 artillerymen with twenty-eight guns, and the cavalry with Munford—but Garnett's Brigade of 260 men and six guns had their hands full with the Union troops moving from the Middle Bridge upon the eastern slope of Cemetery Hill. During the engagement about to open, and almost at its opening, A. P. Hill came upon the field with 3,300 infantry and four batteries of artillery. Batteries, sections of batteries, and single guns—which had been in action earlier in the day on the left and in the center and had been disabled or expended ammunition—were hastened to the threatened point and thrown into position under the supervision of General Lee.

About mid-day Lee had sent this message to Pendleton, commanding the reserve artillery at Shepherdstown Ford: "If you have fifteen or twenty guns, suitable for our purpose, which you can spare, the general desires you to send them, with a sufficiency of ammunition. You must not take them from the fords if essential to their safety. Send up the stragglers. Take any cavalry about there and send up at the point of the sword. We want ammunition, guns, and provisions."[35] Pendleton could not collect the stragglers, he sent up but little ammunition, and it was not until the engagement had closed that one battery arrived at Sharpsburg. Not a battery, not an infantry soldier (save a straggler) did Lee take from his left or center to strengthen his right. He depended alone upon D. R. Jones and A. P. Hill (to whom he gave general directions) and upon such disabled batteries and single guns as could be gathered. To the movement and position of these he gave personal attention.

We know return to the deployment of Willcox's division and the general advance on Sharpsburg. Willcox's head of column had crossed the bridge at two o'clock and, upon arriving where the road leaves the creek and goes to Sharpsburg, he deployed his command. Christ's brigade filed across the hollow on the right under artillery fire and formed under a high bluff, on a narrow strip of low-level ground bordering the Antietam. Captain Devol's company of the 36th Ohio, which had been skirmishing in the advance on the right of the road, fell back and rejoined its regiment. After the formation of the corps line, but before the general advance was ordered, Christ's brigade scaled the steep bluff and drew up on the crest of the high ground, the 79th New York (Lieutenant Colonel David Morrison) deployed in double skirmish line, the 28th Massachusetts, 50th Pennsylvania, and 17th Michigan in line of battle in the order named from left to right.[36] Here it was subjected to a severe fire from Garden's and Squires's guns in front and suffered from a wicked enfilading fire from Brown's and Reilly's guns on the left, and the men, lying down, sought such shelter as the ground afforded (which, on the left, was very slight). Welsh formed on the heights to the left of the road, deploying the 100th Pennsylvania as skirmishers and forming the other three regiments in line: the 45th Pennsylvania on the right, 46th New York in center, and 8th Michigan on the left. In going forward into position, the left of the line passed over the 35th Massachusetts of Sturgis's division, and when halted, waiting for the order to advance, the left regiment was about one hundred feet on the immediate right of the 9th New York—the right

---

[35] Robert H. Chilton to William N. Pendleton, September 17, 1862, reprinted in *OR*, vol. 19, pt. 2, 610.

[36] Carman originally placed the 50th Pennsylvania on the far left. A proofreading mark (presumably made by him) on the manuscript page re-orders the regiments in the manner shown herein.

of Rodman's division—and about sixty feet in its rear. These movements were made under fire from the moment that Christ began to cross the hollow or a man appeared at the crest of the high ground on either side of the road.

The disposition of the corps line being completed about 3:00 p.m., in accordance with instructions received from McClellan, Cox was now directed by Burnside, who had crossed the bridge to assist Cox and hasten matters, to move forward with the whole command (except Sturgis's division, which was held in reserve) in the order in which they were formed and attack Sharpsburg and the heights on the left. Meanwhile, the Confederates kept up an incessant fire of artillery. Having the exact range of the valley and the ravines, their shells came in very fast, causing much annoyance and numerous casualties, notwithstanding the fact that the men were kept lying on the ground near the crests of the hills while the changes in the line and the partially new formation (after the arrival of Willcox's division) were being made.

In the formation as made, Willcox's division was on the right, Christ's brigade north and Welsh's brigade south of the road leading to Sharpsburg, with Crook's brigade in support of Willcox. Rodman's division was on the left, with Ewing's brigade as a support or reserve. Sturgis's division was to hold the crest of the hill above the bridge. It was determined that Willcox, supported by Crook, should move directly upon Sharpsburg, and that Rodman, supported by Ewing, should follow the movement of Willcox, first dislodging the enemy in their immediate front and then inclining to the right, so as to bring the left wing *en echelon* on the left of Willcox.

The order to advance was given by Cox at 3:15 p.m. and was responded to in the most cheerful and gallant manner, officers and men moving with the greatest enthusiasm and, on the right and in the center, carrying everything before them. The movement was made as nearly simultaneously as such movements are generally made, and we follow it from right to left, first accompanying Willcox in his successful advance to the edge of town and the expulsion of the Confederates from Cemetery Hill, and then returning to the advance of Fairchild's brigade of Rodman's division.

We left Christ's brigade on the high ground east of the road, with the 79th New York deployed in double line of skirmishers. When the order was given to advance, this regiment went forward and in its movement came up on the left of Poland's 2d and 10th U.S. Infantry (consolidated), and with their assistance it drove back McMaster's small command (the 17th South Carolina, the Holcombe Legion, and Twiggs's detachment) to the small apple orchard on the southern slope of Cemetery Hill and to the stone house and mill on the road to Sharpsburg. When within three hundred yards of the Confederate guns on Cemetery Hill, they found that the brigade had failed to follow and instead had halted. Poland's orders would not permit the farther advance of the 2d and 10th, upon which the 79th New York was halted and, lying down, continued its fire upon Moody's two guns and their infantry support. (The brigade had halted because of the very severe enfilading fire of the artillery on the left, in addition to the artillery fire on Cemetery Hill and that of Garnett's and Jenkins's infantry.) Welsh had not yet come up on the left, and for a few minutes until he did so Christ was exposed to a fire of round shot, shell, and canister, by which he suffered severely.

Welsh had a greater distance to move, and over much more difficult ground. His brigade, preceded by the 100th Pennsylvania as skirmishers and supported by Crook's Ohio brigade, went forward—the 45th Pennsylvania on the right, 46th New York in the center, and 8th Michigan on the left. The 45th Pennsylvania and the 46th New York swept over the hill in their front, down into a ravine, and then up the hill to the Otto buildings and apple orchard, the 45th Pennsylvania passing on either side of the barn. On the left the 8th Michigan, in starting, became involved with the 9th New York (a few files going with it), but, swinging to the right with its brigade, the entire line, after a short, sharp encounter (assisted by Crook), drove part of the 15th South Carolina of Drayton's Brigade (deployed as skirmishers) from a stone fence beyond the ravine and 130 yards from the Otto barn and then descended into the ravine. Here the troops were somewhat crowded, and the 45th Pennsylvania moved by the right flank out of the ravine to the Rohrbach Bridge Road. The rest of the brigade ascended out of the ravine, crossed the stone fence from which the 15th South Carolina skirmishers had been driven, and the entire brigade became engaged with these, Jenkins's Brigade (which had taken position in the orchard on the slope of Cemetery Hill), and with McMaster's command (which, driven back by Welsh and Poland, had rallied in the orchard and occupied the stone house and stone mill on the road).

Meanwhile, a section of Cook's Massachusetts battery under Lieutenant John N. Coffin was brought forward. The battery had crossed the Antietam with Willcox. Four guns were halted in the road near the bridge and two (under Coffin) went forward up the road "200 yards in advance of the column."[37] They went from the road to the left up the Otto lane and, taking position near the orchard near the barn, opened with shell upon the artillery on Cemetery Hill and upon Jenkins's Brigade and McMaster in the orchard. As we have said in the preceding chapter, Squires's two rifled guns, after shelling Willcox's advance from the bridge, had been withdrawn because they were out of ammunition. Jenkins's Brigade, which was supporting them, then advanced "some 400 yards to an apple orchard, under a heavy fire of artillery and small-arms."[38]

---

[37] John N. Coffin to Asa M. Cook, September 21, 1862, reprinted in *OR*, vol. 19, pt. 1, 435.

[38] Joseph Walker to Robert Johnston, October 24, 1862, reprinted in *OR*, vol. 19, pt. 1, 907.

Colonel Walker threw out the 1st South Carolina Volunteers and the 5th and 6th South Carolina and engaged Christ on the left, while the Palmetto Sharpshooters and the 2d Rifles were sent to the front and to the right to meet Welsh. "From this position," says Walker, "we continued to pour a destructive fire into the ranks of the enemy, at short range."[39]

Garden's (South Carolina) Battery of 12-pounders, which had been placed east of the road, just north of the stone house and in full view of the long-range guns beyond the Antietam, came under an accurate and destructive fire that they could not return, but instead opened upon Willcox's infantry as it crossed the bridge, during its advance up the road, over the hills, and while ascending the elevation on which the battery was posted. Garden's ammunition had now run out. Several men had been wounded (Lieutenant Samuel M. Pringle mortally), many horses were killed, one was dismounted (the carriage being entirely destroyed), another rendered useless by the bursting of a shell, and the remaining guns were run down the hill by hand to a ravine in rear. The disabled guns were then hauled off, the horses attached, and the entire battery entered the road—one gun without wheels, dragging on the ground—and went through Sharpsburg, barely escaping the men of Welsh's brigade (who had now reached the Avey orchard, almost in its rear), some of whom were running forward to the street down which it retired.

Meanwhile, Welsh had pressed forward. The 45th Pennsylvania obliqued across the road and, with the assistance of Christ (who had now advanced to the Sherrick lane) on his right and rear and the forward momentum of the remainder of the brigade on the left, forced Jenkins's Brigade back. The 45th, supported by a part of the 100th Pennsylvania, after a sharp and severe fire from the stone mill and house (by which it lost several men) carried them and took a number of prisoners, among them Captain Twiggs, who had been wounded. At the same time, Fairchild had driven back Kemper and Drayton, and as Jenkins's Brigade was over the hill and out of sight, Welsh moved his entire brigade forward and to the left into the Avey orchard, where he joined a part of Fairchild and prepared to engage the South Carolinians (who were now seen on his right and enfilading him) and to advance into the town. Skirmishers were thrown forward to the first street and some of these went beyond, one of whom was killed in the street running north from the Avey house.

Jenkins's Brigade fell back over the hill about two hundred yards to the edge of the town and changed front to the right, parallel and close to the Rohrbach Bridge Road, his right looking down the first street of the town and the entire brigade overlooking the low ground beyond which was the Avey orchard. Walker gives reasons for falling back to this position: "Perceiving that the enemy had advanced three heavy columns some 400 yards in rear of the brigade and to the right across a ravine leading up from the creek, and was steadily driving back the brigades of Generals Kemper and Drayton, I moved this brigade into line parallel with the turnpike [the Rohrbach Bridge Road—EAC] and ravine and near to the latter, and opened a destructive enfilade fire upon the enemy."[40] This position the brigade maintained. Its losses for the day were 26 killed and 184 wounded. Among the killed were two captains of the Palmetto Sharpshooters; five officers were seriously wounded, two of whom were commanding regiments.

Jenkins's Brigade having been driven out of range, Coffin now directed the fire of his two guns on the right section of Moody's Battery. At the same time, Christ, who had been severely engaged with the South Carolinians and also suffering from the fire of Moody's section and its supporting infantry, charged it with the 17th Michigan (this being the regiment immediately in front), supported by the 50th Pennsylvania and the 28th Massachusetts. But when within one hundred yards of the guns, which were then retiring and covered by a hill that prevented the advance from shooting either the horses or their riders, the artillery escaped. The charging party was ordered back—an order very reluctantly obeyed by the 17th Michigan, who saw that Cemetery Hill had been abandoned, but Christ "did not deem it prudent to advance after [the] artillery had retired, for the reason that the woods were lined with … sharpshooters."[41] He could only have exposed his command without gaining anything, so the charging party was withdrawn and remained with the brigade until the entire command was ordered to fall back.

As stated in the preceding chapter, the pressure of the regular infantry on the Boonsboro Road, and the advance of Willcox's division and Fairchild's brigade from the south and in rear, forced Garnett and S. D. Lee to abandon Cemetery Hill. Both claim that they could have held ground against the advance of the regular infantry, but that the movement to their right and rear endangered their escape.

S. D. Lee made an effort to check this Union movement and to support Jenkins's Brigade. Just before he withdrew Moody's Battery, he requested Captain Carter to take position with his battery about 120 yards in Moody's rear and, facing Cox's advance, open fire upon it. Carter had been engaged earlier in the afternoon at the sunken road and just before receiving Colonel Lee's request had, with three rifled guns of his own battery and the assistance of two rifled guns of Rhett's Battery under Lieutenant Elliott, opened fire upon an "imposing force of Yankees" which had "advanced in fine style" upon

[39] Ibid.

[40] Ibid.

[41] Benjamin C. Christ to Robert A. Hutchins, September 21, 1862, reprinted in *OR*, vol. 19, pt. 1, 439.

the right of Jones's Division.[42] Carter moved to the position designated by Colonel Lee, on the hill about one hundred yards south of the Boonsboro Road and three hundred yards east of the Lutheran church and overlooking Jenkins's Brigade, but before he could get his guns in position there was such a heavy reverse artillery fire poured upon him from the long-range guns beyond the Antietam that he found the position untenable, and Colonel Lee advised him to withdraw. A little later, Colonel Walker, having sent for artillery to assist his brigade, Boyce's (South Carolina) Battery (then on Cemetery Ridge, north of the road) was ordered to report to him. Boyce crossed the road east of the church as ordered, but could find no one there to give him any information as to who gave him the order or what was required. Boyce says, "This was late in the afternoon, and the battle soon after ended."[43]

In its early advance, Willcox's division was closely supported by Crook's brigade, which moved on the left of the road. It assisted in driving skirmishers of the 15th South Carolina from the stone fence beyond the Otto farm, and when Welsh moved forward the 28th and 36th Ohio charged across the ravine under a heavy fire of artillery from the front and left, by which Lieutenant Colonel Melvin Clarke of the 36th was killed. Parts of the two regiments went beyond the stone fence but were soon recalled to it, and the 11th Ohio was halted in the Otto lane (south of the barn) to command the ravine leading to the left, where A. P. Hill's attack was now developing.

We have now accompanied Willcox and Crook to their extreme advance and have seen the artillery and Garnett's Brigade abandon Cemetery Hill and Jenkins's Brigade driven back to the edge of the town. We now return to Fairchild's brigade, which advanced on Willcox's left and of which we have had an occasional glimpse as its movements assisted Welsh and stopped the enfilading artillery fire that temporarily checked Christ.

As mentioned, Fairchild's brigade was composed of the 9th New York (Lieutenant Colonel Edgar A. Kimball), 89th New York (Major Edward Jardine of the 9th New York), and 103d New York (Major Benjamin Ringold). It was a well drilled, disciplined brigade, had seen much and varied service in North Carolina and elsewhere, and carried into the battle about 940 officers and men. In coming upon the field, it took position immediately in rear of the advanced high ridge upon which were the batteries of Clark and Durell, its right about three hundred yards south of the Otto house and about one hundred feet from the left of Willcox's division, its left opposite the northeast corner of the forty-acre cornfield. The 9th New York was on the right, its left in rear of and very close to Clark's battery. Both received a merciless fire of shot and shell that killed and wounded a number of men. Lieutenant Matthew J. Graham of the 9th New York says that Clark's battery

did not appear to be able to do much in the way of firing, as it seemed to me that every time they would get fairly at work the rebels would concentrate such a fire on them as to silence them; and the men would be obliged to lie down in such shelter as they could get until the weight of the enemy's fire was directed to another part of the line. Their "park" was on [a] lower level, and almost in line with, and in rear of, the guns, and it caught a good deal of the fire that missed the battery. The practice of the rebel artillerymen was something wonderful in its accuracy; they dropped shot and shell right into our line repeatedly. They kept the air fairly filled with missiles of almost every variety … The shrapnel or canister was very much in evidence … I watched solid shot—round shot—strike in front of the guns with what sounded like an innocent thud, and, bounding over the battery and park, fly through the tree tops, cutting some of them off so suddenly that it seemed to me they lingered for an instant undecided which way to fall. These round shot did not appear to be in a hurry. They came along slowly and deliberately, apparently, and there appeared no harm in them until they hit something.[44]

Clark's battery and the 9th New York were not the only recipients of this artillery fire. It was received on the left by Durell's battery and the other regiments of the brigade (the 103d New York being in the center of the line, between Clark and Durell, though a little retired under the crest of the ridge, and the 89th New York in rear of Durell's battery, which

---

[42] Daniel H. Hill to Chilton, 1862 [no day or month given], reprinted in *OR*, vol. 19, pt. 1, 1025. Carter reports, "The next movement of the enemy was to advance a heavy column on the extreme right, bearing down on what I supposed to have been the right wing of A. P. Hill's division. Our troops gave way entirely before the column. With three pieces of my battery, aided by two of Lieutenant Elliott's, this column was shattered and driven back without the assistance (so far as I know) of any infantry whatever." Thomas H. Carter to Henry A. Whiting, October 14, 1862, as contained in Daniel H. Hill to Chilton, 1025. [Hill's transcription, which Carman cites, differs slightly from Carter's original text; the original is reprinted in *OR*, vol. 19, pt. 1, 1031.] Hill, who witnessed Carter's practice, says, "The firing was beautiful," the distance about 1,200 yards, and "is the only instance I have ever known of infantry being broken by artillery fire at long range." Daniel H. Hill to Chilton, 1025. This "imposing column" was undoubtedly Fairchild's brigade as it crowned the heights (the only part of the field south of the town that could be seen by Carter) and drove Kemper from them, but it was not broken by this fire. It simply disappeared down a ravine in pursuit of Kemper and Drayton.—EAC

[43] Robert Boyce to Nathan G. Evans, October 20, 1862, reprinted in *OR*, vol. 19, pt. 1, 944.

[44] Matthew J. Graham, *The Ninth Regiment New York Volunteers (Hawkins' Zouaves): Being a History of the Regiment and Veteran Association from 1860 to 1900* (New York: E. P. Coby & Co., 1900), 292–93.

was on the ridge a few yards to the right of the forty-acre cornfield). The fire poured upon this line came from six guns of J. S. Brown's and Reilly's Batteries, on the heights between it and Sharpsburg, and from Richardson's Battery, beyond the Harper's Ferry Road (which earlier in the day occupied the position now held by Clark's battery).

All this time, while the firing was increasing in severity and its range becoming more accurate, the field officers were walking up and down the rear of the line, waiting impatiently for the order to advance. At length Rodman came up and, after surveying the Confederate position for a moment, sent forward a company of each regiment as skirmishers. These had scarcely gone forward and engaged the skirmishers of the 7th Virginia behind a stone fence when Willcox was seen to move on the right, and Rodman ordered Fairchild to advance. The regimental commanders received and repeated the order, the men sprang to their feet, and, under the heavy artillery fire, went on to and down the ridge—the 9th New York being the battalion of direction, the objective point Brown's and Reilly's six guns and the bold elevation upon which they were in position, the distance being about eight hundred yards from Clark's battery. The brigade descended the slope and went over the fences of the Otto lane, the 89th New York on the left passing to the right of the cornfield while the 9th, on the right, became slightly involved with the 8th Michigan of Welsh's brigade (which had advanced at nearly the same time), but this was promptly rectified, the Michigan men swinging to the right. The entire brigade went down into a plowed ravine under fire of artillery and the skirmishers of the 7th Virginia. After advancing about two hundred yards, Fairchild ordered a charge. With a wild hurrah, the men started on a double-quick, ascended out of the ravine, and went over the stone and rail fences that extended along the west edge of the forty-acre cornfield down to the Rohrbach Bridge Road at the Otto farm, captured the skirmishers of the 7th Virginia at the fence, and drove that regiment to the left and back to the Harper's Ferry Road, receiving its fire but not returning it. As they climbed the fence, shells fell fast along the whole line from the batteries in front and from McIntosh's Battery, which had come upon the field and taken position at the Blackford house about 1,500 yards to the left. One shell killed eight men of the 9th New York, and round shot carried away men's heads and crashed through their bodies, reminding one of the officers at the moment of Marshal Lannes's description of the battle of Austerlitz: "I could hear the bones crash in my division like glass in a hailstorm."[45] A few yards beyond the fence and in a depression, the brigade was halted to rest and dress the line, although dressing was not necessary, for the moment the line halted every man was in his place—but it had been much shortened, and its dead and wounded marked the steps of its advance. Fully one-fourth of the brigade had fallen. No enemy, save the 7th Virginia, was yet to be seen, and another elevation was before it. With but a moment to draw breath, it again went forward under the fire of the merciless guns (now using both shell and canister, making great gaps in the line) and descended into a slight vale. Here the brigade halted a minute or two to gather strength for the final struggle with a foe whom they had not yet seen, but who were known to be at the crest of the hill in support to the six guns that were exploding shrapnel into the ranks.

The hill is a broad spur of the plateau along which runs the Harper's Ferry Road and terminates at the spring branch that runs through the town through a ravine to the Antietam. From the spring branch, there was a stone fence running southwest over this hill or spur, bounding the Avey orchard on the east for a distance of three hundred yards to its highest point, which is over eighty feet higher than the spring branch (a stout post-and-rail fence then continued in the same southwest direction). This elevation is some seventy feet higher than the depression where Fairchild's men had now halted to draw breath. Kemper's and Drayton's Brigades had been lying in a ravine beyond this spur and one hundred yards from the fence, well sheltered from artillery fire. J. S. Brown's Battery was still engaging Clark's battery (the fire of which was covering Fairchild's advance) when, knowing that Fairchild was approaching, Kemper and Drayton ordered their men up the hill to the fences.

Kemper was on the right. The left of his brigade, the 11th Virginia (Major Adam Clement), rested at the point where the stone and rail fences united. On its right was the 1st Virginia (Major William H. Palmer[46]), and on the right of the 1st was the 17th Virginia (Colonel Montgomery D. Corse). The three regiments had an aggregate of about 210 officers and men. Drayton's Brigade formed on Kemper's left, with the right of the 51st Georgia at the point where the stone and rail fences united. The left of the brigade, the 15th South Carolina, under Colonel DeSaussure, extended down the hill in skirmishing order and was employed principally in opposing the advance of Welsh. On the immediate left of the 51st Georgia was the 3d South Carolina Battalion, numbering 17 men. (The brigade numbered about 380 men; the aggregate of the two brigades about 590 officers and men.) They came into position under a severe fire from Clark's guns and those of Benjamin beyond the Antietam, by which Captain John T. Burke and Lieutenant Francis B. Littleton of the 17th Virginia were killed. Fairchild's

[45] Ibid., 294.
[46] Carman gives Palmer's rank as "Colonel." The actual colonel of the regiment was Lewis B. Williams, who had been wounded and captured at Williamsburg in May 1862 and did not rejoin the regiment until after the close of the Maryland campaign. Around the time of Williams's return, Major Palmer was transferred from the 1st Virginia to become assistant adjutant general on the staff of A. P. Hill. Palmer ended his military service as a lieutenant colonel, which rank he did not achieve until February 19, 1864. See Lee A. Wallace Jr., *1st Virginia Infantry*, 3d edition (Lynchburg, Va.: H. E. Howard, 1985), 36, 110; Robert E. L. Krick, *Staff Officers in Gray: A Biographical Register of the Staff Officers of the Army of Northern Virginia* (Chapel Hill: University of North Carolina Press, 2003), 236.

brigade was now reported advancing up the hill. Captain Brown of the Wise Artillery was wounded, and his four guns, moving to the right across the field, gained the Harper's Ferry Road and went through Sharpsburg. Reilly's two guns went through a gateway of the fence and through the town, and the Union artillery soon ceased firing. Kemper's men rested their rifles on the lower rails of the fence; Drayton's did so on top of the stone wall. The hill shut out the view, but the commands of the Union officers, the clanking of equipment, and the steady tramp of the approaching line was easily distinguishable.

Fairchild made but a brief halt, and, in beautiful line, as well dressed as on parade, the brigade began the ascent of the hill at a quick step, but the line had been much shortened and did not now number over seven hundred men. Nearly one-third had fallen. Not a shot had been fired, but the muskets were loaded and the bayonets fixed. (The orders were that not a shot was to be fired until the command was given to do so, then to deliver a volley and charge with the bayonet.) Brown's and Reilly's guns were now getting out of the way, but the line was enfiladed by Richardson's Battery on the left, and Clark's friendly guns were firing over the New Yorkers at the enemy on the hilltop. Clark's fire soon ceased, and as the brigade appeared at the crest of the hill and the clear sky showed behind the heads and shoulders of the men, there was a crash of musketry from the commands of Kemper and Drayton that sent down scores of men in every regiment. It was particularly destructive to the 9th New York, coming up in front the stone fence—behind which and about fifty yards distant was the right of Drayton's Brigade. The entire color guard of that regiment went down and the colors lay on the ground. "One or two of the men staggered to their feet and reached for the flags, but were shot down at once. Then there was what seemed a spontaneous rush for them by a dozen or more men from several companies, who were shot down in succession as each one raised his flag … The flags were up and down, up and down, several times in a minute." Lieutenant Sebastian Myers was hit just as he picked up one of them.[47] The men had now lain down and opened fire. At last, Captain Adolph Libaire seized one of the flags and, swinging it around his head, shouted to his company to get up and follow him. Captain Lawrence Leahy seized the other color. The entire regiment rose to its feet and, officers in front, charged to the stone fence, across which there was a short struggle in which bayonets were used. Drayton's men were routed—some of them captured and the rest pursued through the Avey orchard, where Welsh now came up on the right. (A number of Drayton's men escaped by the ravine to the Harper's Ferry Road.) Some of the 9th New York, with others of Welsh's brigade, pushed clear into Sharpsburg. (One was killed in the street and a number were captured.) There were still about one hundred men left in the regiment; these Kimball rallied on the colors at the fence and with difficulty recalled those who had gone down into the ravine. The 103d New York (in the center), in its advance and from the first volley, lost over one-half of its men and did not reach the fence in the final charge, but halted within fifty feet of it when it was seen that the enemy had retreated. On the left, the 89th New York had a severe engagement with the right of Kemper's line, which it overlapped. Colonel Corse, commanding the 17th Virginia (nine officers and forty-six men) on the extreme right, says he "engaged the enemy at a distance of 50 or 60 yards" and that his regiment "came directly opposite the colors of the regiment to which it was opposed, consequently being overlapped by them, as far as I can judge, at least 100 yards."[48] A historian of the 17th says:

> The first thing we saw appear was the gilt eagle that surmounted the pole, then the top of the flag, next the flutter of the Stars and Stripes itself slowly mounting—up it rose; then their hats came in sight; still rising the faces emerged; next a range of curious eyes appeared, then such a hurrah as only the Yankee troops could give broke the stillness, and they surged towards us.
>
> "Keep cool men—don't fire yet," shouted Colonel Corse; and such was their perfect discipline that not a gun replied. But when the bayonets flashed above the hill-top the forty-six muskets exploded at once, and sent a leaden shower full in the breasts of the attacking force, not over sixty yards distant. It staggered them—it was a murderous fire—and many fell; some of them struck for the rear, but the majority sent a stunning volley at us, and but for that fence there would have been hardly a man left alive. The rails, the posts, were shattered by the balls; but still it was a deadly one—fully one half of the Seventeenth lay in their tracks; the balance that is left load and fire again and again, and for about ten minutes the unequal struggle is kept up … the combatants not over thirty yards apart … Our Colonel falls wounded; every officer except five [two—EAC] of the Seventeenth is shot down; of the forty-six muskets thirty-five [twenty-four—EAC] are dead, dying or struck down.[49]

The 89th New York rushed to the fence. Ten of the Virginians were captured; the rest escaped. Corse was taken prisoner but, soon after, was rescued by Toombs's Brigade. All of Kemper's Brigade had now been routed or run over and captured.

As a regiment, the 89th, with its colors, remained at the fence, but many men went over and down into the hollow and up to a rock ledge on the other side. Some pushed forward up the hill to the edge of the town and not much over three hundred

[47] Graham, 296.

[48] Report of Montgomery D. Corse, no date, reprinted in *OR*, vol. 19, pt. 1, 905.

[49] Alexander Hunter, "A High Private's Sketch of Sharpsburg: Conclusion," *Southern Historical Society Papers* 11 (1883): 18–19.

yards from the town square. The entire regiment would have gone forward, but some Confederates were rallying with the apparent intention of turning its left. Major Jardine's men charged with the bayonet and drove the enemy to the Harper's Ferry Road, then fell back under orders and rejoined the brigade, which was ordered to withdraw to the ravine near the Otto farm, about four hundred yards in the rear. The men went back with curses on their lips for those who had mismanaged affairs on this part of the field and, Colonel Kimball reports, "with tears in their eyes at the necessity which compelled them to leave the field they had so dearly won."[50]

From the time of its advance to the rout of the Confederates from the fences, the brigade occupied about thirty minutes and lost nearly half its men. Including the few men lost early in the morning and before the charge, 87 were killed, 321 were wounded, and 47 were missing—an aggregate of 455, or 48.4 percent of the 940 carried into action. The 9th New York had 373 in action and, as officially reported, 45 killed, 176 wounded,[51] and 14 missing—an aggregate of 235, or 63 percent. (The historian of the regiment says it had 54 killed and mortally wounded, 158 wounded, and 28 missing—an aggregate of 240, or 64.34 percent.[52]) The 103d New York lost 117, or 58.5 percent, and the 89th New York 103, or 28 percent. The Confederate loss was not so heavy; the fences were a great protection. The total loss of Drayton and Kemper was about 102 killed and wounded and 20 missing. The greatest loss was that of the 17th Virginia: 8 killed, 23 wounded, and 10 missing[53]—an aggregate of 41, or over 74.5 percent (in killed and wounded alone, 56.33 percent).

D. R. Jones, the Confederate division commander, reports that "the enemy advanced in enormous masses to the assault of the heights. Sweeping up to the crest, they were mowed down by Brown's battery, the heroic commander of which had been wounded but a few moments before. They overcame the tough resistance offered by the feeble forces opposed to them, and gained the heights … Kemper and Drayton were driven back through the town. The Fifteenth South Carolina, Colonel DeSaussure, fell back very slowly and in order, forming the nucleus on which the brigade rallied."[54]

All was now confusion in Sharpsburg. Artillery was dashing to the rear through the rough and narrow streets. Stragglers from the left in squads, men of Garland's and Colquitt's Brigades (who had been driven from Cemetery Ridge by the 4th U.S. Infantry), and portions of Kemper's, Drayton's, and Garnett's commands (who were retreating from Cemetery Hill) filled the streets, broken in organization, as Jones, Kemper, Drayton, Garnett, and other officers endeavored to rally them. Earlier in the afternoon, General Lee had been near the Reel farm directing affairs on the left and at the sunken road. When the advance of the Ninth Corps became serious, he rode to the high ground near his headquarters, where he met A. P. Hill and gave him his instructions, and ordered every gun that had wheels and horses to the south of the town. Now that his right was broken, he directed that every man that could be gathered should be sent out on the Harper's Ferry Road to unite with Toombs (who had been ordered to join Kemper's right), and he rode into town and gave his personal assistance in stopping stragglers and rallying the broken commands. Drayton's men were rallied on the colors of the 15th South Carolina in the road just out of town, a few men of Kemper's Brigade were rallied on their colors (which were conspicuously displayed in the road), and the men of Toombs's Brigade were seen coming down the road as the 8th Connecticut made its appearance on the high ground from which Kemper had been driven, but a little nearer the road and farther south.

When the order was given to Rodman's division to advance, Harland's brigade was on the left of Fairchild's. The 8th Connecticut, on the right, was a little to the left and rear of Fairchild, overlooking the northeast corner of the forty-acre cornfield; the 16th Connecticut was in the cornfield, into which it had entered at the northeast corner; and the 4th Rhode Island was approaching to move on the left of the 16th Connecticut. When making dispositions for the advance, Major Thomas W. Lion of the staff, who had carried instructions to the left of the line, rode up to Harland and reported that he and officers of Ewing's brigade had seen Confederate infantry (Gregg's Brigade) forming on the left, which fact Harland reported to Rodman and then ordered his brigade forward. The 8th Connecticut wheeled slightly to the right and passed to the right of the cornfield, its right in rear of Fairchild's left (which preceded it by a few minutes), but the 16th Connecticut apparently did not hear the order to advance. Harland sent an aide to hasten them and, when moving down the hill, suggested to Rodman that the 8th Connecticut, when at the foot of the hill and under cover from the artillery fire pouring on it,

[50] Edgar A. Kimball to Harrison S. Fairchild, date unknown, reprinted in Graham, 319.

[51] In Carman's original manuscript, the number of wounded in the 9th New York is given as 174. This is obviously a transcription error by Carman, as killed, wounded, and missing totals of 45, 174, and 14, respectively, would yield a sum of 233, not 235 (as Carman writes). A table of casualties compiled by the editors of the OR shows 176 wounded in this regiment, and the rest of the figures agree with Carman's results. "Return of Casualties in the Union forces at the battle of Antietam, Md.," OR, vol. 19, pt. 1, 197. The regimental losses for the other two regiments in the brigade, given later in the paragraph, also match those in the OR tabulation precisely—making it certain that this was Carman's source and that he intended to write "176 wounded."

[52] Graham, 327.

[53] Carman's source for the breakdown of killed and wounded in the 17th Virginia is unclear, but the sum of his figures, and the number of missing that he cites, matches the information provided in the after-action report of the regiment. Report of Corse, 905.

[54] Jones to Gilbert Moxley Sorrel, December 8, 1862, reprinted in OR, vol. 19, pt. 1, 886–87.

should halt and wait for the 16th Connecticut and 4th Rhode Island to come up. Rodman, however, ordered the continued advance of the regiment, saying he would hurry up the latter two regiments, so Harland kept on with the 8th Connecticut and began firing at some skirmishers who appeared on his left. The two regiments not yet coming up, Harland turned to see if they were advancing and saw instead some Confederate infantry (the 7th and 37th North Carolina) rapidly advancing on his left flank, upon which (Rodman having ridden ahead to Fairchild after he ordered the 8th Connecticut to continue its advance) he put spurs to his horse and rode back to hasten the advance of the 16th Connecticut. The 8th Connecticut, under a scattering flank fire from the North Carolina skirmishers, moved on and soon came under the fire of McIntosh's Battery. Although somewhat protected (as it was moving under cover of the hill upon which the battery had just gone into position), it suffered some casualties.

McIntosh's Battery was the advance of A. P. Hill's Division. After crossing the Potomac, it preceded the infantry and came by the road from Shepherdstown Ford. When approaching the Blackford house, near the Harper's Ferry Road, McIntosh left one howitzer and all of his caissons and, with a Napoleon gun and two rifles, took position on the right of and near the house. After firing two or three shots at Fairchild's brigade, moving to the left, the battery was ordered by A. P. Hill to report to Kemper on the left of a cornfield and support the right of Jones's Division. The guns were limbered up and went at a gallop directly across the fields and came into the Harper's Ferry Road at the northeast corner of what is known in the Confederate reports as the "narrow cornfield," and then moved up the road a few yards in the direction of Sharpsburg to a gate in the plank fence, where it waited in the road for J. S. Brown's Battery, leaving the field, to come out. Some of the men suggested that it was not a proper place to put a battery, as another had already been driven out, but McIntosh replied that he had been directed to go in there and fight and ordered the battery forward. It went through the gate as soon as Brown's guns had cleared it and, obliquing to the right, took position one hundred feet on the left of the narrow cornfield and one hundred yards from the road, the guns not quite to the crest of the ridge. When taking this position there was seen, about three hundred yards to the left and front, Kemper's small brigade, huddled together behind a fence and firing upon Fairchild's brigade, which was rapidly advancing. About the time the guns began firing, less than three minutes after they were in position, Kemper's men were run over by Fairchild. In coming into position, McIntosh's Battery came under the fire of the Union artillery posted on the high ground from which Rodman had charged, to which it responded with vigor. McIntosh himself worked one of his guns, for the battery was short-handed. While so engaged, he saw the colors of the 8th Connecticut and, occasionally, the heads of the men as they approached under the hill, moving diagonally across his front from right to left, and opened fire upon them. McIntosh says the advancing column "halted and lay down for some minutes when they began their advance again" and gradually came into view.[55] As they approached to within sixty yards of his guns, McIntosh ordered the men to save themselves and abandon the guns, all but two of the battery's horses having been shot.

It was not the entire 8th Connecticut McIntosh saw approaching him. It had largely passed to his left, but the left company, under the command of Captain Upham, had been detached while advancing to take the battery (from which the gunners had apparently been driven, as at the time the battery was silent). But as the company was crossing the field, ascending the hill, and nearing the guns—apparently at the very moment McIntosh was abandoning them—Upham's attention was called to troops approaching his left and rear through the narrow cornfield, upon which, without reaching the guns, he had his men fall back. Upham says, "They came up company or division front and deployed on reaching the fence at the edge of the field, each division opening fire as soon as in line. We fell back to our regiment, which changed front and engaged them."[56] This Confederate force was the 7th and 37th North Carolina, whose skirmishers had been annoying the 8th Connecticut in its advance.

When Upham rejoined his regiment, it had gained the high ground to the left of where Fairchild's men had fought. Fairchild had swung off to the right and downhill in pursuit of Kemper and Drayton and had then been ordered to fall back, but his dead and wounded marked the ground over which he had fought. Save these dead and wounded, there was not a Union soldier in sight. The regiment was alone, over half a mile in advance of the position from which it had charged, and with no support. It was 120 yards from the Harper's Ferry Road and nearly parallel to it. On its right front, in the road, were small remnants of Kemper's and Drayton's Brigades that had retreated to a deep cut of the road and, looking to the left, Toombs's Brigade could be seen coming at a double-quick down the road.

When Toombs fell back from the bridge to the stone fences, he was joined by the 15th and 17th Georgia of his brigade and five companies of the 11th Georgia (under Major Little) of G. T. Anderson's. The 2d and 20th Georgia were then ordered

---

[55] The source of this statement is not McIntosh but a member of his battery. "The advancing column of Federals halted and lay down for some moments when they advanced again." James L. Napier to Ezra A. Carman, January 13, 1897, typescript copy, "Report of Maj. Gen. A. P. Hill" folder, box 3, Letters and Reports Concerning the Battle of Antietam, 1895–1900 ("Antietam Studies"), Record Group 94, National Archives.

[56] As of this writing, Carman's source for this quotation has not been identified.

to the rear for ammunition, and the two fresh regiments moved into the forty-acre cornfield. Little's battalion was posted by Toombs behind a stone fence on the right of the two regiments, and Little reports that skirmishers were sent out, brisk firing began, and his skirmishers were driven in, the enemy's advancing to within 125 yards of him, a full line of battle drawn up in rear. He quietly awaited their advance, but the efforts of the Union officers to move them forward were unavailing.[57] The skirmishers encountered by Little were those of the 48th Pennsylvania and the movements seen by him of a full line of battle were those of Nagle's brigade taking position after crossing the bridge.

As A. P. Hill's Division was announced as approaching the field, Toombs was directed that, as soon as Gregg's Brigade arrived and relieved him, he was to move his command to the right of his own division in the direction of Sharpsburg. Before Gregg arrived, Toombs received an order to move immediately to meet the enemy, who had already begun his attack on Jones's Division. He quickly put his command in motion and fell back to the Harper's Ferry Road, where he was met by another order to hasten his march, as the enemy had broken the line of Jones's Division and were nearly up to the road with not a Confederate soldier in front. At this point Toombs was joined by the 20th Georgia, and the entire command went double-quick along the road and passed the 7th Virginia, which had fallen back before the advance of Fairchild. In a short time, the head of the line passed the narrow cornfield and saw McIntosh's then-abandoned guns and the 8th Connecticut "standing composedly in line of battle" about 120 yards from the road, apparently waiting for support on the very ground Toombs had been ordered to occupy. Colonel Benning reports that "neither in their front nor far to their right (our left) was a man of ours to be seen, but three abandoned pieces of ours were conspicuous objects about midway between the road and the enemy's line." Little's battalion was in advance, followed by the 17th, 15th, and a large part of the 20th Georgia in rear. All, however, made but a short line, and Benning, when he thought the rear had not quite cleared the cornfield (for he did not desire the enemy to see how short his line was), halted the head of his line opposite the 8th Connecticut and ordered it to begin firing. Benning writes, "The rest of the line as it came up joined in the fire. The fire soon became general. It was hot and rapid. The enemy returned it with vigor, and showed a determination to hold their position stubbornly."[58]

Meanwhile, Rodman had fallen. He had gone forward with the 8th Connecticut, rode ahead to where Fairchild was engaged, saw the 8th Connecticut coming up, and started either to meet it or to go back for the rest of the brigade when he was shot through the breast and fell from his horse. No one saw him fall, but as two of Upham's men (Privates Seth D. Bingham and Timothy E. Hawley) were falling back from the advance on McIntosh's guns to rejoin their regiment, they heard his cry for help, went to him, and took him to a sheltered position under the hill, from which he was removed across the Antietam to the Rohrbach house, where he died some days later.

While Toombs was engaging the 8th Connecticut, the 16th Connecticut and the 4th Rhode Island were heavily engaged a half-mile in rear of the 8th in the forty-acre cornfield, to which, in order to preserve the sequence of events, we now return. This forty-acre cornfield, covered at the time with dense corn, has running through it (from the northwest to the southeast) a deep ravine. From its northeast corner, the ground descends directly to this ravine, but in the southwest part of it there is a plateau, from which the ground descends quite abruptly thirty to forty feet. The west edge of the field was bounded the greater part of its extent by a stone wall, broken in places by rail fences. Beyond this, between it and the high ground on which runs the Harper's Ferry Road, there is quite a valley, lower by nearly fifty feet than the road. In the cornfield, 130 yards from the stone fence on the west and parallel to it, is a stone ledge, upon which was an old board fence, partially thrown down and neglected, and its line was marked by trees. Seen through the dense corn and smoke of combat, it had the appearance of a stone fence, and is so called in the Confederate reports.

The 16th Connecticut, 760 men under Colonel Francis Beach, had entered the cornfield at its northeast corner and moved to the bottom of the ravine, where skirmishers under Captain Frederick M. Barber were thrown out up the hill to the edge of the plateau in the southwest part of the field. It did not advance with the 8th Connecticut, and soon an order was received from Rodman to swing to the left to face Gregg's Brigade of A. P. Hill's Division, then approaching.

Hill had remained at Harper's Ferry until the morning of the seventeenth, when, at half past six, he received orders from Lee to march to Sharpsburg. Leaving Thomas's Brigade to complete the removal of the captured property, he put his division in motion at half past seven, marched up the Virginia side of the river, crossed at Shepherdstown Ford, and—after an exhausting march of seventeen miles—the head of his column arrived on the field at 2:30 p.m. Hill reported in person to Lee, by whom he was warmly greeted and who exclaimed, "General Hill, I was never before so glad to see you. You are badly needed. Put your force in on the right as fast as they come up."[59] Hill next rode to D. R. Jones, who gave him such

[57] Francis H. Little to George T. Anderson, October 7, 1862, reprinted in *OR*, vol. 19, pt. 1, 912.

[58] Benning to DuBose, 164.

[59] As of this writing, Carman's source for this quotation has not been identified, but Hill stated officially that he reported to Lee in person at 2:30 p.m. and that Lee then ordered him to take position on the right. Ambrose P. Hill to Charles J. Faulkner, February 25, 1863, reprinted in *OR*, vol. 19, pt. 1, 981.

information of the character of the ground as was necessary, and then to the Blackford house, where he met the advance of his division coming upon the field by the road leading from the ford. (McIntosh's Battery had already taken position near the Blackford house, where it fired a few shots and was then sent forward to strengthen Jones's right.) The infantry now came up and were rapidly thrown into position: the brigades of Pender and Brockenbrough on the extreme right, looking to the road crossing the Antietam near its mouth, those of Branch, Gregg, and Archer extending to the left to make connection with Jones's Division. Hill says, "Braxton's battery … was placed upon a commanding point on Gregg's right; Crenshaw and Pegram on a hill to my left, which gave them a wide field of fire. My troops were not in a moment too soon. The enemy had already advanced in three lines, had broken through Jones' division, captured McIntosh's battery, and were in the full tide of success."[60]

A. P. Hill's Division did not come upon the field in a body. As soon as one brigade crossed the river and climbed up its slippery bank, it was hurried forward without waiting to allow the men to wring the water from their clothing and socks, or for the brigade immediately following, by which it came that the brigades arrived at the front at varying intervals—not of many minutes, however, for they were small and promptly handled. It is impossible to say in what order the brigades arrived, but we first follow Gregg. The appearance of McIntosh's Battery had attracted the attention of the Union artillery and guns were trained in that direction, so when Gregg's Brigade appeared, passing the Blackford house and nearing the Harper's Ferry Road, it came under artillery fire from the guns beyond the Antietam as well as those west of it, upon which it inclined to the right, went downhill under cover, then, changing direction to the left, crossed the Harper's Ferry Road and formed line about 250 yards beyond it. The 14th South Carolina (Lieutenant Colonel William D. Simpson), the leading regiment, was thrown out to the right behind a stone fence nearly at right angles to the brigade line to protect that flank and was so far beyond the Union left that it was not engaged. Gregg formed three regiments in line: the 1st South Carolina (Provisional Army; Colonel Daniel H. Hamilton) on the right, the 12th South Carolina (Colonel Dixon Barnes) in the center, and the 13th South Carolina (Colonel Oliver E. Edwards) on the left. The 1st South Carolina Rifles (Lieutenant Colonel James M. Perrin) was held in reserve. The four regiments numbered about 750 men.

Pegram's Battery closely supported Gregg and went into position a few yards east of the Harper's Ferry Road and 355 yards a little north of west from the southwest corner of the forty-acre cornfield that Gregg was about to enter. It was on a very commanding position, giving a wide range of fire—which was immediately opened, principally upon the Union infantry on the ridge beyond the cornfield. Braxton's Battery was put in position in rear of Gregg's right, 130 yards east of the Harper's Ferry Road, 450 yards a little south of west of the cornfield, and 270 yards on Pegram's right. It followed Pegram in opening fire upon the Union infantry. (We anticipate in saying that later, about 4:30 p.m., one gun of Pegram's Battery and two rifled guns of Braxton's were moved to the extreme right, on a hill about 280 yards due north of the Snavely barn, giving them an enfilading fire and, as reported by Hill's chief of artillery, were worked, "with beautiful precision and great effect, upon the infantry of the enemy until nightfall closed the engagement."[61]

Gregg's skirmishers, who had been thrown to the front, were now withdrawn, and Gregg ordered his three regiments to advance into the cornfield that crowned a bold hill in his front drive back the enemy, whom the skirmishers had reported advancing through the corn. They advanced, went quickly over an intervening ravine and up the hill, and struck the southwest corner of the cornfield. The 13th South Carolina, under a misapprehension of orders, halted at the stone fence bordering the cornfield on the west, while the 1st and 12th South Carolina went over it, both at the south and west sides of the field, moved northeast about 120 yards (driving back the skirmishers of the 16th Connecticut), and, reaching the highest part of the field, halted and opened fire upon the troops in the ravine at the foot of the hill and also upon those on the high, open ground, who were seen advancing. The 12th South Carolina halted for a few minutes only on the left of the 1st South Carolina when, the Union skirmishers having fallen back to the old fence that ran through the corn, it charged down the hill upon the 16th Connecticut, which was then changing front beyond the low rock ledge and fence. The Connecticut skirmishers were driven from the fence, but the main body, though somewhat disordered, returned the fire with such spirit that the 12th South Carolina was checked and, coming under this fire in front and on both flanks, was compelled (almost immediately after reaching the fence) to fall back to prevent being flanked on the right, and the Union line again advanced to the fence. Colonel Barnes charged once more with his regiment but was again repulsed by the combined fire of the 16th Connecticut and 4th Rhode Island. The movement of the Rhode Island regiment threatening his right, he fell back in some disorder, carrying with him part of the left of the 1st South Carolina, but quickly rallied in the southwest corner of the corn.

We left Colonel Harland riding back to this cornfield to hasten the advance of the 16th Connecticut. His horse was shot from under him before he had gone far, which delayed his arrival. He found that the regiment, by an order of Rodman, had changed front to the left and was heavily engaged, and perceiving that the right of the 12th South Carolina was exposed he

---

[60] Ambrose P. Hill to Faulkner, 981.

[61] Reuben Lindsay Walker to Richard C. Morgan, March 1, 1863, reprinted in *OR*, vol. 19, pt. 1, 984–85.

ordered Colonel Beach to change the front of the 16th Connecticut to strike it. "This change," Harland writes, "was effected, though with some difficulty, owing to the fact that the regiment had been in service but three weeks, and the impossibility of seeing but a small portion of the line at once."[62] It was this change of front of the 16th Connecticut, its attack, and the appearance of the 4th Rhode Island that caused the 12th South Carolina to fall back in some disorder, but almost immediately after this both the 16th Connecticut and 4th Rhode Island were flanked in turn and driven from the field.

The 247 men of the 4th Rhode Island (Colonel William H. P. Steere) entered the cornfield by the right flank, under fire of the Confederate artillery in full view. Descending into the ravine, they came into line on the left of the 16th Connecticut, which was in some confusion, engaging the second advance of the 12th South Carolina and crowding to the left, which compelled the 4th Rhode Island to move to the left, rendering it almost impossible to dress the line, which had become somewhat disordered in advancing through the corn. But their appearance assisted in forcing back the 12th South Carolina and in compelling the 1st South Carolina to move farther to the right and throw back its three right companies, fearing a movement on that flank. In this position the 1st South Carolina opened fire upon the 4th Rhode Island. At this moment the Rhode Island men mistook the colors of the 1st for a Union flag and ceased firing. Lieutenants George E. Curtis and George H. Watts volunteered to go forward through the dense corn and ascertain what was in front. Placing themselves one on each side of the regimental colors, carried by Corporal Thomas B. Tanner, they went up the hill to within twenty feet of the enemy when they were fired upon and Tanner was killed. Curtis seized the colors and ran back, followed by Watts, and the order was given to open fire. Steere sent Lieutenant Colonel Joseph B. Curtis to the 16th Connecticut to see if it would support him in a charge up the hill, but, the corn being very thick and high, Curtis could find no one to whom to apply. He returned to Steere to report that they must depend upon themselves, and Steere sent to the rear for support. Before any could get back, the crisis had come.[63]

The 1st South Carolina, which was engaging the 4th Rhode Island, was running out of ammunition and about to fall back when the 1st South Carolina Rifles, which had been held in reserve, was now sent forward by Gregg to sweep the field on the right. Ascending to the crest of the hill in its front and coming up on the right of the 1st South Carolina, the Rifles saw the 4th Rhode Island, which had turned the right of the 1st South Carolina and was delivering a destructive fire on its flank. The Rifles advanced a short distance beyond the 1st South Carolina, threw forward its right so as to completely turn the left flank of the 4th Rhode Island, and delivered a destructive fire before its presence seemed to be realized. The Rhode Island men attempted to return the fire, but so great was the disorder into which they and the 16th Connecticut had been thrown that, after a short, sharp fire, both were thrown into hopeless confusion, broke, and fell back. The Rifles captured eleven prisoners, among them Captain Caleb T. Brown of the 4th Rhode Island, who had been wounded.

Harland, referring to the action of the 16th Connecticut, says, "The right of the enemy's lines, which was concealed in the edge of the corn-field, opened fire. Our men returned the fire and advanced, but were forced to fall back. Colonel Beach rallied them and returned to the attack, but they were again driven back, this time out of the cornfield, beyond the fence. Here they were again rallied, but as it was impossible to see the enemy, and the men were under fire for the first time, they could not be held."[64] Colonel Curtis reports that the 4th Rhode Island was outflanked and enfiladed:

> The regiment on our right now broke, a portion of them crowding on our line. Colonel Steere ordered the regiment to move out of the gully by the right flank, and I left him to carry the order to the left, of which wing I had charge, the colonel taking the right … The regiment commenced the movement in an orderly manner, but, under the difficulty of keeping closed up in a corn-field, the misconception of the order on the left, and the tremendous fire of the enemy, … the regiment broke. Colonel Steere, as I afterward learned, was severely wounded in the left thigh, immediately after I left him to repeat on the left the order to leave the corn-field.[65]

An attempt was made to rally on Muhlenberg's battery, which, some distance from the cornfield, now opened with shell and canister upon the South Carolinians in the southwest part of the cornfield, but before many could be collected the battery retired, the efforts becoming unavailing. A few men rallied on the left of the 51st Pennsylvania and continued fighting until their ammunition was exhausted, when they recrossed the Antietam and rejoined their regiment and brigade. The loss of the 16th Connecticut was 42 killed and 140 wounded; that of the 4th Rhode Island 21 killed and 77 wounded.

---

[62] Harland to Gardner, 454.

[63] See Joseph B. Curtis to William Sprague, September 22, 1862, reprinted in *OR*, vol. 19, pt. 1, 456–57. Carman originally wrote that Steere sent "to the rear for support," then crossed out "to" and wrote, "sent him [Curtis] to the rear for support. But before he could get back, the crisis had come." Why Carman made this change is unclear, as Curtis's own report (which, based on similarities in word usage, is the basis for this section of the manuscript) suggests that someone else was tasked with carrying the second request for assistance back to the rear and that Curtis remained with the regiment.

[64] Harland to Gardner, 454.

[65] Curtis to Sprague, 457.

As the 4th Rhode Island and the 16th Connecticut were giving way, Ewing's brigade (the 12th, 23d, and 30th Ohio) was charging toward the stone wall in front. This brigade was in support of the left of Rodman's division, and when that division was ordered forward the Ohioans were lying down behind the ridge from which Rodman advanced. Upon the report that the Confederates were massing on the left, the brigade moved in that direction about a quarter of a mile and then directly back to the point from which it had started, and without a halt came into line to the left and charged. The 23d Ohio (Major James M. Comly) and the 30th Ohio (Lieutenant Colonel Theodore Jones) swept over the crest between Clark's and Durell's batteries, then over the fence, down into the valley, and up to the stone fences that ran along the west side of the cornfield and extended far to the north. The 23d Ohio, on the right, made its advance over open ground, 375 yards under fire of artillery and musketry, and came to the fence on the right of the ravine, where it cuts the corner of the forty-acre cornfield, the left of the regiment very near it and the right extending up the hillside to higher ground. The 30th Ohio started over open ground, gained ground to the left, and entered the corn as it went downhill. It passed some men of the 16th Connecticut, who were still in the hollow, passed over their dead and wounded, and, under a severe fire that had been poured upon it from the moment it moved to the charge (and which continued and increased as the regiment advanced), reached the stone fence at the west edge of the corn. It was on a hillside sloping to the north, its left on the highest part of the hill and 240 yards from the southwest corner of the corn, its right at the base of the hill, close to the ravine, beyond which was the 23d Ohio. Its entire front was covered by the stone fence.

Both regiments reached the fence about the same moment and saw in the open field before them the enemy, upon whom they opened fire. Leaving them here for a moment, we return to the 8th Connecticut and the troops now encountered by these two Ohio regiments.

In Benning's desire to front the right of the 8th Connecticut, he had carried his line so far that his rear had passed one hundred yards beyond the narrow cornfield, but he was in an excellent, well sheltered position in the road, which at this point ran in a cut much lower than the bank in front. On the left were parts of Kemper's and Drayton's Brigades. The entire line engaged the 8th Connecticut with some spirit, inflicting upon it much loss. In addition to this fire in their front, the Connecticut men were suffering from a fire upon their left flank and rear, which caused the regiment to change the front of its left wing. This flank and rear fire came from the 7th and 37th North Carolina of Branch's Brigade.

When Branch's Brigade came upon the field by the road passing the Blackford house, a battery opened upon it, forcing the command to turn sharply to the right, downhill, before resuming its first course. The leading regiment, the 7th North Carolina, fired two or three volleys at a regiment beyond the cornfield, crossed the Harper's Ferry Road, and marched east until the 8th Connecticut was seen marching in line northwest, upon which skirmishers were sent out. The 7th North Carolina (Colonel Edward G. Haywood) and the 37th North Carolina (Captain William G. Morris) were detached and sent on the double-quick northward, the 7th on the right. The running skirmishers soon opened fire upon the moving 8th Connecticut, and the two regiments followed by the flank. The 37th, on the left, went through the lower part of the narrow cornfield, the 7th over open ground on its right, and both came into line behind the fence on the northern edge of the cornfield and the fence continuing east from it. The fence was approached as Upham was advancing to seize McIntosh's guns, and it was this force that caused him, as we have seen, to fall back on his regiments. The 37th was a little to the right and front of McIntosh's guns and opened fire upon the left and rear of the 8th Connecticut, not quite three hundred yards distant, which caused it to make a partial change of front. This fire and that of the enemy in the road was more than the Connecticut men could stand. Richardson's Battery across the road now opened upon them and, after an engagement of less than thirty minutes, losing nearly one-half its men (34 killed and 139 wounded) and with no hope of support, the regiment was ordered to retreat. Toombs and Benning say it retreated in confusion, but officers of the 37th North Carolina testify that it "held ground quite stubbornly, fought splendidly, and went off very deliberately, firing back at the 37th and waving its flag."[66] Officers of the 8th Connecticut admit that some of the men retreated without halting to fire but contend that a greater part of them stopped several times to fire at the enemy in the corn. While the 37th North Carolina was engaged, a volley was poured into its right flank and also upon the flank of the 7th North Carolina from the fence of the forty-acre cornfield, by which some men of the latter were killed or wounded and some of the former wounded. The 7th immediately fell back, soon followed by the 37th. We shall see them later.

When the 8th Connecticut was seen leaving the field, Toombs ordered pursuit, and his men, with those of Kemper and Drayton (a mere handful), climbing the bank and the board fence. They advanced to where the regiment had stood and Toombs ordered a charge over the hill, but Benning, who was a better soldier, thought otherwise. He says, "We could not see what was below the crest of the hill, but I knew a very large force of the enemy must be somewhere below it, for I had from our late position seen three or four successive long lines of them march out from the bridge. I therefore suggested to General

---

[66] As of this writing, Carman's source for this quotation has not been identified.

Toombs the propriety of halting the line, as its numbers were so small and it had no supports behind it, just before it reached the crest of the hill, and sending to that crest only the men armed with long-range guns. This suggestion he adopted."[67]

As Toombs was about to leave the road, Archer's Brigade came up on his right. This brigade—composed of the 1st Tennessee (Provisional Army; Colonel Peter Turney), 7th Tennessee (Major Samuel G. Shepard), 14th Tennessee (Colonel William McComb), and 19th Georgia (Major James H. Neal)—reached the field with less than four hundred men. Turning to the left, it marched right in front on the road leading to Sharpsburg, formed line of battle, and faced by the rear rank in the road, with the narrow cornfield, of 150 yards width, extending along its immediate front. (Toombs's Brigade was in the road a few yards to the left and about to go forward.) Skirmishers were immediately thrown into the cornfield, and the brigade, scaling a board fence, went forward, under a scattering fire, through the tall corn 225 yards to its eastern edge overlooking open, plowed ground, but when the two left regiments (the 14th and 7th Tennessee) reached this advanced position, the others were found to have fallen back to the road, from which, meanwhile, Toombs had advanced. The 37th North Carolina, in falling back form the fence under the enfilading fire received by it, had halted in the corn, and Archer's two regiments, hearing the commands of officers of that regiment to fall back, mistook these orders as intended for themselves (the corn was so dense that nothing could be seen) and fell back to the road. Archer, who was ill and very weak, had ridden in an ambulance (assuming command of his brigade only because he was on the soil of his native state) and had not yet left the road. As quickly as possible, he re-formed line in the road, and again the two regiments advanced through the corn to where the 14th and 7th Tennessee had halted, when the entire line, Toombs following on the left, charged over a plowed field of three hundred yards to the stone fence of the cornfield, behind which were the 23d and 30th Ohio. Archer's men were met by a withering fire that caused him much loss. Colonel McComb was wounded and nearly one-third of his brigade stricken down, but with the assistance of Gregg on his right, Archer drove back the 23d and 30th Ohio and halted at the fence.

It was the assistance given by Gregg that caused the retreat of the two Ohio regiments. Without it, they could have held their position against the frontal attack of Archer and Toombs. When the two regiments reached the fence, three of Gregg's regiments were in the southwest part of the cornfield and one was behind the same fence, but on the other side and a few yards to the left of the 30th Ohio. None of them were visible, but one (the 1st South Carolina Rifles) was firing, and as this was so far to the left and supposed to be taken care of by the 12th Ohio (which it was thought was moving on that flank), no attention was paid to it. As the fence was reached, fire was opened upon Archer's men. Major George H. Hildt of the 30th Ohio reports, "Our men were at this time utterly exhausted from the effect of the double-quick step across the plowed field, and their fire was necessarily slow and desultory for several minutes. As soon, however, as our first volley had been given, and our colors erected at the wall, a withering fire was directed upon us from our left flank, and from which we suffered most severely."[68] Its left company was on the crown of the elevated ground, from which there was a rapid descent to the ravine on the right, beyond which was the 23d Ohio on open ground.

Major Comly of the 23d Ohio, from the elevated position where he was standing, saw what he took to be a Union line advancing on the left and toward the rear of the 30th Ohio, and at the same time he saw that the 30th was still in position and that it was opening fire on this supporting Union line. He gave his own men orders not to fire upon it, although it was rapidly approaching and within easy range. But when a volley came down the flank and rear of the 30th and enfiladed the 23d, all doubt vanished. Ewing immediately ordered Comly to change front perpendicularly to the rear, which was quickly done, and Colonel Jones was ordered to fall back with the 30th and form on the left of the 23d. Jones, who was on the right of the 30th, gave the order to move by the right flank and join the 23d, which order was not heard except by the four right companies, which moved in that direction, the remaining companies still holding position at the wall. Lieutenant Reese R. Furbay of Ewing's staff was sent with orders to these companies to fall back but was killed before reaching them, and they remained a few minutes longer, until the enemy's fire upon their flank could not be borne, two color bearers had been killed, and Archer's Brigade was at the fence. It was now discovered that the right of the regiment had gone, and the six companies fell back to the ravine, where they found a few men of the 16th Connecticut.

Archer's men gained the stone fence just as the Ohioans abandoned it. In fact, Archer's left reached the fence abandoned by the right wing of the 30th Ohio before its left fell back, and a few men charged over it and captured Colonel Jones. Archer soon came up and ordered his entire brigade, now reduced to less than three hundred men, to charge into the cornfield, an order to which the men promptly responded, but when less than one hundred yards in the corn they were met by such a severe fire from the six companies of the 30th Ohio and the few Connecticut men who had rallied with them in the ravine that they were driven back with loss and lay down behind the stone fence.

There is a strong probability that some of the loss sustained by Archer's Brigade was inflicted by the 12th South Carolina, which, not perceiving through the dense corn that the Ohio men had fallen back, was still firing in that direction. When the

[67] Benning to DuBose, 164.
[68] George H. Hildt to Hugh B. Ewing, September 20, 1862, reprinted in *OR*, vol. 19, pt. 1, 470.

firing came from the ravine, the 12th charged for the third time and was met by a volley from the Ohio men, who immediately retreated through the corn and up the hill from which they had advanced, the 12th following to the north fence of the corn and firing upon the retreating troops. In this last charge, Colonel Barnes of the 12th was mortally wounded, and the command devolved on Major William H. McCorkle, who remained with his men at the fence until near sunset, when the regiment fell back to the top of the hill and then over the stone fence on the right of the 13th South Carolina, which had maintained its position during the entire engagement.

When the six companies of the 30th Ohio fell back out of the cornfield, the other four companies and the 23d Ohio were not in sight. Their withdrawal had been hastened by the advance of Toombs's Brigade charging on the left of Archer's, and they fell back down the ravine leading to the Rohrbach Bridge Road at the Otto spring. The regiments, when united, bivouacked a little north and west of the bridge and about one hundred yards from it.

We have said that the 23d Ohio was hastened from its position by the advance of Toombs's Brigade. This is true only as to a part of it. At Benning's suggestion, Toombs halted his brigade just before reaching the crest of the hill from which the 8th Connecticut had been driven. Those men who were armed with long-range guns were advanced to the crest and opened fire upon the retreating Connecticut men. Two guns of Richardson's Battery were ordered up and opened fire as well. Coffin's section of the 8th Battery, Massachusetts Light Artillery, which after the retreat of Garnett's Brigade and Moody's guns from Cemetery Hill had moved from the Otto orchard to a position south of it, turned its guns upon Archer's and Toombs's infantry seen in the narrow cornfield and on the open ground north of it. Not deeming this position a good one, Coffin moved farther to the left, "on a high eminence overlooking the enemy's infantry."[69] Here, his section came under the fire of Richardson's guns, about 650 yards distant.

Meanwhile, Garnett had joined Drayton in the road. Having reached the rear of the town and hearing that Toombs had reinforced the right and "restored the fortunes of the day in that quarter," he gathered as many men as he could get to follow him (not over a small company) and joined Drayton in the road just after Toombs advanced from it.[70] Archer was now moving forward. Drayton and Kemper occupied the fence from which Fairchild had driven them. Toombs's 15th and 20th Georgia charged forward to the fence and opened fire upon the retreating infantry (the 23d and 30th Ohio) and Coffin's section of artillery and, with the assistance of Richardson's guns, compelled Coffin to fall back through the ranks of the 35th Massachusetts, which was moving to the front, to the position from which the 9th New York had charged. Coffin says his guns worked "with terrible effect" and fell back when "ammunition was exhausted."[71]

Toombs "desired to pursue the enemy across the river" but had no artillery available, and he was about to content himself with having to occupy the position at the bridge from which he had been driven.[72] However, the Union line forming in his front prevented this, perceiving which Toombs, leaving a small reserve with Colonel Benning, ordered the rest of his command down to the stone fence, following himself, and opened a hot fight with the 35th Massachusetts, on the hill opposite about three hundred yards, during which Colonel Millican of the 15th Georgia was killed. Toombs's men reached the stone fence about the time Archer's Brigade (on his right) was being driven out of the cornfield, and they were soon followed by Branch's Brigade.

We have seen that when Branch's Brigade came upon the field, the 7th and 37th North Carolina were pushed forward, engaged the left and rear of the 8th Connecticut, and then fell back under an enfilading fire on their right (probably from the 23d Ohio) just before Archer charged. After these two regiments went forward, or about the time they were ordered forward, A. P. Hill came down the road from the direction of Sharpsburg. Seeing an unsupported battery west of the road, nearly two hundred yards beyond Toombs's right and nearly opposite the southwest corner of the cornfield, and apparently not knowing that the 7th and 37th were moving or about to move in that direction (for they were below the ridge, out of view), Hill ordered Colonel James H. Lane to take his 28th North Carolina (which was in rear of the brigade and had not crossed the Harper's Ferry Road) and hasten up the road in support of the battery, as Union skirmishers were reported moving on it through the corn. Lane quickly led his regiment up the road until he came to the corner of the cornfield, where he halted in the road and in front of the battery but did not become engaged. (The 7th and 37th were then contending with the 8th Connecticut, though, himself in a deep cut in the road and they at the foot of a hill beyond and screened by the corn, Lane did not see them. At least, he has no recollection of seeing them, but he did see the advance of the 23d and 30th Ohio and the movement of the 12th Ohio. Soon after, Archer passed him and charged through the narrow cornfield.) Though Lane did not see the two North Carolina regiments and has no recollection of seeing Archer's Brigade, Major William J. Montgomery of the 28th North Carolina saw Archer pass and make his charge, and from the high, open ground in front

[69] Coffin to Cook, 435.

[70] Richard B. Garnett to Asbury Coward, November 6, 1862, reprinted in *OR*, vol. 19, pt. 1, 897.

[71] Coffin to Cook, 435.

[72] Toombs to Jones, 892

of the right of the regiment saw the 7th and 37th North Carolina advance from the position to which they had fallen back, cross the trail of Archer's Brigade over the plowed field, and, swinging to the right, go forward. In swinging to the right, they came under artillery fire that threw the left of the 7th into some confusion, but they charged up to the fence on Archer's left. The 7th came in on the right of Toombs's men, at the northwest corner of the corn; the 37th went over the fence on the right of the 7th, into the corn by the right flank, and fired at some retreating troops. The 37th met a warm fire, and Captain Morris immediately fell back, as he saw the 33d North Carolina come up and pass his left flank.

The 18th North Carolina (Lieutenant Colonel Thomas J. Purdie) and the 33d North Carolina (Lieutenant Colonel Robert F. Hoke), which had immediately preceded the 28th, halted two hundred yards east of the Harper's Ferry Road as a reserve. Colonel Hoke, seeing the 7th and 37th going forward the second time, followed without orders. The 33d passed closely in rear of Archer at the fence, crossed the ravine, and came into line on the left of Toombs. The moment it passed the left of the 37th, that regiment came out of the corn, followed the 33d, and formed on its right. The 18th was halted by Branch in a hollow in Archer's rear, and Branch rode forward to the high ground and fence where lay the 12th and 13th South Carolina of Gregg's Brigade and had some conversation with Major McCorkle and Colonel Edwards. Raising his field glass to get a better view of the Union line on the ridge beyond, he was shot in the head and instantly killed.

Meanwhile, Colonel Lane had been ordered to rejoin the brigade. He came up in Archer's rear as Branch was being carried off the field and was notified that, as senior officer, he was in command of the brigade. It was after sunset, and he found the 7th, 37th, and 33d North Carolina posted behind the stone fence and the 18th North Carolina sheltered in the hollow. He ordered the 28th North Carolina to the left of the line, but the order was delivered to the 18th, which in obedience was posted to the left behind a rail fence, a portion of it being broken back to guard against a flank movement. The 28th was placed on the left of the 7th in an opening caused by the withdrawal of Toombs's men, who were ordered to the left and bivouacked on Cemetery Hill.

The remainder of A. P. Hill's Division had come upon the field while all this was occurring. Pender's Brigade followed Branch and was ordered by Hill to the extreme right, "looking to a road which crossed the Antietam near its mouth."[73] It was in an open field on Gregg's right and not actively engaged. During the engagement, it was moved from the right to the center, did not become engaged, and, after sunset, bivouacked on Branch's left. Brockenbrough's Brigade was the last of the infantry to arrive; it thrown to the right and the 40th Virginia sent to support the guns of Pegram and Braxton on the hill near the Snavely farm. It was not engaged and, after dark, was withdrawn and bivouacked south of the town near the stone mill. Crenshaw's was the last of Hill's batteries to reach the field and "took position on a hill in front of Captain McIntosh, from which, disregarding the enemy's artillery, he directed his fire entirely at their infantry."[74]

When McIntosh's guns were saved, the men returned to them (bringing up the one gun that had been left behind) and opened fire. Batteries other than those of A. P. Hill had arrived and were still arriving, and by General Lee's orders were thrown in front of Cox, along the high ground west of the Harper's Ferry Road and south of Sharpsburg. We have seen Eshleman's Battery opposing the advance of Rodman at Snavely's Ford, after which it received orders to hold the enemy in check until Hill arrived. Pender soon came to its support, and the battery "kept up a moderate shelling of the woods near the ford until night."[75] It was on the right of the entire line of batteries and south of the road leading past the Blackford house. Two guns of Miller's Battery had been withdrawn from the engagement at the sunken road because they had run out of ammunition. Miller replenished his ordnance and "was returning to his former position, when he was directed by General Lee to an elevated and commanding position on the right and rear of the town, where General A. P. Hill had but just begun his attack."[76] He was about 170 yards west of the Harper's Ferry Road and opposite the narrow cornfield. Captain Richardson, with his section of Napoleons and a 10-pounder Parrott gun of Squires's Battery under Lieutenant John M. Galbraith, went to the right near the guns under Miller, opened fire, and continued in action until nightfall. (At the same time, Richardson's section of howitzers, as we have seen, was assigned by Toombs to a position near his brigade, opened upon the men of the Ninth Corps, and continued the fire until they were out of range.) At the time Jones's Division was giving way, Lieutenant John A. Ramsay, with two rifled guns of Reilly's Battery, came on the field from the artillery park near Lee's headquarters and hurried into position on the right near Richardson and about 170 yards west of the narrow cornfield. He took position as Hill's men came up. Somewhat later, Captain Squires (who had quit Cemetery Hill after running out of ammunition for his section of rifled guns, refilled his limber chests, and reported to Toombs) was, with his two guns and a section each of the Maryland Light Artillery (Dement's Battery) and Reilly's Battery, sent to the right, but as the Union attack had been repulsed they were not brought into action. About the same time, a gun each of Captain Wilford E. Cutshaw's (Virginia) Battery and

---

[73] Ambrose P. Hill to Faulkner, 981.

[74] Reuben Lindsay Walker to Morgan, 985.

[75] James B. Walton to Sorrel, December 4, 1862, reprinted in OR, vol. 19, pt. 1, 851.

[76] Ibid., 850.

Chew's Battery of horse artillery dashed up. On the outskirts of the town and 450 yards west of the Harper's Ferry Road, Bachman's four guns were placed on a commanding hill. Six hundred yards in Bachman's rear and 450 yards southeast of Lee's headquarters two rifled guns of Read's Battery were placed in position by Lee's order to bear upon the enemy across "some fields over on the right of the road."[77] (Bachman and Read were not engaged, being held in reserve.) Some of these guns were in position when Cox advanced, others came up as Hill arrived, and some came later. Nearly all were engaged, and the judicious posting of this artillery aggregating (with Hill's batteries) forty-three guns made Lee's right very strong.

We return to the 12th Ohio. It had about two hundred men and was commanded by Colonel Carr B. White. By Ewing's orders it was to go forward with the 23d and 30th Ohio to the stone fence. Before moving, however, it was reported that the enemy were moving around the left, and the regiment was ordered to form line at right angles with the 30th, move down to the cornfield, and engage the enemy's flanking column then seen in the southwest part of the cornfield. It reached the northeast corner of the cornfield, but before it could close up on the left of the 30th it came under a heavy fire of shell and spherical case that threatened its destruction, and immediately Gregg's Brigade, about 375 yards distant in the southwest corner of the corn, also opened fire upon it. A Union battery in the rear now opened in reply to the Confederate battery (probably Pegram's), and the regiment was directly in the line of fire of the two batteries and on the highest point of ground between them, receiving shots from both. To add to its discomfiture, a regiment of raw troops that had taken position on the left of the battery apparently mistook it for the enemy, or endeavored to reach the enemy in the corn beyond, and opened fire. (Fortunately, the fire was wild and too high.) The 12th Ohio was ordered to lie down to escape the rain of shot and shell that was sweeping across its position, and Colonel White called for a volunteer to go back to the regiment and battery and explain the situation. Sergeant John M. Snook performed the service, and White undertook to move the regiment to the left, out of the immediate range of the two batteries and less exposed to the fire of Gregg's infantry. The order was misunderstood by the companies on the left and resulted in an oblique move to the southeast (toward the Antietam), which came near resulting in a break of the regiment. It was rallied at a fence, where it was as fully exposed both to the fire of artillery and musketry as in its first position, and after some effort on the part of its officers it advanced to the east edge of the cornfield, about the length of the regiment to the left of its original position. Here it remained, exchanging fire with the 1st South Carolina Rifles, until, being relieved by a regiment of Sturgis's division (which was now taking position on the left of the corps line), it fell back to the brow of the hill in front of the bridge and rejoined its brigade.

When disaster came to Harland's two regiments in the cornfield—the extreme left of the Ninth Corps—Cox was in the center of his line, near Clark's battery, watching the progress of affairs on the right. He saw Willcox's and Crook's successful advance, the brilliant charge of Fairchild's brigade, and the advance of the 8th Connecticut. He saw also the movement of the 7th and 37th North Carolina on the flank and rear of the 8th Connecticut, the advance of Toombs and Archer on the Harper's Ferry Road, the deployment of two regiments of Branch's Brigade in near support to Gregg, and the movement of Pender toward his left. He saw also the Confederate batteries hasten into position on the high ridge near the Harper's Ferry Road and open fire and concluded "that it would be impossible to continue the movement to the right, and sent instant orders to Willcox and Crook to retire the left of their line, and to Sturgis to come forward into the gap made in Rodman's. The troops on the right swung back in perfect order; Ewing's brigade hung on at its stone-wall with unflinching tenacity till Sturgis had formed on the curving hill in rear of them, and Rodman's had found refuge behind."[78]

In his official report, Cox says:

The mass of the enemy on the left still continued to increase; new batteries were constantly being opened upon us, and it was manifest the corps would, without re-enforcements, be unable to reach the village of Sharpsburg, since the movement could not be made to the right whilst the enemy exhibited such force in front of the extreme left, and the attack both to the right and left at once would necessarily separate the wings to such an extent as to imperil the whole movement unwarrantably.

The attack having already had the effect of a most powerful diversion in favor of the center and right of the army, which by this means had been able to make decided and successful advances, and no supports being at the time available for our exhausted corps, I ordered the troops withdrawn from the exposed ground in front to the cover of the curved hill above the bridge, which had been taken from the enemy earlier in the afternoon. This movement was effected shortly before dark, in perfect order and with admirable coolness and precision on the part of both officers and men.[79]

[77] John P. W. Read to Edward P. Alexander, October 20, 1862, reprinted in OR, vol. 19, pt. 1, 866.
[78] Cox, "The Battle of Antietam," 656.
[79] Cox to Richmond, 426.

Let us see how the movement was conducted. Sturgis's division was ordered forward to fill the gap in the line caused by the advance of Rodman. This division, after being relieved by Willcox, had been placed behind the ridge from which Rodman advanced (Ferrero's brigade on the right, Nagle's on the left). Just before and while advancing to the position vacated by Rodman, the 8th Connecticut was attacked and driven back by Toombs, Kemper, Drayton, and a part of Branch, and the 23d and 30th Ohio were forced to retreat from the stone fence by the advance of Toombs, Archer, and Branch on their front and Gregg on their left flank. Ferrero's brigade, nearest Cox, advanced to the position vacated by Fairchild. About this time, Durell's and Clark's batteries, having fired their last round of ammunition, retired, and Coffin's two guns retreated under the fire of Richardson's Battery and Toombs's infantry.

The 35th Massachusetts, on Ferrero's right, was ordered forward by Cox in person. It was lying down one hundred yards in rear of the ridge. It rose to its feet and moved a short distance when Coffin's section came dashing back at full speed, breaking the line for a moment, but the men closed up, obliqued a little to the left, then charged with a hurrah, on the double-quick, over the hill from which the 9th New York had charged, and rushed down the slope, passing some broken commands, to the rail fence of the Otto lane, where it halted in a very exposed position, laid its rifles on the fence rails, and opened fire. In front was a plowed field through which ran a deep ravine sloping up to a stone wall three hundred yards distant, behind which were the enemy; on the left front, 150 to 250 yards distant, was the forty-acre cornfield. Beyond the stone wall on rising ground and at a distance varying from six hundred to twelve hundred yards were Confederate batteries.

The first fire of the 35th Massachusetts was a rattling volley, then at will. The 21st Massachusetts, 51st New York, and 51st Pennsylvania advanced on the left of the 35th, and, having more experience in war, did not descend the west slope of the ridge but lay down just under its crest a few yards back from the lane. The entire brigade line came under heavy artillery fire and a rattling fire of musketry from the stone fence and cornfield in front and on the left. A portion of the 4th Rhode Island rallied on the left of the 51st Pennsylvania. An officer of the brigade says, "It was now nearly dark and the enemy jumped the fence with their colors and endeavored to advance but were driven back."[80] This refers to the 37th North Carolina or Archer's Brigade (probably both).

Of Nagle's brigade, on the left, the 2d Maryland and 6th New Hampshire were held in reserve near the bridge; the 48th Pennsylvania was in rear, as a second line to the 51st Pennsylvania; and the 9th New Hampshire, which had been in the rear, near Muhlenberg's battery, was now advanced nearly to the left of the 51st Pennsylvania, overlooking the cornfield and on the right of the 12th Ohio, which was still engaged. Here it lay down to avoid the heavy artillery fire poured upon it. The brigade was covered by Muhlenberg's battery a few yards in its rear (Muhlenberg being supported by the 11th Connecticut of Harland's brigade, the other regiments of the brigade returning to their bivouac beyond the Antietam.) Soon the ammunition of the 51st Pennsylvania gave out and the 48th, crawling forward, relieved it, and it fell back to the position from which the 48th had advanced and replenished ammunition. Very soon after this, about sunset, the 12th Ohio fell back and the 9th New Hampshire soon followed, both under a heavy artillery fire from the batteries in front and from the three guns of Pegram and Braxton near the Snavely farm. The 9th New Hampshire went back in some disorder, most of its men recrossing the Antietam by the ford below the bridge, the remainder being rallied about halfway between the cornfield and the bridge. It was now dark, and the 2d Maryland and 6th New Hampshire were sent forward as skirmishers on the left, overlooking the corn, and remained all night. On the right of the division line, the 35th Massachusetts, though exposed to a most terrific fire of artillery and musketry (during which it lost 3 officers and 45 men killed and 160 wounded) remained until near dark, when, under orders, it fell back under a shower of musketry, went down to the bridge, then up the road to the left and bivouacked. The 51st Pennsylvania, having replenished ammunition, again went forward and occupied that point of the ridge beyond which the 35th Massachusetts had fought, and the 51st New York was relieved by an Ohio regiment of Crook's brigade, now taking position to relieve Sturgis, who was massing his division on the left. The 21st Massachusetts, after seeing everything on its right fall back and the 51st New York on its left relieved, fell back to the high ground just above the bridge and joined its brigade. Ferrero says of his brigade, "Firing every round they had in their boxes, they quietly placed themselves on the ground in their position, and remained until other regiments had formed in front to relieve them, when by my orders they retired in good order from the field, and again marched to the banks of the creek."[81] In marching to the banks of the creek, Ferrero joined the other brigade of the division, which formed the extreme left, resting on the creek below the bridge. The troops relieving Ferrero and forming the center of the line were Crook's regiments, supported by Ewing's rallied command.

It was under the cover of Sturgis's advance to the ridge vacated by Rodman that Willcox and Crook were withdrawn. It was half-past four. Willcox was about out of ammunition (for the wagons had not been able to accompany the forward

---

[80] As of this writing, Carman's source for this quotation has not been identified.
[81] Edward Ferrero to Samuel D. Sturgis, September 19, 1862, reprinted in *OR*, vol. 19, pt. 1, 449.

movement) and his advance was halted "partly in the town and partly on the hills"[82] to allow his men to take some breath and to fetch up some cartridges when he received Cox's order to fall back, upon which he sent an order to Fairchild, on his left (as we have seen), to withdraw to the ravine near the Otto farm. Here Fairchild, with the 11th Ohio of Crook's brigade, faced to the left to meet the advance of Toombs and Archer, but these being held back by Sturgis (who had now formed on the ridge), Fairchild soon moved down the road to the bridge and halted in the roadway. Willcox then withdrew to the position from which he had made his final advance, every regiment marching back in perfect order. Crook's brigade, which had remained at the stone fence in advance of the Otto farm and was about to advance when Willcox was ordered to withdraw, now fell back and relieved Sturgis, who fell back to the left. The line, as then established, covered the Rohrbach Bridge: Sturgis's division in front (on the left), supported by Fairchild; the Kanawha Division (under Colonel Scammon) in the center, Crook's large brigade in front, supported by Ewing; and Willcox's division on the right. Muhlenberg's battery and the 11th Connecticut recrossed the Antietam and bivouacked with the other three regiments of Harland near the Rohrbach farm. The four guns of Cook's battery, which had been halted in the road when Coffin went forward with his section, countermarched about 4:00 p.m., went up the road to the left of the bridge, and opened fire near the cornfield, where they were subjected to a crossfire from the enemy's batteries and infantry. The fire from the corn was very severe. After firing several rounds, while Sturgis was taking his position on the left, the approach of darkness compelled a cessation of operations, but the guns were charged with canister and the men lay near them.

Cox expressed his satisfaction with the manner in which his divisions were handled: "The movements were accurate as those of a parade, and the systematic order with which they were executed made the spectacle in the heat of the battle a grand and imposing one."[83] No corps commander on the field displayed more tactical ability than Cox, both in the attack and the disposition quickly made when reverse—for which he was not responsible—came to his left. Cox reports that these dispositions were made "shortly before dark,"[84] and elsewhere he says, "The men of the Ninth Corps lay that night upon their arms, the line being one which rested with both flanks near the Antietam, and curved outward upon the rolling hilltops which covered the bridge and commanded the plateau between us and the enemy. With my staff I lay upon the ground behind the troops, holding our horses by the bridles as we rested, for our orderlies were so exhausted that we could not deny them the same chance for a little broken slumber."[85]

An instance of comradeship and thoughtful devotion to duty may here be noted. As the sun was setting, a nineteen-year-old[86] regimental commissary sergeant, who had remained with the trains in camp east of the Antietam, approached the Rohrbach Bridge with a loaded wagon. Loaded ammunition wagons were going forward as far as the bridge and empty ones were returning, empty ambulances were going and loaded ones were coming back, wounded men were finding their way to the rear, and shells were exploding. He was cautioned of the danger and advised not to proceed. A general officer, passing to the rear, ordered him to turn back, but when he had passed by, the young soldier crossed the bridge, went up the road to the left, turned to the right, and, halting at the bivouac of the 23d Ohio—under artillery fire—distributed to his comrades cooked rations and coffee. There was no finer exhibition of thoughtful duty than that given by this youthful soldier—William McKinley. It was recognized by promotion and was the beginning of a brilliant career.

The Confederates did not venture an attack upon Cox's position. Content with having repulsed him, they kept up a brisk artillery and musketry fire until dark, when it gradually ceased. The battle of Antietam was ended.

A. P. Hill's Division rested for the night along the stone fences running northerly from the large cornfield to the Rohrbach Bridge Road, Kemper and Drayton in its rear in the position occupied earlier in the day. Toombs was on Cemetery Hill on Hill's left. Jenkins's Brigade again advanced to the apple orchard and threw out skirmishers beyond the Sherrick lane, and Garnett's small command reoccupied Cemetery Hill. At dark Carter's Battery was sent by Lee to occupy the hill and guard the road leading from the Middle Bridge.

The loss in the Ninth Corps was 24 officers and 414 men killed, 98 officers and 1,698 men wounded, and 2 officers and 113 men missing—an aggregate of 2,349. Rodman's division suffered the most severely, and the heaviest percentage of loss was in Fairchild's brigade. Crook's brigade suffered least; it had 73 killed, wounded, and missing.

The loss in A. P. Hill's Division in its short, sharp, and successful encounter was 66 killed, 332 wounded, and 6 missing—an aggregate of 404. The loss in Jones's Division for the day alone, and including the loss in its engagement with the regular infantry on the Boonsboro Road, was about 75 killed, 450 wounded, and 40 missing—an aggregate of 565. The total

---

[82] Orlando B. Willcox to Gustavus M. Bascom, September 21, 1862, reprinted in *OR*, vol. 19, pt. 1, 431.

[83] Cox to Richmond, 427. In his original manuscript, Carman's text reads "… inspiring one."

[84] Ibid., 426.

[85] Cox, "The Battle of Antietam," 656.

[86] In his original manuscript, Carman lists McKinley's age incorrectly as eighteen. The future president was born on January 29, 1843.

loss in the two divisions was 969; the loss of the artillery not belonging to these divisions would increase the casualties to over 1,000.

The conduct of the battle on the Union left has given rise to much heated discussion, in which McClellan, Porter, and Burnside have been severely condemned, McClellan and his friends contending that, for Burnside's tardiness, the "victory might thus have been much more decisive."[87] In this chapter we have given, in some detail, Burnside's movements; in the preceding chapter we have treated of Porter's. It remains to say a few words of McClellan, who has been criticized for his failure in not uniting what he could spare of Franklin's corps to Porter's and supporting Burnside's attack by a movement along the Boonsboro Road directly toward Sharpsburg.

McClellan passed nearly the entire day on the high ground at the Pry house, where he had his headquarters and where, Palfrey says, he "had some glasses strapped to the fence, so that he could look in different directions."[88] Early in the day Colonel Delos B. Sacket of his staff was sent with an order to Burnside to push across the bridge, and Sacket was directed to remain with Burnside to see that the order was promptly executed and to give him his assistance. Other messengers went from headquarters to Burnside urging haste in the execution of the movement. Before noon McClellan sent Pleasonton across the Antietam by the Middle Bridge to support Sumner's fight at the sunken road and, about noon, sent his batteries of Porter's corps and some of Porter's infantry to support them and drive back the Confederate skirmishers, who had been annoying Pleasonton's guns. Sykes says these were sent against his (Sykes's) judgment,[89] and Porter complained that the infantry were diverted from the service of supporting the batteries and were "employed to drive the enemy's skirmishers to their reserves."[90] At one o'clock information was received that the bridge had been carried, and there was a lull along the whole line from right to left. The fighting on the extreme right had ceased, and that at the sunken road was confined to artillery.

A short time before the bridge was carried, McClellan sent Colonel Thomas M. Key of his staff to inform Burnside that he desired him to push forward with the utmost vigor, take the bridge with the bayonet, and carry the enemy's position on the heights; that the movement was vital to success; that this was the time when he must not stop for loss of life, if a great object could thereby be accomplished; and that if, in his judgment, the attack would fail, to inform him so at once, that his troops might be withdrawn and used elsewhere on the field. The bridge was now carried, and Key quickly returned with Burnside's reply that he would soon advance and go up the hill as far as a battery of the enemy, on the left, would permit. Key was immediately sent back to Burnside with peremptory orders to advance at once.[91] "And *this* time," says William F. Biddle, "Colonel Key *carried an order in McClellan's handwriting relieving Burnside on the spot, and placing General Morell in command, to be used if Burnside did not instantly advance and fight.*"[92]

Captain Dryer was now ordered across the Middle Bridge with additional battalions of regular infantry, with directions to take command of all of Porter's troops there. After sending Key on the second mission to Burnside, McClellan, "towards the middle of the afternoon, proceeding to the right, … found that Sumner's, Hooker's, and Mansfield's corps had met with serious losses … and the aspect of affairs was anything but promising." McClellan says, "At the risk of greatly exposing our centre, I ordered two brigades from Porter's corps, the only available troops, to re-enforce the right." Franklin was chafing to attack with the Sixth Corps, but Sumner had forbidden it and expressed to McClellan "the most decided opinion against another attempt during that day to assault the enemy's position in front, as portions of our troops were so much scattered and demoralized. In view of these circumstances," continues McClellan, "after making changes in the position of some of the troops, I directed the different commanders to hold their positions, and, *being satisfied that this could be done without the assistance of the two brigades from the centre,* I countermanded the order, which was in course of execution [emphasis Carman's]."[93]

While McClellan was absent on the right (where there was no fighting, and where he had determined that on his own part, so far as he could prevent, there should be none), Porter and Sykes were discontinuing movements that would have helped Burnside. We have already stated in the preceding chapter that, about 3:00 p.m., Pleasonton asked McClellan for more infantry. He received this reply:

---

[87] McClellan, *Own Story*, 604.

[88] Palfrey, 119.

[89] George Sykes to Fred T. Locke, September 30, 1862, reprinted in *OR*, vol. 19, pt. 1, 351.

[90] Fitz John Porter to Williams, October 1, 1862, reprinted in *OR*, vol. 19, pt. 1, 339.

[91] McClellan, *Own Story*, 603.

[92] Biddle, 468.

[93] This passage appears in McClellan, *Own Story*, 601, and Carman cites it as such in his original manuscript, but it was first contained in McClellan to Thomas, August 4, 1863, 62.

Headquarters Army of the Potomac
September 17, 1862—3.30 p.m.

Brigadier-General Pleasonton:

General: General McClellan directs me to say he has no infantry to spare.

Confer with Major-General Porter, and if he cannot support your batteries, withdraw them.

I am, general, very respectfully, your obedient servant,

R[andolph] B. Marcy,
Chief of Staff[94]

The tenor of this dispatch and the surrounding circumstances indicate that it was not dictated by McClellan, who was then absent, but that it was made upon the responsibility of the chief of staff, who had remained at headquarters. Certainly it would be very singular that McClellan, if present, would have referred Pleasonton to Porter when Porter himself was at headquarters, a word to whom would have decided the matter, without having the reply go to Pleasonton and then another to Porter, all of which would have consumed nearly an hour of very precious time. It is still more singular that McClellan, Porter, or Marcy would consent to the withdrawal of the batteries at the very moment Burnside was advancing. The natural conclusion would be that all would have united in supporting them strongly to assist Burnside, but it was not so. Both Porter and Sykes had very reluctantly sent their artillery and infantry across the Antietam. They were not disposed to do more, and a half-hour later Pleasonton was ordered by McClellan to send some of his cavalry to the right, where it was employed in gathering stragglers of the First Corps.[95]

Pleasonton saw the weakness of the Confederate line in his front and the advance of Burnside on Sharpsburg, and, believing there was a good opening for him to advance his batteries to Cemetery Hill and Ridge and there assist Burnside, acted upon the suggestion made by the chief of staff in his note of 3:30 p.m., and at 4:00 p.m. sent a request to Porter for a division to support his advance. Porter says he did not receive this request until after Burnside had been repulsed, that he did not have the division and could not, under his orders, imperil the success of the day by diminishing his small command.[96] Not only were troops withheld from Pleasonton, but soon after this, Sykes, who saw the regulars under Dryer advancing in fine style upon Cemetery Hill and Ridge and making close connection with Burnside's right, withdrew them and reprimanded their commander for exceeding his instructions. (In justice to Porter it may be stated that at 5:00 p.m. he sent this dispatch to Sykes, elsewhere quoted: "Burnside is driving the enemy. Please send word to the command you sent to Pleasonton, to support his batteries, and let him drive them."[97])

Colonel Sacket, who had been directed to remain with Burnside, waited until the general's troops were well under way up the heights and then returned to headquarters, where he found Porter, McClellan being away on the right. It was past four o'clock in the afternoon, and it was not long after this that the check and repulse of Burnside was witnessed.[98]

Soon after Sacket's arrival at headquarters, McClellan returned from the right and was a quiet witness to the check given Burnside and his withdrawal to the bridge. (At this time Lee was rallying his broken commands in the streets of Sharpsburg.) McClellan had made such disposition of his troops on the right as to satisfy him that it was safe without the assistance[99] of Porter's two brigades from the center, and, under these circumstances, one would suppose he could have spared some of Porter's troops to assist Burnside, who was seen to be hard pressed, but he did not use a man of them, and

---

[94] Randolph B. Marcy to Alfred Pleasonton, September 17, 1862, 3:30, p.m., reprinted in *OR*, vol. 51, pt. 1, 845.

[95]

Headquarters Army of the Potomac
September 17, 1862—4 p.m.

Brigadier-General Pleasonton:

General: General McClellan directs you to send two squadrons of cavalry to report to Brigadier-General Meade. He will probably be found near the Pennsylvania Reserves, on our right.

I am, general, very respectfully, your obedient servant,

Geo. D. Ruggles,
Colonel and Aide-de-Camp

As reprinted in *OR*, vol. 51, pt. 1, 845.—*EAC*

[96] Porter to Williams, 339.

[97] Porter to Sykes, September 17, 1862, 5:00 p.m., reprinted in *OR*, vol. 19, pt. 2, 316.

[98] Letter of Delos B. Sacket to McClellan, February 20, 1876, reprinted in McClellan, *Own Story*, 610. McClellan misspells the name as "Sackett" in his autobiography, and Carman repeats the error in his original manuscript.

[99] In his original manuscript, Carman presents the phrase *safe without the assistance* as a direct quotation, but it is in fact a paraphrase of McClellan's statement in his autobiography. McClellan, *Own Story*, 601.

when Burnside called for assistance replied that he had no infantry to give him. There was at this time a correspondent of the *New York Tribune* at McClellan's headquarters, who wrote that evening that, while Burnside was being checked and then falling back,

McClellan's glass for the last half-hour has seldom been turned away from the left. He sees clearly enough that Burnside is pressed—needs no messenger to tell him that. His face grows darker with anxious thought. Looking down into the valley where fifteen thousand troops [about ten thousand—*EAC*] are lying, he turns a half-questioning look on Fitz-John Porter, who stands by his side, gravely scanning the field. They are Porter's troops below, are fresh and only impatient to share in this fight. But Porter slowly shakes his head, and one may believe that the same thought is passing through the minds of both generals. "They are the only reserves of the army; they cannot be spared."

McClellan remounts his horse, and with Porter and a dozen officers of his staff rides away to the left in Burnside's direction. Sykes meets them on the road—a good soldier, whose opinion is worth taking. The three Generals talk briefly together …

Burnside's messenger rides up. His message is: "I want troops and guns. If you do not send them, I cannot hold my position half an hour." McClellan's only answer for the moment is a glance at the western sky. Then he turns and speaks very slowly: "Tell Gen. Burnside this is the battle of the war. He must hold his ground till dark at any cost. I will send him Miller's battery [Battery G, 4th U.S. Artillery]. I can do nothing more. I have no infantry." Then as the messenger was riding away he called him back. "Tell him if he *cannot* hold his ground, then the bridge, to the last man!—always the bridge! If the bridge is lost, all is lost."

The sun is already down; not half an hour of daylight is left.[100]

McClellan did not go to Burnside. Miller's battery was sent and took position with Benjamin east of the Antietam to guard the bridge, and this order was sent:

> Headquarters Army of the Potomac
> September 17, 1862—6.10 p.m.

Major-General Burnside:

  General: General McClellan directs me to say that whatever the result of your affair to-night may be, you must so guard the bridge with infantry and artillery as to make it impossible for the enemy to cross it.

  I am, general, very respectfully, your obedient servant,

> R. B. Marcy,
> Chief of Staff[101]

Five minutes after this, upon a report that the enemy was retreating, this dispatch was sent:

> Headquarters Army of the Potomac
> September 17, 1862.—6.15 p.m.

Major-General Burnside:

  General: General McClellan directs me to inclose the accompanying dispatch from signal officer, and to say that if there is any truth in it, he desires you to push the enemy vigorously. Let the general know if the enemy is retreating, and he will push forward with the center.

  I am, general, very respectfully, your obedient servant,

> R. B. Marcy,
> Chief of Staff[102]

McClellan's reasons for not using Porter's corps are given in his official report:

This corps filled the interval between the right wing and General Burnside's command, and guarded the main approach from the enemy's position to our trains of supply. It was necessary to watch this part of our line with the utmost vigilance, lest the enemy should take advantage of the first exhibition of weakness here to push upon us a vigorous assault for the purpose of piercing our center and turning our rear, as well as to capture or destroy our supply

---

[100] George W. Smalley, "New-York *Tribune* Narrative," in Frank Moore, ed., *The Rebellion Record: A Diary of American Events*, vol. 5 (New York: G. P. Putnam, 1863), Documents and Narratives, 472.

[101] Marcy to Burnside, September 17, 1862, 6:10 p.m., reprinted in *OR*, vol. 51, pt. 1, 844.

[102] Marcy to Burnside, September 17, 1862, 6:15 p.m., reprinted in *OR*, vol. 51, pt. 1, 844.

trains. Once having penetrated this line, the enemy's passage to our rear could have met with but feeble resistance, as there were no reserves to re enforce or close up the gap …

… Continually under the vigilant watch of the enemy, this corps guarded a vital point.[103]

Porter shared McClellan's views as to the great importance of his position in guarding the trains, and that any diminution of his force for offensive operations would endanger their safety and imperil the army. It is inconceivable that these two soldiers could seriously suppose that Lee would think of putting a column of attack against McClellan's center—snugly ensconced behind the Antietam with a bold bluff bordering it—a position approachable only over open ground for nearly a mile, covered by a direct and cross-fire of 80 guns (120 if necessary), then, by head of column, crossing a narrow bridge so entirely commanded by the heights looking down upon it from either side of the road that an officer of ordinary spirit with two thousand men could have successfully defended it against twenty thousand of the very best Lee had in his army. It is conceivable only upon the theory that they supposed Lee had such an overwhelming force that he could afford a great sacrifice for the desperate venture. In fact Lee never entertained a thought of McClellan's trains and, in striking contrast to McClellan, cared for and defended his own only by putting every man on the fighting line.

One of the defects of McClellan as a commander was his overestimate of his adversary's numbers. It began with his campaign in western Virginia, it was with him on the Peninsula, and he had not been a week on his Maryland campaign that we find him estimating Lee's army at 120,000. At Antietam he believed that he was greatly outnumbered. If he had substantial reason for this belief, as Palfrey notes, "prudence of the commonest kind would have forbidden any attack at all."[104] Especially is it true that, after Sedgwick's repulse on the right and Franklin's enforced inaction, the persistent urging of Burnside to advance from the high ground at the bridge without supporting him on the line of the Boonsboro Road was a stupendous crime. If it had any justification, it was that such a movement was necessary to save the right from a disastrous defeat. This is the view taken by Cox, who, as commander of the Ninth Corps on the field, was in a position to know, and has thus written of Porter's reserve and the failure of McClellan to use it:

As troops are put in reserve, not to diminish the army, but to be used in a pinch, I am deeply convinced that McClellan's refusal to use them on the left was the result of his continued conviction through all the day after Sedgwick's defeat, that Lee was overwhelmingly superior in force, and was preparing to return a crushing blow upon our right flank. He was keeping something in hand to cover a retreat, if that wing should be driven back. Except in this way, also, I am at a loss to account for the inaction of our right during the whole of our engagement on the left. Looking at our part of the battle as only a strong diversion to prevent or delay Lee's following up his success against Hooker and the rest, it is intelligible. I certainly so understood it at the time, as my report witnesses, and McClellan's preliminary report supports this view. If he had been impatient to have our attack delivered earlier, he had reason for double impatience that Franklin's fresh troops should assail Lee's left simultaneously with ours, unless he regarded action there as hopeless, and looked upon our movement as a sort of forlorn-hope to keep Lee from following up his advantages.[105]

Longstreet says McClellan's plan of battle "was not strong, the handling and execution were less so. Battles by the extreme right and left, divided by a river, gave us the benefit of interior lines, and it was that that saved the Confederate army, for it became manifest early in the day that his reserves were held at the bridge No. 2 [the Middle Bridge], which gave us freer use of our inner lines."[106] He also says, "We were so badly crushed that at the close of the day ten thousand fresh troops could have come in and taken Lee's army and everything it had."[107]

The battle was a succession of disjointed attacks and stubborn resistance to them. It began with the advance of the First Corps at daybreak, and the fighting of this corps was over when the Twelfth Corps became engaged at 7:30 a.m. This corps, without any assistance from the First (except Patrick's small brigade) fought alone and drove the enemy across the Hagerstown Road a little before nine o'clock. At 9:00 a.m., Sumner came up with one division of the Second Corps, went forward, and was repulsed with great loss. (Palfrey says this one division—Sedgwick's—"might as well have been in another country for any direct aid it received from the rest of the Army of the Potomac,"[108] but Palfrey is in error, for support and aid was given it by the greater part of the Twelfth Corps.) The other two divisions of Sumner's corps became engaged later—not simultaneously, and not in close connection with Sedgwick—and not until the fighting was nearly over on the right did Burnside become seriously engaged. Sumner testified before the Committee on the Conduct of the War, "I have

---

[103] McClellan to Thomas, August 4, 1863, 61–62.

[104] Palfrey, 122.

[105] Cox, "The Battle of Antietam," 657.

[106] James Longstreet, *From Manassas to Appomattox: Memoirs of the Civil War in America* (Philadelphia: J. P. Lippincott Co., 1896), 267.

[107] Longstreet, "The Invasion of Maryland," in *Battles and Leaders*, 670.

[108] Palfrey, 120–21.

always believed that, instead of sending these troops into that action in driblets, as they were sent, if General McClellan had authorized me to march these 40,000 men on the left flank of the enemy, we could not have failed to throw them right back in front of the other divisions of our army on our left, Burnside's, Franklin's, and Porter's corps; as it was, we went in, division after division, until even one of my own divisions was forced out. The other two drove the enemy and held their positions."[109]

Franklin's Sixth Corps arrived near Keedysville a little after 10:00 a.m. "It was first intended," McClellan reports, "to keep this corps in reserve on the east side of the Antietam, to operate on either flank or on the center, as circumstances might require, but on nearing Keedysville the strong opposition on the right, developed by the attacks of Hooker and Sumner, rendered it necessary at once to send this corps to the assistance of the right wing."[110] Had Franklin's entire corps, or one division of it, been pushed across the Middle Bridge and seized the ridge overlooking Sharpsburg, as it could have done, Lee would have had his hands full in guarding his center, without any offensive operations against McClellan's right. It is futile, however, to speculate upon what he might have done; McClellan was content in his opinion that he had handled his army with great skill.

Both McClellan and Lee considered Antietam their greatest battle. In a letter home written the day after, McClellan says, "Those in whose judgment I rely tell me that I fought the battle splendidly and that it was a masterpiece of art."[111] History will not accept this view of the battle, in the conduct of which more errors were committed by the Union commander than in any other battle of the war. It will accept the opinion of the Confederate historian William Allan: "Whatever may be thought or said of the strategy which led to the battle of Sharpsburg, the conduct of that battle itself by Lee and his principal subordinates seems absolutely above criticism. Had Lee known all that we know now of the Federal plans and forces, it is difficult to see how he could have more wisely disposed or more effectively used the means he had at hand. The utmost tension existed at different points of his lines during the day. He had no reserves, but so judiciously were the Confederate troops handled that their obstinate courage was sufficient everywhere to prevent any serious loss of position."[112]

Between daybreak and the setting sun of September 17, 1862, was the bloodiest day of American history. Ninety-three thousand men of kindred blood (56,000 Union and 27,000 Confederate) and 520 guns engaged in the desperate struggle, and when the sun went down and mercifully put an end to the strife, 3,654 men were dead and 17,292 wounded.[113] About 1,770 were missing, some of whom were dead, but most of whom were carried as prisoners from the field. Every state from the Great Lakes on the North to the Gulf of Mexico on the South, from the Atlantic to the Mississippi, and (with the exception of Iowa and Missouri) every state watered by the Mississippi contributed to this carnival of death and suffering.

Palfrey has most beautifully written:

As the sun sank to rest on the 17th of September, the last sounds of battle along Antietam Creek died away. The cannon could at last grow cool, and unwounded men and horses could enjoy rest and food, but there were thousands already sleeping the sleep that knows no waking, and many times as many thousands who were suffering all the agonies that attend on wounds. The corn and the trees, so fresh and green in the morning, were reddened with blood and torn by bullet and shell; and the very earth was furrowed by the incessant impact of lead and iron. The blessed night came, and brought with it sleep and forgetfulness and refreshment to many; but the murmur of the night wind, breathing over fields of wheat and clover, was mingled with the groans of the countless sufferers of both armies. Who can tell, who can even imagine, the horrors of such a night, while the unconscious stars shone above, and the unconscious river went rippling by?[114]

---

[109] *Report of the Joint Committee on the Conduct of the War*, 37th Cong., 3d sess., 1863, S. Rep. 108, pt. 1, serial 1152, 368.
[110] McClellan to Thomas, August 4, 1863, 61.
[111] McClellan to Mary Ellen McClellan, September 18, 1862, reprinted in McClellan, *Own Story*, 612.
[112] Allan, 441–42.
[113] Including the losses on the sixteenth, which did not exceed one hundred killed and wounded.—*EAC*
[114] Palfrey, 124–25.

21

General Lee Recrosses the Potomac

September 18–19, 1862

General McClellan intended to renew the battle on the eighteenth. During the afternoon of the seventeenth, while on the right, Franklin called his attention to Nicodemus Hill, commanding the West Woods, and proposed to occupy it by artillery early next morning and then, after shelling the woods, to make an attack upon them by his whole corps from the position held by Sumner's troops. Franklin had no doubt of his ability to seize the hill, as there was plenty of artillery bearing on it from Poffenberger Hill; once occupied, the whole Confederate left would be uncovered and victory assured. There is not the shadow of a doubt that had the hill been occupied by artillery, Lee's left would have been turned and the West Woods rendered untenable, but we very much doubt whether Franklin's entire corps could have succeeded in getting artillery upon it. However, McClellan assented, and it was understood that the attack was to be made early in the morning. During the night, however, the order was countermanded, McClellan giving the reason "because fifteen thousand Pennsylvania troops would soon arrive, and that upon their arrival the attack would be ordered."[1]

When the day closed with Burnside's repulse on the left, the night brought with it grave responsibilities. Whether to renew the attack on the eighteenth or to defer it, even with the risk of the enemy's retirement, was the question McClellan considered, and in its consideration he consulted only with Porter. He says:

> After a night of anxious deliberation, and a full and careful survey of the situation and condition of our army, the strength and position of the enemy, I concluded that the success of an attack on the 18th was not certain. I am aware of the fact that under ordinary circumstances a general is expected to risk a battle if he has a reasonable prospect of success; but at this critical juncture I should have had a narrow view of the condition of the country had I been willing to hazard another battle with less than an absolute assurance of success. At that moment—Virginia lost, Washington menaced, Maryland invaded—the national cause could afford no risks of defeat. One battle lost and almost all would have been lost. Lee's army might then have marched, as it pleased, on Washington, Baltimore, Philadelphia, or New York. It could have levied its supplies from a fertile and undevastated country, extorted tribute from wealthy and populous cities, and nowhere east of the Alleghanies [*sic*] was there another organized force able to arrest its march.[2]

Among the considerations which led him to doubt the certainty of success in attacking before the nineteenth:

> The troops were greatly overcome by the fatigue and exhaustion attendant upon the long-continued and severely contested battle of the 17th, together with the long day and night marches to which they had been subjected during the previous three days. The supply trains were in the rear, and many of the troops had suffered from hunger. They required rest and refreshment. One division of Sumner's and all of Hooker's corps on the right had, after fighting most valiantly for several hours, been overpowered by numbers, driven back in great disorder, and much scattered, so that they were for the time somewhat demoralized. In Hooker's corps, according to the return made by General Meade, commanding, there were but 6,729 men present on the 18th, …
>
> One division of Sumner's corps had also been overpowered, and was a good deal scattered and demoralized. It was not deemed by its corps commander in proper condition to attack the enemy vigorously the next day.
>
> Some of the new troops on the left, although many of them fought well during the battle and are entitled to great credit, were, at the close of the action, driven back and their *morale* impaired.
>
> On the morning of the 18th, General Burnside requested me to send him another division to assist in holding his position on the other side of the Antietam, and to enable him to withdraw his corps as if he should be attacked by a superior force. He gave me the impression that if he were attacked again that morning, he would not be able to make a very vigorous resistance …

1   *Report of the Joint Committee on the Conduct of the War*, 37th Cong., 3d sess., 1863, S. Rep. 108, pt. 1, serial 1152, 627; William B. Franklin, "Notes on Crampton's Gap and Antietam," in *Battles and Leaders of the Civil War*, vol. 2 (New York: Century Co., 1887), 597.—*EAC*
2   George B. McClellan to Lorenzo Thomas, August 4, 1863, reprinted in *OR*, vol. 19, pt. 1, 65.

A large number of our heaviest and most efficient batteries had consumed all their ammunition on the 16th and 17th, and it was impossible to supply them until late on the following day. Supplies of provisions and forage had to be brought up and issued, and infantry ammunition distributed. Finally, re-enforcements to the number of 14,000 men, to say nothing of troops expected from Pennsylvania, had not arrived, but were expected during the day.

The 18th was, therefore, spent in collecting the dispersed, giving rest to the fatigued, removing the wounded, burying the dead, and the necessary preparations for a renewal of the battle.

Of the re-enforcements, Couch's division, marching with commendable rapidity, came up into position at a late hour in the morning. Humphreys' division of new troops, in their anxiety to participate in the battle which was raging when they received the order to march from Frederick about 3.30 p.m. on the 17th, pressed forward during the entire night, and the mass of the division reached the army during the following morning. Having marched more than 23 miles after 4.30 o'clock on the preceding afternoon, they were, of course, greatly exhausted, and needed rest and refreshment. Large re-enforcements expected from Pennsylvania never arrived.[3]

At eight o'clock in the morning, McClellan telegraphed Halleck that he had fought a hard battle with heavy losses, that it would probably be renewed during the day, and requested him to forward all the troops he could by the most expeditious route.[4] Halleck ordered some regiments to him, but they did not arrive until two days later, and the expected Pennsylvania Militia failed him. A large body of them assembled at Hagerstown, but most of them refused to go farther.[5] John Reynolds, who had them in charge, says he had about fourteen thousand men, but much to his surprise, "all the regiments refused to march."[6]

There were some changes of position during the day, which are of no particular interest. McClellan had, by noon, fully seventy-eight thousand men, of whom thirty-five thousand had not been engaged. Orders were given for a renewal of the attack at daylight of the nineteenth, but, before daylight, the watchful pickets reported that the enemy had gone.

Lee's army was too badly crippled to renew the battle on the eighteenth. S. D. Lee gives an interesting statement of a meeting of General Lee and his principal commanders on the night of the seventeenth:

General Lee's headquarters were on the pike leading from Sharpsburg to the Potomac, and about half a mile from the town. About one hour or two after night had set in the weird scene of the great battle-field had changed, in that the firing had ceased everywhere, and more open help was being given to the searching for dead ones, and caring for the dying and wounded. General Lee had summoned his corps and division commanders to meet him. For once during the day he had some of his staff and escort about him, and one by one his commanders began to arrive, generally two or three horsemen with them.

As they came up … General Lee inquired quietly, "General, how is it on your part of the line?" I, too, had been summoned, and was a quiet, intensely interested observer of one of the most remarkable scenes and interviews I ever witnessed. To the inquiry of Lee, Longstreet, apparently much depressed, replied to the effect "that it was as bad as could be; that he had lost terribly, and his lines had been barely held, and there was little better than a good skirmish line along his front," and he volunteered the advice that General Lee should cross the Potomac before daylight. D. H. Hill came next. He said that his division was cut to pieces; that his losses had been terrible, and he had no troops to hold his line against the great odds against him. He, too, suggested crossing the Potomac before daylight. Next came Jackson. He quietly said that he had had to contend against the greatest odds he had ever met. He had lost a good many colonels killed, and several division and brigade commanders were dead or wounded, and his losses in the different commands had been terrible. He, too, suggested crossing the Potomac before daylight. Next came Hood. To General Lee's inquiry, he displayed great emotion, seemed completely unmanned. He replied that he had no division. General Lee, with more excitement than I ever witnessed in him, exclaimed, "Great God! General Hood, where is your splendid division you had this morning?" Hood replied, "They are lying on the field, where you sent them. But few have straggled. My division has been almost wiped out."

After the opinion of all had been given, there was an appalling stillness over the group. It seemed to last several minutes, when General Lee, apparently rising more erect in his saddle, said, "Gentlemen, we will not cross the Potomac to-night. You will go to your respective commands, strengthen your lines; send two officers from each brigade towards the ford to collect your stragglers and get them up. Many others have also come up. I have had the

---

3. Ibid., 66–67.
4. McClellan to Henry W. Halleck, September 18, 1862, 8:00 a.m., reprinted in *OR*, vol. 19, pt. 2, 322.
5. See Israel Vogdes to Halleck, September 18, 1862, reprinted in *OR*, vol. 19, pt. 2, 329.
6. John F. Reynolds to Halleck, September 18, 1862, reprinted in *OR*, vol. 19, pt. 2, 332.

proper steps taken to collect all the men who are in the rear. If McClellan wants to fight in the morning I will give him battle again. Go!"

The above was in substance what occurred and what was said. The group gradually broke up, each going to his command, and, if I read their countenances aright, they said: "This is a rash conclusion, and we fear that the Army of Northern Virginia is taking a great risk in the face of the day's battle and the great numbers opposed to us." The two armies faced each other all the next day (18th of September), the guns unlimbered, the lines of battle and skirmishers in place, but every one being careful not to let a gun go off for fear, apparently, the terrible slaughter and scenes of the day before might be renewed—one army was afraid, the other "daresn't."[7]

Before dawn of the eighteenth, Hood was in the saddle and rode to the front. Jackson came up instantly, asking, "Hood, have they gone?" When Hood answered in the negative, he replied, "I hoped they had," and then passed on to look after his brave but greatly exhausted command.[8]

It will be remembered that on the afternoon of the seventeenth, Lee ordered Jackson to turn the Union right and that Jackson found it so securely posted and held so strongly with artillery that he desisted in the attempt, much to his own disappointment as also to Lee's. From the statement made by S. D. Lee, it would appear that General Lee, on the morning of the eighteenth, ordered Jackson to take fifty guns and crush McClellan's right, to which Jackson responded that it could not be done. Colonel Lee was summoned to headquarters and General Lee sent him to report to Jackson, who was found at his bivouac. Jackson and Colonel Lee then rode to Nicodemus Hill, which was strewn with wrecks of caissons, broken wheels, dead bodies, and dead horses, and Lee was directed to take his glass and carefully examine the Federal position. After noting the batteries unlimbered and prepared for action, supported by heavy masses of infantry, he was asked if he could crush that force with fifty guns. Lee said he could try and that he could do it if anyone could, but Jackson insisted upon a definite answer, yes or no, whether it could be done. He made another careful examination and finally said, "General, it cannot be done with fifty guns and the troops you have near here."[9] Jackson instantly led the way back and upon reaching his bivouac directed S. D. Lee to go to General Lee and tell him all that had occurred, his examination of the Federal position, the conversation about crushing the Federal right and his being forced to give his opinion as to its possibility. Colonel Lee says, "With feelings such as I never had before, nor ever expect to have again, I returned to General Lee and gave a detailed account of my visit to General Jackson, closing with the account of my being forced to give my opinion as to the possibility of success. I saw a shade come over General Lee's face, and he said: 'Colonel, go and join your command.'"[10]

For many years S. D. Lee never fully understood his mission that day or why he was sent to General Jackson. It was only after the official reports were published that he was aware that Jackson had been ordered to turn McClellan's right on the afternoon of the seventeenth and had reported that it could not be done, that General Lee had repeated the order on the eighteenth and directed Jackson to take fifty guns and crush McClellan's right, and that "Jackson having reported

---

7   Dabney H. Maury, "Our Confederate Column," *Richmond Dispatch*, December 20, 1896. In the article, Maury claimed S. D. Lee told the story over a dinner during "the great Confederate reunion in Richmond," and presents the entirety of Lee's account as a direct quotation. Given the length of the passage (the original fills two full newspaper columns) and the unlikelihood of Maury taking copious notes during his meal (in the course of which, one suspects, a bottle or two was opened), such specificity invites doubt. At a minimum, the language does not seem to be in keeping with what is known of the personalities of several of the principals.

In defense of Carman, however, it will be admitted that, as S. D. Lee was still alive at the time of publication, it is unlikely that Maury would have invented the entire episode and then falsely claimed Lee as his source. Further, in his biography of Jackson, G. F. R. Henderson repeats the story, much of it verbatim from the *Dispatch* article. The ambiguity of the citations he presents, however, makes it impossible to confirm whether Henderson took these particular passages from his correspondence with S. D. Lee (who, if this was the case, drew upon the earlier article in writing to Henderson) or simply worked from the *Dispatch* article in drafting that portion of his narrative. See G. F. R. Henderson, *Stonewall Jackson and the American Civil War*, vol. 2, (London: Longmans, Green, and Co., 1898), 323–29.

Regardless of the authorship, Carman's uncritical acceptance of this account is problematic. Not only does it contrast sharply with what is known of Lee's style of command, but a note found among Carman's personal papers states, "Regarding this paper of Gen. S. D. Lee, I had a conversation on the evening of March 9, 1897, with Col. Chas. Marshall, formerly of General [R. E.] Lee's staff ... As to the alleged council of war he was positive that S. D. Lee was in error. He knew nothing of it and such an event would have come under his observation. He knew of but two instances in which Lee held a council. The first was soon after taking command of the army when he called in his division commanders, all of whom, save one, advised a retrograde movement from the Chickahominy and a stand nearer Richmond. The second council was at Appomattox." Memorandum of Ezra A. Carman, no date, folder 15, box 10, Ezra A. Carman Papers, Manuscripts and Archives Division, New York Public Library.

8   John B. Hood, *Advance and Retreat: Personal Experiences in the United States and Confederate States Armies* (n.p., 1880), 45.

9   Maury, "Our Confederate Column."

10   Ibid.

against such an attempt on the 17th, no doubt said if an artillerist in whom General Lee had confidence would say the Federal right could be crushed with fifty guns he would make the attempt."[11]

During the night of the seventeenth and the early morning of the eighteenth, Lee's army was increased by the arrival of about six thousand men who had straggled on the march from Harper's Ferry, but these did not repair much more than half the losses of the seventeenth and gave him not to exceed thirty-five thousand of all arms—entirely too small a force with which to assume the offensive. He had no reserves that he could call upon. McClellan's army was known to be increasing. Finding the Union commander indisposed to attack on the eighteenth, and his own position "being a bad one to hold with the river in rear," Lee determined to cross his army to the Virginia side.[12] He reports:

> On the 18th we occupied the position of the preceding day, except in the center, where our line was drawn in about 200 yards. Our ranks were increased by the arrival of a number of troops, who had not been engaged the day before, and, though still too weak to assume the offensive, we awaited without apprehension the renewal of the attack. The day passed without any demonstration on the part of the enemy, who, from the reports received, was expecting the arrival of re-enforcements. As we could not look for a material increase in strength, and the enemy's force could be largely and rapidly augmented, it was not thought prudent to wait until he should be ready again to offer battle. During the night of the 18th the army was accordingly withdrawn to the south side of the Potomac, crossing near Shepherdstown, without loss or molestation.[13]

Between two and three o'clock in the afternoon, orders were given for the trains to cross the Potomac at Shepherdstown Ford. When night came Longstreet moved from the line and was across the river by two o'clock on the morning of the nineteenth. Jackson followed Longstreet, Gregg's Brigade of A. P. Hill's Division being the last of the infantry to cross, followed by Fitzhugh Lee's cavalry brigade. By ten o'clock in the morning, the Army of Northern Virginia had crossed with all its horses and materiel. Such of the wounded as could be moved went back with the army; those who could not be moved were left in the hands of the Union army and received kind and careful attention.

Pleasonton, who had been engaged on the eighteenth in collecting stragglers and reconnoitering the various roads on the flanks and in rear, started in pursuit when it was ascertained the Confederates had gone, and before reaching the river his men captured 167 prisoners, one abandoned gun, and a color. On nearing the river via the turnpike, the Confederate artillery on the heights below Shepherdstown covering the ford opened a heavy fire upon him. Lee had left as a rear-guard about six hundred infantry of Armistead's and Lawton's Brigades (under Colonels James G. Hodges and John H. Lamar, respectively) and over forty guns (Brown's and Nelson's Battalions and other guns, all under the command of Pendleton). Pleasonton engaged these guns with the batteries of Gibson, Tidball, and Robertson, with such effect that Pendleton withdrew some of his. While thus engaged, Pleasonton received a dispatch from McClellan stating that he did not propose to cross the river and did not desire Pleasonton to do so unless he saw a splendid opportunity to inflict great damage upon the enemy without loss to himself. In about two hours, Porter came up and ordered Pleasonton back to his camp.[14]

Porter's Fifth Corps followed Pleasonton, went through Sharpsburg about noon, and, with the troops that had advanced on the right, was directed to take up a position in line beyond the town. During the afternoon, Porter was ordered to support Pleasonton, who was in advance. He relieved Pleasonton and "determined to clear the fords, and, if possible, secure some of the enemy's artillery."[15] With this in view, he caused the banks of the river and canal at the ford to be well lined with skirmishers and sharpshooters, supported by portions of their respective divisions (Morell's and Sykes's), while their artillery and that of the reserve were posted to control the opposite bank. The batteries brought into action were those of Weed and Van Reed and one gun each of Randol's, Kusserow's, and Langner's.

While these were driving the cannoneers and horses of the Confederate batteries from their guns and silencing the fire of the infantry, an attacking party from Griffin's and Colonel James Barnes's brigades (composed of about sixty men of the 1st U.S. Sharpshooters, the 4th Michigan, and parts of the 118th Pennsylvania and the 18th and 22d Massachusetts), volunteers for the occasion, was formed under the immediate direction of Griffin. Under cover of the fire of the sharpshooters, the remainder were posted along the river bank and in the bed of the canal, then pushed across the ford in the face of a warm fire from the Confederate infantry, who finally gave way, retreating in confusion (Pendleton says in a "state of disorder, akin to panic"[16]) and compelling the abandonment of several of the guns. Through some misunderstanding, an order

---

[11] Ibid.

[12] Robert E. Lee to Jefferson Davis, September 20, 1862, reprinted in *OR*, vol. 19, pt. 1, 142.

[13] Lee to Samuel Cooper, August 19, 1863, reprinted in *OR*, vol. 19. pt. 1, 151.

[14] See Alfred Pleasonton to Randolph B. Marcy, September 19, 1862, reprinted in *OR*, vol. 19, pt. 1, 212; Marcy to Pleasonton, September 19, 1862, 1:15 p.m., reprinted in *OR*, vol. 51, pt. 1, 853.

[15] Fitz John Porter to Seth Williams, October 1, 1862, reprinted in *OR*, vol. 19, pt. 1, 339.

[16] William N. Pendleton to Lee, September 24, 1862, reprinted in *OR*, vol. 19, pt. 1, 833.

for Sykes to move over a similar party did not reach him, but his skirmishers, under the direction of Colonel Gouverneur K. Warren, were engaged in keeping down the fire of the Confederate infantry and, with the artillery, annoyed the enemy's cannoneers and partially prevented them from manning their guns.

It was sunset when Griffin crossed the river. Night was at hand as his men scaled the heights near the water's edge, but the skirmishers, pushing forward, came upon small parties of Confederates, who hastily retired. One body, left in charge of two guns, made some resistance, but was soon put to flight by Corporal Cassius Peck and a few men of the 1st U.S. Sharpshooters, the guns captured and one man taken prisoner. (The guns were removed to a point near the riverbank, from which they were subsequently taken to the Maryland shore.) Some time after dark, Porter ordered a recall to the east side of the Potomac, and the whole corps bivouacked near the ford. Porter's movement during the day was very deliberate; he had marched three miles unopposed, reaching the ford in the afternoon. As he reports, "Darkness concealed the movements of the enemy and enabled them to remove a portion of their artillery before our attacking party scaled the heights."[17]

The result of the day's action, so far as Porter's corps was concerned, was "the capture of 5 pieces, 2 caissons, 2 caisson bodies, 2 forges, and some 400 stand of arms; also 1 battle-flag."[18] Porter again crossed the Potomac on the morning of the twentieth, with disastrous results, but this properly belongs to another chapter.

At 8:30 a.m. on the nineteenth, McClellan dispatched Halleck that the enemy had abandoned his position and that he was in pursuit, but did not know whether Lee was falling back to an interior position or crossing the river. "We may," he said, "safely claim a complete victory."[19] Two hours later he dispatched, "Pleasonton is driving the enemy across the river. Our victory was complete. The enemy is driven back into Virginia. Maryland and Pennsylvania are now safe."[20] Two hours later still we have a glimpse of McClellan: "Porter's corps was passing through the town. McClellan and his staff came galloping up the hill. Porter's men swung their hats and gave a cheer; but few hurrahs came from the other corps—none from Hooker's. A change had come over the army. The complacent look which I had seen upon McClellan's countenance on the 17th, as if all were going well, had disappeared. There was a troubled look instead—a manifest awakening to the fact that his great opportunity had gone by. Lee had slipped through his fingers."[21]

The change that came over the army in two days was very marked. On the morning of the seventeenth, it had great confidence in McClellan, but that confidence began to wane before the close of the day. The inaction of the eighteenth increased the feeling that he was not the man for the occasion. Officers and men alike freely discussed the manner in which they had been used the day before, criticized the failure to use the Fifth Corps (which was the admiration of every West Pointer in the army) to support Burnside instead of holding it in reserve to guard wagon trains, and wondered why the attack was not renewed. In the Ninth Corps, there was very pronounced dissatisfaction, not to say distrust of his honesty of purpose. The First and Twelfth Corps felt that they had been called upon to sacrifice many of their best officers and men, while the Fifth and Sixth Corps were spared the effusion of blood. Even in the latter two corps there was not wanting the opinion that McClellan had not used them to good purpose—that, had he thrown them into action, a great and decisive victory would have followed. When it was found that Lee had escaped, there were those who thought that McClellan was in no wise disappointed, that it was as he wished it should be, that he was not so intent upon driving Lee into the Potomac as he was desirous to see him safely over it. A few, only, shared these extreme views, but the fact remains that confidence in him as a commander on the field was greatly shaken.[22]

---

[17] Porter to Williams, 340. Three of the guns were secured by Griffin on the morning of the twentieth.—*EAC*

[18] Ibid.

[19] McClellan to Halleck, September 19, 1862, 8:30 a.m., reprinted in *OR*, vol. 19, pt. 2, 330.

[20] McClellan to Halleck, September 19, 1862, 10:30 a.m., reprinted in *OR*, vol. 19, pt. 2, 330.

[21] Charles Carleton Coffin, "Antietam Scenes," in *Battles and Leaders of the Civil War*, vol. 2 (New York: Century Co., 1887), 685.

[22] Carman ends this chapter in his original manuscript with three additional pages containing an account, taken from a memorandum written by Lincoln, of the dismissal of Major John J. Key from the U.S. Army. (The last of these three pages was separated from the rest of the chapter at some point, most likely during a processing of the Carman papers by the Library of Congress. On the archival microfilm of the Carman manuscript, the page in question appears instead at the end of the next chapter, originally entitled "Shepherdstown or Boteler's Ford." By sheer coincidence, the numbering at the top of the manuscript page allows it to fit in the sequence of either chapter, but after a careful textual analysis, the editor is convinced that it is in fact the last page of "General Lee Recrosses the Potomac.") A complete version of the memorandum event appears again at the close of "Lincoln and McClellan" (herein Chapter 24). As the redundancy serves no apparent function and the material is more consistent thematically with the tenor of the final chapter, its first appearance has been struck out by the editor.

In Carman's original manuscript, "General Lee Recrosses the Potomac" is followed immediately by chapters dealing with the strengths of and losses in the two armies. These are reprinted herein as Appendices J and L.

22

Shepherdstown Ford

September 20, 1862

The information gained by Fitz John Porter's troops on the evening of the nineteenth was to the effect that Lee had retreated on the Charlestown and Martinsburg roads toward Winchester. To verify this, and to ascertain how far he had retreated, Porter was authorized to send over a reconnoitering force on the morning of the twentieth. Pleasonton was directed to cross the river at daybreak and cooperate with Porter.[1] Porter ordered Morell and Sykes to cross their divisions at 7:00 a.m., preceding their main columns by advance guards thrown well forward on the roads to Shepherdstown and Charlestown.[2] Before these movements were made, and as soon as it was light enough to see, the 4th Michigan and 62d Pennsylvania of Griffin's brigade crossed the river with some horses from Battery D, 5th U.S. Artillery (Lieutenant Charles E. Hazlett), and brought back three guns, several caissons, and one battle-flag (picked up on the field), returning to camp about 8:00 a.m.

Sykes was directed to cross with a brigade and push out on the Charlestown Road. He took Lovell's brigade (the 1st and 6th, the 2d and 10th, the 1st Battalion of the 11th, and the 1st Battalion of the 17th U.S. Infantry), crossed the river at eight o'clock, threw out skirmishers, and advanced Lovell on the Charlestown Road. Lovell went about a mile and, upon approaching a belt of woods, discovered the enemy in force—A. P. Hill's Division—on his right and in front. Sykes was informed, and he ordered Lovell to fall back to the crest of the river bluff. Lovell fell back slowly and in good order, skirmishing lightly until reaching the open ground on the heights near the river, when a heavy fire was opened upon him. The 2d and 6th U.S. Infantry were then thrown into a piece of woods on the left, but soon the Union batteries beyond the river opened fire and much of it fell in and around the two regiments, rendering it absolutely necessary to withdraw them to the crest of the hill. After this, Warren's brigade (composed of just the 5th and 10th New York) formed on Lovell's left. The cavalry, which was to have preceded the infantry at daybreak, came up after Lovell had encountered the enemy, and, being useless, was withdrawn.

The evening before, Pleasonton had been ordered back to his camp by Porter. At 10:45 p.m. he was directed by McClellan to have his cavalry and artillery at the river by daylight and precede Porter's infantry; later, during the night, he was ordered to send two brigades and a battery in the direction of Williamsport. These he started at 6:30 a.m. on the twentieth, at which hour he dispatched McClellan, from his camp near Keedysville, that the remainder of his command was about getting off for Shepherdstown, and complained:

> The order of Maj. Gen. Fitz John Porter of yesterday, sending my command to the rear, by the order of General McClellan, and which was transmitted by [Brigadier] General [John] Buford, has interfered most materially with a proper pursuit of the enemy. Many of the men of my command have had nothing to eat for two days, and last night, in consequence of the movement to the rear, they missed their trains, and are now starting out without anything … I trust, after the past experience of yesterday, the general commanding will not permit corps commanders to interfere with the cavalry under my command, for it breaks up all my system and plans.[3]

Meanwhile, about 9:00 a.m., Barnes's brigade of Morell's division crossed the Potomac under orders to go on the road to Shepherdstown and see what was there. Sykes requested Barnes to occupy the crest on the right of the Charlestown Road and connect with Lovell's right, which was then falling back. Barnes's brigade was composed of the 18th Massachusetts (Lieutenant Colonel Joseph Hayes), 22d Massachusetts (Lieutenant Colonel William S. Tilton), 2d Maine (Colonel Charles W. Roberts), 1st Michigan (Captain Emory W. Belton), 13th New York (Colonel Elisha G. Marshall), 25th New York (Colonel Charles A. Johnson), and 118th Pennsylvania (Colonel Charles M. Prevost)—in all 1,700 officers and men. As soon as the 18th Massachusetts (the leading regiment) had crossed the ford, it was drawn up on the road leading to Shepherdstown and under a bold bluff overlooking the road and river. It was at this moment, and before the other regiments had crossed, that Sykes came up to Barnes with information that the enemy were in strong force less than two miles in front, gave Barnes orders to suspend his march on Shepherdstown, and directed that the 18th Massachusetts take position near but

---

[1] Randolph B. Marcy to Alfred Pleasonton, September 19, 1862, 11:00 p.m., reprinted in *OR*, vol. 51, pt. 1, 853.

[2] Fitz John Porter to Seth Williams, October 1, 1862, reprinted in *OR*, vol. 19, pt. 1, 340.

[3] Pleasonton to Marcy, September 20, 1862, 6:30 a.m., reprinted in *OR*, vol. 19, pt. 2, 334.

below the top of the ridge or bluff (which ran on the left of and parallel to the road). The 25th and 13th New York, as they crossed, were placed on the right of the 18th Massachusetts, but to reach that point it was necessary to pass along the road and beyond the ravine by which the 18th had ascended to another ravine a few rods distant, the interval forming a rocky bluff, nearly perpendicular, up which it was impracticable to advance.[4] Sykes at 9:15 a.m. reported to Porter that he had sent Barnes temporarily to the top of the hill to support Lovell and suggested that more troops be sent over, along with "some one in authority."[5]

A brief description of the ground is necessary. The ford by which the movement was made, and by which Lee recrossed the Potomac, is about a mile below Shepherdstown, and variously known as Shepherdstown, Blackford's, and Boteler's Ford. On the Maryland side, it starts from the Blackford farm and reaches the Virginia side on the Boteler farm. It crosses the river a short distance below the breast of a mill dam constructed to give water to Boteler's large mill. On the Virginia side, the ford road runs along the southern extremity of a high bluff off in the direction of Charlestown; another road extends along the foot of a bluff, between it and the river, in the direction of Shepherdstown. The bluff rises almost perpendicularly and for some distance is scarped to give passage for the road. Boteler's Mill is about 350 yards above the ford, and beyond it, along the lower face of the bluff and on the right of the road, were several kilns or arches for the burning of cement, of which the bluff furnished excellent material. The road to Shepherdstown passed over the kilns, the bluff still continuing to rise precipitately as it passes over, and another road passes down from the northern extremity of the bluff and in front of the kilns. A member of the 118th Pennsylvania writes, "The dam-breast, some ten feet wide, had been long neglected, many of the planks had rotted away or been removed, and water trickled through numerous crevices. The outer face, sloping to its base, was covered with a slippery green slime. On the Virginia side, some twenty feet had been left for a fish-way, through which flowed a rapid current. The river was low, and the fish-way easily fordable."[6]

The operations of Sykes's two brigades were conducted on the Charlestown Road and south of Boteler's Mill, those of Barnes's brigade on the high bluff running north from the mill. The 118th Pennsylvania followed the 25th and 13th New York in crossing and was ordered to follow these two regiments and, Barnes says, "to take a similar position below the top of the ridge and to their left."[7] On the left of the 118th Pennsylvania, the 1st Michigan, 2d Maine, and 22d Massachusetts joined the 18th Massachusetts. Skirmishers were thrown forward, who immediately began firing upon those of the enemy, who had by this time advanced within musket range and were deployed along their whole front in large numbers and at very short intervals. At first Barnes was informed that the enemy were advancing upon the left of the position held by his brigade. It was, however, soon perceived that the Confederates were not only approaching with a greatly superior force from that direction, but that they were also, in equal numbers, advancing in his front and on his right. "Springing as it were from the bushes and corn-fields which had concealed them to this time, and making their first appearance within short musket range, a rapid and vigorous fire commenced immediately, and, notwithstanding the vastly superior numbers of the enemy, every man stood his ground firmly."[8]

The attacking force was A. P. Hill's Division. When Lee heard that Griffin had crossed the river on the evening of the nineteenth and received Pendleton's alarming reports that much of the reserve artillery had been captured and that the Union cavalry were in Shepherdstown, he suspended his movement on Williamsport and returned to Shepherdstown "with the intention of driving the enemy back if not in position with his whole army." (If McClellan was there "in full force," Lee thought "an attack would be inadvisable," and would instead "make other dispositions.")[9] Accordingly, Longstreet was left in bivouac and Jackson was turned back toward Shepherdstown "to rectify occurrences in that quarter."[10]

On the evening of the nineteenth, Jackson moved on the road leading to Martinsburg and early on the twentieth ordered A. P. Hill and Early, who had bivouacked about five miles from Shepherdstown Ford, to return and drive into the river some brigades that had been reported as having crossed and captured some artillery. Hill led the advance at half past six o'clock and as he approached the river by the Charlestown Road threw out a skirmish line. About one and a half miles from the ford, it came in contact with Lovell's skirmishers, upon which Hill formed his division in a woods in two lines, the first composed of the brigades of Thomas, Gregg, and Pender (in order from right to left) under the command of General Gregg, and the second line of Brockenbrough, Branch (under Colonel Lane), and Archer (in order from right to left) under General Archer. Early, with his own brigade and those of Trimble and Hays, took position in a wood on the right and left of the road as a support to Hill. The Union artillery was seen on the opposite heights of the Potomac. A. P. Hill's Division, preceded

4 James Barnes to Francis S. Earle, September 25, 1862, reprinted in OR, vol. 19, pt. 1, 346.
5 George Sykes to Fitz John Porter, September 20, 1862, 9:15 a.m., reprinted in OR, vol. 19, pt. 2, 334–35.
6 [John L. Smith], Antietam to Appomattox with the 118th Penna. Vols., Corn Exchange Regiment (Philadelphia: J. L. Smith, 1892), 54–55.
7 Barnes to Earle, 346.
8 Ibid., 347.
9 Robert E. Lee to Jefferson Davis, September 20, 1862, reprinted in OR, vol. 19, pt. 1, 142.
10 Lee to Davis, September 21, 1862, reprinted in OR, vol. 19, pt. 1, 142.

by a heavy line of skirmishers, advanced. Lovell's men slowly retired to the heights near the ford, and Hill's men now came under a very heavy fire of shot and shell from the batteries across the river. He saw the Union infantry on the bluff and south of it and made a short halt to rectify his lines, but his skirmishers advanced and became severely engaged.

Meanwhile, writes Sykes, "Knowing that the Virginia side of the river was no place for troops until a proper reconnaissance had been made, and several reports from citizens inducing the belief that a large force of the enemy was moving upon us, I expressed my opinion to General Porter, who … directed the immediate recrossing of the troops."[11] Skirmishers were left on the line, the batteries of Weed, Randol, and Van Reed kept up a heavy fire, and Lovell and Warren effected their crossing in excellent order and without loss. Warren, on regaining the Maryland side, threw his two regiments behind the embankment of the canal. The 1st U.S. Sharpshooters were on the right and assisted the other troops to recross by keeping up a fire upon such of the Confederate infantry as appeared on the riverbank opposite. The loss in the two brigades was trifling (one killed and eight wounded), but Barnes was not so fortunate.

While Sykes was withdrawing his two brigades, the skirmishing was growing more severe on Barnes's line, and the Union batteries across the river opened a heavy fire, some of which fell short, struck in his ranks, and inflicted some casualties. All his regiments, save one, were under cover and suffered slight loss from the enemy's fire in front. To this one regiment—the 118th Pennsylvania—we now confine our attention.

The regiment (as we have seen) was ordered to follow the 25th and 13th New York and form on their left. It passed Boteler's Mill and the cement kilns at the foot of the bluff, and as the head of the regiment approached a ravine or glen on the left, by which a path led to the summit, a staff officer dashed up and reported the enemy approaching in heavy force. Barnes, who was riding with Colonel Prevost, asked if he could get his regiment onto the bluff. Prevost, replying that he would try, dismounted and led his column into a narrow, unfrequented path that led from the ravine to the summit, and Barnes rode back to the left of his brigade. As the head of the column reached the summit, it saw before it open country for a mile or more, with occasional cornfields; then the fields changed to forests, and a wide belt of timber skirted the open lands. Farmhouses, barns, and haystacks dotted the plain, and to the right in the distance were the roofs and spires of Shepherdstown. But the beauty of the landscape did not impress them so much as did the musket barrels of A. P. Hill's Division gleaming and glistening in the sunlight in their front, and to the right, "not half a mile away, a whole brigade was sweeping down with steady tread, its skirmishers well in advance, moving with firm front; and ere the head of the regimental column had scarce appeared upon the bluff, they opened a desultory straggling fire." As his men came up Provost brought them by file into line, and Company E, with Lieutenants John V. Hunterson and Samuel N. Lewis, was deployed as a skirmish line. Advancing but a short distance, it was soon severely engaged, and, unable to resist the heavy pressure, very shortly fell back upon the main line.[12]

The time at which the regiment reached the summit of the bluff is fixed by Major George L. Andrews of the 17th U.S. Infantry (Lovell's brigade), which was the last of that brigade to retire. He was on the right of his brigade, under the crest of the southern extremity of the bluff on the Charlestown Road, shut off from view of the rest of the brigade. Hearing that it was falling back, he went to the top of the hill and "noticed a line of battle of our own troops rise as it were out of the ground to my right." He immediately received orders to recross the river.[13] At about the same time, Barnes, who was with the left of his brigade, saw that Lovell and Warren on his left were retiring and had nearly reached the foot of the hill, when he received orders to return in good order and to cross the river. Barnes gave orders to the four regiments on the left of the 118th Pennsylvania to fall back and recross the river (which was quickly done, with small loss), dispatched Lieutenant W. S. Davis of his staff up the road to recall the 25th and 13th New York, and sent an orderly to recall the 118th Pennsylvania. As Davis passed to the right on his mission to recall the two New York regiments he observed that the 118th Pennsylvania was making no movement to withdraw but actually becoming engaged, and he called up the ravine to an officer nearest him to tell Colonel Provost that Barnes's orders were to withdraw his regiment at once. The word was passed to Provost, who had by this time only the right wing of his regiment up the bluff and in position, but he refused to receive an order received in that way, saying, "If Colonel Barnes has any order to give me, let his aid come to me," and he continued to conduct the formation of the regiment.[14] Davis recalled the 13th and 25th New York from the right, and these two regiments retired and crossed the river with a loss of a few wounded, but the orderly sent by Barnes to recall the Pennsylvania regiment did not reach it. It was now alone on the bluff to receive the attack of A. P. Hill's Division.

[11] Sykes to Fred T. Locke, September 30, 1862, reprinted in *OR*, vol. 19, pt. 1, 352.

[12] [Smith], 59–60.

[13] George L. Andrews to Ephraim E. Sellers, September 24, 1862, reprinted in *OR*, vol. 19, pt. 1, 366.

[14] [Smith], 60–61.

In his official report, Barnes states that he ordered the regiment to a position "below the top of the ridge" and that it "advanced it the excitement of the contest from the cover of the ridge."[15] Lieutenant Colonel James Gwyn of the 118th Pennsylvania says it was ordered to "form line of battle on the top of a bluff, and under cover."[16] It was a new regiment, but a few days in service, and crossed the river with 737 officers and men, all of most excellent material but with no experience, and to this fact must be attributed part of the hard fate that befell it. Owing to the nature of the ground, the regiment, in reaching the summit of the bluff, came in line in right by file. Seven companies only had formed line under partial cover when firing was heard on the right flank; two companies on the right were refused to meet it. The other companies had now come up, and Prevost ordered an advance to the crest of the hill. The enemy were seen advancing in heavy force in front and on the left. Provost now led the three left companies to meet the movement on the left, to a knoll on the left of the regiment. These became almost immediately engaged, and about the same time the right was fired on from a heavy force in front and by Colonel Gwyn's orders began firing by file. The engagement was now general along the whole line, this one regiment contending at close quarters with four brigades of A. P. Hill's Division.

Hill's advance along the Charlestown Road was not seriously opposed by Lovell (who fell back before it), but the fire from the Union batteries across the river is described in some of the Confederate reports as the most terrific ever witnessed, tearing great gaps in the ranks, particularly in Gregg's Brigade. Thomas's, on the right, and a part of Gregg's quickly drove back the skirmishers that Lovell had deployed to cover his retreat across the river, and advanced to the high ground covering the ford but did not venture near it, as the artillery fire and that of the sharpshooters on the Maryland shore was very active and very accurate. Pender's Brigade, on Hill's left, became very hotly engaged with Barnes's skirmishers and then with those of the 118th Pennsylvania. Believing that his left was threatened (when he saw the 118th advance), Pender informed Archer of the supposed danger, and that officer promptly moved by the left flank. The left regiment of Archer's Brigade (as soon as it was unmasked by Pender) and the other regiments (as soon as unmasked by the preceding ones) went in on the double-quick and, coming up on Pender's left, opened fire. The Pennsylvanians were poorly armed with Enfield rifles, many of which could not be discharged.[17] Their line began to waiver, when Provost, seizing the colors, advanced and was almost immediately wounded severely in the shoulder and compelled to leave the field. The regiment fell back in some disorder to the position where it had formed and a total rout seemed imminent, when Gwyn, with the assistance of Major Charles P. Herring, succeeded in rallying about two hundred men and charged over the slope of the hill in front. A heavy fire was poured into his left; the enemy was still advancing on his front and extending beyond his right. Captains Courtland Saunders and Joseph W. Ricketts and Lieutenant Joseph M. Moss Jr. were killed, many others were killed or wounded, and Gwyn fell back under the brow of the hill and re-formed his remnants with the intention of repeating the charge. At this moment a regiment of the enemy, with colors displayed, crowned the hill on the left and opened fire. Gwyn ordered a fire in response and was directing it when adjutant James P. Perot came up with an order which had been sent by Barnes that the regiment was to be withdrawn and cross the river, as both the right and left flanks had been turned. (Its left was completely turned, and Branch's and Brockenbrough's Brigades, following the movements of Archer, had extended Hill's line far to the right, and commanded the ravine by which the regiment had reached its position.) Hill's line of five brigades was now advancing. The only line of retreat was over the precipitous bluff. Orders were given to get into the road and retreat across the river. The loss had already been very heavy, and the historian of the regiment says that the scene following the order almost beggars description, the men breaking in wild confusion for the river.[18] Perot remained almost alone upon the bluff, firing his pistol at the enemy, and was severely wounded and taken prisoner. The greater part of the regiment made furiously for the ravine, down which they dashed precipitately. Since the march up, a tree, in a way never accounted for, had fallen across the path. This materially obstructed the retreat. Over and under it, the now thoroughly demoralized crowd jostled and pushed each other, whilst, meanwhile, the enemy, having reached the edge of the bluff, poured upon them a fatal and disastrous plunging fire. The slaughter was fearful; men were shot as they climbed over the tree, and their bodies, suspended from the branches, were clearly visible from the other side of the river. Others, who avoided the route by the ravine, driven headlong over the bluff, were seriously injured or killed outright.

A. P. Hill reports that the final charge on the regiment was made by the brigades of Pender and Archer and "the enemy driven pell-mell into the river. Then commenced the most terrible slaughter that this war has yet witnessed."[19] The plateau on the bluff was very much exposed to the fire of the Union guns, and Hill drew back the greater part of his men, but the

---

[15] Barnes to Earle, 346–47.

[16] James Gwyn to W. S. Davis, September 30, 1862, reprinted in OR, vol. 19, pt. 1, 348.

[17] Gwyn reports that the 118th Pennsylvania had been issued "condemned" rifles, not more than half of which were capable of being discharged. Gwyn to Davis, 348.

[18] [Smith], 66–67.

[19] Ambrose P. Hill to Charles J. Faulkner, February 25, 1863, reprinted in OR, vol. 19, pt. 1, 982.

22d North Carolina of Pender's Brigade and detachments from other commands crept close to the edge of the bluff and kept up a fire upon those in the road and upon those who were struggling in the water to escape. The historian of the 118th Pennsylvania writes:

> An old abandoned mill stood upon the ford road, at the base of the cliff. It completely commanded the ford and the dam-breast. When the last of the fugitives had disappeared from the bluff, the enemy crowded the doors, windows and roof and poured their relentless, persecuting fire upon those who had taken to the water. Numbers, observing the telling effect of the fire upon those who had essayed to the venture of crossing, huddled together and crowded each other in the arches at the base of the bluff; whilst others, hoping to escape the fatal effect of the avenging bullets, took to deeper water and crossed where the stream was deep enough to cover the entire body and leave the head alone exposed …
>
> At this moment a battery from the Maryland side opened heavily. The practice was shameful. The fuses, too short, sent the terrible missiles into the disorganized mass fleeing in disorder before the serious punishment of the enemy's musketry. It was a painful ordeal, to be met in their effort to escape an impending peril by another equally terrible. Shell after shell, as if directly aimed, went thundering into the arches, bursting and tearing to pieces ten or twelve of those who had crowded there for cover. A cry and wail of horror went up, plainly heard above the din and roar of battle. Waiving handkerchiefs fixed to ramrods, they endeavored by their signals to warn the gunners to desist, but to no avail; the fatal work continued. Hoping for better treatment, numbers turned with their white insignia of truce towards the enemy and, again ascending to the hill-top, surrendered …
>
> The dam-breast was still crowded, and here and there across it were the dead, wounded and dying. As the last of the survivors were nearing the Maryland shore, Berdan's [1st U.S.] Sharpshooters appeared. Deploying hurriedly in the bed of the canal, shouting loudly to those still exposed to seek what cover they could, they opened vigorously with their usual unerring and effective aim and soon almost entirely cleared the other bank. Those who had not yet fully accomplished the entire journey across were thus enabled to complete it in comparative safety.[20]

Lieutenant J. Rudhall White was killed as he touched the Maryland shore.[21]

In this disastrous affair, the 118th Pennsylvania lost 63 killed, 101 wounded, and 105 missing—an aggregate of 269;[22] the loss in the entire brigade was 317 killed, wounded, and missing.[23] This was bad enough, but scarcely justifying Hill's extravagant report: "The broad surface of the Potomac was blue with the floating bodies of our foe. But few escaped to tell the tale. By their own account they lost 3,000 men, killed and drowned, from one brigade alone." However, we readily accept Hill's statement that it "was a wholesome lesson to the enemy, and taught them to know that it may be dangerous sometimes to press a retreating army." Hill's loss was 30 killed and 231 wounded[24]—exceeding by 70 that of the Union killed, drowned, and wounded. After the engagement Hill and Early marched from the field and joined the main body of the army, which bivouacked that night on the Opequon near Martinsburg. Robertson's Brigade remained at the ford, observing the Union army.

The Union loss at Shepherdstown Ford on the nineteenth and twentieth was 71 killed, 161 wounded, and 131 missing—an aggregate of 363.[25] The Confederate losses were: A. P. Hill's Division, 30 killed and 231 wounded; Ewell's Division, 9 wounded;[26] Armistead's Brigade, 8 wounded;[27] artillery, 3 killed and 4 wounded[28]—an aggregate of 33 killed and 252 wounded.

Before crossing the Potomac on the nineteenth, Lee, in order to threaten McClellan's right and rear and make him apprehensive for his communications (and thus prevent pursuit), sent Hampton's Brigade up the Virginia side of the Potomac to cross over at Williamsport and put his army in motion for the same point, with the intention of crossing the river and

20 [Smith], 67–69.
21 Ibid., 70.
22 "Return of Casualties in the Union forces in the skirmishes at Sharpsburg, Shepherdstown Ford, and near Williamsport Md., September 19, action near Shepherdstown Va., September 20, 1862, and general summary for the campaign," OR, vol. 19, pt. 1, 204.
23 Carman's source for the brigade total is not known. Barnes's after-action report gives the total as 326. Barnes to Earle, 348. Computing the the aggregate loss for the brigade out of the same return from whence Carman appears to have drawn his figures for the 118th Pennsylvania yields a sum of 321. "Return of Casualties in the Union forces," 204.
24 Hill to Faulkner, 982.
25 "Return of Casualties in the Union forces," 204.
26 Carman's source for this figure is not known. A return produced by the editors of the OR gives the total as eight. "Return of casualties in Ewell's division at Boteler's Ford, September 19, 1862," OR, vol. 19, pt. 1, 975.
27 Carman's source for this figure is not known.
28 William N. Pendleton to Lee, September 24, 1862, reprinted in OR, vol. 19, pt. 1, 834.

moving upon Hagerstown. Hampton crossed into Maryland at Mason's Ford and, on the afternoon of the nineteenth, joined Stuart at Williamsport. Stuart had preceded him and, with a part of the 12th Virginia Cavalry, dashed across the river, drove back a few pickets, and occupied the place. In this movement Stuart was supported and aided by a battalion of infantry under the command of Captain William W. Randolph of the 2d Virginia, a detachment of the 11th Georgia (and, possibly, Stuart says, "by small detachments of other regiments"), a section of the Salem Artillery, and a section of the 2d Company, Richmond Howitzers.[29] Hampton having joined him, Stuart moved out upon the ridges overlooking the town, and active demonstrations were made on the various roads. On the twentieth Hampton, in attempting to advance, was met by a part of Pleasonton's cavalry and Couch's division of infantry. Keeping up a bold front and skirmishing until dark, Stuart ordered his whole force to recross the river at night, which was done without loss.

---

[29] James E. B. Stuart to Robert H. Chilton, February 13, 1864, reprinted in *OR*, vol. 19, pt. 1, 820.

23

The Results of the Maryland Campaign[1]

The battle of Antietam on September 17 and the affair at Shepherdstown Ford on September 20 ended the two week Maryland campaign. The condition of Lee's troops demanded repose, and he marched to the Opequon near Martinsburg, from which position it was his desire "to threaten a passage into Maryland, to occupy the enemy on this frontier" and, if his purpose could not be accomplished, "draw them into the [Shenandoah] Valley," where he could attack them "to advantage."[2] Lee says that when he withdrew from Sharpsburg into Virginia, it was his intention to recross the Potomac at Williamsport and move upon Hagerstown, but the condition of the army prevented this.[3] Resting a few days on the Opequon and seeing that McClellan was not disposed to follow him on that line, he marched to Bunker Hill and Winchester, where on October 2 he issued the following address to his army:

> In reviewing the achievements of the army during the present campaign, the commanding general cannot withhold the expression of his admiration of the indomitable courage it has displayed in battle and its cheerful endurance of privation and hardship on the march. Since your great victories around Richmond, you have defeated the enemy at Cedar Mountain, expelled him from the Rappahanhock [sic], and, after a conflict of three days, utterly repulsed him on the plains of Manassas, and forced him to take shelter within the fortifications around his capital. Without halting for repose, you crossed the Potomac, stormed the heights of Harper's Ferry, made prisoners of more than 11,000 men, and captured upward of seventy-five pieces of artillery, all their small-arms, and other munitions of war. While one corps of the army was thus engaged, the other insured its success by arresting at Boonsborough the combined armies of the enemy, advancing under their favorite general to the relief of their beleaguered [sic] comrades. On the field of Sharpsburg, with less than one third his numbers, you resisted from daylight until dark the whole army of the enemy, and repulsed every attack along his entire front of more than 4 miles in extent. The whole of the following day you stood prepared to resume the conflict on the same ground, and retired next morning without molestation across the Potomac. Two attempts subsequently made by the enemy to follow you across the river have resulted in his complete discomfiture and being driven back with loss. Achievements such as these demanded much valor and patriotism. History records few examples of greater fortitude and endurance than this army has exhibited, and I am commissioned by the President to thank you in the name of the Confederate States for the undying fame you have won for their arms. Much as you have done, much more remains to be accomplished. The enemy again threatens with invasion, and to your tried valor and patriotism the country looks with confidence for deliverance and safety. Your past exploits give assurance that this confidence is not misplaced.[4]

McClellan considered that he was in no condition to follow Lee. He had moved from Washington with the single purpose of expelling Lee from Maryland and considered that purpose fully and finally accomplished by the battle of Antietam. He sums up the objects and results of the campaign:

> In the beginning of the month of September the safety of the National Capital was seriously endangered by the presence of a victorious enemy, who soon after crossed into Maryland and then directly threatened Washington and Baltimore, while they occupied the soil of a loyal State and threatened an invasion of Pennsylvania. The army of the Union, inferior in numbers, wearied by long marches, deficient in various supplies, worn out by numerous battles, the last of which had not been successful, first covered by its movements the important cities of Washington and Baltimore, then boldly attacked the victorious enemy in their chosen strong position and drove them back, with all their superiority of numbers, into the State of Virginia, thus saving the loyal States from invasion and rudely dispelling the rebel dreams of carrying the war into our country and subsisting upon our resources. Thirteen guns and

---

[1] In his original manuscript, Carman opens this chapter with tabular results of the losses on both sides for the entire Maryland campaign. These are presented herein as Appendices M and N.

[2] Robert E. Lee to Jefferson Davis, September 21, 1862, reprinted in *OR*, vol. 19, pt. 1, 143.

[3] Lee to Davis, September 25, 1862, reprinted in *OR*, vol. 19, pt. 2, 626.

[4] Headquarters Army of Northern Virginia, General Orders No. 116, October 2, 1862, reprinted in *OR*, vol. 19, pt. 2, 644–45.

thirty-nine colors, more than 15,000 stand of small-arms, and more than 6,000 prisoners were the trophies which attest the success of our arms.[5]

On November 7 McClellan was removed from command of the Army of the Potomac. In closing an elaborate report of its operations under his command, he paid it this just tribute:

I am devoutly grateful to God that my last campaign with this brave army was crowned with a victory which saved the nation from the greatest peril it had then undergone. I have not accomplished my purpose if, by this report, the Army of the Potomac is not placed high on the roll of the historic armies of the world. Its deeds ennoble the nation to which it belongs. Always ready for battle, always firm, steadfast, and trustworthy, I never called on it in vain; nor will the nation ever have cause to attribute its want of success, under myself or under other commanders, to any failure of patriotism or bravery in that noble body of American soldiers.

No man can justly charge upon any portion of that army, from the commanding general to the private, any lack of devotion to the service of the United States Government and to the cause of the Constitution and the Union. They have proved their fealty in much sorrow, suffering, danger, and through the very shadow of death. Their comrades, dead on all the fields where we fought, have scarcely more claim to the honor of a nation's reverence than the survivors to the justice of a nation's gratitude.[6]

The result of the Maryland campaign was satisfactory neither to the North nor the South. In the North there was great dissatisfaction at the loss of Harper's Ferry and its garrison (which was in no way the fault of McClellan), and this dissatisfaction was intensified by the indecisive result at Antietam and Lee's escape, when his army should have been destroyed. In the South there was criticism of Lee and disgust at the apathy of the people of Maryland. Lee himself was disappointed at the result. Fitzhugh Lee says, "General Lee's Maryland campaign was a failure. He added but few recruits to his army, lost ten thousand men, and fought a drawn battle, which for an invading army is not a success."[7] It was freely admitted that the campaign was both a political and military blunder. It accomplished no change in the political relations of Maryland, so confidently anticipated, and Lee's retreat across the Potomac "after sustaining a loss in battle he could not afford was the first serious damper upon the exuberant and well earned confidence in the invincible prowess of the Army of Northern Virginia." It opened the eyes of the South to the fact that Maryland was not disposed to unite her destinies with the Southern Confederacy, that her people were not disposed to throw off the "Northern yoke" and respond to Lee's noble appeal "in the right way,"[8] and that "the victories of Boonsboro and Sharpsburg, purchased with torrents of blood, have been rendered unprofitable in a military point of view."[9] Longstreet attributes the failure of the campaign to "the great mistake" in dividing the army: "If General Lee had kept his forces together, he could not have suffered defeat." He also admits that "at Sharpsburg was sprung the keystone of the arch upon which the Confederate cause rested."[10]

An accomplished historical critic has well said:

In entering upon the interpretation of the battle of Antietam we are constrained, more perhaps than in the case of any other action in the war, to look away from the mere phenomena of the field itself to those larger considerations in which its true significance is to be sought.

.... We must recall the overwhelming disasters that befel[l] Pope, the blows under which he reeled back from the Rapidan to the Potomac. We must conceive the utter demoralization into which the Union army had fallen in consequence of these untoward experiences of bad generalship, and reflect that only this panic-stricken mob stood between Washington and Lee's victorious legions. We must form to ourselves an image of the terror and dismay that overcame the Government, and the inexpressible humiliation brought home to the heart of the people of the North. We must take into account what fearful augment these sentiments received when it was known that Lee had actually passed the barrier of the Potomac and stood on the soil of the loyal States. We must estimate, not in the light of subsequent events but in the light of existing probabilities, how strong was the likelihood of a secessionist uprising in Maryland, should Lee be able to maintain himself north of the Potomac. We must remember the boldness and vigor of the Confederate movements in Maryland, and the prestige acquired by the capture of Harper's Ferry, with its twelve thousand men.

5 George B. McClellan to Lorenzo Thomas, October 15, 1862, reprinted in *OR*, vol. 19, pt. 1, 33.
6 McClellan to Thomas, August 4, 1863, reprinted in *OR*, vol. 19, pt. 1, 93–94.
7 Fitzhugh Lee, *General Lee* (New York: D. Appleton and Co., 1894), 215.
8 As of this writing, Carman's sources for these unattributed quotations have not been identified.
9 See Edward O. Lord, *History of the Ninth Regiment New Hampshire Volunteers in the War of the Rebellion* (Concord, N.H.: Republican Press Association, 1895), 138. According to Lord, the quotation comes from a September 23, 1862, issue of the *Petersburg Express* (an extant copy of which has not been located) and ends "... in a *material* point of view [emphasis added]."
10 James Longstreet, "The Invasion of Maryland," in *Battles and Leaders of the Civil War*, vol. 2 (New York: Century Co., 1887), 673–74.

Finally, we must add to all the images of dread and fear (vague indeed, and indefinable, but from that very circumstance, all the more powerful) raised in the public mind by the very thought of *invasion*. With these considerations as the data of a judgment, let the reader say of what and of how much was that sanguinary field decisive which saw the insurgent army, after being shattered in the conflict, compelled to abandon the invasion of the North, and with its arrogant assumptions of superior valor brought low, seek refuge behind the barrier of the Potomac.

Nor would it be beyond the warranty of sound reason if we should enlarge the scope of our induction by the reflection of what would have been the result upon the issue of the war, had McClellan suffered defeat at Antietam. It is very certain that had that fate befallen the Union army, there was nothing between Lee and Washington and Baltimore. And even had the national capital not fallen a prey to the Confederate advance, who shall say how different a reception Lee's ragged, hatless, and shoeless soldiers might have met in Eastern Maryland from that they experienced in the loyal section within which their maneuvers were circumscribed. It is not worth while now to discuss how far the mistakes of the national government gave a tinge of plausibility and a flavor of force to the Confederate commander's lofty recitation of the wrongs inflicted upon "down-trodden" Maryland. But imagine the language of Lee's proclamation, held not in the little city of Frederick, before the ordeal of battle, but in the great city of Baltimore, after a defeat of the Union army, and who would venture to forecast what under the circumstances might have been the ultimate upshot of the audacious foray? If the country was spared the experience of whatever of reality might have lain behind the curtain of contingency, it was because Antietam intervened to thrust aside that horror. And under whatever category the pedantry of military classification may range that action, it is very certain that to the present generation of men it can never appear otherwise than as a signal deliverance and a crowning victory.[11]

While Lee was marching northwards toward Pennsylvania, Lincoln made a "solemn vow" to God that if Lee was driven back he would issue the proclamation.[12] He gave the circumstances leading up to it to Francis B. Carpenter, who has preserved the statement:

"It had got to be," said he [Lincoln], "midsummer, 1862. Things had gone on from bad to worse, until I felt that we had reached the end of our rope on the plan of operations we had been pursuing; that we had about played our last card, and must change our tactics, or lose the game! I now determined upon the adoption of the emancipation policy; and, without consultation with, or the knowledge of the Cabinet, I prepared the original draft of the proclamation, and, after much anxious thought, called a Cabinet meeting upon the subject. This was the last of July, or the first part of the month of August, 1862." (The exact date he did not remember.) "This Cabinet meeting took place I think, upon a Saturday. All were present, excepting Mr. Blair, the Postmaster-General, who was absent at the opening of the discussion, but came in subsequently. I said to the Cabinet that I had resolved upon this step, and had not called them together to ask their advice, but to lay the subject-matter of a proclamation before them; suggestions as to which would be in order, after they had heard it read. Mr. Lovejoy," said he, "was in error when he informed you that it excited no comment, excepting on the part of Secretary Seward. Various suggestions were offered. Secretary Chase wished the language stronger in reference to the arming of the blacks. Mr. Blair, after he came in, deprecated the policy, on the ground that it would cost the Administration the fall elections. Nothing, however, was offered that I had not already fully anticipated and settled in my own mind, until Secretary Seward spoke. He said in substance: 'Mr. President, I approve of the proclamation, but I question the expediency of its issue at this juncture. The depression of the public mind, consequent upon our repeated reverses, is so great that I fear the effect of so important a step. It may be viewed as the last measure of an exhausted government, a cry for help; the government stretching forth its hands to Ethiopia, instead of Ethiopia stretching forth her hands to the government.' His idea," said the President, "was that it would be considered our last *shriek*, on the retreat." (This was his *precise* expression.) "'Now,' continued Mr. Seward, 'while I approve the measure, I suggest, sir, that you postpone its issue, until you can give it to the country supported by military success, instead of issuing it, as would be the case now, upon the greatest disasters of the war!'" Mr. Lincoln continued: "The wisdom of the view of the Secretary of State struck me with very great force. It was an aspect of the case that, in all my thoughts upon the subject, I had entirely overlooked. The result was that I put the draft of the proclamation aside, as you do your sketch for a picture, waiting for a victory. From time to time

---

[11] William Swinton, *The Twelve Decisive Battles of the War: A History of the Eastern and Western Campaigns, in Relation to the Actions That Decided Their Issue* (New York: Dick & Fitzgerald, 1867), 173–76.

[12] William O. Stoddard, *Abraham Lincoln: The Man and the War President; Showing His Growth, Training, and Special Fitness for His Work* (New York: Fords, Howard, & Hulbert, 1888), 334. In his original manuscript, Carman presents the second half of this sentence (everything after "Lincoln") as a direct quotation from Stoddard himself, but it is in fact a re-working of what, in the source material, appears as a first-person statement by Lincoln.

I added or changed a line, touching it up here and there, anxiously waiting the progress of events. Well, the next news we had was of Pope's disaster at Bull Run. Things looked darker than ever. Finally, came the week of the battle of Antietam. I determined to wait no longer. The news came, I think, on Wednesday, that the advantage was on our side. I was then staying at the Soldiers' Home (three miles out of Washington). Here I finished writing the second draft of the preliminary proclamation; came up on Saturday; called the Cabinet together to hear it, and it was published the following Monday."[13]

---

[13] F. B. Carpenter, *Six Months at the White House with Abraham Lincoln: The Story of a Picture* (New York: Hurd and Houghton, 1867), 20–23. In his original manuscript, Carman concludes this chapter by citing portions of three letters (without comment) between the British foreign secretary (Lord John Russell) and the prime minister (Viscount Palmerston). These appear herein as Appendix O.

24
Lincoln and McClellan

The outcome of the battle of Antietam was a disappointment to Abraham Lincoln, who expected much more than the mere expulsion of the Confederate army from Maryland. He felt that "the result was not commensurate with the efforts made and the resources employed."[1] McClellan, however, was well satisfied, and after going into camp near Sharpsburg he wrote his wife on September 20, "I feel that I have done all that can be asked in twice saving the country."[2] On the twenty-third he feared that Lee was about to cross the Potomac and attack him, thought that Sumner could hold Harper's Ferry until reinforced, and requested Halleck to dispense with troops around Washington and elsewhere and push them forward by rail to the army at Sharpsburg.[3] On the twenty-seventh he reported, "This army is not now in condition to undertake another campaign nor to bring on another battle, unless great advantages are offered by some mistake of the enemy or pressing military exigencies render it necessary." His present purpose was to act on the defensive against Lee's greatly larger army, and he again requested that other points be stripped to the lowest and more troops be sent to his army.[4]

Two days before he had written, "My plans are not easily given, for I really do not know whether I am to do as I choose or not. I shall keep on doing what seems best until brought up with a round turn … It is very doubtful whether I shall remain in the service after the rebels have left this vicinity. The President's late proclamation, the continuation of Stanton and Halleck in office, render it almost impossible for me to retain my commission and self-respect at the same time."[5] McClellan was opposed to emancipation, and when he saw Lincoln's proclamation in the *Baltimore Sun* he hurled the paper from him, exclaiming, "There! Look at that outrage! I shall resign to-morrow!" He made the same threat to several of his staff.[6] He would restore the Union and save slavery, and he was not in accord with the political views of those who, believing slavery the sole cause of the war, demanded immediate emancipation.

To one who carefully noted McClellan and his surroundings at this time, it was evident that he was subjected to a good deal of pressure by opponents of the administration to make him commit himself to them. He believed that the war would end in the abolition of slavery but feared the effects of haste and thought that the steps to that end should be conservatively careful and not extremely radical. He regarded the president as nearly right in his general views and political purposes but overcrowded by more radical men around him into steps that, as yet, were imprudent and extreme. A few days after the publication of the Emancipation Proclamation, Generals Cox, Burnside, and Cochrane were invited by McClellan to visit his headquarters and discuss with him the course he should pursue respecting it. He stated to the three generals that he was urged to put himself in open opposition to it not only by politicians but by army officers who were near to him, giving no names but intimating that they were of rank and influence, which gave weight to their advice. Knowing that these men were all friends of the administration, he sought their opinion whether he should say anything about the proclamation or maintain silence on the subject, for he assumed that they would oppose any hostile demonstrations on his part. (As for himself, he thought that the proclamation was premature.) His visitors were in accord in advising him that any declaration on his part against the proclamation would be a fatal error, and that any public utterance by him in his official character criticizing the civil policy of the administration would be properly regarded as a usurpation. McClellan intimated that this was his own opinion, but by way of showing how the matter was thrust at him by others said that people had assured him that the army was so devoted to him that they would, as one man, enforce any decision he should make as to any part of

---

[1] John G. Nicolay and John Hay, *Abraham Lincoln: A History,* vol. 6 (New York: Century Co., 1890), 146.

[2] George B. McClellan to Mary Ellen McClellan, September 20, 1862, 9:00 p.m., reprinted in *McClellan's Own Story: The War for the Union, the Soldiers Who Fought It, the Civilians Who Directed It, and His Relations to It and Them* (New York: Charles L. Webster & Co., 1887), 613.

[3] McClellan to Henry W. Halleck, September 23, 1862, 9:30 a.m., as contained in McClellan to Lorenzo Thomas, August 4, 1863, reprinted in *OR,* vol. 19, pt. 1, 70.

[4] McClellan to Halleck, September 27, 1862, 10:00 a.m., as contained in McClellan to Thomas, 70.

[5] McClellan to Mary Ellen McClellan, September 25, 1862, 7:30 a.m., reprinted in McClellan, *Own Story,* 615.

[6] Frank Abial Flower, *Edwin McMasters Stanton: The Autocrat of Rebellion, Emancipation, and Reconstruction* (Akron, Oh.: Saalfield Publishing Co., 1905), 193.

the war policy. Cox, who had already and quite clearly perceived that disloyal influences were at work at McClellan's head-quarters,[7] now said with some emphasis

that those who made such assurances were his worst enemies, and in my judgment knew much less of the army than they pretended; that our volunteer soldiers were citizens as well as soldiers, and were citizens more than soldiers; and that greatly as I knew them to be attached to him, I believed not a corporal's guard would stand by his side if he were to depart from the strict subordination of the military to the civil authority. Burnside and Cochrane both emphatically assented to this, and McClellan added that he heartily believed both that it was true and that it ought to be so. But this still left the question open whether the very fact that there was an agitation in camp on the subject, and intrigues of the sort I have mentioned, did not make it wise for him to say something which would show, at least, that he gave no countenance to any would-be revolutionists. We debated this at some length, with the general conclusion that it might be well for him to remind the army in general orders that whatever might be their rights as citizens, they must as soldiers beware of any organized effort to meddle with the functions of the civil government.[8]

Cochrane, who had been a frequent visitor at McClellan's headquarters and had heard him discuss political matters, and who himself was a radical anti-slavery Democrat, was so much and so favorably impressed with McClellan's advanced views as expressed on this occasion, and so well satisfied also that "the politicians were paltering with General McClellan, injuriously to himself and with danger to the country" for the purpose of carrying the fall elections, that he determined to bring about an understanding between McClellan and the administration. He was also convinced that the radicals wit-tingly misrepresented McClellan and that the general was ignorantly misunderstood by many men. He says, "It was needed that such a change should be made in the administration of the army as, attended with enlarged powers and increased responsibilities to General McClellan, would impress the public with the thorough accord between him and the President, in the principles of conducting the war. This result produced, and it was believed that the conservative interests, which adhered personally to McClellan, would be extricated from the skillfully-pitched toils of the political jugglers, and would quietly relapse into a vigorous support of the Administration and its friends."[9]

Halleck could be displaced, it was thought, without friction in any quarter. "His removal would be significant of noth-ing but a change; but to replace him with General McClellan, would modify events, and perhaps secure to the prosecution of the war that unanimity of support, which selfish machinations were endangering." Cochrane broached the subject to McClellan, and soon after he went to Washington with permission to repeat McClellan's views to those to whom he might address the project of a change in the chief military command.[10]

Other friends of McClellan in the army advised him to have nothing whatsoever to do with politics, among whom was General Franklin. General Smith, when he heard that McClellan had prepared a written protest against the proclamation, is said to have urged him not to put himself on record against it, that such action would be a fatal breach of discipline.[11] There were also friends outside of the army who would save McClellan from his own folly. One of these was William H. Aspinwall of New York, who visited McClellan about October 5, and of whom McClellan says, "Mr. Aspinwall is decidedly of the opinion that it is my duty to submit to the President's proclamation … I presume he is right … I shall surely give his views full consideration."[12]

Meanwhile, Major John J. Key, a brother of Colonel Key of McClellan's staff, came down from the army to Washington with a story current near headquarters that Union generals did not push the advantages they had on the Maryland cam-paign because it was not considered desirable to crush the rebellion at once, if indeed at all, but to so manage affairs as to secure a compromise. There were many who believed that the failure to finish the rebellion at Antietam was evidence of

---

[7] A few days after the battle of Antietam, McClellan invited a number of officers to attend religious services in the parlors of the house where headquarters were. General Cox attended and was standing by himself when a stout man in civilian dress entered and engaged him in con-versation laudatory of McClellan. He spoke of the politicians in Washington as wickedly trying to sacrifice McClellan and added, whisper-ing the words emphatically in Cox's ear, "But you military men have that matter in your own hands, you have but to tell the administration what they must do, and they will not dare to disregard it!" This roused Cox, who turned upon the stranger with a sharp demand of what he meant, upon which the latter, betraying by his look that he had mistaken Cox for another, moved away and was soon seen talking with one of McClellan's corps commanders. Cox says, "I was a good deal agitated, for though there was more or less current talk about disloyal influ-ences at work, I had been skeptical as to the fact, and to be brought face to face with that sort of a thing as a surprise." The stranger was John W. Garrett, president of the Baltimore and Ohio Railroad Company. Jacob D. Cox, *Military Reminiscences of the Civil War*, vol. 1 (New York: Charles Scribner's Sons, 1900), 358–59.—*EAC*

[8] Cox, 360–61.

[9] John Cochrane, *The War for the Union: Memoir of Gen. John Cochrane* (n.p., n.d.), 29–30.

[10] Ibid., 30.

[11] Nicolay and Hay, 180.

[12] McClellan to Mary Ellen McClellan, October 5, 1862, reprinted in *Own Story*, 655.

something more serious than military incompetence, and they were loud in the expression of their views. So when Major Key's confirmatory remarks were brought to Lincoln's attention, he made a personal investigation, of which the following is the record:

Executive Mansion
Washington, Sept. 26. 1862

Major John J. Key

Sir: I am informed that in answer to the question "Why was not the rebel army bagged immediately after the battle near Sharpsburg?'" propounded to you by Major Levi C. Turner, Judge Advocate &c. you answered "That is not the game" [*sic*] "The object is that neither army shall get much advantage of the other; that both shall be kept in the field till they are exhausted, when we will make a compromise and save slavery."

I shall be very happy if you will, within twentyfour [*sic*] hours from the receipt of this, prove to me by Major Turner, that you did not, either literally, or in substance, make the answer stated.

A. Lincoln

[Endorsements]

Copy delivered to Major Key at 10.25 A.M. September 27th. 1862.

John Hay

At about 11 o'clock, A.M. Sept. 27. 1862, Major Key and Major Turner appear before me. Major Turner says: "As I remember it, the conversation was, I asked the question why we did not bag them after the battle at Sharpsburg? Major Key's reply was that was not the game, that we should tire the rebels out, and ourselves, that that was the only way the Union could be preserved, we come together fraternally, and slavery be saved" [*sic*]

On cross-examination, Major Turner says he has frequently heard Major Key converse in regard to the present troubles, and never heard him utter a … sentiment unfavorable to the maintainance [*sic*] of the Union. He has never uttered anything which he Major T. would call disloyalty. The particular conversation detailed was a private one.

A. Lincoln

In my view it is wholly inadmissable [*sic*] for any gentleman holding a military commission from the United States to utter such sentiments as Major Key is within proved to have done. Therefore let Major John J. Key be forthwith dismissed from the Military service of the United States.[13]

A. Lincoln

Two months later, Lincoln wrote in answer to a missive from Key:

Dear Sir:

A bundle of letters including one from yourself, was, early last week, handed me by Gen. Halleck, as I understood, at your request. I sincerely sympathise [*sic*] with you in the death of your brave and noble son.

In regard to my dismissal of yourself from the military service, it seems to me you misunderstand me. I did not charge, or intend to charge you with disloyalty. I had been brought to fear that there was a class of officers in the army, not very inconsiderable in numbers, who were playing a game to not beat the enemy when they could, on some peculiar notion as to the proper way of saving the Union; and when you were proved to me, in your own presence, to have avowed yourself in favor of that "game," and did not attempt to controvert the proof, I dismissed you as an example and a warning to that supposed class. I bear you no ill will; and I regret that I could not have the example without wounding you personally. But can I now, in view of the public interest, restore you to the service, by which the army would understand that I indorse and approve that game myself? If there was any doubt of your having made the avowal, the case would be different. But when it was proved to me, in your presence, you did not deny or attempt to deny it, but confirmed it in my mind, by attempting to sustain the position by argument.

I am really sorry for the pain the case gives you, but I do not see how, consistently with duty, I can change it. Yours, &c.

A. Lincoln[14]

---

[13] Abraham Lincoln, "Record of Dismissal of John J. Key," September 26, 1862. A copy appears in Roy P. Basler, ed., *The Collected Works of Abraham Lincoln*, vol. 5 (New Brunswick, N.J.: Rutgers University Press, 1953), 442–43.

[14] Lincoln to John J. Key, November 24, 1862. A copy of this letter appears in Basler, vol. 5, 508.

[Endorsement]

The within, as appears, was written some time ago. On full re-consideration, I cannot find sufficient ground to change the conclusion therein arrived at.

A. Lincoln

Dec. 27. 1862[15]

Lincoln afterward said to John Hay, one of his secretaries, "I dismissed Major Key because I thought his silly, treasonable expressions were 'staff talk' and I wished to make an example."[16] To another he said that "if there was a 'game' ever among Union men" to have the army "not take an advantage of the enemy when it could, it was his intent to break up that game."[17]

On October 1 McClellan wrote to his wife, "I don't know where we are drifting, but do not like the looks of things; time will show … I do not yet know what are the military plans of the gigantic intellects at the head of the government."[18] The next day he heard that the president had arrived at Harper's Ferry on his way to visit the army, and he wrote, "His ostensible purpose is to see the troops and the battle-field; I incline to think that the real purpose of his visit is to push me into a premature advance into Virginia."[19]

Lincoln had become very impatient at the inaction of the army after the battle of Antietam. What he wanted and what the country demanded was a decisive victory in the field, important in a military point of view and indispensable politically, for the fall elections were now approaching. He felt that he must have another victory and a more decisive one than Antietam to allay political discontent and encourage a greater interest in the prosecution of the war. There were grave misgivings as to the loyalty of some officers of the Army of the Potomac, and there were rumors that the army itself was in a state of demoralization, partly on account of the proclamation of emancipation and partly from a want of confidence in the officers. To satisfy himself on these points and, by a personal interview with McClellan, incite the general to an honest effort to defeat Lee, he left Washington on October 1 and made a visit to the army at Antietam, by which he was warmly and enthusiastically received. The president reviewed the army and went through the camps, and as far as he could see it was fully armed and equipped and prepared to take the field. He urged McClellan to greater activity and tried to impress upon him the necessity for immediate movement. It was during this visit that he said, "General McClellan, if it had been possible for you to resume fighting the morning of the eighteenth, and you had captured or destroyed General Lee's army of Northern Virginia, the nation would never have ceased to sing your praises, and you would be my successor in 1865. I am not saying this complainingly, but I sincerely wish such a result might have been brought about."[20]

Lincoln returned by way of Frederick, Maryland, where on the fourth he made two speeches, one of which follows:

Fellow-Citizens: I see myself surrounded by soldiers, and a little further off I note the citizens of this good city of Frederick, anxious to hear something from me. I can only say, as I did five minutes ago, it is not proper for me to make speeches in my present position. I return thanks to our soldiers for the good service they have rendered, for the energies they have shown, the hardships they have endured, and the blood they have so nobly shed for this dear Union of ours; and I also return thanks not only to the soldiers, but to the good citizens of Maryland, and to all the good men and women in this land, for their devotion to our glorious cause. I say this without any malice in my heart to those who have done otherwise. May our children and our children's children to a thousand generations, continue to enjoy the benefits conferred upon us by a united country, and have cause yet to rejoice under those glorious institutions bequeathed us by Washington and his compeers. Now, my friends, soldiers and citizens, I can only say once more, farewell.[21]

The next day Lincoln returned to Washington, taking but little comfort from his visit to McClellan's headquarters yet much gratified and greatly encouraged at what he had seen of the army, which had received him with unbounded enthusiasm. The feeling exhibited by the Army of the Potomac toward the president was not lost upon McClellan. It opened his eyes to the fact that, as much as the men liked him, they loved their president more, and we believe that it was this, added

---

[15] Lincoln, "Endorsement Concerning John J. Key," December 27, 1862. A copy appears in Basler, vol. 6, 20.

[16] Nicolay and Hay, 188.

[17] Lincoln, "Record of Dismissal of John J. Key," 443. Carman's start to this sentence, "To another," suggests that the statement was made by Lincoln to a secretary other than Hay. However, according to the final paragraph of the "Record of Dismissal" (the original of which Basler states is written entirely in Lincoln's own hand), this statement was the "substance" of his reply to Key in their meeting. See Basler, vol. 5, 443 n. 1.

[18] McClellan to Mary Ellen McClellan, October 1, 1862, 7:30 a.m., reprinted in McClellan, Own Story, 617.

[19] McClellan to Mary Ellen McClellan, October 2, 1862, a.m. [hour not given], reprinted in McClellan, Own Story, 654.

[20] As of this writing, Carman's source for this quotation is not known.

[21] See "The President's Visit to the Army," New York Tribune, October 6, 1862.

to the advice of his true friends (and perhaps somewhat to the efforts then being made to bring harmony between him and the administration), that brought him to a final decision to issue the following:

General Orders,
No. 163.

Headquarters Army of the Potomac
Camp near Sharpsburg, Md., October 7, 1862

The attention of the officers and soldiers of the Army of the Potomac is called to General Orders, No. 139, War Department, September 24, 1862, publishing to the army the President's proclamation of September 22.

A proclamation of such grave moment to the nation, officially communicated to the army, affords to the general commanding an opportunity of defining specifically to the officers and soldiers under his command the relation borne by all persons in the military service of the United States toward the civil authorities of the Government.

The Constitution confides to the civil authorities—legislative, judicial, and executive—the power and duty of making, expounding, and executing the Federal laws. Armed forces are raised and supported simply to sustain the civil authorities, and are to be held in strict subordination thereto in all respects. This fundamental rule of our political system is essential to the security of our republican institutions, and should be thoroughly understood and observed by every soldier. The principle upon which, and the object for which, armies shall be employed in suppressing rebellion, must be determined and declared by the civil authorities, and the Chief Executive, who is charged with the administration of the national affairs, is the proper and only source through which the needs and orders of the Government can be made known to the armies of the nation.

Discussions by officers and soldiers concerning public measures determined upon and declared by the Government, when carried at all beyond temperate and respectful expressions of opinion, tend greatly to impair and destroy the discipline and efficiency of troops, by substituting the spirit of political faction for that firm, steady, and earnest support of the authority of the Government which is the highest duty of the American soldier. The remedy for political errors, if any are committed, is to be found only in the action of the people at the polls.

In thus calling the attention of this army to the true relation between the soldier and the Government, the general commanding merely adverts to an evil against which it has been thought advisable during our whole history to guard the armies of the Republic, and in so doing he will not be considered by any right-minded person as casting any reflection upon that loyalty and good conduct which has been so fully illustrated upon so many battle-fields.

In carrying out all measures of public policy, this army will, of course, be guided by the same rules of mercy and Christianity that have ever controlled its conduct toward the defenseless.

By command of Major-General McClellan:
Ja[me]s A. Hardie,
Lieutenant-Colonel, Aide-de-Camp, and Acting Assistant Adjutant-General[22]

On the morning of the day upon which McClellan issued his orders, Cochrane called on Secretary Chase at his home in Washington and discussed with him the condition of the army, the effect of its inactivity on the country, and "the danger to be apprehended in the conduct of the war, from an expression by the approaching elections in New York and Pennsylvania, of a want of confidence in the administration, and proposed to counteract the malign influences that were bitterly opposing the Administration." Cochrane recommended restoring McClellan to his former position as commander-in-chief of the army, thus displacing Halleck. When Chase objected because of McClellan's views on the slavery question, Cochrane repeated to him what McClellan had said to him and Cox on that subject, upon which Chase said, "Under your assurances, I will accede to the proposal; for no man should suffer personal contention to impede the performance of a public duty. The country's necessities are great, and I will not indulge private inclinations in the selection of the instrument most effective to relieve them ... I will co-operate with his friends in the effort to reinstate him at the head of the armies."[23]

Chase says that he and Cochrane conversed freely about McClellan and that Cochrane

said McClellan would like to retire from active command, if he could do so without disgrace—which could be accomplished, and a more active general secured, by restoring him to the chief command ...

I explained frankly my relations to McClellan—my original admiration and confidence—my disappointment in his inactivity and irresolution—my loss of confidence and conviction that another general should replace him—my constant endeavor to support him by supplies and reinforcements, notwithstanding my distrust, when the President determined to keep him in command—my present belief that I had not judged incorrectly, but my entire willingness

[22] Headquarters Army of the Potomac, General Orders No. 163, October 7, 1862, as contained in McClellan to Lincoln, October 7, 1862, reprinted in OR, vol. 19, pt. 2, 395–96.
[23] Cochrane, 30–31.

also to receive any correction which facts would warrant; and my absolute freedom from personal ill-will, and my entire willingness to do anything which would insure the earliest possible suppression of the rebellion ...

He said he would talk to McClellan, and write me. I answered that I should be glad to hear from him, and was quite willing he should repeat to McClellan what I had said.[24]

On this same day, Aspinwall, who had advised McClellan to submit to the president's proclamation, dined with Chase, spoke of his visit to McClellan, and seemed greatly to desire the secretary's cooperation with the general.[25]

In the evening Cochrane visited the president at the Soldiers' Home and found him so much depressed by the difficulties which beset him that his nights were sleepless. When Cochrane presented to him the matter of McClellan's re-assignment to the chief command, Lincoln "answered that the plan had occurred to him, and that it might, perhaps, supply the proper relief for the troubles [they] were enduring and avert the dangers which menaced. He apprehended no serious inconvenience from the loss of General Halleck's services, ... supposed that a position could readily be found for him," and expressed a willingness to bring the subject to the attention of the cabinet.[26] The secretary of war, when directly approached with an intimation that whatever differences had existed between himself and McClellan could be arranged, declared that he desired no arrangement.

Upon his return to the army, Cochrane had an interview with McClellan, and then on October 10 wrote Chase that McClellan appreciated his support and would gladly communicate with him or see him, and that there was no substantial difference between them on the slavery question.[27] Chase replied to Cochrane on the eighteenth:

My indisposition has prevented me from much intercourse with other members of the Administration, so that I have not been able to ascertain the condition of opinion in relation to the measures you proposed to me.

It has of course been impossible for me to visit headquarters, nor do I think that it would be exactly delicate for me to do so without an invitation.

My judgment in respect to the course demanded by the public interests remains unchanged. No man can lament General McClellan's want of success more than I do. No man has labored more sincerely and earnestly to supply the means of success. No man would more sincerely rejoice if now, by a series of prompt and decisive movements, he might more than retrieve all he has lost in the judgments of sincere and judicious and patriotic men.

My longing and my prayer is ... for the salvation of the country. He whom God may honor as the instrument of its salvation, whoever he may be, shall be my hero. *Magnus mihi erit Apollo.* [He will be for me a great Apollo.]

General McClellan will remember my talks with him of a year ago—how I told him then of the necessity of sharp and decisive action to my ability to provide the means to carry on the war. By miracles almost I have been enabled to get on this far, notwithstanding our disasters. But the miracles cannot be repeated; and I see financial disaster imminent. I dare not say all I feel and fear. My hope is in the prompt and successful use of all the immense resources in men and means now provided.[28]

This letter was never forwarded to Cochrane,[29] but is here given to show the writer's feelings at the time. Negotiations had failed of the desired result. By this time the October elections had occurred, resulting in serious reverses to the administration. Much of the blame for these reverses was laid upon the president for his not dismissing McClellan from command. There was a renewal of the great and intense pressure for his immediate removal not only to save the remaining states, whose elections would take place in November, but to save the country and crush the rebellion. These influences could not be entirely disregarded; they certainly must be considered as being of sufficient weight to prevent McClellan's promotion. Cochrane, who had conducted the negotiations, says the reasons for his failure were never clearly revealed, but supposes that "the delay which continued to detain the Army of the Potomac in its Maryland encampment, and which the President had interposed his own authority to terminate, had at last exasperated the Cabinet beyond any prudential consideration of elections and their results."[30]

---

[24] Robert B. Warden, *An Account of the Private Life and Public Services of Salmon Portland Chase* (Cincinnati: Wilstach, Baldwin & Co., 1874), 499–500.

[25] Ibid., 501.

[26] Cochrane, 31–32.

[27] Warden, 505.

[28] Salmon P. Chase to Cochrane, October 18, 1862, quoted in J. W. Schuckers, *The Life of and Public Services of Salmon Portland Chase, United States Senator and Governor of Ohio; Secretary of the Treasury, and Chief-Justice of the United States* (New York: D. Appleton and Co., 1874), 457.

[29] Cochrane, 32.

[30] Ibid., 33.

During his visit to the army, Lincoln had told McClellan of the general's great over-cautiousness, intimated very plainly that he should insist upon a vigorous prosecution of the campaign against Lee, and discussed with him plans of advance, urging McClellan to operate upon Lee's communications by marching south on the east side of the Blue Ridge. The president was not inclined to force a movement before the army was ready, yet "saw no reason why it should take longer to get ready after Antietam than after Pope's last battle."[31] Nor during his visit had he seen anything that in his opinion should delay the movement longer, so upon his return to Washington he directed the following order:

Washington, D.C., October 6, 1862

Major-General McClellan:

I am instructed to telegraph you as follows: The President directs that you cross the Potomac and give battle to the enemy or drive him south. Your army must move now while the roads are good. If you cross the river between the enemy and Washington, and cover the latter by your line of operations, you can be re-enforced with 30,000 men. If you move up the Valley of the Shenandoah, not more than 12,000 or 15,000 can be sent to you. The President advises the interior line, between Washington and the enemy, but does not order it. He is very desirous that your army move as soon as possible. You will immediately report what line you adopt and when you intend to cross the river; also to what point the re-enforcements are to be sent. It is necessary that the plan of your operations be positively determined on before orders are given for building bridges and repairing railroads.

I am directed to add that the Secretary of War and the General-in-Chief fully concur with the President in these instructions.

H. W. Halleck,
General-in-Chief[32]

This was followed by a letter of Halleck's, written on October 7, in which McClellan was informed that every possible effort was being made to fill up the old regiments in his army, but that he must not delay his operations for more recruits; the army must move. "The country is becoming very impatient at the want of activity of your army, and we must push it on." Halleck was satisfied that the enemy were falling back to Richmond, and the army must follow and punish them. He sharply criticized McClellan's inactivity by saying, "There is a decided want of legs in our troops … They are not sufficiently exercised in marching; they lie still in camp too long … They are not sufficiently exercised to make them good and efficient soldiers."[33] On the same day, he said in a private letter, "Everything would now be satisfactory if I could only get General McClellan to move. He has now lain still *twenty days* since the battle of Antietam, and I cannot persuade him to advance an inch. It puts me out of all patience."[34] To Brigadier General John M. Schofield in St. Louis, Missouri, Halleck wrote, "The famous Army of the Potomac is demoralized and without discipline … You will ask the cause of this. I cannot answer. Probably several causes combined … One thing I think is certain: The rabid Abolitionists and Northern Democrats of secession proclivities have done all in their power to weaken and embarrass the administration and at the same time to discourage and demoralize the Army. We are now reaping the fruits of their accursed work."[35]

It is a just criticism upon Halleck that as general-in-chief he failed to decide upon which line the army should move, and that he did not even express an opinion as to the relative merit of the two lines mentioned in the president's directions of the sixth, wherein the president had advised the interior line, between Washington and the enemy. McClellan, however, in his usual spirit of perversity, decided against Lincoln's suggestion, writing Halleck on the seventh that he had received the president's order and not an hour should be lost in carrying it into effect. He had determined to adopt the line of the Shenandoah for immediate operations against the enemy, then near Winchester, as on no other line north of Washington could the army be supplied and at the same time cover Maryland and Pennsylvania. He saw no objective point of strategic value to be gained by a movement between the Shenandoah and Washington; the line of the Shenandoah was unimportant for ulterior objects and important only so long as the enemy remained at Winchester.[36]

But McClellan did not move. He began a campaign of correspondence with the War Department. He wanted shoes and clothing for the men. He wanted shoes for his horses. He wanted more men and more horses. In fact, he was not prepared to take the field. It was about this time, when the president was becoming impatient at McClellan's slow movements, that he

---

[31] Cox, 371.

[32] Halleck to McClellan, October 6, 1862, reprinted in *OR*, vol. 19, pt. 1, 10–11.

[33] Halleck to McClellan, October 7, 1862, reprinted in *OR*, vol. 19, pt. 2, 395.

[34] Halleck to Elizabeth Halleck, October 7, 1862, reprinted in James Grant Wilson, "Types and Traditions of the Old Army: II. General Halleck—A Memoir," *Journal of the Military Service Institution of the United States* 36, no. 135 (May–June 1905): 559.

[35] Halleck to John M. Schofield, September 20, 1862, reprinted in *OR*, vol. 13, 654.

[36] McClellan to Halleck, October 7, 1862, 1:00 p.m., reprinted in *OR*, vol. 19, pt. 1, 11.

said to a friend of McClellan's who called at the White House (and doubtless with the expectation that it would be repeated), "McClellan's tardiness reminds me of a man in Illinois, whose attorney was not sufficiently aggressive. The client knew a few law phrases, and finally, after waiting until his patience was exhausted by the non-action of his counsel, he sprang to his feet and exclaimed: 'Why don't you go at him with a Fi Fa, demurrer, a *capias*, a *surrebutter* or a *ne exeat*, or something; and not stand there like a *nudum pactum*, or a *non est*?'"[37]

The monotony of camp life in the Army of the Potomac was now broken by a daring Confederate cavalry raid. During the night of October 10, Stuart, at the head of 1,800 selected troopers, crossed the Potomac above Williamsport, went through Chambersburg, Pennsylvania, and despite all efforts to head him off made a circuit in rear and entirely around McClellan's army, recrossing the Potomac near the mouth of the Monocacy on the twelfth, after capturing many horses, destroying much property, and paroling some prisoners. A few days after this raid, Lincoln was returning on a steamer from a review near Alexandria, and somebody remarked, "What about McClellan?" Without looking at his questioner the president drew a ring on the deck with a stick or umbrella and said, "When I was a boy we used to play a game, three times round and out. Stuart has been round him twice; if he goes round him once more, gentlemen, McClellan will be out!"[38]

In making a report to Halleck of Stuart's raid, McClellan called attention to the fact that he needed an increase in his cavalry force to watch the various crossings of the Potomac,[39] to which Halleck replied on the fourteenth, "The President has read your telegram, and directs me to suggest that, if the enemy had more occupation south of the river, his cavalry would not be so likely to make raids north of it."[40] McClellan continued to insist that his cavalry should be increased; he wanted more supplies of every kind. Meanwhile, the fine autumn weather was slipping away. There was discontent in the cabinet and in the country. There was intense and growing impatience at the inactivity of the Army of the Potomac and bitter criticism of the political views of its commander. The result of the October elections plainly showed that the people were, for one reason and another, getting weary of the contest. To reassure these and convince others that there was a prospect of the end of the war, writes James Ford Rhodes, "and to guard against an interference of France and England, who were eager to get cotton, Lincoln felt that he had great need of victories in the field."[41] Believing that the army could win a further victory, Lincoln determined to have McClellan break up his camp in Maryland and seek the army under Lee, and he pointed the way for the movement. He had sent for Vice President Hannibal Hamlin immediately following the Stuart raid, and together they discussed McClellan and the state of military and political affairs. Lincoln was worried over the military situation and the development of the McClellan problem into a political issue. He was disposed to be fair and patient with McClellan and, although he had numerous provocations to remove him, he would not take the last step until he felt sure that he was absolutely justified in the minds of his advisers and the Northern people. Hamlin maintained that McClellan's usefulness had gone, that he would not act vigorously, that he had meddled in politics, and that his removal was not only justified but demanded. Lincoln agreed substantially with Hamlin that, after his delays and his foolish propensity to meddle in politics, there was little guarantee that McClellan would now act with vigor and success. Still, he felt that in all fairness he should give him one more chance.[42] He showed Hamlin the letter that he had prepared, in which he had appealed to McClellan's sense of manliness to go forward:

Executive Mansion
Washington, D.C., October 13, 1862

Major-General McClellan:

My Dear Sir: You remember my speaking to you of what I called your overcautiousness. Are you not overcautious when you assume that you cannot do what the enemy is constantly doing? Should you not claim to be at least his equal in prowess, and act upon the claim? As I understand, you telegraphed General Halleck that you cannot subsist your army at Winchester unless the railroad from Harper's Ferry to that point be put in working order. But the enemy does now subsist his army at Winchester, at a distance nearly twice as great from railroad transportation as you would have to do, without the railroad last named. He now wagons from Culpeper Court-House, which is just about twice as far as you would have to do from Harper's Ferry. He is certainly not more than half as well provided with wagons as you are. I certainly should be pleased for you to have the advantage of the railroad from Harper's Ferry to Winchester, but it wastes all the remainder of autumn to give it to you, and in fact ignores the question of time, which cannot

---

[37] Isaac N. Arnold, *The Life of Abraham Lincoln* (Chicago: Jansen, McClurg, & Co., 1885), 297.

[38] Richard B. Irwin, "Washington Under Banks," in *Battles and Leaders of the Civil War*, vol. 2 (New York: Century Co., 1887), 544.

[39] McClellan to Halleck, October 13, 1862, 7:00 p.m., reprinted in *OR*, vol. 19, pt. 2, 417.

[40] Halleck to McClellan, October 14, 1862, reprinted in *OR*, vol. 19, pt. 2, 421 (first message).

[41] James Ford Rhodes, *History of the United States from the Compromise of 1850*, vol. 4 (New York: Harper & Brothers Publishers, 1899), 186.

[42] Charles Eugene Hamlin, *The Life and Times of Hannibal Hamlin* (Cambridge, Mass.: Riverside Press, 1899), 442–43.

and must not be ignored. Again, one of the standard maxims of war, as you know, is to "operate upon the enemy's communications as much as possible without exposing your own." You seem to act as if this applies against you, but cannot apply in your favor. Change positions with the enemy, and think you not he would break your communication with Richmond within the next twenty-four hours? You dread his going into Pennsylvania, but if he does so in full force, he gives up his communications to you absolutely, and you have nothing to do but to follow and ruin him. If he does so with less than full force, fall upon and beat what is left behind all the easier. Exclusive of the water-line, you are now nearer Richmond than the enemy is by the route that you can and he must take. Why can you not reach there before him, unless you admit that he is more than your equal on a march? His route is the arc of a circle, while yours is the chord. The roads are as good on yours as on his. You know I desired, but did not order, you to cross the Potomac below instead of above the Shenandoah and Blue Ridge. My idea was that this would at once menace the enemy's communications, which I would seize if he would permit.

If he should move northward I would follow him closely, holding his communications. If he should prevent our seizing his communications and move toward Richmond, I would press closely to him; fight him, if a favorable opportunity should present, and at least try to beat him to Richmond on the inside track. I say "try;" if we never try we shall never succeed. If he makes a stand at Winchester, moving neither north nor south, I would fight him there, on the idea that if we cannot beat him when he bears the wastage of coming to us, we never can when we bear the wastage of going to him. This proposition is a simple truth, and is too important to be lost sight of for a moment. In coming to us he tenders us an advantage which we should not waive. We should not so operate as to merely drive him away. As we must beat him somewhere or fail finally, we can do it, if at all, easier near to us than far away. If we cannot beat the enemy where he now is, we never can, he again being within the intrenchments of Richmond.

Recurring to the idea of going to Richmond on the inside track, the facility of supplying from the side away from the enemy is remarkable, as it were, by the different spokes of a wheel extending from the hub toward the rim, and this, whether you move directly by the chord or on the inside arc, hugging the Blue Ridge more closely. The chord-line, as you see, carries you by Aldie, Hay Market, and Fredericksburg; and you see how turnpikes, railroads, and finally the Potomac, by Aquia Creek, meet you at all points from Washington; the same, only the lines lengthened a little, if you press closer to the Blue Ridge part of the way.

The gaps through the Blue Ridge I understand to be about the following distances from Harper's Ferry, to wit: Vestal's, 5 miles; Gregory's, 13; Snicker's, 18; Ashby's, 28; Manassas, 38; Chester, 45; and Thornton's, 53. I should think it preferable to take the route nearest the enemy, disabling him to make an important move without your knowledge, and compelling him to keep his forces together for dread of you. The gaps would enable you to attack if you should wish. For a great part of the way you would be practically between the enemy and both Washington and Richmond, enabling us to spare you the greatest number of troops from here. When at length running for Richmond ahead of him enables him to move this way, if he does so, turn and attack him in the rear. But I think he should be engaged long before such point is reached. It is all easy if our troops march as well as the enemy, and it is unmanly to say they cannot do it. This letter is in no sense an order.

Yours, truly,

A. Lincoln[43]

This elaborate letter, in which Lincoln reminded McClellan of what he said to him at Antietam about his "overcautiousness," temperately and very thoroughly discussed all the strategic lines of McClellan's prospective advance into Virginia. It was in all respects a very remarkable paper, and it proved that the writer had acquired a complete familiarity with the country that the army was to occupy and also a sound judgment upon strategic questions and all the accepted rules of modern warfare. Cox says, "As a mere matter of military comprehension and judgment of the strategic situation, the letter puts Mr. Lincoln head and shoulders above both his military subordinates."[44] G. F. R. Henderson says, "Lincoln's letter … shows that the lessons of the war had not been … lost upon him … [and they had taught him] what an important part is played by lines of supply."[45] Not only was the plan well considered but it was perfectly feasible. Henry Villard writes, "The very fact, however, that the President found it necessary to address such an implied censure to McClellan and to tell him what to do, was conclusive proof of the grievous error he committed in re-appointing him."[46]

---

[43] Lincoln to McClellan, October 13, 1862, reprinted in *OR*, vol. 19, pt. 1, 13–14.

[44] Cox, 373.

[45] G. F. R. Henderson, *Stonewall Jackson and the American Civil War*, vol. 2, (London: Longmans, Green, and Co., 1898), 363.

[46] Henry Villard, *Memoirs of Henry Villard: Journalist and Financier, 1835–1900*, vol. 1 (Boston: Houghton, Mifflin and Co., 1904), 341.

Before sending the letter, Lincoln discussed it, as already stated, with Vice President Hamlin, and expressed the opinion that the letter would do no good and that he would soon be compelled to retire McClellan.[47] Halleck recognized the force of the letter but would not order its intentions to be carried out, shrinking from the responsibility. As for McClellan, he "shrank from the decisive vigor of the plan," though finally accepted it some days later as the means of getting a larger reinforcement than that promised him should he take the route by the Shenandoah Valley.[48]

It was as predicted by Lincoln. His letter of the thirteenth did no immediate good, and McClellan continued to offer excuses for not moving. He still wanted cavalry horses, but on the twenty-first telegraphed that in other respects he was nearly ready to move and inquired whether the president desired him to march on the enemy at once or wait for new horses,[49] to which Halleck replied on the same day, "Your telegram of 12 m. has been submitted to the President. He directs me to say that he has no change to make in his order of the 6th instant. If you have not been and are not now in condition to obey it, you will be able to show such want of ability. The President does not expect impossibilities, but he is very anxious that all this good weather should not be wasted in inactivity. Telegraph when you will move, and on what lines you propose to march."[50]

This plain notice to McClellan that he would be held responsible for the failure to obey the order of the sixth unless he could show good reasons why the order could not be obeyed was taken by McClellan as authority for him to decide for himself whether or not it was possible to move with safety to the army. This responsibility, says McClellan, "I exercised with the more confidence in view of the strong assurances of his trust in me as commander of that army with which the President had seen fit to honor me during his last visit."[51] But the dispatch brought him to a decision as to his line of operations; he replied to Halleck on the twenty-second that he had decided to move upon the line indicated by the president in his letter of the thirteenth, and that he should need all the cavalry and other reinforcements that could be sent him.[52] Halleck answered that, should McClellan move as proposed, he could send twenty thousand men from Washington.[53] In his official report, McClellan says he concluded to select that line east of the Blue Ridge, "feeling convinced that it would secure me the largest accession of force and the most cordial support of the President, whose views from the beginning were in favor of that line."[54]

In several dispatches McClellan continued his appeals for more cavalry, and in one of these he complained of the condition of his horses, that they were fatigued and sore-tongued. This coming under Lincoln's eye, he telegraphed:

War Department
Washington City, October 24 [25—*OR* editors], 1862

Major-General McClellan:

I have just read your dispatch about sore-tongued and fatigued horses. Will you pardon me for asking what the horses of your army have done since the battle of Antietam that fatigues anything?

A. Lincoln[55]

McClellan responded that the cavalry, since the battle of Antietam, performed hard service, six regiments making a trip of two hundred miles (fifty-five miles in one day) while undertaking to reach Stuart's cavalry, and that his remainder had tracked Stuart, making seventy-eight miles in twenty-four hours. If any instance could be found where overworked cavalry had performed more labor than had his since the battle of Antietam, he was not conscious of it.[56]

Lincoln replied:

Executive Mansion, Washington
October 26, 1862 (Sent 11.30 a.m.)

Major-General McClellan:

Yours, in reply to mine about horses, received. Of course, you know the facts better than I; still, two considerations remain. Stuart's cavalry outmarched ours, having certainly done more marked service on the Peninsula and

[47] Hamlin, 443.
[48] Cox, 373.
[49] McClellan to Halleck, October 21, 1862, as contained in McClellan to Thomas, 81.
[50] Halleck to McClellan, October 21, 1862, 3:00 p.m., as contained in McClellan to Thomas, 81.
[51] McClellan to Thomas, 81.
[52] McClellan to Halleck, October 22, 1862, 2:30 p.m., reprinted in *OR*, vol. 19, pt. 2, 464.
[53] Halleck to McClellan, October 23, 1862, 3:30 p.m., reprinted in *OR*, vol. 19, pt. 2, 470.
[54] McClellan to Thomas, 83.
[55] Lincoln to McClellan, October 24 [25], 1862, reprinted in *OR*, vol. 19, pt. 2, 485.
[56] McClellan to Lincoln, October 25, 1862, 6:00 p.m., reprinted in *OR*, vol. 19, pt. 2, 485.

everywhere since. Secondly, will not a movement of our army be a relief to the cavalry, compelling the enemy to concentrate, instead of foraying in squads everywhere? But I am so rejoiced to learn from your dispatch to General Halleck that you begin crossing the river this morning.

A. Lincoln[57]

McClellan took issue with the president on his statement that Stuart's cavalry had outmarched his own, was convinced that someone had given an erroneous impression in regard to the service of the Union cavalry, and then went into a very elaborate explanation of what the cavalry had done since leaving Washington.[58] To all of this, Lincoln replied:

Executive Mansion
Washington, October 27, 1862 (Sent 12.10 p.m.)

Major-General McClellan:

Yours of yesterday received. Most certainly I intend no injustice to any, and if I have done any I deeply regret it. To be told, after more than five weeks' total inaction of the army, and during which period we have sent to the army every fresh horse we possibly could, amounting in the whole to 7,918, that the cavalry horses were too much fatigued to move, presents a very cheerless, almost hopeless, prospect for the future, and it may have forced something of impatience in my dispatch. If not recruited and rested then, when could they ever be? I suppose the river is rising, and I am glad to believe you are crossing.

A. Lincoln[59]

The cavalry question being disposed of, McClellan now requested the president to fill up the old regiments of his army before they were again taken into action, and suggested that the order to fill them up with drafted men be issued at once.[60] This indicated *another* period of delay. Halleck was disgusted,[61] and Lincoln telegraphed:

Executive Mansion
Washington, October 27, 1862 (Sent 3.25 p.m.)

Major-General McClellan:

Your dispatch of 3 p.m. to-day, in regard to filling up old regiments with drafted men, is received, and the request therein shall be complied with as far as practicable.

And now I ask a distinct answer to the question, Is it your purpose not to go into action again until the men now being drafted in the States are incorporated into the old regiments?

A. Lincoln[62]

McClellan made haste to explain that there had been a wrong impression conveyed, that he did not authorize or intend his staff officer to write (as he had) the words "before taking them into action again," and that the dispatch was sent without its being submitted to him. He now wished distinctly to say that he had no idea of postponing the advance until the old regiments were filled by drafted men, and that he was then crossing the river into Virginia and should push forward as rapidly as possible to endeavor to meet the enemy.[63]

To this and other dispatches that followed, Lincoln replied:

Washington, October 29, 1862—11.15 a.m.

Major-General McClellan:

Your dispatches of night before last, yesterday, and last night all received. I am much pleased with the movement of the army. When you get entirely across the river, let me know. What do you know of the enemy?

A. Lincoln[64]

---

[57] Lincoln to McClellan, October 26, 1862, 11:30 a.m., reprinted in *OR*, vol. 19, pt. 2, 490.

[58] McClellan to Lincoln, October 26, 1862, 9:00 p.m., reprinted in *OR*, vol. 19, pt. 2, 490–91.

[59] Lincoln to McClellan, October 27, 1862, 12:10 p.m., reprinted in *OR*, vol. 19, pt. 2, 496.

[60] McClellan to Lincoln, October 27, 1862, 3:00 p.m., reprinted in *OR*, vol. 19, pt. 2, 496.

[61] "I am sick, tired, and disgusted with the condition of military affairs here in the East and wish myself back in the Western army. With all my efforts I can get nothing done. There is an immobility here that exceeds all that any man can conceive of. It requires the lever of Archimedes to move this inert mass. I have tried my best, but without success. I do not yet despair, and shall continue my efforts." Halleck to Hamilton R. Gamble, October 30, 1862, reprinted in *OR*, ser. 3, vol. 2, 703–4.—*EAC*

[62] Lincoln to McClellan, October 27, 1862, 3:25 p.m., reprinted in *OR*, vol. 19, pt. 2, 497.

[63] McClellan to Lincoln, October 27, 1862, 7:15 p.m., reprinted in *OR*, vol. 19, pt. 2, 497–98.

[64] Lincoln to McClellan, October 29, 1862, 11:15 a.m., reprinted in *OR*, vol. 19, pt. 2, 504.

The movement began on the twenty-sixth of October, the army crossing the Potomac at Harper's Ferry and Berlin, seven miles to the east.[65] By the second of November, it was on the south side of the river, moving by way of Lovettsville and Snicker's Gap on Warrenton. The Twelfth Corps, now under the command of Slocum, was left on Maryland, Loudoun, and Bolivar Heights to bar the way into Maryland; Morell, with three brigades, was tasked with guarding the Potomac from Sharpsburg to Cumberland and covering Pennsylvania. There were still left to McClellan about 116,000 men with which to execute the campaign that Lincoln had suggested in his letter of October 13.

As McClellan turned his columns toward Warrenton, Lee's army was divided, Jackson being at and around Winchester with about thirty-six thousand men and Longstreet at and near Front Royal with about thirty-two thousand. When Lee heard of the movement on Warrenton, threatening to interpose between him and Richmond, he ordered Longstreet from Front Royal and through Chester Gap in the Blue Ridge, his corps taking position at Culpeper Court House on November 3. One of Jackson's divisions also was ordered to the east side of the Blue Ridge, and Jackson was left with the remainder of the army between Berryville and Charlestown in the Shenandoah Valley. McClellan saw his opportunity to fall upon and crush the two parts of the divided Confederate army, first Longstreet and then Jackson, and was laying his plan for the purpose by massing his army at Warrenton, when on November 7 he was ordered to turn the command of the army over to Burnside and to report at Trenton, New Jersey. The president's patience had been exhausted; he had been carefully watching McClellan and had become distrustful of his real desire to beat the enemy. His private secretaries write, "He set in his own mind the limit of his forbearance. He adopted for his guidance a test which he communicated to no one until long afterwards, on which he determined to base his final judgment of McClellan. If he should permit Lee to cross the Blue Ridge and place himself between Richmond and the Army of the Potomac he would remove him from command."[66] So when Lincoln heard on November 5 that Lee had crossed the Blue Ridge and was at Culpeper, these orders were issued:

Executive Mansion
Washington, November 5, 1862

By direction of the President, it is ordered that Major-General McClellan be relieved from the command of the Army of the Potomac, and that Major-General Burnside take the command of that army. Also that Major-General [David] Hunter take command of the corps in said army which is now commanded by General Burnside. [Hunter did not take command of the Ninth Army Corps, but no revocation of the order is of record—OR editors.] That Major-General Fitz John Porter be relieved from the command of the corps he now commands in said army, and that Major-General Hooker take command of said corps.

The General-in-Chief is authorized, in [his] discretion, to issue an order substantially as the above, forthwith, or so soon as he may deem proper.

A. Lincoln[67]

Headquarters of the Army
Washington, November 5, 1862

Major-General McClellan, Commanding, &c.:

General: On receipt of the order of the President, sent herewith, you will immediately turn over your command to Major-General Burnside, and repair to Trenton, N.J., reporting, on your arrival at that place, by telegraph, for further orders.

Very respectfully, your obedient servant,

H. W. Halleck,
General-in-Chief

---

[65] Carman appears to have been working from memory in regard to the location of Berlin (modern-day Brunswick), Maryland. In his original manuscript, he placed it south (not east) of Harper's Ferry and left a blank space for the number of miles distant, intending to consult a map at some later date.

[66] Nicolay and Hay, 188. A footnote by Hay states that these "are the President's own words," taken down in Hay's diary "at the time they were uttered."

[67] Order of Lincoln, November 5, 1862, reprinted in OR, vol. 19, pt. 2, 545.

[Enclosure]
General Orders No. 182

War Department, Adjt. Gen's Office
Washington, November 5, 1862

By direction of the President of the United States, it is ordered that Major-General McClellan be relieved from the command of the Army of the Potomac, and that Major-General Burnside take the command of that army.

By order of the Secretary of War:

E. D. Townsend,
Assistant Adjutant-General[68]

Beyond the record in Hay's diary giving the reason for McClellan's removal, no other reason has ever been given as coming from the president for this act at this time. As a purely military reason the action has been criticized, for at the time McClellan was in a position to deal the Confederates a great blow, but he had had other opportunities of the kind, of which he had not availed himself, and it was a fair presumption that he would let the opportunity slip from him here as it had elsewhere. A more satisfactory explanation of his removal is given by a careful writer: "It was the final outcome of the long course of misunderstandings, conflicting views, and heated controversy which had obtained between McClellan and the Washington authorities, and of the political jealousies existing between the Republicans and the Democrats in regard to the command of the army. The hostilities aroused by the Emancipation Proclamation between the Republicans and the Democrats undoubtedly influenced the President, in some degree, in his view of the fitness of Democratic generals to prosecute the war against slavery."[69] Halleck assigns this reason for the removal: "It became a matter of absolute necessity. In a few weeks more he would have broken down the Government."[70]

On the night of November 7, McClellan was much surprised when there was handed to him the order relieving him from command.[71] He issued this farewell:

Headquarters Army of the Potomac
Camp near Rectortown, Va., November 7, 1862

Officers and Soldiers of the Army of the Potomac:

An order of the President devolves upon Major-General Burnside the command of this army.

In parting from you, I cannot express the love and gratitude I bear to you. As an army, you have grown up under my care. In you I have never found doubt or coldness. The battles you have fought under my command will proudly live in our nation's history. The glory you have achieved, our mutual perils and fatigues, the graves of our comrades fallen in battle and by disease, the broken forms of those whom wounds and sickness have disabled—the strongest associations which can exist among men—unite us still by an indissoluble tie. We shall ever be comrades in supporting the Constitution of our country and the nationality of its people.

Geo. B. McClellan,
Major-General, U.S. Army[72]

The Army of the Potomac was devotedly attached to McClellan, who by personal magnetism had captured the hearts of the men, and the news of his removal from command was received with deep regret. The greater part of the men and a majority of the general officers were loud in denunciation of the act. It appeared to them, as it did to a large party in the North, that it was a political act, a punishment meted out to him for his hostility to the political ideas of the administration,

---

[68] Halleck to McClellan, November 5, 1862, reprinted in *OR*, vol. 19, pt. 2, 545.

[69] John W. Burgess, *The Civil War and the Constitution, 1859–1865*, vol. 2 (New York: Charles Scribner's Sons, 1901), 104.

[70] Halleck to Elizabeth Halleck, November 9, 1862, quoted in Wilson, *Journal of the Military Service Institution of the United States* 37, no. 137 (September–October 1905): 334.

[71] "Of course I was much surprised … They have made a great mistake. Alas for my poor country! I know in my inmost heart she never had a truer servant … I have done the best I could for my country; to the last I have done my duty as I understand it. That I must have made many mistakes I cannot deny. I do not see any great blunders; but no one can judge of himself. Our consolation must be that we have tried to do what was right; if we have failed it is not our fault." McClellan to Mary Ellen McClellan, November 7, 1862, 11:30 p.m., reprinted in McClellan, *Own Story*, 660.—EAC

[72] McClellan to "Officers and Soldiers of the Army of the Potomac," November 7, 1862, reprinted in *OR*, vol. 19, pt. 2, 551.

and this idea McClellan encouraged (at least, he did nothing to dispel the false impression).[73] McClellan says that his removal created such a deep feeling in the army that many were in favor of his refusing to obey the order, marching upon Washington, and taking possession of the government.[74] There was a like feeling outside the army in some quarters and wild talk of McClellan as dictator. Henry Villard says, "I even heard talk in the hotel lobbies and bar-rooms [at Washington] about the intention of the deposed commander to lead the army to Washington and take possession of the Government; but that impious wish of not a few never became a real purpose."[75] It is not supposable that McClellan for a single moment ever countenanced such an idea as assuming the reins of government; there was not enough of the Cromwell in him for that. Nevertheless, it is true that he did not discountenance the suggestion as strongly and as promptly as he should have done when upon previous occasions those by whom he was surrounded had heralded the idea. "He must be condemned," observes Jacob Cox, "for the weakness which made such approaches to him possible; but we are obliged to take the fact as he gives it, and to accept as one of the strange elements of the situation a constant stream of treasonable suggestions from professed friends in the army and out of it."[76] James Ford Rhodes says, "While he was too true a patriot to do anything that was questionable, he was nevertheless so influenced by the conviction that the government had not shown him the gratitude and consideration which was his due that he did not rebuke these suggestions as a general subject to the civil power ought to have done."[77]

McClellan's relief from active duty during the war was final. Efforts made to have him given another command in the field failed. Lincoln could not be induced to reinstate him, and it has been said that if history should censure the president for anything in his relations with McClellan it would not be for refusing him active service, but for retaining him in command as long as he did. Lincoln thought highly of him as a soldier and acknowledged his virtues. This is the president's estimate of him, expressed a short time before his final removal and when he was urging him to cross the Potomac: "For organizing an army, for preparing an army for the field, for fighting a defensive campaign, I will back General McClellan against any general of modern times. I don't know but of ancient times, either. But I begin to believe that he will never get ready to go forward!"[78] This estimate of McClellan holds to this day, and it is generally conceded also that from the day he put the Army of the Potomac in the field until the surrender of Lee at Appomattox, that army bore the imprint of his organizing spirit and skill. General Beauregard[79] speaks of it as "that magnificent military machine, which, through all of its defeats and losses, remained sound, and was stronger with readily assimilating new strength, at the end of the war than ever before" and as "the powerful army that, in the end, wore out the South."[79] Charles A. Clark says, "It fulfilled in all things the conception of its first great commander, and it never lost the inspiration it received from him in its formative period, and its earliest campaigns under his guidance and direction."[80] Joshua L. Chamberlain says that, under McClellan's eye and guiding hand, "organized from the *debris* of defeat, and in the presence of a defiant enemy, the Army of the Potomac acquired an earnestness of soldiership, a habitude, discipline and confidence, which made it an Army of veterans before it had struck a blow, and gave it a unity and identity, a tenacity of life and constancy of fraternal regard, which all its strange experiences, its great vicissitudes of ill and good, have never for a moment shaken."[81] It was fortunate for the Army of the Potomac and unfortunate for McClellan that he was its first commander. It was still more unfortunate for McClellan that he was called to high command too early in the war. This and other facts are kindly and appreciatively referred to by Ulysses S. Grant:

> I have entire confidence in McClellan's loyalty and patriotism. But the test which was applied to him would be terrible to any man, being made a major-general at the beginning of the war. It has always seemed to me that the critics of

---

[73] On November 5, the day on which McClellan was relived from command, Lincoln (in writing to Colonel William R. Morrison of Illinois regarding a matter personal to Morrison) said, "In considering military merit, it seems to me the world has abundant evidence that I discard politics." Lincoln to William R. Morrison, November 5, 1862. A copy of this letter appears in Basler, vol. 5, 486.—*EAC*

[74] McClellan, *Own Story*, 652.

[75] Villard, 337.

[76] Cox, 363–64.

[77] Rhodes, 191.

[78] William O. Stoddard, *Abraham Lincoln: The Man and the War President; Showing His Growth, Training, and Special Fitness for His Work* (New York: Fords, Howard, & Hulbert, 1888), 274.

[79] Pierre G. T. Beauregard, "The First Battle of Bull Run," in *Battles and Leaders*, vol. 1, 220, 222.

[80] Charles A. Clark, "General McClellan," in *War Sketches and Incidents as Related by the Companions of the Iowa Commandery, Military Order of the Loyal Legion of the United States*, vol. 2 (Des Moines: n.p., 1898), 14.

[81] Address of Joshua L. Chamberlain, in *Society of the Army of the Potomac: Record of Proceedings at the First Annual Re-Union, Held in the City of New York, July 5th and 6th, 1869* (New York: Pease & Stuyvesant, 1870), 13.

McClellan do not consider this vast and cruel responsibility—the war, a new thing to all of us, the army new, everything to do from the outset, with a restless people and Congress. McClellan was a young man when this devolved upon him, and if he did not succeed, it was because the conditions of success were so trying. If McClellan had gone into the war as Sherman, Thomas, or Meade, had fought his way along and up, I have no reason to suppose that he would not have won as high a distinction as any of us.[82]

---

[82] John Russell Young, *Around the World with General Grant: A Narrative of the Visit of General U. S. Grant, Ex-President of the United States, to Various Countries in Europe, Asia, and Africa, in 1877, 1878, 1879; To Which Are Added Certain Conversations with General Grant on Questions Connected with American Politics and History*, vol. 2 (New York: American New Company, 1879), 216–17.

Appendix A: Organization of the Army of the Potomac in the Maryland Campaign

(k = killed; mw = mortally wounded; w = wounded; c = captured)

Major General George B. McClellan, commanding

GENERAL HEADQUARTERS

escort
Captain James B. McIntyre

Independent Company, Oneida (New York) Cavalry	Captain Daniel P. Mann
Company A, 4th U.S. Cavalry	Lieutenant Thomas H. McCormick
Company E, 4th U.S. Cavalry	Captain James B. McIntyre

[volunteer engineer brigade][1]
[Brigadier General Daniel P. Woodbury]

[15th New York]	[Colonel John M. Murphy]
[50th New York]	[Lieutenant Colonel William H. Pettes]

regular engineer battalion
Captain James C. Duane
Lieutenant Charles E. Cross

provost guard[2]
Major William H. Wood

Companies E, F, H, and K, 2d U.S. Cavalry	Captain George A. Gordon
Companies A, D, F, and G, 8th U.S. Infantry	Captain Royal T. Frank
Company G, 19th U.S. Infantry	Captain Edmund L. Smith
Company H, 19th U.S. Infantry	Captain Henry S. Welton

headquarters guard
Major Granville O. Haller

[Sturges (Illinois) Rifles][3]	[Captain James Steel]
93d New York	Lieutenant Colonel Benjamin C. Butler

quartermaster's guard

Companies B, C, H, and I, 1st U.S. Cavalry	Captain Marcus A. Reno

FIRST CORPS[4]
Major General Joseph Hooker (w, Sept. 17)
Brigadier General George G. Meade

escort

Companies A, B, I, and K, 2d New York Cavalry	Captain John E. Naylor

---

1 "Detached at Washington, D.C., since September 7." "Organization of the Army of the Potomac, Maj. Gen. George B. McClellan, U.S. Army, Commanding, September 14–17, 1862," *OR*, vol. 19, pt. 1, 169 n. †.

2 "The composition of this command is not fully reported on the returns." Ibid., 170 n. *.

3 "Detached at Washington, D.C., since September 7." Ibid., 170 n. †.

4 The numbers assigned to the various corps in this table reflect the redesignation of elements of the former Army of Virginia that occurred on September 12. See "Summary of the Principal Events," *OR*, vol. 19, pt. 1, 157.

First Division

[Brigadier General Rufus King][5]
Brigadier General John P. Hatch (w, Sept. 14)
Brigadier General Abner Doubleday

First Brigade

Colonel Walter Phelps Jr.

22d New York	Lieutenant Colonel John McKie Jr.
24th New York	Captain John D. O'Brian (w, Sept. 17)
30th New York	Colonel William M. Searing
	Captain John H. Campbell
84th New York (14th [Brooklyn] Militia)	Major William H. de Bevoise
2d U.S. Sharpshooters	Colonel Henry A. V. Post (w, Sept. 17)

Second Brigade

Brigadier General Abner Doubleday
Colonel William P. Wainwright (w, Sept. 14)
Lieutenant Colonel John W. Hofmann

7th Indiana	Major Ira G. Grover
76th New York	Colonel William P. Wainwright
	Captain John W. Young
95th New York	Major Edward Pye
56th Pennsylvania	Lieutenant Colonel John W. Hofmann
	Captain Frederick Williams

Third Brigade

Brigadier General Marsena R. Patrick

21st New York	Colonel William F. Rogers
23d New York	Colonel Henry C. Hoffman
35th New York	Colonel Newton B. Lord
80th New York (20th Militia)	Lieutenant Colonel Theodore B. Gates

Fourth Brigade

Brigadier General John Gibbon

19th Indiana	Colonel Solomon Meredith[6]
	Lieutenant Colonel Alois O. Bachman ([mw], Sept. 17)[7]
	Captain William W. Dudley
2d Wisconsin	Colonel Lucius Fairchild (w, Sept. 14)
	Lieutenant Colonel Thomas S. Allen (w, Sept. 17)
	Captain George B. Ely
6th Wisconsin	Lieutenant Colonel Edward S. Bragg (w, Sept. 17)
	Major Rufus R. Dawes
7th Wisconsin	Captain John B. Callis

---

[5] "Brig. Gen. R. King is relieved from duty with Hooker's corps, and will report in person to the Adjutant-general." Headquarters Army of the Potomac, Special Orders No. 25, September 14, 1862, reprinted in *OR*, vol. 51, pt. 1, 831.

[6] "Owing to the fall which Colonel Meredith received in the battle of the 28th of August, and the subsequent fatigue and exposure of the marches up to the 16th instant, he was unable to take command on our movement across the Antietam Creek. The command now fell upon Lieutenant-Colonel Bachman." William W. Dudley to Frank A. Haskell, September 21, 1862, reprinted in *OR*, vol. 19, pt. 1, 251.

[7] "It was at this point that brave Lieutenant-Colonel Bachman fell, mortally wounded, and I took command immediately." Ibid. In Carman's original table of organization, Bachman is listed as "killed."

artillery
Captain John A. Monroe

1st Battery, New Hampshire Light Artillery	Lieutenant Frederick M. Edgell
Battery D, 1st Rhode Island Light Artillery	Captain John A. Monroe
Battery L, 1st New York Light Artillery	Captain John A. Reynolds
Battery B, 4th U.S. Artillery	Captain Joseph B. Campbell (w, Sept. 17)
	Lieutenant James Stewart

Second Division
Brigadier General James B. Ricketts

First Brigade
Brigadier General Abram Duryee

97th New York	Major Charles Northrup
	Captain Rouse S. Egelston[8]
104th New York	Major Lewis C. Skinner
105th New York	[Lieutenant] Colonel Howard Carroll (mw, Sept. 17)[9]
107th Pennsylvania	Captain James MacThomson

Second Brigade
Colonel William A. Christian[10]
Colonel Peter Lyle

26th New York	Lieutenant Colonel Richard H. Richardson
94th New York	Lieutenant Colonel Calvin Littlefield
88th Pennsylvania	[Major George W. Gile (w, Sept. 17)][11]
	Captain Henry R. Myers
90th Pennsylvania	Colonel Peter Lyle
	Lieutenant Colonel William A. Leech

Third Brigade
Brigadier General George L. Hartsuff (w, Sept. 17)
Colonel Richard Coulter

12th Massachusetts	Major Elisha Burbank (mw, Sept. 17)
	Captain Benjamin F. Cook
13th Massachusetts	Major Jacob P. Gould
83d New York (9th Militia)	Lieutenant Colonel William Atterbury
11th Pennsylvania	Colonel Richard Coulter
	Captain David M. Cook
[16th Maine][12]	[Colonel Asa W. Wildes]

---

8 In his original table of organization, Carman gives the name incorrectly as "Eggleston."

9 Although he introduces Carroll in his narrative as "Lieutenant Colonel" (see p. 217), Carman follows the example of the *OR* editors in listing him as "Colonel" in his table of organization. The extant records are confusing. The majority of the returns for this period that are noted in his service record show him as "Colonel," but the highest rank shown on the outside of the record jacket is "Lieutenant Colonel." (One record slip, quoting a regimental return for August 1862, says, "Promoted to Colonel August 2, 1862," yet the same slip says "Lt. Col." at the top.) Compiled Service Record of Howard Carroll, 105th New York, Carded Records Showing Military Service of Soldiers Who Fought in Volunteer Organizations During the American Civil War, 1890–1912, Record Group 94, National Archives. However, careful examination reveals the lower rank to be the one under which Carroll exercised his command on September 17, 1862. See *Official Army Register of the Volunteer Force of the United States Army for the Years 1861, '62, '63, '64, '65*, pt. 2 (Washington, D.C.: Government Printing Office, 1865), 598; *Annual Report of the Adjutant-General of the State of New York for the Year 1902*, serial 33 (Albany: Argus Co., 1903), 1092. An explanation is suggested in Frederick Pfisterer, comp., *New York in the War of the Rebellion, 1861 to 1865*, vol. 4, 3d ed. (Albany: J. B. Lyon Co., 1912), 3234–37. Carroll is credited no higher than lieutenant colonel on the master list of the regiment's officers (p. 3234). In a special category titled "Officer who was Commissioned or Appointed, but did not Serve in the Grade Named" (p. 3236), Pfisterer lists "Howard Carroll, as Colonel." A later entry for Carroll himself (p. 3237) reads, "Colonel, *not mustered*, August 2, 1862, with rank of same date, vice J. M. Fuller, resigned [emphasis added]."

10 Christian panicked under a bombardment by Confederate artillery on September 17 and fled the battlefield, resigning his commission two days later. See Stephen W. Sears, *Landscape Turned Red: The Battle of Antietam* (New Haven, Conn.: Ticknor & Fields, 1983), 187–88.

11 "During the engagement Major George W. Gile was badly wounded in the leg, and the command devolved upon Capt. H. R. Myers." Henry R. Myers to David P. Weaver, September 19, 1862, reprinted in *OR*, vol. 19, pt. 1, 265.

12 "Joined September 9, and detached September 13 as railroad guard." "Organization of the Army of the Potomac," 171 n. †. In his original manuscript, Carman lists it incorrectly as the "19th Maine."

artillery

Battery F, 1st Pennsylvania Light Artillery	Captain Ezra W. Matthews
Battery C, Pennsylvania Light Artillery	Captain James Thompson

Third Division

[Brigadier General John F. Reynolds][13]
Brigadier General George G. Meade
Brigadier General Truman Seymour

First Brigade

Brigadier General Truman Seymour
Colonel Richard B. Roberts

1st Pennsylvania Reserves	Colonel Richard B. Roberts
	Captain William C. Talley
2d Pennsylvania Reserves	Captain James N. Byrnes
5th Pennsylvania Reserves	Colonel Joseph W. Fisher
6th Pennsylvania Reserves	Colonel William Sinclair
13th Pennsylvania Reserves (1st Rifles)	Colonel Hugh W. McNeil (k, Sept. 16)
	Captain Dennis McGee

Second Brigade

[Brigadier General George G. Meade]
Colonel Albert L. Magilton

3d Pennsylvania Reserves	Lieutenant Colonel John Clark
4th Pennsylvania Reserves	[Colonel Albert L. Magilton]
	Major John Nyce
7th Pennsylvania Reserves	Colonel Henry C. Bolinger (w, Sept. 14)
	Major Chauncey A. Lyman
8th Pennsylvania Reserves	Major Silas M. Baily

Third Brigade

Colonel Thomas F. Gallagher (w, Sept. 14)
Lieutenant Colonel Robert Anderson

9th Pennsylvania Reserves	Lieutenant Colonel Robert Anderson
	Captain Samuel B. Dick
10th Pennsylvania Reserves	Lieutenant Colonel Adoniram J. Warner (w, Sept. 17)
	Captain Jonathan P. Smith
11th Pennsylvania Reserves	Lieutenant Colonel Samuel M. Jackson
12th Pennsylvania Reserves	Captain Richard Gustin

artillery

Battery A, 1st Pennsylvania Light Artillery	Lieutenant John G. Simpson
Battery B, 1st Pennsylvania Light Artillery	Captain James H. Cooper
Battery C, 5th U.S. Artillery	Captain Dunbar R. Ransom
[Battery G, 1st Pennsylvania Light Artillery][14]	[Lieutenant Frank P. Amsden]

---

[13] Although he refers in his narrative to Reynolds's participation in the campaign (see pp. 87, 91, 95, 98–99), Carman's original table of organization does not reflect the command billets held by Reynolds, Meade, or Magilton prior to Reynolds's detachment on September 11 at the request Pennsylvania governor Andrew G. Curtin. See George B. McClellan to Henry W. Halleck, September 11, 1862, reprinted in *OR*, vol. 19, pt. 2, 253.

[14] "Detached at Washington, D.C., since September 6." "Organization of the Army of the Potomac," 172 n. †.

SECOND CORPS
Major General Edwin V. Sumner

escort

Company D, 6th New York Cavalry   Captain Henry W. Lyon
Company K, 6th New York Cavalry   Captain Riley Johnson

First Division
Major General Israel B. Richardson (mw, Sept. 17)
Brigadier General John C. Caldwell[15]
Brigadier General Winfield S. Hancock

First Brigade
Brigadier General John C. Caldwell

5th New Hampshire	Colonel Edward E. Cross (w, Sept. 17)
7th New York	Captain Charles Brestel
61st and 64th New York	Colonel Francis C. Barlow (w, Sept. 17)
	Lieutenant Colonel Nelson A. Miles
81st Pennsylvania	Major Henry B. McKeen

Second Brigade
Brigadier General Thomas F. Meagher (w, Sept. 17)
Colonel John Burke

29th Massachusetts	Lieutenant Colonel Joseph H. Barnes
63d New York	Colonel John Burke
	Lieutenant Colonel Henry Fowler (w, Sept. 17)
	Major Richard C. Bently (w, Sept. 17)
	Captain Joseph O'Neill
69th New York	Lieutenant Colonel James Kelly (w, Sept. 17)
	Major James Cavanagh
88th New York	Lieutenant Colonel Patrick Kelly

Third Brigade
Colonel John R. Brooke

2d Delaware	Captain David L. Stricker[16]
52d New York	Colonel Paul Frank
57th New York	Lieutenant Colonel Philip J. Parisen (k, Sept. 17)
	Major Alford B. Chapman
66th New York	Captain Julius Wehle[17]
53d Pennsylvania	Lieutenant Colonel Richards McMichael

artillery

Battery B, 1st New York Light Artillery   Captain Rufus D. Pettit
Batteries A and C, 4th U.S. Artillery   Lieutenant Evan Thomas

---

[15] Caldwell's command of the division was short-lived. "Early in the afternoon, after General Richardson had been removed from the field, I was directed to take command of his division by Major General McClellan in person." Winfield S. Hancock to Joseph H. Taylor, September 29, 1862, reprinted in *OR*, vol. 19, pt. 1, 279.

[16] In his original manuscript, Carman gives the name incorrectly as "Strickler."

[17] The editors of the *OR* list Lieutenant Colonel James H. Bull underneath Wehle in their table of organization. "Organization of the Army of the Potomac," 172. Both men are named as commanders of the regiment on the New York State Monument at Antietam National Battlefield. However, Wehle's report of the battle states that he was in command from September 16 through September 19 and makes no mention of Bull at this time. Report of Julius Wehle, September 21, 1862, reprinted in *OR*, vol. 19, pt. 1, 303. Similarly, the report of the brigade commander makes no mention of Bull being at Antietam. John R. Brooke to William G. Mitchell, September 21, 1862, reprinted in *OR*, vol. 19, pt, 1, 299–300.

Second Division
Major General John Sedgwick (w, Sept. 17)
Brigadier General Oliver O. Howard

First Brigade
Brigadier General Willis A. Gorman[18]

15th Massachusetts	Lieutenant Colonel John W. Kimball
1st Minnesota	Colonel Alfred Sully
34th New York	Colonel James A. Suiter
82d New York (2d Militia)	Colonel Henry W. Hudson
1st Company, Massachusetts Sharpshooters	Captain John Saunders
2d Company, Minnesota Sharpshooters	Captain William F. Russell

Second Brigade
Brigadier General Oliver O. Howard
Colonel Joshua T. Owen[19]
Colonel DeWitt C. Baxter

69th Pennsylvania	Colonel Joshua T. Owen
71st Pennsylvania	Colonel Isaac J. Wistar [(w. Sept. 17)][20]
	Lieutenant Richard P. Smith (adjutant) [(w, Sept. 17)][21]
	Captain Enoch E. Lewis
72d Pennsylvania	Colonel DeWitt C. Baxter
106th Pennsylvania	Colonel Turner G. Morehead

Third Brigade
Brigadier General Napoleon J. T. Dana (w, Sept. 17)
Colonel Norman J. Hall
[Colonel William R. Lee][22]

19th Massachusetts	Colonel Edward W. Hinks (w, Sept. 17)
	Lieutenant Colonel Arthur F. Devereux
20th Massachusetts	Colonel William R. Lee (w, Sept. 17)
7th Michigan	Colonel Norman J. Hall
	Captain Charles J. Hunt
42d New York	Lieutenant Colonel George N. Bomford (w, Sept. 17)
	Major James E. Mallon
59th New York	Colonel William L. Tidball

artillery

Battery A, 1st Rhode Island Light Artillery	Captain John A. Tompkins
Battery I, 1st U.S. Artillery	Lieutenant George A. Woodruff

---

[18] In his original manuscript, Carman gives the name incorrectly as "Willis O. Gorman."

[19] "Colonel Baxter, Seventy-second Pennsylvania, with a portion of his regiment, had fallen back considerably to our left, and did not find me till afternoon. As Colonel Owen, Sixty-ninth Pennsylvania, was the ranking colonel in his absence, he commanded my brigade; Colonel Baxter took command on his return." Oliver O. Howard to "Colonel," September 20, 1862, reprinted in *OR*, vol. 19, pt. 1, 307.

[20] "[The 71st Pennsylvania's] retreat was not effected without sharp fighting and severe loss. Every field and staff officer, including the Colonel[,] was left upon the ground." Isaac J. Wistar, *Autobiography of Isaac Jones Wistar, 1827–1905: Half a Century in War and Peace* (New York: Harper & Brothers Publishers, 1914), 405.

[21] "Adjutant Smith, who had been acting as a field officer …, pushed on, unmindful of disaster, but had scarcely reached the enemy when he also fell." Samuel P. Bates, *History of Pennsylvania Volunteers, 1861–5*, vol. 2 (Harrisburg, Pa.: B. Singerly, 1869), 794. That Lewis was the final regiment's final commander of the day is attested to by Wistar: "Under its surviving Captain ([Enoch E.] Lewis), what was left of [the 71st Pennsylvania] marched to the rear, served fresh cartridges, called its roll and reported to General Meade ready for any duty." Wistar, 405. Carman's reason for placing Lieutenant Smith ahead of Captain Lewis in the sequence of command in not known.

[22] "In a field behind the woods I found Colonel Lee with his regiment, Twentieth Massachusetts Volunteers, in perfectly good order and with very full ranks. I informed Colonel Lee that he was in command of the brigade, being my senior; but he positively declined to relieve me, and repeatedly desired me to give such orders as I saw fit, and he would obey them. I reported this immediately to General Howard, commanding the division, and he directed me to continue in command … Colonel Lee assumed command on the 19th." Norman J. Hall to Eben T. Whittelsey, September 20, 1862, reprinted in *OR*, vol. 19, pt. 1, 321–22.

Third Division

Brigadier General William H. French

First Brigade

Brigadier General Nathan Kimball

14th Indiana	Colonel William Harrow
8th Ohio	Lieutenant Colonel Franklin Sawyer
132d Pennsylvania	Colonel Richard A. Oakford (k, Sept. 17)
	Lieutenant Colonel Vincent M. Wilcox
7th West Virginia	Colonel Joseph Snider

Second Brigade

Colonel Dwight Morris

14th Connecticut	Lieutenant Colonel Sanford H. Perkins
108th New York	Colonel Oliver H. Palmer
130th Pennsylvania	Colonel Henry I. Zinn

Third Brigade[23]

Brigadier General Max Weber (w, Sept. 17)
Colonel John W. Andrews

1st Delaware	Colonel John W. Andrews
	Lieutenant Colonel Oliver Hopkinson (w, Sept. 17)
5th Maryland	Major Leopold Blumenberg (w, Sept. 17)
	Captain Ernest F. M. Faehtz[24]
[4th New York][25]	[Lieutenant Colonel John D. McGregor]

artillery

Battery G, 1st New York Light Artillery	Captain John D. Frank
Battery B, 1st Rhode Island Light Artillery	Captain John G. Hazard
Battery G, 1st Rhode Island Light Artillery	Captain Charles D. Owen

FOURTH CORPS

First Division

Major General Darius N. Couch

First Brigade

Brigadier General Charles Devens Jr.

7th Massachusetts	Colonel David A. Russell
10th Massachusetts	Colonel Henry L. Eustis
36th New York	Colonel William H. Browne
2d Rhode Island	Colonel Frank Wheaton

---

[23] This brigade remained at Washington for some time and was sent to join the Fourth Corps in the midst of the campaign. See Halleck to McClellan, September 11, 1862, 1:00 p.m., reprinted in *OR*, vol. 19, pt. 2, 253.

[24] Carman accepts the determination of the editors of the *OR* that Faehtz succeeded Blumenberg in command of the 5th Maryland. However, the official state history of the war offers this account: "The commanding officer for the time being, Major Leopold Blumenberg, was seriously wounded at the head of the regiment and carried to the rear, when Captain [William] W. Bamberger, of Company B, assumed command of the regiment, who, in turn, was seriously wounded and taken to the rear, when the command of the regiment devolved on Capt. Salome Marsh, of Company F, who commanded the regiment during the remainder of the day." L. Allison Wilmer, J. H. Jarrett, and George W. F. Vernon, *History and Roster of Maryland Volunteers, War of 1861–5*, vol. 1 (Baltimore: Guggenheimer, Weil, & Co., 1899), 179.

[25] Carman omits the 4th New York from his table of organization inadvertently but makes numerous references in his narrative to its participation (see pp. 279–82 passim).

Second Brigade
Brigadier General Albion P. Howe

62d New York	Colonel David J. Nevin
93d Pennsylvania	Colonel James M. McCarter
98th Pennsylvania	Colonel John F. Ballier
102d Pennsylvania	Colonel Thomas A. Rowley
139th Pennsylvania[26]	Colonel Frank H. Collier

Third Brigade
Brigadier General John Cochrane

65th New York	Colonel Alexander Shaler
67th New York	Colonel Julius W. Adams
122d New York	Colonel Silas Titus
23d Pennsylvania	Colonel Thomas H. Neill
61st Pennsylvania	Colonel George C. Spear
82d Pennsylvania	Colonel David H. Williams

artillery

3d Battery, New York Light Artillery[27]	Captain William Stuart
Battery C, 1st Pennsylvania Light Artillery	Captain Jeremiah McCarthy
Battery D, 1st Pennsylvania Light Artillery	Captain Michael Hall
Battery G, 2d U.S. Artillery	Lieutenant John H. Butler

FIFTH CORPS
Major General Fitz John Porter

escort

1st Maine Cavalry (detachment)	Captain George J. Summat

First Division
Major General George W. Morell

First Brigade
Colonel James Barnes

2d Maine	Colonel Charles W. Roberts
18th Massachusetts	Lieutenant Colonel Joseph Hayes
22d Massachusetts	Lieutenant Colonel William S. Tilton
1st Michigan	Captain Emory W. Belton
13th New York	Colonel Elisha G. Marshall
25th New York	Colonel Charles A. Johnson
118th Pennsylvania	Colonel Charles M. Prevost (w, Sept. 20)
	Lieutenant Colonel James Gwyn[28]
2d Company, Massachusetts Sharpshooters	Captain Lewis E. Wentworth

Second Brigade
Brigadier General Charles Griffin

2d District of Columbia	Colonel Charles M. Alexander
9th Massachusetts	Colonel Patrick R. Guiney
32d Massachusetts	Colonel Francis J. Parker
4th Michigan	Colonel Jonathan W. Childs
14th New York	Colonel James McQuade
62d Pennsylvania	Colonel Jacob B. Sweitzer

---

[26] "Joined September 17." "Organization of the Army of the Potomac," 174 n. †.

[27] "Joined September 15." Ibid., 174 n. ‡.

[28] In his original table of organization, Carman—twice—gives the name here incorrectly as "Gynn," but spells it properly in the text.

Third Brigade
Colonel Thomas B. W. Stockton

20th Maine	Colonel Adelbert Ames
16th Michigan	Lieutenant Colonel Norval E. Welch
12th New York	Captain William Huson
17th New York	Lieutenant Colonel Nelson B. Bartram
44th New York	Major Freeman Conner
83d Pennsylvania	Captain Orpheus S. Woodward
Brady's Company, Michigan Sharpshooters	Lieutenant Jonas H. Titus Jr.

artillery
Battery C, Massachusetts Light Artillery	Captain Augustus P. Martin
Battery C, 1st Rhode Island Light Artillery	Captain Richard Waterman
Battery D, 5th U.S. Artillery	Lieutenant Charles E. Hazlett

sharpshooters
1st U.S. Sharpshooters	Captain John B. Isler

Second Division
Brigadier General George Sykes

First Brigade
Lieutenant Colonel Robert C. Buchanan

3d U.S. Infantry	Captain John D. Wilkins
4th U.S. Infantry	Captain Hiram Dryer
1st Battalion, 12th U.S. Infantry	Captain Matthew M. Blunt
2d Battalion, 12th U.S. Infantry	Captain Thomas M. Anderson
1st Battalion, 14th U.S. Infantry	Captain William H. Brown
2d Battalion, 14th U.S. Infantry	Captain David B. McKibbin

Second Brigade
Major Charles S. Lovell

1st and 6th U.S. Infantry	Captain Levi C. Bootes
2d and 10th U.S. Infantry	Captain John S. Poland
11th U.S. Infantry	[Major] DeLancey Floyd-Jones[29]
17th U.S. Infantry	Major George L. Andrews

Third Brigade
Colonel Gouverneur K. Warren

5th New York	Captain Cleveland Winslow
10th New York	Lieutenant Colonel John W. Marshall

artillery
Batteries E and G, 1st U.S. Artillery	Lieutenant Alanson M. Randol
Battery I, 5th U.S. Artillery	Captain Stephen H. Weed
Battery K, 5th U.S. Artillery	Lieutenant William E. Van Reed

---

[29] In his original table of organization, Carman lists Floyd-Jones's rank incorrectly as "Captain." He was appointed major on July 31, 1861 (to rank May 14, 1861) and confirmed five days later. See *Senate Exec. Journal*, 37th Cong., 1st sess., August 2, 1861, 509; August 5, 1861, 555.

Third Division[30]
Brigadier General Andrew A. Humphreys

First Brigade
Brigadier General Erastus B. Tyler

[9]1st Pennsylvania[31]	Colonel Edgar M. Gregory
126th Pennsylvania	Colonel James G. Elder
129th Pennsylvania	Colonel Jacob G. Frick
134th Pennsylvania	Colonel Matthew S. Quay

Second Brigade
Colonel Peter H. Allabach

123d Pennsylvania	Colonel John B. Clark
131st Pennsylvania	Lieutenant Colonel William B. Shaut
133d Pennsylvania	Colonel Franklin B. Speakman
155th Pennsylvania	Colonel Edward J. Allen

artillery
Captain Lucius N. Robinson

Battery C, 1st New York Light Artillery	Captain Almont Barnes
Battery L, 1st Ohio Light Artillery	Captain Lucius N. Robinson

artillery reserve[32]
Lieutenant Colonel William Hays

Battery A, 1st Battalion, New York Light Artillery[33]	Lieutenant Bernhard Wever
Battery B, 1st Battalion, New York Light Artillery	Lieutenant Alfred von Kleiser
Battery C, 1st Battalion, New York Light Artillery	Captain Robert Langner
Battery D, 1st Battalion, New York Light Artillery	Captain Charles Kusserow
5th Battery, New York Light Artillery	Captain Elijah D. Taft
Battery K, 1st U.S. Artillery	Captain William M. Graham
Battery G, 4th U.S. Artillery	Lieutenant Marcus P. Miller

SIXTH CORPS
Major General William B. Franklin

escort

Companies B and G, 6th Pennsylvania Cavalry	Captain Henry P. Muirheid

First Division
Major General Henry W. Slocum

First Brigade
Colonel Alfred T. A. Torbert

1st New Jersey	Lieutenant Colonel Mark W. Collet [(3d New Jersey)][34]
2d New Jersey	Colonel Samuel L. Buck
3d New Jersey	Colonel Henry W. Brown
4th New Jersey	Colonel William B. Hatch

---

[30] "This division was organized September 12, and reached the battle-field September 18." "Organization of the Army of the Potomac," 175 n. *.

[31] In his original manuscript, Carman lists this regiment incorrectly as the "21st Pennsylvania."

[32] "Batteries detached from the reserve are embraced in the roster of the commands with which they served." Ibid., 176 n. *.

[33] Batteries A, B, C, and D, New York Light Artillery, formed a battalion under the command of Major Albert Arndt, who was mortally wounded on September 16.—EAC

[34] Collet signs his official report of Antietam as "Lieut. Col. Third N.J. Vols., in command of First N.J. Vols." Mark W. Collet to H. P. Cooke, September 16, 1862, reprinted in OR, vol. 19, pt. 1, 384. Carman makes note of this fact in his narrative (see p. 138).

Second Brigade
Colonel Joseph J. Bartlett

5th Maine	Colonel Nathaniel J. Jackson
16th New York	Lieutenant Colonel Joel J. Seaver
27th New York	Lieutenant Colonel Alexander D. Adams
96th Pennsylvania	Colonel Henry L. Cake
[121st New York][35]	[Colonel Richard H. Franchot]

Third Brigade
Brigadier General John Newton

18th New York	Lieutenant Colonel George R. Myers
31st New York	Lieutenant Colonel Francis E. Pinto [(32nd New York)][36]
32d New York	Colonel Roderick Matheson (k, Sept. 14)
	Major George F. Lemon (mw, Sept. 14)
95th Pennsylvania	Colonel Gustavus W. Town

artillery
Captain Emory Upton

Battery A, Maryland Light Artillery	Captain John W. Wolcott
Battery A, Massachusetts Light Artillery	Captain Josiah Porter
Battery A, New Jersey Light Artillery	Captain William Hexamer
Battery D, 2d U.S. Artillery	Lieutenant Edward B. Williston

Second Division
Major General William F. Smith

First Brigade
Brigadier General Winfield S. Hancock
Colonel Amasa Cobb

6th Maine	Colonel Hiram Burnham
43d New York	Major John Wilson
49th Pennsylvania	Lieutenant Colonel William Brisbane
137th Pennsylvania	Colonel Henry M. Bossert
5th Wisconsin	Colonel Amasa Cobb

Second Brigade
Brigadier General William T. H. Brooks

2d Vermont	Major James H. Walbridge
3d Vermont	Colonel Breed N. Hyde
4th Vermont	Lieutenant Colonel Charles B. Stoughton
5th Vermont	Colonel Lewis A. Grant
6th Vermont	Major Oscar L. Tuttle

Third Brigade
Colonel William H. Irwin

7th Maine	Major Thomas W. Hyde
20th New York	Colonel Ernest von Vegesack
33d New York	Lieutenant Colonel Joseph W. Corning
49th New York	Lieutenant Colonel William C. Alberger (w, Sept. 17)
	Major George W. Johnson
77th New York	Captain Nathan S. Babcock

---

[35] In his original manuscript, Carman lists the 121st New York incorrectly as part of the division's Third Brigade. See Frederick H. Dyer, *A Compendium of the War of the Rebellion: Compiled and Arranged from Official Records of the Federal and Confederate Armies, Reports of the Adjutant Generals of the Several States, the Army Registers, and Other Reliable Documents and Sources* (Des Moines: Dyer Publishing Co., 1908), 1452.

[36] His official report is presented by the editors of the *OR* as "Report of Lieut. Col. Francis E. Pinto, Thirty-second New York Infantry, commanding Thirty-first New York Infantry, of the battle of Crampton's Pass," *OR*, vol. 19, pt. 1, 398. Carman makes note of Pinto's billet with the 32d New York in his narrative (see p. 138).

<u>artillery</u>[37]

Captain Romeyn B. Ayres

Battery B, Maryland Light Artillery	Lieutenant Theodore J. Vanneman
1st Battery, New York Light Artillery	Captain Andrew Cowan
Battery F, 5th U.S. Artillery	Lieutenant Leonard Martin

NINTH CORPS

Major General Ambrose E. Burnside
Major General Jesse L. Reno (k, Sept. 14)
Brigadier General Jacob D. Cox[38]

<u>escort</u>

Company G, 1st Maine Cavalry   Captain Zebulon B. Blethen

First Division

Brigadier General Orlando B. Willcox

First Brigade

Colonel Benjamin C. Christ

28th Massachusetts	Captain Andrew P. Caraher
17th Michigan	Colonel William H. Withington
79th New York	Lieutenant Colonel David Morrison
50th Pennsylvania	Major Edward Overton (w, Sept. 17)
	Captain William H. Diehl

Second Brigade

Colonel Thomas Welsh

8th Michigan[39]	Lieutenant Colonel Frank Graves
	Major Ralph Ely
46th New York	Lieutenant Colonel Joseph Gerhardt
45th Pennsylvania	Lieutenant Colonel John I. Curtin
100th Pennsylvania	Lieutenant Colonel David A. Leckey

<u>artillery</u>

8th Battery, Massachusetts Light Artillery	Captain Asa M. Cook
Battery E, 2d U.S. Artillery	Lieutenant Samuel N. Benjamin

---

[37] The 3d Battery, New York Light Artillery was transferred to the First Division, Fourth Corps on September 15. "Organization of the Army of the Potomac," 177 n. †.

[38] For a discussion of the Ninth Corps' problematic command structure at Antietam, see p. 333.

[39] "Transferred from First Brigade September 16." Ibid., 177 n. ‖.

Second Division
Brigadier General Samuel D. Sturgis

First Brigade
Colonel[/Brigadier General] James Nagle[40]

2d Maryland	Lieutenant Colonel Jacob E. Duryee
6th New Hampshire	Colonel Simon G. Griffin
9th New Hampshire	Colonel Enoch Q. Fellows
48th Pennsylvania	Lieutenant Colonel Joshua K. Sigfried

Second Brigade
Brigadier General Edward Ferrero

21st Massachusetts	Colonel William S. Clark
35th Massachusetts	Colonel Edward A. Wild (w, Sept. 14)
	Lieutenant Colonel Sumner Carruth (w, Sept. 17)
51st New York	Colonel Robert B. Potter
51st Pennsylvania	Colonel John F. Hartranft

artillery

Battery D, Pennsylvania Light Artillery	Captain George W. Durell
Battery E, 4th U.S. Artillery	Captain Joseph C. Clark Jr. [(w, Sept. 17)][41]
	[Sergeant Christopher F. Merkle][42]

Third Division
Brigadier General Isaac P. Rodman (mw, Sept. 17)
Colonel Edward Harland

First Brigade
Colonel Harrison S. Fairchild

9th New York	Lieutenant Colonel Edgar A. Kimball
89th New York	Major Edward Jardine (9th New York)
103d New York	Major Benjamin Ringold

---

[40] This is the only point in Carman's original manuscript where he lists Nagle's rank, giving it as "Colonel." Nagle began the campaign at the lower rank but was appointed shortly thereafter, during the congressional recess, to brigadier general (to rank September 10, 1862). It appears, however, that notification did not reach him until after the fighting at South Mountain. See Samuel D. Sturgis to "Assistant Adjutant-General, Headquarters Ninth Corps," September 22, 1862, reprinted in *OR*, vol. 19, pt. 1, 443–44. A plaque on the 48th Pennsylvania's monument at Antietam National Battlefield states that Nagle received the commission "on the battlefield of Antietam, September 17, 1862." The editors of the *OR* present a similar timeline, listing him as colonel at South Mountain and as brigadier general at Antietam. "Return of Casualties in the Union forces at the battle of South Mountain (Turner's Pass), Md.," *OR*, vol. 19, pt. 1, 186; "Return of Casualties in the Union forces at the battle of Antietam, Md.," *OR*, vol. 19, pt. 1, 197. The War Department tablet (no. 69) erected for Nagle's brigade, under Carman's supervision, at Antietam National Battlefield also credits him at the higher rank on the seventeenth. The date and signature on Nagle's official reports of both battles demonstrate that the commission reached him before the close of the campaign. James Nagle to Sturgis, September 20, 1862, reprinted in *OR*, vol. 19, pt. 1, 445–47. For the administrative history and subsequent fate of Nagle's commission, see *Senate Exec. Journal*, 37th Cong., 3d sess., January 19, 1863, 60, 87; February 12, 1863, 128; John H. Eicher and David J. Eicher, *Civil War High Commands* (Stanford, Calif.: Stanford University Press, 2001), 403.

[41] According to Carman's own narrative, "Captain Clark [was] severely wounded and compelled to leave the field [p. 337]."

[42] Carman continues, "The command devolved upon Sergeant Christopher F. Merkle, who fought the battery the rest of the day with skill and courage [p. 337]."

Second Brigade
Colonel Edward Harland

8th Connecticut	Lieutenant Colonel Hiram Appelman (w, Sept. 17)[43]
	Major John E. Ward
11th Connecticut	Colonel Henry W. Kingsbury (mw, Sept. 17)
	Lieutenant Colonel Griffin A. Stedman Jr.
16th Connecticut[44]	Colonel Francis Beach
4th Rhode Island	Colonel William H. P. Steere (w, Sept. 17)
	Lieutenant Colonel Joseph B. Curtis

artillery

Battery A, 5th U.S. Artillery	Lieutenant Charles P. Muhlenberg

Kanawha Division
Brigadier General Jacob D. Cox
Colonel Eliakim P. Scammon

First Brigade
[Colonel Eliakim P. Scammon][45]
Colonel Hugh Ewing

12th Ohio	Colonel Carr B. White
23d Ohio	Lieutenant Colonel Rutherford B. Hayes (w, Sept. 17)
	Major James M. Comly
30th Ohio	[Colonel Hugh Ewing]
	Lieutenant Colonel Theodore Jones (w, c, Sept. 17)
	Major George H. Hildt
1st Battery, Ohio Light Artillery	Captain James R. McMullin
Gilmore's Company, West Virginia Cavalry	Lieutenant James Abraham
Harrison's Company, West Virginia Cavalry	Lieutenant Dennis Delaney

Second Brigade
[Colonel Augustus Moor (c, Sept. 12)][46]
Colonel George Crook

11th Ohio	Lieutenant Colonel Augustus H. Coleman (k, Sept. 17)
	Major Lyman J. Jackson
28th Ohio	Lieutenant Colonel Gottfried Becker
36th Ohio	[Colonel George Crook]
	Lieutenant Colonel Melvin Clarke (k, Sept. 17)
	Captain Hiram F. Devol
Schambeck's Company, Chicago Dragoons	Captain Frederick Schambeck
Simmonds's Battery, Kentucky Light Artillery	Captain Seth J. Simmonds

unattached

6th New York Cavalry (eight companies)	Colonel Thomas C. Devin
3d Independent Company, Ohio Cavalry	Lieutenant Jonas Seamen
Batteries L and M, 3d U.S. Artillery	Captain John Edwards Jr.
Battery L, [2]d New York Artillery[47]	Captain Jacob Roemer

---

[43] In his original table of organization, Carman gives the name incorrectly as "Appleman."

[44] Newly accepted into Federal service, the 16th Connecticut was assigned to the Ninth Corps on September 6 and joined Harland's brigade on September 16. Headquarters Washington, Special Orders No. 3, September 6, 1862, reprinted in OR, vol. 19, pt. 2, 197; "Organization of the Army of the Potomac," 178 n. †.

[45] Carman omits the command billets held by Scammon and Ewing prior to the changes necessitated on account of Reno's death at Fox's Gap. However, these assignments are described correctly in the text (see pp. 91 and 144, respectively).

[46] Although Carman omits Moor from his table of organization, his command of the brigade and subsequent capture is described in Carman's narrative (see p. 91).

[47] Carman lists this battery incorrectly as belonging to the "3d New York Artillery" at this point in his original manuscript, but gives its proper designation elsewhere (see p. 458).

TWELFTH CORPS
[Brigadier] General Joseph K. F. Mansfield (mw, Sept. 17)[48]
Brigadier General Alpheus S. Williams[49]

escort

Company L, 1st Michigan Cavalry   Captain Melvin Brewer

First Division
Brigadier General Alpheus S. Williams
Brigadier General Samuel W. Crawford (w, Sept. 17)
Brigadier General George H. Gordon

First Brigade

Brigadier General Samuel W. Crawford
Colonel Joseph F. Knipe

5th Connecticut[50]	Captain Henry W. Daboll
10th Maine	Colonel George L. Beal
28th New York	Captain William H. H. Mapes
46th Pennsylvania	Colonel Joseph F. Knipe
	Lieutenant Colonel James L. Selfridge
124th Pennsylvania	Colonel Joseph W. Hawley (w, Sept. 17)
	Major Isaac L. Haldeman
125th Pennsylvania	Colonel Jacob Higgins
128th Pennsylvania	Colonel Samuel Croasdale (k, Sept. 17)
	Lieutenant Colonel William W. Hammersly (w, Sept. 17)
	Major Joel B. Wanner

---

[48] In Carman's original manuscript, the section of his table of organization covering the command billet for the Twelfth Corps consists of an excerpt from the *OR* table that he cut from its binding and pasted onto the page. Here and elsewhere, the editors of the *OR* designate Mansfield as a major general. See "Summary of the Principal Events," 157; "Organization of the Army of the Potomac," 179; "Return of Casualties in the Union forces at the battle of Antietam," 202. Carman himself calls Mansfield "Major General" at one point in his original narrative, and the War Department tablet (no. 27) erected for the Twelfth Corps, under Carman's supervision, at Antietam National Battlefield likewise refers to him in this manner.

At the time of his death at Antietam, however, Mansfield held a commission in the regular Army as a brigadier general. On March 5, 1863, Lincoln submitted Mansfield's name to the Senate for posthumous promotion to major general of volunteers (to rank July 18, 1862) "as a token of the Government's appreciation" of his "distinguished merit." The nomination was confirmed four days later. See *Senate Exec. Journal*, 38th Cong., special sess., March 5, 1863, 206; March 9, 1863, 261–62.

It appears that in the compilation of the *OR*, the editors chose to use the July 18, 1862, effective date of Mansfield's final commission as justification for designating him at the higher rank. This decision has resonated throughout the historiography of Antietam ever since. Compounding the confusion is the fact that the one document that appears in the *OR* over Mansfield's signature with rank after that date does in fact read "Major General." Joseph K. F. Mansfield to Halleck, August 17, 1862, reprinted in *OR*, vol. 51, 1, 742. This error is not the product of the *OR* editors; it is contained in the original document. See Telegrams Collected by the Office of the Secretary of War (Bound), 1861–1882 (National Archives Microfilm Publication M473, reel 17), Record Group 107, National Archives. As this is the received copy of the telegram, it is impossible to know where in the transmission process (which involved the services of a third party) the mistake was made.

Nevertheless, the evidence is overwhelming that Mansfield neither held the rank of nor was believed to be a major general in September 1862. The orders assigning him to command of the corps (see p. 182) refer to him as a brigadier general. A previous order, placing him under McClellan's authority, reads the same way. Headquarters of the Army, Adjutant General's Office, Special Orders No. 229, September 8, 1862, reprinted in *OR*, vol. 19, pt. 2, 214. Of the three after-action reports published in the *OR* that give a complete rank for Mansfield, all refer to him as a brigadier general. Alpheus S. Williams to Taylor, September 29, 1862, reprinted in *OR*, vol. 19, pt. 1, 474; James L. Selfridge to "the Commanding Officer, First Brigade, First Division, Banks' Army Corps [Joseph F. Knipe]," September 22, 1862, reprinted in *OR*, vol. 19, pt. 1, 489; George S. Greene to Williams, September 29, 1862, reprinted in *OR*, vol. 19. pt. 1, 505.

[49] Williams served as acting commander of the corps prior to Mansfield's assumption of command on September 15, with the same effect upon lower command billets in the First Division as occurred immediately after Mansfield's wounding.

[50] "Detached at Frederick, Md., since September 15." "Organization of the Army of the Potomac," 179 n. §.

Third Brigade
Brigadier General George H. Gordon
Colonel Thomas Ruger

27th Indiana	Colonel Silas Colgrove
2d Massachusetts	Colonel George L. Andrews
13th New Jersey	Colonel Ezra A. Carman
107th New York	Colonel Robert B. Van Valkenburgh
Zouaves D'Afrique (Pennsylvania)	————————[51]
3d Wisconsin	Colonel Thomas H. Ruger

Second Division
Brigadier General George S. Greene

First Brigade
Lieutenant Colonel Hector Tyndale (w, Sept. 17)
Major Orrin J. Crane

5th Ohio	Major John Collins
7th Ohio	Major Orrin J. Crane
	Captain Frederick A. Seymour
29th Ohio[52]	Lieutenant Theron S. Winship
66th Ohio	Lieutenant Colonel Eugene Powell (w, Sept. 17)
28th Pennsylvania	Major Ario Pardee Jr.

Second Brigade
Colonel Henry J. Stainrook

3d Maryland	Lieutenant Colonel Joseph M. Sudsburg
102d New York	Lieutenant Colonel James C. Lane
109th Pennsylvania[53]	Captain George E. Seymour
111th Pennsylvania	Major Thomas M. Walker

Third Brigade
Colonel William B. Goodrich (k, Sept. 17)
Lieutenant Colonel Jonathan Austin

3d Delaware	Major Arthur Maginnis (w, Sept. 17)
	Captain William J. McKaig[54]
Purnell Legion (Maryland)	Lieutenant Colonel Benjamin L. Simpson
60th New York	Lieutenant Colonel Charles R. Brundage
78th New York	Lieutenant Colonel Jonathan Austin
	Captain Henry R. Stagg

artillery
Captain Clermont L. Best

4th Battery, Maine Light Artillery	Captain O'Neil W. Robinson Jr.[55]
6th Battery, Maine Light Artillery	Captain Freeman McGilvery
Battery M, 1st New York Light Artillery	Captain George W. Cothran
10th Battery, New York Light Artillery	Captain John T. Bruen
Battery E, Pennsylvania Light Artillery	Captain Joseph M. Knap
Battery F, Pennsylvania Light Artillery	Captain Robert B. Hampton
Battery F, 4th U.S. Artillery	Lieutenant Edward D. Muhlenberg

---

[51] "No officers present; enlisted men of company attached to Second Massachusetts." Ibid., 179 n. ‖.

[52] "Detached September 9." Ibid., 179 n. **.

[53] "Detached September 13." Ibid., 179 n. ††.

[54] In his original table of organization, Carman gives the name incorrectly as "McCaig."

[55] In his original table of organization, Carman gives the name incorrectly as "O'Neill W. Robinson."

cavalry division

Brigadier General Alfred Pleasonton

First Brigade

Major Charles J. Whiting

5th U.S. Cavalry	Captain Joseph H. McArthur
6th U.S. Cavalry	Captain William P. Sanders

Second Brigade

Colonel John F. Farnsworth

8th Illinois Cavalry	Major William H. Medill
3d Indiana Cavalry	Major George H. Chapman
1st Massachusetts Cavalry	Colonel Robert Williams[56]
8th Pennsylvania Cavalry	Lieutenant Colonel Amos E. Griffiths

Third Brigade

Colonel Richard H. Rush

4th Pennsylvania Cavalry	Colonel James H. Childs (k, Sept. 17)
	Lieutenant Colonel James K. Kerr
6th Pennsylvania Cavalry	Lieutenant Colonel C. Ross Smith

Fourth Brigade

Colonel Andrew T. McReynolds

1st New York Cavalry	Major Alonzo W. Adams
12th Pennsylvania Cavalry	Major James A. Congdon

Fifth Brigade[57]

Colonel Benjamin F. Davis

8th New York Cavalry	Colonel Benjamin F. Davis
3d Pennsylvania Cavalry	Lieutenant Colonel Samuel W. Owen

artillery

Battery A, 2d U.S. Artillery	Captain John C. Tidball
Batteries B and L, 2d U.S. Artillery	Captain James M. Robertson
Battery M, 2d U.S. Artillery	Lieutenant Peter C. Hains
Batteries C and G, 3d U.S. Artillery	Captain Horatio G. Gibson

unattached

15th Pennsylvania Cavalry (detachment)	Colonel William J. Palmer

---

[56] Carman initially listed the commanding officer as "Capt. Casper Crowninshield"—whom the editors of the *OR* designate in their table of organization—but later crossed him out and inserted Williams. "Organization of the Army of the Potomac," 180.

[57] Apparently formed upon Davis's junction with the Army of the Potomac following his escape from Harper's Ferry, the composition and participation of this unit at Antietam is attested to in Pleasonton's official report. Alfred Pleasonton to Randolph B. Marcy, September 19, 1862, reprinted in *OR*, vol. 19, pt. 1, 211, 213. As late as the first week of October, however, McClellan was still uncertain as to whether or not Davis and the 8th New York Cavalry were part of his command. See McClellan to Halleck, October 5, 1862, 1:00 p.m., reprinted in *OR*, vol. 19, pt. 2, 384.

Appendix B: Organization of the Army of Northern Virginia in the Maryland Campaign

(k = killed; mw = mortally wounded; w = wounded; c = captured)

General Robert E. Lee, commanding

LONGSTREET'S COMMAND[1]
Major General James Longstreet

McLaws's Division
Major General Lafayette McLaws

Kershaw's Brigade
Brigadier General Joseph B. Kershaw

2d South Carolina	Colonel John D. Kennedy (w, Sept. 17)
	Major Franklin Gaillard
3d South Carolina	Colonel James D. Nance
7th South Carolina	Colonel David W. Aiken (w, Sept. 17)
	Captain John S. Hard
8th South Carolina	[Colonel John W. Henagan (w, Sept. 13)][2]
	Lieutenant Colonel Axalla J. Hoole

Cobb's Brigade
Brigadier General Howell Cobb[3]
Lieutenant Colonel Christopher C. Sanders
Lieutenant Colonel William MacRae

16th Georgia	Lieutenant Colonel Henry P. Thomas
24th Georgia	Lieutenant Colonel Christopher C. Sanders
	Major Robert E. McMillan (w, Sept. 17)
Cobb's (Georgia) Legion (infantry battalion)	[Lieutenant Colonel Jefferson M. Lamar (mw, c, Sept. 14)][4]
	[Captain] Luther J. Glenn[5]
15th North Carolina	Lieutenant Colonel William MacRae

---

[1] Confederate law did not allow for any formal military unit larger than a division until September 18, 1862, when Davis approved the amendatory act creating corps. See Adjutant and Inspector General's Office, General Orders No. 93, November 22, 1862, reprinted in *OR*, ser. 4, vol. 2, 198. Carman's assertion at this point in his original manuscript that a corps formation was not adopted in the Army of Northern Virginia until the spring of 1863 is gravely in error. The re-organization of Lee's army into two corps was announced formally on November 6, 1862. Headquarters Army of Northern Virginia, Special Orders No. 234, November 6, 1862, reprinted in *OR*, vol. 19, pt. 2, 698–99.

[2] D. Augustus Dickert, *History of Kershaw's Brigade, with Complete Roll of Companies, Biographical Sketches, Incidents, Anecdotes, Etc.* (Newbury, S.C.: E. H. Aull Co., 1899), 148–49; Compiled Service Record of John Williford Henagan, Compiled Service Records of Confederate Soldiers Who Served in Organizations from the State of South Carolina (National Archives Microfilm Publication M267, reel 231), Record Group 109, National Archives.

[3] "I was necessarily absent for two days from the command, and reached it the morning after the battle [of Sharpsburg]. Howell Cobb to Lafayette McLaws, September 22, 1862, reprinted in *OR*, vol. 19, pt. 1, 871. In the most comprehensive study to date of the health of Confederate general officers, no mention is made of Cobb's absence during the Maryland campaign, but it is noted that various ailments sidelined him for a number of weeks during July and again in October 1862. Jack D. Welsh, *Medical Histories of Confederate Generals* (Kent, Ohio: Kent State University Press, 1995), 42.

[4] For evidence of Lamar's presence and mortal wounding at Crampton's Gap, see Compiled Service Record of Jefferson M. Lamar, Compiled Service Records of Confederate Soldiers Who Served in Organizations from the State of Georgia (National Archives Microfilm Publication M266, reel 585), Record Group 109, National Archives.

[5] In his original table of organization, Carman gives Glenn's rank incorrectly as "Lieutenant Colonel." At the time of the Maryland campaign, Glenn was only a captain, receiving promotion to major on October 7, 1862. See *Journal of the Senate of the First Congress of the Confederate States of America*, vol. 2 of *Journal of the Congress of the Confederate States of America, 1861–1865*, 58th Cong., 2d sess., 1904, S. Doc. 234, serial 4611, 440–41. Glenn did not gain a lieutenant colonelcy until March 26, 1863. See *Journal of the Senate*, vol. 3 of *Journal of the Congress*, serial 4612, 214–15.

Semmes's Brigade
Brigadier General Paul J. Semmes

10th Georgia	Major Willis C. Holt (w, Sept. 14)
	Captain William F. Johnston (w, Sept. 17)
	Captain Philologus H. Loud [(w, Sept. 17)][6]
53d Georgia	Lieutenant Colonel Thomas Sloan (w, Sept. 17)
	Captain Samuel W. Marshborne
15th Virginia	Captain Emmett M. Morrison (w, Sept. 17)
	Captain Edward J. Willis
32d Virginia	Colonel Edgar B. Montague

Barksdale's Brigade
Brigadier General William Barksdale

13th Mississippi	Lieutenant Colonel Kennon McElroy
17th Mississippi	Lieutenant Colonel John C. Fiser
18th Mississippi	Major James C. Campbell (w, Sept. 17)
	Lieutenant Colonel William H. Luse[7]
21st Mississippi	Captain John H. Sims Jr.
	Colonel Benjamin G. Humphreys

artillery
[Major Samuel P. Hamilton]
Colonel Henry C. Cabell[8]

Manly's (North Carolina) Battery	Captain Basil C. Manly
Pulaski (Georgia) Artillery	Captain John P. W. Read
Richmond Fayette (Virginia) Artillery	Captain Miles C. Macon
1st Company, Richmond (Virginia) Howitzers	Captain Edward S. McCarthy
Troup (Georgia) Artillery	Captain Henry H. Carlton

Anderson's Division
Major General Richard H. Anderson (w, Sept. 17)
Brigadier General Roger A. Pryor

Wilcox's Brigade
Colonel Alfred Cumming [(w, Sept. 17)][9]
Major Hilary A. Herbert
Captain James M. Crow

8th Alabama	Major Hilary A. Herbert
9th Alabama	Major Jeremiah H. J. Williams (w, Sept. 17)
	Captain James M. Crow
	Lieutenant Alexander C. Chisolm
10th Alabama	Captain George C. Whatley (k, Sept. 17)
11th Alabama	Major John C. C. Sanders

---

6 "[Among] the officers wounded were … Capt. P. H. Loud, of Company H, assisting in command." Philologus H. Loud to Edmund B. Briggs, September 23, 1862, reprinted in *OR*, vol. 19, pt. 1, 878.

7 Colonels Luse and Humphreys "reached the field just as the battle was closing" on the seventeenth. "Their timely presence not only cheered and animated their own regiments, but the entire brigade." William Barksdale to James M. Goggin, October 12, 1862, reprinted in *OR*, vol. 19, pt. 1, 884.

8 "Col. Henry Coalter Cabell, chief of artillery, who had been absent, sick, joined me on the field [at Sharpsburg], and remained during the rest of the engagement." McLaws to "the Adjutant-General, Headquarters General Longstreet [Gilbert Moxley Sorrel]," October 20, 1862, reprinted in *OR*, vol. 19, pt. 1, 860.

9 "On September 17 [Cumming] was wounded at Sharpsburg; hospitalization was required through October." Welsh, 50.

<u>Mahone's Brigade</u>[10]

Lieutenant Colonel William A. Parham

6th Virginia	Captain John R. Ludlow
12th Virginia	[Captain Richard W. Jones][11]
	Captain John R. Lewellyn [(w, Sept. 14)][12]
16th Virginia	Major Francis D. Holliday [(c, Sept. 14)][13]
41st Virginia	<u>not known</u>

Featherston's Brigade

[Brigadier General Winfield S. Featherston][14]

Colonel Carnot Posey

12th Mississippi	Colonel William H. Taylor
16th Mississippi	Captain Abram M. Feltus
19th Mississippi	[not known][15]
2d Mississippi Battalion	Major William S. Wilson (w, Sept. 17)

<u>Armistead's Brigade</u>

Brigadier General Lewis A. Armistead (w, Sept. 17)

Colonel James G. Hodges

9th Virginia	Captain William J. Richardson
	Captain James J. Phillips[16]
14th Virginia	Colonel James G. Hodges
38th Virginia	Colonel Edward C. Edmonds
53d Virginia	Captain William G. Pollard (k, Sept. 17)
	Captain Joseph C. Harwood
57th Virginia	[Captain William H. Ramsey][17]

---

10 Other tables of organization for the Army of Northern Virginia during this period (including the one published in the *OR*) include the 61st Virginia as the fifth regiment of the brigade. See "Organization of the Army of Northern Virginia, General Robert E. Lee, commanding, during the Maryland Campaign," *OR*, vol. 19, pt. 1, 804. However, this <u>regiment was not brigaded with the rest of Mahone's command until November 1862.</u> See Benjamin H. Trask, <u>*61st Virginia Infantry*</u> (Lynchburg, Va.: H. E. Howard, 1988), 8.

11 "I should mention that since the foregoing has been set in type a letter received by me from …. Richard W. Jones, … who gallantly led the Twelfth at the Crater and in several other engagements, recalls the fact that, on the morning after the battle of Second Manassas, he took command of it, and was in command until about the 14th of September, 1862, when Capt. Lewellyn, who had been slightly wounded in that battle, reported for duty in time to participate in the action of Crampton's Gap." George S. Bernard, "The Maryland Campaign of 1862," in Bernard, comp. and ed., *War Talks of Confederate Veterans* (Petersburg, Va.: Fenn & Owen, 1892), 42 n. Although officially absent from duty, sick, for the duration of the campaign, the regiment's commanding officer, Lieutenant Colonel Fielding L. Taylor, accompanied his men into Maryland. Too ill to resume his post, he nevertheless stood with his men in an unofficial capacity at Crampton's Gap and was mortally wounded in the fighting. See Bernard, 25, 41, 42 n.

12 See Compiled Service Record of John R. Lewellyn, Compiled Service Records of Confederate Soldiers Who Served in Organizations from the State of Virginia (National Archives Microfilm Publication M324, reel 524), Record Group 109, National Archives.

13 "[On September 14], the Fourth [Vermont] proceeded on the crest of the mountain about a mile, and captured another party of prisoners, all belonging to the Sixteenth Virginia. In the last party was the major of the regiment, who commanded." William T. H. Brooks to "the Assistant Adjutant-General, Division Headquarters," September 1862 [no day given], reprinted in *OR*, vol. 19, pt. 1, 408. See also Compiled Service Record of Francis M. Holliday, Virginia (M324, reel 523).

14 Featherston was plagues by illnesses during the campaign, relinquishing his command as necessary. He appears to have been in command during the operations against Harper's Ferry on the fourteenth but was incapacitated again by the seventeenth. See McLaws to Robert H. Chilton, October 18, 1862, reprinted in *OR*, vol. 19, pt. 1, 855; Welsh, 66.

15 In his original table of organization, Carman lists the commanding officer as "Colonel Nathaniel H. Harris" and states that he was wounded on the seventeenth. Both of these statements are in error. He sustained a wound of some severity at Second Manassas and took a twenty-day leave beginning on September 15. It is likely that Harris commanded the regiment only on paper at any point during the campaign. As to his rank, Harris was not appointed lieutenant colonel until December 20, 1862 (to rank November 24, 1862); he was appointed colonel on April 2, 1863 (to rank May 5, 1862). See Welsh, 94; Richard J. Sommers, "Nathaniel Harrison Harris," in William C. Davis, ed., *The Confederate General*, vol. 3 (n.p.: National Historical Society, 1991), 65.

16 He appears in Carman's original table of organization as "Jasper J. Phillips."

17 "In the battle [of Sharpsburg] the Regiment was on the left under General Jackson, but did not participate in the fight. Capt. Wm. H. Ramsey of Company 'E' was commanding at this time." C. R. Fontaine, *A Complete Roster of the Field and Staff Officers of the 57th Virginia Regiment of Infantry during the Civil War, Including Commissioned and Non-commissioned Officers* (n.p, n.d.), 11. Carman leaves this space blank.

<u>Pryor's Brigade</u>
Brigadier General Roger A. Pryor
Colonel John C. Hately

14th Alabama	Major James A. Broome
2d Florida	[Captain] William D. Ballantine (w, Sept. 17)[18]
	Lieutenant Geiger [*sic*][19]
5th Florida	Colonel John C. Hately
	Lieutenant Colonel Thomas B. Lamar (w, Sept. 17)
	Major Benjamin F. Davis
8th Florida	Lieutenant Colonel Georges A. G. Coppens (k, Sept. 17)
	Captain Richard A. Waller (k, Sept. 17)
	Captain William Baya
3d Virginia	Colonel Joseph Mayo (w, Sept. 17)
	Lieutenant Colonel Alexander D. Callcote

<u>Wright's Brigade</u>
Brigadier General Ambrose R. Wright (w, Sept. 17)
Colonel Robert H. Jones (w, Sept. 17)
Colonel William Gibson

44th Alabama	Lieutenant Colonel Charles A. Derby (k, Sept. 17)
	Major William F. Perry
3d Georgia	[Lieutenant Colonel] Reuben B. Nisbet (w, [c] Sept. 17)[20]
	Captain John F. Jones
22d Georgia	Colonel Robert H. Jones
	Captain Lawrence D. Lallerstedt [(w, Sept. 17)][21]
48th Georgia	Colonel William Gibson

---

[18] For a discussion of Ballantine's rank, see p. 286 n. 30.

[19] Carman's source for this assertion is a telegram from Ballantine, in which he states, "I was succeeded on the Battlefield by 1st Lieut. Geiger of Co. C (who was afterward killed July 3rd at Gettysburg). He was succeeded on the morning of the 18th by Capt. Ali. Manly of Co. b." William D. Ballantine to Ezra A. Carman, July 27, 1898, "Misc." folder, box 1, Letters and Reports Concerning the Battle of Antietam, 1895–1900 ("Antietam Studies"), Record Group 94, National Archives. No such officer appears in any regimental listing for the period of September 1862. The closest match is Sergeant Henry C. Geiger of Company E. See David W. Hartman, comp., *Biographical Rosters of Florida's Confederate and Union Soldiers, 1861–1865*, vol. 1 (Wilmington, N.C.: Broadfoot Publishing Co., 1995), 183; Florida Board of State Institutions, *Soldiers of Florida in the Seminole Indian, Civil and Spanish-American Wars* (Live Oak, Fla.: Democrat Book and Job Print, n.d.), 87. Sergeant Geiger was captured on September 17, 1862, and later exchanged. On January 5, 1864, he was elected captain. Compiled Service Record of Henry C. Geiger, Compiled Service Records of Confederate Soldiers Who Served in Organizations from the State of Florida (National Archives Microfilm Publication M251, reel 37), Record Group 109, National Archives. If Ballantine is correct about the death of his temporary successor at Gettysburg, Henry C. Geiger is not the man in question. Furthermore, neither Company B nor any other company of the regiment carried a captain resembling the name Ballantine provides as the commander on the 18th. Given these inconsistencies, coupled with his dubious claims to higher rank, Ballantine's trustworthiness as a source is questionable.

[20] "They [the 132d Pennsylvania and the Irish Brigade] drove the enemy from their stronghold and captured some 300 prisoners, including a number of officers, among them Lieutenant-Colonel Nisbet, of Macon, Ga." Vincent M. Wilcox to Nathan Kimball, September 19, 1862, reprinted in *OR*, vol. 19, pt. 1, 331. Carman lists him as "Captain" in his original table of organization, but this is clearly an inadvertent error, as he speaks of "Colonel" Nisbet in the body of the text (see p. 283 n. 22). At the same point in the text, he also makes reference to Nisbet's capture.

[21] In his original table of organization, Carman began to write "wounded" next to Lallerstedt's name, but then scratched it out. However, evidence of his wounding is provided in Lawrence D. Lallerstedt to Samuel Cooper, June 10, 1863, Compiled Service Record of Lallerstedt, Georgia (M266, reel 344).

<u>artillery</u>
Major John S. Saunders[22]
[Captain Cary F. Grimes (mw, Sept. 17)][23]

Donaldsonville (Louisiana) Artillery	Captain Victor Maurin
Huger's (Virginia) Battery	Captain Frank Huger
Moorman's (Virginia) Battery	Captain Marcellus N. Moorman
Grimes's (Virginia) Battery [Portsmouth Artillery]	Captain Cary F. Grimes
	[Lieutenant John H. Thompson][24]

Jones's Division
Brigadier General David R. Jones

<u>Toombs's Brigade</u>
Brigadier General Robert A. Toombs[25]
Colonel Henry L. Benning

2d Georgia	Lieutenant Colonel William R. Holmes (k, Sept. 17)
	[Major William T. Harris (w, Sept. 17)][26]
	Captain Abner M. Lewis
15th Georgia	Colonel William T. Millican ([mw, c], Sept. 17)[27]
	Captain Thomas H. Jackson
17th Georgia	Captain John A. McGregor
20th Georgia	Colonel John B. Cumming

<u>Drayton's Brigade</u>
Brigadier General Thomas F. Drayton

50th Georgia	Lieutenant Colonel Francis Kearse
51st Georgia	not known
3d South Carolina Battalion	[Lieutenant Colonel] George S. James [(k, Sept. 14)][28]
15th South Carolina	Colonel William D. DeSaussure
[Phillips's (Georgia) Legion][29]	[not known]

---

[22] Carman lists only Saunders in command of this battalion in his original table of organization, but in his narrative (see p. 283) and on the War Department tablet (no. 280) erected for this unit, under Carman's supervision, at Antietam National Battlefield, Grimes is credited as being in command on the seventeenth. Indeed, it is unclear whether Saunders was present at any point in the campaign. By the first week of December, Saunders was declared "unfit for service in the field" due to "typhoid fever." Surgeon's certificate [signer illegible], December 3, 1862, Compiled Service Record of John S. Saunders, Compiled Service Records of Confederate General and Staff Officers, and Non-Regimental Enlisted Men (National Archives Microfilm Publication M331, reel 219), Record Group 109, National Archives.

[23] Grimes's mortal wounding is described by Carman in his narrative (see p. 290).

[24] Carman states that Grimes continued to command his own battery on the seventeenth while simultaneously acting as battalion commander (see p. 283). As Grimes was killed on the seventeenth, however, Thompson unquestionably commanded the battery by day's end.

[25] During the fighting at Antietam, Toombs exercised overall command of the Confederate defense of the Rohrbach Bridge, ceding immediate control of his brigade to Benning. See pp. 173–74, 332, 337, 341.

[26] Both Carman and the editors of the *OR* list "Maj. Skidmore Harris" as Holmes's replacement in their respective tables of organization. "Organization of the Army of Northern Virginia," 804. Skidmore Harris had served previously as lieutenant colonel of the 2d Georgia, but at the time of the Maryland campaign was serving in the Western theater with the 43d Georgia. Compiled Service Record of Skidmore Harris, Georgia (M266, reels 154, 462).

"At this time [the afternoon of September 17] Lieut. Col. William R. Holmes, commanding, was killed, the command falling upon Maj. W. T. Harris." Abner M. Lewis to Henry L. Benning, September 23, 1862, reprinted in *OR*, vol. 51, pt. 1, 165. "My two regiments having been constantly engaged from early in the morning up to 1 o'clock with a vastly superior force of the enemy, … the commanding officer, Lieutenant-Colonel Holmes, of the Second, having been killed in the action, and the only remaining field officer, Major … Harris, being painfully wounded, … I deemed it my duty, in pursuance of your original order, to withdraw my command." Robert A. Toombs to David R. Jones, October 25, 1862, reprinted in *OR*, vol. 19, pt. 1, 890. The editors of the *OR* err once again by inserting "Skidmore" in square brackets after "Major."

[27] In Carman's original table of organization, Millican is listed as "killed." See Compiled Service Record of William T. Millican, Georgia (M266, reel 294).

[28] In his original table of organization, Carman gives James's rank as "Major" and makes no mention of his death at South Mountain. See Compiled Service Record of George S. James, South Carolina (M267, reel 180).

[29] This unit does not appear in any known tables of organization for the Maryland campaign. Indeed, it seems to vanish from all recorded history between the Second Manassas and Fredericksburg campaigns. However, new research demonstrates convincingly that the unit was both present and active during the fighting of September 1862. Kurt D. Graham, "Lost Legion - The Phillip's [sic] Legion Infantry Battalion at Fox's Gap, Maryland, Sept. 14th, 1862," http://www.angelfire.com/ga2/PhillipsLegion/lostlegion.html (last accessed June 18, 2007). See also the various compiled service records of members of the battalion. Georgia (M266, reels 592–600).

Garnett's Brigade
[Colonel Eppa Hunton][30]
Brigadier General Richard B. Garnett

8th Virginia	Colonel Eppa Hunton
18th Virginia	Major George C. Cabell
19th Virginia	Colonel John B. Strange (k, Sept. 14)
	Captain John L. Cochran
	Lieutenant William N. Wood[31]
28th Virginia	Captain William L. Wingfield
56th Virginia	Colonel William D. Stuart
	Captain John B. McPhail[32]

Kemper's Brigade
Brigadier General James L. Kemper

1st Virginia	Captain George F. Norton[33]
	Major William H. Palmer
7th Virginia	Major Arthur Herbert (17th Virginia)
	Captain Philip S. Ashby
11th Virginia	Major Adam Clement
17th Virginia	Colonel Montgomery D. Corse (w, Sept. 17)
24th Virginia	Colonel William R. Terry

Jenkins's Brigade
Colonel Joseph Walker

1st South Carolina Volunteers	Lieutenant Colonel Daniel Livingston (w, Sept. 17)
2d South Carolina Rifles	Lieutenant Colonel Robert A. Thompson
5th South Carolina	Captain Thomas C. Beckham
6th South Carolina	[Lieutenant Colonel John M. Steedman][34]
	Captain E. B. Cantey (w, Sept. 17)
4th South Carolina Battalion	Lieutenant W. T. Field
Palmetto (South Carolina) Sharpshooters	Captain Alfred H. Foster (w, Sept. 17)
	Captain Franklin W. Kilpatrick[35]

[30] Arrested by Jackson on April 1, 1862, on highly dubious charges relating to his alleged mismanagement of the First (Stonewall) Brigade at the battle of Kernstown, Garnett was released in September and transferred to Longstreet's command. Headquarters Department of Northern Virginia, Special Orders No. 188, September 5, 1862, reprinted in *OR*, vol. 19, pt. 2, 595. As senior colonel, Hunton was acting commander for a brief period at the opening of the campaign.

[31] In his original table of organization, Carman reverses the order of succession, placing Wood above Cochran. However, the official reports for the regiment state clearly, "The command fell upon Capt. John L. Cochran after the fall of Colonel Strange" at South Mountain, and, "The Nineteenth Regiment, ... commanded by Lieut. William N. Wood, acting adjutant, ... [was] attacked in the evening of the 17th." Reports of Benjamin Brown, October 15, 1862, reprinted in *OR*, vol. 19, pt. 1, 901–2. The whereabouts of Cochran on the seventeenth are unknown, but illness is suggested in a letter he penned to the secretary of war shortly after the battle, in which he asserts, "Nearly eighteen months of continuous service in the line has satisfied me that my health will not admit of my longer continuing in the Army under the fatigue and exposure of infantry service." John L. Cochran to the "Hon. Secretary of War [George W. Randolph]," September 26, 1862, Compiled Service Record of John L. Cochran, Virginia (M324, reel 618).

[32] Stuart was not able to command on the seventeenth due to "severe illness." John B. McPhail to Richard B. Garnett, October 26, 1862, reprinted in *OR*, vol. 19, pt. 1, 903.

[33] In his original table of organization, Carman gives the name incorrectly as "Geo. F. Newton."

[34] Steedman's presence in command of the regiment at South Mountain is noted in Walker's after-action report. Joseph Walker to Robert Johnston, October 24, 1862, first report, reprinted in *OR*, vol. 19, pt. 1, 906. No mention is made here or in his report of Antietam of Steedman's wounding, but Walker concludes the latter report by stating that "Captain Cantey, commanding Sixth Regiment ... [was] seriously wounded." Walker to Johnston, October 24, 1862, second report, reprinted in *OR*, vol. 19, pt. 1, 908. Steedman had been wounded previously in the Seven Days and again at Second Manassas, and this might account for his inability to retain command throughout the entirety of the Maryland campaign. See Compiled Service Record of John M. Steedman, South Carolina (M267, reel 211).

[35] In his original table of organization, Carman gives the name incorrectly as "Kirkpatrick."

G. T. Anderson's Brigade
Colonel George T. Anderson

1st Georgia (Regulars)	Colonel William J. Magill (w, Sept. 17)
	Captain Richard A. Wayne
7th Georgia	Colonel George H. Carmical[36]
8th Georgia	Colonel John R. Towers
9th Georgia	Lieutenant Colonel John C. L. Mounger
11th Georgia	Major Francis H. Little

artillery[37]

Wise (Virginia) Artillery	Captain James S. Brown [(w, Sept. 17)][38]

Walker's Division
Brigadier General John G. Walker

[Manning's] Brigade[39]
Colonel Van H. Manning (w, Sept. 17)
Colonel Edward D. Hall

3d Arkansas	Captain John W. Reedy
27th North Carolina	Colonel John R. Cooke
46th North Carolina	Colonel Edward D. Hall
	Lieutenant Colonel William A. Jenkins
48th North Carolina	Colonel Robert C. Hill
	Lieutenant Colonel Samuel H. Walkup
30th Virginia	Lieutenant Colonel Robert H. Chew (w, Sept. 17)

Ransom's Brigade
Brigadier General Robert Ransom Jr.

24th North Carolina	Lieutenant Colonel John L. Harris
25th North Carolina	Colonel Henry M. Rutledge
35th North Carolina	Colonel Matt W. Ransom
49th North Carolina	Lieutenant Colonel Lee M. McAfee

artillery

French's (Virginia) Battery	Captain Thomas B. French[40]
Branch's (Virginia) Battery	Captain James R. Branch[41]

---

[36] In his original table of organization, Carman gives the name incorrectly as "G. H. Carmichael."

[37] Three additional Virginia batteries—the Fauquier, Loudoun, and Turner Artillery (commanded respectively by Captains Robert M. Stribling, Arthur L. Rogers, and Walter D. Leake)—were left at Leesburg and did not enter Maryland. "Organization of the Army of Northern Virginia," 805 n. *.

[38] "I was wounded at Sharpsburg." James S. Brown to Samuel Cooper, May 7, 1864, Compiled Service Record of James S. Brown, Virginia (M324, reel 267).

[39] This unit is listed as "Walker's Brigade" in Carman's original table of organization, but he refers to it as "Manning's Brigade" throughout his narrative. For a full discussion, see p. 275 n. 84.

[40] However, French's Battery is listed as part of Manning's Brigade on the War Department tablet (no. 367) erected for that unit, under Carman's supervision, at Antietam National Battlefield.

[41] As above, Branch's Battery is listed as part of Ransom's Brigade on the latter's tablet (no. 362).

Hood's Division[42]
Brigadier General John B. Hood

[Wofford's] Brigade[43]
Colonel William T. Wofford

18th Georgia	Lieutenant Colonel Solon Z. Ruff
Hampton (South Carolina) Legion	Lieutenant Colonel Martin W. Gary
1st Texas	Lieutenant Colonel Philip A. Work
4th Texas	Lieutenant Colonel Benjamin F. Carter
5th Texas	Captain Isaac N. M. Turner

Law's Brigade
Colonel Evander M. Law

4th Alabama	Lieutenant Colonel Owen K. McLemore (mw, Sept. 14)
	Captain Lawrence H. Scruggs (w, Sept. 17)[44]
	Captain William M. Robbins
2d Mississippi	Colonel John M. Stone (w, Sept. 17)
	Lieutenant William C. Moody[45]
11th Mississippi	Colonel Philip F. Liddell ([mw], Sept. 16)[46]
	Lieutenant Colonel Samuel Butler ([mw], Sept. 17)[47]
	Major Taliaferro S. Evans (k, Sept. 17)
6th North Carolina	Major Robert F. Webb (w, Sept. 17)

artillery
Major Bushrod W. Frobel

German (South Carolina) Artillery	Captain William K. Bachman
Palmetto (South Carolina) Artillery	Captain Hugh R. Garden
Rowan (North Carolina) Artillery	Captain James Reilly

---

[42] For the fluctuating status of this division and its commander at the start of the campaign, see p. 42 n. 99.

[43] In Carman's original table of organization, this unit is listed as "Hood's Brigade," but (with one exception) it is designated as "Wofford's Brigade" throughout his narrative. For a full discussion, see p. 155 n. 24.

[44] In his original table of organization, Carman gives the name incorrectly as "H. L. Scruggs."

[45] In his original table of organization, Carman simply gives the name as "Lieut. Moody." The regiment carried two lieutenants named "William Moody" on its rolls during the war. Private William C. Moody of Company B was elected second lieutenant on April 21, 1862, while Private William M. Moody of Company A was not brevetted second lieutenant until March 21, 1863. See Compiled Service Record of William C. Moody, Compiled Service Records of Confederate Soldiers Who Served in Organizations from the State of Mississippi (National Archives Microfilm Publication M269, reel 119), Record Group 109, National Archives; Compiled Service Record of William H. [*sic*] Moody, Mississippi (M269, reel 119).

[46] In Carman's original table of organization, Liddell is listed as "killed." See Compiled Service Record of Philip F. Liddell, Mississippi (M269, reel 195).

[47] In Carman's original table of organization, Butler is listed as "killed." See Compiled Service Record of Samuel Butler, Mississippi (M269, reel 192).

Evans's [Independent] Brigade
Colonel Peter F. Stevens
Brigadier General Nathan G. Evans[48]

17th South Carolina	Colonel Fitz W. McMaster
18th South Carolina	Colonel William H. Wallace
22d South Carolina	Lieutenant Colonel Thomas C. Watkins ([mw, c], Sept. 14)[49]
	Major Miel Hilton
23d South Carolina	Captain S. A. Durham [(w, Sept. 14)][50]
	Lieutenant Edwin R. White
Holcombe (South Carolina) Legion	Colonel Peter F. Stevens
Macbeth (South Carolina) Artillery	Captain Robert Boyce

[Longstreet's reserve] artillery

Washington (Louisiana) Artillery
Colonel James B. Walton

1st Company	Captain Charles W. Squires
2d Company	Captain John B. Richardson
3d Company	Captain Merritt B. Miller
4th Company	Captain Benjamin F. Eshleman

Lee's Battalion
Colonel Stephen D. Lee

Ashland (Virginia) Artillery	Captain Pichegru Woolfolk Jr.
Bedford (Virginia) Artillery	Captain Tyler C. Jordan
Brooks (South Carolina) Artillery [Rhett's Battery]	Lieutenant William Elliott
Eubank's (Virginia) Battery	Captain John L. Eubank
Madison (Louisiana) Light Artillery	Captain George V. Moody
Parker's (Virginia) Battery	Captain William W. Parker

---

[48] In his original manuscript, Carman follows the format adopted by the editors of the *OR*, placing Evans above Stevens. As a matter of chronology, this is incorrect. It is true that, by the afternoon of September 17, Evans's provisional division (see p. 42 n. 99) consisted of little more than his own brigade and an assortment of rallied survivors from broken commands, but Evans's did not assume direct command of his own brigade until September 20, at which point Stevens returned to his regiment. Nathan G. Evans to Gilbert Moxley Sorrel, October 13, 1862, reprinted in *OR*, vol. 19, pt. 1, 939–40; Peter F. Stevens to Asa L. Evans, October 13, 1862, reprinted in *OR*, vol. 19, pt. 1, 941–42.

[49] In Carman's original table of organization, Watkins is listed as "killed." See Compiled Service Record of Thomas C. Watkins, South Carolina (M267, reel 330).

[50] "Having been wounded in the fight of Sunday, the 14th, I was not able to command the regiment the whole of Wednesday, and left it in charge of Lieut. E. R. White." S. A. Durham to Nathan G. Evans, October 16, 1862, reprinted in *OR*, vol. 19, pt. 1, 949.

JACKSON'S COMMAND
Major General Thomas J. Jackson

Ewell's Division
Brigadier General Alexander R. Lawton (w, Sept. 17)
Brigadier General Jubal A. Early

Lawton's Brigade
Colonel Marcellus Douglass (k, Sept. 17)
Major John H. Lowe
[Colonel John H. Lamar][51]

13th Georgia	Captain D. A. Kidd
26th Georgia	[Colonel Edmund N. Atkinson (w, Sept. 17)][52]
31st Georgia	Lieutenant Colonel John T. Crowder (w, Sept. 17)
	Major John H. Lowe
38th Georgia	Captain William H. Battey (k, Sept. 17)
	Captain Peter Brennan
	Captain John W. McCurdy
60th Georgia	Major Waters B. Jones
61st Georgia	[Colonel John H. Lamar]
	Major Archibald P. McRae (k, Sept. 17)
	Captain James D. Van Valkenburg [(w, Sept. 17)][53]

Trimble's Brigade
Colonel James A. Walker (w, Sept. 17)

15th Alabama	Captain Isaac B. Feagin [(w, Sept. 20)][54]
12th Georgia	Captain James G. Rodgers (k, Sept. 17)
	Captain John T. Carson
21st Georgia	Major Thomas C. Glover (w, Sept. 17)
	Captain James C. Nisbet [(w, Sept. 17)][55]
21st North Carolina	Captain Francis P. Miller (k, Sept. 17)
1st North Carolina Battalion	—————————[56]

---

[51] Carman neglects to include Lamar in his table of organization, yet does state correctly in the text (p. 368) that the colonel was in command of Lawton's Brigade as it covered the withdrawal of the army at Shepherdstown Ford—a fact attested to in numerous sources. See William N. Pendleton to Robert E. Lee, September 24, 1862, reprinted in *OR*, vol. 19, pt. 1, 831; Thomas J. Jackson to Lee, April 23, 1863, reprinted in *OR*, vol. 19, pt. 1, 957; Jubal A. Early to Alexander S. Pendleton, January 12, 1863, reprinted in *OR*, vol. 19, pt. 1, 972. Lamar's whereabouts on September 17 are unstated but can be surmised from the official report of the brigade's actions that day, submitted by Lowe: "After a severe engagement, the brigade was compelled to fall back a short distance. Re-enforcements then came, and with them we made a charge in the most gallant manner. During that time (before the charge) *the brigade lost its commander, and nearly every regiment lost its regimental commander*; also the greater portion of the different companies lost their company commanders ... Finding that I was senior officer present, I reformed the brigade and reported to Brigadier-General Early [emphasis added]." Report of John H. Lowe, October 13, 1862, reprinted in *OR*, vol. 19, pt. 1, 975. It would appear that Lamar sustained a wound (around the same time that Douglass was killed) sufficient to remove him from further command that day, yet light enough for him to assume command of the brigade by the morning of the nineteenth.

[52] See Compiled Service Record of Edmund N. Atkinson, Georgia (M266, reel 371). Carman leaves this space blank.

[53] See Compiled Service Record of James D. Van Valkenburg, Georgia (M266, reel 561).

[54] "Next morning [September 20] I was ordered to move back to the vicinity of Shepherdstown Ford with the three brigades which were with me ... In this position they remained until late in the afternoon, ... being in range of the enemy's shells, by one of which Captain Feagin, in command of the Fifteenth Alabama Regiment, was seriously wounded." Early to Alexander S. Pendleton, 973.

[55] "As I threw my leg over the top rail of the last fence, a minnie ball went through the rail, the folds of my blanket and oil cloth, striking me squarely on the sword clasp. I fell into the road unconscious, lying upon elevated ground." James Cooper Nisbet, *Four Years on the Firing Line* (Chattanooga: Imperial Press, n.d.), 153. "Our surgeon, after examining my wound, ordered me to the hospital at Shepperdstown [*sic*], across the river, as I was unfit for duty, and it was expected the fight would be renewed next day." Ibid., 161–62.

[56] The 1st North Carolina Battalion was attached to the 21st North Carolina.—*EAC*

Hays's Brigade
Brigadier General Harry T. Hays

5th Louisiana	Colonel Henry Forno
6th Louisiana	Colonel Henry B. Strong (k, Sept. 17)
7th Louisiana	[Colonel Davidson B. Penn (w, Sept. 17)][57]
8th Louisiana	Lieutenant Colonel Trevanion D. Lewis [(w, Sept. 17)][58]
14th Louisiana	[Lieutenant Colonel David Zable (w, Sept. 17)][59]

Early's Brigade
Brigadier General Jubal A. Early
Colonel William Smith (w, Sept. 17)

13th Virginia	Captain Frank V. Winston
25th Virginia	Captain Robert D. Lilley
31st Virginia	not known[60]
44th Virginia	Captain David W. Anderson
49th Virginia	Colonel William Smith
	Lieutenant Colonel John C. Gibson
52d Virginia	Colonel Michael G. Harman
58th Virginia	[Major John G. Kasey][61]
	[Captain Henry W. Wingfield][62]

artillery[63]
Major Alfred R. Courtney

Johnson's (Virginia) Battery	Captain John R. Johnson
Louisiana Guard Artillery	Captain Louis E. D'Aquin
1st Maryland Battery	Captain William F. Dement
Staunton (Virginia) Artillery	Lieutenant Asher W. Garber
[Brown's (Maryland) Battery][64]	[Captain William D. Brown]
[Latimer's (Virginia) Battery]	[Captain Joseph W. Latimer]

---

[57] See Compiled Service Record of David B. Penn, Compiled Service Records of Confederate Soldiers Who Served in Organizations from the State of Louisiana (National Archives Microfilm Publication M320, reel 182), Record Group 109, National Archives. Carman leaves this space blank.

[58] See Compiled Service Record of Trevanion D. Lewis, Louisiana (M320, reel 194).

[59] See Compiled Service Record of David Zable, Louisiana (M320, reel 263). Carman leaves this space blank.

[60] Returns for the regiment show its colonel, John S. Hoffman, absent, sick, for the month of September 1862. Compiled Service Record of John S. Hoffman, Virginia (M324, reel 775).

[61] "September 6, 1862. Started early this morning and after we had proceeded to within sight of Buckey Town Major Kasey being sick gave up the command of the Regt. to me and went back." Diary of Henry W. Wingfield, reprinted in W. W. Scott, ed., "Two Confederate Items," *Bulletin of the Virginia State Library* 16, no. 2 and 3 (July 1927): 16. Carman leaves this space blank.

[62] "September 14, 1862 … Still in command of Regt." Ibid. "September 17, 1862 … The 58th Va. which I commanded behaved quite gallantly." Ibid., 17.

[63] "The Charlottesville Artillery, left at Richmond in August, did not rejoin the Army till after the battle of Sharpsburg." "Organization of the Army of Northern Virginia," 807 n. *.

[64] Carman omits Brown's and Latimer's Batteries from his table of organization but credits them properly in his narrative as having participated in the bombardment of Harper's Ferry (see pp. 122, 125–26).

A. P. Hill's (Light) Division
[Brigadier General Lawrence O'Bryan Branch]
Major General Ambrose P. Hill[65]

Branch's Brigade
Brigadier General Lawrence O'Bryan Branch (k, Sept. 17)
Colonel James H. Lane

7th North Carolina	Colonel Edward G. Haywood
18th North Carolina	Lieutenant Colonel Thomas J. Purdie
28th North Carolina	Colonel James H. Lane
	Major William J. Montgomery
33d North Carolina	Lieutenant Colonel Robert F. Hoke
37th North Carolina	Captain William G. Morris

Gregg's Brigade
Brigadier General Maxcy Gregg (w, Sept. 17)

1st South Carolina (Provisional Army)	Colonel Daniel H. Hamilton[66]
1st South Carolina Rifles	Lieutenant Colonel James M. Perrin
12th South Carolina	Colonel Dixon Barnes ([mw], Sept. 17)[67]
	Major William H. McCorkle
13th South Carolina	Colonel Oliver E. Edwards
14th South Carolina	Lieutenant Colonel William D. Simpson

Archer's Brigade
Brigadier General James J. Archer[68]
Colonel Peter Turney

5th Alabama Battalion	Captain Charles M. Hooper
19th Georgia	Major James H. Neal
	Captain Tilghman W. Flynt [(w, Sept. 17)][69]
	Captain Frank M. Johnston
1st Tennessee (Provisional Army)	Colonel Peter Turney
7th Tennessee	Major Samuel G. Shepard
	Lieutenant George A. Howard
14th Tennessee	Colonel William McComb (w, Sept. 17)
	Lieutenant Colonel James W. Lockert

---

[65] Prior to crossing into Maryland, Hill was placed under arrest arrested by Jackson, only to be released "temporarily" on September 10 due to the exigencies of the campaign. A copy of Jackson's charges against Hill appears as an appendix in William Woods Hassler, *A. P. Hill: Lee's Forgotten General* (Richmond: Garrett & Massie, 1957), n.p.

[66] Hamilton was not with his unit for the opening phase of the campaign. "I was not present with my regiment [at Second Manassas and Chantilly], being on sick leave, in consequence of a severe and protracted illness, contracted by exposure and fatigue in the battles of June 26, 27, and 30, and July 1, around Richmond … At Frederick City, Md., I rejoined my regiment and resumed command of it." Daniel H. Hamilton to Alexander C. Haskell, September 30, 1862, reprinted in *OR*, vol. 19, pt. 1, 991. The compilers of the table of organization in the *OR* state that Maj. Edward McCrady Jr. commanded in Hamilton's absence. However, McCrady was wounded in the head at Second Manassas, and as late as September 1 he had not yet returned to duty. Hamilton to Haskell, September 30, 1862, reprinted in *OR*, vol. 12, pt. 2, 684.

[67] In Carman's original table of organization, Barnes is listed as "killed." See Compiled Service Record of Dixon Barnes, South Carolina (M267, reel 254).

[68] "The next morning after the capture of Harper's Ferry, being too unwell for duty, I turned over the command of the brigade to Colonel Turney (First Tennessee), under whom, with the exception of the Fifth Alabama, it marched to the battle-field of Sharpsburg, while I followed in an ambulance … I resumed command just as the brigade was forming into line on the ground assigned to it by General Hill … The next morning about 9 o'clock, the little strength with which I entered the fight being completely exhausted, I turned over the command to Colonel Turney, reported to the major-general commanding, and left the field." James J. Archer to Richard C. Morgan, March 1, 1863, reprinted in *OR*, vol. 19, pt. 1, 1001.

[69] Carman's reason for including Flynt (whom he styles "Capt. T. W. Flynnt" in his original table of organization) is unclear. Neal writes that he turned the command over to Johnston on the nineteenth and resumed it on the twenty-third. Report of James H. Neal, November 19, 1862, reprinted in *OR*, vol. 19, pt. 1, 1003. It must be noted, however, that this is not a formal report; it is not addressed to any particular officer and bears the sub-title (given by the editors of the *OR*) "Abstract of march made and actions engaged in by Nineteenth Georgia Volunteers from September 4, 1862, to October 19, 1862." Whatever Flynt's role on the seventeenth, it drew the attention of his brigade commander. "My loss in this action was 15 killed and 90 wounded; among the latter Colonel [William] McComb, Fourteenth Tennessee, severely, and Captain [T. W.] Flynt, Nineteenth Georgia, dangerously. The gallant conduct of both these officers attracted my attention, though where all who were engaged behaved so gallantly it is difficult to select examples of particular merit." Archer to Morgan, 1001.

[Brockenbrough's] Brigade[70]
Colonel John M. Brockenbrough

40th Virginia	Lieutenant Colonel Fleet W. Cox
47th Virginia	Lieutenant Colonel John W. Lyell
55th Virginia	Major Charles N. Lawson
22d Virginia Battalion	Major Edward P. Tayloe

Thomas's Brigade
Colonel Edward L. Thomas

14th Georgia	Colonel Robert W. Folsom
35th Georgia	not known[71]
45th Georgia	Major Washington L. Grice
49th Georgia	Lieutenant Colonel Seaborn M. Manning

Pender's Brigade
Brigadier General William Dorsey Pender[72]

16th North Carolina	Lieutenant Colonel William A. Stowe
22d North Carolina	Major Christopher C. Cole
34th North Carolina	Lieutenant Colonel John L. McDowell
38th North Carolina	[Lieutenant Colonel Robert F. Armfield (w, Sept. 20)][73]

artillery[74]
Major Reuben Lindsay Walker

Crenshaw's (Virginia) Battery	Captain William G. Crenshaw
Fredericksburg (Virginia) Artillery	Captain Carter M. Braxton
Pee Dee (South Carolina) Artillery	Captain David G. McIntosh
Purcell (Virginia) Artillery	Captain William J. Pegram
Letcher (Virginia) Artillery	Captain Greenlee Davidson

---

[70] In his original manuscript, Carman refers to this unit as "Field's Brigade" in his table of organization, but as "Brockenbrough's Brigade" throughout the narrative.

[71] The commanding officer was most likely Lieutenant Colonel Bolling C. Holt, but the editor has not found any evidence to verify his presence. In his report of the campaign, Thomas commends the other three regimental leaders by name but makes no reference at all to the 35th Georgia. Edward L. Thomas to Morgan, October 26, 1862, reprinted in *OR*, vol. 19, pt. 1, 1006. See also John J. Fox, III, *Red Clay to Georgia: Trail of the 35th Georgia Infantry Regiment, C.S.A.* (Winchester, Va.: Angel Valley Press, 2004), 122–23.

[72] In his narrative, Carman states that Pender had overall command of three brigades during one stage of the operations against Harper's Ferry, during which time his own brigade was temporarily commanded by Lieutenant Richard H. Brewer (see p. 119).

[73] "Lieutenant-Colonel Armfield took command as soon as Colonel Hoke was wounded [at Mechanicsville, June 26, 1862] ... On 27 December Colonel William J. Hoke rejoined the regiment. Lieutenant-Colonel Armfield, while at home on furlough, *on account of a wound received at Shepardstown* [sic], was elected solicitor, and resigned his position in the army [emphasis added]." George W. Flowers, "Thirty-Eighth Regiment," in Walter Clark, ed., *Histories of the Several Regiments and Battalions from North Carolina in the Great War 1861–65*, vol. 2 (Goldsboro, N.C.: Nash Brothers, 1901), 681, 687. See also Compiled Service Record of Robert F. Armfield, Compiled Service Records of Confederate Soldiers Who Served in Organizations from the State of North Carolina (National Archives Microfilm Publication M270, reel 408), Record Group 109, National Archives. Carman leaves this space blank.

[74] Two additional Virginia batteries—the Branch (North Carolina) and Middlesex (Virginia) Artillery (commanded respectively by Captains A. C. Latham and William C. Fleet—were left at Leesburg and did not enter Maryland. "Organization of the Army of Northern Virginia," 807 n. †.

Jackson's Division
Brigadier General John R. Jones (w, Sept. 17)[75]
Brigadier General William E. Starke (k, Sept. 17)
Colonel Andrew J. Grigsby

Winder's Brigade
Colonel Andrew J. Grigsby
Lieutenant Colonel Robert D. Gardner (w, [Sept. 17])[76]
Major Hazael J. Williams

[2d Virginia]	[Captain Raleigh T. Colston][77]
4th Virginia	Lieutenant Colonel Robert D. Gardner
5th Virginia	Major Hazael J. Williams
	Captain Edwin L. Curtis (w, Sept. 17)
27th Virginia	Captain Frank C. Wilson
33d Virginia	Captain Jacob B. Golladay (w, Sept. 17)
	Lieutenant David H. Walton

Jones's Brigade
Colonel Bradley T. Johnson[78]
Captain John E. Penn (w, Sept. 17)
Captain Archer C. Page (w, Sept. 17)
Captain Robert W. Withers

21st Virginia	Captain Archer C. Page
42d Virginia	Captain Robert W. Withers
48th Virginia	Captain John H. Candler
1st Virginia Battalion	Lieutenant Charles A. Davidson

Taliaferro's Brigade
Colonel Edward T. H. Warren
Colonel James W. Jackson (w, Sept. 17)
[Lieutenant Colonel John F. Terry (w, Sept. 17)][79]
Colonel James L. Sheffield

47th Alabama	Colonel James W. Jackson
	Major James M. Campbell
48th Alabama	Colonel James L. Sheffield
[10th Virginia]	[Colonel Edward T. H. Warren][80]
23d Virginia	[Lieutenant Colonel Simeon T. Walton (w, Sept. 17)][81]
37th Virginia	Lieutenant Colonel John F. Terry

---

[75] Jones had been on sick leave since late July and reunited with the army in Frederick around the sixth of September. See Welsh, 123; Bradley T. Johnson, *Maryland*, vol. 2 of *Confederate Military History*, ed. Clement A. Evans (Atlanta: Confederate Publishing Co., 1899), 91.

[76] In his original manuscript, Carman does not give a date for Gardner's wounding. See Compiled Service Record of Robert M. Gardner, Virginia (M324, reel 406).

[77] "On the 13th, marched to Martinsburg, halted two hours, and moved toward Harper's Ferry, the Second Regiment, Captain Colston commanding, having been detached as provost guard, remaining in town encamped for the night within sight of the enemy's tents." Hazael J. Williams to Warner T. Taliaferro, January 15, 1863, reprinted in *OR*, vol. 19, pt. 1, 1011. The 2d Virginia was retained in Martinsburg for the remainder of the campaign. See Dennis E. Frye, *2d Virginia Infantry* (Lynchburg, Va.: H. E. Howard, 1984), 43–44.

[78] "After the occupation of Frederick City ... Colonel Johnson was relieved of the command of the Second Brigade. Colonel Johnson was then ordered to Richmond, and appointed Colonel of Cavalry, and assigned for duty on the military court stationed in Richmond, here to await promotion." W. W. Goldsborough, *The Maryland Line in the Confederate Army, 1861–1865* (Baltimore: Guggenheimer, Weil, & Co., 1900), 71.

[79] "I was knocked down by a ball just before the retreat began & seeing me fall was the cause of [Taliaferro's Brigade] giving way too soon. As I came to my senses I found I was wounded in the right arm, the ball penetrating to the bone. I hobbled off the field & rallied my men behind a hill & turned over command to Col. Terry who was wounded allmost [*sic*] immediately." James W. Jackson to Jennie Cloud Jackson, September 21, 1862, reprinted in "Providence has been kind ...," *Military Images* 20, no. 4 (January/February 1999): 22.

[80] Colonel Warren and the 10th Virginia were retained at Martinsburg for the remainder of the campaign. See D. H. Lee Martz, "A History of the 10th Virginia Regiment, Volunteer Infantry," in John W. Wayland, *A History of Rockingham County* (Dayton, Va.: Ruebush-Elkins Co., 1912), 138. Carman included this regiment in his original table of organization, then crossed it out.

[81] See Compiled Service Record of Simeone [*sic*] T. Walton, Virginia (M324, reel 670). Carman leaves this space blank.

Starke's Brigade

Brigadier General William E. Starke
Colonel Jesse M. Williams (w, Sept. 17)
Colonel Leroy A. Stafford (w, Sept. 17)
Colonel Edmund Pendleton

1st Louisiana	Lieutenant Colonel Michael Nolan (w, Sept. 17)
	Captain William E. Moore
2d Louisiana	Colonel Jesse M. Williams
9th Louisiana	Colonel Leroy A. Stafford
	Lieutenant Colonel William R. Peck
10th Louisiana	Captain Henry D. Monier
15th Louisiana	Colonel Edmund Pendleton
Coppens's (Louisiana) Battalion	not known

artillery

Major Lindsay M. Shumaker

Alleghany (Virginia) Artillery	Captain [John C.] Carpenter [(w, Sept. 17)][82]
Brockenbrough's (Maryland) Battery	Captain John B. Brockenbrough
Danville (Virginia) Artillery	Captain George W. Wooding
Lee (Virginia) [Artillery]	Captain Charles I. Raine
Rockbridge (Virginia) Artillery	Captain William T. Poague
[Hampden (Virginia) Artillery][83]	[Captain William H. Caskie]

D. H. Hill's Division

Major General Daniel H. Hill

Ripley's Brigade

Brigadier General Roswell S. Ripley (w, Sept. 17)
Colonel George Doles

4th Georgia	Colonel George Doles
	Major Robert S. Smith (k, Sept. 17)
	Captain William H. Willis
44th Georgia	Captain John C. Key
1st North Carolina	Lieutenant Colonel Hamilton A. Brown
3d North Carolina	Colonel William L. DeRosset (w, Sept. 17)
	Major Stephen D. Thruston (w, Sept. 17)

---

[82] In his original table of organization, Carman lists the commanding officer as Captain Joseph Carpenter. Joseph was the battery commander until August 8, 1862, when he was mortally wounded at Cedar Mountain. See C. A. Fonerden, *A Brief History of the Military Career of Carpenter's Battery: From Its Organization as a Rifle Company Under the Name of the Alleghany Roughs to the Ending of the War between the States* (New Market, Va.: Henkel & Co., 1911), 30. His brother John was elevated to the command and led the battery in the Maryland campaign until he too was wounded. "Ordered to report to General Jeb Stuart for detached duty at daylight the next morning [September 17], . . . we became engaged fiercely, and Captain John Carpenter was severely wounded, being entirely incapacitated for duty, his knee being crushed so badly by a shell that the synovial fluid was discharged." Ibid., 38.

[83] "This [the Federal fire] was vigorously replied to by the batteries of Poague, Carpenter, Brockenbrough, Raine, *Caskie*, and Wooding [emphasis added]." Jackson to Lee, 956. But a modern unit history states, "Whether or not the Hampden Artillery joined the battalion [in the Maryland campaign] is unclear . . . The only indication that is given of [the battery's] participation is a metal marker [no. 382] on the field [at Antietam] that actually refers to the entire battalion. Maps made in postwar years give no further clue to the location of the Hampden Battery's guns." Robert H. Moore, II, *The Richmond Fayette, Hampden, Thomas, and Blount's Lynchburg Artillery* (Lynchburg, Va.: H. E. Howard, 1991), 29–30. As part of a major reorganization of the army's artillery in early October 1862, the battery received the men and guns of the disbanded Thomas (Virginia) Artillery. It is possible, therefore, that the Hampden Artillery was another of those understrength batteries left behind in Leesburg when the army crossed into Maryland.

Rodes's Brigade

Brigadier General Robert E. Rodes (w, Sept. 17)

3d Alabama	Colonel Cullen A. Battle
5th Alabama	Major Edwin L. Hobson
6th Alabama	Colonel John B. Gordon (w, Sept. 17)
	Lieutenant Colonel James N. Lightfoot (w, Sept. 17)
12th Alabama	Colonel Bristor B. Gayle (k, Sept. 14)
	Lieutenant Colonel Samuel B. Pickens (w, Sept. 14)
	Captain Exton Tucker (k, Sept. 17)
	Captain William L. Maroney (k, Sept. 17)
	Captain Adolph Proskaner (w, Sept. 17)
26th Alabama	Colonel Edward A. O'Neal (w, Sept. [14])[84]

Garland's Brigade

Brigadier General Samuel Garland Jr. (k, Sept. 14)

Colonel Duncan K. McRae (w, Sept. 17)

5th North Carolina	Colonel Duncan K. McRae
	Captain Thomas M. Garrett
12th North Carolina	Captain Shugan Snow
13th North Carolina	Lieutenant Colonel Thomas Ruffin Jr.[85]
	Captain Joseph H. Hyman
20th North Carolina	Colonel Alfred Iverson Jr.
23d North Carolina	Colonel Daniel H. Christie
	[Lieutenant Colonel Robert D. Johnston][86]

---

[84] Carman gives the date of O'Neal's wounding inadvertently as the seventeenth. Rodes's official report, which Carman quotes at great length, specifically mentions O'Neal being wounded at Turner's Gap (see p. 158).

[85] "Owing to an accident, I was not able to command the regiment on the 17th, and, therefore, have the honor to call your attention to the accompanying report from Captain Hyman, who commanded on that day." Thomas Ruffin Jr. to James M. Taylor, October 12, 1862, reprinted in *OR*, vol. 19, pt. 1, 1047. In his original table of organization, Carman lists him as having been wounded on the fourteenth.

[86] This omission of Johnston is likely inadvertent, as Carman mentions in his narrative that Johnston was commanding the regiment at the sunken road (see p. 277). See also n. 87 below.

G. B. Anderson's Brigade

Brigadier General George B. Anderson (mw, Sept. 17)
Colonel Charles C. Tew (k, Sept. 17)
Colonel Risden T. Bennett (w, Sept. 17)
[Colonel Daniel H. Christie][87]

2d North Carolina	Colonel Charles C. Tew
	Major John Howard (w, Sept. 17)
	Captain George M. Roberts
4th North Carolina	Colonel Bryan Grimes[88]
	Captain William T. Marsh (k, Sept. 17)
	Captain Edwin A. Osborne (w, Sept. 17)
	Captain Daniel P. Latham (k, Sept. 17)
	[Lieutenant Franklin H. Weaver (k, Sept. 17)][89]
14th North Carolina	Colonel Risden T. Bennett
	Lieutenant Colonel William A. Johnston (w, Sept. 17)
	[Captain] Andrew J. Griffith[90]
30th North Carolina	Colonel Francis M. Parker (w, Sept. 17)
	Major William W. Sillers

[87] "The 18th [of September] was spent in line of battle ready for the attack which did not come. Lieutenant-Colonel R. D. Johnston was now in command of the Twenty-third, Colonel Christie having been placed in command of General Anderson's brigade." V. E. Turner and H. C. Wall, "Twenty-third Regiment," in Clark, vol. 2, 223.

[88] "On the 5th, when crossing the Potomac ..., I received a very severe hurt from the kick of a horse, which incapacitated me from active duty, not being able to either walk or ride, but had myself carried in an ambulance in anticipation and hopes of a speedy recovery ... On the 14th of September ..., I had myself placed upon my horse and took the command of my regiment ... Here my horse was killed under me on the mountain and to my own and the surprise of my command I commanded my troops in the battle until nightfall, when I threw myself down to rest by my brigade commander, Gen. G. B. Anderson, who seeing me so exhausted after the excitement of the day, insisted upon my going to the rear, and called up four litter bearers and had me carried to the hospital." Bryan Grimes, *Extracts of Letters of Major-Gen'l Bryan Grimes to His Wife: Written While in Active Service in the Army of Northern Virginia; Together with Some Personal Recollections of the War, Written by Him After Its Close, etc.*, comp. Pulaski Cowper (Raleigh, N.C.: Edwards, Broughton & Co., 1883), 19–20.

[89] "One by one the other company officers fell, either killed or wounded, until Second Lieutenant Weaver, of Company H., was in command of the handful of men who were left, and then he was killed bearing the colors of the regiment in his hand. The regiment was left without a commissioned officer; but the men needed none, except for general purposes." Edwin A. Osborne, "Fourth Regiment," in Clark, vol. 1, 247.

[90] In his original table of organization, Carman lists him incorrectly as "Major A. J. Griffiths." See Compiled Service Record of Andrew J. Griffith, North Carolina (M270, reel 224).

Colquitt's Brigade

Colonel Alfred H. Colquitt

13th Alabama	Colonel Birkett D. Fry (w, Sept. 17)[91]
	[Lieutenant Colonel William H. Betts (w, Sept. 17)][92]
	[Captain] Algernon S. Reaves (w, Sept. 17)[93]
6th Georgia	Lieutenant Colonel James M. Newton (k, Sept. 17)
	Major Philemon Tracy (k, Sept. 17)
	Lieutenant Eugene P. Burnet[94]
23d Georgia	Colonel William P. Barclay (k, Sept. 17)
	Lieutenant Colonel Emory F. Best (w, Sept. 17)
	Major James H. Huggins (w, Sept. 17)[95]
27th Georgia	Colonel Levi B. Smith (k, Sept. 17)
	Lieutenant Colonel Charles T. Zachry (w, Sept. 17)
	Captain William H. Rentfro
28th Georgia	Major Tully Graybill (w, Sept. 14)
	Captain Nehemiah J. Garrison (w, Sept. 17)
	Captain George W. Warthen

artillery

Major Scipio F. Pierson

Hardaway's (Alabama) Battery	Lieutenant John W. Tullis[96]
Jeff Davis (Alabama) Artillery	Captain James W. Bondurant
Jones's (Virginia) Battery	Captain William B. Jones
King William (Virginia) Artillery	Captain Thomas H. Carter

[general] reserve artillery

Brigadier General William N. Pendleton

Cutts's Battalion

Lieutenant Colonel Allen S. Cutts

Blackshear's (Georgia) Battery	Captain James A. Blackshear
Irwin (Georgia) Artillery	Captain John Lane
Lloyd's (North Carolina) Battery	Captain Whitmel P. Lloyd
Patterson's (Georgia) Battery	Captain George M. Patterson
Ross's (Georgia) Battery	Captain Hugh M. Ross

---

[91] In his original table of organization, Carman gives the name incorrectly as "D. B. Fry."

[92] "Lieutenant-Colonel Betts, Thirteenth Alabama, was slightly wounded." Daniel H. Hill to Chilton, 1862 [no day or month given], reprinted in *OR*, vol. 19, pt. 1, 1027. Although Carman omits him from his original table of organization, Betts is referenced in the text (see p. 324).

[93] In his original table of organization, Carman gives Reaves's rank incorrectly as "Major." See Compiled Service Record of Algernon S. Reaves, Compiled Service Records of Confederate Soldiers Who Served in Organizations from the State of Alabama (National Archives Microfilm Publication M374, reel 225), Record Group 109, National Archives.

[94] The name is given incorrectly in many records as "Burnett," which is how Carman styles him in his original table of organization. See Compiled Service Record of Eugene P. Burnet, Georgia (M266, reel 205).

[95] However, the director of Georgia's Confederate Pension and Record Department asserts that Huggins was "wounded in both legs at South Mountain, Md. Sept. 14, 1862." Lillian Henderson, comp., *Roster of the Confederate Soldiers of Georgia, 1861–1865*, vol. 2 (Hapeville, Ga.: Longino & Porter, n.d.), 1018. Huggins's service record provides no evidence to favor one date over the other. Compiled Service Record of James H. Huggins, Georgia (M266, reel 351).

[96] The editors of the *OR* list Captain Robert A. Hardaway as the commander during the Maryland campaign. "Organization of the Army of Northern Virginia," 809. According to his compiled service record, Hardaway was hospitalized for fever on August 6, but returned to duty on September 1. Compiled Service Record of Robert A. Hardaway, Alabama (M374, reel 75). In a letter to Carman, however, Tullis stated that "Hardway [*sic*] was sick and left behind, and I commanded the Battery all through the Maryland campaign." John W. Tullis to Carman, April 6, 1900, "Gen. D. H. Hill's Report—Pierson's Artillery Battalion, Hill's Division" folder, box 3, "Antietam Studies."

Jones's Battalion
Major Hilary P. Jones

Morris (Virginia) Artillery	Captain Richard C. M. Page
Orange (Virginia) Artillery	Captain Thomas J. Peyton[97]
Turner's (Virginia) Battery	Captain William H. Turner
Wimbish's (Virginia) Battery	Captain Abram Wimbish

Brown's Battalion
Colonel John Thompson Brown

✔ Powhatan (Virginia) Artillery	Captain Willis J. Dance —
2d Company, Richmond (Virginia) Howitzers	Captain David Watson
3d Company, Richmond (Virginia) Howitzers	Captain Benjamin H. Smith Jr.
Salem (Virginia) Artillery	Captain Abraham Hupp
Williamsburg (Virginia) Artillery	Captain John A. Coke

Nelson's Battalion[98]
Major William Nelson

Amherst (Virginia) Artillery	Captain Thomas J. Kirkpatrick
Fluvanna (Virginia) Artillery	Captain John J. Ancell
Huckstep's (Virginia) Battery	Captain Charles T. Huckstep
Johnson's (Virginia) Battery	Captain Marmaduke Johnson
Milledge (Georgia) Artillery	Captain John Milledge Jr.

miscellaneous[99]

Cutshaw's (Virginia) Battery	Captain Wilford E. Cutshaw
Magruder (Virginia) Artillery	Captain Thomas J. Page Jr.
Rice's (Virginia) Battery	Captain William H. Rice
Dixie (Virginia) Artillery	Captain William H. Chapman[100]

cavalry division
Major General James E. B. Stuart

Hampton's Brigade
Brigadier General Wade Hampton

1st North Carolina Cavalry	Colonel Lawrence S. Baker
2d South Carolina Cavalry	Colonel Matthew C. Butler
Cobb's (Georgia) Legion (cavalry battalion)	[Lieutenant Colonel Pierce M. B. Young (w, Sept. 13)][101]
	Major William G. Delony
Jeff Davis (Mississippi) Legion	Lieutenant Colonel William T. Martin
[10th Virginia Cavalry][102]	[Colonel James L. Davis]

---

97   Carman styles him "Jefferson Payton" is his original table of organization.

98   Brown's and Nelson's Battalions were not engaged at Antietam; they remained on the Virginia side of the Potomac, near Shepherdstown Ford.—*EAC*

99   One additional Virginia battery—the Thomas Artillery (Captain Edwin J. Anderson)—was left at Leesburg and did not enter Maryland. "Organization of the Army of Northern Virginia," 809 n. **.

100   In his original table of organization, Carman gives the name incorrectly as "G. B. Chapman."

101   "Our loss was 4 killed and 9 wounded, among … the latter Lieutenant-Colonel Young." James E. B. Stuart to Chilton, February 13, 1864, reprinted in *OR*, vol. 19, pt. 1, 817–18. Although Carman omits him from his original table of organization, Young is referenced in the text (see p. 95).

102   The 10th Virginia Cavalry spent almost the entire campaign on the Virginia side of the Potomac, crossing briefly only after the fighting at Sharpsburg had concluded. See Robert J. Driver Jr., *10th Virginia Cavalry* (Lynchburg, Va.: H. E. Howard, 1992), 23–24.

Lee's Brigade
Brigadier General Fitzhugh Lee

1st Virginia Cavalry	Lieutenant Colonel Luke Tiernan Brien
3d Virginia Cavalry	Lieutenant Colonel John T. Thornton (k, Sept. 17)
	Captain Thomas H. Owen
4th Virginia Cavalry	Colonel Williams C. Wickham
5th Virginia Cavalry	Colonel Thomas L. Rosser
9th Virginia Cavalry	Colonel William H. F. Lee (w, Sept. 15)[103]

[Robertson's] Brigade[104]
[Brigadier General Beverly H. Robertson][105]
Colonel Thomas T. Munford

2d Virginia Cavalry	Lieutenant Colonel Richard H. Burks (12th Virginia Cavalry)
7th Virginia Cavalry	Captain Samuel B. Myers
12th Virginia Cavalry	Colonel Asher W. Harman
17th Virginia Cavalry Battalion[106]	not known

Stuart Horse Artillery
Captain John Pelham

Chew's (Virginia) Battery	Captain Roger P. Chew
Hart's (South Carolina) Battery	Captain James F. Hart
Pelham's (Virginia) Battery	Captain John Pelham

---

[103] In his original table of organization, Carman lists the name inadvertently as "W. H. H. Lee," but renders it properly in the narrative.

[104] Carman designates this as "Munford's Brigade" in his original table of organization. For a full discussion, see p. 46 n. 6.
An additional regiment of the brigade, the 6th Virginia Cavalry, was left at Centreville, Virginia, to collect arms and equipment. Stuart to Chilton, 816.

[105] Robertson commanded the brigade in one of the opening skirmishes of the campaign before being relieved from duty with Lee's army (see pp. 43–44).

[106] "The seventeenth Virginia Battalion was detached before crossing the Potomac on an expedition to Berkeley." Stuart to Chilton, 816.

The despot's heel is on thy shore,
  Maryland!
His torch is at thy temple door,
  Maryland!
Avenge the patriotic gore
That flecked the streets of Baltimore,
And be the battle queen of yore,
  Maryland, my Maryland!

Hark to an exiled son's appeal,
  Maryland!
My mother State, to thee I kneel,
  Maryland!
For life or death, for woe or weal,
Thy peerless chivalry reveal,
And gird thy beauteous limbs with steel,
  Maryland, my Maryland!

Thou wilt not cower in the dust,
  Maryland!
Thy beaming sword shall never rust,
  Maryland!
Remember Carroll's sacred trust,
Remember Howard's warlike thrust,
And all thy slumberers with the just,
  Maryland, my Maryland!

Come! 'Tis the red dawn of the day,
  Maryland!
Come with thy panoplied array,
  Maryland!
With Ringgolds' spirit for the fray,
With Watson's blood at Monterey,
With fearless Lowe and dashing May,
  Maryland, my Maryland!

Dear mother, burst the tyrant's chain,
  Maryland!
Virginia should not call in vain,
  Maryland!
She meets her sisters on the plain,
"*Sic semper*!" 'tis the proud refrain

That baffles minions back amain,
  Maryland!
Arise in majesty again,
  Maryland, my Maryland!

Come! for thy shield is bright and strong,
  Maryland!
Come! for thy dalliance does thee wrong,
  Maryland!
Come to thine own heroic throng
Stalking with liberty along,
And chant thy dauntless slogan-song,
  Maryland, my Maryland!

I see the blush upon thy cheek,
  Maryland!
But thou wast ever bravely meek,
  Maryland!
But lo! There surges forth a shriek,
From hill to hill, from creek to creek,
Potomac calls to Chesapeake,
  Maryland, my Maryland!

Thou wilt not yield the Vandal toll,
  Maryland!
Thou wilt not crook to his control,
  Maryland!
Better the fire upon thee roll,
Better the shot, the blade, the bowl,
Than crucifixion of the soul,
  Maryland, my Maryland!

I hear the distant thunder-hum,
  Maryland!
The "Old Line's" bugle, fife, and drum,
  Maryland!
She is not dead, nor deaf, nor dumb;
Huzza! she spurns the Northern scum—
She breathes, she burns! She'll come!
She'll come!
  Maryland, my Maryland![1]

---

[1] Reprinted in Louis Albert Banks, *Immortal Songs of Camp and Field* (Cleveland: Burrow Brothers Co., 1898), 205–7.

The author of this stirring and popular song is James R. Randall, who at the time of writing was a professor of English literature at Poydras College in Louisiana. On April 26, 1861, he read in a New Orleans paper an account of the attack on the 6th Massachusetts as it passed through Baltimore. Randall says:

This account excited me greatly … I had long been absent from my native city, and the startling event there inflamed my mind. That night I could not sleep, for my nerves were all unstrung, and I could not dismiss what I had read in the paper from my mind. About midnight I arose, lit a candle, and went to my desk. Some powerful spirit appeared to possess me, and almost involuntarily I proceeded to write the song of "My Maryland." I remember that the idea appeared to take shape first as music in the brain—some wild air that I cannot now recall. The whole poem of nine stanzas, as originally written, was dashed off rapidly when once begun.[2]

The manner in which the words were wedded to music is told by Hattie Cary of Baltimore, afterwards the wife of Professor H. M. Martin of Johns Hopkins University:

The Glee Club was to hold its meeting in our parlors one evening early in June … and my sister Jennie, being the only musical member of the family, had charge of the program on the occasion. With a schoolgirl's eagerness to score a success, she resolved to secure some new and ardent expression of feelings that were by this time wrought up to the point of explosion. In vain she searched through her stock of songs and airs—nothing seemed intense enough to suit her. Aroused by her tone of despair, I came to the rescue with the suggestion that she should adapt the words of "Maryland, My Maryland," which had been continuously on my lips since the appearance of the lyric a few days before in the South. I produced the paper and began declaiming the verses. "*Lauriger Horatius*," she exclaimed, and in a flash the immortal song found a voice in the stirring air so perfectly adapted to it. That night when her contralto voice rang out the stanzas, the refrain rolled forth from every throat without pause or preparation; and the enthusiasm communicated itself with such effect to the crowd assembled beneath our windows as to endanger seriously the liberties of the party.[3]

---

[2] Ibid., 208.

[3] Ibid., 211–12. Both "O Tannenbaum" and "Maryland, My Maryland" are set to the score of the traditional students' song "Lauriger Horatius Quam Dixisti Verum" ("Laurel-bearing Horatius, How Truly You Spoke").

Appendix D: Union Losses at Maryland Heights and Harper's Ferry[1]

September 12–15, 1862

	Killed		Wounded		Captured or Missing		Aggregate[2]
	Officers	Enlisted Men	Officers	Enlisted Men	Officers	Enlisted Men	
general and staff	—	—	1	—	6	—	7
12th Illinois Cavalry	—	—	—	2	4	153	159
Battery M, 2d Illinois Light Artillery	—	—	—	—	3	97	100
65th Illinois	—	—	1	6	32	778	817
15th Indiana [von Sehlen's] Battery	—	—	—	3	4	114	121
Rigby's (Wilder) Indiana Battery	—	—	—	—	4	109	113
1st Maryland Cavalry (detachment)	—	—	1	2	1	19	23
Cole's Battalion, Maryland Cavalry[3]	—	—	—	—	—	—	—
1st Maryland, Potomac Home Brigade	—	6	—	6	32	747	791
3d Maryland, Potomac Home Brigade	1	2	1	8	24	510	546
8th New York Cavalry	—	—	—	—	5	87	92
Batteries A and F, 5th New York Heavy Artillery	—	2	—	—	9	256	267
12th New York Militia	—	—	—	—	30	530	560
39th New York	—	—	—	15	10	520	545
111th New York	—	5	—	6	36	934	981
115th New York	—	—	1	10	28	950	989
125th New York	—	2	—	1	38	881	922
126th New York	1	12	4	38	30	946	1,031
Potts's Ohio Battery (Co. F, 32d Ohio Infantry)	—	—	—	—	2	82	84
32d Ohio	1	9	3	55	31	643	742
60th Ohio	—	2	1	5	38	867	913
87th Ohio	—	1	—	—	38	976	1,015
7th Squadron, Rhode Island Cavalry[4]	—	—	—	—	—	—	—
9th Vermont	—	—	—	3	30	714	747
unattached, in hospitals, etc.	—	—	—	—	—	1,172	1,172
Total	3	41	13	160	435	12,085	12,737

OFFICERS KILLED—Captain Jacob Sarbaugh, 3d Maryland, Potomac Home Brigade; Captain Samuel R. Breese, 32d Ohio; and Lieutenant Alfred R. Clapp, 126th New York.

DIED OF WOUNDS—Colonel Dixon S. Miles, 2d U.S. Infantry; and Lieutenant Daniel C. Hiteshew, 1st Maryland Cavalry.

---

[1] "Return of Casualties in the Union Forces at Maryland Heights and Harper's Ferry," *OR*, vol. 19, pt. 1, 549.

[2] A number of the wounded fell into the enemy's hands and are also counted with the captured—*OR* editors.

[3] No loss reported—*OR* editors.

[4] No loss reported—*OR* editors.

Appendix E: The Surrender of Harper's Ferry

On the twenty-third of September, 1862, a military commission was organized to investigate and report upon the conduct of certain officers connected with and the circumstances attending the abandonment of Maryland Heights and the surrender of Harper's Ferry. The commission, after a session of forty days and the examination of many witnesses, reported on November 3 that the conduct of Brigadier General Julius White merited approbation. It called attention to the "disgraceful behavior of the One hundred and twenty-sixth New York Infantry"[1] and therein did a gross injustice. As to Colonel Thomas H. Ford, commanding on Maryland Heights, it was perfectly clear that he should not have been placed in that command, and that he had a "discretionary power to abandon the heights or not, as his better judgment might dictate, with the men and the means then under his command; and it is believed from the evidence, circumstantial and direct, that the result did not, to any great extent, surprise, nor in any way displease, the officer [Colonel Dixon S. Miles] in command at Harper's Ferry."[2] It found that under these discretionary powers, Ford had mismanaged affairs; that he conducted the defense of the heights without ability, and abandoned them prematurely and without sufficient cause; and that throughout he displayed such a total lack of military capacity as to disqualify him for a command in the service. Ford was dismissed on November 8, 1862, as also was Major William Baird of the 126th New York. In the case of Baird, it was subsequently proven that his conduct, far from being disgraceful, was most meritorious; he was restored to command, and fell in front of Petersburg on June 16, 1864.

In the case of Miles, the following report was made:

The Commission has approached a consideration of this officer's conduct, in connection with the surrender of Harper's Ferry, with extreme reluctance. An officer who cannot appear before any earthly tribunal to answer or explain charges gravely affecting his character, who has met his death at the hands of the enemy, even upon the spot he disgracefully surrendered, is entitled to the tenderest care and most careful investigation. These this Commission has accorded Colonel Miles, and, in giving an opinion, only repeats what runs through our nine hundred pages of evidence, strangely unanimous upon the fact that Colonel Miles' incapacity, amounting to almost imbecility, led to the shameful surrender of this important post.

Early as the 15th of August he disobeys orders of Major-General [John E.] Wool to fortify Maryland Heights. When it is attacked by the enemy, its naturally strong positions are unimproved, and, from his criminal neglect, to use the mildest term, the large force of the enemy is almost upon an equality with the few men he throws out for their protection.

He seemed to have understood and admitted to his officers that Maryland Heights was the key to the position, and yet he placed Colonel Ford in command with a feeble force; made no effort to strengthen him by fortifications, although, between the 5th and the 13th of September, there was ample time to do so; and to Colonel Ford's repeated demands for means to intrench and re-enforcements to strengthen the position, he made either inadequate return or no response at all. He gave Colonel Ford discretionary power as to when he should abandon the heights, the fact of the abandonment having, it seems, been determined on in his own mind, for, when the unhappy event really occurred, his only exclamations were to the effect that he feared Colonel Ford had given them up too soon. This, too, when he must have known that the abandonment of Maryland Heights was the surrender of Harper's Ferry. This leaving the key of the position to the keeping of Colonel Ford, with discretionary power, after the arrival of the capable and courageous officer who had waived his rank to serve wherever ordered, is one of the more striking facts illustrating the utter incapacity of Colonel Miles.

Immediately previous to and pending the siege of Harper's Ferry he paroled rebel prisoners, and permits, indeed, sends them to the enemy's headquarters. This, too, when he should have known that the lack of ammunition, the bad conduct of some of our troops, the entire absence of fortifications, and the abandonment of Maryland Heights were important facts they could, and undoubtedly did, communicate to the enemy. Sixteen of these prisoners were paroled on the 12th, and a pass given them in the handwriting of Colonel Miles, and some of them left as late as the 14th; while a rebel officer, by the name of Rouse, after an escape, is retaken, and subsequently has a private interview with

---

[1] Report of the Harper's Ferry Military Commission, November 3, 1862, reprinted in *OR*, vol. 19, pt. 1, 798.

[2] Ibid.

Colonel Miles, is paroled, and after the surrender appears at the head of his men, among the first to enter Harper's Ferry.

It is not necessary to accumulate instances from the mass of evidence that throughout scarcely affords one fact in contradiction to what each one establishes, that Colonel Miles was unfit to conduct so important a defense as that of Harper's Ferry.

This Commission would not have dwelt upon this painful subject were it not for the fact that the officer who placed this incapable in command should share in the responsibility, and in the opinion of the Commission Major-General Wool is guilty to this extent of a grave disaster, and should be censured for his conduct.[3]

It is safe to say that, at the time, ninety-nine out of every hundred Union men in the North believed that Ford was an arrant coward and Miles a designing traitor; the conclusions of the commission were approved, and it would have been commended had it suggested that Ford be shot and the body of the unfortunate Miles exposed as food for vultures. Time has softened the asperities of these hot hours. A clearer light leads to a calmer judgment, and there are many who doubt whether the finding of the commission was a just one. They have come to the conclusion that it was unduly severe. While Miles committed a blunder in abandoning Maryland Heights, the blunder was exceeded by that of Halleck in retaining the garrison at Harper's Ferry after it was known that Lee had crossed into Maryland.

Having covered Ford and Miles with disgrace and justly censured Wool, the commission proceeded to give its opinion of McClellan and his share of the blame:

The Commission has remarked freely on the conduct of Colonel Miles, an old officer, killed in one of the battles of our country, and it cannot, from any motives of delicacy, refrain from censuring those in high command when it thinks such censure deserved. The General-in-Chief [Halleck] has testified that General McClellan, after having received orders to repel the enemy invading the State of Maryland, marched only 6 miles per day on an average when pursuing the invading enemy. The General-in-Chief also testifies that, in his opinion, General McClellan could, and should, have relieved and protected Harper's Ferry, and in this opinion the Commission fully concur.

The evidence thus introduced confirms the Commission in the opinion that Harper's Ferry, as well as Maryland Heights, was prematurely surrendered. The garrison should have been satisfied that relief, however long delayed, would come at last, and that 1,000 men killed in Harper's Ferry would have made a small loss had the post been secured, and probably save 2,000 at Antietam. How important was this defense we can now appreciate. Of the 97,000, composing at that time the whole of Lee's army, more than one-third were attacking Harper's Ferry, and of this the main body was in Virginia. By reference to the evidence, it will be seen that at the moment Colonel Ford abandoned Maryland Heights his little army was in reality relieved by Generals Franklin's and Sumner's corps at Crampton's Gap, within 7 miles of his position, and that after the surrender of Harper's Ferry no time was given to parole prisoners even, before 20,000 troops were hurried from Virginia, and the entire force went off on the double-quick to relieve Lee, who was being attacked at Antietam. Had the garrison been slower to surrender or the Army of the Potomac swifter to march, the enemy would have been forced to raise the siege or have been taken in detail, with the Potomac dividing his forces.[4]

The findings of the commission were cordially approved by Halleck. He cared little for the censure of Wool and the condemnation of Miles and Ford but was more than pleased at the censure of McClellan. The commission had done what it was organized to do—condemn McClellan. It had failed to declare that which the evidence proved: that the guilty party was Henry W. Halleck.

A curious and caustic commentary upon the animus of the commission and its findings is made by one of its members, Donn Piatt, who says:

We had not been in session twenty-four hours before it was understood at the Executive Mansion, and in the War Department it was well known, that the fault was in McClellan. How this came to be the opinion of the board no one could explain. It seemed to pervade the atmosphere. Now we all know, as well as facts could control conviction, that Harper's Ferry was lost, not through any fault of McClellan, but from the treachery, cowardice, and stupidity of the officers left there for the defense. Had not Maryland Heights been abandoned …, the place could easily have been held until McClellan came to the rescue. McClellan was not only a Democrat, but he had forced his political opinions into the army, and instead of fighting the country's battles with some sense and a little success, he had impudently elevated his shallow mind to the post of advisor on political subjects. This was enough to brush aside Miles's treachery and

---

[3] Ibid., 799–800.
[4] Ibid., 800.

Ford's cowardice. The writer of this, the younger member, was called on to write the opinion of the court. It was not his opinion, and so he embodied in the judgment Halleck's testimony, which said, truly enough, that had McClellan marched an hour more or a mile further a day, he would have reached Harper's Ferry in time to rescue the garrison. The fact was that McClellan, after advising the evacuation of the place, was feeling his way along in utter ignorance of the enemy's whereabouts or intentions. The finding of the board, as far as McClellan was concerned, is an historical infamy, and so impressed with such a conclusion was he that he inserted a sentence in the finding that rendered the entire judgment a ludicrous absurdity. It read: "By reference to the evidence, it will be seen that, at the very moment Colonel Ford abandoned Maryland Heights, *his little army was in reality relieved* by Generals Franklin's and Sumner's corps at Crampton's Gap, within seven miles of his position."[5]

It will be observed in the report of the commission that it made no effort to ascertain through McClellan or any of his experienced officers the condition of the army on its march, or why it made short marches or slow ones, but accepted, without question, Halleck's testimony that "General McClellan, after having received orders to repel the enemy invading the State of Maryland, marched only 6 miles per day on an average when pursuing the invading army." This testimony, given by a man jealous of McClellan and desiring to placate and please his enemies, invites comparison.

On the second of September, McClellan was assigned to the command of the forces for the defense of Washington; on the third, he was ordered to prepare an army for active operations in the field. By the evening of the fifth, in less than four days, the defeated, disorganized, and partially demoralized army lying around Washington was ready for the field. On the morning of the sixth, McClellan was verbally assigned to the command of the army in the field; on the morning of the nineteenth, after marching seventy miles and fighting the battles of Crampton's Gap, Turner's Gap, and Antietam, he telegraphed to Halleck, "I have the honor to report that Maryland is entirely freed from the presence of the enemy who have been driven across the Potomac."[6]

The battle of Shiloh was fought by Major Generals Ulysses S. Grant and Don Carlos Buell on April 6–7, 1862 and resulted in a Confederate defeat. On the tenth, Halleck arrived and assumed command. It took him until the thirtieth—twenty days—to get his victorious army in readiness to pursue the defeated Confederates. On the thirtieth, at the head of a grand army of one hundred thousand men, he began an advance on Corinth, distant about twenty miles, digging entrenchments and creeping along behind them. He threw up works every few hundred yards and occupied seven strongly entrenched camps. For thirty days he so marched and entrenched, making not to exceed two-thirds of a mile a day. During the last week of the campaign, when everybody in the army except Halleck knew that Beauregard was getting out of Corinth as rapidly as possible with his immense supplies, the most arduous work was done in entrenching. On the twenty-ninth of May, Beauregard evacuated Corinth, and Halleck, ignorant of the fact, on the morning of May 30 announced in orders that an attack by the enemy all along the line was expected.[7] When the place was occupied, it was found that Beauregard had carried away everything except a few Quaker guns made of wood. This was the extent of Halleck's service in the field.

In view of the snail-like pace of Halleck at the head of a powerful, victorious army, at the rate of two-thirds of a mile a day, it ill became him—who never commanded an army in battle and was never under fire during the war—to criticize McClellan or any other officer for not marching more than six miles a day against a victorious army commanded by Robert E. Lee.

The commission reported, "The General-in-Chief also testifies that, in his opinion, General McClellan could, and should, have relieved and protected Harper's Ferry, and in this opinion the Commission fully concur."[8] There is no question that up to September 12, McClellan was in no way responsible for the situation of affairs at Harper's Ferry; on the contrary, he had made honest effort to impress upon Halleck the danger at that point. He had, on more than one occasion, protested against the bad judgment that kept a garrison there after Lee had crossed the Potomac, and had suggested that it be withdrawn by way of Hagerstown to cover the Cumberland Valley or concentrated on Maryland Heights, as it was in imminent danger of capture, but to these suggestions Halleck gave a flat and contemptuous refusal. Finally, on September 11, McClellan requested that Miles be ordered to leave Harper's Ferry and join the army in the field by the most practicable route,[9] to which Halleck replied that there was no way for Miles to join him. "His only chance is to defend his works till you can open

---

5   Donn Piatt, *General George H. Thomas: A Critical Biography* (Cincinnati: Robert Clarke & Co., 1893), 349–50.

6   George B. McClellan to Henry W. Halleck, September 19, 1862, as contained in McClellan to Lorenzo Thomas, August 4, 1863, reprinted in *OR*, vol. 19, pt. 1, 68.

7   For evidence of Halleck's beliefs regarding Confederate intentions at Corinth, see his numerous dispatches reprinted in *OR*, vol. 10, pt. 2, 227–29.

8   Report of the Harper's Ferry Military Commission, 800.

9   McClellan to Halleck, September 11, 1862, reprinted in *OR*, vol. 19, pt. 2, 254.

communication with him. When you do so he will be subject to your orders."[10] Had Halleck given a candid reply to McClellan's request, it would read, "In defiance of all sound military principles, we have kept Colonel Miles so long at Harper's Ferry to hold an indefensible position that he is now surrounded and cannot escape, and is peremptorily ordered not to escape if he could, but if you can relieve him from the trap in which we have placed him you are welcome to his services."

Halleck could not have been of more service to the Confederates had he been Lee's chief of staff, with authority to issue orders from the head of the Union army.

---

[10] Halleck to McClellan, September 11, 1862, as contained in "Record of the Harper's Ferry Military Commission," October 17, 1862, reprinted in *OR*, vol. 19, pt. 1, 758.

Appendix F: Union Losses at Crampton's Gap[1]

September 14, 1862

	Killed		Wounded		Captured or Missing		Aggregate
	Officers	Enlisted Men	Officers	Enlisted Men	Officers	Enlisted Men	
general and staff	—	—	1	—	—	—	1
5th Maine	—	4	1	27	—	—	32
1st New Jersey	—	7	3	31	—	—	41
2d New Jersey	—	10	1	44	—	—	55
3d New Jersey	—	11	2	27	—	—	40
4th New Jersey	1	9	3	23	—	—	36
16th New York	—	20	1	40	—	—	61
18th New York	1	10	1	40	—	2	54
27th New York	—	6	2	25	—	—	33
31st New York	—	1	—	3	—	—	4
32d New York	1	10	3	37	—	—	51
95th Pennsylvania	—	1	—	14	—	—	15
96th Pennsylvania	2	18	—	71	—	—	91
2d Vermont	—	—	—	5	—	—	5
4th Vermont	—	1	—	10	—	—	11
6th Vermont	—	—	1	2	—	—	3
Total	5	108	19	399	—	2	533

---

[1] "Return of Casualties in the Union forces at the battle of Crampton's Pass Md. [*sic*]," *OR*, vol. 19, pt. 1, 183.

Appendix G: Confederate Losses at Crampton's Gap

September 14, 1862

	Killed	Wounded	Missing	Aggregate
2d Virginia Cavalry[1]	1	2	—	3
12th Virginia Cavalry[2]	2	3	—	5
Mahone's Brigade[3]	5	74	124	203
10th Georgia (Semmes's Brigade)[4]	3	21	37	61
Troup Artillery [Carlton's Battery][5]	1	3	—	4
Cobb's Brigade[6]	58	186	442	686
Total	70	289	603	962

---

[1] Thomas T. Munford to James T. W. Hairston, October 3, 1862, reprinted in *OR*, vol. 19, pt. 1, 827.

[2] From information given by survivors of the regiment.—*EAC*

[3] From the best attainable information, Mahone's Brigade had about 550 officers and men at Crampton's Gap. A statement accompanying Longstreet's after-action report gives its losses for September 14–17, 1862, as 8 killed, 92 wounded, and 127 missing—an aggregate of 227. "Statement of losses in the corps commanded by Maj. Gen. J. Longstreet in the engagements at Crampton's Gap, Maryland Heights, Sharpsburg, and South Mountain," *OR*, vol. 19, pt. 1, 843. At Antietam, September 17, the brigade had 3 killed, 18 wounded, and 3 missing, thus leaving the loss at Crampton's Gap as stated. The muster roll of the 12th Virginia (October 31, 1862) shows its loss as 86.—*EAC*

[4] Willis C. Holt to Edmund B. Briggs, September 22, 1862, reprinted in *OR*, vol. 19, pt. 1, 877.

[5] "Return of casualties in McLaws' division at the battle of Crampton's Gap," *OR*, vol. 19, pt. 1, 861.

[6] Ibid.

Appendix H: Union Losses at Turner's Gap and Fox's Gap[1]

September 14, 1862

	Killed		Wounded		Captured or Missing		Aggregate
	Officers	Enlisted	Officers	Enlisted	Officers	Enlisted	
First Army Corps							
First Division							
general and staff	—	—	1[2]	—	—	—	1
First Brigade	—	20	4	63	—	8	95
Second Brigade	—	3	4	48	—	4	59
Third Brigade	—	3	—	19	—	1	23
Fourth Brigade	1	36	6	245	—	30	318
Second Division							
First Brigade	—	5	1	15	—	—	21
Second Brigade	—	2	1	5	—	—	8
Third Brigade	—	2	—	4	—	—	6
Third Division							
First Brigade	4	34	7	126	—	—	171
Second Brigade	1	24	1	62	—	1	89
Third Brigade	2	30	8	92	—	—	132
Total First Corps	8	159	33	679		44	923
Ninth Army Corps							
general and staff	1[3]	—	—	—	—	—	1
First Division							
First Brigade	—	26	5	131	—	—	162
Second Brigade	2	36	8	147	—	—	193
Second Division							
First Brigade	—	—	—	34	—	7	41
Second Brigade	1	9	5	78	—	23	116
Third Division							
First Brigade	—	2	1	17	—	—	20
Kanawha Division							
First Brigade	1	62	11	190	—	8	272
Second Brigade	—	17	3	61	—	3	84
Total Ninth Corps	5	152	33	658	—	41	889
cavalry division	—	1	—	—	—	—	1
Grand Total	13	312	66	1,337	—	85	1,813

---

[1] "Return of Casualties in the Union forces at the battle of South Mountain (Turner's Pass), Md.," *OR*, vol. 19, pt. 1, 184–87.

[2] Brigadier General John P. Hatch.

[3] Major General Jesse L. Reno.

Appendix I: Confederate Losses at Turner's Gap and Fox's Gap

September 14, 1862

	Killed	Wounded	Missing	Aggregate
D. H. Hill's Division				
general and staff	1	—	—	1[1]
Rodes's Brigade[2]	61	157	204	422
Ripley's Brigade	—	—	—	—
G. B. Anderson's Brigade[3]	7	54	29	90
Garland's Brigade[4]	37	168	154	359
Colquitt's Brigade[5]	18	74	17	109
Bondurant's Battery[6]	—	3	—	3
Total	124	456	404	984
Jones's Division				
G. T. Anderson's Brigade[7]	—	3	4	7
Garnett's Brigade[8]	35	142	19	196
Drayton's Brigade[9]	49	164	176	389
Kemper's Brigade[10]	11	57	7	75
Jenkins's Brigade[11]	3	29	—	32
Total	98	395	206	699
Hood's Division				
Wofford's Brigade[12]	—	3	2	5
Law's Brigade[13]	3	11	5	19
Total	3	14	7	24
Evans's Brigade[14]	23	142	45	210

Recapitulation				
	Killed	Wounded	Missing	Aggregate
D. H. Hill's Division	124	456	404	984
Jones's Division	98	395	206	699
Hood's Division	3	14	7	24
Evans's Brigade	23	148	45	210
Total	248	1,013	662	1,923

Not included in this recapitulation is the loss sustained by the 5th Virginia Cavalry and the artillery acting with it. It was not large but would probably increase the aggregate to 1,950 men.

---

[1] Brigadier General Samuel Garland Jr.

[2] Robert E. Rodes to James W. Ratchford, October 13, 1862, reprinted in *OR*, vol. 19, pt. 1, 1036

3 In the casualty figures accompanying D. H. Hill's official report of the entire Maryland campaign, the loss in G. B. Anderson's Brigade is stated as 64 killed, 299 wounded, and 202 missing. Daniel H. Hill to Robert H. Chilton, 1862 [no day or month given], reprinted in *OR*, vol. 19, pt. 1, 1026. Colonel Bennett, who commanded the brigade following the mortal wounding of Anderson on the seventeenth, gives the loss at Antietam as 57 killed and 245 wounded, but does not report the number missing, which was very large. Risden T. Bennett to Ratchford, December 6, 1862, reprinted in *OR*, vol. 19, pt. 1, 1048. Hill says Anderson had 29 missing at Turner's Gap, and this estimate we accept, making the loss at Turner's Gap as tabulated. Hill, "The Battle of South Mountain, or Boonsboro'," in *Battles and Leaders of the Civil War*, vol. 2 (New York: Century Co., 1887), 579.—*EAC*

4 In Hill's official report, the loss in Garland's Brigade in the entire campaign is given as 46 killed, 210 wounded, and 187 missing—an aggregate of 443. Hill to Chilton, 1026. It is known that at Antietam this brigade was not long or severely engaged, while at Turner's Gap the opposite was the case. We estimate that four-fifths of its loss, as recorded for the entire campaign, was sustained at Turner's Gap, which gives the result as tabulated.—*EAC*

5 In Hill's official report, the loss in Colquitt's Brigade for the entire campaign is given as 129 killed, 518 wounded, and 184 missing. Hill to Chilton, 1026. Hill, after an extended correspondence with the officers of the brigade, estimates its loss at Turner's Gap as 92 killed and wounded and 7 missing, in which estimate is not included 10 missing of the 6th and 27th Georgia and 13th Alabama. Hill, "The Battle of South Mountain," 579. This estimate we believe to be approximately correct and adopt. Allowing 1 killed for every 4 wounded and adding the 10 missing in the 6th and 17th Georgia and 13th Alabama, we have 18 killed, 74 wounded, and 17 missing.—*EAC*

6 In Hill's official report, the loss of artillery in the division is given as 4 killed, 30 wounded, and 3 missing for the entire campaign. Hill to Chilton, 1026. Of this number, Bondurant's Battery had 3 wounded. We cannot learn that the other batteries had any casualties.—*EAC*

7 General Anderson informs us that his loss at Turner's Gap was 6 or 7 men wounded or missing; another officer of the brigade says it was 3 wounded and 4 missing.—*EAC*

8 For Garnett's Brigade, the report of the 8th Virginia gives 11 killed and wounded. Eppa Hunton to Richard B. Garnett, 1862 [no day or month given], reprinted in *OR*, vol. 19, pt. 1, 898. The 18th Virginia had 7 killed, 27 wounded, and 7 missing. George C. Cabell to "General Garnett's assistant adjutant-general," October 14, 1862, reprinted in *OR*, vol. 19, pt. 1, 901. The 19th Virginia had 63 killed, wounded, and missing. Report of Benjamin Brown, October 15, 1862, reprinted in *OR*, vol. 19, pt. 1, 901. The 56th Virginia had 40 killed and wounded and 5 missing. William D. Stuart to Garnett, October 25, 1862, reprinted in *OR*, vol. 19, pt. 1, 903. There are no reports from the 28th Virginia, but its strength was about 95 men. Assuming that its loss was in the same proportion as the other regiments of the brigade would give 41 killed, wounded and missing. Estimating the ratio of 1 killed for every 4 wounded, the 8th Virginia had 2 killed and 9 wounded. Assuming that the 19th Virginia had the same proportion of missing as had the 18th and 56th Virginia, and that the ratio of killed to wounded was 1:4, the loss in the 19th Virginia was 11 killed, 46 wounded, and 6 missing. The 56th Virginia reports 40 killed and wounded, of which (in the usual ratio) 8 were killed and 32 wounded. Of the 41 killed, wounded, and missing of the 28th Virginia, we estimate that 7 were killed, 28 wounded, and 6 missing.—*EAC*

9 Longstreet's official report of the campaign shows a loss in Drayton's Brigade during the Maryland campaign of 82 killed, 280 wounded, and 179 missing—an aggregate of 541. James Longstreet to Chilton, October 10, 1862, reprinted in *OR*, vol. 19, pt. 1, 843. An extensive correspondence with survivors of the brigade indicates that its loss at Antietam was 33 killed, 106 wounded, and 3 missing—an aggregate of 142. Deduct these figures from those given as the loss in the entire campaign and we have the loss at Turner's Gap as 49 killed, 164 wounded, and 176 missing—an aggregate of 389 out of the 650 men taken into action.—*EAC*

10 Kemper's Brigade carried about 400 men into action; there are no official reports of its losses. The muster rolls of the 1st Virginia note a loss of 1 lieutenant and 4 men wounded and 1 captured. From a history of the 7th Virginia [which Carman incorrectly titles *History of Co. D, 7th Virginia*] and correspondence with survivors of the regiment, we put its loss at 5 killed, 24 wounded, and 3 missing. David E. Johnston, *Four Years a Soldier* (Princeton, W. Va.: n.p., 1887), 202. The 11th Virginia was very small, and its loss, as gleaned by correspondence with survivors, was 1 killed, 7 wounded, and 2 missing. The history of the 17th Virginia gives the names, in eight companies, of 3 killed and 10 wounded. George Wise, *History of the Seventeenth Virginia Infantry, C.S.A.* (Baltimore: Kelly, Piet & Co., 1870), 124. The 24th Virginia was a small regiment and sustained a severe loss, which from information derived from its members was 2 killed, 11 wounded, and 1 missing.—*EAC*

11 Joseph Walker to Robert Johnston, October 24, 1862, reprinted in *OR*, vol. 19, pt. 1, 906.

[12] The muster rolls of the 18th Georgia give 1 man wounded; of the 1st Texas, 1 man wounded and 1 missing; and of the 4th Texas, 1 wounded and 1 missing.—*EAC*

[13] Hood's official report gives 3 killed and 11 wounded. John B. Hood to Gilbert Moxley Sorrel, September 27, 1862, reprinted in *OR*, vol. 19, pt. 1, 925. The muster rolls of the 4th Alabama note 5 men captured.—*EAC*

[14] There are official reports from three regiments of Evans's Brigade. The 17th South Carolina had 7 killed, 37 wounded, and 17 missing. Fitz W. McMaster to Nathan G. Evans, October 20, 1862, reprinted in *OR*, vol. 19, pt. 1, 945. The 22d South Carolina had 10 killed, 51 wounded [in his original manuscript, Carman copies this incorrectly as "57," resulting in a brigade total of 216 casualties], and 4 missing. Miel Hilton to Asa L. Evans, October 15, 1862, reprinted in *OR*, vol. 19, pt. 1, 949. According to the statistics compiled by the medical director of the Army of Northern Virginia, the Holcombe Legion had 18 men wounded in the entire campaign. "Report of Surg. Lafayette Guild, C. S. Army, Medical Director Army of Northern Virginia, of killed and wounded at Boonsborough (South Mountain or Turner's Pass), Crampton's Gap, Harper's Ferry, Sharpsburg (Antietam), and Shepherdstown (Blackford's or Boteler's) Ford," no date, reprinted in *OR*, vol. 19, pt. 1, 811. Assuming that two-thirds of this number is chargeable to Turner's Gap would give 12 as the number there wounded. In the same tally, the 18th South Carolina is reported to have had 3 killed and 39 wounded during the entire campaign; two-thirds of this loss is fairly chargeable to Turner's Gap, which gives 2 killed and 26 wounded. The missing in the 18th South Carolina is estimated by us, from incomplete data, as 13, and in the Holcombe Legion as 7, thus making an aggregate in the brigade of 210.—*EAC*

Appendix J: Strength of the Union and Confederate Armies at Antietam

The Union Army

In his official report of the Maryland campaign, General McClellan says:

Our own forces at the battle of Antietam were as follows:

First Corps	14,856
Second Corps	18,813
Fifth Corps (one division not arrived)	12,930
Sixth Corps	12,300
Ninth Corps	13,819
Twelfth Corps	10,126
cavalry division	4,320
Total in action	87,164[1]

That these figures correctly state the number reported as "present for duty" is not questioned; that they correctly give the number "in action" is an error. Every old soldier who served in the War of 1861–65 knows the difference between the number of those who answered roll-call in camp or were accounted for as present and the number of those who went onto the fighting line—a difference of from 20 to 40 percent, depending upon the discipline of the organization. (Some of the very best in the Union Army considered themselves very fortunate in getting four-fifths of their men in action.)

We propose to test these figures and endeavor to arrive at a reasonably correct conclusion as to the number of men in action at Antietam and shall depend upon the official reports of the division, brigade, and regimental commanders, regimental histories, and other authentic sources of information.

First Corps: This corps is reported as having 14,856 in action. Hooker says that he crossed the Antietam on the afternoon of September 16 with between 12,000 and 13,000, having lost nearly 1,000 at South Mountain.[2] How many of these left the ranks before the morning of the seventeenth we do not know, but he began the engagement that morning with about 9,438 officers and men (infantry and artillery).

Ricketts reports that he carried into action 3,158 officers and men.[3] Meade reports that his division "went into action under 3,000 strong, and lost in killed and wounded over 570 [571—*EAC*]—20 per cent."[4] If 571 was 20 percent of the number engaged, he had 2,855 officers and men, and a close examination convinces us that these figures are correct. (The artillery is included in the figures given for the two divisions.)

Ricketts's division had two batteries of artillery of four guns each, and they were short-handed on the morning of the seventeenth and obliged to get details from the infantry. As nearly as we can estimate, the two batteries had an aggregate of 6 officers and 115 men.

Meade's division had two Pennsylvania batteries of four guns each and Ransom's Battery C, 5th U.S. Artillery, of six guns. The Pennsylvania batteries had 3 officers each and about 16 men to a gun. The regular battery had 4 officers and (we estimate) 110 men—an aggregate of 114 officers and men. The aggregate of the three batteries of the division is 248.

Hatch reports that his division, commanded by Doubleday at Antietam, had not to exceed 3,500 at South Mountain.[5] Its loss at South Mountain was 496, so it should have had at Antietam about 3,000 men. Doubleday, who commanded at South Mountain the brigade led by Colonel Hofmann at Antietam, says he had at South Mountain about 1,000 men.[6] The loss at South Mountain was 59 men; the brigade should have had over 900 at Antietam, but Hofmann informs us that he had

---

[1] George B. McClellan to Lorenzo Thomas, August 4, 1863, reprinted in *OR*, vol. 19, pt. 1, 67.

[2] Joseph Hooker to Seth Williams, November 8, 1862, reprinted in *OR*, vol. 19, pt. 1, 217.

[3] James B. Ricketts to Hooker, September 21, 1862, reprinted in *OR*, vol. 19, pt. 1, 259.

[4] George G. Meade to Joseph Dickinson, September 22, 1862, reprinted in *OR*, vol. 19, pt. 1, 270–71.

[5] John P. Hatch to Dickinson, September 15, 1862, reprinted in *OR*, vol. 19, pt. 1, 220.

[6] Abner Doubleday to Dickinson, September 23, 1862, reprinted in *OR*, vol. 19, pt. 1, 222.

454 • The Maryland Campaign of September 1862

about 750 men, not including the battery attached to the brigade.[7] At Antietam the 7th Indiana had 175 men and the 56th Pennsylvania 220 officers and men.[8] The strength of the 76th and 95th New York is not definitely known, but we accept Hofmann's statement that his brigade numbered about 750.

Colonel Phelps says in his official report that his brigade went into action with 425 officers and men.[9] Gibbon's brigade had four regiments: the 19th Indiana had 202 officers and men in action,[10] the 2d Wisconsin, 265,[11] the 6th Wisconsin, 314,[12] and the 7th Wisconsin, 190[13]—a total of 971 officers and men for the brigade.

Patrick's brigade had four New York regiments. The 23d New York had 238 officers and men in action.[14] The 80th New York reported less than 150[15] (in reality, 136). Information from the survivors of the 21st New York is that it had in action about 225 officers and men, and that the 35th New York was about the same size (say, 230 officers and men)—thus making the strength of the brigade 829 officers and men.

This would make the aggregate strength of the four brigades of Doubleday's division as follows:

Hofmann's brigade	750
Phelps's brigade	425
Gibbon's brigade	971
Patrick's brigade	829
Total	2,975

This is a very close approximation to what there should have been, according to Hatch's report of what it had at South Mountain. To this aggregate of infantry must be added the strength of the four batteries of artillery of the division, which, from a careful and liberal estimate, we place at 450 officers and men—making the aggregate of the division (infantry and artillery) 3,425 officers and men.

The corps had forty-six pieces of artillery, all of which were more or less engaged.

First Corps

	Infantry	Artillery	Aggregate
Ricketts's division	3,037	121	3,158
Meade's division	2,607	248	2,855
Doubleday's division	2,975	450	3,425
Total	8,619	819	9,438

Second Corps: This corps is reported by McClellan as having 18,813 engaged. Of the fourteen regiments in Richardson's division, but four officially report the number engaged. Colonel Cross, in a report to the governor of New Hampshire, said the 5th New Hampshire went into the fight with 300 rifles and 19 commissioned officers,[16] but his official report mentions by name 21 officers engaged;[17] we put the strength of the regiment at 21 officers and 300 men. The 88th New York had 302

[7] John W. Hofmann to Ezra A. Carman, June 25, 1896, "1st Corps—Doubleday—Hooker" folder, box 1, Letters and Reports Concerning the Battle of Antietam, 1895–1900 ("Antietam Studies"), Record Group 94, National Archives.

[8] In his original manuscript, Carman cites Hofmann's official report of South Mountain as his source for the 56th Pennsylvania's strength at Antietam. According to that report, however, the regiment had 247 officers and men present for duty on the morning of September 14 and lost 15 at South Mountain, which should leave 231. Hofmann to Eminel P. Halstead, September 15, 1862, reprinted in *OR*, vol. 19, pt. 1, 238–39. If Carman had reason to lower this figure to 220, he did not make reference to it.

[9] Walter Phelps to Halstead, September 23, 1862, reprinted in *OR*, vol. 19, pt. 1, 234.

[10] William F. Fox, *Regimental Losses In The American Civil War, 1861–1865: A Treatise on the Extent and Nature of the Mortuary Losses in the Union Regiments, with Full and Exhaustive Statistics Compiled from the Official Records on File in the State Military Bureaus and at Washington* (Albany, N.Y.: Randow Printing Co., 1889), 343.

[11] Letter of Colonel T. S. Allen [not found].—*EAC*

[12] Rufus R. Dawes, *Service with the Sixth Wisconsin Volunteers* (Marietta, Ohio: E. R. Alderman & Sons, 1890), 92.

[13] John B. Callas to Frank A. Haskell, September 18, 1862, reprinted in *OR*, vol. 19, pt. 1, 258.

[14] Henry C. Hoffman to Marsena R. Patrick, September 20, 1862, reprinted in Pound Sterling [William P. Maxson], *Camp Fires of the Twenty-third: Sketches of the Camp Life, Marches, and Battles of the Twenty-third Regiment, N.Y.V., during the Term of Two Years in the Service of the United States* (New York: Davies & Kent, 1863), 102.

[15] Theodore B. Gates to Patrick, September 21, 1862, reprinted in *OR*, vol. 19, pt. 1, 246.

[16] *Report of the Adjutant General of the State of New Hampshire for the Year Ending May 20, 1865*, vol. 1 (Concord: Amos Hadley, 1865), 456.

[17] Edward E. Cross to George H. Caldwell, September 18, 1862, reprinted in *OR*, vol. 19, pt. 1, 288.

men,[18] the 52d New York had 119 officers and men,[19] and the 57th New York had 309 officers and men.[20] William F. Fox says the 63d New York had 341 engaged and the 69th New York had 317.[21] (With its officers, the 69th had 331.) The 29th Massachusetts had about 20 officers and 360 men—an aggregate of 380.[22] Survivors of the 2d Delaware inform us that the regiment had about 310 officers and men. The 66th New York, according to the recollection of a number of its survivors, was about the same strength as the 2d Delaware and 57th New York, which would give it 310 officers and men. The acting adjutant of the 61st New York informs us that the regiment carried into action 23 officers and 205 muskets—making an aggregate of 228.[23] An officer of the 64th New York says the regiment had in action 214 officers and men.[24] These eleven regiments average 288 each. In the absence of reliable data from the 53d and 81st Pennsylvania and the 7th New York (all of whom had seen the same service as the other regiments), we estimate that these had the average strength of the eleven regiments enumerated (288 each); this agrees very closely with the meager data we have been able to gather from these three regiments. The summing up shows an infantry strength in Richardson's division of 4,029 officers and men.

The two batteries of the division—Pettit's Battery B, 1st New York Light Artillery and Thomas's Batteries A and C (consolidated), 4th U.S. Artillery—had six guns each. We estimate 3 officers to each battery and 20 men to a gun—a total of 6 officers and 240 men.

Sedgwick's division had three brigades and two batteries. In Gorman's brigade, the 15th Massachusetts had 606 officers and men,[25] the 1st Minnesota, 435,[26] the 34th New York, 311,[27] and the 82d New York, 339[28]—and aggregate of 1,691 officers and men. In Dana's brigade, the 42d New York had 345,[29] the 59th New York, 381,[30] and the 19th Massachusetts, by the most reliable estimates of its survivors), 26 officers and 392 men—an aggregate of 418. A narrative report of the adjutant general of Massachusetts for 1862 states, "The Twentieth [Massachusetts] took about four hundred men into the battle of Antietam."[31] (James L. Bowen, in his *Massachusetts in the War*, adopts these figures.[32]) The 7th Michigan, according to statements made by seven of its surviving officers, had 27 officers and 375 men present (an aggregate of 402), and this agrees substantially with the statement made in *Michigan in the War* that the regiment lost over one-half its number at Antietam.[33] (It lost 221; its strength, then, must have been about 400.) The aggregate strength of Dana's brigade foots up 1,946 officers and men. For Howard's brigade our information is fragmentary and conflicting. Its survivors claim that it lost about one-third of those taken into action. Its loss was 545; by this measure, it had 1,635 officers and men. We think it exceeded this number by nearly 200 and have estimated its strength at 1,800.

The infantry strength of Sedgwick's division was as follows:

Gorman's brigade	1,691
Dana's brigade	1,946
Howard's brigade	1,800
Total	5,437

The two batteries (Tompkins's Battery A, 1st Rhode Island Light Artillery, and Woodruff's Battery I, 1st U.S. Artillery) aggregated twelve guns. Captain Tompkins informs us he had 3 officers and 117 men.[34] Battery I had 4 officers engaged,[35] and we estimate that it had 20 men to a gun—an aggregate of 124 officers and men. The strength of the two batteries was 244.

[18] Patrick Kelly to Thomas F. Meagher, October 5, 1862, reprinted in *OR*, vol. 19, pt. 1, 298.

[19] Paul Frank to Charles P. Hatch, September 20, 1862, reprinted in *OR*, vol. 19, pt. 1, 301.

[20] Alford B. Chapman to Hatch, September 24, 1862, reprinted in *OR*, vol. 19, pt. 1, 303.

[21] Fox, 31.

[22] Major John M. Deane.—*EAC*

[23] As of this writing, no textual source for this statement has been found. (This may be the product of one of Carman's many oral interviews and informal conversations with veterans.)

[24] Ibid.

[25] John W. Kimball to J. W. Gorman, September 20, 1862, reprinted in *OR*, vol. 19, pt. 1, 313.

[26] Alfred Sully to Gorman, September 20, 1862, reprinted in *OR*, vol. 19, pt. 1, 315

[27] Fox, 31.

[28] Ibid.

[29] Ibid.

[30] Ibid.

[31] *Annual Report of the Adjutant-General, of the Commonwealth of Massachusetts, with Reports from the Quartermaster-General, Surgeon-General, and Master of Ordnance, for the Year Ending December 31, 1862* (Boston: Wright & Potter, 1863), 233.

[32] James L. Bowen, *Massachusetts in the War, 1861–1865* (Springfield, C. W. Bryan & Co., 1889), 317.

[33] *Michigan in the War* (Lansing: W. S. George & Co., 1882), 271.

[34] As of this writing, no textual source for this statement has been found.

[35] Report of George A. Woodruff, September 21, 1862, reprinted in *OR*, vol. 19, pt. 1, 310.

French's division had three brigades. In Kimball's brigade the 14th Indiana had 320 officers and men,[36] the 8th Ohio, 341,[37] and the 132d Pennsylvania, 750.[38] Several inquiries to officers of the 7th West Virginia elicit the information that it had about 340 officers and men—an aggregate in the brigade of 1,751. In Weber's brigade the 1st Delaware was 708,[39] the 4th New York, 540,[40] and we are informed by George R. Graham that the 5th Maryland had about 550 officers and men[41]—making the aggregate of the brigade 1,798. Morris's brigade consisted of three new regiments. The 14th Connecticut had 31 officers and 720 men—an aggregate of 751. (This estimate is made by Henry S. Stevens, the chaplain and historian of the regiment.[42]) The 108th New York was organized at the same time as the 14th Connecticut, was a full regiment, and had seen the same amount of marching service; we estimate it had the same effective strength, 750 officers and men. Our information from survivors of the 130th Pennsylvania is that it had 690 officers and men—thus making 2,191 as the strength of the brigade.

The infantry strength of French's division was as follows:

Kimball's brigade	1,751
Weber's brigade	1,798
Morris's brigade	2,191
Total	5,740

The unattached artillery of the Second Corps consisted of Frank's Battery G, 1st New York Light Artillery (six guns), Hazard's Battery B, 1st Rhode Island Light Artillery (six guns), and Owen's Battery G, 1st Rhode Island Light Artillery (six guns)—in all, eighteen guns. There were no returns of the strength of these batteries. We estimate that each had 3 officers and that the guns had 20 men each—an aggregate of 9 officers and 360 men.

The corps had forty-two pieces of artillery, all of which were engaged.

Second Corps

	Infantry	Artillery	Aggregate
Richardson's division	4,029	246	4,275
Sedgwick's division	5,437	244	5,681
French's division	5,740	—	5,740
unattached artillery	—	369	369
Total	15,206	859	16,065

Fifth Corps: McClellan reports that the two divisions (Sykes's and Morell's) of the Fifth Corps had 12,930 officers and men. This includes not only the six batteries of those two divisions, but also the seven batteries of the reserve artillery of the army. Morell's division was not engaged, not a man of it crossing the Antietam. Of Sykes's division, but five small battalions of United States regular infantry were engaged. All the artillery of the corps (thirteen batteries) was in action; three batteries—Randol's, Van Reed's, and Graham's—west of the Antietam, the others on the bluff east of the stream. After reporting the movements of the five battalions that crossed the Antietam, Sykes says, "The remainder of my division was unengaged on the 17th."[43] The five battalions were the 2d and 10th (consolidated; twelve companies), the 1st Battalion of the 12th (eight companies), the 1st Battalion of the 14th (eight companies), the 2d Battalion of the 14th (eight companies), and the 4th U.S. Infantry. None of these battalions report the number present. The late John S. Poland, who commanded the 2d and 10th U.S. Infantry, informed us in 1896 that he had 402 men.[44] The battalion of the 12th had 280 men.[45] We are informed by survivors that the companies of the 14th U.S. Infantry averaged about 40 men; there were sixteen companies in the

---

[36] William Harrow to Nathan Kimball, September 19, 1862, reprinted in *OR*, vol. 19, pt. 1, 329. Carman's manuscript, typed at this point, reads "330." This is clearly a typographical error. Harrow's report says 320, and the aggregate Carman provides for the entire brigade comes to 10 men less than would be the case if the 14th Indiana were credited with 330.

[37] Franklin Sawyer to Nathan Kimball, September 18, 1862, reprinted in *OR*, vol. 19, pt. 1, 330.

[38] Vincent M. Wilcox to Nathan Kimball, September 19, 1862, reprinted in *OR*, vol. 19, pt. 1, 331.

[39] John W. Andrews to William H. French, September 20, 1862, reprinted in *OR*, vol. 19, pt. 1, 336.

[40] Ibid.

[41] As of this writing, no textual source for this statement has been found.

[42] Ibid.

[43] George Sykes to Fred T. Locke, September 30, 1862, reprinted in *OR*, vol. 19, pt. 1, 351.

[44] As of this writing, no textual source for this statement has been found.

[45] Letter from an officer [not found].—*EAC*

two battalions, so their strength would be 640 men. William H. Powell, an officer of the 4th U.S. Infantry and the brigade adjutant general, says the two battalions had between 600 and 700 men.[46] The 4th, when it went into bivouac on the night of September 15, had 318 men; we assume it had that number on the seventeenth. (Powell says it had about 320.[47]) The total is 1,640. The companies averaged 1 officer each, or 44 in all—an aggregate in the five battalions of 1,684 officers and men.

The seven batteries of reserve artillery reported, on November 1, 1862, 31 officers and 931 men.[48] Add to this their loss at Antietam, which was 11, and we get the number on the seventeenth as 973, of whom we may safely estimate about 950 were engaged. The six batteries of Sykes's and Morell's divisions are estimated to have had 3 officers and 115 men each. Five of these batteries were engaged, with an aggregate of 15 officers and 575 men. We thus have 1,540 officers and men as the strength of the artillery of the Fifth Corps, which includes the reserve artillery of the army.

The number of guns in the corps proper was thirty, in the reserve artillery, forty-two—an aggregate of seventy-two.

Fifth Corps

	Infantry	Artillery	Aggregate
five battalions	1,684	590	2,274
reserve artillery	—	950	950
Total	1,684	1,540	3,224

Sixth Corps: Of the six brigades of this corps, only one (Irwin's) was engaged. It had five regiments. The 7th Maine had 181 officers and men.[49] The 77th New York had 175 men "all told."[50] The 33d New York, judging from the estimates of seven company officers, had about 380 officers and men. Lieutenant Colonel William C. Alberger says the 49th New York had 268.[51] The 20th New York had, according to estimates of many survivors, 680. The aggregate of the five regiments foots up 1,684. The corps had seven batteries, six of six guns each and one of eight guns—an aggregate of forty-four guns, all of which were engaged. These batteries were fully manned, and we estimate that each had 3 officers and each gun 20 men, making an aggregate of 21 officers and 880 men. The infantry strength of the corps, engaged, was 1,684, the artillery, 901—an aggregate of 2,585.

Ninth Corps: This corps had four divisions. Willcox's division had eight regiments. The 28th Massachusetts had less than 200 men in line;[52] we conclude that, with the officers, it had full 200. The 17th Michigan went into the fight with about 525 officers and men.[53] The 79th New York had 300 engaged.[54] The 50th Pennsylvania had 370 officers and men. The 8th Michigan, taking the average estimate of its surviving officers, had 435 officers and men engaged. The 46th New York had 278 officers and men,[55] the 45th Pennsylvania had about 20 officers and 540 men,[56] and the 100th Pennsylvania had 350 officers and men.[57] The aggregate strength of the eight regiments was 3,002 officers and men. Attached to this division were the two batteries of Benjamin and Cook, of six guns each, with an estimated strength of 6 officers and 240 men—a division aggregate (infantry and artillery) of 3,248.

Sturgis's division had eight regiments and two batteries. The 2d Maryland had engaged 162 officers and men.[58] The 6th New Hampshire had 150 men, and its historian says the 2d Maryland had the same number.[59] The 9th New Hampshire had been in service three weeks only, had lost some by straggling, and its officers estimate it had 30 officers and 680 men in action. The 48th Pennsylvania we estimate to have had 390 officers and men (this estimate based on information from

[46] As of this writing, no textual source for this statement has been found.

[47] Ibid.

[48] "Report of the number of officers and enlisted men, the number of horses and other means of transportation, and the number of cavalry and artillery horses in each regiment or battery, and at brigade and division headquarters, in the Army of the Potomac on November 1, 1862," reprinted in *OR*, vol. 19, pt. 1, 98. Carman misdated the return as having been conducted on October 1.

[49] Thomas W. Hyde to Charles Mundee, September 19, 1862, reprinted in *OR*, vol. 19, pt. 1, 413.

[50] Nathan S. Babcock to William H. Irwin, September, 20, 1862, reprinted in *OR*, vol. 19, pt. 1, 415.

[51] As of this writing, no textual source for this statement has been found.

[52] Fox, 169.

[53] Frederick W. Swift.—*EAC*

[54] History of the regiment [source not identified].—*EAC*

[55] Joseph Gerhardt to Thomas Welsh, September 18, 1862, reprinted in *OR*, vol. 19, pt. 1, 442.

[56] As of this writing, Carman's source for this statement has not been identified.

[57] Ibid.

[58] Ibid.

[59] Lyman Jackman, *History of the Sixth New Hampshire Regiment in the War for the Union* (Concord: Republican Press Association, 1891), 104.

Oliver C. Bosbyshell and other surviving members).[60] The 21st Massachusetts had about 150 engaged.[61] John D. Cobb, historian of the 35th Massachusetts, informs us that it had 30 officers (including surgeons) and about 750 muskets.[62] The morning report of the 51st Pennsylvania dated September 17, 1862 (a retained copy of which has been furnished us[63]), shows 336 present for duty, and we assume all were engaged. The 51st New York was of about the same strength as the 51st Pennsylvania (say, 335). The aggregate strength of the eight regiments foots up 3,013. The two batteries—Clark's and Durell's—had six guns each, with 5 officers and 236 men—an aggregate of 241. The strength of the division (infantry and artillery) was 3,254 officers and men.

Rodman's division consisted of seven regiments and two batteries. The 9th New York had 373 engaged.[64] The 89th New York was about the same strength as the 9th (say, 370), and the 103d New York had but six companies numbering about 200 (four companies having been left in North Carolina). Two officers of the 8th Connecticut give the regiment 23 officers and 398 men, while another says 396 men. (We give it 421 officers and men.) The 11th Connecticut had 430 officers and men.[65] The 16th Connecticut was a new regiment, and our information is that it took about 750 officers and men into action. Our best information gives the 4th Rhode Island 247. The seven regiments of the division aggregated 2,791. C. P. Muhlenberg's battery of six guns is estimated to have had 3 officers and 120 men (an aggregate of 123); the battery of five guns attached to the 9th New York was manned by Company K of that regiment.

The Kanawha Division had six Ohio regiments and two batteries of six guns each. Scammon's brigade (the 12th, 23d, and 30th Ohio) had 1,455 in action at South Mountain.[66] Of this number 272 were lost in that action[67]; it should have had about 1,180 at Antietam (under Ewing), but it had over 200 less than this. The 12th Ohio had about 200 engaged. George H. Hildt has a memorandum of the strength of the 30th Ohio, made on the morning of September 17, 1862, showing the number of each company—the aggregate being 22 officers and 321 men.[68] The 23d Ohio was about the same size as the 30th; our information is that it had 360 officers and men. The aggregate for the brigade is 903. Crook's brigade had the 11th, 28th, and 36th Ohio. The 11th Ohio was the smallest regiment in the brigade, and from the best information numbered about 430 officers and men. From a memorandum furnished by one of its officers, the 28th Ohio had 25 officers and 750 men[69]—an aggregate of 775. Hiram F. Devol writes us that the 36th Ohio was quite full when it passed through Parkersburg to join the Army of the Potomac, and that it entered the battle of Antietam with at least 800 officers and men.[70] The aggregate in the brigade was 2,005; in the division, it was 2,908. The two batteries (McMullin's and Simmonds's) had six guns each, and we estimate they had 6 officers and 240 men. There were attached to the corps—but unassigned to any division—Batteries L and M (consolidated; Captain John Edwards Jr.), 3d U.S. Artillery, and Battery L, 2d New York Artillery (Captain Jacob Roemer). Only Roemer's battery was engaged; it had six guns and (we estimate) 3 officers and 120 men. The corps had thirty-two guns in action.

Ninth Corps

	Infantry	Artillery	Aggregate
Willcox's division	3,002	246	3,248
Sturgis's division	3,013	241	3,254
Rodman's division	2,791	123	2,914
Cox's division	2,908	246	3,154
unattached artillery	—	123	123
Total	11,714	979	12,693

[60] As of this writing, no textual source for this statement has been found.

[61] Charles F. Walcott, *History [of] the Twenty-first Regiment Massachusetts Volunteers in the War for the Preservation of the Union, 1861–1865, with Statistics of the War and of Rebel Prisons* (Boston: Houghton, Mifflin and Co., 1882), 206.

[62] As of this writing, no textual source for this statement has been found.

[63] Not found.

[64] Fox, 31.

[65] As of this writing, Carman's source for this statement has not been identified.

[66] Eliakim P. Scammon to G. M. Bascom, September 20, 1862, reprinted in *OR*, vol. 19, pt. 1, 462.

[67] "Return of Casualties in the Union forces at the battle of South Mountain (Turner's Pass), Md.," *OR*, vol. 19. pt. 1, 187.

[68] Not found.

[69] Ibid.

[70] Ibid.

Twelfth Corps: This was the smallest corps in the army. McClellan gives its strength engaged as 10,126; in reality it was about 7,600. Williams reports that the loss in the corps (1,746) was "at least one-fourth of the number actually engaged."[71] Assuming the correctness of this statement would give 6,984 as engaged. This is less than the number taken into action, yet more by a thousand than those who fired a shot. Greene reports that his division had an "aggregate present on the day of the action" of 2,504.[72] We assume that he carried that number into the fight, though it is doubtful if he did so. Gordon, who initially commanded one of the two brigades of Williams's division, reports he went into action with 2,210 officers and men.[73] Knipe, who succeeded to the command of the division's other brigade (Crawford's), does not give the number engaged, nor do any of the regimental commanders. John M. Gould says that the 10th Maine went into action with 21 officers and 276 enlisted men—a total of 297.[74] The acting adjutant of the 28th New York, Frank B. Seely, informs us that the regiment had 68 in action;[75] this statement is confirmed by others of the regiment as well as those of other commands near it, who thought at the time it was but a skirmish party of about 40 men. Several survivors of the 46th Pennsylvania agree that it had not to exceed 150 men in action, and the general estimate is 135 to 140 (say, 150). The three new regiments (the 124th, 125th, and 128th Pennsylvania) were quite full when the army left Washington, but hot weather and unaccustomed marching had caused much straggling and sickness, and the regiments did not array more than 670 each, or 2,010 in the three. This would make the aggregate of Crawford's brigade 2,525 officers and men. The aggregate infantry strength of the corps was 7,239. There were nominally attached to the corps seven batteries of artillery. Of these, but four were engaged: Cothran's, Bruen's, Knap's, and E. D. Muhlenberg's—an aggregate of twenty-two guns. From the best attainable information, these four batteries had 10 officers and 382 men engaged. The aggregate strength of the corps (infantry and artillery) was 7,631. This is 2,495 less than McClellan reports (by nearly 25 percent), and yet it is a very credible showing when compared with some other corps.

Twelfth Corps

	Infantry	Artillery	Aggregate
Greene's division	2,504		2,504
Williams's division	4,735		4,735
unattached artillery		392	392
Total	7,239	392	7,631

cavalry division: Pleasonton's cavalry division is reported by McClellan as having 4,320. This includes its artillery (Tidball's, Robertson's, Hains's, Gibson's batteries) aggregating twenty-two guns—all of which were engaged, and which we estimate had 12 officers and 480 men (an aggregate of 492). We have no means of verifying the figures given by McClellan, but shall accept them. It cannot be said that Pleasonton's cavalrymen were actively engaged in fighting (and the same is true as regards the Confederate cavalry) but we shall consider them as engaged.

Aggregate Engaged Strength of the Union Army, September 17, 1862

	Infantry	Artillery	Aggregate
First Corps	8,619	819	9,438
Second Corps	15,206	859	16,065
Fifth Corps	1,684	1,540	3,224
Sixth Corps	1,684	901	2,585
Ninth Corps	11,714	979	12,693
Twelfth Corps	7,239	392	7,631
Total	46,146	5,490	51,636
	Cavalry	**Artillery**	**Aggregate**
cavalry division	3,828	492	4,320

[71] Alpheus S. Williams to Joseph H. Taylor, September 29, 1862, reprinted in *OR*, vol. 19, pt. 1, 477.

[72] George S. Greene to Alpheus S. Williams, September 29, 1862, reprinted in *OR*, vol. 19, pt. 1, 504.

[73] George H. Gordon to Alpheus S. Williams, September 24, 1862, reprinted in *OR*, vol. 19, pt. 1, 497–98.

[74] John M. Gould, *History of the First-Tenth-Twenty-Ninth Maine Regiment: In Service of the United States from May 3, 1861, to June 21, 1866* (Portland: Stephen Berry, 1871), 258.

[75] See Frank B. Seely to Gould, October 27, 1892, John M. Gould Collection of Papers Relating to the Battle of Antietam (preservation microfilm, reel 2), Rauner Special Collections Library, Dartmouth College, Hanover, N.H.

The number engaged in the battle on the Union side, as shown by these figures, was 46,146 infantry, 5,982 artillery, and 3,828 cavalry—an aggregate of 55,956. The number of guns in action was 301.

The Confederate Army

General Lee reports, "The arduous service in which our troops had been engaged, their great privations of rest and food, and the long marches without shoes over mountain roads, had greatly reduced our ranks before the action began. These causes had compelled thousands of brave men to absent themselves, and many more had done so from unworthy motives. This great battle was fought by less than 40,000 men on our side, all of whom had undergone the greatest labors and hardships in the field and on the march."[76] In 1865 Thomas White, who had been chief clerk in the office of the adjutant general of the Army of Northern Virginia, and who had charge of the field returns, prepared for Lee an estimate of the effective strength of the army at several dates, according to his recollection. At Sharpsburg, the effective infantry was 33,000; cavalry, 4,500; artillery, 4,000—a total of 41,500.[77] Armistead L. Long says that "the Confederates, including the division of A. P. Hill … amounted to 40,000."[78] Walter H. Taylor of Lee's staff says the effective strength of the infantry was 27,255, and estimates the cavalry and artillery at 8,000, thus making the entire strength 35,255.[79] Taylor says, "Every man was engaged. We had no reserve … These thirty-five thousand Confederates were the very flower of the Army of Northern Virginia."[80] Fitzhugh Lee adopts Taylor's figures. He says that after McLaws, R. H. Anderson, and A. P. Hill arrived, Lee had 27,255 infantry, "which, with eight thousand cavalry and artillery, would make Lee's army at Sharpsburg 35,255," and he adds in a footnote, "General Lee told the writer he fought the battle with 35,000 troops."[81] R. L. Dabney says that Lee had 33,000 men.[82] D. H. Hill says the battle "was fought with less than 30,000 men," and that the straggling preceding the battle was enormous. "Had all our stragglers been up, McClellan's army would have been completely crushed or annihilated. Doubtless the want of shoes, the want of food, and physical exhaustion had kept many brave men from being with the army; but thousands of thieving poltroons had kept away from sheer cowardice."[83] Hill elsewhere says that Lee's strength (infantry and artillery) was about 27,000.[84] Adding to this 4,500 for the cavalry makes a total of 31,500.

It is seen from these figures that the estimate of Lee's strength, from a Confederate standpoint, runs from 41,500 (as given by Thomas White) to 31,500 (as given by D. H. Hill), and there are others who make the number much less. It may not be possible to get at the correct figures, but it is possible to get at a close approximation. With such official reports as are available and the assistance of many survivors of the organization, who have placed their retained papers at our disposal and otherwise assisted, we present what we consider a very close approximation to the number actually engaged.

Longstreet's command: McLaws reports that the four brigades of his division had 64 officers and 2,629 men engaged.[85] This includes two batteries, but does not include Carlton's Battery or the officers of Cobb's Brigade of 357 men. Carlton had 1 officer and 30 men at Crampton's Gap, where he lost 4, leaving its probable strength at Antietam at 1 officer and 26 men.[86] Assuming that the officers of Cobb's Brigade bore the same ratio to the men in the other brigades (1 officer to 8⅔ men) gives 41 officers to the 357 men of the brigade. Add to this the 1 officer and 26 men of Carlton's Battery and we have 306 officers and 2,655 men—an aggregate of 2,961 officers and men in the division. McLaws accounts for the small number carried into action by the sleepless nights for two or three days preceding and "the straggling of men wearied beyond further endurance, and of those without shoes."[87] Kershaw says his men had been under arms or marching nearly the whole of the night of Monday and Tuesday. "As a consequence, many had become exhausted and fallen out on the wayside, and all were worn

---

[76] Robert E. Lee to Samuel Cooper, August 19, 1863, reprinted in *OR*, vol. 19, pt. 1, 151.

[77] Walter H. Taylor, *Four Years with General Lee: Being a Summary of the More Important Events Touching the Career of General Robert E. Lee, in the War between the States, Together with an Authoritative Statement of the Strength of the Army Which He Commanded in the Field* (New York: D. Appleton and Co., 1877), 157–58.

[78] Armistead L. Long, *Memoirs of Robert E. Lee: His Military and Personal History, Embracing a Large Amount of Information Hitherto Unpublished* (New York: J. M. Stoddard & Co., 1886), 217.

[79] Taylor, 73.

[80] Ibid., 69, 73.

[81] Fitzhugh Lee, *General Lee* (New York: D. Appleton and Co., 1894), 208–9.

[82] R. L. Dabney, *Life and Campaigns of Lieut.-Gen. Thomas J. Jackson, (Stonewall Jackson.)* (New York: Blelock & Co., 1866), 572.

[83] Daniel H. Hill to Robert H. Chilton, 1862 [no day or month given], reprinted in *OR*, vol. 19, pt. 1, 1026.

[84] Address of Daniel H. Hill, contained in "Reunion of the Virginia Division Army of Northern Virginia Association," *Southern Historical Society Papers* 13 (1885): 272.

[85] Lafayette McLaws to "the Adjutant-General, Headquarters General Longstreet [Gilbert Moxley Sorrel]," October 20, 1862, reprinted in *OR*, vol. 19, pt. 1, 860.

[86] "Return of casualties in McLaws' division at the battle of Crampton's Gap, September 14, 1862," *OR*, vol. 19, pt. 1, 861.

[87] McLaws, "The Capture of Harper's Ferry," *Philadelphia Weekly Press*, September 19, 1888.

and jaded."[88] Barksdale says a portion of his men "had fallen by the wayside from loss of sleep and excessive fatigue, having been constantly on duty for five or six days, and on the march for almost the whole of the two preceding nights."[89] These statements are borne out by information from surviving officers of the command, who write us that the greater part of the straggling was on the march from Harper's Ferry to Sharpsburg, and that in that march some of the companies lost one-half of their men, others one-third. By the morning of the eighteenth, most of the absentees had joined, more than enough to make good the losses of the seventeenth.

The number of guns of McLaws's Division on the field was nineteen. Of these, but nine were engaged—four of Read's Battery, three of Carlton's, and two of McCarthy's.

Anderson's Division followed McLaws from Harper's Ferry and suffered much from straggling. D. H. Hill reports that it came to his support "with some 3,000 or 4,000 men."[90] We have official reports from only one regiment of this division and partial information from other sources, but conclude that the number engaged, including officers and Saunders's artillery battalion of four batteries, was 4,000 officers and men (infantry, 3,672; artillery, 328). The division had sixteen guns and all were engaged.

D. R. Jones reports that, on the morning of the seventeenth, his "entire command of six brigades comprised only 2,430 men."[91] We have but partial official returns from the brigades of this division. Of Toombs's Brigade, but two regiments (the 2d and 20th Georgia) were at that time on the field. The 2d Georgia had 18 officers and 89 men;[92] the 20th Georgia had not more than 250 officers and men[93]—an aggregate in the two regiments of 357 officers and men. Garnett's Brigade had an aggregate of 234 muskets, thus divided: the 8th Virginia, 22 men;[94] 18th Virginia, 75;[95] 19th Virginia, 50;[96] 28th Virginia, 47 (estimated); and 56th Virginia, 40.[97] No report is given of the strength of the 28th Virginia, but assuming that it had the strength of the average of the other four regiments gives it 47 men. Assuming further that the officers bore the same ratio to the men as in McLaws's Division (1 officer to 8⅔ men) would give 27 officers, combined with 234 men for an aggregate of 261. In explanation of the very small number of men of this brigade with their colors in the Maryland campaign, Eppa Hunton informs us that the brigade had suffered quite heavily in the summer campaign and that, upon nearing the Potomac, came into the section of the country where they had been recruited. The men had been away from their homes a long time, left the ranks to see their old folks, wives, and sweethearts, and did not rejoin until the army had recrossed into Virginia.[98] William H. Palmer informs us that Kemper's Brigade did not number more than half a regiment, and that his own regiment (the 1st Virginia) had but 40 men.[99] The 7th Virginia had 113 men.[100] The 11th Virginia, we are informed by some of its survivors, had about 100 men. The 17th Virginia had 9 officers and 46 men;[101] the 24th Virginia, 95 men (as estimated by three of its survivors). Assuming 1 officer to 8⅔ men in the 1st, 7th, 11th, and 24th Virginia, we get the strength of the regiments in officers and men as follows: 1st Virginia, 45; 7th Virginia, 126; 11th Virginia, 111; 17th Virginia, 55; 24th Virginia, 106—an aggregate strength for the brigade of 443 officers and men. We are informed by G. T. Anderson that, exclusive of the 11th Georgia (which was on detached duty on the morning of the seventeenth), he had between 520 and 550 men (say, 535).[102] Assuming that it had the same complement of officers as had McLaws's Division would give it 62 officers—an aggregate of 597 officers and men. Drayton's Brigade suffered severely at South Mountain and was very small at Antietam. The 3d South Carolina Battalion had but 17 men. The 50th Georgia had about 100.[103] We have no definite data relating to the 15th South Carolina and 51st Georgia, but from incomplete data estimate that the former had 200 and the latter 100—an aggregate in the brigade of 417 men. Adding to this the officers in the usual proportion (48) would give an aggregate of 465. There is but one official return from Jenkins's Brigade, that of the 1st South Carolina Volunteers, which

[88]   Joseph B. Kershaw to James M. Goggin, October 9, 1862, reprinted in *OR*, vol. 19, pt. 1, 864–65.

[89]   William Barksdale to Goggin, October 12, 1862, reprinted in *OR*, vol. 19, pt. 1, 883.

[90]   Daniel H. Hill to Chilton, 1023.

[91]   David R. Jones to Sorrel, December 8, 1862, reprinted in *OR*, vol. 19, pt. 1, 886.

[92]   Abner M. Lewis to Henry L. Benning, September 23, 1862, reprinted in *OR*, vol. 51, pt. 1, 165.

[93]   Benning to Dudley M. DuBose, October 13, 1862, reprinted in *OR*, vol. 51, pt. 1, 162.

[94]   Eppa Hunton to Robert B. Garnett, 1862 [no day or month given], reprinted in *OR*, vol. 19, pt. 1, 898.

[95]   George C. Cabell to "General Garnett's assistant adjutant-general," October 14, 1862, reprinted in *OR*, vol. 19, pt. 1, 900.

[96]   Report of Benjamin Brown, October 15, 1862, reprinted in *OR*, vol. 19, pt. 1, 901.

[97]   John B. McPhail to Garnett, October 26, 1862, reprinted in *OR*, vol. 19, pt. 1, 904.

[98]   As of this writing, no textual source for this statement has been found.

[99]   Ibid.

[100]   David E. Johnston to Henry Heth, September 18, 1897, typescript copy, "Maj. Gen. David R. Jones' Division Report—Artillery of Jones' Division" folder, box 2, "Antietam Studies."

[101]   Report of Montgomery D. Corse, no date, reprinted in *OR*, vol. 19, pt. 1, 905.

[102]   As of this writing, no textual source for this statement has been found.

[103]   Robert Toombs to David R. Jones, October 25, 1862, reprinted in *OR*, vol. 19, pt. 1, 889.

says the regiment had 106 rank and file in action and lost 40.[104] The *Charleston Courier* says the brigade had 755 men in action.[105] We accept these figures and consider that the officers are included. This makes for Jones's Division, on the morning of the seventeenth: Toombs's Brigade, 357; Garnett's Brigade, 261; Kemper's Brigade, 443; G. T. Anderson's Brigade, 597; Drayton's Brigade, 465; and Jenkins's Brigade, 755—an aggregate of 2,878. This does not include J. S. Brown's Battery of four guns, which was on the field, nor does it include five companies of the 11th Georgia of G. T. Anderson's Brigade or the 15th and 17th Georgia of Toombs's (all of which joined late in the day and were engaged). Francis H. Little, commanding the five companies of the 11th Georgia, reports that he carried into action about 140 men;[106] the complement of officers was about 12. The 15th Georgia had 13 officers and 112 men.[107] The 17th Georgia was about one-fourth larger than the 15th (say, 16 officers and 140 men). J. S. Brown's Battery had 3 officers and 78 men. Adding these numbers to those already given as present in the morning (2,878) gives 3,311 infantry and 81 artillery—an aggregate of 3,392 for the strength of Jones's Division. This is a small showing for a division of six brigades, but it must be borne in mind that Drayton's Brigade had suffered severely at South Mountain, Garnett's and Kemper's had lost many by straggling, and all had seen exceptionally hard service in the four months preceding. The four guns of the division were on the field and engaged.

Walker's Division had two brigades, with a battery attached to each. Ransom reports that the strength of his brigade present "was about 1,600 aggregate."[108] The strength of Walker's old brigade (commanded by Colonel Manning) is not officially reported. A roll call of nine companies of the 30th Virginia before going into action showed 236 officers and men. One company, left on picket near Snavely's Ford, joined during the engagement; estimating that this company had the strength of the average of the other nine companies gives 26, and makes the strength of the regiment 262. The 27th North Carolina had 325 officers and men.[109] Our information from the 46th North Carolina is meager, but indicates that it had 320 officers and men. The 48th North Carolina was very large. Seven survivors have answered our inquiries: two say the regiment was very full, had many recruits, and that it numbered a full 1,000; one says it had 950 men; two, 850; and one, 750—an average of 907, which we take as the strength of the regiment. The 3d Arkansas had 350 men in action.[110] The aggregate of the five regiments is 2,164 officers and men. The two batteries of the division had a fairly full complement of men (230, including officers). In total, Ransom had 1,600, Manning, 2,164, and the artillery, 230—an aggregate in the division of 3,994. The twelve guns of the two batteries were actively engaged.

Hood's Division consisted of two brigades—Law's and Wofford's—and three batteries. Wofford reports that the strength of his brigade was 854.[111] Law does not give the strength of his brigade. Hood made no report of the strength of the division, but in his memoirs says he had not far from 2,000 effectives,[112] and this is the generally accepted strength of his division (officers and men). The three batteries of the division had eighteen guns, and from partial data we estimate for them 8 officers and 296 men—an aggregate of 304. Infantry and artillery, the division had 2,304 officers and men. All eighteen guns of the batteries were engaged.

Evans's Brigade had about 550 men engaged at South Mountain, where its loss was 210; therefore, it should have had at Sharpsburg over 300 men. Colonel Stevens, temporarily in command of the brigade, says, "At the battle of Sharpsburg sickness, fatigue, and the casualties of battle had reduced the brigade to a mere skeleton."[113] Colonel McMaster of the 17th South Carolina reports that his regiment had 6 officers and 53 men at Sharpsburg,[114] and he informs us that his was the largest regiment of the brigade.[115] We cannot present any detailed data regarding the other four regiments of the brigade, but estimate from incomplete data that the entire brigade had 29 officers and 255 men—an aggregate of 284, which we consider a very close approximation. Boyce's Battery of six guns, attached to this brigade, had 3 officers and 112 men, and was very active.

[104] Joseph Walker to Robert Johnston, October 24, 1862, reprinted in *OR*, vol. 19, pt. 1, 908.

[105] "Casualties in Jenkins' Brigade," *Charleston Courier*, October 1, 1862. Carman's estimate is probably high, likely due to a misreading of his source. The *Courier*'s return covers the fighting at South Mountain as well, and the figure of 755 presumably refers to the number carried into action on the fourteenth, in which engagement Carman himself attributes 32 casualties to the brigade (see Appendix G).

[106] Francis H. Little to George T. Anderson, October 7, 1862, reprinted in *OR*, vol. 19, pt. 1, 912.

[107] Thomas H. Jackson to Benning, no date, reprinted in *OR*, vol. 51, pt. 1, 166.

[108] Robert Ransom Jr. to William A. Smith, September 22, 1862, reprinted in *OR*, vol. 19, pt. 1, 919.

[109] Lieutenant James A. Graham.—*EAC*

[110] "Casualties: List of Casualties in the 3d Regiment Arkansas Vols. at the Battle of Sharpsburg, on the 17th of Sept. 1862. Capt. J. W. Ready Commanding the Regiment," *Richmond Enquirer*, October 14, 1862.

[111] William T. Wofford to William H. Sellers, reprinted in *OR*, vol. 19, pt. 1, 929.

[112] John B. Hood, *Advance and Retreat: Personal Experiences in the United States and Confederate States Armies* (n.p., 1880), 43.

[113] In his original manuscript, Carman attributes the quotation incorrectly to Colonel McMaster of the 17th South Carolina. See Peter F. Stevens to Asa L. Evans, October 13, 1862, reprinted in *OR*, vol. 19, pt. 1, 942.

[114] Fitz W. McMaster to Nathan G. Evans, October 20, 1862, reprinted in *OR*, vol. 19, pt. 1, 946.

[115] As of this writing, no textual source for this statement has been found.

With regard to Longstreet's reserve artillery, Colonel Lee reports that about 300 men of his battalion of six batteries (twenty-four guns) went into action.[116] This seems a very low figure for twenty-four guns, and does not include the officers, of whom there were 18 present. Colonel Walton's Washington Artillery had four batteries of four guns each, and our estimate of its strength, based upon information from survivors of three of the battalions, is that it had 15 officers and 263 men[117]—an aggregate of 278. The aggregate number of guns in the two battalions was forty, and all were engaged.

Longstreet had 115 guns on the field, 105 of which were in action.

Recapitulation

	Infantry	Artillery	Aggregate
McLaws's Division	2,823	138	2,961
R. H. Anderson's Division	3,672	328	4,000
D. R. Jones's Division	3,311	81	3,392
Walker's Division	3,764	230	3,994
Hood's Division	2,000	304	2,304
Evans's Brigade	284	115	399
S. D. Lee's Battalion		318	
Washington Artillery		278	
Total	15,854	1,792	17,646

Jackson's command: Jackson's command consisted of the divisions of Ewell, A. P. Hill, Jackson, and D. H. Hill. Early reports that Ewell's Division went into action at Sharpsburg with less than 3,500,[118] of which Lawton's Brigade had 1,150, Hays's, 550, and Trimble's, less than 700.[119] We have no official report of the strength of Early's Brigade, but Confederate writers have generally placed it at 1,100 men, and this estimate we adopt, which makes the strength of the division about 3,500 men. The officers are not included in these figures. Assuming 8⅔ men to 1 officer gives us 404 officers—an aggregate of 3,904 officers and men of the infantry of the division. There were four batteries in the division on the field, and their aggregate (officers and men), as estimated by the survivors, was 223. The batteries aggregated fifteen guns present, all of which were engaged.

A. P. Hill reports that the three brigades of his division actually engaged—Branch's, Gregg's, and Archer's—did not number 2,000 men.[120] Pender's and Brockenbrough's Brigades were on the extreme right and not engaged (though having some casualties); they are not to be included in the estimate of the fighting strength of the division. The three brigades named by Hill as engaged were very much larger when they marched from Harper's Ferry, and they left many stragglers by the wayside. How many, none can say, and we have no other course than to accept Hill's statement that he did not have over 2,000 men engaged. To this estimate we add 231 officers, making an aggregate of 2,231 infantry. The division batteries of McIntosh, Crenshaw, Braxton, and Pegram were engaged. Information from survivors is that they aggregated 337 officers and men. The strength of the division (infantry and artillery) was 2,568. The number of guns engaged was eighteen.

Jackson's old division was commanded by J. R. Jones, who reports that the division did not number over 1,600 men at the beginning of the fight.[121] Walter H. Taylor writes, "The route from Harper's Ferry was strewed with foot-sore and weary men, too feeble to keep up with the stronger and more active; and, instead of going into battle with full ranks, the brigades were but as regiments, and in some cases no stronger than a full company."[122] Not included in the 1,600 are the commissioned officers, which, in the proportion we have followed, gives 184—an aggregate of 1,784 officers and men. There were five batteries with the division, which were engaged, aggregating twenty-one guns. We have information from three of these batteries, indicating that they had 9 officers and 177 men, or 3 officers and 59 men to a battery. Assuming that the other two had the same gives the strength of the five batteries as 15 officers and 295 men—an aggregate of 310.

[116] Stephen D. Lee to Sorrel, October 11, 1862, reprinted in *OR*, vol. 19, pt. 1, 846.

[117] No textual evidence has been found regarding the number of men, but the names of all fifteen officers are given in James B. Walton to Sorrel, December 4, 1862, reprinted in *OR*, vol. 19, pt. 1, 848.

[118] Jubal A. Early to Alexander S. Pendleton, January 12, 1863, reprinted in *OR*, vol. 19, pt. 1, 973.

[119] Ibid., 968.

[120] Ambrose P. Hill to Charles J. Faulkner, February 25, 1863, reprinted in *OR*, vol. 19, pt. 1, 981.

[121] John R. Jones to Pendleton, January 21, 1863, reprinted in *OR*, vol. 19, pt. 1, 1008.

[122] Taylor, 68.

D. H. Hill says, "My ranks had been diminished by some additional straggling, and the morning of the 17th I had but 3,000 infantry."[123] These figures are entirely too low. D. H. Hill's Division consisted of five brigades of infantry and four batteries. We consider each organization. No official report is made of the strength of Ripley's Brigade. The adjutant's report of the 3d North Carolina, made early in the morning of September 17, showed 27 officers and 520 men—an aggregate of 547.[124] Hamilton A. Brown, who commanded the 1st North Carolina, writes us that he carried into action about 300 men, of whom 36 were killed and 140 wounded.[125] Other survivors confirm Brown's statement, and all agree that the number of officers was very small. We estimate the number of officers and men at 315. Seven survivors of the 4th Georgia have given us estimates in which there is a substantial agreement that the regiment had about 325 officers and men. Captain John C. Key, commanding the 44th Georgia, writes us that he had the smallest regiment of the brigade, and carried into action 162 officers and men.[126] The aggregate of the four regiments is 1,349 men. Rodes reports that his effective force was less than 800 men.[127] This does not include the officers; with these, he had fully 850 in his brigade. Colquitt made no report of the strength of his brigade at Sharpsburg. He had 1,250 men engaged at South Mountain, of whom he lost 109 killed, wounded, and missing. Without addition to his force, he should have had 1,141 men at Sharpsburg, but his force was increased after South Mountain by those who had been left on picket and camp guard near Boonsboro on the fourteenth—enough to more than make good the losses on that day—and therefore should have had over 1,250 at Sharpsburg. James M. Folsom says that the 6th Georgia went into battle with not more than 250 men.[128] We have had correspondence with many survivors of this regiment, and there is substantial agreement among them that it took into action about 260 officers and men, of whom about 200 were killed and wounded, and many missing. The 23d Georgia had about 280 officers and men in action, according to estimates made by survivors. The testimony of seven survivors of the 27th Georgia shows that it had 290 officers and men in action. The 28th Georgia called into action, as estimated by several of its survivors, about 180. Our information from the 13th Alabama is that it had in action about 310 officers and men.[129] This would make the aggregate strength of the brigade 1,320 officers and men. This exceeds the number at South Mountain, after deducting the losses on that field, by 179, but we are confident that 1,320 is substantially correct. In his official report, Colquitt says, "In this sharp and unequal conflict [Antietam] I lost many of my best officers and one-half of the men in the ranks."[130] As definitely as can be ascertained, his loss was 111 killed, 444 wounded, and 167 missing—an aggregate of 722. If this loss was one-half of the brigade, it had 1,444 officers and men. However, we retain the figures as given by the detailed information from the five regiments—1,320 officers and men. Garland's Brigade had five North Carolina regiments and at South Mountain numbered about 1,000; its complement of officers was 115—giving an aggregate of 1,115. Its loss at South Mountain was 359 killed, wounded, and missing,[131] which, deducted from 1,115, gives 756 present at Sharpsburg, and this agrees substantially with information obtained from the several regiments of the brigade. G. B. Anderson's Brigade consisted of four North Carolina regiments. Daniel W. Hurtt writes us that the 2d North Carolina had from 220 to 260 muskets;[132] three other survivors estimate the number of men at 240, and this estimate we adopt. The complement of officers was small and did not exceed 15, thus giving an aggregate of 255. Five estimates from survivors of the 4th North Carolina vary from 160 to 190, the average being 182 muskets. It had but 12 officers, making an aggregate of 194 officers and men. Captain Andrew J. Griffith of the 14th North Carolina reports that the regiment had 213 killed, wounded, and missing,[133] and our information from survivors is that it lost nearly half its men. Colonel Risden T. Bennett, who commanded the regiment at the start of the battle, writes us that, according to his recollection and that of several officers from various companies of the regiment, he took into action 475 officers and men.[134] These figures we adopt. Major William W. Sillers of the 30th North Carolina

[123] Daniel H. Hill to Chilton, 1022.

[124] William L. DeRosset to Daniel H. Hill, June 22, 1885, typescript copy, "Gen. D. H. Hill's Report—Pierson's Artillery Battalion, Hill's Division" folder, box 3, "Antietam Studies."

[125] Hamilton A. Brown to Carman, August 27, 1897, typescript copy, "Gen. D. H. Hill's Report" folder, "Antietam Studies."

[126] John C. Key to Carman, September 29, 1897, typescript copy, "Gen. D. H. Hill's Report" folder, "Antietam Studies."

[127] Robert E. Rodes to James W. Ratchford, October 13, 1862, reprinted in OR, vol. 19, pt. 1, 1038.

[128] James M. Folsom, Heroes and Martyrs of Georgia: Georgia's Record in the Revolution of 1861, vol. 1 (Macon, Ga.: Burke, Boykin &Co., 1864), 26.

[129] However, a note by Carman found among his papers says, "A. S. Reaves commanding 13th Ala writes that he carried into action Sep 17 1862 612 men." Memorandum of Carman, folder 2, box 9, Ezra A. Carman Papers, Manuscripts and Archives Division, New York Public Library.

[130] Alfred H. Colquitt to Ratchford, October 13, 1862, reprinted in OR, vol. 19, pt. 1, 1054.

[131] Colonel McRae, who succeeded to the command of the brigade after Garland's death, reports that "the brigade numbered scarce 1,000 men" at South Mountain. Duncan K. McRae to "Major," October 18, 1862, reprinted in OR, vol. 19, pt. 1, 1041. For Carman's methodology in computing the brigade's casualties in that battle, see p. 450 n. 4.

[132] Not found.

[133] Report of Andrew J. Griffith, 1862 [no day or month given], reprinted in OR, vol. 19, pt. 1, 1050.

[134] Not found.

reports, "The regiment before the fight numbered about 250, all told."[135] This gives an aggregate strength of 1,174 for the brigade. The five infantry brigades numbered as follows: Ripley's, 1,349; Rodes's, 850; Colquitt's, 1,320; Garland's, 756; and G. B. Anderson's, 1,174—an aggregate of 5,449 infantry for D. H. Hill's Division. The artillery of the division consisted of four batteries—Hardaway's, Bondurant's, Jones's, and Carter's—in all twenty-one guns. Hill reports that he had twenty-six guns, evidently an error.[136] (He probably included a battery not properly belonging to his division, but temporarily serving with it.) Information from Thomas H. Carter and others connected with the batteries named enable us to estimate that they had in action 11 officers and 335 men—an aggregate of 346. The entire strength of D. H. Hill's Division was 5,449 infantry and 346 artillery—an aggregate of 5,795.

Jackson's command had seventy-five guns engaged.

Recapitulation

	Infantry	Artillery	Aggregate
Ewell's Division	3,904	223	4,227
A. P. Hill's Division	2,231	337	2,568
Jackson's Division	1,784	310	2,094
D. H. Hill's Division	5,449	346	5,795
Total	13,368	1,216	14,584

reserve artillery: The reserve artillery of the Army of Northern Virginia consisted of four battalions aggregating nineteen batteries. The battalions of Brown and Nelson were on the Virginia side of the Potomac; only those of Cutts and H. P. Jones were on the field and engaged on the seventeenth. Cutts's Battalion had four batteries (Blackshear's, Ross's, Patterson's, and Lane's) of six guns each. Lane was engaged on the evening of the sixteenth, but not at all on the seventeenth. Lloyd's Battery was temporarily attached to Cutts's Battalion, but was not engaged. Blackshear's, Ross's, and Patterson's Batteries had 9 officers and 310 men in action. Of the five batteries under Cutts's command, aggregating thirty guns (all of which were on the field), only eighteen were engaged on the seventeenth. Jones's Battalion consisted of four batteries of four guns each, and our information from Jones and other survivors of the battalion is that it had 12 officers and 290 men—an aggregate of 302. All the guns of this battalion were engaged.

cavalry division: We have no official data showing the strength of Stuart's cavalry division. Confederate writers generally agree that it numbered 4,500. We adopt these figures, and include the horse artillery of the division, of which but four guns of Pelham's battery were engaged.

Aggregate Engaged Strength of the Confederate Army, September 17, 1862

	Infantry	Artillery	Aggregate
Longstreet's command	15,854	1,792	17,646
Jackson's command	13,368	1,216	14,584
reserve artillery		621	621
Total	29,222	3,629	32,851
			Aggregate
cavalry division			4,500

The number engaged in the battle on the Confederate side, as shown by these figures, was 29,222 infantry, 3,629 artillery, and 4,500 cavalry (including the horse artillery)—an aggregate of 37,351. Longstreet had 105 guns in action; Jackson, 75; Stuart, 4; and the reserve artillery, 35—an aggregate of 219 guns engaged by the Confederate army on the seventeenth.

There are some who will think these figures of the Confederate strength too high; there are others who will believe them to be far too low. We believe they do not vary by 500 either way from the number actually engaged.

In all, on both the Union and Confederate side, there were engaged 75,368 infantry, 9,611 artillery, and 8,328 cavalry—an aggregate of 93,307. The number of guns brought into action was 520.

---

[135] William W. Sillers to William P. Bynum, October 13, 1862, reprinted in *OR*, vol. 19, pt. 1, 1052.
[136] Hill to Chilton, 1022.

Appendix K: The Mortal Wounding of General Mansfield

There has been much discussion, showing a wide divergence of opinion, as to where Brigadier General Joseph K. F. Mansfield was mortally wounded. At least seven places have been indicated on the field where it occurred. Colonel William F. Rogers of the 21st New York states that he saw him killed beyond the D. R. Miller barn in the West Woods.[1] As Mansfield never crossed the Hagerstown Road, Rogers is in error, probably mistaking Colonel William B. Goodrich for Mansfield. Another statement is that he was shot in the D. R. Miller orchard, but he was not on that part of the field after he had led his corps forward. Two places have been indicated that, at the time, were 250 yards inside the Confederate lines. Brigadier General George H. Gordon reports that Mansfield was wounded "while making a bold reconnaissance of the woods through which we had just dashed."[2] If Gordon refers to the North Woods, through which his own brigade advanced, he is in error; if he refers to the East Woods, through which a part of Crawford's brigade deployed, he is nearer the fact. Colonel Jacob Higgins of the 125th Pennsylvania, whose regiment was in line fronting the East Woods and north of the Smoketown Road, reports that some of his men carried the general "off the field on their muskets until a blanket was procured,"[3] and these men say that where they saw him wounded was at a point in front of and to the left of the 128th Pennsylvania in the edge of the East Woods and about 120 yards west of the Smoketown Road. John M. Gould, adjutant of the 10th Maine, says Mansfield was wounded about 35 yards east of the Smoketown Road, and in his history of the 10th Maine he gives a circumstantial account of the event:

> The rebels in our front showed no colors. They appeared to be somewhat detached from and in advance of the main rebel line, and were about where the left of Gen. [Abram] Duryée's brigade might be supposed to have retreated. To Gen. Mansfield we appeared to be firing into Duryée's troops, therefore he beckoned to us to cease firing, and as this was the very last thing we proposed to do, the few who saw him did not understand what his motions meant, and so no attention was paid to him. He now rode down the hill from the 128th Penn., and passing quickly through H, A, K, E, I, G, and D, ordering them to cease firing, he halted in front of C, at the earnest remonstrances of Capt. [William P.] Jordan and Sergt. [Henry A.] Burnham, who asked him to see the gray coats of the enemy, and pointed out particular men of them who were then aiming their rifles at us and at him! The general was convinced, and remarked "Yes, yes, you are right," and was almost instantly hit. He turned and attempted to put his horse over the rails, but the animal had also been severely wounded and could not go over. Thereupon the General dismounted, and a gust of wind blowing open his coat we saw that he was wounded in the body. Sergt. Joe Merrill, [Private] Storer Knight and I took the General to the rear, assisted for a while by a negro cook from Hooker's corps. We put the General into an ambulance in the woods in front of which we had deployed, and noticed that Gen. Gordon was just at that moment posting the 107th New York in their front edge.[4]

1   William F. Rogers, "Movement of the Twenty-first Regiment New York Volunteers at the Battle of Antietam September 17th, 1862," no date, typescript copy, "1st Corps—Doubleday—Hooker" folder, box 1, Letters and Reports Concerning the Battle of Antietam, 1895–1900 ("Antietam Studies"), Record Group 94, National Archives.
2   George H. Gordon to Alpheus S. Williams, September 24, 1862, reprinted in OR, vol. 19, pt. 1, 495.
3   Jacob Higgins to Joseph F. Knipe, September 22, 1862, reprinted in OR, vol. 19, pt. 1, 492.
4   John M. Gould, *History of the First-Tenth-Twenty-ninth Maine Regiment, in Service of the United States from May 3, 1861, to June 21, 1866* (Portland: Stephen Berry, 1871), 240–41.

Appendix L: Casualties in the Union and Confederate Armies at Antietam

Union Losses at Antietam, September 17, 1862[1]

	Killed	Wounded	Missing	Aggregate
First Corps	417	2,051	122	2,590
Second Corps	883	3,859	396	5,138
Fifth Corps	17	90	2	109
Sixth Corps	71	335	33	439
Ninth Corps	438	1,796	115	2,349
Twelfth Corps	275	1,386	85	1,746
cavalry division	7	23	—	30
Total	2,108	9,540	753	12,401

Of the 55,956 engaged, this is a little more than 3.76 percent in killed, over 20.82 percent in killed and wounded, and 22.16 percent in killed, wounded, and missing.

The First Corps had 26.14 percent killed and wounded of the number engaged; the Second Corps, 29.51 percent; the Fifth Corps, 3.63 percent; the Sixth Corps, 15.70 percent; the Ninth Corps, 17.60 percent; the Twelfth Corps, 21.76 percent; and the cavalry division, less than 1.00 percent. Ricketts's division of the First Corps leads in the severity of loss, losing 35.40 percent in killed and wounded, Sedgwick's division of the Second Corps being next, with 34.60 percent. The regiment showing the highest percentage of loss is the 12th Massachusetts, Hartsuff's brigade, Ricketts's division.[2]

* * *

Confederate Losses at Antietam, September 16–18, 1862

	Killed	Wounded	Missing	Aggregate
McLaws's Division				
Kershaw's Brigade[3]	57	292	6	355
Cobb's Brigade[4]	17	129	10	156
Semmes's Brigade[5]	53	255	6	314
Barksdale's Brigade[6]	33	257	4	294
Total[7]	160	933	26	1,119

(continued on next page)

---

[1] "Return of Casualties in the Union forces at the battle of Antietam, Md.: Recapitulation," *OR*, vol. 19, pt. 1, 200. These figures do not include the losses from Couch's division of the Fourth Corps, which sustained 1 officer and 8 men wounded on the eighteenth.

[2] A comprehensive study of such data places the casualties sustained by this regiment at Antietam in excess of 22 percent. See William F. Fox, *Regimental Losses in the American Civil War, 1861–1865: A Treatise on the Extent and Nature of the Mortuary Losses in the Union Regiments, with Full and Exhaustive Statistics Compiled from the Official Records on File in the State Military Bureaus and at Washington* (Albany, N.Y.: Albany Publishing Co., 1889), 36.

[3] "Return of casualties in McLaws' division at the battle of Sharpsburg, Md., September 17, 1862," *OR*, vol. 19, pt. 1, 862.

[4] Ibid.

[5] Ibid.

[6] Ibid., 861.

[7] Including artillery.—*EAC*

	Killed	Wounded	Missing	Aggregate
Anderson's Division				
Wilcox's Brigade[8]	34	181	29	244
Mahone's Brigade[9]	3	18	3	24
Featherston's Brigade[10]	45	238	36	319
Armistead's Brigade[11]	5	29	1	35
Pryor's Brigade[12]	48	285	49	382
Wright's Brigade[13]	32	192	34	258
artillery battalion[14]	5	11	—	16
Total	172	954	152	1,278
Jones's Division				
Toombs's Brigade[15]	16	122	22	160
Drayton's Brigade[16]	33	106	3	142
Garnett's Brigade[17]	9	69	—	78
Kemper's Brigade[18]	10	43	16	69
Jenkins's Brigade[19]	26	184	6	216
G. T. Anderson's Brigade[20]	8	77	2	87
J. S. Brown's Battery[21]	1	4	1	6
Total	103	605	50	758

(continued on next page)

8   "Statement of losses in the corps commanded by Maj. Gen. J. Longstreet in the engagements at Crampton's Gap, Maryland Heights, Sharpsburg, and South Mountain," *OR*, vol. 19, pt. 1, 843.

9   Mahone's Brigade numbered 84 men at Antietam. The losses here given are from survivors of the brigade and names given in John W. H. Porter, *A Record of Events in Norfolk County, Virginia, from April 19th, 1861, to May 10th, 1862, with a History of the Soldiers and Sailors of Norfolk County, Norfolk City and Portsmouth Who Served in the Confederate States Army or Navy* (Portsmouth: W. A. Fiske, 1892), 130–31, 138–40, 144–46, 148–50, 152–53, 155–56, 159–60, 162–63, 166–68, 171–72, 264–65, 267–68, 273–75, 277–78.—*EAC*

10   "Statement of losses in the corps commanded by Maj. Gen. J. Longstreet," 843.

11   Ibid.

12   Ibid.

13   Ibid.

14   Grimes's Battery had 3 killed and 2 wounded. Porter, 44–45. Huger's Battery had 1 killed and 2 wounded. Ibid., 257–58. Moorman's Battery had 1 killed and 7 wounded, of which the names have been given by survivors.—*EAC*

15   "Statement of losses in the corps commanded by Maj. Gen. J. Longstreet," 843; "Return of casualties in Brig. Gen. D. R. Jones' division, September 14–18, 1862," *OR*, vol. 19, pt. 1, 888.

16   "Return of casualties in Brig. Gen. D. R. Jones' division," 888. There are no official reports of the loss of Drayton's Brigade at Antietam. The figures here given have been estimated on information received from survivors of the brigade.—*EAC*

17   Eppa Hunton to Richard B. Garnett, 1862 [no day or month given], reprinted in *OR*, vol. 19, pt. 1, 898; George C. Cabell to "General Garnett's assistant adjutant-general," October 14, 1862, reprinted in *OR*, vol. 19, pt. 1, 901; Report of Benjamin Brown, October 15, 1862, reprinted in *OR*, vol. 19, pt. 1, 902; John B. McPhail to Garnett, October 26, 1862, reprinted in *OR*, vol. 19, pt. 1, 904. The 28th Virginia is estimated to have suffered 2 killed and 18 wounded.—*EAC*

18   The muster roll of the 1st Virginia (October 31, 1862) shows 2 missing. David E. Johnston, in his *Four Years a Soldier* [Carman again titles this incorrectly as *History of Co. D, 7th Virginia*], says, "Our regiment lost a few men in killed and wounded." David E. Johnston, *Four Years a Soldier* (Princeton, W. Va.: n.p., 1887), 202. Johnston informs us that he thinks the loss was 2 killed, 9 wounded, and 2 missing. Muster rolls of the 11th Virginia show 9 wounded and 2 missing. The 17th Virginia reports 31 killed and wounded and 10 missing. Report of Montgomery D. Corse, no date, reprinted in *OR*, vol. 19, pt. 1, 905. The history of the regiment gives a nominal list of 8 killed and 12 wounded. George Wise, *History of the Seventeenth Virginia Infantry, C.S.A.* (Baltimore: Kelly, Piet & Co., 1870), 124–25. The 24th Virginia was detached to the extreme right, was not actively engaged, and had 2 men wounded.—*EAC*

19   Joseph Walker to Robert Johnston, October 24, 1862, reprinted in *OR*, vol. 19, pt. 1, 907.

20   G. T. Anderson's Brigade lost 8 killed, 80 wounded, and 6 missing during the entire campaign. "Return of casualties in Brig. Gen. D. R. Jones' division," 888. Its loss at Turner's Gap was 3 wounded and 4 missing. Deduct this from the loss during the entire campaign and we have the figures as tabulated.—*EAC*

21   Muster roll of October 31, 1862.—*EAC*

	Killed	Wounded	Missing	Aggregate
Walker's Division				
Manning's Brigade[22]	140	684	93	917
French's Battery[23]	1	1	—	2
Ransom's Brigade[24]	41	141	4	186
Branch's Battery[25]	2	13	—	15
Total	184	839	97	1,120
Hood's Division				
Wofford's Brigade[26]	69	417	62	548
Law's Brigade[27]	50	379	25	454
Reilly's Battery[28]	2	8	—	10
Garden's Battery[29]	—	9	—	9
Bachman's Battery[30]	2	2	—	4
Total	123	815	87	1,025
Evans's Brigade				
infantry[31]	11	43	11	65
Boyce's Battery[32]	2	17	—	19
Total	13	60	11	84
Longstreet's reserve artillery				
Washington Artillery[33]	4	28	2	34
S. D. Lee's Battalion[34]	10	75	—	85
Total	14	103	2	119
Ewell's Division				
general and staff[35]	—	2	—	2
Lawton's Brigade[36]	106	440	21	567

(continued on next page)

---

22 "Statement of losses in the corps commanded by Maj. Gen. J. Longstreet," 843.

23 "Report of Surg. Lafayette Guild, C. S. Army, Medical Director Army of Northern Virginia, of killed and wounded at Boonsborough (South Mountain or Turner's Pass), Crampton's Gap, Harper's Ferry, Sharpsburg (Antietam), and Shepherdstown (Blackford's or Boteler's) Ford," no date, reprinted in *OR*, vol. 19, pt. 1, 811.

24 "Statement of losses in the corps commanded by Maj. Gen. J. Longstreet," 843.

25 Muster roll of October 31, 1862.—*EAC*

26 John B. Hood to Gilbert Moxley Sorrel, September 27, 1862, reprinted in *OR*, vol. 19, pt. 1, 925.

27 Ibid.

28 "Report of Surg. Lafayette Guild," 811.

29 Ibid.

30 Ibid.

31 The official report of the 17th South Carolina gives 4 killed, 12 wounded, and 3 missing. Fitz W. McMaster to Nathan G. Evans, October 20, 1862, reprinted in *OR*, vol. 19, pt. 1, 946. The 23d South Carolina reports 6 killed, 6 wounded, and 1 missing. S. A. Durham to Evans, October 16, 1862, reprinted in *OR*, vol. 19, pt. 1, 950. The losses in the 18th South Carolina are arrived at by assuming that the loss at Antietam was one-third the loss of the entire campaign (3 killed and 39 wounded), or a loss at Antietam of 1 killed and 13 wounded. "Report of Surg. Lafayette Guild," 811. The loss in missing, estimated from incomplete data, was 5. The 22d South Carolina gives 2 by name as being wounded. [One of these, according to the report, was actually sustained on September 15.] Miel Hilton to Asa L. Evans, October 15, 1862, reprinted in *OR*, vol. 19, pt. 1, 949. From other sources we learn that 4 more were wounded and 2 missing. The Holcombe Legion reports 18 men wounded in the entire campaign. "Report of Surg. Lafayette Guild," 811. Assuming that one-third is chargeable to Antietam would give 6 as its loss in wounded.—*EAC*

32 Robert Boyce to Nathan G. Evans, October 20, 1862 (first report), reprinted in *OR*, vol. 19. pt. 1, 944.

33 "Statement of losses in the corps commanded by Maj. Gen. J. Longstreet," 843; James B. Walton to Sorrel, December 4, 1862, reprinted in *OR*, vol. 19, pt. 1, 851.

34 "Statement of losses in the corps commanded by Maj. Gen. J. Longstreet," 843.

35 The division commander, Brigadier General Alexander R. Lawton, was one of the two wounded. "Return of casualties in Ewell's division at the battle of Sharpsburg, September 17, 1862," *OR*, vol. 19, pt. 1, 974.

36 Ibid.

	Killed	Wounded	Missing	Aggregate
Early's Brigade[37]	18	167	9	194
Trimble's Brigade[38]	27	202	8	237
Hays's Brigade[39]	45	289	2	336
Garber's Battery[40]	—	2	—	2
Total[41]	196	1,102	40	1,338
A. P. Hill's Division				
Branch's Brigade[42]	21	79	4	104
Gregg's Brigade[43]	28	135	2	165
Archer's Brigade[44]	15	90	—	105
Pender's Brigade[45]	2	28	—	30
artillery[46]	4	9	—	13
Total	70	341	6	417
D. H. Hill's Division				
Rodes's Brigade[47]	50	132	21	203
Ripley's Brigade[48]	121	531	124	776
Garland's Brigade[49]	9	42	33	84
G. B. Anderson's Brigade[50]	57	245	173	475
Colquitt's Brigade[51]	111	444	167	722
Hardaway's Battery[52]	—	9	—	9

(continued on next page)

---

[37] Ibid.

[38] Ibid. These figures include J. R. Johnson's Battery.—*EAC*

[39] Ibid. These figures include D'Aquin's Battery.—*EAC*

[40] Muster roll of October 31, 1862.—*EAC*

[41] In his official report, Early says, "Its loss [Ewell's Division] at Sharpsburg alone was 199 killed, 1,115 wounded, and 38 missing, being an aggregate loss of 1,352 out of less than 3,500, with which it went into that action." Jubal A. Early to Alexander S. Pendleton, January 12, 1863, reprinted in *OR*, vol. 19, pt. 1, 973.—*EAC*

[42] James H. Lane to Richard C. Morgan, November 14, 1862, reprinted in *OR*, vol. 19, pt. 1, 986.

[43] Samuel McGowan to Morgan, February 9, 1863, reprinted in *OR*, vol. 19, pt. 1, 989.

[44] James J. Archer to Morgan, March 1, 1863, reprinted in *OR*, vol. 19, pt. 1, 1001.

[45] William Dorsey Pender to "General [Ambrose P. Hill]," October 14, 1862, reprinted in *OR*, vol. 19, pt. 1, 1005.

[46] Crenshaw's Battery had 1 killed and 3 wounded. *Richmond Enquirer*, September 22, 1862 [article not located]. McIntosh's Battery had 1 killed and 2 wounded. We have no definite information as to the losses in Braxton's and Pegram's Batteries. Both were actively engaged, and we judge that they suffered equally with Crenshaw's and McIntosh's (say, 1 killed and 2 wounded each).—*EAC*

[47] Robert E. Rodes to James W. Ratchford, October 13, 1862, reprinted in *OR*, vol. 19, pt. 1, 1038.

[48] Daniel H. Hill to Robert H. Chilton, 1862 [no day or month given], reprinted in *OR*, vol. 19, pt. 1, 1026. The losses in the 4th and 44th Georgia are as given in the *OR*: 22 killed and 119 wounded in the 4th, 17 killed and 65 wounded in the 44th. "Report of Surg. Lafayette Guild," 813. The 1st North Carolina is reported as having 18 killed and 142 wounded, and the loss in the 3d North Carolina is given as 46 killed and 207 wounded. Ibid. However, a nominal list of the 1st North Carolina in our possession shows 36 killed and 140 wounded—an aggregate of 176. The muster rolls of the 3d North Carolina say, "The regiment suffered severely, losing over 300 officers and men." Colonel DeRosset says there was a loss of 330 men and 23 of the 27 officers, of whom 7 were killed. William L. DeRosset to Daniel H. Hill, June 22, 1885, typescript copy, "Gen. D. H. Hill's Report—Pierson's Artillery Battalion, Hill's Division" folder, box 3, Letters and Reports Concerning the Battle of Antietam, 1895–1900 ("Antietam Studies"), Record Group 94, National Archives. To be entirely within the probability of correctness, we adopt for the 3d North Carolina the figures as given by Surgeon Guild.—*EAC*

[49] The loss in Garland's Brigade is given as 46 killed, 210 wounded, and 187 missing for the entire campaign. Daniel H. Hill to Chilton, 1026. We have estimated the loss at Turner's Gap as four-fifths of that incurred during the entire campaign, leaving one-fifth as the loss at Antietam.—*EAC*

[50] The loss in G. B. Anderson's Brigade is given as 64 killed, 299 wounded, and 202 missing for the entire campaign. Daniel H. Hill to Chilton, 1026. Colonel Bennett gives the loss of the brigade at Antietam as 57 killed and 245 wounded, but does not report the number missing (which is known to be large). Risden T. Bennett to Ratchford, December 6, 1862, reprinted in *OR*, vol. 19, pt. 1, 1048. In a postwar article, Hill says G. B. Anderson had 29 missing at Turner's Gap, and this estimate we accept. Daniel H. Hill, "The Battle of South Mountain, or Boonsboro'," in *Battles and Leaders of the Civil War*, vol. 2 (New York: Century Co., 1887), 579. Deducting the 29 from the number reported missing during the entire campaign leaves 173 for the number missing at Antietam.—*EAC*

[51] The loss in Colquitt's Brigade is given as 129 killed, 518 wounded, and 184 missing for the entire campaign. Daniel H. Hill to Chilton, 1026. In the battle at Turner's Gap, its loss was 18 killed, 74, wounded, and 17 missing, leaving for Antietam the loss as here given.—*EAC*

[52] Letter of John W. Tullis [not found].—*EAC*

	Killed	Wounded	Missing	Aggregate
Bondurant's Battery[53]	1	8	—	9
Jones's Battery[54]	1	25	—	262
Carter's Battery[55]	2	3	1	6
Total	352	1,439	519	2,310
Jackson's Division				
Winder's Brigade[56]	11	77	—	88
Jones's Brigade[57]	9	62	—	71
Starke's Brigade[58]	81	189	17	287
Taliaferro's Brigade[59]	41	17	—	168
Wooding's Battery[60]	2	3	—	5
Poague's Battery[61]	—	6	—	6
Raine's Battery[62]	—	5	—	5
Brockenbrough's Battery[63]	—	8	—	8
Carpenter's Battery[64]	1	9	—	10
Total	145	486	17	648

Only two battalions of the Army of Northern Virginia's reserve artillery were engaged, those of Cutts and Jones. The records are silent as to their losses. Malcolm B. Council, the adjutant of Cutts's Battalion, writes us that the battalion suffered severely.[65] Captain Hugh M. Ross says his battery had 18 wounded and none killed.[66] In Blackshear's Battery, Lieutenant Thomas A. Maddox was wounded, and the men suffered 1 killed and 6 wounded, for a total of 8 casualties. Lane's Battery had 2 men wounded. Information from Patterson's Battery is very conflicting; our best estimate is that it had 1 killed and 5 wounded—making an aggregate in the four batteries of 2 killed and 32 wounded.[67] In Jones's Battalion, R. C. M. Page's Battery had 2 killed and 7 wounded.[68] Peyton's Battery had 8 wounded.[69] We can give no information as to the Virginia batteries of Captains William H. Turner and Abram Wimbish. We place the loss in the battalion as 2 killed and 15 wounded.

The official reports give no table of casualties in the cavalry. Stuart says that at Sharpsburg he was "several times subjected to severe shelling."[70] From surviving officers of the cavalry division, we have received data from which we estimate that it had 10 killed, 28 wounded, and 11 missing.

[53] Letter of John Purifoy.—*EAC*

There are a number of such letters in several collections of Carman's papers, but the only one the editor has been able to locate that specifies casualties for the battery at Antietam says, "Our losses were much heavier at Sharpsburg, being two killed and six or eight wounded." Purifoy to Ezra A. Carman, August 7, 1900, "The Maryland Campaign of September 1862, Related Material, Correspondence, 1897–1902, n.d." folder, container 16, Manuscript Division, Library of Congress.

[54] "Report of Surg. Lafayette Guild," 813.

[55] Thomas H. Carter to Henry A. Whiting, October 14, 1862, reprinted in *OR*, vol. 19, pt. 1, 1031.

[56] Hazel J. Williams to Warner T. Taliaferro, January 15, 1863, reprinted in *OR*, vol. 19, pt. 1, 1013.

[57] There are no reports of the loss in Jones's Brigade. It had about 200 men in action; Winder's Brigade, which had 250 in action, lost 88. As it was engaged with Winder's, it probably suffered in the same ratio, and we have so estimated.—*EAC*

[58] "Return of casualties in the Second Louisiana Brigade at the battle of Sharpsburg, September 17,1862," *OR*, vol. 19, pt. 1, 1015.

[59] "Return of casualties in Taliaferro's brigade at the battle of Sharpsburg, September 17, 1862," *OR*, vol. 19, pt. 1, 1009.

[60] "Report of Surg. Lafayette Guild," 813.

[61] William T. Poague to William H. Thomas, September 22, 1862, reprinted in *OR*, vol. 19, pt. 1, 1010.

[62] Muster roll of October 31, 1862.—*EAC*

[63] "Report of Surg. Lafayette Guild," 813.

[64] Estimated.—*EAC*

[65] Malcolm B. Council to Carman, March 26, 1900, "Reserve Artillery, Army of Northern Virginia" folder, box 3, "Antietam Studies."

[66] As of this writing, no textual source for this statement has been found.

[67] As of this writing, Carman's source for the casualties in these three batteries has not been identified.

[68] *Richmond Dispatch*, October 15, 1862 [article not located].—*EAC*

[69] Letter of M. Tabb [not found].—*EAC*

[70] James E. B. Stuart to Chilton, February 13, 1864, reprinted in *OR*, vol. 19, pt. 1, 821.

Recapitulation of Confederate Losses

	Killed	Wounded	Missing	Aggregate
McLaws's Division	160	933	26	1,119
Anderson's Division	172	954	152	1,278
Jones's Division	103	605	50	758
Walker's Division	184	839	97	1,120
Hood's Division	123	815	87	1,025
Evans's Brigade	13	60	11	84
Longstreet's reserve artillery	14	103	2	119
Ewell's Division	196	1,102	40	1,338
A. P. Hill's Division	70	341	6	417
D. H. Hill's Division	352	1,439	519	2,310
Jackson's Division	145	486	17	648
reserve artillery	4	47	—	51
cavalry division	10	28	11	49
Total	1,546	7,752	1,018	10,316

This is 4.13 percent in killed, 24.89 percent in killed and wounded, and 27.62 percent in killed, wounded and missing of the 37,351 engaged. The division showing the greatest percentage of loss in killed and wounded was Hood's, with 40.71 percent; McLaws's was second with 36.90 percent. Wofford's Brigade lost 64.10 percent in killed, wounded, and missing, and the 1st Texas of this brigade suffered 86.25 percent in killed and wounded. Hays's Brigade lost 60.72 percent in killed and wounded. It is probable that the 6th Georgia of Colquitt's Brigade lost nearly 90 percent in killed and wounded.

* * *

On September 17, 1862, at Antietam, there were more men killed and wounded on either side than on any other single day in the War of the Rebellion; more on the Union side than in the two days of Shiloh, Fair Oaks, Second Corinth, Stones River, or Chickamauga; more than in the three days' battles of Fredericksburg, Chancellorsville, Chattanooga, or Cold Harbor; more than in the five days of Groveton, Second Manassas, and Chantilly; as many as in the five days around Spotsylvania; more than in the Seven Days battles on the Peninsula; more than in the twelve-day[71] campaign ending at Appomattox; more than in all the battles around Atlanta; and more than in all the operations around Vicksburg, including the siege, from May 1 to July 4, 1863. Only two battles of the war show greater Union losses: Gettysburg, with 17,684 killed and wounded, and the Wilderness, with 14,283 killed and wounded. In both these battles the forces engaged were larger, and both extended over three days, while the work at Antietam was done between daybreak and sunset of one day—the bloodiest day in American history.[72]

The severity of the contest is best shown by the percentage of loss in killed and wounded in one day, which was greater at Antietam than in any other single day's battle, excepting Olustee and Cedar Mountain, and greater than all the battles of the war extending over two days and more, excepting Stones River and Gettysburg:

Numbers and Losses of Union Forces in Some Principal Engagements of the War[73]

			Days	Engaged	Killed	Wounded	Aggregate	Percent
1864	Feb. 20	Olustee	1	5,115	203	1,152	1,355	26.49
1862–63	Dec. 31–Jan. 1	Stones River	2	41,400	1,677	7,543	9,220	22.26
1862	Aug. 9	Cedar Mountain	1	8,030	314	1,445	1,759	21.90
1863	July 1–3	Gettysburg	3	83,289	3,155	14,529	17,684	21.20
1862	**Sept. 17**	**Antietam**	**1**	**55,956**	**2,108**	**9,540**	**11,648**	**20.82**
1863	Sept. 19–20	Chickamauga	2	58,222	1,657	9,756	11,413	19.60
1864	May 12–16	Drewry's Bluff	5	15,800	390	2,380	2,770	17.53
1861	Aug. 10	Wilson's Creek	1	5,400	223	721	944	17.47
1862	April 6–7	Shiloh	2	62,682	1,754	8,408	10,162	16.21

(continued on next page)

[71] Carman says "eleven" in his original manuscript. It has been changed herein to agree with the data source Carman cites in the chart that follows.

[72] Thomas L. Livermore, *Numbers and Losses in the Civil War in America, 1861–65* (Boston: Houghton, Mifflin, and Co., 1900), 102, 110.

[73] Ibid, 77–136. All except Antietam is from Livermore's book.—*EAC*

			Days	Engaged	Killed	Wounded	Aggregate	Percent
1864	May 5–7	Wilderness	3	101,895	2,246	12,037	14,283	14.01
1862	Aug. 27–Sept. 1	Groveton/ Manassas/ Chantilly	5	75,696	1,724	8,372	10,096	13.34
1864	Oct. 19	Cedar Creek	1	30,829	644	3,430	4,074	13.21
1864	Sept. 19	Third Winchester	1	37,711	697	3,983	4,680	12.41
1862	June 27	Gaines's Mill	1	34,214	894	3107	4,001	11.66
1863	May 1–4	Chancellorsville/ Second Fredericksburg	4	97,382	1,575	9,594	11,169	11.46
1864	May 10	Spotsylvania	1	37,822	753	3,347	4,100	10.84
1862	June 25–July 1	Seven Days campaign	7	91,169	1,734	8,062	9,796	10.74
1862	May 31–June 1	Fair Oaks	2	41,797	790	3,594	4,384	10.49
1862	October 3–4	Second Corinth	2	21,147	355	1,841	2,196	10.38
1864	June 1–3	Cold Harbor	3	107,907	1,844	9,078	10,922	10.12
1862	Mar. 7	Pea Ridge	1	11,250	203	980	1,183	10.05
1862	October 8	Perryville	1	36,940	845	2,851	3,696	10.00
1863	Nov. 23–25	Chattanooga	3	56,359	753	4,722	5,475	9.67
1862	Feb. 12–16	Fort Donelson	5	27,000	500	2,108	2,608	9.66
1862	Dec. 11–13	Fredericksburg	3	113,987	1,284	9,600	10,884	9.55
1865	Mar. 29–Apr. 9	Appomattox campaign[74]	n/a	112,892	1,316	7,750	9,066	8.03
1864	July 20	Peachtree Creek	1	21,655	n/a	n/a	1,600	7.38
1864	July 22	Atlanta	1	34,863	430	1,559	1,989	5.70
1861	July 21	Bull Run	1	28,452	481	1,011	1,492	5.24
1864	Nov. 30	Franklin	1	27,939	189	1,033	1,222	4.31

Numbers and Losses of Confederate Forces in Some Principal Engagements of the War[75]

			Days	Engaged	Killed	Wounded	Aggregate	Percent
1863	July 1–3	Gettysburg	3	75,054	3,903	18,735	22,638	30.16
1862–63	Dec. 31–Jan. 1	Stones River	2	34,732	1,294	7,945	9,239	26.87
1863	Sept. 19–20	Chickamauga	2	66,326	2,312	14,674	16,986	25.61
1862	**Sept. 17**	**Antietam**	**1**	**37,351**	**1,546**	**7,752**	**9,298**	**24.89**
1862	April 6–7	Shiloh	2	40,335	1,723	8,012	9,735	24.13
1862	June 25–July 1	Seven Days campaign	7	95,481	3,478	16,261	19,739	20.67
1864	Nov. 30	Franklin	1	26,897	1,750	3,800	5,550	20.63
1862	Oct. 8	Perryville	1	16,000	510	2,635	3,145	19.65
1862	Aug. 27–Sept. 1	Groveton/Manassas/ Chantilly	5	48,527	1,481	7,627	9,108	18.77
1863	May 1–4	Chancellorsville/ Second Fredericksburg	4	57,352	1,665	9,081	10,746	18.73
1864	July 22	Atlanta	1	36,934	n/a	n/a	7,000	18.30
1864	February 20	Olustee	1	5,200	93	841	934	18.00
1862	June 27	Gaines's Mill	1	57,018	n/a	n/a	8,751	15.34
1862	May 31–June 1	Fair Oaks	2	41,816	980	4,749	5,729	13.70
1864	July 20	Peachtree Creek	1	18,832	n/a	n/a	2,500	13.27
1864	May 12–16	Drewry's Bluff	5	18,025	355	1,941	2,296	12.73
1864	May 5–7	Wilderness	3	61,025	n/a	n/a	7,750	12.69
1864	Sept. 19	Third Winchester	1	17,103	276	1,827	2,103	12.30
1862	Oct. 3–4	Second Corinth	2	22,000	473	1,997	2,470	11.23

(continued on next page)

[74] Carman's original manuscript gives the number engaged as 114,826. Given his comment in n. 73, this is mostly likely an error in transcription. As the rest of the data cited for the Appomattox campaign matches that found in Livermore to the man, the number engaged has been changed herein to reflect the total given in Livermore, 136.

[75] Livermore, 77–132 (excepting the Antietam data, as before).

			Days	Engaged	Killed	Wounded	Aggregate	Percent
1862	Sept. 14	South Mountain[76]	1					
1864	Oct. 19	Cedar Creek	1	18,410	320	1,540	1,860	10.00
1862	Feb. 12–16	Fort Donelson	5	21,000	n/a	n/a	2,000	9.47
1861	August 10	Wilson's Creek	1	11,600	257	9000	1,157	9.09
1862	Dec. 11–13	Fredericksburg	3	72,497	595	4,061	4,656	6.42
1861	July 21	Bull Run	1	32,232	387	1,582	1,969	6.11
1863	Nov. 23–25	Chattanooga	3	46,165	361	2,160	2,521	5.46

* * *

William F. Fox enumerates seventy-three Union regiments whose losses in one engagement (killed, wounded, and missing) reached 50 percent. Excluding those whose missing brought the percentage to this figure, there were forty-seven such regiments. Of these, fifteen met their losses at Gettysburg, eight at Antietam, four at [Second] Manassas, four at Fredericksburg, two at Cold Harbor, and one each at Chickamauga, Shiloh, Bethesda Church, Petersburg, Milliken's Bend, Spotsylvania, the Wilderness, Salem Church, Missionary Ridge, Cedar Mountain, the Opequon [Third Winchester], Chaffin's Farm, Fort Donelson, and Cedar Creek.[77]

Union Regiments at Antietam with Losses in Killed and Wounded Exceeding 50 Percent[78]

	Engaged	Killed	Wounded	Percent
12th Massachusetts[79]	334	49	165	64.07
69th New York	317	44	152	61.83
9th New York	373	45	176	59.25
3d Wisconsin	340	27	173	58.82
63d New York	341	35	165	58.65[80]
14th Indiana	320	30	150	56.25
15th Massachusetts	606	65	255	52.81
59th New York	381	48	153	52.76

Fox gives a list of fifty-three Confederate regiments whose loss in any one battle reached 50 percent. Forty-seven of these lost 50 percent and over in killed and wounded. Of these, twelve met their loss at Chickamauga, nine at Antietam, seven at [Second] Manassas, four at Gettysburg, three at Stones River, three in the Seven Days campaign, two at Seven Pines, two at Fair Oaks, and one each at Shiloh, Glendale, Mechanicsville, Gaines's Mill, and Raymond.[81]

Confederate Regiments at Antietam with Losses in Killed and Wounded Exceeded 50 Percent[82]

	Engaged	Killed	Wounded	Percent
1st Texas[83]	226	45	141	82.30
16th Mississippi	228	27	117	63.16

(continued on next page)

---

[76] Carman has an entry for South Mountain marked at this point in his chart, but the remaining fields in the row are left blank. Given the battle's specific placement by Carman between Second Corinth and Cedar Creek, it is surmised that he calculated a percentage of loss and then neglected to copy his figures into the chart. From the data given in Appendices G and I, the Confederates suffered 318 killed and 1,302 wounded—an aggregate of 1,620. If Carman is correct in where he positions South Mountain relative to other engagements, the percentage of loss was no greater than 11.23 and no less than 10.00, yielding an engaged force of between 14,426 to 16,200 men.

[77] Fox, 36–37.

[78] Ibid. Because Fox also included the number of missing in his table, his percentages are not used.

[79] A revised statement shows that the 12th Massachusetts had nine companies (comprising 262 officers and men) engaged, of whom 49 were killed and 163 wounded—80.92 percent of those engaged.—*EAC*

[80] In his original manuscript, Carman makes an error in division. He gives the loss as 59 percent and places the 63d New York ahead of the 3d Wisconsin as a result.

[81] Fox, 556–58.

[82] Ibid. Per n. 78, the percentages are recalculations.

[83] A revised statement gives the 1st Texas 211 engaged, of whom 50 were killed and 132 wounded—23.70 percent killed and 86.26 percent killed and wounded. Philip A. Work to Robert Burns, February 13, 1891, "Report Brig. Gen. J. B. Hood's Division—Artillery Battalion, Major F. W. Frobel" folder, box 2, "Antietam Studies"; "1st Texas Infantry," no date, "Report Brig. Gen. J. B. Hood's Division" folder, "Antietam Studies."—*EAC*

	Engaged	Killed	Wounded	Percent
27th North Carolina	325	31	168	61.23
15th Virginia	128	11	64	58.59
10th Georgia	148	15	69	56.76
17th Virginia	55	7	24	56.36
4th Texas	200	10	97	53.50
7th South Carolina	268	23	117	52.24
18th Georgia	170	13	72	50.00

In addition to these nine regiments given by Fox, there were at least eleven others whose losses in killed and wounded exceeded 50 percent. These were:

	Engaged	Killed	Wounded	Percent
6th Georgia[84]	250	81	115	78.40
2d Mississippi[85]	210	27	127	73.33
13th Georgia[86]	312	59	166	72.12
Hampton Legion[87]	77	6	49	71.43
30th Virginia[88]	236	39	121	67.80
12th Georgia[89]	100	13	49	62.00
38th Georgia[90]	123	18	52	56.91
3d Arkansas[91]	350	27	155	52.00
61st Georgia[92]	191	16	81	50.79
44th Georgia[93]	162	17	65	50.62
27th Georgia[94]	206	15	89	50.49

Hays's Brigade had about 550 engaged, of whom 45 were killed and 289 wounded—a loss of 60.73 percent.[95] Wofford's Brigade had 854 engaged, of whom 69 were killed and 417 wounded—a loss of 56.91 percent.[96]

---

[84] James M. Folsom, *Heroes and Martyrs of Georgia: Georgia's Record in the Revolution of 1861*, vol. 1 (Macon, Ga.: Burke, Boykin & Co., 1864), 26.

[85] Carman's source for the number engaged is not known. He states earlier that even the strength of the brigade to which the regiment was attached (Law's) is not known (see p. 462). The losses appear in "Report of Surg. Lafayette Guild," 811.

[86] Carman's source for these figures is not known. The only citation he gives for this item is "Return of casualties in Ewell's division," 974. This document does not provide the number engaged, however, and it gives the total killed as 48.

[87] Both the number engaged and the losses are given in Martin W. Gary to William T. Wofford, September 23, 1862, reprinted in *OR*, vol. 19, pt. 1, 931.

[88] For the number engaged, see p. 462. Carman does not explain why he uses the total strength of only nine of the regiment's companies, given his earlier assertion that the tenth, which had been on picket duty during the cited roll call, rejoined the regiment "during the engagement." For the losses, see "Report of Surg. Layfayette Guild," 811.

[89] Carman's source for the number engaged is not known, but he gives the figure in his narrative (see p. 217). The losses appear in "Report of Surg. Lafayette Guild," 813.

[90] Carman's source for the number engaged is not known, but he gives the figure in his narrative (see p. 225). The losses appear in "Return of casualties in Ewell's division," 974.

[91] The number engaged is given in "Casualties: List of Casualties in the 3d Regiment Arkansas Vols. at the Battle of Sharpsburg, on the 17th of Sept. 1862. Capt. J. W. Ready Commanding the Regiment," *Richmond Enquirer*, October 14, 1862. The losses appear in "Report of Surg. Lafayette Guild," 811.

[92] Carman's source for the number engaged is not known. The losses appear in "Report of Surg. Lafayette Guild," 813.

In his original manuscript, Carman makes an error in division. He gives the loss as 50.6 percent and places the 61st Georgia below the 44th Georgia as a result.

[93] The number engaged is given in John C. Key to Carman, September 29, 1897, "Gen. D. H. Hill's Report" folder, "Antietam Studies." The losses appear in "Report of Surg. Lafayette Guild," 813.

[94] Carman's source for the number engaged is not known. It contradicts his earlier embrace of claims by seven survivors of the regiment that the unit went into action on the seventeenth with 290 officers and men (see p. 464). The losses appear In "Report of Surg. Lafayette Guild," 813.

[95] The number engaged is given in Jubal A. Early to Alexander S. Pendelton, January 12, 1863, reprinted in *OR*, vol. 19, pt. 1, 968. The losses appear in "Return of casualties in Ewell's division," 974.

[96] Wofford to William H. Sellers, September 29, 1862, reprinted in *OR*, vol. 19, pt. 1, 929.

Appendix M: Union Losses in the Maryland Campaign

			Killed	Wounded	Captured/ Missing	Aggregate
September	5	Poolesville	—	8	31	39
	8	Poolesville and Monocacy Church	1	12	—	13
	10–11	Sugar Loaf	1	4	—	5
	12	Frederick	2	1	12	15
	13	Catoctin, Middletown, Jefferson, and South Mountain	5	22	5	32
	14	Crampton's Gap	113	418	2	533
	14	Turner's Gap	325	1,403	85	1,813
	15	Boonsboro	1	15	3	19
	17	Antietam	2,108	9,549[1]	753	12,410
	19–20	Shepherdstown Ford	71	161	131	363
		Total (Army of the Potomac)	2,627	11,593	1,022	15,242
September	11–15	Maryland Heights and Harper's Ferry	44	173	12,520	12,737
		Grand Total	2,671	11,766	13,542	27,979

---

[1] Includes 9 casualties sustained on September 18 (see p. 469 n. 1).

Appendix N: Confederate Losses in the Maryland Campaign

			Killed	Wounded	Captured/ Missing	Aggregate
September	5	Poolesville	3	4	—	7
	7	Poolesville	—	—	2	2
	8	Monocacy Church	1	10	4	15
	9	Barnesville	—	—	27	27
	9	Monocacy Viaduct	1	—	2	3
	11–15	Maryland Heights and Harper's Ferry	41	247	—	288
	12	Monocacy Bridge	2	—	—	2
	12	Frederick	2	3	—	5
	13	Fairview	—	8	3	11
	13	Near Burkittsville	4	9	—	13
	14	Crampton's Gap	70	289	603	962
	14	Turner's Gap	248	1,013	662	1,923
	15	Boonsboro	28	20	15	63
	17	Antietam	1,546	7,752	1,018	10,316
	19–20	Shepherdstown Ford	33	252	—	285
	Total		1,979	9,607	2,336	13,922

These figures do not represent the full loss to Lee's army in its unsuccessful campaign. All reports agree that there was much straggling in the army, and it is known that large numbers of stragglers were left on the roads from South Mountain to the Antietam. Pleasonton reports that he picked up hundreds of them.[1] McClellan writes that during the campaign he captured 6,000 prisoners,[2] in which, we conclude, are the 2,336 (as calculated above) and probably from 750 to 1,000 of the most severely wounded that could not be removed—in all, 3,100 to 3,300 men, the remaining 2,700 to 2,900 being stragglers. Add these captured stragglers to our table of casualties and we have a loss in the campaign of over 16,600. Longstreet says it was more: "Lee's army on entering Maryland was made up of nearly 57,000 men, exclusive of artillery and cavalry. As we had but 37,000 at Sharpsburg, our losses in the several engagements after we crossed the Potomac, *including stragglers*, reached nearly 20,000"[3]—and in this 20,000 are not included the losses at Sharpsburg. But not all these 33,922 men were lost to the Confederacy; quite 17,000 of them rejoined the ranks soon after Lee recrossed the Potomac (in fact, many preceded him). However, the importance of the campaign and its results are not to be measured by the losses on either side.

[1] Alfred Pleasonton to Randolph B. Marcy, September 19, 1862, reprinted in *OR*, vol. 19, pt. 1, 210.

[2] George B. McClellan to Lorenzo Thomas, October 15, 1862, reprinted in *OR*, vol. 19, pt. 1, 33.

[3] James Longstreet, "The Invasion of Maryland," in *Battles and Leaders of the Civil War*, vol. 2 (New York: Century Co., 1887), 674.

Appendix O: The British Perspective

94 Piccadilly: September 14, 1862

My dear Russell,— The detailed accounts given in the 'Observer' to day of the battles of August 29 and 30 between the Confederates and the Federals show that the latter got a very complete smashing; and it seems not altogether unlikely that still greater disasters await them, and that even Washington or Baltimore may fall into the hands of the Confederates.

If this should happen, would it not be time for us to consider whether in such a state of things England and France might not address the contending parties and recommend an arrangement upon the basis of separation? …

—Yours sincerely,

Palmerston[1]

Gotha: September 17, 1862

My dear Palmerston, —Whether the Federal army is destroyed or not, it is clear that it is driven back to Washington, and has made no progress in subduing the insurgent States. Such being the case, I agree with you that the time is come for offering mediation to the United States Government, with a view to the recognition of the independence of the Confederates. I agree further, that, in the case of failure, we ought ourselves to recognize the Confederate States as an independent State. For the purpose of taking so important a step, I think we must have a meeting of the Cabinet. The 23rd or 30th would suit me for the meeting.

We ought then, if we agree on such a step, to propose it first to France, and then, on the part of England and France, to Russia and the other powers, as a measure decided upon by us.

We ought to make ourselves safe in Canada, not by sending more troops there but by concentrating those we have in a few defensible posts before the winter sets in …

—Yours truly,

J. Russell[2]

Broadlands: September 23, 1862

My dear Russell,—Your plan of proceedings about the mediation between the Federals and Confederates seems to be excellent. Of course, the offer would be made to both the contending parties at the same time; for though the offer would be as sure to be accepted by the Southerns as was the proposal of the Prince of Wales by the Danish Princess, yet, in the one case as in the other, there are certain forms which it is decent and proper to go through.

A question would occur whether, if the two parties were to accept the mediation, the fact of our mediating would not of itself be tantamount to an acknowledgement of the Confederates as an independent State.

Might it not be well to ask Russia to join England and France in the offer of mediation? …

We should be better without her in the mediation, because she would be too favorable to the North; but on the other hand her participation in the offer might render the North more willing to accept it.

The after communication to the other European powers would be quite right, although they would be too many for mediation.

As to the time of making the offer, if France and Russia agree,—and France, we know, is quite ready, and only waiting for our concurrence—events may be taking place which might render it desirable that the offer should be made before the middle of October.

It is evident that a great conflict is taking place to the north-west of Washington, and its issue must have a great effect on the state of affairs. If the Federals sustain a great defeat, they may be at once ready for mediation, and the iron should be struck while it is hot. If, on the other hand, they should have the best of it, we may wait awhile and see what may follow …

—Yours sincerely,

Palmerston[3]

---

[1] Henry John Temple, Viscount Palmerston, to John Russell, September 14, 1862, reprinted in Spencer Walpole, *The Life of Lord John Russell*, vol. 2 (London: Longmans, Green, and Co., 1889), 349.

[2] Russell to Palmerston, September 17, 1862, reprinted in Walpole, 349–50.

[3] Palmerston to Russell, September 23, 1862, reprinted in Walpole, 350.

J

Jackson, Lt. Benjamin W., 147
Jackson, Col. James W., 208, 428
Jackson, Maj. Lyman J., 334, 410
Jackson, Col. Nathaniel J., 138, 407
Jackson, Lt. Col. Samuel M., 231, 400
Jackson, Capt. Thomas H., 419
Jackson, Maj. Gen. Thomas J. "Stonewall," 424
  advance through Maryland, and, 45–46
  Antietam, at
    9th Va. Cav., and, 247
    attempts to rally men, 244, 247, 256
    attends council of war, 366
    Brockenbrough's Battery, and, 246
    D'Aquin's Battery, and, 220, 246
    describes fighting on left, 226
    Hays's Brigade, and, 220
    inquires about progress of Hood's Division, 229
    Lee's attempted counterattack, and, 272, 309–312, 367–368
    orders support from McLaws, 259, 272n69, 275
    promises Early reinforcements if Ewell's Division will hold, 248
    rebukes Branch's Battery, 282
    Sept. 16, on, 187, 201–202, 206, 208, 210
  arrests A. P. Hill, 426n65
  arrests Garnett, 420n30
  commands at Harper's Ferry in 1861, 16, 101
  desirous of invading Maryland, 23, 26–27, 45–46
  Harper's Ferry operation, and, 55–56, 108–110, 115, 117–118, 120–122, 125–127, 135, 165, 173, 186
  ordered to cover Lee's retreat following South Mountain defeat, 168–169
  Peninsula campaign, and, 27, 59
  rejects union with McLaws against Sixth Corps, 190, 193–194
  Second Manassas campaign, and, 29–30, 89
  Special Orders No. 191, and, 131
  Valley campaign of, 26–27, 37–38, 59, 78
Jackson, Col. William L., 117
Jackson's Brigade. See Taliaferro's Brigade
Jackson's command/wing, 424–434
  advance through Maryland, and, 45–47, 52, 82, 84–86, 127, 129
  advance to Potomac, 41
  Antietam, at, 127, 201–202, 210, 463–465

Harper's Ferry operation, and, 55, 57, 86, 92–93, 95, 106–109, 115, 118–119, 127, 189
  march to rejoin Lee, and, 127
  ordered to cover Lee's retreat following South Mountain defeat, 168–169
  post-campaign, 392
  retreat from Maryland, and, 368, 372
  Second Manassas campaign, and, 29–30
  straggling in, 463
Jackson's Division, 424–425
  advance through Maryland, and, 45
    fighting on left, and, 215, 218–220, 224, 234, 247–249, 253, 256, 260–261, 269, 272
    final position of, 312
    losses incurred in, 316, 473–474
    Sept. 16, on, 201–202, 206, 208, 219
    strength of, 316, 463, 465
    targeted by artillery beyond creek, 317
  Harper's Ferry operation, and, 110, 117, 119
James, Lt. Col. George S., 419
James River, 47, 89
Jardine, Maj. Edward, 344, 409
Jeff Davis Artillery. See Alabama units— Bondurant's Battery
Jeff Davis Legion. See Mississippi units
Jefferson, Md., 47, 92, 94–95, 105, 109, 130–133, 135–136, 169
Jenkins, Lt. Col. William A., 421
Jenkins's Brigade, 420
  Antietam, at, 173, 188, 323, 325, 332, 339–340, 342–344, 358, 461–462, 470
  South Mountain, at, 155, 160, 162–163, 166–167, 175, 449
Jetton, Charles P., 304
Johnson, Col. Bradley T., 5, 8, 14, 16, 39, 46–47, 52–53, 428
Johnson, Col. Charles A., 371, 404
Johnson, Maj. George W., 407
Johnson, Capt. John R., 425
Johnson, Capt. Marmaduke, 433
Johnson, Reverdy, 5, 10
Johnson, Capt. Riley, 401
Johnson's Battery, J. R. See Virginia units (C.S.)
Johnson's Battery, M. See Virginia units (C.S.)
Johnson's Brigade. See Jones's Brigade
Johnston, Capt. Frank M., 426
Johnston, Gen. Joseph E., 21–23, 26, 101, 195
Johnston, Lt. Col. Robert D., 277, 430–431n87

Johnston, Lt. Col. William A. (14th N.C.), 431
Johnston, Capt. William F. (10th Ga.), 416
Jones, Brig. Gen. David R., 160, 169, 172, 340–341, 347, 349–350, 419, 461
Jones, Maj. Hilary P., 288–289, 321, 433
Jones, Capt. John F., 418
Jones, Brig. Gen. John R., 53, 117, 119, 208, 219–220, 428, 463
Jones, Capt. Richard W., 417
Jones, Col. Robert H., 283–284, 418
Jones, Lt. Col. Theodore, 352–353, 410
Jones, Maj. Waters B., 424
Jones, Capt. William B., 432
Jones's Battalion, 197, 288, 318, 321–322, 433, 465, 473
Jones's Battery. See Virginia units (C.S.)
Jones's Brigade, 46, 208, 219, 222–223, 428
Jones's Cross-Roads, Md., 171, 180
Jones's Division, D. R., 419–421
  advance through Maryland, 109–110
  advance to Potomac, 41–42
  Antietam, at
    assault by Ninth Corps, and, 334, 340, 344, 347–350, 355
    losses incurred in, 358, 470, 474
    positioned on right of Lee's line, 119
    Sept. 15, on, 173–174
    strength of, 461–463
  South Mountain, at, 160, 449
Jones's Division, J. R. See Jackson's Division
Jordan, Capt. Tyler C., 216, 423
Jordan, Capt. William P., 467
Jordan's Battery. See Virginia units (C.S.)

K

Kanawha Division. See Cox's division; Scammon's division
Kane, George P., 18
Kasey, Maj. John G., 425
Kavanagh, Capt. John, 286
Kearneysville, Va., 102, 107, 122
Kearse, Lt. Col. Francis, 332, 419
Keedysville, Md., 111, 121, 123, 125, 169, 171–174, 177–178, 189, 192, 195, 202, 204, 284, 300, 308, 317, 320, 326, 364, 371
Keedysville–Sharpsburg Road. See Boonsboro Road
Keitt, Lawrence M., 31, 33
Kelley, Capt. Elisha S., 177
Kellogg, Capt. John A., 221, 223
Kelly, Lt. Col. James, 285, 401
Kelly, Lt. Col. Patrick, 286, 401
Kemper, Brig. Gen. James L., 160, 345, 347–348, 420
Kemper's Brigade, 420